WHO'S WHO IN ROCK MUSIC

WHO'S WHO IN ROCK MUSIC

WILLIAM YORK

CHARLES SCRIBNER'S SONS · NEW YORK

Library of Congress Cataloging in Publication Data

York, William.
Who's who in rock music.

1. Rock music — Bio-bibliography. 2. Rock Music — Discography.
I. Title.
ML102.R6Y7 784.5'4'00922 [B] 81-21368
ISBN 0-684-17342-5 (cloth) AACR2
ISBN 0-684-17343-3 (paper)

This book published simultaneously in the
United States of America and in Canada—
Copyright under the Berne Convention.

1 3 5 7 9 11 13 15 17 19 V/C 20 18 16 14 12 10 8 6 4 2
1 3 5 7 9 11 13 15 17 19 V/P 20 18 16 14 12 10 8 6 4 2

Printed in the United States of America.

PREFACE

Who's Who in Rock Music is an attempt to compile in one volume the essential facts about the recording career of every individual and group in the history of rock music. In over 13,000 alphabetical entries, this book lists virtually every rock group that has recorded an album released by a "major" label and every individual who has performed on a rock album — whether as a member of a rock band, a solo performer, or a session artist.

Each individual's entry tells what instruments that person plays, bands he has been a member of, people or groups he has done session work for, and albums he has recorded. Entries for groups list their members over the years, instruments played by each member, and the albums recorded by the group. Brief essays place the more important individuals and groups within the history of rock music and describe their origins, evolution, and influence.

My intention in writing this book is to credit everyone who has contributed to rock music, from the best-known performers to unknown session artists and producers, and to provide a more complete reference to the field than is currently available. For purposes as diverse as simply looking up the albums recorded by a given group, tracing an individual's development through careers with several bands or changes in a band's sound through several personnel changes, discovering what groups a favorite artist has performed with, tracking down trivia, and just for browsing, *Who's Who in Rock Music* is intended to include more hard facts and pertinent information than any other publication in the field.

The term "rock and roll" has been defined many times, with varying degrees of accuracy and pretension. Rather than attempt to redefine rock here,

I will simply say that *Who's Who* is strongest in its coverage of those artists, from the 1960s onward, who would have called their music rock and roll — in particular, American artists and those British performers whose music succeeded in crossing the Atlantic. Cross-references into other areas of music are inevitable and essential, though. Since it was from the work of blues performers like Muddy Waters, Howlin' Wolf, Mississippi John Hurt, and Blind Lemon Jefferson that rock (not to mention other musical genres) evolved, many of the influential blues artists are included. Jazz, country and western, soul, and folk artists whose work affected rock musicians are credited also. Some "middle of the road" performers whose songs are often on the charts alongside those of rock-and-roll bands are not included, at editorial discretion.

The information in this book is derived almost entirely from album jackets, a method of compilation that is not without limitations. Though most of the music we are exposed to on the radio is brought to us by major record companies with massive distribution, many artists began on remote labels with limited local distribution. Situations like that hinder complete documentation of many artists' careers, and account, to a certain degree, for the less thorough coverage of early rock artists.

Also limiting complete coverage of artists is the sometimes whimsical distribution techniques of these major labels. Some recordings become discontinued within weeks of their debut. If popularity blossoms at a later date, these same recordings may be reissued as new. In recent years, many small labels have been absorbed by larger conglomerates, which may also reissue old "new" material; other small labels disappear due to commercial failure. Whenever possible, original record labels, numbers, and issue dates have been recorded here. It is important to remember that the dates represent the dates of album issue, not necessarily when the material was performed.

Another hindrance to the accumulation of data is the random thoroughness of the credits on rock albums. Some detail the participation of those responsible for their creation to the minutest detail, including the names of managers, road crews, secretaries, on down to who delivered what particular refreshments, while other albums list no credits whatsoever. In some circumstances, certain artists are unable to use their real names because of contractual obligations to other companies; others use pseudonyms to create an image, to keep their personal identities separate from their public life, or for other reasons. In addition, typographical errors are inevitable from album to album. In compiling *Who's Who*, every attempt has been made to resolve these contradictions.

Some biographical data has been supplied for the better-known artists, but the actual music is the focus of this book. Each album is a musical work of art and should be viewed as a unit. For this reason anthology albums have been purposely neglected, as they represent a marketer's idea of commercial appeal, rather than the artist's conception.

I would like to take this opportunity to thank my friends at the Seattle branches of Tower Records and Peaches Records, at Bozotronics and Atomic Press, Michael Pietsch of Scribners, and the countless others whose faith in rock music and encouragement made *Who's Who* a reality.

Notice of errors, oversights, and additions will be welcomed. Please write the author, enclosing substantiating material if possible, at 1421 N. 34th St., Seattle, WA 98103.

A NOTE ON THE ORDER OF ENTRIES

Entries for both groups and individuals appear in alphabetical order. This method is simple enough in most cases; individuals are alphabetized under their last names, and groups with made-up names under the first word in the name. When a group is named after an individual in the group, we have chosen to place the group's entry immediately following the entry for the individual after whom the group is named. For example, you will find "Eric Burdon Band" immediately after "Burdon, Eric."

As can be seen from the example just given, we have also chosen to retain normal word order in the headings for group entries, including those for groups named after individuals. In this way we avoid bizarre inversions like "Baker's Air Force, Ginger." We trust that readers will not be confused because an entry alphabetized under one letter begins with another; we have tried to be guided by common sense, for increased ease of use.

WHO'S
WHO
IN
ROCK
MUSIC

A'S Rocco Notte; Richard Bush; Rick Difonzo; Terry Bortman; Michael Snyder. *Album:* The A's (ARI 4238) 1979.

A-440 Ted Neely—vocal; Yvonne Werson—vocal; Michael Rapp—keyboards; Carlos Luevano—guitar; Craig Meacham—bass; Ian Hoffman—percussion. *Album:* Ulysses, the Greek Suite (TCF 1101) 1978.

AABERG, PHIL Piano, clarinet. Member of the Elvin Bishop Band, 1974-76. Session for Henry Gross (1975-77); Mark Farner (1977); Elvin Bishop (1978).

AALON Guitar. Member of the Eric Burdon Band, 1974-75.

AALTONEN, VESA Drums, percussion. Member of Tasavallan Presidenti, 1974.

AARON, MARC Guitar. Session for John Cale (1979).

AARONS, AL Trumpet. Session for B. B. King (1977).

AARONSON, KENNY Bass. Member of Stories, 1972-73.

ABBA Annifred Lygnstad—vocal; Agnetha DeWhart—vocal; Bjorn Ulvaeus—guitar, vocal; Benny Anderson—keyboards, vocal. Pop vocal group from Sweden. *Albums:* Abba (ATC 18146) 1975; The Abba Album (ATC 19164); Arrival (ATC 19115); Gift of Song (POL 2-6214); Greatest Hits (ATC 19114) 1976; Greatest Hits, Vol. II (ATC 16009); Voulez-Vous (ATC 16000) 1979; Waterloo (ATC 18101) 1974; Super Trouper (ATC 16023) 1980.

ABBOTT, DREW Guitar, vocal. Original member of the Silver Bullet Band, 1974-present.

ABBOTT, TIM Guitar, vocal, flute, harmonica. *Album:* Time and Space (GPR 768) 1980.

ABEL, MARK Bass, vocal, guitar. Member of Silent Dancing, 1975. Session for Tom Verlaine (1979).

ABENE, MIKE Organ. Session for Pavlov's Dog (1976).

ABERNATHY, ROD Guitar. Member of Arrogance, 1980.

ABLER, DUANE Keyboards. Member of the Sunblind Lion, 1976.

ABLER, KEITH Guitar, vocal. Member of the Sunblind Lion, 1976-78.

ABRAHAM, LOU Guitar. Member of Barooga, 1980.

ABRAHAMS, ALAN Drums, vocal. Member of Pig Iron.

ABRAHAMS, MICK Guitar, mandolin, pedal steel guitar, vocal. Born 4/7/43. After his departure from Jethro Tull in 1968, Abrahams formed Blodwyn Pig, 1969-70, a rock-jazz combo featuring Jack Lancaster on reeds, which failed to catch public attention. He was the founder and namesake of the Mick Abrahams Band, 1971-72. Session for Gary Wright (1970).

MICK ABRAHAMS BAND Mick Abrahams—guitar, mandolin, pedal steel guitar, vocal; Ritchie Dharma—drums, percussion; Bob Sargent—keyboards, guitar, vocal; Walt Monaghan—bass, vocal; Jack Lancaster—saxophone, clarinet (1972). Formed by ex-Jethro Tull member Abrahams, the Mick Abrahams Band was less dynamic than Tull, but not without its enjoyable moments, such as Lancaster playing two saxes simultaneously. *Albums:* Mick Abrahams (AAM 4312) 1971; At Last (CHR 1005) 1972.

ABRAHAMS, PAUL Bass. Member of the Reels, 1980.

ABRAMS, LESTER Vocal, drums, piano, percussion. Member of Crackin, 1975. Session for the Doobie Brothers (1978).

AC/DC Angus Young—guitar; Malcolm Young—guitar; Bon Scott—vocal; Phil Rudd—drums; Mark Evans—bass (1976-78); Brian Johnson—vocal (1980); Cliff Williams—bass (1978-present). Hard rock Australian quintet that suffered the loss of singer Scott in 1980, as their popularity began to crest. Scott was competently replaced by Johnson, and they continued their "bad boy" image and hard rock popularity. *Albums:* Back in Black (ATC 16018) 1980; High Voltage (ACO 36-142) 1976; Highway to Hell (ATC 19244) 1979; If You Want Blood You've Got It (ATC 19212) 1978; Let There Be Rock (ACO 36-151) 1979; Powerage (ATC 19180) 1978; Dirty Deeds Done Dirt Cheap (Import) 1976.

ACE Frank Byrne—drums; Bam King—guitar, vocal; Paul Carrack—keyboards, vocal; Tex Comer—bass, vocal; Phil Harris—guitar; Jon Woodhead—vocal, guitar (1977). *Albums:* Five a Side, 1974; Time for Another, 1975; No Strings (ANC) 1977.

ACE THE BASS Bass. Member of Wedge, 1980.

ACE, MARTIN Bass. Session for the Motors (1980).

ACEVES, HAROLD Drums, vocal. Session for Barry Melton (1978).

ACKER, STEVE Guitar. Member of Law, 1977.

ACKERMAN, WILLIAM Guitar, vocal. *Album:* It Takes a Year, 1977.

ACKERMAN, WILLIE Drums. Session for Doug Kershaw (1972); Waylon Jennings (1973).

ACKLES, DAVID Vocal, piano. California based songwriter-singer. His "Road to Cairo" was used by Julie Driscoll as her second single in 1968. *Album:* David Ackles (ELK) 1968.

ACQUAYE, SPEEDY Percussion. Session for Wings (1979).

ACROBAT Bob Lehnert—vocal, guitar; Billy Jones—guitar, vocal; Mel Senter—bass, piano, vocal; Greg Davis—percussion, guitar, vocal; Richie Simpson—drums; Barry Johnson—drums. *Album:* Acrobat, 1972.

ACUNA, ALEX Drums. Member of Weather Report. Session for Lee Ritenour (1978-79).

ACUNA, JESS Vocal, percussion. Member of Hiroshima, 1980.

ADAIR, REGGIE Keyboards. Session for Levon Helm (1980).

ADAM, LARRY Guitar. Member of David Peel's Lower East Side, 1969.

ADAMEK, STEVE Drums, vocal. Member of Bighorn, 1978.

ADAMORE, CARL Vocal. Member of Joey Dee and the Starlighters.

ADAMS, CHRIS Vocal, guitar. Original member of the String Driven Thing, 1972-73.

ADAMS, DAVID Keyboards, vocal. Member of Glass Moon, 1980.

ADAMS, DAVID Vocal. Member of Screams, 1980.

ADAMS, DONN Trombone. Member of the Whole Wheat Horns, and the Johnny Average Dance Band, 1980. Session for Martin Mull (1974).

ADAMS, GREG Trumpet, trombone, piano, vocal, arranger. Member of the Tower of Power horn section. Session for Roy Buchanan (1974); Ron Gardner (1974).

ADAMS, JEFF Guitar. Member of Face Dancer since 1979.

ADAMS, JIMMY Vocal. Session for Ry Cooder (1979).

ADAMS, JUSTIN Guitar. Session for Fats Domino (1956).

ADAMS, MARK Harmonica. Session for Mike Bloomfield (1979).

ADAMS, PAULINE Vocal. Original member of the String Driven Thing, 1972-73.

ADAMS, PEPPER Saxophone. Session for Martin Mull (1974).

ADAMS, RICK Guitar. Replaced Dave Wellbelove in the Groundhogs, 1976.

ADAMS, TERRY Keyboards. Member of NRBQ.

ADAMSON, BARRY Bass, vocal. Member of Magazine since 1978. Session for Visage (1980).

ADAMSON, STUART Guitar. Member of the Skids, 1979.

ADAY, MARVIN LEE Real name of Meatloaf. See Meatloaf.

ADDABBO, STEVE Guitar, vocal. Member of Arbuckle, 1972.

ADELMAN, RICHARD Drums, conga. Session for Martin Mull (1972, 75, 77); Jonathan Edwards (1971-74).

ADELSTEIN, DAVID Keyboards. Session for Bob Welch (1979).

ADER, ROYSE Bass. Member of the Rubinoos, 1977-79.

ADERHOLD, K. Saxophone. Session for Triumvirat (1973).

ADKINS, ALAN Vocal, guitar. Member of Tears, 1979.

ADKINS, JOHN RAINEY Guitar. Member of the Candymen.

ADLER, LOU Producer. Founder of Ode and Dunhill Record Companies. Produced the Mamas and the Papas, Spirit, and others.

ADNOPOZ, ELLIOTT Real name of Ramblin' Jack Elliott. See Ramblin' Jack Elliott.

ADRIAN, DEAN Conga, vocal. Session for Martin Mull (1972); Jonathan Edwards (1972, 74).

AERIEL Laurie Currie—drums, vocal; Malcolm Buchanan—keyboards; Brian Miessner—bass, guitar, vocal; Gary O'Conner—guitar, bass, vocal. *Album:* In the Middle of the Night (CAP SW 11828) 1978.

AEROSMITH Tom Hamilton—bass; Joey Kramer—drums; Joe Perry—guitar; Steve Tyler—vocal; Brad Whitford—guitar. Rootless New England band whose talent was inversely proportionate to their success. *Albums:* Aerosmith (COL JC 32005) 1973; Draw the Line (COL JC 34856) 1977; Get Your Wings (COL JC 32847) 1974; Live Bootleg (COL JC 2 35564); Night in the Ruts (COL FC 36050) 1979; Rocks (COL JC 34165) 1976; Toys in the Attic (COL JC 33479) 1979; Greatest Hits (COL FL 36865) 1980.

AFDEM, JEFF Flute. One-time leader of the Springfield Rifle. *Album:* Magic Flute (FSM 7702).

AFFOLTER, TED Drums. Replaced Steve Williams in the Sand, 1976.

AGCAOILI, DEMO RAY Drums, percussion. Member of Laurie and the Sighs, 1980.

AGIUS, ALFIE Bass, vocal. Member of Interview since 1979.

AGNELLI, LAUREN Keyboards, vocal, guitar. Member of Nervus Rex, 1980.

AGNEW, PETE Bass, vocal. Original member of Nazareth, since 1972.

AGUBELLA, FRANCISCO Percussion. Session for the Doors' "Other Voices" (1971); Santana (1980).

AHERN, BRIAN Guitar. Session for Jonathan Edwards (1976, 77).

AHLADIS, JOE Guitar. Member of Mom's Apple Pie, 1973.

AHLADIS, PAT Drums. Member of Mom's Apple Pie, 1973.

AHRENDT, DIETER Drums, percussion. Member of Lake since 1977.

AHWAI, ROBERT Guitar. Session for Hummingbird (1976).

AIELLO, FRANCESCO Vocal. Member of Bedlam, 1973.

AIELLO, JERRY Keyboards. Member of the Stills-Young Band, 1976. Session for Steve Stills (1975-76); Firefall (1977).

AIKELS, RUDY Bass. Session for B. B. King (1975).

AIM Michael Overly—guitar, flute, vocal; Patrick O'Conner—bass; Warren Pemberton—drums; Loren Newkirk—keyboards. *Album:* Aim (BTM) 1974.

AINSWORTH, IAN Bass. Member of Quick,1976.

AIR FORCE Ginger Baker—drums, percussion; Steve Winwood—guitar, keyboards, vocal; Denny Laine—guitar; Chris Wood—saxophone, flute; Rick Grech—bass, violin; Graham Bond—saxophone; Jeanette Jacobs—vocals; Remi Kabaka—percussion. After the collapse of Blind Faith, Baker organized some of the most respected names in British jazz-rock circles. Like Faith, Air Force did not get off the ground. *Albums:* Ginger Baker's Air Force, Vol. I (ACO); Ginger Baker's Air Force, Vol. II (ACO) 1971.

AIR SUPPLY Russell Hitchcock—vocal; Graham Russell—vocal, guitar; Ralph Cooper—drums; David Moyse—guitar, vocal; Criston Baker—bass, vocal. *Albums:* Love and Other Bruises, 1977; Lost in Love (ARI 4268) 1980.

AIRBORNE Larry Stewart—vocal, guitar, keyboards, reeds; Beau Hill—vocal, guitar, keyboards; John Pierce—vocal, bass; David Zychek—vocal, guitar; Mike Baird—drums. *Album:* Airborne (COL JC 36076) 1979.

AIREY, DON Keyboards. Replaced David Stone in Rainbow, 1979. Member of the Michael Schenker Group, 1980.

AIROLDI, TONY Guitar, vocal. Member of Greezy Wheels.

AIRTO Drums, percussion, vocal, writer. Real name: Airto Moreira. Jazz percussionist popularizing the usage of the voice as a percussive instrument in modern jazz, in addition to supplying some excellent latin percussives as backing to many current jazz greats. Session for Stanley Clarke (1974); Paul Simon (1972-73); George Duke (1975); Full Moon (1972); Deodato; Santana (1974); Flora Purim (1978). *Albums:* Free (CTI 8000); Virgin Land, 1974; Fingers (CTI Q-6041); Natural Feelings (BUD 21); Seeds on the Ground (BUD 5085); Touching You . . . Touching Me (WBR K 3279).

AIRWAVES Ray Martinez—vocal, guitar, keyboards, horns; John David—vocal, bass, keyboards; Dave Charles—drums, percussion, vocal. *Albums:* New Day (AAM 4689) 1978; Next Stop (AAM 4763) 1979.

AITCHISON, IAN Saxophone, percussion. Member of the Greatest Show On Earth, 1970.

AITL, DAVE Drums. Member of the Suicide Commandos, 1978.

AKKERMAN, JAN Guitar, bass, lute, piano. First made his mark as guitarist of Holland-based Focus before soloing, working classical pieces into his own guitar compositions. *Albums:* Profile (SIR) 1972; Jan Akkerman (ATC 19159) 1977; Eli (ATC 18210) 1976; Live (ATC 19241) 1979; Sunshower (ATC 19193); Tabernakel (ACO 7032) 1973.

AKPAN, SONNY Percussion. Session for Phil Manzanera (1975).

ALABAMA Randy Owen—vocal, guitar; Jeff Cook—guitar, keyboards, vocal, fiddle; Teddy Gentry—bass, vocal; Mark Herndon—drums, vocal. *Album:* My Home's in Alabama (VIC AHLI-3644) 1980.

ALAMO Ken Woodley—organ, vocal; Larry Raspberry—guitar; Richard Rosebrough—drums; Larry Davis—bass. *Album:* Alamo (ACO 50 8279) 1971.

ALAN Drums. Member of Devo since 1978.

ALBANI, RIK Horns, vocal. Member of the Sunship, 1974.

ALBAUGH, BILL Drums. Member of the Lemon Pipers, 1968.

ALBERICO, SALVATORE, JR. Saxophone, clarinet. Member of Sail.

ALBERS, EEF Guitar. Member of Medusa, 1978. Session for Alan Price and Rob Hoeke (1977).

ALBIN, PETER Bass, vocal. Original member of Big Brother and the Holding Company.

ALBRECHT, JOEY Guitar, vocal. Member of Karthago, 1974.

ALBRECT, NORRIS Guitar. Member of Joy Division, 1979-80.

ALBRIGHT, NED Keyboards, guitar, vocal.Member of Tidbits.

ALBRIGHT, RICHIE Drums. Member of the Waylors, Waylon Jenning's backup band.

ALBRIGHTON, ROYCE Guitar, vocal. Member of Nektar, 1972-78.

ALBUM, PAUL Bass. Member of Chrysalis, 1968.

ALCIVAR, JAMES Keyboards. Member of Montrose, 1975-78, and Gamma since 1979. Session for 1994 (1979).

ALDA RESERVE Brad Ellis—keyboards, vocal, writer; Matthew "Chips" Patuto—drums, vocal; Tony Shanahan—bass, vocal; Mark Suall—guitar, vocal. *Album:* Love Goes On (SIR K-6079) 1979.

ALDCROFT, RANDY Trombone. Session for Ry Cooder (1978).

ALDER, CHUCK Bass. Member of Illusions.

ALDER, JOHN Guitar, keyboards. Member of the Jags, 1980.

ALDRIDGE, TOMMY Drums. Member of the Pat Travers Band.

ALESSI, BILLY Vocal. Half of the Alessi Brothers duo since 1976.

ALESSI, BOBBY Vocal. Half of the Alessi Brothers duo since 1976.

ALESSI BROTHERS Billy Alessi—vocal; Bobby Alessi—vocal. Session for Art Garfunkel (1979). *Albums:* Alessi (AAM 4608) 1976; All for a Reason (AAM 4657) 1977; Driftin' (AAM 4713) 1978; Words and Music (AAM 4776) 1979.

ALEXANDER, ARTHUR Guitar. Member of the Sorrows, 1980.

ALEXANDER, CHERYL Vocal. Member of Medusa, 1978.

ALEXANDER, DAVE Bass. Original member of the Stooges, 1968-69.

ALEXANDER, GARY Guitar, vocal. Original member of the Association. Session for Russ Giguere (1971).

ALEXANDER, GEORGE Bass. Member of the Flamin' Groovies, 1971.

ALEXANDER, JAMES Vocal. Member of the reformed Bar-Kays.

ALEXANDER, JOE Guitar, vocal. Member of Emperor, 1977.

ALEXANDER, LARRY Vocal. Member of Tornader, 1977.

ALEXANDER, WILLIE Piano, vocal. Member of Bagatelle, 1968, and the Arthur Gee-Whiz Band, 1971-72, before forming Willie Alexander and the Boom Boom Band, 1978. Session for Moon Martin (1978).

ALEXIS Randy Reeder—drums; Larry Braden—bass, vocal; Dave Peters—saxophone, synthesizer; Robbie Falberg—guitar; Eddie Ullibarri—vocal, keyboards; Dave Walker—keyboards, vocal. *Album:* Alexis, 1977.

ALIAS Dorman Cogburn; Jimmy Dougherty; Jo Jo Billingsley. *Album:* Contraband (MER SRM 1-3800) 1979.

ALIAS, DON Drums. Session with Carlos Santana—John McLaughlin's "Love, Devotion and Surrender" (1973); Ian Hunter (1976); Jaco Pastorius (1976); the Pages (1979).

ALIBI Nick Graham—vocal, bass, keyboards; Charlie Morgan—drums, vocal; Mark Fisher—keyboards, vocal; Geoff Sharkey—guitar, vocal. *Albums:* Friends (POL 16292) 1980.

ALINKOFF, ARTIE Drums. Member of the Floating Opera, 1971.

ALIVE 'N' KICKIN' Personnel not listed. *Album:* Alive 'n' Kickin', 1969.

ALL STARS See Cyril Davies and the All Stars.

ALLEN, ANGELA Vocal, keyboards. Member of Carmen, 1974. Session for Jethro Tull (1976).

ALLEN, ARVEE Recording name for Ritchie Valens on "Fast Freight" (1959).

ALLEN, BARRY Guitar, vocal. Member of Painter, 1973, and the Atlanta Rhythm Section since 1973. Session for Ironhorse (1979).

ALLEN, BRIAN Guitar. Member of Toronto,1980.

ALLEN, BRUCE B. C. Guitar, vocal. Member of the Suburbs, 1980.

ALLEN, CHAD Vocal, piano, guitar, mandolin, accordion, writer. Original member of Brave Belt, 1971.

ALLEN, CHARLES Vocal. Member of the reformed Bar-Kays.

ALLEN, CHARLIE Vocal, guitar. Member of Pacific Gas and Electric, 1973.

ALLEN, COLIN Drums. Replaced Jon Hiseman in John Mayall's Bluebreakers, 1969, before joining Stone the Crows, 1971-72. A member of Focus, 1973-75. Session for Mike Vernon; Gary Wright (1971); Donovan (1977); Rod Stewart (1980).

ALLEN, DAVE Guitar. Member of the Gang of Four, 1980.

ALLEN, DAVID Vocal, guitar. Member of the Soft Machine, and Carmen, 1974.

ALLEN, DEE Conga, percussion. Original member of War.

ALLEN, GARY Drums. Member of the Charlie Daniels Band.

ALLEN, JOE Bass. Session for Doug Kershaw (1972, 74); Waylon Jennings (1974-75).

ALLEN, LAURA Percussion, zither. Session for David Crosby (1970); Crosby and Nash (1976).

ALLEN, LAURIE Drums. Member of Formerly Fat Harry, 1971. Session for Robert Wyatt (1974).

ALLEN, LEE Tenor saxophone. Session for Fats Domino (1955-57); Dr. John (1972); Little Richard.

ALLEN, PETER Piano, vocal. *Albums:* All That Jazz (CAS 7198), 1976; Continental American (AAM 3643) 1979; It Is Time for Peter Allen (AAM 3706) 1977; I Could Have Been a Sailor (AAM 3706) 1979; Taught by Experts (AAM 4584) 1978; Bi-Coastal (AAM SP 4825) 1980.

ALLEN, RAY Saxophone, percussion, vocal. Member of the Contenders, 1979.

ALLEN, RICHARD Drums. Session for the Temptations, 1973.

ALLEN, RICK Drums. Member of Def Leppard, 1980.

ALLEN, RUSTEE Bass. Took over for James Dewar in Robin Trower's backup band, 1977-79.

ALLEN, SANDY Vocal, guitar, bass. Member of Free Beer, 1976.

ALLEN, SKIP Drums. Member of the Pretty Things.

ALLEN, STEVE Vocal. Member of the Original Mirrors, 1980.

ALLEN, STEVE Vocal, guitar. Member of 20/20, 1979. Session for the Tremblers (1980).

ALLEN, T. R., JR. Drums. Backup for Mink de Ville, 1977.

ALLEN, VERDEN Organ. Original member of Mott the Hoople, 1969-73.

ALLERHAND, PETE Guitar, vocal, keyboards. Member of Interview since 1979.

ALLISON, JERRY Drums, Vocal. Member of the Crickets, 1958-73. Session for Eric Clapton (1970).

ALLISON, KEITH Guitar. Session for Nilsson (1976).

ALLISON, VERN Vocal. Member of the Dells.

ALLMAN, DUANE "SKYDOG" Guitar, slide guitar, dobro. Born 11/20/46. With brother Gregg, a founder of the Allman Joys, Hourglass, 1968, and the Allman Brothers Band, which became the "Macon, Georgia sound" of Capricorn records. Equally at home on acoustic or electric guitar, he is most remembered for his mastery of the slide guitar. A motorcycle mishap led to his death, 10/29/71. Session for Boz Scaggs (1969); Wilson Pickett (1968-69); Clarence Carter (1967); Aretha Franklin (1969-70); King Curtis (1969); John Hammond (1969); Johnny Jenkins (1970); Delaney and Bonnie (1970-71); Cowboy (1971); Eric Clapton (1970); Otis Rush (1969); Ronnie Hawkins (1971); Sam Samudio (1971); Arthur Conley (1969); Lulu (1970); Herbie Mann (1971); Derek and the Dominoes (1970); Barry Goldberg Reunion (1969). *Albums:* Anthology of Duane Allman (CPN 2 CP 0108) 1972; Anthology, Volume 2 (CPN 2 CP 0139) 1973.

ALLMAN, GREGG Piano, guitar, vocal. Born 12/8/47. With brother Duane, he co-founded the Allman Joys, Hourglass, 1968, and the Allman Brothers Band. Since his brother's death in 1971, he has emerged from his brother's shadow as a songwriter in his own right, further refining the Macon sound of rock. With former wife Cher Bono, he recorded "Two the Hard Way," 1977, before forming the Gregg Allman Band, 1977, and re-forming the Allman Brothers, 1979 to present. *Albums:* Two the Hard Way (CPN) 1977; Laid Back (CPN 0116) 1973; Gregg Allman Tour (CPN 2C 0141) 1974.

GREGG ALLMAN BAND Gregg Allman—guitar, keyboards, vocal; Bill Stewart—drums; Neil Larsen—keyboards, synthesizer; Ricky Hirsch—guitar; Steve Beckmeier—guitar; John Hug—guitar; Willie Weeks—bass. *Album:* Playin' Up a Storm (CPN 0181) 1977.

ALLMAN BROTHERS BAND Duane Allman—slide guitar (until 1971); Gregg Allman—keyboards, vocal, guitar; Richard Betts—guitar; Berry Oakley—bass (until 1972); Jaimoe (Jai Johnny Johanson)—drums, percussion; Butch Trucks—drums, percussion; Chuck Leavell—keyboards (1973-76); Lamar Willams—bass (1972-76); Dan Toler—guitar (1979); David Goldflies—bass (1979). The Allman Brothers slid onto the rock scene rather precariously after an abortive attempt as Hourglass in Los Angeles. Duane Allman went to Florida to discover Betts and Oakley in Second Coming, returning with them to form his new group, the Allman Brothers. Their first two albums caused a quiet undercurrent before they exploded on the scene with a live double record in 1971. Duane Allman's unmistakable slide and lead guitar work, which he previously used as a session man for artists Wilson Pickett, Clarence Carter, Aretha Franklin and others, blended perfectly with brother Gregg's keyboard work and country flavored vocals. Then tragedy hit, with Duane's death in a motorcycle accident. "Eat a Peach" (1972) displayed his final work, some of his best with the group. Betts stepped into Duane's spot and to the delight of the critics hesitant to predict his success, Betts' guitar work was equally engaging. A year later, tragedy again struck the band when Oakley died. Williams replaced him, and Leavell was added to the lineup. Despite these tragedies the band released better and better music under the hands of Betts and Gregg Allman, altering their much-imitated "Macon sound" subtly toward country and western. Personality disputes led to the band's breakup in 1976, which were later resolved as the group re-formed in 1979. *Albums:* Allman Brothers Band (CPN 0196) 1970; Allman Brothers Band at the Fillmore East (CPN 2 CX 0131) 1971; Beginnings (ACO SD 2-805) 1973; Brothers and Sisters (CPN 0111) 1973; Eat a Peach (CPN 2-0102) 1972; Enlightened Rogues (CPN 0218) 1979; Idlewild South (CPN 0197) 1970; Reach for the Sky (ARI 9535) 1980; Win, Lose or Draw (CPN 0156) 1973; Wipe the Windows, Check the Oil, Dollar Gas (CPN 0177) 1976.

ALLMARK, DANNY Trombone. Session for the Keef Hartley Band (1971).

ALLRED, BYRON Keyboards. Session for Steve Miller (1977).

ALLSUP, MIKE Guitar. Member of Three Dog Night. Session for Kim Fowley.

ALLSUP, TOMMY Guitar, producer. Member of the Crickets. Session for Doug Kershaw; Leon Russell (1975); Bill Medley (1978). Produced Asleep at the Wheel (1976).

ALMAAS, STEVE Bass. Member of the Suicide Commandos, 1978.

ALMOND, JOHNNY Flute, saxophone. Became well known on John Mayall's "Turning Point" (1969), though he had been in the industry for several years previously. He joined Jon Mark to form Mark-Almond 1970-73, 1976. Session for Chicken Shack; the Keef Hartley Band (1971); Ben Sidran; Fleetwood Mac (1969); John Mayall's Bluesbreakers (1967); John Mayall (1977). *Album:* Johnny Almond's Music Machine (DRM).

ALOMAR, CARLOS Guitar. Member of Iggy Pop's backup band, 1977. Session for David Bowie (1977).

ALONGI, PETER Guitar, vocal. Member of Banchee, 1969.

ALOYA, RANDY Bass. Member of Kalapanna, 1973.

ALPHA BAND David Mansfield; "T-Bone" J. Henry Burnett; Steven Soles—vocal, guitar, keyboards. *Albums:* Spark in the Dark, 1977; Alpha Band, 1976; Statue Makers of Hollywood (ARI 4179).

ALPHONSO, RICK Trumpet. Session for Joe

Cocker (1972).

ALQUIN Ferdinand Bakker—guitar, piano, vocal; Ronald Ottenhoff—saxophone, flute; Dick Franssen—keyboards; Michael Van Dijk—vocal; Hein Mars—bass; Paul Westrate—drums, percussion; Job Tarenskeen—drums, percussion, saxophone, vocal. *Album:* Nobody Can Wait Forever (VIC) 1975.

ALQUIRE, DARRYL Guitar, vocal. Member of the Cooper Brothers Band since 1978.

ALTHEIMER, JOSHUA Piano. Session with Lonnie Johnson (1939).

ALTMAN, KENNY Bass. Member of White Horse, 1977. Session for John Sebastian (1971, 74, 76); Jules and the Polar Bears (1979).

ALTON, KENNY Bass, vocal. Member of the Fingerprintz, 1980.

ALTON, SHERON Guitar. Member of Toronto, 1980.

ALTRIELD, DON Percussion. Session for Jan and Dean (1963).

ALTSCHUL, MIKE Woodwinds. Session for the Mothers of Invention (1972); Frank Zappa (1972).

ALTSCHULER, RICK Drums. Member of the Rockicks, 1977.

ALVAREZ, DINO Drums. Member of the Jimmy Johnson Band, 1977.

ALVAREZ, RUBEN Drums, vocal. Session for John Mayall (1979).

ALVES, JOEY Guitar, vocal. Member of Yesterday and Today, 1976.

ALYWARD, MICHAEL Guitar, vocal. Member of Tin Huey, 1979.

AMANOR, COMPTON Guitar. Member of the Selecter, 1980.

AMAO, LOUGHTY Percussion, reeds, vocal. Member of Zzebra, 1974-75.

AMARAL, ROBERTO Vocal, percussion. Member of Carmen, 1974.

AMARANTHA, JORDON Percussion. Member of the Dija Rhythm Band, 1976.

AMARFIO, SOL Drums, percussion. Member of Osibisa. Session for the Hollies (1978).

AMARO, DAVID Guitar. Session for Airto (1974).

AMAZING BLONDEL Paul Kossoff—guitar; Eddie Baird—piano, vocal; Terry Wincott—guitar, vocal; Willy Murrey—drums; Mick Feat—bass. *Album:* Mulgrave Street, 1974.

AMAZING RHYTHM ACES Barry Burton—guitar, steel guitar, dobro, mandolin, vocal; Billy Earheart—keyboards; Butch McDade—drums, percussion, vocal; James Hooker—piano, vocal; Russell Smith—guitar, harmonica, vocal; Jeff Davis—bass, vocal. *Albums:* Stacked Deck, 1975; Too Stuffed To Jump, 1976; Amazing Rhythm Aces (COL JC 36083); Amazing Rhythm Aces (MCA AA-1123); How The Hell Do You Spell Rhythum (WBR BSK 3476).

AMAZING, STEPHEN Bass. Member of Upp, 1975-76.

AMBOY DUKES Ted Nugent—guitar; Steve Farmer—guitar; Dave Palmer—drums; Greg Arama—bass; Andy Solomon—keyboards; Rusty Day—vocal; Vic Mastrianni—drums, vocals (1974-75); Rob Grange—bass (1974-75); Derek St. Holmes—guitar (1975); Cliff Davies—drums, percussion, vocals. Hard rock group from Detroit. After struggling through personnel and label changes, they hit the charts in 1968 with "Journey to the Center of Your Mind," and quickly faded into the background. In 1974, Nugent resurfaced with some of the best rock 'n' roll of the year. In 1975, he dropped the Amboy Dukes name to start a solo career. See Ted Nugent. *Albums:* Amboy Dukes; Journey to the Center of Your Mind (MST) 1968; Journeys and Migrations; Nuggets (ELK); Dr. Slingshot, 1974.

AMBROSE, DAVE Bass. Member of Julie Driscoll, Brian Auger and the Trinity, 1968-69.

AMBROSIA Joe Puerta—bass, vocal; David Pack—guitar, vocal; Christopher Worth—keyboards, vocal (1975-78); Burleigh Drummond—drums; Royce Jones—vocal; David Lewis—keyboards. Formerly called the Sentrys. *Albums:* Ambrosia (WBR K-3181) 1975; Life Beyond L.A. (WBR I-3135) 1978; One Eighty (WBR K-3368) 1980; Somewhere I've Never Travelled (WBR K-3182) 1976.

AMBROSIA, JERRY Accordion. Session for Foghat (1979).

AMERICA Dewey Bunnell—guitar, vocal; Dan Peek—guitar, vocal (1971-78); Gerry Beckley—guitar, vocal. As the Beatles were imitated in the 1960s, so were the vocal harmonies of Crosby, Stills, Nash and Young in the 1970s. America was one of the more successful CSNY imitators. *Albums:* Alibi (CAP SOO-12098); America (WBR B-2576) 1971; America Live (WBR I-3136) 1977; Harbor (WBR BK-3017) 1977; Hat Trick (WBR B-2728) 1973; Hearts (WBR B-2852) 1975; Hideaway (WBR 2932) 1976; History (America's Greatest Hits) (WBR K-3110) 1975; Holiday (WBR 2808) 1974; Homecoming (WBR B-2655) 1972; Silent Letter (CAP SO-11950) 1979.

AMERICAN BREED Chuck Colbert; Gary Loizzo; Lee Graziano, Al Ciner. Rockers from the Midwest, they hit the national charts in 1968 with "Bend Me, Shape Me." Despite their patriotic names, they faded from the charts shortly thereafter. *Albums:* American Breed, 1967; Bend Me, Shape Me, 1968; Pumpkin, Powder, Scarlet and Green, 1968; Lonely Side of the City (PMT) 1968.

AMERICAN EAGLE Robert Lowery—vocal; Fred Zuefeldt—drums; Greg Beck—guitar; Gene Hubbard—keyboards. Pacific Northwest band that got their start as the Surprise Package in 1970. *Album:* American Eagle (COL).

AMERICAN TEARS Tommy Gunn—drums; Greg Baze—bass, guitar; Mark Mangold—keyboards. *Albums:* Branded, 1974; Tear Gas, 1975; Power, 1977.

AMEY, IAN Tich of Dave Dee, Dozy, Beaky, Mick

and Tich.

AMIS, DAVE Trombone. Member of Centipede, 1971.

AMOEBA Early name of the Seeds.

AMON DUUL Renate Knaup—vocal; Robby Heibl—vocal, bass, guitar, violin; Chris Karrer—vocal, guitar, banjo, violin; Peter Leopold—drums, percussion; Falk Rogner—keyboards; Nando Tischer—vocal, guitar; John Weinzierc—guitar. *Albums:* Carnival in Babylon; Dance of the Lemmings; Vive La Trance; Wolf City; Amon Duul (UAR) 1975.

AMOROSO, JERRY Drums, percussion, vocal. Member of Potliquor, 1979.

AMY, CURTIS Saxophone. Session for the Doors (1969).

ANAMAN, RON Bass, vocal. Member of Trillion, 1978-80.

ANDERLE, DAVID Producer. Produced Marc Benno; Rita Coolidge, 1972; the Ozark Mountain Daredevils, 1976; and others.

ANDERSEN, JOHN Drums. Member of Fludd, 1971, and the Silver Tractors, 1976.

ANDERSEN, SIGNE Vocal. Original vocalist of the Jefferson Airplane, replaced by Grace Slick.

ANDERSON, AL Guitar. Member of Bob Marley's Wailers, 1980.

ANDERSON, AL Guitar, vocal. Member of NRBQ. Session for Jonathan Edwards (1973); Martin Mull (1974).

ANDERSON, ANGRY Vocal. Member of Rose Tattoo, 1980.

ANDERSON, BENNY Vocal, guitar. Member of Abba since 1974.

ANDERSON, BLAIR Vocal, drums. Member of Whole Wheat, 1977, and Passion, 1979.

ANDERSON, BOB Bass. Original member of the James Cotton Blues Band and Charlie Musselwhite's Southside Band.

ANDERSON, BOB Saxophone, vocal. Member of Texas, 1973.

ANDERSON, CHARLEY Bass. Member of Selecter, 1980.

ANDERSON, CLEAVE Drums. Member of Battered Wives.

ANDERSON, DAVID D. Drums. Replaced Tony Gooden in the Son Seals Blues Band, 1980.

ANDERSON, DOUG Bass, guitar. Member of Tim Weisberg's backup band, 1973-76.

ANDERSON, ERIC Vocal, guitar. He came from the same school as Dylan, Phil Ochs and Judy Collins, a singer of his own songs. Unlike the others, he did not convert to electric sound in the 1960s, or become as famous. *Albums:* 'Bout Changes and Things (VAN 79206) 1966; Take 2 (VAN 79236) 1967; Best of Eric Anderson (VAN VSD 7/8); Blue River (COL C-31062); Country Dream (VAN 6540); More Hits from Tin Can Alley (VAN 79271) 1968; Today Is the Highway (VAN 79157) 1965; Be True to You (VAN).

ANDERSON, GARY Real name of Gary "U.S." Bonds.

ANDERSON, IAN Saxophone, guitar, mandolin, flute, piano, percussion, vocal, writer, producer. Born 8/10/47. Organizer and head of Jethro Tull since 1968. Session for Maddy Prior (1980).

ANDERSON, IKE Bass. Member of the Jimmy Johnson Band, 1977.

ANDERSON, JOHN Bass, vocal. Member of the Fugs, 1965-67, and Charlie since 1976.

ANDERSON, JON Vocal, writer. Founding member and lyricist for Yes, 1970-80. Like the other members of the group, he released a solo album, based on the group's reputation. Teamed up with keyboard soloist Vangelis for an album in 1979. Session for King Crimson; Colin Scot (1971). *Albums:* Olias of Sunhillow (ATC 18180) 1976; Short Stories (POL 1 6272) 1979; Song of Seven (ACO SD 16021) 1980.

ANDERSON, MAXINE Vocal. Session for Art Garfunkel (1979).

ANDERSON, MILLER Guitar, vocal. Original member of the Keef Hartley Band, 1969-71. Released a solo LP that remained virtually unknown. Came back into the limelight as a member of Savoy Brown's "Boogie Brothers," 1974, before teaming up with Hartley again in Dog Soldier, 1975. Resurfaced as a member of the Dukes, 1979. Session for Broken Glass (1976). *Album:* Bright City (LON) 1972.

ANDERSON, RICK Bass. Member of the Tubes, 1975 to present.

ANDERSON, ROBERTA JOAN Real name of Joni Mitchell.

ANDERSON, SHONA Vocal. Session for Maddy Prior (1980).

ANDERSON, TODD Reeds, piano, accordion. Member of the Loading Zone, 1968.

ANDES, MARK Bass, vocal. Started in Canned Heat, before becoming a member of Spirit, 1967-72, 1976. Bassist for Jo Jo Gunne, 1972-73. Member of Firefall since 1976. Session on John Fahey's "Regina."

ANDES, MATTHEW Guitar, vocal. Member of Jo Jo Gunne, 1972-73, and Spirit, 1976. Session for John Fahey.

ANDINO, REINOL Conga. Member of the Fabulous Rhinestones, 1972-73. Session for Doors (1969); John Sebastian (1970); Jim Morrison (1978).

ANDRE, WAYNE Trombone. Session for Eumir Deodato; Bruce Springsteen (1975); Steely Dan (1980).

ANDREJEWSKI, PAT Real name of Pat Benatar.

ANDREW, SAM Guitar, vocal. Original member of Big Brother and the Holding Company. Session for Janis Joplin (1969).

ANDREWS, BARRY Keyboards. Member of XTC, 1976-78. Session for Iggy Pop (1980).

ANDREWS, BOB Piano. Member of the Rumour, 1977. Session for Dave Edmunds (1975, 77);

Roy Sundholm (1979); Bram Tchaikovsky (1980); Carlene Carter (1980).

ANDREWS, BOB "DERWOOD" Guitar, vocal. Member of Generation X, 1978-79.

ANDREWS, DAVID Kazoo. Member of the Temple City Kazoo Orchestra, 1978.

ANDREWS, IDA Bassoon, flute, fife, vocal. Member of Wind in the Willows, 1968.

ANDREWS, MARK Guitar, vocal. Namesake of Mark Andrews and the Gents, 1980.

MARK ANDREWS AND THE GENTS Mark Andrews—guitar, vocal; Martin Sawtell—bass, vocal; Larry Tolfree—drums; Barry Lines—guitar, vocal; Brian Kemp—keyboards, vocal. *Album:* Big Boy (AAM SP 4812) 1980.

ANDRIDGE, RICK Drums. Original member of the Seeds, 1966.

ANGEL, DAVID Bass. Member of Boyzz, 1978.

ANGEL Punky Meadows—guitar; Mickie Jones—bass (1976-78); Greg Giuffria—keyboards; Barry Brandt—drums; Frank Dimlin—vocal; Not to be confused with the vocal group who recorded "My Boyfriend's Back" (1963)," these Angels first appeared in 1976, from the remnants of Bux. *Albums:* Angel (CAS 7021); Bad Publicity (CAS 7127); Helluva Band (CAS 7028) 1976; Live Without a Net (CAS 2-7203); On Earth As It Is in Heaven (CAS 7043) 1977; White Hot (CAS 7085) 1977; Sinful, 1979.

ANGEL CITY Doc Neeson—vocal; John Brewster—guitar, vocal; Rick Brewster—guitar, keyboards; Buzz Throckman—drums (1977-78); Graham Bidstrup—drums (1978-present); Chris Bailey—bass, vocal. Early name: the Angels. Australian hard rock in the AC/DC tradition. *Albums:* Face to Face (EPC NJE 36344) 1980; No Exit (Import) 1979; The Angels (Import) 1979; Dark Room (EPC JE 36543) 1980.

ANGELO Vocal, keyboards. Member of Flash Cadillac.

ANGELS Early name of Australian rockers Angel City.

ANGELS Recorded "My Boyfriend's Back," 1963.

ANGEROSA, PAUL Guitar. Member of Sail.

ANIMALS Eric Burdon—vocal (1962-68, 77); Alan Price—piano, vocal (until 1962); Andy Somers—guitar (1968); John Weider—guitar, violin, bass (1967-68); Luke Francis—guitar, vocal (until 1962); Hilton Valentine—guitar; Charles Chandler—bass (until 1967, 77); Dave Rowberry—organ (until 1967, 77); John Steele—drums (1962-66, 77); Barry Jenkins—drums, percussion (1968); Vic Briggs—guitar, bass (1967); Danny McCullough —bass, guitar, vocal (1968); George Bruno (Zoot Money)—keyboards, vocal (1967-68). The Alan Price Combo gained a new member, Eric Burdon, in 1962, and shortly thereafter became known as the Animals. Burdon's raspy black-sounding blues vocals contrasted greatly with the current fad of Beatlemania, but hits like "House of the Rising Sun" (1962), and "Don't Let Me Be Misunderstood" (1965) established the group's popularity. By then, Price had left with most of the group's original members. Burdon's name was featured, and with just cause, considering the length and magnitude of their success: "San Franciscan Nights," (1967), "Monterey," (1968), and "Sky Pilot," (1968). After a dynamic double release in 1968, on which the Animals expanded their blues style through jazz and country-western, the group broke apart. McCulloch and Briggs did unsuccessful solo work, while Burdon allegedly disappeared to do movies. He returned with War, however, in the 1970s. Price enjoyed some popularity with the release of his movie soundtrack, "O Lucky Man" in 1973. In a period of nostalgia when other "old" groups re-formed with updated sounds for their new audiences, the Animals re-formed in 1977, again demonstrating the sound that made them famous through the 1960s. *Albums:* The Animals (MGM) 1964; On Tour (MGM) 1965; Animal Tracks (MGM) 1965; Best of the Animals (MGM 4324) 1966; Animalization, 1966; Animalism (MGM) 1966; Eric Is Here (MGM) 1967; Best of Eric Burdon and the Animals, Vol. 2 (MGM 4454) 1967; Winds of Change (MGM 4484) 1967; Twain Shall Meet (MGM 4537) 1968; Every One of Us (MGM 4553) 1968; Love Is (MGM 4591) 1968; Before We Were So Rudely Interrupted (UAR JT-LA790-H) 1977.

ANISETTE Vocal. Featured vocalist of Savage Rose, 1969-71.

ANKA, PAUL Vocal. At the age of 15, he wrote his first hit, "Diana," in 1958. A puppy lover and a beach blanket bingo star, Canadian-born Anka penned hit after hit through the 1960s. Session for Jackie DeShannon (1979). *Albums:* Paul Anka—His Best (UAR LO-922); Anka Sings His Favorites (VIC ANLI- 1584) 1976; Anka's 21 Golden Hits (VIC AFLI- 2691) 1973; Best of Paul Anka (BUD 5704) 1977; 50 Years of Hit Songs (CDN ADL2-0779); Headlines (VIC AFLI-3382) 1979; Listen To Your Heart (VIC AFLI-2892) 1978; My Way (CDN ACLI-0616); Remember Diana (VIC ANLI-0896) 1975; Times of Your Life (UAR LO-569); Vintage Years 1957-1961 (SIR X-6043); Anka (UAR UA LA314G); Paul Anka (BUD 5093); Paul Anka Gold (SIR H-3704) 1974; Feelings (UAR UA-LA 03367-G); Jubilation (BUD 5114); The Painter (UAR LA653-G) 1976; The Musicman (UAR LA746-H) 1977; Big Hits, Vol. 2; Diana; Songs I Wish I'd Written; Strictly Nashville, 1966; Paul Anka Live, 1967; Anka at the Copa; Our Man around the World; Let's Sit This One Out; Young, Alive, and In Love; My Heart Sings; Paul Anka Swings for Young Lovers; 15 Songs, 1963.

ANNAN, TOM Drums. Member of R.A.F., 1980.

ANNIS, JOHN Bass. Member of the Holy Modal Rounders.

ANTHILL, DANNY Organ. Member of the Stingray, 1979.

ANTHONY, JOHN Tenor saxophone. Member of the Andy Bown group.

ANTHONY, JOHN Guitar, keyboards. Member of Wet Willie, 1972-79.

ANTHONY, MARK Vocal, guitar. Member of Hollywood Stars, 1977.

ANTHONY, MICHAEL Member of the Illinois Speed Press, 1969.

ANTHONY, MICHAEL Guitar. Session for Nilsson (1976).

ANTHONY, MICHAEL Bass. Member of Van Halen since 1978.

ANTONELLI, BOB Drums, percussion, vocal. Member of the Robbin Thompson Band, 1980.

ANTONI, ROBERT Keyboards, vocal. Member of Nazz, 1968-69.

ANY TROUBLE Clive Gregson—vocal, guitar, keyboards; Phil Barnes—bass, vocal; Chris Parks—guitar; Mel Harley—drums. *Album:* Where Are All the Nice Girls (STF USE 6) 1980.

APHRODITE'S CHILD Vangelis Papathanassiou—keyboards, flute, percussion, vibes, vocal; Demis Roussos—bass, vocal; Lucas Sideras—drums, vocal; Silver Koulouris—guitar, percussion. Jazz-rock Greek entry in the rock field. *Albums:* Aphrodite's Child (VTG 2-500) 1970; Rain and Tears, 1968; The Best of Aphrodite's Child, 1972.

APLANALP, RICHARD Flute, oboe, saxophone. Session for Shuggie Otis (1971).

APPEL, MARTIN J. Guitar. Member of Sweetbottom, 1978-79.

APPEL, MIKE Vocal. Session for Bruce Springsteen (1975).

APPICE, CARMINE Drums, vocal. Original member of Vanilla Fudge 1967-69, and Cactus, 1970-73. Also a member of the ill-received Beck, Bogart and Appice tour, 1973. In 1975, he was a member of the studio band KGB, and since 1978, Rod Stewart's backup band. Session for Jan Akkerman (1973); Jeff Beck (1973); Rod Stewart (1977); Ray Gomez (1980).

APPICE, VINNY Member of Axis, 1978.

APPLEBY, GEOFF Bass, harmonica, vocal. Session for Ian Hunter (1975).

APPLEJACK Harmonica. Early member of the Elvin Bishop Band. Session for Stephen Miller.

APRIL WINE Myles Goodwyn—vocal, guitar; Steve Lang—bass (1975-79); Gary Moffet—guitar, vocal; Brian Greenway—guitar, vocal; Jerry Mercer—drums (1971-79); David Henman—vocal, guitar, sitar; Ritchie Henman—percussion, keyboards; Jim Henman—vocal, bass, guitar; Jim Clench—bass (1974). Canadian rockers whose underground popularity in the U.S. has recently begun to grow. *Albums:* First Glance (CAP SW-11852) 1978; Harder . . . Faster (CAP ST-12013); Whole World's Goin' Crazy (LON PS-675) 1976; April Wine; Electric Jewels; Stand Back, 1974; April Wine, Live, 1974; Forever, For Now, 1976; Live at the El Macambo, 1977.

AQUAYE, NEEMOI Percussion. Session for the Faces (1973).

ARAMA, GREG Bass, vocal. Member of the Amboy Dukes, and Ursa Major, 1972.

ARBUCKLE Ronnie Fierstein—vocal, keyboards, guitar; Jan Flato—keyboards, vocal; Steve Addabbo—guitar, vocal; Gil Bowen—guitar, flute, vocal; Rolf Bernstein—drums; Joe de Chaves—bass. *Album:* Arbuckle (MSR 3243) 1972.

ARC Bobby Savene—bass, vocal; Wayne George—keyboards, vocal; Eddie Kosowski—guitar, vocal; Steve Szczesnaik—drums, vocal. *Album:* Arc (LFS JZ 35413) 1978.

ARCHER, CLIFFORD Bass. Member of Atlantic Starr, 1978-79.

ARCHER, JAMES Violin. Session for Mott the Hoople (1971).

ARDITO, RONALD Guitar, vocal, keyboards. Member of the Shirts, 1978-80.

ARDOLINI, TOM Drums. Member of NRBQ.

AREA CODE 615 Kenneth Buttrey—drums, percussion, vocal; David Briggs—keyboards; Mac Gayden—guitar, french horn, vocal; Charlie McCoy—harmonica, percussion, vocal; Wayne Moss—guitar, percussion; Weldon Myrick—steel guitar; Norbert Putnam—bass, cello; Buddy Spicher—fiddle, viola, cello, percussion; Bobby Thompson—banjo, guitar, percussion. After years of playing as session men to the most famous Nashville country and western stars, they banded together under a single name for two albums. Rarely played on radio, they were technically perfect, indicating why each member of that group was and is still playing as the best session men in their field and in their separate ventures. *Albums:* Area Code 615 (POL) 1968; Trip in the Country (POL) 1969.

AREAS, JOSE "CHEPITO" Timbales, percussion, conga. Original member of Santana 1969-74. Session for It's a Beautiful Day (1961); Santana (1977). *Album:* Jose Chepito Areas (COL) 1972.

AREKLEW, MICHAEL Guitar. Member of Blue Swede.

ARELLAND, DAVE Keyboards. Member of the Ides of March.

ARGENT, ROD Keyboards, vocal. After he left the Zombies in 1968, he co-founded the group bearing his name. Session for Trapeze (1972-73); Splinter (1977); Phoenix (1979).

ARGENT Rod Argent—keyboards, vocal, writer; Russ Ballard—guitar, piano, vocal (1970-75); Jim Rodford—bass, vocal, guitar; Robert Henrit—drums, percussion; Jim Grimaldi—guitar (1975-76); John Verity—guitar, vocal (1975-76). When the Zombies died in the wake of the English invasion, Rod Argent lent his name to a new group, which held together through the years with few personnel changes, demonstrating their musical determination with a unique brand of jazz-rock instrumentation. Ballard, who shouldered most of the songwriting chores from album to album, left on a solo career in 1975, to be replaced by Verity and Grimaldi. *Albums:* All Together Now (EPC 31556) 1972; Argent, 1970; Encore 1974; In Deep (EPC 32195) 1973; Nexus, 1974; Ring of Hands (EPC 30128) 1971; Circus, 1975; Argent Anthology (EPC 33955) 1975; Counterpoint, 1976.

ARIZONA Mary Dobbins—vocal; Ken Ashby—vocal, guitar; Willie Knowles—vocal, guitar; Doug Holzwarth—keyboards; Bob Huff—guitar, vocal; Pat Murphy—bass, vocal; Pete Kuch—drums. *Album:* Arizona, 1976.

ARMAGEDDON Keith Relf—vocal, harmonica; Martin Pugh—guitar; Bobby Caldwell—drums, percussion, vocal; Louis Cennamo—bass. Fresh from Renaissance, Relf joined Steamhammer's Martin Pugh, and Bobby Caldwell, from Johnny Winter and Captain Beyond, for his last recordings before his death in 1976. *Album:* Armageddon (AAM 4513) 1975.

ARMAND, RICK Guitar, vocal, piano. Member of 1994, 1979.

ARMATRADING, JOAN Vocal, guitar. *Albums:* Joan Armatrading (AAM 4588) 1976; Back to the Night (AAM 4525) 1975; Me Myself I (AAM 4809) 1980; Show Some Emotion (AAM S4663) 1977; Steppin' Out (AAM 4789) 1979; To the Limit (AAM 4732) 1978; Whatever's for Us (AAM 4382) 1972; Wild Geese (AAM 4730); How Cruel (AAM 3302) 1979.

ARMIGER, MARTIN Guitar, vocal. Member of the Sports since 1979.

ARMITT, IAN Keyboards. Session for Long John Baldry (1971-72).

ARMSTEAD, JOSHIE Vocal. Session for B. B. King (1971); Taj Mahal (1978).

ARMSTRONG, BILL Trumpet. Session for the Doobie Brothers (1980).

ARMSTRONG, DERRICK Bass, vocal. Member of Dayton, 1980.

ARMSTRONG, DAN Sitar. Session for the Doobie Brothers (1977).

ARMSTRONG, HERBIE Guitar, vocal. Member of Fox.

ARMSTRONG, JIM Guitar, sitar, drums. Replaced Billy Harrison in Them.

ARMSTRONG, LIL HARDIN Piano. Session with Lonnie Johnson (1941).

ARMSTRONG, PAUL Bass, percussion. Member of Country Joe and the Fish, 1966.

ARMSTRONG, TIPPY Guitar. Session for Don Nix (1971); Tony Joe White (1972); Roy Orbison (1979).

ARNESEN, PETE Piano. Member of the Rubettes. Session for Ian Hunter (1975); the Hollies (1978-79).

ARNEZ, DESI, JR. Drums. Son of Lucille Ball and Desi Arnez and original member Dino, Desi and Billy, 1965-67.

ARNOLD, HARVEY Bass, vocal. Member of the Outlaws, 1975-79.

ARNOLD, JEROME Bass. Member of Paul Butterfield's Blues Band, 1965-67.

ARNOLD, JIM Guitar. Member of the Jonathan Cain Band, 1977.

ARNOLD, JOE Tenor saxophone. Session for Boz Scaggs (1969); Wilson Pickett; Clarence Carter (1967).

ARNOLD, LEONARD Guitar. Member of Blue Steel, 1980.

ARNOLD, PAT Vocal. Session for Nils Lofgren (1967); Sky (1970); Gary Wright (1971); Freddie King (1974); Small Faces (1977); Eric Burdon (1977).

ARNOLD, ROBERT Bass, tuba, percussion, vocal. Member of Sod, 1971.

ARNOLD, VANCE One time recording name of Joe Cocker.

ARNOT, CURT Bass, vocal. Member of Edge, 1980.

ARNOTT, RAY Drums. Member of Flash and the Pan since 1979.

ARROGANCE Don Dixon—vocal, bass, percussion, guitar; Robert Kirkland—vocal, guitar, percussion; Scott Davidson—drums, percussion; Marty Stout—keyboards; Rod Abernathy—guitar (1980). *Albums:* Suddenly (WBR K-3429) 1980; Rumors (VAN) 1976.

ARS NOVA Wyatt Day—guitar; Jon Pierson—vocal, trombone; Sam Brown—guitar; Jimmy Owens—horns; Art Koenig—bass; Joe Hunt—drums; Maury Baker; Bill Folwell; Giovanni Papalia; Jonathan Raskin. The merger of rock and classical music was an inevitable experiment of the 1960s. Ars Nova was a group of classical musicians who mixed rock with baroque and medieval settings in their compositions. Though extremely unique and technically professional, their short career proved that even tasteful novelty is not always commercial. *Albums:* Ars Nova (ELK) 1968; Sunshine and Shadows (ELK) 1969.

ART Mike Harrison—keyboards, vocal; Greg Ridley—bass; Mike Kellie—drums, percussion; Luther Grosvenor—guitar. Original name of Spooky Tooth, prior to Gary Wright's membership. *Album:* Supernatural Fairy Tale (Import) 1967.

ARTFUL DODGER Steve Grigida—drums; Gary Cox—guitar (1975-79); Steve Cooper—bass; Gary Herrewig—guitar; Billy Paliselli—vocal; Peter Bonita—piano (1980). *Albums:* Rave On (ARA 1503) 1980; Artful Dodger (COL) 1975; Honor Among Thieves (COL PC 34273) 1976; Babes on Broadway, 1977.

ARTHUR, JEFFREY Guitar, vocal. Member of Arthur, Hurley and Gottlieb, 1975.

ARTHUR, HURLEY AND GOTTLIEB Jeffrey Arthur—guitar, vocal; Michael Hurley—vocal; Neil Gottlieb—vocal. *Album:* Sunlight Shinin' (AAM) 1975.

ARTHURS, LEAM Bass. Session for Bill Nelson (1971).

ARTHURWORRY, LOUISE Vocal. Session for Ginger Baker (1977).

ARVANITAS, GEORGE Piano. Session for T-Bone Walker (1973).

ARVIZU, ERSI Vocal, percussion. Member of El Chicano.

ASCHER, KENNY Keyboards, mellotron. Session for John Lennon (1973); Nilsson (1974); the Plastic Ono Band (1974); Carly Simon (1974); Johnny Winter (1974); Dr. John (1975); Leslie West (1976).

ASH, LESLIE Vocal. Session for Donovan (1973).

ASHBY, KEN Vocal, guitar. Member of Arizona, 1976.

ASHER, JAMES Drums. Session for Pete Townsend (1980).

ASHER, PETER Vocal, producer. Born 6/22/44. Half of the 1960s Peter and Gordon team, and manager for James Taylor. Producer for Tony Joe White (1971); Linda Ronstadt. Session for James Taylor (1976).

ASHETON, RON Guitar. Original member of the Stooges, 1967-69.

ASHETON, SCOTT Drums. With brother Ron, an original member of the Stooges, 1967-69.

ASHFORD, JACK Trombone, percussion. Session for Bob Seger (1973); the Temptations (1973).

ASHFORD, NICKLAS Vocal. Half of the husband-wife duet Ashford and Simpson, since 1973.

ASHFORD, ROSALIND Vocal. Original member of Martha and the Vandellas.

ASHFORD, TED Organ. Session for Country Joe McDonald (1975); Mike Bloomfield (1978).

ASHFORD AND SIMPSON Nicklas Ashford —vocal; Valerie Simpson—vocal. Husband and wife vocal duet. *Albums:* Come As You Are (WBR B-2858) 1976; Gimme Something Real (WBR 8-2739) 1973; I Wanna Be Selfish (WBR B-2789) 1974; Is It Still Good to Ya (WBR K-3319) 1977; Musical Affair (WBR HS-3458) 1980; Send It WBR B-3008) 1977; So So Satisfied (WBR 2992) 1977; Stay Free (WBR HS-3357) 1979.

ASHLEE, BILL Bass, vocal. Session for Barry Melton (1978).

ASHLEY, DEL One time pseudonym for David Gates.

ASHTON, MARK Drums, guitar, vocal. Member of Rare Bird, 1969-72, and Headstone, 1974-75. *Album:* Mark Ashton, 1976.

ASHTON, TONY Keyboards. Member of Medicine Head, 1973, Ox, 1975, and Paice, Ashton, Lord, 1977. Session for George Harrison (1968); John Entwhistle (1972); Chicken Shack (1973); Jerry Lee Lewis (1973); Deep Purple; Broken Glass (1976); Wings (1979).

ASHTON, WILLIAM HOWARD Real name of Billy J. Kramer.

ASKEW, ADRIEN Keyboards, vocal. Member of Lucifer's Friend, 1978-80.

ASLEEP AT THE WHEEL Chris O'Connell—vocal, guitar; Ray Benson—vocal, guitar; Link Davis, Jr.—saxophone, fiddle; Floyd Domino—keyboards; Tony Garnier—bass; Scott Hennige—drums; Danny Levin—fiddle, mandolin; Bill Mabry —fiddle; Lucky Oceans—pedal steel guitar; Leroy Preston—vocal, guitar. Popular country-swing band. *Albums:* Collision Course (CAP SW-11726); Comin' Right At Ya (UAR LW-038) 1973; Fathers and Sons (EPC BG-33782); Framed (MCA 5131); Served Live (CAP ST-11995) 1979; The Wheel (CAP ST-11620) 1977; Wheelin' and Dealin' (CAP ST-11546) 1976; Texas Gold (CAP ST-11441) 1975.

ASPERY, RON Saxophone, flute, piano. Member of Back Door, 1972-73. Session for Roger Glover (1968); Frankie Miller (1979); Oxendale and Shephard (1979); the Who (1980); Alibi (1980).

ASSOCIATION Russ Giguere—vocal; Brian Cole —vocal, bass; Ted Bluechel—vocal, drums; Gary Alexander—guitar, vocal; Terry Kirkman—vocal; Jim Yester—vocal, guitar. Originally called Men. Group vocal techniques began refining through the 1960s in rock. Outside of the Beach Boys, the fresh sounds of the Association's harmony in "Windy," "Cherish" and "Along Comes Mary" (1967) were the best around. The group, however, disappeared in 1968. In 1976 a rumor was circulated about their reunion, but was unrealized. *Albums:* Association's Greatest hits; Waterbeds in Trinidad; Along Comes Mary (VLT 25002); Renaissance.

ASTON, JOHN Guitar. Member of the Psychedelic Furs, 1980.

ASYLUM CHOIR Leon Russell—vocals, guitar, keyboards; Marc Benno—vocals, drums. Two man band that served as a starting place for two separate, more successful solo careers. *Albums:* Look Inside the Asylum Choir (SMS) 1968; Asylum Choir II (SMS) 1969.

ATAMANUIK, PETER Member of Seatrain.

ATCHISON, DAN Bass. Member of Stonebolt, 1978-80.

ATHEY, DIANNE Bass. Member of Nervus Rex, 1980.

ATHLETICO SPIZZ 80 Spizz—vocal, guitar; Jim Solar—bass; Mark Coalfield—keyboards, vocal; C. P. Snare—drums; Dave Scott—guitar. *Album:* Do a Runner (AAM 4838) 1980.

ATILLO Synthesizer. Member of the Sand, 1976.

ATKINS, DON Guitar. Member of the Music Explosion, 1967.

ATKINSON, PAUL Guitar, violin, harmonica. Member of the Zombies, 1965-68.

ATLANTA RHYTHM SECTION Ronnie Hammond—vocal; Barry Allen—guitar; Dean Daugherty—keyboards; J. R. Cobb—guitar; Robert Nix—drums (1972-78); Roy Yeager—drums (1979-present); Paul Goodard—bass. Originally started as the backup band for Roy Orbison. *Albums:* Are You Ready (POL 2-6236); Atlanta Rhythm Section (MCA 2-4114) 1973; Boys from Doraville (POL 1-6285) 1980; Champagne Jam (POL 1-6134) 1978; Dog Days (POL 6041) 1975; Red Tape (POL 6060) 1976; Rock and Roll Alternatives (POL S-1-6080) 1976; Third Annual Pipe Dream (POL 6027) 1974; Undergod (POL 1-6200).

ATLANTIC STARR Clifford Archer—bass; Sharon Bryant—vocal, percussion; Porter Carroll, Jr.—drums, vocal; Joseph Phillips—percussion, flute; David Lewis—guitar, vocal; Jonathan Lewis—trombone, percussion; Wayne Lewis—keyboards, vocal; Damon Rentte—reeds; William Sudderth—trumpet. *Albums:* Atlantic Starr (AAM 4711) 1978; Straight to the Point (AAM 4764) 1979.

ATLANTICS Ray Fernandez—drums, vocal, percussion; Tom Hauck—guitar, vocal; B. Wilkinson—bass, vocal, keyboards; Fred Pineau—guitar; Bobby Marron—vocal. *Album:* Big City Rock (MCA AA-1134) 1979.

ATLANTIS PHILHARMONIC Joe di Fazio—keyboards, bass, vocal; Royce Gibson—percussion, vocal. *Album:* Atlantis Philharmonic (DHM 802) 1974.

ATOMIC ROOSTER Vincent Crane—keyboards, vocal; John Cann—guitar, vocal (1972); Paul Hammond—drums, percussion (until 1971); Carl Palmer—drums, percussion; Pete Frenchy—vocal (1971); Chris Farlowe—vocal (1971-73); Ric Parnell—drums, percussion (1972); Steve Bolton—guitar (1972); Johnny Mandala—guitar (1973). Most knowledgeable rockers remember Arthur Brown's classic "Fire" in 1967. Arranger and mastermind of Brown's show was keyboard man Vincent Crane, who formed Atomic Rooster with drummer Carl Palmer (of Emerson, Lake and Palmer) after the Brown tour. Various personnel changes led to the acquisition of premier vocalist, Chris Farlowe, from Colosseum. Though very talented, personnel changes forced the disbanding of the group. *Albums:* Death Walks Behind You (EKS 74094) 1971; In Hearing of Atomic Rooster (EKS 74109) 1971; Made in England (EKS 75039) 1972; IV (EKS 75074) 1973.

ATTITUDES Jim Keltner—drums; Paul Stallworth—bass; Danny Kootch—guitar; Dave Foster—keyboards. Studio band formed of session men from George Harrison's Dark Horse record company. *Albums:* Good News (DKH 3021) 1976; Attitudes II (DKH) 1976.

ATTRACTIONS Steve Nieve—keyboards; Bruce Thomas—bass; Pete Thomas—drums. Elvis Costello's backup band.

ATWOOD, BILL Trumpet. Original member of the Sir Douglas Quintet 1965-68. Session for It's a Beautiful Day (1971); Lamb (1971).

AUDIENCE Keith Gemmell—saxophone, clarinet, flute; Howard Werth—guitar, vocal; Trevor Williams—bass; Tony Conner—percussion, vibes. *Albums:* House on the Hill (ELK 74100) 1971; Lunch (ELK 75026) 1972.

AUGER, BRIAN Keyboards, vocal. Began in Steam Packet, 1965. An original member of the Trinity, with Julie Driscoll, 1968-69, (when he was voted "Brightest Hope" in music by Melody Maker) before realizing his jazz inclinations by forming Oblivion Express, 1971-77. See Oblivion Express.

AUGER, FRANCOIS Drums, percussion. Member of Heldon, 1976. Session for Richard Pinhas (1977).

AUGUST, JACK Bass, vocal. Member of Moonquake, 1975.

AUGUSTINE, CHRISTOPHER Drums. Member of Every Mother's Son, 1967-68.

AULDRIDGE, MIKE Dobro, pedal steel guitar. Session for Jonathan Edwards (1977). *Albums:* Mike Auldridge (FLF 029) 1976; Auldridge and Old Dog (FLF 054) 1977; Blues and Blue Grass (TKM 1062) 1974; Critic's Choice (TKM 1062); Dobro (TKM 1033); Slidin' Smoke (FLF 080).

AULDRIDGE, TOMMY Drums. Member of the Pat Travers Band.

AURACLE Richard Braun—trumpet, flugelhorn; Stephen Fujala—reeds; Biff Hannon—keyboards (1979); Steven Rehbein—percussion; Jerry Serry, Jr.—keyboards (1978); Ron Wagner—drums; Bill Staebell—bass. *Albums:* City Slickers (CYS 1210) 1979; Glider (CYS 1172) 1978.

AURRA Curt Jones—vocal, guitar, percussion; Charles Carter—keyboards, reeds, percussion, vocal; Starleana Young—vocal; Buddy Hank—bass. *Album:* Aurra (WIZ 1302) 1980.

AUSTIN, DEREK Keyboards. Session for the Keef Hartley Band (1971); the Alvin Lee Band (1980).

AUSTIN, PATTI Vocal. Session for Marshall Tucker (1980); the Blues Brothers (1980); Steely Dan (1980).

AUSTIN, PAUL Vocal. Session for Paul Simon (1980).

AUSTIN, STUART Drums, vocal. Member of Tin Huey, 1979.

AUSTRIA, JAIME Bass. Original member of Stardrive, 1974.

AUTOMATIC MAN Pat Thrall—guitar; Bayette—vocal, keyboards; Jerome Rimson—bass (1977); Doni Harvey—bass (1976); Glenn Symmonds—drums (1977); Michael Shrieve—drums (1976). *Albums:* Automatic Man (ISL 9397) 1976; Visitors (ISL 9429) 1977.

AUTOSALVAGE Thomas Danaher—vocal, guitar; Darius LaNoue Davenport—vocal, oboe, keyboards, drums, trombone, guitar, bass, percussion; Rick Turner—guitar, banjo; Skip Booge—bass, piano. The flood of no-talent groups cashing in on the music scene of 1968 often times obscured the talented groups. Autosalvage was one of the talented groups to be drowned by the deluge. *Album:* Autosalvage, 1968.

AVALANCHE Tony Naylor—guitar, vocal; Clive Harrison—bass, vocal; Geoff Cox—drums; Adrian Campbell—vocal. *Album:* Avalanche, 1976.

AVALON, FRANKIE Vocal. By the time the surf fad hit in the 1960s, Avalon had been a star for years. First appeared in 1959 with "Venus." *Albums:* Venus (DLT 2020); You're My Life (DLT DSR-9504).

AVANT, FRANK Guitar. Member of the Other Side.

AVENGERS Penelope Houston—vocal; John Wilsy—bass, vocal; D. Furious—drums, vocal; Greg Ingraham—guitar. *Album:* Avengers (WNR 002) 1979.

AVERAGE, JOHNNY Vocal, guitar, keyboards. Head of the Johnny Average Dance Band, 1980.

JOHNNY AVERAGE DANCE BAND Johnny Average—vocal, guitar, keyboards; Frank Campbell —bass; Billy Mundi—drums; Gary Windo—saxophone; Ian Bennett—saxophone; Donn Adams—trombone. *Album:* Some People (BSV 3514) 1980.

AVERAGE WHITE BAND Alan Gorrie—vocal, bass; Hamish Stuart—vocal, guitar, bass; Roger Ball—keyboards, saxophone; Onnie McIntyre—vocal, guitar; Malcom Duncan—saxophone; Robbie McIntosh—drums, percussion; Steve Ferrone—drums, percussion (1978-present). Scottish white soul band that rode the crest of the funk rage that began in 1974. *Albums:* Average White Band (ATC 19116) 1974; Average White Band, Volume 8 (ATC 19266) 1980; Benny and Us (ATC 19105) 1977; Cut the Cake (ATC 18140) 1975; Feel No Fret (ATC 19207); Person to Person (ATC 2-1002); Put It Where You Want It (MCA 475) 1975; Shine (ARI 9523) 1980; Soul Searching (ATC 18179) 1976; Warmer Communications (ATC 19162) 1978.

AVERRE, BERTON Guitar. Member of the Knack, 1979-80.

AVERY, BOB Drums, harmonica. Member of the Music Explosion, 1967.

AVERY, ELLA Vocal. Member of Wet Willie, 1974-79.

AVIARY Brad Love—keyboards, vocal; Paul Madden—keyboards; Ken Steimonts—bass, vocal; Toby Bowen—guitar; Richard Bryans—drums, vocal. *Albums:* Aviary (EPC IE 35716) 1979.

AVIATOR Mick Rogers—guitar, vocal; Clive Bunker —drums, percussion; John G. Perry—bass, vocal; Jack Lancaster—reeds, keyboards. Little known group of talent collected from some of the finest British bands: Rogers from Manfred Mann; Bunker from Jethro Tull; Lancaster from Blodwyn Pig. *Albums:* Aviator (EIA 17012) 1979; Turbulence (EIA SW-17028).

AVORY, MICK Drums. Born 2/15/44. Original member of the Kinks, since 1964.

AVSEL, MARK Keyboards, vocal. Member of Breathless, 1979.

AXE Teddy Mueller—drums; Michael Osborne—guitar; Michael Turpin—bass; Bobby Barth—guitar; Edgar Riley, Jr.—vocal. *Albums:* Axe (MCA 3171) 1979; Living on the Edge (MCA 3224) 1980.

AXIS Vinny Appice; Danny Johnson; Jay Davis. *Album:* Circus World (RCA AFL1-2950) 1978.

AXTON, HOYT Vocal, guitar. Freelance folk singer/writer influenced by country blues roots. *Albums:* Fearless (AAM 4571) 1976; Free Sailin; (MCA 2319) 1978; Less Than the Song (AAM 4376) 1973; Life Machine (AAM 3604) 1974; My Griffin is Gone (COL C-33103); Rusty Old Halo (JER 5000) 1979; Snowblind Friend (MCA 2233); Southbound (AAM 4510); Where Did the Money Go (JH 50001) 1980.

AYERS ROCK Jimmy Doyle—guitar; Duncan McGuire—bass; Col Loughman—saxophone, flute, keyboards, vocal; Chris Brown—guitar, vocal; Mark Kennedy—drums, percussion. Australia's 1975 entry into the United States' rock markets. *Albums:* Big Red Rock (AAM) 1975; Beyond (AAM) 1976.

AYERS, KEVIN Guitar, vocal. Original member of the Soft Machine. Session with Eno, John Cale, Nico (1974). *Albums:* Bananamour (SAS 7406) 1973; Confessions of Dr. Dream (ILS 9263) 1974; Yes, We Have No Mananas (ABC 1021) 1977; Rainbow Takeaway; June 1, 1974 (ILS 9291) 1974; Whatever She Brings, We Sing; Joy of a Toy.

AYERS, MARK Keyboards. Member of Mariah, 1976.

AYERS, VIRGINIA Vocal. Session for Joe Cocker (1972).

AYIVOR, KOFI Congas, percussion. Member of Osibisa.

AYKROYD, DAN Vocal, harmonica. Recording name: Elwood Blues. "Saturday Night Live" comedian whose parody of blues musicians (with John Belushi as Joliet Jake Blues) became a success of its own as the Blues Brothers.

AYLMER, CHRIS Bass. Member of Samson, 1980.

AYOUB, JAMES Drums, percussion. Original member of Mahogany Rush, 1974-present.

AZEVEDO, MIKE Percussion. Member of Caldera, 1976-78.

AZTEC TWO STEP Rex Fowler; Neal Shulman. *Albums:* Two's Company, 1976; Aztec Two Step (ELK 75031) 1972; Second Step (VIC AFLI-1161); Times of Our Lives (WH 9) 1979.

B-52'S Cindy Wilson—vocal, percussion, guitars; Kate Pierson—vocal, keyboards, guitar; Fred Schneider—vocal, keyboards; Keith Strickland—drums; Ricky Wilson—guitar. Eccentric appearance coupled with dance music from Athens, Georgia. *Albums:* The B-52's (WBR K-3355) 1980; Wild Planet (WBR BSK 3471) 1980.

B., STEVIE Guitar. Member of the Tom Robinson Band since 1978.

B. J. Guitar, vocal. Member of Sweathog, 1973.

BA-FA BAND Michael Parker—keyboards; Randall Foote—percussion, vocal; Barry Pullman—organ, moog; Peter Lyon—guitar. Backup band for the Hudson Brothers, 1976.

BAAC, ROCKY Drums. Member of Bux, 1976.

BAAH, REBOP KWAKU See Rebop.

BABB, MIKE Bass. Member of High Cotton, 1975.

BABBINGTON, ROY Acoustic bass, bass. Member of Centipede, 1971, and the Soft Machine. Session for Chris Youlden (1973).

BABBIT, BOB Bass. Played on posthumous Hendrix albums, "Crash Landing" and "Midnight Lightning" (1975). Session for the Temptations (1973); Alice Cooper (1976); Mark Farner (1977); Taj Mahal (1978); John Mayall (1979); Elton John (1979); Nils Lofgren (1979); the Michael Zager Band; the Euclid Beach Band (1979).

BABBOZZA, TYRONE Vocal. Session for Henry Gross (1973).

BABE RUTH Janita "Jenny" Haan—vocals, percussion (until 1976); Alan Shacklock—guitar, keyboards, vocal, percussion (until 1976); Ed Spevock—drums, percussion; Dave Hewitt—bass (until 1976); Steve Gurl—keyboards, moog; Ellie Hope—vocal (1976); Bernie Marsden—guitar; Ray Knott—bass (1976); Dick Powell—violin. *Albums:* Amar Caballero (HAR); Babe Ruth (HAR ST 11367); First Base (HAR SW-11151); Kids Stuff, 1976; Stealin' Home, 1975.

BABY Brian Keenan—drums; John Platana—guitar; Mitch Styles—guitar; Nick Oliva—keyboards; Peter Hodgson—bass; Bernard Williams—percussion. Backup band for Genya Ravan on her solo debut.

BABY Johnny Lee Schell—guitar, organ, vocal; John Camp—guitar, vocal; Stephen Crane—bass, vocal; Woody Putnam—drums. *Albums:* Baby, 1975; Where Did All the Money Go, 1976.

BABY GRAND David Kagan—vocal; Rob Hyman—keyboards, vocal; Eric Bazilian—guitar, vocal. *Albums:* Ancient Medicine (ARI 4200) 1978; Baby Grand (ARI 4148) 1977.

BABY RAY AND THE FERNS Early name for Frank Zappa and the Mothers of Invention.

BABYS John Waite—vocal, bass; Michael Corby—guitar, keyboard; Wally Stocker—guitar; Tony Brock—drums, vocal; Ricky Phillips—bass (1980). *Albums:* The Babys (CYS 1129) 1976; Broken Heart (CYS 1150) 1977; Head First (CYS 1195) 1978; Union Jacks (CYS 1267) 1979.

BACCHIOCCHI, RON Keyboards. Session for the Randle Chowning Band (1978).

BACH, BYRON T. Cello. Session for Waylon Jennings (1973).

BACHMAN, RANDY Guitar, vocal, producer. Mastermind behind Bachman-Turner Overdrive, 1973-78. He broke into the pop field in the Guess Who in 1969. He left in 1971 to form Brave Belt with Chad Allen. After poor public reception, Bachman changed the format of Belt, dropping Allen, to capture the spotlight of hard rock with Overdrive. Retiring from the BTO formula for a brief solo attempt he returned in 1979 with Ironhorse. *Album:* Survivor, 1978.

BACHMAN, ROB Drums, percussion. Brother of Randy Bachman and original member of Brave Belt, 1971, and Bachman-Turner Overdrive, 1973-79.

BACHMAN, TIM Guitar, vocal. Brother of Randy Bachman, and original member of Bachman-Turner Overdrive, 1973-74.

BACHMAN–TURNER OVERDRIVE Randy Bachman—guitar, vocal, producer (1973-78); Rob Bachman—drums, percussion; C.F. Turner—bass, guitar, vocal (1973-74); Blair Thornton—guitar, vocal (1974-79); Jim Clench—bass, vocal (1978-79). After retiring from the commercial success of Guess Who, and suffering through the poor reception of Brave Belt, Canadian Randy Bachman returned to the drawing board and returned with a masterfully engineered group and sound to cash in on the rock market. Featuring alternating lead guitars and Turner's gruff vocals, Bachman tailored the group's output to a specific formula aimed at the popular market. *Albums:* BTO (MER ML-8011) 1973; Bachman-Turner Overdrive II (MER SRM-1-696) 1973; Best of Bachman-Turner Overdrive (MER SRM-1-696); Best Of Bachman-Turner Overdrive (MER SRM-1-1101); Not Fragile (MER SRM-1-1004) 1974; Rock 'N' Roll Nights (MER SRM-1-3748) 1979; Street Action (MER SRM-1-3713) 1978; Four Wheel Drive (MER) 1974; Head On (MER) 1975; Freeways (MER) 1977.

BACK DOOR Ron Aspery—saxophone, flute, piano; Colin Hodgkinson—vocal, bass; Tony Hicks—drums. *Albums:* Back Door (WBR) 1972; 8th

Street Nites (WBR) 1973.

BACKSTREET CRAWLER Paul Kossoff—guitar (1975-76); Terry Wilson—bass; Mike Montgomery—keyboards, vocal (1975-76); Tony Braunagle—drums; Terry Wilson-Slesser—vocal; John Bundrick—keyboards, vocal (1976). The formation of super group Bad Company brought much attention to some of its member's roots. Kossoff, as a member of Free with Paul Rodgers and Simon Kirke, began to get some of his due publicity as a formidable guitarist with the release of his solo album "Back Street Crawler," 1973, featuring various English session men. He remained in the undercurrents, his name always popping up, until he formed the group bearing the title of his solo album in 1975, showcasing Wilson-Slesser's haunting vocals. Writer Montgomery left in 1976, to be replaced by former Free member Bundrick. That same year Kossoff died. "2nd Street" features his final work. See Crawler. *Albums:* The Band Plays On (ATC 36 125) 1975; 2nd Street (ATC) 1976.

BACKUS, DONNIE Keyboards. Member of the Rockets, 1979-present.

BACON, BILL Drums, percussion. Member of Flying Island, 1976.

BACON, MAURICE Drums. Member of Love Affair.

BACUS, DON Vocal. Member of the Del Vikings.

BACUS, RICK Guitar, keyboards, chimes, vocal. Member of Morningstar, 1979.

BAD BOY Steve Grimm—guitar, vocal; Joe La Vie—guitar, vocal; Lars Hanson—drums; John Marcelli—bass. *Albums:* Back to Back (UAR LT 869) 1978; Band That Milwaukee Made Famous (UAR LT 781).

BAD COMPANY Paul Rodgers—vocal, piano, guitar; Simon Kirke—drums, percussion; Boz Burrell—bass; Mick Ralphs—guitar, keyboards. The first group to record on Led Zeppelin's own record label, Swan Song (1974). According to publicity, Bad Company was the supergroup of 1974. They had obviously paid their dues: Rodgers and Kirke were former members of Free, Burrell was from King Crimson (both groups that were less than commercially successful) and Ralphs was from Mott the Hoople. Behind all the publicity, Bad Company carefully constructed a hard rock sound in a commercially salable package, utilizing the same formula on all of their albums. *Albums:* Bad Company (SWN 8501) 1974; Burnin' Sky (SWN 8500) 1977; Desolation Angels (SWN 8506) 1979; Run with the Pack (SWN 8503) 1976; Straight Shooter (SWN 8502) 1975.

BADANJEK, JOHNNY "BEE" Drums, vocal. Member of Mitch Ryder's Detroit Wheels. Member of the Rockets since 1977. Session for Dr. John (1975); Alice Cooper (1975).

BADELLA, PHIL Vocal. Session for Janis Joplin (1969).

BADFINGER Mike Gibbons—drums; Pete Ham—guitar; Tom Evans—guitar, vocal; Joey Molland—guitar, vocal. Originally Beatles sound alikes, Badfinger started with a Beatles' song "Come and Get It" (1970) for the movie "The Magic Christian," with Ringo Starr, before progressing to their own identity. Session for Bangladesh (1971); George Harrison (1972); John Palumbo (1978). *Albums:* Ass (APL SW-3411); Badfinger (WBR B-2762); Magic Christian Music (APL SW-3364); No Dice (APL ST-3367); Straight Up (APL SW-3387); Wish You Were Here (WBR B-2827); Air Waves (ELK 6E 175) 1979.

BAERENWALD, SCOTT Bass, vocal. Member of Robin Lane and the Chartbusters, 1980.

BAEZ, JOAN Vocal, guitar. Female folk-blues legend whose career parallels Bob Dylan's. First appeared in 1965, gaining recognition with her recording of Dylan's "It's All Over Now, Baby Blue." Performed at Woodstock, 1969. *Albums:* Any Day Now (VAN 79306-7); Joan Baez (VAN 2077) 1967; Joan Baez (VAN 2097) 1967; Joan Baez (VAN 79160); Joan Baez Ballad Book (VAN VSD-41/42) 1972; Joan Baez in Concert (VAN 2122); Joan Baez in Concert, Vol. 2 (VAN 2123); Joan Baez Love Song Album (VAN VSD-79/80) 1976; Baptism (VAN 79275) 1978; Best of Joan C. Baez (AAM 4668) 1977; Blessed Are (VAN 6570-1); Blowin' Away (POR PR-34697) 1977; Carry It On (VAN 79313); Come from the Shadows (AAM 4339) 1972; David's Album (VAN 79308) 1969; Diamonds and Rust (AAM 4527) 1975; Farewell, Angelina (VAN 79200); First 10 Years (VAN 6560-61); From Every Stage (AAM 3704) 1975; Gracias A La Vida (AAM 3614) 1974; Greatest Songs of Woody Guthrie (VAN VSD-35/36); Hits/Greatest and Others (VAN 79332) 1973; Honest Lullaby (POR JR-35766); Joan (VAN 79240) 1967; Newport Folk Festival (VAN 79148); Noel (VAN 79230) 1966; One Day at a Time (VAN 79310) 1969; Tribute to Woody Guthrie (WBR 2W-3007); Joan Baez (POR JR 35766) 1979; Joan Baez Country Music Album (VAN VSD 105/106); Gulf Winds (AAM SP 4603) 1976; Celebration (ODE X77008); Where Are You Now, My Son (AAM 4390) 1973.

BAEZA, ANDRE Conga, percussion, vocal. Member of El Chicano, 1971-75, and Tierra, 1980.

BAGATELLE Lee Mason—drums, vocal; Fred Griffith—vocal; Steve Schrell—reeds; Willie Alexander—piano, vocal; David Thomas—vocal; David Bynoe—bass, drums, harmonica, flute; Mark Gould—horns, keyboards; Rodney Young—drums, percussion, vocal; Marshall O'Connell—guitar. *Album:* 11 PM Saturday, 1968.

BAGLEY, BILL Organ. Member of the Jitters, 1980.

BAHULA, JULIAN African drums. Session for Mike Oldfield (1975).

BAIER, WALLY Organ. Session for Peter C. Johnson (1980).

BAILEY, BARRY Guitar. Member of the Atlanta Rhythm Section.

BAILEY, CHRIS Vocal. Member of the Saints, 1977.

BAILEY, CHRIS Bass, vocal. Member of Angel City since 1977.

BAILEY, COLIN Drums. Session for Martin Mull (1977-78).

BAILEY, RICHARD Keyboards, flute, vocal. Member of Magnum, 1979.

BAILEY, RICHARD Drums, percussion. Session for Jeff Beck (1975-76); Mick Taylor (1979).

BAILIN, DEAN Guitar. Session for Gilda Radner (1979).

BAILLIE, MIKE Member of the Skids, 1979.

BAIN, JIMMY Bass. Replaced Craig Gruber in Ritchie Blackmore's Rainbow, 1976-77. Session for David Kubinec (1979).

BAINBRIDGE, HARVEY Bass, vocal. Member of Hawklords, 1978.

BAIRD, ALEX Drums. Member of the Jags, 1980.

BAIRD, EDDIE Piano, vocal. Member of the Amazing Blondel, 1974.

BAIRD, MIKE Drums. Member of Ironhorse, 1979, and Airborne, 1979. Session for Steve Marriot (1976); Bob Wier (1978); Art Garfunkel (1979); the Marc Tanner Band (1979).

BAIRD, TOM Vocal, keyboards. Member of Hub, 1975-76.

BAIRINSON, IAN Guitar. Member of the Alan Parsons Project since 1976.

BAKER, BILL Saxophone. Member of the Righteous Brothers Band, 1966.

BAKER, CRISTON Bass, vocal. Member of Air Supply.

BAKER, EARL Vocal. Member of the Fugs chorus, 1965-66.

BAKER, GARY Vocal, bass. Member of Boatz, 1979.

BAKER, GINGER Drums, percussion, vocal. Born 8/19/40. Received his training in Blues Incorporated and the Graham Bond Organization, before achieving international fame as drummer in the legendary Cream. His complicated rhythms were matched only by his improvisational mastery. "Toad" (1967) was the first drum solo in rock history to be imitated internationally. A member of Blind Faith, 1969, before forming Ginger Baker's Air Force, 1970-71. (See Air Force.) He emerged from retirement to form the Baker-Gurvitz Army, 1975-76. *Albums:* Stratavarious; Live Africa (ACO) 1970; Ginger Baker and Friends (SIR SA 7532) 1977.

GINGER BAKER'S AIR FORCE See Air Force.

BAKER, JEFF Guitar, piano, harmonica, vocal. Member of Taos.

BAKER, JO Vocal. Member of the Elvin Bishop Band, 1968-72, and Stoneground. Session for Elvin Bishop (1974-75).

BAKER, JOSEPH Guitar. Member of Sly and the Family Stone, 1979.

BAKER, KEITH Drums, percussion. Session for Uriah Heep (1970).

BAKER, KEN Guitar, keyboards, vocal. Member of Unicorn, 1974-77.

BAKER, LEFTY Guitar, vocal. Member of Spanky and Our Gang, 1967-69.

BAKER, LENNIE Saxophone, vocal. Member of Sha Na Na, 1971-present, and one-time member of Danny and the Juniors.

BAKER, MAURY Drums. Member of Ars Nova, 1968-69. Session for Janis Joplin (1969).

BAKER, MAX Guitar, vocal. Member of Mama's Pride, 1975.

BAKER, RICHARD Moog. Session for Gary Wright (1977).

BAKER, ROB Drums. Member of Red Rider, 1980.

BAKER, RONNIE Bass. Session for B. B. King (1973-74).

BAKER, ROY THOMAS Producer. Produced Hustler (1975); Reggie Knighton (1978); Queen; the Cars (1979-80); Journey (1979); Ron Wood (1979); Ian Hunter; Foreigner (1979).

BAKER-GURVITZ ARMY Ginger Baker—drums, percussion, vibes, vocal; Adrian Gurvitz—guitar, vocal; Paul Gurvitz—bass, vocal; John Norman-Mitchell—keyboards, synthesizer, vibes (1975); Snips—vocals (1975-76); John Lemer—keyboards (1975-76). Teaming with Adrian Gurvitz from Gun and Three Man Army, Baker attempted a repeat performance of the success he enjoyed with Cream in the 1960s. The sound, however, was not as fresh in 1975 as it was then. *Albums:* Baker-Gurvitz Army (JNS 7015) 1975; Elysian Encounters (ACO) 1975; Hearts on Fire (ACO) 1976.

BAKKER, FERDINAND Guitar, piano, vocal. Member of Alquin, 1975, and the Meteors, 1980.

BALANCE, RICHIE Kazoo. Member of the Temple City Kazoo Orchestra, 1978.

BALAZ, MICHAEL Guitar. Member of Blue Swede.

BALCONES FAULT Steve Blodgett—percussion; A. Fetcher Clark—guitar; Michael Christian—drums; Don Elam—saxophone; Jack Jacobs—guitar; Kerry Kimbrough—trumpet; Mike McGreary—drums, piano; Riley Osborne—keyboards, guitar; Dean Stimulus—bass. *Album:* It's All Balcones Fault, 1977.

BALDACCI, ARTE Drums, synthesizer, vocal. Member of Heartsfield, 1973-75.

BALDOCK, LARRY Bass, vocal. Replaced Steve Olschesky in Sunblind Lion, 1978.

BALDOS, STEVE Bass. Member of Overland Stage, 1972.

BALDRY, LONG JOHN Vocal, guitar. A former

disc jockey, Baldry began his reputation in early British blues groups like Blues Incorporated, Cyril Davies and the All-Stars, the Hoochie Coochie Men, Steam Packet and Bluesology before striking out on his own. Session with Alexis Korner and Cyril Davies (1954-61). *Albums:* Long John's Blues; Everything Stops for Tea (WBR 2614) 1972; Baldry's Out (EIA SW-17015) 1979; Good To Be Alive (CAS NBLP 7012) 1975; It Ain't Easy (WBR WS 1921); Long John Baldry (EMI SW 17038) 1980.

BALDURSSON, THOR Keyboards, orchestral arranger. Session for Elton John (1979).

BALDWIN, DON Drums, vocal. Member of the Elvin Bishop Band, 1974-77, and Snail, 1978-79.

BALIN, DIXIE D. Vocal. Member of the Catfish Hodge Band, 1979.

BALIN, MARTY Vocal, writer. Real name: Martin Buchwald. Born 1/30/45. Original member of the Jefferson Airplane, 1965-75, and Starship, 1975-78. *Album:* Rock Justice (EMI SWAK 17036) 1980.

BALIN, TRACY Vocal. Session for Long John Baldry (1979).

BALKIN, JOHN Keyboards. Member of Menage A Trois, 1970-72.

BALL, ANDY Keyboards. Member of Candlewick Green, 1974.

BALL, DAVID Guitar. Replaced Robin Trower in Procol Harum, 1972. Member of Bedlam, 1973. Session for Long John Baldry (1975).

BALL, DENNIS Bass. Member of Bedlam, 1973. Session for Long John Baldry (1975); David Byron (1975).

BALL, MAX Saxophone. Member of Kenny and the Kasuals.

BALL, ROGER Saxophone, keyboards. Member of the Average White Band since 1974. Session for Bryan Ferry (1974).

BALL, SCOTT Acoustic bass. Session for Nils Lofgren (1976).

BALLARD, BUCKNER Vocal, guitar, bass. Member of the Werewolves, 1978.

BALLARD, FLORENCE Vocal. Original member of the Supremes until she left to go solo in 1968. Died in 1976.

BALLARD, HANK Organizer of the Midnighters and author of "The Twist," "Work With Me Annie," "Annie Had a Baby" and other rock classics. *Albums:* Hank Ballard and the Midnighters; Hank Ballard's Biggest Hits, 1963; Those Lazy, Lazy Days; Biggest Hits, 1963; Glad Songs, Sad Songs; One and Only, 1960; Spotlight, 1960; Dance Away, 1961; Greatest Jukebox Hits; Mr. Rhythm and Blues, 1960. Jumpin', 1962; Let's Go Again, 1961; Sound of 1963; Singin' and Swingin', 1959; Twistin' Fools, 1962; You Can't Keep a Good Man Down; A Star in Your Eyes.

BALLARD, RUSS Guitar, piano, vocal. Original member of Argent, 1970-75. *Albums:* Danger Zone; Russ Ballard, 1975; You Can Do Voodoo (EPC); At the Third Stroke (EPC JE 35035) 1979; Barnet Dogs (EPC JE 36186) 1980.

BALLERINI, FREDDIE Violin. Session for Hapshash and the Coloured Coat.

BALLIN, PETER Tenor saxophone. Member of the Boneroos, 1977.

BALLIN' JACK Jim Coile—reeds, vocal; Ronnie Hammon—drums, vocal; Timmy McFarland—-trombone, vocal; Glenn Thomas—guitar, mandolin; Luther Rabb—bass, vocal. *Albums:* Ballin' Jack (COL C 30344); Special Pride (MER SRM 1 672) 1973.

BALLINGER, PHIL Drums. Session for Van Wilks (1980).

BALOUGH, BILL Guitar. Member of the Royal Guardsmen, 1969.

BALSANO, PHIL Keyboards. Member of Tantrum, 1978-79.

BALZALL, KEN Trumpet. Session for Jerry Garcia and Howard Wales (1970).

BANANA Piano, guitar, vocal, mandolin. Took his name from a line in Donovan's "Mellow Yellow," referring to an "Electrical Banana." Original member of the Youngbloods, 1967-72.

BANCHEE Jose Miguel de Jesus—guitar, vocal; Victor Di Gilio—drums, vocal; Michael Marino—bass, vocal; Peter Alongi—guitar, vocal. *Album:* Banchee (ATC 8240) 1969.

THE BAND Richard Manuel—vocal, keyboards; Levon Helm—vocal, drums, keyboards; Rick Danko—vocal, bass; Garth Hudson—vocal, keyboards, saxophone, accordion, piccolo; Robbie Robertson—vocal, guitar. Early name: Levon and the Hawks. First received notoriety as Bob Dylan's backup band before striking out on their own in 1968. After 16 years of consistently first rate music composition and performance, the group retired in a filmed concert "The Last Waltz" with friends Van Morrison, Joni Mitchell, Neil Young, Neil Diamond and others. *Albums:* Anthology (CAP SKBO-11856) 1979; The Band (CAP STAO-132) 1976; Best of the Band (CAP St-11553) 1977; Cahoots (CAP SMAS-651); Islands (CAP SO-11602) 1977; Last Waltz (WBR 3WS-3146) 1978; Moondog Matinee (CAP SW-11214); Music from Big Pink (CAP SKAO-255); Northern Lights-Southern Cross (CAP ST-11440); Planet Waves (ASY 7E-1003); Rock of Ages (CAP SABB-11045) 1972; Stage Fright (CAP SW-425).

BAND OF THIEVES Napolean Crayton—vocal, keyboards; Donald Breedlove—guitar, bass, vocal; Wilbur Cole—organ, vocal; James Vasquez—drums; Orville Shannon—guitar, vocal; Jeffrey McRauch—bass; Bill Haskell—saxophone; Gary McKeen—trumpet; Mark Maxwell—trombone. *Album:* Band of Thieves (OVA 1727) 1976.

BANDIT Jim Diamond—vocal; Danny McIntosh,

Jr.—guitar; James Litherland—guitar; Cliff Williams —bass; Graham Broad—drums. *Albums:* Bandit, 1976; Hit and Run (ARA SW-50067); Partners in Crime (ARA SW-50042).

BANDIT Joey Newman—guitar, vocal; Kevin Barnhill—bass, steel guitar, vocal; Tommy Eaton—vocal; David Della Rosa—guitar, vocal; Danny Gorman—drums, percussion. *Album:* Bandit, 1975.

BANG Frank Ferrara—bass, vocal, piano; Frank Gilcken—guitar. *Album:* Bang Music (CAP ST 11190) 1973.

BANGLA DESH A special concert held August 1, 1971, at Madison Square Garden, sponsored by George Harrison and friends for the relief of refugees from that country during their civil war. Harrison's friends included Eric Clapton, Bob Dylan, Leon Russell, Ringo Starr, Billy Preston, Klaus Voorman, Badfinger, Ravi Shankar and others. *Album:* Bangla Desh (APL STCX 3385) 1971.

BANGOR, LARRY Vocal. Member of Human Sexual Response, 1980.

BANGOR FLYING CIRCUS Michael Tegza—drums; David Wolinski—vocal, bass, keyboards, percussion; Alan de Carlo—guitar, vocal, percussion. *Album:* Bangor's Flying Circus.

BANKS, BRENTON Violin. Session for Waylon Jennings (1973, 75).

BANKS, HAMP Guitar. Member of Sly and the Family Stone, 1979.

BANKS, PETER Guitar, vocal. Member of Yes, 1970-71, and Flash, 1972 .

BANNISTER, JEFF Keyboards. Member of Andy Bown. Session for Bronco.

BANTON, HUGH Keyboards, bass, vocal. Member of Van der Graff Generator, 1970-77.

BAR-KAYS James Alexander; Charles Allen; Vernon Burch; Ben Cauley; Larry Dodson; Darnell Hagan; Harvey Henderson; Winston Stewart; Ron Caldwell; Carl Cunningham; Phalin Jones; Jimmy King. Originally known as the six man backup group to the late Otis Redding. Four of them died in Redding's plane crash, December 10, 1967. The survivors regrouped in 1968. *Albums:* Soul Finger, 1968; Flying High on Your Love (MER SRM-1181); Gotta Groove (STX 4130); Injoy (MER SRM-1-3781); Light of Life (MER SRM-1-3732); Money Talks (STX 4106); Too Hot To Stop (MER ML-8010).

BARAJAS, GEORGE Bass, vocal. Member of Duke Jupiter since 1978.

BARANDWSKI, BOBBY Drums. Member of the Werewolves, 1978.

BARBALACE, FRANK Guitar, vocal. Member of Trillion, 1978-80.

BARBARIANS Jerry Causi—bass; Jeff Morris—guitar; Bruce Benson—guitar; Victor Moulton—drums. *Album:* The Barbarians (RHI 008) 1979.

BARBATA, JOHN Drums, percussion. Original member of the Turtles, 1965-69. Replaced Dallas Taylor in Crosby, Stills, Nash and Young, 1970-71. Member of the Jefferson Starship, 1974-78. Session for Lee Michaels (1968); Dave Mason (1970); Steve Stills (1970); Ry Cooder (1970); John Sebastian (1971); Neil Young (1973).

BARBATO, EDDIE Drums. Member of Flame, 1977.

BARBER, BILL Keyboards. Member of the Jan Park Band, 1979.

BARBER, CHRIS Member of the Ken Colyer Skiffle Group, 1952-54.

BARBER, JACK Bass. Session for Willie Nelson (1973).

BARBIERI, RICHARD Keyboards, synthesizer. Member of Japan since 1979.

BARBOUR, J. Vocal, percussion. Member of Chrysalis, 1968.

BARCLAY JAMES HARVEST John Lees—guitar, vocal; Les Holroyd—bass, vocal; Wooly Wolstenholme—keyboards, vocal; Mel Pritchard—drums, percussion. *Albums:* Time Honored Ghosts, 1975; Everyone Is Everybody Else (POL); Eyes of the Universe (POL 1-6267); Gone to Earth (MCA 2302) 1977; XII (POL 1-6173); Barclay James Harvest; Once Again; Baby James Harvest.

BARCLAY, NICHOL Vocal, keyboards. Member of Joe Cocker's Greatest Show on Earth, 1970, and Fanny, 1974.

BARDEN, GARY Vocal. Member of the Michael Schenker Group, 1980.

BARDENS, PETER Keyboards, moog, mellotron, vocal. An original member of Them before forming Camel in 1975. Session for Peter Green (1970).

BARE, DOUG Keyboards. Member of Whiteface, 1979. Session for John Mayall (1977).

BARG, JOHN Guitar, vocal. Member of Kak.

BARGERON, DAVE Trombone. Session for Ian Hunter (1976).

BARGERON, LEE Keyboards, guitar, vocal. Member of Hotel since 1978.

BARHAM, JOHN Piano, flugelhorn, harmonica, string arranger. Session for John Lennon (1971); George Harrison (1967, 72, 73).

BARISH, JESSE Vocal, guitar, flute. *Albums:* Barish (RCA AFLI-2555) 1978; Mercury Shoes (RCA AFL 1-3420) 1980.

BARKEIN, GENE Guitar, vocal. Member of Glider, 1977.

BARKER, CRISTON Bass, vocal. Member of Air Supply, 1980.

BARKER, GUY Horns. Session for the Jags (1980).

BARKER, KENNY Guitar, vocal. Member of Two Guns, 1979.

BARKER, ROLAND Vocal, saxophone, synthesizer. Member of the Blackouts, 1980.

BARKSDALE, CHUCK Vocal. Member of the Dells.

BARLOW, BARRIEMORE Drums, percussion. Replaced Clive Bunker in Jethro Tull, 1971-80.

Session for Maddy Prior (1980); Kerry Livgren (1980).

BARLOW, BRUCE Bass. Member of Commander Cody's Lost Planet Airmen.

BARNABAS Percussion. Member of Dillinger, 1976.

BARNACLE, PETE Drums, percussion, vocal. Member of Broken Home, 1980.

BARNES, BARRY Guitar, vocal. Member of the Charlie Daniels Band.

BARNES, BILLY Vocal. Session for Taj Mahal (1978).

BARNES, BOB Bass. Member of the Yellow Payges, 1969.

BARNES, CLAY Guitar, vocal, piano. Member of Lowry Hamner and the Cryers, 1978-79. Session for Willie Nile (1980).

BARNES, DAVID Drums. Member of Limousene, 1972, and the Faith Band, 1977.

BARNES, DON Guitar, vocal. Member of 38 Special since 1977.

BARNES, JIM Vocal. Member of Cold Chisel, 1979.

BARNES, JOHN Keyboards. Session for Jim Capaldi (1979).

BARNES, PATRICK Guitar, vocal. Member of Dirty Looks, 1980.

BARNES, PHIL Bass, vocal. Member of Any Trouble, 1980.

BARNES, TIM Guitar, bottleneck guitar, vocal. Original member of Stoneground, 1971.

BARNETT, MARCUS Percussion. Session for B. B. King (1975).

BARNHILL, KEVIN Bass, steel guitar, vocal. Member of Bandit, 1975.

BARNS, REBECCA Vocal. Session for John Mayall (1978).

BARNWELL, CARL Guitar. Member of Matthew's Southern Comfort.

BARON, JACK Reeds. Member of the Numa Band, 1980.

BARONE, MICHAEL Drums. Member of Critical Mass, 1980.

BARONS Early name for Jan and Dean.

BAROOGA Bruce Mecham—vocal, guitar; Mat de Raad—keyboards, vocal; Franz de Raad—drums, vocal; Chuck Moses—bass, vocal; Lou Abraham—guitar. *Album:* Running Alone (CAP ST 12105) 1980.

BARR, CHRIS Keyboards, guitar, vocal. Member of Rock Rose, 1979.

BARR, RALPH Guitar, clarinet, cello. Original member of the Nitty Gritty Dirt Band.

BARRABAS Jo Tejada—vocal; Ricky Morales—guitar; Miquel Morales—guitar, bass; Juan Vidal—keyboards; Daniel Louis—drums, percussion; Ernest Duarte—percussion, brass, bass. *Albums:* Barrabas, 1974; Heart of the City, 1975; Watch Out, 1976; Power (ACO); Mejor De (ARC 3268).

BARRACLOUGH, ELIZABETH Vocal. *Albums:* Elizabeth Barraclough (BSV K-6978); Hi (BSV K-6992) 1979.

BARRATT, NORMAN Guitar, vocal. Member of the Alwyn Wall Band, 1977.

BARRE, MARTIN Guitar. Replaced Mick Abrahams in Jethro Tull, 1969-71. Session for Chick Churchill (1974); Maddy Prior (1980).

BARRE, PAUL Guitar. Member of Little Feat, 1971-77. Session for Tom Johnston (1979).

BARRELHOUSE SAMMIE One time performing name of Blind Willie McTell.

BARRET, BUCKY Guitar. Session for Neil Young (1978).

BARRETT, ASTON Bass, guitar, percussion. Member of Bob Marley's Wailers. Session for Taj Mahal.

BARRETT, CARLTON Drums, percussion. Member of Bob Marley's Wailers.

BARRETT, RICHARD Vocal. Member of the Cleftones.

BARRETT, SYD Vocal, guitar. An original member of Pink Floyd, he broke into the market in 1967 with highly progressive space-electronic sounds and imaginative lyrics. He disappeared from the group in 1968 and lived in obscurity until the release of his solo albums. Unfortunately, his albums did not add as much to his reputation as his work with the group. *Albums:* Barrett; Madcap Laughs (HAR SABB-11314).

BARRETTO, RAY Percussion. Session for Eumir Deodato; Full Moon (1972); Crosby, Stills and Nash (1977). *Albums:* Can You Feel It (ATC 19198); Carnival (FSY 324713) 1973; Eye of the Beholder (ATC 19140); Midnight Blue (BLN 84123); Tomorrow: Barretto Live (ATC 1-509) 1976.

BARRON, RONNIE Keyboards, percussion, vocal. Member of Paul Butterfield's Better Days Band, 1973. Session for Dr. John (1972, 75, 78, 79); Gene Clark (1974); Ry Cooder (1974, 79); Tony Joe White (1972); John Mayall (1977-78); B. B. King (1977); Colin Winski (1980).

BARROW, ARTHUR Synthesizer, bass, vocal. Session on Jim Morrison's "American Prayer" (1978); Frank Zappa (1979).

BARRY, DAN Bass. Member of Stone Country, 1968.

BARRY, LEN Vocal. Member of the Dovells 1963, before going solo in 1965 with his recording of "1-2-3." *Album:* 1-2-3 (MCA).

BARSON, MIKE Keyboards. Member of Madness, 1979.

BARTA, TAMAS Guitar, harmonica, vocal. Member of Locomotive GT, 1974-75.

BARTEL, ANDY Guitar, vocal. Member of Yipes, 1979-80.

BARTH, BOBBY Guitar. Member of Axe since 1979.

BARTH, STEVE Vocal. Session for Private Lines (1980).

BARTHOL, BRUCE Bass, harmonica. Original member of Country Joe and the Fish, 1965-68. Member of Formerly Fat Harry, 1971. Session for Country Joe McDonald (1975).

BARTHOLOMEW, DAVE Trumpet. Session for Fats Domino (1949-56).

BARTLE, JOHN Guitar, vocal. Member of the Jan Park Band, 1979.

BARTLET, ROGER Guitar. Member of the Coral Reefer Band, 1974.

BARTLETT, BILL Guitar. Member of the Lemon Pipers, 1968.

BARTLETT, BILL Vocal, percussion. Member of Ram Jam, 1977-78.

BARTLETT, BRIAN Guitar, vocal. Member of the Choice, 1980.

BARTLETT, RICH Guitar, vocal. Member of the Fools, 1980.

BARTLETT, RICHIE Guitar. Member of Brother Fox and the Tar Baby, 1969.

BARTLEY, JOCK Guitar, pedal steel guitar, slide guitar. Member of Firefall since 1976.

BARTNOF, MORLEY Keyboards, vocal. Member of Bugs Tomorrow, 1980.

BARTOLIN, BILL Guitar, vocal. Member of Blue Ash, 1973.

BARTON, CLIFF Bass. Member of Cyril Davies' All Stars. Session for Donovan (1967).

BARTON, GORDON Drums. Session for John Entwhistle (1972).

BARTOS, KARL Percussion. Replaced Klaus Roeder in Kraftwerk, 1975 to present.

BASCOMBE, WILBUR Bass, trumpet. Session for Barry Goldberg (1969); Martin Mull (1974); Jeff Beck (1976).

BASHER, A. "KUNG FU" Drums, percussion. Replaced Tommy Ruger in Root Boy Slim and the Sex Change Band, 1979.

BASHO, ROBBIE Guitar. *Albums:* Voice of the Eagle (VAN 79321); Zarthus (VAN 79339) 1974; Art of the Steel String Guitar (WHS C-1010) 1979; Visions of the Country (WHS C-1005) 1978.

BASKIN, LLOYD Keyboards, vocal, percussion. Member of Seatrain. Session for Martin Mull (1975).

BASKIN, RICHARD Keyboards, vocals. Performed the soundtrack in the movie "Welcome To L.A." *Album:* Welcome to L.A. (UAR UA-LA703-H).

BASNIGHT, JIM Guitar, vocal. Member of the Moberlys, 1979.

BASORE, STU Steel guitar. Session for Doug Kershaw (1972, 74).

BASS, CARVEL Guitar. Original member of Country Joe and the Fish, 1965.

BASS, STELLA Bass, vocal. Member of Isis, 1974-75.

BASSINI, RUBENS Percussion. Session for Roy Buchanan (1976); John Mayall (1979).

BATDORF, JOHN Guitar, vocal, piano. Half of the Batdorf and Rodney duet since 1971.

BATDORF AND RODNEY John Batdorf—guitar, vocal, piano; Mark Rodney—guitar, vocal, piano. *Albums:* Life Is You (ARI) 1975; Batdorf and Rodney (ASY 5056) 1971; Off the Shelf (ATC 8298).

BATERA, CHICO Congas, percussion. Session for Cat Stevens (1976).

BATES, HOWARD Bass, vocal. Member of Slaughter, 1980.

BATES, KENNETH Vocal. Early member of the Fugs Chorus.

BATES, PHIL Guitar, vocal. Member of Trickster, 1978-79.

BATEY, KEVIN Bass, percussion. Member of Junkyard Angel.

BATH, WILLIE Bass. Member of Rough Diamond, 1977.

BATHELT, HANS Drums, percussion. Member of Triumvirat, 1973-76.

BATORS, STIV Vocal. Member of the Dead Boys, 1977.

BATSTONE, BILLY Bass. Session for Richie Furay (1978).

BATT, MIKE Piano, accordion, keyboards, producer. Member of Hapshash and the Coloured Coat. Produced Steeleye Span (1976). *Album:* Tarot Suite, 1980.

BATTAGLIA, TONY Guitar. Session for Jay Ferguson (1977-80); Blackjack (1979).

BATTEAU, ROBIN Violin. Session for Peter C. Johnson (1980).

BATTELENE, RUSS Drums. Member of the Pages, 1978.

BATTERED WIVES Toby Swann—guitar, vocal; John Gibb—guitar, vocal; Jasper—bass; Cleave Anderson—drums. *Album:* Battered Wives (BMP 7028).

BATTIN, SKIP Bass, vocal, percussion. Member of the Byrds. Replaced Dave Torbert in the New Riders of the Purple Sage. Member of the Flying Burrito Brothers, 1976. *Album:* Skip Battin, 1972.

BATTISTE, HAROLD Saxophone, clarinet. Session for Dr. John (1972).

BATTON, JAMES Keyboards, vocal. Member of Medusa, 1978.

BATTRAY, BOB Piano. Session for Frut (1972).

BAUER, JOE Drums. Original member of the Youngbloods, 1967-72.

BAUER, MIREILLE Percussion. Member of Gong since 1975.

BAUMAN, JOHN Piano. Member of Sha Na Na, 1971.

BAUMANN, PETER Keyboards, synthesizer, flute, electronics. Original member of Tangerine Dream, 1973-74. *Album:* Romance 76 (VGN PZ-34897)

1976.

BAUMANN, RAINER Guitar, steel guitar. Member of Frumpy, 1973.

BAUMBACH, BERT Guitar. Member of the Dixie Flyers.

BAUTISTA, ROLAND Guitar. Session for Gary Wright (1979). *Album:* Heat of the Wind (MCA 1071).

BAXTER, JEFF "SKUNK" Pedal steel guitar, guitar. From Steely Dan, 1972-75, he joined the Doobie Brothers, 1975-80. Member of Four on the Floor, 1979. Session for Navasota (1972); Cashman and West (1972); Joni Mitchell (1975); John Sebastian (1976); Commander Cody (1978); Gene Simmons (1978); Production and session for Nazareth (1978); Terrance Boylan (1980).

BAXTER, LES Keyboards. Member of Neil Norman's Cosmic Orchestra, 1975-80.

BAY CITY ROLLERS Leslie McKeown—vocal, guitar; Stuart Wood—vocal, guitar, bass, piano; Derek Longmuir—drums, percussion; Eric Faulkner—vocal, guitar, violin, mandolin; Alan Longmuir—vocal, bass, piano, accordion; Ian Mitchell—guitar, vocal (1976); Duncan Favre—vocal, keyboards (1979). 1970s pop-rock. *Albums:* Bay City Rollers (ARI 4049) 1975; Greatest Hits (ARI 4158) 1977; It's a Game (ARI 7004) 1977; Rock 'n' Roll Love Letter (ARI 4071) 1976; Strangers in the Wind (ARI 4194); Elevator (ARI AB4241) 1979.

BAYERS, EDDIE Drums. Member of the Rock Killough Group, 1980.

BAYETTE Keyboards, vocal. Member of the Automatic Man, 1976. Session for Wilding-Bonus (1978).

BAYLESS, PETER Vocal, bass, guitar. Member of the Bottles, 1979.

BAZALGETTE, EDWARD Guitar. Member of the Vapors, 1980.

BAZE, GREG Bass, guitar. Member of American Tears.

BAZILIAN, ERIC Guitar, vocal. Member of Baby Grand, 1977-78.

BE-BOP DELUXE Andrew Clark—vocal, keyboards (1974-78); Charles Tumahai—bass (1975-78); Bill Nelson—guitar, vocal; Simon Fox—drums (1974-78); Ian Parkin—guitar (until 1975); Nicholas Chatterton-Dew—drums (until 1974). Progressive rock music with intelligent social commentary, led by Bill Nelson. A musically talented and challenging effort that failed to catch on commercially. *Albums:* Axe Victim (HAR SM-11689) 1974; Best of . . . and the Rest of Be-Bop Deluxe (HAR SKBO-11870) 1978; Drastic Plastic (HAR SW 11750) 1978; Futurama (HAR ST 11432) 1975; Live in the Air Age (CAP SKB-11666) 1977; Modern Music (HAR ST 11575) 1976; Sunburst Finish (HAR ST 11478) 1976.

BEACH BOYS Al Jardine—guitar, vocal; Mike Love—vocal; Brian Wilson—bass, keyboards, vocal; Dennis Wilson—drums, vocal; Blondie Chaplin—drums, vocal (1972); Ricky Fataar—vocal, guitar, bass (1972); Bruce Johnston—bass (1964-65). Early names: The Pendletones; Kenny and the Cadets; Carl and the Passions. As the beach movies indicated, the beaches of Southern California were the place to be in the early 1960s. Waves, sun, bikinis and dreams come true were waiting there, and that is what the Beach Boys sang about. Brian Wilson was the main writer for the group, except during his self-imposed exile with Van Dyke Parks from 1964-66. In 1966, years after their initial success, they released "Pet Sounds," an album featuring more matured lyrics in their distinctive vocal harmonies with additional orchestral music. For the next 5 years they were constantly on the charts, yet without smash hits. They re-emerged in 1973 with "Holland" (after "Surf's Up," 1971) featuring "Sail On Sailor," which shot them into the limelight once again. *Albums:* Surfin' Safari (CAP 1808) 1962; Shut Down, Vol. II, 1964; The Beach Boys Today (CAP 2209) 1965; Summer Days And Summer Nights (CAP 2354); The Beach Boys Party (CAP 2398) 1965; Best of the Beach Boys, Volume III (CAP 2945) 1968; Close Up (CAP 263) 1969; Beach Boys (CAP) 1977; All Summer Long (CAP STBB-500) 1964; Beach Boys Christmas Album (CAP SM-2164); Beach Boys Concert (CAP SM-2198) 1964; Beach Boys in Concert (RPS 2RS-6484) 1973; '69 (CAP SN-12011) 1969; Best of the Beach Boys (CAP DT-2545) 1966; Best of the Beach Boys, Vol. II (CAP DT-2706) 1967; Beach Boys—Good Vibrations (RPS K-2280) 1975; California Girls (CAP STBB-500); Carl and the Passions—So Tough (RPS 2-2083) 1972; Dance, Dance, Dance (CAP STBB-701); Endless Summer (CAP SVBB-11307) 1974; 15 Big Ones (RPS 2251) 1976; Friends (RPS 2MS-2167) 1968; Fun, Fun, Fun (CAP STBB-701); Holland (RPS 2118) 1973; Keepin' the Summer Alive (CRB FZ-36283); L.A. (Light Albums) (CRB JZ-35752); Little Deuce Coupe (CAP SM-1998) 1963; Love You (RPS K-2258); M.I.U. Album (RPS K-2268); Pet Sounds (RPS 2-2083) 1966; Pet Sounds (RPS 2197); Smiley Smile (RPS 2MS-2167) 1967; Spirit of America (CAP SVBB-11384) 1975; Sunflower (RPS 6382) 1970; Surfer Girl (CAP SM-1981) 1963; Surfin' U.S.A. (CAP SM-1890) 1963; Surf's Up (RPS 6453) 1971; 20/20 (RPS 2MS-2166) 1969; Wild Honey (RPS 2MS-2166) 1967.

BEACH BUMS Early name for Bob Seger's band.

BEACON STREET UNION Paul Tartachny—guitar, vocal; Wayne Ulaky—bass, vocal; John Wright—vocal, percussion; Richard Weisberg—drums; Robert Rhodes—keyboards, bass. Part of the Boston Sound (with Ultimate Spinach, and others) that was highly promoted in 1968. Their original songs, like the Boston Sound, faded from popularity quickly. *Albums:* Eyes of the Beacon

Street Union (MGM) 1968; Clown Died in Marvin Gardens (MGM) 1968.

BEACON, KIMBERLEY Vocal. Replaced Pauline Adams in the String Driven Thing, 1974-75.

BEADLE, BUDDY Saxophone. Session for Chicken Shack; Steve Howe (1975); Freddie King (1974-75).

BEAKY Nickname of John Dymond. Member of Dave Dee, Dozy, Beaky, Mick and Tich.

BEAL, CHUCK Guitar, mandolin. Original member of the Paupers, 1966-69.

BEAR Vocal, harmonica. Nickname for Robert Hite, Jr. of Canned Heat. See Robert Hite, Jr.

BEAR, RICHARD T. Vocal. Session for the Blues Brothers (1980); Billy Squier (1980). *Albums:* Bear (VIC AFLI-3313) 1979; Red Hot and Blue (VIC AFLI-2927).

BEARD, FRANK Drums. Member of Z. Z. Top since 1971.

BEARD, SNOYD Saxophone. Session for the Catfish Hodge Band (1979).

BEARD, STAN Vocal. Session for Martin Mull (1978).

BEASLEY, ALFRED Vocal, percussion. Half of the Watson-Beasley duet, 1980.

BEAT, NICKY Drums. Original member of Venus and the Razor Blades, 1977, replaced by Kyle Raven before their recording debut.

BEAT Paul Collins—guitar, vocal, writer; Steven Huff—bass, vocal; Larry Whitman—guitar, vocal; Michael Ruiz—drums. *Album:* The Beat (COL JC 36195) 1979.

BEAT BROTHERS Early name of the Beatles.

BEATLES Paul McCartney—piano, bass, guitar, vocal; John Lennon—harmonica, guitar, piano, vocal; George Harrison—sitar, guitar, vocal; Ringo Starr (Richard Starkey)—drums, percussion, vocal; Tony Sheridan—vocal (1961); Peter Best—drums (1961); Stu Sutcliffe—guitar (1961). Early names: Silver Beatles; Beat Brothers; Johnny and the Moondogs. The 1930s and 1940s had Benny Goodman and Glenn Miller; the 1940s and 1950s saw Crosby, Como, Nat King Cole, Bill Haley and Elvis Presley; and the 1960s saw the Beatles. McCartney and Lennon had been writing together since 1956. They were with Tony Sheridan and the Silver Beatles, 1959-61, before they recruited Ringo Starr from Rory Storme and the Hurricanes. In 1962 they released "Love Me Do" which became #1 in 4 weeks. The rest is history. Without underestimation, the Beatles have had a greater effect on rock music than any other individual or group. Because of the Beatles, general rock lyrics evolved from "bop-bop-sha-do-wop" into many types of beautiful and humorous ballads, love songs, and social commentaries. Their instrumentation and arrangements matured as they aged, forcing their less talented imitators to mature or fall by the wayside. Due to internal personality struggles, the group disbanded (1970) on an unpleasant note. Each member pursued his respective career with equal success. *Albums:* This Is Where It Started; This Is the Savage Young Beatles with Tony Sheridan and Peter Best, 1961; Ain't She Sweet, 1964; Very Together, 1961; Live at the Star Club . . . '62, 1977; Abbey Road (CAP SO-383, SEAX 11900) 1969; Beatles at Hollywood Bowl (CAP SMAS-11638) 1977; Beatles 2nd Album (CAP ST-2080) 1964; Beatles VI (CAP ST-2358) 1965; Beatles 1962-1966 (CAP SKBO-3403, SEBX-11842) 1973; Beatles 1967-1970 (CAP SKBO-3404, SEBX-11843) 1973; Beatles '65 (CAP ST-2228) 1965; The Beatles Story (CAP STBO-2222) 1965; The Beatles (White Album) (CAP SWBO-101, SEBX-11841) 1968; Early Beatles (CAP ST-2309) 1965; Hard Day's Night (UAR LO-6366) 1964; Help (CAP SMAS-2336) 1965; Hey Jude (CAP SW-385) 1970; Let It Be (CAP SW-11922) 1970; Love Songs (CAP SKBL-11711) 1977; Magical Mystery Tour (CAP SMAL-2835) 1967; Meet the Beatles (CAP ST-2047) 1964; Rarities (CAP SHAL 12060) 1980; Revolver (CAP SW-2576) 1966; Rock 'n' Roll Music (CAP SKBO-11537); Rubber Soul (CAP SW-2442) 1965; Sgt. Pepper's Lonely Hearts Club Band (CAP SMAS 2653, SEAX-11840) 1967; Something New (CAP ST-2108) 1964; Yellow Submarine (CAP SW-153) 1969; Yesterday and Today (CAP ST-2553) 1966.

BEATTIE, DORIAN Vocal. Voice of Painter, 1973, and Hammersmith, 1973-76.

BEAU BRUMMELS Sal Valentino—vocal; Ron Meagher—bass; Ron Elliot—guitar; John Peterson; Dellon Mulligan. Early name: The Irish Americans. Originally Beatles imitators who arrived in the U.S. in 1966, but developed their own identity. Behind Valentino's vocals, called by many the best in the business, their first album, a collage of other people's hits, was a big hit itself. *Albums:* Beau Brummels (RPS) 1966; Best of Beau Brummels (RPS) 1967; Bradley's Barn (RPS) 1967; Triangle (RPS).

BEAU, TOBY See Toby Beau.

BEAUDRY, TOM Bass. Co-founder of Frijid Pink, 1970-71.

BEAUVIOR, JEAN Bass. Member of the Plasmatics, 1980.

BEAVER, DAVID Keyboards. Member of the Gentrys.

BEAVER, PAUL Moog, organ. Half of the Beaver and Krause duet, 1970-71.

BEAVER AND KRAUSE Paul Beaver—moog, organ; Bernard Krause—moog. *Albums:* In a Wild Sanctuary (WBR) 1970; Ganohawa (WBR) 1971.

BEAVIS, RAY Tenor saxophone. Member of the Rumor Brass Section, 1979.

BECH, PHIL Piano. Session for Mahogany Rush (1975, 77).

BECHAMIN, MOE Vocal. Session for Dr. John

(1972).

BECHER, CURT Vocal. Session for Elton John (1980).

BECK, DON Banjo, guitar, mandolin, bass. Member of Stone Country, 1968, and the Dillard and Clark Expedition. Session for Russ Giguere (1971).

BECK, DONNA Vocal. Member of the Jitters, 1980.

BECK, GREG Guitar. Member of Surprise Package, 1969, and American Eagle, 1970.

BECK, JEFF Guitar, writer. Born 6/22/44. Started in Cyril Davies' All Stars before he replaced Eric Clapton in the Yardbirds, 1964-67. In 1968 he formed the Jeff Beck Group, specializing in blues, featuring Rod Stewart on vocals. Personality upheavals forced the group to break up after two albums. Beck reappeared in 1971 with a new Jeff Beck Group featuring Max Middleton on piano and Bobby Tench at vocals. The new music was more jazz and rhythm oriented. In 1973 he disbanded that group for a brief fling with heavy rock in Beck, Bogart and Appiece. He returned in 1975 to a jazz-rock format as a soloist. See the Jeff Beck Group. Session for Lord Sutch. *Albums:* Beck, Bogert, Appice (EPC KE-32140) 1973; Jeff Beck Group (EPC PE-31331) 1972; Jeff Beck Live/Jan Hammer Group (EPC PE-34433) 1977; Beck—Ola (EPC BXN-26478, BG-33779) 1969; Blow by Blow (EPC PE-33409) 1975; Rough and Ready (EPC PE-30973) 1971; There and Back (EPC FE-35684) 1980; Truth (EPC PE-26413, BG-33779) 1968; Wired (EPC PE-33849) 1976.

JEFF BECK GROUP Jeff Beck—guitar, bass; Rod Stewart—vocal (1968-69); Ron Wood—bass; Mick Waller—drums (1968); Tony Newman—drums (1969); Nicky Hopkins—piano (1969); Clive Chaman—bass (1971-72); Max Middleton—piano (1971-72); Cozy Powell—drums (1971-72); Bob Tench—vocal (1971-72). Formed in 1968 after Beck left the Yardbirds, featuring Rod Stewart on vocal and Nicky Hopkins on piano. Personnel disputes led to the group's breakup in 1969. The group was re-formed by Beck in 1971 with Bobby Tench and Max Middleton and became more jazz oriented. Just as they began becoming popular again they disbanded. Chaman and Tench formed Hummingbird, Powell formed Cozy Powell's Hammer, and Beck achieved even greater fame as a soloist. See Jeff Beck. Session for Donovan (1968).

BECK, JOE Guitar. Session for Paul Simon (1975-80). *Albums:* Beck Guitar Album; Beck and Sanborn (CTI 8002).

BECK, MIKE Percussion. Member of Happy the Man, 1977.

BECK, RONNIE Drums. Member of Tower of Power, 1976.

BECK, BOGERT AND APPICE Jeff Beck—guitar; Tim Bogert—bass, vocals; Carmine Appice—drums, percussion. Meeting of heavy metal Cactus members Appice and Bogert with Beck, after the dissolution of his group and before his more successful debut as a jazz soloist. *Albums:* Beck, Bogert and Appice (EPC KE 32140) 1973; Beck, Bogert and Appice Live (Import).

BECKER, CAROL Vocal. Session for Long John Baldry (1979).

BECKER, STEVE Drums, vocal. Replaced Kenny Pentifallo in Southside Johnny and the Asbury Jukes, 1978-present.

BECKER, WALTER Bass, guitar, vocal, harmonica. Began as part of touring backup band for Jay and the Americans before becoming half of the song-writing team of Steely Dan with Don Fagen (1972-present). Session for Navasota (1972).

BECKER, WERNER Keyboards, vocal. Member of Randy Pie, 1975-77.

BECKERLEE, FRANZ Vocal, guitar, moog. Member of Gasolin', 1974.

BECKETT, BARRY Keyboards, producer. Member of Traffic, 1973, and the Muscle Shoals Rhythm Section. Session and production for Southside Johnny and the Asbury Jukes (1979); Bob Dylan (1979-80); Joan Baez (1979); Paul Kossoff (1974); Joe Cocker (1978); Art Garfunkel (1978); Willie Nelson (1974); Kim Carnes (1976). Produced John Prine (1980). Session for Boz Scaggs (1969, 72); Wilson Pickett (1968); Clarence Carter (1967); King Curtis (1969); John Hammond (1969); Jim Capaldi (1971, 73, 75); Art Garfunkel; Leon Russell (1971); Bob Seger (1973, 75); Paul Simon (1973); Rod Stewart (1975-76); Barry Goldberg (1974); Mike Harrison (1972); Don Nix (1971); Tony Joe White (1972).

BECKETT, HARRY Trumpet. Member of the Keef Hartley Band horn section, 1969. Session for Jack Bruce (1969); Memphis Slim (1971); Lo and Behold (1972).

BECKETT, PETER Guitar, vocal. Member of Player, 1977.

BECKHAM, VIRGIL Guitar, vocal. Session for Richie Furay (1978).

BECKIES Michael Brown—keyboards, vocal; Mayo James McAlister; Gary Hodgden; Scott Trusty. *Album:* Beckies (SIR SASO 7579) 1976.

BECKLEY, GERRY Guitar, vocal. Born 9/12/52. Member of America, 1971-present.

BECKMEIER, FRED Bass. Member of Paul Butterfield's Blues Band, 1969, and Full Moon, 1972. Session for Mike Pindar (1976).

BECKMEIER, STEVE Guitar. Member of the Gregg Allman Band, 1977. Session for Mike Pindar (1976); John Palumbo (1978).

BEDFORD, DAVID Composer. Riding on the crest of friend Mike Oldfield's success with "Tubular Bells," Bedford released a fully orchestrated composition, featuring Oldfield on bass and guitar, and the Royal Philharmonic Orchestra, "Star's End." Session for Roy Harper (1975); Mike Oldfield

(1974). String arrangement for Kevin Ayers (1977). *Albums:* Star's End (VIR) 1974; Rhyme of the Ancient Mariner.

BEDFORD, KIT Bass, piano, vocal. Member of Taos.

BEDFORD, MARK Bass. Member of Madness, 1979.

BEDLAM Cozy Powell—drums; Francesco Aiello—vocal; Dennis Ball—bass; Dave Ball—guitar. Produced by Felix Pappalardi, Bedlam made their short-lived debut after Powell left the Jeff Beck Group. *Album:* Bedlam (WBR) 1973.

BEE GEES Barry Gibb—vocal, guitar; Robin Gibb—vocal; Maurice Gibb—vocal, keyboards, guitar, bass. Australian brothers who began singing in 1956 while still in their teens, the Bee Gees rose to prominence in their native land approximately at the same time as the Beatles. Excellent arrangers and masters of string accompaniment to commercial lyrics, they achieved popular notoriety with their contributions to the musical soundtrack of the movie "Saturday Night Fever" (1977). Session for Andy Gibb (1980). *Albums:* First (ACO 33-223) 1967; Idea (ACO 33253) 1968; Horizontal (ACO 33233) 1968; Best of the Bee Gees, Vol. I and II (ACO); Rare, Precious and Beautiful Vol. I and II (ACO); Two Years On (ACO 33-353) 1971; Trafalgar (ACO 7003) 1971; To Whom It May Concern (ACO 7012) 1972; Life In a Tin Can (RSO SO870) 1973; Mr. Natural (RSO 4800) 1974; Cucumber Castle (ATC) 1976; Bee Gees Gold, Vol. I (RSO 1-3006) 1976; Bee Gees Greatest (RSO 2-4200) 1979; Children to the World (RSO 1-3003) 1976; Gift of Song (POL 1-6214); Here At Last (RSO 2-3901) 1977; Main Course (RSO 1-3024) 1975; Odessa (RSO 1-3007) 1969; Saturday Night Fever (RSO 2-4001) 1977; Spirits Having Flown (RSO 1-3041) 1979.

BEE, JOHNNY See Johnny Badanjek.

BEEBE, DAVID Drums. Member of Jules and the Polar Bears since 1979.

BEECH, WES Guitar. Member of the Plasmatics, 1980.

BEECHAM, JOHN Trombone, tuba. Member of the Kinks, 1971-72. Session for Chris Youlden (1974); the Kinks (1975).

BEECHER, FRANCIS Member of Bill Haley and the Comets.

BEECHMAN, LAURIE Vocal. Namesake of Laurie and the Sighs, 1980.

BEEFHEART, CAPTAIN See Captain Beefheart.

BEERS, STEVE Drums. Member of the Cretones, 1980.

BEINFIELD, LOLLY Trombone, vocal. Member of Isis, 1974-75.

BELCHAM, BRIAN Bass. Session for Ronnie Lane (1975).

BELCHER, ARTHUR Tenor saxophone. Session for Junkyard Angel (1972).

BELEW, ADRIAN Guitar. Member of Photoglo, 1980, and the Talking Heads, 1980. Session for Frank Zappa (1979).

BELFIELD, DENNIS Bass. Member of Osamu, 1977, C.O.D., 1979, and Photoglo, 1980. Session for Richard Tate (1977); John Palumbo (1978); Art Garfunkel (1979); Neil Young (1980).

BELFIORE, JOEY Drums. Member of Centaurus.

BELGRAVE, MARCUS Trumpet. Session for Joe Cocker (1978).

BELL AND JAMES Casey James—keyboards, guitar, bass, percussion, vocal. LeRoy Bell—drums, percussion, guitar, vocal. *Albums:* Bell and James (AAM 4728) 1978; Only Make Believe (AAM 4784) 1979.

BELL, ANN Vocal. Session for Leon Russell (1974).

BELL, ARCHIE Vocal. Namesake of Archie Bell and the Drells.

ARCHIE BELL AND THE DRELLS James Wise—vocal; Archie Bell—vocal; Lee Bell—vocal; Lucious Larkins—vocal. *Albums:* Archie Bell and the Drells (PHL PZ-33844) 1978; Hard Not To Like It (PHL PZ-34855) 1977; Strategy (PHL JZ-36096) 1979; Where Will You Go When the Party's Over (PHL PZ-34323) 1976.

BELL, CHRISTOPHER Guitar, vocal. Member of Big Star, 1972.

BELL, DEREK Harp. Session for Art Garfunkel (1978).

BELL, ERIC Guitar. Member of the Noel Redding Band, 1975.

BELL, GLEN Drums, vocal. Member of the Cooper Brothers Band since 1978.

BELL, GLEN Vocal, guitar. Member of Sam the Band.

BELL, GRAHAM Vocal. Session on "Tommy" (1972).

BELL, KENNY Guitar. Session for Bob Seger (1975).

BELL, LAURIE Drums, percussion, vocal. Member of the Orchids, 1980.

BELL, LEE Vocal. Member of Archie Bell and the Drells since 1976.

BELL, LEROY Guitar. Session for Elton John (1979).

BELL, MACH Vocal. Member of Thundertrain, 1977.

BELL, MAGGIE Vocal. Featured vocalist of Blue Mink, and Stone the Crows, 1971-72, before going solo. Session for Long John Baldry (1971-72); Rod Stewart (1973); "Tommy" (1972); Joe Cocker (1968); the Rolling Stones (1970); Kim Fowley (1973); Gary Wright (1970-71); Chris de Burgh (1975); Climax Blues Band (1978). *Album:* Touch of Class.

BELL, MARC Bass, vocal. Member of Richard Hell and the Voidoids, 1977.

BELL, MIC Vocal. Replaced Billy Davis in the Fifth Dimension.

BELL, PETER Guitar. Member of the James Montgomery Band, 1976.

BELL, RICHARD Keyboards. Member of the Full Tilt Boogie Band, 1969-70. Session for Paul Butterfield (1975); John Sebastian (1976).

BELL, THOM Keyboards, producer. Production and session for Elton John (1979) and others.

BELL, TONY Guitar. Session for Elton John (1979).

BELL, VINCENT Bellzouki, guitar. Session for Barry Goldberg (1969); Bob Dylan (1975); Scarlet Rivera (1978).

BELLAMY, DAVID Guitar, vocal. Member of the Bellamy Brothers since 1976.

BELLAMY, HOWARD Guitar, vocal. Member of the Bellamy Brothers since 1976.

BELLAMY, TONY Vocal, guitar. Original member of Redbone.

BELLAMY BROTHERS David Bellamy—guitar, vocal; Howard Bellamy—guitar, vocal. *Albums:* Beautiful Friends (WBR K-3176) 1978; Bellamy Brothers (WBR B-2941) 1976; Plain and Fancy (WBR K-3347) 1979; You Can Get Crazy (WBR K-3408) 1980.

BELLINE, DENNIS Guitar, piano, vocal. Member of Man.

BELLINGER, DENNIS Vocal, bass. Member of the Mark Farner Band, 1978. Session for Mark Farner (1977).

BELLIS, BOB Drums, vocal. Member of the Yachts since 1979.

BELLOTTE, PETE Producer. Half of the Trax duet. Produced Elton John (1979).

BELMONT, MARTIN Guitar. Member of the Ducks DeLuxe, 1972-75, and the Rumour, 1977.

BELOW, FRED, JR. Drums. Member of Charlie Musselwhite's Southside Band. Session for Chuck Berry (1956-59).

BELSHAM, CHRIS Bass. Session for Andy Bown (1972).

BELSHAW, BRIAN Bass. Member of Centipede, 1971.

BELUSHI, JOHN Vocal. Under the name Joliet Jake Blues, a member of the Blues Brothers, a satire-turned-reality for one of the original members of television's "Saturday Night Live."

BEMBRIDGE, CHARLEY Drums. Member of the Selecter, 1980.

BEMENT, DWIGHT Tenor saxophone. Member of Gary Puckett and the Union Gap, 1967-68.

BENAIR, DANNY Drums. Member of Quick, 1976.

BENATAR, PAT Female vocalist. Real name: Pat Andrejewski. Backup band: Neil Geraldo—guitar, keyboards, vocal; Scott St. Claire-Sheets—guitar; Roger Capps—bass, vocal; Glen Alexander Hamilton—drums (1979); Myron Grombacher—drums (1980). *Albums:* Crimes of Passion (CYS 1275) 1980; In the Heat of the Night (CYS 1236) 1979.

BENAY, BEN Guitar, harmonica. Member of the Marketts, 1973, and the Fun Zone, 1977. Session for Billy Strange; Delaney and Bonnie (1970); Steve Marriott (1976); Neil Sedaka (1975), Steely Dan (1973, 74); Kim Fowley (1972); Cashman and West (1972); Russ Giguere (1971); Arthur, Hurley and Gottlieb; Glen Campbell (1976); John Mayall (1979); Hoyt Axton (1976); David Blue (1975); Cher Bono (1976, 1979); Yvonne Elliman (1978); the Marc Tanner Band (1979); Terrence Boylan (1980).

BENBERG, BOB Drums. Member of Supertramp.

BENDER, ARIEL Guitar, harp. Alternate name of Luther Grosvenor. Replaced Mick Ralphs in Mott the Hopple, 1973. Member of Widowmaker, 1976.

BENDIT, DAVE Keyboards. Session for Vapour Trails (1980).

BENGE, ALFREDA Vocal. Session for Robert Wyatt (1974).

BENICK, RICK Guitar, vocal. Member of Roadmaster since 1978.

BENJAMIN, BOB Bass, vocal. Member of Breathless, 1979.

BENJAMIN, NIGEL Vocal. Member of Mott the Hopple, 1976.

BENJAMIN, WILLIAM Drums, vocal. Member of the Elevators, 1980.

BENKO, LASZLO Keyboards, vocal. Member of Omega, 1975-78.

BENNETT, BRIAN Horns. Session for Sassafras (1975).

BENNETT, BRIAN Drums. Session for Olivia Newton-John (1976); Chris Spedding (1976).

BENNETT, CHUCK Trombone. Session for Mike Bloomfield (1978).

BENNETT, CRUSHER Percussion. Session for Sea Level (1978); Art Garfunkel (1979); Steely Dan (1980).

BENNETT, DAVID Guitar. Member of Limousene, 1972, and the Faith Band, 1977.

BENNETT, DUSTER Harmonica, guitar, drums, percussion, vocal, writer. Protege of John Mayall, he started as a one-man blues band, playing high-hat cymbals, bass drum, guitar, harmonica, and singing at the same time. In addition to his one-man barrage, he recorded with some of the best English blues musicians. Session for Fleetwood Mac (1969); B. B. King (1971); Memphis Slim (1971). *Albums:* Smiling Like I'm Happy (BLH 7701) 1968; Justa Duster (BLH 4804) 1969; 12DB (BLH 4812) 1970.

BENNETT, ERROL Percussion. Session for Martin Mull (1977); Taj Mahal (1978); John Mayall (1979).

BENNETT, HAROLD Flute. Session for Jan Akkerman (1973).

BENNETT, IAN Saxophone. Member of Pam Windo and the Shades, 1980, and the Johnny Average Dance Band, 1980.

BENNETT, MALCOLM Flute. Session for Steve Howe (1975).

BENNETT, MAX Bass. Member of Tom Scott's LA Express, and Neil Norman's Cosmic Orchestra, 1975. Session for Art Garfunkel; Ry Cooder (1970); Henry Gross (1972); Frank Zappa (1969-70); Joni Mitchell (1975); Austin Roberts (1973).

BENNETT, NIGEL Guitar, vocal. Member of the Members, 1979-80.

BENNETT, PATRICIA Vocal. Member of the Chiffons.

BENNETT, PAUL Vocal. Session for Luther Grosvenor.

BENNETT, RAY Member of Flash, 1972.

BENNETT, RICHARD Guitar. Session for Ringo Starr (1974); Neil Diamond (1976).

BENNETT, ROB Drums, percussion. Original member of the Sonics.

BENNETT, TERRY Vocal. Member of Sassafras, 1975.

BENNETT, WILLIE Harmonica. Member of the Dixie Flyers.

BENNIE, ANDY Bass. Session for Sean Tyla (1980).

BENNO, MARC Writer, guitar, vocals, keyboards. Started in the late 1960s with Leon Russell in the Asylum Choir, before embarking on his solo career. He has written songs for Rita Coolidge and others. Session for the Doors (1971); Rita Collidge (1972). *Albums:* Ambush (AAM 4363) 1971; Asylum Choir (MCA 52010) 1968; Asylum Choir II (SMS); Marc Benno (AAM 4273) 1969; Lost in Austin (AAM 4767) 1979; Minnows (AAM 4303) 1970.

BENSON, BRUCE Guitar. Member of the Barbarians, 1979.

BENSON, CARLA Vocal. Session for Elton John (1979).

BENSON, RAY Vocal, guitar. Member of Asleep at the Wheel since 1973.

BENSON, RENALDO Vocal. Original member of the Four Tops.

BENTLEY, DAVID Keyboards. Member of Python Lee Jackson, 1972.

BENTLEY, JOHN Bass. Replaced Harry Kakoulli in Squeeze, 1979-present.

BENTON, EVETTE Vocal. Session for Elton John (1979).

BENTON, TIM Drums. Member of Cargoe, 1972.

BERBERICH, BOB Drums, vocal. Original member of Nils Lofgren's Grin.

BERENZY, JOHN Guitar, vocal. Member of Silent Dancing, 1975.

BERETTA, ROCKY Bass. Member of the Coon Elder Band, 1977.

BERG, BILL Drums. Session for Mike Pindar (1976).

BERG, RON Drums. Member of Mick Abraham's Blodwyn Pig, 1969-70. Replaced Dave Bidwell in Savoy Brown, 1973. Session for Alvin Lee (1975).

BERGAMO, JOHN J. Percussion. Session for Nilsson (1975).

BERGANTE, MERLE Drums. Member of Loggins and Messina backup band, 1973-77.

BERGE, BOB Drums. Original member of Zephyr, 1971. Session for Tommy Bolin (1975).

BERGER, ALAN Bass. Member of Southside Johnny and the Asbury Jukes, 1976-79.

BERGER, BUCKY Drums. Session for Chilliwack (1980).

BERGER, RONNIE Drums, percussion. Member of Sunship, 1974.

BERGHOFFER, CHUCK Bass. Session for Ry Cooder (1978).

BERGI, CHUCK Drums. Member of Brand X, 1978.

BERGLAND, BOB Bass, vocal. Member of the Ides of March.

BERGLUND, TOMMY Trumpet. Member of Blue Swede.

BERGMAN, STAN Flute. Session for Bo Hansson.

BERGSTEN, GUNNAR Saxophone. Session for Bo Hansson.

BERKE, KARL Keyboards, vocal. Replaced Steve Hardin in Point Blank, 1980.

BERLEU, SOREN Drums. Member of Gasolin', 1974.

BERLIN Jo Julian—synthesizer, vocal; Dan Van Patten—drums; Chris Velasco—guitar, vocal; John Crawford—bass, vocal; Virginia Macolino—vocal. *Album:* Information (VYL 624340) 1980.

BERLIN, JEFF Bass, vocal. Member of Bruford, 1979.

BERLINE, BYRON Vocal, fiddle. Member of the Flying Burrito Brothers, and founder of Sundance, 1976. Session for Bob Dylan (1973); Jonathan Edwards (1976); the Rolling Stones (1970); Gram Parsons (1973-74); Bill Wyman (1974), Navasota (1972); Elton John (1980); the Doobie Brothers (1978); Stuart Margolin (1980). *Albums:* Festival Tapes (FLF 068); Live at McCabes (TKM 1061).

BERLINER, JAY Guitar. Session for Eumir Deodato. *Albums:* Bananas Are Not Created Equal (MST 394); Guitar Players (MST 410).

BERLY, KIM Member of the Stampeders, 1973-76.

BERMANI, MIKE Drums. Member of Duane Eddy's Rebels, 1961.

BERMUDEZ, NANCY Vocal, percussion, saxophone. Member of the Heaters, 1978-present.

BERNARD, ANDREW Baritone saxophone. Member of John Fred and the Playboy Band, 1968.

BERNARD, BARRY Bass. Member of Jigsaw, 1975-77.

BERNFIELD, TEX Vocal. Session for Barry Goldberg (1974).

BERNFIELD, TOM Vocal. Session for Eric Clapton (1974); Barry Goldberg (1974).

BERNHARD, BARRIE Bass. Member of Jigsaw,

1977.

BERNHARDT, WARREN Member of Jeremy and the Satyrs, 1967-68.

BERNSTEIN, JOEL Guitar. Session for Terry Reid (1976).

BERNSTEIN, PETER Bass, vocal. Member of the Cretones, 1980.

BERNSTEIN, ROLF Drums. Member of Arbuckle, 1972.

BERRETTA, ROCKY Bass, vocal. Member of Larry Raspberry and the High-Steppers.

BERRY, CHUCK Guitar, vocal, writer. Born: 10/18/26. Full name: Charles Edward Berry. St. Louis-born Berry first hit the charts in 1955 with the much-imitated and still unequaled "Maybelline." Then, it was not fashionable or profitable to be black, playing rock'n'roll to white audiences. But his ability to deliver a wide range of songs, from "Roll Over Beethoven," "Johnny B. Goode," "Little Queenie," and others to the blues- based "Wee Wee Hours" and "Deep Feeling" kept his name constantly on the charts. Today, no rock band does not know at least five of his songs, due to popular demand of audiences young and old. *Albums:* Chuck Berry's Greatest Hits (EVR 321); Best of Chuck Berry (GUS 0004); 16 Greatest Hits (TRP TOP-16-55); After School Sessions (CSS 1426); Back Home (CSS 1550); Chuck Berry (CSS 60032); Chuck Berry Golden Decade (CSS 1514) 1965; Chuck Berry's Golden Decade, Vol. 2 (CSS); Golden Decade, Vol. 3 (CSS); Chuck Berry's Golden Hits (MER 61103); Chuck Berry Greatest Hits (CSS 1485); Chuck Berry Is On Top (CSS 1435); Chuck Berry On Stage (CSS 1480); Chuck Berry's One Dozen Berrys (CSS 1432); Chuck Berry's Twist (CSS 1465); Bio (CSS 50043); London Chuck Berry Sessions (CSS 6001) 1972; St. Louis to Frisco to Memphis (MER SRM-2-6501); St. Louis to Liverpool (CSS 1488); San Francisco Dues (CSS 50008); Two Great Guitars (CHK 2991); Rock It (ACO SD 3818) 1979.

BERRY, JAN Vocal, writer, producer. Half of the original surf sound of Jan and Dean, 1958-63.

BERRY, MARTHA Vocal. Session for Chuck Berry (1961).

BERRY, MIKE Guitar, vocal. *Albums:* I'm a Rocker (EPC JE 36071) 1979; Rocks in My Head (SIR SASD 7524) 1976.

BERRY, RICHARD Vocal. Originally recorded "Louie, Louie," 1957.

BERRY, WAYNE Guitar, vocal. Member of Volunteers, 1976. *Album:* Home At Last, 1974.

BERRYHILL, BOB Guitar. Member of the Surfaris, 1963-65.

BERTLES, BOB Reeds, vocal. Member of Ian Carr's Nucleus since 1975.

BERWALD, LARRY Guitar. Session for Jimmy Hall (1980).

BESEDICK, STEVE Piano, vocal. Member of Highwind, 1980.

BESHOURI, JOE Drums. Member of Wild Oats, 1977.

BEST, HENRY Bass. Session for Leon Russell (1974).

BEST, JOHN Bass. Session for B. B. King (1971); Lightnin' Slim (1978).

BEST, PETER Drums. Replaced by Ringo Starr in the Silver Beatles in 1961.

BETHELMY, ROGER Drums. Session for Rod Stewart (1978-80).

BETHESDA, JOHNNY Bass, vocal. Member of the Rubber City Rebels, 1980.

BETINIS, MIMI Vocal, guitar, piano. Member of the Pezband, 1977.

BETTS, RICHARD Guitar, slide guitar, vocal, producer, writer. Born: 12/12/43. Playing second lead behind Duane Allman in the Allman Brothers was not a particularly advantageous spot in which to display his talents. With Duane's untimely death, it was unknown whether the Allman Brothers could continue, and when they announced they would, and without a replacement, i.e., keeping Betts as the only guitarist, fans anxiously awaited. Surprisingly, the sound of the group changed very little, proving his wealth of talent. Personnel disputes within the group led to Betts' departure as a soloist, backed by Great Southern, displaying his country-western roots. In 1979, the Allman Brothers reunited, with Betts handling most of the writing duties. Session for the Charlie Daniels Band (1976); the Marshall Tucker Band (1976); Elvin Bishop (1974); Bobby Whitlock (1975). *Albums:* Atlanta's Burning Down (ARI 4168) 1978; Dickey Betts and Great Southern (ARI 4123) 1977; Highway Call (CPN 0123) 1975.

BEVAL, ROGER Drums, vocal. Member of Offenbach, 1976.

BEVAN, BEV Drums. Original member of the Move, and of the Electric Light Orchestra since 1973.

BEYER, ED Keyboards. Member of Canned Heat, 1973, and Gary Myrick and the Figures, 1980.

BIANCO, GEORGE Harmonica. Session for Henry Gross (1973).

BIANCO, GINGER Drums. Member of Isis, 1974-75.

BICHEL, KENNETH Keyboards. Member of the Stories, 1972-73. Session for Roy Buchanan (1976).

BICKLER, DAVE Vocal, keyboards. Member of Survivor, 1979.

BIDEWELL, JOE Keyboards, vocal. Session for John Cale (1979).

BIDSTRUP, GRAHAM Drums. Replaced Buzz Throckman in Angel City, 1978-present.

BIDWELL, DAVE Drums, percussion. Original member of Stan Webb's Chicken Shack through the late 1960s. He replaced Roger Earle in Savoy

Brown, 1971-73, and returned to Savoy Brown again in 1975 for one album, "Wire Fire."

BIELA, GREG Bass, vocal. Member of Heartsfield, 1973-75.

BIFF Vocal, percussion. Member of Saxon, 1980.

BIG BLACK Congas. Member of Paul Butterfield's Blues Band, 1971.

BIG BOPPER Vocal. Real name: Jiles Perry Richardson. Disk jockey from Beaumont, Texas, who wrote and recorded the third most popular record played in the U.S. in 1958 (also released in 37 other countries), "Chantilly Lace." Died in a plane crash with Buddy Holly and Ritchie Valens, February 3, 1959.

BIG BROTHER AND THE HOLDING COMPANY Janis Joplin—vocal; Peter Albin—bass, vocal; Sam Andrew—guitar, vocal; James Gurley—guitar, vocal; David Getz—drums, vocal. A more unlikely combination never existed. A psychedelic rock band from San Francisco, specializing in volume, with a Texan, Southern Comfort-drinking female vocalist with a voice as gruff as Joe Cocker's. It seemed she was most comfortable singing the blues, "Summertime," "Ball and Chain (1968)," etc., but whatever she sang was a Joplin song. In 1968, she left the group, as did Andrew, to begin a solo career, which was cut short by her death of a drug overdose on October 4, 1970. Andrew returned to the group for two more albums, neither of which was as dynamic as with the legendary Joplin. *Albums:* Be a Brother (COL); How Hard It Is (COL); Cheap Thrills (COL PC 9700) 1968; Big Brother and the Holding Company (COL 6099) 1967.

BIG FIGURE Member of Dr. Feelgood, 1975.

BIG SONNY AND THE LOWBOYS Band formed by former Mother of Invention, Jimmy Carl Black.

BIG STAR Christopher Bell—guitar, vocal; Alex Chilton—guitar, vocal; Andy Himmel—bass, piano, vocal; Jody Stephens—drums, vocal. *Albums:* Number One Record, 1972; Radio City.

BIG THING Early name for Chicago.

BIG THREE Cass Elliot; Tim Rose; Denny Doherty. The group that evolved into Mugwumps, which developed into the Mamas and the Papas.

BIG WHA-KOO Danny Douma—vocal, guitar; Don Francisco—drums, vocal, percussion; David Palmer—vocal, percussion; Nick Van Maarth—guitar, vocal; Richard Kosinski—keyboards, vocal; Andy Silvester—bass; John Mack—drums; Peter Freiberger—bass; Claude Pepper—drums. Evolved into Wha-Koo after their first album. See Wha-Koo. *Album:* Big Wha-Koo (MCA 971) 1977.

BIGHORN Joe Shikany—guitar, vocal; Michael Ipsen—bass, vocal; Steve Adamek—drums, vocal; Bob Marcy—reeds, vocal; Peter Davis—keyboards, vocal. *Album:* Bighorn (COL JC-35618) 1978.

BIGLIN, MARTIN Bass. Member of Fireballet, 1975-76.

BIGLIN, SPIKE Bass. Member of Private Lines, 1980.

BIKIALO, GERALD Keyboards. Member of Magma.

BILAN, DANNY Drums. Replaced Bill Wade in Moxy, 1978.

BILDT, LUTHER Vocal, guitar. Original member of Stoneground, 1971.

BILLINGS, BUD Trumpet. Session for the Steve Miller Band (1970).

BILLINGS, DAN Drums. Replaced Bill Larson in Missouri, 1979.

BILLINGSLEY, JO JO Member of Alias, 1979.

BILLION DOLLAR BABIES Bob Dolin—keyboards, vocal; Neal Smith—drums, vocal; Dennis Dunaway—bass, vocal; Michael Bruce—vocal, guitar; Mike Marconi—vocal, guitar. Alice Cooper's backup band on their own. *Album:* Battle Axe (POL 1-6100) 1977.

BILLIVEAU, TOM Bass. Member of Brother Fox and the Tar Baby, 1969.

BILYEA, MALANI Guitar. Member of Kalapanna, 1977.

BINGHAM, STEVE Bass. Session for Matthew Fisher (1974); Ronnie Lane (1975).

BINKLEY, GEORGE, III Violin. Session for Waylon Jennings (1973, 75).

BINKS, LES Drums. Member of Fancy, 1976. Replaced Alan Moore in Judas Priest, 1977-80.

BIONDO, GEORGE Bass. Member of Steppenwolf, 1971-76. Session for John Kay (1973).

BIRCH, DAVID Guitar. Member of Bruce Wooley and the Camera Club, 1980.

BIRCH, DIANE Vocal. Session for Alvin Lee (1974); Bryan Ferry (1977); Manfred Mann (1979-80); Marianne Faithfull (1979).

BIRCH, GAYLORD Drums. Accompanied the Pointer Sisters, 1973-75.

BIRCH, MARTIN Guitar, producer, engineer. Engineered Fleetwood Mac (1971-73); Deep Purple (1969-76); the Faces (1970). Produced Whitesnake (1978-80); Roger Glover (1978); Blue Oyster Cult; Black Sabbath (1980); and others. Session for Fleetwood Mac (1973).

BIRCH, WILL Drums, vocal. Member of the Records, 1979-present.

BIRDSONG, CINDY Vocal. Replaced Florence Ballard in the Supremes.

BIRELL, PETE Member of Freddie and the Dreamers, 1962-66.

BIRKETT, CHRIS Vocal, guitar. Member of Omaha Sheriff, 1977.

BIRKIN, CHRIS Bass. Member of Sniff 'n' the Tears, 1978.

BIRMINGHAM JAM Early name for John Lee Hooker.

BIRTHA Shele Pinizzotto—guitar, vocal; Liver Favela—percussion, harmonica, vocal; Sherry Hagler—keyboards; Rosemary Butler—bass, vocal. *Album:* Can't Stop the Madness (DHL 50136)

1973.

BIRTLES, BEEB Guitar, vocal. Member of the Little River Band since 1977.

BIRTLES AND GOBLE Beeb Birtles—guitar, vocal; Graham Goble—guitar, vocal. Joint venture by the nucleus of the Little River Band. *Album:* Last Romance (BMI ST 21078) 1980.

BISCHOF, INGO Keyboards, vocal. Member of Karthago, 1974, and Kraan, 1975.

BISCUITS, CHUCK Drums. Member of D.O.A. since 1979.

BISETTI, VICTOR Drums. Member of the Heaters, 1978-present.

BISHOP, CHRISTOPHER Vocal, bass. Member of McKendree Spring.

BISHOP, ELVIN Guitar. Member of the Paul Butterfield Blues Band, 1965-68. He went solo, releasing two little-known albums on Fillmore Records. After breaking with his lead singer and girlfriend, Jo Baker, and the old record label, he resurfaced on Capricorn Records with a new group, and a matured sound featuring intricate guitar duets with Johnny Vernazza. See the Elvin Bishop Band. Session for the Marshall Tucker Band (1974); Super Session (1969).

ELVIN BISHOP BAND Elvin Bishop—guitar, slide guitar, vocal, writer; Applejack—harmonica (until 1972); Stephen Miller—keyboards (until 1972); Kip Maercklein—bass (until 1972); Bill Meeker—drums (until 1972); Johnny Vernazza—guitar, dobro, vocal (1974-78); Don Baldwin—drums, vocals (1974-78); Michael Brooks—bass (1974-77); Phil Aaberg—piano, clarinet (1974-76); Mickey Thomas—vocals (1975-78); Melvin Seals—keyboards (1977-78); Maurice Criolin—bass (1978). After leaving Paul Butterfield in 1968, Bishop formed his own group, which achieved little fame. On the Epic label, he released "Rock My Soul," 1972, a delightful album featuring better production. A self-imposed retirement lasted almost two years, at which time Bishop moved to record on the Allman Brothers' Capricorn label. His all-new group featured a tighter, more commercial sound, away from his blues roots. His popularity soared with "Juke Joint Jump," an album featuring more group participation, with Vernazza's echoing guitar lines, reminiscent of the Allman Brothers, and Aaberg's haunting piano solos. Thomas was added to the line-up on "Stuff," giving the group a new voice to further explore their new direction. Part of Fillmore (1972). Session for Mickey Thomas (1977). *Albums:* Best of Elvin Bishop/Crabshaw Rising (EPC PE 33693); Hog Heaven (CPN 0215) 1978; Hometown Boy Makes Good (CPN 0176) 1977; Juke Joint Jump (CPN 0151) 1975; Let It Flow (CPN 0134) 1974; Raisin' Hell (CPN 2CP-0185) 1977; Rock My Soul (EPC KE-31563) 1972; Struttin' My Stuff (CPN 0165) 1975.

BISHOP, STEPHEN Vocal. Session for Art Garfunkel (1974, 78, 79); Randy Newman (1979). *Albums:* Bish (MCA 1082) 1978; Careless (MCA D-954); Red Cab to Manhattan (WBR BSK 3473) 1980.

BITELLI, PETER Drums. Member of Riot, 1980.

BITTAN, ROY Keyboards, vocal, producer. Member of the E Street Band. Production and session for Jimmie Mack and the Jumpers, 1980. Session for Ian Hunter (1979); Dire Straits (1980).

BITZER, GEORGE Keyboards, vocal. Member of Network, 1977.

BIZARROS Nick Nichols—vocal; Gerald Parkins—guitar; Donald Parkins—guitar, bass; Terry Walker—keyboards, viola, guitar, bass; Rick Garberson—drums. *Album:* Bizarros (MER SRM-1-3776) 1979.

BIZEAU, BILLY Keyboards, vocal. Member of Quick, 1976.

BLACK, BARRY Drums, percussion. Member of the John Miles Band.

BLACK, BOBBY Pedal steel guitar. Member of Commander Cody's Lost Planet Airmen. Member of the New Commander Cody Band, 1977. Session for Alvin Lee (1973); Commander Cody (1978).

BLACK, CHARLES Horns. Session for Steppenwolf (1974).

BLACK, CILLA Vocals. Real name: Priscilla White. One of the many discoveries of Beatles manager Brian Epstein who few people discovered on record. *Album:* It Is Love, 1968.

BLACK, DAVE Guitar. Member of the Spiders from Mars, 1976.

BLACK, DOUG Bass. Member of the Group Image, 1968.

BLACK, FLOYD Drums. Member of Ted Nugent's backup band, 1978.

BLACK, HAROLD C. Tambourine. Member of David Peel's Lower East Side, 1969.

BLACK, JAY Vocal. Namesake of Jay and the Americans, 1963-68, and less successful soloist.

BLACK, JIMMY CARL Drums, vocal. Original member of the Mothers of Invention, 1966-70, Geronimo Black, until 1973, Big Sonny and The Low Boys, and the Grandmothers, 1980.

BLACK, PAULINE Vocal. Member of Selecter, 1980.

BLACK, PHIL Guitar, fiddle, vocal. Member of the Coon Elder Band, 1977.

BLACK, ROBIN Producer, engineer. Production and engineering for Jethro Tull (1978-present).

BLACK, SHERYL Vocal. Member of S.C.R.A., 1972.

BLACK CAT BONES Early English band that brought together Paul Kossoff and Simon Kirke, who later formed Free.

BLACK FLAG Greg Ginn—guitar; Charles Dukowski—bass; Robo—drums; Chavo Pederast—vocal. *Album:* Jealous Again (STF 003).

BLACK GRASS Rev. Patrick Henderson—keyboards, vocal; Nawsa Crowder—vocal; Phyliss Lindsey—vocal; Mary Ann Lindsey—vocal. Vocal backup group for Leon Russell, 1972.

BLACK OAK ARKANSAS Jim "Dandy" Mangrum —vocal; Wayne Evans—drums; Stan Knight—guitar, organ, vocal; Harvey Jett—guitar, banjo, piano, vocal; Pat Daugherty—bass, vocal; Ricky Reynolds—guitar, vocal. Hard rock group, featuring Jim "Dandy" Magrum's hoarse, screaming vocals, that saturated the market before they faded from the public eye. *Albums:* Ten Year Overnight Success, 1976; Balls of Fire, 1976; Street Party, 1974; High on the Hog, 1973; Ain't Life Grand, 1975; Early Times, 1974; Keep the Faith; If an Angel Came To See You; Race With the Devil (ACO) 1977; Best of Black Oak Arkansas (ACO 36-150); Black Oak Arkansas (ACO 354) 1971; Live, Mutha (ACO 36-128) 1976; Raunch 'N' Roll (ACO SD-7019) 1973; X—Rated (MCA 2155) 1975.

BLACK PLAGUE Early name of Johnny Winter's backup group.

BLACK RUSSIAN Serge Kapustin—keyboards, synthesizer, vocal, guitar; Natasha Kapustin—vocal, keyboards, synthesizer; Vladimir Shneider —vocal. First Russian rock group signed to an American label, they renounced their Soviet citizenship and moved to the U.S. in 1976. *Album:* Black Russian (MTN 942RI) 1980.

BLACK SABBATH Tony Iommi—guitar, keyboards; Terry Geezer Butler—bass; Bill Ward—drums; John "Ozzy" Osbourne—vocal, harmonica (1970-80); Ronnie James Dio—vocal (1980). Original name: Earth. As the devil gave an image to the Stones, so he gave an image to Black Sabbath. A quartet, they first appeared in 1970, and gained an underground reputation with heavy metal lovers. After a three year retirement, Osbourne left to go solo and was replaced by Rainbow vocalist Dio. *Albums:* Black Sabbath (WBR 1871) 1970; Black Sabbath—Vol. 4 (WBR B-2602) 1972; Heaven and Hell (WBR 3372) 1980; Master of Reality (WBR B-2562) 1971; Never Say Die (WBR K-3186) 1978; Paranoid (WBR K-3104) 1970; Sabbath, Bloody Sabbath (WBR B-2695) 1974; Sabotage (WBR B-2822) 1975; Technical Ecstasy (WBR B-2969) 1976; We Sold Our Soul for Rock 'n' Roll (WBR B-2923) 1976.

BLACK SHEEP Donald Mancuso—guitar; Louis Grammatico—vocal; Mike Bonafede—drums; Larry Cruzier—keyboard; Bruce Turson—bass. *Album:* Encouraging Words, 1975.

BLACKBURN, MONK Saxophone, flute, vocal. Member of Razmataz, 1972.

BLACKFOOT, J. D. Guitar, vocal. *Albums:* Song of Crazy Horse (FSY 9468) 1974; Southbound and Gone, 1975.

BLACKFOOT Greg Walker—bass, vocal; Charlie Hargrett—guitar; Jackson Spires—drums, vocals; Rick Medlocke—vocal, guitar. *Albums:* Flyin' High (EPC) 1976; Strikes (ACO 38-112) 1979; Tomcattin' (ACO 32-101) 1980; No Reservations (ISL AN-7076) 1975.

BLACKJACK Michael Bolotin—vocal; Bruce Kulick —guitar; Sandy Gennard—drums; Jimmy Haslip —bass. *Albums:* Blackjack (POL 1-6215) 1979; Worlds Apart (POL 1-6279) 1980.

BLACKMAN, BRUCE Vocal, keyboards. Member of Starbuck, 1977-78.

BLACKMORE, RITCHIE Guitar, vocal, writer. Born 4/14/45. Co-founder of Deep Purple, 1968-75, he left to form Rainbow, 1975-present. Session for Lord Sutch.

BLACKOUTS Bill Rieflin—drums; Erich Werner —vocal, guitar; Mike Davidson—bass; Roland Barker—vocal, saxophone, synthesizer. *Album:* Men in Motion (ENG 0001) 1980.

BLACKSMOKE HORNS Buddy McDaniel—tenor saxophone; Cliff Ervin—trumpet; Bradford Henry Thoelke, III—trombone; Trevor Lawrence—tenor saxophone; Steve Madio—trumpet; Jim Price—trombone. Studio horn group. Session for John Mayall (1978).

BLACKWELL, CHRIS Producer. English producer for Free, Traffic, the B-52's (1980), and others.

BLACKWELL, CHUCK Drums, percussion. Part of Joe Cocker's Greatest Show on Earth, 1970. Session for Taj Mahal; Freddie King (1971-73); Leon Russell (1971, 72, 74).

BLACKWELL, RICHARD Percussion. Session for Bruce Springsteen (1973).

BLADD, STEPHEN JO Drums, percussion, vocals. Original member of the J. Geils Band, since 1970.

BLADE, VICKI RAZOR Vocal. Namesake of Vicki and the Razor Blades, 1977.

BLADES, JACK Bass. Member of Rubicon, 1978-79. Session for Mike Bloomfield (1978).

BLAIN, BOBBY Piano. Session for Sylvain Sylvain (1979).

BLAINE, HAL Drums, percussion. Session for Art Garfunkel; Billy Strange; Jon Mark (1974); Paul Simon (1972); Jan and Dean (1963); Simon and Garfunkel (1970); Martin Mull (1979); Steven T. (1978).

BLAIR, CRAIG Guitar. Member of Hammersmith, 1975-76.

BLAIR, EDDIE Saxophone, keyboards, vocal. Member of Nantucket since 1978.

BLAIR, EDDIE Trumpet. Session for Savoy Brown (1969).

BLAIR, JOHN Guitar. Member of Jon and the Nightriders, 1980.

BLAIR, RON Bass. Member of Tom Petty's Heartbreakers since 1977. Session for the Tremblers (1980).

BLAKE, ALEX Bass. Session for Airto (1974); Blast (1979).

BLAKE, GINGER Vocal. Session for Bob Seger

(1980).

BLAKE, NORMAN Session for Bob Dylan (1969).

BLAKELY, ALAN Guitar. Original member of the Tremeloes.

BLAKELY, JOHN Guitar, bass. Original member of Stoneground, 1971. Session for Sammy Hagar (1975); Country Joe McDonald (1979).

BLAKELY, RONEE Vocal. Country-western star of the movie "Nashville," whose singing talents were put to disk after the movie. Session for Bob Dylan (1975). *Album:* Ronee Blakely 1975.

BLAKEMORE, RICK Guitar, vocal. Member of Fandango.

BLAKESLEY, MICHAEL Trombone. Session for McDonald and Giles (1971).

BLAKESON, DON Trumpet. Session for Mike Oldfield (1975).

BLAMIRE, ROBERT Member of Penetration, 1979.

BLAND, BOBBY "BLUE" Rhythm and blues vocalist. *Albums:* Ain't Nothing You Can Do (MCA X-78); Barefoot Rock and You Got Me (MCA X-72); Best of Bobby "Blue" Bland (MCA X-84); Best of Bobby "Blue" Bland, Vol. II (MCA X-86); Call On Me (MCA X-77); Come Fly with Me (MCA 1075); Here's the Man (MCA X-75); I Feel Good, I Feel Fine (MCA 3157); Introspective of the Early Years (MCA D-92); Reflections in Blue (MCA 1018); Soul of the Man (MCA X-79); Spotlighting the Man (MCA X-89); Together Again —Live (MCA 9317); Together for the First Time (MCA Y-50190); Touch of the Blues (MCA X-88); Two Steps from the Blues (MCA X-74).

BLANDAMER, STEVE Tenor saxophone. Session for Status Quo (1973).

BLANKENFIELD, PETER Real name of Peter Wolf.

BLASQUIZ, KLAUS Vocal. Voice of Magma.

BLAST Ula Hedwig—vocal; Garoslav Jakubovic—keyboards, saxophone, vocal. *Album:* Blast (COL JC-36012) 1979.

BLAUVELT, HOWIE Bass. Member of Ram Jam, 1977-78.

BLEND Jim Brown—guitar; Steven Dore—guitar, piano; Ken Holt—bass; Skip Smith—drums; Donnie Pomber—keyboards. *Albums:* The Blend (MCA 3058) 1978; Anytime Delight (MCA 3175) 1979.

BLESSING, LYNN Keyboards, vibes, writer. Co-author and performer with Tim Weisberg, 1971-79.

BLIFFERT, FRED Member of Jelly, 1977.

BLIND FAITH Eric Clapton—guitar, vocal, writer; Steve Winwood—guitar, vocal, keyboards, writer; Ginger Baker—drums, percussion, writer; Rick Grech—bass, violin. The dissolve of Cream and Traffic in 1968 left Clapton and Baker (of the former) and Winwood (of the latter) to join in the formation of Blind Faith. Perhaps the first supergroup in rock, their union, with ex-Family member Grech, was expected to make at least a million dollars on their first U.S. tour of twenty-four cities in 1969. Their only album (issued in a censored and uncensored jacket), though interesting and listenable, was less dynamic than any of their works in their parent groups. *Album:* Blind Faith (ACO 33-3048) 1969.

BLIND SAMMIE Early performing name of Blind Willie McTell.

BLIND WILLIE Early performing name of Blind Willie McTell.

BLISS, JOHN Drums. Member of the Reels, 1980.

BLISS, PAUL Bass, vocal, writer. Original member of Dog Soldier, 1975, and namesake of the Bliss Band, 1977-78.

BLISS, PHILLIP Steel guitar. Session for Bob Seger (1973).

BLISS BAND Paul Bliss—vocal, keyboards; Andy Brown—bass, vocal; Phil Palmer—guitar, vocal; Alan Park—keyboards; Nigel Elliott—drums, percussion. *Albums:* Neon Smiles (COL JC-36070); Dinner with Raoul (COL JC-35511) 1978.

BLITZ, JOHNNY Drums. Member of the Dead Boys, 1977-78.

BLITZ, URBAN Guitar. Member of Doctors of Madness, 1977.

BLIZZARD OF OZZ Ozzy Osbourne—vocal; Bob Daisley—bass, vocal, percussion; Lee Kerslake—drums, percussion; Randy Rhodes—guitar. *Album:* Blizzard of Ozz (Import) 1980.

BLOCH, GREGORY Violin. Replaced Mauro Pagni in P.F.M., 1977. Session for the Dwight Twilley Band (1979); Gilda Radner (1979).

BLOCK, RORY Guitar, vocal. *Albums:* Intoxication (CYS 1157) 1977; You're the One (CYS 1233) 1979; I'm in Love (BLG 2022) 1976.

BLOCKER, JO Session for Steve Hillage (1977).

BLOCKHEADS See Ian Dury and the Blockheads.

BLOCKI, ED Vocal, bass. Member of the Numbers, 1980.

BLODGETT, STEVE Drums. Member of Balcones Fault, 1977.

BLODWYN PIG Mick Abrahams—vocal, guitar, writer; Jack Lancaster—saxophone, violin, coronet; Andy Pyle—bass; Ron Berg—drums, percussion. After leaving Jethro Tull, Abrahams formed Blodwyn Pig, in which he could experiment more himself, rather than behind the dynamic Ian Anderson. "Ahead Rings Out," 1969, featuring a cigarette-smoking pig with headphones, sunglasses, and a ring in his nose on the cover, showed jazz inclinations and featured the reed and horn work of Lancaster. "Getting to This" was a continuation of the same. Despite the accessibility of the sound, Pig never made it to the radio, or to the end of the year. *Albums:* Ahead Rings Out (AAM 4210) 1969; Getting to This (AAM 4243) 1970.

BLONDIE Deborah Harry—vocal; Chris Stein—guitar, bass (1979-present); Gary Valentine—bass, guitar (1979-present); Clement Burke—drums;

James Destri—keyboards; Frank Infante—guitar (1977-78); Nigel Harrison—bass (1978). *Albums:* Blondie (CYS 1166); Eat to the Beat (CYS 1225) 1979; Parallel Lines (CYS 1165) 1978; Plastic Letters (CYS 1166) 1977.

BLOOD, SWEAT AND TEARS Lou Soloff—trumpet; Alan Rubin—trumpet; Chuck Winfield—trumpet (1968-69); Fred Lipsius—saxophone, piano; Steve Katz—guitar, harmonica, vocal; Jerry Hyman—trombone; Dick Nalligan—keyboards; Jim Fielder—bass; Bobby Colomby—drums; David Clayton-Thomas—vocals; William Tillman—saxophone; Dave Bergeron—trombone, tuba; Ron McClure—bass; George Wadenius—guitar; Jerry LaCroix—saxophone, vocal; Tom Klatka—trumpet; Larry Willis—keyboard; Greg Herbert. The band was the brainchild of Al Kooper, who formed it and left before their first album was released. Clayton- Thomas, a Canadian blues singer, replaced him. Blood, Sweat and Tears continued with what was then experimental in a rock band, a horn section. The goal was to merge rock and jazz, and no one can argue with their much-imitated success. When Clayton-Thomas left, the group disbanded, only to be re-formed by Colomby with totally new personnel in the 1970s. But the novelty was gone, as was the original talent. *Albums:* Brand New Day, 1977; Blood, Sweat and Tears (COL PC-9720); Blood, Sweat and Tears Greatest Hits (COL PC-31170); Child Is Father to the Man (COL PC-9619) 1968; Heavy Sounds (COL CS-9952); No Sweat (COL C-32180); Mirror Image (COL PCQ-32929) 1974; New Blood (COL KC-31780); New City (COL PCQ-33484) 1975.

BLOODROCK Warren Ham—saxophone, flute, vocal (until 1972); Lee Pickens—guitar; Nick Taylor—guitar; Steve Hill—keyboard; Ed Grundy—bass; Rick Cobb—drums; Jim Rutledge—vocal (1972-73). Hard rock specialists. *Albums:* Bloodrock (CAP ST-435); Bloodrock 2 (CAP ST-491) 1970; Bloodrock 3 (CAP ST-765) 1971; Bloodrock—Bloodrock 'N' Roll (CAP SM-11417); Bloodrock Live (CAP SVBB-11038) 1972; Bloodrock U.S.A. (CAP SMAS-645); Passage (CAP SW-11109); Whirlwind Tongues (CAP SMAS-11259).

BLOOME, ERIC Vocal, guitar, keyboards. Member of the Blue Oyster Cult. Session for Ian Hunter (1979).

BLOOMFIELD, BRETT Bass, vocal. Member of Snail, 1978-79.

BLOOMFIELD, MICHAEL Guitar, bass, drums, banjo, keyboards. Organized the Electric Flag, 1967-68. Member of Paul Butterfield Blues Band, 1965-68; Fathers and Sons, 1969; Triumvirat, with John Hammond and Dr. John, 1974; KGB, 1975; and most recently, a soloist recording traditional American blues. Session for John Hammond (1965, 68); Sleepy John Estes (1963); Yank Rachel. *Albums:* It's Not Killing Me (COL); Analine (TKM 1059) 1977; Between the Hard Place and the Ground (TKM 7070) 1979; Michael Bloomfield (TKM 1063) 1978; Count Talent and the Originals (CLD 8805) 1978; Live Adventures of Mike Bloomfield and Al Kooper (COL PG-6) 1969; Super Session (COL CS-9701) 1968; Bloomfield—Harris (TKM 164) 1980.

BLOOMFIELD, STEVE Guitar, mandolin, harmonica, vocal. Member of Matchbox, 1979.

BLOONTZ Tony Braunagle—drums; Andy Chapman—vocal; David Kealey—guitar; Mike Montgomery—keyboards; Terry Wilson—bass, guitar. *Album:* Bloontz (EVN 3020) 1973.

BLOTTO, BOWTIE Vocal, guitar. Member of Blotto, 1980.

BLOTTO, BROADWAY Vocal, guitar. Member of Blotto, 1980.

BLOTTO, CHEESE Vocal, bass. Member of Blotto, 1980.

BLOTTO, CHEVROLET Vocal, keyboards. Member of Blotto, 1980.

BLOTTO, LEE HARVEY Vocal, drums. Member of Blotto, 1980.

BLOTTO, SERGEANT Vocal, percussion. Member of Blotto, 1980.

BLOTTO Broadway Blotto—vocal, guitar; Bowtie Blotto—vocal, guitar; Sergeant Blotto—vocal, percussion; Cheese Blotto—vocal, bass; Lee Harvey Blotto—vocal, drums; Chevrolet Blotto—vocal, keyboards. *Album:* Across and Down (BLT 002) 1980.

BLOUGH, BILLY Bass. Member of George Thorogood and the Destroyers since 1977. Session for Preacher Jack (1980).

BLOXSOM, IAN Percussion. Member of S.C.R.A., 1972.

BLT Paul West—piano, vocal; Gail Clements—guitar, vocal; Rolf Brye—bass, vocal. *Album:* BLT, 1977.

BLUE, AMANDA Vocal. Member of Spider, 1980.

BLUE, BARRY Vocal, guitar, bass, percussion. Member of Javaroo.

BLUE, BILL Guitar, vocal. Namesake of the Bill Blue Band since 1979.

BILL BLUE BAND Bruce Courson—keyboards (1979); Sharon Garland—vocal (1979); Glenn Pavone—guitar, vocal (1979); David Carey—bass, vocal; David Poole—drums, vocal (1979); Zip Irvin—saxophone, vocal (1980); Ricky White—guitar, vocal (1980); Steve Snyder—trumpet, trombone, vocal (1980); Mark Crump—drums (1980); Bill Blue—guitar, vocal. *Albums:* Sing Like Thunder (ADP 4109) 1979; Giving Good Boys a Bad Name (DP 4118) 1980.

BLUE, DAVID Vocal, guitar. *Albums:* Singer—Songwriter Project (ELK); Comin' Back for More (ASY 7E-1043) 1975; Cupid's Arrow (ASY 7E-1077) 1976; Stories (ASY 5052) 1971.

BLUE, SUGAR Harmonica. Session for the Rolling Stones (1978).

BLUE, VICKI Member of the Runaways, 1976-77.

BLUE ANGEL John Turi—keyboards, saxophone; Johnny Morelli—drums; Cyndi Lauper—vocal; Lee Brovitz—bass; Arthur Neilson—guitar. *Album:* Blue Angel (POL PD 1-6300) 1980.

BLUE ASH Jim Kendzor—vocal, guitar; Frank Secich—bass, vocal; David Evans—drums, vocal; Bill Bartolin—guitar, vocal. *Album:* No More, No Less (MER) 1973.

BLUE CHEER Leigh Stephens—guitar, vocal; Dick Peterson—bass, vocal, writer; Paul Whaley—drums; Randy Holden—guitar (1968). Bay Area rockers from the psychedelic 1960s, specializing in high volume. Their first album included an Owsley poem for liner notes and an electrified rendition of "Summertime Blues." The unavoidable comparison of their heavy trio format to Cream and Hendrix left them at odds and resulted in little popularity outside of the West Coast. *Albums:* Outsideinside, 1968; Improved! Blue Cheer (PHI) 1969; Vincebus Eruptum (PHI PL-9001) 1968.

BLUE GOOSE Nick Hogarth—keyboards; Mike Dodman—guitar; Alan Callan—guitar, synthesizer, vocal; Sean Locke—percussion; Chris Perkey—drums; Nick South—bass. *Album:* Blue Goose (ANC) 1975.

BLUE JAYS Justin Hayward—guitar, vocals, writer; John Lodge—bass, vocals, writer; Graham Deakin—drums; Kirk Duncan—piano; Jim Cockney—violin; Tim Tompkins—cello; Tom Tompkins—viola. Group formed by ex-Moody Blues members Justin Hayward and John Lodge. *Album:* Blue Jays (THS 14) 1975.

BLUE JUG Ed Ratzeloff—guitar, vocal; Clint de Long—guitar, vocal; Bill Little—keyboards, vocal; Bill Burnett—bass; Paul Walkley—drums. *Album:* Blue Jug (CPN) 1975.

BLUE MINK Madeline Bell—vocal; Roger Cook—vocal; Barry Morgan—drums; Herbie Flowers—bass; Alan Parker—guitar; Roger Coulam—keyboards. *Album:* Real Mink (PHL 600 339).

BLUE OYSTER CULT Donald Roeser—guitar, vocal; Eric Bloome—vocal, guitar, keyboards; Albert Bouchard—drums, vocal; Joe Bouchard—bass, vocal; Allen Lanier—guitar, keyboards. Jazz-rock artists who debuted in 1973. *Albums:* Agents of Fortune (COL PC-34164) 1976; Blue Oyster Cult (COL PC-31064) 1973; Cultosaurus Erectus (COL JC-36550, 1980); Mirrors (COL JC-36009, 1979); On Your Feet or On Your Knees (COL PG-33371) 1975; Secret Treaties (COL PC-32858) 1974; Some Enchanted Evening (COL JC-35563); Spectres (COL JC-35019) 1977; Tyranny and Mutation (COL KC-32017).

BLUE RIDGE RANGERS Collective name of John Fogerty's one-man recording debut after leaving Credence Clearwater Revival. *Album:* Blue Ridge Rangers (FSY 9415) 1973.

BLUE STEEL Leonard Arnold—guitar; Richard Borden—guitar; Howard Burke—guitar; Marc Durham—bass; Mickey McGee—drums; Michael Huey—drums. *Album:* No More Lonely Nights (INF 9018) 1980.

BLUE SWEDE Bjorn Skefs—vocal; Jan Guldback—drums; Bosse Liljedahl—bass; Michael Areklew—guitar; Ladislau Balaz—keyboard; Tommy Berglund—trumpet; Hinke Ekestubble—saxophone, flute. International rock 'n' roll played with the Swedish touch. *Albums:* Hooked on a Feeling (EMI ST-1128); Out of the Blue (EMI ST-11346).

BLUECHEL, TED Drums. Original member of the Association.

BLUES BAND Paul Jones—vocal, harmonica; Tom McGuiness—guitar, vocal; Hughie Flint—drums; Dave Kelly—guitar, vocal; Gary Fletcher—bass. Traditional 1960s English blues updated for the 1970s. *Album:* The Official Blues Band Bootleg Album (Import) 1979.

BLUES BROTHERS Joliet Jake Blues (John Belushi)—vocal; Elwood Blues (Dan Aykroyd)—harmonica, vocal. Originally a satire of old rhythm and blues by two of television's "Saturday Night Live" comedy troupe, the Brothers played their parody to perfection and popularity, using original R & B artists from Booker T.'s M.G.s in their back-up band. *Albums:* Blues Brothers (ATC 16017) 1980; Briefcase Full of Blues (ATC 19217) 1978; Made in America (ACO SD 16025) 1980.

BLUES INC. According to Long John Baldry, the first white electric blues band. Formed in 1961. Members from 1961 to 1967 included: Charlie Watts, Mick Jagger, Ginger Baker, Brian Jones, Jack Bruce, Keith Richards, Eric Burdon, Long John Baldry, Dick Heckstall-Smith, Graham Bond, Cyril Davies, Duffy Power, Zoot Money, Nigel Strangler, Lee Jackson, Danny Thompson, Terry Cox, Dave Holland, Herbie Goins, Paul Williams, Phil Seaman, Paul Jones, John Marshall, Dave Castle, Jack Bruce, Art Themen, Spike Heatley, Johnny Parker, John Surman, Ray Warleigh, Chris Pyne, Malcolm Cecil, Save Stevens, Alan Skidmore, Keith Scott, Andy Hoogenboom, Brian Smith, Mike Scott, Tony Roberts, Barry Booth, Barry Howten, Bernard George, Colin Bowden, Dave McIver, Sylvia McNeil, Ronnie Dunn, Mike Pyne, Ronnie Jones, and Davy Graham, among others.

BLUES MAGOOS Ralph Scala—vocals, organ; Ron Gilbert—bass; Geoff Daking—drums; Mike Esposito—guitar; Emil Thielheim—vocal, guitar. A New York Group with a misleading name. Based in the blues, their specialty was electric rock. *Albums:* Psychedelic Lollipop, 1966; Electric Comic Book, 1967; Basic Blues Magoos, 1968; Gulf Coast Bound; Never Goin' Back to Georgia; Nuggets (ABC and ELK).

BLUES PROJECT Andy Kulberg—flute, bass, piano; Roy Blumenfeld—drums; John Gregory—guitar, vocals; Donald Gretman—bass, saxophone; Richard Greene—violin; Tommy Flanders—vocals (1966-67); Danny Kalb—guitar; Steve Katz; Al Kooper—organ. New York's contribution to the rock scene of the mid 1960s. Actually, they could play anything, as Kalb was considered to be the best folk guitarist around. Kalb disappeared in 1967, as the then-unknown Kooper was planning other projects, so the band collapsed. Kulberg organized the remaining members in Seatrain, while Kooper started Blood, Sweat and Tears. *Albums:* Blues Project Live at the Cafe A Go-Go, 1966; Projections, 1967; Live at Town Hall, 1967; Planned Obsolescence (ELK) 1968; Blues Project (ELK 7264) 1966; Reunion in Central Park (MCA).

BLUES SYNDICATE Early name for John Mayall's group, 1962, before changing it to the Bluesbreakers.

BLUESBREAKERS See John Mayall's Bluesbreakers.

BLUESOLOGY See Steam Packet.

BLUMBERG, STU Trumpet. Session for Joe Cocker (1974).

BLUMENFELD, ROY Drums. Member of Blues Project, 1966-68, before joining Seatrain in 1968.

BLUNSTONE, COLIN Guitar, percussion, vocal, writer. Original member of the Zombies, 1965-68, he retired for a few years before making his solo debut. Session for the Alan Parsons Project (1978); Mike Batt (1979). *Albums:* Journey; One Year (EPC).

BLUNT, ROBBIE Guitar, slide guitar, writer. Member of Bronco with Jess Roden. Cofounded Broken Glass with Stan Webb, 1976. Member of the Steve Gibbons Band, 1979 to present.

BOATMAN, BILL Guitar. Session for Taj Mahal; J. J. Cale (1972).

BOATMAN, JIM Vocal. Session for Leon Russell and Willie Nelson (1979).

BOATRIGHT, GRANT Guitar. Session for Neil Young (1978).

BOATZ Thom Flora—vocal, keyboards; Gary Baker—vocal, bass; Pete Carr—guitar; Rick Powell—drums; Steve Nathan—keyboards; Roger Clark—drums. *Album:* Boatz (CPN 0222) 1979.

BOB 1 Guitar, vocal. Recording name of Devo's Bob Mothersbaugh.

BOB 2 Guitar, vocal. Member of Devo.

BOBBE, LELAND Drums, percussion. Member of Silent Dancing, 1975.

BOBBIDAZZLER James Divsek—drums; George Marinell, Jr.—guitar; Brian Whitcomb—keyboards; Grant Gullickson—vocal; Lance Gullickson—vocal. *Album:* Bobbidazzler, 1977.

BOBO, WILLIE Percussion. Session for Terry Reid (1973). *Albums:* Drum Session (CTI 6051); Hell of an Act to Follow (COL JC-35374); Bobo (COL JC-36108) 1979.

BOCHNER, RICK Vocal, guitar. Member of Mad River, 1968.

BOD, ARTHUR Guitar, vocal. Member of Iguana, 1977.

BODDICKER, MIKE Keyboards. Session for Flora Purim (1978); Gary Wright (1979); Randy Newman (1979); Adam Mitchell (1979); Rock Rose (1979); Platinum Hook (1979); J. Michael Reed (1979); Paul Waroff (1979); the Marc Tanner Band (1979); the Strand (1980).

BODENHAMER, DAVID Bass, vocal. Member of Porrazzo, 1980.

BODINE, BILL Bass, vocal. Member of the Funky Kings, 1976.

BODMAR, ANDREW Bass. Member of Rumour, 1977.

BODNER, PHIL Clarinet, saxophone. Session for Martin Mull (1974); Grace Slick (1980).

BOGAN, ANN Vocal. Replaced Gladys Horton in the Marvelettes.

BOGERT, JOHN VOORHIS "TIM" Bass. Original member of the Vanilla Fudge, 1967-69, Cactus, 1970-73, and Beck, Bogert and Appice, 1973. Session for Jan Akkerman (1973); Jeff Beck (1973); Rod Stewart (1980).

BOGIE, DOUGLAS A. Guitar. Member of R.A.F., 1980.

BOGLE, BOB Bass. Original member of the Ventures, 1960-71.

BOHANAN, GEORGE Trombone. Session for the Doors (1969); Ry Cooder (1972, 78, 80); James Taylor (1976).

BOHANNON, JIM Keyboards, percussion. Replaced Roger Crissinger in Pearls Before Swine, 1968.

BOHLE, PAT Drums. Member of the Skyboys, 1979 to present.

BOHN, CARSTEN Drums, percussion. Member of Frumpy, 1973.

BOILERHOUSE Band that Danny Kirwan left to join Fleetwood Mac, 1968.

BOISEN, PAYLES Guitar, saxophone, vocal. Member of Viktor Koncept, 1979.

BOLAN, MARC Guitar, vocal, writer. Real name: Marc Feld. Head of Tyrannosaurus Rex, 1968-74. Died 9/16/77. Session for Ringo Starr (1973).

BOLDER, TREVOR Bass. Member of Spiders from Mars, 1976. Replaced John Wetton in Uriah Heep, 1977-78. Session for David Bowie.

BOLEN, PATRICK Guitar, vocal. Replaced Tim Goshorn in Pure Prarie League, 1979.

BOLES, CHARLIE Organ. Session for B. B. King (1969).

BOLES, ELLARD Bass, vocal. Session for Lou Reed (1979-80).

BOLIN, TOMMY Guitar, vocal, writer, piano, synthesizer. An original member of Zephyr, 1971, he became better known in jazz and rock circles before becoming a member of the James Gang, replacing Joe Walsh, 1973-74, and replacing Ritchie Blackmore in Deep Purple, 1975. Released his solo debut in 1975, incorporating several different aspects of rock, from reggae and funk to heavy metal, and jazz. Died 12/4/76. *Albums:* Private Eyes (COL C 34329) 1976; Teaser (NMP 436) 1975.

BOLOGNESI, JACQUES Trombone. Session for Elton John (1971-72).

BOLOTIN, MICHAEL Vocal, guitar. Member of Blackjack since 1979. *Album:* Every Day of My Life, 1976.

BOLTON, MICK Organ. Session for Mott the Hoople (1973).

BOLTON, STEVE Guitar. Replaced John Cann in Atomic Rooster, 1972. Member of Headstone, 1974-75. Session for Zaine Griff (1980).

BOMMARIUS, KONNI Drums. Replaced Norbert Lehman in Karthago, 1974-76.

BONAFEDE, MIKE Drums. Member of Black Sheep, 1975.

BONAR, JOHN Member of Zuider Zee, 1975.

BONAROO Bill Cuomo—keyboards, vocal; Michael Hossack—drums; Robert Lichtig—bass, vocal; Jerry Weems—guitar, vocal; Bobby Winkelman—guitar, vocal. *Album:* Bonaroo (WBR) 1975.

BONAS, PETER Guitar. Member of the Contenders, 1979. Session for Jim Capaldi (1979).

BOND, GRAHAM Saxophone, keyboards. A founding father of English blues as a soloist, he was a member of Blues Incorporated before forming the Graham Bond Organization. A member of Ginger Baker's Air Force, 1970-71. Session for Dr. John (1971); Harvey Mandel.

GRAHAM BOND ORGANIZATION Graham Bond—saxophone, vocal, keyboards; Dick Heckstall-Smith—saxophone; Ginger Baker—drums; Jack Bruce—bass; Neil Hubbard—guitar. Blues was the new music in England in the 1960s. But Graham Bond threw a curve into the formula by mixing it with jazz and with the best musicians in both fields.

BOND, JIM Bass, acoustic bass. Member of the Righteous Brothers Band, 1966. Session for Jan and Dean (1963); Fred Neil (1968); Joe Walsh (1974).

BOND, MACEO Keyboards. Member of Osiris, 1978.

BOND, RONNIE Drums, percussion. Original member of the Troggs.

BOND, SON Guitar. Session with Sleepy John Estes (1941).

BONDS, GARY "U.S." Vocal. Recorded the hit "Quarter to Three," 1961.

BONE, JACK Bass. Session for Martin Mull (1972).

BONEBRAKE, D. J. Drums. Member of X, 1980.

BONEROO Peter Graves—trombone; Whit Sidener—baritone saxophone (1974-76); Ken Faulk—trumpet; David Muse—tenor saxophone (1974-76); Mark Colby—saxophone (until 1974); Neal Bonsouth—saxophone, English horn (until 1974); Peter Ballin—tenor saxophone; Jeff Kievit—trumpet; Stan Webb—baritone saxophone; Bill Purse. Studio horn section. Session for Firefall (1976); Bill Wyman (1974); the Bee Gees (1977); Foxy (1978); Andy Gibb (1980).

BONES Jimmy Faragher—vocal, bass, saxophone, guitar; Danny Faragher—keyboards, vocal, horns; Greg Tornquist—guitar, vocal, flute; Patrick McClure—guitar, vocal; Casey Cunningham—drums. *Albums:* Waitin' Here (MCA) 1973; Bones (SNP 8402) 1973.

BONFIRE, MARS Guitar. Real name: Dennis Edmonton. Brother of Steppenwolf drummer Jerry Edmonton. Member of Steppenwolf, 1968, and Rainbow Red Oxidizer, 1980. Session for Kim Fowley (1972).

BONHAM, JOHN Drums. Born 5/31/48. Replaced Jim McCarty in the Yardbirds, 1969. Original member of Led Zeppelin, 1969-80. Died 9/24/80. Session for Lord Sutch; Ron Wood (1979).

BONILLA, DON ARMANDO Percussion. Member of Dr. Buzzard's Original Savannah Band, 1976-78.

BONITA, PETER Piano. Added to the Artful Dodger lineup, 1980.

BONNER, JUKE BOY Guitar, vocal, harmonica. Grass-roots blues. *Albums:* Blues Roots (TMT 2-7006) 1972; Legacy of the Blues (CRS 10010); Legacy, Vol. 5 (CRS 10015).

BONNIWELL, SEAN Guitar. Original member of the Music Machine, 1966.

BONO, CHER Vocal. Born 5/20/45. Early recording name: Bonnie Jo Mason. Maiden name: Cheryl LaPere. Began as the wife of Sonny Bono in the Sonny and Cher duet of the mid sixties. After the initial successes of the team's numerous hits (see Sonny and Cher), she released solo albums, as she represented the melodic half of the team, while Sonny was mainly the writer/business half. Television opportunities came in the 1970s, as did her divorce and brief marriage to Gregg Allman of the Allman Brothers Band. Session for Gene Simmons (1978). *Albums:* All I Really Want To Do, 1965; Sonny Side of Cher, 1966; Cher, 1967; With Love, 1968; Backstage, 1968; Cher's Golden Greats, 1968; Two The Hard Way (MCA) 1977; Cher (MCA 2020); Cherished (WBR B-3046); Greatest Hits (MCA 2127); I'd Rather Believe in You (WBR B-2898) 1976; Night at Studio 54 (CAS 2-7161); Prisoner (CAS 1-7184); Roller Boogie (CAS 2-7194); Stars (WBR B-2850); Take Me Home (CAS 7133/PIX 7133) 1979; Bittersweet White Light (MCA 210); Dark Lady (MCA 2113); Foxy Lady (MCA 2019); Half Breed (MCA 2104); Very Best of Cher (UAR UA-377-E); Very Best of Cher, Volume II (UAR UA-LA435F); Cher's Greatest Hits (SPB 4028).

BONO, SONNY Vocal, Writer. Early recording

names: Don Christy; Ronnie Sommers. Former husband of Cher, in the rock team of Sonny and Cher, 1965-76.

BONOFF, KARLA Piano, vocal. *Albums:* Karla Bonoff (COL PC-34672) 1977; Restless Nights (COL JC-35799) 1979.

BONOMO, TOMMY LEE Drums, percussion, vocal. Member of the Granati Brothers, 1979.

BONSOUTH, NEAL Saxophones, English horn. Member of Boneroo until 1974.

BONUS, JACK Reeds. Session for the Rowans (1975).

BONUS, PETE Guitar. Half of the Wilding-Bonus duet of 1978.

BONZO DOG DOO-DAH BAND Vivian Stanshall—vocal; "Legs" Larry Smith—drums; Neil Innes—piano; Rodney Slater—saxophone; Roger Ruskin Spear—percussion; David Claque. America had the Fugs and the Mothers of Invention for comedy rock in the 1960s; England had the Bonzos. Outrageous costumes and stage antics were their specialty. *Albums:* Gorilla, 1968; Keynsham; Tad Poles; Urban Spaceman (IMP); Let's Make Up and Be Friendly (UAR); Beast of the Bonzos (UAR LKAO-5517) 1978; History of the Bonzos (UAR LWB-321).

BOOGE, SKIP Bass, piano. Member of Autosalvage, 1968.

BOOGIE BROTHERS Kim Simmonds—guitar, vocal, writer; Stan Webb—guitar, vocals, writer; Jimmy Leverton—bass; Eric Dillon—drums. Brief name for Savoy Brown in 1974. See Savoy Brown.

BOOKER, JAMES Piano. Session for Ringo Starr (1973); the Doobie Brothers (1974).

BOOKER T. Keyboards, vocal, bass, writer. Real name: Booker T. Jones. Head of Booker T. and the MGs. Session for Marc Benno; Willie Nelson (1978); Bob Dylan; Steve Stills (1970); Rita Coolidge (1972); Mickey Thomas (1977). *Albums:* Best of You (AAM 4798); Evergreen (EPC KE-33143) 1974; Try and Love Again (AAM 4720) 1978.

BOOKER T. AND THE MGS Booker T. Jones—keyboards; Steve Cropper—guitar; Donald Dunn—bass; Willie Hall—drums. Since recording "Green Onions" in 1962, Booker T and his Memphis Group have survived the rock boom as a group and as individual studio musicians. Session for Pakalameredith (1977). *Albums:* Best of Booker T. and the MGs (ATC 8202); Free Rider (STX 4104); Soul Years (ATC 2-504); Universal Language (ASY 7E-1093); Booker T. and the MGs Greatest Hits; Melting Pot; Green Onions, 1962; And Now; In the Christmas Spirit; Hip Hug Her; Back to Back; Doin' Our Thing.

BOOM BOOM BAND Willie Alexander—vocal, keyboards; Severin Grossman—bass; Billy Loosigian—guitar, vocal; David McLean—Drums. Backup band for Willie Alexander. *Albums:* Willie Alexander and the Boom Boom Band (MCA 2323) 1978; Meanwhile . . . Back in the States (MCA 3052) 1978.

BOOMTOWN RATS Bob Geldorf; Gerry Cott; Garry Roberts; Pete Briquette; Johnnie Fingers. *Albums:* Boomtown Rats (MER SRM-1-1188) 1977; Fine Art for Surfacing (COL JC-36248) 1979; Tonic for the Troops (COL JC-35750) 1979.

BOONE, DEBBIE Vocal. One of Pat's singing daughters who struck it big with the title track of the movie, "You Light Up My Life." *Albums:* Debbie Boone (WBR K-3301) 1979; Love Has No Reason (WBR K-3419) 1980; Midstream (WBR K-3130) 1978; With My Song (LLN 1046) 1980; You Light Up My Life (WBR B-3118) 1977.

BOONE, JOBRAITH Vocal. Namesake of Jobraith, 1973-74.

BOONE, PAT Vocal. From his religious and country-western roots, Pat Boone sang "acceptable" rock as far as parents who censored their children's music in the 1950s and 1960s were concerned. *Albums:* Hymns We Love, 1957; Star Dust, 1958; Pat's Greatest Hits, 1959; Pat's Greatest Hits, Vol. II, 1959; Side by Side, 1959; Tenderly, 1959; Great, Great, Great, 1961; My God and I, 1961; Golden Hits, 1962; Moody River, 1961; Days of Wine and Roses, 1963; Sing Along Without, 1963; Touch of Your Lips, 1964; Pat Boone, 1964; 12 Greatest Hits, 1964; Boss Beat, 1964; Golden Era of Country Hits, 1965; Memories, 1966; Wish You Were Here, 1966; True Love, 1967; I Was Kaiser Bill's Batman, 1967; Golden Hits, 1967; At the Hop (MCA AA-1111); Pat Boone/First Nashville Jesus Band (LLN 1004); S-A-V-E-D (LLN 1013); Pat Boone Sings Golden Hymns (LLN 1001); Pat Boone Sings the New Songs of the Jesus People (LLN 1002); Born Again (LLN 1007); Christian People, Vol. I (LLN 1005); Cross and the Switchblade (LGT 5550); Down Home (LLN 1024); He Leadeth Me (WOR 8664) 1950; Just the Way I Am (LLN 1039); Miracle Merry-Go-Round (LLN 1029); Great Performances (MCA DP-4006); Something Supernatural (LLN 1017); Songs from the Inner Court (LLN 1016); Star Spangled Banner (WOR 8725) 1963; Greatest Hits (PMT 2-1043); Greatest Hymns (PMT 1024); Crisis—America (BBV 7076); How Great Thou Art (DOT 25798) 1967; Lord's Prayer (DOT 25582) 1964.

BOONE, SKIP Bass, piano. Member of Autosalvage, 1966-68. His brother, Steve, played bass for the Lovin' Spoonful.

BOONE, STEVE Bass. Original member of the Lovin' Spoonful, 1965-69.

BOOTH, BARRY Began in Blues Incorporated.

BOOTH, DOUG Drums, percussion. Member of the Ron Gardner Group, 1974.

BOOTH, HENRY Member of Hank Ballard's Midnighters.

BOOTSMAN, PETER Guitar, vocal. Member of

the New Adventures, 1980.

BOPP, REINHARD Vocal, guitar. Added to the Karthago lineup, 1976.

BORCH, MIKE Drums, vibes, vocal. Member of the Ides of March.

BORDEN, GEORGE WEATHERS, JR. Bass, vocal. Member of Oak, 1980.

BORDEN, B. B. Drums. Member of Mothers Finest since 1976.

BORDEN, RICHARD Guitar. Member of Dan Hicks and His Hot Licks, 1978, and Blue Steel since 1980.

BORDY, BOB Guitar, vocal. Member of Crackin', 1975-78.

BORGE, DALE Bass, vocal. Member of Fat Chance, 1972.

BORGERS, BERTUS Saxophone. Session for Golden Earring (1974-75); George Kooymans.

BORNEMANN, FRANK Guitar, vocals, percussion. Member of Eloy, 1975-76.

BORNHOLD, HERBERT Drums. Member of Lucifer's Friend.

BORO, JAMES Guitar, vocal. Member of Porrazzo, 1980.

BORTMAN, TERRY Member of the A's, 1979.

BORTZ, DANIEL Guitar, cello. Member of Kittyhawk, 1980.

BOSHELL, BIAS Member of the Kiki Dee Band, 1973-74.

BOSTON Tom Scholz—guitar, bass, keyboards; Brad Delp—guitar, vocal, percussion; Barry Goudreau—guitar; Fran Sheehan—bass; Sib Hashian—drums, percussion. Surprise hit group of 1976 that was slow to follow their initial success, "More Than A Feeling." *Albums:* Boston (EPC HE-34188) 1976; Don't Look Back (EPC FE-35050) 1978.

BOSTON, ANNE Vocal. Session for the Brains (1980).

BOSWELL, SIMON Guitar, keyboards, vocal. Replaced Chris Cutler in Live Wire, 1980.

BOTNICK, BRUCE Producer. Produced the Doors' "L.A. Woman" (1971); the Beat (1979); Laughing Dogs (1979) and others.

BOTTLES Peter Bayless—vocal, bass, guitar; Jefery Levy—guitar, bass, keyboards; Andy Dworkin—drums; Ken Roclord Schmidt—keyboards. *Album:* The Bottles (MCA 3177) 1979.

BOTTS, MIKE Drums, vocal. Member of Bread. Session for the Ozark Mountain Daredevils (1980).

BOUCHARD, ALBERT Drums, vocal. Member of the Blue Oyster Cult.

BOUCHARD, JOE Bass, vocal. Member of the Blue Oyster Cult.

BOUCHER, BOB Bass. Session for Neil Diamond (1976).

BOUDREAUX, JOHN Drums. Session for Dr. John (1975); Robbie Robertson (1980).

BOULDER Bob Harris—vocal; Stan Bush—guitar, vocal; Zeke Zirngiebel—guitar, bass, vocal; Marty Stinger—drums; Mithran Cabin—percussion, vocal. *Album:* Boulder (ELK 6E-238) 1979.

BOULET, GERRY Vocal, keyboards, guitar. Member of Offenbach, 1976.

BOULWARE, WILL Keyboards. Session for B. B. King (1974).

BOUNSAL, DOUG Guitar, bass, vocal. Member of the Dillards, 1979.

BOUNTY BILL Keyboards, vocal. *Album:* Rain in My Life (CRB 3316) 1979.

BOURGE, TONY Guitar. Member of Budgie, 1975-77.

BOUTERSE, CURT Dulcimer. Session for Ry Cooder (1980).

BOUTTE, LILLIAN Vocal. Session for Mylon LeFevre (1979).

BOUVIER, DOMINQUE Percussion. Member of Transit Express, 1976.

BOVA, JEFF Keyboards, trumpet. Member of Flying Island, 1976.

BOWDEN, COLIN Began in Blues Incorporated.

BOWDER, STONEY, JR. Guitar, piano, vocal. Member of Dr. Buzzard's Original "Savannah" Band, 1976-78.

BOWEN, ANN Vocal, guitar, percussion. Member of Deadly Nightshade, 1975.

BOWEN, GIL Guitar, flute, vocal. Member of Arbuckle, 1972.

BOWEN, PAUL Member of Starjets, 1980.

BOWEN, TOBY Guitar. Member of Aviary, 1979.

BOWIE, DAVID Writer, vocal, guitar, saxophone, keyboards, harmonica, producer. Real name: Davey Jones. English rock 'n' roll stylist, proponent of the degenerate and "glitter" aspects of rock performance, also the author of many sensitive ballads. He was essential in the rediscovery of Iggy Pop in 1977, and made his acting debut as "The Man Who Fell To Earth." Session for Mott the Hoople (1972); Lou Reed (1972); Iggy Pop (1977, 78, 80). *Albums:* Aladdin Sane (VIC AFLI-4852) 1973; Bowie Pin Ups (VIC AFLI-0291) 1973; Changes One (VIC AFLI1732) 1976; David Live (VIC CPL2-0771) 1974; Diamond Dogs (VIC AFLI-0576) 1974; Hunky Dory (VIC AFLI-4623) 1971; Lodger (VIC AQLI-3254) 1979; Rise and Fall of Ziggy Stardust (VIC AFLI-4702) 1972; Scary Monsters (VIC AQLI-3647) 1980; Space Oddity (VIC AFLI-4813) 1972; Station to Station (VIC AFLI-1327) 1976; Young Americans (VIC AFLI-0998); Images (LON BP-628/29); Man Who Sold the World (LON BP 628/29 LSP-4816) 1972; Heroes (VIC) 1977; Low, 1977.

BOWKETT, ROD Member of Stackridge, 1974.

BOWN, ANDY Guitar, bass, keyboard, trumpet. Member of the Herd, 1967. Head of the Andy Bown, and soloist. Session for Long John Baldry (1975); Status Quo (1973, 76, 78); Peter Frampton (1972, 75); Jerry Lee Lewis (1973). *Album:* Sweet William (MER).

THE ANDY BOWN Andy Bown—trumpet; Geoff Bannister—organ; John Anthony—tenor saxophone; Steve Haldane—bass; Jess Roden—guitar, vocal; Vic Sweeny—drums; Tony Catchpole—guitar. Horn lineups in rock never attracted English audiences as well as American audiences. Bown also failed to attract much attention with his group (after being in the Herd, with Peter Frampton) or as a soloist. *Album:* The Andy Bown (MGM).

BOWNE, DOUG Drums, vocal. Session for John Cale (1979).

BOWSER, MIKE Bass. Member of the Downchild, 1979.

BOWZER Vocal. Member of Sha Na Na since 1972.

BOX, MICK Guitar, writer. Original member of Uriah Heep, 1970-78. Session for David Byron (1975).

BOX TOPS Alex Chilton—vocal; Billy Cunningham—bass; Gary Talley—guitar; Danny Smythe—drums; John Evans—organ, guitar. They had been playing for two years in the Memphis area before they hit the big time with their number one hit, "The Letter." Chilton's vocals were reminiscent of the black sound of the Righteous Brothers and their first album included three hits: "The Letter," "Neon Rainbow," and "Trains and Boats and Planes." It was a tasty sampling, but future albums were not too numerous or dynamic. *Albums:* Box Tops (BEL) 1967; Cry Like a Baby (BEL) 1968; Non-Stop (BEL) 1968.

BOXER Mike Patto—vocal, keyboards; Ollie Halsall—guitar, keyboards; Keith Ellis—bass; Tony Newman—drums. *Album:* Below the Belt (VIR) 1975.

BOY, JON Guitar, vocal, organ. Member of the Flyboys, 1980.

BOYAN, JEFFERY Bass. Replaced Jerry McGeorge in H. P. Lovecraft, 1968.

BOYCE, KEITH Drums, percussion. Member of the Heavy Metal Kids, 1974, Kids, 1975, and Bram Tchaikovsky, 1979.

BOYCE, TOMMY Vocal, writer. Half of the Boyce and Hart writing/performing team of the 1960s who wrote many of the Monkees' hits, and member of Dolenz, Jones, Boyce and Hart, 1976.

BOYD, REGGIE, JR. Guitar. Member of Captain Sky's Band since 1979.

BOYER, JODIE Vocal. Session for Joe Walsh (1974-78).

BOYER, SCOTT Guitar, piano, producer. Original member of the 31st of February, 1968, and Cowboy, 1971-73, 77. Produced the Skyboys. Session for Martin Mull (1974); Greg Allman (1973-74).

BOYLAN, JOHN Guitar, producer. Produced the Ozark Mountain Daredevils (1980). Session for Russ Giguere (1971).

BOYLAN, TERENCE Vocal. *Album:* Terence Boylan (ASY 7E-1091) 1977; Suzy (ASY 6E-201) 1980.

BOYLE, EDDIE Bass. Member of the Stingray, 1979.

BOYLE, GARY Guitar. Member of Python Lee Jackson, 1972, and Isotope, 1974-75.

BOYNSTON, PETER Vocal, keyboards. Member of Red Rider, 1980.

BOYNTON, JEFF Keyboards. Member of the Wazband, 1979.

BOYTER, GEORGE Bass, vocal. Member of the Headboys, 1979.

BOYZZ Mike Tafoya—guitar; "Dirty" Dan Buck—vocal, percussion, harmonica; Gil Pini—guitar, vocal; Anatole Halinkovich—keyboards; Kent Cooper—drums; David Angel—bass. *Album:* Too Wild To Tame (EPC JE-35440) 1978.

BOZ See Boz Burrell.

BOZZIO, DALE Vocal. Session for Frank Zappa (1979).

BOZZIO, TERRY Drums, percussion. Replaced Bill Bruford in U.K., 1979. Session for Frank Zappa (1975, 76, 79).

BRACKETT, AL Bass. Member of the Peanut Butter Conspiracy, 1967-68.

BRADAC, MARC Guitar, vocal. Member of the Teaze, 1979.

BRADBURY, JOHN Drums. Member of the Specials since 1979.

BRADBURY, PHILLIP Vocal. Session with Arthur Brown (1975).

BRADEN, LARRY Bass, vocal. Member of Alexis, 1977.

BRADFORD, CHRIS Vocal, guitar. Member of the Heroes, 1980.

BRADLEY, HAROLD Guitar, bass. Session for Doug Kershaw; Leon Russell (1973); J. J. Cale (1974).

BRADLEY, JULES Vocal. Session for Paul Butterfield (1980).

BRADLEY, MICKEY Bass. Member of the Undertones, 1979.

BRADLEY, PAM Vocal. Member of Tantrum, 1978-79.

BRADLEY, TOMI LEE Vocal. Member of Cottonwood South, 1974.

BRADSHAW, IAIN Keyboards. Member of Supercharge, 1976-77.

BRADSHAW, JIM Vocal, harmonica. Session for Shuggie Otis (1971).

BRADSHAW, KYM Bass. Member of the Saints, 1977.

BRADY, JIM Vocal. Born 1944. Member of the Sandpipers.

BRAIN, ALAN Guitar, vocal. Member of Interview since 1979.

BRAINS Tom Gray—keyboards, vocal; Rick Price—guitar, vocal; Bryan Smithwick—bass; Charles Wolff—drums, vocal. *Album:* Brains (SRM 1-3835) 1980.

BRAITHWAITE, DARYL Vocal, percussion. Member of Sherbet, 1976-80.

BRAMAH, MARTIN Guitar, vocal. Member of the Fall, 1979.

BRAMALL, PETER Real name of Bram Tchaikovsky.

BRAMBLETT, RANDALL Keyboards, vocal, vibraphone, saxophone. Member of Sea Level, 1978-present. Session for John Hammond (1975); Martin Mull (1974); Greg Allman (1974); Elvin Bishop (1974); Hydra (1974); Robbie Robertson (1980). *Albums:* Light of the Night (POL) 1976; The Other Mile (POL 6045) 1975.

BRAMLETT, BONNIE Vocal, writer. Former wife half of Delaney and Bonnie, gospel rock artists. Like her husband, after the divorce, she attempted a solo career with little success. Session for Dave Mason (1970); Eric Clapton (1970); Carly Simon (1972); the Allman Brothers (1979); Great Southern (1978); Jimmy Hall (1980). *Albums:* Sweet Bonnie Bramlett; It's Time (COL) 1974.

BRAMLETT, DELANEY Guitar, vocal, writer, producer. Husband half of Delaney and Bonnie, gospel rock artists. After the divorce he attempted a solo career with little success. Session for John Hammond (1972); Dave Mason (1970); Elvin Bishop (1972); Eric Clapton (1970); Free Creek (1972); Jerry Lee Lewis (1973). *Albums:* Delaney and Friends—Class Reunion (PRG P7-10017); Mobius Strip (COL KC 32420) 1973; Some Things Coming (COL KC 31631).

BRANCH, MARGARET Vocal. Session for Barry Goldberg (1974).

BRAND X John Goodsall—guitar; Percy Jones—bass; Robin Lumley—keyboards; Phil Collins—drums, vocal; Morris Pert—percussion; Peter Robinson—keyboards (1979-present); Mike Clarke—drums (1979-present); Chuck Bergi—drums (1978); John Gilbin—bass (1979-present). *Albums:* Livestock (PST 9824) 1977; Masques (PST 9829) 1978; Product (PST 9840) 1979; Do They Hurt (PST 9845) 1980; Unorthodox Behavior (PST 9819) 1976; Moroccan Roll (PST 9822) 1977.

BRAND, RICK Banjo, mandolin. Member of the Left Banke, 1967.

BRANDES, MICHIEL Guitar. Member of the Tapes, 1980.

BRANDIS, HARRY Guitar, vocal. Member of Growl, 1974.

BRANDT, BARRY Drums. Member of the Angels, 1977.

BRANDT, PAMELA Vocal, bass, percussion. Member of Deadly Nightshade, 1975.

BRANN, ERIK Guitar, vocal, writer. Original member of Iron Butterfly, 1967-69. Five years after the group fell apart, he and Ron Bushy resurrected a poor excuse for the original band for the nostalgia craze.

BRANYAN, DAVE Guitar, vocal. Member of the Scruffs, 1977.

BRANYAN, RICK Bass, piano, vocal. Member of the Scruffs, 1977.

BRASHEAR, OSCAR Horns. Session for James Taylor (1976); Ry Cooder (1978-80); Dr. John (1979).

BRAUN, AL Bass. Member of the Kracker, 1978.

BRAUN, MIKE Drums. Session for Elliott Murphy (1976).

BRAUN, RICHARD Trumpet, flugelhorn. Member of Auracle, 1978-79.

BRAUNAGLE, TONY Drums, percussion. Original member of Bloontz, 1973, Backstreet Crawler, 1975-76, Clover, 1977, and Crawler, 1977. Session for John "Rabbit" Bundrick (1974).

BRAVE BELT Chad Allen—vocal, piano, guitar, mandolin, accordion, writer; Randy Bachman—vocal, guitar, bass; Rob Bachman—drums, percussion; C. F. Turner—bass. After leaving the Guess Who, Randy Bachman organized a group around Chad Allen's lyrical compositions. Public reception was cool. He abandoned the group's format, dissolved the group formally to replace Allen and reorganized a new group under a carefully produced hard rock format. The new name became Bachman-Turner Overdrive. *Album:* Brave Belt (RPS 6447) 1971.

BRAWLEY, CHRIS Guitar. Member of High Cotton, 1975.

BRAY, JIM String bass. Session with Cyril Davies and Alexis Korner (1954-61).

BRAYFIELD, BUDDY Keyboards, vocal, percussion. Original member of the Ozark Mountain Daredevils, 1973-75.

BRAYLEY, REX Guitar. Member of Love Affair.

BREAD Mike Botts—drums, vocal; David Gates—guitar, keyboards, vocal, producer; James Griffen—bass, vocal; Larry Knechtel—guitar, vocal (1972-77); Robb Royer (1971). Originally called Pleasure Faire. Featuring the creditable experience of Knechtel and writing/production of Gates, Bread produced some of the most marketable vocal harmonies since Crosby, Stills, Nash and Young. *Albums:* Baby, I'm-A Want You (ELK 75015, EQ-5015); Best of Bread (ELK 6E-108, EQ-5056) 1973; Best of Bread, Vol. II (ELK 6E-110) 1974; Bread (ELK 74044); Bread on the Waters (ELK 74076); Guitar Man (ELK 75047) 1972; Lost Without Your Love (ELK 7E-1094) 1977; Manna (ELK 74086) 1971.

BREATHLESS Mark Avsec—keyboards, vocal; Bob Benjamin—bass; Alan Greene—guitar; Jonah Koslen—guitar, vocal; Rodney Psyka—percussion, vocal; Kevin Valentine—drums. *Album:* Nobody Leaves This Song Alive (EMI SW 17041) 1980; Breathless (EIA 17013) 1979.

BREBNER, ASA Bass, vocal, guitar. Replaced Curly Keranen in the Modern Lovers, 1978. Member of Robin Lane and the Chartbusters, 1980.

BRECKENFELD, BRUCE Keyboards. Member of Gambler since 1979.

BRECKENFELD, DEL Bass, vocal. Member of Gambler since 1979.

BRECKER, MIKE Horns, tenor saxophone. Began in Dreams, 1970. Session for James Taylor (1976); Pavlov's Dog (1976); Lou Reed (1973); Johnny Winter (1974); Roy Buchanan (1976); John Lennon (1973); Bruce Springsteen (1975); Carly Simon (1974); Frank Carillo (1978); Ray Gomez (1980); Art Garfunkel (1979); John Mayall (1979); Ian Lloyd (1979).

BRECKER, RANDY Trumpet. Began in Dreams, 1970. Member of Larry Coryell's Eleventh House, 1974. Session for Full Moon (1972); Lou Reed (1973); Johnny Winter (1973-74); Bruce Springsteen (1975); Roy Buchanan (1976); Scarlet Rivera (1978); John Mayall (1979); Ray Gomez (1980).

BRECKER BROTHERS Randy Brecker—trumpet; Mike Brecker—saxophone. Jazz session men who formed their own group for credit in the jazz-rock field. Session for the Fabulous Rhinestones (1973); Pacific Gas and Electric (1973); Randall Bramblett (1975); Jaco Pastorius (1976); the Pages (1978); Roger Voudouris (1979); Steely Dan (1980). *Albums:* Back to Back (ARI 4061); Brecker Brothers (ARI 4037) 1976; Don't Stop the Music (ARI 4122); Heavy Metal Be-Bop (ARI 4185); Detente (ARI 4272) 1980.

BREDICE, RICHARD Guitar. Member of Jules and the Polar Bear since 1979.

BREEDLOVE, DONALD Guitar, bass, vocal. Member of Band of Thieves, 1976.

BREEDUS, PAUL Vocal, keyboards, guitar, percussion. Member of Javaroo.

BREGANTI, MERLE Drums, vocal. Member of the Sunshine Company, 1967-69, and the Dirt Band since 1978. Session for Steve Martin (1978).

BREGG, DON Vocal. Member of the Cooper Brothers band since 1978.

BREMNER, BILLY Guitar. Member of Rockpile since 1979. Session for Dave Edmunds (1978-79); Carlene Carter (1980).

BRENDELL, STEVE Bass. Session for John Lennon (1971).

BRENNAN, MARK Drums. Member of the Thumbs, 1979.

BRETT, ADRIAN Flute. Session for Mike Batt (1979).

BRETT, PAUL Guitar, vocal. Namesake of the Paul Brett Sage.

PAUL BRETT SAGE Bob Voice—drums; Nicky Higginbottom—flute, saxophone; Paul Brett—guitar, vocal; Dick Dufall—bass. *Album:* Paul Brett Sage (JNS JLS 3026).

BREWER, DON Drums, vocals, writer, producer. Produced the Godz, 1979. Original member of Grand Funk Railroad, 1968-75, and Flint, 1978.

BREWER, MIKE Guitar, vocal. Half of the Brewer and Shipley team.

BREWER AND SHIPLEY Mike Brewer—guitar, vocal; Tom Shipley—guitar, vocal. *Albums:* Brewer and Shipley Down in L.A. (AAM); Rural Space (KMS 2058); Shake Off the Demon (KMS 2039); Tarkio (KMS 2024); Weeds (KMS 2016); Welcome to Riddle Bridge (CAP ST 11402).

BREWINGTON, RAY Guitar. Member of High Cotton, 1975.

BREWSTER, JOHN Guitar, vocal. Member of Angel City since 1977.

BREWSTER, KIRK Bass, guitar, vocal. Member of the Werewolves, 1978.

BREWSTER, RICK Guitar, keyboards. Member of Angel City since 1977.

BREWTON, BEN Keyboards. Session for Robbie Robertson (1980).

BREZEZICKE, MARK Drums. Session for Pete Townsend (1980).

BRIAN, DAVE Guitar. Chicago blues man of the mid 1960s who worked with Barry Goldberg.

BRIDGEFORD, GEOFF Drums. Member of the Bee Gees backup band, 1971-72.

BRIDGES, GIL Woodwinds, percussion, vocal. Member of Rare Earth.

BRIDGES, WILLIE Saxophone. Session for John Hammond (1968).

BRIGATTI, DAVID Vocals. Member of Joey Dee and the Starlighters, and half of the Brigatti duet, 1976. Session for Roy Buchanan (1976).

BRIGATTI, EDDIE Vocals. Half of Brigatti, 1976. Original member of the Rascals, 1965-69. Session for Roy Buchanan (1976).

BRIGATTI Eddie Brigatti—vocal; David Brigatti—vocal. *Album:* Lost in the Wilderness (ELK 7E-1074) 1976.

BRIGGS, BRIAN Keyboards, guitars, vocal, percussion. *Album:* Brain Damage (BSV BRK 6996) 1980.

BRIGGS, DAVID Keyboards, strings, arranger, producer, vocal. First became known in the rock field through the success of Neil Young. A former member of Area Code 615. Producer for Grin; Spirit (1971-72); Nils Lofgren (1975-76); Neil Young (1969, 70, 75); and others. Session for Ian Matthews (1976); Donovan (1974, 76); Tom Rapp (1972); Willie Nelson (1973); Pearls Before Swine (1970); Waylon Jennings (1973); Pointer Sisters (1974); Leon Russell (1973); Bob Seger (1974); J. J. Cale (1971, 79); the James Gang (1975); Buddy Spicher (1976).

BRIGGS, DAVID Guitar. Member of the Little River Band since 1977.

BRIGGS, VIC Guitar, vocal. First became known in Steam Packet in 1965, before joining the Animals, 1967.

BRIGGS, WILLIAM Keyboards. Member of the Remains, 1965-67.

BRIGHAM, PHIL Guitar, vocal. Member of

Clinic, 1973.

BRIGHT, BETTE Vocal. Member of Deaf School, 1979-80.

BRIGHTON, SHAUN Vocal, guitar. Member of Nervus Rex, 1980.

BRIGHTON, THOMAS RICHARD Guitar, vocal. Member of Russia, 1980.

BRIGIDA, STEVE Drums. Member of Artful Dodger, 1975-present.

BRILEY, MARTIN Bass. Session for Ian Hunter (1980).

BRILLEAUX, LEE Member of Dr. Feelgood, 1975.

BRILLION, PETER Drums, percussion. Member of the Rockspurs, 1978-79.

BRIQUETTE, PETE Member of the Boomtown Rats since 1977.

BRITISH LIONS John Fiddler—vocal, guitar; Buffin—drums; Overend Watts—bass, vocal; Ray Major—guitar, vocal; Morgan Fisher—keyboards, vocal. Re-formed Mott the Hoople centered around Ian Hunter replacement, Fiddler. *Albums:* British Lions (RSO 1-3032) 1978.

BRITNEL, TONY Saxophone. Session for Golden Earring (1980).

BRITT, EDDIE Guitar, vocal. Member of the Iron City Houserockers since 1979.

BRITTAIN, PETER Guitar, vocal. Member of the Wind in the Willows, 1968.

BRITTON, CHRIS Guitar. Original member of the Troggs.

BRITTON, GEOFF Drums, saxophone. Member of the Rough Diamond, 1977. Replaced Chris Slade in Manfred Mann, 1979. Session for Danny Kirwan; Wings (1975).

BROAD, GRAHAM Drums. Member of Bandit, 1976.

BROADBENT, MICKEY Bass, guitar, keyboards, vocal. Member of Bram Tchaikovsky since 1979.

BROCCO, CHARLIE Guitar. Member of Pam Windo and the Shades, 1980.

BROCK, DAVE Guitar, organ, vocal, strings. Member of the Dharma Blues Band, Hawkwind, and Hawklords, 1978 to present. Session for Iggy Pop (1979).

BROCK, NAPOLEAN MURPHY Reeds, vocal. Member of the Mothers of Invention, 1974-75. Session for Frank Zappa (1974-76, 79).

BROCK, TONY Drums, vocal. Member of the Babys since 1976. Session for Rod Stewart (1980).

BROCKBANK, NEIL Bass. Member of the Hitmen, 1980.

BROCKETT, JAMIE Guitar, vocal. Country folk artist. *Albums:* Remember The Wind and The Rain (CAP ST-678) 1969; #2 (CAP) 1970.

BROCKS, GARY Trombone. Session for the Paul Butterfield Blues Band (1973).

BRODIE, BRUCE Keyboards, synthesizer. Member of the Patti Smith Group since 1978. Session for Tom Verlane, 1979; Peter C. Johnson (1980).

BROGAN, BEN Bass, vocal. Member of the Rio Grande Band.

BROKEN GLASS Stan Webb—vocal, guitar, dobro, slide guitar, writer; Robbie Blunt—guitar, writer, slide guitar; Rob Rawlinson—bass; Mac Poole—drums. After the dissolve of Chicken Shack and an unsuccessful stint as one of Savoy Brown's "Boogie Brothers," Webb returned to his blues roots, forming Glass with Robbie Blunt. Capably produced (by Tony Ashton) and musically competent, lack of promotion kept the album from achieving any prominence. *Album:* Broken Glass (CAP ST 11510) 1976.

BROKEN HOME Dicken—vocal, guitar; Pete Crowther—bass, keyboard, guitar; Rory Wilson—guitar, vocal; Pete Barnacle—drums, percussion, vocal. *Album:* Broken Home (ATC 19274) 1980.

BROKENSHA, JACK Drums, bells, percussion. Session for the Temptations (1973).

BROMBERG, DAVID Guitar, dobro. Session for Bob Dylan (1970); Jonathan Edwards (1973); Gordon Lightfoot (1972); Rick Derringer (1973); Sha Na Na (1971); Ringo Starr (1973, 77); Willie Nelson (1973); Phoebe Snow (1976). *Albums:* Bandit in a Bathing Suit (FSY 9555); David Bromberg (COL C-31104); Demon in Disguise (COL C-31753); Hillybilly Jazz (FLF 101); How Late'll Ya Play Til (FSY 79007) 1976; Midnight on the Water (COL PC-33397) 1975; My Own House (FSY 9572) 1978; Out of the Blues (Best of D. Bromberg) (COL C-34467); Reckless Abandon (FSY 9540) 1974; Wanted/Dead or Alive (COL KC-32717) 1974; You Should See the Rest of the Band (FSY 9590) 1980.

BROMBERG, STEVEN Drums, percussion. Member of Upepo.

BROMHAM, DEL Guitar, keyboards. Member of Stray, 1970-75.

BRONCO Jess Roden—vocal, guitar, percussion, producer, writer; Robbie Blunt—vocal, guitar; John Pasternak—bass, vocal; Pete Robinson—drums, harmonica, vocal. English born Bronco failed to capture much attention with their original, competent uncommercial songs. *Album:* Country Home (ISL# 9300).

BRONOWSKI, KEN Guitar, bugle, vocal. Member of Skafish, 1980.

BRONSON, HAROLD Vocal. Member of the Low Numbers, 1977-78.

BRONSTEIN, STAN Saxophone, flute, clarinet. Original member of Elephant's Memory. Session for Yoko Ono and John Lennon.

BROOD, HERMAN Piano, vocal. Namesake of Herman Brood and his Wild Romance.

HERMAN BROOD AND HIS WILD ROMANCE Herman Brood—piano, vocal; Ferdie Karmelk—guitar, harmonica, vocal (1979); Gerrit Veen—bass; Peter Walrecht—drums; Danny Lademacher—guitar; Kees Meerman—drums (1980). *Albums:*

Herman Brood and His Wild Romance (ARA SW-50059); Go Nutz (ARA OL 1500) 1980.

BROOKER, GARY Vocal, keyboards, writer, harmonica, percussion. Original member and co-founder of Procol Harum, 1966-77. Session for George Harrison (1972); Frankie Miller (1977); Tim Renwick (1980); Wings (1979); the Hollies (1979). *Album:* No More Fear of Flying (CYS 1224) 1979.

BROOKINS, STEVE Drums, percussion. Member of 38 Special, 1977-present.

BROOKLYN BRIDGE Johnny Maestro—vocal; Tommy Sullivan—saxophone, flute, vocal; Jimmy Rosica—bass, vocal; Joe Ruvio—saxophone, vocal; Les Cauchi—vocal, piano; Richie Maclore—guitar; Artie Catanzarita—drums, trumpet; Fred Ferrara—vocal, guitar, trumpet; Mike Gregorio—vocal, organ; Carolyn Wood—organ; Shelly Davis—trumpet, piano. *Albums:* Brooklyn Bridge (BUD); Second Brooklyn Bridge (BUD).

BROOKLYN DREAMS Joe Esposito—guitar; Eddie Hokenson—drums; Bruce Sudano—keyboards. *Albums:* Brooklyn Dreams (MLN 8002) 1977; Joy Ride (CAS 7165); Sleepless Nights (CAS 7135).

BROOKS, CLIVE COLIN Drums. Born 12/28/49. Member of Egg, 1970. Replaced Ken Pustelnik in the Groundhogs, 1972-74. Member of Liar, 1980.

BROOKS, CRAIG Guitar, vocal. Member of the Touch, 1980.

BROOKS, DIANE Vocal. Session for Jonathan Edwards (1977).

BROOKS, DON Harmonica. Member of the Waylors. Session for Waylon Jennings (1973); the James Gang (1975).

BROOKS, DOUG Guitar. Member of Stone Country, 1968.

BROOKS, ELKIE Vocal. *Albums:* Rich Man's Woman (AAM 4554) 1975; Shooting Star (AAM 4695); Two Days Away (AAM 4631) 1977.

BROOKS, ERNIE Bass. Session for Elliott Murphy (1976).

BROOKS, HARVEY Bass. Original member of the Electric Flag, 1967-68, the Fabulous Rhinestones, 1972-73, and the Rhinestones, 1975. Session for the Doors (1969); Bob Dylan (1970); John Sebastian (1970); Super Session (1968).

BROOKS, JOANNA Vocal. Session for Steve Hunter (1977).

BROOKS, MICHAEL Bass. Member of the Elvin Bishop Band, 1974-77.

BROOKS, RAY Bass. Member of Gasmask.

BROOKS, REG Trombone, vocal. Member of Rick Wakeman's backup group in 1976. Session for Paice, Ashton, Lord (1977).

BROOME, TOM Keyboards. Member of Great Southern, 1977.

BROONZY, BIG BILL Vocal, guitar, writer. Real name: William Lee Conley Broonzy. From the '30s through the '50s, Broonzy was well known to the public for the diversity of music he played, from country to his specialty, the blues. Died in 1958. *Albums:* Best of the Blues (SQN 103); Blues (FLW 3817); Blues Tradition 1927-1932 (MLS 2016); Big Bill Broonzy (EVR 213) 1967; Big Bill Broonzy Sings Country Blues (FLW 31005); Big Bill Broonzy Sings Folk Songs (FLW 2328) 1962; Feelin' Low Down (CRS 10004); From Spirituals to Swing (VAN VSD-47-48); Lonesome Road Blues (CRS 10009) 1975; Roots (MCR 8805); Big Bill Broonzy Songs and Stories; Big Bill Broonzy with Washboard Sam.

BROTHER FOX AND THE TAR BABY Joe Santangelo—keyboards; Richie Bartlett—guitar; Tom Billiveau—bass; Bill Garr—drums; Steve High—vocal, percussion; Dave Christiansen—guitar. *Album:* Brother Fox and the Tar Baby (OVA DRS 703) 1969.

BROTHER JAMES Congas. Member of Hanson, 1974. Session for Alvin Lee (1975); Steve Winwood (1977); Annette Peacock (1979).

BROTHERWOOD, NICK Drums. Member of the Alwyn Wall Band, 1977.

BROTMAN, STUART A. Bass, vocals, cymbalum. Replaced Christopher Darrow in Kaleidoscope, 1968. Session for Ry Cooder (1978).

BROUDIE, IAN Guitar. Member of the Original Mirrors, 1980.

BROUGHTON, STEVE Vocal, guitar, mandolin. Member of City Boy, 1976.

BROUGHTON, STEVE Drums. Session for Roy Harper (1975); Mike Oldfield (1973).

BROUSSARD, JULES Saxophone. Session for Santana (1974); Boz Scaggs (1972); Art Garfunkel; Elvin Bishop (1978).

BROUSSARD, TONY Bass. Session for Mylon Le Fevre (1979).

BROVITZ, LEE Bass. Member of Blue Angel, 1980.

BROWDER, BILL Guitar, keyboards, vocal. Member of Denim, 1977, and Traveller.

BROWN, ANDY Bass. Replaced Phil Curtis in the Tiger, 1976. Session for the Rutles (1978).

BROWN, ARTHUR Vocal. A PhD graduate from Cambridge (philosophy), Brown was tagged "The God of Hell Fire" with his hit, "Fire" (1968). He disappeared shortly thereafter, retiring from the theatrical costumes and makeup that made his show one of a kind. He reappeared in 1973 as the head of Arthur Brown's Kingdom Come, refining his already dynamic voice, but still in an ethereal format. In 1975, he went solo with an album of original compositions and ballads, something new, yet not beyond his range and talents. See Kingdom Come. Session for the Alan Parsons Project (1976). *Album:* Dance (GUL-405S1) 1975.

BROWN, CHARLIE Guitar. Member of the White Cloud, 1972.

BROWN, CHRIS Guitar, vocal. Member of Ayer's Rock, 1975-78.

BROWN, DANNY JOE Vocal. Born 8/24/51. Member of Molly Hatchett, 1978-80.

BROWN, DAVE Guitar, bass. Member of Tucky Buzzard, 1973.

BROWN, DAVID Bass, flute, saxophone. Original member of the 31st of February, 1968, and Santana, 1974. Session for Daddy Cool (1971); Martin Mull (1974); Boz Scaggs (1972); Greg Allman (1973); Elvin Bishop (1974); Gordon Lightfoot (1972).

BROWN, DAVID WARNER Bass, vocal. Member of Mistress, 1979.

BROWN, DESMOND Keyboards. Member of Selecter, 1980.

BROWN, EDDIE Congas, percussion. Session for Bob Seger (1973); the Temptations (1973); B. B. King (1977).

BROWN, ELLA Vocal. Session for the Marshall Tucker Band (1973).

BROWN, ESTELLE Vocal. Member of the Sweet Inspirations, 1967-69.

BROWN, FREEMAN Percussion. Session for Dr. John (1975).

BROWN, GARNETT Trombone. Session for Eumir Deodato; Barry Goldberg (1969); B. B. King (1972, 1977); Muddy Waters (1972).

BROWN, GARY Saxophone. Session for Andy Gibb (1980).

BROWN, GERRY Drums, percussion. Member of the Chris Hinze Combination, 1974, Return to Forever, 1978, and Medusa, 1978.

BROWN, GLORIA Vocal. Replaced Cissy Houston in the Sweet Inspirations.

BROWN, HAROLD Drums. Original member of War.

BROWN, HUKS Guitar. Session for Paul Simon (1972).

BROWN, J. T. Tenor saxophone. Session for Fleetwood Mac (1969).

BROWN, JAMES Keyboards, vocal. Member of the Stanky Brown Group, 1975-77.

BROWN, JENNIFER Vocal. Early member of the Fugs Chorus.

BROWN, JIM Guitar. Member of the Blend, 1978-79.

BROWN, JOHN Bass. Session for Wreckless Eric.

BROWN, JUDY Vocal. Session for John Mayall (1978).

BROWN, LAURIE Vocal. Member of the Kinks, 1973-76.

BROWN, MEL Guitar. Session for B. B. King (1972).

BROWN, MIKE Keyboard. Member of the Left Banke, 1967, and the Beckies, 1976.

BROWN, MORRIE E. Bass. Session for Pearls Before Swine (1971).

BROWN, OLLIE Drums, percussion. Session for Joe Cocker (1974); the Rolling Stones (1976-77); Sly and the Family Stone (1979); Ozz (1980).

BROWN, PAULETTE Vocal. Session for Nazareth (1980); Boz Scaggs (1980); the Ozark Mountain Daredevils (1980).

BROWN, PETE Lyrics. Lyrical partner of Jack Bruce.

BROWN, PHIL Bass, vocal. Member of the Records, 1979-present.

BROWN, RAY String bass. Session for Marc Benno; Martin Mull (1973); Steely Dan (1973).

BROWN, RICHARD Drums, harmonium. Session for Bill Nelson (1971).

BROWN, RICK Bass. Session for Lord Sutch; Long John Baldry.

BROWN, ROGER Vocal. Session for Gerry Rafferty (1970).

BROWN, RON Bass. Session for B. B. King (1972).

BROWN, SAM Guitar. Member of Ars Nova, 1968-69.

BROWN, SUE Vocal. Session for the Kinks (1973-74).

BROWN, TOM Drums. Member of Wedge, 1980.

BROWN, TONI Keyboards, steel guitar, vocal. Member of Joy of Cooking, 1970-77, and Joy, 1977.

BROWN, TONY Bass. Session for Bob Dylan (1974).

BROWN, TONY Percussion, harmonica, vocal. Session for Alibi (1980).

BROWN, VICKI Vocal. Session for Bryan Ferry (1974); Manfred Mann (1973); Olivia Newton-John (1971); Carly Simon (1972); the Small Faces (1977-78); Elton John (1978); Eric Burdon (1977); Oxendale and Shephard (1979).

BROWN, WILLIAM Vocal. Session for Martin Mull (1978).

STANKY BROWN GROUP James Brown—keyboards, vocal; Jeffrey Leynor—guitar, vocal; Richard Bunkiewicz—bass; Jerry Cordasco—drums, vocal; Allan Ross—reeds; Frank Greene—lyrics. *Albums:* Our Pleasure To Serve You, 1976; Stanky Brown (SIR K 6053) 1977; If the Lights Don't Get You, 1975.

BROWNE, DUNCAN Vocal, guitar. Member of Metro, 1977. *Albums:* Streets of Fire (SIR K-6080) 1979; Wild Places (SIR K-6065) 1978.

BROWNE, IVAN Guitar, vocal. Member of the Lemon Pipers, 1968.

BROWNE, JACKSON Guitar, banjo, mandolin, percussion, piano, vocal, writer. Born 10/9/48. Started in the Nitty Gritty Dirt Band before going solo. Part of "No Nukes," 1979. Session for Nico; Steve Noonan (1968); Warren Zevon (1980). *Albums:* Jackson Browne (ASY 5051) 1972; For Every Man (ASY 5067) 1973; Hold Out (ASY 5E-511) 1980; Late for the Sky (ASY 7E-1017) 1974; The Pretender (ASY 6E-107) 1977; Running on Empty (ASY 6E-113A) 1977.

BROWNE, MARK Bass. Member of the Tremblers,

1980.

BROWNE, THOMAS F. Drums, vocal, producer. *Album:* Thomas F. Browne (VRV) 1972.

BROWNING, CHUCK Drums. Session for J. J. Cale (1971).

BROWNING, JOHN Trumpet. Session for B. B. King (1972).

BROWNING, MISTY Vocal. Session for Freddie King (1974); Trapeze (1974).

BROWNSVILLE STATION Henry Weck—drums, percussion; Michael Lutz—bass, guitar, vocal, keyboards; Cub Koda—guitar, vocal, steel; Bruce Mazarian—keyboards (1977). Heavy rock trio that enjoyed a brief fling with notoriety in 1974. *Albums:* Motor City Connection, 1975; School Punks, 1974; Yeah, 1974; Brownsville Station (BGT) 1977; Night on the Town, 1972.

BROX, ANNETTE Vocal. Wife of Victor Brox. Played in "Jesus Christ Superstar," 1970. Session for Lord Sutch; Aynsley Dunbar's Retaliation (1970).

BROX, VICTOR Organ, vocal, writer. Member of Aynsley Dunbar's Retaliation, 1968-70. Played Caiaphas in "Jesus Christ Superstar," 1970. Session for Dr. John (1971); Lord Sutch.

BRUBECK, DAN Drums. Session for Roy Buchanan (1980).

BRUCE, BOBBY Fiddle. Session for Elvin Bishop (1972); Ry Cooder (1970).

BRUCE, BRUCE Vocal. Member of Samson, 1980.

BRUCE, DENNY Producer. Produced the Fabulous Thunderbirds (1979-80).

BRUCE, JACK Bass, vocal, harmonica, writer, piano, organ, cello. Born 5/14/43. Originally with Blues Incorporated before a brief affiliation with Manfred Mann. Through 1966 he traveled with the Graham Bond Organization and John Mayall to achieve international acclaim as the voice of Cream, 1967-69. After three years of experimenting with jazz as a soloist he formed the Cream-like West, Bruce and Laing, 1972-74. Formed the Jack Bruce Band, 1977. Session for Donovan (1967); Lou Reed (1973); Aynsley Dunbar's Retaliation; Frank Zappa (1974); Les Dudek (1978). *Albums:* Songs for a Tailor (ACO 33 306) 1969; Things We Like (ACO 33 349) 1971; Harmony Row (ACO 33 365) 1971; Out of the Storm (RSO 4805) 1974; I've Always Wanted To Do This (EPC JE 36827) 1980.

JACK BRUCE BAND Jack Bruce—vocal, bass, harmonica; Hughie Burns—guitar, vocal; Tony Hymas—keyboards, vocal; Simon Phillips—drums, vocal. *Album:* How's Tricks (RSO 1-3021) 1977.

BRUCE, MICHAEL Vocal, guitar. Member of Billion Dollar Babies, 1977. Session for Bob Seger; Long John Baldry (1979).

BRUCE, WAYNE Vocal, guitar, writer. Member of Hydra, 1975-77.

BRUCE-DOUGLAS, IAN Vocal, bell, chimes, writer. Original member of Ultimate Spinach, 1968-69.

BRUCK, THOMAS Bass. Member of Satin Whale, 1975.

BRUFORD, BILL Drums, percussion. Original member of Yes, 1970-72. Replaced Ian Wallace in King Crimson, 1973-75. Member of U.K., 1978, before forming Bruford, 1979. Session for Chris Squire (1975); Steve Howe (1975); Pavlov's Dog (1976); Rick Wakeman (1972); Roy Harper (1975); Annette Peacock (1979). *Albums:* Feels Good To Me (POL 1-6149) 1977; One of a Kind (POL 1-6205).

BRUFORD Bill Bruford—drums; Dave Stewart—keyboards; Jeff Berlin—bass, vocal; John Clark—guitar. *Album:* Gradually Going Tornado (POL 1-6261) 1979.

BRUMLEY, TOM Steel guitar. Member of the Stone Canyon Band.

BRUNKERT, OLA Drums. Member of Abba's backup band since 1974. Session for John "Rabbit" Bundrick (1974).

BRUNNING, BOB Bass. Session for Fleetwood Mac (1968).

BRUNO, AL Guitar, vocal. Session for Phillip Walker (1977).

BRUNO, BOB Guitar, keyboards, vocal, writer. Original member of Circus Maximus, 1967-68.

BRUNO, GEORGE Keyboards, vocal. Member of the Animals, 1967. Also records under the name Zoot Money. See Zoot Money.

BRUNO, STEVE Bass, keyboards. Member of Elizabeth, 1968.

BRUNSON, TYRONE Bass. Member of Osiris, 1978.

BRUNTON, RICHARD Guitar. Session for Gerry Rafferty (1978).

BRUSH ARBOR Joe Rice; Jim Rice; Dave Rose; Mike Holtzer. *Album:* Straight (MDN 7613) 1977.

BRUTON, STEVE Guitar. Session for Gene Clark (1974); Geoff Muldaur (1978).

BRUZZESE, JIM Tambourine. Session for Bob Seger.

BRYAN, DOGGIE Guitar. Member of Dillinger, 1976.

BRYAN, ROBERT Vocal, bass. Original member of Be Bop Deluxe, 1974.

BRYANS, RICHARD Drums, vocal. Member of Aviary, 1979.

BRYANT, AB Bass. Member of Prism, 1977-78. Replaced Glenn Miller in Chilliwack, 1980.

BRYANT, BOBBY Trumpet. Session for B. B. King (1972, 77).

BRYANT, BRENDA Vocal. Session for Barry Goldberg (1974).

BRYANT, DUANE Drums. Member of the Candle, 1972.

BRYANT, JOHN Drums, percussion. Member of

Phyrework, 1978.

BRYANT, PHIL Bass, vocal. Member of 707, 1980.

BRYANT, SHARON Vocal, percussion. Member of Atlantic Starr, 1978-79.

BRYANT, TERRI Vocal. Replaced Marilyn McCoo in the Fifth Dimension.

BRYANT, WARREN Percussion. Session for John Mayall (1977).

BRYCE, RODNEY Violin, mandolin, synthesizer. Member of the Bob Meighan Band, 1976.

BRYE, ROLF Bass, vocal. Member of BLT, 1977.

BRYERS, BRENT Conga, vocal. Member of Tower of Power.

BRYMER, BRUCE Vocal, drums, percussion. Member of the Ducks, 1973.

BRYSON, WALLY Guitar, vocal. Member of Raspberries, 1972-74, Tatoo, 1976, and Fotomaker, 1978-79.

BUCHANAN, BUZ Drums. Member of the Jeremy Spencer Band, 1979.

BUCHANAN, DON Guitar. Member of the Plastic Rhino Band, 1977.

BUCHANAN, JIMMY Fiddle. Session for the Doors (1969); Ringo Starr (1971); Leon Russell (1973).

BUCHANAN, MALCOLM Keyboards. Member of Aeriel, 1978.

BUCHANAN, NEIL Guitar. Member of Marseille, 1980.

BUCHANAN, ROY Vocal, writer. It was rumored that when Eric Clapton was looking for a second guitarist for his new group, Derek and the Dominoes in 1970, he offered East Coaster Roy Buchanan the job. Roy Buchanan politely refused, saying he had his own group (The Snakestretchers). Indeed, Buchanan's mastery of the guitar easily rivals or surpasses Clapton's. Buchanan's first album (1972) had a country-western flair, while his second leaned more heavily on blues. The third was largely rock, featuring a tribute to Jimi Hendrix ("Hey Joe"), that would have done even that master justice. "In the Beginning" (1974), featured rhythm and blues, and he has expanded his style through jazz as well. His refusal to travel beyond his native environs has limited his popularity. *Albums:* Roy Buchanan (POL 5033) 1972; In the Beginning (POL 6035) 1974; Live Stock (POL 6048) 1975; Loading Zone (ATC 19138) 1977; Second Album (POL 5046) 1973; Street Called Straight (ATC 18170) 1976; You're Not Alone (ATC 19170) 1978; That's What I'm Here For (POL 6020) 1973; My Babe (WTH 12) 1980.

BUCHANAN, RUSTY Vocal, bass, guitar. Member of Thieves, 1979.

BUCHHOLZ, FRANCIS Bass. Member of the Scorpions since 1974.

BUCHNER, DAN Drums. Member of Hammersmith since 1975.

BUCHWALD, MARTIN Real name of Marty Balin.

BUCK, "DIRTY" DAN Vocal, percussion, harmonica. Member of Boyzz, 1978.

BUCK, MIKE Drums. Member of the Fabulous Thunderbirds since 1979.

BUCK, NICK Keyboards, vocal. Member of Hot Tuna, 1978, and SVT, 1980. Session for Peter Green (1970); Hot Tuna (1972, 75-76); Peter Kaukonen (1972); Roy Loney and the Phantom Movers (1979).

BUCKACRE Alan Thacker—guitar, slide guitar; Dick Halley—bass; Dick Verruchi—drums, percussion; Darrel Data—guitar; Les Lockridge—guitar. *Albums:* Morning Comes, 1976; Buckacre (MCA 2365).

BUCKEYE Ronn Price—vocal, bass, guitar; Thom Fowle—guitar, vocal; Gabriel Katona—keyboards, vocal; Beaver Parker—drums, percussion, vocal. *Album:* Buckeye (POL I 6213) 1979.

BUCKINGHAM, LINDSAY Guitar, vocals, writer, producer. With partner Stevie Nicks, he replaced Bob Welsh and Bob Weston in Fleetwood Mac, 1975-present. Produced Warren Zevon. Session for Bob Welch (1977); Danny Douma (1979). *Album:* Buckingham/Nicks (POL 5058) 1975.

BUCKINGHAM AND NICKS See individual listings for Lindsay Buckingham, Stevie Nicks.

BUCKINGHAMS Denny Tufano—vocals; Carl Giammarese—guitar; Jon-Jon Poulas—drums; Nick Fortune—bass; Marty Grebb—organ; Dennis Miccoli—organ. Early names: the Centuries; the Falling Pebbles. Well tailored rock band that grew out of Chicago in 1966. James William Guerrco's first experiments and compositions were with them. *Albums:* Kind of a Drag; Made in Chicago; Buckingham's Greatest Hits (COL CS-9812); In One Ear and Gone Tomorrow (COL CS-9703) 1968; Portraits (COL CS-9598) 1968; Time and Changes (COL CS 9469) 1967.

BUCKINS, MICKEY Percussion. Session for Roy Orbison (1979); Bob Dylan (1979).

BUCKLER, RICK Drums. Member of the Jam, 1978-80.

BUCKLEY, BOB Saxophone, keyboards. Member of the Straight Lines, 1980. Session for Chilliwack (1972).

BUCKLEY, TIM Vocal, guitar, writer. From the child in the garden image in 1966, his folk songs matured into testimonies of experience and sometimes disillusion; but they were all sung in his pleasant manner. Died 1975. *Albums:* Tim Buckley, 1968; Happy/Sad, 1969; Look at the Fool (ELK); Goodbye and Hello (ELK 74028) 1967; Starsailor; Lorca; Blue Afternoon; Sefronia.

BUCKMASTER, PAUL Orchestral arranger, cello. Worked with Elton John, 1969-78. Member of the Hill, 1975. Session for Mott the Hoople (1973); Nilsson (1972); Carly Simon (1972-74).

BUCKWHEAT Timmy Harrison—vocal; Michael

Smotherman—keyboards, vocal; D. Durham; D. Campbell. *Album:* Movin On (LON PS 609).

BUDA, MAXWELL Harmonica, organ. Original member of Kaleidoscope. Session for the Rank Strangers (1977).

BUDGIE Tony Bourge—guitar; Steve Williams—drums; Burke Shelley—bass, vocal. *Albums:* Bandolier (AAM 4618) 1975; If I Were Brittania I'd Waive The Rules (AAM 4593) 1976; Impeckable (AAM 4675) 1977.

BUDIHAS, RANDY Drums, vocal. Member of Emperor, 1977.

BUDIMIR, DENNIS Guitar. Session for Nilsson (1975-76); Arthur, Hurley and Gottlieb.

BUDWIG, MONTY Bass. Session for Martin Mull (1978).

BUFFALO CHIPS Early name of the Ozark Mountain Daredevils.

BUFFALO SPRINGFIELD Stephen Stills—guitar, piano, vocal, writer; Richie Furay—guitar, vocal, writer; Bruce Palmer—bass (1966-67); Neil Young—guitar, vocal, writer; Dewey Martin—drums; Jim Messina—bass, vocal, engineer (1967-68); Doug Hastings—vocals (1966). The joining of teams Stills and Furay with Canadians Palmer and Young in L.A. in 1966 led to the makings of what could have been the biggest country rock group since the Byrds. Indeed, their talent was not as limited as the moniker suggests, and their vocal harmonies were the birth of what developed to their peaks in Poco; Crosby, Stills, Nash and Young; and Loggins and Messina. Two years after their big hit "For What it's Worth," personality rifts led to the group's disbanding. *Albums:* Buffalo Springfield/Neil Young (ACO 2-806); Buffalo Springfield (ACO 200) 1967; Buffalo Springfield (ACO 2-806); Buffalo Springfield Again (ACO 226) 1967; Last Time Around (ACO 256) 1968; Retrospective (ACO 38-105) 1969.

BUFFALO, MAD MISSISSIPPI Keyboard, vocal. Member of Duke and the Drivers, 1975.

BUFFALO, NORTON Harmonica. Session for the Doobie Brothers (1977-78); Steve Miller (1977); Chris Montan (1980). *Albums:* Desert Horizon (CAP SW-11847) 1978; Lovin' in the Valley of the Moon (CAP ST-11625) 1977.

BUFFET, JIMMY Vocal, guitar, writer. A blend of pop-folk with a country flavor from Florida. Received his initial fame with "Margaritaville," backed by the Coral Reefer Band. Session for the Eagles (1979). *Albums:* A-1-A (MCA D-50183) 1974; Changes in Latitudes, Changes in Attitudes (MCA 990); Havana Daydreamin' (MCA D-914); Living and Dying in 3/4 Time (MCA D-50132) 1974; Son of a Sailor (MCA D-50132) 1978; Volcano (MCA 5102) 1979; White Sport Coat and Pink Crustacean (MCA X-50150); You Had To Be There (MCA AK-1108).

BUFFIN See Dale Griffin.

BUGS TOMORROW David Vaught—bass; Morley Bartnoff—keyboards, vocal; Bugs Tomorrow—guitar, vocal; Andrew Campbell-Hare—drums, vocal. *Album:* Bugs Tomorrow (CAS 7199) 1980.

BUHLER, CRAIG Reeds. Member of Honk, 1973-74.

BULL, JOHN Drums. Session for the Inmates (1979).

BULL, SANDY Guitar, banjo, oud, bass, percussion, vocal, writer. When recording studios were still in their Stone Ages (1963), long before one-man studio bands like Dave Edmunds and others, Bull was laying down track after track of instrumental parts in compositions lasting the length of album sides. Everything from Eastern influences to classical guitar, and jazz to rock were covered in his compositions, and he laid the studio groundwork for rock musicians for years to come. *Albums:* Sandy Bull (VAN 79119) 1963; Demolition Derby (VAN 6578) 1972; E Pluribus Unum (VAN 6513) 1969; Essential (VAN VSD-59/60); Inventions (VAN 79191) 1965.

BULLENS, CINDY Vocal, guitar. Session for Gene Clark (1964); the Alpha Band (1972); Rory Block (1979). *Albums:* Desire Wire (UAR LKAO-933) 1978; Steal the Night (CAS 7185) 1979.

BULLFROG Sebastian Leitner—guitar; Gerd Hoch—vocal; Harald Kaltenecker—keyboards; Vincent Trost—bass; Bruno Perosa—percussion. *Album:* Bullfrog (SKY AC 1003) 1976.

BULLFROG BHEER Early name for Kiss.

BULLOCK, ANNIE MAY Real name of Tina Turner.

BULLOCK, HIRAM Guitar. Session for the Blues Brothers (1980); Rob Stoner (1980); Paul Simon (1980); Steely Dan (1980).

BULSARA, FREDDIE Real name of Freddie Mercury.

BUMPUS, CORNELIUS Saxophone, vocal, keyboards. Joined the Doobie Brothers, 1980.

BUNCE, DAVID Guitar. Member of Upp, 1975-76.

BUNCH, VERNON Keyboards. Session for Dick St. Nicklaus (1979).

BUNDRICK, JOHN "RABBIT" Keyboards, vocals, writer. In 1972 when Free started to fall apart, Bundrick appeared on the album called "Kossoff, Kirke, Tetsu and Rabbit." He continued as a member of the re-formed Free through 1973. Replaced Mike Montgomery in Backstreet Crawler, 1976. Member of Crawler, 1977, and traveled with the Who, 1980. Session for Donovan (1973); Jim Capaldi (1971, 73); the Sutherland Brothers (1973); "Rough Mix" (1977); Eric Burdon (1977); Frankie Miller (1977); the Who (1980); the Only Ones (1979); Pete Townshend (1980). *Albums:* Broken Arrow (ISL SMAS 9328) 1973; Dark Saloons (ISL ILPS 9289) 1974.

BUNDY, CHARLIE Bass, vocals. Member of

Randy California's Kapt. Kopter and the Fabulous Twirly Birds, 1972.

BUNKER, CLIVE Drums, percussion. Member of Jethro Tull, 1968-71, and Aviator, 1978-present.

BUNKIEWICZ, RICHARD Bass. Member of the Stanky Brown Group, 1975-77.

BUNNELL, DEWEY Guitar, vocal. Member of America.

BUNNELL, GEORGE Bass. Member of the Strawberry Alarm Clock, 1968.

BUNNYMEN See Echo and the Bunnymen.

BUNTEN, BOBBY Member of Nan Mancini and JDB, 1979.

BUNTING, LORD TED Saxophone. Session for Crawler (1977).

BUONO, MIKE Drums. Member of Starwood, 1976-77.

BURCH, DARYL Drums. Member of Mephistopheles.

BURCH, VERNON Member of the re-formed Bar-Kays.

BURCHER, MIKE Guitar, vocal. Member of the Elton Motello band, 1980.

BURCHILL, CHARLES Guitar, violin, vocal. Member of the Simple Minds since 1979.

BURDEN, GARY Session for David Crosby (1971).

BURDETT, JOHN Drums. Member of the Royal Guardsmen, 1969.

BURDON, ERIC Vocal, writer. Born 5/11/41. Began in Blues Incorporated. Original member of the Animals, 1962 (then known as the Alan Price Combo), of "House of the Rising Sun," "We've Gotta Get Out of This Place," and "Don't Let Me Be Misunderstood" fame. After their demise (1968) he retired, only to re-emerge with War, an all-black (except for him and Lee Oskar) soul group, which went on to even greater fame after he left them in 1972. He again went into retirement and after two more years came back with the Eric Burdon Band, 1974-75. In all the bands, his gravelly blues style was the distinguishing trademark. Without a doubt he is one of the best vocalists in that area. Member of the regrouped Animals, 1977. See the Animals, Eric Burdon Band.

ERIC BURDON BAND Eric Burdon—vocal, writer; Aalon—guitar; Alvin Taylor—drums, percussion (1974); Randy Rice—bass (1974); John Sterling—guitar (1975); George Suranough—drums (1975); Kim Kesterson—bass (1975); Terry Ryan—key-1boards (1975); Moses Wheelock—percussion (1975). Ex-Animal Burdon's effort after his discovery of War. *Albums:* Sun Secrets (CAP) 1974; Stop (CAP) 1975.

BUREK, ED Bass. Member of Mariah, 1976.

BURGER, ALAN Bass. Member of Southside Johnny and the Asbury Jukes, 1976-80.

BURGESS, DARYL Drums, percussion. Member of the Straight Lines, 1980.

BURGESS, PAUL Drums, percussion. Member of 10 CC, 1980.

BURGH, STEVE Guitar. Session for Willie Nelson (1973); Elkie Brooks (1975).

BURGI, ESTHER Violin. Member of Centipede, 1971.

BURGON, HAROLD Synthesizer. Session for Alvin Lee (1975).

BURK, MIKE Member of the Wailers.

BURKE, CLEMENT Drums. Member of Blondie since 1977.

BURKE, GARY Drums. Session for Scarlet Rivera (1978).

BURKE, HOWARD Guitar. Member of Blue Steel since 1980.

BURKE, KENI Bass. Member of Sly and the Family Stone, 1979.

BURKE, PAT Tenor saxophone. Member of the Foundations, 1968.

BURKE, SONNY Keyboards. Session for Freddie King (1975); B. B. King (1977).

BURKE, VAL Bass, vocal. Took over for Chris Stewart in Gary Wright's re-formed Spooky Tooth, 1974.

BURNEL, JEAN JACQUES Bass, vocal. Member of the Stranglers.

BURNETT, "T BONE" J. HENRY Member of the Alpha Band, 1977.

BURNETT, BEN Percussion. Session for the Marshall Tucker Band (1980).

BURNETT, BILL Bass. Member of Blue Jug, 1975.

BURNETT, CHESTER Real name of Howlin' Wolf.

BURNETT, JAMES Guitar, banjo, vocal. Member of El Roachos, 1973.

BURNETT, LARRY Guitar, vocal, writer. Member of Firefall, 1976-present.

BURNETT, RICK Drums, percussion. Member of Grinderswitch, 1974-76.

BURNETTE, BILLY Vocal, guitar. *Albums:* Between Friends (POL 1-6242) 1979; Billy Burnette (POL PD 6187) 1979; Billy Burnette (COL NJC 36792) 1980.

BURNEVIK, TOM Saxophone. Member of the Lamont Cranston Band, 1977.

BURNHAM, HUGO Bass. Member of the Gang of Four, 1980.

BURNIP, JOHN Drums, percussion. Member of Mr. Big, 1975.

BURNS, AUGUST Cello. Member of Sweetwater.

BURNS, BECKY Vocal. Session for John Mayall (1979).

BURNS, BOB Drums. Member of Lynyrd Skynyrd, 1973-77.

BURNS, HARVEY Drums, percussion. Original member of Sweet Thursday, 1967-70. Session for Cat Stevens (1970-71); Shawn Phillips.

BURNS, HUGHIE Guitar, vocal. Member of Prelude, 1976, and the Jack Bruce Band, 1977. Session for Phillip Rainbow (1979).

BURNS, JAKE Guitar, vocal. Member of Stiff Little

Fingers, 1980.

BURNS, KARL Drums. Member of the Fall, 1979.

BURNS, KIM Piano, vocal. Member of the Other Side.

BURNS, MICK Drums. Session for Tim Renwick (1980).

BURNS, MURRAY Keyboards, vocal. Member of Mi-Sex, 1980.

BURNS, RANDY Vocal, guitar. Soloist and head of the Sky Dog Band, 1973. *Albums:* Evening of the Magician; Of Love and War; Songs for an Uncertain Lady (ESP).

RANDY BURNS AND THE SKY DOG BAND Randy Burns—vocal, guitar; Matt Kastner—guitar, vocal; David Tweedy—keyboards, vocal; Bruce Samuels—bass, vocal; David Mohn—drums, vocal; A. J. Mulhern—vocal, percussion. *Album:* Still on Your Feet (POL) 1973.

BURNS, RUSTY Guitar, vocal. Member of Point Blank, 1976.

BURNS, STEPHEN Guitar, vocal, piano, synthesizer. Member of the Scruffs, 1977.

BURNSIDE, DONALD Keyboards. Member of Captain Sky's Band since 1979.

BURNZ, CHA Vocal, guitar. Member of Fingerprintz, 1980.

BURR, CLIVE Drums. Member of Iron Maiden, 1980.

BURR, GARY Guitar, vocal. *Album:* Matters of the Heart (LIF JZ-35362).

BURRE, PAT Tenor saxophone. Member of the Foundations, 1968.

BURRELL, BOZ Bass, vocal. Member of Centipede, 1971. After a less than commercially rewarding stint with the highly progressive rock/jazz oriented King Crimson in 1972 (replacing Gorden Haskell), and Snape, in 1972, he became a member of Bad Company, 1974 to present. Session for Alvin Lee (1973, 75); Ted Nugent (1977).

BURRILO, JAY Percussion. Member of Chase, 1971-73.

BURROUGHS, ALAN Guitar. Member of Captain Sky's Band since 1979.

BURROWS, BRYN Drums, percussion. Member of the Fabulous Poodles, 1978-79.

BURROWS, CLIVE Saxophone, drums, flute. Member of the Alan Price Set, 1965-68.

BURROWS, TONY Vocal. Session for Long John Baldry (1971); Chris Spedding (1976).

BURRUSS, MONICA Vocal. Session for Johnny Winter (1974).

BURSTIN, JEFF Guitar. Member of Jo Jo Zep and the Falcons, 1980.

BURT, JO Bass. Member of the Tom Robinson Band since 1978.

BURTIS, JAMES Harmonica, vocal. Born 1928. Cousin of Sonny Terry. *Albums:* Anthology of the Blues—Arkansas Blues (KNT 9007).

BURTIS, SAM Trombone. Session for Paul Butterfield's Better Days (1973).

BURTNICK, GLENN Guitar, keyboards, harmonica, vocal. Member of Helmet Boy, 1980.

BURTON, BARRY Guitar, steel guitar, dobro, mandolin, vocal. Member of the Amazing Rhythm Aces.

BURTON, DAVE Vocal, guitar. Member of Liar, 1980.

BURTON, GARY Vibraphone. Founder and mastermind of the Gary Burton Quartet of the late 1960s, he has since developed as a jazz soloist. Session for Chick Corea (1972). *Albums:* Gary Burton and Keith Jarrett (ATC 1577) 1971; Crystal Silence (ECM 1024) 1973; Dreams, So Real (ECM 1072) 1976; Hotel Hello (ECM 1055) 1974; Matchbook (ECM 1056); New Quartet (ECM 1030); Paris Encounter (ATC 1597) 1972; Passengers (ECM 1-1092); Ring (ECM 1051) 1974; Seven Songs (ECM 1040) 1974; Times Square (ECM 1-1111) 1978; Turn of the Century (ATC 2-321); Alone At Last (ATC 1598) 1971; Duster (VIC LSP-3835); Good Vibes (ATC 1560) 1970; In the Public Interest (POL); Norwegian Wood (CDN); Throb (ATC 1531).

GARY BURTON QUARTET Gary Burton—vibraharp; Jerry Hahn—guitar; Bob Moses—drums; Steve Swallow—bass; Larry Coryell—guitar; Roy Haynes—drums. Burton's field is actually jazz, but he is responsible for a large audience of rock listeners who would never have listened to jazz under normal circumstances in their formative music-listening years. His original group featured one of the fastest guitar players of the time, Larry Coryell, who has since built a large jazz audience around himself as a soloist. See Gary Burton. *Albums:* The Time Machine, 1966; Tennessee Firebird, 1967; Lofty Fake Anagram, 1968.

BURTON, JAMES Guitar, dobro. Session for Doug Kershaw; Elvis Presley; Rick Nelson; Jonathan Edwards (1976); Buffalo Springfield (1967).

BURTON, JOE Trombone. Session for B. B. King (1972, 75).

BURTON, KEVIN Organ. Session for Harvey Mandel (1972).

BURTON, TREVOR Bass, vocal, guitar. Original member of the Move, 1967. Member of the Steve Gibbons Band, 1976. Session for Luther Grosvenor; Gary Wright (1970).

BUSCEMI, DOMINIC Guitar, vocal. Member of Citizen, 1980.

BUSCH, JAMES N. Drums, percussion. Member of the Invaders, 1980.

BUSEY, GARY Vocal, guitar, drums. Actor/musician who starred in "The Buddy Holly Story" where he and his costars performed all the music, rather than overdub the original Holly hits. Also records under the name Teddy Jack Eddy. See Teddy Jack Eddy. Session for Leon Russell (1975-76); Robbie Robertson (1980).

BUSH, KATE Vocal. *Albums:* Kick Inside (EIA SW-17003) 1978; Kite (EIA 8003); Man with the Child in His Eyes (EIA 8006); Moving (EIA 8006); Wuthering Heights (EIA 8003).

BUSH, RICHARD Member of the A's, 1979.

BUSH, ROGER Drums. Member of the Flying Burrito Brothers before their dissolve. Session for Gene Parsons (1979).

BUSH, STAN Guitar, vocal. Member of Boulder, 1979.

BUSHY, RON Drums. Original member of the Iron Butterfly, 1967-69. Five years after the group fell apart, he and Erik Brann resurrected a poor excuse of the original band for the nostalgia craze.

BUSLOWE, STEVE Bass. Replaced Alan Berger in Southside Johnny and the Asbury Jukes, 1980. Session for Ian Lloyd (1979); Blackjack (1980).

BUTALA, TONY Vocal. Member of the Lettermen.

BUTANI, BOBBY Guitar. Member of the Tuff Darts, 1978.

BUTCH Vocal, bass. Member of Flash Cadillac.

BUTCHER, DAMON Keyboards. Member of Rough Diamond, 1977.

BUTLER, ARTIE Piano. Session for Joe Cocker (1968).

BUTLER, BILLY Guitar. Session for John Hammond (1964, 68); Barry Goldberg (1969).

BUTLER, BRIAN Member of Quincy, 1980.

BUTLER, CHRIS Guitar, vocal, percussion. Member of Tin Huey, 1979.

BUTLER, HAL Vocal, keyboards. Member of the Creed, 1978.

BUTLER, JERRY Vocal. Original member of the Impressions before going solo. *Albums:* All Time Jerry Butler Hits (TRP 8011); Best of Jerry Butler (MER 61281); It All Comes Out in Song (MTN M7-892) 1977; Just Beautiful (KNT 536); Love's on the Menu (MTN M7-850) 1976; Nothing Says I Love You Like I Love You (PHL JZ-35510); 16 Greatest Hits (TRP TOP-16-45); Starring Betty Everett (TRD 2073); Suite for the Single Girl (MTN M7-878); Thelma and Jerry (MTN M7-887) 1977; Two to One (MTN M7-903) 1978; Jerry Butler's Golden Hits-Live (MER 61151); Curtis in Chicago (CTM 8018); First Generation-Soul (BUD 7504); 14 Golden Recordings (ABC X-785); Ice Man Cometh (MER 61198); Infinite Style of Jerry Butler (TRP X-9516); Just Beautiful (KNT 536); Power of Love (MER SRM-1-689); Together (BUD 7507); Tribute to Burt Bacharach (SEP 5100); Very Best of Jerry Butler (BUD 4001).

BUTLER, JESSE Organ. Session for the Doobie Brothers (1976).

BUTLER, JOE Drums. Original member of the Lovin' Spoonful, 1965-69.

BUTLER, MARTIN Guitar. Member of the Demons, 1977.

BUTLER, PAUL Guitar. Session for Mike Vernon, B. B. King (1971).

BUTLER, RICHARD Lyrics. Member of the Psychedelic Furs, 1980.

BUTLER, ROSEMARY Vocal, bass. Member of Birtha, 1973. Session for the Doobie Brothers (1978); Richie Furay (1979); the Marc Tanner Band (1979); Boz Scaggs (1980); the Ozark Mountain Daredevils (1980); Jackson Browne (1980).

BUTLER, STEVE Member of Quincy, 1980.

BUTLER, TERRY "GEEZER" Bass. Original member of Black Sabbath, since 1970.

BUTLER, TIM Bass. Member of the Psychedelic Furs, 1980.

BUTLER, TONY Bass. Session for Pete Townshend (1980).

BUTORAC, FRANK Guitar, vocal. Member of Gabriel, 1975.

BUTTERFIELD, PAUL Writer, harmonica, guitar, flute, piano. Born 12/17/42. From Chicago, one of America's most well-known old school blues stylists. Many of America's finest blues musicians, such as Mike Bloomfield, Elvin Bishop and others, received their first break in his Blues Band before striking out on their own. His Better Days Band lasted from 1971 to 1973 before he began his solo career with "Put It in Your Ear," 1975. See Paul Butterfield's Better Days and Blues Band. Member of Fathers and Sons, 1969. Session for Creation (1976); Nick Jameson (1977); the Band (1978); Elizabeth Barraclough (1979). *Albums:* Put It in Your Ear (BSV 6960) 1975; North South (BSV 6995) 1980.

PAUL BUTTERFIELD'S BETTER DAYS Paul Butterfield—keyboards, harmonica, vocal; Geoff Muldaur—vocal, slide guitar, keyboards; Ronnie Barron—keyboard; Christopher Parker—drums; Billy Rich—bass; Amos Garrett—guitar, bass, vocal. Formed by Paul Butterfield between the Paul Butterfield Blues Band and his solo career in 1975. See Paul Butterfield Blues Band. *Albums:* Paul Butterfield's Better Days (BSV 2119) 1974; It All Comes Back (BSV 2170) 1975.

PAUL BUTTERFIELD BLUES BAND Paul Butterfield—harmonica, guitar, flute, piano; Mike Bloomfield—guitar (1965-67); Elvin Bishop—guitar (1965-67); Mark Naftalin—keyboards (1966-68); Billy Davenport—drums (1966); Bugsy Maugh—bass, vocals (1967); Gene Dinwiddie—saxophone, flute, mandolin (1967); Dave Sanborn—saxophone (1967); Keith Johnson—trumpet, piano (1967); Buzzy Feiten—guitar, keyboard (1968); Rod Hicks—bass, cello, vocal (1969); Steve Madaio—trumpet (1969); Ted Harris—keyboards (1969); George Davidson—drums (1971); Dennis Whitted—drums (1971); Phil Wilson—drums, congas, percussion (1967-69); Trevor Lawerence—saxophone; Fred Beckmeier—bass; Ralph Walsh—guitar (1971); Big Black—congas (1971). Out of Chicago in the early 1960s, Butterfield split from his blues companions, Barry Goldberg, Harvey Mandel and others, to form his first band. For the next six years, Butterfield was the focal point of blues in the United States. He dissolved his Blues Band in 1972 to form Better Days, a return to his roots, with old Chicago blues friends. This lasted for three years, after which he went solo without the aid of a band (in name only), to pursue a new direction in his career; that of a vocalist. Part of Woodstock, 1969. *Albums:* Butterfield Blues Band Live (Elk 7E-2001) 1971; Paul Butterfield Blues Band (ELK 7294) 1965; East-West (ELK 7315) 1966; Golden Butter (ELK 7E-2005) 1972; In My Own Dream (ELK 74025) 1968; Resurrection of Pigboy Crabshaw (ELK) 1967; What's Shakin' (ELK 74002).

BUTTREY, KENNETH Drums, percussion, producer. First heard on Dylan's "Blonde On Blonde" album. Member of the Stray Gators, 1972, after a session as a member of Area Code 615. Produced the Wilson Brothers (1979). Session for Donovan (1974, 76); Bob Dylan (1969); John Hammond (1975); Harvey Mandel; Pearls Before Swine (1970); Neil Young (1975); Ian and Sylvia; the Pointer Sisters (1974); Bob Seger (1974); J. J. Cale (1972, 79); Levon Helm (1980); Mike Harrison (1975); Splinter (1977); John Stewart.

BUX Ralph Morman—vocal; Punky Meadows—guitar; James Newlon—guitar; Mickey Jones—bass; Rocky Isaac—drums. *Album:* We Come To Play (CAP) 1976.

BUZZCOCKS Pete Shelley—guitar, keyboards, vocal; Steve Garvey—bass; John Mahler—drums, vocal; Steve Diggle—guitar, vocal. *Albums:* Different Kind of Tension (IRS 001) 1979; Singles Going Steady (IRS 001) 1979; Another Music in a Different Kitchen (Import) 1978; Love Bites (Import) 1978.

BYERS, BILL Trombone. Session for the Mothers of Invention (1972); Frank Zappa (1972).

BYERS, JIM Guitar. Member of Touchstone, 1971.

BYNOE, DAVID Bass, harmonica, flute, drums. Member of Bagatelle, 1968.

BYRD, BILLY Guitar. Session with Leon Russell (1973).

BYRD, CARL Drums. Member of Zulu.

BYRD, JOSEPH Synthesizer. Member of the United States of America, 1968. *Albums:* Christmas Yet To Come (TKM 1046); Yankee Transcendoodle (TKM 1051); American Metaphysical Circus (COL MC 7317) 1969.

BYRD, RICKY Guitar, vocal. Member of Susan, 1979.

BYRD, STEVE Guitar. Replaced Terry Smith in Zzebra, 1975.

BYRDS Roger McGuinn—guitar, vocal, writer, keyboards; Jay York—bass; Clarence White—guitar; Gene Parsons—drums; Red Rhodes—pedal steel guitar; Gene Clark—guitar, vocal, writer, harmonica; David Crosby—guitar, vocal, writer; Mike Clark—drums; Gram Parsons—guitar, vocal (until 1969); Chris Hillman—bass, mandolin, guitar, vocal; Skip Battin—drums, vocal. Early name: the Beefeaters. In 1965 the Byrds released "Mr. Tambourine Man," the first successful synthesis of folk and rock, bringing them as much notoriety as the Beatles. After establishing themselves as innovators of the first magnitude, they expanded together, and in their subsequent solo careers, into the realms of country music until 1969. A short-lived reunion in 1974 resulted in a meeting of the solo stars they had become, rather than the collective innovators they had been. *Albums:* Best of the Byrds, Vol. II (COL KC 31795) 1972; Byrds (COL) 1974; Ballad of Easy Rider (COL KCS-9942); Best of the Byrds (COL C-31795); Byrd's Greatest Hits (COL PC-9516); Byrds (Untitled) (COL CG-30127); Byrds Play Dylan (COL PC-36293); Dr. Byrds and Mr. Hyde (COL CS-9755); Fifth Dimension (COL CS-9349); Mr. Tambourine Man (COL CS-9172); Notorious Byrd Brothers (COL CS-9575); Preflyte (COL C-32183); Sweetheart of the Rodeo (COL CS-9670); Turn, Turn, Turn (COL CS-9254, CG-33645); Younger Than Yesterday (COL CS-9442).

BYRNE, DAVID Guitar, vocal, writer. Leader of the Talking Heads since 1977.

BYRNE, FRANK Drums. Member of Ace, 1974-78. Session for Danny Kirwan (1979); Frankie Miller (1979); Sean Tyla (1980).

BYRNE, ROBERT Guitar. Session for Roy Orbison (1979).

BYRNE, SIMON Drums, vocal. Member of Gringo, 1971.

BYRON, D. L. Vocal, guitar. Songwriter-soloist backed by the Protector 4. *Album:* This Day and Age (ARI 4258) 1980.

BYRON, DAVID Vocal, writer. Original member of heavy metal Uriah Heep, 1970-76. The international fame of the band commercially guaranteed the feasibility of solo albums for its group members, though they sounded more like group outtakes. Voice of Rough Diamond, 1977. *Album:* Take No Prisoners (MER) 1975.

BYRON, DENNIS Drums. Session for the Bee Gees (1975, 77); Andy Gibb (1980).

BYRON, LARRY Guitar. Member of Time, 1968-69, before he replaced Mars Bonfire in Steppenwolf, 1970. Session for Joe Cocker (1978); Roy Orbison (1979).

BYTNAR, RIC Guitar, vocal. Session for the Pop (1977).

C., RICHIE Guitar. Member of Network, 1977.

C.O.D. Joe Falsia—guitar; Bill Cuomo—keyboards; Ralph Humphrey—drums; Dennis Bellfield—bass; John Raines—percussion. *Album:* Tears (CSB 7193) 1979.

CABAZA, LUIS Keyboards, vocal. Member of Stray Dog, 1974. Session for Gene Parsons (1979).

CABIN, MITHRAN Percussion, vocal. Member of Boulder, 1979.

CACTUS Carmine Appice—drums, vocal (1970-73); Tim Bogert—bass, vocal (1970-73); Rusty Day—vocal, harpsichord (1970-72); Jim McCarty —guitar (1970-72); Werner Fritzschings—guitar (1972); Peter French—vocal (1972); Duane Hitchings—keyboards, vocal (1972-73); Roland Robinson —bass, vocal (1973); Mike Pinera—guitar, vocal (1973); Jerry Norris—drums, vocal (1973). Cactus began in 1970 and took heavy rock to its furthest extreme, with dominating rhythm lines equally as loud and intricate as the highly electrified guitar and raunchy vocals, much as Appice and Bogert demonstrated earlier as members of Vanilla Fudge. Day and McCarty left in 1972 to be replaced by Fritzschings, French and a new addition to their sounds, a keyboard, played by Hitchings. While the energy came through on "Ot 'n' Sweaty," enthusiasm was lacking. Bogert and Appice left after that to do a stint with Jeff Beck in Beck, Bogert and Appice. That left Hitchings with no original members of the band. He tried to hold the group together with friend Mike Pinera, but the original sound had vanished to be replaced by the more commercial effort of "The New Cactus Band." *Albums:* Cactus (ACO SD 33-340) 1970; One Way or Another (ACO SD 33-356), 1971; Restrictions (ACO SD 33-377) 1971; 'Ot 'N' Sweaty (ACO SD-7011) 1972; Son of Cactus (ACO 50-7017) 1973.

CADENHEAD, MICHAEL Drums, percussion, vocal. Member of Hotel since 1978.

CADETS Early backup band for Paul Anka. Recorded "Stranded in the Jungle," 1956.

CADILLAC JACK Guitar, vocal. Member of Duke and the Drivers, 1975.

CADILLAC, ENRICO Vocal. Member of Deaf School, 1979-80.

CAESAR AND CLEO Early name of Sonny and Cher.

CAFE JACQUES Peter Veitch; Chris Thompson—vocal, guitar; Mike Ogletree. *Albums:* International (COL JC-35697) 1979; Round the Back (COL JC 35294) 1977.

CAGE, BUDDY Pedal steel guitar, vocal. Member of the New Riders of the Purple Sage. Session for Bob Dylan (1974).

CAHAN, ANDY Drums. Session for Jimmy Carl Black and Bunk Gardner (1971).

CAHILL, TONY Drums. Replaced Snowy Fleet in the Easybeats. Member of Python Lee Jackson, 1972.

CAHN, ELLIOT Guitar, vocal. Original member of Sha Na Na, 1970-71. Session for Henry Gross.

CAIN Jiggs Lee—vocal, percussion; Dave Elmeer —bass, guitar, keyboards; Lloyd Forsberg—guitar; Kevin De Remer—drums. Minnesota based hard rockers. *Albums:* A Pound of Flesh, 1975; Stinger, 1977.

CAIN, JONATHAN Vocal, keyboards. Namesake of the Jonathan Cain Band, 1977. Replaced Michael Corby in the Babys, 1980.

JONATHAN CAIN BAND Jonathan Cain—vocal, keyboard; Jim Arnold—guitar; Gary Richwine—bass; Tommy Cain—drums. *Album:* Windy City Breakdown (BSV 6969) 1977.

CAIN, MARK "DIODE" Drums. Member of Sham 69, 1978-79.

CAIN, TOMMY Drums, vocal. Member of the Jonathan Cain Band, 1977. Session for the Allman Brothers (1980).

CAINE, BUDDY Guitar. Member of Moxy, 1976.

CAIRNS, DAVID Guitar, vocal. Member of Secret Affair, 1980.

CALABRIA, BARBARA Vocal. Member of the Fugs Chorus.

CALAMISE, CHARLES Bass. Session for the Steve Miller Band (1976).

CALDERA Jorge Stranz—guitar, percussion; Eduardo del Barrio—keyboards, vocal; Steve Tavaglione—saxophone, flute, bass; Mike Azevedo —percussion; Carlos Vega—drums; Dean Cortez —bass. *Albums:* Caldera (CAP ST-11571) 1976; Dreamer (CAP ST-11952) 1979; Sky Islands (CAP SW-11658) 1977; Time and Chance (CAP SW-11810) 1978.

CALDWELL, BOBBY Drums, percussion, vocal, piano, vibes, writer. Original member of Johnny Winter's backup group, 1970-72, Captain Beyond, 1972, and Armageddon, 1975. Session for Rick Derringer (1973); Johnny Winter (1973). *Albums:* Bobby Caldwell (CLD 8804) 1978; Cat in the Hat (CLD 8810) 1980.

CALDWELL, CHARLES Drums. Member of the Son Seals Blues Band, 1973.

CALDWELL, RON Vocal. Original member of the Bar-Kays. Died in the Otis Redding plane crash

12/10/67.

CALDWELL, SONNY Vocal, guitar, percussion. Member of Tir Na Nog, 1973.

CALDWELL, TOM Bass, percussion, vocal, drums. Original member of the Marshall Tucker Band, 1973. Died 1980.

CALDWELL, TOY Guitar, pedal steel guitar, vocal, writer. Featured guitarist, writer and organizer of the Marshall Tucker Band, 1973-present. Session for Elvin Bishop (1974).

CALE, J. J. Guitar, vocal, writer, bass. Debuting in 1971 on Leon Russell's Shelter label, Cale's quiet voice hints a country flavor in his unique brand of rock-blues. Session for Art Garfunkel; Leon Russell (1973-75); Bob Seger (1973); Neil Young (1975). *Albums:* 5 (SLT 3163) 1979; Naturally . . . J. J. Cale (MCA 52009) 1971; Okie (MCA 52015) 1974; Really J. J. Cale (MCA 52012) 1972; Troubador (MCA 52002) 1976.

CALE, JOHN Vocal, viola, keyboards, bass, guitar, writer, producer. With Lou Reed and Nico, an original member of Andy Warhol's Velvet Underground, 1967-69. He left to produce his own and others' albums. His droning voice and eerie lyrics give an otherworldly dimension to his mesmerizing music. Released "June 1, 1974" with friends Nico, Eno, and Kevin Ayers. Produced the Stooges. Production and session for Nico (1967, 68, 70, 74); Patti Smith (1975). Session for Ian Hunter (1979); David Kubinec (1979). *Albums:* Fear, 1974; Slow Dazzle, 1975; Helen of Troy, 1973; Guts (ISL 9459) 1977; Sabotage (IRS 004) 1979; Vintage Violence (COL CS-1037) 1970; Mercenaries (IRS 9008); Rosegarden Funeral of Sores (IRS 9008); Academy in Peril (WBR MS 2079) 1972; Paris, 1919 (WBR MS 2131) 1973; June 1, 1974, (ISL) 1974; Church of Anthrax (with Terry Riley) (COL) 1970.

CALHOUN, GERALD Bass, vocal. Member of Phyrework, 1978.

CALHOUN, JIMMY Bass. Member of Creation, 1974. Session for Dr. John (1972); Robbie Robertson (1980).

CALHOUN, KEVIN Percussion. Session for Les Dudek (1977).

CALHOUN, MOON Drums. Session for Leon Russell (1975).

CALHOUN, RICK Vocal. Member of the Strand, 1980.

CALICO Jerry Oates—guitar, vocal; Keith Impellitier—guitar, vocal; Bill Miner—drums; Tom Morrell—pedal steel guitar; John McClure—keyboards; Mike Redden—bass; Dave Kirby—guitar. *Albums:* Calico (UAR); Calico, Vol. II (UAR) 1976.

CALIFORNIA, RANDY Guitar, vocal, writer. Original member the Rainflowers, and Spirit, 1968-72, 1976-79. During the interim of Spirit's disbandment (1972-75), he organized Kapt. Kopter and the Fabulous Twirly Birds, 1972. *Album:* Kapt. Kopter and the Fabulous Twirly Birds (EPC E 31755) 1972.

CALIMAN, HADLEY Saxophone, flute. Session for Carlos Santana and Buddy Miles Live (1972); Santana (1972).

CALIMISE, CHARLES Bass. Session for Steve Miller (1977).

CALIUTO, VINCE Drums. Session for Rozetta (1980).

CALL, ALEX Vocal, guitar. Member of Clover, 1977.

CALL, JIM Keyboards. Member of the Penetrators, 1980.

CALL, JOHN Steel guitar. Member of Pure Prairie League, 1972-78.

CALLA, JOHNNY Guitar, saxophone, vocal. Member of Huey Lewis and the News, 1980.

CALLAN, ALAN Guitar, synthesizer, vocal. Member of Blue Goose, 1975.

CALLENDER, GEORGE "RED" String bass, horns, tuba. Session for B. B. King (1972); Martin Mull (1973); Donovan (1974); Ry Cooder (1974); James Taylor (1976).

CALLOWAY, GREG Bass, vocal. Member of No Slack, 1978.

CALLOWAY, HARRISON Trumpet. Member of the Muscle Shoals Horns. Session for Mike Harrison (1972); Barry Goldberg (1974); Bob Seger (1975); Tim Weisberg (1977); Joe Cocker (1978); Roy Orbison (1979); Bob Dylan (1979); Boatz (1979).

CALVER, STUART Vocal. Session for Danny Kirwan (1979).

CALVERT, BERNARD Bass, keyboards. Member of the Hollies, 1965-present, replacing Eric Haydock.

CALVERT, JIMMY Guitar. Session for Ringo Starr (1973).

CALVERT, ROBERT Vocal. Voice of Hawkwind, 1977 to present, and Hawklord, 1978.

CAMARENA, ROBERT Guitar, vocal. Member of Ruben and the Jets, 1973. Session for Frank Zappa (1974).

CAMEL Doug Fergusson—bass; Andy Ward—drums, percussion; Peter Bardens—keyboards, moog, mellotron, vocal; Andy Latimer—guitar, flute, vocal. Extended instrumental space journeys with occasional distant lyrics. *Albums:* Mirage, 1975; Moonmadness, 1976; Snow Goose, 1975; Breathless (ARI 4206); I Can See Your House from Here (ARI 4254); Rain Dances (INS 9X5 7035) 1977.

CAMERA CLUB See Bruce Wooley and the Camera Club.

CAMERON, CASEY Vocal. Member of Human Sexual Response, 1980.

CAMERON, CHRIS Keyboards. Session for John Mayall (1979).

CAMERON, GEORGE Vocal. Member of the Left Banke, 1967.

CAMERON, JOHN Guitar, vocal. Session for Donovan (1973).

CAMERON, TOM Harmonica. Member of the Resurrection Band, 1978.

CAMILLERI, JOE Vocal, saxophone, guitar. Member of Jo Jo Zep and the Falcons, 1980.

CAMP, JOHN Guitar, vocal. Member of Baby, 1975.

CAMP, JON Bass, vocal. Member of Renaissance.

CAMPBELL, ADRIAN Vocal. Voice of Avalanche, 1976.

CAMPBELL, AMBROSE Congas. Session for Leon Russell (1972, 75); Leon Russell and Willie Nelson (1979).

CAMPBELL, BRAD Bass. Replaced Denny Gerrard in the Paupers, 1968-69. Member of the Full Tilt Boogie Band, 1969-70.

CAMPBELL, CHRIS Bass, vocal. Original member of the Silver Bullet Band, since 1974.

CAMPBELL, D. Member of Buckwheat.

CAMPBELL, DUANE Bass. Member of the Catfish Hodge Band, 1979.

CAMPBELL, FRANK Bass. Member of the Johnny Average Dance Band, 1980.

CAMPBELL, GLEN Guitar, vocal. Spending his apprenticeship as a session guitarist in the '60s, Campbell went solo with "Gentle on My Mind," 1967, and "Wichita Lineman," 1969, and evolved into a successful Nevada and television showman. Session for Jan and Dean (1963); Billy Strange. *Albums:* Astounding 12-String Guitar of Glen Campbell (CAP SM-2023); Basic (CAP ST-11722); Best of Glen Campbell (CAP ST-11577); Christmas (CAP STBB-2979); Vol. I (CAP SM-11833); Bloodline (CAP SM-11821) 1976; By the Time I Get to Pheonix (CAP SM-12040); Glen Campbell, Greatest Hits (CAP SW-752); Live at Royal Festival Hall (CAP SWBC-11707) 1977; Travis (CAP SW-11117); Country Hits of the '60s (CAP SM-886); Gentle On My Mind (CAP SM-11960); Highwayman (CAP SOO-12008); In the Heat of the Night (UAR LT-290); Last Time I Saw Her (CAP SM-733); Rhinestone Cowboy (CAP SW-11430); Somethin' 'bout You Baby I Like (CAP SOO-12075) 1980; Southern Nights (CAP SO-11601) 1977; That Christmas Feeling (CAP SM-2978); Try a Little Kindness (CAP SM-389); Wichita Lineman (CAP SM-103).

CAMPBELL, GLENN ROSS Pedal steel guitar, mandolin, vocal, writer. Head of Juicy Lucy, 1970-71.

CAMPBELL, LARRY Pedal steel guitar. Session for Rob Stoner (1980).

CAMPBELL, MIKE Guitar. Member of Tom Petty's Heartbreakers, since 1977.

CAMPBELL, MIKE Drums. Member of the Ravers.

CAMPBELL, MONT Bass, vocal. Member of Egg, 1970.

CAMPBELL, TONY Guitar. Member of Jigsaw, 1975-77.

CAMPBELL, WILGAR Drums, percussion. Session for Rory Gallagher (1971-72).

CAMPBELL-HARE, ANDREW Drums, vocal. Member of Bugs Tomorrow, 1980.

CAMPERS Early name of the Crickets.

CAMPIGOTTO, JOHN Percussion. Member of McGuffey Lane, 1980.

CAMPO, BOBBY Percussion, vocal. Member of Le Roux since 1979.

CAN Irwin Schmidt—keyboards; Jacki Liebezeit—drums; Michael Karoli—vocal, guitar; Holgar Czukay—bass. *Albums:* Soon Over Babaluma, 1975; Egg Bamyasi (UAR).

CANADY, STEVE Guitar, drums, vocal. Member of the Ozark Mountain Daredevils, 1977-78.

CANDLE Jeffrey David Hooven—piano, guitar, vocal; Robert Verne—guitar, vocal; Davey Wison—bass, vocal; John Skeeton—flute, vocal; L. J. Wolken—accordion; Don Peake—guitar; Duane Bryant—drums; Richard Roberts—percussion; Andy Narell—steel drums, keyboards; Doug Kraatz—violin, viola. *Album:* Candle (GNB 1003) 1972.

CANDLESTICK BRASS Ian Hamer—trumpet, flugelhorn; Stan Sultzmann—tenor saxophone; Alan Skidmore—tenor saxophone; Jeff Dacy—baritone and alto saxophones; Derek Wadsworth—trombone; Eddie Morove—baritone saxophone; Wally Smith—trombone. Session for Ginger Baker (1977).

CANDLEWICK GREEN Terry Webb—vocal; Jimmy Nunnen—bass, vocal; Derek Cleary—guitar, vocal; Andy Ball—keyboards; Alan Leyland—drums, percussion. *Album:* What Kind of Songs (BSF) 1974.

CANDYMEN John Rainey Adkins—guitar; Rodney Justo—vocal; Dean Daughtry—keyboards; Bill Gilmore—bass; Bob Nix—drums. Former backup group for Roy Orbison from Alabama, they went solo in 1967 in New York, handling other people's material with greater success than their own. *Albums:* Candymen, 1967; Candymen Bring You Candypower (1968).

CANDYSTORE PROPHETS Group that originally played the music for the Monkees on their television series.

CANFIELD, KERRY Member of Wheatfield, 1980.

CANG, MARTIN Keyboards, guitar, vocal. Member of the Sensational Alex Harvey Band.

CANN, JOHN Guitar, vocal. Member of Atomic Rooster, 1971, and Hard Stuff, 1973.

CANN, WARREN Drums, vocal. Member of Ultra Vox, since 1977.

CANNATA, RICHIE Saxophone. Session for Elton John (1980).

CANNED HEAT Robert "Bear" Hite—vocal, harp, writer, percussion (1965-73, 1979); Alan Wilson

—harmonica, vocal, guitar, writer (1965-70); Adolfo de la Parra—drums, percussion (1965-73, 1979); Henry Vestine—guitar (1965-69, 1972-73); Larry Taylor—bass (1965-70); Harvey Mandel—guitar, writer (1969); Antonio de la Barreda—bass (1970-73); James Shane—bass (1973); Ed Beyer—keyboards (1973); Richard Hite—bass (1973, 1979); Chris Morgan—guitar (1979); Mark Skyer—guitar, vocal (1979). Los Angeles' Canned Heat had formed, played, and broken apart before the blues were popular (1965). So, when the blues came into vogue around 1967, Canned Heat reformed and was knocking on the door to success. Shortly after Wilson's death in 1970, John Lee Hooker credited him for being "the greatest harmonica player ever." Harvey Mandel replaced Vestine in 1969, before joining John Mayall with Larry Taylor in 1970. In the transition period, they released America's answer to the Yardbirds and Sonny Boy Williamson's album by releasing a double set with old time boogier, John Lee Hooker. In 1973, the group retired until 1979, when they released "Human Condition." Session with John Lee Hooker (1970); Woodstock (1969). *Albums:* Canned Heat, 1967; Best of Canned Heat (SEP 18017); Boogie with Hooker and Heat (UAR UA-LA049) 1970; One More River To Cross, 1973; Very Best of Canned Heat (UAR UA-LA431); Vintage (JNS 3009); Historical Figures and Ancient Heads; Future Blues (LIB LST 11002) 1969; Boogie with Canned Heat (UAR LM-1015) 1968; Livin' the Blues (LIB LST 27200) 1968; Human Condition (TAK 7066) 1979; The New Age (UAR UA LA049 F) 1973.

CANNON, FREDDIE Vocal. Real name: Frederick Anthony Picariello. Recorded "Tallahassee Lassie," 1959, and "Palisades Park" in the '60s.

CANNON, PAUL Guitar. Member of Target, 1976-77.

CANOFF, RICK Saxophone. Member of the Flock.

CANSFIELD, TIM Guitar. Session for Elton John (1979).

CANTRELLI, T. JAY Reeds. Former member of Love. Session for James Sherwood.

CAPALDI, JIM Drums, percussion, vocal, writer. Born 8/2/44. An original member of Traffic, 1967-75. The group's unstable status did not hinder his development as a soloist, starting in 1971. In 1979 he began recording with the Contenders. Session for Dave Mason; Alvin Lee (1973); the Rainbow Concert (1973); Luther Grosvenor; Paul Kossoff (1974); Steve Winwood (1977). *Albums:* Daughter of the Night (RSO 1-3037) 1979; Electric Nights (RSO 1-3050) 1979; Short Cut Draw Blood (ISL 9336) 1975; Oh How We Danced (ISL SW 9314) 1971; Whale Meat Again (ISL ILPS 9254) 1973.

CAPALDI, PHIL Drums, vocal. Brother of Jim Capaldi, and member of the Contenders, 1979.

CAPITAL CITY ROCKETS Jamie Lyons—vocal; Robert Hill—guitar, vocal, writer; Michael Warner—guitar, vocal, writer; Eric Moore—bass; Jerry Hertig—drums. Good time rock group made their debut and exit in 1973, not lacking in talent but in distinction. *Album:* Capital City Rockets (ELK) 1973.

CAPON, CHRIS String bass. Session with Alexis Korner and Cyril Davies (1954-61).

CAPP, FRANKIE Drums. Session for Frank Zappa (1967).

CAPPICK, GENE Bass, vocal. Member of the Slick Band, 1976.

CAPPS, JIMMY Guitar. Session for J. J. Cale (1972); Waylon Jennings (1973); Bill Medley (1978).

CAPPS, ROGER Bass, vocal. Member of Pat Benatar's backup band since 1979.

CAPTAIN AND TENILLE Darryl Dragon—keyboards; Toni Tenille—vocal, keyboards. Husband and wife team breaking into the pop market and television through rock. *Albums:* Captain and Tenille's Greatest Hits (AAM 4667) 1977; Dream (AAM 4707) 1978; Love Will Keep Us Together (AAM 4552) 1975; Come In from the Rain; Keeping Our Love Warm (CAS NBLP 7250) 1980; Song of Joy (AAM SP 4570) 1976.

CAPTAIN BEEFHEART Vocal, harmonica, bass, clarinet, saxophone, producer. Founder of Captain Beefheart and His Magic Band, 1965-74, and soloist. His abstract, avant garde lyrics and unique delivery established him on the fringes of the rock community, though he is equally capable at writing and arranging commercial material. Session for Frank Zappa (1969, 1975-76).

CAPTAIN BEEFHEART AND HIS MAGIC BAND Don Van Vliet (Captain Beefheart)—vocal, harmonica; Alex St. Claire—guitar (1965-69, 1974); Antennae Jimmy Simmons—guitar (1965-69); Jerry Handsley—bass (1965-69); Drumbo (John French)—drums (1965-68); Jeff Cotton—guitar (1968); Zoot Horn Rollo—guitar, flute (1969-72, 1974); Rockette Morton—bass, vocal, guitar (1969-72, 1974); the Mascara Snake—bass, clarinet, vocal (1969-72); Ed Marimba—drums, percussion (1972); Orejon—bass (1972); Dean Smith—guitar (1974); Ira Ingber—bass (1974); Michael Smotherman—keyboards, vocal (1974); Mark Gibbons—keyboards (1974); Gene Pello—drums (1974); Ty Grimes—percussion (1974); Jimmy Caravan—keyboards (1974); Mark Marcellino—keyboards (1974-75); Art Tripp—drums, percussion (1974); Richard Reons—guitar, vocal (1978); Robert Arthur Williams—drums (1978-present); Eric Drew Feldman—bass, keyboards (1975-present); Jeff Morris Tepper—guitar (1978-present); Bruce Fowler—trombone (1978-present). They were around Southern California in 1965, but no one took them seriously. They offered avant garde jazz vocals and instrumentals in a seemingly structureless mode. In 1969, at the hands of Frank Zappa, a former schoolmate and partner of Captain Beefheart, they released the double set "Trout Mask Replica," rumored to be the most outrageous album of the year. A temporary fallout with Zappa led to the group's split from Bizarre Records. They recorded sporadically until 1972. On the "Spotlight Kid," the Captain made some concessions to structure and melody. In 1975 he reunited with Zappa for a live concert, and has since continued with his re-formed Magic Band. *Albums:* Blue Jeans and Moon Beams (SRM1 1018) 1974; Clear Spot (RPS MS 2115) 1972; Lick My Decals Off, Baby (RPS 6420) 1970; Safe As Milk (BUD 5001) 1967; Trout Mask Replica (STS 1053) 1969; Unconditionally Guaranteed (MER SRM 1 709) 1974; Mirror Man (BUD 5077) 1968; Strictly Personal (BTS 1) 1968; The Spotlight Kid (MS 2050) 1972; Bongo Fury (DCT 2234) 1975; Shiny Beast (WBR) 1978; Doc at the Radar Station (VIR 13148) 1980.

CAPTAIN BEYOND Rod Evans—vocal, writer; Bobby Caldwell—drums, percussion, writer, vocal, piano, vibes, bells; Rhino—guitar, slide guitar; Lee Dorman—bass, vocal, piano, writer; Guille Garcia—congas, percussion (1973); Marty Rodriguez—drums, vocal (1973); Reese Wynans—piano (1973); Willy Daffern—vocal. Their first album appeared in 1972 with a 3-D cover photo, not unlike the Stones' "Their Satanic Majesty's Request." Evans had been Deep Purple's first lead vocalist, Dorman and Rhino had both been in the Iron Butterfly, and Caldwell had respectable credits from Johnny Winter. The first album was a smooth concept album and the second record featured some tasty ballads, but all in all, they could not motivate any buying enthusiasm. They reorganized with a new vocalist, Daffern, in 1977 in another futile attempt to make their talent known. *Albums:* Captain Beyond (CPN 0105) 1972; Dawn Explosion (WBR B-3047) 1977; Sufficiently Breathless (CPN 0115) 1973.

CAPTAIN GLASSPACK AND HIS MUFFLERS Early name for the band that developed into the Mothers of Invention.

CAPTAIN SENSIBLE Guitar, vocal, keyboards. Member of the Damned, 1980.

CAPTAIN SKY Captain Sky—vocal; Ed Gosa—drums; Larry Kimpel—bass; Alan Burroughs—guitar; Reggie Boyd Jr.—guitar; Donald Burnside—keyboards; Herbie Walker—guitar (1980). *Albums:* Adventures of Capt. Sky (AVI 6042A) 1979; Pop Goes the Captain (AVI 6077) 1979; Concerned Party #1 (TEC 1202) 1980.

CARABELLO, MICHAEL Conga. Original member of Santana, 1969-71; and Giants, 1978. Session for Carlos Santana-Buddy Miles Live (1972).

CARABILLO, BOB Saxophone, vocal. Member of Sunship, 1974.

CARAS, IRENE Vocal. Session for Peter C. Johnson (1980).

CARAVAN, JIMMY Keyboards. Member of Captain Beefheart and His Magic Band, 1974.

CARAVAN Richard Sinclair—bass, guitar, vocal; Pye Hastings—guitar, vocal; David Sinclair—keyboards, vocal; Richard Coughlan—drums, percussion; Jimmy Hastings—flute, saxophone; David Grinsted—percussion; Mike Wedgewood—bass, vocal, percussion (1976); Geoffery Richardson—viola, guitar, flute (1976); Jan Schelhaas—keyboards (1976). *Albums:* In the Pink, 1971; Waterloo Lilly, 1972; Plump in the Night, 1973; Blind Dog at St. Dunstans (ARI 4088) 1976; In the Land of Grey and Pink (LON PA-593).

CARDENS, RICHIE Bass, vocal. Member of Man.

CARDINALE, DOMINIC Keyboards. Session for Scarlet Rivera (1978).

CAREY, DAVE Vibes, marimba. Session for Taj Mahal (1978).

CAREY, DAVID Bass, vocal. Member of the Bill Blue Band, 1979-present.

CAREY, TONY Keyboards. Replaced Mickey Lee Soule in Ritchie Blackmore's Rainbow, 1976-78.

CARGOE Tommy Richard—guitar; Tim Benton—drums; Max Wisely—bass; Bill Phillips—keyboards. *Album:* Cargoe, 1972.

CARILLO, FRANK Vocal, guitar. Member of the T-Bones, and Hamilton, Joe Frank and Reynolds. Session for Peter Frampton (1972-73). *Albums:* Street of Dreams (ACO SD 19235) 1979; Rings around the Moon (ACO SD 19176) 1978.

CARL AND THE PASSIONS Early name for the Beach Boys.

CARLE, RONNIE Bass, harmonica, vocal. Member of the Laughing Dogs, 1979-present.

CARLIN, BOBBY Drums, vocal. Member of Coal Kitchen, 1977.

CARLIN, JOANNA Vocal, guitar. Session for Gerry Rafferty (1978).

CARLISI, JEFF Guitar. Member of 38 Special since 1977.

CARLOS, BUN E. Drums. Member of Cheap Trick, 1977-present. Session for John Lennon (1980).

CARLSON, CHAS Keyboards, vocal. Member of Couchois since 1979.

CARLSON, DAVID Guitar. Member of the Tazmanian Devils, 1980.

CARLSSON, RUNE Session for Bo Hansson.

CARLTON, LARRY Guitar. Session for Art Garfunkel; Austin Roberts (1973); Ray Manzarek; Steely Dan (1976, 1980); Seals and Crofts (1976); Joni Mitchell (1975); Glen Campbell (1976); David Blue (1975); Hoyt Axton (1976); Terence Boylan (1980); Christopher Cross (1980). *Albums:* Larry Carlton (OBR K-3221); Strikes Twice (WBR BSK-3380) 1979.

CARLTON, TOMMY Guitar, vocal. Member of

Hotel since 1978.

CARLUCCI, BILL Vocal. Member of Danny and the Juniors.

CARMASSI, DENNIS Drums. Member of Montrose, 1973-75, and St. Paradise, 1979. Replaced Skip Gillette in Gamma, 1980. Session for Sammy Hagar (1977-78).

CARMELLA, DENNIS Vocal, drums. Member of Sam the Band.

CARMEN David Allen—vocal, guitar; Roberto Amaral—vocal, percussion; Angela Allen—vocal, keyboards; John Glascock—vocal, bass; Paul Fenton—drums, percussion. Retrospectively, noted as having spawned Jethro Tull member John Glascock. *Album:* Fandangos in Space (ABC) 1974.

CARMEN, ERIC Guitar, keyboards, vocal, producer. Member of the Raspberries, 1972-74. Production and session for the Euclid Beach Band, 1979. *Albums:* Boats against the Current (ARI 4124) 1977; Eric Carmen (ARI 4057) 1975; Change of Heart (ARI 4184) 1978; Tonight You're Mine (ARI 9513) 1980.

CARMEN, PAULIE Vocal. Voice of Coal Kitchen, 1977.

CARMICHAEL, PETER Percussion. Member of the Dija Rhythm Band, 1976.

CARMICHAL, EVANGELINE Vocal. Session for Paul Butterfield (1975).

CARMICHEL, CAROL Vocal. Session for Seals and Crofts (1976).

CARNES, KIM Vocal, piano. *Albums:* Kim Carnes (AAM 4548) 1975; Romance Dance (EIA SW-17030) 1980; St. Vincent's Court (EIA SW-17004) 1979.

CARNEY, ALAN Bass. Member of Prelude, 1976.

CARNEY, RALPH Reeds, keyboards, vocal, percussion. Member of Tin Huey, 1979. Session for Randy Vanwarmar (1979).

CARON, DANNY Drums. Member of Oak, 1980.

CARP, CHARLIE Guitar, vocal. Member of the Dirty Angels, 1978.

CARP, JEFFREY Harmonica. Session for Howlin' Wolf (1972).

CARPENDER, DAVID Guitar. Member of the Greg Kihn Band since 1976.

CARPENTER, BOB Guitar, keyboards, vocal. Member of Starwood, 1976-77.

CARPENTERS Karen Carpenter—vocal, drums; Richard Carpenter—vocal, piano. Brother-sister pop vocal team. Albums; Carpenters (AAM 3502); Christmas Portrait (AAM 4726) 1978; Close To You (AAM 4271); Horizon (AAM 4581) 1976; Kind of Hush (AAM 4581) 1976; Now and Then (AAM 3519) 1973; Passage (AAM 4703); Singles 1969-1973 (AAM 3601) 1973; Song for You (AAM 3511) 1972; Ticket to Ride (AAM 4205).

CARR, C. Keyboards, vocal. Member of the Sneakers, 1980.

CARR, DAVID Guitar. Member of Rich Mountain Tower, 1976.

CARR, EAMON Drums, percussion. Original member of Horslips, 1970-present.

CARR, IAN Trumpet, flugelhorn. Member of Centipede, 1971, and founder of Ian Carr's Nucleus, 1975-present.

IAN CARR NUCLEUS Ian Carr—horns, keyboards; Brian Smith—reeds (1979); Geoff Castle—keyboards; Billy Kristian—bass (1979); Roger Sellers—drums; Bob Bertles—reeds, vocal (1975); Ken Shaw—guitar (1975); Roger Sutton—bass (1975). *Album:* Out of the Long Dark (CAP ST-11916) 1979; Shakehips Etcetera (SIR SASD 7508) 1975; In Flagrante Delicto (CAP ST 11771) 1977.

CARR, JOHN Conga, bongo. Session for Donovan (1967, 70).

CARR, MIKE Vibraphone. Session for Donovan (1967).

CARR, PETE Guitar. First gained public attention as a member of Hourglass, 1968. Half of the LeBlanc and Carr duet, 1977. Member of the Muscle Shoals Studio Band, 1978, and Boatz, 1979. Session for Boz Scaggs (1972); Johnny Jenkins (1970); Jim Capaldi (1973); Art Garfunkel; Bob Seger (1973, 75); Barry Goldberg (1974); Paul Simon (1973); Rod Stewart (1975); Mike Harrison (1972); Willie Nelson (1974); Paul Kossoff (1974); Richard Tate (1977); Joe Cocker (1978). *Album:* Not a Word of It (BTR 89518) 1976.

CARR, TONY Drums, percussion. Session for Donovan (1968, 73); Bryan Ferry (1974); Ken Tobias (1973); Chris Spedding (1976); Crawler (1977); Wings (1979); Mike Batt (1979); Justin Hayward (1980); the Who (1980).

CARRACK, PAUL Keyboards, vocal. Member of Ace, 1974-76, and Roxy Music, 1979. Session for Frankie Miller (1979); Roxy Music (1980).

CARRADINE, KEITH Guitar, vocal. Actor John Carradine's son, he entered the music field with his contributions to the movies "Welcome to L.A." and "Nashville." *Albums:* I'm Easy (ASY 7E-1066) 1977; Lost and Found (ASY 6E-114) 1978.

CARRIGAN, JERRY Drums. Session for Doug Kershaw (1972); Waylon Jennings (1973); Leon Russell (1973); Bill Medley (1978); Levon Helm (1980).

CARRINGTON, VALERIE Vocal. Session for Donovan (1973).

CARROLL, DAVE Guitar, vocal. Member of the Steve Gibbons Band, 1976.

CARROLL, JIM Vocal. Namesake of the Jim Carroll Band, 1980.

JIM CARROLL BAND Jim Carroll—vocal; Brian Linsley—guitar; Steve Linsley—bass; Terrell Winn—guitar; Wayne Woods—drums. *Album:* Catholic Boys (ACO SD 38-132) 1980.

CARROLL, JON Guitar, vocal. Member of the Starland Vocal Band, 1976.

CARROLL, PORTER, JR. Drums, vocal. Member of Atlantic Starr, 1978-79.

CARROLL, STEVE Guitar. Member of Lonely Boys, 1979.

CARS Rik Ocasek—vocal, guitar, writer, producer; Benjamin Orr—bass, vocal; David Robinson—drums, percussion, vocal; Elliot Easton—guitar, vocal; Greg Hawkes—keyboards, percussion, saxophone, vocal. *Albums:* Candy-O (ELK 5E-507) 1979; The Cars (ELK 6E-135) 1978; Panorama (ELK 5E-514) 1980.

CARTER Producer. Produced Sammy Hagar (1975-79); Bob Welch (1979-80) and others.

CARTER, CARLENE Vocal. Soloist daughter of Johnny Cash. Session for Sean Tyla (1980). *Albums:* Carlene Carter (WBR K-3204) 1978; Two Sides to Every Woman (WBR K-3375) 1979; Musical Shapes (WBR BSK 3465) 1980.

CARTER, CHARLES Keyboards, reeds, percussion, vocal. Member of Aurra, 1980.

CARTER, CLARENCE Vocal, guitar, writer. *Albums:* Real; 60 Minutes with Clarence Carter; The Dynamic Clarence Carter (1967).

CARTER, COLIN Member of Flash, 1972.

CARTER, ERNEST Drums. Session for Bruce Springsteen (1975); Billy Squier (1980).

CARTER, FRED, JR. Guitar, producer. Production and session for Levon Helm (1980). Session for Paul Butterfield (1975); Art Garfunkel; Waylon Jennings (1973); Simon and Garfunkel (1970); Willie Nelson (1974).

CARTER, GREGG G. Member of Hammer, 1979.

CARTER, JERRY Member of Smith.

CARTER, JOHNNY Vocal. Member of the Dells.

CARTER, RON Bass. Jazz star who has recorded with a few rock artists. Session for Larry Coryell; Eumir Deodato; Paul Simon (1972); Jon Mark (1974); Martin Mull (1977). *Albums:* All Blues (CTI 6037) 1974; Blues Farm (CTI 6027); Out Front (PRS 7397); Where (PRS 7843); Alone Together (MLS 9045); Magic (PRS 24053); New York Slick (MLS 9096) 1980; Out Front (PRS 7397); Parade (MLS 9088) 1979; Pastels (MLS 9073); Peg Leg (MLS 9082) 1978; Piccolo (MLS 55004) 1977; Pick 'Em (MLS 9092) 1980; The Quintet (COL C2-34976); Song for You (MLS 9086) 1978; Spanish Blue (CTI 6051) 1975; Yellow and Green (CTI 6064); Anything Goes (KUD 25-51) 1975.

CARTER, VALERIE Vocal. Session for James Taylor (1976); Randy Newman (1979); Adam Mitchell (1979). *Albums:* Just a Stone's Throw Away (COL PC-34155); Wild Child (COL JC-35084) 1978.

CARTHY, MARTIN Vocal, guitar, banjo, organ. Member of Steeleye Span, 1976-78. Session for Dave Swarbrick (1976).

CARTHY, RON Trumpet. Session for Freddie King (1974-75).

CARTMELL, TOM Saxophone, flutes. Session for Bob Seger (1973-75).

CARTWRIGHT, ALAN Bass. Member of Procol Harum, 1972-75.

CARTWRIGHT, ERIK Guitar, vocal. Member of Tears, 1979.

CARTWRIGHT, JOHN Bass. Member of the Jess Roden Band, 1976. Session for Jess Roden (1977).

CARUSO, JOHN Bass. Session for Gilda Radner (1979).

CARVER, SIEGFRIED Violin, sitar, viola. Original member of Pavlov's Dog, 1975.

CARVIN, MICHAEL Drums. Session for Martin Mull (1977).

CASADY, JACK Bass. Born 4/13/44. Original member of the Jefferson Airplane, 1965-73, he left with guitarist Jorma Kaukonen in 1970 for Hot Tuna, 1970-77. A member of SVT, 1980. Session for Jimi Hendrix (1968); David Crosby (1971).

CASALE, GERALD Bass, vocal. Member of Devo since 1978.

CASANOVA, RICH Fiddle. Member of the Moonlighters, 1977.

CASAVANI, DANNY Guitar. Member of Graham Shaw and the Sincere Serenaders, 1980.

CASCELLA, JOHN Saxophone, keyboards, vocal. Member of Limousene, 1972, and Faith Band, 1977.

CASE, DAVID Keyboards. Member of the James Montgomery Band, 1976.

CASE, ED Drums, vocal. Member of 999, 1978-80.

CASE, PETER Vocal, guitar. Member of the Plimsouls, 1980.

CASEY Vocal. Member of Gringo, 1971.

CASEY, AL Piano. Session for Duane Eddy's Rebels (1961).

CASEY, CORKEY Guitar. Session for Duane Eddy's Rebels (1961).

CASEY, HOWIE Saxophone. Member of Ox, 1975. Session for John Entwhistle (1972); Mike Vernon; Kevin Ayers (1973); Wings (1976); Paice, Ashton, Lord (1977); Wings (1979).

CASH, FRED Vocal. Original member of the Impressions.

CASH, JOHNNY Guitar, vocal, writer. Cash began singing at the same time as Elvis and to much the same audiences. While he was always considered a country balladeer, that was when the distinction did not really matter in the pop industry. His affiliation with Bob Dylan and his influences on bands like the Byrds and the Band made him a vital part of the rock industry, not to mention the scores of songs he has penned. Session with Bob Dylan (1969). *Albums:* Best of Johnny Cash (TRP 8500); Blood, Sweat and Tears (COL CS-8781) 1963; John R. Cash (COL KC 33370); Johnny Cash and

His Woman (COL KC 32443); Children's Album (COL C32898); Country Hymns (COL C30324); Everybody Loves a Nut (COL C59292) 1966; Greatest Country and Western Hits (COL CS 8881); Five Feet High and Rising (COL C 32951); Holy Land (COL KCS 9726); Johnny Cash, Hymns from the Heart; Junkie and the Juicehead Minus Me (COL KC 33086); Man in Black (COL C 30550); Ragged Old Flag (COL KC 32917); True West (COL C25838) 1965; Johnny Cash with His Red and Blue Guitar; Johnny Cash Sings the Songs That Made Him Famous; Johnny Cash Sings Hank Williams; Greatest Johnny Cash; All Aboard the Blue Train with Johnny Cash; Original Sun Sound of Johnny Cash; Songs of Our Soil, 1959; Fabulous Johnny Cash, 1959; There Was a Song, 1960; Sound of Johnny Cash, 1962; Bitter Tears, 1964; That's What You Get for Lovin' Me, 1966; Carryin' On, 1967; From Sea to Shining Sea, 1968; Family at Christmas; Sing Precious Memories; Look At Them Beans; Strawberry Cake; Any Old Wind That Blows (COL C-32091); Banded Together (EPC JE-36177); Believer Sings The Truth (CCT 9001); Johnny Cash (EVR 278); Johnny Cash and Jerry Lee Lewis Sing Hank Williams (SUN 125); At Folsom Prison (COL KC-9639, CG-33639) 1978; At San Quentin (COL CS-9827, CG-33639); Get Rhythm (SUN 105); Greatest Hits (COL PC-9478); Greatest Hits, Vol. II (COL KC-30887); The Legend (SUN 2-118); Original Golden Hits, Vol. I (SUN 100); Original Golden Hits, Vol. II (SUN 101); Original Golden Hits, Vol. III (SUN 127); Story Songs of the Trains and Rivers (SUN 104); Christmas (COL C 31754); Christmas Album (COL CG-30763); Christmas Spirit (COL CS-8917) 1963; Gone Girl (COL KC-35646) 1978; Gospel Road (COL CG-32253) 1973; Greatest Hits, Vol. I (PPK 248); Greatest Hits, Vol. 2 (PPK 249); Volume 3 (COL KC-35637); Greatest Hits of the '60s (COL G3P-23); Harper Valley PTA (PLN 700); Hymns by Johnny Cash (COL CS-8125); I Walk the Line (COL CS-8990); I Would Like To See You Again (COL PC-35313); Man, the World, His Music (SUN 126); Mean As Hell (COL CS-9246) 1966; Memphis Country (SUN 120); Nashville Skyline (COL KC-9825) 1969; Old Time Religion (PPK 254); One Piece at a Time (COL KC-34193); Orange Blossom Special (COL CS-9109) 1965; Original Johnny Cash (SUN 1006); Precious Memories (COL C-33087) 1975; Ride This Train (COL KCS-8255) 1963; Ring of Fire (COL CS-8853) 1963; Rough Cut King of Country Music (SUN 122); Show Time (SUN 106); Silver (COL JC-36086) 1979; Singing Story Teller (SUN 115); Souvenirs of Music City, U.S.A. (PLN 506); Sunday Down South (SUN 119); Sunday Morning Coming Down (COL C-32240); Superbilly (SUN 1002); World of Johnny Cash (COL CG-29); World's Favorite Hymns (COL C-32246).

CASH, NICK Vocal, guitar. Member of 999, 1978-present.

CASH, ROSANNE Guitar, vocal. *Album:* Right or Wrong (COL JC 36155) 1979.

CASH, STEVE Vocal, harpsichord, percussion, writer. Original member of the Ozark Mountain Daredevils, 1973-80. *Album:* White Mansions (AAM 6004).

CASHMAN, TERRY Vocal, guitar, writer. Half of the Cashman and West duet. Session for Henry Gross (1977).

CASHMAN AND WEST Terry Cashman—vocal, guitar, writer; Tommy West—vocal, writer, keyboards. Pop-folk duet that formed Lifesong records to further perfect their tight production techniques for themselves and others, like Henry Gross. Session and production for Henry Gross (1973, 75). *Albums:* Lifesong; Moondog Serenade; Song or Two (DHL) 1972.

CASON, BUZZ Vocal. Session for Levon Helm (1980).

CASSIDY, ED Drums, percussion. A drummer of 15 years experience before forming Spirit with his son-in-law, Randy California, 1968-72, 1975-79. Member of Rainbow Red Oxidizer, 1980. Session for Kapt. Kopter (1972); Zoot Sims; Roland Kirk; Ry Cooder; Taj Mahal.

CASSIDY, SHAUN Guitar, vocal. Television pop star. *Albums:* Born Late (WBR K-3126) 1977; Shaun Cassidy (WBR K-3351) 1977; Room Service (WBR K-333067) 1979; That's Rock 'N' Roll (WR HS-3265) 1979; Under Wraps (WBR K-3222) 1978; Wasp (WBR K-3451) 1980.

CASSOTTO, ROBERT Real name of Bobby Darin.

CASTELUCCI, BRUNO Drums. Session for Jan Akkerman (1977).

CASTILLE, LONNIE Drums. Original member of Mother Earth, 1968. Session for Janis Joplin (1969).

CASTILLO, EMILIO Tenor saxophone, vocal. Member of the Tower of Power horn section. Session for Bill Wyman (1976); Roy Buchanan (1974); Ron Gardner (1974).

CASTLE, DAVID Vocal. Started in Blues Incorporated. *Albums:* Castle in the Sky (PCH 9002) 1977; Love You Forever (PCH 9015) 1979; Midnight Express (CAS 7114).

CASTLE, GEOFF Keyboards. Member of Ian Carr's Nucleus since 1975.

CASTRO, LENNY Percussion. Session for Gary Wright (1979); Randy Newman (1979); Gordon Lightfoot (1980); Boz Scaggs (1980); the Strand (1980); Elton John (1980); Christopher Cross (1980).

CASTRO, PEPPY Vocal, percussion. Member of Wiggy Bits.

CASWELL, DAVE Trumpet, flugelhorn. Member of Ox, 1975. Session for the Keef Hartley Band

(1970-71); Kevin Ayers (1973); Chris Youlden (1974); Paice, Ashton, Lord (1977).

CASWELL, JOHNNY Vocal, piano. Member of Crystal Mansion.

CAT MOTHER AND THE ALL NIGHT NEWSBOYS Bob Smith—keyboards; Larry Packer—violin; Charley Chinn—guitar, banjo, bass; Roy Michaels—banjo, guitar, bass; Mike Equine—drums, guitar, bass, cello, keyboard, percussion. Multi-instrumental five piece rock band from New York that was received well with and under Jimi Hendrix's management, but faded quietly. *Albums:* Cat Mother and the All Night Newsboys (POL) 1967; Vol. II (POL); Albion Doo Wah, 1972; Last Chance Dance, 1973.

CATALANO, TOM Producer. Produced Neil Diamond (1966-1976).

CATALDO, STEVE Vocal, guitar, writer. Member of the Nervous Eaters, 1980.

CATALINE, GLEN Drums, vocal. Member of the Godz, 1978-79.

CATANZARITA, ARTIE Drums, trumpet. Member of the Brooklyn Bridge.

CATCHPOLE, TONY Guitar. Member of the Andy Bown group.

CATE, EARL Guitar, vocal. Member of the Cate Brothers since 1975.

CATE, ERNIE Vocal, keyboards. Member of the Cate Brothers since 1975.

CATE BROTHERS Ernie Cate—vocal, keyboards; Earl Cate—guitar, vocal. *Albums:* Cate Brothers (ASY 7E-1050) 1975; Cate Brothers Band (ASY 7E-1116) 1977; Fire on the Tracks (ATC 19240); In One Eye and Out the Other (ASY 7E-1080) 1980.

CATES, RANDY Bass. Replaced Doni Larsen in Gypsy, 1973.

CATFISH Bob Hodge—vocal; Dallas Hodge—guitar; Dennis Cranner—bass; Jim Demers—drums; Harry Phillips—keyboards. Late '60s rock and blues band built around the vocals of Bob "Catfish" Hodge. *Albums:* Catfish (EPC); Live Catfish (EPC E-30361).

CATFISH HODGE BAND Bob Hodge—vocal, guitar; John Lee—drums; Jimmy Powers—harmonica; Diana Crawford—vocal; Dixie D. Balin—vocal; Duane Campbell—bass; David Namerdy—guitar. *Album:* Eyewitness Blues (ADL AD4113) 1979.

CATHCART, CARTER Keyboards, guitar, vocal. Member of the Laughing Dogs, 1979-present.

CATHERINE, PHILLIP Guitar. Member of the Chris Hinze Combination, 1974. *Albums:* Spendid (ELK 6E-153); Twin House (ELK 6E-123); Young Django (PAU 7041).

CATHEY, TOM Bass. Member of Target, 1976-77.

CATLEY, BOB Guitar, vocal. Member of Magnum, 1979.

CATON, ROY Brass. Session for Russ Giguere (1971).

CATS Danny Weston—guitar; Dennis Tilli—bass; Fred Zarra—keyboards, vocal; Michael Corr—vocal; Peter Keltz—guitar; Tommy Stewart—drums, vocal. *Album:* Cats (ELK 6E-275) 1980.

CATTINI, CLEM Drums. Member of Bee Gees, 1972. Session for Joe Cocker (1968); Lou Reed (1972); Chris Spedding (1976).

CATTO, JOHN Guitar. Member of the Diodes, 1978.

CAUCHER, PETER Keyboard, vocal. Member of Gruppo Sportivo, 1978.

CAUCHI, LES Vocal, piano. Member of the Brooklyn Bridge.

CAUGHLAN, JIM Drums. Member of Pure Prairie League, 1972-75.

CAULEY, BEN Trumpet. Member of the Bar-Kays. Session for Boz Scaggs (1969); Tim Weisberg (1977); the Doobie Brothers (1978).

CAULFIELD, SANDY Vocal. Member of the Tantrum, 1978-79.

CAUSEY, DAVIS Guitar. Member of Sea Level, 1978-present. Session for Robbie Robertson (1980).

CAUSEY, MIKE Guitar. Member of Stillwater, 1977.

CAUSI, JERRY Bass. Member of the Barbarians, 1979.

CAVALIERE, FELIX Keyboards, vocal, writer. Born 11/29/44. Original member of the Rascals, 1965-69, before starting his solo career. Member of Treasure, 1977. *Albums:* Felix Cavaliere, 1974; Destiny (BSV); Castles in the Air (EPC 35990) 1979.

CAVALLARI, TONY Guitar, vocal. Original member of H. P. Lovecraft, 1967-68.

CAVARI, JACK Guitar. Session for Felix Pappalardi (1979).

CAVE, NORMAN Piano. Session for "Jesus Christ Superstar" (1970).

CECIL, MALCOM Synthesizer, producer. Began in Blues Incorporated. Session for Nilsson (1976); Steve Hillage (1977).

CECILIO AND KAPONO *Albums:* Cecilio and Kapono (COL PC-32928) 1974; Eulua (COL PC-33689) 1975; Night Music (COL PC-34300).

CEDRANE, DANNY Member of Bill Haley and the Comets.

CENNAMO, LOUIS Bass. Creator of the electric bowed bass. Member of Steamhammer, Colosseum, 1971, Armageddon, 1975, and Illusion, 1977.

CENTANO, FRANKIE Bass. Session for John Mayall (1979).

CENTAURUS Nick Paine—guitar; Joey Belfiore—drums; Louis Merlind—vocal; Nick Costello—bass. *Album:* Centaurus (AZR).

CENTIPEDE Wendy Treacher—violin; John

Trussler—violin; Wilf Gibson—violin; Carol Slater—violin; Louise Jopling—violin; Garth Morton—violin; Channa Salononson—violin; Steve Towlandson—violin; Mica Gomberti—violin; Colin Kitching—violin; Philip Saucer—violin; Esther Burgi—violin; Michael Hurwitz—cello; Timothy Kramer—cello; Suki Towb—cello; Katherine Thulborn—cello; Catherine Finnis—cello; Peter Parkes—trumpet; Rick Collins—trumpet, flugelhorn; Mongesi Fesa—trumpet; Mark Charig—coronet; Elton Dean—alto saxophone; Jan Steel—alto saxophone, flute; Ian MacDonald—alto saxophone; Dudu Pukwana—alto saxophone; Larry Stabbins—tenor saxophone; Gary Windo—tenor saxophone; Brian Smith—tenor saxophone; Alan Skidmore—tenor saxophone; David White—baritone clarinet; Karl Jenkins—baritone, oboe; John Williams—baritone, bass, soprano saxophone; Nick Evans—trombone; Dave Perrottet—trombone; Paul Rutherford—trombone; Paul Weiman—trombone; John Marshall—drums; Tony Fennell—drums; Robert Wyatt—drums; Brian Godding—guitar; Brian Belshaw—bass; Roy Babbington—bass; Jill Lyons—bass; Harry Miller—bass; Jeff Clyne—bass; Dave Markee—bass; Maggie Nicholls—vocal; Julie Tippet—vocal; Mike Patto—vocal; Zoot Money—vocal; Boz—vocal; Keith Tippett—piano. An English studio band consisting of over fifty members, including strings and horns, who released one experimental jazz album under the production of Robert Fripp. *Album:* Septober Energy (Import) 1971.

CENTURIES Early name for the Buckinghams.

CEPPIC, GENE Bass, vocal. Member of the Slick Band, 1976.

CERNEY, TODD Vocal. Session for Levon Helm (1980).

CERNIGLIA, RICK Guitar. Member of the Illusions, and the Wiggy Bits.

CETERA, PETER Bass, vocals. Born 9/13/44. Original member of Chicago, since 1969.

CHAD AND JEREMY Chad Stuart—vocal, guitar, banjo, keyboards, sitar; Jeremy Clyde—vocal, guitar. Vocal duet from England. Having survived the Beatle era with their inoffensive soft vocals, they failed to establish a distinctive public identity between 1964 and 1968, despite having participated in movie sound tracks and producing well-planned concept LPs. *Albums:* I Don't Want To Lose You, Baby, 1965; More Chad and Jeremy, 1966; Cabbages and Kings, 1967; Yesterday's Gone (COL); Best of Chad and Jeremy (CAP SN-12057) 1966; The Arc (COL LS 9699) 1968; Before and After (COL CL 2374) 1964; Distant Shores (COL CS 9364) 1966.

CHADWICK, LES Bass. Born 5/11/43. Member of Gerry and the Pacemakers, 1962-65.

CHADWICK, RUSS Drums. Original member of the Siegel-Schwall Band, until 1970.

CHAGRIN, MARGINAL Saxophone. Session for Frank Zappa (1979).

CHAKOUR, MITCH Guitar. Session for Joe Cocker (1978).

CHALKER, CURLEY Pedal steel guitar. Session for Doug Kershaw (1972); Leon Russell (1973).

CHALMERS, CHARLES Tenor saxophone, vocal. Member of RCR, 1980. Session for Boz Scaggs (1969); Jackie de Shannon (1972); Tony Joe White (1972); Andy Gibb (1980).

CHAMAN, CLIVE Bass, flute. First received public attention as a member of the re-formed Jeff Beck Group, 1971-72. Replaced Barry Dean in Brian Auger's Oblivion Express, 1975-77, while becoming an original member of Hummingbirds with Max Middleton and Bobby Tench, both ex-Jeff Beck members, 1975-76. Session for Donovan (1973).

CHAMBERLAIN, DEAN Guitar, vocal. Member of Code Blue, 1980.

CHAMBERS, CRAIG Guitar, vocal. Member of the Rio Grande Band.

CHAMBERS, DAVE Saxophone. Session for Annette Peacock (1979).

CHAMBERS, GEORGE Bass. Original member of the Chambers Brothers.

CHAMBERS, JERRY Guitar, vocal. Member of Morningstar, 1979.

CHAMBERS, JOE Vocal, guitar. Original member of the Chambers Brothers. Session for Ry Cooder (1980). *Albums:* Almoravid (MUS 5035); Double Exposure (MUS 5165).

CHAMBERS, JOHN Drums. Early member of the Elvin Bishop Band. Session for Elvin Bishop (1972); Stephen Miller.

CHAMBERS, LESTER Vocal, percussion, harmonica. Original member of the Chambers Brothers. Session for Ry Cooder (1980).

CHAMBERS, MARTIN Drums, vocal. Member of the Pretenders, 1980.

CHAMBERS, ROLAND Guitar. Session for B. B. King (1973-74).

CHAMBERS, SCOTT Bass. Member of the Romeos, 1980. Session for Jay Ferguson (1979).

CHAMBERS, TERRY Drums. Member of XTC since 1979.

CHAMBERS, WILLIE Vocal, guitar. Original member of the Chambers Brothers.

CHAMBERS BROTHERS George Chambers—bass; Willie Chambers—vocal, guitar; Joe Chambers—vocal, guitar; Lester Chambers—vocal, percussion, harmonica; Brian Keenan—drums. Mississippi born, the Chambers Brothers played gospel music before adding a drummer, 1965, four years after turning professional. Their big hit "Time Has Come," 1967, was a psychedelic Afro-rock venture coming in an edited and an unedited version. Session for Canned Heat (1979). *Albums:* Best Of The Chambers Brothers (COL); Chambers Brothers Live at Bill Graham's Fillmore East (COL KGP-20); Love, Peace and Happiness; Right Move (AVC 69003) 1976; Unbonded (AVC 11013) 1973; Chambers Brothers Shout, 1968; Now People Get Ready; New Time—New Day, 1968; New Generation (COL); Best of the Chambers Brothers (FSY 24718) 1973; Chambers Brothers Greatest Hits (COL C-30871); Barbara Dane/ Chambers Brothers (FLW 2468); Groovin' Time (FLW 31008); Time Has Come (COL CS-9522 CG 33642) 1967.

CHAMPLIN, BILL Vocal, keyboards, guitar. Namesake of the Sons of Champlin. Member of the Dinettes, 1976. Session for Bob Weir (1978); Vapour Trails (1980); Boz Scaggs (1980); Elton John (1980).

CHAMPS Made the hit "Tequila," 1968.

CHANCE, LARRY Vocal. Member of the Earls, 1959.

CHANCLER, LEON "NDUGU" Drums. Member of Santana, 1976. Session for Santana (1974); George Duke (1975).

CHANDLER, CHARLES Producer, bass, vocal. Original member of the Animals until 1966 and the re-formed Animals, 1977. Manager of Jimi Hendrix. Produced Eric Burdon (1977).

CHANDLER, CHUCK Vocal, keyboards. Member of the Lavender Hill Mob, 1977-78.

CHANDLER, DYANNE Vocal. Session for Terry Reid (1979).

CHANDLER, GENE Vocal. Real name: Eugene Dixon. Recorded "Duke of Earl," 1962. *Albums:* Gene Chandler (TWC 605) 1980; Get Down (TWC 578) 1978; Girl Don't Care (BRU 754124); Great Soul Hits of Gene Chandler (BRU 754129); There Was a Time (BRU 754131); Two Sides of Gene Chandler (BRU 754149); When You're No. 1 (TWC 598) 1979; Situation (MER); Gene Chandler (CKR) 1967.

CHANDLER, GEORGE Vocal. Member of the Olympic Runners, 1974-79.

CHANDLER, JOE Saxophone. Member of the Lamont Cranston Band, 1977.

CHANDLER, STEPHEN Guitar, vocal. Member of the States, 1979.

CHANEY, BLAINE JOHN Vocal, percussion. Member of the Suburbs, 1980.

CHANEY, WAYNE Vocal, percussion. Member of FCC, 1980.

CHANTER, DOREEN Vocal. Session for John Entwhistle (1975); Manfred Mann (1973); Paul Manzanera (1975); Bryan Ferry (1977); Sad Cafe (1978); Justin Hayward (1980).

CHANTER, IRENE Vocal. Session for John Entwhistle (1975); Manfred Mann (1973); Sad Cafe (1978); Justin Hayward (1980).

CHANTEREAU, MARK Vocal, keyboards, percussion. Member of Voyage.

CHANTLER, ROGER Drums. Member of Fresh, 1980.

CHANTRY, MARVIN Viola. Session for Waylon Jennings (1973, 75).

CHAP, FRIENDLY Guitar. Member of Junior Wells Chicago Blues Band.

CHAPIN, ANDY Keyboards. Replaced Goldy McJohn in Steppenwolf, 1975.

CHAPIN, HARRY Guitar, vocal, writer. Born 12/7/42. A folk singer for the 1970s, following in the style of Dylan, with distinctive lyrical stories. Died, 1981 in a car accident. *Albums:* Dance Band on the Titanic (ELK 9E-301) 1977; Greatest Stories—Live (ELK 6E-6003); Heads and Tales (ELK 75023) 1972; Legends of the Lost and Found (ELK BB-703) 1979; Living Room Suite (ELK 7E-1082); On the Road to Kingdom Come (ELK 7E-1082) 1976; Portrait Gallery (ELK 7E-1041) 1975; Short Stories (ELK 75065) 1973; Sniper and Other Love Songs (ELK 75042) 1972; Verities and Balderdash (ELK 7E-1012) 1974; Sequel (BDW FW 36872) 1980.

CHAPLIN, BLONDIE Drums, vocal. Member of the Beach Boys, 1972-73. *Album:* Blondie Chaplin (ASY 7E-1095) 1977.

CHAPMAN, ANDY Vocal. Member of Bloontz, 1973.

CHAPMAN, JON Drums, vocal. Member of D. B. Cooper, 1980.

CHAPMAN, MARGOT Vocal. Member of the Starland Vocal Band, 1976.

CHAPMAN, MARSHALL Vocal, guitar. *Albums:* Jaded Virgin (EPC JE-35341) 1978; Marshall (EPC JE-36192) 1979; Me, I'm Feelin' Fine (EPC PE-34422) 1977.

CHAPMAN, PAUL Guitar. Member of Lone Star, 1977. Added to the UFO lineup, 1980.

CHAPMAN, ROGER Vocal, percussion, saxophone, harmonica. Member of Family, and the Streetwalkers, 1973-77. Session for Mike Batt (1979).

CHAPPELL, RAY Bass. Original member of Savoy Brown, 1967.

CHAPPELL, RUELL Keyboards, vocal. Replaced Buddy Brayfield in the Ozark Mountain Daredevils, 1977.

CHAPPELLE, HELEN Vocal. Session for Ray Thomas (1976); Bryan Ferry (1974-77); Dan McCafferty (1975); Roger Glover (1978); the Small Faces (1978); the Climax Blues Band (1978); Oxendale and Shephard (1979).

CHAPTER THREE See Manfred Mann.

CHAQUICO, CRAIG Guitar. Member of Jefferson Starship since 1974.

CHARIG, MARK Trumpet, coronet. Member of Centipede, 1971. Session for the Soft Machine (1970); King Crimson (1971, 72, 74).

CHARLES, BOBBY Vocal. Session for Paul Butterfield's Better Days Band (1973).

CHARLES, CHARLIE Drums. Member of Loving

Awareness, Ian Dury's Blockheads, 1979, and the Planets, 1980. Session for Arthur Brown (1975).

CHARLES, CHILLI Drums. Member of Headstone, 1974. Session for Nilsson (1976).

CHARLES, DAVE Drums, percussion, vocal. Member of the Neutrons, 1974, and Airwaves, 1978-79.

CHARLES, DENNIS Hand drums. Session for Sandy Bull (1972).

CHARLES, EVAN Pianos. Member of the Cowboys International, 1979.

CHARLES, PEE WEE Pedal steel guitar. Session for Gordon Lightfoot (1975, 76, 80).

CHARLES, PETER Drums. Member of Ram Jam, 1977-78.

CHARLES, RAY Vocal, piano, writer. Born 9/23/32. Real name: Ray Charles Robinson. Blind from age 6, he began recording in 1954, moving through rhythm and blues and jazz into pop. He even branched out into country and western in 1962, with equal popularity. His moving vocals are without classification. He is said to have created soul, because of the honesty and depth of any song he sang, pop, rhythm and blues, or country and western. Session for the Blues Brothers (1980). *Albums:* Blues in Modern Jazz (ATC 1337); Ray Charles-Stidham-Wayne-Jackson (MST 310); Definitive Jazz Scene (IPE 100); Genius After Hours (ATC 1369) 1961; Recorded Live at Newport in New York (BJD 5616); Yes Indeed, 1958; Ray Charles at Newport, 1958; What'd I Say, 1959; In Person, 1960; Great Hits of Ray Charles; Dedicated To You, 1961; Genius Plus Soul Equals Ray Charles, 1961; Ray Charles Sings the Blues, 1961; Ray Charles and Betty Carter, 1961; Modern Sounds in Country and Western Music, 1962; Greatest Hits, Vol. 1, 1962; Ray Charles Story, Vol. 1, 1962; Ray Charles Story, Vol. 2, 1962; Sweet and Sour Years, 1963; Have a Smile with Me, 1964; Ray Charles Live in Concert, 1965; Together Again, 1965; Crying Time, 1966; Ray's Moods, 1966; A Man and His Soul, 1967; Listen, 1967; A Portrait of Ray, 1968; Ain't It So (ATC 19251) 1979; All Time Great Country and Western Hits (MCA X-781); Best of Ray Charles (ATC 1543) 1970; Brother Ray's At It Again (ACO SD 19281) 1980; Ray Charles (EVR 244); Ray Charles, Vol. 2 (EVR 292); Live (ATC 2-502); Come Live With Me (CRO 9000); Do The Twist with Ray Charles (ATC 8054); 14 Original Greatest Hits (KGO 5011); Genius of Ray Charles (ATC 1312) 1959; Golden Soul (ATC 18198); Great Ray Charles (ATC 1259); Greatest Ray Charles (ATC 8054) 1963; In the Heat of the Night (UAR LT-290); Jazz Years (ATC 2-316); Love and Peace (ATC 19199); My Kind of Jazz (PT CRO 9007); Renaissance (CRO 9005); Soul Brothers (ATC 1279); Soul Meeting (ATC 1360); Soul Years (ATC 2-504); True to Life (ATC 19142).

CHARLES, RON Vocal. Session for Kim Fowley (1973).

CHARLES, STEVE Drums, vocal. Member of Brent Maglia's backup band, 1977.

CHARLES, VINCE Steel drums. Session for Loggins and Messina (1973).

CHARLIE Steve Gadd—drums, percussion; Martin Smith—vocal, guitar; John Anderson—vocal, bass; Terry Thomas—vocal, guitar. *Albums:* Fantasy Girls (COL PC-34081) 1976; Fight Dirty (ARI 4239) 1979; Lines (JNS 7036) 1978; No Second Chance (JNS 7032) 1977.

CHARLTON, MANUEL Guitar, vocal, writer, producer. Founder and original member of Nazareth, 1977-present. Produced Sweetheart (1979), and Marseilles (1980). Session for Dan McCafferty (1975).

CHARRINGTON, VALERIE Vocal. Session for the Keef Hartley Band (1971).

CHARTBUSTERS See Robin Lane and the Chartbusters.

CHARTER, ANDY Guitar. Member of Marseille, 1980.

CHASE, BILL Trumpet. Member of Woody Herman Band and head of Chase, 1971-73. Session on Free Creek (1973).

CHASE, JEANETTE Vocal. Member of Storm, 1979.

CHASE Bill Chase—trumpet; Ted Piercefield—trumpet, vocal; Alan Ware—trumpet; Jarry Van Blair—trumpet, vocal; Phil Porter—keyboards; Dennis Johnson—bass, vocal; Jay Burrilo—percussion; Terry Richards—vocal; Angel South—guitar. *Albums:* Chase (EPC BG-33737); Ennea (EPC 4-31097, BG-33737) 1972; Pure Music (EPC KE-32572) 1973.

CHATER, KERRY Bass. Member of Gary Puckett and the Union Gap, 1967-68, before going solo. *Albums:* Love on a Shoestring (WBR K-3179); Part Time Love (WBR B-3008).

CHATFIELD, MARK Guitar, vocal. Member of the Godz, 1978-79.

CHATTERTON, SIMON Drums, vocal. Replaced Ted McKenna in the Sensational Alex Harvey Band.

CHATTERTON-DEW, NICHOLAS Drums. Original member of Be Bop Deluxe, until 1975.

CHATTON, BRIAN Clarinet, moog, vocal. Member of Jackson Heights, 1974. Session for the Baker-Gurvitz Army (1976); Jack Green (1980); John Miles (1980).

CHAUDHURI, AUSHIM Percussion. Member of the Dija Rhythm Band, 1976.

CHAULK, VINCE Drums, vocal. Member of Mr. Big, 1975.

CHAULKIE Drums, percussion. Member of the Streetband, 1980.

CHAUNCEY, DANNY Guitar, vocal. Member of Mistress, 1979.

CHAUTEMPS, JEAN-LOUIS Saxophone. Session for Elton John (1972).

CHAVIN, CHINGA Vocal, guitar. *Albums:* Jet Lag (JTR 777) 1978; Country Porn (CPR 666) 1976.

CHEAP TRICK Robin Zander—vocal, guitar; Rick Nielsen—guitar, vocal; Tom Peterson—bass, vocal (1977-80); Bun E. Carlos—drums; Pete Comita—bass (1980). Formed in Illinois, 1972. Reminiscent of the early Who and Rolling Stones, Trick's vocal harmonies sometimes bear striking resemblances to the Beatles. *Albums:* At Budokan (EPC JE-35795) 1979; Cheap Trick (EPC PE-34400) 1977; Dream Police (EPC FE-35773) 1979; Found All the Parts (EPC 4E-36453) 1980; Heaven Tonight (EPC JE-35312) 1978; In Color (EPC PE-34884) 1977.

CHECKER, CHUBBY Vocal. Real name: Ernest Evans. Recorded Hank Ballard's "Twist" in 1960, starting an international dance craze that lasted until Beatlemania. Imitators invented new dances and new songs but they were variations on his theme. *Albums:* Twist, 1962; Don't Knock the Twist, 1962; For Teen Twisters Only, 1962; It's Pony Time, 1962; Let's Twist Again, 1962; Twistin' Round the World, 1962; Your Twist Party, 1962; Limbo Party, 1963; Let's Limbo More, 1963; Beach Party, 1963; Twist It Up; Chubby Checker and Bobby Rydell; Chubby Checker Discoteque; Chubby Checker's Folk Album, 1964; Chubby Checker's Greatest Hits (AKO 4219).

CHEMAY, JOE Vocal. Session for Leon Russell (1979); Pink Floyd (1979); Elton John (1980).

CHEN, PHILLIP Bass. Member of the Keef Hartley Band, Headstone, 1974, and the Rod Stewart Band, 1978-present. Session for Donovan (1973); Jeff Beck (1975); Rod Stewart (1977).

CHENIER, JOE Drums, vocal. Member of Fist, 1980.

CHENIER, RON Guitar, vocal. Member of Fist, 1980.

CHER See Cher Bono.

CHEROKEE David Donaldson—guitar, harmonica; George Donaldson—guitar, saxophone; Robert Donaldson—keyboards; Craig Kampf—drums, percussion, accordion; Tom La Tondre—piano, trumpet, percussion. *Album:* Cherokee, 1971.

CHERRY, DON Trumpet, vocal, percussion. Session for Steve Hillage (1976); Lou Reed (1979). *Albums:* Gato Barbieri and Don Cherry (ICT 1009); Complete Communion (BLN LT-84226); Hear and Now (ATC 18217); New York Eye and Ear Control (ESP 1016); Old and New Dreams (ECM 1-1154) 1977; Something Else (CTP 7551); Where Is Brooklyn (BLN LT-84311); World of Don Cherry (MTN MP-8601).

CHERRY, VIVIAN Vocal. Session on posthumous Hendrix albums, "Crash Landing" and "Midnight Lightning" (1975); Henry Gross (1978); John Mayall (1979); Marshall Tucker (1980); the Blues Brothers (1980).

CHESBORO, BILLY Congas. Session on Free Creek (1973).

CHICAGO Daniel Seraphine—drums; James Pankow—trombone; Peter Cetera—bass, vocal; Walter Parazaider—woodwinds, vocal; Lee Loughnane—trumpet, vocal; Terry Kath—guitar, vocal (1968-78); Robert Lamm—keyboards, vocal, writer; Laudier de Oliveira. Originally called Big Thing. Formerly Chicago Transit Authority, until 1969. The notoriety Blood, Sweat and Tears received using a full horn section was surpassed when Chicago (then the Chicago Transit Authority) took their horn section and made it the focal point of the group. Since then, horns have become less of a novelty, but Chicago has always been the leader of the genre. *Albums:* Greatest Hits (COL PC-33900) 1976; Chicago, Vol. 2 (COL PG-24) 1969; Vol. 3 (COL C2-30110) 1970; Vol. 5 (COL PC-31002) 1972; Vol. 6 (COL PC-32400) 1973; Vol. 7 (COL C2-32810) 1974; Vol. 8 (COL PC-33100) 1975; Vol. 10 (COL PC-34200) 1976; Vol. 11 (COL JC-34860) 1977; Vol. 13 (COL FC-36105) 1979; Vol. 14 (COL FC-36517) 1980; At Carnegie Hall (COL K4X-30865) 1971; Chicago Transit Authority (COL PG-8) 1968; Hot Streets (COL FC-35512) 1978.

CHICAGO BLUES BAND Junior Wells—harmonica, vocal; Friendly Chap—guitar; Jack Myers—bass; Billy Warren—drums. See Junior Wells.

CHICHLIDS Debbie Mascaro—guitar; Susan Robins—bass, guitar; Allan Portman—guitar; Bobby Tak—drums. *Album:* Be True to Your School (BLD 306) 1980.

CHICKEN SHACK Stan Webb—vocal, guitar, writer; Dave Bidwell—drums (1966-71); Andy Silvester—bass (1966-71); Christine Perfect—vocal, piano (1966-69); Paul Raymond—vocal, keyboards, guitar, writer (1969); John Glascock—bass; Paul Hancox—drums, percussion (1969); Bob Daisley—bass (1973); Chris Mercer—saxophone; Tony Ashton—piano. Chicken Shack was the vehicle Stan Webb chose to showcase his various musical inclinations. As a top notch British blues band, they changed personnel often, as did Webb's moods. Though not as popular as his talent deserved, Webb never failed to have the best supporting blues musicians, who more often than not achieved greater notoriety after leaving him. Session for Christine McVie (1969). *Albums:* 40 Blue Fingers Freshly Packed and Ready To Serve (BLH); O.K. Ken? (BLH); Accept Chicken Shack (BLH); 100 Ton Chicken (BLH 7706) 1969; Imagination Lady (DER 18063) 1973; Unlucky Boy (LON XPS 632) 1973.

CHIFFONS Patricia Bennett—vocal; Judy Craig—vocal; Barbara Lee—vocal; Sylvia Peterson—vocal; Pat Stelley—vocal. Early name: the Four

Pennies. Recorded "He's So Fine," 1963. *Albums:* He's So Fine, 1963; One Fine Day, 1963; Sweet Talking Guy, 1966; My Secret Love.

CHILDS, PETER Guitar, dobro. Session for Fred Neil (1968).

CHILLIWACK Bill Henderson—guitar, piano, vocal, writer; Ross Turney—drums, organ, percussion (1971-80); Claire Lawrence—flute, saxophone, bass, organ, writer (1971-73); Glenn Miller—bass, vocal, writer (1972-80); Howard Froese—guitar, keyboards, vocal (1973-80); Brian MacLeod—drums (1978-present); John Roles—guitar (1980); Ab Bryant—bass (1980). Their single "Lonesome Mary" (1971) received little airplay, yet after a double-record album debut, Canadian-born Chilliwack continued making albums almost as frequently as they changed record labels. In 1972, the original trio format, specializing in distinctive vocal harmonies, adopted Glenn Miller and a heavier rock format. Lawrence left shortly thereafter for a brief return to a trio format that was abandoned once again with the addition of Froese. Despite pleasant vocal harmonies and competent musicianship, they have yet to break the AM pop market. *Albums:* All Over You (AAM 4375) 1972; Breakdown in Paradise (MSH 5015) 1980; Dreams, Dreams, Dreams (MSH 5006) 1976; Lights from the Valley (MSH 5011) 1978; Chilliwack (AAM SP3509) 1971; Chilliwack (PAR PAS 71040); Chilliwack (SIR SASO 7506) 1974; Rockerbox (SIR SASO 7511) 1975.

CHILTON, ALEX Vocal, guitar. Voice of the Box Tops, 1965-68, and Star, 1972.

CHIMES, TERRY Drums, percussion. Original member of the Clash, until 1978, and Cowboys International, 1979.

CINDRICH, RON Bass, vocal. Member of the L. A. Jets, 1976.

CHINN, CHARLIE Banjo, guitar, bass. Member of Cat Mother and the All Night Newsboys. Session for Buffalo Springfield (1967).

CHINN, EDDIE Bass. Member of the Tourists since 1980.

CHIROWSKI, JOSEF Keyboards. Original member of Mandala, 1968. Session for Alice Cooper (1975); Steve Hunter (1977).

CHITWOOD, ROBERT Bass. Member of El Rochos, 1973, and the Bugs Henderson Group, 1975.

CHLANDA, RYCHE Guitar, vocal. Member of Fireballet, 1975-76, and Private Lines, 1980.

CHOICE Bruce Dremer—keyboards, vocal; Brian Bartlett—guitar, vocal; Mark Paxon—keyboards, vocal; Steve Fecker—drums; Paul Roethlinger—vocal; Dave Miller—bass, vocal. *Album:* Choice Cuts (POL PD1-6296) 1980.

CHOIR Early name of the Raspberries.

CHOUNIARD, BOB Drums. Member of Orphan, 1974. Session for Billy Squier (1980).

CHOWNING, RANDLE Guitar, pedal steel guitar, mandolin, vocal, harpsichord, writer. Original member of the Ozark Mountain Daredevils, 1973-75, before forming his own band in 1978.

RANDLE CHOWNING BAND Randle Chowning—vocal, guitar, mandolin, harmonica; Ken Shephard—vocal, guitar; Larry Van Fleet—bass, vocal; Lloyd Hicks—drums, vocal. *Album:* Hearts On Fire (AAM SP 4715) 1978.

CHRISTENSEN, ROY Cello. Session for Waylon Jennings (1975); J. J. Cale (1979).

CHRISTENSON, STACY Keyboards, vocal. Member of Gabriel, 1975.

CHRISTIAN, MICHAEL Drums. Member of Balcones Fault, 1977.

CHRISTIANSEN, DAVE Guitar. Member of Brother Fox and the Tar Baby, 1969.

CHRISTIANSON, BOB Keyboards, conductor. Member of Hammer, 1979. Session for Gilda Radner (1979).

CHRISTIE, JOEL Bass. Session for Lee Michaels.

CHRISTINA, FRAN Drums. Session for the Fabulous Thunderbirds (1980).

CHRISTMAN, J. B. Vocal, keyboards. Member of FCC, 1980.

CHRISTOPHER, GRETCHEN Vocal, writer. Member of the Fleetwoods, 1959.

CHRISTOPHER, GAVIN Keyboards, vocal. *Albums:* Gavin Christopher (ISL 9398) 1976; Gavin Christopher (RSO 13052) 1979.

CHRISTOPHER, JOHNNY Guitar. Session for Donovan (1974-76); Doug Kershaw (1972, 74); Jackie DeShannon (1972); Neil Young (1978).

CHRISTY, DON Early recording name of Sonny Bono.

CHROME, CHEETAH Guitar. Member of the Dead Boys, 1977-78.

CHRYSALIS Paul Album—bass; J. Barbour—vocal, percussion; Ralph Kotkov—keyboards, vocal; Nancy Nain—vocal; John Sabin—guitar; Dahaud Shaar—percussion. New York rock group of the late 1960s. *Album:* Definition, 1968.

CHUCK AND THE TIGERS Chuck Dean—vocal, guitar, organ; Butch Clydale—drums, vocal; Don McKenzie—bass, vocal; Bruce Crossley—guitar, vocal. *Album:* Chuck and the Tigers (WEP 1004) 1980.

CHUDACOFF, RICK Bass, percussion, vocal. Member of Crackin', 1977-78. Session for Tom Johnston (1979).

CHUNKY Nickname of Lauren Wood.

CHUNKY, ERNIE AND NOVI Lauren "Chunky" Wood—vocal, keyboards; Novi Novag—viola, synthesizer; Ernie Eremita—bass, percussion. After their debut failed to attract attention, this same group dropped their name and reappeared on Lauren Wood's solo debut album. *Album:* Chunky, Ernie and Novi (WBR 3030).

CHURCH, BILL Bass. Original member of Montrose, 1973. Session for Sammy Hagar (1975, 77, 80).

CHURCHILL, CHICK Keyboards, vocal, writer. With the disbandment of England's Ten Years After, 1967-72, Churchill began a somewhat less successful career as producer and solo artist. *Album:* You and Me (CYS).

CIAMBOTTI, JOHN Bass. Member of Clover, 1977. Session for Carlene Carter (1980).

CIAPPA, ALBIE Drums, percussion, vocal. Member of Taos.

CINDRICH, RON Bass, vocal. Member of the L. A. Jets, 1976.

CINER, AL Member of the American Breed, 1965-68.

CIPOLLINA, JOHN Guitar, vocal. Original member of Quicksilver Messenger Service. Session for Rocky Sullivan (1978).

CIPOLLINA, MARIO Bass. Member of Huey Lewis and the News, 1980. Session for Rocky Sullivan (1978).

CIPRIANO, GENE Saxophone. Session for Russ Giguere (1971); Nilsson (1975-76).

CIRCUS MAXIMUS Jerry Jeff Walker—guitar, vocal, writer; Bob Bruno—guitar, keyboards, vocal, writer; David Scherstrom—drums; Gary White—bass, vocal; Peter Troutner—guitar, vocal. Starting place for "Mr. Bojangles," Jerry Jeff Walker, who was a soloist before joining and after leaving the group. *Albums:* Circus Maximus (VAN 79260) 1967; Neverland Revisited (VAN 79274) 1968.

CISZON, ROGER Member of Scott Wilk and the Walls, 1980.

CITIZEN Ernst Waitrowski—keyboards, vocal; Craig Gillespie—bass, vocal; Donn Marier—vocal; Robert Horn—drums, vocal; Dominic Buscemi—guitar, vocal. *Album:* Sex and Society (OVA 1758) 1980.

CITY BOY Lol Mason—vocal, percussion; Steve Broughton—vocal, guitar, mandolin; Max Thomas—keyboards, vocal, guitar, percussion; Mike Slammer—vocal, guitar, percussion; Chris Dunn—vocal, guitar, bass; Roger Kent—drums, percussion. *Albums:* Book Early (MER SRM-1-3737); City Boy (MER SRM-1-1098) 1976; Day the Earth Caught Fire (ATC 19249) 1979; Dinner at the Ritz (MER SRM-1-1182); Young Men Gone West (MER SRM-1-1182); Heads Are for Rolling (ATC SD 19285) 1980.

CLAGGETT, JAMES Keyboards. Member of Wax, 1980.

CLANTON, IKE Bass. Member of Duane Eddy's Rebels, 1961.

CLANTON, K. Vocal. Voice of the Waves, 1977.

CLAPTON, ERIC Guitar, vocal, writer. Born 3/30/45. The young guitarist everyone heard about from the Yardbirds, 1962-64, and John Mayall's Bluesbreakers, 1965-67, carved an international reputation with his classic blues in Cream. In 1968, the group split apart. With Ginger Baker he joined Traffic's Steve Winwood in the ill-fated supergroup Blind Faith, 1969. He formed Derek and the Dominoes, 1970-1972. After the group's disbandment and a highly publicized one-time-only super concert jam with Steve Winwood, Ron Wood, Pete Townshend and others, the Rainbow Concert (1973), he shed his electric cocoon for a new image as a balladeer. Some critics held it was a step down, but in 1975 he released a live electric album showing he had not lost his touch with the blues. Session with Beatles (1968); Joe Cocker (1976); Delaney and Bonnie; Dr. John (1971); Jackie Lomax, Steve Stills (1970-71); Freddie King (1972); the Mothers of Invention (1967); Bangla Desh (1971); George Harrison (1972, 79); Kinky Friedman (1973); the Plastic Ono Band (1969); Howlin' Wolf (1972); "Rough Mix" (1977); Rick Danko (1977); Danny Douma (1979). *Albums:* Backless (RSO 1-3039) 1978; Eric Clapton (RSO 1-3008) 1970; Eric Clapton and Yardbirds (MER ML-8003); 461 Ocean Blvd. (RSO 1-3023) 1974; History of Eric Clapton (ACO 2-803) 1972; Just One Night (RSO 4202) 1980; No Reason To Cry (RSO 1-3004) 1976; On Tour (ACO 326); Slowhand (RSO 1-3030) 1977; There's One in Every Crowd (RSO SO 4806) 1975; Rainbow Concert (RSO SO 877) 1973; Eric Clapton Was Here (RSO SO 4809) 1975.

CLAQUE, DAVID Original member of the Bonzo Dog Doo-Dah Band.

CLARK, A. FLETCHER Guitar. Member of Balcones Fault, 1977.

CLARK, ANDREW Vocal, keyboards. Member of Upp, 1975-76, Be Bop Deluxe, 1976-78, and Red Noise, 1979. Session for Zaine Griff (1980).

CLARK, DAVE Drums. Namesake of the Dave Clark Five, 1964-68. Session for the Tremblers (1980).

DAVE CLARK 5 Dave Clark—drums; Lenny Davidson—guitar; Rick Huxley—guitar, banjo; Dennis Payton—saxophone, guitar, clarinet, harmonica; Mike Smith—vocal, piano, vibes. The Dave Clark 5 were hot on the heels of the Beatles in 1964 with their hits "Glad All Over" and "Bits and Pieces." They wore matching tailored outfits, and their brand of rock was equally as infectious. In short, they were as good and as salable as the Beatles but they were not as durable. *Albums:* Greatest Hits (EPC LN 24185) 1966; Glad All Over, 1964; American Tour, 1964; Dave Clark 5 Return, 1964; Dave Clark 5 Coast to Coast, 1965; Having a Wild Weekend, 1965; I Like It Like That, 1966; Try Too Hard, 1966; Satisfied with You, 1969; More Greatest Hits, 1966; 5 x 5, 1967; Everybody Knows, 1968; Weekend in London, 1968.

CLARK, FRANK Bass, guitar. Session for Elton John (1969).

CLARK, GENE Guitar, vocal, writer, harpsichord, keyboards. Original member of the Byrds, 1965-66. Cofounder of the Dillard and Clark Band, 1968. Since then he has soloed with discretion and not much publicity, singing his ballads in the space-country spirit of the Byrds. In 1979 he rejoined the Byrds alumni in McGuinn, Hillman and Clark. *Albums:* Two Sides to Every Story (RSO 1-3011) 1977; White Light (AAM 4292) 1974; No Other (ASY FE-1016) 1974.

CLARK, GEORGE Bass, vocal. Original member of Cowboy, 1971-73.

CLARK, IAN Drums. Replaced Alex Napier in Uriah Heep, 1971.

CLARK, JACKIE Guitar. Session for Bill Wyman (1974, 76).

CLARK, JOHN Guitar. Member of Bruford, 1979.

CLARK, JOHN Vocal, guitar. Member of the Elevators, 1980.

CLARK, MICHAEL Guitar, vocal. *Albums:* Free As A Bird, 1977; Save The Night (CAP ST-11982) 1979.

CLARK, MICK Guitar. Session for Long John Baldry (1979).

CLARK, PETULA Vocal. European vocalist who hit the charts in the United States in 1964 with her hit "Downtown." After her followup "I Know A Place" (1965), she began her film career and edged into the role of pop performer. *Albums:* Petula Clark Live at the Royal Albert Hall (CRS 2069); Petula Clark Sings for Everybody (LAU 2043); This Is Petula Clark (MGM 4859) 1966; Color My World, 1967; These Are My Songs, 1967; Other Man's Grass Is Always Greener, 1968; Petula, 1968; Petula Clark's Greatest Hits, 1968; Petula Clark, 1965; Downtown; I Couldn't Live Without Your Love; I Know a Place, 1965; My Love, 1966.

CLARK, ROBIN Vocal. Session for Full Moon (1972); Roy Buchanan (1976).

CLARK, ROGER Drums. Member of Boatz, 1979. Session for the Steve Miller Band (1972); Roy Orbison.

CLARK, STEVE Drums. Session for Colin Wolinski (1980).

CLARK, STEVE Guitar. Member of Def Leppard, 1980.

CLARKE, ALLAN Vocal. Born 4/15/42. Original member of the Hollies, 1963-78. Session for the Alan Parsons Project (1977). *Albums:* I Wasn't Born Yesterday (ATC 19175) 1978; I've Got Time (ASY 7E-1056) 1976; Legendary Heroes (ELK 6E-267) 1980.

CLARKE, BERNIE Keyboards. Member of Ten Years Later, 1978.

CLARKE, BRUCE Bass, vocal. Member of Sha Na Na, 1970-73.

CLARKE, JON Saxophone, flute, oboe, clarinet. Member of the Loggins and Messina backup band, 1971-77.

CLARKE, MARK Bass, keyboards, vocal. Member of Tempest, 1973-74, and Natural Gas, 1976. Replaced Jimmy Bain in Rainbow, 1977.

CLARKE, MICHAEL Drums. Member of the Byrds, Flying Burrito Brothers, 1968-74, and Firefall, since 1976. Session for Gram Parsons (1973).

CLARKE, MICK Bass, vocal. Member of the Rubettes.

CLARKE, MIKE Drums. Member of Brand X, 1979-present.

CLARKE, PETER Vocal, bass. Member of the Straight Lines, 1980.

CLARKE, PHIL Guitar. Member of Motorhead, 1979-present.

CLARKE, STANLEY Bass, producer, piano, vocal, writer. After playing with several jazz greats, he achieved national prominence as a member of Chick Corea's Return to Forever, demonstrating lightning fingers, articulately and melodically placed. Session for Santana (1974); Eumir Deodato; Airto (1974); Roy Buchanan (1977). *Albums:* The Bass (MCA 9284); Stanley Clarke (IMP 431) 1974; I Wanna Play for You (NMP KZ2-35680) 1979; Individuals (COL CG-36213); Journey to Love (NMP 433) 1975; Rocks, Pebbles and Sand (EPC JE-36506) 1980; School Days (NMP 900); Modern Man (COL 9Z 35303) 1978.

CLARKIN, TONY Guitar, vocal. Member of Magnum, 1979.

CLASH Nicky Headon—drums (1978-present); Terry Chimes—drums (1978); Mick Jones—guitar, vocal; Paul Simonon—bass, vocal; Joe Strummer—guitar, vocal. Preeminent among the bands emerging from the British new wave, the Clash have proven themselves capable in numerous musical styles, especially reggae, and lyrically infuse their political stance in their arrangements. *Albums:* The Clash (EPC JE-36060) 1979; Give 'Em Enough Rope (EPC JE-35543) 1979; London Calling (EPC E2-36328) 1980; Black Market Clash (COL 4E 36846) 1980.

CLAUSMAN, DUNCAN Bass. Member of the Johnny Van Zant Band, 1980.

CLAWSON, E. G. Drums. Member of S.R.C.

CLAY, FRANCIS Drums. Member of the James Cotton Blues Band.

CLAYTON, CHRIS Horns. Session for Leon Russell (1974).

CLAYTON, EDDIE Guitar. Session for George Harrison (1967).

CLAYTON, JOE Percussion. Session for Art Garfunkel.

CLAYTON, MERRY Vocal. Session for Joe Cocker (1968, 74); Grin (1973); Taj Mahal (1974); Lee Michaels; Neil Young (1969); B. B. King (1970); the Rolling Stones (1970); Russ Giguere (1971); "Tommy" (1972); Ringo Starr (1973). *Albums:* Emotion (MCA 3200); Keep Your Eye on the

Sparrow (ODE SP7030) 1975.

CLAYTON, SAM Congas, vocal. Member of Little Feat, 1971-77. Session for Freddie King (1975); Rory Block (1979); Bob Seger (1980).

CLAYTON-THOMAS, DAVID Vocal. Voice of Blood, Sweat and Tears, 1968-69. *Album:* Clayton (MCA 1104).

CLEAR LIGHT Cliff de Young—vocal; Doug Lubahn—bass; Mike Ney—drums; Bob Seal—guitar; Ralph Schuckett—keyboards; Dallas Taylor—drums. Los Angeles based rock band featuring dual drummers, a novelty in rock at the time. Disbanded in 1968. *Album:* Clear Light (ELK) 1967.

CLEARY, DEREK Guitar, vocal. Member of Candlewick Green, 1974.

CLEFTONES Richard Barrett—vocal; Warren Corbin—vocal; Herbie Cox—vocal; Charlie James—vocal; William McClain—vocal; Berman Patterson—vocal; Eugene Pearson—vocal; Gene Phison—vocal. Made the hit "Little Girl of Mine" (1956). *Albums:* Heart and Soul, 1961; For Sentimental Reasons, 1962.

CLEMENT, LEE Percussion. Session for the Mothers of Invention (1972).

CLEMENTS, GAIL Guitar, vocal. Member of BLT, 1977.

CLEMENTS, RON Bass. Replaced Thomas Duffy in Lindisfarne, 1978.

CLEMENTS, TERRY Guitar, vocal. Session for Gordon Lightfoot since the late 1960s.

CLEMENTS, TERRY Tenor saxophone. Member of the Electric Flag, 1967-68, and Buddy Miles Express, 1968-69. Session for Janis Joplin (1969).

CLEMENTS, VASSAR Fiddle, strings. Session for Richard Betts (1974); Elvin Bishop (1974); J. J. Cale (1972). *Albums:* Southern Country Waltzes; 701; Vassar Clements (MER SRM-1-1022); Band (MCA 2270) 1980; The Bluegrass Sessions (FLF 038); Crossing the Catskills (RND 0016) 1972; Hillbilly Jazz (FLF 101); Nashville Jam (FLF 073) 1979; Superbow (MER SRM-1-1058); Vassar (FLF 232).

CLEMINSON, ZAL Guitar. Member of Sahb, 1976, the Sensational Alex Harvey Band, Nazareth, 1979-80. Session for Dan McCafferty (1975).

CLEMONS, CLARENCE Saxophone. Member of the E Street Band, 1973-present. Session for Flame (1977).

CLEMONS, GREGG Vocal. *Album:* Gregg Clemons (NMP JZ-36536) 1980.

CLEMPSON, DAVE "CLEM" Guitar, vocal. Member of Colosseum, 1970-71. He left Colosseum to replace Peter Frampton in Humble Pie, 1971-75. Member of Rough Diamond, 1977.

CLENCH, JIM Bass, vocal. Replaced Jim Henman in April Wine, and Randy Bachman in Bachman-Turner Overdrive, 1978.

CLESSER, COL Saxophone. Session for Jay Ferguson (1979)

CLIBURN, JAMES Member of Smith.

CLIC, BUZZ Guitar, vocal. Member of the Rubber City Rebels, 1980.

CLIFFORD, DOUG Drums. Original member of Creedence Clearwater Revival, 1968-72, and the Don Harrison Band, 1976.

CLIFTON, DENNIS Vocal, guitar. Member of FCC, 1980.

CLIMAX CHICAGO BLUES BAND Colin Cooper—vocal, harmonica, saxophone, flute; Peter Haycock—guitar, slide guitar, vocal; Arthur Wood—keyboards (1968-71); Derek Holt—guitar, bass, organ; Richard Jones—bass (1968); George Newsome—drums (1968-73); Humpty Farmer—keyboards (1970); John Cuffely—drums, vocal, percussion (1973-present); Richard Jones—keyboards, vocal, bass, guitar (1975); Peter Filleul—vocal, keyboards (1979-present). Though they did not have a popular hit until 1974, Climax's origins go back to the early days in London, competing with bands like Savoy Brown, Ten Years After and Fleetwood Mac. Peter Haycock was the focal point in their blues format, but slowly their sound changed to focus on the tight interplay between Haycock and Colin Cooper's reeds. In 1970 they shortened their name to the Climax Blues Band. As other blues bands dropped by the wayside, Climax continued on, gradually phasing out old blues tunes, though not completely, and doing their own songs, mixing ballads with up tempo tunes, all tightly produced. Session for Tarney and Spencer (1978). *Albums:* Climax Chicago Blues Band (SIR K-6003) 1970; Plays On (SIR K-6033) 1969; FM Live (SIR 2XS-6013) 1973; Lot of Bottle (SIR 6004); Real to Reel (WBR K-3334) 1979; Shine On (SIR K-6056) 1978; Stamp Album (SIR 6016) 1975; Tightly Knit (SIR 6008) 1972; Gold Plated (SIR SASO 7523) 1976; Sense of Direction (SIR SAS 7501); Rich Man (SIR SAS 7402) 1972; Climax Chicago Blues Band (SIR SES 97013) 1968; Flying the Flag (WBR BSK 3493) 1980.

CLINGINGBEARD, LES Saxophone, percussion, vocal. Member of Junior Cadillac since 1979. Session for Lance Romance.

CLINIC Gerry Murphy—drums; Phil Trainer—bass, vocal; Phil Brigham—guitar, vocal; Alan Reeves—keyboards, vocal. *Album:* Now We're Even (ROU 3010) 1973.

CLINTON, GEORGE Keyboards, vocal. Born 7/23/42. Member of Crackin', 1975, and Volunteers, 1976.

CLOUD, NEIL Drums. Member of Rabbitt, 1976.

CLOVER Alex Call—vocal, guitar; Huey Lewis—vocal, harpsichord; John McFee—guitars; John Ciambotti—bass; Sean Hopper—keyboards; Tony Braunagel—drums; Mitch Howie—drums. *Album:* Love on the Wire, 1977; Clover, 1971; Forty Niner, 1972.

CLUB, BILLY Bass, vocal. Member of the Dickies

since 1978.

CLUNEY, HENRY Guitar, vocal. Member of Stiff Little Fingers, 1980.

CLYDALE, BUTCH Drums, vocal. Member of Chuck and the Tigers, 1980.

CLYDE, JEREMY Vocal, guitar, writer. Half of the English soft vocal duet, Chad and Jeremy.

CLYNE, JEFF Bass. Member of Centipede, 1971, and Isotope, 1974. Session on "Jesus Christ Superstar" (1970).

COAL KITCHEN Bobby Carlin—drums, vocal; Rob Newhouse—guitar, vocal; Carla Peyton—vocal, percussion; Andre Mossotti—bass; Paulie Carmen—vocal. *Album:* Thirsty or Not, 1977.

COALFIELD, MARK Keyboards, vocal. Member of Athletico Spizz 80, 1980.

COALITION See Chuck Rainey.

COBAR, GLEN Kazoo. Member of the Temple City Kazoo Orchestra, 1978.

COBB, J. R. Guitar. Member of the Atlanta Rhythm Section since 1973.

COBB, JIMMY Vocal, bass. Member of Starbuck, 1977-78.

COBB, JOHNNY Keyboards, vocal. Half of the Lawler and Cobb duet, 1980. Session for the Allman Brothers (1980).

COBB, RICK Drums. Member of Bloodrock.

COBB, SHERRY Vocal. Session for the Allman Brothers (1980).

COBERT, JON Keyboards. Session for Henry Gross (1978).

COBHAM, BILLY Drums, producer. Member of Dreams, 1970. Produced Airto (1974). Session with Carlos Santana and John McLaughlin on "Love Devotion Surrender" (1973); Eumir Deodato; Roy Buchanan (1976); Carly Simon (1974); Richard Davis (1977); Jack Bruce (1980). *Albums:* Alivemutherforya (COL JC-35349); B.C. (COL JC-35993) 1979; Best of Billy Cobham (ATC 19238) 1979; Crosswinds (ATC 7300) 1974; Funky Thide of Sings (ATC 18149) 1975; Individuals (COL CG-36213); Inner Conflicts (ATC 19174) 1978; Life and Times (ATC 18166) 1976; Live on Tour in Europe (ATC 18194); Magic (COL JC-34939); Shabazz (ATC 18139) 1975; Simplicity of Expression-Depth of Thought (COL JC-35457); Spectrum (ATC 7268); Total Eclipse (ATC 18121) 1974.

COBIAN, ELPIDIO Percussion. Member of Sweetwater.

COCHRAN, BOBBY Drums, vocal. Member of Ruby, 1976.

COCHRAN, BOBBY Guitar, vocal. Member of Steppenwolf, 1974-76.

COCHRAN, CHUCK Keyboards. Session for Doug Kershaw; Tom Rapp; Waylon Jennings (1975).

COCHRAN, DAVE Bass. Session for Roy Harper; Chris Spedding (1976).

COCHRAN, DAVE Drums, vocal. Session for Robert Johnson (1978).

COCHRAN, EDDIE Vocal, writer. Rock star of the 1950s and author of "Summertime Blues," which was a hit for the Who and Blue Cheer years after his death in an auto accident, April, 1960, with Gene Vincent. *Albums:* Singing to My Baby, 1957; Eddie Cochran, 1960; Never To Be Forgotten, 1963; Summertime Blues, 1958; Very Best of Eddie Cochran (UAR).

COCHRANE, TOM Vocal, guitar. Member of Red Rider, 1980.

COCKER, JOE Vocal. Born 5/20/44. With the voice of a gravel pit and the mannerisms of a person with a short circuited central nervous system, he sang his way into the hearts of the children of the Woodstock era with "With a Little Help from My Friends," 1968. After exchanging his Grease Band for Leon Russell and a troupe called "The Greatest Show on Earth," he made one more extravaganza tour before taking a brief sabbatical, 1970-72. *Albums:* Joe Cocker (AAM 4224) 1969; Joe Cocker (AAM 4368) 1972; Joe Cocker's Greatest Hits (AAM 4670) 1977; I Can Stand a Little Rain (AAM 3633) 1975; Jamaica Say You Will (AAM 4529) 1975; Luxury You Can Afford (ASY 6E-145) 1978; Mad Dogs and Englishmen (AAM 6002) 1970; With a Little Help from My Friends (AAM 4182) 1968.

COCKNEY, JIM Violin. Member of the Blue Jays, 1975.

COCKNEY REBEL See Steve Harley and Cockney Rebel.

COCKRELL, BUD Bass, vocal. Member of Pablo Cruise since 1975.

COCKS, MICHAEL Guitar. Member of the Rose Tattoo, 1980.

CODE BLUE Dean Chamberlain—guitar, vocal; Gary Tibbs—bass, vocal; Randall Marsh—drums, vocal. *Album:* Code Blue (WBR BSK 3461) 1980.

COE, CHARLIE Bass, guitar. Replaced Philip Volk in Paul Revere and the Raiders until 1969.

COE, DAVID ALLEN Vocal, guitar. Session for Willie Nelson (1976). *Albums:* David Allen Coe, Rides Again (COL PC-34310) 1977; Compass Point (COL JC-36277) 1979; Family Album (COL KC-35306) 1978; Greatest Hits (COL PC-35627) 1978; Human Emotions (COL KC-35535) 1978; I've Got Something To Say (COL JC-36489) 1980; Longhaired Redneck (COL KC-32942); Mysterious Rhinestone Cowboy (COL KC-33085) 1974; Once Upon a Rhyme (COL KC-33085) 1975; Penitentiary Blues (SSS 9); Souvenirs of Music City U.S.A. (PLN 506); Spectrum VII (COL KC-35789) 1979; Tattoo (COL KC-34870) 1977; Texas Moon (PLN 507); 20 Greatest Hits (PLN 521).

COE, TONY Saxophone. Session for the Hollies (1978).

COFFEY, DENNIS Guitar, vocal. Session for Ringo Starr (1974); *Albums:* Back Home (WSB 300); Sweet Taste of Sin (WSB 6105) 1978.

COGBILL, TOMMY Bass. Member of the Coral Reefer Band. Session for John Hammond (1975); Doug Kershaw (1972); Bob Seger (1974); J. J. Cale (1974); Wilson Pickett; Aretha Franklin.

COGBURN, DORMAN Member of Alias, 1979.

COGNITION Phil Hudson—vocal; Jerry Hudson —guitar, vocal; Nick Di Stefano—vocal, drums; Don "Jake" Jakubowski—organ; Joe Hesse—bass. *Album:* The Road (KMS 2052) 1971.

COHEN, ALAN Bass. Member of Missouri.

COHEN, BOB Guitar. Session for Long John Baldry (1975-79); Mike Harrison (1975).

COHEN, BRUCE Keyboards. Member of the Reds, 1979.

COHEN, DAVID Guitar, organ. Original member of Country Joe and the Fish, 1966-69. Session for Joe Cocker (1968); Arthur, Hurley and Gottlieb.

COHEN, JEFF Drums. Member of Proof, 1980.

COHEN, JOHN Guitar. Member of the New Lost City Ramblers.

COHEN, LAURIE Vocal. Member of Giants, 1976.

COHEN, LEONARD Guitar, vocal, writer. Born 9/21/35. Writing poems instead of lyrics, Cohen sings in a distinctive drone. *Albums:* Songs of Leonard Cohen, 1968; Live Songs; Best of Leonard Cohen; (COL CS-9535) 1975; Leonard Cohen (COL CS-9535); Death of a Ladies' Man (WBR B-3125) 1977; New Skin for the Old Ceremony (COL C-33167); Recent Songs (COL CS-9767) 1969; Songs from a Room (COL CS-9767) 1969; Songs of Love and Hate (COL C-30103).

COHEN, NAOMI Real name of Cass Elliot.

COHEN, PAUL Guitar. Member of Guns and Butter, 1972.

COHEN, PETER Bass. Member of Guns and Butter, 1972.

COHEN, TOM Vocal, guitar. Member of Proof, 1980.

COILE, JIM Saxophone. Member of Ballin' Jack. Session for Richie Furay (1978).

COLA, JOEY Guitar. Member of the Sorrows, 1980.

COLA, NICK Keyboards, vocal. Member of the Tigers, 1980.

COLAVITA, VINCE Drums. Member of the Christopher Morris Band, 1977. Session for Frank Zappa (1979).

COLBATH, DICK Piano. Replaced Duane Abler in Sunblind Lion, 1978.

COLBECK, JULIAN Guitar, vocal. Replaced Martin Smith in Charlie, 1977.

COLBERT, CHUCK Member of the American Breed, 1965-68.

COLBURN, KRAIG Guitar. Member of Ted Nugent's backup band, 1978.

COLBY, MARK Saxophone. Member of Boneroo until 1974. Session for Bill Wyman (1976); Jay Ferguson (1979).

COLCORD, RAY Keyboards. Session for Lou Reed (1974).

COLD BLOOD Lydia Pense—vocal; Raul Matute —piano, organ; Larry Jonutz—trumpet; Jerry Jonutz—alto and baritone saxophone; Rod Ellicott —bass; Frank J. Davis—drums; Danny Hull—tenor saxophone; David Padron—trumpet; Larry Field—guitar. San Franciscan horn band from the heydays of the Fillmore. *Albums:* Thriller; First Taste of Sin (RPS 2074); Sisyphus; Cold Blood.

COLD CHISEL Jim Barnes—vocal; Ian Moss—guitar, vocal; Don Walker—keyboards; Phil Small —bass; Steve Prestwich—drums. *Album:* Breakfast at Sweet Heart (ELK 90001) 1979.

COLE, B. J. Pedal steel guitar. Session for Ray Thomas (1975); Nazareth (1972); Procol Harum (1974); Elton John (1971, 79); Dave Edmunds (1971); Jerry Lee Lewis (1973); Ken Tobias (1973); Trapeze (1972-73); Uriah Heep (1972); Chris de Burgh (1975); Gay and Terry Woods (1976); Olivia Newton-John (1976); the Alan Parsons Project (1977); Kevin Ayers (1977); the Graham Edge Band (1977); Kevin Lamb (1978); Gerry Rafferty (1978); Gary Brooker (1979); Mike Batt (1979); Maddy Prior (1980); Oxendale and Shephard (1979).

COLE, BRIAN Vocal, bass. Original member of the Association.

COLE, JERRY Guitar. Session for Sonny Terry and Brownie McGhee (1973).

COLE, JON Guitar, slide guitar, vocal. Member of Movies.

COLE, JUDE Guitar, vocal. Member of the Ravens, 1979. Replaced Huw Gower in the Records, 1980.

COLE, KENNY Vocal. Session for Trapeze (1974).

COLE, RICH Member of the Romantics, 1980.

COLE, RITCHIE Drums. Member of Stray, 1970-75.

COLE, WILBUR Organ, vocal. Member of the Band of Thieves, 1976.

COLEMAN, CORNELIUS Drums. Session for Fats Domino (1951-59).

COLEMAN, GARY Percussion. Session for Greg Sutton (1975); Nilsson (1975); Steely Dan (1976); Cashman and West (1972); Martin Mull (1979); Tim Weisberg and Dan Fogelberg (1978); the Ozark Mountain Daredevils (1980).

COLEY, JOHN FORD Keyboards, guitar, vocal. Half of the England Dan and John Ford Coley duet since 1974.

COLIS, ED Harmonica. Session for J. J. Cale (1971).

COLLEN, PHIL Guitar, vocal. Member of Girl, 1980.

COLLETTE, BUDDY Saxophone. Session for Nilsson (1976).

COLLETTI, COURTNEY Guitar, bass. Member of Johnny's Dance Band, 1977.

COLLIER, PAT Bass, vocal. Member of the Vibrators, 1977.

COLLIER, TOM Marimba. Session for Ry Cooder (1978).

COLLINGE, CRAIG Drums. Member of Manfred Mann, 1971, and Shoot, 1973.

COLLINS, ALBERT Guitar, vocal. Classic blues guitarist in the traditional style. *Albums:* Frostbite (ALG 4719) 1980; Ice Pickin' (ALG 4713) 1978.

COLLINS, ALLEN Guitar. Member of Lynyrd Skynyrd, 1973-77, and the Rossington-Collins Band, 1980.

COLLINS, ANSEL Keyboards. Member of Dillinger, 1976.

COLLINS, BURT Horns. Session for John Sebastian (1970).

COLLINS, CARTER Conga. Session for Harvey Mandel.

COLLINS, CHARLES Drums. Session for Elton John (1979).

COLLINS, DENNIS Bass. Session for Johnny Winter (1970).

COLLINS, FRANK Vocal. Session for Alvin Lee (1974); Marianne Faithfull (1979).

COLLINS, JUDY Vocal, guitar, writer. Born 5/1/39. Began singing in the folk boom of the late 1950s and survived the 1960s achieving her most widespread fame with Joni Mitchell's "Both Sides Now" (1968). *Albums:* Bread and Roses (ELK 7E-1076) 1976; Judy Collins Concert (ELK 7280) 1964; 5th Album (ELK 7300) 1964; No. 3 (ELK 7243) 1963; Colors of the Day (ELK 75030) 1972; Golden Apples of the Sun (ELK 7222); Hard Times for Lovers (ELK 6E-171); In My Life (ELK 74027) 1966; Judith (ELK 6E-111) 1975; Living (ELK 75014) 1971; Maid of Constant Sorrow (ELK 7209); Recollections (ELK 74055) 1965; Running for My Life (ELK 6E-253) 1980; So Early in the Spring (ELK 8E-6002) 1977; True Stories and Other Dreams (ELK 75053) 1973; Whales and Nightingales (ELK 75010); Who Knows Where The Time Goes (ELK 74033) 1968; Wildflowers (ELK 74012) 1967.

COLLINS, LEWIS Alto saxophone, flute. Member of the Memphis Horns.

COLLINS, MEL Horns, saxophone. Member of King Crimson, replacing Ian McDonald, 1970-72. Member of Snape, 1972. Session for Splinter (1974-75); Chris Squire (1975); Bad Company (1973); Alvin Lee (1974-75); Bryan Ferry (1977-79); "Rough Mix" (1977); the Small Faces (1977); the Rolling Stones (1978); Richard Wright (1978); Mike Batt (1979); Vapour Trails (1980); Anthony Phillips (1980).

COLLINS, MIKE Washboard. Session with Cyril Davies and Alexis Korner (1954-66).

COLLINS, MITCH Vocal. Session for the Bill Blue Band (1980).

COLLINS, PAUL Guitar, vocal, writer. Member of the Beat, 1979.

COLLINS, PHIL Percussion, drums, vocal. Member of Genesis, and Brand X since 1977. Session for Colin Scot (1971); Tommy Bolin (1975); John Cale (1975); Elliott Murphy (1977); Anthony Phillips (1977); Robert Fripp (1979); Cafe Jacques (1977-79).

COLLINS, RAY Vocal, harmonica. Original member of the Mothers of Invention, 1966-70. Session for Frank Zappa (1974).

COLOMBIER, MICHAEL Keyboards. Session for Flora Purim (1978). *Albums:* Michel Colombier (CYS 1212) 1979: Nadia's Theme (AAM 3412).

COLOMBY, BOBBY Drums, producer. Member of Blood, Sweat and Tears, 1967-68. Produced Jaco Pastorius (1976). Production and session for the Pages (1978-79).

COLOSSEUM Jon Hiseman—drums; Dick Heckstall-Smith—saxophones; Dave Greenslade—keyboards, vocal; Tony Reeves—bass (1968); James Litherland—vocal, guitar (1968-69); Dave Clempson—guitar, vocal (1970); Mark Clarke—bass (1970); Chris Farlow—vocals (1970); Barbara Thompson—reeds, vocal; Louis Cennamo—bass. With the British blues explosion of the late 1960s, came several talented musicians who expanded into more progressive areas. Colosseum flirted with jazz in a rock format. *Albums:* Daughter of Time (DHL DSX 50101) 1970; Grass is Greener; Live (WBR 2XS 1942) 1971; Those Who Are About to Die Salute You, 1969; Valentyn Suite (Import) 1969.

COLOSSEUM II Gary Moore—guitar, vocal; Don Airey—keyboard; Jon Hiseman—drums, percussion; John Mole—bass. Formed by Ex-Colosseum member Hiseman, Colosseum II resurrected Colosseum's jazz format after a 6 year absence. *Albums:* Electric Savage (MCA) 1977; Wardance (MCA 2310) 1977.

COLTON, TONY Percussion, vocal. Voice of Heads, Hands and Feet, 1970-71.

COLTRANE, ALICE Keyboards, writer. Coauthor of "Illuminations" with Carlos Santana, 1974. *Albums:* Cosmic Music (MCA 9148); 9272); Elements (MLS 9053); Illuminations (COL PC-32900); Radha-Krishna Nama Sanbkirtana (WBR B-2986); Transcendence (WBR B-3077); Transfiguration (WBR 2B-3218); World Galaxy (MCA 9218).

COLUMBIER, MICHAEL Keyboards, producer. Session for John Palumbo (1978).

COLVARD, JIMMY Guitar. Session for Doug Kershaw (1972); Tom Rapp (1972); Waylon Jennings (1975).

COLWELL, BILL Guitar. Member of the Colwell-

Winfield Blues Band, 1968.

COLWELL-WINFIELD BLUES BAND Moose Sorrento—vocal; Chuck Purro—drums; Jack Schroder—saxophone; Bill Colwell—guitar; Mike Winfield—bass; Collin Tilton—saxophone, flute. Blues band that jumped on the train of the blues boom in 1968. *Album:* Cold Wind Blues, 1968.

COLYER, KEN Namesake and founder of the Ken Colyer Skiffle Group, 1952-54.

KEN COLYER SKIFFLE GROUP Alexis Korner —guitar, vocal; Lonnie Donegan; Chris Barber; Ken Colyer. Early group for Alexis Korner, 1952-54.

COMER, TEX Bass, vocal. Member of Ace, 1974-78. Session for Danny Kirwan (1979); Frankie Miller (1979); Sean Tyla (1980).

COMETS See Bill Haley and the Comets.

COMITA, PETE Bass. Replaced Tom Petersson in Cheap Trick, 1980.

COMMANDER CODY Piano, vocal. Real name: George Frayne. Founder of Commander Cody's Lost Planet Airmen. Returning to rock 'n' roll, he formed the New Commander Cody Band, 1977. Session for the New Riders of the Purple Sage.

COMMANDER CODY AND HIS LOST PLANET AIRMEN Bruce Barlow—bass; Bill Kirchen—gutar, vocal; Lance Dickerson—drums; John Tichy —guitar, vocal; Andy Stein—fiddle, saxophone; Commander Cody (George Frayne)—piano, vocal; Bill Farlow—vocal, harpsichord; Bobby Black—pedal steel guitar. Proving country music is alive and well, Commander Cody continues to mix old country favorites with a few of his own songs. *Albums:* Commander Cody and His Lost Planet Airmen, 1971; Tales from the Ozone, 1975; Country Casanova (MCA 6054); Flying Dreams (ARI 4183) 1978; Hot Licks, Cold Steel and Trucker's Favorites (MCA 6031); Live from Deep in the Heart of Texas (MCA 1017); Lost in the Ozone (MCA 6017); We've Got a Live One Here (WBR 2LS-2939) 1976.

NEW COMMANDER CODY BAND Commander Cody—piano, vocal; Bobby Black—pedal steel guitar; Darius Janaher—guitar; Fred Meyer—drums; Rob Greer—bass. *Album:* Rock 'n' Roll Again (ARI 4125) 1977.

COMO, JIM Vocal, drums, percussion. Member of Fireballet, 1975-77.

COMPTON, TOM Drums. Member of Ten Years Later, 1978-79, and the Alvin Lee Band, 1980.

CONAWAY, JEFF Vocal. *Album:* Jeff Conaway (COL JC-36111) 1979.

CONDON, CHIP Keyboards. Member of Cowboy, 1977, replacing Bill Pillmore.

CONDON, GEOFF Horns, saxophone, flute, oboe, percussion. Member of Mark-Almond, 1972.

CONDON, MIKE Guitar. Member of the Jan Park Band, 1979.

CONLEY, ARTHUR Vocal, writer. Protege of Otis Redding in 1965 at the age of sixteen. Enjoyed some fame in 1968 with his single "Sweet Soul Music." *Albums:* Shake, Rattle and Roll; Soul Directions; Sweet Soul Music.

CONLY, PAUL Guitar, keyboards. Member of Lothar and the Hand People, 1966-68. Session for Zephyr (1971).

CONN, MARTY Keyboards. Session for St. Paradise (1979).

CONNELL, MAGGIE Keyboards, vocal. Member of the Heaters, 1978-present.

CONNELL, MISSY Bass, vocal. Member of the Heaters, 1978-present.

CONNER, GEORGE Guitar, vocal. Member of the Tremblers, 1980.

CONNER, MIKE Keyboards. Member of Pure Prairie League, 1975-80.

CONNER, TONY Drums, percussion, vibes. Member of Audience, 1971.

CONNERS, BILL Guitar. Original member of Chick Corea's Return To Forever, 1973-74. Session for Stanley Clarke (1974).

CONNEXION Andy Fernbach—guitar, vocal, writer; J. D. Fanger—guitar; Bob Rowe—bass; Phil Crowther—drums. Fernbach's group effort, based on his solo blues career, that never crossed the ocean from England to the United States in the 1960s.

CONNOLLY, BRIAN Vocal, keyboards. Member of Sweet, 1975-present.

CONNOLLY, PAT Vocal, bass. Member of the Surfaris, 1963-65.

CONNORS, DAVE Saxophone, flute. Session for Jade Warrior (1971).

CONRAD, DAVE Bass. Member of Orphan, 1974.

CONRAD, JACK Bass, guitar. Session on the Doors "Other Voices" (1971), "Full Circle" (1972); the Babys (1978).

CONSTANTEN, TOM Organ. Member of the Grateful Dead, 1967-69, and Touchstone, 1971.

CONTARDO, JOHNNY Vocal. Member of Sha Na Na, 1971 to present.

CONTE, BRUCE Guitar, vocal. Replaced Willie Fulton in Tower of Power, 1973.

CONTE, VICTOR Bass. Member of the Pure Food and Drug Act, and Tower of Power, 1978. Session for Harvey Mandel.

CONTENDERS Peter Bonas—guitar; Chris Parren —keyboards; Ray Allen—saxophone, percussion, vocal; Phil Capaldi—drums, vocal. Backup band for Jim Capaldi, 1979.

CONTI, ALEX Guitar, vocal. Member of Lake since 1977.

CONWAY, DENNIS Drums, percussion. Member of Stone Country, 1968.

CONWAY, GERRY Drums, percussion, vocal. First appeared in Eclection, 1968. Member of

Fotheringay, 1971, and the Thieves, 1979. Session for John Cale (1974); Cat Stevens (1971-78); Mike Berry (1976); Jim Capaldi (1979).

COODER, RY Bottleneck guitar, vocal, writer, mandolin, bass. In the same tradition as Woodie Guthrie, Cooder plays traditional 1920s and 1930s folk and blues songs, telling stories of the dust bowl days under FDR, why a "Married Man's A Fool," "Vigilante Man" and others. He has also recorded songs in numerous other American genres, from gospel to rock. His arrangements are always fresh and current. What distinguishes him most is his authentic bottleneck guitar and vocals. When major names require authentic blues backing, it is easy to see why they call on Cooder, as his list of session credits show. Released the first all digitally produced album, 1979. Session for Marc Benno; Crazy Horse (1971); Taj Mahal; Randy Newman; the Rolling Stones (1970); John Sebastian (1974); Maria Muldaur (1973); Rodney Crowell (1978); Little Feat (1971). Part of "No Nukes," 1979. *Albums:* Boomer's Story (RPS 2117) 1972; Bop Till You Drop (WBR K-3358) 1979; Chicken Skin Music (RPS 2254) 1976; Ry Cooder (RPS 6402) 1970; Into the Purple Valley (RPS MS-2052) 1972; Jazz (WBR K-3197) 1978; Paradise and Lunch (RPS 2179) 1974; Show Time (WBR B-3059) 1977; Long Riders (Soundtrack) (WBR HS 3448) 1980.

COOK, ALLISON Drums. Member of the Pousette-Dart Band, 1976-77.

COOK, BETSY Vocal. Session for Gerry Rafferty (1979-80); Vapour Trails (1980).

COOK, JEFF Guitar, keyboards, vocal, fiddle. Member of Alabama, 1980.

COOK, JOHN Organ, vocal. Played on "Joseph and the Amazing Technicolor Dreamcoat," 1967. Member of Stretch, 1977. Session for Danny Kirwan (1979).

COOK, MICK Drums. Replaced Clive Brooks in the Groundhogs, 1976.

COOK, PAUL Drums. Member of the Sex Pistols, 1977.

COOK, ROGER Vocal. Member of Blue Mink. Session for Long John Baldry, 1971.

COOK, STU Bass. Original member of Creedence Clearwater Revival, 1968-72, and the Don Harrison Band, 1976.

COOK, WAYNE Keyboards. Replaced Andy Chapin in Steppenwolf, 1976. Member of the L.A. Jets, 1976, and Player, 1977.

COOKE, CURLEY Guitar. Member of Tim Bavis and the Chordairs, 1966, before joining Steve Miller, 1966-68. Formed Curley Cooke's Hurdy Gurdy Band, 1968. Session for Ben Sidran; Steve Miller (1970, 76, 77); Jerry Garcia and Howard Wales (1972).

CURLEY COOKE'S HURDY GURDY BAND Early band of Curley Cooke after the Steve Miller Band, 1968.

COOKE, JOHN Vocal. Session for Janis Joplin (1969).

COOKE, SAM Vocal. Contemporary of Otis Redding. His first record "You Send Me" (1957) was a smash, and was followed by others like "Chain Gang" (1960), "Bring It On Home" (1962), and "Send Me Some Lovin'" (1962). He was accidentally killed December 16, 1964, a victim of what the courts ruled as justifiable homicide. *Albums:* Ain't That Good News (SPE 2115) 1964; Best of Sam Cooke (VIC LSP-2625) 1962; Golden Sound of Sam Cooke; Gospel Soul of Sam Cooke (SPE 2116); Gospel Soul of Sam Cooke, Vol. 2 (SPE 2128); That's Heaven to Me (SPE 2146); This Is Sam Cooke (VIC VPS 6027); Two Sides of Sam Cooke (SPE 2119); You Send Me (CON ACLI-0445); Twistin' the Night Away, 1962; Mr. Soul, 1963; Night Beat, 1963; Sam Cook at the Copa (VIC ANLI 2658) 1964; Shake, 1965; Best of Sam Cooke, Vol. 2, 1965; Unforgettable Sam Cooke, 1966; The Man Who Invented Soul, 1968.

COOKER Slide guitar. Member of the Seeds, 1967.

COOLAN, ROGER Organ. Session for Nilsson (1971).

COOLBAUGH, WES Guitar, vocal. Member of the Love Affair, 1980.

COOLEY, FLOYD Tuba. Session for the Pointer Sisters (1974); Bill Wyman (1976).

COOLEY, MIKE Guitar. Session for John Mayall (1977).

COOLIDGE, RITA Vocal. Born 5/1/44. Got her start singing in a backup troupe headed by Leon Russell for Joe Cocker, 1975, and has since developed her own folk style. Session with Marc Benno; Delaney and Bonnie; Dave Mason (1970); David Blue (1971); Steve Stills (1970); Eric Clapton (1970); Johnny Cash (1973); Glen Campbell (1980). *Albums:* Full Moon; Anytime Anywhere (AAM 4616) 1977; Rita Coolidge (AAM 4291); Fall into Spring (AAM 3627) 1974; It's Only Love (AAM 4531) 1975; Lady's Not for Sale (AAM 4370) 1972; Love Me Again (AAM 4699) 1978; Nice Feelin' (AAM 4325); Satisfied (AAM 4781) 1979.

COOMBES, PEET Vocal, guitar, writer. Member of the Tourists since 1980.

COOMBES, ROD Drums, percussion. Replaced Pete Dobson in Juicy Lucy, 1970-71. Member of Stealer's Wheel, 1972-75, and the Strawbs. Session for John Entwhistle (1972).

COONCE, RICK Drums, percussion. Member of the Grass Roots.

COOPER, ALAN Vocal. Member of Sha Na Na, 1970.

COOPER, ALICE Vocal, writer. Born 2/5/44. Namesake and founder of the group "Alice Cooper," 1970-73, he masterminded the most bizarre stage show in the history of rock, incorporating masochism, sadism, self-abuse, murder, suicide and general degeneracy. Meanwhile, he wrote catchy songs for radio, like "I'm Eighteen," 1971, "School's Out," 1972, "Elected," 1971, and others. Continued as a soloist after the group's demise in 1973. In 1979 he released a movie backed by his new group, Ultra-Latex. *Albums:* Welcome to My Nightmare (ATC 19157) 1975; Goes to Hell (WBR 2896) 1976; Billion Dollar Babies (WBR 2685) 1973; Alice Cooper's Greatest Hits (WBR K-3107); Easy Action (WBR 1845) 1970; From the Inside (WBR K-3263); Killer (WBR B-2567) 1971; Love It to Death (WBR 1883) 1971; Muscle of Love (WBR B-2748) 1973; Pretties for You (WBR 1840) 1970; School's Out (WBR 2623) 1972; Alice Cooper Show (WBR K 3138) 1977; Flush the Fashion (WBR BSK 3436) 1980; Lace and Whiskey (WBR BK-3027) 1976.

ALICE COOPER BAND Alice Cooper—vocal, harmonica, writer; Neal Smith—drums, vocal; Dennis Dunaway—bass, vocal; Glen Buxton—guitar; Mike Bruce—guitar, vocal, keyboards; Dick Wagner—guitar, vocal; Prakash John—bass; Steve Hunter—guitar; Penti Glan—drums; Fred Mandel—keyboards. One of Zappa's many discoveries of the 1960s was Alice Cooper. Originally a novelty act, Alice (a he who believed he was the reincarnation of a 16th century she) refined one of the most bizarre theatrical stage acts in the history of rock, while cranking out top 40 hits. In addition, the group had one of the most original album packaging designers, including albums that looked like giant wallets, complete with giant money and group pictures, an old-fashioned school desk which, when the top was swung open included a pair of lady's disposable panties, and a calendar, with a portrait of Alice swinging at the end of a rope. *Albums:* Billion Dollar Babies (WBR 2685) 1973; Alice Cooper's Greatest Hits (WBR K-3107); Easy Action (WBR 1845) 1970; From the Inside (WBR K-3263); Killer (WBR B-2567) 1971; Love It to Death (WBR 1883) 1971; Muscle of Love (WBR B-2748) 1973; Pretties for You (WBR 1840) 1970; School's Out (WBR 2623) 1972.

COOPER, BILL Bass. Session for John Kay (1973).

COOPER, BRIAN Bass, vocal. Member of the Cooper Brothers band since 1978.

COOPER, COLIN Vocal, harmonica, saxophone, flute. Original member of Climax Blues Band, 1968 to present.

COOPER, D. B. Vocal. Namesake of the group D. B. Cooper, 1980.

D. B. COOPER Jon Chapman—drums, vocal; Roger Heath—guitar, vocal; Robby Scharf—bass, vocal; Ric Streeter—guitar, vocal; D. B. Cooper—vocal. *Album:* Buy American (WBR BSK-3444) 1980.

COOPER, JOEY Vocal, guitar. Session for Freddie King (1971); Leon Russell (1971, 72, 74); Don Nix (1971).

COOPER, KENT Drums. Member of Boyzz, 1978.

COOPER, LEROY Baritone saxophone. Session for Dr. John (1975).

COOPER, LINDSAY String bass. Session for Mike Oldfield (1973-74).

COOPER, RALPH Drums. Member of Air Supply.

COOPER, RAY Percussion. Began with Elton John in 1971, before becoming a full time member of his backup group, 1974-78. Session for Long John Baldry (1972); Donovan (1973); Nilsson (1972); Rod Stewart (1974); the Rolling Stones (1974); Rick Wakeman (1972); Jon Kongos (1972); Vigrass and Osborne (1972); Carly Simon (1972); Pilot (1972); Bryan Ferry (1977); Chris Spedding (1977-78); Kevin Lamb (1978); Mike Batt (1979); Wings (1979); George Harrison (1979); Runner (1979); Anthony Phillips (1979).

COOPER, RICHARD Guitar, vocal. Member of the Cooper Brothers band since 1978.

COOPER, STEVE Bass. Member of Artful Dodger, 1975 to present.

COOPER BROTHERS Brian Cooper—bass, vocal; Richard Cooper—guitar, vocal; Terry King—steel guitar, vocal; Glen Bell—drums, vocal; Darryl Alquire—guitar, vocal; Charles Robertson III—flute, vocal (1979); Al Serwa—keyboards; Don Bregg—vocal (1978). *Albums:* Cooper Brothers (CPN 0206) 1978; Pitfalls of the Ballroom (CPN 0226) 1979.

COPELAND, STEWART Drums. Member of the Police since 1978.

COPELY, AL Piano. Member of Roomful of Blues, 1977.

COPLEY, JAMES Drums. Member of Upp, 1976.

COPPING, CHRIS Bass, organ. Replaced David Knights in Procol Harum in 1970 and remained on organ when Alan Cartwright joined the group, 1972-79.

COPPOLA, TOM Keyboards. Half of the Googie and Tom Coppola duet, 1980.

CORAL REEFER BAND Jimmy Buffett—guitar, vocal; Reggie Young—guitar; Doyle Gresham—pedal steel guitar; Tommy Cogbill—bass; Mike Utley—keyboards; Sammy Taylor—harmonica; Ferrel Morris—percussion; Sammy Creason—drums; Larry Fiel—guitar (1974); Steve Goodman—guitar (1974); Roger Bartlett—guitar (1974). Backup band for Jimmy Buffett. See Jimmy Buffett.

CORBETT, MIKE Flute, percussion, vocal. Half of the Corbett and Hirsch team, 1971. Session for Henry Gross (1976).

CORBETT AND HIRSCH Mike Corbett—flute, percussion; Jay Hirsch—guitar, keyboards, mandolin, accordion. Vocal duet of 1971, assisted by John Siomos on drums and Hugh McCracken. *Album:* Corbett and Hirsch with Hugh McCracken (ACO) 1971.

CORBETTA, JERRY Keyboards, vocal, writer. Original member of Sugarloaf. *Album:* Jerry Corbetta (WBR K-3230) 1978.

CORBIN, WARREN Vocal. Member of the Cleftones.

CORBITT, JERRY Guitar, bass. Original member of the Youngbloods, 1967-68.

CORBY, MICHAEL Guitar, keyboards. Member of the Babys, 1977 to present.

CORDASCO, JERRY Drums, vocal. Member of the Stanky Brown Group, 1975-76.

CORDELL, DENNY Producer. Produced Procol Harum (1968); Leon Russell (1970); Tom Petty (1978). Session for Freddie King.

COREA, CHICK Keyboards, writer, producer. Prior to organizing "Return To Forever," 1972-78, he was one of the most sought after jazz pianists in the business, and for good reason. His ability is matched only by his imagination and innovation. He is recognized internationally as one of the foremost pianists to bridge the gap between rock and jazz. See Return To Forever. Session for Stanley Clarke (1975); Richard Davis (1975). *Albums:* Chick Corea Is (SLS 18055); Outback (CTI 6014); Crystal Silence (ECM 1024 ST) 1973; Romantic Warrior, 1976; Round Trip, 1971; Arc (ECM 1-1009) 1971; Bliss (MUS 5011); Circle/Paris Concert (ECM 1018/19); Circling In (BLN LWB-472) 1975; Circulus (BLN LWB-882); Chick Corea (BLN LWB-395) 1975; Chick Corea/Bill Evans—Sessions (VRV 2-2510); Chick Corea, Herbie Hancock, Keith Jarrett, McCoy Tyner (ATC 1696); Delphi, Vol. 1 (POL 1-6208) 1979; Duet (ECM 1-1140); Evening with Herbie Hancock and Chick Corea (COL PC1-35663); Friends (POL 1-6160); Mad Hatter (POL 1-6130) 1978; My Spanish Heart (POL 2-9003) 1976; Piano Giants (PRS 324052); Piano Improvisations, Vol. 1 (ECM 1014) 1971; Piano Improvisations, Vol. 2 (ECM 1020) 1972; Secret Agent (POL K-6176) 1978; Song of Singing (BLN LT-84353); Tap Step (WBR K-3425) 1980; Leprechaun (POL 606Z) 1976; Inner Space (ACO SD 2-305); Live in New York (DXF 3005) 1974.

CORI, GEORGE Washtub bass. Member of David Peel's Lower East Side, 1969.

CORLEY, ROBIN DAVID Saxophone, vocal. Member of Platinum Hook since 1979.

CORNELISON, BUZZ Keyboards, trumpet, vocal. Member of Exile since 1973.

CORNELIUS, RON Guitar. Session for Bob Dylan (1970).

CORNICK, GLENN Bass, keyboards, producer. Original member of Paris, 1975, with Fleetwood Mac's Robert Welch. Began in Jethro Tull, 1968-71, went to Wild Turkey, 1972, and replaced Gerald Luciano in Karthago, 1974. Produced April Wine, 1974.

CORNISH, GENE Guitar, bass. Original member of the Rascals, 1965-69, and Fotomaker, 1978-79.

CORNWELL, HUGH Guitar, vocal. Member of the Stranglers.

CORONADO, JULIO Member of Seatrain.

CORR, MICHAEL Vocal. Member of the Cats, 1980.

CORRACCIO, RICK Bass. Member of DMZ, 1978.

CORREA, DONNA Vocal. Session for George Duke (1975).

CORREA, MAILTO Congas. Session for Ray Manzarek.

CORREA, WILLIE Drums. Session for Rod Stewert (1975).

CORRERO, JOE Drums. Replaced Jim Valley in Paul Revere and the Raiders, until 1969. Session for Jennifer Warnes (1976); the Alpha band (1977).

CORRIGAN, BRIAN Guitar, vocal. Member of the New York Rock and Roll Ensemble, 1968-69.

CORSO, GREGORY Harmonium. Session for the Fugs (1967).

CORTESE, DOM Mandolin, accordion. Session for Bob Dylan (1975).

CORTEZ, DAVE "BABY" Keyboards. Recorded "The Happy Organ," 1959.

CORTEZ, DEAN Bass. Member of Caldera, 1976-78, and the Strand, 1980.

CORWIN, TOM Drums. Member of the Ohio Express, 1968-69.

CORY, JOHN Keyboards, vocal. Session for St. Paradise (1979).

CORYELL, LARRY Guitar, bass, vocal, writer. Are the fingers faster than the eye? Listening to Coryell, one is convinced. He was an original member of the Gary Burton Quartet before going out on his own. After several solo albums, he formed the Eleventh House to showcase his jazz talents. *Albums:* Barefoot Boy (FLD 10139) 1971; Fairyland (MEG 607) 1974; Back Together Again (ATC 18220); Basics (VAN 79375); Blue Montreux (ARI 4224); Coryell (VAN 6547) 1969; Larry Coryell and the Brubeck Brothers (DOR 109); Larry Coryell and the Eleventh House at Montreux (VAN 79410) 1974; Coryell at the Village Gate (VAN 6573); Eleventh House Larry Coryell (VAN 79342); Essential (VAN VSD-75/76) 1975; Guitar Player (MCA 8012); Lady Coryell (VAN 6509); Offering (VAN 79319) 1972; Real Great Escape (VAN 79329) 1973; Restful Mind (VAN 79353) 1975; Return (VAN 79426) 1979; Spaces (VAN 79345); Splendid (ELK 6E-153) 1978; Twin House (ELK 6E-123) 1977; Two for the Road (ARI 4156); Young Django (PAU 7041); Planet End (VAN 79367) 1975.

COSENTINO, CURT Bass, synthesizer. Member of Polyrock, 1980.

COSGROVE, TOMMY Vocal. Session for the Congregation.

COSKER, PETE Guitar, vocal, bass. Member of Wally, 1975.

COSMIC ORCHESTRA See Neil Norman and his Cosmic Orchestra.

COSMO Guitar. Member of Kids, 1975.

COSMO, FRAN Vocal. Session for Barry Goudreau (1980).

COSMOLOGY Dawn Thomson—vocal; Bob Jospe—drums; John D'Earth—horns; Dave Glenn—trombone; Armen Donelian—keyboards; Rick Kilburn—bass. *Album:* Cosmology (VAN 79394) 1977.

COSSA, LOU Keyboards, vocal. Member of Dakota, 1980.

COSTA, RUDY Saxophone, flute. Session for Taj Mahal (1977).

COSTELLO, ELVIS Guitar, vocal. Real name: Declan McManus. With Presley's name and Buddy Holly's glasses, this prolific writer/performer began his climb to fame in 1977 with abundant publicity. See the Attractions. *Albums:* Armed Forces (COL JC-35709) 1978; Get Happy (COL JC-36347) 1980; My Aim Is True (COL JC-35037) 1977; This Year's Model (COL JC-35331) 1978; Taking Liberties (COL JC-36839) 1980.

COSTELLO, NICK Bass. Member of Centaurus, and Toronto, 1980.

COSTER, TOM Keyboards, vocal, writer, producer. Member of Santana, 1972 to present. Session for Santana (1979).

COTINOLA, FRANK Drums, percussion. Member of the Funky Kings, 1976.

COTT, GERRY Member of the Boomtown Rats since 1977.

COTTEN, MIKE Synthesizer. Member of the Tubes, 1975 to present.

COTTON, JAMES Harmonica, vocal. Founder of the blues band that bears his name since 1966. See James Cotton Blues Band. Session for Otis Spann; Muddy Waters (1954-66, 1979); Steve Miller (1976). *Albums:* Best of the Blues, Vol. 2 (SQN 124); Chicago Breakdown (TKM 7071); Cut You Loose (VAN 79283); Taking Care of Business (CAP SM-814).

JAMES COTTON BLUES BAND James Cotton—harmonica, vocal; Luther Tucker—guitar; Bob Anderson—bass; Albert Gianquinto—piano; Francis Clay—drums. Mississippi born, Cotton ran away from home at the age of nine and wound up in Memphis. He played with Muddy Waters until 1966, when he formed his own band for the very popular blues market. An example of the citified country blues, he is a respected member of the second generation blues artists. *Albums:* Cut You Loose (VAN 79283); 100 Per Cent Cotton (BUD 5620); Chicago/the Blues/Today (VAN 792217); James Cotton Blues Band (BUD) 1967; Pure Cotton (BUD) 1968.

COTTON, JEFF Guitar. Member of Captain Beefheart and His Magic Band, 1968.

COTTON, MIKE Trumpet. Member of the Kinks, 1971-72. Session for Chris Youlden (1974).

COTTON, PAUL Guitar, vocal. Member of the Illinois Speed Press, 1969-70, and Poco.

COTTONWOOD SOUTH Tomi Lee Bradley—vocal; Jackie Danzat—vocal; Gary Walker—vocal; Angel South—guitar; Eddy Reynolds—keyboards; Dan Dorion—bass; Dexter Girourard—drums. *Album:* Cottonwood South (COL) 1974.

COUCHLAN, RICHARD Drums, percussion. Member of Caravan, 1971-73.

COUCHOIS, CHRIS Vocal, percussion. Member of Couchois since 1979.

COUCHOIS, MICHAEL Drums, vocal. Namesake of Couchois since 1979.

COUCHOIS, PAT Drums, guitar, vocal. Replaced Steve Rumph in T.I.M.E., 1968. Member of Couchois since 1979.

COUCHOIS Chas Carlson—keyboards, vocal; Howard Messer—bass, vocal; Pat Couchois—guitar, vocal; Chris Couchois—vocal, percussion; Michael Couchois—drums, vocal. *Albums:* Couchois (WBR K-3289) 1979; Nasty Hardware (WBR BSK 3420) 1980.

COUGAR, JOHN Vocal. *Albums:* John Couger (RVA 7401); Nothin' Matters and What If It Did (RVA 7403) 1980.

COUGHLAN, JAMES Drums. Original member of Status Quo, 1965-present.

COUGHLIN, JACK LINCOLN Real name of Preacher Jack.

COULAM, ROGER Keyboards. Member of Blue Mink.

COULSON, DENNIS Keyboards, vocal. Original member of McGuiness Flint, and Lo and Behold, 1972.

COULTER, ALAN Drums, percussion. Session for Matthew Fisher (1974).

COULTER, CLIFF Tambourine. Session for B. B. King (1972).

COUNTRY JOE AND THE FISH Joe McDonald—vocal, guitar, percussion, writer; Barry Melton—vocal, guitar, writer; David Cohen—guitar, organ; Bruce Barthol—bass, harpsichord; Chicken Hirsh—drums; Paul Armstrong—bass, percussion (1965); Carvel Bass—guitar (1965); John Francis Gunning—drums (1966); Mark Ryan—bass (1968); Greg Dewey—drums (1969); Doug Metzer—bass (1969); Mark Kapner—keyboards (1969). 1969: Haight-Ashbury, Timothy Leary, the draft, and Country Joe and the Fish. From Berkeley to Woodstock, one of the great underground bands that managed fame with their uncommercial image. *Albums:* C. J. Fish (VAN 6555); Electric Music for the Mind and Body (VAN 79244); Greatest Hits (VAN 6545); Here We Are Again (VAN 79299); I Feel Like I'm Fixin' to Die (VAN 79266); Life and Times of Country Joe and the

Fish (VAN VSD-27/28); Reunion (FSY 9530) 1977; Together (VAN 79277); Tonight I'm Singing Just for You (VAN 6557); Essential (VSD 85/86) 1976; Love Is a Fire (FSY 9511) 1976; Rock 'N' Roll Music from the Planet Earth (FSY 9544) 1978; Early Years (AMR 3309) 1978; Incredibler Live (VAN 79316) 1972; Goodbye Blues (FSY 9925) 1977; Leisure Sweet (FSY 9586) 1979.

COURSON, BRUCE Keyboards. Member of the Bill Blue Band, 1979.

COURTNEY, LOU Vocal. Replaced Ron Townson in the Fifth Dimension.

COURY, JOHN Guitar, keyboards, flute, vocal. Original member of Sky, 1970-71.

COUSINS, DAVID Vocal, guitar, banjo. Member of the Strawbs. Session for Rick Wakeman (1972); Def Leppard (1980). *Album:* Two Weeks Last Summer.

COUSINS, RICHARD Bass. Member of the Robert Cray Band, 1980.

COVERDALE, DAVID Vocal. Replaced Ian Gillan in Deep Purple, 1974-75. Founded Whitesnake, 1978 to present. *Album:* Snakebite (UAR LT 915) 1978.

COVINGTON, JOEY Drums, percussion. Session for the Jefferson Airplane (1969); Peter Kaukonen (1977).

COWART, HAROLD Bass. Member of John Fred and the Playboy Band, and Elephant, 1975. Session for the Bee Gees (1979); Andy Gibb (1980).

COWBOY Scott Boyer—guitar, vocal, violin; Bill Pillmore—piano, guitar, vocal (1971-73) Tommy Talton—guitar, vocal; George Clark—bass, vocal (1971-73); Tom Wynn—drums (1971-73); Pete Kowalkie—guitar, vocal; Arch Pearson—bass (1977); Chip Condon—keyboards (1977); Chip Miller—drums (1977); *Albums:* Cowboy, 1973; Five'll Getcha Ten, 1971; Why Quit While Yer Ahead; Cowboy, 1977.

COWBOYS INTERNATIONAL Terry Chimes—drums; Jimmy Hughes—bass; Evan Charles—piano; Rick Jacks—guitar; Ken Lockie—vocal. *Album:* The Original Sin (VIR 13138) 1979.

COWLING, PETER "MARS" Bass. Member of Pat Traver's Band, 1979.

COWSILL, BARRY Vocal, bass. Member of the Cowsills.

COWSILL, BILL Vocal, guitar. Member of the Cowsills.

COWSILL, BOB Vocal, guitar. Member of the Cowsills.

COWSILL, JOHN Vocal, drums. Member of the Cowsills.

COWSILL, SUSAN Vocal. Member of the Cowsills.

COWSILLS John Cowsill—vocal, drums; Bob Cowsill—vocal, guitar; Barry Cowsill—vocal, bass; Bill Cowsill—vocal, guitar; Susan Cowsill—vocal. Uninspired, wholesome family rock, a predecessor of the Brady Bunch, Partridge Family and others. *Albums:* Cowsills (MGM) 1967; We Can Fly (MGM) 1968; Captain Sad and His Ship of Fools (MGM) 1968; Best of the Cowsills (MGM) 1968; On My Side (MGM).

COX, ANDY Member of the English Beat, 1980.

COX, BILLY Bass. Replaced Noel Redding as bassist in the Jimi Hendrix's Experience, 1970. Session for J. J. Cale (1979).

COX, GARY Guitar. Member of Artful Dodger, 1975-present.

COX, GEOFF Drums. Member of Avalanche, 1976.

COX, HERBIE Vocal. Member of the Cleftones.

COX, IRV Saxophone. Session for the Jefferson Starship (1975).

COX, MICHAEL Guitar. Member of Eire Apparent, 1969.

COX, PETER Vocal. Session for Backstreet Crawler (1975); Jim Capaldi (1979).

COX, SAM Drums. Session for Taj Mahal.

COX, TERRY Drums. Original member of Pentangle, 1968-72. Started in Blues Incorporated. Session for Long John Baldry (1975); Bert Jansch; John Renbourn; Elton John (1969, 71).

COXTON, MIKE Keyboards. Member of Network, 1977.

CRABTREE, LEE Keyboards, flute. Member of the Fugs, 1966-67. Session for Pearls Before Swine (1968).

CRABTREE, ROGER Harmonica. Session for Waylon Jennings (1974-75).

CRACK THE SKY Jim Griffiths—guitar, vocal; Joe Macre—bass, vocal; John Palumbo—keyboards, guitar, vocal; Rick Witkowski—guitar, percussion; Joey d'Amico—drums. *Albums:* Crack the Sky (LFS) 1975; Safety in Numbers (LFS) 1977; Animal Notes, 1976.

CRACKIN Rick Chudacoff—bass, percussion, vocal; Bob Bordy—guitar, vocal; Leslie Smith—vocal, percussion; Arno Lucas—vocal, drums, percussion; George Clinton—keyboards, vocal; Brian Ray—guitar (1978). *Albums:* Crackin' (WBR B-3123) 1975; Makings of a Dream (WBR B-2989) 1977; Special Touch (WBR K-3235) 1978.

CRADDOCK, KEN Keyboards, guitar, vocal, percussion. Replaced Tommy Eyre in Mark-Almond, 1972. Member of Lindisfarne.

CRAFTSMEN Early name of Johnny and the Hurricanes.

CRAIG, JUDY Vocal. Member of the Chiffons.

CRAIG, PAT Keyboards, vocal. Member of the Tazmanian Devils, 1980.

CRAIN, BILL Guitar, vocal. Member of the Henry Paul Band since 1979.

CRAIN, TOM Guitar, vocal. Replaced Barry Barnes in the Charlie Daniels Band, 1975-80.

CRAMPS Lux Interior—vocal; Poison Ivy—guitar; Brian Gregory—guitar; Nick Knox—drums. *Album:* Songs the Lord Taught Us (IRS SP 007) 1980.

CRAMPTON, JEFFREY Guitar. Member of Rick Wakeman's backup group, 1975.

CRANE, JOE Piano. Member of the Hoodoo Rhythm Devils, 1973. Session for Sammy Hagar (1975).

CRANE, STEPHEN Bass, vocal. Member of Baby, 1975.

CRANE, VINCENT Keyboards, vocal, writer, arranger. Arranger and organist for the Crazy World of Arthur Brown, 1967, before forming Atomic Rooster, 1970-73. Session for Rory Gallagher (1971).

CRANEY, MARK Drums. Replaced Barriemore Barlow in Jethro Tull, 1980.

CRANNER, DENNIS Bass. Member of Catfish.

CRANSHAW, BOB Bass. Session for Paul Simon (1973).

LAMONT CRANSTON BAND Pat Hayes—vocal, harmonica; Larry Hayes—guitar; Bruce McCabe—keyboards; Tom Burneik—saxophone; Joe Chandler—saxophone; Joe Sheromahn—bass; Jim Novak—drums. *Album:* Specials, 1977.

CRARY, DAN Guitar. Member of Sundance, 1976.

CRAVIOTTO, JOHN Drums. Session for Ry Cooder (1972).

CRAWFORD, BILL Bass. Member of Crystal Mansion.

CRAWFORD, DAVE Keyboards, producer. Session and production for B. B. King (1973-74).

CRAWFORD, DIANA Vocal. Member of the Catfish Hodge Band, 1979.

CRAWFORD, JOHN Bass, vocal. Member of Berlin, 1980.

CRAWFORD, MICHAEL Guitar, vocal. Member of Wireless, 1979.

CRAWFORD, TONY Bass. Session for Junior Wells.

CRAWLER Geoff Whitehorn—guitar; Terry Wilson-Slesser—vocal; Terry Wilson—bass; Tony Braunagle—drums; John Bundrick—keyboard. Replacing cult hero Paul Kossoff in Backstreet Crawler was no easy task, but Geoff Whitehorn rose to the occasion. See Backstreet Crawler. *Albums:* Crawler (ACO) 1977; Snake, Rattle and Roll, 1978.

CRAWLEY, MARK Bass, vocal. Member of Limousene, 1972, and the Faith Band, 1977-79.

CRAY, ROBERT Guitar, vocal. Namesake of the Robert Cray Band, 1980.

ROBERT CRAY BAND Robert Cray—guitar, vocal; Curtis Salgado—harmonica, vocal; Richard Cousins—bass; David Olson—drums. *Album:* Who's Been Talkin' (TMT 7041) 1980.

CRAYTON, NAPOLEAN Vocal, keyboards. Member of the Band of Thieves, 1976.

CRAZY HORSE Ralph Molina—drums, vocal; Billy Talbot—bass; Jack Nitschke—piano, vocal; Danny Whitten—guitar (1971-72); Nils Lofgren—guitar, vocal; Greg Leroy—vocal, guitar; George Whitsell—vocal, cello, keyboards, harpsichord; Rick Curtis—vocal, guitar, banjo; Michael Curtis—vocal, keyboards, guitar; Karl Himmell—drums (1977); Tim Drummond—bass (1977); Ben Keith—dobro, guitar (1977); Frank Sampedro—guitar (1978-present). Originally Neil Young's backup band, they struck out on their own. Unfortunately, they did not gather an adequate following to stay together profitably. They re-formed in 1977 again to support Neil Young. *Albums:* Crazy Horse (REP 6431) 1971; Loose (RPS); American Stars 'n' Bars (RPS 2261) 1972; Crazy Horse at Crooked Lake (EPC E-31710); Crazy Moon (VIC AFLI-3054); Everybody Knows This Is Nowhere (RPS 6349) 1969; Zuma (RPS 2242) 1975.

CRAZY WORLD OF ARTHUR BROWN Vincent Crane—organ, writer; Drachian Theaker—drums; Sean Nicholas—bass; Arthur Brown—vocal, writer. In 1968, Brown appeared as the head of a highly electrified group, wearing maniacal costumes, makeup, and a hat of flames. He pranced on stage like an overactive stick man, screaming one moment and melodically crooning the next. With his hit "Fire," he was tagged the "God of Hell Fire," but burned out quickly. In 1972, Brown resurfaced as head of Arthur Brown's Kingdom Come. Crane had since become head of Atomic Rooster. See Arthur Brown. *Album:* Crazy World of Arthur Brown (TRK) 1968.

CREACH, PAPA JOHN Fiddle, vocal, writer. Discovered late in life by the Jefferson Airplane, he played on their albums as a member of the group in addition to building his solo career and accompanying Hot Tuna, 1971-72. *Albums:* Papa John Creach (GNT 1003) Filthy (GNT 1009) 1972; Playing My Fiddle for You (GNT 0418); Rock Father, 1976; I'm the Fiddle Man, 1975; Best of Papa John Creach (BUD 5707); Cat and the Fiddle (DJM 11) 1977; Inphasion (DJM 18) 1978.

CREAM Ginger Baker—drums, vocal, writer; Jack Bruce—bass, harpsichord, vocal, writer; Eric Clapton—guitar, vocal. 1967 saw the birth of heavy music and superstardom in the band known as Cream. A blending of talents that had "paid their dues" with the blues and jazz, they synthesized their combined knowledge with several watts to create an unequalled niche in rock history with their interpretive blues that literally lasted for hours. Their farewell concert was given 11/26/69. *Albums:* Disraeli Gears (ACO 33 232) 1967; Fresh Cream (ACO 33 206) 1967; Goodbye (ACO 7001) 1969; Live Cream (RSO 1-3014) 1968; Live Cream, Vol. 2 (RSO 1-3015) 1968; Wheels of Fire (RSO 2-3802) 1968.

CREAMER, LINDA Vocal. Session for Bob Seger (1980).

CREASMAN, GEORGE Bass, vocal. Member of Hotel since 1978.

CREASON, SAMMY Drums. Member of the Coral

Reefer Band. Session for Tony Joe White (1971); Rita Coolidge (1972); Geoff Muldaur (1978).

CREATION Carol Stallings—violin, vocal; Orlando Stallings—guitar, vocal; Gerry Peterson—reeds; Billy Gerst—trumpet; Jimmy Calhoun—bass; Leon Patillo—keyboards, vocal; Lenny Goldsmith—keyboards, vocal; Barry Frost—percussion. *Album:* Creation (ACO) 1974.

CREATION Shigeru Matsumoto—bass; Masayuki Higuchi—drums; Kazuo Takeda—guitar; Yoshiaki Iijima—guitar. After Mountain crumbled, Felix Pappalardi traveled to Japan to explore the Japanese rock scene. With his return to the States, he brought Creation, and recorded an album displaying the usual hard rock Pappalardi formula. *Album:* Felix Pappalardi and Creation (AAM) 1976.

CREED Chip Thomas—drums; Steve Ingle—vocal, guitar; Hal Butler—vocals, keyboards; James Flynn—bass; Luther Maben—guitar. *Album:* Creed (ASY 6E-146) 1978.

CREEDENCE CLEARWATER REVIVAL Doug Clifford—drums; Stu Cook—bass; John Fogerty—guitar, harpsichord, vocal, writer; Tom Fogerty—guitar. Early name: the Golliwogs. In 1968, Creedence exploded on the scene with "Suzie Q." Until 1972 they were constantly on the charts with their basic rock 'n' blues. *Albums:* Bayou Country (FSY 8387); Chronicle (FSY CCR-2); Cosmo's Factory (FSY 8402); Creedence Clearwater Revival (FSY 8382); Creedence Clearwater Revival—1968-1969 (FSY CCR-68) 1978; Creedence Clearwater Revival 1969 (FSY CCR-69) 1978; Creedence Clearwater Revival 1970 (FSY CCR-70) 1978; Creedence Gold (FSY 9418); Green River (FSY 8393); The Golliwogs (FSY 9474) 1975; Live in Europe (FSY CCR-1); Mardi Gras (FSY 9404) 1972; More Creedence Gold (FSY 9430); Pendulum (FSY 8410); Willie and the Poor Boys (FSY 8397).

CREEK, COSMO Pedal steel guitar. Member of Root Boy Slim's Sex Change Band, 1978.

CREGAN, JIM Guitar, vocal. Replaced Jean Paul Crocker in Cockney Rebel. Session for Rod Stewart (1977); the Rod Stewart Band (1978).

CREME, LOL Guitar, vocal. Member of 10 CC, 1974-76, before dueting with partner Kevin Godley, 1977-present. Session for Neil Sedaka (1975).

LOL CREME/KEVIN GODLEY Lol Creme—guitar, vocal; Kevin Godley—drums, percussion, vocal. Half of 10 CC who broke away in 1977. *Albums:* Consequences (MER SRM-3-1700) 1977; Freeze Frame (POL 1-6257) 1980; "L" (POL 1-6177) 1978.

CRESPO, JIMMY Guitar. Member of Flame, 1977. Session for Ian Lloyd.

CRESS, CURT Drums. Replaced Hans Bathelt in Triumvirat, 1977.

CRESSWELL, TONY Drums. Member of the Mandala Band, 1975, and Sad Cafe, 1978.

CRETONES Steve Beers—drums; Peter Bernstein—bass, vocal; Mark Goldenberg—guitar, vocal; Steve Leonard—keyboards, vocal. *Album:* Thin Red Line (PLA P-5) 1980.

CREWSON, ROY Member of Freddie and the Dreamers, 1962-66.

CRICKETS Jerry Allison—drums; Joe B. Mavloin—bass; Nick Sullivan—guitar. Buddy Holly's backup band. *Album:* Chirping Crickets, 1958.

CRICKETS Albert Lee—keyboards; Rick Grech—bass; Jerry Allison—drums; Sonny Curtis—guitar; Rick Van Maarth—guitar; Steve Krikorian—vocal. Post Buddy Holly band. *Album:* Remnants (VRV) 1973.

CRIDLIN, MAC Bass. Session for Taxxi (1980).

CRIGGER, DAVID Drums. Session for Julie Tippets and Brian Auger (1978).

CRIMSON TIDE Dale Perkins; Greg Straub; Richard Wolf; Bobby Delander; J. Jackson; Wayne Perkins—guitar. *Albums:* Crimson Tide (CAP SW-11806) 1978; Reckless Love (CAP ST-11939) 1979.

CRIOLIN, MAURICE Bass. Member of Elvin Bishop's Band, 1978.

CRISCIONE, JOHN Vocal, drums, percussion. Member of the Shirts, 1978-80.

CRISS, PETER Drums, vocal. Real name: Peter Crisscoula. Born 12/20/45. Member of Kiss, 1973-80. *Albums:* Kiss (CAS 7122/PIX-7122); Out of Control (CAS NOLP 7240) 1980.

CRISSINGER, ROGER Keyboards. Original member of Pearls Before Swine, 1967.

CRITICAL MASS Mick Fazz—vocal, guitar; David Owen—guitar; Henri Laplume—bass; Michael Barone—drums. *Album:* It's What's Inside That Counts (MCA 3260) 1980.

CRITTERS Chris Darway—autoharp; Kenny Gorka—bass; Jeff Pelosi—drums; Jim Ryan—guitar; Bob Spinella—organ. Original recorders of the John Sebastian song "Younger Girl," 1966. *Albums:* Younger Girl, 1966; Touch 'n' Go with the Critters.

CROCE, JIM Guitar, vocal, writer. Born 1/10/43. Country folk artist who died in an airplane crash at the peak of his popularity, 9/20/73. *Albums:* Jim Croce's Greatest Character Songs (LIF JZ-35571); Faces I've Been (LIF 900); I Got a Name (LIF JZ-35009); Life and Times (LIF JZ-35008); Photographs and Memories (LIF JZ-35010); Time in a Bottle (LIF JZ-35000); You Don't Mess Around with Jim.

CROCKER, JEAN PAUL Strings, mandolin, guitar. Member of Steve Harley's Cockney Rebel.

CROCKER, JOHN Clarinet. Session for Elton John (1978).

CROFT, CHARLES Guitar, percussion, vocal. Member of Upepo.

CROFTS, DASH Mandolin, vocal, writer. Half of Seals and Crofts.

CROMBIE, NOEL Percussion. Member of Split Enz.

CRONK, CHAS Bass, vocal. Member of the Strawbs. Session for Rick Wakeman (1972).

CROOKS, RICHARD Drums, percussion. Member of Dr. John's Band, and White Cloud, 1972. Session on Free Creek (1973); Roy Buchanan (1980).

CROON, DREW Guitar. Session for Jerry Lee Lewis (1973).

CROPPER, STEVE Guitar, producer. Original member of Booker T. and the MGs since 1962. Produced John Cougar, 1980. Session for Art Garfunkel; Otis Redding; Leon Russell (1975); Neil Sedaka (1975-76); Rod Stewart (1975-77); the Richie Furay Band (1976); Ringo Starr (1973-74); Mickey Thomas (1977); Roy Buchanan (1977); Yvonne Elliman (1978).

CROSBY, DAVID Vocal, guitar. An original member of the Byrds before becoming part of Crosby, Stills, Nash and Young, 1969-71. Member of the Seastones, 1976. Session for Jefferson Airplane (1969); Dave Mason; Steve Stills (1971, 75); Neil Young (1972, 73, 75); James Taylor (1976); Art Garfunkel; Hot Tuna (1972); John Sebastian (1970); Joni Mitchell (1975). *Album:* If I Could Only Remember My Name (ACO SO 7203) 1971.

CROSBY, ETHAN Vocal. Session for David Crosby (1971).

CROSBY AND NASH David Crosby—guitar, vocal, writer; Graham Nash—guitar, vocal, writer. The dissolve of Crosby, Stills, Nash and Young left the individuals to their solo careers and occasional partnerships, like Crosby and Nash's. *Albums:* Best of David Crosby and Graham Nash (MCA 1102); Graham Nash/David Crosby (ATC 72280) 1976; Wind on the Water (MCA D-902) 1976.

CROSBY, STILLS, NASH AND YOUNG David Crosby—guitar, vocal, writer; Steven Stills—piano, guitar, vocal, writer, bass; Graham Nash—guitar, vocal, writer; Neil Young—guitar, piano, vocal, writer; Dallas Taylor—drums, percussion (1969-70); Greg Reeves—bass (1970-71); John Barbata—drums, percussion (1970-71). Not since Cream had there been so much fuss over a supergroup. Crosby, from the Byrds, Stills from Buffalo Springfield, and Nash from the Hollies, teamed up to set standards for vocal harmonies that are still being followed today. They performed electrically and acoustically, most notably in the latter. Their first album (1969) was without Neil Young and laid the groundwork for their eagerly awaited "Deja Vu" in 1970. By then, the mere mention of their name meant a sold-out concert date. The dynamic individuality in the group, however, cut their longevity as a band, and in 1971 they disbanded in favor of solo careers, not without helping each other in session roles. They regrouped in 1977 for an audience that had not forgotten them. Performed at Woodstock, 1969. Part of "No Nukes," 1979. *Albums:* Crosby, Stills and Nash (ATC 19117) 1977; Crosby, Stills and Nash (ATC 19104) 1969; Deja Vu (ATC 19118) 1970; Four Way Street (ATC 2-902) 1971; So Far (ATC 19119); Replay (ATC SD 16026) 1980.

CROSS, BILLY Guitar. Member of Topaz, 1977. Session for Bob Dylan (1978-79); Link Wray (1979); Hilly Michaels (1980).

CROSS, CHRIS Bass, vocal. Member of Ultra Vox since 1977.

CROSS, CHRISTOPHER Vocal, guitar. *Album:* Christopher Cross (WBR K-3383) 1980.

CROSS, DAVID Violin, viola, mellotron. Replaced Mel Collins in King Crimson, 1972-75.

CROSSFIRES Early name of the Turtles.

CROSSLEY, BRUCE Guitar, vocal. Member of Chuck and the Tigers, 1980.

CROSSLEY, CHARLOTTE Vocal. Session for Boz Scaggs (1980).

CROSSLEY, KEVIN Keyboards. Session for Mark-Almond (1973).

CROSSWINDS Mike Selvidge—drums, percussion; Don Mock—guitar, vocal; Arthur Dunn—keyboards; Tom Peck—vocal; Melinda Mohn—vocal. *Album:* Crosswinds.

CROUCH, SANDRA Tambourine. Session for Janis Joplin (1969).

CROW, JERRY Bass. Member of Denim, 1977, and Traveller.

CROWE, GEORGE Bass, percussion. Member of the Invaders.

CROWDER, GAYLE Vocal. Session for Skafish (1980).

CROWDER, NAWSA Vocal. Member of Black Grass, 1972.

CROWE, DAVE Drums. Member of the Public Image since 1979.

CROWE, GEORGE Bass, percussion. Member of the Invaders, 1980.

CROWELL, RODNEY Guitar, vocal. Session for Jonathan Edwards (1976-77). *Albums:* Ain't Living Long Like This (WBR K-3228) 1978; But What Will the Neighbors Think (WBR K-3407) 1980; Honky Tonkin' (VIC AHLI-3422).

CROWL, CHUCK Member of Jay and the Techniques.

CROWLEY, J. C. Keyboards, vocal, guitar. Member of Player since 1977.

CROWTHER, PETE Bass, keyboards, guitar. Member of Mr. Big, 1975, and Broken Home, 1980.

CROWTHER, PHIL Drums. Member of the Andy Fernbach Connexion.

CROY, DENNIS Bass. Member of the Ravens since 1979.

CROY, RICK Drums. Member of the Ravens since 1979.

CRUDUP, ARTHUR "BIG BOY" Guitar, vocal, writer. Blues singer and writer of the 1930s and

1940s. Died 1974.

CRUIKSHANK, PETER ROLAND Bass. Born 7/2/45. Original member of the Groundhogs, 1968-74.

CRUMP, BRUCE Drums. Born 7/17/47. Member of Molly Hatchet since 1978.

CRUMP, MARK Drums. Replaced Dave Poole in the Bill Blue Band, 1980.

CRUNCHY CRYSTALS Guitar. Member of Fruit, 1970-72.

CRUZ, JAVIER Keyboards, synthesizer, vocal. Member of Skafish, 1980.

CRUZ, LITO Horns, vocal. Member of Please, 1976.

CRUZ, RAFAEL Percussion. Member of Raices, 1975. Session for Tommy Bolin (1975); Frank Carillo (1978); Ray Gomez (1980).

CRUZER, BEEGIE Keyboards. Session for J. J. Cale (1974).

CRUZIER, LARRY Keyboards. Member of Black Sheep, 1975.

CRYERS Lowry Hamner—vocal, guitar, piano; Lee Townsend—vocal, guitar, piano, saxophone; Clay Barnes—vocal, guitar; Tom Ethridge—bass; Billy Mintz—drums. See Lowry Hamner and the Cryers. *Album:* Cryers (MER SRM 1 3734) 1978.

CRYSLER, KEN Drums. Member of Starbuck, 1977-78.

CRYSTAL, LEE Drums. Session for Sylvain Sylvain (1979).

CRYSTAL MANSION Rick Morley—percussion; Sal Rota—keyboards, vocal; Ronnie Gentile—guitar; Mario Sanchez—conga, vocal; Bill Crawford—bass; Johnny Caswell—vocal, piano; Peter Tannetti—keyboards; Dave White—vocal, keyboards; Tom Herzer—guitar. *Albums:* Crystal Mansion, 1972; Crystal Mansion (TWC 588) 1979.

CSERNITS, BILLY Keyboards. Backup for Mitch Ryder, 1978-79.

CUA, RICK Bass, vocal. Replaced Harvey Arnold in the Outlaws, 1980.

CUBER, RONNIE Saxophone. Session for Dr. John (1978); John Mayall (1979); Grace Slick (1980); Steely Dan (1980).

CUCURULLO, WARREN Guitar, vocal. Session for Frank Zappa (1979).

CUFFLEY, JOHN Drums, percussion, vocal. Replaced George Newsome in the Climax Blues Band, 1973 to present.

CUKRAS, WAYNE Bass, vocal. Member of the Love Affair, 1980.

CULLEN, WAYNE Drums, vocal. Member of the Dudes, 1975.

CUMMING, BRYAN Bass, guitar, saxophone, trumpet, percussion, vocal. Session for Martin Mull (1975, 77).

CUMMINGS, BURTON Vocal, keyboards, writer. Born 12/31/47. Original member of the Guess Who, 1969-76. *Albums:* California Dreaming (AIE 3001); Burton Cummings (POR PR-34261) 1976; Dream of a Child (POR JR-35481) 1978; My Own Way To Rock (POR PR-34698) 1977; Voices (PNT 9002).

CUMMINGS, DONNIE Bass. Member of Doucette, 1979.

CUMMINGS, GEORGE Vocal, guitar. Born 7/28/38. Member of Dr. Hook.

CUMMINGS, STEPHEN Vocal. Member of the Sports since 1979.

CUMMINS, DAVID Guitar, vocal. Member of Taxxi, 1980.

CUNNINGHAM, BILLY Bass. Member of the Box Tops, 1965-68.

CUNNINGHAM, BLAIR Drums, vocal. Session for Robert Johnson (1978).

CUNNINGHAM, CARL Vocal. Original member of the Bar-Kays. Died in the Otis Redding plane crash, 12/10/67.

CUNNINGHAM, CASEY Drums. Member of the Bones, 1973.

CUNNINGHAM, DAVID Vocal, keyboards, bass, drums. Records under the name the Flying Lizards since 1979.

CUNNINGHAM, MATTHEW Dulcimer. Session for John Lennon (1980).

CUNNINGHAM, RON Vocal, keyboards. Member of Law, 1977.

CUNNINGHAM, RONNIE LEE Keyboards. Session for Phoenix (1979).

CUOMO, BILL Keyboards, vocal. Member of Bonaroo, 1975, C.O.D., 1979, Photoglo, 1980, and In Transit, 1980. Session for Gene Clark (1974).

CUOMO, JIM Session for Marianne Faithfull (1979); Magnet (1979).

CURE Robert Smith—guitar, vocal; Michael Dempsey—bass, vocal; Lol Tolhurst—drums. *Album:* Boys Don't Cry (PVC 7916) 1980.

CURNVITE, JIM Guitar, keyboard, vocal. Member of Phaze Shifter, 1980.

CURRIE, BILLY Violin, keyboards. Member of Ultravox, 1977-present, and Visage, 1980.

CURRIE, CHERIE Vocal, piano. Member of the Runaways, 1976, and half of the Currie Sisters, 1979.

CURRIE, GEORGE Vocal. Member of the Darts since 1978.

CURRIE, LAURIE Drums, vocal. Member of Aeriel, 1978.

CURRIE, MARIE Vocal. Half of the Currie Sisters, 1979.

CURRIE SISTERS Cherie Currie—vocal; Marie Currie—vocal. *Album:* Messin' with the Boys (CAP ST-12022) 1979.

CURRY, MICKEY Drums. Member of the Yankees, 1978.

CURRY, STEVE Session for Chris Spedding (1978).

CURRY, TIM Vocal. *Albums:* Fearless (AAM 4773); Read My Lips (AAM 4717) 1978.

CURTIS, CED Member of Rare Bird, 1972.

CURTIS, CHRIS Original member of the Searchers 1960-64.

CURTIS, CLEM Vocal. Member of the Foundations, 1968.

CURTIS, IAN Vocal. Voice of Joy Division, 1979-80. Committed suicide, 1980.

CURTIS, JOHN Guitar. Member of the Pousette-Dart Band since 1977.

CURTIS, KING Saxophone. Real name: Curtis Ousley. Died 1971. Session for Aretha Franklin (1970); John Lennon (1971); Gary Wright (1971). *Albums:* Best of King Curtis (ACO 266) 1968; Best of King Curtis (CAP SM-11963); Best of King Curtis (PRS 7775) 1968; Blues at Montreux (ATC 1637); King Curtis Live at Fillmore West (ACO 359); Golden Soul (ATC 18198); Jazz Groove (PRS 7789) 1967; Soul Meeting (PRS 7833) 1970; Soul Serenade (CAP SM-11798).

CURTIS, MICHAEL Vocal, keyboards, guitar. Member of Crazy Horse.

CURTIS, NICK Vocal. Session for Donovan (1973).

CURTIS, PHIL Bass. Member of the Kiki Dee Band, 1973-74, the Tiger, 1976, and the Vapour Trails, 1980.

CURTIS, RICK Vocal, guitar, banjo. Member of Crazy Horse.

CURTIS, SONNY Guitar, vocal. Member of the Crickets, 1973. Session for Eric Clapton (1970). *Albums:* Sonny Curtis (ELK 6E-227); Love Is All Around (ELK 6E-283).

CURTIS A Guitar, vocal. *Album:* Courtesy (TTR 8015) 1980.

CURULEWSKI, JOHN Guitar, synthesizer, autoharp, vocal. Original member of Styx, 1970-79.

CURVED AIR Sonja Kristina—vocal; Darryl Way —violin, vocal (1970-73); Francis Monkman—guitar, keyboards; Robert Martin—bass; Florian Pilkington—drums. *Albums:* Air Conditioning (WBR) 1970; 2nd Album (WBR) 1971; Phantasmagoria (WBR); Air Cut; Live; Midnight Wire; Airborne; The Very Best of Curved Air.

CUSANO, VINNIE Guitar, vocal. Member of Treasure, 1977.

CUTHALL, DICK Flugelhorn. Member of the Specials since 1979. Session for XTC (1979).

CUTLER, CHRIS Drums. Member of Henry Cow, 1973.

CUTLER, CHRIS Guitar, vocal. Original member of Live Wire, 1977.

CUTLER, IVOR Vocal. Session for Robert Wyatt (1974).

CUTLER, RICK Drums, percussion. Member of Show of Hands, 1970.

CYRKLE Don Dannemann—guitar; Tom Dawes —guitar, banjo, harmonica, sitar; Marty Fried—drums; Mike Losekamp—keyboards. They had been together since 1962 but under the management of Brian Epstein, and with a song co-written by Paul Simon, the Cyrkle hit the charts in 1966 with "Red Rubber Ball." "Turn Down Day" (1966), their follow-up, kept their names on the charts, but not for long. *Albums:* Red Rubber Ball, 1966; Neon, 1967.

CZUKAY, HOLGER Bass. Member of Can, 1975.

D'ABO, MIKE Keyboards, vocal. Born 3/1/44. Replaced Paul Jones as a member of Manfred Mann in 1966. Played King Herod in "Jesus Christ Superstar," 1970. Session for Rod Stewart (1970). *Albums:* Broken Rainbows (AAM) 1974; Down at Rachel's Place.

D'ALEO, ANGELO Original member of Dion and the Belmonts.

D'AMATO, MARIA Vocal, percussion. Maiden name of Maria Muldaur. Original member of the Even Dozen Jug Band before going into Jim Kweskin's Jug Band, 1962-68. See Maria Muldaur.

D'AMICO, JOEY Drums. Member of Crack the Sky, 1975-77.

D'AMICO, TONY Vocal. Session for Steve Hunter (1977).

D'AMORE, JACK Drums, vocal. Member of Rock Rose, 1979.

D'ARROW, PHILIP Vocal. *Albums:* Phillip D'Arrow (POL 1-6210) 1979; Sub Zero (POL 1-6271) 1980.

D'EARTH, JOHN Horns. Member of Cosmology, 1977.

D'ELIA, JOE Piano. Session for Grace Slick (1980).

D.O.A. Chuck Biscuits—drums; Joe Shithead—guitar; Randy Rampage—bass. Canadian punk trio. *Albums:* Live Triumph (FRS 001) 1979; Something Better Change (FRS 003) 1980.

DA COSTA, PAULINHO Percussion. Session for Rod Stewart (1977, 78, 80); Robin Trower (1978); Lee Ritenour (1978); Gary Wright (1979); Martin Mull (1979); Dr. John (1979); Elton John (1979); Nazareth (1980); Vapour Trails (1980). *Albums:* Agora (PAB 2310785) 1977; Pablo Today—Happy People (PAB 2312102) 1979; Tudo Bem (PAB 2310824) 1978.

DACUS, DONNIE Guitar, vocal, writer. Session for Steve Stills (1975-76).

DACY, JEFF Member of the Candlestick Brass, 1977.

DAD FROM MEMPHIS One-string fiddle. Session with Poor Joe Williams (1935).

DADDY COOL Ross Wilson—vocal, harmonica, guitar, writer; Ross Hannaford—vocal, guitar; Wayne Duncan—vocal, bass; Gary Young—vocal, drums; Ian Winters—guitar (1972). Australian rock group that made a dent in the rock field with their infectious original 1950-ish songs. *Albums:* Daddy Who? Daddy Cool (RPS RS6471) 1971; Teenage Heaven (RPS MS 1088) 1972.

DADDY, GRAHAM Vocal. Member of the Ravers.

DAFFERN, WILLY Vocal. Member of Hunger before replacing Rod Evans in Captain Beyond, 1977.

DAGGER, MIKE Vocal, flute. Member of the Thunderhead, 1976.

DAGREAZE, DEWEY Drums, vocal. Member of Marty Balin's Jefferson Airplane on "Bodacious."

DAHAN, PIERRE-ALAIN Vocal, drums, percussion. Member of Voyage.

DAHME, JIM Vocal, flute, guitar. Member of Elizabeth, 1968.

DAISLEY, BOB Bass, vocal. Member of Stan Webb's Chicken Shack, 1973, Widowmaker, 1976, and Ritchie Blackmore's Rainbow, replacing Mark Clarke, 1978. Member of the Blizzard of Ozz, 1980. Session for Sean Tyla (1980).

DAKING, GEOFF Drums. Member of the Blues Magoos.

DAKOTA Jerry Hludzik—guitar, vocal; Bill Kelly—guitar, vocal; Lou Cossa—keyboards, vocal; Jeff Mitchell—keyboards, vocal; Bill McHale—bass, vocal. *Album:* Dakota (COL JC-36261) 1980.

DAKOTAS Backup band for Billy J. Kramer, 1963-65. See Billy J. Kramer and the Dakotas.

DALBY, ANDY Guitar, writer. Member of Arthur Brown's Kingdom Come, 1973-74, and Vapour Trails, 1980. Session for Arthur Brown (1975).

DALE, ERIC ALLEN Trombone. Member of the Foundations, 1968.

DALE, PAUL Vocal. Member of Marseille, 1980.

DALE, ROBIN Bass, vocal. Member of S.R.C.

DALER, BOBBY Drums. Member of Hollywood Stars, 1977.

DALL'ENESE, GILBERT Reeds. Session for Paice, Ashton, Lord (1977).

DALTON, GARY Guitar, bass, vocal, clarinet. Member of Dalton and Dubarri since 1973.

DALTON, JOHN Bass. Replaced Peter Quaife in the Kinks, 1970-79.

DALTON, LACY J. Vocal. *Albums:* Lacy J. Dalton (COL NJC-36322) 1980; Hard Times (COL JC-36763) 1980.

DALTON AND DUBARRI Kent Dubarri—percussion, vocal; Gary Dalton—guitar, bass, vocal, clarinet. *Albums:* Dalton and Dubarri, 1973; Good Head, 1974; Success and Failure (CHC HKT 19226) 1979.

DALTRY, DAVID Guitar, vocal. Played on "Joseph and the Amazing Technicolor Dreamcoat," 1971.

DALTRY, ROGER Vocal. Born 3/1/44. Original member of the Who, since 1965, and soloist. Session for "Tommy" (1972). *Albums:* Daltry (MCA

2349); McVicar (POL 1-6284) 1980; One of the Boys (MCA 2271); Ride a Rock Horse (MCA 2147).

DALY, JEFF Baritone and alto saxophones. Member of Candlestick Brass, 1977. Session for Kevin Lamb (1979).

DALY, JOSEPH Tuba, trombone. Session for Taj Mahal.

DAMBRA, JOEY Vocal. Session for John Lennon (1974).

DAMERST, MARCUS Vocal, guitar. Member of the Arthur Gee-Whiz Band, 1971-72.

DAMIANI, CHIP Drums. Member of the Remains, 1965-67.

DAMMERS, JERRY Keyboards, producer. Member of the Specials since 1979.

DAMNED Captain Sensible—guitar, vocal, keyboards; Rat Scabies—drums, vocal, guitar; Paul Grey—bass; David Vanian—vocal. *Album:* The Damned (IRS SP 70012) 1980.

DAMRELL, JOSEPH Bass, sitar, percussion, vocal. Member of Kak.

DANAHER, THOMAS Vocal, guitar. Co-founder of Autosalvage, 1966-68.

DANCE BAND See the Johnny Average Dance Band.

DANCER Carl Dante—vocal, bass; Jonathan Doglas—vocal, keyboards; Ian Espinoza—vocal, guitar. *Album:* Dancer (AAM) 1976.

DANCHO, DANTE Guitar. Member of Jay and the Techniques, 1967-68.

DANDY, JIM See Jim Mangrum.

DANELLI, DINO Drums, producer. Original member of the Rascals, 1965-69, and member of Fotomaker, 1978-79. Produced April Wine, 1974.

DANGEL, RICHARD Member of the Wailers.

DANIEL, GREGG Bass. Member of Kenny and the Kasuals.

DANIEL, KENNY Vocal, harmonica, guitar, bass. Member of Kenny and the Kasuals, 1965.

DANIELS, CHARLIE Bass, guitar, fiddle, writer, vocal, banjo. Born 10/28/36. Country western sideman of the 1960s who rose to star stature with the popularity of Southern rock in the 1970s as a soloist and with his own band. See Charlie Daniels Band. Session for Bob Dylan (1969-70); Marshall Tucker Band (1974-77); Elvin Bishop (1974); Ringo Starr (1971). *Albums:* Charlie Daniels (CAP ST-11414); Uneasy Rider (EPC E-34369).

CHARLIE DANIELS BAND Charlie Daniels—guitar, banjo, fiddle, vocal; Earl Grigsby—bass (1972); Jeffrey Meyer—drums (1972); Barry Barnes—guitar, vocal (1976-79); Joel di Gregorio—keyboards, vocal (1972-78); Mark Fitzgerald—bass (1976); Fred Edwards—drums (1975-79); Gary Allen—drums (1975); Tom Crain—guitar, vocal (1975-80); Don Murray—drums (1975-79); Charlie Hayward—bass (1977-80); James W. Marshall—drums (1979-80). With the popularity of the Allman Brothers country sound came a host of closely related sounds. One of them was the Charlie Daniels Band. Charlie Daniels, though, had been playing country music as a session man for years. *Albums:* Charlie Daniels (KMS 2060); Charlie Daniels (CAP ST 11414); Fire on the Mountain (KMS 2063) 1974; Honey in the Rock; Way Down Yonder (KMS 2067); Banded Together (EPC JE-36177); Fire on the Montain (EPC PE-34365); Full Moon (EPC FE-36571) 1980; High Lonesome (EPC PE-34377) 1976; Midnight Wind (EPC PE-34970) 1977; Million Mile Reflections (EPC JE-35751) 1979; Night Rider (EPC PE-34402) 1975; Saddle Tramp (EPC PE-34150) 1976; Te John, Grease and Wolfman (EPC JE-34665) 1978; Uneasy Rider (EPC 34369) 1976; Whiskey (EPC PE-34664) 1977.

DANIELS, EDDIE Clarinet. Session for Airto (1974). *Albums:* Brief Encounter (MUS 5154); Morning Thunder (COL JC-36290) 1980; Street Wind (MAR 2214); A Flower for All Seasons (CHS CRS 1002) 1973.

DANIELS, GIDEON Vocal. Session for Elvin Bishop (1974).

DANIELS, HALL Keyboards. Member of Neil Norman's Cosmic Orchestra, 1975-80.

DANIELS, JESS Guitar. Session for B. B. King (1975).

DANIELS, LES Vocal. Session for Martin Mull.

DANIELS, STEPHEN Drums, percussion. Member of the Platinum Hook since 1979.

DANIELSON, AKE Keyboards. Member of the Meteors, 1980.

DANKO, RICK Vocal, bass. Born 12/29/42. Member of the Band, 1963-78. Session for Neil Young (1973); Ringo Starr (1973). *Album:* Rick Danko (ARI 4141) 1977.

DANNEMAN, DON Guitar. Member of the Cyrkle, 1966-67.

DANNY AND THE JUNIORS Bill Carlucci—vocal; Frank Maffe—vocal; Danny Rapp—vocal; Joe Terranora—vocal; Jimmy Testa—vocal; Dave White—vocal. Recorded the hit "At The Hop," 1958. *Albums:* At The Hop (MCA AA-1111); Rock and Roll Is Here To Stay (GUS 0065).

DANOFF, BILL Vocal. Member of the Starland Vocal Band, since 1976.

DANOFF, TAFFY Vocal. Member of the Starland Vocal Band since 1976.

DANTE, CARL Vocal, bass. Member of Dancer, 1976.

DANTE, RON Vocal. One man vocalist who recorded under the group name the Cuff Links, and the Detergents, for "Leader of the Laundromat," 1964.

DANTER, BRIAN Vocal, bass, moog. Member of the Teaze, 1979.

DANUS, MICHAEL LUIS VICENS Bass. Member of Los Bravos, 1966-68.

DANYLS, BOB Bass, vocal. Member of Fandango since 1979.

DANZAT, JACKIE Vocal. Member of Cottonwood South, 1974.

DARBY Member of the Germs, 1979.

DARIN, BOBBY Vocal. Real name: Robert Cassotto. Made a hit of "Mack the Knife" in 1959 and from there rose in importance in the pop folk field. Only after his death in 1973 was he recognized as a formidable white rhythm and blues singer. *Albums:* Bobby Darin (MTN MS753); Bobby Darin Story (ACO 131); Darin 1936-1973 (MTN M5-813).

DARLA, SHEILA Vocal. Member of the Group Image, 1968.

DARLING Alice Spring—vocal; Hal Lindes—guitar; Mike Howard—bass; Paul Varley—drums. *Album:* Put It Down to Experience (CMA 1-2204) 1979.

DARNELL, AUGUST Bass, vocal. Member of Dr. Buzzard's Original Savannah Band, 1976-78.

DAROU, ALEX Bass. Member of Kensington Market, 1968-69.

DARREN, JENNY Vocal. Pop country vocalist. *Album:* Queen of Fools (DJM 21) 1978.

DARROW, CHRIS Fiddle, guitar, bass, vocal, banjo, mandolin. Original member of the Critters, 1966, and Kaleidoscope until 1968. Replaced Bruce Kunkel in the Nitty Gritty Dirt Band. Member of Rank Strangers, 1977. Session for James Taylor; Free Creek (1973); Jelly (1977); Steven T. (1978); Colin Winski (1980). *Album:* Fretless (PFA 132) 1979.

DARRYL Vocal. Credited as a member of the Silicon Teens, 1980.

DARTS George Currie—guitar; Den Hegarty—vocal; Horatio Hornblower—saxophone; Griff Fender—vocal; Thump Thompson—bass; Rita Ray—vocal; Hammy Howell—piano; Bob Fish—vocal; John Dummer—drums. *Album:* Darts (UAR UA-LA850) 1978.

DARWAY, CHRIS Keyboards, vocal. Member of Johnny's Dance Band, 1977, and Nan Mancini and JDB, 1979.

DASHIEL, RUSSELL Guitar, vocal. Member of the Don Harrison Band, 1976. Session for Harvey Mandel; John Sebastian (1974). *Album:* Elevator (EPC JE 35074) 1978.

DATA, DARRELL Guitar. Member of Buckacre, 1976.

DAUGHERTY, DEAN Keyboards. Member of the Candymen, and the Atlanta Rhythm Section since 1973.

DAUGHERTY, JAY DEE Drums. Member of the Patti Smith Group since 1975. Session for Tom Verlaine (1979); the Roaches (1980); Willie Nile (1980).

DAUGHERTY, PAT Bass, vocal. Member of Black Oak Arkansas, 1971-78.

DAUGHTERS, KENNY Keyboards. Member of Hustler.

DAVE DEE, DOZY, BEAKY, MICK AND TICH David Harmon (Dave Dee); Trevor Davies (Dozy); John Dymond (Beaky); Michael Wilson (Mick); Ian Amey (Tich). Formerly Dave Dee and the Bostons, they changed to their schooldays nicknames to appeal to rock audiences of the 1960s. Unlike their innocent name, their first single "Bend It" (1966) was banned for its lewd references, which were staged in their live show. *Albums:* Dave Dee, Dozy, Beaky, Mick and Tich, 1967; Time to Take Off.

DAVENPORT, BILLY Drums. Member of Paul Butterfield Blues Band, 1966-67.

DAVENPORT, DARIUS LaNOUE Vocal, oboe, piano, drums, trombone, guitar, bass, recorder. Co-founder of Autosalvage, 1966-68.

DAVID, CARLOS Guitar, vocal. Member of Please, 1976.

DAVID, GAVIN Vocal. Added to the Sailor lineup, 1980.

DAVID, JAY Drums. Session for Chinga Chavin.

DAVID, JOHN Vocal, bass, keyboards. Member of the Airwaves, 1978-79.

DAVID, KAL Guitar, vocal. Member of the Illinois Speed Press, 1969-70, the Fabulous Rhinestones, 1972-73, and the Rhinestones, 1975.

DAVID, ROY Keyboards, vocal. Member of Please, 1976.

DAVID, VIRGINIA Vocal. Added to the Sailor lineup, 1980.

DAVIDSON, BILL Guitar. Member of Gasmask.

DAVIDSON, DIANNE Guitar, vocal. Session for J. J. Cale (1971); Leon Russell (1973).

DAVIDSON, GEORGE Drums. Member of Paul Butterfield Blues Band, 1971.

DAVIDSON, HOWARD Bass. Member of Network, 1977.

DAVIDSON, LENNY Guitar. Member of the Dave Clark 5, 1964-68.

DAVIDSON, MIKE Bass. Member of the Blackouts, 1980.

DAVIE, HUTCH Keyboards. Session for Pearls Before Swine (1970).

DAVIES, ALUN Guitar, vocal, writer. Member of Sweet Thursday, 1970, and Mark-Almond, 1973. Accompanist for Cat Stevens, 1970-77. Session for Martin Mull (1978). *Album:* Alun Davies (COL).

DAVIES, CHRIS Guitar, vocal. Member of the Penetrators, 1980.

DAVIES, CLIFF Drums, percussion, vocal, producer. Replaced Vic Mastrianni in the Amboy Dukes, 1974-75, before becoming a permanent member of Ted Nugent's backup band, 1975-present.

DAVIES, CLIVE Drums, synthesizer, vocal. Replaced Dennis Elliott in If, 1974.

DAVIES, CYRIL Guitar, vocal. Founder of Cyril

Davies and the All Stars, and reported by Jimmy Page to be the man responsible for bringing Chicago blues to England. Played with Alexis Korner as a duet, 1954-61. Played with Big Bill Broonzy, Otis Spann, John Lee Hooker, Muddy Waters, Memphis Slim, Champion Jack Dupree, Sonny Terry and Brownie McGhee.

CYRIL DAVIES AND THE ALL STARS Carlo Little—drums; Nicky Hopkins—piano; Cliff Barton —bass; Cyril Davies—guitar, vocal; Jeff Beck—guitar; Long John Baldry—vocal (1962). English blues band featuring the Chicago blues sound, which inspired such bands as the Rolling Stones, the Yardbirds, and John Mayall's Bluesbreakers in the early 1960s.

DAVIES, DAVE Vocal, keyboards, bass, drums, guitar. Born 2/3/47. With brother Ray, co-founder of the Kinks, 1964-present. *Album:* Dave Davies (AFLI 3603) 1980.

DAVIES, NEAL Guitar. Member of Selecter, 1980.

DAVIES, PAUL Vocal. Played Peter in "Jesus Christ Superstar," 1970.

DAVIES, RAY Harmonica, vocal, guitar, writer. Born 6/21/44. With brother Dave, co-founder of the Kinks, 1964-present.

DAVIES, RICHARD Vocal, keyboards. Member of Supertramp.

DAVIES, RICK Drums. Session for Chick Churchill (1974).

DAVIES, ROY Keyboards. Session for Freddie King (1974-75); Elton John (1979).

DAVIES, TREVOR Dozy of Dave Dee, Dozy, Beaky, Mick and Tich, 1967.

DAVIS, ANDY Vocal, keyboards, mandolin, drums. Member of Stackridge, 1974, and the Korgis since 1979.

DAVIS, ANTHONY Bass, vocal. Member of Ruby, 1976.

DAVIS, BILLY Guitar, vocal. Member of the Fifth Dimension.

DAVIS, BILLY Member of Hank Ballard's Midnighters.

DAVIS, BLIND JOHN Piano, vocal. Born 12/7/13. Mississippi blues man who moved to west Chicago. Contemporary of Big Bill Broonzy, Tampa Red and others. *Albums:* Incomparable (OLB 2803) 1974; Stompin on a Saturday (ALG 4790) 1977.

DAVIS, BUDDY Guitar, organ. Member of Target, 1976-77.

DAVIS, CLIFF Saxophone. Chicago blues man whose credits include backing Barry Goldberg and Harvey Mandel.

DAVIS, DAVID Keyboards. Member of the Winters Brothers Band.

DAVIS, DENNIS Drums. Session for David Bowie (1977).

DAVIS, FRANK Drums. Member of Cold Blood. Session for Lee Michaels (1968).

DAVIS, GARY Organ. Session for Lee Michaels (1968).

DAVIS, GREG Percussion, guitar, vocal. Member of Acrobat, 1972.

DAVIS, HENRY Bass. Session for Freddie King (1975).

DAVIS, HUBIE Vocal, guitar. Member of the Edge, 1980.

DAVIS, JAY Member of Axis, 1978.

DAVIS, JEFF Bass, vocal. Member of the Amazing Rhythm Aces.

DAVIS, JESSE ED Guitar, piano. Session for Marc Benno; Taj Mahal; Donovan (1976); Keith Moon (1975); Nilsson (1974-76); the Pointer Sisters (1974); Leon Russell (1971); Rod Stewart (1975-76); Bangla Desh (1971); Gene Clark (1974); George Harrison (1975); B. B. King (1972); John Lennon (1974); the Steve Miller Band (1972); Ringo Starr (1974).

DAVIS, JOE Baritone saxophone. Session for Ry Cooder (1972); Freddie King (1975).

DAVIS, KIM Guitar, vocal. Member of Point Blank, 1976-78.

DAVIS, L. C. Tenor saxophone. Session for Chuck Berry (1959-61).

DAVIS, LARRY Bass. Member of Alamo, 1971.

DAVIS, LINK, JR. Saxophone, fiddle. Member of Asleep at the Wheel since 1973.

DAVIS, MARK Keyboards. Member of Sly and the Family Stone, 1979.

DAVIS, MARTHA Vocal, guitar. Member of the Motels, 1979-80.

DAVIS, MAURICE Trumpet. Session for the Temptations (1973).

DAVIS, MICHAEL Bass. Member of the MC 5, 1968-69.

DAVIS, MIKE Trumpet. Member of the Keef Hartley Band horn section, 1969-71.

DAVIS, NED Drums. Member of the Snakestretchers, 1972-73.

DAVIS, ORVILLE Bass. Member of Hydra, 1975-77, and the Rex, 1977.

DAVIS, PAUL Guitar. Session for J. J. Cale (1974).

DAVIS, PAUL Synthesizer. Member of Raw Milk, 1970.

DAVIS, PETER Keyboards, vocal. Member of Bighorn, 1978.

DAVIS, RAY Flugelhorn. Session for Savoy Brown (1969).

DAVIS, RICHARD Acoustic bass. Session for Martin Mull (1975); Jonathan Edwards (1973); Bruce Springsteen (1973); Paul Simon (1973); Free Creek (1973); Sha Na Na (1971); Carly Simon (1974). *Albums:* As One (MUS 5903) 1976; Black Fire (BLN LT-84151); Dealin' (MUS 5027) 1973; Epistrophy and Now's the Time (MUS 5002) 1972; Harvest (MUS 5115) 1979; Judgement (BLN LT-84159); Muses of Richard Davis (PAU 7002) 1970; Strike Up the Band (FLD BDLI-0829); Way Out West (MUS 5180)

1977; With Understanding (MUS 5083) 1975; Fancy Free (GXY 5102) 1977.

DAVIS, SHELLY Trumpet, piano. Member of the Brooklyn Bridge.

DAVIS, SPENCER Guitar, vocal. Born 7/17/41. Organizer and namesake of the Spencer Davis Group, 1964-68. Session for Dave Mason.

SPENCER DAVIS GROUP Spencer Davis—guitar, vocal, harmonica; Steve Winwood—keyboards, guitar, vocal, harmonica, writer (1964-68); Muff Winwood—bass (1964-68); Pete York—drums; Eddie Hardin—keyboards, vocal (1968); Ray Fenwick—guitar, vocal (1968); Dee Murray—bass (1968); Dave Hynes—drums (1968). In 1963, college man Davis teamed up with the Winwood brothers, featuring Steve, then 15 years old. By 1966 they hit the charts with "Keep On Running," followed the next year by the classics "Gimme Some Lovin'," and "I'm a Man." Both songs were typical of the group, with Steve's blues vocals and organ in the front. He dropped out in 1968, and Davis reorganized a new group which did not enjoy as much popularity as the previous group. *Albums:* Gimme Some Lovin' (UAR UA-XW115-A) 1967; I'm a Man (UAR UA-XW116-A) 1967; Keep On Running (UAR UA-XW115-A); Somebody Help Me (UAR UA-XW116-A); Spencer Davis Band Greatest Hits, 1968; With Their New Face On, 1968.

DAVIS, TERRY Bass. Member of Stoneground, 1971-78.

DAVIS, THOM Keyboards, trumpet. Member of the Jaggerz.

DAVIS, TIM Congas, drums. Member of the Steve Miller Band, 1968-70. Session for Ben Sidran.

TIM DAVIS AND THE CHORDAIRS Early band of Tim Davis and Curley Cooke before joining the Steve Miller Band, 1966.

DAVIS, WALTER Piano. Session for Dr. John (1971).

DAVIS, WILLIE Vocal. Member of Joey Dee and the Starlighters.

DAVIS, WINDLE Vocal. Member of Human Sexual Response, 1980.

DAVISON, BRIAN Drums, percussion. Original member of the Nice until 1970, and Refugee, 1972.

DAVISON, SCOTT Drums, percussion. Member of Arrogance, 1976.

DAVY, COLIN Drums. Member of the Hill, 1975.

DAVY, STEVE Bass. Original member of Steamhammer, 1969.

DAWBER, RUSSELL Drums. Member of Flight, 1976-79.

DAWE, MICHAEL Drums. Replaced Allison Cook in the Pousette-Dart Band, 1978-79.

DAWES, TOM Guitar, banjo, harmonica, sitar. Member of the Cyrcle, 1966-67.

DAWSON, JIM Guitar, vocal, writer, bass. Member of the Siegel-Schwall Band until 1970. Original member of the New Riders of the Purple Sage.

DAWSON, LARRY Keyboards. Member of Fandango.

DAWSON, STEVE Bass. Member of Saxon, 1980.

DAY, BOBBY Vocal. Began in the Hollywood Flames before recording "Rockin' Robin." 1958.

DAY, DAVE Member of Bill Haley and the Comets.

DAY, JAMES CLAYTON Dobro, pedal steel guitar. Session for Willie Nelson (1973).

DAY, RUSTY Vocal. Lead singer for the Amboy Dukes, and Cactus, 1970-72.

DAY, WYATT Guitar. Original member of Ars Nova, 1968-69.

DAYE, STU Vocal, guitar. Session for Nils Lofgren (1979).

DAYRON, NORMAN Producer. Produced Mike Bloomfield (1977-79).

DAYS, GUY Guitar, vocal. Member of 999, 1978 to present.

DAYTON Dean Hummons—keyboards, percussion; Chris Jones—vocal, trumpet, percussion; Shawn Sandridge—vocal, guitar, keyboards, percussion; Derrick Armstrong—bass, vocal; Jenny Douglas—vocal; John Hardin—drums, vocal. *Album:* Dayton (UAR LT 1025) 1980.

DE AGUERO, JOE Percussion. Session for Nilsson (1975).

DE ALBUQUERQUE, MIKE Vocal, guitar. Member of Violinski, 1979.

DE ATH, ROD Drums, percussion. Replaced Wilgar Campbell as backup to Rory Gallagher, 1973-75.

DE BOER, MICKEY Bass. Member of the Tumbleweeds, 1975.

DE BOIS, RICHARD Drums. Session for Jan Akkerman and Kaz Lux (1976).

DE BOLT, KEITH Vocal. Member of Snopek, 1980.

DE BUHR, ALICE Drums. Member of the Peter Ivers Band, 1974.

DE BURGH, CHRIS Vocal, guitar, piano. *Albums:* At the End of a Perfect Day (AAM 4647) 1977; Crusader (AAM 4746) 1979; Eastern Winds (AAM 4815) 1980; Far Beyond These Castle Walls (AAM 4516) 1975; Spanish Train and Other Stories (AAM 4568) 1979.

DE CARLO, ALAN Guitar, vocal, percussion. Member of the Bangor Flying Circus.

DE CARO, BOB Drums. Member of the Truth, 1975.

DE CARO, NICK Accordion, piano, mellotron, producer, orchestral arranger. Produced Livingston Taylor (1979). Session for Marc Benno; Harvey Mandel; James Taylor (1976); Neil Diamond (1976); Gordon Lightfoot (1972, 74, 80); Montrose (1974); the Steve Miller Band (1972); Adam Mitchell (1979).

DE CHAVES, JOE Bass. Member of Arbuckle, 1972.

DE FREITAS, PETE Drums. Member of Echo and the Bunnymen, 1980.

DE FUENTES, RUBEN Guitar. Member of the Hollywood Stars, 1977.

DE GEWERES, TOMMY Organ. Member of John Fred and the Playboy Band.

DE GUEVARA, RUBEN Vocal. Session for Frank Zappa (1974, 76).

DE JESUS, JOSE MIGUEL Guitar, vocal. Member of Banchee, 1969.

DE JONCKHEERE, JAAP Guitar. Member of the Urban Heroes, 1980.

DE JONG, THEO Bass. Replaced Bert Veldkamp in Kayak, 1977.

DE LA BARREDA, ANTONIO Bass. Replaced Larry Taylor in Canned Heat, 1970-73. Session for Harvey Mandel (1972).

DE LA PARRA, ADOLFO Drums. Original member of Canned Heat, 1965-73, 1979. Session for Harvey Mandel (1972); Free Creek (1973).

DE LA PAZ, CARLOS Guitar. Member of the Heaters, 1978-present.

DE LEEUWE, PETER Drums, vocal. Member of Ekseption.

DE LOACH, DARRYL Original member of Iron Butterfly, 1967-68.

DE LONG, CLINT Guitar, vocal. Member of Blue Jug, 1975.

DE LORME, GABRIEL Guitar. Session for Airto (1974).

DE LUNA, JOHN Drums, percussion. Member of El Chicano.

DE MARTINEZ, BILL Keyboards, vocal. Member of Iron Butterfly, 1974.

DE MASO, JOHN Bass. Member of Jukin' Bone, 1972.

DE MEUR, TONY Vocal, guitar, harmonica. Member of the Fabulous Poodles, 1978-79.

DE NICOLA, JOHN Bass, vocal. Replaced John Ray in Flight, 1980.

DE NUNZIO, VINNY Drums, vocal. Session for Richard Lloyd (1979).

DE OLIVEIRA, LAUDIER Member of Chicago.

DE OLIVERA, GERALDO Percussion. Member of the Numa Band, 1980.

DE PHILLIPS, STEVE Bass, vocal. Member of Wind in the Willows, 1968.

DE POE, PETE Drums. Original member of Redbone, 1970-77.

DE RAAD, FRANZ Drums, vocal. Member of Barooga, 1980.

DE RAAD, MAT Keyboards, vocal. Member of Barooga, 1980.

DE REMER, KEVIN Drums. Member of Cain, 1975-77.

DE ROBERTS, JOHN Vocal. Voice of Hammer, 1970.

DE ROSA, VINCENT Horns. Session for Boz Scaggs (1976).

DE SALVO, JOHN Bass. Member of the Tuff Darts, 1978.

DE SHANNON, JACKIE Vocal, writer, guitar. Song stylist of the country pop genre, DeShannon enjoyed some notoriety on the pop charts with her classic, "Wishin' and Hopin'" in the 1960s. *Albums:* Jackie (ATC 7231) 1972; Your Baby Is a Lady (ATC 7303); You're the Only Dancer (AMH 1010); New Arrangement (COL PC 33500) 1975; Together (VIC ABLI-3541) 1979.

DE SILVA, CONSUELO Synthesizer. Member of Vivabeat, 1980.

DE SOUZA, BARRY Drums. Session for Lou Reed (1972); Rick Wakeman (1972); Shawn Phillips (1973); Chris de Burgh (1975); Brian Protheroe (1976); Elliott Murphy (1977); Kevin Ayers (1978); the Dukes (1979); Ian Gomm (1979); Justin Hayward (1980); Matthew Fisher (1980).

DE SYKES, STEPHANIE Vocal. Session for Gary Brooker (1979).

DE TEMPLE, MIKE Session for Dave Mason.

DE VILLE, WILLY "MINK" Vocal, guitar, harmonica. *Albums:* Le Chat Bleu (CAP ST-11955); Mink De Ville (CAP ST 11631); Return to Magenta (CAP SW 11780) 1978.

DE VITO, DON Producer. Produced Bob Dylan since 1975.

DE VITO, HANK Pedal steel guitar. Session for Jonathan Edwards (1976-77); Hoyt Axton (1976); Martin Mull (1977).

DE VITO, HOWARD Vocal, writer. Member of Magazine since 1978.

DE VITO, RALPH Vocal. Member of the Happenings, 1966-68.

DE VITO, TOMMY Vocal. Original member of the Four Seasons.

DE WHART, AGNETHA Vocal. Member of Abba since 1974.

DE WINTER, HARRY Bass, vocal, keyboards. Member of the New Adventures, 1980.

DE YOUNG, CLIFF Vocal. Member of Clear Light, 1967-68.

DE YOUNG, DENNIS Keyboards, synthesizer, vocal, writer. Original member of Styx, 1970-present.

DE ZWAAN, ERIC Guitar, vocal. Member of the Meteors, 1980.

DEACON, MICK Keyboards. Member of the Greatest Show on Earth, 1970. Session for Ginger Baker (1977).

DEAD BOYS Stiv Bators—vocal; Cheetah Chrome—guitar; Jeff Magnum—bass; Johnny Blitz—drums. *Album:* We Have Come for Your Children (SIR K-6054) 1978; Young, Loud and Snotty (SIR 6038) 1977.

DEADLY NIGHTSHADE Helen Hooke—vocal, guitar, fiddle, keyboards; Anne Bowen—vocal, guitar, percussion; Pamela Brandt—vocal, bass, percussion. *Album:* Deadly Nightshade (PTM)

1975.

DEAF SCHOOL Bette Bright—vocals (1979-80); Eric Shark—vocals; Max Ripple—keyboards; Clive Langer—guitar (1979-80); Enrico Cadillac—vocals; Steve Lindsey—bass; Ian Ritchie—saxophone; Tim Whittaker—drums; Paul Pilnick—guitar. *Albums:* Don't Stop the World (WBR 2LS-3011) 1979; English Boys/Working Girls (WBR K-3169) 1980; 2nd Honeymoon (WBR 2LS-3011) 1979.

DEAKIN, GRAHAM Drums. Member of the Blue Jays, 1975, Ox, 1975, and Full House, 1977-78. Session for John Entwhistle (1972); Ray Thomas (1976).

DEAL, STUART Bass. Member of the Plastic Rhino Band, 1977.

DEAN, BARRY Bass, vocal. Original member of Brian Auger's Oblivion Express, 1971-74. Session for Shawn Phillips.

DEAN, BOBBY Trombone. Member of Woody Herman Band. Session for Free Creek (1973).

DEAN, CHUCK Vocal, guitar, organ. Member of Chuck and the Tigers, 1980.

DEAN, DIXIE Bass, harmonica, coronet, percussion, vocal. Member of Lo and Behold, 1972.

DEAN, ELTON Alto saxophone, saxcello. Credited with supplying half of Elton John's adopted name. Member of the Soft Machine, 1970, and Centipede, 1971.

DEAN, JOHNNY Chimes. Session with Memphis Slim (1971).

DEAN, PAUL Guitar, vocal. Member of Loverboy, 1980.

DEAN, RICHARD Keyboards, vocal. Member of One Hand Clapping, 1977-79.

DEAN, ROB Guitar. Member of Japan since 1979.

DEAN, ROGER Guitar. Member of John Mayall's group before it became the Bluesbreakers, 1964.

DEANE, ED Guitar, bass, harpsichord. Member of the Woods Band.

DEANE, J. A. Trombone, synthesizer. Member of the Indoor Life, 1980.

DEANE, SANDY Vocal. Member of Jay and the Americans, 1963-68.

DEANS, KENNY Drums. Member of the Heats, 1980.

DEANS, ROBERT Keyboards. Replaced Frank Ludwig in Trooper.

DEBRECENI, FERENC Drums. Member of Omega, 1975-78.

DECCHIO, DAN Bass, guitar, flute, vocal. Member of Glass Harp, 1970-72.

DEDICATIONS Early name for the Soul Explosions until 1966.

DEE, BRYAN Organ. Session for Elton John (1969-71).

DEE, DAVE Nickname of David Harmon. Member of Dave Dee, Dozy, Beaky, Mick and Tich.

DEE, JOEY Vocal. Real name: Joey di Nacola. Namesake of Joey Dee and the Starlighters. *Album:* Joey Dee (ROU) 1963.

JOEY DEE AND THE STARLIGHTERS Carl Adamore—vocal; David Brigatti—vocal; Willie Davis—vocal; Joey Dee (Joey di Nacola)—vocal; Carlton Latimer—vocal; Larry Vernieri—vocal. Chubby Checker may have invented the Twist, but that was secondary at the Peppermint Lounge, home of the "Peppermint Twist" (1961), and Joey Dee and the Starlighters. *Albums:* Hey Let's Twist (ROU) 1962; All the World's Twistin' (ROU) 1962; Two Tickets for Paris (ROU) 1962; Doin' the Twist at the Peppermint Lounge (ROU) 1962; Twistin' Live Back to the Peppermint (ROU) 1962; Dance, Dance, Dance (ROU) 1963; The Peppermint Twister (SPR); Joey Dee (ROU) 1963.

DEE, KIKI Vocal. Born 3/6/47. Real name: Pauline Matthews. Elton John protege introduced in 1973. Session for Elton John (1973, 75); Yvonne Elliman (1978). *Albums:* I've Got The Music In Me, 1974; Loving and Free, 1975; Kiki Dee, 1977.

KIKI DEE BAND Roger Pope—drums; Bias Boshell; Phil Curtis—bass; Jo Partridge. Backup band for Kiki Dee. See Kiki Dee.

DEE, KOKO Bass. Member of Duke and the Drivers, 1975.

DEE, ROBIN Member of the Now, 1979.

DEEP PURPLE Rod Evans—writer, vocal (1968-70); John Lord—keyboards, vocal, writer; Nic Simper—bass, vocal, writer (1968-70); Richie Blackmore—guitar, vocal, writer; Ian Paice—drums, writer; Ian Gillan—vocal, writer (1970-74); Roger Glover—bass, vocal, writer (1970-74); David Cloverdale—vocal (1974); Glenn Hughes—bass, vocal (1974); Tommy Bolin—guitar (1975). Once rated as the loudest rock 'n' roll band, Deep Purple could always be counted upon to deliver the loudest hard rock music wherever they travelled. Their debut, "Hush," 1968, was the first of many heavy hits such as "Smoke on the Water," 1972, and "Woman From Tokyo," 1973. *Albums:* Deep Purple—and the Royal Philharmonic, 1971; Deep Purple (TET T-119) 1968; Shades of Deep Purple (TET T-102) 1968; Book of Taliesyn (TET T-107) 1969; Burn (WBR 2768) 1974; Come Taste the Band (WBR 1877) 1970; Deep Purple in Rock (WBR K-3100) 1970; Fireball (WBR 2564) 1971; Machine Head (WBR K-3100) 1972; Made in Europe (WBR B-1995) 1976; Made in Japan (WBR SWS-2701) 1973; Purple Passages (WBR 2LS-2644) 1972; Stormbringer (WBR PR-2832) 1974; When We Rock, We Rock and When We Roll, We Roll (WBR K-3223) 1978; Who Do We Think We Are (WBR B-2678) 1973; Deepest Purple (WBR PRK-3486) 1980.

DEERFRANCE Percussion, vocal. Session for John Cale (1979); Tom Verlaine (1979).

DEF LEPPARD Steve Clark—guitar; Rick Savage

—bass; Pete Willis—guitar; Rick Allen—drums; Joe Elliot—vocal. *Album:* On Through the Night (MER SRM-1-3828) 1980.

DEKKER, COR Bass. Member of Ekseption.

DEL BARRIO, EDUARDO Keyboards, vocal. Member of Caldera, 1976-78.

DEL DIN, ROBERT Vocal. Member of the Earls, 1959.

DEL RAY, MARINA Keyboards. Member of Vivabeat, 1980.

DEL VIKINGS Don Bacus—vocal; Don Jackson—vocal; Chuck Jackson—vocal; Corin Johnson—vocal; David Lerchey—vocal; Clarence Quick—vocal; Norman Wright—vocal. Recorded the hit "Come Go With Me," 1957. *Albums:* Del Vikings; Swinging Singing Record Session; They Sing, They Swing, 1957; Best of the Del Vikings.

DEL ZOPPO, ALEX Keyboards, harmonica, vocal. Member of Sweetwater.

DELANDER, BOBBY Member of Crimson Tide 1978-79.

DELANEY AND BONNIE Delaney Bramlett—guitar, vocal, writer; Bonnie Bramlett—vocal, writer. Delaney and Bonnie, a husband and wife team, brought gospel music to the rock public more successfuly than any other rock artists. Their list of famous backup musicians includes Leon Russell, Jerry McGee, Bobby Whitlock, Eric Clapton, Jim Keltner, Jim Price, Carl Radle, Bob Keys, Dave Mason and a host of others. After their separation, both tried solo careers with little success. Session for Elvin Bishop (1972); Doris Troy (1972). *Albums:* The Original Delaney and Bonnie; On Tour with Eric Clapton (ACO 326); Genesis (CRS 2054).

DELAWARE DESTROYERS See George Thorogood and the Destroyers.

DELGADO, VINCE Percussion. Member of the Dija Rhythm Band, 1976.

DELGATTO, LOUIS Tenor saxophone, trombone, oboe. Member of the Buddy Rich Band. Session for Johnny Winter (1973-74); Free Creek (1973); Roy Buchanan (1976); Ian Hunter (1979); the Blues Brothers (1980).

DELLA GALA, MICHAEL Bass, vocal. Member of Sail.

DELLER, MARTIN Drums, percussion. Member of FM, 1979.

DELLMAN, GERALD Keyboards. Member of Satin Whale, 1975.

DELLS Chuck Barksdale—vocal; Marvin Junior—vocal; Vern Allison—vocal; Mike McGill—vocal; Johnny Carter—vocal. Recorded "Love Is Blue," 1969. *Albums:* Face to Face (MCA AA-1131); I Touched a Dream (TWC 618) 1980; New Beginnings (MCA 1100); Like It Is (CAD LPS 837) 1969; No Way Back (MER SRM 1-1084) 1976.

DELMAR, MARCO Guitar, vocal. Member of the Electrics, 1980.

DELP, BRAD Guitar, vocal, percussion. Member of Boston, 1976-78. Session for Sammy Hagar (1979); Barry Goudreau (1980).

DELTAS Early name of the Hollies.

DELTON JOHN Early recording name of John Lee Hooker.

DELUX, SAM Guitar, vocal. Member of Duke and the Drivers, 1975.

DEMERS, JIM Drums. Member of Catfish.

DEMME, FRANK Bass, vocal. Member of Rock Rose, 1979.

DEMONS Mike Rappoport—drums; Rob Twyford—bass; Martin Butler—guitar; Bob Jones—guitar; Elliot Kidd—vocal. *Album:* Demons, 1977.

DEMPSEY, MARTIN Bass, vocal. Member of the Yachts since 1979, and the Cure, 1979.

DEMPSEY, RAY Guitar. Session with Memphis Slim (1971).

DENIM Bill Browder—guitar, keyboards, vocal; David Moerbe—drums; Richard Mullen—guitar; Jerry Crow—bass. *Album:* Denim, 1977.

DENNARD, DAVID Bass. Member of the Ravers, the Low Numbers, 1977-78, and Gary Myrick and the Figures, 1980.

DENNEN, BARRY Vocal. Played Pontius in "Jesus Christ Superstar," 1970.

DENNEY, DIX Guitar. Member of the Wierdos, 1979-80.

DENNIS, CAROLYN Vocal. Session for Bob Dylan (1978-79); Art Garfunkel (1979).

DENNIS, CHRISTOPHER Percussion. Session for Firefall (1980).

DENNY, DAVID Guitar. Session for Steve Miller (1977).

DENNY, JOHN Vocal. Member of the Wierdos, 1979-80.

DENNY, SANDY Vocal. Voice of Fotheringay, 1971, and Fairport Convention. Died 1978. Session for Led Zeppelin (1971); "Tommy" (1972). *Albums:* North Star Grassman and the Ravens (AAM 4317); Sandy (AAM 4371); Like an Old Fashioned Waltz.

DENOV, ERNIE Guitar. Member of the Numa Band, 1980.

DENSMORE, JOHN Drums. Born 12/1/44. Original member of the Doors, until their dissolve in 1972. Member of the Butts Band.

DENTITH, JOHN Drums. Session for Long John Baldry (1972).

DENTON, JIM Bass, guitar, vocal. Member of the Resurrection Band, 1978.

DENTWEILER, CRAIG Horns. Session for Bill Wyman (1976).

DENTZ, WALLY Bass, harmonica, vocal. Member of the Henry Paul Band since 1979.

DENVER, JOHN Vocal, guitar. Folk singer turned pop/lounge star with his "Rocky Mountain High," 1972. *Albums:* Aerie (VIC AFLI-4607) 1971; Autograph (VIC AQLI-3449) 1980; Back Home

Again (VIC AFLI-0548) 1974; Beginnings (MER SRM-1-704) 1965; Christmas Together (VIC AFLI-3451); John Denver (VIC AQLI-3075) 1978; John Denver's Greatest Hits (VIC AFLI-0374) 1973; John Denver's Greatest Hits, Vol. 2 (VIC CPLI-2195) 1977; Evening with John Denver (VIC CPL2-0764) 1975; Farewell Andromeda (VIC AFLI-0101) 1973; Gift of Song (POL 1-6214); I Want to Live (VIC AFLI-2521) 1977; Poems, Prayers and Promises (VIC AFLI-4499) 1971; Rhymes and Reasons (VIC AFLI-4207) 1969; Rocky Mountain Christmas (VIC AFLI-1201) 1975; Rocky Mountain High (VIC AFLI-4731) 1972; Spirit (VIC AFLI-1694) 1976; Take Me to Tomorrow (VIC AFLI-4278) 1970; Whose Garden Is This (VIC AFLI-4414) 1970; Windsong (VIC AFLI-1183) 1975.

DEODATO, EUMIR Keyboards, writer. Jazz artist who helped popularize jazz to the rock audience with his Latin interpretation of "Also Sprach Zarathustra" (Space Odyssey: 2001 theme), 1973. *Albums:* Artistry (MCA 457) 1974; Fire Into Music (CTI 2); First Cuckoo (MCA 491) 1975; In Concert (CTI 6041); Knights of Fantasy (WBR K-3321) 1979; 2001 (CTI 7081); Very Together (MCA 410) 1976; Prelude (CTI 6021); Whirlwinds (MCA 410) 1974.

DEREK AND THE DOMINOES Eric Clapton—guitar, vocal, writer; Bobby Whitlock—keyboards, guitar, vocal, writer; Jim Gordon—drums, percussion, piano; Carl Radle—bass, percussion. Eric Clapton's much awaited group between Blind Faith (1969) and his serious pursuits in his solo career (1974). Unfortunately, the group did not last much longer than Faith, and their second album, a live double set, was issued almost a year after the group's demise. "Layla," however, is still an often played FM record, ten years after its initial release. See Eric Clapton. *Albums:* Layla (ACO 2-790) 1970; In Concert (ACO 502-8800) 1973.

DERMER, LAURENCE Keyboards, vocal. Replaced Charlie Murciano in Foxy, 1980.

DEROSIER, MIKE Drums. Member of Heart.

DERRINGER, RICK Guitar, vocal, writer, producer, synthesizer, sitar, percussion. Real name: Rick Zehringer. Born 8/5/47. Original member of the McCoys, 1965-68, before becoming famous as a member of the Johnny Winter Band, 1971-73, from which he went solo, and into production. Session for Steely Dan (1973, 80); Johnny Winter (1974-76); Blast (1979). *Albums:* All American Boy (BSY KZ 32481) 1973; Outside Stuff (MER SRM 2-7506); Spring Fever (BSY PZQ 33423) 1974; Sweet Evil, 1977; Face to Face (BSY JZ 36551) 1980; Guitars and Women (BSY JZ 36092) 1979; Glass Derringer (LAI GG 58009) 1976; If I Weren't So Romantic, I'd Shoot You (BSY JZ 35075) 1978.

DES BARRES, MICHAEL Vocal. Voice of Detective, 1977. Session for Gene Simmons (1978); Phoenix (1979).

DESAUTELS, JOHN Drums. Member of the L.A. Jets, 1976, and 1994, 1978-79.

DESMARIAS, MICHAEL Drums. Member of the Tyla Gang, 1977-79. Session for the Motors (1980); Sean Tyla (1980).

DESMOND, PAUL Saxophone. Session for Art Garfunkel (1978).

DESPOMMLER, PHIL Drums. Session for John Mayall (1977).

DESTRI, FRANK Keyboards. Member of Blondie since 1977.

DESTROYERS See George Thorogood and the Destroyers.

DESTRY, JOHNNY Guitar, vocal. *Album:* Girls, Rock 'n' Roll and Cars (MIL BXL 17753) 1980.

DETECTIVE Michael des Barres—vocal; Michael Monarch—guitar; Jon Hyde—drums; Bobby Picket—bass; Tony Kaye—keyboards. *Albums:* Detective (SWN 8417); It Takes One to Know One (SWN 8504) 1977.

DETERMEIUER, CLEEM Keyboards. Member of Finch, 1975.

DETRICK, RICHIE Vocal. Member of the Nuns, 1980.

DETROIT FALCONS Group from which Wilson Pickett made his solo debut, 1963.

DETROIT WHEELS See Mitch Ryder and the Detroit Wheels.

DETTMAR, DEL Keyboards. Member of Hawkwind, 1978 to present.

DETWEILER, CAROL Drums, vocal. Member of the Pink Section, 1980.

DEUTSCH, STU Drums. Member of the Plasmatics, 1980.

DEVENS, GEORGE Percussion. Session for Henry Gross (1973, 76, 78); Grace Slick (1980).

DEVERS, LARRY Drums, vocal. Member of Sod, 1971.

DEVLIN, BARRY Bass, vocal, writer. Original member of Horslips.

DEVO Mark Mothersbaugh—vocal, guitar; Gerald Casale—bass, vocal; Bob Mothersbaugh (Bob 1)—guitar, vocal; Bob (Bob 2)—guitar, vocal; Alan—drums. Produced by Brian Eno, Devo evolved in 1978 in a brief wave of publicity with a Devo-ised version of the Rolling Stones' "Satisfaction." *Albums:* Duty Now for the Future (WBR K-3337) 1979; Freedom of Choice (WBR 3435) 1980; Q: Are We Not Men? A: We Are Devo (WBR K-3239) 1978.

DEVON, DAVID Drums. Member of Storm, 1979.

DEVONPORT, MICK Vocal, guitar. Member of Nutz, 1974-77.

DEWALD, ROBERT Bass, vocal. Member of the U. S. Radio Band, 1976.

DEWAR, JAMES Bass, vocal, writer. Original member of Stone the Crows, 1971-72, and Robin

Trower's group, 1973-present. Session for Matthew Fisher (1980).

DEWEY, GEORGE Vocal, drums, percussion, recorder. Member of Mad River, 1968.

DEWEY, GREG Drums. Member of Country Joe and the Fish, 1969.

DEY, RICK Vocal, bass. Member of Melton, Levy and the Dey Brothers, 1972.

DEY, TONY Vocal, drums. Member of Melton, Levy and the Dey Brothers, 1972.

DFK BAND See Dudek, Finnegan, Kruger Band.

DHARMA, RITCHIE Drums. Original member of the Mick Abrahams Band, 1971-72. Session for Lou Reed (1972-74).

DHARMA BLUES BAND Dave Brock—guitar, vocals; Luke Francis—guitar, vocals; Mike King—piano. British blues band of the 60s.

DI ANNE, PAUL Vocal. Member of Iron Maiden, 1980.

DI BARTELLO, JOEL Bass. Session for Mike Pindar (1976).

DI CHIRO, ROBERT LOUIS Bass. Member of Sumner, 1980.

DI CIOCCIO, FRANZ Drums, percussion. Member of P.F.M., 1973-77.

DI FAZIO, JOE Keyboards, bass, vocals. Half of the Atlantis Philharmonic duet, 1974.

DI GILIO, VICTOR Drums, vocal. Member of Banchee, 1969.

DI GREGORIO, JOEL Keyboards, vocals. Member of the Charlie Daniels Band.

DI MEOLA, AL Guitar, percussion. Replaced Bill Conners in Return to Forever, 1975-76, before going solo. *Albums:* Casino (COL JC-35277) 1978; Elegant Gypsy (COL JC-34461); Go—Live from Paris (ISL 10); Land of the Midnight Sun (COL PC-34074) 1976; Splendido Hotel (COL C2X-36270) 1980; Al DiMeola, 1976.

DI MUCCI, DION Vocal, guitar. Namesake of Dion and the Belmonts, he was an early rock idol of the '60s, with teen tunes like "Teenager in Love." Personnel problems resulted in his eventual soloing. In 1968 he had the smash hit, "Abraham, Martin and John." *Albums:* Dion (LAU 2047); Dion Sings the 15 Million Sellers (LAU 2019); Dion's Greatest Hits (COL C-31942) 1973; Dion's Greatest Hits (LAU 2013); Donna the Prima Donna (COL C-35995); More of Dion's Greatest Hits (LAU 2022); Ruby Baby (COL C-35577) 1963; The Wanderers (WBR K-3359); Everything You Always Wanted to Hear by Dion and the Belmonts (LAU 4002).

DI NACOLA, JOEY Recorded under the name Joey Dee with the Starlighters.

DI STEFANO, NICK Vocal, drums. Member of Cognition, 1971.

DI VARCO, WAYNE Drums. Member of Mariah, 1976.

DIAMOND, DAVID Member of the Kings, 1980.

DIAMOND, DINKY Drums. Replaced Harvey Feinstein in the Sparks, 1973-76.

DIAMOND, DYAN Vocal, guitar, percussion. Member of Venus and the Razor Blades, 1977. *Album:* In the Dark (MCA 3053) 1978.

DIAMOND, GODFREY Vocal. Session for Lou Reed (1976).

DIAMOND, GREGG Drums, percussion, piano. Member of Five Dollar Shoes, 1972. *Albums:* Gregg Diamond's Starcruiser (MAR 2217); Hardware (MER SRM-1-3757); Hot Butterfly (POL 1-6162).

DIAMOND, JIM Vocal. Member of Bandit, 1976.

DIAMOND, MICHAEL Bass. Member of Legs Diamond, 1977-78.

DIAMOND, NEIL Vocal, guitar, writer. Born 1/24/44. In 1966, Diamond, a songwriter for the Monkees, struck out on his own and has since become one of the most popular male vocalists around. Produced and starred in "The Jazz Singer," 1980. Session for the Band (1978). *Albums:* And the Singer Sings His Song (MCA 2227) 1976; Bang and Shout Super Hits (BNG 220); Beautiful Noise (COL JC-33965) 1976; Neil Diamond Gold (MCA 2007); Neil Diamond's Greatest Hits (BNG 219); Neil Diamond, His 12 Greatest Hits (MCA 2016); Do It (BNG 224); Double Gold (BNG 2-227); Feel of Neil Diamond (BNG 214); Gang at Bang (BNG 215); Hot August Night (MCA 8000) 1972; I'm Glad You're Here with Me Tonight (COL KC-32550) 1973; Just for You (BNG 217); Jonathan Livingston Seagull (COL KC-32550) 1973; Love at the Greek (COL KC2-34404) 1977; Moods (MCA 2005) 1973; Rainbow (MCA 2103) 1973; September Morn (COL PC 32919) 1974; Shilo (BNG 221); Stones (MCA 2008); Sweet Caroline (MCA 2011); Tap Root Manuscript (MCA 2013); Touching You, Touching Me (MCA 2006); Velvet Gloves and Spit (MCA 2010); You Don't Bring Me Flowers (COL FC-35625) 1978; The Jazz Singer (CAP SWAN 12120) 1980.

DIAMOND REO Norm Nardini; Warren King; Frank Zuri; Robert Johns. *Album:* Ruff Cuts (PIC 3311) 1979.

DIAMONDE, DICK Bass. Member of the Easybeats, 1967-68.

DIAMONDS Mike Douglas—vocal; John Felton—vocal; Evan Fisher—vocal; Ted Kowalski—vocal; Phil Leavitt—vocal; Bill Reed—vocal; Dave Sommerville—vocal. Recorded "Little Darlin," 1957. *Albums:* Wrap Your Troubles in Dreams (MER); Songs from the Old West (MER); All New Songs (MER) 1957; America's Famous Song Stylists (WNG) 1957; Pop Hits (WNG) 1960.

DIANE Synthesizer. Credited as a member of the Silicon Teens, 1980.

DIAPER, LAUREN Trumpet. Member of Isis, 1974-75.

DIAS, DENNY Guitar. Original member of Steely Dan, 1972-76.

DICKEN Vocal, guitar. Member of Mr. Big, 1975, and Broken Home, 1980.

DICKENS, ERIN Vocal. Session for Gregg Allman (1974); Paul Butterfield (1975); Ian Hunter (1976).

DICKENSON, JIM Keyboards. Session for Ry Cooder (1980).

DICKERSON, B. B. Bass, vocal. Original member of War.

DICKERSON, BILL Bass. Session for Splinter (1975).

DICKERSON, LANCE Drums. Member of Commander Cody's Lost Planet Airmen.

DICKEY, DAVE Bass. Session for America (1977).

DICKIE, CHARLES Cello, piano, synthesizer. Member of Van Der Graaf, 1978.

DICKIE, TOM Guitar, vocal. Member of Susan, 1979.

DICKIES Leonard Graves Phillips—vocal, keyboards; Stan Lee—guitar, vocal; Chuck Wagon—keyboards, guitar, saxophone, harmonica, percussion, vocal; Billy Club—bass, vocal; Karlos Kaballero—drums. *Albums:* Dawn of the Dickies (AAM 4796) 1980; Incredible Shrinking Dickies (AAM 4742) 1979.

DICKINSON, JIM Piano, celeste, producer. Session for Ry Cooder (1972).

DICKINSON, PAUL Guitar, vocal. Member of the Hunt, 1980.

DICKSON, ARTHUR Drums. Session for the Blues Brothers (1980).

DICKSON, BARBARA Vocal. Session for Gerry Rafferty (1978-79). *Albums:* Barbara Dickson (COL JC-36495) 1980; Evita (MCA 2-11003); Morning Comes Quickly (RSO 1-3022).

DICTATORS Dick Manitoba—vocal; Ross the Boss—guitar, vocal; Top Ten—guitar, vocal; Adny Shernoff—bass, keyboards, vocal; Ritchie Teeter—drums, vocal; Mark Mendoza—bass (1977). *Albums:* Bloodbrothers (ASY 6E-147) 1978; Manifest Destiny (ASY 7E-1109) 1977.

DIDDLEY, BO Guitar, vocal, writer. Born 12/23/28. Ellas McDaniel, alias Bo Diddley, began playing rhythm and blues on Willie Dixon's Chess label. His animated tales reached all the way to England where they were even more popular than in his native U.S. Easily observable as influential on early Rolling Stones, the Who, and others. Session for Chuck Berry (1958). *Albums:* Another Dimension (CSS 50001); Big Bad Bo (CSS 50047); Bo Diddley (CHK 3007); Bo Diddley and Company (CHK 2985); Bo Diddley in the Spotlight (CHK 2976); Bo Diddley Is a Lover (CHK 2980); Bo Diddley, London Sessions (CSS 50029); Bo Diddley 16 All Time Greatest Hits; 500 Per Cent More Man (CHK 2996); Go Bo Diddley (CHK 3006); Got My Own Bag of Tricks; Have Guitar, Will Travel (CHK 2974); Origination (CHK 3001); Road Runner (CHK 2982); Bo Diddley Is a Gunslinger (CHK 2997); Where It All Began (CSS 50016).

DIEFENDERFER, DAN Guitar, vocal. Member of the Romeos, 1980.

DIETRICHSON, TOR Percussion. Member of the Dija Rhythm Band, 1976.

DIETZ, FRANK Guitar. Session for Eric Burdon (1977).

DIFFORD, CHRIS Guitar, vocal. Added to the Squeeze lineup, 1980.

DIFONZO, RICK Member of the A's, 1979.

DIGGLE, JULIAN Percussion. Member of Movies since 1976. Session on "Rough Mix" (1977).

DIGGLE, STEVE Guitar, vocal. Member of the Buzzcocks since 1977.

DIJA RHYTHM BAND Jim Loveless—percussion; Ray Spiegel—vibes; Jordan Amarantha—percussion; Vince Delgado—percussion; Mickey Hart—drums; Tor Dietrichson—percussion; Aushim Chaudhuri—percussion; Zakir Hussain—percussion; Arshad Syed—percussion; Joy Schulman—percussion; Peter Carmichael—percussion. *Album:* Dija Rhythm Band (UAR) 1976.

DIJON, ROCKY Congas. Session with Steve Stills (1971).

DIK Percussion, harmonica, vocal. Member of Fashion, 1979.

DILEMA, PETER Drums, vocal. Member of the Doctors of Madness, 1977.

DILL, BOB Trumpet. Member of Stanley Steamer, 1973.

DILLARD, DOUG Banjo. Co-founder of the Dillard and Clark Expedition with Gene Clark, which became the Doug Dillard Expedition. Session for Nilsson (1975); Mistress (1979). *Album:* Heaven (FLF 086) 1979.

DILLARD, RODNEY Guitar, dobro, pedal steel guitar. Original member of the Dillards.

DILLARD AND CLARK EXPEDITION Gene Clark—guitar, vocal, keyboards, writer; Doug Dillard—banjo, vocal, writer; Bernie Leadon—banjo, guitar; Don Beck—dobro, mandolin; Dave Jackson—bass. First venture of former Byrd Gene Clark and Doug Dillard of the Dillards, when both left their respective groups. *Albums:* Fantastic Expedition of Dillard and Clark, 1968; Through the Morning, Through the Night (AAM 4203); Genuine, 1971; Duelin' Banjo (TWC T-409); You Don't Need a Reason to Sing (TWC).

DILLARDS Rodney Dillard—guitar, dobro, pedal steel guitar; Herb Pedersen—guitar, banjo; Dean Webb—mandolin; Buddy Emmons—pedal steel guitar; Mitch Jayne—acoustic bass (until 1977); Joe Osborn—electric bass; Toxey French—drums; Jim Gordon—drums; Doug Dillard—guitar, banjo; Paul York—drums; Jeff Gilkinson—bass, cello, vocal (1977-80); Billy Ray Latham—banjo, guitar, vocal (1977); Ray Parks—fiddle (1979); Doug

Bounsal—guitar, bass, vocal (1979). Emulating the success of the Byrds, the Dillards brought country and bluegrass music to rock audiences. *Albums:* Roots and Branches (ANT 5901); Tribute to the American Duck (POP PPLA 175); Wheatstraw Suite (ELK 74035) 1968; Back Porch Bluegrass (ELK 7232) 1963; Decade Waltz (FLF 082) 1979; Dillards—Copperfields (ELK 74054); Dillards Live (ELK 7265) 1964; Dillards Vs. the Incredible L. A. Time Machine (FLF 040) 1972; Pickin' and Fiddlin' (ELK 7285) 1965; Mountain Rock (CCS 5007) 1979.

DILLINGER Vocal. Namesake of Dillinger, 1976.

DILLINGER Dillinger—vocal; Sly—drums; Ranchie—bass; Ansel Collins—keyboards; Doggie Bryan—guitars; Sticky—percussion; Barnabas—percussion. *Albums:* Bionic Dread (MNG 9455) 1976; C.B. 200 (MNG 9385) 1976.

DILLON, ERIC Drums. After being a member of Noel Redding's short lived Fat Mattress, 1969-70, he became a member of Savoy Brown's Boogie Brothers, 1974. Member of Lion, 1980.

DILLON, JIM Guitar, vocal. Session for Mike Pindar (1976).

DILLON, JOHN Guitar, fiddle, mandolin, vocals, autoharp, dulcimer, percussion, writer. Original member of the Ozark Mountain Daredevils since 1973.

DILLON, PAUL Drums, percussion, guitar, vocal. Member of Earth Opera, 1968-69.

DILTZ, HENRY Vocal. Session for Steve Stills (1971); David Crosby (1971).

DIMLIN, FRANK Vocal. Voice of the Angels, 1976-79.

DINES, PETE Keyboards. Original member of the Keef Hartley Band, 1969.

DINETTES Waddy Wachtel—guitar, vocal; David Foster—keyboards; Bill Champlin—organ, vocal; Dee Murray—bass, vocal; Nigel Olsson—drums, vocal. Backup band for Michael Dinner, 1976.

DINNER, MICHAEL Guitar, vocal. *Albums:* Great Pretender (FSY 9454) 1974; Tom Thumb the Dreamer (FSY 9502) 1976.

DINNING, MARK Vocal. Rose to fame with "Teen Angel," 1959. *Albums:* Teen Angel (MGM) 1960; Wanderin' (MGM) 1960.

DINO, DESI AND BILLY Dino Martin, Jr.—guitar, vocal; Desi Arnez, Jr.—drums, vocal; Billy Hinsche—guitar. Dean Martin's son Dino, and Desi Arnez's son, Desi, were discovered by Frank Sinatra, who enabled them to record their hit "I'm a Fool," 1967. *Album:* Dino, Desi and Billy (RPS).

DINWIDDIE, GENE Saxophone, flute, mandolin, vocal. Member of Paul Butterfield Blues Band, 1967-71, and Full Moon, 1972. Session for B. B. King (1972); Paul Butterfield's Better Days (1973); Nilsson (1975).

DINWOODIE, STEVE Bass. Member of Marseille, 1980.

DIO, RONNIE JAMES Vocal, writer. Formerly from Elf. With Ritchie Blackmore, he co-founded Ritchie Blackmore's Rainbow, 1975, until he left to replace Ozzy Osbourne in Black Sabbath, 1980.

DIODES Paul Robinson—vocal; John Catto—guitar; Ian MacKay—bass, keyboards, vocal; Mike Lengyell—drums. *Album:* Permanent Wave (EPC JE-36136) 1978.

DION AND THE BELMONTS Dion Di Mucci—vocal, guitar; Angelo d'Aleo; Fred Milano—piano; Carlo Mastrangelo—drums. Recorded the hit "Runaround Sue," 1961. *Albums:* Presenting Dion and the Belmonts; Dion and the Belmonts, 1960; When You Wish Upon a Star, 1960; Dion Alone; Runaround Sue; Lovers Who Wander; Love, Come to Me; Together with the Belmonts, 1966; Songs to Sandy, 1966; 15 Million Sellers, 1966; Greatest Hits, 1966; Together Again, 1967; Dion, 1968; Everything You Always Wanted to Hear by Dion and the Belmonts (LAU 4002).

DIPPOLITO, BERNARDO Vocal, percussion. Member of Sam the Band.

DIRBY, DAVE Guitar. Session for Waylon Jennings (1974).

DIRE STRAITS Mark Knopfler—vocal, guitar; David Knopfler—guitar (1978-79); John Illsley—bass, vocal; Pick Withers—drums. *Albums:* Communique (WBR HS-3330) 1979; Dire Straits (WBR K-3266) 1978; Making Movies (WBR BSK-3480) 1980.

DIRT BAND Merle Bregante—drums; John McEuen—banjo, guitar, mandolin, fiddle; Richard Hathaway—bass; Jeff Hanna—vocal, guitar; Al Garth—saxophone, fiddle. See Nitty Gritty Dirt Band. *Albums:* American Dream (UAR LO-974) 1979; Dirt Band (UAR LO-854) 1978; Make a Little Magic (UAR LT-1042) 1980.

DIRTY ANGELS Charlie Carp—guitar, vocal; David Hull—bass, vocal, keyboards; Jimmy Maher—drums, vocal; George Maher—guitars. *Albums:* Dirty Angels (AAM 4716) 1978; Kiss Tomorrow Goodbye (PRS PS2020) 1976.

DIRTY LOOKS Patrick Barnes—guitar, vocal; Marco Sin—bass, vocal; Peter Parker—drums, vocal. *Album:* Dirty Looks (SSF JE-36434) 1980.

DIRTY TRICKS Terry Horbury—bass; Johnny Fraser-Binnie—guitar, keyboards; John Lee—drums, percussion; Kenny Stewart—vocal. *Album:* Night Man (POL) 1976.

DIVEN, MALCOLM Vocal. Member of the Ruts, 1979.

DIVSEK, JAMES Drums. Member of Bobbidazzler, 1977.

DIX, DAVID Drums. Replaced Monte Yoho in the Outlaws, 1979-present.

DIXIE CUPS Barbara Ann Hawkins—vocal; Rosa Lee Hawkins—vocal; Joan Marie Hawkins—vocal; Joan Johnson—vocal. Sang "Chapel of Love,"

1964. *Albums:* Ridin' High (ABC) 1964; Iko, Iko (RBD); Chapel of Love (RBD) 1965.

DIXIE DREGS Steve Morse—guitar, banjo, pedal steel guitar; Andy West—bass; Allen Sloan—violin, viola; Rod Morganstein—drums, percussion; T. Lavitz—keyboards. *Albums:* Dregs of the Earth (ARI 9528) 1980; Free Fall (CPN 1089); Night of the Living Dregs (CPN 0216); What If (CPN 0203).

DIXIE FLYERS Bert Baumbach—guitar; Ken Palmer—mandolin; David Zoriluk—bass; Willie Bennett—harmonica; Dennis Le Page—banjo; David Jack—banjo. *Albums:* Cheaper to Lease (BOO 6002); For Our Friends (BOO 6007); Just Pickin' (BOO 6004) 1978; Light, Medium Heavy (BOO 6000).

DIXON, DON Vocal, bass, percussion, guitar. Member of Arrogance, 1976.

DIXON, EUGENE Real name of Gene Chandler.

DIXON, GARY Vocal, guitar. Member of T.M.G., 1979.

DIXON, SAMUEL Trumpet. Session for the Marshall Tucker Band (1973).

DIXON, WILLIE String bass, vocal, writer. Executive producer with Chess Records and became popular with Chuck Berry and his Combo, 1956, but most noted for his singular blues performance and writing. "Little Red Rooster," "Seventh Son" and "Wang Dang Doodle" are just a few of his songs that were standards for any young blues band trying to make the charts in the '60s. Session for Chuck Berry (1956-60); Muddy Waters; Bo Diddley. *Albums:* Blues from "Big Bill's" Copa Cabana; Blues Jam (BUD 7510); Catalyst (OVA QD-1433); I Am the Blues (COL CS-9987); Memphis Slim and Willie Dixon at Village Gate (FLW 32986); Songs of Memphis Slim and Willie Dixon (FLW 23985); What Happened to My Blues (OVA 1705).

DJAVAS, PATRICK Bass, moog. Member of P.F.M., 1973-77.

DMOCHOWSKI, ALEX Bass. Played with John Mayall, 1970, after being a member of Aynsley Dunbar's Retaliation, 1968-70. Session for Peter Green (1970); John Mayall (1977).

DMZ Paul Murphy—drums; J. Rassler—guitar; Mono Mann—vocal, organ; Rick Corraccio—bass; Peter Greenberg—guitar. *Album:* DMZ (SIR K 6051) 1978.

DOBBINS, MARY Vocal. Member of Arizona, 1976.

DOBBS, FRED Guitar, banjo, vocal. Member of Heartsfield, 1973-75.

DOBBS, RONNIE Guitar. Member of the Thunderhead, 1976.

DOBEK, TOMMY Drums, percussion. Member of the Michael Stanley Band since 1977.

DOBSON, LYNN Saxophone, flute. Member of the Keef Hartley Band horn section, 1969-71.

DOBSON, PETE Drums, percussion. Member of Juicy Lucy, 1970, and the Tigers, 1980.

DOCTORS OF MADNESS Kid Strange—vocal, guitar, harmonica, saxophone; Urban Blitz—guitar; Stoner—bass; Peter di Lema—drums, vocal. *Album:* Doctors of Madness (UAR LA-871-12) 1977.

DODD, RORY Vocal. Session for Ted Nugent (1977); Ian Hunter (1979).

DODGERS Paul Hooper—drums, vocal; Bob Jackson—keyboards, guitar, vocal; Roger Lomas—guitar, bass, vocal; John Wilson—guitar, bass, vocal. *Album:* Love on the Rebound (POL 1 6174) 1978.

DODMAN, MIKE Guitar. Member of the Blue Goose, 1975.

DODSON, LARRY Member of the re-formed Bar-Kays.

DODSON, MARK Vocal. Session for Sean Tyla (1980).

DODSON, RICH Member of the Stampeders, 1973-76.

DODT, DAVID Guitar. Member of the Bob Meighan Band, 1976.

DOE, JOHN Bass, vocal. Member of X, 1980.

DOERGE, CRAIG Keyboards. Member of the Section, 1972 and 1977. Session for Donovan (1973); James Taylor; Gene Clark (1974); Crosby and Nash (1976); Russ Giguere (1971); Crosby, Stills and Nash (1977); Yvonne Elliman (1978); Richie Furay (1979); Jackson Browne (1980).

DOERING, GEORGE Guitar. Session for Julie Tippets and Brian Auger (1978); Robbie Robertson (1980).

DOG SOLDIER Mel Simpson—keyboards, vocal, writer; Miller Anderson—guitar, vocal, writer; Keef Hartley—drums, writer; Paul Bliss—bass, vocal, writer; Derek Griffiths—vocal, writer, guitar. The Keef Hartley Band was never as famous as they deserved to be, so it was no surprise when Dog Soldier went virtually unnoticed. Hartley formed the band, with old partner Miller Anderson. Soldier concentrated on instrumental backing to the different soloist/writers in the group, for a mutually complementary blend of rock and blues. *Album:* Dog Soldier (UAR UA-LA405) 1975.

DOGGETT, ALAN Moog synthesizer. Session on "Jesus Christ Superstar," 1970.

DOHENY, NED Guitar, vocal. *Album:* Prone (COL PC-34889).

DOHERTY, BILLY Drums. Member of the Undertones, 1979.

DOHERTY, DENNY Vocal. Starting with Cass Elliot in the Mugwumps, he moved with her in 1966 to join the Mamas and the Papas.

DOLBY, TOM Keyboards. Member of Bruce Wooley and the Camera Club, 1980.

DOLENZ, MICKEY Guitar, vocal, drums. Singer-turned-actor, from the Missing Link to the Monkees,

1966-69. Resurfaced in 1976 in Dolenz, Jones, Boyce and Hart.

DOLENZ, JONES, BOYCE AND HART Mickey Dolenz—guitar, vocal, drums; Davy Jones—vocal, percussion; Tommy Boyce—vocal; Bobby Hart—vocal. An attempted nostalgia resurrection of the Monkees with Boyce and Hart, who wrote the early hits for the Monkees, 1976.

DOLIN, BOB Keyboards, vocal. Member of the Billion Dollar Babies, 1977. Session for Alice Cooper (1973).

DOLITZSCH, HANNA Vocal. Session for Triumvirat (1973).

DOLLARHIDE, ROGER Vocal. Session for George Duke (1975).

DOMANICO, CHUCK Acoustic bass. Session for Marc Benno; Harvey Mandel (1972); Martin Mull (1977); Ry Cooder (1978); Robbie Robertson (1980).

DOMINO, ANTOINE "FATS" Piano, vocal, writer. At an early age, Antoine had an accident in which his hands were crushed. He was told he would never play the piano again. Years of practice and perseverance overcame this tragedy to establish him as the king of pre-Elvis rock. His crooning of ballads "Blueberry Hill" (1956), "My Blue Heaven" (1956), "I'm in the Mood For Love" (1957), and so many more, including "Walking to New Orleans" (1960), set blues ballad standards for years to come. Few of his contemporaries have survived with his stature. *Albums:* Fats Domino (IMP 12103) 1956; Fats Domino Rock and Rollin' (IMP 12387); Fats Domino Swings (IMP 12091); Here Stands Fats, 1957; I Miss You So (IMP 12398) 1961; This Is Fats (IMP 12391) 1958; Very Best of Fats Domino (UAR UA-LA233); Walking to New Orleans (IMP 12227); Mr. D., 1958; Let's Play Fats Domino, 1959; Fats Domino Sings Million Record Hits, 1960; 12,000,000 Records, 1959; Lots of Dominos; Let's Dance with Domino, 1963; Here He Comes Again, 1963; Here Comes Fats Domino, 1973; Fats on Fire, 1963; Getaway with Fats Domino, 1966; Stompin' Fats Domino, 1967; Trouble in Mind; Fats Is Back, 1968; Fabulous Mr. Domino, 1958; Let the Four Winds Blow, 1961; What a Party, 1961; Twisting the Stomp, 1961; Just Domino, 1963; Cooking with Fats (UAR LWB-122) 1966; Fats Domino (EVR 280) 1966; Fats Domino, Vol. 2 (EVR 330); Million Sellers by Fats (UAR LM-1027) 1962; When I'm Walking (COL C-35996).

DOMINO, FLOYD Keyboards. Member of Asleep at the Wheel since 1973.

DOMINOES See Derek and the Dominoes.

DON Member of the Germs, 1979.

DONAHUE, JERRY Guitar, slide guitar, vocal. Member of Fotheringay, 1971. Replaced Simon Nichol in Fairport Convention, 1975. Member of the Thieves, 1979. Session for Gary Wright (1971); Thomas F. Browne (1972); Gerry Rafferty (1978-80).

DONALD, CHRIS Guitar. Replaced Henry Gross in Sha Na Na, 1971.

DONALD, TIM Drums. Session for John Cale (1974-75); David Kubinec (1979).

DONALDSON, BOBBY Drums. Session for John Hammond (1964, 68).

DONALDSON, DAVID Guitar, harmonica. Member of Cherokee, 1971.

DONALDSON, GEORGE Guitar, saxophone. Member of Cherokee, 1971.

DONALDSON, PAT Bass. Member of Fotheringay, 1971, and Medicine Head, 1973. Session for John Cale (1975); the Sutherland Brothers (1973); Thomas F. Browne (1973); Jess Roden (1974); John Cale (1975); Gay and Terry Woods (1976-78); David Kubinec (1979).

DONALDSON, ROBERT Keyboards. Member of Cherokee, 1971.

DONALDSON, STARR Guitar, vocal. Member of Sawbuck, 1971.

DONEGAN, LONNIE Vocal. Real name: Anthony James Donegan. Member of the Ken Colyer Skiffle Group, 1952-54. Recorded "Does Your Chewing Gum Lose It's Flavor," 1961. *Albums:* Skiffle Folk Music (ACO); Grand Coulee Dam (DAM DOT); Lonnie Donegan (DOT).

DONELIAN, ARMEN Keyboards. Member of Cosmology, 1977.

DONELLY, JOHN Trumpet. Session for Mike Vernon.

DONNELLY, ALBIE Saxophone, flute, vocal. Member of Supercharge, 1976-77. Session for Bram Tchaikovsky (1980).

DONNELLY, BEN Bass. Member of the Inmates since 1979.

DONNELLY, PHILLIP Guitar. Session for Donovan (1976).

DONOHUE, DANE Guitar, vocal. *Album:* Dane Donohue (COL JC-34278) 1978.

DONOVAN Guitar, vocal, writer. Real name: Donovan Leitch. Born 5/10/46. The Dylan sound-alikes of 1965 were more plentiful than the cast of a Cecil B. de Mille movie. Probably most famous of the survivors is Donovan. About the time hippies were discovering themselves, Donovan arrived in a sea of flowers, singing his songs of love, peace and happiness in fairylands. *Albums:* 7-Tease, 1975; Fairy Tale (HIK LPM 127); Like It Is with the Real Donovan (HIK LP135); Slow Down World, 1976; Cosmic Wheels (EPC KE 32156) 1973; Catch the Wind (HIK); Mellow Yellow (EPC LN 24239); Barabajagal (EPC 26481) 1968; Donovan (ARI 4143) 1977; Donovan in Concert (EPC 26386) 1967; Donovan's Greatest Hits (EPC PE-26439); Essence to Essence (EPC KE-32800) 1973; Gift from a Flower to a Garden (EPC 171) 1967; Hurdy Gurdy Man (EPC 26420) 1968;

Sunshine Superman (EPC 26217); HMS Donovan (Import) 1971; Open Road (EPC E 30125) 1970.

DOOBIE BROTHERS Tom Johnston—guitar, harp, keyboards, vocal, writer (1971-78); Pat Simmons—guitar, vocal, writer; John Hartman—drums (1971-80); Dave Shogren—bass, keyboards, vocal (until 1971); Tiran Porter—vocal, bass (1972-present); Michael Hossack—drums (1972-74); Keith Knudsen—drums (1974-present); Jeff "Skunk" Baxter—pedal steel guitar, guitar (1975-80); Michael McDonald—keyboards, vocal, writer (1976-present); Chet McCracken—drums (1980); Cornelius Bumpus—saxophone, keyboards, vocal (1980). As a local band, the Doobies were popular with California's Hell's Angels MC. After their first acoustic album, the Doobies surprised everyone with an electric album, demonstrating that instead of following trends, they would be setting them. They became most popular upon the acquisition of writer McDonald (from Steely Dan) and their popularity continues to this day. Part of "No Nukes," 1979. *Albums:* Best of the Doobie Brothers (WBR K-3112) 1978; Captain and Me (WBR B-2694) 1973; Doobie Brothers (WBR 1919) 1971; Livin' on the Fault Line (WBR K-3045) 1977; Minute by Minute (WBR K-3193) 1978; Stampede (WBR B-2835) 1975; Takin' It to the Streets (WBR B-3899) 1976; Toulouse Street (WBR B-2634) 1972; What Were Once Vices Are Now Habits (WBR 2750) 1974.

DOOLARD, FRANZ Pedal steel guitar. Session for George Kooymans (1973).

DOORS Jim Morrison—vocal, writer (1967-71); Ray Manzarek—keyboards, bass, vocal, writer; Robbie Krieger—guitar; John Densmore—drums. Originally called the Psycedelic Rangers. With unusually good production from their debut in 1967, chief lyricist Morrison's songs ranged the gamut from songs of love to songs of loneliness. They all carried a hidden current of violence and/or terror. With Morrison's death in 1971, the remaining Doors fumbled through two more albums, "Full Circle," and "Other Voices." The talent was there, but the inspiration was gone. *Albums:* The Best of the Doors (ELK); Full Circle (ELK); Absolutely Live (ELK 9002) 1970; American Prayer (ELK 5E-502) 1978; Doors (ELK 74007) 1967; L. A. Woman (ELK 75011) 1971; Morrison Hotel/Hard Rock Cafe (ELK 75007) 1970; Soft Parade (ELK 75005) 1969; Strange Days (ELK 74014) 1967; 13 (ELK 74079) 1970; Waiting for the Sun (ELK 74024) 1968; Weird Scenes Inside the Gold Mine (ELK 8E-6001) 1972; Other Voices (ELK 75017) 1971; Greatest Hits (ELK 5E 515) 1980.

DORAN, DAVE Guitar. Session for Bob Seger (1974).

DORE, CHARLIE Vocal, guitar. *Album:* Where to Now (ISL 9559) 1979.

DORE, STEVEN Guitar, piano. Member of the Blend, 1978-79.

DORION, DAN Bass. Member of Cottonwood South, 1974.

DORMAN, LEE Bass, vocal, piano, writer. Born 9/15/42. Original member of the Iron Butterfly, 1967-69, and Captain Beyond, 1972-73.

DOROUGH, BOB Drums, vocal. Early member of the Fugs Chorus. Session for Pearls Before Swine (1971); Art Garfunkel (1978).

DORSEY, LESLEY Vocal. Early member of the Fugs Chorus.

DORSEY, "GEORGIA" TOM Piano. Session with Ma Rainey (1928); Tampa Red (1934).

DORSEY, TONY Horns. Session for Wings (1976-79).

DOUBLEDAY, MARCUS Trumpet. Original member of the Electric Flag, 1967-68, and the Buddy Miles Express, 1968-69.

DOUCETTE, JERRY Vocal, guitar, drums. Namesake of Doucette, 1979.

DOUCETTE Jerry Doucette—vocal, guitar, drums; Duris Maxwell—drums, keyboards; Donnie Cummings—bass; Mark Olson—keyboards. *Albums:* Douce is Loose (MSH 5013) 1979; Mama Let Him Play (MSH 5009).

DOUCHETTE, THOM Harmonica. Session for the Allman Brothers (1971).

DOUD, EARL Congas, percussion, vocal. Session for Free Creek (1973). *Albums:* Honest To God, We Really Mean It, Very Last Nixon Album (BRU 754201).

DOUGHERTY, JIMMY Member of Alias, 1979.

DOUGHERTY, NEIL Keyboards. Born 7/29/46. Member of R. E. O. Speedwagon since 1971.

DOUGHERTY, TOM Percussion. Member of Tim Weisberg's backup band, 1977.

DOUGLAS, BRUCE Bass, guitar. Session for Roy Sundholm (1979).

DOUGLAS, GREG Slide guitar. Session for Steve Miller (1977); Rocky Sullivan (1978).

DOUGLAS, JENNY Vocal. Member of Dayton, 1980.

DOUGLAS, JONATHAN Vocal, keyboards, guitar. Member of Dancer, 1976.

DOUGLAS, MIKE Vocal. Member of the Diamonds.

DOUGLAS, PAM Vocal. Session for Peter Green (1980).

DOUGLAS, PAUL Member of Wheatfield, 1980.

DOUGLAS, ROBERT Keyboards, vocal. Member of Platinum Hook since 1979.

DOUGLAS, STEPHEN Harmonica, keyboards, vocal. Member of McGuffey Lane, 1980.

DOUGLAS, STEVE Tenor saxophone. Member of Duane Eddy's Rebels, 1961. Session for Nilsson (1975); Jan and Dean (1963); Bob Dylan (1978-79); Sammy Hagar (1979).

DOUKAS, JOHN Vocal, guitar. Member of Earthquake since 1966.

DOUMA, DANNY Vocal, guitar. Original member of Big Wha-Koo, 1977. *Album:* Night Eyes (WBR K-3326) 1979.

DOVE, GLENN Drums, percussion. Member of Speedway Blvd., 1980.

DOVER, DAVE Bass. Session for Eric Burdon (1977).

DOWD, TOM Percussion, producer, piano. Produced the Marshall Tucker Band, Blackjack (1979), and Kenny Loggins (1979), among others. Session for the James Gang (1975).

DOWLE, DAVE Drums. Replaced Steve Ferrone in Brian Auger's Oblivion Express, 1975. Member of Whitesnake, 1978-79, and Runner, 1979. Session for Kevin Lamb (1978).

DOWLER, STEVE Guitar. Member of the Loading Zone, 1968.

DOWNBEATS Early name for Paul Revere and the Raiders, 1962-65.

DOWNCHILD Don Walsh—guitar, harmonica; Rick Walsh—vocal; Tony Flaim—vocal; Jane Vasey—keyboards; Mike Bowser—bass; Wayne Wilson—drums; Michael O'Connell—trombone. *Album:* So Far (ADP 4114) 1979.

DOWNES, GEOFF Keyboards, vocal. Replaced Rick Wakeman in Yes, 1980.

DOWNEY, BRIAN Drums. Member of Thin Lizzy since 1973.

DOWNIE, TYRONE Keyboards, bass, percussion, vocal. Member of Bob Marley's Wailers.

DOWNING, K. K. Guitar. Member of Judas Priest since 1974.

DOWNING, MARK Guitar. Member of Nantucket since 1978.

DOYLE, JIMMY Guitar. Member of Ayer's Rock, 1975-77.

DOYLE, JOHN Drums. Replaced Martin Jackson in Magazine, 1979-present.

DOYLE, MARK Guitar. Member of Jukin' Bone, 1972. Session for Far Cry (1980).

DOZIER, LAMONT Vocal. *Albums:* Bittersweet (WBR K-3282) 1979; Peddlin' Music on the Side (WBR B-3039); Right There (WBR B-2929).

DOZY Nickname of Trevor Davis. Member of Dave Dee, Dozy, Beaky, Mick and Tich.

DR. BUZZARD'S ORIGINAL SAVANNAH BAND Stoney Bowder, Jr.— guitar, piano, vocal; August Darnell—bass, vocal; Mickey Sevilla—drums; Andy Hernandez—vibes; Don Armando Bonilla—percussion. *Albums:* Dr. Buzzard's Original Savannah Band (VIC AFLI-1504); Dr. Buzzard Goes to Washington (ELK 6E-218); Dr. Buzzard Meets King Penett (VIC AFLI-2402) 1976.

DR. FEELGOOD John B. Sparks—bass; Lee Brilleaux—vocal, harmonica; Wilko Johnson—guitar (1975-80); Big Figure—drums, percussion, vocal. *Album:* Malpractice (COL PC 34098) 1978.

DR. HOK Guitar. Member of the Group Image, 1968.

DR. HOOK Pseudonym for Ray Sawyer. See Dr. Hook and the Medicine Show.

DR. HOOK AND THE MEDICINE SHOW Ray Sawyer—vocal, piano; Dennis Locorriere—vocal, guitar, bass, harmonica; George Cummings—vocal, guitar (until 1980); Bill Francis—keyboards, vocal; John Wolters—drums, vocal; Jance Garfat—bass; Rick Elswit—guitar, vocal; Rod Smarr—guitar (1980). *Albums:* Sloppy Seconds (COL C-31622) 1972; Belly Up (COL C-32270) 1973; Bankrupt (CAP ST-11397) 1975. Little Bit More (CAP ST-11522) 1976; Revisited, 1976; Makin' Love and Music (CAP ST 11632) 1977; Sometimes You Win (CAP SOO-12023) 1978; Rising (CAS NBLP 7251) 1980; Pleasure and Pain (CAP SW-11849); Dr. Hook and the Medicine Show (COL C-30898); Best of Dr. Hook (COL C-34147); Dr. Hook's Greatest Hits (CAP 500 12122) 1980.

DR. JOHN Piano, vocal, writer, guitar. Real name: Malcolm Rebennack. Alias: John Creux. Born 11/21/40. A registered priest of voodoo in Louisiana, Dr. John has been composing songs with mystical lyrics and voodoo rhythms, directly related to the blues, since the 1960s. The world was not then ready for his "Gris-Gris" music, but when funk became popular in the '70s, the history behind it became known and people realized Dr. John had been playing it for years. Leon Russell is said to have styled his voice after the Doctor. After achieving some degree of notoriety, he was a member of the short-lived Triumvirat with Mike Bloomfield and John Hammond. Session for Canned Heat (1969); Steve Stills (1971); B. B. King (1971); John Sebastian (1971); the Rolling Stones (1972); Maria Muldaur (1973); Free Creek (1973); Bill Wyman (1974-76); Carly Simon (1974); Ringo Starr (1974); Nilsson (1975-76); Neil Diamond; the Band (1978); Rodney Crowell (1978); Joe Cocker (1978); Robbie Robertson (1980); Bob Seger (1980); Professor Longhair (1980). *Albums:* Babylon (ACO SD 33270) 1968; Remedies (ACO SD 33316) 1970; The Sun, Moon and Herbs (ACO SD 7018); Gumbo (ACO SD 7006) 1972; Desitively Bonaroo (UAR UA LA552G) 1972; In the Right Place (ACO SD 7018) 1973; Triumvirat (COL) 1974; Hollywood Be Thy Name (UAR UA LA552-G) 1975; Gris Gris (ACO 234); City Lights (AAM 7321) 1978; Nite Tripper at His Best (PPK 263); Tango Palace (AAM 740) 1979.

DR. ROSS Drums, guitar, harmonica, vocal. Born 10/21/25. Blues-boogie from the John Lee Williamson school of Mississippi blues. *Album:* Dr. Ross (ARH 1065) 1972.

DRAGON, DARRYL Piano. The Captain of the Captain and Tenille. Session for the Beach Boys (1965); John Kay (1973); the Tremblers (1980).

DRAGON, DENNIS Drums, vocal, percussion, producer. Member of the Surf Punks, 1980.

DRAKE, DOUGLAS P. Reeds, piano, strings, percussion. Member of Viktor Koncept, 1979.

DRAKE, NICK Vocal, guitar. *Album:* Five Leaves Left (ANT AN7010) 1973.

DRAKE, OMA Vocal. Session for Neil Diamond (1976).

DRAKE, PETE Pedal steel guitar. Session for Bob Dylan (1969); Harvey Mandel; Waylon Jennings (1973); Leon Russell (1973-74); George Harrison (1972); Ringo Starr (1971); the Earl Scruggs Revue (1976); Bill Medley (1978).

DRAPER, LAUREN Trumpet. Member of Isis, 1974-75.

DRAPER, RAY Tuba, percussion, vocal. Session for Dr. John (1971).

DRAPER, TERRY Member of Klaatu since 1976.

DREAMS Michael Brecker—saxophone, flute; Randy Brecker—trumpet, flugelhorn; Bill Cobham—drums; Jeff Kent—guitar, keyboards, vocal; Doug Lubahn—bass, vocal; Barry Rogers—trombone, tuba; Edward Vernon—vocal. *Album:* Dreams (COL C-30225) 1970.

DREJA, CHRIS Guitar, percussion, piano, bass. Original member of the Yardbirds, 1962-69, and Renaissance, 1969-77.

DREMER, BRUCE Keyboards, vocal. Member of the Choice, 1980.

DRESHER, PAUL Guitar, flute. Member of Touchstone, 1971.

DREW, BOB Keyboards, vocal. Member of the Electrics, 1980.

DREWD, KARL Saxophone. Session for Triumvirat (1973).

DREYFUSS, MICHAEL Violin, viola. Member of McKendree Spring.

DRIFTERS Rhythm and blues group who had a string of hits, including "Save the Last Dance for Me" (1962), "Up on the Roof" (1963), and "Under the Boardwalk" (1964), featuring the lead vocals of Clyde McPhatter. Other former lead singers included Ben E. King and Bobby Hendricks. *Albums:* Stardust (ARI 5000); Rockin' and Drifting, 1958; Save the Last Dance for Me, 1962; Up on the Roof, 1963; Under the Boardwalk, 1964; Good Life with the Drifters, 1965; I'll Take You Where the Music's Playing, 1966; Drifters' Golden Hits (ATC 8153) 1963; Golden Soul (ATC 18198); Greatest Hits (GUS 0063) 1960; Soul Years (ATC 2-504); Their Greatest Recordings (ACO 375) 1971.

DRIGGS, CARL Vocal, percussion. Member of Foxy, 1979.

DRINK SMALL Guitar, vocal. Blues artist born in South Carolina. *Album:* Drink Small (SLD SLP-1).

DRINKARD, CISSY Vocal. Real name for Cissy Drinkard Houston of the Sweet Inspirations, 1967-69.

DRISCOLL, GARY Drums. Original member of Ritchie Blackmore's Rainbow, 1975-76.

DRISCOLL, JULIE Vocal. With Brian Auger, she was the focal point of the Trinity, 1968-69. Started in Steam Packet in 1965. *Album:* Encore (WBR BSK 3153) 1976.

JULIE DRISCOLL, BRIAN AUGER AND THE TRINITY Julie "Jools" Driscoll—vocal; Brian "Auge" Auger—organ, vocal, writer, piano; Clive Thacker—drums, percussion; Dave Ambrose—bass, guitar, vocal. "Jools" was called the Janis Joplin of Great Britain, because of her frizzy hair and casual psychedelic dress. "Auge" was voted the "Brightest Hope," 1964, by British pop magazines. Driscoll's voice was cool and haunting and fit perfectly with Auger's flowing, progressive organ lines and compositions, a blend of rock and jazz. That was the basis for their "Best New Group of the Year" award in 1968. Their first two albums preceded a dynamic double set, "Street Noise," 1969, the pinnacle of their career. Auger left shortly thereafter, moving to the U.S. and forming the Oblivion Express. *Albums:* Jools and Brian (CAP DT136) 1968; Open (ACO 5D 33258) 1968; Street Noise (ACO JD 20701) 1969.

DRISCOLL, MIKE Drums. Session for Long John Baldry (1975); Mick Taylor (1979).

DRIVE, DAVE Drums. Member of the Gears, 1980.

DROVER, MARTIN Trumpet. Session for the Keef Hartley Band (1971); Bryan Ferry (1977-78).

DRUMBO Drums. Real name: John French. Original member of Captain Beefheart and his Magic Band, 1965.

DRUMMOND, BURLEIGH Drums. Member of Ambrosia since 1975. Session for the Alan Parsons Project (1976).

DRUMMOND, DENNY Drums. Member of the Flyboys, 1980.

DRUMMOND, TIMOTHY Bass, drums. Member of the Stray Gators, 1972, and Crazy Horse, 1977. Session for Paul Butterfield (1975); Neil Young (1973, 75, 77, 78, 80); J. J. Cale (1974-76); Crosby and Nash (1976); Crosby, Stills and Nash (1977); Rick Danko (1977); John Mayall (1979); Ry Cooder (1979-80); Bob Dylan (1979-80).

DRYDEN, SPENCER Drums. Replaced Skip Spence in Jefferson Airplane, 1965-74, before joining the New Riders of the Purple Sage. Member of Seastones, 1976.

DUARTE, ERNESTO Percussion, brass, bass. Member of Barrabas.

DUBARRI, KENT Percussion, vocal. Half of Dalton and Dubarri since 1973.

DUBE, JOE X. Drums. Member of Starz since 1976.

DUCK, IAN Harmonica, vocal, writer. Member of Hookfoot, 1972. Session for Elton John (1970); Nilsson (1971).

DUCKS Bruce Brymer—vocal, drums, percussion; Kent Housman—vocal, guitar, percussion; Dennis

Lanigan—vocal, reeds, keyboards; Donald Luther—vocal, bass. *Album:* Ducks (SNS J55 6) 1973.

DUCKS DELUXE Sean Tyla—guitar, vocal; Nick Garvey—bass (1972-75); Tim Roper—drums; Andy McMasters—organ (1974-75); Mick Groom—bass, vocal (1975). *Albums:* Ducks Deluxe (Import) 1974; Taxi to the Terminal Zone (Import) 1975; Don't Mind Rockin' Tonight (RCA AFL 1-3025) 1978.

DUCONGE, WENDELL Alto saxophone. Session for Fats Domino (1951-58).

DUDEK, LES Guitar, slide guitar, vocal, producer. Soloist and member of the Dudek, Finnigan, Krueger Band, 1980. Session for the Allman Brothers Band (1973); the Steve Miller Band (1976-77). *Albums:* Les Dudek (COL PC-33702) 1976; Ghost Town Parade (COL JC-35088) 1978; Say No More (COL PC-34397) 1977.

DUDEK, FINNIGAN, KRUEGER BAND Les Dudek—vocal, guitar; Mike Finnigan—keyboards, vocal; Jim Kruger—guitar, vocal; Bill Meeker—drums; Trey Thompson—bass. *Album:* Dudek, Finnigan, Krueger Band (COL JC-35770) 1980.

DUDES Brian Greenway—guitar, vocal; David Henman—guitar, vocal; Wayne Cullen—drums, vocal; Bob Segarini—guitar, vocal; Ritchie Henman—drums, vocal; Kootch Trochim—bass. *Album:* We're No Angels, 1975.

DUDGEON, GUS Producer, engineer. Session for Ten Years After (1967-68); Elton John (1969-78); Audience (1971); John Kongos (1972).

DUFALL, DICK Bass. Member of the Paul Brett Sage.

DUFAY, RICK Guitar. *Album:* Tender Loving Abuse (POL PD 1 6294) 1980.

DUFFY, ROY Drums. Member of Matthew's Southern Comfort.

DUFFY, THOMAS Bass, vocal. Member of Lindisfarne, 1971-76.

DUGGAN, DUGG Guitar, mandolin, harmonica, vocal. Member of Timberline, 1977.

DUGGAN, JIMMY Guitar, vocal. Member of the Trigger, 1978.

DUGMORE, DAN Pedal steel guitar. Member of Ronin, 1980. Session for Pablo Cruise; Randy Newman; James Taylor; Richie Furay (1979); Adam Mitchell (1979).

DUHIG, DAVID Guitar. Session for Jade Warrior (1972).

DUHIG, TONY Guitar. Member of July, and Jade Warrior, 1970-72.

DUKE, DAVID French horn. Session for Martin Mull (1973); Arthur, Hurley and Gottlieb; Peter Frampton (1979).

DUKE, GEORGE Moog, keyboards, percussion, vocal, writer. First gained notoriety as a member of the Mothers of Invention, 1971-75, adding a concrete jazz direction to Zappa's inclinations. Since then he has worked as a session man and soloist, specializing in jazz. Session for Stanley Clarke (1975); Shuggie Otis (1971); Flora Purim (1976). *Albums:* Faces in Reflection; Feel; I Love the Blues—She Heard My Cry (BSF MC 25671) 1975; After You've Gone (CCJ 6); Aura Will Prevail (PAU 7042); Brazilian Love Affair (EPC FE-36483) 1979; Don't Let Go (EPC JE-35366) 1978; George Duke (PCJ LT-891) 1976; Follow the Rainbow (EPC JE-35701) 1979; From Me to You (EPC PE-34469); Live on Tour in Europe (ATC 18194); Master of the Game (EPC JE-36263) 1979; Reach for It (EPC JE-34883) 1977; Taste of Jazz (CCJ 93); Liberated Fantasies (ADF G22835) 1976.

DUKE, JOHN Oboe, flute, bass. Session for Pearls Before Swine (1970); Ry Cooder (1974).

DUKE, MICHAEL Vocal, keyboards. Added to Wet Willie, 1976-79. Session for Jimmy Hall (1980).

DUKE AND THE DRIVERS Sam Delux—guitar, vocal; Mad Mississippi Buffalo—keyboards, vocal; Cadillac Jack—guitar, vocal; Rhinestone Mudflaps III—saxophone, vocal; Koko Dee—bass; Bobby Blue Sky—drums. *Albums:* Cruisin, 1975; Rollin' On, 1975.

DUKE JUPITER Greg Walker—guitar, vocal; George Barajas—bass, vocal; Marshall Styler—keyboards, vocal; Earl Jetty—drums (1978); Don Maracle—guitar; David Hanlon—drums (1979-present). *Albums:* Sweet Cheeks (MER SRM 1-3718) 1978; Taste the Night (MER SRM 1-3756) 1979; Band in Blue (MER SRM 1-3815) 1980.

DUKES Miller Anderson—vocal, guitar; Ronnie Leahy—keyboards; Jimmy McCulloch—guitar, vocal; Charlie Tumahai—bass, vocal. English band formed from members of Keef Hartley (Anderson), Wings (McCulloch), and Be Bop Delux (Tumahai). *Album:* The Dukes (WBR R-3376) 1979.

DUKOWSKI, CHARLES Bass. Member of the Black Flag.

DULAINE, TIMMY Vocal, guitar, writer. Member of Stray Dog, 1974.

DULMER, EARL Woodwinds. Session for the Mothers of Invention (1972).

DUMMER, JOHN Drums. Member of the Darts since 1978.

DUNAWAY, DENNIS Bass, vocal. Member of the Alice Cooper Band, and Billion Dollar Babies, 1977.

DUNBAR, AYNSLEY Drums. Replaced Hughie Flint in John Mayall's Bluesbreakers, 1966-67. Formed Aynsley Dunbar's Retaliation, 1968-70, a blues band featuring Victor Brox on vocal. Member of the Mothers of Invention, 1971-72. In 1975, he was an original member of Journey with Santana alumni Neal Schon and Greg Rolie, before leaving in 1979 to replace John Barbata in the Jefferson Starship. Session for David Bowie; Ian Hunter (1975); Sammy Hagar (1975); Shuggie Otis

(1971); Lou Reed (1973); Nils Lofgren (1975-76); Frank Zappa (1970, 72, 74). *Albums:* Blue Whale (Import) 1970.

AYNSLEY DUNBAR'S RETALIATION Aynsley Dunbar—drums; Victor Brox—guitar, keyboards, coronet, vocal; Alex Dmochowski—bass; John Moorshead—guitar; Tommy Eyre—keyboards (1970). From John Mayall's Bluesbreakers, Dunbar left to form his own group with Victor Brox. Their arrangements and compositions were keyed down, less electric than their contemporaries in the blues field, and especially unique with Brox's deep vocal. Without the aid of a hit single, they cultivated a loyal underground following. Dunbar left in 1970. The group's fourth and last album, one side recorded without a drummer, was an exercise in basic blues and jazz vocal. *Albums:* Aynsley Dunbar's Retaliation, 1968; Dr. Dunbar's Prescription (BTM 8136), 1969; To Mum, From Aynsley and the Boys (BTM BTS 16) 1970; Remains To Be Heard (Import) 1970.

DUNBAR, CHARLIE Drums. Member of Skin, Flesh and Bone, 1975.

DUNBAR, ROBBIE Guitar, vocal. Member of Earthquake since 1966.

DUNBAR, TOMMY Guitar, keyboards. Member of the Rubinoos, 1977-79.

DUNCAN, GARY Guitar, writer. Original member of the Quicksilver Messenger Service, 1965-70.

DUNCAN, KIRK Piano. Member of the Blue Jays, 1975. Session for Trapeze (1972).

DUNCAN, LESLIE Vocal. Composer of Elton John's first hit that he and Taupin did not pen, "Love Song," 1970. Session for Long John Baldry (1971); Donovan (1973); Pink Floyd (1973).

DUNCAN, MALCOM Tenor saxophone. Session for Bryan Ferry (1974).

DUNCAN, WAYNE Bass, vocal. Original member of Daddy Cool, 1971-72.

DUNFORD, MICHAEL Guitar, vocal. Member of Renaissance.

DUNLOP, FRANKIE Drums. Session for Martin Mull (1974).

DUNLOP, RUSSELL Drums. Member of S.C.R.A., 1972.

DUNMORE, TONY Bass, vocal. Member of Supercharge, 1976-77.

DUNN, ARTHUR Keyboards. Member of Crosswinds.

DUNN, CHRIS Vocal, bass, guitar. Member of City Boy, 1976.

DUNN, DON Vocal. Member of In Transit, 1980.

DUNN, DONALD "DUCK" Bass, producer. Original member of Booker T. and the MGs, since 1962. Member of Fathers and Sons, 1969. Produced Crimson Tide (1979). Session for Otis Redding; Don Nix (1971); Freddie King (1971-72); Leon Russell (1975); Rod Stewart (1975-76); Mickey Thomas (1977); Roy Buchanan (1977).

DUNN, JOYCE Vocal. Session for Boz Scaggs (1969).

DUNN, KELLY Keyboards, vocal. Member of the Lost Gonzo Band, 1978.

DUNN, ROBBIE Member of Blues Incorporated.

DUNNE, MURPHY Keyboards. Session for the Blues Brothers (1980).

DUNSFORD, MARTIN Bass. Session for Christine Perfect (1969).

DUNSMOOR, DALE Drums. Member of the Kracker, 1978.

DUNSTERVILLE, JOHN Guitar, mandolin, vocal. Replaced Jeffrey Crampton in Rick Wakeman's backup band.

DUPREE, CHAMPION JACK Piano, vocal. Born 1910. Popular founding blues artist. *Albums:* Blues at Montreux (ATC 1637); Blues for Everybody (KGO 1084); Champion Jack Dupree (EVR 217); Finest of Champion Jack Dupree—Folk Bluesmen (BET BCP-6017); Happy To Be Free (CRS 10006) 1973; Legacy of the Blues (CRS 10010); Legacy of the Blues, Vol. 2 (CRS 10013) 1976; Raw Blues (LON PS-543); Tricks (CRS 10001) 1973; Women Blues of Champion Jack Dupree (FLW 33825) 1968.

DUPREE, CORNELL Guitar. Backup for Joe Cocker, 1975-76. Session for Ian Hunter (1976); Paul Simon (1973); B. B. King (1972); Pacific Gas and Electric; Ringo Starr (1977); Joe Cocker (1978); John Mayall (1979); Andy Gibb (1980). *Albums:* Teasin' (ATC 7311) 1974; Saturday Night Fever (VER MSG 6001) 1977.

DUPREE, ROBBIE Vocal. *Album:* Robbie Dupree (ELK 6E-273) 1980.

DURAN, TONY Guitar. Member of Ruben and the Jets, 1973. Session for the Mothers of Invention (1972); Frank Zappa (1972).

DURANT, DAVID Vocal. Member of the Mandala Band, 1975.

DURHAM, D. Member of Buckwheat.

DURHAM, JUDITH Vocal. Member of the Seekers, 1965-67.

DURHAM, MARC Bass. Member of Blue Steel since 1980.

DURILL, JOHN Keyboards. Added to the Ventures.

DURKEE, NORMAN Piano. Session for Bachman-Turner Overdrive (1973).

DUROCS Ron Nagle—keyboards, percussion; Scott Mathews. *Albums:* Durocs (CAP 11981) 1979.

DURY, IAN Vocal. Soloist and namesake of Ian Dury and the Blockheads, 1979. *Album:* New Boots and Panties (STF 0002) 1978.

IAN DURY AND THE BLOCKHEADS Ian Dury—vocal; Charley Charles—drums; Norman Watt-Roy—bass; Davey Payne—saxophone; John Turnbull—guitar; Chaz Jankel—guitar, keyboards; Mickey Gallagher—keyboards. *Album:* Do It Yourself (SFF JE-36104) 1979.

DUSSAULT, THOM Guitar. Member of the Flyer.

DUVIVIER, GEORGE Bass. Session for Martin Mull (1974).

DWIGHT, REGINALD Elton John's real name, before combining the monikers of Elton Dean, an English saxophone player, and Long John Baldry, vocalist, both from Steam Packet.

DWIRE, STEVE Bass. Member of the Rivets, 1980.

DWORKIN, ANDY Drums. Member of the Bottles, 1979.

DWYER, BERNIE Member of Freddie and the Dreamers, 1962-66.

DWYER, P. K. Guitar, vocal. Member of the Jitters, 1980.

DYCHE, MICK Slide guitar, guitar, vocal. Member of Wild Turkey, 1972, and Sniff 'n' the Tears, 1978-80.

DYE, DEBBIE Vocal. Session for Bob Dylan (1979).

DYER, DES Vocal, percussion. Member of Jigsaw, 1975-77.

DYER, PETE Vocal, guitar. Member of Stray, 1970-75.

DYKE, ROY Drums. Member of Medicine Head, 1973. Session for George Harrison (1967).

DYLAN, BOB Guitar, vocal, writer, harmonica, keyboards. Real name: Robert Zimmerman. Born 5/24/41. Began in the early 1960s as a street singer with contemporaries Joan Baez, Joni Mitchell, John Sebastian, Cass Elliot and other New Yorkers, crooning his songs of social criticism. His acoustic style became the focal point of the folk music boom. Reclusive in nature, his habits added an air of mystery to his popularity. The voice of the "hippy generation," he received much criticism for "selling out," or more appropriately "going electric" with his affiliation with the Band, a then unknown Canadian group that carved a legend of their own after separating from Dylan. Withstanding the criticism, his lyrical content remained as poignant, yet his style began to broaden to more melodic ends. Marital difficulties in 1978 led to his "born-again" Christian image, again the subject of critical controversy. His talent and popularity, however, survive intact. Made his acting debut in the movie "Pat Garrett and Billy The Kid," 1973. Session for Bangla Desh (1971); Barry Goldberg (1974); Earl Scruggs; David Blue (1975); the Band (1978). *Albums:* Another Side of Bob Dylan (COL JC-8993) 1964; At Budokan (COL PC2-36067) 1979; Basement Tapes (COL C2-33682) 1975; Before the Flood (ASY 201) 1974; Blonde on Blonde (COL C2S-841) 1966; Blood on the Tracks (COL JC-33235) 1974; Bringing It All Back Home (COL JC-9128) 1965; Desire (COL JC-33893) 1975; Dylan (COL JC-32747) 1974; Bob Dylan (COL JC-9463) 1967; Bob Dylan's Greatest Hits (COL JC-9463) 1967; Bob Dylan's Greatest Hits, Vol. 2 (COL PG-31120) 1971; Freewheelin' Bob Dylan (COL JC-8786) 1963; Hard Rain (COL JC-34349) 1977; Highway 61 Revisited (COL JC-9189) 1965; John Wesley Harding (COL JC-9604) 1968; Nashville Skyline (COL JC-9825) 1968; New Morning (COL JC-30290) 1969; Pat Garrett and Billy the Kid (COL JC-32460) 1973; Planet Waves (ASY 7E-1003) 1974; Saved (COL FC-36553) 1980; Self Portrait (COL C2X-30050); Slow Train Coming (COL FC-36120) 1979; Street Legal (COL JC-35453) 1978; Times They Are A-Changin' (COL JC-8905) 1964.

DYMOND, JOHN Beaky of Dave Dee, Dozy, Beaky, Mick and Tich, 1966-67.

DYSON, BOBBY Bass. Session for Waylon Jennings (1973).

DYSON, KATHLEEN Guitar. Session for Watson-Beasley (1980).

DZIDZORNU, KWASI "ROCKI" Percussion. Session for Joe Walsh (1976); Taj Mahal (1977).

E STREET BAND Bruce Springsteen—guitar, vocal, harmonica; Gary Tallent—bass; Max Weinberg—drums; Roy Bittan—keyboard, vocal; Clarence Clemons—saxophone; Danny Federik—organ (1978-present); Steve Van Zant—guitar (1978-present). Backup band for Bruce Springsteen. See Bruce Springsteen.

EADES, RON Baritone saxophone. Session for Mike Harrison (1972); Barry Goldberg (1974); Bob Seger (1975); Tim Weisberg (1977); Joe Cocker (1978); Roy Orbison (1979); Boatz (1979).

EAGAN, ED Keyboards. Member of Fist, 1980.

EAGLE, ROBERT Guitar. Member of Stanley Steamer, 1973.

EAGLES, STEVE Guitar, vocal. Member of the Photos, 1980.

EAGLES Don Henley—vocal, drums; Glenn Frey—vocal, guitar, piano; Randy Meisner—vocal, bass (1972-80); Bernie Leadon—vocal, guitar, banjo (until 1976); Don Felder—guitar; Joe Walsh—guitar, vocal (1976-present); Timothy B. Schmit—bass, vocal (1980). Early name: Teen King and the Emergencies. Popular Los Angeles based vocal harmonists joined by Joe Walsh in 1976. Concentrated efforts on production and commercial lyrics elevated them beyond their initial folk rock image. *Albums:* Desperado (ASY 5068) 1973; Eagles (ASY 5054) 1972; Hotel California (ASY 6E-103) 1976; Long Run (ASY 5E-508) 1979; On the Border (ASY 7E-1004) 1974; One of These Nights (ASY 7E-1039) 1975; Their Greatest Hits (ASY 6E-105) 1976; Eagles Live (ASY BB 705) 1980.

EARHART, BILLY Keyboards. Member of the Amazing Rhythm Aces.

EARL, COLIN Keyboards. Session for Foghat (1979).

EARL, ROGER Drums, percussion. Replaced Leo Mannings in Savoy Brown, 1968-71, before forming Foghat with Dave Peverett and Tony Stevens, also from Savoy Brown, 1972-present.

EARLE, JOHN Baritone saxophone. Member of the Rumor Brass Section, 1979. Session for Sean Tyla (1980).

EARLS Larry Chance—vocal; Robert Del Din—vocal; Eddie Harder—vocal; Larry Palumbo—vocal. Made the hit "Remember Then" in 1959. *Album:* Remember Me, Baby.

EARLY FROST Recording debut of Dick Wagner. Other personnel unknown. *Albums:* Early Frost (VAN 79392); Frost Music, 1970; Through The Eyes Of Love, 1971.

EARTH Early name of Black Sabbath.

EARTH BAND See Manfred Mann.

EARTH OPERA Peter Rowan—guitar, saxophone, vocal; David Grisman—mandolin, piano, vocal, saxophone; Paul Dillon—drums, vocal, percussion, guitar; John Nagy—bass, cello; Bill Stevenson—vibes, keyboards. Part of the Boston wave in rock, 1968. Despite their talent, they faded quickly. *Albums:* Earth Opera, 1968; The Great American Eagle Tragedy, 1969.

EARTHQUAKE John Doukas—vocal, guitar; Robbie Dunbar—guitar, vocal; Stan Miller—bass, vocal; Steve Nelson—drums, vocal. San Francisco band that began in 1966. *Albums:* Chartbusters (BES 0044) 1975; 8.5 (BES 0047) 1976; Leveled (BES 0054) 1976; Rocking The World (BES 0045) 1975; Two Years in a Padded Cell (BES BZ-10065) 1979; Earthquake (AAM SP 4308).

EASLEY, MIKE Guitar, vocal. Member of the Waves, 1977.

EAST, DENNIS Vocal. Member of Stingray, 1979.

EASTER, LARRY Woodwinds. Began in Linn County, 1968-69. Session for Harvey Mandel; Stephen Miller.

EASTON, ELLIOT Guitar, vocal. Member of the Cars since 1978.

EASYBEATS Stevie Wright—vocal; Dick Diamonde—bass; Tony Cahill—drums; George Young—guitar, vocal; Harry Vanda—guitar, vocal. Native Europeans Vanda and Young migrated from Australia back to England to hit the big time amidst Beatlemania. Their biggest single, "Friday on My Mind" (1966) fared better in England than the States. *Albums:* Friday on My Mind, 1967; Falling Off the Edge of the World, 1968.

EATON, STEVE Vocal, guitar, harmonica. Member of Fat Chance, 1972.

EATON, TIMMY Vocal. Voice of Bandit, 1975.

EBERT, DENNIS Drums, percussion. Member of the Eddie Boy Band, 1975.

ECHITO, MARTIE Keyboards. Member of the Waves, 1977.

ECHO AND THE BUNNYMEN Ian McCulloch—vocal, guitar; Will Sergeant—guitar; Lee Pattinson—bass; Pete de Freitas—drums. *Album:* Crocodiles (SIR 6096) 1980.

ECHOLS, JOHN Guitar. Member of Love, 1967-69.

ECKERT, JOHN Trumpet. Member of Ten Wheel Drive, 1970.

ECKLER, GREG Member of Rubicon, 1978-79.

ECKLUND, PETER Trumpet, coronet. Session

for Martin Mull (1972); Gregg Allman. *Album:* Paula Lockheart with Peter Ecklund.

ECKSTEIN, RICK Drums. Session for Bobby Whitlock (1975).

ECLECTIN Michael Rosen—guitar, vocal, trumpet; Trevor Lucas—bass, vocal; Kerrilee Male—vocal; Gerry Conway—drums; George Hultgreen—guitar, vocal. *Album:* Eclectin, 1968.

EDDIE Drums. Member of the Vibrators, 1977.

EDDIE AND THE EVERGREENS Early name of Sha Na Na.

EDDIE AND THE HOT RODS Barrie Masters—vocal; Dave Higgs—guitar, vocal; Steve Nichols—drums; T. C.—bass; Paul Gray—bass (1976). *Albums:* Live on the Line (ISL 9509); Teenage Depression (ISL 9457) 1976; Fish 'n' Chips (EMC SW 17037) 1980.

EDDIE BOY BAND Josh Leo—guitar, vocal; Mark Goldenberg—guitar, vocal, piano; Tim Walkoe—bass, vocal; John Paruolo—vocal, keyboards; Dennis Ebert—drums, percussion; Mike Lerner—drums, percussion. *Album:* Eddie Boy Band (MCA) 1975.

EDDY, DUANE Guitar. Discovered by Lee Hazelwood, he was one of the first rockers to use an electric guitar as the main attraction of his group. His style was known as the "Twang," and it was the starting point for many future rockers. *Albums:* Especially for You, 1961; Have Twangy Guitar, Will Travel, 1961; Million Dollars Worth of Twang, 1961; Twangs the Thang, 1961; Twangy Guitar, 1962; Duane Eddy Plays Songs of Our Heritage, 1964; Lonely Guitar, 1964; Girls, Girls, Girls, 1964; Duane Eddy with the Rebels—In Person, 1964; Million Dollars Worth of Twang, Vol. 2, 1964; Surfin', 1964; Twangin' the Golden Hits, 1965; Twangsville, 1965; Best of Duane Eddy, 1966; Biggest Twang of All, 1966; Roaring Twangies, 1967.

DUANE EDDY AND THE REBELS Duane Eddy—guitar; Steve Douglas—saxophone; Mike Bermani—drums; Ike Clanton—bass. Backup group for Duane Eddy. See Duane Eddy.

EDDY, TEDDY JACK Drums. Recording name of actor Gary Busey. See Gary Busey.

EDELMAN, RANDY Keyboards, vocal. *Albums:* If Love Is Real (ARI 4139); You're the One (ARI 4210); Prime Cuts (TWC T448) 1974; Laughter and the Tears (MGM LN1013) 1972.

EDEN, BILL Reeds, vocal. Member of Phyrework, 1978.

EDEN'S CHILDREN Richard Schamach—guitar; Jimmy Sturman—drums; Larry Kiely—bass. Heavy metal trio from Boston. *Albums:* Eden's Children, 1968; Sure Looks Real, 1968.

EDENTON, RAY Guitar, vocal. Session for Leon Russell (1973); Neil Young (1978); Bill Medley (1978).

EDGAR, RON Drums. Original member of the Music Machine, 1966.

EDGE, GRAEME Drums, vocal. Born 3/30/80. Original member of the Moody Blues, since 1965. Formed the Graeme Edge Band in 1975.

GRAEME EDGE BAND Graeme Edge—drums, vocal, producer; Adrian Gurvitz—vocal, guitar; Paul Gurvitz—bass; Mick Gallagher—keyboard. Brief solo distraction from Edge's role in the Moody Blues. *Albums:* Kick Off Your Muddy Boots (THS 15) 1976; The Paradise Ballroom (THS) 1978.

EDGE Bruce Tibbits—vocal, guitar; Hubie Davis—vocal, guitar; Bob Fink—keyboards, vocal; Curt Arnot—bass, vocal; Butch Raymond—drums. *Album:* The Edge (CSB 7214) 1980.

EDISON ELECTRIC BAND Mark Jordan—keyboards, guitar; T. J. Tindall—vocal, guitar; Dan Friedberg—bass, guitar; David Stock—drums, vocal. *Album:* Bless You, Dr. Woodward.

EDMONTON, DENNIS Real name of Mars Bonfire.

EDMONTON, JERRY Drums, percussion. Original member of Steppenwolf, 1965-79.

EDMUNDS, DAVE Guitar, drums, keyboards, percussion, producer. Unsuccessful in Love Sculpture, Edmunds opted for a solo career, in the literal sense of the word. Besides production, he played most of the instruments on his first album. Like Sculpture, he is equally comfortable with the blues as well as 1950s rock and roll. His own compositions reflect his admiration for the Everly Brothers. Produced Man. Session and production for Foghat (1972); Ducks Deluxe (1974); Carlene Carter (1980). *Albums:* Get It (SWN 8418) 1977; Repeat When Necessary (SWN 8507) 1979; Tracks on Wax (SWN 8505) 1978; Seconds of Pleasure (COL JC-36886) 1980; Subtle as a Flying Mallet (RCA LPI-5003) 1975; Rockpile (MAM 3) 1971.

EDMUNDS, MICHAEL Guitar, vocal. Member of Morningstar, 1979.

EDWARDS, BILL Trombone. Session for Jules and the Polar Bears (1979).

EDWARDS, BOBBY Drums. Member of Thundertrain, 1977.

EDWARDS, CINDY Vocal. Member of the Rank Strangers, 1977.

EDWARDS, CLIVE Drums. Member of Electric Sun, 1979.

EDWARDS, DANIEL Bass, guitar. Session for Lord Sutch.

EDWARDS, DAVID "HONEY BOY" Guitar. Born 4/28/15 in Mississippi and moved to Chicago. Contemporary of Robert Johnson, Big Joe Williams, Walter Horton and others. Session with Fleetwood Mac (1969). *Albums:* Drop Down Mama (CHS); Ramblin' on My Mind (MLS 3002).

EDWARDS, DENNIS Vocal. Replaced David Ruffin in the Temptations in 1968.

EDWARDS, DOUG Guitar. Member of the Hometown Band, 1976.

EDWARDS, FRED Drums. Member of the Charlie Daniels Band, 1975-79.

EDWARDS, GEORGE Guitar, bass, vocal. Original member of H. P. Lovecraft, 1967-68.

EDWARDS, GORDON Bass. Session for the Plastic Ono Band (1973); Pacific Gas and Electric (1973); Paul Simon (1973-75); Joe Cocker (1976); John Mayall (1979).

EDWARDS, JOHN Bass. Session for Peter Green (1980).

EDWARDS, JOHN Trumpet. Session for Savoy Brown (1969).

EDWARDS, JONATHAN Vocal, guitar, harmonica, bass, percussion. His first single, "Sunshine," appeared in 1971. It was hard to tell whether his catchy lyrics, melodic voice, or superb musicianship of his backup band, Orphan, were the true stars, but they complemented one another quite well. In 1975, Edwards changed recording labels and backup bands without sacrifice to his country rooted style. *Albums:* Jonathan Edwards (CPN 50862) 1971; Honky Tonk Stardust Cowboy (ACO SO 7015) 1972; Have a Good Time for Me (ACO 7036) 1973; Lucky Day (ACO 36-104) 1974; Rockin' Chair (RPS 2238) 1975; Sailboat (WBR B-3020) 1977.

EDWARDS, JUMA Percussion. Session on Hendrix's "Rainbow Bridge," 1970.

EDWARDS, KEN Guitar. Member of the Stone Poneys, 1967-68.

EDWARDS, MIKE Vocal, guitar. Member of Live Wire since 1979.

EDWARDS, NOKIE Guitar. Original member of the Ventures.

EDWARDS, PAUL Chapman stick, vocal. Member of Kittyhawk, 1980.

EDWARDS, ROD Vocal. Session for Ken Tobias (1973).

EDWARDS, RON Bass. Member of the Marc Tanner Band since 1979.

EDWARDS, RON Keyboards, synthesizer. Session for Ken Tobias (1973).

EDWARDS, SCOTT Bass. Session for Greg Sutton (1975); B. B. King (1977); Small Wonder (1977); Commander Cody (1978).

EDWARDS, SKIP Piano. Session for Firefall (1977).

EFAW, TERRY Steel guitar, guitar. Member of McGuffey Lane, 1980.

EFFETE, STEVE Bass. Member of F-Word, 1978.

EFFORD, BOB Tenor saxophone. Session for Savoy Brown (1969).

EGAN, JOE Vocal, keyboard. Member of Stealer's Wheel, 1972-75. *Album:* Out of Nowhere (ARA SW-50064).

EGAN, MARY Fiddle, vocal. Member of Greezy Wheels, 1976.

EGAN, MIKE Guitar. Session for Rick Wakeman (1972-74).

EGAN, RUSTY Member of Visage, 1980.

EGAN, WALTER Guitar, vocal. *Albums:* Fundamental Roll (COL PC-34679) 1977; Hi Fi (COL JC-35796) 1979; Last Stroll (COL JC-36513) 1980; Not Shy (COL JC-35077) 1978.

EGG Dave Stewart—keyboards; Mont Campbell—bass, vocal; Clive Brooks—drums. *Album:* Egg (DRM 18039) 1970.

EGGERMONT, JAAP Drums. Original member of the Golden Earring until 1970.

EGILSON, ARNI Bass. Session for Martin Mull (1978).

EGO, BOB Drums. Member of Painter, 1973.

EGOSARIAN, GEORGE Guitar. Member of Jukin' Bone, 1972.

EHART, PHIL Drums. Born 2/4/50. Original member of Kansas since 1974.

EICHHORN, EDIE LEHMANN Vocal. Member of the Ron Hicklin Singers.

EIDE, JOEL Harmonica. Member of One Hand Clapping, 1977.

EILLEDGE, GARETH Bass. Session for Bill Nelson (1971).

EIRE APPARENT Michael Cox—guitar; Chris Stewart—bass; Dave Lutton—drums; Ernie Graham—bass. Irish heavy metal band that toured with producer Jimi Hendrix in 1968. *Album:* Sunrise, 1969.

EISEN, STANLEY Real name of Kiss's Paul Stanley.

EISEN, STEVE Saxophone. Session for Styx (1979).

EISENBERG, NAOMI Vocal, percussion, fiddle. Member of Dan Hicks and His Hot Licks until 1974.

EISENSTEIN, NANCY Vocal. Session for Martin Mull (1975).

EKESTUBBLE, HINKE Saxophone, flute. Member of Blue Swede.

EKSEPTION Rein van den Broek—trumpet; Rob Kruisman—saxophone, flute, guitar, vocal; Rick van der Linden—keyboards; Huib van Kampen—guitar, saxophone; Cor Dekker—bass; Peter de Leeuwe—drums, vocal. Dutch rock group, serving as the starting point for van der Linden, who later formed Trace. *Album:* Ekseption (PHI).

EL CHICANO Bobby Espinosa—organ; Andre Baeza—conga, percussion, vocal; Ersi Arvizu—vocal, percussion; Freddie Sanchez—vocal, bass; Mickey Lespron—guitar; John de Luna—drums, percussion. Ethnic Latin rock on the heels of the fame of Santana. *Albums:* Revolution, 1971; Pyramid, 1975; Celebration (MCA 74); Cinco (MCA 401); Best of Everything (MCA 437) 1975; El Chicano (MCA 69) 1974; This Is El Chicano (SHB 33005) 1975; Viva Tirado (MCA 548).

EL ROACHOS John Hoff—drums, percussion; Curtis Massey—saxophone; Edd Lively—guitar, vocal; Hugh Laravea—keyboards, vocal; Robert

Chitwood—bass; James Burnett—guitar, banjo, vocal. *Album:* El Roachos Greatest Hits (COL) 1973.

ELAM, DON Saxophone. Member of Balcones Fault (1977).

ELASTIQUE Steve Emery—bass, guitar; Kirby—guitar; Elmer Gantry—guitar, vocal. *Album:* Stretch (ANC) 1976.

ELDER, COON Vocal, guitar. Namesake of the Coon Elder Band, 1977.

COON ELDER BAND Brenda Patterson—vocal; Coon Elder—vocal, guitar; Phil Black—guitar, fiddle, vocal; Mark Sallings—reeds, harmonica, vocal; Bill Marshall—drums, vocal; Rocky Beretta—bass. *Album:* Coon Elder Band (MER SRM 1-1140) 1977.

ELDORADO, FRANKIE Vocal, percussion. *Album:* Frankie Eldorado (EPC JE-36291) 1980.

ELECTRIC FLAG Mike Bloomfield—guitar (1967-68); Harvey Brooks—bass; Buddy Miles—drums, vocal; Barry Goldberg—organ; John Simon—piano; Terry Clements—tenor saxophone; Marcus Doubleday—trumpet; Nick Gravenites—guitar, vocal; Virgil Gonsalves—saxophone, flute; Stemsy Hunter—saxophone, vocals; Hoshal Wright—guitar; Herbie Rich—organ. Brainchild of Bloomfield, who formed the band in 1967 from the top Chicago blues session men, backed by a horn section. The arrangements were fresh, snappy and diversified but distant from the blues, which is probably why Bloomfield and Goldberg left the group, leaving Miles at the helm. *Albums:* A Long Time Coming (COL CS 9597) 1968; The Electric Flag (COL) 1968; Band Kept Playing (COL).

ELECTRIC LIGHT ORCHESTRA Roy Wood—vocal, cello, oboe, guitar, bass, bassoon, clarinet (until 1974); Jeff Lynne—vocal, piano, guitar, bass, percussion; Bev Bevan—drums, percussion; Steve Woolam—violin, vocal; Kelly Groucutt—bass, vocal (1974- present); Mik Kaminsky—violin, vocal (1974-78); Hugh McDowell—cello; Melvin Gale—cello (1974-present). Formed from the ashes of the Move, ELO featured Wood, before he left to go solo. Lynn and Bevan then took the helm, spiriting their experimental rock with electrified strings to AM stations. *Albums:* Night the Lights Went On in Long Beach (UAR-VALA 318); Discovery (JET FZ-35769) 1979; Eldorado (JET JZ 35526) 1974; Electric Light Orchestra (JET JZ-35533) 1972; ELO's Greatest Hits (JET FZ 36310) 1979; Face the Music (JET JZ-35527) 1975; New World Record (JET JZ-35529) 1976; No Answer (JET JZ-35524); Ole ELO (JET JZ-35528) 1976; On the Third Day (JET JZ 35525); Out of the Blue (JET JZ-35530) 1977.

ELECTRIC PRUNES Jim Lowe—vocal, guitar, percussion; Weasel—vocal, guitar; Ken Williams—guitar; Mark Tulin—bass, keyboards; Preston Ritter—drums, percussion; John Herren—keyboards (1967); Ron Morgan—guitar (1967); Mark Kincaid—guitar, vocal (1967); Richard Whetstone—drums, guitar, vocal (1967); Brett Wade—bass, flute, vocal (1967). "I Had Too Much To Dream Last Night" was an overnight hit in the drug oriented pop market of 1967. The Prunes were revered for their insight to the soul and timeless spirituality, as demonstrated by their "Mass in F Minor" (1967). By the end of that same year, the band had changed personnel completely and no one had noticed their passing. *Albums:* Electric Prunes (RPS) 1967; Underground (RPS) 1967; Mass in F Minor (RPS) 1967; Just Good Old Rock and Roll, 1969.

ELECTRIC SUN Ulrich Roth—guitar, vocal; Clive Edwards—drums; Ule Ritgen—bass. Ex-Scorpion Roth's solo effort. *Album:* Earthquake (Import) 1979.

ELEKTRICS Marco Delmar—guitar, vocal; Bob Drew—keyboards, vocal; Chris James—bass, vocal; Carl Worner—vocal; Andrew Papa—drums. *Album:* Current Events (CAP ST-12093) 1980.

ELEPHANT Dick Glass—vocal, guitar; Harold Cowart—bass; Ron Ziegler—drums; Geoff Levin—guitar. *Album:* Elephant (BTR) 1975.

ELEPHANT'S MEMORY Steve Bronstein—woodwinds; Richard Frank—drums; Michael Shapiro—vocal; Richard Sussman—keyboards; John Ward—bass; Myron Yules—bass, trombone. Experimental rock-jazz group from New York that John Lennon picked up for session work in 1972. *Albums:* Elephant's Memory, 1969; Angels Forever; Sometime in New York City (With John Lennon and Yoko Ono) (CAP 5VBB-3392) 1972.

ELEVATORS William Benjamin—drums, vocal; John Clark—vocal, guitar; Jerry Ellis—bass; Zonder Kennedy—vocal, guitar; Tom Myers—vocal, keyboards. *Album:* Frontline (ARI 4270) 1980.

ELEVENTH HOUSE Larry Coryell—guitar; Michael Lawrence—trumpet, flugelhorn (1978); John Lee—bass (1974); Mike Mandel—keyboards; Randy Brecker—trumpet (1974); Alphonse Mouzon—percussion; Danny Trifan—bass. Jazz quartet organized by Larry Coryell. *Albums:* The Eleventh House (ARI) 1975; Aspects (ARI) 1976; Larry Coryell and the Eleventh House at Montreaux (VAN 79410) 1978; Eleventh House/Larry Coryell (VAN 79342) 1974.

ELEWY Guitar. Member of Shakin' Street, 1980.

ELGART, BILLY Drums. Session for Martin Mull (1972).

ELI, BOBBY Guitar. Session for Elton John (1979); Atlantic Starr (1979).

ELIAS, MANNY Drums, percussion. Member of Interview since 1979.

ELIZABETH Harmony vocal. Worked with Tom Rapp and Pearls Before Swine, 1969-71.

ELIZABETH Steve Weingarten—guitar, organ; Jim Dahme—vocal, flute, guitar; Bob Patterson—

guitar, vocal; Steve Bruno—keyboards, bass; Hank Ransome—drums, bass, guitar. Short-lived Philadelphia group of 1968. *Album:* Elizabeth, 1968.

ELLICOTT, ROD Bass. Member of Cold Blood. Session for the Pointer Sisters (1973).

ELLIMAN, KEVIN Percussion. Member of Utopia.

ELLIMAN, YVONNE Vocal. Played Mary Magdalene in "Jesus Christ Superstar," 1970, before launching her solo career. Session for Deep Purple; Eric Clapton (1974-75). *Albums:* Food of Love (DCA); Yvonne Elliman (RSO 1-3038) 1972; Love Me (RSO 1-3018); Night Flight (RSO 1-3031) 1978.

ELLIOT, "MAMA" CASS Vocal. Real name: Naomi Cohen. Born 9/19/43. Started with the Mugwumps in 1964 before she graduated to the Mamas and the Papas (1965) and international stardom. Ventured out on her solo career in 1968. Died in 1971. Session for Dave Mason; Steve Stills (1970). *Albums:* Don't Call Me Mama Anymore (VIC); Cass Elliot (VIC) 1972; The Road Is No Place for a Lady (VIC) 1972; Mama's Big Ones (MCA 50093); Cass.

ELLIOT, BILL Keyboards, vocal. Member of Orphan, 1971-74. Session for Martin Mull (1972); Andy Pratt (1973).

ELLIOT, BILL Vocal. Part of the English duet Splinter, 1974-76.

ELLIOT, BOBBY Drums. Member of the Hollies since 1963.

ELLIOT, DENNIS Drums, percussion. Original member of If, and Foreigner since 1977. Session for Ian Hunter (1975); Ian Lloyd (1979).

ELLIOT, RAY Organ. Replaced Peter Bardens in Them.

ELLIOT, RICHARD Lyricon, saxophone. Member of Kittyhawk, 1980.

ELLIOT, RON Guitar. Original member of the Beau Brummels. Member of Giants, 1976. Session for Randy Newman.

ELLIOTT, DON Bass. Member of Mandala, 1968.

ELLIOTT, DON Vibes. Session for Paul Simon (1973).

ELLIOTT, JOE Vocal. Member of Def Leppard, 1980.

ELLIOTT, KEN Keyboards, percussion. Member of the Seventh Wave, 1974-75. Session for Arthur Brown (1975).

ELLIOTT, MIKE Tenor saxophone. Member of the Foundations, 1968.

ELLIOTT, NIGEL Drums, percussion. Member of the Bliss Band, 1977-78.

ELLIOTT, PAUL Drums, percussion. Member of Trickster, 1978-79.

ELLIOTT, RAMBLIN' JACK Guitar, vocal, harmonica. Real name: Elliott Adnopoz. A student of Woody Guthrie, he ran away from New York to meet and travel with his idol in the West. Elliott adopted many traits of the late Guthrie and in turn was a major influence on Bob Dylan and other troubadors. *Albums:* Jack Elliott Sings Woody Guthrie Songs, 1961; Bull Durham Sacks and Railroad Tracks; Ramblin' Cowboy, 1962; Hootenany, 1964; Talking Woodie Guthrie, 1966; Jack Elliott, 1967; Young Brigham, 1968; Country Style (PRS 7804); Jack Elliott (PRS 7453) 1964; Essential (VAN VSD-89/90); Greatest Songs of Woody Guthrie (VAN VSD-35/36); Hard Travelin' (FSY 24720) 1977; Newport Folk Festival (VAN 79148); Ramblin' Jack Elliott (PRS 7721) 1961; Ramblin' Jack Elliott Sings Woody Guthrie and Jimmie Rodgers (MTR 380); Songs To Grow On (FLW 7501); Tribute to Woody Guthrie (WBR 2W-3007) 1962.

ELLIOTT, STUART Drums, percussion. Member of Cockney Rebel. Session for Kate Bush (1978); the Alan Parsons Project (1978-80); the Dukes (1979); the Who (1980); Justin Hayward (1980).

ELLIS, ALLAN Trumpet. Session for Chicken Shack.

ELLIS, ART Flute, congas, vocal. Session for Tom Rapp.

ELLIS, BARBARA Vocal. Member of the Fleetwoods, 1959.

ELLIS, BRAD Keyboards, vocal, writer. Member of Alda Reserve, 1979.

ELLIS, DAVE Bass. Member of S.C.R.A., 1972.

ELLIS, DICK Saxophone. Session for Willie Alexander and the Boom Boom Band (1979).

ELLIS, DON Horns. Session for Steppenwolf (1974).

ELLIS, IAN Vocal. Member of Savoy Brown, 1976-78.

ELLIS, JERRY Bass. Member of the Elevators, 1980.

ELLIS, JOCK Horns. Member of the Fun Zone, 1977.

ELLIS, JOHN Guitar, vocal. Member of the Vibrators, 1977.

ELLIS, KEITH Bass, vocal. Member of Juicy Lucy, 1970, and Boxer, 1975. Session for Bobby Whitlock.

ELLIS, MUNDI Vocal. Session for Mike Oldfield (1973).

ELLIS, STEVE Vocal. Original member of Love Affair, and Widowmaker, 1976.

ELLISON, MEL Tenor saxophone. Session for Elvin Bishop (1972).

ELMEER, DAVE Bass, guitar, keyboards. Member of Cain, 1975-77.

ELMORE, GREGORY Drums. Original member of the Quicksilver Messenger Service.

ELOFSON, JULIAN Vocal, percussion. Member of Overland Stage, 1972.

ELOY Frank Bornemann—guitar, vocal, percussion; Fritz Randow—drums, guitar, flute, percussion; Manfred Wieczorke—keyboards, guitar, vocal, percussion; Wolfgang Stocker—bass (1976);

Luitjen Janssen—bass (1975). German group specializing in long, space-oriented compositions, much like countrymen Camel. Bornemann's vocals are at times mistakable for Ian Anderson's of Jethro Tull. *Albums:* Floating (JNS 915 7018) 1975; Inside (JNS) 1976.

ELSEY, JOANN Vocal. Session for the Brains (1980).

ELSTAR, JOHN Harmonica. Session for Kim Fowley (1973).

ELSWIT, RICK Guitar, vocal. Member of Dr. Hook.

ELY, VINCE Drums. Member of the Psychedelic Furs, 1980.

EMBLOW, JACK Accordion. Session for Donovan (1973); Elton John (1971); Chris Spedding (1977).

EMELIN, JOHN Theremin. Member of Lothar and the Hand People, 1966-68.

EMERICK, GERALD Member of Quincy, 1980.

EMERSON, KEITH Keyboards, arranger, writer. Born 11/2/44. Original member of the Nice, 1967-70, and foremost rock keyboardist, as demonstrated in the works of Emerson, Lake and Palmer, 1971-80. As a member of the Nice, he was banned from playing the Royal Albert Hall in London for burning an American flag on stage. Session for Rod Stewart (1970); Free Creek (1973). *Albums:* Keith Emerson/the Nice (MER SRM-2-6500); Inferno (Soundtrack) (Import) 1980.

EMERSON, VIC Keyboards. Member of the Mandala Band, 1975, and Sad Cafe, 1978-79.

EMERSON, LAKE AND PALMER Keith Emerson—keyboards, writer, arranger; Greg Lake—vocal, bass, guitar, production, writer; Carl Palmer—drums, percussion. The humble beginnings of ELP are found in the dissolution of the Nice (Emerson), King Crimson (Lake), and Atomic Rooster (Palmer). They joined forces in 1971, and from close examination of the parent groups, nothing seemed to be beyond the new group's range. Emerson's talent and stage antics, like knifing his keyboards or turning the organ on himself while playing it lying on the floor, added yet another dimension to their awesome 360 degree sound show. Lake's lyrics conjure images of demons and love in the same breath, while Palmer concocts intricate rhythms on one of the most impressive drum kits in the business. *Albums:* Brain Salad Surgery (ATC 19124) 1973; Emerson, Lake and Palmer (ATC 19120) 1971; In Concert (ATC 19255) 1979; Ladies and Gentlemen (MNC 3-200) 1974; Love Beach (ATC 19211) 1978; Pictures at an Exhibition (ATC 19122) 1972; Tarkus (ATC 19121) 1971; Trilogy (ATC 19123) 1972; Works, Vol. 1 (ATC 2-7000) 1977; Works, Vol. 2 (ATC 19147) 1977.

EMERY, STEVE Bass, vocal. Member of Ross, Elastique, 1976, and Stretch, 1976-77.

EMERY, TERRY Percussion. Session for Vigrass and Osborne (1972).

EMIGRE Willi Morrison—vocal, guitar; Ian Guenther—violin. *Album:* Emigre (CYS 1228) 1979.

EMMETT, RIK Guitar, vocal. Member of Triumph since 1979.

EMMONS, BOBBY Keyboards. Session for John Sebastian (1970, 74); Jackie DeShannon (1972); Doug Kershaw (1972, 74).

EMMONS, BUDDY Pedal steel guitar. Original member of the Dillards. Session for Russ Giguere (1971); Buddy Spicher (1976); the Ozark Mountain Daredevils (1980); Levon Helm (1980). *Albums:* Buddies (FLF 041); Buddy Emmons Sings Bob Wills (FLF 017); Minors Aloud (FLF 088) 1978; Steel Guitar (FLF 007) 1975.

EMPEROR Joe Marques—bass, vocal; Mike Lobbett—keyboards, vocal; Joe Alexander—guitar, vocal; Steve Watts—drums, vocal; Randy Budihas—drums, vocal. *Album:* Emperor, 1977.

ENGEL, SCOTT Bass, vocal. Member of the Walker Brothers, 1966-67, before performing as a soloist under the name Scott Walker.

ENGEMANN, BOB Vocal. Original member of the Lettermen.

ENGLAND DAN AND JOHN FORD COLEY England Dan (Seals)—saxophone, guitar; John Ford Coley—keyboards, guitar. *Albums:* England Dan and John Ford Coley; Big and Best of England Dan and John Ford Coley (BIG 76018); Dr. Heckle and Mr. Jive (BIG 76000) 1977; Fables (AAM 4350) 1972; Nights Are Forever (BIG 89517) 1976; Some Things Don't Come Easy (BIG 76006).

ENGLER, RIK Vocal, violin, clarinet, percussion, bass. Member of the Fifth Estate, 1967.

ENGLISH, JOE Drums, percussion, vocal. Member of Wings, 1975-78. Replaced Jai Johanny Johanson in Sea Level, 1978-present.

ENGLISH, PAUL Drums. Session for Willie Nelson (1973-79); Leon Russell and Willie Nelson (1979).

ENGLISH BEAT Saxa; Andy Cox; David Steele; Everett Moreton; Roger Rankins; Dave Wakeling. *Album:* I Just Can't Stop It (SIR SRK-6091) 1980.

ENNIS, RAY Guitar, vocal. Member of the Racing Cars, 1976-78.

ENO, BRIAN Synthesizer, vocal, producer. Original member of Roxy, 1972, he left in 1973 for his solo career. Produced Ultravox (1977); Devo (1978); the Talking Heads (1979-80); and others. Session for Nico (1974); John Cale (1975); Phil Manzanera (1975); David Bowie (1977); Robert Fripp (1979). *Albums:* Eno and Robert Fripp; Another Green World (ISL 9351) 1975; Before and After Science (ISL 9478) 1977; Here Come the Warm Jets (ISL 9268) 1973; Taking Tiger Mountain by Strategy (ISL 9309) 1974; Fripp and Eno/No Pussyfooting (ANT AN7001) 1973.

ENTNER, WARREN Guitar. Member of the Grass Roots.

ENTWHISTLE, JOHN Bass, vocal, trumpet, piano, synthesizer. Born 9/10/44. Original member of the Who and the first member of that group to release a solo effort. Session on "Tommy" (1972); "Rough Mix" (1977); Dave Lambert (1979). *Albums:* Smash Your Head Against the Wall (DEC DL 79183) 1971; Whistles and Rhymes (MCA) 1972; Rigor Mortis Sets In (MCA 321) 1973; Mad Dog (MCA) 1975.

EPPLE, KAT Flute. Session for the Randle Chowning Band (1978).

EPSTEIN, BRIAN Manager. Born 9/19/34. Became manager of the Silver Beatles (later to become the Beatles) in 1961. By 1962, he had arranged for the hit "Love Me Do" to be released, which started that chapter of rock history known as Beatlemania. A careful network of bands, including Gerry and the Pacemakers, the Cyrkle, Billy J. Kramer and the Dakotas, and others was set up under his management, but fell apart with his death.

EPSTEIN, JAY Drums. Member of Gypsy, 1971.

EQUINE, MIKE Drums, guitar, bass, cello, keyboards, percussion. Member of Cat Mother and the All Night Newsboys, 1967-68.

ERBER, BARB Vocal. Member of Tantrum, 1978-79.

ERELWINE, MIKE Harmonica. Session for the Bob Seger System.

EREMITA, ERNIE Bass, percussion. Member of Chunky, Ernie and Novi, which became Lauren Wood's backup band in 1979.

ERICKSON, RORY Vocal. Member of the 13th Floor Elevators.

ERICKSON, RED Vocal, guitar. Member of One Hand Clapping.

ERLANDER, LOUIS X. Guitar. Backup for Mink DeVille, 1977.

ERNST, JERDEN Keyboards. Member of the Urban Heroes, 1980.

EROKAN, JOHNNY Guitar. Session for Chinga Chavin.

ERRICO, GREGG Drums. Original member of Sly and the Family Stone, and Giants, 1978. Session for Santana (1971); Carlos Santana-Buddy Miles Live (1972).

ERRONEOUS Bass, vocal. Session for Frank Zappa (1972, 74).

ERWIN, TEDDY Guitar. Session for Donovan (1974).

ESCOVEDO, ALEJANDRO Drums, percussion. Member of the Nuns, 1980.

ESCOVEDO, PETE "COKE" Timbales, vocal. Member of Santana, 1978, and Giants, 1978. Session for Santana (1971); It's a Beautiful Day (1971); Carlos Santana-Buddy Miles Live (1972).

ESPERANTO Tony Mallson—drums; Gino Mallson—bass; Bruno Libert—keyboards; Roger Meakin—vocal; Kim Moore—vocal. *Album:* Last Tango, 1975.

ESPINOSA, BOBBY Organ. Member of El Chicano.

ESPINOSA, IAN Vocal, guitar. Member of Dancer, 1976.

ESPOSITO, JOE Guitar, vocal. Member of Brooklyn Dreams.

ESPOSITO, MIKE Guitar. Member of the Blues Magoos.

ESPOSITO, VINCENT C. Keyboards, vocal. Member of Sail.

ESSERY, JIM Harmonica. Session for the Allman Brothers (1977-80).

ESSEX, DAVID Vocal, guitar. Born 7/23/47. English pop-rock and film star. *Albums:* David Essex, 1974; Rock On (COL C32560) 1973; All the Fun of the Fair (COL PC 33813) 1975; Hold Me Close (COL) 1979.

ESTES, ALAN Percussion, vibes. Session for Frank Zappa (1967); the Mothers of Invention (1972); Steve Marriott (1976); Firefall (1977); Art Garfunkel (1979); Nazareth (1980).

ESTES, GENE Percussion. Session for Frank Zappa (1967); Arthur, Hurley and Gottlieb; Nilsson (1975).

ESTES, SLEEPY JOHN Guitar, vocal. Tennessee bluesman Estes was first recorded in 1929. Though a performer and singer for most of his life, he did not receive wide public attention until his appearance at the 1964 Newport Folk Festival. Born in 1904, he played the Delta blues through the depression and had to be rediscovered through rumor (by Big Bill Broonzy) in 1950. By then, he was blind in one eye, but he was still writing classic blues songs like "Key to the Highway," "Going Down Slow" and numerous others, which bluesmen Big Joe Williams, John Lee Hooker, Muddy Waters and others made famous. Blues owes no small debt to the legend of Sleepy John Estes. *Albums:* Legend of Sleepy John Estes (DEL DS 9603); Broke and Hungry (DEL DS 9608) 1964.

ESTRADA, ROY Bass, vocal. Original member of the Mothers of Invention, 1966-70. Session for Ry Cooder (1970); Frank Zappa (1976).

ETHERIDGE, JOHN Guitar. Member of the Wolf, 1974.

ETHOS Will Sharpe—guitar, vocal; Brad Stephenson—bass, vocal; Mark Richards—percussion; Michael Ponczek—keyboards. *Album:* Open Up, 1977.

ETHRIDGE, CHRIS Bass, piano. Original member of the Flying Burrito Brothers. Session for Ry Cooder (1970, 72, 74); Russ Giguere (1971); David Blue (1971); David Mason; the Doors' "Full Circle" (1972); Maria Muldaur (1973); Willie Nelson (1978); Willie Nelson and Leon Russell (1979).

ETHRIDGE, TOM Bass. Member of Lowry Hamner and the Cryers, 1978-79. Session for

Willie Nile (1980).

EUBANK, MIKE Piano. Session for Jimmy Hall (1980).

EUBANKS, JERRY Saxophone, flute, percussion, vocal. Original member of the Marshall Tucker Band, 1973-present.

EUCLID BEACH BAND Pete Hewlett—vocal, guitar; Richard Reising—vocal, guitar, keyboards. *Album:* Euclid Beach Band (EPC JE 35619) 1979.

EUPHONIUS WALL Bart Libby—keyboards; Steve Tracy—guitar, vocal; Gary Violetti—bass, vocal; Suzanne Rey—vocal, percussion; Doug Hoffman—drums, vocal. *Album:* Euphonius Wall (KAP) 1973.

EVAN, JOHN Keyboards. Born 3/28/48. Member of Jethro Tull, 1971-79.

EVANS, BOB Member of Smith, 1970.

EVANS, DAVID Drums, vocal. Member of Blue Ash, 1973.

EVANS, ERNEST Real name of Chubby Checker. See Chubby Checker.

EVANS, FURVUS Drums, percussion. Member of the Fifth Estate, 1967.

EVANS, GUY Drums, percussion, piano. Member of Van der Graff Generator, 1970-77, and Van der Graaf, 1978.

EVANS, JIMMY Drums. Member of FCC, 1980. Session for Barry Goldberg (1974).

EVANS, JOHN Organ, guitar. Member of the Box Tops, 1965-68.

EVANS, MARK Bass. Member of AC/DC, 1976-78.

EVANS, MIKE Member of Stackridge, 1974.

EVANS, NATE Vocal. Member of the Impressions.

EVANS, NICK Trombone. Member of Centipede, 1971. Session for the Soft Machine (1970); King Crimson (1971); Memphis Slim (1971).

EVANS, PAUL Vocal. Session for Robert Gordon (1979).

EVANS, PETE Vocal, guitar, keyboards. Member of the Numbers, 1980.

EVANS, RALPH Guitar, vocal. Member of Sassafras, 1975.

EVANS, ROD Vocal. Original member of Deep Purple, 1968-70, and Captain Beyond, 1972.

EVANS, TOM Guitar, vocal. Member of Badfinger. Session for John Lennon (1971).

EVANS, WAYNE Drums. Member of Black Oak Arkansas, 1971-78.

EVEN DOZEN JUG BAND Maria d'Amato—vocal; Steve Katz—harmonica, guitar, vocal; Pete Siegel; Josh Rifkin; John Sebastian—guitar, vocal, harmonica. *Album:* Even Dozen Jug Band, 1964.

EVERLY, DON Vocal, guitar. Half of the Everly Brothers with brother Phil. *Album:* Don Everly (ODE).

EVERLY, PHIL Guitar, vocal. With brother Don, half of the Everly Brothers. Session for John Sebastian (1974). *Album:* Star Spangled Springer (RCA); Every Which Way But Loose (ELK 5E-503); Living Alone (ELK 6E-213) 1979.

EVERLY BROTHERS Don Everly—guitar, vocal; Phil Everly—guitar, vocal. Surviving the golden days of rock, through the psychedelic era and English invasions, are the Everly Brothers. Popular with country-western and pop audiences, the Everlys began in 1957 with "Bye Bye Love." Other Everly hits include "Wake Up Little Susie" (1957) and "Bird Dog" (1958), among countless others. Personal disputes led to their separate solo careers. *Albums:* Chained to a Memory (HMY 11388); Christmas with the Everly Brothers (HMY 11350); Everly Brothers (HMY 11304); Everly Brothers Sing Great Country Hits (WBR 1513) 1963; Pass the Chicken and Listen (RCA LSP 4781); Gone, Gone, Gone, 1965; Yanks in England, 1965; Rock 'n' Soul, 1965; Beat 'n' Soul, 1965; In Our Image, 1966; Hit Sounds of the Everly Brothers, 1967; Everly Brothers Sing, 1967; Roots, 1968; Date with the Everly Brothers, 1961; Both Sides of an Evening, 1961; Instant Party, 1962; Golden Hits of the Everly Brothers (WBR 1471) 1962; Silver Meteor (SIE 8706); Very Best of the Everly Brothers (WBR 1554) 1962.

EVERS, GEORGE Vocal, bass. Member of Sam the Band.

EVERY MOTHER'S SON Larry Larden—vocal, guitar; Dennis Larden—guitar, vocal; Bruce Milner—keyboards, vocal; Christopher Augustine—drums; Schuyler Larsen—bass (1968); Don Kerr—bass (1967). Attempting to spoil the long-haired, unrespectable image of rock in 1967, Son appeared in all their manicured wholesomeness singing "Come On Down to My Boat." *Albums:* Every Mother's Son (MGM) 1967; Every Mother's Son's Back (MGM) 1968.

EVES, MICK Tenor saxophone. Session for Freddie King (1974); Steve Howe (1975).

EVETS, ZTAK Tambourine. Session for Horslips (1979).

EWING, FRANK Guitar, bass, vocal. Member of Tilt, 1980.

EXELL, JAMES Bass, vocal. Replaced Colin Wilson in the String Driven Thing, 1974-75.

EXENE Vocal. Member of X, 1980.

EXILE Jimmy Stokely—vocal; Billy Luxon—vocal, percussion, trumpet; Buzz Cornelison—keyboards, trumpet, vocal; Bernie Faulkner—keyboards, guitar, saxophone, vocal (1973-78); Jimmy Pennington—guitar, vocal; Kenny Weir—bass, vocal (1973-78); Bobby Johns—drums (1973-78); Marlon Hargis—keyboards, vocal (1978-80); Sonny Le Maire—bass, vocal (1978-80); Steve Goetzman—drums (1978-80). *Albums:* All There Is (WBR K-3323) 1979; Exile (VIC AFLI-3086) 1973; Mixed Emotions (WBR K-3205); Stage Pass (VIC AFLI-3087) 1978; Don't Leave Me This Way (WBR 3437) 1980.

EXPLORER See Paul Warren and Explorer.
EXTREMES See Duke Williams and the Extremes.
EYRE, GEOFF Drums. Member of the Hometown Band, 1976.
EYRE, TOMMY Keyboards. Member of the Aynsley Dunbar Retaliation, 1970, Mark-Almond, 1971, and Zzebra, 1975, replacing Gus Yeadon. Replaced Hugh McKenna in the Sensational Alex Harvey Band. Session for Joe Cocker (1968); Aynsley Dunbar (1970); Jon Mark (1974); Gerry Rafferty (1978-79).
EYRICH, JEFF Bass. Member of Glider, 1977.
EZRIN, BOB Ondioline, keyboards, percussion, vocal, producer. Production and session for Nils Lofgren (1979). Produced Alice Cooper (1971-73); Ursa Major (1972); Richard Wagner (1978); and others. Session for Lou Reed (1973); Dr. John (1975); Alice Cooper (1975-76); Steve Hunter (1977).

F-WORD Rick L. Rick—vocal; Dim Wanker—guitar; Steve Effete—bass; Dutch Schultz—drums. *Album:* Like It or Not (PBS 101) 1978.

FABIAN Vocal. Philadelphia born Fabian Forte was a commercial creation of the Elvis era of 1959. Guesting on television and in the movies, he invariably had a singing number in which his voice betrayed his pretty face. *Album:* Sixteen Greatest Hits (ABC).

FABRES, SHELLY Vocal. Television teenage actress who made a hit of "Johnny Angel," 1962.

FABULOUS POODLES Tony de Meur—vocal, guitar, harmonica; Richie Robertson—bass, guitar, keyboards, percussion; Bobby Valentino—violin, vocal, mandolin; Bryn Burrows—drums, percussion. *Albums:* Mirror Stars (EPC JE 35666) 1978; Think Pink (EPC JE 36256) 1979.

FABULOUS RHINESTONES Harvey Brooks—bass, guitar; Kal David—guitar, vocal; Marty Grebb—keyboards, bass, vocal, saxophone; Greg Thomas—drums; Reinol Andino—percussion. *Albums:* The Fabulous Rhinestones, 1972; Free Wheelin', 1973.

FABULOUS THUNDERBIRDS Jimmy Vaughn—guitar; Kim Wilson—vocal, harmonica; Keith Ferguson—bass; Mike Buck—drums. Return to authentic American blues by a Texas quartet. *Albums:* Fabulous Thunderbirds (TKM 7068) 1979; What's the Word (CYS 1287) 1980.

FACE DANCER Jeff Adams—guitar; Michael Milsap—piano, vocal, synthesizer (1980); Billy Trainor—drums; Scott McGinn—bass, synthesizer, vocal; Carey Kress—vocal (1979); David Utter—guitar, vocal (1979). *Albums:* This World (CAP ST-11934) 1979; About Face (CAP ST 12082) 1980.

FACES Steve Marriott—vocal, guitar, writer (1965-68); Ronnie Lane—bass, guitar, writer; Ian McLagen—keyboards; Kenny Jones—drums, percussion; Rod Stewart—vocal, banjo (1971-76); Ron Wood—guitar, harmonica (1971-76). A part of the British rock invasion, the Faces hit the American charts in 1968 with "Itchycoo Park." The group was then a Steve Marriott vehicle. Because of management and personnel problems, he left in 1969 (to form Humble Pie) and was replaced by ex-Jeff Beck Group member recently turned soloist, Rod Stewart, and by Ronnie Lane a year later. Their raunchy rock sound was a popular alternative reminiscent of the Stones. Consequently, their solo careers became equally commercial. See Small Faces. *Albums:* These Are But Four Small Faces (IMD 21251 001) 1968; Ogden's Nut Gone (IMD 4225) 1968; Long Player (WBR WS 1892) 1971; A Nod's as Good as a Wink (WBR 2574) 1971; Ooh La La (WBR B 2665) 1973; The First Step (WBR 1851) 1970.

FADDEN, JIMMIE Drums, percussion, trombone. Replaced Hanna in the Nitty Gritty Dirt Band.

FADDIS, JOHN Horns. Session for Lou Reed (1974); John Mayall (1979); Paul Simon (1980).

FAEHSE, TONY Guitar, vocal. Member of Jo Jo Zep and the Falcons, 1980.

FAGAN, RICHARD Vocal. *Album:* Richard Fagan (MER SRM-1-3811).

FAGEN, DONALD Keyboards, vocal, writer. Began playing backup for Jay and the Americans. With Walter Becker, he writes for Steely Dan, 1972-present. Session for Navasota (1972).

FAGEN, DOUG Tenor saxophone. Session for Junior Wells; Catfish Hodge Band (1979).

FAHEY, JOHN Guitar, writer. Maryland-born guitarist and founder of Takoma records. He specializes in taking his classical and Spanish guitar knowledge and applying it to traditional blues themes. *Albums:* Requia (VAN VSD 79259); Voice of the Turtle (TKM C 1019) 1968; Great San Bernadino Birthday Party (TKM); John Fahey, 1966; John Fahey, 1968; Days Have Gone By, 1967; Best of John Fahey 1959-77 (TKM 1058) 1977; Blind Joe Death (TKM 1002) 1967; Christmas with John Fahey, Vol. 2 (TKM 1045) 1975; Dance of Death and Other Plantation Favorites (TKM 1004) 1967; Death Chants, Breakdowns and Military Waltzes (TKM 1003); Essential (VAN VSD-55/56) 1974; John Fahey Guitar (VAN 79259) 1968; John Fahey, Leo Kottke, Peter Lang (TKM 1040); John Fahey Visits Washington D.C. (TKM 7069) 1979; Fare Forward Voyagers (TKM 1035) 1973; New Possibility (Xmas Album) (TKM 1020); Old Fashioned Love (TKM 1043) 1979; Transfiguration of Blind Joe Death (TKM 7015) 1967; Yellow Princess (VAN 79293); Yes! Jesus Loves Me (TAK 7085) 1980.

FAIELLA, BENNY Guitar, bass, vocal. Member of the Jaggerz.

FAILLA, RICK Vocal. Voice of Trouble, 1977.

FAIRBAIRN, BRUCE Vocal. Session for Ian Lloyd (1979).

FAIRLY, COLIN Drums, percussion, vocal. Member of the String Driven Thing, 1972-75. Session for the Climax Blues Band (1978).

FAIRPORT CONVENTION Simon Nicol—guitar (until 1974); Dave Swarbrick—violin, viola, vocal, writer; Richard Thompson—guitar (until 1974); Sandy Denny—vocal; Dave Mattacks—drums; Ashley Hutchings—bass (until 1974); Dave Pegg —bass (until 1974); Jerry Donahue—guitar, slide guitar (1974); Trevor Lucas—vocal, guitar, harmonica (1974); Bruce Rowland—drums, percussion (1974). While other English groups were emulating American blues in the late 1960s, Fairport chose to study their own domestic blues. Old English ballads and traditional musical tales were updated in a quasi-electric/acoustic format and mixed with their own material. The group's sound was centered around vocalists Denny and Swarbrick. *Albums:* Rising for the Moon (ISL 9313) 1975; Gottle 'O' Gear (ISL 9389); Angel Delight (AAM 4319); Barbbacombe Lee (AAM 4339); Full House (AAM 4265); Liege and Lief (AAM 4257); Moveable Feast (ISL 9285) 1974; Nine (AAM 3603) 1973; Rosie (AAM 4386); Unhalfbricking (AAM 4206); Fairport Chronicles (AAM 3530) 1972; Fairport Convention (AAM 4185); What We Did on Our Holidays.

FAIRS, JIM Guitar, vocal, percussion. Member of Pearls Before Swine, 1969.

FAIRWEATHER-LOWE, ANDY Guitar, drums. Session for Dave Edmunds (1971); Foghat (1972); the Who (1978); Gerry Rafferty (1978). *Albums:* La Booga Rooga, 1975; Spider Jiving (AAM); Mega She Bang (WBR BSK 3450) 1980.

FAITH BAND Dave Barnes—drums; Dave Bennett —guitar; John Cascella—saxophone, keyboards; Mark Crawley—bass, vocal; Carl Storie—vocal, harmonica. *Albums:* Face to Face (MER SRM-1-3770) 1979; Rock 'n' Romance (MER SRM 1-3759) 1978; Vital Signs (MER SRM 1-3807) 1979; Excuse Me I Just Cut an Album (VIL VR 7703) 1977.

FAITH, CHRISSY Vocal. Session for Lou Reed (1979).

FAITHFULL, MARIANNE Vocal. Blonde English folksinger who first became noticed in 1964 with "Come and Stay With Me" and "Go Away from My World." A highly publicized relationship with Mick Jagger kept her name circulating even though she dropped singing for the movies. By 1970, she had faded from the public eye, but in 1979 she returned to recording. *Albums:* Marianne Faithful (LON LS 3423) 1965; Go Away from My World (LON PS 452) 1965; Faithfull Forever, 1966; Greatest Hits (LON PS 547) 1964; Broken English (ISL 9570) 1979.

FAKIR, ABDUL Vocal. Original member of the Four Tops.

FALBERG, ROBBIE Guitar. Member of Alexis, 1977.

FALCON, BILLY Guitar, vocal. *Albums:* Falcon Around (MCA 3238); Improper Attire (UAR LT-967); Billy Falcon (UAR LA 967-4) 1979; Burning Rose (UAR MR-LA-8320G) 1977.

FALCON, FELIX Percussion. Session for Joe Cocker (1972); Dave Mason (1974).

FALCONER, RODERICK Vocal, guitar. *Albums:* New Nation (UAR UA-LA-651-G) 1976; Victory in Rock City (UAR UA LA777-G) 1977.

FALK, DON Guitar, bass, vocal. Member of Iguana, 1977.

FALL Mark E. Smith—vocal; Yvonne Pawlett—piano; Mark Riley—bass; Martin Bramah—guitar, vocal; Karl Burns—drums. *Album:* Live at the Witch Trails (IRS 003) 1979.

FALLING PEBBLES Early name of the Buckinghams.

FALLING SPIKES Early name for the Velvet Underground, 1965.

FALOMIR, STEVE Bass. Member of Tierra, 1980.

FALSIA, JOE Guitar. Member of C.O.D., 1979.

FALSINI, FRANCO Vocal, guitar, synthesizer. Member of the Sensations Fix.

FALZONE, SAM Horns. Session for Steppenwolf (1974).

FAME, GEORGIE Organ, vocal. British jazz-rock stalwart virtually unknown by American listeners. *Album:* Georgie Fame (ILS 9293) 1975.

FAMILY Jim King—harmonica; Rob Townsend—drums; Rick Grech—bass, violin, cello; John Witney—guitar, sitar; Roger Chapman—vocal, saxophone, harmonica. Experimental English rock group most famous for spawning Rick Grech, who went on to become a member of Blind Faith. *Albums:* Music in a Doll's House, 1968; Anyway; Bandstand; Fearless; It's Only a Movie (UAR); Family Entertainment; A Song for Me.

FANCY Mo Foster—bass; Les Binks—drums, percussion; Ray Fenwick—guitar; Annie Kavanaugh —vocal. *Albums:* Turns You On, 1976; Wild Thing (VIC).

FANDANGO Joe Lynn Turner—vocal, guitar; Rick Blakemore—guitar, vocal; Bob Danyls—bass, vocal; Larry Dawson—keyboards; Abe Spellmore —drums; Santos—percussion. *Albums:* Cadillac (VIC AFLI-3591) 1980; One Night Stand (VIC AFLI-3245) 1979.

FANGER, J. D. Guitar. Member of the Andy Fernbach Connexion.

FANNON, JOHN Guitar, vocal. Member of New England, 1980.

FANNY Patti Quatro—guitar; Jean Millington—bass; Brie Howard—drums; Nicole Barclay—keyboards. *Album:* Rock 'n' Roll Survivors (CSB NBLP 7007) 1974.

FAR CRY Peter Thom; Phil Galdston—keyboards, vocal. *Album:* More Things Change (COL JC-36286) 1980.

FAR EAST FAMILY BAND Fumio Miyashta—vocal, guitar, flute, keyboards; Hirohito Fukushima —guitar, koto, vocal; Yushin Harada—drums, percussion; Akira Fukakasha—bass. *Album:* Tenkujin (AER 11479) 1977.

FARAGHER, DAVEY Bass, vocal. Member of the Faragher Brothers, 1978-79.

FARAGHER, DANNY Keyboards, organ, harmonica, vocal, horns. Member of the Bones, 1973, and the Faragher Brothers, 1978-79.

FARAGHER, JIMMY Vocal, bass, saxophone, guitar. Member of the Bones, 1973, and the Faragher Brothers, 1978-79.

FARAGHER, MARTY Drums. Member of the Faragher Brothers, 1978-79.

FARAGHER, TOMMY Keyboards, vocal. Member of the Faragher Brothers, 1978-79.

FARAGHER BROTHERS Tommy Faragher—keyboards, vocal; Davey Faragher—bass, vocal; Marty Faragher—drums; Jimmy Faragher—guitar, vocal; Danny Faragher—organ, vocal, harmonica. *Albums:* The Faraghers (POL 1-6232) 1979; Open Your Eyes (POL 1-6167) 1978.

FARBER, STAN Vocal. Member of the Ron Hicklin Singers, 1979. Session for John Kay (1973); Tin Huey (1979); Pink Floyd (1979).

FARGUS, JEFF Keyboards, vocal. Member of the Ravens, 1980.

FARINA, MIMI Joan Baez's younger sister, and solo folksinger. See Richard and Mimi Farina.

MIMI FARINA AND TOM JANS *Album:* Take Heart (AAM 4310) 1971.

FARINA, RICHARD See Richard and Mimi Farina.

RICHARD AND MIMI FARINA Folk husband and wife duet of the 1960s, including Joan Baez's younger sister. Richard handled the writing, arranging and production (not to mention writing the classic period novel, "Been Down So Long It looks Like Up to Me") with his wife harmonizing. He died in a motorcycle accident in 1966. She retired from the industry, except for occasional cameo roles with her sister and one with Tom Jans. *Albums:* Best of Mimi and Richard Farina (VSD 21/22); Celebrations for a Grey Day (VAN 79174); Greatest Folksingers of the Sixties (VAN VSD-17/18); Memories (VAN 79263); Reflections in Crystal Wind (VAN 79204).

FARIS, JOHN Keyboards, reeds, vocal. Member of Zephyr, 1971.

FARLEY, FRANK Drums. Member of the Pirates.

FARLOW, BILL Vocal, harmonica. Member of Commander Cody's Lost Planet Airmen.

FARLOWE, CHRIS Vocal. Mick Jagger once commented that the best male vocalist in England was Chris Farlowe. Farlowe first gained notoriety in Colosseum, 1970-71, before he left to replace Pete French in Atomic Rooster, 1972-73. After a year out of sight, he returned with the Hill for a lone album. *Albums:* Chris Farlowe–From Here to Mama Rosa with the Hill (POL 24-4041) 1975; Chris Farlowe Band (Import) 1975; Chris Farlowe's Greatest Hits (Import).

FARMER, HUMPTY Keyboards. Member of Climax Blues Band, 1970.

FARMER, JULIUS Bass. Session for Dr. John (1975).

FARMER, STEVE Guitar. Member of the Amboy Dukes.

FARNDON, PETE Bass, vocal. Member of the Pretenders, 1980.

FARNELL, TOMMY Drums, percussion. Replaced Eric Dillon in Savoy Brown, 1976-78.

FARNER, MARK Guitar, keyboards, vocal, writer. Born 9/29/48. Bare chested guitarist of Grand Funk Railroad. Produced one solo album before forming the Mark Farner Band, 1978. *Album:* Mark Farner (ACO SD 18232) 1977.

MARK FARNER BAND Mark Farner—guitar, keyboards, vocal; Dennis Bellinger—bass, vocal; Andy Newmark—drums. *Album:* No Frills (ACO SD 19196) 1978.

FARNER, RICKY Vocal. Session for Mark Farner (1977).

FARR, GARY Vocal. Member of Lion, 1980.

FARR, STEVE Alto saxophone. Session for Status Quo (1973).

FARRAR, JIMMY Vocal. Replaced Danny Joe Brown in Molly Hatchet, 1980.

FARRAR, JOHN Guitar, vocal. Session for Olivia Newton-John (1976); the Tremblers (1980). *Album:* John Farrar (COL JC 46375) 1980.

FARRAR, PAT Vocal. Session for Olivia Newton-John (1976).

FARRELL, JOE Saxophone, English horn, French horn, flute. Member of Elvin Jones Trio, and Return to Forever. Session for the Band (1972); the Bee Gees (1975); Martin Mull (1974); Pearls Before Swine (1968); Santana (1974); Free Creek (1973); Art Garfunkel (1978). *Albums:* Benson and Farrell (CTI 6059); Cathedral Y El Toro (WBR B-3121); Moon Germs (CTI 6023); Night Dancing (WBR K-3225) 1978; Outback (CTI 6014); Penny Arcade (CTI Q-6034); Song of the Wind (CTI 6067); Sonic Text (CON 14002) 1980; Skate Board Park (XAN 174) 1979.

FARRELL, LOUIS Drums, percussion. Original member of Gun.

FARYAR, CYRUS Guitar. Session for Fred Neil (1968).

FASHION Dik—percussion, harmonica, vocal; Luke—guitar, vocal; Mulligan—bass, synthesizer, vocal. *Album:* Product Perfect (IRS 002) 1979.

FAST, LARRY Synthesizer. One-man group known as Synergy since 1978. See Synergy. Session for Ian Lloyd (1979).

FAT CHANCE Bill La Bounty—vocal, keyboards; Fred Sherman—horns; Phil Garonzik—reeds; Dale Borge—bass, vocal; Gordon Hirsch—drums; Steve Eaton—vocal, guitar, harmonica. *Album:* Fat Chance (VIC LSP 4626) 1972.

FAT MATTRESS Eric Dillon—drums, percussion; Jimmy Leverton—bass, keyboards, vocal, writer; Neil Landon—vocal, writer; Noel Redding—guitar, vocal, writer. After working with Jimi Hendrix as a bass player, Redding returned to his initial instrument, lead guitar, and formed Mattress in 1969. The pace slowed to encompass ballads and three-part vocal harmonies. A dynamic change, but not successful. *Albums:* Fat Mattress (ACO SD 33 309) 1969; Fat Mattress II (ACO SD 33 347) 1970.

FATAAR, RICKY Vocal, drums. Member of Sweetwater, the Beach Boys, 1972-73, and the Rutles, 1978, under the name Stig O'Hara. Session for Henry Gross (1975).

FATHERS AND SONS Muddy Waters—vocal, guitar; Otis Spann—piano; Mike Bloomfield—guitar; Paul Butterfield—harmonica; Donald "Duck" Dunn—bass; Sam Lay—drums. As it happens in jazz, several big blues names often get together not with the intention of staying together. Such was the case in Chicago in April, 1969. Old timers Muddy Waters and Otis Spann teamed up with some members of the newer wave of blues musicians for a little fun and some old blues. *Album:* Fathers and Sons, 1969.

FAUCETTE, LARRY Congas. Session for Jimi Hendrix (1968).

FAUERSO, PAUL Vocal, keyboards. Member of the Loading Zone, 1968.

FAULK, KEN Trumpet. Member of the Boneroos since 1976.

FAULKNER, BERNIE Keyboards, guitar, saxophone, vocal. Member of Exile, 1973-78.

FAULKNER, ERIC Vocal, guitar, mandolin, violin. Member of the Bay City Rollers.

FAURE, DUNCAN Keyboards. Member of Rabbitt, 1976-77, and the Bay City Rollers, 1979.

FAUST, BOB Trumpet. Member of the Righteous Brothers Band, 1966.

FAVELA, LIVER Percussion, harmonica, vocal. Member of Birtha, 1973.

FAY, MARTIN Fiddle. Session for Art Garfunkel (1978).

FAYE, DANIELLE Bass. Member of Venus and the Razor Blades, 1977.

FAYER, ART Violin. Member of Touchstone, 1971.

FAZZ, MICK Vocal, guitar. Member of the Critical Mass, 1980.

FCC Wayne Chaney—vocal, percussion; J. B. Christman—vocal, keyboards; Dennis Clifton—vocal, guitar; Jimmy Evans—drums; Steve Gooch—vocal, guitar; Lonnie Ledford—bass. *Album:* Do You Believe in Magic (VIC AFLI 3582) 1980.

FEALDMAN, ALAN Keyboards. Member of Sniff 'n' the Tears, 1978.

FEAN, JOHN Guitar, banjo, vocal. Original member of Horslips.

FEAT, MICK Bass, vocal. Member of the Amazing Blondel, 1974, Runner, 1979, and the Alvin Lee Band, 1980. Session for Kevin Ayers (1977); Kevin Lamb (1978).

FECKER, STEVE Drums. Member of Choice, 1980.

FEDERICI, DANNY Organ. Member of the E Street Band, 1978-present. Session for Bruce Springsteen (1975).

FEE See Fee Waybill.

FEGY, DICK Guitar. Session for Ringo Starr (1977).

FEIDMAN, DAVID Percussion. Session for Grace Slick (1980).

FEINBERG, JEANNIE Saxophone, flute. Member of Isis, 1974-75.

FEINGOLD, ALAN Keyboards. Session for Les Dudek (1977).

FEINSTEIN, HARLEY Drums. Member of Halfnelson, 1971, and Sparks, 1972.

FEISTER, DAVID Guitar, vocal. Replaced Jim Fish in the Henry Paul Band, 1980.

FEITEN, BUZZY Guitar, keyboards, bass. Member of Paul Butterfield Blues Band, 1969. Founder of Full Moon, 1972. Session for Bob Dylan (1970); Gregg Allman (1973); Gene Clark (1974); Free Creek (1973); Commander Cody (1978); Adam Mitchell (1979); Gary Wright (1979); Randy Newman (1979).

FEJARANG, ALVIN Drums. Member of Kalapanna, 1977.

FELD, MARC Real name of Marc Bolan.

FELDER, DON Guitar, vocal. Born 9/21/47. Original member of the Eagles, since 1972. Session for David Blue (1975); Joe Walsh (1976); Bob Seger (1978); Terence Boylan (1980).

FELDER, WILTON Bass. Session for Donovan (1976); Shuggie Otis (1971); Steely Dan (1974); Henry Gross (1972); Seals and Crofts (1973, 76); Steven T. (1978). *Album:* We All Have a Star (MCA AA-1109).

FELDMAN, BILL Guitar, vocal. Member of Johnny and the Distractions, 1980.

FELDMAN, DENNIS Bass, vocal. Member of Speedway Blvd., 1980.

FELDMAN, ERIC DREW Keyboards. Member of Captain Beefheart's Magic Band since 1975, replacing Mark Marcellino.

FELDMAN, MIKE Vocal, guitar. Member of Halloween, 1979.

FELDMAN, POPE Bass. Session for the Rank Strangers (1977).

FELDMAN, VICTOR Bells, vibes, percussion, piano, congas. Session for James Taylor (1976); Jon Mark (1974); Steely Dan (1972-76, 80); B. B. King (1972); Frank Zappa (1967); Joni Mitchell (1975); Seals and Crofts (1971); the Doobie Brothers (1977); Lee Ritenour (1977); Randy Newman (1979); Adam Mitchell (1979); Alan O'Day (1979); Terence Boylan (1980); Elton John (1980); Christopher Cross (1980). *Albums:* Arrival of Victor Feldman (CTP 7549); Latinsville (CTP

9005); Sonny Rollins and Contemporary Leaders (CTP 7564); Suite Sixteen (CTP 3541); Your Smile (CHR CRS 1005) 1974; Artful Dodger (CND CJ 38) 1977; In My Pocket (CHR CJR 1001) 1977; Love Me with All Your Heart (VJY VJ 1096).

FELDTHOUSE, SOLOMON Guitar, oud, clarinet, vocal. An original member of Kaleidoscope, 1967-68, 1976.

FELICIANO, JOSE Guitar, vocal, writer. Feliciano made his name with Latin arrangements of rock songs for the pop market, beginning with "Light My Fire," 1968. *Albums:* Compartments (VIC APDI 0141); En Mi Soledad No Flores Mas (ARC 3060); Jose Feliciano (Xmas) (VIC LSP 4421); For My Love . . . Mother Music (VIC APLI 0266); Just Wanna Rock 'N' Roll (VIC APLI 1005); And the Feelin's Good (VIC AFLI-0407) 1974; Angela (PVS 2010) 1976; Canta Otra Vez (ARC 3145); Encore (VIC AFLI-2824) 1971; Fantastico (ARC 3058); Feliciano (VIC AFLI-4185) 1969; Feliciano/10 to 23 (VIC AFLI-3957); Jose Feliciano-January '71 (ARC 3065); Jose Feliciano Sings (CDN 2563) 1972; Felicidades (ARC 3061); Fireworks (VIC AFLI-4370); Mas Exitos De Jose Feliciano (ARC 3063); Sentimiento La Voz Y La Guitarra De Jose Feliciano (ARC 3006); Sombras . . . Una Voz, Una Guitarra (ARC 3007); Sweet Soul Music (PVS 2022).

FELIOUS, ODETTA Full name of Odetta. See Odetta.

FELIX, JULIE Vocal, guitar. American folk singer who moved to England to enjoy more popularity. *Albums:* Julie Felix; Julie Felix Second Album; Strangers (BEO) 1975.

FELTON, JOHN Vocal. Member of the Diamonds.

FENCIL–WALLACE, GEORGE Guitar, keyboards, percussion, vocal. Member of the Invaders, 1980.

FENDER, GRIFF Vocal. Member of Darts since 1978.

FENELLY, MIKE Guitar. Session for Ray Manzarek.

FENN, RICK Guitar, vocal. Member of 10 CC, 1980.

FENNEL, TONY Drums. Member of Centipede, 1971.

FENNELL, KEVIN Guitar. Session for Colin Winski (1980).

FENT, LANCE Guitar, harmonica. Original member of the Peanut Butter Conspiracy, 1967.

FENTON, DAVID Guitar, vocal. Member of the Vapors, 1980.

FENTON, GRAHAM Vocal. Member of Matchbox, 1979.

FENTON, PAUL Drums, percussion. Member of Carmen, 1974.

FENWICK, RAY Guitar, slide guitar, vocal. Member of Fancy, 1975-76, and the Ian Gillan Band, 1976. Session for Chris Youlden (1973).

FERGUSON, DAN Guitar. Replaced Ray Monette in Rare Earth, 1977.

FERGUSON, DAVID Keyboards. Member of Random Hold, 1980.

FERGUSON, DOUG Bass. Original member of Camel, since 1975.

FERGUSON, JANET Vocal. Session for Frank Zappa (1972).

FERGUSON, JAY Keyboards, vocal, writer, guitar. Half of the songwriting team that made Spirit one of the best American bands of the 1960s, he went on to form Jo-Jo Gunne, 1972-74. After Gunne's four commercially dubious albums, he toured with Joe Walsh, 1976, before beginning his solo career. Session for John Fahey; Joe Walsh (1978). *Albums:* All Alone in the End Zone (ASY 7E-1063) 1976; Real Life Ain't This Way (ASY 6E-158) 1979; Terms and Conditions (CAP ST-12083) 1980; Thunder Island (ELK 7E-1115) 1977.

FERGUSON, KEITH Bass. Member of the Fabulous Thunderbirds since 1979.

FERGUSON, STEVE Bass, vocal, harmonica. Replaced Al Anderson in NRBQ.

FERNANDEZ, MANUEL Organ. Member of Los Bravos, 1966-68.

FERNANDEZ, RAY Drums, vocal, percussion. Member of the Atlantics since 1979.

FERNANDEZ, TONY Drums, percussion. A member of Ross, 1974, before he replaced Barney James in Rick Wakeman's backup band, 1976. Session for Rick Wakeman (1977).

FERNBACH, ANDY Guitar, vocal. Part of the English blues wave of the 1960s that did not make it commercially in the United States, as a soloist or as founder of the Andy Fernbach Connexion. See Connexion.

FERRANTE, CAROL Vocal, percussion, piano. Member of Larry Raspberry and the Highsteppers.

FERRANTE, DENNIS Vocal. Session for Johnny Winter (1974).

FERRANTELLA, NICK Drums, percussion. Session for Leslie West (1975).

FERRAR, DUCK Vocal, guitar, bass. Member of the Fifth Estate, 1967.

FERRARA, FRANK Bass, vocal, piano. Member of Bang, 1973.

FERRARA, FRED Vocal, guitar, trumpet. Member of the Brooklyn Bridge.

FERRARO, JOHN Drums. Session for Vapour Trails (1980).

FERREIRA, BOB Alto saxophone. Session for It's a Beautiful Day (1971); Boz Scaggs (1972).

FERRELL, JAMES Guitar. Member of Roy Loney and the Phantom Movers, 1979-80.

FERRERO, ROBERT Vocal, guitar. Member of the Scooters, 1980.

FERRIS, ROGER "PEACHES" Vocal. Member

of No Dice, 1978-79.

FERRONE, STEVE Drums. Replaced Godfrey MacLean in Brian Auger's Oblivion Express, 1973-75. Joined the Average White Band, 1978-present. Session for Freddie King (1974-75).

FERRONE, TOMMY Guitar. Session for Dr. John (1971).

FERRY, BRYAN Vocal, writer, piano. Voice of Roxy, an experimental English rock group, 1972-present. Temporary vacations as a soloist allow him greater freedom as an arranger and performer. *Albums:* Another Time, Another Place (ATC 18113) 1974; Bride Stripped Bare (ATC 19205) 1978; In Your Mind (ATC 18216) 1978; Let's Stick Together (ATC 18187) 1976; These Foolish Things (ATC 7304) 1974.

FESI, MONGESI Trumpet. Member of Centipede, 1971. Session for Robert Wyatt (1974).

FESTA, MICHAEL Guitar, vocal, piano, pedal steel guitar. Member of the Rockspurs, 1978-79.

FETTA, JOHN PAUL Bass. Member of the Flame, 1977.

FEVER TREE Dennis Keller—vocal; John Tuttle—percussion; Michael—guitar; E. E. Wolfe—bass; Rob Landes—keyboards, cello, flute, harmonica. Psychedelic Texas group that scored in 1968 with "San Francisco Girls." *Albums:* Creation; Fever Tree (MCA 551) 1968.

FEY, DONALD Tenor saxophone. Session for Chicken Shack.

FEY, RITA Autoharp. Session for Neil Young (1978).

FICCA, BILLY Drums. Member of Television, 1977-78.

FICTION BROTHERS Alan Senauke—guitar; Howie Tarnower—mandolin. *Albums:* Things Are Coming My Way (FLF 204) 1979; Country Cooking (FLF 019) 1975.

FIDDLER, JOHN Vocal, guitar. Member of Medicine Head, 1973, and the British Lions, 1978.

FIEDERER, LENNY Violin, viola. Member of Guns and Butter, 1972.

FIEGER, DOUG Bass, guitar, vocal, writer, producer. Original member of Sky, 1970-71, and the Knack, 1979-present. Produced the Rubber City Rebels, 1980.

FIEL, LANNY Guitar. Member of White Duck, 1971, and the Coral Reefer Band, 1974.

FIEL, RICK Guitar, keyboards, vocal. Member of White Duck, 1971.

FIELD, GRAHAM Organ. Member of Rare Bird, 1969-72.

FIELD, JERRY Bass. Member of Whole Wheat, 1977, and Passion, 1979.

FIELD, JOHN Fiddle, banjo, mandolin. Session for Long John Baldry (1975).

FIELD, JON Flute, conga, percussion. Member of July, and Jade Warrior, 1970-72.

FIELD, LARRY Guitar. Member of Cold Blood.

FIELDER, JAMES "JIM" Bass. Member of Blood, Sweat and Tears, 1967-68, who began playing with Frank Zappa, pre-Mothers of Invention. Session for Buffalo Springfield (1967).

FIELDS, FRANK Bass. Session for Fats Domino (1949-57).

FIELDS, GIL Drums. Member of Wind in the Willows, 1968.

FIELDS, VENETTA Vocal. Session for Marc Benno; Joe Cocker (1974); Dr. John (1975); Neil Diamond (1976); Steve Marriott (1976); Shuggie Otis (1971); Steely Dan (1972, 76); the Rolling Stones (1972); Bill Wyman (1976); Elvin Bishop (1972); Roy Buchanan (1974); Gene Clark (1974); Rita Coolidge (1972); John Kay (1973); B. B. King (1970); Joe Walsh (1973); Russ Giguere (1971); Country Joe McDonald (1975); Bob Seger (1978); Gary Wright (1979); Richie Furay (1979); the Marc Tanner Band (1979); Nazareth (1980); Boz Scaggs (1980); the Ozark Mountain Daredevils (1980).

FIERRO, MARTIN Saxophone. Member of Sir Douglas Quintet, 1966-68, and Mother Earth, 1968. Session for Jerry Garcia and Howard Wales (1972).

FIERSTEIN, RONNIE Vocal, keyboards, guitar. Member of Arbuckle, 1972.

FIESTER, DAVID Guitar, vocal. Replaced Jim Fish in the Henry Paul Band, 1980.

FIFTH DIMENSION Ron Townson—vocal; Lamonte Lemore—vocal; Marilyn McCoo—vocal; Florence La Rue—vocal; Billy Davis—guitar, vocal; Mic Bell—vocal; Lou Courtney—vocal; Terri Bryant—vocal. Black quintet that emerged in 1966 with the single "Go Where You Wanna Go," a pop arrangement of a John Phillips song. They recorded "Up, Up and Away" (1967), which was closely imitated in an airline commercial. *Albums:* Greatest Hits on Earth; Soul and Inspiration; Up, Up and Away, 1967; The Magic Garden, 1967; Stoned Soul Picnic, 1968; High on Sunshine (MTN M7-914) 1978.

FIFTH ESTATE Rik Engler—vocal, violin, clarinet, percussion, bass; Duck Ferrar—vocal, guitar, bass; Wads Wadhams—keyboards; Furvus Evans—drums, percussion; D. William Shute—mandolin, guitar. *Album:* Ding Dong the Witch Is Dead, 1967.

FIG, ANTON Drums, vocal. Member of Spider, 1980. Session for Link Wray (1979-80).

FIGUEROA, SAMMY Percussion, vocal. Member of Raices, 1975. Session for Tommy Bolin (1975).

FILLEUL, PETER Keyboards, vocal. Added to the Climax Blues Band lineup, 1979. Session for the Climax Blues Band (1978).

FILLMORE Gala concert farewell for the closing date of Bill Graham's Fillmore Auditorium, most famous concert hall on the West Coast, February 1966 — July 4, 1972. Guest artists included Lamb, the Elvin Bishop Group, Malo, the Sons of Champlin, It's a Beautiful Day, the Quicksilver Messenger Service, Tower of Power, Boz Scaggs, Cold Blood, Stoneground, the New Riders of the Purple Sage, the Grateful Dead, Hot Tuna, and Santana. *Album:* Fillmore–The Last Days (FIL E3X 31390) 1972.

FINCH Cleem Determeiuer—keyboards; Joop Van Nimwegen—guitar; Peter Jink—bass; Beer Klaasse—drums. *Album:* Glory of the Inner Force (ACO) 1975.

FINCHAM, JOHN Member of Trickster, 1979.

FINDLEY, BOB Horns. Session for Steely Dan (1976).

FINDLEY, CHUCK Horns. Session for Boz Scaggs (1976); Donovan (1976); Neil Diamond (1976); Nilsson (1974); Neil Sedaka (1975); Steely Dan (1976); the Rolling Stones (1973); George Harrison (1974-75); B. B. King (1971); Ringo Starr (1973-74); Joni Mitchell (1975); Glen Campbell (1976); Cher Bono (1976); Yvonne Elliman (1978); Richie Furay (1978); Jerry Corbetta (1978); Randy Newman (1979); Dick St. Nicklaus (1979); Adrian Gurvitz (1979); Elton John (1980); Johnny Rivers (1980); Stuart Margolin (1980); Christopher Cross (1980).

FINERTY, BARRY Guitar. Session for Taj Mahal (1978).

FINGERPRINTZ Jimmy O'Neill—vocal, guitar; Cha Burnz—vocal, guitar; Kenny Alton—bass, vocal; Bob Shilling—drums. *Albums:* The Very Dab (VIR 2119) 1980; Distinguishing Marks (VIR 31136) 1980.

FINGERS, JOHNNIE Member of the Boomtown Rats since 1977.

FINK, BOB Keyboards, vocal. Member of the Edge, 1980.

FINK, MIKE Drums. Member of 3-D, 1980.

FINKLE, CARL Bass. Member of Martha and the Muffins, 1980.

FINLAYSON, WILLY Vocal. Session for Manfred Mann (1980).

FINLEY, JOHN Vocal. Voice of Rhinoceros, 1968.

FINN, MICKEY Guitar. Session for Steve Marriott (1979).

FINN, NEIL Guitar, vocal. Member of the Split Enz.

FINN, STEVE Bass, vocal. Member of Sassafras, 1975.

FINN, TIM Vocal. Member of the Split Enz.

FINN, TOM Bass. Member of the Left Banke, 1967.

FINNEGAN, OWEN Congas. Session for Savoy Brown (1970).

FINNERTY, DAVID Guitar. Session for Peter C. Johnson (1980).

FINNIGAN, MICHAEL Keyboards, vocal. Member of the Dudek, Finnigan, Kruger Band, 1980. Session for Big Brother and the Holding Company; Jimi Hendrix (1968); Dave Mason (1974-80); Peter Frampton (1977); Les Dudek (1978); Steve Stills (1978); Rod Stewart (1978); the Marc Tanner Band (1979).

FINNIS, CATHERINE Cello. Member of Centipede, 1971.

FINOCCHIARO, TONY Tenor saxophone. Member of Stanley Steamer, 1973.

FIORINO, BOB Vocal. Member of Mom's Apple Pie, 1973.

FIORY, VITO Drums, percussion. Member of the Lavender Hill Mob, 1977-78.

FIREBALLET Jim Como—vocal, drums, percussion; Bryan Howe—keyboards; Ryche Chlanda—guitar, vocal; Martin Biglin—bass; Frank Petto—keyboards, vocal. *Albums:* Night on Bald Mountain (PST) 1975; Two Too (PST) 1976.

FIREFALL Mark Andes—bass; Jock Bartley—vocal, guitar, pedal steel guitar; Larry Burnett—guitar, vocal, writer; Michael Clarke—drums; Rick Roberts—guitar, vocal, writer; David Muse—woodwinds, keyboards (1978-present). The reunited Byrds fell apart in 1974. The Souther/Hillman/Furay Band had broken apart for solo careers in 1975, and the Flying Burritos had long since been a band of the past. Country rock was low on stars to follow. Firefall attempted to fill the bill. They were not newcomers; Andes was in Spirit and Jo Jo Gunne, Clarke was a Byrd, and Roberts and Burnett came from the Burritos. The talent is there and it shows. *Albums:* Elan (ATC 19183) 1978; Firefall (ATC 19125) 1976; Luna Sea (ATC 19101) 1974; Undertow (ATC 16006) 1980; Clouds Across the Sun (ATC SD 16024) 1980.

FIRESTONE, ROD Guitar, vocal. Member of the Rubber City Rebels, 1980.

FIRST NATIONAL BAND John Ware—drums; John London—bass; Michael Nesmith—guitar, vocal, writer. Former Monkee Michael Nesmith's attempt with his own career. *Albums:* And the Hits Just Keep on Comin' (PFA 116); Compilation (PFA 106); From a Radio Engine to the Photon Wing (PFA 107); Infinite Rider on the Big Dogma (PFA 130); Live at the Palais (PFA 118); Pretty Much Your Standard Ranch Stash (PFA 117); The Prison (PFA 101); Wichita Train Whistle Sings (PFA 113).

FISCHER, ANDRE Drums. Session for Dr. John (1979).

FISCHER, LARRY "WILD MAN" Vocal, writer. Los Angeles based counterculture singer, discovered and produced by Frank Zappa in 1968. He was found selling and singing his original songs for dimes on the streets in Hollywood. Besides his songs, he narrates his autobiography, full of indirect social commentary of dubious importance. His 1977 comeback was backed by the Plastic Rhino Band. *Albums:* Evening with Wild Man Fischer (BIZ 2XS-6332) 1968; Wildmania (RHI

001) 1977.

FISCHER, VALERIE JEAN Vocal. Member of Viktor Koncept, 1979.

FISCHER-Z Steve Skolnik—keyboards; Steve Liddle—percussion; John Watts—guitar, vocal; David Graham—bass. *Albums:* Word Salad (UAR UA-LA975-H) 1979; Going Deaf for a Living (UAR LT 1048) 1980.

FISH, BOB Vocal. Member of the Darts since 1978.

FISH, JAMES LEE Bass. Session for Long John Baldry (1979).

FISH, JIM Guitar, vocal. Member of the Henry Paul Band, 1979.

FISHELL, STEVE Pedal steel guitar. Member of the Moonlighters, 1977.

FISHER, ADRIAN Guitar. Member of Sparks, 1972-76.

FISHER, CLARE Piano. Session for Santana (1979).

FISHER, EVAN Vocal. Member of the Diamonds.

FISHER, HAROLD Bass. Session for Watson-Beasley (1980).

FISHER, HAROLD Drums. Session for Mike Batt (1979).

FISHER, MARK Vocal, keyboards. Member of Alibi, 1980.

FISHER, MATTHEW Organ, vocal, writer, producer. Original member of Procol Harum, 1966-69, he left to embark on his solo career, which received next to no attention despite excellent material and production. Produced Procol Harum (1969), and Robin Trower (1973-75). Session for Joe Cocker (1968); Lord Sutch; Jerry Lee Lewis (1973). *Albums:* Journey's End (VIC) 1973; Mathew Fisher (AAM 4801) 1980; I'll Be There (VIC APLI-0325) 1974.

FISHER, MORGAN Keyboards, vocal. Replaced Lynton Guest in Love Affair. Member of Mott The Hoople, 1974-77, and British Lions, 1976. Session for Mike Harrison (1975); Slaughter (1980). *Album:* Brown Out, 1976.

FISHER, NANCY Vocal. Session for Mylon Le Fevre (1979).

FISHER, ROGER Guitar. Member of Heart, 1975-78.

FIST Ron Chenier—guitar, vocal; Ed Eagan—keyboards; Joe Chenier—drums, vocal; Jeff Nystrom—bass, vocal. *Album:* Hot Spikes (AAM SP 4823) 1980.

FITCHET, BETH Guitar. Member of Honk, 1973.

FITZGERALD, ALAN Bass, synthesizer. Replaced Bill Church in Montrose, 1974-75. Member of Gamma, 1979-80. Session for Sammy Hager (1977-78).

FITZGERALD, ED Bass. Member of Pam Windo and the Shades, 1980.

FITZGERALD, MARK Bass. Replaced Jeff Meyer in the Charlie Daniels Band, 1976.

FITZPATRICK, RAY Bass. Session for Taj Mahal (1977).

FIVE AMERICANS Jim—guitar; John; Norman—bass; Mike—guitar; Jimmy—vocal. Their only hit, "I See the Light," 1966, was an exciting debut. A good album followed, showing a mix of rock, rhythm and blues, and ballads, but they faded into obscurity. *Album:* I See the Light (HBR HBS 9503) 1966.

FIVE DOLLAR SHOES Gregg Diamond—drums, percussion, vocal; Tom Graves—keyboards, vocal; Jim Gregory—bass, vocal; Mike Millius—vocal, harmonica; Scott Woody—guitar, vocal. *Album:* Five Dollar Shoes (NBD) 1972.

FLACK, ROBERTA Piano, vocal, writer. Jazz-soul vocalist who first became known with "The First Time Ever I Saw Your Face," 1971. *Albums:* Blue Lights in the Basement (ATC 19149) 1977; Chapter Two (ATC 1569) 1970; Feel Like Makin' Love (ATC 18131) 1971; First Take (ATC 8230) 1969; Roberta Flack (ATC 19186); Roberta Flack Featuring Donny Hathaway (ATC 16013) 1979; Golden Soul (ATC 19198); Killing Me Softly (ATC 19154) 1973; Quiet Fire (ATC 1594) 1971; Roberta Flack and Donny Hathaway (ATC 7218) 1972.

FLACKE, RAY Guitar. Member of the Tiger, 1976.

FLACO Percussion. Member of Root Boy Slim's Sex Change Band, 1978.

FLAIM, TONY Vocal. Member of the Downchild, 1979.

FLAME Jimmy Crespo—guitar; Frank Ruby—guitar; Marge Raymond—vocal; John Paul Fetta—bass; Bob Leone—keyboards; Eddie Barbato—drums. *Album:* Queen of the Neighborhood (VIC APLI 2160) 1977.

FLAMIN' GROOVIES Roy Loney—vocal; Cyril Jordan—guitar (1971-79); Danny Mihn—drums (1971-79); Tim Lynch—guitar (1971-79); George Alexander—bass; Chris Wilson—guitar, harpsichord (1979); Mike Wilhelm—guitar (1979); David Wright—drums (1979). *Albums:* Flamin' Groovies, 1971; Flamin' Groovies Still Shakin', 1976; Jumpin' in the Night (SIR K-6067) 1979.

FLAMINGOS Recorded "Lovers Never Say Goodbye," 1958.

FLANDERS, TOMMY Vocal. Original member of the Blues Project, 1966-67, before starting his solo career.

FLANNERY, TERRY Tenor trombone. Session for Savoy Brown (1969).

FLASH Vocal, guitar. Member of Flash Cadillac.

FLASH Peter Banks—guitar, vocal; Colin Carter; Ray Bennett; Mike Hough. *Album:* Flash in the Can (CAP SM-11115) 1972.

FLASH AND THE PAN Harry Vanda—guitar, vocal; George Young—guitar, keyboards, vocal; Ray Arnott—drums; Les Karski—bass; Warren Morgan—keyboards. The nucleus of the 1960s

Easybeat, re-formed with a new sound for the 1980s. *Albums:* Flash and the Pan (EPC JE-36018) 1979; Lights in the Night (EPC JE-36432) 1980.

FLASH CADILLAC AND THE CONTINENTAL KIDS Flash—guitar; Angelo—vocal, keyboards; Spider—saxophone; Spike—vocal, guitar; Butch—vocal, bass; Wally—vocal, percussion. 1950s rock interpreters, complete with motorcycle jackets and greasy hair. *Albums:* There's No Face Like Chrome (EPC) 1974; Flash Cadillac and the Continental Kids (EPC E-31787) 1972; Rock and Roll Forever (EPC PEG-33465); Flashman (VAN 79403); Sons of the Beaches (IPS PS 2003) 1975.

FLASHER Guitar, vocal. Member of Jimmie Mack and the Jumpers, 1980.

FLATO, JAN Keyboards, vocal. Member of Arbuckle, 1972.

FLEET, SNOWY Drums. Original member of the Easybeats, 1967-68.

FLEETWOOD, MICK Drums, percussion, producer. Born 6/24/47. Began in John Mayall's Bluesbreakers, 1963-66, and left that group with Peter Green and John McVie to become half of the namesake of Fleetwood Mac, 1967. With McVie, he survived the group's several personnel changes and continues to be the cornerstone of the group's ever-changing sound. Produced Turley Richards (1979). Session for Alvin Lee (1973); Duster Bennett (1968); Gordon Smith; Jeremy Spencer (1970); Bob Welch (1977); Ron Wood (1979); Danny Douma (1979).

FLEETWOOD, MIKE Vocal, guitar. Member of Whole Wheat, 1977, and Passion, 1979.

FLEETWOOD MAC Peter Green—guitar, vocal, writer (1967-70); John McVie—bass; Mick Fleetwood—drums; Jeremy Spencer—guitar, vocal, writer, piano (1967-71); Danny Kirwan—guitar, vocal, writer (1967-73); Christine Perfect—keyboards, vocal, writer (1970-present); Bob Welch—guitar, vocal, writer (1971-74); Bob Weston—guitar, banjo, harmonica (1973); Lindsey Buckingham—guitars, vocal (1975-present); Stevie Nicks—vocal (1975-present). When they started in 1967, they were one of the finest British blues bands. Green, McVie and Fleetwood all came from John Mayall's Bluesbreakers. After three classic blues albums, they began experimenting with their own sound. They were one of the first groups to feature three lead guitars; Green, and his intricate guitar riffs ranging from the blues to progressive rock and jazz; Spencer and his Elvis parodies; and straight pop songs and ballads by Kirwan. Then, in 1969, it was rumored Green and Spencer had both found a higher calling of religious duties. Green's last album "Then Play On," 1969, was an unusual blend of rock and blues, bordering on jazz. A year later, Spencer left for "The Children of God," after "Kiln House." Bob Welch filled in, 1971-74. The group then seemed to sever their blues roots in favor of more progressive rock, with Welch at the helm. The next major change came when Welch left in 1974, to be replaced by Buckingham and Nicks. A new album zoomed to number one and continued as a top selling album for months, demonstrating their new commercial sound to be a tremendous and overdue success. "Rumours" was the number one album of 1977, staying at #1 longer than any rock album of recent years. *Albums:* English Rose (EPC BN 26446) 1969; Black Magic Woman (EPC EG 30632); Mr. Wonderful (Import) 1968; Greatest Hits (Import) 1971; Bare Trees (RPS K-2278) 1972; Fleetwood Mac (RPS K-2281) 1975; Fleetwood Mac in Chicago (SIR 2XS-6009) 1969; Future Games (RPS K-2279) 1971; Heroes Are Hard to Find (RPS 2196) 1974; Kiln House (RPS 6408) 1970; Mystery to Me (RPS K-2279) 1973; Original Fleetwood Mac (SIR 6045) 1968; Penguin (RPS 2138) 1973; Rumours (WBR B-3010) 1977; Then Play On (RPS 6368) 1969; Tusk (WBR 2HS-3350) 1979; Live (WBR 2WB 3500) 1980.

FLEETWOODS Gretchen Christopher—vocal; Barbara Ellis—vocal; Gary Troxel—vocal. No relation to Fleetwood Mac, the Fleetwoods were a vocal trio, two women and a man, who enjoyed some popularity in April, 1959, with their hit, "Come Softly To Me." Their harmonies and lyrics were typical of the sock hop days. *Albums:* Mr. Blue; Fleetwoods; Softly; Deep in a Dream (DOL).

FLEISCHER, PAUL Saxophone, vocal. Member of Randall's Island, 1971-72. Session for Zephyr (1971); Lou Reed (1974).

FLEISCHMAN, ROBERT Vocal. Original vocalist of Journey. *Album:* Perfect Stranger (ARI 4220).

FLEMING, DEBBIE Vocal. Session for Nils Lofgren (1979).

FLEMING, GORDON Piano, accordion. Session for John Hammond (1968); Cat Stevens (1976); Steve Winwood (1980).

FLESHTONES Bill Milhizer; Jan Marek Pakulski; Keith Streng; Peter Zaremba. *Album:* Up Front (IRS SP 70402) 1980.

FLETCHER, CHRIS Percussion. Session for Danny Kirwan (1979).

FLETCHER, GARY Bass, vocal. Member of the Blues Band, 1979.

FLETCHER, JERRY Vocal, piano. Member of Liberty, 1975.

FLETT, DAVE Guitar, vocal. Replaced Mic Rogers in Manfred Mann, 1976.

FLIGHT Pat Vidas—brass, vocal; Ted Karczewski—guitar; John Ray—bass (1976-79); Russell Dawber—drums (1976-79); Jim Yaeger—keyboards; Steve Shebar—drums, vibes, vocal (1980); John de Nicola—bass, vocal (1980). *Albums:* Incredible Journey (CAP) 1976; Excursion Beyond (MTN M7-932) 1980.

FLINT Craig Frost—keyboards; Mel Schacher—bass; Don Brewer—drums, vocal. Unsuccessful resurrection of Grand Funk Railroad. *Album:* Flint (COL JC-35574) 1978.

FLINT, HUGHIE Drums, percussion. First became known with John Mayall's Bluesbreakers, 1964-67. Co-namesake of McGuiness Flint. Member of Lo and Behold, 1972, and the Blues Band, 1979.

FLINT, JIM Keyboards. Member of the Overland Stage, 1972.

FLO AND EDDIE Howard Kaylan—vocal, writer, producer; Mark Volman—guitar, vocal, writer, producer. Original members of the Turtles, these satiric rock writers and arrangers were rediscovered in the Mothers of Invention, 1971. Produced the Good Rats, 1978, and DMZ, 1978. Session for Ray Manzarek; Keith Moon (1975); Navasota (1972); Frank Zappa (1970); Bruce Springsteen (1980). *Albums:* Moving Targets, 1976; Illegal, Immoral, and Fattening (COL) 1975; California Dreaming (AIR 3001).

FLOATING OPERA John Nemerovski—piano; Steve Welkom—guitar; Carol Lees—keyboards; Gary Munce—bass; Artie Alinkoff—drums. From Michigan, the Floating Opera made their brief debut in rock in 1971. *Album:* The Floating Opera, 1971.

FLOCK Fred Glickenstein—guitar, vocal; Jerry Goodman—violin, vocal, guitar; Ron Karpman—drums; Jerry Smith—bass; Rick Canoff—saxophone; Frank Posa—trumpet; Tom Webb—saxophone. Bay area rock band of the 1960s most noted for the electric violin work of Goodman. *Album:* The Flock (COL CS-9911); Dinosaur Swamps.

FLOEGEL, RON Guitar, vocal. Member of Redwing.

FLORA, THOM Vocal, keyboards. Member of Boatz, 1979.

FLOWERS, CORNELIUS Baritone saxophone, vocal. Session for Janis Joplin (1969).

FLOWERS, HERBIE Bass. Member of Blue Mink. Session for Elton John (1971); Nilsson (1971); Lou Reed (1972); Ginger Baker (1977); Chris Spedding (1977); Bryan Ferry (1978); Elton John (1978); Justin Hayward (1980); the Who (1980); Ian Gomm.

FLOYD, EDDIE Vocal, writer. Writer and vocalist who has written for Wilson Pickett, Otis Redding and other soul greats. *Albums:* Knock on Wood, 1968; Baby Lay Your Head Down; Soul Street, (STX); Chronicle (STX 4122); Experience (MAL 6352); His Greatest Hits (STX 4122) 1979.

FLOYD, FRANK Vocal. Session for Steely Dan (1980).

FLOYD, NEALE Member of Penetration, 1979.

FLUDD Greg Godovitz—bass, vocal; Mick Walsh—guitar; Ed Pilling—vocal, percussion; Brian Pilling—guitar, vocal; John Andersen—drums. *Album:* Fludd (WBR) 1971.

FLUR, WOLFGANG Percussion. Member of Kraftwerk, 1975 to present.

FLURIE, BOB Guitar, vocal. Session for Barry Melton (1978).

FLYBOYS Jon Boy—guitar, vocal, organ; Scott Towels—bass, vocal; Thames—guitar, vocal; Denny Drummond—drums. *Album:* Flyboys (FRT FLP 1001) 1980.

FLYE, TOM Drums. Member of Lothar and the Hand People, 1966-68.

FLYER Lou Rerra—vocal; Bob Weisner—drums; Bill Torrico—vocal; Thom Dussault—guitar. *Album:* Send a Little Love (INF 9021).

FLYING BURRITO BROTHERS Gram Parsons—guitar, vocal (until 1972); Chris Hillman—guitar, mandolin; Sneaky Pete—pedal steel guitar; Chris Ethridge—bass, piano; Michael Clarke—drums; Bernie Leadon—guitar; Rick Roberts—guitar, vocal; Al Perkins—pedal steel guitar; Bryon Berlin—fiddle; Kenny Wertz; Roger Bush—drums; Gib Gilbeau—guitar, mandolin, fiddle, vocal; Joel Scott—guitar, bass, vocal; Greg Harris—guitar, banjo, vocal; Ed Ponder—drums. A continuation of the country folk sound of the Byrds. Session for Gram Parsons (1973). *Albums:* Airborne, 1976; Burrito Deluxe (AAM 4258); Close Up the Honky Tonks (AAM 3631) 1974; Flying Burrito Brothers (AAM 4295); Gilded Palace of Sin (AAM 4175) 1969; Last of the Red Hot Burritos (AAM 4343); Sleepless Nights (AAM 4578); Live from Tokyo (REG 79001) 1979.

FLYING ISLAND Jeff Bova—keyboards, trumpet; Bill Bacon—drums, percussion; Faith Fraioli—violin, flute; Thom Preli—bass; Ray Smith—guitar. *Album:* Another Kind of Space (VAN) 1976; Flying Island (VAN 79359) 1975.

FLYING LIZARDS David Cunningham—vocal, keyboards, bass, drums. One man band of new wave rock. *Albums:* Flying Lizards (VGN 13137) 1979.

FLYNN, GEORGE Keyboards, glockenspiel. Session for Jan Akkerman (1973).

FLYNN, JAMES Bass. Member of the Creed, 1978.

FLYNN, MALCOLM Congas. Session for Arthur Brown (1975).

FLYNT, RON Vocal, bass. Member of 20/20, 1979.

FM Catherine Hawkins—vocal, bass, synthesizer, piano; Ben Mink—violin, mandolin, vocal; Martin Deller—drums, percussion. *Album:* Surveillance (ARI 4246) 1979.

FOCUS Thijs Van Lear—keyboards, flute, percussion; Bert Ruiter—bass, percussion; Colin Allen—drums, percussion; Jan Akkerman—guitar; Pierre van der Linden—drums (1973). Progressive jazz rockers from Holland featuring future solo artists Van Leer and Akkerman. *Albums:* Ship of Memories (SIR 7531) 1977; Focus (SIR) 1973; Live at the Rainbow (SIR) 1973; Hamburger (SIR) 1974; Mother (SIR) 1975; In and Out (SIR SAS 7404) 1973.

FOGEL, MARTY Saxophone. Member of Pig Iron. Session for Lou Reed (1978-79).

FOGELBERG, DAN Guitar, percussion, keyboards, vocal, writer, arranger. Born 8/13/51. Session for Joe Walsh (1974). *Albums:* Captured Angel (EPC PE-33499) 1976; Home Free (COL PC-31751) 1972; Nether Lands (EPC PE-34185) 1977; Phoenix (EPC FE-35634) 1974; Souvenirs (EPC 33137) 1974; Twin Sons of Different Mothers (EPC JE-35339) 1978.

FOGERTY, JOHN Guitar, vocal. Born 5/18/45. With brother, Tom, founder of Creedence Clearwater Revival. Soloed as the Blue Ridge Rangers. *Albums:* John Fogerty (ASY 7E-1046) 1975.

FOGERTY, LEN Guitar, vocal. Member of Mariah, 1976.

FOGERTY, MICHAEL Vocal. Member of Rich Mountain Tower, 1976, and the Jeremy Spencer Band, 1979.

FOGERTY, TOM Guitar. Born 11/9/41. Founder of Creedence Clearwater Revival, 1968-72, he left the group to start a solo career which sounded more like a rehash of the old material than a new expansion. Formed Ruby, 1976. *Albums:* Excalibur (FSY); Tom Fogerty (FSY); Myopia (FSY 9469); Zephyr National (FSY).

FOGHAT Lonesome Dave Peverett—vocal, guitar, writer; Rod Price—vocal, slide guitar, guitar (1972-80); Tony Stevens—bass, vocal (1972-74); Roger Earl—drums, percussion; Nick Jameson—bass, keyboards (1975); Craig MacGregor—bass, vocal, guitar (1975-present). As Savoy Brown finally began to be noticed with a relatively stable personnel, Lonesome Dave Peverett took drummer Earl and bassist Stevens to organize Foghat, 1972. A dynamite first album set the pace for their mixed bag of heavy rock and old blues. *Albums:* Boogie Motel (BSV BHS-6990) 1979; Energized (BSV 6950) 1974; Foghat (BSV 2077) 1973; Foghat (BSV 2136) 1972; Foghat Live (BSV K-6971) 1977; Fool for the City (BSV K-6980) 1975; Night Shift (BSV 6962) 1976; Rock and Roll Outlaws (BSV 6956) 1971; Stone Blue (BSV K-6977) 1978; Tight Shoes (BSV BHS-6999) 1980.

FOLEY, ELLEN Vocal. Session for Ian Hunter (1979-80); Iron City House Rockers (1980); the Sorrows (1980); Hilly Michaels (1980). *Albums:* Nightout (EPC JE-36052) 1979.

FOLTZ, MARTY Drums, percussion, congas. Member of Pig Iron, and Tim Weisberg's backup band, 1974-75.

FOLWELL, BILL Member of Ars Nova, 1968-69.

FONFARA, MICHAEL Keyboards, guitar, producer. Original member of Rhinoceros, and Tycoon. Session for Lou Reed (1974, 78, 80).

FONTANA, RICHIE Drums, percussion, vocal. Member of the Piper, 1977.

FONTANA, WAYNE Vocal. Original head of the Mindbenders, 1966.

FOOLS Rich Bartlett—guitar, vocal; Doug Forman—bass, vocal; Mike Girard—vocal; Chris Pedrick—drums; Stacey Pedrick—guitar. *Album:* Sold Out (EIA SW-17024) 1980.

FOOLS GOLD Tom Kelly—guitar, vocal, bass; Denny Henson—guitar, vocal; Ron Grinel—drums; Doug Livingston—keyboards, guitar. *Album:* Fools Gold (ARI) 1976.

FOOS, RON Bass. Replaced John Pierce in Ironhorse, 1980. Travelled with Paul Revere and the Raiders, 1980.

FOOTE, RANDALL Percussion, vocal. Member of the Ba-Fa Band, 1976.

FORBERT, STEVE Guitar, vocal. *Albums:* Alive on Arrival (NMP JZ-35538); Jackrabbit Slim (NMP JZ-36191) 1979; Little Stevie Orbit (COL JC-36595) 1980.

FORBES, DENNIS Bass, keyboards, vocal. Member of Bram Tchaikovsky, 1980.

FORBES, DEREK Bass, vocal. Member of the Simple Minds since 1979.

FORBES, RAND Bass. Member of the United States of America, 1968.

FORCE, ROGER Saxophone, flute. Member of Mom's Apple Pie, 1973.

FORD, BARRY Drums. Session for B. B. King (1971).

FORD, CLARENCE Alto saxophone. Session for Fats Domino (1955-59).

FORD, DEAN Vocal. Session for the Alan Parsons Project (1978).

FORD, EARL Trombone. Session for Martin Mull (1974); the Marshall Tucker Band (1974); Hydra (1974).

FORD, FRANKIE Vocal. Recorded "Sea Cruise."

FORD, GEORGE Bass, vocal. Replaced Paul Jeffries in Cockney Rebel.

FORD, JOHN Bass, vocal. Member of the Strawbs, 1970-71, and half of the namesake for Hudson-Ford, 1974-75.

FORD, LITA Guitar. Member of the Runaways, 1976-77.

FORD, RICK Bass. Member of Red Noise, 1979.

FORD, ROBBEN Guitar. Member of Tom Scott's L. A. Express. Session for George Harrison (1974); Joni Mitchell (1975). *Album:* Inside Story (ELK 6E-169).

FORD, RUSTY Bass. Member of Lothar and the Hand People, 1966-68.

FORDHAM, KEN Saxophone. Session for David Bowie.

FOREIGNER Lou Gramm—vocal; Ian McDonald—guitar, keyboards, horns, vocal (1977-80); Al Greenwood—keyboards, synthesizer (1977-80); Ed Gagliardi—bass, vocal (1977-80); Dennis

Elliott—drums; Rick Wills—bass, vocal (1980-present). *Albums:* Double Vision (ATC 19999) 1978; Foreigner (ATC 19109) 1977; Head Games (ATC 29999) 1979.

FOREMAN, CHRIS Guitar. Member of Madness, 1979.

FOREMAN, KIM Member of Zuider Zee, 1975.

FOREMAN, STEVE Percussion. Session for Ray Manzarek; Mickey Thomas (1977); Firefall (1978); Lee Ritenour (1978-79); Art Garfunkel (1979); Bob Welch (1979); John Mayall (1979); Peter Frampton (1979); J. Michael Reed (1979); Paul Waroff (1980).

FOREST, JOHN Bass. Member of the Tufana-Giammarese Band.

FORGIONE, JOEY Drums. Member of the Soul Explosion, 1966-68.

FORMAN, DOUG Bass, vocal. Member of the Fools, 1980.

FORMAN, HOWARD Guitar. Session for Watson-Beasley (1980).

FORMERLY FAT HARRY Phil Greenberg—vocal, guitar, writer; Gary Peterson—vocal, keyboards, guitar, percussion, writer; Bruce Barthol—bass; Laurie Allen—drums. Mellow acoustic ballads were the feature of this group, 1971, which totally slipped by the radio stations. *Album:* Formerly Fat Harry (CAP ST 877) 1971.

FORMULA, DAVE Keyboards. Member of Magazine since 1978, and Visage, 1980.

FORREST, JIMMY Tenor saxophone. Session for B. B. King (1977). *Album:* Sit Down and Relax (PRS 7235).

FORSBERG, LLOYD Guitar. Member of Cain, 1975-77.

FORSEY, KEITH Drums. Half of the Trax duet, 1977. Session for Elton John (1979).

FORSEY, KEN Drums. Replaced Dinky Diamond in Sparks, 1979.

FORSSI, KEN Bass. Member of Love.

FORSYTHE, JULIE Vocal. Session for Donovan (1973).

FORTE, BOBBY Tenor saxophone. Session for B.B. King (1972, 75).

FORTE, FABIAN Full name of Fabian.

FORTINA, CARL Harmonium. Session for Bob Dylan (1973); Ringo Starr (1974).

FORTUNE, GEORGE Keyboards. Session for Muddy Waters (1972).

FORTUNE, NICK Bass. Member of the Buckinghams, 1967-69.

FORTUNES Early name for the Hollies.

FOSSEN, STEVE Guitar. Member of Heart, 1975 to present.

FOSTER, ALEX Horns. Session for Lou Reed (1974).

FOSTER, BRUCE Keyboards. Session for Status Quo (1971); Elkie Brooks (1975).

FOSTER, BYRD Drums, vocal. Session for Roy Buchanan (1974-76).

FOSTER, DAVID Keyboards, producer. Member of the Dinettes, 1976, and Attitudes, 1976. Produced Ray Kennedy (1980). Session for Donovan (1976); Steve Marriott (1976); Neil Sedaka (1975); Rod Stewart (1976-77); Tommy Bolin (1975); George Harrison (1975-76); Ringo Starr (1974, 77); Kim Carnes (1975); Gary Wright (1975, 77); Lee Ritenour (1978); Bob Weir (1978); Steven T. (1978); Boz Scaggs (1980).

FOSTER, FRANK Saxophone. Session for Martin Mull (1977).

FOSTER, GARY Flute, recorder. Session for Bob Dylan (1973).

FOSTER, GREG Trombone, percussion. Member of S.C.R.A., 1972.

FOSTER, JIM Horns, vocal. Member of Phyrework, 1978.

FOSTER, JOHN Bass. Replaced George Weathers Borden, Jr., in Oak, 1980.

FOSTER, MO Bass. Member of Fancy, 1975-76, and the Michael Schenker Group, 1980. Session for Gerry Rafferty (1979-80); Jeff Beck (1980); Tim Renwick (1980); Matthew Fisher (1980).

FOSTER, RON Drums. Session for Roy Buchanan (1980).

FOTHERINGAY Sandy Denny—vocal, piano, guitar; Trevor Lucas—vocal, guitar; Jerry Donahue—guitar, vocal; Gerry Conway—drums, vocal; Pat Donaldson—bass, vocal. Debut of future Fairport Convention members Denny and Lucas. *Album:* Fotheringay (AAM 4269) 1971.

FOTOMAKER Wally Bryson—guitar, vocal; Gene Cornish—bass, vocal; Dino Danelli—drums; Lex Marchesi—guitar, vocal; Frankie Vinci—keyboards, vocal. *Albums:* Fotomaker (ATC 19165) 1978; Transfer Station (ATC 19246) 1979; Vis-A-Vis (ATC 19208) 1978.

FOUNDATIONS Clem Curtis—vocal; Tim Harris—drums; Peter Macbeth—bass; Eric Allen Dale—trombone; Allan Warner—guitar; Tony Gomez—organ; Pat Burre—tenor saxophone; Mike Elliott—tenor saxophone. English group who achieved some fame in 1968 with "Baby Now That I've Found You." *Album:* Baby Now That I've Found You, 1968.

FOUR GRADUATES Early name of the Happenings.

FOUR LOVERS Early name of the Four Seasons.

FOUR ON THE FLOOR Jeff Baxter—guitar, synthesizer; Al Kooper—keyboards; Neil Stubenhaus—bass; Rich Schlosser—drums. *Album:* Four on the Floor (CAS 7180) 1979.

FOUR PENNIES Early name of the Chiffons.

FOUR SEASONS Frankie Valli—vocal; Bob Saudio—vocal; Tommy De Vito—vocal; Joe Long—vocal. Early names: the Four Lovers; Larry and the Legends. After hits like "Sherry" (1962) and "Big Girls Don't Cry" (1963), the Four Seasons became identified with the early 1960s. From then on, it was a matter of perfecting the stage act behind Valli's soprano falsetto. Valli attempted a less successful solo career before rejoining the group. *Albums:* Born to Wander, 1964; Dawn, 1964; Rag Doll, 1964; Four Seasons Entertain You, 1965; Four Seasons Sing Big Hits, 1965; Working My Way Back to You, 1965; Looking Back, 1966; Four Seasons Christmas Album, 1966; Four Seasons Second Vault of Hits, 1967; Four Seasons New Gold Hits, 1967; Genuine Imitation Life, 1968; Charisma; Hickory; How Come; Life and Breath; Helicon (WBR B-3016); Who Loves You (WBR B-2900).

FOUR TOPS Levi Stubbs, Jr.—vocal; Renaldo Benson—vocal; Abdul Fakir—vocal; Lawrence Payton—vocal. Early pacesetters of the soul movement in rock from 1965, with "I Can't Help Myself," through the 1970s. *Albums:* Best of the Four Tops (MTN MS 764); Four Tops Greatest Hits, Vol. 2 (MTN M5 740); In Loving Memory (MTN M5 642); Keeper of the Castle (DHL 50129); Live and in Concert (DHL D-50188); Main Street People (DHL X50144) 1973; Meeting of the Minds (DHL 50166) 1974; Nature Planned It (MTN M5-748); Night Lights Harmony (ABC 862) 1975; Four Tops, 1965; Four Tops Second Album, 1965; On Top, 1966; Four Tops Live, 1966; Four Tops on Broadway, 1967; Anthology (MTN M9-809) 1974; At the Top (MCA AA-1092); Four Tops Greatest Hits (MTN M7-662) 1967; Catfish (ABC 968) 1976; Reach Out, 1967; Yesterday's Dreams, 1968.

FOUR WINDS Early name of the Tokens.

FOWLE, THOM Guitar, vocal. Member of Buckeye, 1979.

FOWLER, BRUCE Trombone. Member of the Mothers of Invention, 1973-74, and Captain Beefheart's Magic Band since 1978. Session for George Duke (1975); Frank Zappa (1974-75).

FOWLER, REX Half of the Aztec Two Step duet, 1972-79.

FOWLER, TOM Bass. Replaced Michael Holman in It's a Beautiful Day, 1971-72. Member of the Mothers of Invention, 1973-75. Session for George Duke (1975); Frank Zappa (1974-75).

FOWLER, WALT Trumpet. Member of the Mothers of Invention, 1974.

FOWLEY, KIM Keyboards, percussion, producer, vocal, writer. Somewhat of a legend in the Southern California area for his poetry and songs, he achieved his fame in the drug music scene of the late 1960s. Produced Venus and the Razor Blades (1977); Joan Jett; Steven T. (1978), the Orchids (1980); and others. Session for the Mothers of Invention (1966). *Albums:* I'm Bad (CAP ST 11075) 1972; International Heroes (CAP ST 11159) 1973; Outrageous (IPR-LP 12423); Snake Document Masquerade (ANT AN 7075) 1979; Sunset Boulevard (PUC 7906) 1979; Hollywood Confidential (LRS GUPS 2132) 1980.

FOX Early name of Wet Willie.

FOX, ART Drums. Member of the Wierdos, 1979-80.

FOX, DEREK Piano. Member of Laurie and the Sighs, 1980.

FOX, JACKI Bass, vocal. Member of the Runaways, 1976-77.

FOX, JIM Drums, piano. Original member of the James Gang, 1969-77.

FOX, JIMMY Drums. Member of Toronto, 1980.

FOX, LUCAS Drums. Session for Motorhead (1979).

FOX, NOOSHA Vocal. Session for Tim Renwick (1980).

FOX, PAUL Guitar, vocal, organ. Member of the Ruts, 1979.

FOX, RICK Guitar, vocal. Member of the Highwind, 1980.

FOX, SIMON Drums. Replaced Nicholas Chatterton-Dew in Be Bop Deluxe, 1975-78.

FOX Herbie Armstrong—guitar, vocal; Kerry Young—guitar, vocal; Pete Solley—keyboards, vocal; Jim Frank—drums, vocal; Gary Taylor—bass, vocal; Roosha—vocals. *Album:* Fox (ARA).

FOXTON, BRUCE Vocal, bass. Member of the Jam, 1977-78.

FOXX, JOHN Vocal. Member of Ultravox, 1977-79.

FOXX, LEIGH Bass. Session for the Paley Brothers (1978).

FOXY Joe Galdo—drums, vocal; Arnold Paseiro—bass; Richie Puente—guitar, percussion; Laurence Dermer—keyboards, vocal (1980); Ish Ledesma—guitar, vocal; Carl Driggs—vocal, percussion (1979); Charlie Murciano—keyboards, woodwinds, vocal, vibes (1979). *Albums:* Foxy (DHS 30001); Get Off (DSH 30005) 1978; Hot Numbers (DSH 30010); Party Boys (DSH 30015); Live (DSH 30016) 1980.

FRAGA, JOHNNY Bass. Member of the Rockets since 1977.

FRAIOLI, FAITH Violin. Member of the Flying Island, 1976.

FRAMPTON, PETER Guitar, vocal, writer. Born 4/22/50. After debuting in the Herd, 1967, he cofounded Humble Pie, 1969 (with Steve Marriott). He left in 1971 to work at his solo career (he formed Camel in 1972, then went solo again later), which rocketed in 1976 with the release of a double live album that showed his multifaceted abilities. "Frampton Comes Alive" proved to be the most successful live rock album ever recorded. Session for Doris Troy (1970); Donovan (1973); John Entwhistle (1972); Nilsson (1972); Jerry Lee Lewis (1973); Andy Bown (1972); Jobraith (1973); Martin Mull (1979). *Albums:* Frampton (AAM 4512) 1975; Frampton Comes Alive

(AAM PR-3703) 1976; Peter Frampton (AAM 3710); I'm in You (AAM 4704) 1977; Something's Happening (AAM 3619) 1972; Wind of Change (AAM 4848) 1972; Where I Should Be (AAM SP 3710) 1979.

FRAMPTON'S CAMEL Rick Wills—bass; Mick Gallagher—keyboards; John Siomos—drums, percussion; Peter Frampton—guitar, vocal, writer, keyboards. Peter Frampton's first solo appearance. *Album:* Frampton's Camel (AAM 4389) 1972.

FRANCE, LINDA Member of the Urban Verbs, 1980.

FRANCIS, ARCHIE Drums. Session for Phillip Walker (1977).

FRANCIS, BILL Keyboards, vocal. Member of Dr. Hook.

FRANCIS, CONNIE Vocal. Real name: Concetta Franconcero. Teen idol of the 1960s who first appeared on the charts with "My Heart Has a Mind of Its Own," 1960. *Albums:* Connie Francis Sings Jewish Favorites (MGM 3869); Italian Favorites (MGM 379K); More Greatest Hits (MGM 3942); Very Best of Connie Francis (MGM 4167).

FRANCIS, KEVIN Bass. Member of Fresh, 1970.

FRANCIS, LUKE Guitar, vocal. Original member of the Dharma Blues Band and early member of the Animals, prior to Eric Burdon's membership.

FRANCIS, MAMIE Member of the Now, 1979.

FRANCIS, PAUL Drums. Member of Tranquility, 1972.

FRANCIS, STEWART Drums. Member of Glencoe, 1972.

FRANCISCO, DON Drums, vocal. Member of Highway Robbery, 1972, and Big Wha-Koo, 1977. Session for Bob Welch (1979).

FRANCO, BISMARCK, JR. Timbales. Session for Taj Mahal (1977).

FRANCO, JOE Drums. Member of the Good Rats since 1978.

FRANCOIS, HELENE Vocal. Session for Lou Reed (1972).

FRANCOIS, RON Bass, vocal. Member of the Sinceros, 1979.

FRANCONCERO, CONCETTA Real name of Connie Francis.

FRANCOUR, CHUCK *Album:* Under the Boulevard Lights. (EIA SW-17032).

FRANGENBURG, DICK Bass. Member of Triumvirat, 1976.

FRANGIPANE, RON Synthesizer. Session for Grace Slick (1980).

FRANK, BOB Vocal. *Album:* Bob Frank (VAN 6582).

FRANK, JIM Drums. Member of Fox. Session for Matthew Fisher (1974); Ronnie Lane (1975).

FRANK, RICHARD, JR. Drums. Member of Elephant's Memory. Session for Yoko Ono and John Lennon.

FRANKE, CHRIS Moog, keyboards, electronics. Original member of Tangerine Dream, 1973-74. Session for Edgar Froese (1974).

FRANKEL, DANNY Member of the Urban Verbs, 1980.

FRANKLIN, ARETHA Vocal, writer. First lady of soul. *Albums:* Aretha, 1961; Electrifying; Tender, Moving, Swinging, 1962; Runnin' Out of Fools, 1964; Yeah, 1965; Soul Sister, 1966; Take It Like You Give It, 1967; Lady Soul, 1968; Now, 1968; In Paris, 1968; Best of Aretha Franklin (ATC QD 8305); Great Aretha Franklin (First 12 Sides) (COL KC 31953); Hey Now Hey (The Other Side of the Sky) (ATC 7265); Laughing on the Outside (COL CS 8879) 1963; Let Me in Your Life (ATC 7292); Recorded Live at Newport in New York (BUD 5616); Soft and Beautiful (COL CS 9776); Spirit in the Dark (ATC 8265); Stardust (ARI 5000); With Everything I Feel in Me (ATC 18116); Almighty Fire (ATC 19161); Amazing Grace (ATC 2-906); Aretha–Greatest Hits (ATC 8295) 1967; Aretha Live at Fillmore West (ATC 7205); Aretha's Gold (ATC 8227) 1969; La Diva (ATC 19248) 1979; Aretha Franklin's Greatest Hits, Vol. 2 (COL CS-9601) 1967; Golden Soul (ATC 18198); I Never Loved a Man (ATC 8139) 1967; Sparkle (ATC 18176); Sweet Passion (ATC 19102); Ten Years of Gold (ATC 18204); Unforgettable (COL CS-9863) 1964; Young, Gifted and Black (ATC 7213) 1972; Aretha (ARI 9538) 1980.

FRANKLIN, BONNIE Vocal, guitar. *Albums:* Applause (MCA OC 11).

FRANKLIN, DOUG Vocal. Member of the Fugs Chorus.

FRANKLIN, ERMA Vocal. Sister of Aretha Franklin, she released "Piece of My Heart" in 1967, one year before Janis Joplin recorded it. *Albums:* Bend and Shout Super Hits (BNG 220); Soul Sister (BRU 754147).

FRANKLIN, IRENE Vocal. Sister of Aretha Franklin. *Album:* They Stopped the Show (AUR 32290).

FRANKLIN, JUANITA Vocal. Session for John Entwhistle (1975).

FRANKLIN, MEL Vocal. Original member of the Temptations.

FRANKS, CLIVE Vocal, bass. Member of Elton John's backup band, 1978. Session for Elton John (1975-80).

FRANKS, MICHAEL Guitar, vocal, piano. Session for Sonny Terry and Brownie McGhee (1973). *Albums:* Art of Tea (RPS 2230); Burchfield Nines (WBR K-3167) 1978; Sleeping Gypsy (WBR B-3004) 1977; Tiger in the Rain (WBR K-3294) 1979.

FRANSEN, RON Keyboards. Replaced Frank Westbrook in Rare Earth, 1977. Member of Wha-Koo since 1979. Session for Tommy Bolin (1975).

FRANSSEN, DICK Keyboards. Member of Alquin, 1975.

FRANTZ, CHRIS Drums. Member of the Talking Heads since 1977. Session for Robert Palmer (1980).

FRANTZ, RODDY Member of the Urban Verbs, 1980.

FRASER, ANDY Bass, keyboards, vocal, writer. First became known with John Mayall, 1968, before joining Free, 1968-72, after which he formed Sharks in 1973, and the Andy Fraser Band. Session for Robert Palmer (1980).

FRASER-BINNIE, JOHNNY Guitar, keyboards. Member of Dirty Tricks, 1976.

FRAYNE, GEORGE Real name of Commander Cody.

FRAZIER, L. C. Real name of Memphis Slim.

FRED, JOHN Vocal, harmonica. Founder and namesake of John Fred and the Playboy Band.

JOHN FRED AND HIS PLAYBOY BAND John Fred—vocal, harmonica; Andrew Bernard—baritone saxophone; Ronnie Goodson—trumpet; Charlie Spin—trumpet; Jimmy O'Rourke—guitar; Howard Cowart—bass; Tommy de Geweres—organ; John Micely—drums. Louisiana based pop band with a horn section that saturated the market with three albums in one year after their hit "Judy In Disguise," 1968. *Albums:* Agnes English (PLA 2197) 1968; John Fred and His Playboys, 1968; Judy in Disguise, 1968; Permanently Stated.

FREDDIE AND THE DREAMERS Pete Birrell; Roy Crewson; Bernie Dwyer; Freddie Gerrity; Derek Quinn. Early name: the Red Sox. Reviving the dance creation craze started by Chubby Checker and "The Twist," Freddie and his Dreamers created "The Freddy." Competing with the Beatles, they released "I'm Telling You Now" in 1966. Despite their talent (they'd been together since 1962), they were unable to survive. *Albums:* Frantic Freddie, 1966; Best of Freddie and the Dreamers (CAP SM-11896) 1979.

FREDERICKS, CAROLE Vocal. Session for Taj Mahal (1977-78).

FREDERIKSEN, DENNIS Vocal. Member of Trillion, 1978.

FREDIANA, STEVE Saxophone, flute. Member of the Sons of Champlin.

FREDRICKS-WILLIAMS, HENRY SAINTE Real name of Taj Mahal.

FREE Paul Rodgers—vocal, writer; Paul Kossoff—guitar, writer; Andy Fraser—bass, piano, writer; Simon Kirke—drums; John "Rabbit" Bundrick—keyboards, vocal, writer (1973); Tetsu Yamauchi—bass, percussion (1973). First became known in 1968. Rodgers' wide-ranging vocals and Kossoff's wailing guitar quietly built up to their only single, "All Right Now," after two years. On again, off again breakup reports reduced the impact of future albums, though not the quality. By 1973 (after "Kossoff, Kirke, Tetsu and Rabbit" in 1972) the final Free album, "Heartbreaker," was released without Kossoff, who had gone solo, and Fraser, who formed Sharks, ending an English tradition. Rodgers and Kirke moved to greater notoriety as half the membership of Bad Company. *Albums:* Tons of Sobs (AAM 4198) 1969; At Last (AAM SP 4349) 1972; Best of Free (AAM 3663); Fire and Water (AAM 4268) 1970; Free (AAM 4204); Free Live (AAM 4306) 1971; Heartbreaker (ISL 9217) 1973; Highway (AAM 4287) 1970.

FREE BEER Sandy Allen—vocal, guitar, bass; Michael Packer—vocal, guitar, bass; Robert Potter—vocal, guitar, bass. *Albums:* Highway Robbery (VIC) 1976; Free Beer (SOW 6402) 1972.

FREE CREEK Todd Rundgren—guitar; Buzzy Feiten—guitar; Harvey Mandel—guitar; Jack Wilkins—guitar; Carol Hunter—guitar; King Cool—guitar; Delaney Bramlett—guitar; Dougie Rodrigues—guitar; Elliot Randall—guitar; Bernie Leadon—guitar; Dr. John—guitar, piano; Stu Woods—bass; Chuck Rainey—bass; Larry Taylor—bass; Richard Davis—bass; John London—bass; Roy Markowitz—drums; Fito de la Parra—drums; Richard Crooks—drums; John Ware—drums; Moogy Klingman—keyboard, harmonica; Keith Emerson—keyboards; Jimmy Greenspoon—keyboards; Bob Smith—keyboards; Chris Wood—flute; Joe Farrell—flute; Lou Delgatto—trombone, oboe; Bobby Keller—trombone; Meco Monardo—trombone; Lou Soloff—trumpet; Alan Rubin—trumpet; Bill Chase—trumpet; Bobby Dean—trombone; Tom Malone—bass; Harry Hall—trumpet; Larry Packer—violin; Chris Darrow—violin; Red Rhodes—pedal steel guitar; Billy Chesboro—percussion; Didymus—percussion; Earl Doud—percussion, vocal; Tommy Cosgrove—vocal; Linda Ronstadt—vocal; Timmy Harrison—vocal; Eric Mercury—vocal; Maretha Stewart—vocal; Hilda Harris—vocal; Valerie Simpson—vocal; Geri Miller—vocal. Seldom heard New York jam of allstars with members from Neil Diamond's band, Michael Nesmith's band, the Nitty Gritty Dirt Band, Three Dog Night, Blood, Sweat and Tears, and the Woody Herman and Buddy Rich bands. *Album:* Music from Free Creek (CHR GAD 101-2) 1973.

FREEBO Bass, producer. Production and session for the Catfish Hodge Band, 1979. Session for Peter C. Johnson (1980).

FREED, ALAN Disc jockey. Born 12/15/22, died 1/20/65. Commonly attributed with coining the term "rock 'n' roll."

FREEDMAN, LARRY Drums, vocal. Member of the U. S. Radio Band, 1976.

FREEDOM Bobby Harrison—vocal, drums, percussion; Roger Saunders—vocal, guitar, piano; Peter Vennis—vocal, bass, synthesizer. *Album:* Through the Years (COT 9048) 1971.

FREELAND, RUSS Trombone. Session for Andy Gibb (1980).

FREEMAN, CHARLIE Guitar. Session for Rita Coolidge (1972).

FREEMAN, KEN Synthesizer. Session for the Baker-Gurvitz Army (1976); Justin Hayward (1980); the Who (1980).

FREEMAN, LEE Vocal, drum, flute, saxophone, harmonica. Member of the Strawberry Alarm Clock, 1968.

FREEMAN, ROB Vocal. Session for Vigrass and Osborne (1972).

FREEMAN, SONNY Drums. Session for B. B. King (1969-72).

FREEMAN, TAFF Keyboards, vocal. Member of Nektar, 1972-77.

FREEMAN, WHITNEY Bass. Original member of the Sir Douglas Quintet, 1965-58.

FREEMAN, WILBERT Bass. Session for B. B. King (1972).

FREESE, TEDDY Drums. Member of Yipes, 1979-80.

FREHLEY, PAUL "ACE" Guitar, vocal. Member of Kiss since 1973. *Album:* Kiss (CAS 7121 PIX-7121) 1978.

FREIBERG, DAVID Bass, keyboards, vocals. Member of the Jefferson Starship since 1974, and of Seastone, 1976. Original member of the Quicksilver Messenger Service, 1965-70. Session for David Crosby (1971). *Album:* Baron Von Tollbooth and the Chrome Nun (GNT BXLI-0148) 1973.

FREIBERGER, PETER Bass. Original member of Big Wha-Koo, 1977.

FRENCH, JOHN "DRUMBO" Drums. Member of Captain Beefheart and His Magic Band, 1965-68. Session for Peter C. Johnson (1980).

FRENCH, MIKE Fiddle. Session for Long John Baldry (1975).

FRENCH, PAUL Vocal, keyboards, harmonica. Member of Voyager, 1979-80.

FRENCH, PETE Vocal. Member of Atomic Rooster, 1971. He replaced Rusty Day in Cactus in 1972.

FRENCH, TOXEY Drums. Original member of the Dillards.

FRENETTE, MATTHEW Drums, vocal. Member of Streetheart, 1979, and Loverboy, 1980.

FRENZY, TOMMY Vocal. Member of the Tuff Darts, 1978.

FRESH Roger Chantler—drums; Kevin Francis—bass; Bob Gorman—guitar. Satirical rock trio who released their London recorded album in 1970. *Album:* Fresh Today (VIC LSP 4427) 1970.

FREY, GLENN Vocal. Born 11/6/48. Original member of the Eagles since 1972. Session for Joe Walsh (1974-78); Bob Seger (1968-78); Elton John (1980); Warren Zevon (1980).

FRICKER, SYLVIA Maiden name of Sylvia Tyson.

FRIDE, JAN Drums. Member of Kraan, 1975.

FRIED, MARTY Drums. Member of the Cyrkle, 1966-67.

FRIEDBERG, DAN Bass, guitar. Member of the Edison Electric Band, 1970.

FRIEDBERG, PETER Bass. Session for Aynsley Dunbar (1970).

FRIEDEL, MARIO Bass, keyboards, guitar, vocal. Member of White Duck, 1971.

FRIEDMAN, KAREN Vocal. Session for Pilot (1972).

FRIEDMAN, KINKY Guitar, vocal. *Albums:* Lasso from El Paso (EPC PE-34304) 1976; Sold American (VAN 79333) 1973.

FRIEDMAN, STEVE Bass. Session for Lou Reed (1978).

FRIESEN, JOHN Drums. Member of Player since 1977.

FRIJID PINK Tom Beaudry—bass, writer; Rich Stevers—drums; Kelly Green—vocal, percussion; Gary Thompson—guitar, writer. After releasing a heavy metal version of "House of the Rising Sun," 1970, Frijid Pink quickly faded into obscurity. *Albums:* Frijid Pink (PAR ST 93137); Defrosted (PAR PAS 71041); All Pink Inside.

FRIPP, ROBERT Guitar, producer, writer, mellotron. Mainstay of King Crimson, 1969-75. Producer of Centipede (1971). Session for Colin Scot (1971); David Bowie (1977); Peter Gabriel (1977); the Talking Heads (1979). *Albums:* Exposure (POL 1-6201) 1979; God Save the Queen (POL 1-6266) 1980; No Pussyfooting (with Brian Eno) (ANT AN 7001) 1973.

FRISDE, JOHN Vocal, guitar. Member of Starbuck, 1978.

FRITH, FRED Guitar, violin, viola. Member of Henry Cow, 1973. Session for Robert Wyatt (1974).

FRITZ, JURGEN Keyboards, synthesizer, vocal, writer, producer. Original member of Triumvirat, since 1973. Session for Eric Burdon (1977).

FRITZSCHINGS, WERNER Guitar. Replaced Jim McCarty in Cactus, 1972. Session for Stanky Brown (1977).

FROESE, EDGAR Mellotron, guitar, bass, organ, synthesizer, electronics. Original member of Tangerine Dream, 1973-74. *Albums:* Aqua (VIR VA 1053) 1974; Stuntman (VIR VI2139) 1979.

FROESE, HOWARD Guitar, keyboards, vocal. Replaced Claire Lawrence in Chilliwack, 1973.

FROMHOLZ, STEVEN Vocal. Session for Willie Nelson (1976). *Albums:* Jus' Playin' Along (LNS 4601); Six Pak, Vol. 1 (LNS 4600).

FROST, BARRY Percussion. Member of Creation, 1974, and Rare Earth, 1975.

FROST, CRAIG Keyboards, vocals, writer. Member of Grand Funk Railroad, 1974-75.

FROSTY Nickname of Bartholomew Smith-Frost.

FRUMPY Carsten Bohn—drums, percussion; Karl-

Heinz Schott—bass; Rainer Baumann—guitar, steel guitar; Inga Rumpf—vocal, guitar; Jean-Jacques Kravetz—keyboards; Erwin Kania—keyboards. *Album:* By the Way (BLR 1003) 1973.

FRUT Crunchy Crystals—guitar; Snidely Whiplash—skins; John Kozmo—bass (1970); Panama Red—vocal; Steve Lee—bass (1972); Kellogg—guitar (1972). From the Motor City, Frut updated old classics such as "Chiffon Baby" and "Running Bear," while mixing in naughty ditties of their own. *Albums:* Keep on Truckin' (WSB 2008) 1970; Spoiled Rotten (WSB WB 21005) 1972.

FRY, MIKE Percussion. Session for Mike Batt (1979).

FRY, TRISTAN Percussion. Session with Memphis Slim (1972); Kevin Ayers (1973); Gay and Terry Woods (1976).

FRYER, TERRY Keyboards. Session for the Blues Brothers (1980).

FUENTES, VAL Drums, percussion, vocal. Original member of It's a Beautiful Day, 1969-72.

FUGS Ed Sanders—vocal, guitar, percussion, writer; Ken Weaver—vocal, drums; Tuli Kupferberg—vocal, percussion, writer; John Anderson—bass, vocal (until 1967); Vinny Leary—guitar, vocal (until 1967); Pete Stampfel—guitar, vocal, fiddle, harmonica (until 1966); Steve Weber—guitar, vocal (until 1966); Lee Crabtree—piano, celeste, bells (1966-67); Pete Kearney—guitar (1966-67); Charles Larkey—bass (1967-68); Dan Kootch—guitar, violin, percussion, vocal (1967); Ken Pine—guitar, organ, percussion, vocal (1967-68); Bill Wolf—bass (1968); Bob Mason—drums (1968); Carl Lynch—guitar (1968); Richard Lee—organ (1968); Howard Johnson—tuba, saxophone (1968); Julius Watkins—french horn (1968). The Fugs Chorus (1965-66): Lesley Dorsey; Bob Dorough; Barbara Calabria; Maryls Trunkill; Bob Hanson; James Jarvis; Kenneth Bates; Earl Baker; Jennifer Brown; Doug Franklin. Reminiscent of beat poets, they started in New York in 1965. The Fugs were the Sanders-Weaver-Kupferberg trio (with some musicians) who set their abstract lyrics of explicit sex, drugs and anti-establishment protest to music. They were classifiable somewhere between beatniks and hippies, along the same lines as beat poet friend, Allen Ginsberg. Beautiful ballads were not beyond them, though they were scattered sparsely from album to album. They set standards for outrageousness in rock still unrivaled today. *Albums:* It Crawled into My Hand, Honest (RSP RS 6305); Tenderness Junction (RSP RS 6280) 1967; Belle of Avenue A (RSP RS 6359) 1968; The Fugs (ESP 1028) 1966; Fugs First Album (ESP 1018) 1965; Golden Filth (RPS 6396) 1970; Virgin Fugs (ESP 1038) 1965.

FUJALA, STEPHEN Reeds. Member of Auracle, 1978-79.

FUKAKASHA, AKIRA Bass. Member of the Far East Family Band, 1977.

FUKUSHIMA, HIROHITO Guitar, koto, vocal. Member of the Far East Family Band, 1977.

FULL HOUSE Jim Hall—keyboards; Ray Minhinnet—guitar (1977); Chris Stewart—bass; Graham Deakin—drums; Ray Russell—guitar (1978). Backup band for Frankie Miller, 1977-78.

FULL MOON Buzz Feiten—guitar, percussion, writer, vocal; Neil Larsen—keyboards, vibes, writer; Gene Dinwiddie—saxophone, flute, vocal; Phillip Wilson—drums, percussion, vocal; Freddie Beckmeier—bass. Comprised of Paul Butterfield Blues Band alumni, Full Moon undertook a commercial, jazz oriented deviation from the blues. *Album:* Full Moon (DOU KZ 31904) 1972.

FULL TILT BOOGIE BAND Brad Campbell—bass; Clark Pierson—drums; Ken Pearson—organ; John Till—guitar; Richard Bell—piano. Backup band for Janis Joplin, 1969-70.

FULLER, ANDY Percussion. Session for Ken Tobias (1973).

FULLER, CRAIG Vocal, guitar, bass. Member of Pure Prairie League, 1972-78.

FULLER, JESSE Vocal, harmonica, guitar, kazoo, washboard. One man blues band of the 1920s. *Albums:* Blues Roots (TMT 2-7006); Brother Lowdown (FSY 24707); San Francisco Bay Blues (PRS 7718).

FULLER, JIM Guitar. Member of the Surfaris, 1963-65.

FULSOM, LOWELL Guitar, vocal. Born in Oklahoma, 1931. A traveling blues soloist. *Albums:* Lowell Fulsom Now (KNT 531); Let's Go Get Stoned (KNT 558); Memphis Slim With Lowell Fulsom (ICT 1011); Rhythm and Blues Christmas (UAR LW-654); Soul (KNT 516); Tramp (KNT 520).

FULTERMAN, MARTIN Drums. Member of the New York Rock and Roll Ensemble, 1968-69.

FULTON, DON Bass, vocal. Member of the Shakers.

FULTON, WILLIE JAMES Guitar, vocal. Member of Tower of Power until 1972. Session for the Pointer Sisters (1973).

FUN ZONE Ben Benay—guitar; Don Poncher—drums; Wolfgang Meltz—bass; John Rubinstein—keyboards, vocal; Gary Garone—horns; Tim McIntyre—vocal, guitar, fiddle; Jock Ellis—horns. *Album:* Fun Zone (FSA FA 4000) 1977.

FUNARD, ARTI Guitar, vocal. Member of the Rhinestones, 1975.

FUNK, RINGO Drums. Replaced Konni Bommarius in Karthago, 1976.

FUNKY KINGS Frank Cotinola—drums, percussion; Richard Stekol—vocal, guitar, piano; Bill Bodine—bass, vocal; Jules Shear—vocal, guitar; Greg Leisz—pedal steel guitar, guitar, vocal; Jack Tempchin—vocal, guitar, harmonica. *Album:* Funky Kings (ARI) 1976.

FURAY, RICHIE Vocal, guitar, writer. Born 5/9/44. He first appeared in 1966, as a founding member of Buffalo Springfield until 1968. Co-founder and member of Poco, he left in 1974 to form the Souther/Hillman/Furay Band, until 1975, before going solo with the Richie Furay Band, 1976-79.

RICHIE FURAY BAND Richie Furay—vocal, guitar, writer; Ron Stipe—keyboards, vocal; Jay Truax—bass, vocal; John Mehler—drums. Solo debut of Richie Furay. *Albums:* Dance a Little Light (ASY 6E-115) 1978; I Still Have Dreams (ASY 6E-231) 1979; I've Got a Reason (ASY 7E-1067) 1976.

FURIOUS, D. Drums, vocal. Member of the Avengers, 1979.

FURLONG, TERRY Guitar. Member of the Grass Roots.

FURLOW, DICK Bass. Member of the Bob Meighan Band, 1976.

FURSDON, PHIL Vocal. Session for Chris Spedding (1980).

FYSON, LESLEY Vocal. Session for Donovan (1973).

G.T.O.'S Initials that stood for "Girls Together Outrageously, or Organically, or All Those O's," as one member of this all feminine Frank Zappa release of the 1960s stated. *Album:* Permanent Damage (BIZ).

GABOURY, STEVE Piano. Session for Country Joe McDonald (1975).

GABRIEL, PETER Vocal, flute, oboe, percussion. Born 5/13/50. Member of Genesis, 1971-74. Session for Colin Scot (1971); Cat Stevens (1976); Robert Fripp (1979). *Albums:* Peter Gabriel (MER SRM-1-3848); Peter Gabriel (ACO 36-147 ATC 19181) 1977.

GABRIEL, WAYNE "TEX" Guitar. Session for Yoko Ono and John Lennon; Mitch Ryder (1978).

GABRIEL Frank Butorac—guitar, vocal; Stacy Christenson—keyboards, vocal; Michael Kinder—drums, percussion; Terry Lauber—guitar, pedal steel guitar, vocal; Gary Ruhl—bass. Seattle band that scored a major contract in 1975. *Album:* This Star on Every Heel (ABC) 1975.

GADD, STEVE Drums. Member of Charlie since 1976. Session for Joe Cocker (1975-76); Stanley Clarke (1975); Paul Simon (1975-76); Henry Gross (1973, 76); Ringo Starr (1977); Mark–Almond (1978); Joe Cocker (1978); Dr. John (1978-79); Art Garfunkel (1978-79); Lee Ritenour (1978); Steely Dan (1980); Kate and Anna McGarrigle (1977-78); Andy Gibb (1980).

GADLER, FRANK Vocal, percussion. Added to the NRBQ lineup.

GADSEN, JAMES Drums. Member of the Joy, 1977. Session for Freddie King (1975); Terry Reid (1976).

GADSEN, JANICE Vocal. Session for Taj Mahal (1978).

GAFA, ALEXANDER Guitar. Session for Paul Simon (1973).

GAFF, WILLIAM Whistle. Session for Rod Stewart (1971).

GAFFEY, MIKE Drums, vocal. Member of the Hitmen, 1980.

GAGLIANO, FRANK Keyboards. Member of Mama's Pride, 1975-77.

GAGLIARDI, ED Bass, vocal. Member of Foreigner, 1977-80.

GAGNON, BRIAN Bass, guitar, keyboards, vocal. Member of the Hunt, 1980.

GAINES, CASSIE Vocal. Died in 1977. Session for Lynyrd Skynyrd (1976-77).

GAINES, STEVE Guitar. Member of Lynyrd Skynyrd, 1975-77. Died with his sister and Ronnie Van Zandt, also of Skynyrd, in a plane crash 10/20/77.

GALBRAITH, BARRY Guitar. Session for Martin Mull.

GALDO, JOE Drums, vocal. Member of Foxy since 1978.

GALDSTON, PHIL Keyboards, vocal. Member of Far Cry, 1980.

GALE, ERIC Guitar. Session for Paul Butterfield (1975); Joe Cocker (1975-76); Barry Goldberg (1969); Felix Pappalardi (1979); Paul Simon (1979-80). *Albums:* Best of Eric Gale (COL JC-36363) 1980; Forecast (KDU 11); Ginseng Woman (COL PC-34421) 1977; Individuals (COL CG-36213); Multiplication (COL JC-34938) 1977; Part of You (COL JC-35715) 1979; Touch of Silk (COL JC-36570) 1980.

GALE, KEN Half of the Gale Force duet, 1977-78.

GALE, LEN Vocal, drums, piano. Half of the Gale Force duet, 1977-78.

GALE, MELVIN Cello, vocal. Member of the Electric Light Orchestra since 1974.

GALE FORCE Len Gale—vocal, drums, piano; Ken Gale—guitar, vocal. *Albums:* Gale Force (FSY F-9527) 1977; Gale Force Two (FSY F-9551) 1978.

GALES, LARRY String bass. Session for John Mayall (1977).

GALINDO, DAN Member of the 13th Floor Elevators.

GALLAGHER, BENNY Guitar, bass, keyboards, vocal, writer. Original member of McGuiness-Flint. Half of the Gallagher and Lyle duet since 1974. Session for Ronnie Lane (1975).

GALLAGHER, MICHAEL Guitar, vocal. Member of Loving Awareness.

GALLAGHER, MICK Keyboards, vocal. Member of Frampton's Camel, 1973, the Graeme Edge Band, 1975, Ian Dury's Blockheads, 1979, and the Planets, 1980. Session for the Clash (1980).

GALLAGHER, RORY Guitar, mandolin, dobro, vocal, writer. First came to America as the leader of Taste, 1969, before starting his solo career. His remarkable guitar work is deeply rooted in the blues. Session for Mike Vernon; Jerry Lee Lewis (1973); Muddy Waters (1972); Mike Batt (1979). *Albums:* Blueprint (POL 5522) 1973; Irish Tour (POL 2-9501) 1974; Gallagher Live (POL 5513); Tatoo (POL 5539); Against the Grain (CYS 1098) 1975; Calling Card (CYS 1124) 1976; Photo-Finish (CYS 1170) 1978; Sinner (POL 6510);

Top Priority (CYS 1235) 1979; Best Years (POL 2383 414) 1973; Take It Easy Baby (SPG SPB 4056) 1976; Stage Struck (CYS 1280) 1980; Deuce (ACO SD 7004) 1972; Rory Gallagher (ACO SD 33-368) 1971.

GALLAGHER AND LYLE Benny Gallagher—guitar, bass, keyboards, vocal, writer; Graham Lyle—guitar, mandolin, bass, vocal, writer. Multitalented duet that formed following the dissolution of McGuiness-Flint. Session on "Rough Mix" (1977); Eric Clapton (1978). *Albums:* Seeds (AAM SP 3605) 1973; Willie and the Lapdog (AAM SP 4384) 1973; Gallagher and Lyle (EMI SM 11016); Last Cowboy (AAM SP 3665) 1974; Breakaway (AAM); Love on the Airwaves (AAM SP 4620) 1977; Showdown (AAM SP 4679) 1978.

GALLES, ALLEN J. Drums, percussion, vocal. Member of the Nu Kats, 1980.

GALLEY, MEL Guitar, writer. Original member of Trapeze, since 1970.

GALLIE, JOHN Organ. Session for Freddie King (1971-72); Leon Russell (1971, 72, 74); Leon Russell and Willie Nelson (1979).

GALLO, MIKE Drums. Member of 20/20, 1979.

GALLUP, CLIFF Guitar. Member of Gene Vincent and His Hub Caps, 1956-61.

GALUTEN, ALBHY Keyboards, producer. Produced Andy Gibb (1977-present); Network (1977); and Frannie Golde (1979). Production and session for the Bee Gees (1977-79). Session for Rod Stewart (1975); Bill Wyman (1976); Eric Clapton (1974); Jackie DeShannon; Steve Stills (1978).

GAMBLER Nathan Shaffer—vocal, guitar; Del Breckenfeld—bass, vocal; Bruce Breckenfeld—keyboards; Warren Mays—guitar, vocal; Chuck Schwartz—drums. *Albums:* Teenage Magic (CAP SW-17009) 1979; Love and Other Crimes (EMI SW 17017) 1980.

GAMMA Ronnie Montrose—guitar; Jim Alcivar—synthesizer; Alan Fitzgerald—bass (1979); Davey Pattison—vocal; Skip Gillette—drums (1979); Glen Letsch—bass (1980); Denny Carmassi—drums (1980). Formed from the ashes of Montrose. *Albums:* Gamma (ELK 6E-219) 1979; Gamma II (ELK 6E-288) 1980.

GAMMOND, KEVYN Guitar, vocal. Original member of Bronco.

GANCHER, CHRISTINA Piano, vocal. Member of Dan Hicks and His Hot Licks.

GANDY, FREDDY Bass. Member of Hookfoot, 1972, and Howard Werth and the Moonbeams, 1975.

GANE, MARK Guitar, synthesizer. Member of Martha and the Muffins, 1980.

GANG OF FOUR Dave Allen—guitar; Hugo Burnham—bass; Andy Gill—vocal; Jon King—drums. *Album:* Entertainment, 1980.

GANNON, JOE Vocal. Session for Alice Cooper (1976).

GANTEK, RAY Steel guitar. Session for the Randle Chowning Band (1978).

GANTRY, CHRIS Guitar, vocal. *Album:* Chris Gantry, 1975.

GANTRY, ELMER Guitar, vocal. Member of Elastique, 1976, and Stretch, 1976. Session for the Alan Parsons Project (1980).

GARANT, RON Bass. Session for Long John Baldry (1980).

GARAU, JEAN-PIERRE Piano. Session for Paul Waroff (1980).

GARAY, VAL Producer. Produced Richie Furay (1979).

GARBERSON, RICK Drums. Member of the Bizarros, 1979.

GARCIA, ARCELIO, JR. Vocal. Member of Malo, 1972.

GARCIA, GUILLE Percussion. Member of Captain Beyond, 1973. Session for Joe Walsh (1974); Bill Wyman (1976).

GARCIA, ISAAC Drums. Session for Ry Cooder (1977).

GARCIA, JERRY Guitar, pedal steel guitar, vocal, writer, keyboards. Born 8/1/42. Original member of the Grateful Dead, 1967-present, and Seastones, 1975. The stature of the Dead guaranteed the success of his progressive rock and jazz solo albums. Session for the Jefferson Airplane (1969); Art Garfunkel; the New Riders of the Purple Sage; Crosby, Stills, Nash and Young (1970); David Crosby (1971); It's a Beautiful Day (1970); Lamb (1971); Merl Saunders (1973). *Albums:* Cats under the Stars (ARI 4160) 1978; Garcia (WBR B-2582) 1972; Live at Keystone (FSY 79002).

GARCIA, MIKE Vibes. Member of Giants, 1979.

GARCIA, VAL Vocal. Voice of Kid Dynamite, 1976.

GARDINER, RICKY Guitar. Member of Iggy Pop's backup band, 1977.

GARDNER, BEVERLY Vocal. Session for Joe Cocker (1972).

GARDNER, BUNK Saxophone, reeds, percussion. Member of the Mothers of Invention, 1967-70, Menage A Trois, 1970-72, and Grandmothers, 1980.

GARDNER, BUZZ Horns, composer. Member of the Mothers of Invention, Menage A Trois, 1970-72, and Grandmothers, 1980.

GARDNER, CHUCK Guitar. Member of the Dixon House Band, 1979.

GARDNER, EARL Trumpet. Member of Southside Johnny and the Asbury Jukes until 1977.

GARDNER, HIRSH Drums, vocal. Member of New England, 1980.

GARDNER, KIM Bass. Session for Danny Spanos (1980).

GARDNER, KOSSIE Organ. Session for J. J. Cale (1972).

GARDNER, MIKE Drums. Member of the Gentrys.

GARDNER, RON Vocal, keyboards. Member of the 1960s Wailers, and namesake of the Ron Gardner Group, 1974.

RON GARDNER GROUP Ron Gardner—vocal, keyboards; Doug Booth—drums, percussion; David Immer—keyboards, vibes, percussion, vocal; David P. Shogren—bass, vocal; Dennis Weaver—guitar. Short-lived Pacific Northwest group. *Album:* Ron Gardner (MCA) 1974.

GARDNER, STU Vocal. Session for Nils Lofgren (1975).

GARFAT, JANCE Bass. Member of Dr. Hook.

GARFIELD, HARRY Keyboards. Member of Simon Stokes and the Black Whip Band, 1973.

GARFIELD, WAYNE Vocal. Session for Taj Mahal (1978).

GARFUNKEL, ART Vocal. Half of the Simon and Garfunkel team. Session for James Taylor (1976). *Albums:* Angel Clare (COL PC-31474) 1973; Breakaway (COL PC-33700) 1975; Fate for Breakfast (COL JC-35780) 1979; Watermark (COL JC-34975) 1978.

GARIBALDI, DAVID Drums. Member of Tower of Power until 1975. Session for Roy Buchanan (1977); Tom Johnston (1979).

GARLAND, SHARON Vocal, percussion. Member of the Bill Blue Band, 1979-80.

GARMAN, CLARK Guitar, vocal. Member of In Transit, 1980.

GARMEN, LAURENCE Harmonica. Session for Mike Vernon; the Inmates (1979).

GARNER, KAY Vocal. Session for Long John Baldry (1971, 75); Lou Reed (1972).

GARNIER, TONY Bass. Member of Asleep at the Wheel since 1973.

GAROFALO, BRYAN Bass, vocal. Session for Doug Kershaw; B. B. King (1970, 72); Joe Walsh (1974).

GARON, LENNY Keyboards. Member of Polyrock, 1980.

GARONE, GARY Horns. Member of the Fun Zone, 1977.

GARONZIK, PHIL Reeds. Member of Fat Chance, 1972.

GARR, ARTIE Early name used by Art Garfunkel.

GARR, BILL Drums. Member of Brother Fox and the Tar Babys, 1969.

GARRETT, AMOS Guitar, bass, vocal. Part of Paul Butterfield's Better Days Band, 1973. Member of the Elvin Bishop Band, 1978. Session for Martin Mull (1974, 77); Pearls Before Swine (1971); John Sebastian (1974); Maria Muldaur (1973); Rodney Crowell (1978); Danny Douma (1979); Chris Montan (1980). *Albums:* Geoff Muldaur/Amos Garrett (FLF 061) 1978; Go Cat Go (FLF FF 226) 1980.

GARRETT, DAVE Keyboards. Member of Quiet Sun, 1975.

GARRETT, DAVID Vocal. Original member of Sha Na Na, 1970.

GARRETT, GERALD Vocal. Session for Neil Diamond (1976).

GARRETT, JAN CAMP Vocal, mandolin, piano, guitar. Member of Liberty, 1975.

GARRETT, LEIF Vocal. *Albums:* Feel the Need (STB 7100) 1978; Leif Garrett (ATC 19152) 1977; Same Goes for You (STB 16008) 1979; Can't Explain (STB SB 7111) 1980.

GARRETT, VIC Bass, vocal, guitar. Member of Liberty, 1975.

GARRISON, JIMMY Bass. Session for Larry Coryell. *Album:* Love Supreme (MCA 77).

GARRISON, RINUS Producer, arranger, vocal. Half of the Garrison and Van Dyke duet, 1979.

GARRISON AND VAN DYKE Rinus Garrison—producer, arranger, vocal; Michael Van Dyke—lyrics, vocal. *Album:* Garrison and Van Dyke (ACO 38-119) 1979.

GARRITY, EDDIE Vocal. Member of Slaughter, 1980.

GARSON, MICK Keyboards. Session for David Bowie.

GARTH, AL Saxophone, clarinet, violin. Member of the Loggins and Messina backup band, 1972-77, and the Dirt Band since 1978.

GARTHWAITE, DAVID Bass, guitar. Member of the Joy of Cooking, 1970-73.

GARTHWAITE, TERRI Guitar, vocal, clarinet. Member of the Joy of Cooking, 1970-73, and Joy, 1977. *Albums:* Hand in Glove (FSY 9664) 1978; Terry Garthwaite, 1975.

GARVEY, NICK Guitar, bass, piano, vocal. Member of the Ducks Deluxe, 1972-75, and the Motors since 1977. Session for Bram Tchaikovsky (1979); Sean Tyla (1980).

GARVEY, STEVE Bass. Member of the Buzzcocks since 1977.

GARY, BRUCE Drums, percussion. Member of the Giants, 1976, and the Knack since 1979.

GASCA, LUIS Trumpet. Member of Malo, 1972. Session with Carlos Santana—Buddy Miles Live (1972); Santana (1971); Janis Joplin (1969). *Albums:* Fantasy Born to Love; Luis Gasca (BTM).

GASDA, RICK Trumpet. Member of Southside Johnny and the Asbury Jukes.

GASKIN, VICTOR Backed John Mayall, 1972-73.

GASMASK Ray Brooks—bass; Bill Davidson—guitar; Nick Oliva—keyboards; Richard Grando—reeds; Bobby Osborne—vocal; James Strassburg—drums; David Gross—saxophone; Enrico Raja—trumpet. *Album:* Their First Album (TSL 4001).

GASOLIN' Kim Larsen—vocal, guitar; Franz Beckerlee—vocal, guitar, moog; Wili Jonsson—bass, keyboards, vocal; Soren Berleu—drums. *Album:* Gasolin' (EPC) 1974.

GASPAR, JEAN PAUL Percussion, vocal. Member of Network, 1977.

GASPAR, STEVEN Organ. Session for the Randle

Chowning Band (1978).

GATCHEL, JOHN Horns. Member of Ten Wheel Drive, 1970.

GATES, DAVID Keyboards, vocal, guitar. Member of Bread and soloist. Session for the Ventures. *Albums:* Falling in Love Again (ELK 6E-2511) 1980; Goodbye Girl (ELK 64-148) 1978; Never Let Her Go (ELK 7E-1028) 1975; First (ELK 75066) 1973; Seconds (ELK) 1975.

GATLING, FREEMAN Drums. Session for B. B. King (1969).

GATTI, JOHN Keyboards, flute, vocal. Member of the Truth, 1975.

GATTO, JOHN Guitar. Member of the Good Rats since 1978.

GAUDIO, BOB Vocal. Original member of the Four Seasons.

GAUVENDA, TOMMY Guitar. Member of Pezband, 1977.

GAVIN, PETE Drums, percussion, vibes, vocal. Member of Heads, Hands and Feet, 1970-71. Session for Jerry Lee Lewis (1974).

GAY, CARL Guitar. Session for Waylon Jennings (1974).

GAY, ROBBIE Guitar. Member of the Johnny Van Zant Band, 1980.

GAYDEN, MAC Guitar. Member of Area Code 615, 1968-69. Session for Pearls Before Swine (1970); J. J. Cale (1971-72, 74).

GAYDON, JAMES Drums. Member of Joy, 1977.

GAYE, MARVIN Vocal. From the church choir to the Moonglows to a solo artist in 1961, Gaye has weathered the years of soul evolution as artist, arranger, performer and writer. *Albums:* Anthology (MTN M9-790) 1974; Marvin Gaye's Greatest Hits (TML T7-252) 1964; Marvin Gaye's Greatest Hits (TML T7); Here, My Dear (TML T-364) 1978; In Loving Memory (TML T7-329) 1973; Love Man (TML T8-369); Pops We Love You (MTN M7-921); What's Going On (TML T7-310) 1971; Super Hits (TML T5-300) 1970; It Takes Two (NR 4012T1) 1978; Soulful Moods (MTN NR 4007T1); Marvin Gaye Live (TML T6-333); Save the Children (MTN M7-800); Trouble Man (TML TS-322); Greatest Hits, Vol. 2, 1967; You're All I Need to Get By, 1968; In The Groove, 1968; Live On Stage, 1963; When I'm Alone, I Cry, 1964; Soulful Sound of Marvin Gaye, 1961; That Stubborn Kinda Fellow, 1963; Hello Broadway, 1964; How Sweet It Is, 1965; Tribute to Nat King Cole, 1965; Moods of Marvin Gaye, 1966; Take Two, 1966; United, 1967.

MARVIN GAYE AND TAMMI TERRELL See Marvin Gaye. *Albums:* Anthology (MTN M9-791); Greatest Hits (TML T7-302) 1970; Marvin Gaye and Tammi Terrell (MTN M5-V102-1) 1980.

GAYNA Vocal. Session for Iggy Pop (1977).

GAYNOR, DAVE Drums. Member of Girl, 1980.

GEARHEART, CHARLIE Vocal, guitar. Member of Goose Creek Symphony, 1971-74.

GEARS Dave Drive—drums; Brian Redz—bass; Kid Spike—guitar; Axxel G. Reese—vocal. *Album:* Rockin' at Ground Zero (PGM GS 6471) 1980.

GEDDES, TOMMY Drums. Member of the Reds, 1979.

GEE, ARTHUR Vocal, guitar, harmonica. Namesake of the Arthur Gee-Whiz Band, 1971-72.

ARTHUR GEE-WHIZZ BAND Arthur Gee—vocal, guitar, harmonica; Bill Alexander—vocal, keyboards; Steven Van Gelder—vocal, guitar, keyboards, fiddle, banjo; Marcus Damerst—vocal, guitar; Don Riggs—vocal, drums; Richard Hathaway—vocal, bass. *Albums:* Arthur Gee, 1971; City Cowboy, 1972.

GEE, ROSCOE Bass. Session for Chris Youlden (1974); Jim Capaldi (1979).

GEESIN, RON Co-author of "Music from the Body," 1970, with Pink Floyd's Roger Waters. *Album:* Music from the Body (IMP 1002) 1970.

GEFFEN, DAVID Producer, vocal. Production and session for John Lennon (1980). Session for David Crosby (1971).

GEILS, JEROME Guitars, mandolin. Born 2/20/46. Guitarist and namesake of the J. Geils Band since 1970.

J. GEILS BAND Peter Wolf—vocal, writer; Seth Justman—keyboards, writer; Magic Duck (Real name: Richard Salwitz)—harmonica; J. Geils—guitar; Danny Klein—bass; Stephen Jo Bladd—drums, vocal; Juke Joint Jimmy—rhythm guitar (1970). Early name: the Hallucinations. The "Bad Boy" image of rock 'n' roll has had several interpreters since the Rolling Stones, but few bands have sustained such high energy with their gut level attack as the J. Geils Band. *Albums:* Best of the J. Geils Band (ATC 19234) 1979; Bloodshot (ATC 7260) 1973; Blow Your Face Out (ATC 507) 1976; Full House (ATC 7241) 1972; J. Geils Band (ATC 8275) 1970; Love Stinks (EIA SOO-17016) 1980; Monkey Island (ATC 19103) 1977; Morning After (ATC 8297) 1971; Nightmares (ATC 10107) 1974; Sanctuary (EIA SO-17006) 1978; Hot Line (ATC) 1975; Ladies Invited (ATC) 1973; Best of the J. Geils Band Two (ATC SD 19248) 1980.

GEILS Abbreviated name adopted by the J. Geils Band in 1977 for their "Monkey Island" album.

GEISINGER, JACK Bass. Member of Influence, 1967-68.

GELBER, BILL Bass. Session for Leslie West (1975-76).

GELDORF, BOB Member of the Boomtown Rats since 1977.

GELLING, EELCO Guitar. Member of the Golden Earring, 1976-78. Session for the Golden Earring (1974-75); George Kooymans (1973).

GELLOTTE, GUNNAR Drums, percussion. Session for Jimmy Hall (1980).

GELSINGER, JACK Bass. Member of Influence, 1968.

GEMMELL, KEITH Saxophone, clarinet, flute. Member of Audience, 1971, and Stackridge, 1974.

GENDEL, MARC Guitar. Session for Long John Baldry (1980).

GENERATION X Billy Idol—vocal; Bob "Derwood" Andrews—guitar, vocal; Mark Laff—drums, vocal; Tony James—bass, vocal. *Albums:* Generation X (CYS 1169) 1978; Valley of the Dolls (CYS 1193) 1979.

GENESIS Phil Collins—drums, percussion, vocal; Michael Rutherford—guitar, bass, sitar; Stephen Hackett—guitar; Tony Banke—keyboards, guitar; Peter Gabriel—vocal, flute, oboe, percussion (1971-74); Anthony Phillips—guitar, vocal, keyboards. Progressive jazz-rock synthesis. *Albums:* Foxtrot (CMA 1058); From Genesis to Revelation (LON 1052); Genesis Live (ACO 2401) 1974; Nursery Cryme (LON CMA 1052); And Then There Were Three (TAC 19173) 1978; Duke (ATC 16014) 1980; Genesis (CMA 2-2701); Lamb Lies Down on Broadway (ACO 2-401) 1974; Seconds Out (ATC 2-9002) 1977; Trespass (MCA X-816); Trick of the Tail (ACO 38-101) 1976; Wind and Wuthering (ACO 38-100) 1976; Selling England by the Pound (CMA 6060) 1973; Trick of the Hat (CMA) 1976.

GENNARD, SANDY Drums. Member of Blackjack since 1979.

GENOCKEY, LIAM Drums. Member of Zzebra, 1974-75. Session for Gerry Rafferty (1979-80); Ian Gillan (1979).

GENT, CHRIS Tenor saxophone. Session for Slaughter (1980).

GENTILE, RONNIE Guitar. Member of Crystal Mansion.

GENTLE GIANT Derek Schulman—vocal, saxophone; Ray Schulman—bass, vocal, violin; Kerry Minnear—keyboards, cello, vocal; Gary Green—guitar; John Weathers—drums, percussion, vocal. Progressive British rock band of the 1970s. *Albums:* Acquiring the Taste (VTG 1005) 1971; Civilian (COL JC-36341) 1980; Free Hand (CAP ST-11428) 1975; Giant for a Day (CAP SW-11813) 1978; Interview (CAP ST-115342) 1976; Missing Piece (CAP ST-11696) 1977; Octopus (COL PC-32022) 1973; Official "Live" Gentle Giant (CAP SKBB-11592) 1977; Power and the Glory (CAP ST-11337) 1974; Three Friends (COL PC-31649) 1972; Pretentions (CAP) 1977.

GENTLEMAN, SIR HORACE Bass. Member of the Specials since 1979.

GENTRY, BOBBIE Vocal. Real name: Roberta Streeter. Her only hit, "Ode to Billy Joe" (1967), was a reminder of the place country and western music once had in the rock field. *Albums:* Bobby Gentry's Greatest (CAP SM-381); Ode to Billy Joe (CAP SM-2830) 1967; Delta Sweetie, 1968; Bobbie Gentry and Glen Campbell (CAP SM 2928).

GENTRY, TEDDY Bass, vocal. Member of Alabama, 1980.

GENTRYS Steve Speer—bass; Jimmy Tarbutton—guitar; David Beaver—keyboards; Jimmy Heart—vocal; Mike Gardner—drums. *Album:* Gentrys (SUN 117).

GEORDIE Early band of Bon Scott's replacement in AC/DC, Brian Johnson. *Album:* Hope You Like It (MGM 4903) 1973.

GEORGE, BERNARD Member of Blues Incorporated.

GEORGE, LOWELL Guitar. Original member of Little Feat, 1971-75. Died 1979. Session for the Mothers of Invention (1970); Nilsson (1972); Carly Simon (1972); Bill Wyman (1974); John Sebastian (1974); Jimmy Webb (1977); Yvonne Elliman (1978); Mick Taylor (1979). *Album:* Thanks I'll Eat It Here (WBR K-3194).

GEORGE, RUSSELL Bass. Session for Paul Simon (1972).

GEORGE, SIDNEY Saxophone, harmonica, flute. Session for Steve Stills (1970); Dr. John (1972).

GEORGE, STEVE Keyboards, synthesizer, vocal. Member of the Pages, 1978-79.

GEORGE, WAYNE Keyboards, vocal. Member of Arc, 1978.

GEORGIA BILL See Blind Willie McTell.

GEORGIADES, MIKE Vocal, guitar. Co-namesake of the Bernie Leadon-Mike Georgiades Band, 1977.

GERALDO, NEIL Guitar, keyboards, vocal. Member of Pat Benatar's backup band since 1979.

GERBER, ALAN Piano. Member of Rhinoceros, 1968.

GERBER, DON Banjo. Session for Richie Furay (1976).

GERBER, JON Saxophone. Session for Sylvain Sylvain (1979).

GERICH, GEORGE Organ. Session for Pavlov's Dog (1976).

GERMANO, DOMINIC Bass. Member of the States, 1979.

GERMS Pat; Darby; Lorna; Don. *Album:* (G) (SLH SR 103) 1979.

GERONIMO BLACK Group formed by ex-Mother of Invention member, Jimmy Carl Black.

GERRARD, DENNY Bass, drums, vocal. Member of the Paupers, 1966-67.

GERRARD, DONNY Vocal. Session for Neil Sedaka (1975).

GERRETT, PAUL Keyboards, vocal. Member of Wally, 1974.

GERRITSEN, RINUS Bass, piano. Original member of Golden Earring.

GERRITY, FREDDIE Vocal. Namesake of Freddie

and the Dreamers, 1962-66.

GERRY AND THE PACEMAKERS Gerry Marsden—vocal; Freddy Marsden—drums; Les Chadwick—bass (1962-65); Les Maguire—piano (1962-65). Originally called the Mars Bars, until 1959. The original "Ferry Cross the Mersey" boys (1965) had been together since 1959. They signed with Brian Epstein and George Martin in 1962. *Albums:* Best of Gerry and the Pacemakers (CAP SM-11898) 1979; Don't Let the Sun Catch You Crying (LAU 2024); Girl on a Swing (LAU 2037); Greatest Hits (LAU 2031); Hits of the Mersey Era (CAP M-11690); I'll Be There (LAU 2030); Laurie Golden Goodies (LAU 2041); Second Album (LAU 2027).

GERST, BILLY Trumpet. Member of Creation, 1974.

GETZ, DAVID Drums, vocal. Original member of Big Brother and the Holding Company.

GETZ, JANE Piano. Session for the Bee Gees (1973); Nilsson (1974-76).

GHEZZI, SUZI Guitar. Member of Isis, 1974-75.

GIALLOMBARDO, PHIL Keyboards, vocal. Member of the James Gang, 1976.

GIAMMARESE, CARL Guitar, vocal. Member of the Buckinghams before co-founding the Tufana-Gimmarese Band, 1973-77.

GIANNI, EDDY B. Guitar. Member of Jon and the Nightriders, 1980.

GIANQUINTO, ALBERT Piano. Member of the James Cotton Blues Band. Session for the Son Seals Blues Band (1978).

GIANTS Greg Errico—drums, synthesizer, producer; Carlos Santana—guitar; Herbie Hancock—piano; Lee Oskar—harmonica; Neal Schon—guitar; Mike Carabello—organ, congos; Greg Rollie—organ; Chepito Areas—percussion; Rico Reyes—percussion; Doug Rauch—bass; Mike Garcia—vibes; Wendy Haas—piano, vocal; Victor Pantoja—congas; Robert Vega—bass; Doug Rodriguez—guitar; Bianca Thornton-Oden—vocal; Freddie Pool—vocal; Gene Washington—vocal; Jody Moreing—vocal; Linda Tillery—vocal; Coke Escovedo—vocal. *Album:* Giants (MCA 3188) 1978.

GIANTS Karl Rucker—bass, guitar; John Plantana—guitar, vocal; Laurie Cohen—vocal; Bruce Gary—drums, percussion; Ron Elliott—guitar. *Album:* Thanks for the Music (CAS) 1976.

GIBB, ANDY Vocal, guitar. Real name: Andrew Roy Gibb. Born 3/5/58. Younger brother of the Bee Gee Gibbs who went solo in 1977, using the same formula with equal success. Session for Steve Stills (1979). *Albums:* Flowing Rivers (RSO 1-3019) 1977; Gift of Song (POL 1-6214); Shadow Dancing (RSO 1-3034) 1978; Greatest Hits (RSO RX 13090) 1980; After Dark (RSO RS 1-3069) 1980.

GIBB, BARRY Vocal, guitar, producer. With brothers Maurice and Robin, founder and namesake of the Bee Gees. With Maurice, he released a duet album, "Cucumber Castle." Produced Network (1977), and Andy Gibb (1980).

GIBB, JOHN Guitar, vocal. Member of Battered Wives.

GIBB, MAURICE Vocal, keyboards, guitar, bass. With brother Barry, he released a duet album, "Cucumber Castle," and with his third brother, Robin, they founded the Bee Gees. Session for Ringo Starr (1977).

GIBB, ROBIN Vocal, writer. With brothers Maurice and Barry, founder of the Bee Gees. He also released a solo album. *Album:* Robin's Reign (ACO).

GIBBONS, BILLY Guitar, vocal, harmonica. Member of the Moving Sidewalks, and ZZ Top since 1971.

GIBBONS, IAN Keyboards, vocal. Member of the Kinks, 1980.

GIBBONS, MARK Keyboards. Member of Captain Beefheart and His Magic Band, 1974.

GIBBONS, MIKE Drums. Member of Badfinger.

GIBBONS, STEVE Vocal. Voice and namesake of the Steve Gibbons Band, 1976-78.

STEVE GIBBONS BAND Steve Gibbons—vocal; Dave Carroll—guitar, vocal; Bob Wilson—guitar, vocal; Trevor Burton—bass, vocal; Bob Lamb—drums; Harry Rix—drums (1979-present); Robbie Blunt—guitar (1979-present). *Albums:* Caught in the Act (MCA 2305) 1977; Down in the Bunker (POL 1-6154) 1978; Any Road Up (MCA 2187); Street Parade (POL PD 16293) 1980; Rollin' On (MCA 2243) 1977.

GIBBS, JERRY Saxophone. Session for Memphis Slim (1971).

GIBLIN, JOHN Bass. Member of Metro, 1977.

GIBSON, BILL Drums, vocal. Member of Huey Lewis and the News, 1980.

GIBSON, COLIN Bass, vocal. Replaced Roger Sutton in Mark-Almond, 1972. Member of Snafu, 1973-75. Replaced Dave Quinn in Movies, 1980. Session for Steve Howe (1975); Alvin Lee (1975).

GIBSON, FRANK Drums, percussion. Session for Rick Wakeman (1979).

GIBSON, LACY Guitar. Member of the Son Seals Blues Band (1978).

GIBSON, LUKE Vocal. Voice of Kensington Market, 1968-69.

GIBSON, PETE Vocal, trombone. Member of Brett Marvin and the Thunderbolts.

GIBSON, ROYCE Percussion, vocal. Half of the Atlantis Philharmonic duet, 1974.

GIBSON, STEVE Guitar. Session for Splinter (1977); Neil Young (1978); Levon Helm (1980).

GIBSON, WILF Violin. Member of Centipede, 1971.

GIFFORD, JOHN Guitar, vocal. Member of the Streetband, 1980.

GIGLIO, JANA Vocal. Member of White Lightnin', 1978.

GIGLIOTTI, TONY Vocal. Member of Mom's Apple Pie, 1973.

GIGUERE, RUSS Vocal. Member of the Association before making his less successful solo debut. *Album:* Hexagram 16 (WBR) 1971.

GILBERT, B. C. Guitar. Member of Wire, 1980.

GILBERT, DAVE Vocal. Member of Rockets since 1977.

GILBERT, EILEEN Vocal. Session for Zephyr (1971); Gregg Allman (1973).

GILBERT, RICH Guitar. Member of Human Sexual Response, 1980.

GILBERT, RON Bass. Member of the Blues Magoos.

GILBERT, WARWICK Bass. Member of Radio Birdman, 1978.

GILBIN, JOHN Bass. Member of Brand X, 1979-present.

GILBRETH, PHIL Bass, vocal. Member of the Twisters, 1980.

GILCKEN, FRANK Guitar. Member of Bang, 1973.

GILDER, NICK Vocal, producer. Namesake of Nick Gilder and Band.

NICK GILDER AND BAND Nick Gilder—vocal, producer; James McCulloch—guitar; Eric Nelson—bass; Steve Halter—keyboards (1977); Chet McCracken—drums (1977); Craig Krampf—drums (1978-79); Jamie Herndon—keyboards, guitar (1978-present). *Albums:* City Nights (CYS 1202) 1978; Frequency (CYS 1219) 1979; Rock America (CAS 7243) 1980; You Know Who You Are (CYS 1147) 1977.

GILDERSLEEVE, JONATHAN LEE Drums. Member of Nervus Rex, 1980.

GILES, GARY Bass. Member of Stray, 1970-75.

GILES, MIKE Drums, vocal. Original member of King Crimson, 1969-70, McDonald and Giles, 1971, and Grimms, 1973. Session for Luther Grosvenor; Ken Tobias (1973); Anthony Phillips (1979).

GILES, PETER Bass. Replaced Greg Lake in King Crimson, 1970. Member of McDonald and Giles, 1971.

GILGAMESH Phil Lee—guitar; Hugh Hopper—bass; Trevor Tomkins—drums; Alan Gowen—keyboards. *Album:* Another Fine Tune You've Got Me Into (CRL 5009).

GILKINSON, JEFF Bass, cello, vocal. Replaced Mitchell Jayne in the Dillards, 1977-80.

GILL, ANDY Vocal. Member of the Gang of Four, 1980.

GILL, BOB Guitar. Session for Maddy Prior (1980).

GILL, PETE Drums. Member of Saxon, 1980.

GILL, VINCE Guitar, banjo, dobro. Replaced Larry Goshorn in Pure Prairie League, 1979.

GILLAN, IAN Vocal, writer. Replaced Rod Evans in Deep Purple, 1970-75. After leaving the group, he formed the Ian Gillan Band, 1976-78 and Gillan, 1979 to present. Played Jesus in "Jesus Christ Superstar," 1970.

IAN GILLAN BAND Ian Gillan—vocal, writer; Ray Fenwick—guitar, slide guitar, vocal; John Gustafson—bass, vocal; Mike Moran—keyboards (1976); Mark Nauseef—drums, percussion; Colin Towns—keyboards (1977). First spinoff group from former Deep Purple member, Gillan. *Albums:* Ian Gillan Band (CYS 1-1602); Scarabus (ISL 9511) 1977; Child in Time (OYS 11602) 1976.

GILLAN Ian Gillan—vocal; Colin Towns—keyboards; John McCoy—bass; Bernie Torme—guitar; Mick Underwood—drums. Former vocalist of Deep Purple, Gillan's attempt to revive the Purple formula. *Albums:* Mr. Universe (Import) 1979; Glory Road (VIR VR-1-1001) 1980.

GILLESPIE, CRAIG Bass, vocal. Member of Citizen, 1980.

GILLESPIE, DANA Vocal. Session for Danny Kirwan (1979).

GILLETTE, MICK Trumpet, trombone. Member of Tower of Power horn section. Session for Roy Buchanan (1974); Ron Gardner (1974); Bill Wyman (1976).

GILLETTE, SKIP Drums. Member of Gamma, 1979.

GILLIS, BRADLEY Member of Rubicon, 1978-79.

GILMORE, BOB Bass. Member of the Candymen, 1967-68.

GILMORE, GARY Bass. Session for Taj Mahal; J. J. Cale (1972).

GILMOUR, DAVID Guitar. Replaced Syd Barrett in Pink Floyd, 1968-present. Session for Syd Barrett; Roy Harper (1975); Kate Bush (1978); Wings (1979). *Album:* Dave Gilmour (COL JC-35388) 1978.

GILPIN, STEVE Vocal. Member of Mi-Sex, 1980.

GILSTRAP, JAMES Vocal. Session for Sonny Terry and Brownie McGhee (1973); Ringo Starr (1974); Neil Diamond (1976); Dr. John (1979); Art Garfunkel (1979).

GIMBLE, JOHNNY Guitar, fiddle. Session for Leon Russell (1973); Willie Nelson (1973-74); Waylon Jennings (1975); Asleep at the Wheel (1976).

GIMLETS Early name for Kansas.

GINFFRIA, GREG Keyboards. Member of the Angels.

GINN, GREG Guitar. Member of the Black Flag.

GINSBERG, ALLEN Vocal, poet. Session for the Fugs (1967).

GINSBERG, JEFF Kazoo. Member of the Temple City Kazoo Orchestra, 1978.

GINSBERG, KIEV Guitar, vocal. Member of 3-D, 1980. Session for the Blues Brothers (1980).

GIORDANO, STEVE Guitar. Session for Rob Stoner (1980). *Album:* Daybreak (MUS 5211) 1979.

GIOVANELLI, VITO Bass, vocal. Member of Brent Maglia's backup band, 1977.

GIRARD, CHUCK Guitar, vocal. *Albums:* Chuck Girard (GDN 8102); Glow in the Dark (GDN 8103); Jubilation (MYR A-6555); Jubilation Too (MYR A-6580); Take It Easy (GDN 8108); Written on the Wind (GDN 8106) 1977.

GIRARD, MIKE Vocal. Member of the Fools, 1980.

GIRAUDY, MIQUETTE Vocal, vibes, synthesizer. Session for Steve Hillage (1975-77).

GIRL Phil Collen—guitar, vocal; Simon Laffy—bass; Gerry Laffy—guitar, vocal; Phillip Lewis—vocal; Dave Gaynor—drums. *Album:* Sheer Greed (JET JZ-36490) 1980.

GIRLANDO, PHIL Guitar, vocal. Member of the Truth, 1975.

GIROURARD, DEXTER Drums. Member of Cottonwood South, 1974.

GIRTON, A. Vocal. Session for the Kinks (1974).

GIRTON, JOHN Guitar. Member of Dan Hicks and His Hot Licks, 1978.

GISMONDI, MICHAEL Bass, synthesizer. Replaced Daniel Pecchio in the Michael Stanley Band, 1980.

GITTLSHON, JUDY Vocal, synthesizer, keyboards. Member of the Pink Section, 1980.

GIUDOTTI, BOB Drums. Member of the Night, 1979-80.

GIVENS, CANDY Keyboards, vocal, harmonica. Member of Zephyr, 1971.

GIVENS, CLIFF Vocal. Session for Ry Cooder (1979).

GIVENS, DAVID Bass, vocal. Member of Zephyr, 1971.

GLAISTER, TOM Drums. Member of Jukin' Bone, 1972.

GLAN, PENTI (WHITNEY) Drums. Member of Mandala, 1968, the Alice Cooper Show, 1977, and Ultra Latex, 1979. Session for Alice Cooper (1975); Lou Reed (1974); John Kay (1973).

GLASCOCK, BRIAN Drums. Member of Trouble, 1977, and the Motels, 1979-80. Session for Iggy Pop (1977).

GLASCOCK, JOHN Bass, vocal. Member of the Gods, 1968, Stan Webb's Chicken Shack, 1970-71, and Carmen, 1974. Replaced Jeffrey Hammond in Jethro Tull, 1976-80.

GLASS, DICK Vocal, guitar. Member of Elephant, 1975.

GLASS, NAPOLEAN Drums. Session for Oxendale and Shephard (1979).

GLASS, PHILLIP Keyboards. Session for Polyrock (1980). *Album:* North Star (VIR VI-2085) 1977.

GLASS HARP Phil Keaggy—guitar, vocal; Dan Decchio—bass, guitar, flute, vocal; John Sferra—drums, guitar, vocal. Ohio born hard rock featuring Keaggy. *Albums:* Glass Harp, (MCA 293) 1970; Synergy, 1971; It Makes Me Glad, 1972; Live at Carnegie Hall, 1972.

GLASS MOON David Adams—keyboards, vocal; Nestor Nunez—bass, vocal; Chris Jones—drums. *Album:* Glass Moon (RAD 2003) 1980.

GLAUB, BOB Bass. Session for Rod Stewart (1975-76); Dave Mason (1974, 80); Steve Miller (1977); Jim Morrison's "American Prayer" (1978); Cher Bono (1979); Jackson Browne (1979); Tom Johnston (1979); the Marc Tanner Band (1979); Gordon Lightfoot (1980).

GLAZE, RED HOT WILLIE See Blind Willie McTell.

GLEASON, PATRICK Moog. Session for Jon Mark (1974).

GLEN, CHRIS Bass. Member of the Sensational Alex Harvey Band, 1972-75, and Sahb, 1976.

GLENCOE Graham Maitland—keyboards, vocal; Norman Watt-Roy—bass, vocal; John Turnbull—guitar, vocal; Stewart Francis—drums. *Album:* Glencoe (GTW) 1972.

GLENISTER, PETE Guitar, vocal. Member of the Hitmen, 1980.

GLENN, DAVE Trombone. Member of Cosmology, 1977.

GLICKSTEIN, FRED Guitar, vocal. Member of the Flock.

GLIDER Tom Myers—guitar, sitar, autoharp, percussion; Gene Barkein—guitar, vocal; Steve Halter—keyboards; Jeff Stillman—vocal; Scott McCarl—vocal; Jeff Eyrich—bass; Eddie Tuduri—drums. *Album:* Glider (UAR UA LA814-G) 1977.

GLOUD, VENETTE Vocal. Session for Elton John (1980).

GLOVER, DAVE Bass. Member of Elton John's band, 1970-72. Session for Long John Baldry (1971); John Kongos (1972).

GLOVER, HENRY Keyboards. Session for Paul Butterfield (1975).

GLOVER, ROBERT Bass. Member of the Sports since 1979.

GLOVER, ROGER Bass, vocal, synthesizer, guitar, percussion, writer, producer. Replaced Nic Simper in Deep Purple, 1970-74, and Bob Daisley in Rainbow, 1979 to present. Produced the Ian Gillan Band (1976); Young and Moody (1977); Rainbow (1979-present); and the Michael Schenker Group (1980). Session for Dan McCafferty (1975). *Album:* Elements (POL PD 1-6137) 1978.

GLOVER, SUZY Vocal. Session for Frank Zappa (1974); Long John Baldry (1975).

GO See Steve Winwood, Stomu Yamashta.

GOALBY, PETE Vocal, guitar. Member of Trapeze, 1980.

GOBLE, GRAHAM Guitar, vocal. Member of Mississippi, 1973, and the Little River Band since

1977.

GODCHAUX, DONNA Vocal. Member of the Grateful Dead since 1972.

GODCHAUX, KEITH Piano. Member of the Grateful Dead, 1972 until his death in July, 1980.

GODDING, BRIAN Guitar. Member of Centipede, 1971, and Magma, 1972-75. Session for Annette Peacock (1979).

GODLEY, KEVIN Drums, percussion, vocal. Member of 10 CC, 1974-76, and Godley-Creme since 1977. Session for Neil Sedaka (1975).

GODLEY-CREME Kevin Godley—drums, percussion, vocal; Lol Creme—guitar, vocal. Duet spinoff from 10 CC. *Albums:* Consequences (MCR SRM 3-1700) 1977; Freeze Frame (POL POl-6257) 1980; L (POL POl-6177) 1978.

GODOVITZ, GREG Bass, vocal. Member of Fludd, 1971.

GODS Ken Hensley—keyboards, guitar, percussion, vocal; Lee Kerslake—drums; Joe Konas—guitar, vocal; John Glascock—bass, vocal. Retrospectively released in the U.S. after the success of Uriah Heep, the Gods were originally formed in 1968 and released two albums before breaking up. *Album:* Gods (IMP 1012).

GODWIN, PETER Vocal, saxophone, moog. Member of Metro, 1977.

GODZ Eric Moore—bass, vocal, producer; Bob Hill—guitar, keyboards, vocal; Glen Cataline—drums, vocal; Mark Chatfield—guitar, vocal. *Albums:* The Godz (MLN 8003) 1978; Nothing Is Sacred (CAS 7134) 1979.

GOEDERT, RON Vocal. Voice of White Witch, 1973-74. *Album:* Breaking All the Rules (POL 1-6265) 1980.

GOERDIE Retrospectively noted for having spawned Brian Johnson, replacement vocalist for Bon Scott in AC/DC. *Album:* Hope You Like It (MGM SE 4903) 1973.

GOETZMAN, STEVE Drums. Replaced Bobby Johns in Exile, 1978-80.

GOFF, DUKE Guitar. Session for Waylon Jennings (1974-76).

GOFFIN, LOUISE Vocal. *Album:* Kid Blue (ASY 6E-203) 1979.

GOIN, JOHN Guitar. Session for the Ozark Mountain Daredevils (1980); Jimmy Hall (1980).

GOINS, HERBIE Member of Blues Incorporated.

GOLD, ANDREW Keyboards. Session for Art Garfunkel; Karla Bonoff (1977). *Albums:* All This and Heaven Too (ASY 6E-116) 1978; Andrew Gold (ASY 7E-1047) 1976; What's Wrong With This Picture (ASY 7E-1086) 1976; Whirlwind (ASY 6E-264) 1980.

GOLD, HARVEY Keyboards, guitar, vocal. Member of Tin Huey, 1979.

GOLDBERG, ANDREW Keyboards, vocal. Member of Elton Motello, 1980.

GOLDBERG, BARRY Keyboards, vocal, writer, guitar. Started in Chicago playing with Harvey Mandel and Charlie Musselwhite in the 1960s. Headed the Barry Goldberg Blues Band and Barry Goldberg Reunion before returning to session and solo work. Worked with Paul Butterfield and the Electric Flag, 1967-68. In 1975 he was a member of KGB. Session for Harvey Mandel; Super Session (1968); Mike Bloomfield (1979). *Albums:* Barry Goldberg and Friends; Recorded Live (BUD BOS 5684) 1976; Barry Goldberg (ACO SD 740) 1974; Two Jews B'ues (BUD BDS 5029) 1969.

BARRY GOLDBERG BLUES BAND Barry Goldberg—keyboards, vocal, writer; Maurice McKinley—drums; Charlie Musselwhite—harmonica; Harvey Mandel—guitar; Roy Ruby—guitar, bass. See Barry Goldberg. *Album:* Blowing My Mind (EPC BN 26199).

BARRY GOLDBERG REUNION Barry Goldberg—keyboards, guitar, vocal, writer; Eddie Hoh—drums; Charlie Musselwhite—harmonica; Harvey Mandel—guitar; Don McCallister—bass (1968); Ron Woods—percussion; David Hood—bass (1969). A re-formation of the Barry Goldberg Blues Band. Received AM play with the single "Hole In My Pocket," but Goldberg's name was quickly forgotten outside of blues circles shortly thereafter. *Albums:* There's No Hole in My Soul, 1968; Barry Goldberg Reunion (BUD BOS 5012).

GOLDE, FRANNIE Piano, vocal. *Albums:* Frannie (POR JR-36048) 1979; Restless (POR NJR 36594) 1980.

GOLDEN EARRING George Kooymans—guitar, vocal, writer; Rinus Gerritsen—bass, piano; Jaap Eggermont—drums (until 1970); Frans Krassenburg—vocal (until 1970); Barry Hay—vocal, flute, guitar (1970-present); Cesar Zuiderwijk—drums, percussion (1970-present); Jan Stips—keyboards (1974-76); Eelco Gelling;—guitar (1976-78). Though they sounded like the Beatles in the 1960s, it took until 1974 for Holland's Golden Earring to solidify their own identity and to achieve a nationwide hit single, "Radar Love." *Albums:* Golden Earring (CAP); Golden Earring Live (MCA 2-8009) 1977; Grab It for a Second (MCA 3057) 1978; Mad Love (MCA 2254) 1977; Moontan (MCA 2352) 1974; No Promises–No Debts (POL 1-6223) 1079; Switch (MCA 2139) 1975; To the Hilt (MCA 2183) 1976; Eight Miles High (ACO SD 8244) 1969; Golden Earring (DWF POL P2000) 1970; Hearing Earring (Import) 1973; Long Blond Animal (POL PO 1-6303) 1980; 12 Gold Bars (Import).

GOLDEN, ANNIE Vocal. Member of the Shirts, 1978-80.

GOLDEN, BOB Guitar. Member of Stillwater, 1977.

GOLDENBERG, MARK Guitar, vocal, piano. Member of the Eddie Boy Band, 1975, and the Cretones, 1980. Session for Chris Montan (1980).

GOLDFLIES, DAVE Bass. Replaced Ken Tibbets in Great Southern, 1978. Member of the Allman Brothers since 1979.

GOLDING, LYNVAL Guitar, vocal. Member of the Specials since 1979.

GOLDIRON, BILL Guitar, vocal. Member of the JTS Band, 1977.

GOLDMAN, BOB Drums. Member of the Spy, 1980.

GOLDRICH, STEVE Keyboards, vocal, percussion. Member of Gun Hill Road.

GOLDSBORO, BOBBY Vocal, guitar. Began recording with Roy Orbison's Candymen as a guitarist before entering the pop and western charts as a vocalist with "Honey." *Albums:* Gator (UAR LT-646); Bobby Goldsboro's Greatest Hits (UAR LMAS-5502); Bobby Goldsboro's 10th Anniversary Album (UAR LWS-311); Bobby Goldsboro (CRB JZ 36822) 1980; Goldsboro (EPC 34703) 1977; Summer (UAR VALA124F) 1978; Bobby Goldsboro (UAR VAS-5516) 1971.

GOLDSCHMIDT, TOMY Percussion. Member of Karthago, 1974.

GOLDSMITH, LENNY Keyboards, vocal. Member of Creation, 1974.

GOLDSMITH, LENNY LEE Vocal, percussion. Member of Stoneground.

GOLDSTEIN, ANDREW Trombone. Session for Mike Bloomfield (1978).

GOLDSTEIN, ELIJAH Kazoo. Member of the Temple City Kazoo Orchestra, 1978.

GOLDSTEIN, RICKY Drums. Replaced Mark Cain in Sham 69, 1979-80.

GOLDSTEIN, ROBERT Member of the Urban Verbs, 1980.

GOLDSTEIN, STEVE Keyboards. Member of the Bernie Leadon-Mike Georgiades Band, 1977, and Thieves, 1979.

GOLDSWAIN, ALLAN Keyboards. Member of Stingray, 1979.

GOLLIWOGS Early name for Creedence Clearwater Revival. *Album:* Golliwogs: Pre-Creedence (FSY 9474) 1975.

GOLUB, MIKE Vocal. Session for Peter C. Johnson (1980).

GOMBERTI, MICA Violin. Member of Centipede, 1971.

GOMEZ, EDDIE Member of Jerry and the Satyrs, 1967-68. *Albums:* Outlaws (ICT 3015) 1977; New Directions (ECM 1-1128) 1978.

GOMEZ, RAY Guitar, keyboards, percussion, vocal. Session for Roy Buchanan (1977). *Albums:* Sunshower (ATC 19193); Volume (COL JC-36143) 1980.

GOMEZ, TONY Organ. Member of the Foundations.

GOMM, IAN Guitar, vocal. *Album:* Gomm with the Wind (SFF JE-36103) 1979.

GONE, MICHAEL Guitar. Member of the Invaders, 1980.

GONG Didier Malherbe—saxophone, flute; Mike Howlete—bass, vocal; Mireille Bauer—percussion; Pierre Moerlin—drums, percussion; Patrick Lemoine—keyboards. *Albums:* Shamal (VIR) 1975; You (VIR) 1976; Downwind (ARI 4219) 1979; Expresso II (ARI 4204) 1978; Time Is the Key (ARI 4255) 1979; Live (ARI AB 4279) 1980.

GONSALVES, VIRGIL Saxophone, flute. Original member of the Electric Flag, 1967-68, and the Buddy Miles Express, 1968-69.

GONZALES, GERMAN Drums. Member of the Live Wire since 1979.

GOOCH, RICH Bass, vocal. Member of Sand, 1973-76.

GOOCH, STEVE Vocal, guitar. Member of the FCC, 1980.

GOOD, BILLY Guitar, piano. Member of the Panic Squad, 1980.

GOOD, BRUCE Autoharp. Session for Gordon Lightfoot (1972-80).

GOOD, LARRY Banjo. Session for Gordon Lightfoot (1972).

GOOD RATS Lenny Kotke—bass, vocal; John Gatto—guitar; Peppi Marchello—vocal; Micky Marchello—guitar, vocal; Joe Franco—drums. *Albums:* Birth Comes to Us All (PST 9830) 1978; From Rats to Riches (PST 9825) 1978; Tasty (RCR 8002) 1978; Live at Last (RCR 998) 1979.

GOODALL, LEE Saxophone. Session for the Rivets (1980).

GOODARD, PAUL Bass. Member of the Atlanta Rhythm Section since 1973.

GOODE, DENNIS Trombone. Session for J. J. Cale (1974).

GOODEN, SAMUEL Vocal. Original member of the Impressions.

GOODEN, TONY Drums. Replaced Charles Caldwell in the Søn Seals Blues Band, 1978.

GOODHAND-TAIT, PHILLIP Piano, vocal. *Albums:* Oceans Away (CYS 1113) 1976; Teaching an Old Dog New Tricks (CYS 1146) 1977.

GOODLY, RONNIE Member of Jay and the Techniques.

GOODMAN, JERRY Violin, vocal, guitar. Member of the Flock. Session for Blast (1979). *Album:* Like Children (NMP 430) 1974.

GOODMAN, SHIRLEY Vocal. Session for Dr. John (1971-72); the Rolling Stones (1972).

GOODMAN, STEVE Guitar, vocal, writer. Member of the Coral Reefer Band before going solo. *Albums:* High and Outside (ASY 6E-174) 1979; Jessie's Jig (ASY 7E-1037) 1975; Say It in Private (ASY 7E-1118) 1977; Words We Can Dance To (ASY 7E-1061) 1976; Somebody Else's Trouble; Steve Goodman; Hot Spot (ASY 6E-297) 1980.

GOODNIK, BILLY Drums. Member of Simon Stokes and the Black Whip Band, 1973.

GOODRICH, BARBIE Guitar, vocal. Member of

Skafish, 1980.

GOODROE, MICHAEL Bass. Member of the Motels, 1979-80.

GOODSALL, JOHN Guitar. Member of Brand X since 1977. Session for Wilding-Bonus (1978).

GOODSON, RONNIE Trumpet. Member of John Fred and the Playboy Band.

GOODWIN, CLIFF Guitar. Session for Joe Cocker (1978).

GOODWIN, JAMES Trumpet. Session for the Pointer Sisters.

GOODWYN, MYLES Guitar, vocal. Member of April Wine, 1976-79.

GOOGIE Half of the Googie and Tom Coppola duet, 1980.

GOOGIE AND TOM COPPOLA Tom Coppola —keyboards; Googie. *Album:* Shine the Light of Love (COL JC 36194) 1980.

GOOLIAK, BO Bass, piano. Member of Peddler, 1976.

GOOSE CREEK SYMPHONY Charlie Gearheart —vocal, guitar; Paul Spradlin—vocal, guitar; Bob Henke—guitar, vocal, keyboards; Pat Moore—bass; Ellis Schweid—fiddle; Dennis Kenmore—drums; Chris Mostert—saxophone. *Albums:* Do Your Thing, But Don't Touch Me (COL KC 3291) 1974; Goose Creek Symphony (CAP SM-444); Welcome to Goose Creek (CAP ST-690); Words of Ernest (CAP ST-11044).

GORDAN, GREG Kazoo. Member of the Temple City Kazoo Orchestra, 1978.

GORDON, BOB Bass, vocal. Original member of Nils Lofgren's Grin, 1971-73.

GORDON, BRENDA Vocal. Session for Neil Sedaka (1975).

GORDON, JIM Drums, piano, reeds. Member of the Dillards, Joe Cocker's Greatest Show On Earth, 1970, Derek and the Dominoes, 1970-72, Traffic, 1972, and the Souther-Hillman-Furay Band, 1974. Session for Delaney and Bonnie; Donovan (1973); Dr. John (1971); Dave Mason; Ben Sidran; Art Garfunkel; Carly Simon (1972); Neil Diamond (1976); Alice Cooper (1976); Waylon Jennings (1976); Freddie King (1972, 75); Gordon Lightfoot (1974-75); Randy Newman; Nilsson (1971); Eric Clapton (1970); Leon Russell (1971); Steely Dan (1974); Elvin Bishop (1972); Tim Weisberg (1973); Jack Bruce (1974); George Harrison (1972-73, 75); B. B. King (1971); John Lennon (1971); Nils Lofgren (1976); John Sebastian (1974); Gary Wright (1971); B. W. Stevenson (1973); Frank Zappa (1974); Cashman and West (1972); Seals and Crofts (1973); Steve Hunter (1976); the Band (1977); Terance Boylan (1977); Jimmy Webb (1977); Jules and the Polar Bears (1979); Rod Stewart (1980); Johnny Rivers (1980).

GORDON, JON Guitar, synthesizer, strings. Member of Tycoon.

GORDON, PETER Keyboards, reeds. Member of the Love of Life Orchestra since 1979.

GORDON, ROBERT Vocal. Rock-a-billy vocalist in the Elvis tradition backed by Link Wray and the Wildcats on his debut. *Albums:* Bad Boy (VIC AFLI-3523) 1980; Rock-A-Billy Boogie (VIC AFLI-3294) 1979; Fresh Fish Special (VIC AFLI-3299) 1979; Robert Gordon/Link Wray (VIC AFLI-3296).

GORDON, SHEP Vocal. Session for Alice Cooper (1976).

GORDON, STUART Violin. Member of the Neutrons, 1974. Session for Arthur Brown (1975).

GORDY, EMORY Bass. Session for Gram Parsons (1973); Jonathan Edwards (1976-77); Neil Diamond (1976).

GORDY, GORDON Vocal. Session for Steely Dan (1980).

GORE, LESLEY Vocal. The boy-meets-girl theme of the early 1960s was handled by Lesley Gore with such hits as "It's My Party" (1963) and "Judy's Turn To Cry" (1963). *Albums:* Lesley Gore Sings of Mixed-Up Hearts, 1963; Boys, Boys, Boys, 1964; Lesley Gore Sings All About Love, 1966; California Nights, 1967; Girl Talk, 1967; Golden Hits of Lesley Gore, Vol. 2 (MER) 1968; Golden Hits of Lesley Gore (MER 61024) 1965; I'll Cry If I Want To (MER ML-8016) 1963.

GORHAM, SCOTT Guitar. Member of Thin Lizzy.

GORIN, REX Drums. Member of Magnum, 1979.

GORKA, KENNY Bass. Member of the Critters, 1966-67.

GORMAN, DAN Drums. Member of the Yellow Payges, 1969, and Bandit, 1975.

GORMAN, JOHN Vocal, percussion. Member of Scaffold, 1968, and Grimms, 1973.

GORMAN, MIKE Bass. Member of Pezband, 1977. Replaced John Pazdan in Off Broadway, 1980.

GORMAN, TIM Keyboards, vocal. Member of Lazy Racer since 1979. Session for Tim Renwick (1980); Taxxi (1980).

GORMAN, TIMOTHY Keyboards, vocal. Member of Lazy Racer since 1979.

GORMON, BOB Guitar. Member of Fresh, 1970.

GORNALL, STEVE Guitar, vocal. Member of Paul Warren and Explorer, 1980.

GORODETZKY, CARL Violin. Session for Waylon Jennings (1975).

GORRIE, ALAN Vocal, bass. Member of the Average White Band since 1974.

GORTON, JIM Vocal, bass. Member of Snopek since 1979.

GOSA, ED Drums. Member of Captain Sky's Band since 1979.

GOSHORN, LARRY Guitar. Member of Pure Prairie League, 1975-78.

GOSHORN, TIM Guitar, vocal. Member of Pure

Prairie League, 1978.

GOSLING, JOHN Keyboards. Member of the Kinks, 1970-79.

GOSLING, PETE Guitar. Session for Wreckless Eric.

GOTHAM Gary Herb; Michael Pace; David McDaniel. *Album:* Void Where Prohibited (AVR AV0002) 1979.

GOTOBED, ROBERT Drums. Member of the Wire, 1980.

GOTTEHRER, RICHARD Piano. Session for Link Wray (1979).

GOTTHELF, ERIC Member of Wha-Koo since 1979.

GOTTHOFER, CATHERINE Harmonica. Session for Harvey Mandel.

GOTTLIEB, LARRY Bass, pedal steel guitar. Member of Liberty, 1975.

GOTTLIEB, NEIL Vocal. Member of Arthur, Hurley and Gottlieb, 1975.

GOUDREAU, BARRY Guitar, vocal, producer. Member of Boston, 1976-78. Session for Sammy Hager (1979). *Album:* Barry Goudreau (EPC NJR 36542) 1980.

GOUGEON, MARK Bass, flute. Backup for Mitch Ryder, 1978-79.

GOULD, AL Fiddle. Session for Steve Stills (1978).

GOULD, MARK Horns, keyboards. Member of Bagatelle, 1968.

GOULD, PHILIP Drums. Member of M, 1980.

GOULD, STEVE Bass, vocal. Member of Rare Bird, 1972-77, Runner, 1979, and the Alvin Lee Band, 1980. Session for Kevin Lamb (1978).

GOULDING, STEVE Percussion. Member of the Rumour, 1977. Session for Dave Edmunds (1977).

GOULDMAN, GRAHAM Bass, vocal. Member of the Mindbenders, 1966, and the Mockingbirds. He wrote "Look Through Any Window" for the Hollies, 1966, before forming 10 CC, 1974-present. Session for Neil Sedaka (1975). *Album:* Animalympics (AAM 4810) 1980.

GOWEN, ALAN Keyboards. Member of Gilgamesh, and the National Health Band, 1977.

GOWER, CHRIS Trombone. Member of the Jess Roden Band, 1976. Session for Jess Roden (1977).

GOWER, HUW Guitar, vocal. Member of the Records, 1979-80.

GOWER, RICHARD Session for Chris Spedding (1980).

GRABERT, FRED Guitar, keyboards, vocal. Member of the Wedge, 1980, and the Twisters, 1980.

GRABHAM, MICK Guitar. Replaced David Ball (who replaced Robin Trower) in Procol Harum, 1973-78. Session for Matthew Fisher (1980).

GRACE, GREG Vocal. Session for Wireless (1979).

GRACE, ROCKY Washboard, vocal. Session for Joe Walsh (1973).

GRADNEY, KEN Bass. Member of Little Feat, 1971-77. Session for Delaney and Bonnie (1970).

GRADY, GORDON Vocal. Session for Peter C. Johnson (1980).

GRAHAM, ALAN Percussion. Session for Vigrass and Osborne (1972).

GRAHAM, BILL Promoter, manager. Real name: Wolfgang Grajonka. Organizer of the Fillmore concert halls and Fillmore Records, he handled prominent San Francisco Bay Area bands of the 1960s and 1970s, like the Jefferson Airplane, Hot Tuna, the Quicksilver Messenger Service, Elvin Bishop, Lamb, Santana, and others.

GRAHAM, BILLY Fiddle. Session for Waylon Jennings (1976); Glen Campbell (1976); Mike Vernon.

GRAHAM, BRYSON Drums. Member of Mainhorse, 1971. Replaced Mike Kellie in Spooky Tooth, 1974-75. Session for John "Rabbit" Bundrick (1974); Alvin Lee (1975).

GRAHAM, DAVID Bass. Member of Fischer-Z since 1979.

GRAHAM, DAVY Guitar. Member of Blues Incorporated. Session for Alexis Korner and Cyril Davies (1954-61).

GRAHAM, ERNIE Bass. Member of Eire Apparent, 1969.

GRAHAM, LARRY Bass, vocal. Member of Sly and the Family Stone before forming Graham Central Station and going solo. *Albums:* My Radio Sure Sounds Good to Me (WBR K-3175); One in a Million You (WBR BSK-3447) 1980; Star Walk (WBR K-3322).

GRAHAM, MIKE Guitar. Member of the Subhumans, 1979.

GRAHAM, NICK Bass, keyboards, flute, vocal. Member of Skin Alley, 1973, and Alibi, 1980.

GRAILLIER, MICHEL Piano. Member of Magma.

GRAINGER, GARY Guitar. Member of Strider, 1973, and the Rod Stewart Band since 1978. Session for Rod Stewart (1977).

GRAJONKA, WOLFGANG Real name of Bill Graham.

GRAMM, LOU Voice of Foreigner since 1977. Session for Ian Lloyd (1979).

GRAMMATICO, BENNY Drums. Session for Gilda Radner (1979).

GRAMMATICO, LOUIS Vocal. Voice of Black Sheep, 1975.

GRAMOLINI, JOEL Guitar, vocal. Member of Southside Johnny and the Asbury Jukes, 1979-present.

GRANATI, DAVID Guitar, bass, vocal. Member of the Granati Brothers, 1979.

GRANATI, HERMIE Keyboards, bass, vocal. Member of the Granati Brothers, 1979.

GRANATI, JOEY Keyboards, bass, vocal. Member of the Granati Brothers, 1979.

GRANATI, RICKY Drums, percussion, vocal. Member of the Granati Brothers, 1979.

GRANATI BROTHERS Hermie Granati—keyboards, bass, vocal; Ricky Granati—drums, percussion, vocal; David Granati—guitar, bass, vocal; Joey Granati—keyboards, bass, vocal; Tommy Lee Bonomo—drums, percussion, vocal. *Album:* G Force (AAM 4748) 1979.

GRAND FUNK RAILROAD Don Brewer—drums, vocal, writer; Mark Farner—guitar, keyboards, vocal, writer; Mel Schacher—bass; Craig Frost—keyboards, vocal, writer (1974-77). Formula band that weathered critical abuse by keeping a constant eye upon the marketability of their music package. Disbanded in 1977. See Flint and Mark Farner. *Albums:* All the Girls in the World Beware (CAP SO 11356) 1975; Shinin' On (CAP SWAE 11278) 1974; Born to Die (CAP) 1975; Caught in the Act (CAP SABB 11445); Closer to Home (CAP SKAO-471) 1970; E Pluribus Funk (CAP SW-853) 1971; Grand Funk (CAP SKAO-406); Grand Funk Hits (CAP SN-12010) 1976; Live Album (CAP SWBB-633); Mark, Don and Mel—1969-71 (CAP SABB-11042) 1972; On Time (CAP ST-307); Phoenix (CAP SMAS-11099) 1973; Survival (CAP SW-764); We're an American Band (CAP SMAS-11207) 1973.

GRANDA, MICHAEL Bass, vocal, percussion. Original member of the Ozark Mountain Daredevils, 1973-75, 1980.

GRANDE, JOHN Member of Bill Haley and the Comets.

GRANDMOTHERS Don Preston—keyboards; Jimmy Carl Black—drums, vocal; Bunk Gardner—reeds, vocal; Elliot Ingber—guitar; Buzz Gardner—horns; James Sherwood—saxophone. Mothers of Invention alumni. *Album:* The Grandmothers (RHI 302) 1980.

GRANDO, RICHARD Reeds. Member of Gasmask.

GRANGE, ROB Bass. Member of the re-formed Amboy Dukes, 1974, and Ted Nugent's side man, 1975-78. Member of St. Paradise, 1979.

GRANMAX Tim McCorkle—bass, vocal; Steve Meyers—guitar, vocal; Lewis McCorkle—drums. *Album:* A Ninth Alive (PAN 1001) 1976.

GRANT, BARRY Guitar. Member of Sunship, 1974.

GRANT, GARY Horns. Session for Jerry Corbetta (1978); the Marshall Tucker Band (1979).

GRANT, GORDON Keyboards. Member of Mephistopheles.

GRANTHAM, GEORGE Drums, vibes, vocal. Member of Poco. Session for Jonathan Edwards (1973).

GRAPPELLI, STEPHANE Violin. Established jazz artist. Session for Paul Simon (1972). *Albums:* Django '35-'39 (CRS 9019) 1976; Fascinating Rhythm (ANG 37156); Stephane Grappelli (EVR 311); Stephane Grappelli and Bill Coleman (CLI 24) 1976; Homage to Django (CLI 23); Jalousie—Music of the '30s (ANG 36968); Pablo Live—Tivoli Gardens (PAB 2308220); Paris Encounter (ATC 1597); Parisian Swing (CRS 9002); Parisian Thoroughfare (ARI 1033); Oscar Peterson, Featuring Stephane Grappelli (PRS 24041); Jean-Luc Ponty and Stephane Grappelli (ICT 1005) 1976; QHCF/Reinhardt/Grappelli (ANG 36985); The Reunion (PAU 7049); Satin Doll (VAN VSD-81/82) 1975; Strictly for the Birds (ANG DS-37710); Tea for Two (ANG SQ-37533); Uptown Dance (COL JC-35415) 1978; Violin Summit (EVR 355); Young Django (PAU 7041); Afternoon in Paris (MPS 20876).

GRASS ROOTS Rick Coonce—drums, percussion; Rob Grill—bass; Warren Entner—guitar; Dennis Provisor—keyboards; Terry Furlong—guitar. Early name: the Thirteenth Floor. The success of "Midnight Confessions" in the 1960s only confirmed the fact that the Roots had accumulated a large, loyal following. *Albums:* Alotta Mileage (DHL X-50137); Big Hits Now (DHL 50047); Feelings (DHL 50027); Golden Grass (DHL 50047); Leaving It All Behind (DHL 50067); Let's Live for Today (DHL 50020); Lovin' Things (DHL 50052); More Golden Grass (DHL 50087); Move Along (DHL X-50112); Original Hits of Right Now (DHL 50070); Their 16 Greatest Hits (DHL X-50107); Where Were You When I Needed You.

GRASSEL, DOUGLAS Guitar. Member of the Ohio Express, 1968-69.

GRASSI, CHRIS Drums. Member of Pam Windo and the Shades, 1980.

GRASSO, CHERIE Vocal. Member of Root Boy Slim and the Sex Change Band, 1978.

GRATEFUL DEAD Jerry Garcia—guitar, vocal, pedal steel guitar, piano, writer; Phil Lesh—bass, piano, writer; Ron "Pig Pen" McKernan—percussion, harmonica, vocal (1967-73); Bob Weir—guitar, writer; Mickey Hart—drums, percussion; Bill Kruetzman—drums; Tom Constantan—organ; Robert Hunter—writer; Bill Sommers—drums; Keith Godchaux—piano (1972-80); Donna Godchaux—vocals (1972-present). Peace in Ashbury in the 1960s was musically accommodated with free concerts by the Dead. While their reputation grew in the drug-oriented culture, so did their music, which was very much rooted in the blues, and expanded into the realms of progressive rock and jazz (with compositions and improvisations lasting over 30 minutes) and country. The loyalty of Dead fans is unequaled by any group's following. Part of Fillmore, 1972. *Albums:* American Beauty (WBR 1893) 1970; Anthem of the Sun (WBR 1749) 1968; Aoxomoxoa (WBR 1790) 1971; Best of Grateful Dead — Skeletons from the Closet (WBR 2764) 1974; Blues for Allah (GRD LO-494) 1975; Europe '72 (WBR 3WX-2668) 1972; Go to Heaven (ARI 9508) 1980; Grateful Dead (WBR 1689) 1967; Grateful Dead (WBR 1935)

1971; Grateful Dead from the Mars Hotel (GRD 102) 1974; History of the Grateful Dead—Vol. 1 (WBR B-2721) 1973; Live/Dead (WBR 1830); Shakedown Street (ARI 4198) 1978; Steal Your Face (GRD LWB-620) 1976; Terrapin Station (ARI 7001); Wake of the Flood (GRD 01) 1979; What a Long, Strange Trip It's Been (WBR 2W-3091) 1977; Working Man's Dead (WBR 1869) 1970.

GRATTON, RICK Drums. Session for Long John Baldry (1980).

GRATZER, ALAN Drums. Member of REO Speedwagon, 1972-present.

GRAVATT, ERIC Drums. Born 11/9/48. Member of Weather Report, 1972-present, replacing Alphonze Mouzon.

GRAVEL, JEAN Guitar, vocal. Member of Offenbach, 1976.

GRAVENITES, NICK Vocal, guitar. Original member of the Electric Flag, 1967-68. Session for Big Brother and the Holding Company; Janis Joplin (1969); Mike Bloomfield (1977-78).

GRAVES, JOSH Dobro. Session for J. J. Cale (1972).

GRAVES, PETER Trombone. Member of the Boneroos. Session for Bill Wyman (1974).

GRAVES, TOM Keyboards, vocal. Member of the Five Dollar Shoes, 1972.

GRAY, ANDY Guitar, vocal. Member of the Panic Squad, 1980.

GRAY, CHAS Synthesizer. Member of the Wall of Voodoo, 1980.

GRAY, DIVA Vocal. Session for the Marshall Tucker Band (1980); Ray Gomez (1980); Steely Dan (1980). *Album:* Hotel Paradise (COL NJC-36265).

GRAY, DOBIE Vocal, percussion. Member of Pollution, 1971. *Albums:* Dobie Gray (INF 9016); Greatest Hits of Dobie Gray (PPK 313); Midnight Diamond (INF 9001); New Ray of Sunshine (CPN CP 0163) 1975.

GRAY, DOUG Vocal, percussion. Voice of the Marshall Tucker Band, 1973-present.

GRAY, PAUL Bass. Member of Eddie and the Hot Rods, 1976.

GRAY, TOM Keyboards, vocal. Member of the Brains, 1980.

GRAYDON, JAY Guitar, string arranger, producer. Produced Steve Kipner, 1979. Session for Joe Cocker (1974); Jennifer Warnes (1976); Terance Boylan (1977); Pakalameredith (1977); Lee Ritenour (1977-78); Jerry Corbetta (1978); Flora Purim (1978); the Marc Tanner Band (1979); Roger Voudouris (1979); Alan O'Day (1979).

GREASE BAND Henry McCullough—guitar, vocal, writer; Neil Hubbard—guitar; Alan Spenner—bass, vocal; Bruce Rowland—drums, percussion; Chris Stainton—keyboards. One of the first bands to record on Leon Russell's Shelter records, the Grease Band achieved their fame as the backup band for Joe Cocker in his rise to fame. As a solo band, they did not fare as well. *Album:* Grease Band (SHR SHE 8904) 1971.

GREAT SOCIETY Grace Slick—vocal; Darby Slick—guitar; Jerry Slick—drums; David Minor—guitar; Peter Vandegilder—bass. The explosion of psychedelic sound from San Francisco in the 1960s had been nurtured in groups such as the Great Society. A family affair, Grace Slick left it in 1965 to join the Jefferson Airplane. Only in retrospect did the Great Society become nationally known. *Albums:* Conspicuous Only in Its Absence; How It Was (COL) 1968.

GREAT SOUTHERN "Dangerous" Dan Toler—guitar, vocal; Ken Tibbets—bass (1977); Tom Broome—keyboards (1977); Jerry Thompson—drums (1977); Doni Sharbono—drums; Dave Goldflies—bass (1978); David Toler—drums (1978); Topper Price—harmonica (1978); Michael Workman—keyboards, vocal (1978). Backup band for Richard Betts, 1977-78.

GREATEST SHOW ON EARTH Leon Russell—vocal, keyboards, guitar; Chris Stainton—keyboards; Don Preston—guitar, vocal; Carl Radle—bass; Jim Gordon—drums; Jim Keltner—drums; Chris Blackwell—drums, percussion; Bobby Torres—congas; Jim Price—trumpet; Bobby Keys—tenor saxophone. Choir: Rita Coolidge, Claudia Linnear, Daniel Moore, Donna Weiss, Pam Pollard, Matt Moore, Donna Washburn, Nicol Barklay, Bobby Jones. Joe Cocker's traveling show of 1970.

GREATEST SHOW ON EARTH Colin Horton-Jennings—vocal, flute, guitar; Garth Watt-Roy—vocal, guitar; Norman Watt-Roy—vocal, bass; Mick Deacon—keyboards, vocal; Ron Prudence—percussion; Dick Hanson—horns, percussion; Tex Phillpotts—saxophone, percussion; Ian Aitchison—saxophone, percussion. *Album:* The Going's Easy (Import) 1970.

GREAVES, JOHN Bass, piano. Member of Henry Cow, 1973.

GREBB, MARTY Keyboards, saxophone, bass, vocal, guitar. Member of the Fabulous Rhinestones, 1972-73, and the Tufana-Giamarese Band, 1973-77. Replaced Dennis Miccoli in the Buckinghams. Session for Leon Russell (1979); Willie Nelson and Leon Russell (1979).

GRECH, RICK Bass, violin. Member of Family, 1968, before joining Steve Winwood, Eric Clapton and Ginger Baker in Blind Faith, 1969. Member of Ginger Baker's Air Force, 1970-71, KGB, 1975, Traffic, 1972, and the Crickets, 1973. Session for the Rainbow Concert (1973); Muddy Waters (1972); the Bee Gees (1973); Rod Stewart (1974); Ginger Baker. *Album:* Five Long Years (ACO) 1972.

GREEDUS, PAUL Vocal, keyboards, guitar, percussion. Member of Javaroo.

GREELY, MATT Percussion, vocal. Added to the Sea Level lineup, 1980. Session for Robbie Robertson (1980).

GREEN, AL Vocal. Born 4/13/46. Rhythm and blues vocalist on the pop charts since the 1960s. *Albums:* Belle Album (HIR 6004) 1977; Al Green's Greatest Hits (HIR 32089) 1975; Al Green's Greatest Hits, Vol. 2 (HIR 32105) 1977; Green Is Blues (HIR 32055); Have a Good Time (HIR 32103) 1976; I'm Still in Love with You (HIR X-32074); Let's Stay Together (HIR 8007); Love Ritual (LON PS-710) 1978; Stardiscs (LON BP-704); Tired of Being Alone (HIR 8000); Truth 'n' Time (HIR 6009) 1978.

GREEN, CHRIS Cello. Session for Chris Spedding (1980).

GREEN, CLARENCE Member of Hank Ballard's backup group, the Midnighters.

GREEN, COLIN Guitar. Session for Elton John (1969); Alan Price (1973).

GREEN, DAN Guitar. Member of Kenny and the Kasuals.

GREEN, DANNY Guitar, harmonica, vocal. *Album:* Night Dog (MCA 1085) 1978.

GREEN, EUNICE Vocal. Session for Ginger Baker (1977).

GREEN, FREDERICK Vocal. Original member of Sha Na Na, since 1970.

GREEN, GARY Guitar. Member of Gentle Giant, 1970-present.

GREEN, GUITAR SLIM Vocal, guitar, piano. Real name: James Stephenson. Over 60 years old, Guitar Slim still plays weekly for local house parties in his native North Carolina, and at church. *Album:* Guitar Slim Green's Stone Down Blues (KNT 549).

GREEN, JACK Guitar, vocal. *Album:* Humanesque (VIC AFLI 1-3639) 1980.

GREEN, JEROME Percussion. Member of Chuck Berry and his Combo, 1955.

GREEN, JOE Vocal. Session for the Rolling Stones (1972).

GREEN, JOEL Bass. Session for J. J. Cale (1974).

GREEN, KARL Guitar, harmonica. Member of Herman's Hermits, 1965-68.

GREEN, KELLY Vocal, percussion. Member of Frijid Pink, 1970-71.

GREEN, MALCOLM Drums. Member of the Split Enz.

GREEN, MARC Keyboards. Session for the Marc Tanner Band (1980).

GREEN, MICHAEL Horns, percussion, vocal. Member of Sod, 1971.

GREEN, MICK Guitar. Member of the Pirates.

GREEN, PETER Guitar, harmonica, vocal, writer. Born 10/29/46. Replaced Eric Clapton in John Mayall's Bluesbreakers, 1967, where he developed a reputation of being the finest blues guitarist in England. In 1967 he left to form Fleetwood Mac, which he molded into the premier British blues band. As the years progressed, so did Green's guitar playing and before he left in 1969 (to devote more time to religious activity), he was bordering on jazz. After his departure, he did release a solo album which was entirely jazz oriented, before successfully disappearing from the rock scene. His blues based style dominated his recorded reappearance in 1979. Session for Jeremy Spencer (1970); Duster Bennett (1968); the Aynsley Dunbar Retaliation; B. B. King (1971); Memphis Slim (1971). *Albums:* End of the Game (REP RS 6436) 1970; In the Skies (SAL 0110) 1979; Little Dreamer (SAL 0112) 1980.

GREEN, ROBERT Vocal. Session for Robert Gordon (1979).

GREEN, WILLIAM Saxophone. Session for Nilsson (1976).

GREEN, WILLIE, JR. Vocal. Session for Ry Cooder (1980).

GREENBERG, CHUCK Saxophone, flute, clarinet. Member of Shadowfax, 1976.

GREENBERG, PETER Guitar. Member of DMZ, 1978.

GREENBERG, PHIL Vocal, guitar, writer. Member of Formerly Fat Harry, 1971.

GREENE, ALAN Guitar. Member of Breathless, 1980.

GREENE, CALVIN Member of Hank Ballard's Midnighters.

GREENE, DAVE Vocal, guitar, banjo. Member of Shoot, 1973.

GREENE, EDDIE Drums. Session for Sonny Terry and Brownie McGhee (1973); Greg Sutton (1979); Seals and Crofts (1976); Glen Campbell (1976); Phoebe Snow (1976); B. B. King (1977); Jeff Beck (1976); Small Wonder (1977); Far Cry (1980); Terence Boylan (1977); Bobby Caldwell (1978); Commander Cody (1978); Adrian Gurvitz (1979); Jim Capaldi (1979); Cher Bono (1979).

GREENE, FRANK Lyricist. Lyricist for the Stanky Brown Group, 1975-77.

GREENE, JEANIE Vocal. Session for Bangla Desh (1971); Boz Scaggs (1969); Willie Nelson (1974).

GREENE, JOSEPH Vocal. Session for Bangla Desh (1971); Ringo Starr (1973-74); Neil Diamond (1976).

GREENE, MARILYN Vocal. Session for Bangla Desh (1971).

GREENE, MIKE Vocal, keyboards, reeds, percussion. Namesake of the Mike Greene Band, 1975-76.

MIKE GREENE BAND Mike Greene—vocal, keyboards, reeds, percussion; David Michael—guitar; Rande Powell—drums; Mike Holbrook—bass. *Albums:* Pale, Pale Moon (GRC GA 10013) 1975; Midnight Mirage (MER SRM 1-1100) 1976.

GREENE, RICHARD Violin. Began in Jim Kweskin's Jug Band before becoming a member of the

Blues Project, 1966-68. Member of Seatrain, 1968. Session for Pearls Before Swine (1969); Gene Clark (1974); Maria Muldaur (1973); Jonathan Edwards (1977); Rod Stewart (1977); Peter Rowan (1978).

GREENFIELD, DAVE Keyboards, vocal. Member of the Stranglers.

GREENHILL, MITCH Vocal. Session for Ry Cooder (1980).

GREENHOUSE, MARK Vocal. Session for Bill Blue (1980).

GREENIDGE, ROBERT Steel drums. Session for Nilsson (1975-76); Bill Wyman (1976); Taj Mahal (1977-78); John Lennon (1980).

GREENSLADE, DAVE Keyboards, vocal. Original member of Colosseum, 1968-71, and founder of Greenslade.

GREENSLADE Andrew McCulloch—drums; Dave Lawson—keyboards; Dave Greenslade—guitar; Tony Reeves—bass. Rock-jazz venture from former Colosseum member, Greenslade. *Albums:* Time and Tide (MER SRM 1-1025); Greenslade; Spyglass Guest (WBR K 56055).

GREENSPOON, JIMMY Keyboards. Member of Three Dog Night. Session for Free Creek (1973); Kim Fowley; Beck, Bogert and Appice (1973).

GREENWAY, BRIAN Guitar, vocal. Member of the Dudes, 1975, and April Wine, 1976-79.

GREENWICH, ELLIE Vocal. Session for Henry Gross (1976).

GREENWOOD, AL Keyboards, synthesizer. Member of Foreigner, 1977-80.

GREENWOOD, CHICO Drums. Original member of Moonrider, 1975.

GREENWOOD, NICK Bass, vocal. Member of Khan, 1972.

GREER, KEN Vocal, guitar, keyboards. Member of Red Rider, 1980.

GREER, MARETTA Vocal. Session for the Fugs (1967).

GREER, ROB Bass. Member of the New Commander Cody Band, 1977.

GREETHAM, CHARLES Saxophone. Session for Aynsley Dunbar (1970).

GREEZY WHEELS Tony Airoldi—guitar, vocal; Mary Egan—fiddle, vocal; Cleve Hattersley—guitar, vocal; Lissa Hattersley—mandolin, vocal; Tony Laier—drums; Pat Pankratz—guitar, vocal; Mike Pugh—bass; Madrile Wilson, Jr.—percussion. *Album:* Radio Radials (LON) 1976.

GREGG, BOBBY Drums. Session for Barry Goldberg (1969).

GREGG, BRUCE Horns. Session for Long John Baldry (1980).

GREGORIO, MIKE Vocal, organ. Member of the Brooklyn Bridge.

GREGORY, BILLY Guitar. Replaced Hal Wagenett in It's a Beautiful Day, 1971-72.

GREGORY, BRIAN Guitar. Member of the Cramps, 1980.

GREGORY, DAVE Guitar, vocal. Replaced Barry Andrews in XTC, 1978 to present.

GREGORY, JIM Bass. Member of the Five Dollar Shoes, 1972, and Jobraith, 1973-74.

GREGORY, JOHN Vocal, guitar. Member of the Blues Project, 1966-68, and Seatrain, 1968.

GREGORY, STEVE Tenor saxophone, flute. Member of the Alan Price Set, 1965-68. Session for Chicken Shack; Freddie King (1974-75); Jeremy Spencer (1970).

GREGSON, CLIVE Vocal, guitar, keyboards. Member of Any Trouble, 1980.

GRENNAN, WINSTON Drums. Session for Paul Simon (1972).

GRESHAM, DOYLE Pedal steel guitar. Member of the Coral Reefer Band.

GRETMAR, DON Bass, saxophone. Member of Blues Project, 1966-68, before replacing Andy Musar in Seatrain, 1968.

GREY, PAUL Bass. Member of the Damned, 1980.

GREY, STEVE Keyboards. Session for Olivia Newton-John (1976).

GRIERSON, RALPH Synthesizer. Session for Robbie Robertson (1980).

GRIFF, ZAINE Vocal, bass. *Album:* Ashes and Diamonds (WBR BSK 3488) 1980.

GRIFFIN, BILL Vocal. Member of Smokey Robinson and the Miracles.

GRIFFIN, BOB Piano. Session for Jim Capaldi (1971).

GRIFFIN, DALE Drums. Original member of Mott the Hoople, 1969-77, and British Lions, 1978.

GRIFFIN, JAMES Bass, vocal. Member of Bread.

GRIFFIN, PAUL Organ, piano. Session for Paul Simon (1973); Bob Dylan (1974); Steely Dan (1976).

GRIFFIN, THOM Guitar, vocal. Replaced Dennis Fredericksen in Trillion, 1980.

GRIFFITH, FRED Vocal. Member of Bagatelle, 1968.

GRIFFITH, JOHN Organ. Session for the Temptations (1973).

GRIFFITHS, CLIVE Bass. Member of Patto, 1970-72, and Timebox, 1976.

GRIFFITHS, DEREK Guitar, vocal, writer. Original member of Dog Soldier, 1975. Session for Mike Vernon; Chuck Berry (1972); Chris Youlden (1974).

GRIFFITHS, JIM Guitar, vocal. Member of Crack the Sky, 1975-77.

GRIFFITHS, MARCIA Vocal. Member of I Threes.

GRIFFITHS, MARK Guitar. Member of Matthew's Southern Comfort.

GRIGGS, CHRISTY Vocal. Session for Johnny Winter (1980).

GRIGGS, NIGEL Bass. Member of the Split Enz.

GRIGSBY, EARL Bass. Member of the Charlie Daniels Band, 1972.

GRILL, ROB Member of the Grass Roots. *Album:* Rob Grill (MER SRM 1-3798) 1979.

GRIMALDI, JIM Guitar. Replaced Russ Ballard in Argent, 1975.

GRIMES, TY Drums, percussion. Member of Captain Beefheart and His Magic Band, 1974, and the Stone Canyon Band. Replaced Marty Foltz in Tim Weisberg's backup group in 1975.

GRIMM, STEVE Guitar, vocal. Member of Bad Boy

GRIMMS John Megginson—piano, bass; Michael Giles—drums; Neil Innes—piano, guitar; Zoot Money—piano, guitar; Adrian Henri—vocal, percussion; Brian Patten—vocal, percussion; Roger McGough—vocal, percussion; Michael McGear—vocal, percussion. Grimms had talent and big names (Money from the Animals, and McGear, Paul McCartney's brother), but no audience in the U.S. *Album:* Grimms (ISL) 1973.

GRIN Nils Lofgren—guitar, keyboards, vocal, writer; Bob Gordon—bass, vocal; Bob Berberich—drums, vocal; Tom Lofgren—guitar. After associating with David Briggs and Neil Young, in Crazy Horse, Nils Lofgren formed the rocking trio, Grin, that could compete with any major group, and dedicated their first album to guitar virtuoso Roy Buchanan. Nils Lofgren dissolved the group in 1973 and started his solo career in 1975. *Albums:* 1 & 1; All Out; Gone Crazy (AAM 4415) 1973; Grin (SZY Z-30321).

GRINDELL, SUSAN Vocal. Session for Rod Stewart (1980).

GRINDERSWITCH Dru Lombar—guitar, vocal; Joe Dan Petty—bass, vocal; Larry Howard—guitar, vocal; Rick Burnett—drums, percussion; Steve Miller—keyboards (1977). *Albums:* Redwing (ACO 152) 1977; Macon Track (CAP) 1975; Honest to Goodness (CAP) 1974.

GRINDLE, STEVE Bass, vocal. Member of the Moberlys, 1979.

GRINEL, RON Drums. Replaced Jim Gordon in the Souther-Hillman-Furay Band, 1975. Member of Fool's Gold, 1976. Session for Joe Walsh (1974).

GRINGO Casey—vocal; Simon Byrne—drums, vocal; Henry Marsh—guitar, keyboards, vocal; John Perry—bass, vocal. *Album:* Gringo (MCA 75314) 1971.

GRINNELL, JEFF Keyboards, vocal. Member of No Slack, 1978.

GRINSTED, DAVID Percussion. Member of Caravan, 1971-73.

GRISMAN, DAVE Mandolin, piano, saxophone, vocal. Member of Earth Opera, 1968-69. Session for Martin Mull (1973); James Taylor (1976); Jonathan Edwards (1976); the Pointer Sisters (1974); Maria Muldaur (1973). *Albums:* David Grisman Quintet '80 (WBR BSK-3469); David Grisman Rounder Album (RND 0069); Hot Dawg (AAM 731) 1979; Early Dawg (SGH 3713) 1980; David Grisman Quintet (KAL) 1977; Rockin' Duck (ANT 7012) 1976.

GROLNICK, DAN Keyboards. Session for Steely Dan (1976, 80); Ringo Starr (1977); Boz Scaggs (1980); Paul Simon (1980).

GROMBACHER, MYRON Drums. Replaced Glen Alexander Hamilton in Pat Benatar's backup band, 1980.

GRONDIN, JACK Drums, percussion. Member of 38 Special, 1977.

GRONENTHAL, MAX Keyboards, vocal. Session for Les Dudek (1978); Rod Stewart (1978); Molly Hatchett (1979); the Marc Tanner Band (1979); the Dudek-Finnigan-Kruger Band (1980); Elton John (1980). *Albums:* Max (CYS 1278); Whistling in the Dark (CYS 1231).

GROOM, MICK Bass, vocal. Replaced Andy McMasters in Ducks Deluxe, 1975. Session for Sean Tyla (1980).

GROPP, JERRY Guitar. Member of the Waylors. Session for Waylon Jennings (1973).

GROSS, DAVID Saxophone. Member of Gasmask.

GROSS, HENRY Guitar, vocal, writer. An original member of Sha Na Na in 1970, he achieved individual fame in 1976 with "Shannon." *Albums:* Release (LFS 6002) 1976; Show Me to the State (LFS LS 6010) 1977; Plug Me Into Something (AAM 4502) 1975; Henry Gross (ABC X-747); Henry Gross (AAM SP 4416) 1973; Love Is the Stuff (LFS JZ 35280) 1978.

GROSSMAN, ALBERT Manager. Managed Bob Dylan, Gordon Lightfoot, Peter, Paul and Mary, Janis Joplin, Big Brother and the Holding Company, the Band, Richie Havens, Odetta, Paul Butterfield, and others.

GROSSMAN, RICHARD Bass, vocal. Member of Helmet Boy, 1980.

GROSSMAN, SEVERIN Bass. Member of Willie Alexander's Boom Boom Band, 1978-79.

GROSSMAN, STEFAN Bottleneck guitar. Session for Paul Simon (1972). *Album:* Perspective (ATC 19230).

GROSVENOR, LUTHER Guitar, vocal, writer, producer, bass. Founder of Art, 1967, which changed its name to Spooky Tooth, 1968-71. Formed Widowmaker in 1976 under his assumed name, Ariel Bender. See Ariel Bender. Session for Mike Harrison (1972). *Album:* Under Open Skies (ISL SMAS 9312).

GROTH, MICHAEL Member of Trickster, 1979.

GROUCUTT, KELLY Bass, vocal. Member of the Electric Light Orchestra since 1974.

GROUNDHOGS Tony McPhee—guitar, vocal, writer; Steve Rye—vocal, harmonica (1968); Pete Cruikshank—bass (1968-74); Ken Pustelnik—drums (1968-72); Clive Brooks—drums, percussion (1972-74); Martin Kent—bass (1976); Mick Cook—drums (1976); Dave Wellbelove—guitar

(1976); Rick Adams—guitar (1976). In the 1960s McPhee was an English acoustic blues man, singing old American blues before forming the Groundhogs (first called John Lee's Groundhogs, after John Lee Hooker) with Steve Rye, of similar inclinations. In 1969, Rye dropped from the group and McPhee signaled his departure from the blues on "Blues Obituary." The focal point of the group in future years was the dynamic electricity of McPhee. After disappearing for two years, McPhee resurfaced with a new Groundhogs in 1976 for two albums before he dropped from sight once again. *Albums:* Scratching the Surface (LIB 83199E) 1968; Blues Obituary (LIB LP 12452) 1969; Thank Christ for the Bomb (LIB LST 7644) 1970; Split (UAR UAS 5513) 1971; Who Will Save the World (UAR UAS 5570) 1972; Hogwash (UAR UA LA008F) 1972; Cross Cut Saw (UAR UA LA605G) 1976; Black Diamond (UAR UA LA680G) 1976; Solid (Import) 1974.

GROUP 87 Patrick O'Hearn—bass; Peter Maunn—guitar, keyboards, violin; Mark Isham—keyboards, electronics. *Album:* Group 87 (COL JC-36338) 1980.

GROUP IMAGE Dr. Hok—guitar; Freddy Knuckles—guitar; William Merrill—guitar; Doug Black—bass; Leon Rix—drums; Sheila Darla—vocal. A New York multi-media community of 1968. *Album:* A Mouth in the Clouds.

GROVES, LANI Vocal. Session for Johnny Winter (1973); Rick Derringer (1973); Carly Simon (1974); the Pages (1978); Henry Gross (1978); Golden Earring (1978); Paul Simon (1980); Ray Gomez (1980); Steely Dan (1980).

GROWL Mick Small—guitar; Dennis Rodriguez—vocal; Richard Manuputi—vocal; Danny McBride—drums; Harry Brandis—guitar, vocal; Gene Lucero—bass. *Album:* Growl (DIS) 1974.

GRUBER, CRAIG Bass. Original member of Ritchie Blackmore's Rainbow, 1975.

GRUEN, PETER Drums, percussion. Member of Point Blank, 1976.

GRUMBACHER, MYRON Drums. Session for Pat Benatar (1980); Rick Derringer.

GRUNDY, ED Bass. Member of Bloodrock.

GRUNDY, HUGH Drums. Member of the Zombies, 1965-68.

GRUPP, PAUL Percussion. Session for the Ozark Mountain Daredevils (1980).

GRUPPO SPORTIVO Eric Wehrmeyer—bass; Hans Vandenburg—guitar, vocal; Max Mollinger—drums, vocal; Josee Van Iersel—vocal; Peter Caucher—keyboards, vocal; Meike Tonw—vocal. *Album:* Mistakes (SIR K 6066) 1978.

GRUSHECKY, JOE Vocal, guitar. Member of the Iron City Houserockers since 1979.

GRUSIN, DAVE Horns. Session for Paul Simon (1980).

GUARD, DAVE Original member of the Kingston Trio, 1958-64.

GUARNERI, MARIO Coronet. Session for Ry Cooder (1978).

GUENTHER, IAN Violin. Member of Emigre, 1979.

GUERCIO, JAMES WILLIAM Guitar, producer. Former member of the Mothers of Invention. Produced the Buckinghams (1967); Chicago (since 1968); and others. Session for the Souther-Hillman-Furay Band (1975).

GUERIN, JOHN Drums. Member of Hammer, 1970, Tom Scott's L. A. Express, and Neil Norman's Cosmic Orchestra, 1975, 1980. Session for Art Garfunkel; Frank Zappa (1967, 69, 70, 74); Joni Mitchell (1975); Seals and Crofts (1973); David Blue (1975).

GUERRA, JOEY Keyboards, vocal. Member of Tierra, 1980.

GUERRERO, MARK Vocal, guitar, keyboards. Member of Tango, 1974.

GUESS WHO Randy Bachman—guitar, vocal, writer (until 1972); Burton Cummings—vocal, keyboards, writer (until 1976); Jim Kale—bass; Gary Peterson; Kurt Winter; Dominic Troiano—guitar, vocal (1972-76); Greg Leskin—guitar (1972); Bill Wallace; David Inglis—guitar (1979); Vance Masters—vocal, drums (1979); Don McDougall—vocal, guitar (1979). Canadian rock group that served as the starting point for Randy Bachman. Recorded "American Woman," 1969. When Bachman left to form Brave Belt (and later Bachman-Turner Overdrive), Cummings assumed control and kept the group familiar to underground and AM audiences. *Albums:* Artificial Paradise (VIC) 1973; Canned Wheat (VIC ANLI-0983); Flavours (VIC APDI-0636) 1974; Guess Who–Live at the Paramount (VIC LSP 4779) 1972; No. 10 (VIC APDI 0130) 1973; Road Food (VIC APDI 0405); Share the Land (VIC LSP 4359); Wheatfield Soul (VIC LSP 4141); All This for a Song (HTK 19227) 1979; American Woman (VIC AYLI-3673) 1969; Best of the Guess Who (VIC AYLI 3662) 1971; Greatest of the Guess Who (VIC AFLI-2253) 1977; Power in the Music, 1975; The Way We Were, 1976; Rockin', 1972; Best of the Guess Who, Vol. II (VIC AFLI 7066) 1979.

GUEST, LYNTON Organ. Original member of Love Affair.

GUEST, WILLIAM Vocal. Original member of Gladys Knight and the Pips.

GUEVARA, RUBEN Vocal, percussion. Namesake of Ruben and the Jets, 1973.

GUFFEY, BILL Keyboards. Member of Shooting Star, 1979.

GUIDRY, BONNIE Vocal. Member of White Lightnin', 1978.

GUILBEAU, GIB Guitar, mandolin, fiddle, vocal. Replaced Chris Hillman in the Flying Burrito Brothers. Session for Crazy Horse (1971). *Albums:*

Gib Guilbeau (ALS 5355); Gib Guilbeau Sings (ALS 5287); Toe Tappin' Music (SLD SLP 4085).

GUILBEAU, PHILLIP Trumpet. Session for Joe Cocker (1978).

GUILIANO, TOM Vocal. Member of the Happenings.

GUILLORY, ISAAC Guitar. Session for Donovan, (1977).

GUISHARD, JEFFREY Percussion. Member of Hi Tension, 1978.

GUITAR BUDDY Guitar. Session with Fleetwood Mac (1969).

GUITAR SLIM Guitar, vocal. Real name: Eddie Jones. Born in Mississippi, 1926. Died 1959. Recorded "The Things I Used to Do," 1954.

GULDBACK, JAN Drums. Member of Blue Swede.

GULILLEROY, ADRIAN Member of Jeremy and the Satyrs, 1967-68.

GULLEY, DENNIS Vocal, guitar, keyboards. Member of Jackson Highway.

GULLEY, RUSSELL Bass, vocal. Member of Jackson Highway.

GULLICKSON, GRANT Vocal. Member of Bobbidazzler, 1977.

GULLICKSON, LANCE Vocal. Member of Bobbidazzler, 1977.

GUN, RANDY Guitar, mandolin. Member of the Love of Life Orchestra since 1979.

GUN Adrian Gurvitz—guitar, vocal, writer; Paul Gurvitz—bass, vocal, writer; Louis Farrell—drums, percussion. First group of the Gurvitz brothers, a hard rock trio. Their second album was received less favorably than their virtually unknown first album. *Albums:* The Gun (EPC 26468); Gun II (EPC).

GUN HILL ROAD Glen Leopolo—vocal, guitar; Gil Roman—bass, guitar, percussion; Steve Goldrich—keyboards, vocal, percussion. *Album:* First Step (MER SRM 61341).

GUNN, PETER Guitar, vocal. Member of the Inmates since 1979.

GUNN, TOMMY Guitar, vocal. Member of the Piper, 1977.

GUNN, TOMMY Drums. Member of American Tears, 1974-77.

GUNNARSON, RUTGER Bass. Member of Abba's backup band since 1974.

GUNNING, JOHN FRANCIS Drums. Member of Country Joe and the Fish, 1966.

GUNS AND BUTTER Jeff Lyons—vocal, guitar; Lenny Fiederer—viola, violin; Paul Cohen—guitar; Peter Cohen—bass; Richard Ploss—saxophone, flute; Peter Tucker—drums. *Album:* Guns and Butter (COT) 1972.

GURL, STEVE Keyboards, moogs. Original member of Wild Turkey, 1971, and Babe Ruth.

GURLEY, JAMES Guitar, vocal. Original member of Big Brother and the Holding Company.

GURVITZ, ADRIAN Guitar, vocal, writer, producer. Underground English guitar player who, with his brother Paul, formed Gun, 1968-69, Three Man Army, 1971-74, and the Baker-Gurvitz Army, 1975. Member of the Graeme Edge Band, 1976-78. Went solo in 1979. *Album:* Sweet Vendetta (JET JZ-35782) 1979.

GURVITZ, PAUL Bass. With brother Adrian, he formed Gun 1968-69, and Three Man Army, 1971-74. A member of the Parrish and Gurvitz Duet, 1972, Baker-Gurvitz Army, 1975, and the Graeme Edge Band, 1976-78. Session for Adrian Gurvitz (1979).

GUS Guitar, vocal. *Album:* Convicted (NMP NJZ 36502) 1980.

GUSELLIT, JEAN-CLAUDE Bass. Member of the Transit Express, 1976.

GUSEVS, ROBERT Piano. Session for Long John Baldry (1980).

GUSTAFSON, JOHNNY Bass, vocal. Original member of Quatermass, 1970, Hard Stuff, 1973, Roxy, 1974-76, and the Ian Gillan Band, 1976. Played Simon in "Jesus Christ Superstar," 1970. Session for Ian Hunter (1975); Jerry Lee Lewis (1973).

GUSTAFSON, OLNE Bass. Session for Bo Hansson.

GUTC, JOE Guitar. Backup for Mitch Ryder, 1978-79.

GUTCHEON, JEFF Piano. Session for Willie Nelson (1973); Ringo Starr (1977).

GUTHEIL, DARYL Keyboards, vocal. Member of Streetheart, 1979.

GUTHRIE, ARLO Harmonica, guitar, vocal, writer. Born 7/10/42. Son of Woody Guthrie. Began recording in 1967 and made his name with "Alice's Restaurant." Session for the Doobie Brothers (1974); Sonny Terry and Brownie McGhee (1973); Woodstock (1970). *Albums:* Alice's Restaurant (RPS 6267); Amigo (RPS 2239) 1976; Arlo (RPS 6299); Best of Arlo Guthrie (WBR K-3117); Arlo Guthrie (RPS 2183); Hobo's Lullaby (RPS 2060) 1972; Last of the Brooklyn Cowboys (RPS MS4-2142) 1973; One Night (WBR K-3232) 1978; Running Down the Road (RPS 6346); Tribute to Leadbelly (TMT 2-7003); Tribute to Woody Guthrie (WBR 2W-3007); Washington County (RPS 6411) 1970.

GUTHRIE, WOODY Guitar, vocal, writer. Wandering minstrel of the early 20th century and hero of Dylan. He traveled the country, taking the cause of the worker, the under-privileged, and the discriminated against and putting it to song. His songs became a part of every folk singer's repertoire. The reputed father of folk, he died in New York 10/3/67. *Albums:* Anthology of Folk Music (SQN 102); Anthology, Vol. 2 (SQN 126); Cowboy Songs (STI 32); Dust Bowl Ballads (FLW 5212); Early Years (TRD 2088); Flamenquistas — Vol. 1 (STI 33); Folk Songs by Woody Guthrie and Cisco

Houston, Vol. 1 (STI 44); Greatest Songs of Woody Guthrie (VAN VSD-35/36); Woody Guthrie (EVR 204) 1965; Woody Guthrie (ELK 271/272) 1964; Woody Guthrie (WBR B-2999); Woody Guthrie Sings Folk Songs (FLW 2483); Immortal Woody Guthrie (OLR 7101); Legendary Performer (VIC CPLI-2099); Legendary Woody Guthrie (TRD 2058) 1967; Lonesome Valley (FLW 2010); Poor Boy (FLW 31010) 1968; Songs of the Spanish Civil War (FLW 4327); Songs to Grow On, Vol. 1 (FLW 7005, 31502); Songs to Grow On, Vol. 3 (FLW 37027); Southern Mountain Hoedowns (STI 54); This Land Is Your Land (FLW 31001); Bonneville Dam, 1966; Bed on the Floor, 1965; Library of Congress Recordings, 1964; Woody Guthrie Sings with Leadbelly, 1962; Bound for Glory, Chain Gang Songs, Cowboy Songs; More Songs by Woody Guthrie and Cisco Houston; Soil and the Sea; Ballads of Sacco and Vanzetti.

GUTKOWSKI, MARK Vocal, organ. Member of the 1910 Fruitgum Company, 1968-69.

GUTMAN, JIM Bass. Session for Peter C. Johnson (1980).

GUY, ATHOL Vocal. Member of the Seekers, 1965-67.

GUY, BOB Early recording name for Frank Zappa.

GUY, BUDDY Guitar, vocal. Noted blues guitarist from Chicago and protege of B. B. King. Session for Junior Wells; Muddy Waters; Howlin' Wolf; Willie Dixon. *Albums:* I Was Walking Through the Woods (CHS); Best of the Chicago Blues(VAN VSD 1/2); Hold That Plane (VAN 79323) 1972; Man and the Blues (VAN 79272) 1968; This Is Buddy Guy (VAN 79290) 1968.

GUZMAN, ED Conga, percussion. Member of Rare Earth.

GWYNN, MARTY Vocal. Session for John Mayall (1978).

GYAN, KIKI Keyboards, vocal. Member of Osibisa.

GYPSY DAVE Kazoo. Before Donovan was known for "Catch the Wind," he used to sing on street corners with partner Gypsy Dave, who blew the kazoo and passed the hat.

GYPSY James Walsh—vocal, keyboards, percussion; Enrico Rosenbaum—vocal, guitar, percussion; Jay Epstein—drums (1971); James C. Johnson—vocal, guitar; Doni Larsen—bass (1971-72); Bill Lordan—drums (1972-73); Randy Cates —bass (1973). *Albums:* Gypsy, 1971; In the Garden, 1972; Antithesis, 1972; Unlock the Gates, 1973.

HAAN, JANITA "PENNY" Vocal, percussion. Member of Babe Ruth until 1976.

HAAS, ANDY Saxophone. Member of Martha and the Muffins, 1980.

HAAS, JIM Vocal. Session for Tin Huey (1979).

HAAS, JOHN Vocal. Session for Pink Floyd (1979).

HAAS, WENDY Piano, vocal. Member of Giants, 1978. Session for Santana (1972); Martin Mull (1978).

HABAN, ANDY Bass, vocal. Member of Wilderness Road.

HABAN, TOM Drum, oboe, vocal. Member of Wilderness Road.

HACKETT, STEPHEN Guitar. Born 2/12/50. Member of Genesis until 1976. *Albums:* Voyage of the Acolyte (CYS 1112) 1976; Please Don't Touch (CYS 1176) 1978; Spectral Morning (CYS 1223) 1979; Defector (CMA CL-1-3103) 1980.

HACON, WALTER Guitar. Session for Wreckless Eric.

HADLOC, JOE Piano. Member of the Jitters, 1980.

HAEHL, STEVE Vocal, guitar. Member of the Shanti, 1971.

HAFFY'S WHISKEY SOUR Harry Vanda—guitar, vocal; George Young—guitar, vocal. AC/DC producer's band formed from Paintbox before becoming the Marcus Hook Roll Band and Flash in the Pan.

HAGAN, DARNELL Vocal. Member of the reformed Bar-Kays.

HAGAR, SAMMY Vocal, guitar, writer, producer. Gained notice as lead singer for Montrose, 1973-74, before going solo in 1975. *Albums:* Nine on a Ten Scale (CAP ST-11489) 1975; Sammy Hagar (CAP ST-11599) 1976; Musical Chairs (CAP ST-11706) 1977; Sammy Hagar Live (CAP SMAS-11812) 1978; Street Machine (CAP ST-11983) 1979; Danger Zone (CAP ST-12069) 1980.

HAGEN, NINA Vocal. Head of the Nina Hagen Band, 1980.

NINA HAGEN BAND R. Heil—keyboards; H. Mitteregger—drums, vocal, percussion; B. Potschka—guitar, vocal; M. Praeker—bass, guitar, vocal; Nina Hagen—vocal. *Albums:* Nina Hagen Band (Import) 1978; Unbehagen (Import) 1979; Nina Hagen Band (COL 3C 36817) 1980.

HAGENS, BUDDY Tenor saxophone. Session for Fats Domino (1955).

HAGGERTY, TERRY Guitar. Member of the Sons of Champlin, 1973-76.

HAGLER, SHERRY Keyboards. Member of Birtha, 1973.

HAGLER, STEPHEN Guitar, vocal. Member of Starcastle, 1972-78.

HAGLEY, BERNARD Guitar. Member of Tranquility, 1972.

HAGOPIAN, HOVANESS Guitar, vocal. Member of Moonquake, 1975.

HAGUE, STEPHEN Keyboards. Member of Jules and the Polar Bears, 1978 to present. Session for the Tremblers (1980).

HAHN, JERRY Guitar. Replaced Larry Coryell in the Gary Burton Quartet. Namesake of the Jerry Hahn Brotherhood. Session for Paul Simon (1972).

HAIGHT, LENNIE Violin. Session for Waylon Jennings (1973).

HAKALA, DON ARP programmer. Session for Tim Weisberg (1974-75).

HAKANSSON, KENNY Guitar. Session for Bo Hansson.

HALCOX, PAT Trumpet. Session for Elton John (1978).

HALDANE, STEVE Bass. Member of the Andy Bown Group.

HALE, JACK Trombone. Member of the Memphis Horns.

HALE, JACK, JR. Trumpet, flugelhorn. Member of the Memphis Horns, 1978.

HALE, MALCOLM Guitar, trombone, vocal. Member of Spanky and Our Gang, 1967-69.

HALES, GEOFFREY Drums. Member of Osamu, 1977.

HALEY, BILL Guitar, vocal. Born 7/6/27. Namesake of Bill Haley and the Comets, and the first international rock star. Died 2/9/81.

BILL HALEY AND THE COMETS Francis Beecher; Danny Cedrane; Dave Day; John Grande; Bill Haley; Nick Mastos; Rudy Pompelli; Dan Raymond; Al Rex; Billy Williamson. 1954 saw Haley and his Comets sing "Rock Around the Clock" and the world has not been the same since. As part of the soundtrack of the movie "Blackboard Jungle," it became a battlecry of teenagers world wide. He opened the doors for Fats Domino, Jerry Lee Lewis, Buddy Holly and even Elvis. *Albums:* Razzle Dazzle (JNS JX25-7003); Travlin' Band (JNS 3035); Bill Haley and His Comets' Rock 'n' Roll Stage Show; Rock Around the Clock, 1962; Rockin' the Joint; Golden Hits (MCA 2-4010); Grandes Hits De Bill Haley/Comets (ORF 12-897); Bill Haley, Greatest Hits (MCA 161) 1968; Bill Haley, King of Rock and Roll (ALS 5313);

R-O-C-K (SUN 143); Rock and Roll (CRS 2077) 1973; Rock and Roll Is Here to Stay (GUS 0065); Rock Around the Country (CRS 2097) 1976; Rockin' (COR 20015).

HALFNELSON Harley Feinstein—drums; Earle Mankey—guitar; Jim Mankey—bass, guitar; Russell Mael—vocal; Ron Mael—keyboards. Brother teams in rock are not uncommon but Halfnelson had two brother teams. Produced by Todd Rundgren, this was the first appearance of the Mael brothers before they became Sparks. *Album:* Halfnelson (WBR) 1971.

HALFORD, BOB Vocal, harmonica. Member of Judas Priest since 1974.

HALINKOVICH, ANATOLE Keyboards. Member of the Boyzz, 1978.

HALL, BOB Piano. Full-time lawyer and part-time pianist, he was a member of Savoy Brown, 1968-69. Session for Savoy Brown (1967, 1969).

HALL, BOBBYE Percussion. Member of the Tim Weisberg Band, 1977. Session for Janis Joplin (1969); Tim Weisberg (1971-79); the Capital City Rockets (1973); B. W. Stevenson (1973); Seals and Crofts (1973); John Sebastian (1974); the Babys (1978); Tim Weisberg and Dan Fogelberg (1978); Bob Dylan (1978-79); the Tears (1979); the Dudek-Finnigan-Kruger Band (1980).

HALL, BRUCE Bass. Member of R.E.O. Speedwagon, 1979.

HALL, CARL Vocal. Session for B. B. King (1971); Gregg Allman (1973); Rick Derringer (1973); Johnny Winter (1973-74); Carly Simon (1974); Leslie West (1976).

HALL, CHRIS Keyboards. Session for Frankie Miller (1979).

HALL, CLARENCE Tenor saxophone. Session for Fats Domino (1949).

HALL, DARRYL Vocal, keyboards, mandolin. Born 10/11/46. Half of the Hall and Oates team since 1973. Session for Robert Fripp (1979). *Album:* Sacred Songs (VIC AFLI-3573) 1980.

HALL, DEBBIE Vocal. Member of the Ron Hicklin Singers, 1979.

HALL, DELORES Vocal. Part of the concert for Bangla Desh, 1971.

HALL, DONNA Vocal. Member of Wet Willie, 1974-79. Session for the Marshall Tucker Band (1973).

HALL, DOUG Keyboards. Session for Van Wilks (1980).

HALL, HARRY Trumpet. Member of Woody Herman Band. Session for Free Creek (1973).

HALL, JACK Bass, vocal. Member of Wet Willie, 1972-79. Session for Jimmy Hall (1980).

HALL, JIM Vocal. Voice of Stillwater, 1977.

HALL, JIM Keyboards. Member of Frankie Miller's Full House, 1977-78.

HALL, JIMMY Vocal, harmonica, saxophone, percussion. Member of Wet Willie, 1972-79. Session for Flint (1978). *Album:* Touch You (EPC JE-36516) 1980.

HALL, JOHN Keyboards. Member of Prism, 1977. Session for Bachman-Turner Overdrive (1978).

HALL, JOHN Vocal, guitar, percussion, mandolin, piano. Member of Kangaroo, 1968, and Orleans, 1973-76. Part of "No Nukes," 1979. Session for Taj Mahal. *Albums:* John Hall (ASY 6E-117) 1978; Power (COL JC-35790) 1979.

HALL, LARRY Trumpet. Session for Elton John (1980).

HALL, LEX Guitar. Member of T.M.G., 1979.

HALL, ROBERT Member of Zuider Zee, 1975.

HALL, SUSAN Percussion. Session for Moon Martin (1978).

HALL, TERRY Vocal. Member of the Specials since 1979.

HALL, TOMMY Member of the 13th Floor Elevators.

HALL, WILLIE Drums. Member of Booker T. and the MGs. Session for the Blues Brothers (1980).

HALL AND OATES Darryl Hall—vocal, keyboards, mandolin; John Oates—vocal, guitar. Vocal duet whose talented session help behind their commercial arrangements and lyrics, captured the hearts of radio listeners in 1975. *Albums:* Darryl Hall and John Oates (VIC ANLI-3463); No Goodbyes (ATC 18213); X-Static (VIC AFLI-3494); Abandoned Luncheonette (ATC 19139) 1973; War Babies (ATC 18109) 1974; Whole Oates (ATC 7242) 1975; Bigger than Both of Us (VIC AFLI-1467) 1976; Beauty on a Back Street (VIC AFLI-2300) 1977; Along the Red Ledge (VIC AFLI-2804) 1978; Livetime (VIC AFLI-2802) 1978; Voice (VIC AQLI-3646) 1980.

HALLEY, DICK Bass. Member of Buckacre, 1976.

HALLIDAY, MICHAEL Bass. Member of the Suburbs, 1980.

HALLIGAN, DICK Keyboards. Member of Blood, Sweat and Tears, 1968.

HALLING, PAT Violin. Session for Donovan (1973).

HALLOWEEN Dave Swanson—vocal, keyboards; Gene Marcellino—vocal, bass; Adrienne Williams—vocal, percussion; Roderick Rancifer—keyboards, vocal; Mike Feldman—vocal, guitar; Jerome Kimsey—drums. *Album:* Come See What It's All About (MER SRM 1-3801) 1979.

HALLUCINATIONS Early name of the J. Geils Band.

HALPIN, SCOTT Drums. Once replaced Keith Moon in a live performance in San Francisco, 1973.

HALSALL, PETER "OLLIE" Guitar, keyboards, vocal. Member of Patto, 1970-72. Replaced Alan Holdsworth in Tempest, 1974. Member of Boxer, 1975, and Timebox, 1976. Session for Kevin Ayers (1977-78); David Kubinec (1979).

HALSEY, JOHN Drums. Member of Patto, 1970-72, Timebox, 1976, and the Rutles, 1978, under the name of Barry Wom. Session for Lou Reed (1972); Annteete Peacock (1979); Maddy Prior (1980).

HALTER, STEVE Keyboards. Member of Nick Gilder's backup band, 1977, and Glider, 1977.

HAM, BILL Guitar. Member of the Yellow Payges, 1969.

HAM, PETE Guitar. Member of Badfinger. Died 4/25/75.

HAM, WARREN Saxophone, flute, vocal. Original member of Bloodrock, until 1972.

HAMBURG, DAN Guitar. Session for the Fugs (1968).

HAMER, IAN Trumpet, flugelhorn. Member of Candlestick Brass, 1977.

HAMES, FRANK Keyboards. Member of Phyrework, 1978.

HAMILTON, DAN Original member of the T-Bones, and Hamilton, Joe Frank and Reynolds.

HAMILTON, DAVID Keyboards. Original member of Pavlov's Dog, 1975-76.

HAMILTON, DIRK Guitar, vocal. *Albums:* Alias (ABC AB 976) 1977; Meet Me at the Crux (ELK 6#-125) 1978; Thug of Love (ELK 6E-249) 1980.

HAMILTON, GLEN ALEXANDER Drums. Member of Pat Benatar's backup band, 1979.

HAMILTON, TOM Bass. Member of Aerosmith, 1971-79.

HAMILTON, JOE FRANK AND REYNOLDS Dan Hamilton; Joe Frank Carillo—vocal, guitar; Tom Reynolds. *Album:* Hamilton, Joe Frank and Reynolds.

HAMMAN, KEN Synthesizer. Session for the James Gang (1975).

HAMMER, CHUCK Guitar. Session for Lou Reed (1980).

HAMMER, JAN Drums, synthesizer, piano, organ. Jazz rock soloist who organized Hammer, 1979 to present. Session with Carlos Santana—John McLaughlin on "Love, Devotion and Surrender," 1973; Stanley Clarke (1974); Tommy Bolin (1975); Jeff Beck (1976-80); Roy Buchanan (1977). *Albums:* Jeff Beck/Jan Hammer Group Live (EPC PE-34433); Like Children (NMP 430) 1974; First Seven Days (NMP 432) 1975; Oh Yeah (NMP 437) 1976; Time Is Free (VAN 79401); Timeless (ECM 1047).

HAMMER, RALPH Guitar. Session for Joe Cocker (1974).

HAMMER, ROBERT Session for David Crosby (1971).

HAMMER Jack O'Brien—guitar; Norman Landsberg—keyboards; John de Roberts—vocal; Richie McBride—bass; John Guerin—drums. *Album:* Hammer (ACO) 1970.

HAMMER Jan Hammer—drums, keyboards; Colin Hodgkinson—bass; Gregg G. Carter; Bob Christianson—keyboards. *Albums:* Black Sheep (ASY 6E-173) 1979; Hammer (ASY 6E-249) 1980.

HAMMERSMITH Dan Lowe—guitar; Dorian Beattie—vocal; Craig Blair—guitar; Royden Morice—bass; Dan Buchner—drums. *Albums:* Hammersmith, 1975; Us for You, 1976.

HAMMILL, PETER Vocal, piano, guitar. Member of Van der Graff Generator 1972-73. Session for Colin Scott (1971); Robert Fripp (1979). *Albums:* Chameleon in the Shadow (CMA) 1973; Vision (IMP 1016) 1977; Over (CMA) 1977; Future Now (CMA 1-2202) 1978; PH7 (CMA 1-2205) 1979; Black Box (IMP) 1980.

HAMMON, RONNIE Drums, vocal. Member of Ballin' Jack.

HAMMOND, JOHN Guitar, vocal, writer. White blues artist known for his honest renditions of black blues, without compromise to white commercial standards. He continues today as much in the vanguard of the blues field as he was 15 years ago. Teamed up with Mike Bloomfield and Dr. John for one album, Triumvirat. Session for Sonny Terry and Brownie McGhee (1973). *Albums:* Country Blues (VAN 79198) 1965; Can Tell, 1968; Mirrors (VAN 79245) 1968; Sooner or Later (USD 8206) 1968; Hot Tracks (VAN 79424) 1969; I'm Satisfied (COL KC-31318) 1972; Can't Beat the Kid (CPN 0153) 1975; John Hammond Solo (VAN 79380) 1976; Footwork (VAN 79400) 1978; Best of John Hammond (VAN VSD-11/12); Big City Blues (VAN 79153); John Hammond (VAN 2148); Blues at Newport (VAN 79145); So Many Roads (VAN 79178); Southern Fried (ATC 8251); Source Point (COL KC 31318); Mileage (RDR 3042) 1980.

HAMMOND, LAWRENCE Vocal, bass. Member of Mad River, 1968.

HAMMOND, PAUL Drums, percussion. Member of Atomic Rooster, 1971, and Hard Stuff, 1973.

HAMMOND, RONNIE Vocal. Voice of the Atlanta Rhythm Section since 1973.

HAMMOND, STEVE Guitar, writer. Member of the Hill, 1975.

HAMMOND-HAMMOND, JEFFREY Bass, vocal, recorder. Born 7/30/46. Replaced Glenn Cornick in Jethro Tull, 1971-75.

HAMNER, LOWRY Vocal, guitar, piano. Namesake of Lowry Hamner and the Cryers since 1979.

LOWRY HAMNER AND THE CRYERS Lee Townsend—vocal, guitar, keyboards (1978); Lowry Hamner—vocal, guitar, piano; Tom Ethridge—bass; Darrell Verdisco—drums, vocal (1979); Clay Barnes—guitar, vocal, piano; Billy Mintz—drums (1978). *Albums:* The Cryers (MER SRM 1-3734) 1978; Midnight Run (MER SRM 1-3785) 1979.

HAMPHILL, ALVIN Organ. Session for Freddie King (1975).

HAMPTON, IAN Bass. Member of Sparks, 1974-78.

HANCK, TERRY Tenor saxophone. Session for Elvin Bishop (1975-78).

HANCOCK, HERBIE Keyboards. Jazz stalwart who became a member of Giants, 1978. Session for the Pointer Sisters (1974); Jaco Pastorius (1976); Flora Purim (1978); Santana (1980). *Albums:* Prisoner (BLN LT-84231) 1969; Best of Herbie Hancock (BLN LT-84232) 1971; Sextant (COL C-32212) 1973; Thrust (COL PC-32965) 1974; Man-Child (COL PC-33812) 1975; Chick Corea, Herbie Hancock, Keith Jarrett, McCoy Tyner (ATC 1696) 1976; Secrets (COL JC 34280) 1976; V.S.O.P. (COL PG-34688) 1977; Quintet (COL C-2-34976) 1977; Evening with Herbie Hancock and Chick Corea (COL PC2-35663) 1978; Sunlight (COL JC 34907) 1978; Feets Don't Fail Me Now (COL JC-35764) 1979; Best of Herbie Hancock (COL JC 36309) 1979; Monster (COL JC 36415) 1980; Mr. Hands (COL JC 36578) 1980; Adam's Apple (BLN LT-84232); Contours (BLN LT-84206); Crossing (WBR B-2617); Empyrean Isles (BLN LT-84175); Evening with Herbie Hancock and Chick Corea (POL 2-6238); Fat Albert Rotunda (WBR 1834); Free Form (BLN LT-84118); Happenings (BLN LT-84231); Love Me By Name (AAM 4564); Maiden Voyage (BLN LT-84195); Mwandishi (WBR 1898); My Point of View (BLN LT-84126); Piano Giants (PRS 24062); Speak Like a Child (BLN LT-84279); Takin' Off (BLN LT-84109); Una Mas (BLN LT-84127).

HANCOX, PAUL Drums, percussion, guitar. Member of the Mindbenders, 1966, and Chicken Shack, 1970-73.

HAND, ROGER Vocal. Session for Ken Tobias (1973).

HANDSLEY, JERRY Bass. Original member of Captain Beefheart and His Magic Band, 1965-69.

HANESS, GAIL Vocal. Member of Jo Mama, 1970. Session for Bill Wyman (1974); Neil Sedaka (1975).

HANK, BUDDY Bass. Member of Aurra, 1980.

HANKINS, MARK Guitar, vocal. Member of the Heroes, 1980.

HANLON, DAVID Drums. Member of Duke Jupiter, 1979-present.

HANNA Percussion, drums, trombone. Member of the Nitty Gritty Dirt Band.

HANNA, JEFF Guitar. Original member of the Nitty Gritty Dirt Band, and the Dirt Band since 1978. Session for Richard Betts (1974); Steve Martin (1978).

HANNAFORD, ROSS Vocal, guitar. Original member of Daddy Cool, 1971-72.

HANNAH, JOHN Guitar, vocal. Member of Streetheart, 1979.

HANNON, BIFF Keyboards. Member of Auracle, 1978-79.

HANSEN, RANDY Guitar, vocal. Began in Seattle as a Hendrix impersonator, before expanding to his original material for his debut in 1980. *Album:* Randy Hansen (CAP ST 12119) 1980.

HANSEN, RONNI Bass. Member of Storm, 1979.

HANSEN, STEVE Member of Hunger.

HANSON, BOB Vocal. Member of the Fugs Chorus.

HANSON, DAVE Drums, vocal. Member of Overland Stage, 1972.

HANSON, DICK Trumpet. Member of the Greatest Show On Earth, 1970, and the Rumour Brass Section, 1979.

HANSON, JUNIOR Vocal, guitar. Member of Hanson, 1974.

HANSON, LARS Drums. Member of Bad Boy.

HANSON, LARS Guitar, keyboards, vocal. Member of Rex, 1977.

HANSON, SILVER Guitar, vocal. Member of the L.A. Jets, 1976.

HANSON Brother James—congas; Glen Le Fleur—drums; Junior Hanson—vocal, guitar; Neil Murray—bass. *Album:* Magic Dragon (MER) 1974.

HANSSON, BO Keyboards, guitar, bass, mellotron, synthesizer, writer. Scandinavian instrumentalist synthesizing jazz and rock. *Albums:* Lord of the Rings (PVC 7907) 1972; Magician's Hat (PVC); Attic Thoughts (CAS 1113); Watership Down (SIR K-6044) 1977.

HAPPENINGS Ralph de Vito—vocal; Bob Miranda—vocal; Tom Guiliano—vocal; Dave Libert—organ. Early name: Four Graduates (until 1966). Recorded, "I Got Rhythm," 1967. *Albums:* The Happenings, 1966; Back to Back; Psycle; Happenings Golden Hits.

HAPPY THE MAN Mike Beck—percussion; Rick Kennell—bass; Stan Wittaker—guitar, vocal; Frank Wyatt—keyboards, reeds; Kim Watkins—keyboards. *Albums:* Happy the Man (ARI 4120) 1977; Crafty Hands (ARI 4191) 1978.

HAPSHASH AND THE COLOURED COAT Michael Mayhew—guitar, writer; Mike Batt—piano, accordion; Waymouth—bass. Avant garde English group specializing in extended rhythmic passages in the late 1960s. After a totally uncommercial first effort, session man Tony McPhee teamed with the group for their second and final album, adding a bit of cohesion and depth to their sound. *Albums:* Featuring the Human Host and the Heavy Metal Kids (IMP LP 12340); Western Flyer (IMP LP 12377).

HARADA, KUMA Bass. Session for Ginger Baker (1977); Mick Taylor (1979); Annette Peacock (1979); Peter Green (1979-80).

HARADA, YUSHIN Drums, percussion. Member of the Far East Family Band, 1977.

HARBOR LIGHTS Early name of Jay and the Americans.

HARCK, KEN Drums. Member of Off Broadway

since 1979.

HARCOURT, KEITH Guitar. Member of Lindisfarne.

HARD STUFF John Gustafson—vocal, bass, keyboards; Paul Hammond—drums; John Cann—vocal, guitar, cello. *Album:* Bolex Dementia (MER SRM 1 663) 1973.

HARDAWAY, STEVELAND MORRIS Real name of Stevie Wonder.

HARDEN, JOHN Horns. Session for Iggy Pop (1977-79).

HARDER, EDDIE Vocal. Member of the Earls, 1959.

HARDESTY, HERB Tenor saxophone, trumpet. Session for Fats Domino (1949-58); B. B. King (1975).

HARDIN, EDDIE Keyboards, vocal. Replaced Steve Winwood in the Spencer Davis Group, 1968. Session for the Sweet (1979).

HARDIN, GLENN Keyboards. Session for Jonathan Edwards (1976-77).

HARDIN, JACKI Vocal. Session for Pilot (1972).

HARDIN, JOHN Drums, vocal. Member of Dayton, 1980.

HARDIN, STEVE Keyboards, vocal. Added to the Point Blank lineup, 1979.

HARDIN, TIM Guitar, vocal, writer. Author of the folk classic, "Don't Make Promises," 1966. His song "If I Were a Carpenter" was a hit under the wholesome treatment of Barry Darin that same year. Died 12/29/80. *Albums:* Tim Hardin (ELK) 1966; Tim Hardin Vol. 2 (ELK) 1967; This Is Tim Hardin (ELK) 1967; Tim Hardin 3 Live in Concert (ELK) 1968; Tim Hardin 4 (ELK) 1969; Tim Hardin—Suite for Susan Moore, 1969; Archetypes; Painted Head (ELK); Tim Hardin 9, 1973.

HARDING, CHRIS Drums, percussion. Session for Christine Perfect (1969).

HARDING, ROB Guitar, vocal. Member of Off Broadway since 1979.

HARDWICK, STEVE Guitar, vocal. Member of Whiteface, 1979.

HARDY, EDDIE Drums. Session for Chuck Berry (1958, 60-61).

HARDY, GERALD Vocal, reeds. Member of the Lavender Hill Mob, 1977-78.

HARGIS, MARLON Keyboards, vocal. Replaced Bernie Faulkner in Exile, 1978-80.

HARGRETT, CHARLIE Guitar. Member of Blackfoot, 1976.

HARGROVE, LINDA Guitar. Session for Leon Russell (1974).

HARKER, ROLAND Guitar, banjo. Session for Elton John (1969); Cat Stevens (1975).

HARKIN, BRENDEN Guitar. Member of Starz since 1976.

HARKIN, GLEN Piano. Session for Gram Parsons (1973).

HARLEY, MEL Drums. Member of Any Trouble, 1980.

HARLEY, STEVE Vocal. English rocker backed by Cockney Rebel. See Steve Harley and Cockney Rebel. Session for the Alan Parsons Project (1977). *Album:* Hobo with a Grin (CAP SW-11770) 1978.

STEVE HARLEY AND COCKNEY REBEL Paul Jeffries—bass; Jean Paul Crocker—strings, mandolin, guitar; Stuart Elliott—drums, vocal; Milton Reame-James—keyboards; Steve Harley—vocal, guitar; George Ford—bass; Jim Cregan—guitar; Duncan Mackay—keyboards. *Albums:* Human Menagerie (EMI ST 11294) 1975; Psychomondo (EMI ST 11330) 1975; Love's a Prima Donna (EMI ST 11596) 1976; Face to Face (HAR SKBB 11661) 1977; Closer Look (HAR ST 11456); Best Years of Our Lives (EMI ST 11394).

HARLOW, ALLAN Bass, vocal. Replaced Ab Bryant in Prism, 1979-80.

HARMONSON, DAVE Guitar, vocal. Member of Lance Romance.

HARMS, JESSE Synthesizer. Session for Ry Cooder (1980).

HARNER, MIKE Guitar, vocal. Member of Tilt, 1980.

HARPER'S BIZARRE Ted Templeton—drums, trumpet; Dick Scoppettone—guitar; Eddie James—guitar; John Peterson—drums; Dick Yount—guitar. Early name: the Other Tikis. Their selection for their debut of a Paul Simon song, "Feelin' Groovy," was an initial step toward success in 1967. Their harmonies were pleasant and nonoffensive, but rock was moving in different directions. *Albums:* Feelin' Groovy, 1967; Anything Goes, 1967; Secret Life of Harper's Bizarre, 1968; Harper's Bizarre 4 (WBR) 1969.

HARPER, DELISLE Bass. Member of Olympic Runners, 1974-79. Session for Freddie King (1974-75); Pete Wingfield (1975); Ginger Baker (1977); Art Garfunkel (1979).

HARPER, LYLE Bass. Session for Art Garfunkel (1979).

HARPER, ROY Guitar, vocal, writer. English solo act who acquired an impressive list of session men, including Pink Floyd's Dave Gilmour, Led Zeppelin's John Paul Jones, Yes's Bill Bruford, Chris Spedding and others for his original material. On "Led Zeppelin III," they played a song dedicated to him. Session for Pink Floyd (1975). *Albums:* Flat Baroque and Beserk (CYS 1160) 1970; Roy Harper, 1970; Stormcock (CYS 1161) 1971; Lifemask (CYS 1162) 1972; Flashes from the Archives of Oblivion (CYS 1164) 1974; Valentine (CYS 1163) 1974; When an Old Cricketer Leaves the Crease (CYS 1105) 1975; One of Those Days in England (CYS 1138) 1977; 1970-1975 (CYS 1188).

HARPO, SLIM Vocal, harmonica. Southern blues player with country overtones. Died 1970. *Albums:* Slim Harpo Knew the Blues, Vol. 2 (EXC 8030);

Baby, Scratch My Back (EXC 8003); Best of Slim Harpo (EXC 8010); Rainin' in My Heart; Real Blues (EXC 8011); Tip On In with Slim Harpo (EXC 8008).

HARRAH, WALTER Vocal. Session for Martin Mull (1978).

HARRELL, BE-BOP Drums. Member of Gene Vincent and His Hub Caps, 1956-61.

HARRELL, TOM Horns. Session for Boz Scaggs (1972).

HARRINGTON, MONALISA Vocal. Session for Neil Diamond (1976).

HARRINGTON, CAREY BELL Harmonica. Session with Muddy Waters (1972).

HARRIS, ANDREW Bass. Session with Lonnie Johnson (1941).

HARRIS, BOB Keyboards, vocal. Member of the Mothers of Invention, 1971.

HARRIS, BOB Vocal. Member of Boulder, 1979.

HARRIS, DON "SUGARCANE" Violin, vocal, writer. Member of the Mothers of Invention, 1969-70. Played with Harvey Mandel in the Pure Food and Drug Act, and with John Mayall, 1971-77. He has since developed into one of the best blues/jazz violinists in the business. Session for Harvey Mandel; Sonny Terry and Brownie McGhee (1973); Frank Zappa (1974). *Albums:* Cup Full of Dreams (MPS MB 2179); Fiddler on the Rock (MPS 20878); I'm On Your Case (BAS 21912); Sugarcane (EPC E 30027); Sugarcane's Got the Blues (MPS 21283).

HARRIS, EMMY LOU Vocal, guitar. Country-folk soloist. Session for Gram Parsons (1973-74); John Sebastian (1974); Bob Dylan (1976); Jonathan Edwards (1976-77); Neil Young (1977); the Band (1978); Rosanne Cash (1979). *Albums:* Elite Hotel (RPS K-2286) 1975; Pieces of the Sky (RPS K-2284) 1975; Luxury Liner (WBR K-3115) 1977; Quarter Moon in a Ten Cent Town (WBR BSK 3454) 1978; Profile (WBR K-3258) 1978; Blue Kentucky Girl (WBR K-3318) 1979; Light of the Stable (WBR BSK 3454) 1979; Roses in the Snow (WBR BSK 3454) 1980; Honky Tonkin' (VIC AHLI 3422).

HARRIS, GOODGE Keyboards, moog. Member of Arthur Brown's Kingdom Come, 1973.

HARRIS, GREG Drums, percussion. Member of Morningstar, 1979.

HARRIS, GREG Guitar, banjo, mandolin, vocal. Member of the Flying Burrito Brothers. Half of the Raines and Harris duet, 1977.

HARRIS, HIGHTIDE Guitar. Played with John Mayall, 1973.

HARRIS, HILDA Vocal. Session for Bob Dylan (1970); Gregg Allman (1973); Free Creek (1973); Jimi Hendrix "Midnight Lightning" (1975); Leslie West (1976).

HARRIS, JACK Vocal. Session for the Alan Parsons Project (1976-78).

HARRIS, JERRY Bass. Member of Nitzinger, 1973-76.

HARRIS, JETT Drums. Member of the Sorrows, 1980.

HARRIS, JOANNE Vocal. Session for Bob Dylan (1978-79).

HARRIS, JOE Alto saxophone. Session for Fats Domino (1949).

HARRIS, JOHN Organ. Session for Bob Seger (1974).

HARRIS, KENT Drums. Member of the Winters Brothers Band.

HARRIS, NORMAN Guitar. Session for B. B. King (1973-74). *Albums:* Dodge City, Hit City (PHL ZS9-3744); Harris Machine (PHL JZ-36313) 1980.

HARRIS, PAUL Keyboards. Member of the Souther-Hillman-Furay Band, 1974-75, and McGuinn, Hillman, Clark, 1979. Session for B. B. King (1969-70, 72); John Sebastian (1970-71); Steve Stills (1971); Henry Gross (1972); Joe Walsh (1972); Rick Derringer (1973); the Michael Stanley Band (1975); Bill Wyman (1976); Terence Boylan (1977); Firefall (1980); Bob Seger (1980); Andy Gibb (1980).

HARRIS, PHIL Guitar, vocal. Member of Ace, 1974-78.

HARRIS, RICHARD Vocal. Session on "Tommy" (1972).

HARRIS, STEVE Bass, vocal. Member of Iron Maiden, 1980.

HARRIS, TED Keyboards. Member of the Paul Butterfield Blues Band, 1969-70.

HARRIS, TIM Drums. Member of the Foundations, 1968.

HARRIS, WESLEY Harmonica. Member of Texas, 1973.

HARRIS, WOODY Guitar. *Albums:* American Guitar Solos (ARH 4008) 1976; After Dinner Mints (KKM 133); Show of Hands (KKM 158) 1978; Bloomfield/Harris (KKM 164) 1980.

HARRISON, BEN Organ. Session for Henry Gross (1978).

HARRISON, BILLY Guitar. Original member of Them.

HARRISON, BOBBY Drums, percussion, vocal. Born 6/28/43. Original member of Procol Harum in 1966, replaced by B. J. Wilson. Member of Freedom, 1970, and Snafu, 1973-75.

HARRISON, BRIAN Keyboards, guitar, bass, vocal. Member of Longdancer, 1973.

HARRISON, CHARLIE Bass. Session for Tim Renwick (1980).

HARRISON, CLIVE Bass, vocal. Member of Avalanche, 1976.

HARRISON, DON Vocal, guitar, keyboards, writer. Namesake of the Don Harrison Band, 1976. *Album:* Not Far From Here (MER SRM 1185) 1975.

DON HARRISON BAND Stu Cook—bass, vocal; Russell Da Sheill—guitar, vocal; Doug Clifford—drums, vocal; Don Harrison—vocal, guitar, keyboards. When the Fogerty brothers left Creedence Clearwater Revival, the rhythm section of Cook and Clifford reappeared behind Don Harrison in 1976, using the same patterns that had made Creedence a sensation, but without the success. *Albums:* Don Harrison Band (ATC) 1976; Red Hot (ATC 18208) 1976.

HARRISON, GEORGE Guitar, vocal, sitar, dobro, mandolin, writer, producer. Born 2/25/43. After leaving the Rebels in 1958, he joined the Quarrymen, which included the personnel who would later become the Beatles. Contrasting the Lennon-McCartney lyrics, Harrison's songs were more ethereal, an added dimension to the group. When he used a sitar on "Norwegian Wood" (1966), it immediately became "in" to listen to Indian music, which spawned a new dimension to the rock scene. Always socially conscious, he sponsored the gala Bangla Desh benefit concert, 1971, including guests Bob Dylan and Ravi Shankar, for that country's refugees. Production and session for Splinter, 1974-75. Session for Doris Troy (1970); John Lennon (1971); Nilsson (1972); Alvin Lee (1973); Ringo Starr (1973); Splinter (1977); Donovan. *Albums:* Wonderwall (APL ST 3350) 1968; Concert for Bangla Desh (CAP STCS-3385) 1971; Living in the Material World (CAP SMAS-3410) 1973; Dark Horse (CAP SMAS-3418) 1974; Extra Texture (CAP SW-3420) 1975; All Things Must Pass (APL STCH-639) 1975; Thirty Three and 1/3 (DKH 3005) 1976; Best of George Harrison (CAP ST-11578) 1977; George Harrison (DKH K-3255) 1979.

HARRISON, JAMES HOPKINS Vocal. Member of Lake since 1977.

HARRISON, JERRY Guitar, keyboards, vocal. Member of the Talking Heads since 1977.

HARRISON, JOHN Bass, vocal. Session for Roy Buchanan (1973-74, 1976).

HARRISON, MIKE Vocal, keyboards, harmonica, writer. Began as a member of Art (1967), before being featured singer of Spooky Tooth, 1968-72. He reorganized Spooky Tooth, for what appeared to be a comeback, 1974-75, but again left to pursue his solo career. *Albums:* Mike Harrison and Junkyard Angel (ISL SMAS 9313) 1972; Smokestack Lightning (ISL SW 9321) 1972; Rainbow Rider (ISL 9359) 1975.

HARRISON, NICKY Strings. Session for Donovan (1973).

HARRISON, NIGEL Bass. Original member of Blondie, 1977-78.

HARRISON, NOEL Vocal. Singing son of actor Rex Harrison whose coincidental acting career was a boost to his less than adequate singing career. *Albums:* Noel Harrison, 1966; Collage, 1967; Santa Monica Pier, 1968.

HARRISON, OLLY Drums, percussion. Member of the Photos, 1980.

HARRISON, PAULA Vocal. Session for Bill Wyman (1976).

HARRISON, STAN Saxophone, flute. Replaced Bob Malach in Southside Johnny and the Asbury Jukes, 1979-present.

HARRISON, TIMMY Vocal. Member of Buckwheat. Session for Free Creek (1973).

HARRISON, WILBUR Vocal. Made a hit of "Kansas City" in 1959.

HARRISSON, JACQUES Keyboards, vocal. Session for the Hunt (1980).

HARRY, DEBORAH Vocal. Member of Wind in the Willows, 1968, and head of Blondie since 1976.

HART VALLEY DRIFTERS Early name for the Grateful Dead.

HART, BOBBY Vocal, writer. Half of the Boyce and Hart writing/performing team of the 1960s, and member of Dolenz, Jones, Boyce and Hart, 1976.

HART, CHARLIE Keyboards, violin, accordian. Session for Ronnie Lane (1975); "Rough Mix" (1977).

HART, MARTIN Played with John Mayall, 1962.

HART, MICKEY Drums, percussion. Replaced Bill Sommers in the Grateful Dead, 1967-75. Member of the Dija Rhythm Band, 1976, and Seastones, 1976. Session for the New Riders of the Purple Sage; David Crosby (1971). *Album:* Rolling Thunder.

HART, MIMI Vocal. Session for the Allman Brothers (1979).

HART, RAY Percussion. Session for Randy Newman.

HART, TIM Guitar, vocal. Member of Steeleye Span, 1970-78.

HARTFORD, JOHN Guitar, vocal, banjo. Replaced Dave Guard in the Kingston Trio, 1964-66, before going solo. He made frequent television appearances on the Smothers Brothers Show. Session for James Taylor. *Albums:* Aero-plain (WBR 1916) 1971; All in the Name of Love (FLF 044) 1972; Mark Twang (FLF 063) 1978; Slumberin' on the Cumberland (FLF 095) 1979; You and Me at Home (FLF 228) 1980; Critic's Choice (TKM 1062); Festival Tapes (FLF 068); Glitter Grass from Nashwood Hollyville Strings (FLF 036); Headin' Down into the Mystery Below (FLF 063); Nobody Knows What You Do (FLF 028); Tennessee Jubilee (FLF 012); Walnut Valley Spring Thing (TKM 1054).

HARTLEY, KEEF Drums, writer. After working with John Mayall, 1967-68, he founded the Keef Hartley Band, 1968-71, before returning to Mayall, 1972-73, and forming Dog Soldier, 1975.

KEEF HARTLEY BAND Miller Anderson—guitar, vocal, writer (1969); Keef Hartley—drums; Gary

Thain—bass (1969-71); Spit James—guitar (1969-70); Peter Dines—keyboards (1969); Mick Taylor—guitar (1969-70); Junior Kerr—guitar, vocal; Mick Weaver—keyboards (1969-71); Jess Roden—vocal; Pete Wingfield—keyboards, vocal (1970); Jean Rousselle—keyboards; Chris Mercer—saxophone (1969-70); Phillip Chen—bass; Nick Newell—saxophone, flute. English blues band from the John Mayall tree that established its own identity, though the talent that passed through the group achieved greater fame in subsequent ventures: Miller (The Boogie Brothers), Thain (Uriah Heep), Taylor (The Rolling Stones). *Albums:* Half Breed (DRM) 1969; Battle of the Northwest (DRM 18035) 1969; The Time is Near (DRM 18047) 1970; Seventy Second Brave (DRM) 1970; Overdog (DRM 18057) 1971; Little Big Band (DRM) 1971; Lancaster Hustler (Import).

HARTMAN, DAN Bass, vocal, keyboards, percussion. Member of the Edgar Winter Group. Session for Johnny Winter (1973); Montrose (1976); Johnny and Edgar Winter (1976); Hilly Michaels (1980). *Albums:* Instant Replay (BSK JZ-35641) 1978; Night at Studio 54 (CAS 2-7161); Relight My Fire (BSK JZ-36302) 1979.

HARTMAN, JOHN "LITTLE JOHN" Drums, percussion. Co-founder of the Doobie Brothers, 1971-80.

HARTMAN, WARREN Piano, harpsichord, vocal. Member of Stanley Steamer, 1973.

HARTNAGLE, BOBBY Guitar. Member of Duke Williams and the Extremes, 1973.

HARTSFIELD, J. C. Guitar, mandolin, banjo, fiddle, vocal. Namesake of Heartsfield, 1973-75.

HARTWIG, GERALD Bass. Replaced Glenn Cornick in Karthago, 1976.

HARVARD, GLYN Vocal, bass, guitar. Member of Jade Warrior.

HARVEY, ALEX Vocal, guitar. Namesake of the Sensational Alex Harvey Band since 1972.

SENSATIONAL ALEX HARVEY BAND Alex Harvey—vocal, guitar; Zal Cleminson—guitar; Chris Glen—bass; Hugh McKenna—keyboards; Ted McKenna—drums; Gordon Sellar—bass, vocal; Don Weller—reeds, vocal; Simon Chatterton—drums, vocal; Tommy Eyre—keyboards; Martin Cang—keyboards, guitar, vocal. English hard rock with as much energy in the music as in the performance. *Albums:* Souveniours, 1972; The Impossible Dream, 1974; Tomorrow Belongs to Me, 1975; Live (ATC 18148) 1975; Purple Crush (BUD 5696); Next.

HARVEY, DAVID Drums. Replaced John McAuley in Them.

HARVEY, DONI Bass, vocal. Member of Automatic Man, 1976.

HARVEY, LES Guitar. Brother of Alex Harvey and member of Stone the Crows until his death in 1972.

HARVEY, RICHARD Keyboards, whistle. Session for Gerry Rafferty (1970-80).

HARVEY, TED Drums. Member of Hound Dog Taylor's Houserockers.

HARWOOD, BARRY Guitar, vocal. Member of the Rossington-Collins Band, 1980.

HARWOOD, PAUL Bass. Original member of Mahogany Rush, 1974-present.

HASELDEN, TONY Guitar. Member of Le Roux since 1979.

HASHIAN, SIB Drums, percussion. Born 9/17/49. Member of Boston, 1976-78. Session for Sammy Hagar (1979), Barry Goudreau (1980).

HASKELL, BILL Saxophone. Member of the Band of Thieves, 1976.

HASKELL, GORDON Vocal. Replaced Peter Giles in King Crimson, 1971. Session for King Crimson (1970).

HASKELL, HERMAN Bass. Member of J. B. Hutto's Hawks.

HASKELL, JIMMY String arranger, conductor, piano, accordion. Session for Simon and Garfunkel (1970); B. B. King (1971); Cashman and West (1972); Austin Roberts (1973); B. W. Stevenson (1973); Art Garfunkel (1978); Dwight Twilley (1979); the Doobie Brothers (1980).

HASKETT, MAX Member of Rubicon, 1978-79.

HASLAM, ANNIE Vocal. Member of Renaissance, 1976-78. Session for Roy Wood (1979). *Album:* Alice in Wonderland (SIR 6046) 1977.

HASLIP, JIMMY Bass. Member of Blackjack since 1979. Session for Crosby, Stills and Nash (1977); Frank Carillo (1978); the Paley Brothers (1978); Ray Gomez (1980); Rod Stewart (1980).

HASON, JOHN Keyboards. Session for the Blues Brothers (1980).

HASSINGER, DAVE Percussion. Member of the Sunblind Lion, 1976.

HASTINGS, DOUG Vocal, guitar. Member of Buffalo Springfield, 1966, and Rhinoceros, 1968.

HASTINGS, JIMMY Flute, saxophone. Member of Caravan, 1971-73, and the National Health Band, 1977. Session for the Soft Machine (1970); Trapeze (1972, 1974); Bryan Ferry (1974); Chris Squire (1975).

HASTINGS, PYE Guitar, vocal. Member of Caravan, 1971-73.

HATA, PETER Guitar. Member of Hiroshima, 1980.

HATFIELD, BOBBY Vocal, writer. Half of the original Righteous Brothers, 1962-68, 1974-75. *Album:* Messin' in Muscle Shoals (MGM) 1969.

HATFIELD, ROGER Reeds, keyboards. Member of Link, 1980.

HATHAWAY, RICHARD Bass. Member of the Arthur Gee-Whizz Band, 1971-72, and the Dirt Band since 1978. Session for Steve Martin (1978).

HATLELID, DOUGLAS Bass. Session for Fred Neil.

HATLEY, STEPHEN Keyboards, guitar, vocal. Member of Sawbuck, 1971.

HATOT, ALAN Saxophone. Member of Magma. Session for Elton John (1972).

HATTERSLEY, CLEVE Guitar, vocal. Member of Greezy Wheels, 1976.

HATTERSLEY, LISSA Mandolin, vocal. Member of Greezy Wheels, 1976.

HATTLER, HELMUT Bass. Member of Kraan, 1975.

HATZIPAULI, ANGELOS Bouzoukia. Session for Cat Stevens (1971).

HAUCK, N. Trombone. Session for Triumvirat (1973).

HAUCK, TOM Guitar, vocal. Member of the Atlantics since 1979.

HAUGHEY, BOBBY Flugelhorn. Session for Savoy Brown (1969).

HAUSER, TIM Vocal. Member of Manhattan Transfer since 1971.

HAVENS, RICHIE Guitar, vocal, writer. Born 1/21/41. His soulful renditions added another dimension to other people's country and folk songs, like Leon Russell's "Tightrope." Session on Woodstock (1970); "Tommy" (1972). *Albums:* Mixed Bag (MGM 4698) 1967; Electric Richie Havens, 1968; Somethin' Else Again (MGM 4699) 1968; Alarm Clock (STG 6005); Great Blind Degree (STF 6010); Richard P. Havens (MGM 4700); Richie Havens on Stage (MGM); Mixed Bag II (STF 6013); Portfolio (STF 6013).

HAVENSTEIN, KURT Vocal, bass, keyboards, guitar. Member of Supermax, 1979.

HAVIS, REGINA Vocal. Session for Bob Dylan (1979-80).

HAWK Nickname of Jerry Lee Lewis, and Ronnie Hawkins.

HAWKEN, JOHN Piano. Member of the Strawbs, and Illusion, 1977. Session for Luther Grosvenor; the Sutherland Brothers (1973).

HAWKES, GREG Reeds, percussion, keyboards. Member of the Cars since 1978. Session for Martin Mull (1975); Hilly Michaels (1980).

HAWKES, LEN Bass. Member of the Tremeloes.

HAWKINS, BARBARA ANN Vocal. Member of the Dixie Cups, 1964-65.

HAWKINS, BUDDY BOY Guitar, vocal. Blues troubador born between 1895 and 1900. *Album:* Blues Tradition, 1927-1932 (MLS 32016).

HAWKINS, CAMERON Vocal, bass, synthesizer, piano. Member of FM, 1979.

HAWKINS, GEORGE Bass. Session for Paul Waroff (1980).

HAWKINS, IRA Vocal. Session for Ringo Starr (1974).

HAWKINS, JIMMY Drums. Member of Strider, 1973.

HAWKINS, JOAN MARIE Vocal. Member of the Dixie Cups, 1964-65.

HAWKINS, ROGER Percussion, drums. Replaced Jim Gordon in Traffic, 1973, and member of the Muscle Shoals Rhythm Section. Session for Jackson Highway; Clarence Carter (1967); Wilson Pickett (1968); John Hammond (1969, 75); Boz Scaggs (1969, 72); King Curtis (1969); Aretha Franklin (1970); Don Nix (1971); Jim Capaldi (1971, 73, 75); Leon Russell (1971); J. J. Cale (1972); Mike Harrison (1972); Tony Joe White (1972); Bob Seger (1973, 75); Paul Simon (1973, 75); Barry Goldberg (1974); Rod Stewart (1975-76); Richard Tate (1977).

HAWKINS, RONNIE Vocal, harmonica. Nickname: the Hawk. Featured vocalist of the band that became the Band after leaving him. Session for the Band (1978). *Album:* Hawk (UAR LT-968) 1979.

HAWKINS, ROSA LEE Vocal. Member of the Dixie Cups, 1964-65.

HAWKINS, ROY Vocal, piano. Blues pianist whose date of birth is unknown. Approximate date of death, 1973, at estimated age of 40-42. No photos exist. *Album:* Anthology of the Blues—West Coast Blues (KNT 9012).

HAWKINS, "SCREAMIN" JAY Vocal. Recorded "Spell,"1954.

HAWKLORDS Robert Calvert—vocal, percussion; Dave Brock—guitar, vocal, synthesizer; Harvey Bainbridge—bass, vocal; Steve Swindells—keyboards; Simon King—drums. *Album:* Hawklords (CMA 1-2203) 1978.

HAWKS Lee Jackson—guitar; Don Myers—bass; Junior Pettis—bass; Herman Haskell—bass; Frank Kirkland—drums; Maurice McIntyre—saxophone. J. B. Hutto's backup band. See J. B. Hutto.

HAWKSHAW, ALAN Keyboards. Session for Donovan (1968); Vigrass and Osborne (1972).

HAWKSWORTH, MICK Bass. Member of Ten Years Later, 1978-79. Session for Matthew Fisher (1973).

HAWKWIND Dave Brock—guitar, organ, vocal; Lemmy—bass, vocal; Simon House—keyboards, violin; Nik Turner—saxophone, oboe, flute; Del Dettmar—keyboards; Simon King—drums, percussion; Robert Calvert—vocal; Adrian Shaw—bass. The overdue fame of Pink Floyd in the 1970s brought many new entries to the space-rock field. Hawkwind was one of the more successful entries. Personnel changes led to the group's evolution as Hawklords, 1978. *Albums:* Doremi Fosol Latido (UAR UA-LA001-F); Hawkwind (UAR LT-5519); In Search of Space (UAR LW-5567); Hall of the Mountain Grill (UAR JA LA328G) 1974; Quark Strangeness and Charm (SIR K-6047) 1977; Space Ritual Alive (UAR LWB-120) 1978.

HAWORTH, BRYN Guitar. Session for Ian Matthews (1978); Gerry Rafferty (1980).

HAY, BARRY Flute, guitar, vocal, writer. Member of Golden Earring, 1970-present.

HAY, IVOR Drums. Member of the Saints, 1977-79.

HAYCOCK, PETER Guitar, slide guitar, vocal. Original member of the Climax Blues Band, 1968-present.

HAYDOCK, ERIC Bass. Original member of the Hollies, 1963-65.

HAYES, CHRIS Guitar, vocal. Member of Huey Lewis and the News, 1980.

HAYES, DAVID Bass. Session for Country Joe McDonald (1975); the Rowans (1975).

HAYES, GORDON Bass. Session for Pearls Before Swine (1972).

HAYES, LARRY Guitar. Member of the Lamont Cranston Band, 1977.

HAYES, MICHAEL Real name of producer Mickie Most.

HAYES, SHAW Guitar. Member of Iguana, 1977.

HAYES, SLOAN Vocal, flute, keyboards. Member of Starbuck, 1977.

HAYNES, RICK Bass, vocal. Session for Gordon Lightfoot since 1966.

HAYNES, ROY Drums. Original member of the Gary Burton Quartet.

HAYNES, STEVE Vocal. Member of Hustler.

HAYNES, WALTER Dobro. Session for J. J. Cale (1971).

HAYS, PAT Vocal, harmonica. Member of the Lamont Cranston Band, 1977.

HAYS, SHERMAN Bass. Session for Waylon Jennings (1976).

HAYWARD, CHARLES Drums, percussion, keyboards, vocal. Member of Quiet Sun, 1975, and Mainstream, 1976. Session for Phil Manzanera (1975).

HAYWARD, CHARLIE Bass. Replaced Mark Fitzgerald in the Charlie Daniels Band, 1977-80. Session for Gregg Allman (1973).

HAYWARD, JUSTIN Guitar, sitar, percussion, keyboards, bass, vocal, writer. Replaced Denny Laine in the Moody Blues, 1967, and with group partner John Lodge, released a joint album "Blue Jays," 1975. See Blue Jays. *Albums:* Songwriter (DER 18075) 1977; Night Flight (DER DRL-1-4801) 1980.

HAYWARD, PRESTON Session for Bryan Ferry (1977).

HAYWARD, RICK Guitar. Session for Christine McVie (1969); Lightnin' Slim (1978).

HAYWARD, RITCHIE Drums, vocal. Member of Little Feat, 1971-77. Session for Ry Cooder (1970); Elliot Ingber (1971); Rick Nelson; Robert Palmer (1976); the Doobie Brothers (1976); Pakalameredith (1977); Peter Frampton (1977).

HAYWOOD, DOUG Vocal. Session for Jackson Browne (1980).

HAZE, LEONARD Drums, vocal. Member of Yesterday and Today, 1976.

HAZZARD, TONY Vocal. Session for Long John Baldry (1971); Elton John (1972).

HEAD, COLEMAN Guitar. Member of the Pure Food and Drug Act. Session for Harvey Mandel.

HEAD, MURRAY Vocal. Played Judas Iscariot in "Jesus Christ Superstar," 1970. *Album:* Jesus Christ Superstar (MCA 2-10000).

HEAD, STEVE Drums, keyboards. Member of the Sensations Fix.

HEADBOYS Lou Lewis—guitar, vocal; George Boyter—bass, vocal; Calum Malcolm—keyboards, vocal; Davy Ross—drums, vocal. *Album:* The Headboys (RSO 1-3068) 1979.

HEADLEY-DOWN, JOHN Drums, percussion. Session for Peter Frampton (1974).

HEADON, NICKY "TOPPER" Drums. Replaced Terry Chimes in the Clash, 1978 to present.

HEADS, HANDS AND FEET Ray Smith—guitar, vocal; Pete Gavin—drums, percussion, vibes, vocal; Albert Lee—guitar, dobro, moog, vibes, vocal; Mike O'Neill—keyboards, vocal; Tony Colton—vocal; Chas Hodges—bass, banjo, fiddle, vocal. Multifaceted group composed of some of the best English session men of the early 1970s. Equally at home with rock, jazz and courntry, their double album debut contained a sampling of it all. *Albums:* Heads, Hands and Feet (CAP SUDB-680) 1971; Old Soldiers Never Die (ATC SD 7025) 1973.

HEADSTONE Mark Ashton—vocal, guitar; Steve Bolton—guitar; Phillip Chen—bass (1974); Chilli Charles—drums (1974); Joe O'Donnell—vocal, piano (1975); Jerome Rimson—bass (1975); Peter Van Hooke—drums (1975). *Albums:* Bad Habits (ABC DSD 50174) 1974; Headstone (TWC T-438) 1975.

HEALEY, DENNIS Trumpet. Session for John Mayall's Bluesbreakers (1967).

HEARD, HUBIE Organ. Session for Bill Wyman (1974, 76).

HEART, JIMMY Vocal. Member of the Gentrys.

HEART Ann Wilson—vocal, percussion; Nancy Wilson—guitar, vocal; Steve Fossen—guitar; Roger Fisher—guitar (1975-78); Mike Derosier—drums; Howard Leese—guitar (1980). *Albums:* Dreamboat Annie (MSH 5005) 1975; Little Queen (POR PR-34799) 1977; Magazine (MSH 5008) 1978; Dog and Butterfly (POR FR-35555); Bebe Le Strange (EPC FE-36371) 1980.

HEARTBEATS Early name of Herman's Hermits.

HEARTBREAKERS See Tom Petty and the Heartbreakers.

HEARTSFIELD Arte Baldacci—drums, synthesizer, vocal; Greg Biela—bass, vocal; Fred Dobbs—guitar, banjo, vocal; J. C. Hartsfield—guitar, mandolin, banjo, fiddle, vocal; Perry Jordan—guitar, vocal; Phil Lucafo—guitar, vocal, pedal steel guitar. *Albums:* Heartsfield (MER SRM-1-688) 1973; Wonder of It All (MER SRM-1-003) 1974; Foolish Pleasures, 1975; Collectors Item, 1976.

HEATERS Mercy Bermudez—vocal, percussion, saxophone; Missy Connell—bass, vocal; Carlos de la Paz—guitars; Maggie Connell—keyboards, vocal; Victor Bisetti—drums. *Albums:* Heaters (ARA SW 50032) 1978; Energy Transfer (COL JC 36486) 1980.

HEATH, FRANK Drums, vocal. Member of the JTS Band, 1977.

HEATH, ROGER Guitar, vocal. Member of D. B. Cooper, 1980.

HEATH, TOMMY Vocal, guitar, keyboards. Namesake of Tommy Tutone, 1980.

HEATLEY, SPIKE Upright bass. Member of Blues Incorporated. Session for Rod Stewart (1972, 74).

HEATLIE, BOB Saxophone. Session for the Headboys (1979); Trevor Rabin (1980).

HEATS Steve Pearson—guitar, vocal; Don Short—guitar, vocal; Kenny Deans—drums; Keith Lilly—bass, vocal. Seattle-based new wave band from the management of Heart. *Album:* Have an Idea (ALB 1001) 1980.

HEAVY METAL KIDS Ronnie Thomas—bass, vocal; Keith Boyce—drums, percussion; Danny Peyronel—keyboards, vocal; Mickey Waller—guitar; Gary Holton—vocal. *Album:* Heavy Metal Kids (ACO) 1974.

HEBB, BOBBY Vocal. A single hit, "Sunny" (1966), made him a brief star. *Album:* Sunny, 1966.

HECHT, PETER Keyboards. Member of Lucifer's Friend, 1974-75.

HECKSTALL-SMITH, DICK Tenor saxophone. Original member of John Mayall's Bluesbreakers, 1968, Alexis Korner's Blues Incorporated, the Graham Bond Organization, and Colosseum, 1968-71. Session for Chicken Shack; Jack Bruce (1968-69).

HEDGEHOPPERS ANONYMOUS Assumed group name of Jonathan King for his single "It's Good News Week," 1966.

HEDLUND, DICK Bass. Member of the Jan Park Band, 1979.

HEDWIG, ULA Vocal. Member of Blast, 1979.

HEFFERN, GARY Vocal. Member of the Penetrators, 1980.

HEGARTY, DEN Vocal. Member of Darts since 1978.

HEGEL, ROB Vocal. *Album:* Hegel (VIC AFLI-3605) 1980.

HEIBERG, ERIC Keyboards, vocal. Member of the Robbin Thompson Band, 1980.

HEIBL, ROBBY Vocal, bass, guitar, violin. Member of Amon Duul.

HEIBS, DANNY Percussion. Session for Phil Manzanera (1975).

HEIL, R. Keyboards. Member of Nina Hagen Band.

HEINRICH, STUART Guitar, vocal. Session for Lou Reed (1978-80).

HEINTZE, DICK Keyboards. Member of the Snakestretchers, 1972-73.

HEIS, STU Guitar, keyboards. Member of the Resurrection Band, 1978.

HELDON Richard Pinhas—synthesizer, guitar, electronics; Francois Auger—drums, percussion. *Albums:* Dream Without Reason (ICT 1021) 1976; Aural Explorer (AXR 5001) 1976.

HELIUM KIDS Early band of XTC's Colin Moulding and Terry Chambers.

HELL, RICHARD Bass, vocal. Member of Richard Hell and the Voidoids, 1977.

RICHARD HELL AND THE VOIDOIDS Robert Quine—guitar, vocal; Richard Hell—bass, vocal; Ivan Julian—guitar, vocal; Marc Bell—drums. *Album:* Blank Generation (SIR 6037) 1977.

HELLFIELD, MITCH Drums, percussion, guitar, vocal. Namesake of Hellfield, 1978.

HELLFIELD Rick Lamb—keyboards, guitar, vocal; Dave Hovey—guitar, vocal; Mitch Hellfield—drums, percussion, guitar, vocal; Jamie Larsen—bass, vocal; Bill Smith—vocal. *Album:* Hellfield (EPC JE-36005) 1978.

HELLIWELL, JOHN Reeds, vocal. Member of Supertramp.

HELM, HOWARD Keyboards, vocal. Member of Zon, 1979.

HELM, LEVON Drums, percussion. Member of the Band, 1963-78, formed Levon Helm and the RCO All-Stars, including Don Dunn, Booker T., Steve Cropper and others, for a brief tour in 1977. Co-starred in the movie "Coal Miner's Daughter," 1980. Session for John Hammond (1965-68); Martin Mull (1972); Neil Young (1973); Ringo Starr (1973); Paul Butterfield (1975); Rick Danko (1977). *Albums:* Levon Helm (MCA 1017); Levon Helm (MCA 1089) 1978; American Son (MCA 5120) 1980.

HELMET BOY David Leon—keyboards, guitar, vocal; Paul Trugman—guitar, vocal; Glenn Burtnick—guitar, keyboards, harmonica, vocal; Richard Grossman—bass, vocal. *Album:* Helmet Boy (ASY 6E-280) 1980.

HENDERSON, ALAN Bass. Original member of Them.

HENDERSON, BILL Guitar, piano, vocal, writer, producer. Original member of Chilliwack, since 1971. Co-produced Toronto, 1980.

HENDERSON, HARVEY Member of the re-formed Bar-Kays.

HENDERSON, JIMMY Vocal, harmonica. Member of Tucky Buzzard, 1973.

HENDERSON, JOAN Vocal. Session for Chilliwack (1972).

HENDERSON, KIM "BUGS" Guitar. Namesake of the Texas based Bugs Henderson Group until his death, 1975.

BUGS HENDERSON GROUP Ron Thompson—drums; Kim Henderson—guitar; Robert Chitwood—bass. Retrospective release after Henderson's death in 1975. *Album:* At Last (ARM AR-LP 78-1) 1978.

HENDERSON, KYLE Bass, vocal. Member of Whiteface, 1979.

HENDERSON, MIKE Saxophone. Member of the Marketts, 1973. Session for Jules and the Polar Bears (1979).

HENDERSON, REV. PATRICK Keyboards. Member of Black Grass, 1972. Session for Leon Russell (1972, 75); Freddie King (1973); Nils Lofgren (1977); Ry Cooder (1979); the Doobie Brothers (1980).

HENDERSON, TIM Bass. Member of the Pop since 1977.

HENDERSON, TOMMY Vocal. Session for Taj Mahal.

HENDRICKS, JAMES Guitar, vocal, writer. Original member of the Lamp of Childhood before he and wife Cass Elliott co-founded the Mugwumps, which dissolved into Cass Elliot's joining the Mamas and the Papas and his embarking on a solo career.

HENDRICKSON, ARTHUR Vocal. Member of Selecter, 1980.

HENDRIX, JIMI Guitar, vocal, writer. Real name: James Marshall Hendrix. (Changed from Johnny Allen Hendrix 9/11/46.) Born 11/27/42. Died 9/18/70. Besides the guitar, he played with pure sound as if it were another instrument, opening a hitherto unknown dimension to rock. Behind the volume were some of the most original blues lines played in the day, which became even more apparent on the instances he used an acoustic guitar. He was a respected peer of such greats as Clapton and Townshend for his original material and unlikely arrangements of "Wild Thing," Dylan's "All Along the Watchtower" and "The Star Spangled Banner." To date, four posthumous albums have been released, one of which, "War Heroes," contains the original Experience. "Crash Landing" and "Midnight Lightning" were completed with studio musicians at later dates, and "Nine to the Universe" was a collection of recorded jam sessions. See Jimi Hendrix Experience. Played at Woodstock, 1969. Session work for Little Richard; Sam Cooke; Joey Dee; Wilson Pickett; Solomon Burke; Jackie Wilson; Ike and Tina Turner; Tommy Tucker; the Isley Brothers.

JIMI HENDRIX EXPERIENCE Jimi Hendrix—guitar, vocal, writer (1967-72); Noel Redding—bass (1967-71); Mitch Mitchell—drums (1967-72); Buddy Miles—drums, vocals (1972-75); Billy Cox—bass; Alan Schwartzberg—drums (1975); Jeff Mirinov—guitar (1975); Bob Babbit—bass (1975). In the summer of 1967, backing the Monkees on a tour was a shot at the big time. For Hendrix's Experience, it meant getting fired after the first concert. Not since Chuck Berry has someone made sexual advances to a guitar, and never before had a group incorporated suicidal pyromaniacs behind a wall of sound. Ex-Animal Chas Chandler managed the Experience and led Hendrix to the first step toward super-stardom, taking him from New York to England, where he was admired by already great guitarists like Clapton and Townshend. After Hendrix died, 9/18/70, posthumous albums continued to be best sellers. *Albums:* Are You Experienced (RPS 6261) 1967; Get the Feeling, 1967; Axis: Bold as Love (RPS 6281) 1968; Electric Ladyland (RPS 6307) 1968; Jimi Hendrix/Otis Redding at Monterey, 1970; Smash Hits (RPS K-2276) 1969; Cry of Love (RPS MS-2034) 1970; Band of Gypsys (CAP STAO-472) 1970; Rainbow Bridge (RPS MS 2040) 1971; In the West (RPS MS 2049) 1971; War Heroes (RPS MS 2103) 1972; Jimi Hendrix (RPS 2RS-6481) 1973; Crash Landing (RPS 2204) 1975; Midnight Lightning (RPS 2229) 1975; Essential (RPS 2RS-2245) 1978; Essential, Vol. 2 (RPS HS-2293) 1979; Nine to the Universe (RPS HS-2299) 1980; Over the Edge (WBR K-3335); Jimi Hendrix Experience (RPS 2029); I Woke Up This Morning and Found I Was Dead (Import) 1980; Hendrix at His Best, Vols. I, II, and III, (Import); Before London (ACD 2002) 1980; Free Spirit (ACD 7112) 1980.

HENDRY, ROB Guitar, mandolin. Replaced Jim McCarty in Renaissance, 1972.

HENKE, BOB Guitar, vocal, keyboards. Member of Goose Creek Symphony.

HENLEY, DON Vocal. Born 7/22/46. Original member of the Eagles, since 1972. Session for Joe Walsh (1974, 76); Terence Boylan (1977); Tim Weisberg and Dan Fogelberg (1978); Bob Seger (1980); Elton John (1980); Waren Zevon (1980); Christopher Cross (1980).

HENMAN, DAVID Guitar, vocal. Member of April Wine, and the Dudes, 1975.

HENMAN, JIM Bass, guitar. Member of April Wine.

HENMAN, RITCHIE Drums, vocal. Member of April Wine, and the Dudes, 1975.

HENNES, MITCH Bass. Member of the Numa Band, 1980.

HENNIGE, SCOTT Drums. Member of Asleep at the Wheel since 1973.

HENRI, ADRIAN Vocal, percussion. Member of Grimms, 1973.

HENRIT, ROBERT Drums, percussion. Original member of the Zombies, Argent, 1970-75, and Phoenix, 1976, 1979.

HENRY COW Geoff Leigh—saxophone, flute; Tim Hodgkinson—keyboards, flute, vocal; Fred Frith—guitar, violin, viola; John Greaves—bass, piano; Chris Culter—drums. *Album:* Henry Cow (VIR) 1973.

HENRY, KENT Guitar. Replaced Larry Byron in Steppenwolf, 1971. Session for Lord Sutch; John Kay (1973).

HENRY, PIERRE Electronics. Classical French electronic composer. Co-authored "Ceremony" with Spooky Tooth in 1970.

HENRY, SAM Keyboards. Session for Myron Le Fevre (1979).

HENRY, SAM Drums. Member of the Wipers, 1980.

HENRY, TERRY Original member of the Sir Douglas Quintet.

HENSHAW, DAVID Synthesizer. Session for Carly Simon (1972).

HENSKE, JUDY Vocal. Wife of Lovin' Spoonful's Jerry Yester, she was a minor sensation in 1963 as a folk singer. Session for Russ Giguere (1971). *Albums:* Death Defying Judy Henske, 1963; Judy Henske, 1963; High Flying Bird, 1963.

HENSLEY, KEN Keyboards, guitar, vocal, percussion, synthesizer, writer. Member of the Gods, 1968, before becoming an original member of heavy metal Uriah Heep, 1970-78. Like Heep lead singer David Byron, he embarked on a solo career as a result of the group's international status. Session for David Byron (1975). *Albums:* Proud Words on a Dusty Shelf, 1973; Eager to Please (BRZ 85-2863) 1975.

HENSLEY, TOM Piano. Member of the Marketts, 1973. Session for Ringo Starr (1973-74).

HENSON, DENNY Guitar, vocal. Member of Fool's Gold, 1976.

HENTSCHEL, DAVID Synthesizer. Author of a cut-for-cut interpretation of Ringo Starr's album "Ringo." Session for Elton John (1972-75); Pilot (1972); Nazareth (1972). *Album:* Startling Music, 1975.

HERB, GARY Member of Gotham, 1979.

HERBERT, GREG Member of Blood, Sweat and Tears. Died 1978.

HERBERT, IAN Guitar, keyboards, vibes, vocal. Member of Junkyard Angel, 1972.

HERBIG, GARY Flute. Session for Rod Stewart (1978); the Marshall Tucker Band (1979); Dr. John (1979); Robbie Robertson (1980).

HERD Andy Bown—guitar, keyboards, bass, harmonica; Andrew Steele—drums; Gary Taylor—bass; Peter Frampton—vocal, guitar, bass, keyboards, drums, harmonica. First appearance of Peter Frampton in the U.S. *Album:* Lookin' Thru You, 1968.

HERMAN, ALLEN Drums, percussion, vibes. Member of Ten Wheel Drive, 1970, and Randall's Island, 1971-72.

HERMAN, NATE Guitar, mandolin, dobro, vocal. Member of Wilderness Road.

HERMAN, TOM Guitar, bass. Member of Pere Ubu, 1979.

HERMAN'S HERMITS Peter Noone—piano, guitar, vocal; Keith Hopwood—guitar; Karl Green—guitar, harmonica; Derek Leckenby—guitar; Barry Whitwam—drums. Combining banal lyrics of the fifties with the Beatles sounds of the 1960s gave the rare result of Peter Noone as Herman in Herman's Hermits. Their hits included "I'm Henry the Eighth," "Mrs. Brown You've Got a Lovely Daughter," and others. Noone was cute enough for a fling at the movies, but his face could not overcome his mediocre talent. He resurfaced in 1980 as head of the Tremblers. *Albums:* Introducing Herman's Hermits (MGM) 1965; Herman's Hermits on Tour (MGM) 1965; Best of Herman's Hermits (MGM) 1965; Hold On (MGM) 1966; Both Sides of Herman's Hermits (MGM) 1966; Best of Herman's Hermits, Vol. 2 (MGM) 1966; There's a Kind of Hush (MGM) 1967; Blaze (MGM) 1967; Best of Herman's Hermits, Vol. 3 (MGM) 1968; Herman's Hermits (XX: AKO 4227).

HERMANN, BOB Bass. Session for Chinga Chavin.

HERMANS, RUDD Vocal, guitar. Member of the Tumbleweeds, 1975.

HERMSEN, ROLF Vocal, guitar. Member of the Tapes, 1980.

HERNANDEZ, ANDY Vibes. Member of Dr. Buzzard's Original Savannah Band, 1976-78.

HERNANDEZ, ERNIE Drums, vocal. Member of Tango, 1974.

HERNDON, JAMIE Keyboards, slide guitar. Member of Neil Merryweather's Space Rangers, 1974-75, and Nick Gilder's backup band, 1978-present, replacing Steve Halter.

HERNDON, MARK Drums, vocal. Member of Alabama, 1980.

HEROES Chris Bradford—vocal, guitar; Pete Lennon—guitar; Mark Hankins—guitar, vocal; Brian Wallis—bass, vocal; Dave Powell—drums. *Album:* Border Raiders (POL 1-6264) 1980.

HEROLD, CHRIS Drums, percussion. Member of Kingfish, 1973.

HERON, MIKE Vocal, guitar, sitar, keyboards, percussion, dulcimer, writer. Replaced Clive Palmer as half of the Incredible String Band in 1967. *Album:* Mike Heron (CAS 7186) 1979.

HERRARA, FRED Bass, vocal. Member of Sweetwater.

HERREN, JOHN Keyboards. Member of Electric Prunes, 1967.

HERREWIG, GARY Guitar. Member of Artful Dodger, 1975-present.

HERRIN, JOHN Drums. Member of the Resurrection Band, 1978.

HERRING, ROY, JR. Vocal, percussion, piano. Member of Speedway Blvd., 1980.

HERSH, HOWIE Bass. Session for Joe Cocker (1978).

HERTIG, JERRY Drums. Original member of the Capital City Rockets, 1973.

HERZBERG, LAWRENCE Violin. Session for Waylon Jennings (1973).

HERZER, TOM Guitar. Member of the Crystal Mansion.

HESS, DEREK Drums, percussion. Member of the

Rossington-Collins Band, 1980.

HESSE, JOE Bass. Member of Cognition, 1971.

HESSLEIN, PETER Guitar, vocal. Member of Lucifer's Friend.

HESTER, HOOT Fiddle, vocal. Member of the Rio Grande Band.

HEWETT, PAT Bass. Member of One Hand Clapping, 1977.

HEWINSON, COLIN Keyboards, synthesizer, vocal. Member of Trickster, 1978-79.

HEWITT, DAVE Bass. Member of Babe Ruth until 1976.

HEWLETT, PETE Vocal, guitar. Member of the Euclid Beach Band, 1979.

HEWSON, RICHARD Strings. Session for Art Garfunkel.

HEY, JERRY Flugelhorn, trumpet. Member of Seawind. Session for Mark-Almond (1978); Adrian Gurvitz (1979); the Pages (1979); J. Michael Reid (1979); Elton John (1980).

HEYDON, STACEY Guitar, producer. Production and session for Long John Baldry, 1980. Session for Iggy Pop (1977).

HEYWOOD, BISHOP Drums, percussion. Session for Jackie DeShannon (1972).

HI TENSION David Joseph—keyboards, synthesizer, vocal; Kenneth Joseph—bass, vocal; Paul Phillips—guitar, vocal; Leroy Williams—percussion; Jeffrey Guishard—percussion; Paul McLean—guitar, vocal; Patrick McLean—saxophone; David Reid—drums; Paapa Mensah—drums. *Album:* Hi Tension (ISL 9564) 1978.

HI-FI's Early name for the Fifth Dimension.

HIATT, JOHN Guitar, vocal. Session for Ry Cooder (1980). *Album:* Slug Line (MCA 3088).

HICKLIN, RON Vocal. Namesake of the Ron Hicklin Singers.

RON HICKLIN SINGERS Edie Lehman Eichhorn—vocal; Debbie Hall—vocal; Ron Hicklin—vocal; Stan Farber—vocal; Gene Morford—vocal. Session for Martin Mull (1979).

HICKMAN, JASON Guitar, vocal. Member of the Twisters, 1980.

HICKMAN, JOHN Banjo. Member of Sundance, 1976.

HICKOX, CHARLIE Keyboards, vocal. Member of Marty Balin's Jefferson Airplane on "Bodacious."

HICKS, CLIVE Twelve string guitar. Session for Elton John (1969); "Jesus Christ Superstar" (1970); Vigrass and Osborne (1972).

HICKS, DAN Vocal, guitar. Leader of Dan Hicks and His Hot Licks.

DAN HICKS AND HIS HOT LICKS Dan Hicks—guitar, vocal; Mary Ann Price—vocal, percussion (1975); Naomi Eisenberg—vocal, percussion, fiddle; Sid Page—violin, mandolin, vocal; Jaimie Leopold—acoustic bass; Jon Weber—guitar; Sherry Snow—vocal; Christina Gancher—vocal, piano; John Girton—guitar (1978); Richard Borden—drums (1978); Lyle Ritz—bass (1978). Acoustic jazz-pop artists. *Albums:* Where's the Money (BTM 29) 1971; Dan Hicks and His Hot Licks (EPC 26464); It Happened One Bite (WBR K-3158) 1978; Last Train to Hicksville (MCA 51); Striking It Rich (MCA 36).

HICKS, LLOYD Drums, vocal. Member of the Randle Chowning Band, 1978.

HICKS, ROD Bass, cello, vocal. Member of Paul Butterfield Blues Band, 1968-71.

HICKS, TOMMY Real name of Tommy Steele.

HICKS, TONY Drums. Member of the Back Door, 1972-73.

HICKS, TONY Guitar, vocals. Original member of the Hollies, 1963-present.

HIERONYMI, WOLFGANG Drums, percussion. Member of the Satin Whale, 1975.

HIGGENBOTHAM, ROBERT Real name of Tommy Tucker.

HIGGERSON, JOHN Bass. Member of Trouble, 1977.

HIGGINBOTHAM, RICK Vocal, guitar. Member of the Moonlighters, 1977.

HIGGINBOTTOM, NICKY Flute, saxophone. Member of the Paul Brett Sage.

HIGGINS, BILLY Drums. Session for Sandy Bull (1963-65), after working with jazz artists Sonny Rollins, Thelonius Monk, Dexter Gordon, Ornette Coleman, Jackie McLean and others.

HIGGS, DAVE Guitar, vocal. Member of Eddie and the Hot Rods since 1976.

HIGGS, ROD Drums. Member of Prism, 1977-78.

HIGH, STEVE Vocal, percussion. Member of Brother Fox and the Tar Baby, 1969.

HIGH COTTON Todd Logan—trumpet, vocal; Jeff Logan—trombone, vocal; Mike Babb—bass; Phil Myers—drums; Chris Brawley—guitar; William Lee—keyboards, vocal; Ray Brewington—guitar. *Album:* High Cotton (ISL 9395) 1975.

HIGHNUMBERS Original name of the Who in 1963.

HIGHSTEPPERS See Larry Raspberry and the Highsteppers.

HIGHTOWER, ROSETTA Vocal. Session for Muddy Waters (1972).

HIGHWAY ROBBERY Don Francisco—drums, vocal; John Tunison—bass, vocal; Michael Stevens—guitar, vocal. *Album:* For Love or Money (VIC) 1972.

HIGHWIND Rick Fox, guitar—vocal; Ray Yancey—bass, vocal; Bruce Stull—drums, percussion, vocal; Steve Besedick—piano, vocal; Greg Shaffer—keyboards, vocal. *Album:* Highwind (FRM FR 1001) 1980.

HIGUCHI, MASAYUKI Drums. Original member of Creation, 1976.

HILL, BEAU Vocal, guitar, keyboards. Member of Airborne, 1979.

HILL, BOB Guitar, keyboards, vocal. Member of

the Godz, 1978-79.

HILL, DAN Vocal, guitar. *Albums:* Dan Hill (TWC 500) 1975; Hold On (TWC 526) 1976; Longer Fuse (TWC 547) 1977; Frozen in the Night (TWC 558) 1978; If Dreams Had Wings (EPC FE-36441) 1980.

HILL, DAVE Guitar, vocal. Original member of Slade, 1972 to present.

HILL, DUDLEY Guitar, vocal. Member of Skyboys since 1979.

HILL, DUSTY Bass, vocal. Member of Z Z Top since 1971.

HILL, IAN Bass. Member of Judas Priest since 1974.

HILL, JEFF Guitar, vocal. Member of the Wazband, 1979.

HILL, JOHN Guitar, keyboards, percussion, producer. Member of Pacific Gas and Electric, 1973. Production and session for Catfish.

HILL, ROBERT Guitar, vocal, writer. Original member of the Capital City Rockets, 1973.

HILL, STEVE Keyboards. Member of Bloodrock.

HILL, VICTOR Drums. Session for Phillip Walker (1977).

HILL, WAYNE Trumpet. Session for Barry Goldberg (1974).

HILL Steve Hammond—guitar, writer; Bruce Waddell—bass, writer; Colin Davy—drums; Peter Robinson—keyboards; Paul Buckmaster—cello. Backup group for Chris Farlowe for a lone album in 1975. Formerly named the Thunderbirds, they added Buckmaster, a cello player, and renamed themselves the Hill. See Chris Farlowe.

HILLAGE, STEVE Guitar, synthesizer, vocal. Jazz-rock space guitarist, who worked in Kahn, and Gong, before his solo career. Session for Kevin Ayers (1973). *Albums:* Fish Rising (VIR VI2031) 1975; L (ATC 18205) 1976; Motivation Radio (ATC 19144) 1977; Aura (VIR AUR 1) 1979.

HILLMAN, CHRIS Bass, mandolin, guitar, vocal. Born 12/4/42. Member of the Byrds until 1969, when he co-founded the Flying Burrito Brothers. He surfaced again as a member of the Souther-Hillman-Furay Band, 1974-75, before going solo. In 1979, he joined Byrd alumni Roger McGuinn and Gene Clark in McGuinn, Hillman and Clark. Session for Cherokee (1971); Gram Parsons (1973). *Albums:* Slippin' Away (ASY 7E-1062) 1976; Clear Sailin' (ASY 7E-1104) 1977.

HILTON, THOMAS Guitar, vocal. Member of Jiva, 1975.

HIMMEL, ANDY Bass, piano, vocal. Member of Big Star, 1972.

HIMMEL, KARL Drums. Member of Crazy Horse, 1977. Session for J. J. Cale (1971, 74); Doug Kershaw (1972); Leon Russell (1974-75); Neil Young (1977-78).

HIMMELMAN, PETER Guitar, vocal. Member of the Sussman Lawrence Band, 1980.

HINCH, JOHN Drums. Member of Judas Priest, 1974.

HINDS, BILL Guitar. Session for Roy Orbison (1979).

HINDS, NEVILLE Organ. Session for Paul Simon (1972).

HINDS, WILLIAM Drums. Member of the Pure Prairie League since 1972.

HINES, GRAHAM Vocal, guitar. Part of the British blues invasion of the 1960s that didn't make it to the U.S. as a soloist or as member of Brett Marvin and the Thunderbolts.

HINKLE, KEN Bass. Session for Leslie West (1975).

HINKLEY, TIM Keyboards. Session for Snape (1972), Alvin Lee (1973-75).

HINSCHE, BILLY Guitar, vocal. Original member of Dino, Desi and Billy, 1966-68. Session and production for Ricci Martin (1977). Session for Elton John (1974).

HINTON, EDDIE Guitar, piano, vocal. Session for the Barry Goldberg Reunion (1969); Boz Scaggs (1969, 72); Waylon Jennings (1973); Barry Goldberg (1974); John Hammond (1975); the Nighthawks (1980).

HINZE, CHRIS Flute. Namesake of the Chris Hinze Combination, 1974.

CHRIS HINZE COMBINATION Chris Hinze—flute; Phillip Catherine—guitar; John Lee—bass; Gerry Brown—drums, percussion; Rob Van Den Broek—piano; Haspar Van't Hof—keyboards; Jan Huydts—keyboards; Robert Jan Stips—organ; Henry Vonk—vocal. Experimental jazz-rock keyboard combination headed by Hinze. *Album:* Sister Slick (COL) 1974.

HIRAYAMA, MASAKO Biwa. Session for Leon Russell (1975).

HIROSHIMA Dan Kuramoto—reeds, vocal, percussion; Teri Kusumoto—vocal, percussion; Okida Kuramoto—koto; Johnny Mori—percussion; Jess Acuna—vocal, percussion; Danny Yamamoto—drums; Dane Matsumura—bass; Peter Hata—guitar; Richard Mathews—keyboards, synthesizer. *Album:* Hiroshima (ARI 4252) 1980.

HIRSCH, CHICKEN Drums. Original member of Country Joe and the Fish, 1965-68, and Touchstone, 1971.

HIRSCH, GORDON Drums. Member of Fat Chance, 1972.

HIRSCH, LARRY Vocal, production. Session for Jules and the Polar Bears (1979).

HIRSCH, PAUL Vocal, keyboards, guitar. Member of Voyager, 1979-80.

HIRSCH, RICKY Guitar, vocal. Member of Wet Willie, 1972-77, and the Gregg Allman Band, 1977.

HIRSH, JAY Guitar, keyboards, mandolin, accordion. Half of the Corbett and Hirsh team of 1971.

HISEMAN, JOHN Member of John Mayall's Bluesbreakers, replacing Keef Hartley, 1968, and of Tempest, 1973-74. Co-founder of Colosseum, 1968-71, and Colosseum II, 1977. Session for Jack Bruce (1968-69); the Keef Hartley Band (1971).

HITCHCOCK, RICKY Guitar. Session for Mike Batt (1979); Oxendale and Shephard (1979); the Who (1980).

HITCHCOCK, RUSSELL Vocal. Member of Air Supply.

HITCHINGS, DUANE Keyboards, mellotron, vocal. Member of Cactus, 1972-73, and Thee Image, 1975. Session for Beck, Bogart and Appice (1973); Danny Spanos (1980).

HITCHINS, PAUL Drums. Member of the Sports since 1979.

HITE, RICHARD Bass. Member of the Canned Heat, 1973 and 1979.

HITE, ROBERT "BEAR" JR. Vocal, harmonica, percussion, writer. Founder of Canned Heat, 1965 until his death, 4/81.

HITMEN Mike Gaffey—drums, vocal; Neil Brockbank—bass; Stan Shaw—keyboards; Ben Watkins—vocal, guitar; Pete Glenister—guitar, vocal. *Album:* Aim for the Feet (COL NJC 36874) 1980.

HLUBECK, DAVE Guitar. Born 8/28/51. Member of Molly Hatchet since 1978.

HLUDZIK, JERRY Guitar, vocal. Member of Dakota, 1980.

HOBART, TED Trumpet. Session for Mike Oldfield (1974).

HOBBS, RANDY JO Bass. Original member of the McCoys, 1965-68. Member of Johnny Winter Band, 1971-75, and Edgar and Johnny Winter Together, 1976. Session with Jimi Hendrix (1968).

HOBBS, WILL Member of Wheatfield, 1980.

HOBIACA, RICHARD Keyboards. Member of the Marketts, 1973.

HOBSON, TOM Guitar, vocal. Co-author of an acoustic blues album with Jorma Kaukonen, 1974. *Album:* Quah (GNT BFLI-0209) 1974.

HOCH, GERD Vocal. Member of the Bullfrog, 1976.

HODDER, JIM Drums. Original member of Steely Dan, 1972-75. Session for Sammy Hagar (1975).

HODDINOTT, ROBBY Guitar, slide guitar. Member of Kingfish, 1976.

HODGDEN, GARY Member of the Beckies, 1976.

HODGE, BOB "CATFISH" Vocal. Gravel-voiced vocalist of Catfish before attempting his unsuccessful solo career. Returned in 1979 as head of the Catfish Hodge Band. *Album:* Soap Operas (EPC) 1975.

HODGE, DALLAS Guitar. Member of Catfish.

HODGEKINSON, J. W. Vocal, percussion. Original member of If.

HODGEKINSON, COLIN Vocal, bass. Member of Back Door, 1972-73, and Hammer, 1979.

HODGES, CHAS Bass, keyboards. Member of Heads, Hands and Feet, 1970-71. Session for Jerry Lee Lewis (1973); Mike Berry (1976).

HODGES, KENNY Bass, vocal. Replaced Geoffrey Myers in Spanky and Our Gang, 1968.

HODGKINS, DAVE Guitar. Added to the Sunshine Company, 1968.

HODGKINSON, TIM Keyboards, flute, vocal. Member of Henry Cow, 1973.

HODGKINSON, RICHARD Drums, vocal. Member of Mi-Sex, 1980.

HODGSON, JOHN Drums, percussion. Member of Violinski, 1979.

HODGSON, PETER Bass. Member of Baby.

HODGSON, ROGER Vocal, guitar, keyboards, bass. Member of Supertramp. Session for Chick Churchill (1974).

HODSON, JOHN Percussion. Member of Rick Wakeman's backup band, 1975.

HOEFER, DOUG Snare drum. Session for Nilsson (1974, 76).

HOEKE, ROB Keyboards, harmonica. Half of a duet with Alan Price, 1977. See Alan Price.

HOENIG, MICHAEL Keyboards. *Album:* Departure from the Northern Wasteland (WBR K-3152) 1978.

HOFF, JANET FERGUSON Vocal. Session for George Duke (1975).

HOFF, JOHN Drums, percussion. Member of El Roachos, 1973.

HOFFMAN, BILL Drums. Member of the Henry Paul Band since 1979.

HOFFMAN, DOUG Drums, vocal. Member of the Euphonius Wall, 1973.

HOFFMAN, GREGG Guitar, vocal. Member of Speedway Blvd., 1980.

HOFFMAN, IAN Percussion. Member of A-440, 1978.

HOFFMAN, KARL Bass, guitar. Member of the Thumbs, 1979.

HOFFMAN, MICHAEL Guitar, vocal, percussion. Member of Yipes, 1979-80.

HOFFMAN, PETER Guitar. Session for Willie Nile (1980).

HOFFNAR, BOB Bass, vocal. Member of Indoor Life, 1980.

HOGAN, DENNIS Guitar, vocal Member of the Tazmanian Devils, 1980.

HOGAN, GERRY Pedal steel guitar. Session for Mott the Hoople (1971); Dave Edmunds (1978).

HOGAN, PETER JOHN Harmonica. Session for Chuck Berry (1965).

HOGARTH, NICK Keyboards. Member of Blue Goose, 1975.

HOGG, SMOKEY Guitar, vocal. Texas blues singer of the 1930s and 1940s. *Album:* Finest of Folk Bluesmen (BET BCP-6017).

HOGG, STEVE Bass, vocal. Member of the Ian Thomas Band, 1976.

HOGINS, ROBERT Keyboards, vocal. Session for Barry Melton (1978).

HOGINS, ROGER Organ. Session for Carlos Santana-Buddy Miles Live (1972).

HOH, EDDIE Drums, percussion. Member of the Barry Goldberg Reunion. Session for Harvey Mandel; Lee Michaels (1968); Kim Fowley; Super Session (1968).

HOKENSON, EDDIE Drums, vocal. Member of Brooklyn Dreams.

HOLBROOK, MIKE Bass. Member of the Mike Greene Band, 1975-76.

HOLD, RANDOM Vocal. Member of Random Hold, 1980.

HOLDEN, BOB Member of Quincy, 1980.

HOLDEN, RANDY Guitar. Replaced Leigh Stephens in Blue Cheer, 1969.

HOLDER, JACK Guitar, keyboards. Session for the Hot Dogs (1973).

HOLDER, NODDY Vocal, guitar. Original member of Slade, 1972-76.

HOLDING COMPANY See Big Brother and the Holding Company.

HOLDRIDGE, LEE Strings. Session for John Mayall (1979).

HOLDSWORTH, ALAN Guitar, violin, vocal. Member of Tempest, 1973, the New Tony Williams Lifetime, 1975-77, and U.K., 1978.

HOLIDAY, MARY Vocal. Session for Boz Scaggs (1969).

HOLIDAY, MIKE Bass. Member of Paul Revere and the Raiders, 1965.

HOLLAND, BERNIE Guitar, writer. Original member of Hummingbird, 1975-76.

HOLLAND, DAVE Drums, percussion. Member of Trapeze since 1974. Session for Justin Hayward (1980).

HOLLAND, JOEY Guitar. Member of Badfinger, and Natural Gas, 1976. Session for John Lennon (1971).

HOLLAND, JOOLS Vocal, keyboards. Member of the Squeeze since 1978.

HOLLAND, MILT Percussion, chimes, drums. Session for Ry Cooder (1970, 72, 74, 79-80); Captain Beefheart (1972); Elvin Bishop (1972); Nilsson (1972, 75); Tim Weisberg (1973); Ringo Starr (1973); Loggins and Messina (1973, 77); Gordon Lightfoot (1974); John Sebastian (1974); Neil Sedaka (1975); Seals and Crofts (1976); James Taylor (1976); Randy Newman.

HOLLAND, PAUL Member of Rare Bird, 1972.

HOLLAND, STEVE Guitar. Member of Molly Hatchet since 1978.

HOLLBROOK, JOHN Guitar. Session for Roger Powell (1980).

HOLLEMAN, MICHAEL J. Drums, percussion, vocal. Member of the Lost Gonzo Band, 1978.

HOLLESTELLE, HANS Guitar, synthesizer. Member of Spin, 1976. Session for Barry Hay; George Kooymans.

HOLLESTELLE, JAN Bass, synthesizer, piano. Member of Spin, 1976.

HOLLIES Graham Nash—guitar, vocal (1963-66); Allan Clarke—vocal, writer (1966-present); Tony Hicks—guitar, vocal (1965-present); Bernard Calvert—bass, keyboards (1965-present); Bobby Elliott—drums (1963-present); Eric Haydock—bass (1963-65); Terry Sylvester—guitar, vocal (1972-present). Early names: the Deltas; the Fortunes. From their very beginnings, the Hollies were the pacesetters for harmony vocals. Since the early 1960s under Graham Nash, their three-part choir-like harmonies were pleasant and distinctive. Nash left in 1966 to develop on his own and Clarke assumed the lead duties. He, too, went solo, though less successfully. The group disbanded, to re-form in 1972, releasing "Long Cool Woman." It revitalized their pop interest (along with the historical value from Nash, now a hit after Crosby, Stills and Nash) luring them a new audience from old memories. "The Air I Breathe" (1974), won over further fans and assured them of popularity long overdue. *Albums:* Hear, Here (IMP) 1965; Here I Go Again (IMP) 1965; Beat Group (IMP) 1966; Bus Stop (IMP) 1966; Stop, Stop, Stop (IMP) 1967; Evolution (IMP) 1967; Dear Eloise/King Midas in Reverse (IMP) 1967; Hollies' Greatest Hits (EPC PE-32061) 1967; The Hollies—Words and Music by Bob Dylan (IMP) 1969; Distant Light (EPC E-30958) 1972; Hollies (EPC KE 32574); Another Night (EPC PE 33387) 1975; Hollies (EPC PE 34714) 1977; Crazy Steal (EPC JE 35334) 1978; Five-Three-One-Double Seven-O-Four (EPC PEC 90551) 1979; He Ain't Heavy (CSP EN-13092).

HOLLOWAY, BRENDA Vocal. Session for Joe Cocker (1968); Neil Young (1969).

HOLLOWAY, RED Tenor and alto saxophones, flute. Played with John Mayall, 1973. Session for B. B. King (1972); John Mayall (1977). *Album:* Forecast: Sonny and Red (CLT 7608).

HOLLOWAY, RON Member of Osiris, 1978.

HOLLY, CHARLES HARDIN "BUDDY" Vocal, guitar, writer. Born 9/7/36. In the 1950s, the commercial phenomenon known as stage presence was essential. It was therefore unlikely for pop singer Holly, clad in a blazer and thick black-rimmed glasses, to become successful. But from 1956 to 1958, he broke that rule with a list of rock classics that included Bill Haley's "Shake, Rattle and Roll," Little Richard's "Rip It Up," and his own "Peggy Sue" (1957), "That'll Be The Day," "Oh Boy," and others. He was one of the biggest stars of the day until his death, February 3, 1959, in a plane crash in Mason City, Iowa. Also killed were Richie Valens and the Big Bopper. Paul McCartney now controls the rights to his songs. *Albums:* That'll Be the Day, 1957; Buddy Holly Story (EPC SE-35412) 1957; Buddy Holly (CRL) 1958; Buddy Holly Story, Vol. 2 (CRL) 1960; Buddy Holly and the Crickets (CRL) 1962; Reminiscing (CRL)

1963; Buddy Holly Showcase (CRL) 1964; Holly in the Hills (CRL) 1965; Best of Buddy Holly (CRL) 1966; Buddy Holly's Greatest Hits (CRL) 1967; Great Buddy Holly, 1967; Brown-Eyed Handsome Man; Giant (CRL) 1969; Good Rockin' Tonight, 1971; Great Buddy Holly (MCA) 1975; Buddy Holly Lives (MCA) 1978.

HOLLY, STEVE Drums. Member of Elton John's backup band, 1978. Replaced Joe English in Wings, 1979. Session for the Vapour Trails (1980).

HOLLYWOOD ARGYLES Recorded "Alley Oop," 1960. Early band for Gary Paxton.

HOLLYWOOD STARS Terry Rae—drums, vocal; Michael Rummens—bass, vocal; Mark Anthony—vocal, guitar; Ruben De Fuentes—guitar; Bobby Daier—drums. *Album:* Hollywood Stars, 1977.

HOLMAN, MICHAEL Bass, vocal. Original member of It's a Beautiful Day, 1969-71.

HOLMES, ALAN Baritone saxophone, clarinet. Member of the Kinks, 1972. Session for the Kinks (1975).

HOLMES, CLIVE Keyboards. Member of Timebox, 1976.

HOLMES, GENE Guitar, vocal. Member of the Waves, 1977.

HOLMES, PHIL Keyboards, vocal. Member of the Alwyn Wall Band, 1977.

HOLMES, RUPERT Vocal. Session for the Strawbs (1976). *Albums:* Rupert Holmes, 1975; Singles, 1976; Partners in Crime (INF 9020); Pursuit of Happiness (MCA 3241) 1978; Adventure (MCA 5129) 1980.

HOLMES, SHERMAN Bass. Session for John Hammond (1980).

HOLROYD, LES Bass, vocal. Member of the Barclay James Harvest.

HOLSTER, DAVID Guitar. Member of Starwood, 1976-77.

HOLT, ASHLEY Vocal. Member of Rick Wakeman's backup band, 1974-77.

HOLT, DEREK Guitar, bass, vibes, vocal. Original member of the Climax Blues Band, 1968-present.

HOLT, HARRY Bass. Session for Sonny Terry and Brownie McGhee (1973).

HOLT, KEN Bass. Member of the Blend, 1978-79.

HOLT, STEVE Session for the Hot Dogs (1973).

HOLTON, GARY Vocal. Voice of the Heavy Metal Kids, 1974, and Kids, 1975.

HOLTZE, ERIC Guitar. Member of the Jan Park Band, 1979.

HOLTZER, MIKE Member of Brush Arbor, 1977.

HOLY MODAL ROUNDERS John Annis—bass; Steve Webber—guitar; Richard Tyler—piano; Sam Shepard—drums; Peter Stampfel—banjo. Experimental rock group combining everything from country and western and jug band music to existential and nonsense lyrics. Their song, "If You Wanna Be a Bird," was used in the movie "Easy Rider." After the initial novelty of the group had passed, the Rounders personnel had settled to the Weber and Stampfel nucleus while the material had become bluegrass based. *Albums:* Moray Eels Eat the Holy Modal Rounders (ELK) 1968; Holy Modal Rounders, Vol. 1 (PRS 7720); Indian War Whoop (ESP 1068); Last Round (ADP 1030) 1978; Stampfel and Weber (FSY 24711); Alleged in Their Own Time (RDR 3004).

HOLZWARTH, DOUG Keyboards. Member of Arizona, 1976.

HOMBRES Recorded "Let It All Hang Out," late 1960s.

HOMESICK JAMES Guitar, vocal. One of the first traditional bluesmen to go electric. *Album:* Goin' Back Home (TRX 3315) 1976.

HOMETOWN BAND Shari Ulrich—vocal, violin, flute; Claire Lawrence—saxophone, flute; Geoff Eyre—drums; Robbie King—keyboards; Doug Edwards—guitar. *Album:* Flying, 1976.

HOMMEL, MICHAEL Bass, vocal. Member of Proof, 1980.

HONAKER, DAN Bass, vocal. Original member of the Bob Seger System.

HONEYWELL, DON Baritone saxophone. Session for Savoy Brown (1969).

HONIGMAN, JERRY Vocal, guitar. Member of the Romeos, 1980.

HONK Tris Imboden—drums; Beth Fitchet—guitar; Don Whaley—bass; Richard Stekol—guitar; Steve Wood—keyboard; Craig Buhler—reeds. *Albums:* Honk (TWC) 1973; Honk (EPC).

HOOCHIE COOCHIE MEN Early band featuring Rod Stewart and Long John Baldry on vocals.

HOOD, BILL Saxophone. Session for Ry Cooder (1978).

HOOD, DAVID Bass. Member of Traffic, 1973, and the Muscle Shoals Rhythm Section. Replaced Dan Keylon in the Rockets, 1979 to present. Session for Jackson Highway; Boz Scaggs (1969, 72); King Curtis (1969); John Hammond (1969); Barry Goldberg Reunion (1969); Don Nix (1971); Jim Capaldi (1971, 73, 75); Leon Russell (1971); Mike Harrison (1972); Tony Joe White (1972); J. J. Cale (1972); Bob Seger (1973, 75); Paul Simon (1973, 75); Barry Goldberg (1974); Paul Kossoff (1974); Willie Nelson (1974); Rod Stewart (1975-76); Richard Tate (1977); Joe Cocker (1978); Art Garfunkel (1978).

HOODOO RHYTHM DEVILS Joe Crane—piano; John Rewind—guitar; Dexter C. Plates—bass; Jerome Kimsey—drums; Skip Mesquite—saxophone. Session for the Pointer Sisters (1973). *Album:* Too Hot to Handle (BTM) 1973.

HOOGENBOOM, ANDY Member of Blues Incorporated.

HOOK, CHRIS Bass. Member of Voyager, 1979-80.

HOOK, PETER Bass. Member of the Joy Division,

1979-80.

HOOKE, HELEN Vocal, guitar, fiddle, keyboard. Member of Deadly Nightshade, 1975.

HOOKER, JAMES Piano, vocal. Member of the Amazing Rhythm Aces.

HOOKER, JOHN LEE Guitar, vocal, writer. Born 7/22/17. Recorded under the names of Texas Sun, Johnny Williams, Delton John, Birmingham Sam, and others. Southern blues guitarist and singer who popularized "Boogie" music, his trademark. Though he had been playing since the 1940s, he did not receive national (and international) recognition until the 1960s, with his appearance at the Newport Folk Festival, which coincided with the beginnings of the British pop invasions. Then, the Animals, the Rolling Stones and others recorded some of his material, and one group even named themselves after him: John Lee's Groundhogs. Since his "discovery" he has been one of the most prolific recording bluesmen. *Albums:* Big Band Blues (BUD 7506); Boogie with Hooker 'n' Heat (TRP 360); Born in Mississippi, Raised Up in Tennessee (ABC XQ 768); Free Beer and Chicken (ABC QD 838); John Lee Hooker's Detroit (UAR UA-LA127-93); John Hooker's Endless Boogie (ABC 720); It Serves You Right To Suffer (IPE 8103) 1966; Live at Soledad Prison (ABC XQ 761); Mad Man Blues (CSS 2-60111); Never Get Out of These Blues Alive (ABC XQ 736); On the Waterfront (WND 689); Very Best of John Lee Hooker (BUD 4002); Whiskey and Wimmen (TRP X-9504); House of the Blues, 1960; John Lee Hooker Plays and Sings the Blues, 1961; Don't Turn Me From Your Door, 1963; And Seven Nights, 1966; Live at the Cafe A Go Go, 1966; Urban Blues, 1968; Real Folk Blues, 1968; John Lee Hooker Alone (SPE 2125) 1972; Sittin' Here Thinkin' (MUS 5205) 1979; That's Where It's At (STX 4134); Real Blues (TRD 2089); Moanin' and Stompin' Blues (KGO 1085); John Lee Hooker (KNT 525); John Lee Hooker (EVR 222); Hooked on the Blues (EVR 347); Greatest Hits of John Lee Hooker (INT 559); Dark Muddy Bottom Blues (SPE 2149); Cryin' in the Morning (MUS 5212); The Cream (TMT 7009); Boogie Chillun (FSY 24706); Black Snake (FSY 24722); Best of John Lee Hooker (CRS 10007).

HOOKFOOT Ian Duck—harmonica, vocal; Caleb Quaye—guitar, piano; Roger Pope—drums, percussion; Freddy Gandy—bass. Early Elton John session men displaying the talent that helped make John famous. The dynamic songwriting however, was lacking. *Album:* Communication (AAM) 1972.

HOOPER, CRAIG Guitar. Member of the Reels, 1980.

HOOPER, DARYL Keyboards. Original member of the Seeds, 1966-67.

HOOPER, PAUL Drums, vocal. Member of the Dodgers, 1978.

HOOPER, TONY Vocal, guitar, percussion. Member of the Strawbs, 1970-72.

HOORELBEKE, PETER Vocal, drums, percussion. Member of Hub, 1975-76, and Rare Earth, 1975-77. Session for Doucette (1979).

HOOVEN, JEFFREY DAVID Piano, guitar, vocal. Member of the Candle, 1972.

HOPE, DAVE Bass, vocal. Born 10/7/49. Original member of Kansas, since 1974.

HOPE, ELLIE Vocal. Replaced Janita Haan in Babe Ruth, 1976.

HOPE-EVANS, PETE Harmonica. Member of Medicine Head, 1973. Session on "Rough Mix" (1977); Pete Townshend (1980).

HOPKIN, MARY Vocal. First artist to record on the Beatles' Apple label in 1969. Her innocent blond looks and vocals made "Those Were the Days" a big and unfollowed hit. *Album:* Postcard (APL) 1969.

HOPKINS, "LIGHTNIN" Guitar, vocal, bottleneck guitar, writer. One of the most underexposed and prolific blues minstrels on record, Hopkins is rarely known outside of the circle of his blues contemporaries. *Albums:* Autobiography in Blues (EVR 342) 1960; Lightnin' Hopkins (EVR 241) 1960; King of the Blues, 1962; Lightnin' Hopkins, Vol. 2 (EVR 313) 1962; Double Blues (FSY 24702); First Meetin' (WPP 1847) 1964; Hootin' the Blues (PRS 7806) 1964; My Life in the Blues, 1965; Roots of Lightnin' Hopkins (FLW 31011) 1965; Lightnin' (PRS 7811) 1965; Lightnin' Blues (UPF 158); Lightnin' Strikes Again (TRP 7502) 1965; Soul Blues, 1966; Something Blue, 1967; Best of Lightnin' Hopkins (PRS 7714) 1967; Talkin' Some Sense, 1968; And the Blues (IMP 12211); Sounder (Movie Soundtrack) (COL 5-31944); Lightnin' Hopkins Greatest Hits (PRS 7592) 1968; Anthology of the Blues—Lightnin' Hopkins—Legend in His Own Time (KNT 9008); Blues Roots (TMT 2-7006); Dark Muddy Bottom Blues (SPE 2149); Double Blues (FSY 24702); Gotta Move Your Baby (PRS 7831); Lightnin' Hopkins (KNT 523); Lightnin' (TMT 2-7004); Lightnin' Strike (TRD 2103).

HOPKINS, KENNY Guitar, vocal. Member of Mistress, 1979.

HOPKINS, MILTON Guitar. Session for B. B. King (1972, 75, 77).

HOPKINS, NICKY Piano, vocal, writer. Born 2/24/44. Began with Cyril Davies and His All Stars, before joining the Jeff Beck Group, 1969, with Rod Stewart. A brief member of the Quicksilver Messinger Service, 1969, he went on to join Sweet Thursday, 1970, and the Rolling Stones, 1972. Sessions for the Rolling Stones (1967, 68, 70, 73, 74, 76, 80); Jeff Beck (1968); the Jefferson Airplane (1969); the Steve Miller Band (1970); Lord Sutch; the Who (1971, 75); John Lennon

(1971, 74); Art Garfunkel; the New Riders of the Purple Sage; Nilsson (1972); Carly Simon (1972); Donovan (1973); George Harrison (1973-75); Mark-Almond (1973); Ringo Starr (1973-74); Joe Cocker (1974-76); McGuiness-Flint; Peter Frampton (1974); Bill Wyman (1976); Jennifer Warnes (1976); Rod Stewart (1977-78); Rocky Sullivan (1978); Night (1979).

HOPPEN, LANCE Bass, vocal. Member of Orleans, 1973-76.

HOPPEN, LARRY Vocal, keyboards, guitar, trumpet. Member of Orleans, 1973-76.

HOPPER, HUGH Bass. Member of the Soft Machine, 1970, and Gilgamesh, before replacing Jeff Clyne in Isotope, 1975. Session for Robert Wyatt (1974).

HOPPER, SEAN Keyboards. Member of Clover, 1977, and Huey Lewis and the News, 1980. Session for Carlene Carter (1980).

HOPPS, ROGER Trumpet. Session for the Memphis Horns.

HOPWOOD, KEITH Guitar. Member of Herman's Hermits, 1965-68.

HORBURY, TERRY Bass. Member of Dirty Tricks, 1976-77.

HORD, ERIC Guitar. Session for Fred Neil (1968).

HORN, JIM Saxophone, flute. Session for Marc Benno; Bangla Desh (1971); Joe Cocker (1972, 74); Donovan (1973); the Rolling Stones (1973); George Harrison (1973-75); Nicky Hopkins (1974); Nilsson (1974, 76); Leon Russell (1975); Neil Sedaka (1975-76); Steely Dan (1976); Carol King; Boz Scaggs (1976); Seals and Crofts (1976); Jennifer Warnes (1976); Glen Campbell (1976); Yvonne Elliman (1978); Richie Furay (1978); Gary Wright (1979); Roy Orbison (1979); Dick St. Nicklaus (1979); Alan O'Day (1979); 1994 (1979); Jay Ferguson (1980); the Strand (1980); Elton John (1980); Johnny Winter (1980); Stuart Margolin (1980); Christopher Cross (1980). *Album:* Through the Ears of a Horn (SLR).

HORN, ROBERT Drums, vocal. Member of Citizen, 1980.

HORN, TREVOR Vocal, bass. Replaced Jon Anderson in Yes, 1980 to present.

HORNBLOWER, HORATIO Saxophone. Member of the Darts since 1978.

HORNS, DIETER Bass, vocal. Member of Lucifer's Friend.

HORNSBY, PAUL Organ, piano, moog, producer. Member of Hourglass, 1968. Session and production for the Marshall Tucker band, 1973-79, and Two Guns, 1979. Session for Johnny Jenkins (1970); Gregg Allman (1973); Captain Beyond (1973); Elvin Bishop (1974).

HOROWITZ, JIMMY Keyboards. Session for Long John Baldry (1972, 75).

HORSLIPS Jim Lockhart—keyboards, flute, vocal, whistle; Eamon Carr—drums, percussion; Barry Devlin—bass, vocal; Charles O'Connor—fiddle, mandolin, concertina, vocal; John Fean—guitar, banjo, vocal. Early specialists in Irish ballads and traditionals, Horslips soon became comfortable with their own unique, underexposed brand of rock. *Albums:* The Tain (ACO SD 7039); Happy To Meet, Sorry To Part (ACO SD 7030) 1973; Dancehall Sweethearts (VIC CPLI-0709) 1974; Book of Invasions (DJM 10) 1976; Aliens (DJM 16) 1977; The Man Who Built America (DJM 20) 1978; Short Stories/Tall Tales (MER SRM-1-3809) 1980.

HORTON, GLADYS Vocal. Original member of the Marvelettes.

HORTON, WALTER "SHAKEY" Harmonica, vocal. Session for Chicken Shack; Fleetwood Mac (1969). *Albums:* Fine Cuts (BPG 006-48) 1972; Big Walter Horton/Carey Bell (ALG 4702).

HORTON–JENNINGS, COLIN Vocal, flute, guitar. Member of the Greatest Show on Earth, 1970.

HORTTER, DAN Vocal, harmonica. Voice of the Yellow Payges, 1969.

HOSKO, BOB Saxophone. Member of Junior Cadillac.

HOSONO, HARJOMI Bass, keyboards. Member of the Yellow Magic Orchestra, 1979-80.

HOSSACK, MICHAEL Drums. Member of the Doobie Brothers, 1972-74, and Bonaroo, 1975.

HOT DOGS Bill Rennie—vocal, bass; Greg Reding—piano, guitar, vocal. *Album:* Say What You Mean, 1973.

HOT LEGS Early name of 10 CC.

HOT LICKS See Dan Hicks and His Hot Licks.

HOT TUNA Jorma Kaukonen—guitar, vocal, writer; Jack Casady—bass; Will Scarlett—harmonica (1970-72); Papa John Creach—violin (1971-72); Sammy Piazza—drums (1971-73); Bob Steeler—drums, percussion (1974-79); Nick Buck—keyboards (1978-79). Hot Tuna's first album was a set of live, acoustic blues and considered a sideline for Kaukonen and Casady from their usual chores in the Jefferson Airplane. Their second album, totally electric, marked a change in atmosphere, and indicated Kaukonen's and Casady's serious intentions about continuing the group, which became official in 1973, when Kaukonen and Casady quit the Airplane. Though the electricity remained (considered a shortcoming by many critics), it was unarguable that Kaukonen and Casady were a unique and extraordinarily talented team, augmenting the best in each other. Part of Filmore, 1972. *Albums:* Hot Tuna (VIC AFLI-4353) 1970; Electric Hot Tuna (VIC AFLI-4550) 1971; Burgers (GNT BXLI-2591) 1972; Phosphorescent Rat (GNT BXLI-0348) 1973; America's Choice (GNT BXLI 0820) 1974; Yellow Fever (GNT BXLI-1238) 1975; Hoppkrov (GNT BXLI-1920) 1976; Double Dose (GNT CYL2-2545)

1978; Final Vinyl (GNT BXLI-3357) 1979.

HOTEL Marc Phillips—guitar, keyboards, vocal; George Creasman—bass, vocal; Lee Bargeron—keyboard, guitar, vocal; Tommy Carlton—guitar, vocal; Michael Reid—guitar, vocal; Michael Cadenhead—drums, percussion, vocal. *Albums:* Hotel (MCA 3158); Half Moon Silver (MCA 5113) 1980.

HOUGH, MIKE Member of Flash, 1972.

HOUGHTON, DAVE Drums. Session for Joe Jackson (1979).

HOURGLASS Duane Allman—guitar, writer; Gregg Allman—keyboards, vocal, writer; Pete Carr—bass; Paul Hornsby—organ; Johnny Sandlin —drums. The recording debut of the Allman Brothers. *Albums:* Hourglass (LIB) 1968; Power of Love (LIB) 1968.

HOUSE, DIXON Keyboards. Namesake of the Dixon House Band, 1979.

DIXON HOUSE BAND Dixon House—keyboards; Chrissy Shefts—guitar; Chuck Gardner—guitar; James Kenfield—bass; Fred Zeufeldt—drums. *Album:* Dixon House Band (INF 9008) 1979.

HOUSE, EDDIE J. "SON" Bottleneck guitar, vocal, writer. Mississippi blues man who recorded during the 1930s, of which only four of nine sides remain. Moved to New York in 1943 and quit playing guitar in 1948. For the Newport Folk Festival in 1964, he was coaxed from retirement to play with other bluesmen, like John Lee Hooker, Sleepy John Estes, Bukka White, and others. *Albums:* Delta Blues (FLW 31928) 1963; Father of the Folk Blues (COL CS-9217); Legendary Son House (COL CS 9217).

HOUSE, RICHIE Guitar, vocal. Member of the Trigger, 1978.

HOUSE, SIMON Keyboard, violin. Member of Hawkwind, 1978 to present.

HOUSEROCKERS See Hound Dog Taylor and the Houserockers.

HOUSMAN, KENT Vocal, guitar, percussion. Member of the Ducks, 1973.

HOUSTON, CISSY DRINKARD Vocal. Member of the Sweet Inspirations, 1967-69. Session for Paul Simon (1972); Jackie DeShannon (1972). *Albums:* Step Aside for a Lady (COL JC-36193); Surprises (ATC 1682); Warning–Danger (COL JC-36112); Cissy Houston (PRS PS 2031) 1977; Think It Over (PRS PS 7015) 1977.

HOUSTON, EMILY Vocal. Session for Gregg Allman (1973).

HOUSTON, PENELOPE Vocal. Member of the Avengers, 1979.

HOVEY, DAVE Guitar, vocal. Member of Hellfield, 1978.

HOWARD, BRIE Drums. Member of Fanny, 1974.

HOWARD, CEPDAS Played with John Mayall, 1971.

HOWARD, DAVE Alto saxophone. Session for Fleetwood Mac (1969).

HOWARD, DOUG Bass, vocal. Member of the Touch, 1980.

HOWARD, JAMES NEWTON Keyboards, synthesizer, mellotron, producer. Produced Valerie Carter (1978). Session for Fanny (1974); Ringo Starr (1974); Elton John (1975-80); Neil Diamond (1976); Melissa Manchester; Nilsson (1976); Neil Sedaka (1976); Yvonne Elliman (1978); the Dudek-Finnigan-Kruger Band (1980); Boz Scaggs (1980).

HOWARD, LARRY Guitar, vocal. Member of Grinderswitch.

HOWARD, MICK Bass. Member of Darling, 1979.

HOWARD, RICHARD Keyboards. Member of the Bob Meighan Band, 1976.

HOWARD, STEVE Horns. Session for Wings (1976).

HOWE, BONES Percussion. Session for Martin Mull (1979).

HOWE, BRYAN Keyboards, vocal. Member of Fireballet, 1975-77.

HOWE, DAN Keyboards, vocal. Member of the Max Demian Band, 1979-80.

HOWE, DAYTON Percussion. Session for Jan and Dean (1963).

HOWE, STEVE Guitars, vocal, writer, bass, steel guitar, moog. Born 4/8/47. Replaced Peter Banks in Yes, 1971 to present. Session for Lou Reed (1972); Rick Wakeman (1972). *Albums:* Beginning (ATC 18154) 1975; Steve Howe Album (ATC 19243) 1979.

HOWELL, ANGELA Vocal, percussion. Session for Lou Reed (1979).

HOWELL, HAMMY Piano. Member of the Darts since 1978.

HOWELL, PEG LEG Guitar, vocal. Real name: Joshua Barnes Howell. Georgia born blues man who first recorded in 1926. *Album:* Story of the Blues (COL CG-30008).

HOWIE, MITCH Drums. Member of Clover.

HOWLAND, BILL Keyboards, vocal. Member of the Timberline, 1977.

HOWLETT, MIKE Bass, vocal. Member of Gong since 1975.

HOWLIN' WOLF Vocal, harmonica, guitar, writer. Born 6/10/10. Chester Burnett, alias Howlin' Wolf, had the most distinct vocals of any major blues artist. He wrote "Smokestack Lightnin'," that was made a rock hit by the Yardbirds and the Rolling Stones. Appeared at the 1966 Newport Folk Festival. He was one of the major sources for the British blues invasion of the 1960s. Died 1976. *Albums:* The Back Door Wolf (CSS 50045); Evil (CSS 1540); Howlin' Wolf Album (CSS 319); Howlin' Wolf (KNT 526); Howlin' Wolf aka Chester Burnett (CSS 60016); Howlin' Wolf Live and Cookin' (CSS 50015); London Howlin' Wolf Sessions (CSS 60008) 1972; London Revisited

(CSS 60026); Message to the Young (CSS 50002); Real Folk Blues (CSS 1502) 1966; More Real Folk Blues, 1967; Tune Box; Moanin' in the Moonlight.

HOWTEN, BARRY Member of Blues Incorporated.

HOY, TOM Vocal, guitar. Member of Magna Carta, 1976.

HOYLE, PIP Keyboards. Member of Radio Birdman, 1978.

HUB Peter Hoorelbeke—vocal, drums, percussion; Mike Urso—vocal, bass; Tom Baird—vocal, keyboards. *Album:* Hub (CAP) 1975.

HUB CAPS See Gene Vincent and His Hub Caps.

HUBBARD, GENE Piano, organ. Member of American Eagle, 1970-71.

HUBBARD, NEIL Guitar. Former member of Bluesology and the Graham Bond Organization. Member of Juicy Lucy, 1970, and the Grease Band, 1971. Session for "Jesus Christ Superstar" (1970); Joe Cocker (1972); Donovan (1973); Alvin Lee (1974); Pete Wingfield (1975); Bryan Ferry (1977-78); Roxy Music (1980).

HUBBARD, PRESTON Bass, fiddle. Member of Roomful of Blues, 1977.

HUBERT, LOUIS Tenor saxophone. Session for B. B. King (1972).

HUBINSON, PAUL Horns. Session for Boz Scaggs (1976).

HUDAK, MICHAEL Drums, vocal. Member of the Love Affair, 1980.

HUDSON, BARBARA Vocal, guitar, percussion. Original member of Ultimate Spinach, 1968-69.

HUDSON, BILL Guitar, vocal. Born 10/17/49. One-third of the Hudson Brothers.

HUDSON, BRETT Bass, guitar, vocal. Born 1/18/53. One-third of the Hudson Brothers.

HUDSON, BUTCH Trumpet. Session for Savoy Brown (1969).

HUDSON, ERIC Organ. Session for John Hammond (1965, 68).

HUDSON, GARTH Keyboards, piccolo, accordion. Born 8/2/37. Member of the Band, 1963-78. Session for Ringo Starr (1973); Paul Butterfield (1975); Neil Diamond (1976); Rick Danko (1977); Danny Douma (1979).

HUDSON, JERRY Guitar. Member of Cognition, 1971.

HUDSON, MARK Piano, drums, vocal. Born 8/23/51. One-third of the Hudson Brothers.

HUDSON, PHIL Vocal. Member of Cognition, 1971.

HUDSON, RICHARD Vocal, guitar, drums, sitar. Member of the Strawbs, 1970-71, and half of the namesake for Hudson-Ford, 1974-75.

HUDSON, TONY Bass. Member of the Alwyn Wall Band, 1977.

HUDSON Abbreviated name for the Hudson Brothers. See the Hudson Brothers. *Album:* Damn Those Kids (ELK 6E-299) 1980.

HUDSON BROTHERS Bill Hudson—guitar, vocal; Mark Hudson—piano, drums, vocal; Brett Hudson—bass, guitar, vocal. *Albums:* Totally Out of Control (MCA) 1974; Ba Fa (MCA) 1976; TV's The Hudson Brothers (FSM 7708) 1978; Truth About Us (ARI 4199); Hollywood Situation (CAS 7004).

HUDSON-FORD Richard Hudson—vocal, guitar; John Ford—vocal, bass; Micky Keene—guitar; Chris Parren—keyboards; Ken Laws—drums, percussion. *Albums:* Free Spirit (AAM) 1974; Nickelodeon (AAM).

HUEY, MICHAEL Drums. Member of Blue Steel since 1980.

HUFF, BOB Guitar, vocal. Member of Arizona, 1976.

HUFF, STEVEN Bass, vocal. Member of the Beat, 1979.

HUFSTETER, STEVE Guitar. Member of Quick, 1976.

HUG, JOHN LESLIE Guitar, mandolin. Member of Osamu, 1977, and the Gregg Allman Band, 1977. Replaced Todd Robinson in the Tim Weisberg Band, 1979. Session for Greg Sutton (1975); Waylon Jennings (1975); Tim Weisberg and Dan Fogelberg (1978).

HUGG, MIKE Drums, percussion, vibes. Cofounder and original member of Manfred Mann, 1963-71. Session for Lo and Behold (1972).

HUGHES, CHRIS Saxophone. Session for Pilot (1972); Long John Baldry (1975); Def Leppard (1980).

HUGHES, DANA Horns. Session for Jerry Corbetta (1978).

HUGHES, GLENN Bass, vocal, writer. Member of Trapeze until 1973. Replaced Roger Glover in Deep Purple, 1973-75.

HUGHES, JIMMY Bass. Member of the Cowboys International, 1979.

HUGHES, LYNNE Vocal. Original member of Stoneground, 1971.

HUGHES, RICHARD Drums. Replaced Bobby Caldwell in the Johnny Winter Band, 1973-present. Session for Edgar Winter (1973-79).

HUGHES, STEVE Guitar. Session for Mylon LeFevre (1979).

HUGHES, VAN Trombone. Session for It's a Beautiful Day (1971).

HUGHEY, JOHN Steel guitar. Session for Tony Joe White (1972); Willie Nelson (1974); Richard Betts (1974).

HUHN, CHARLIE Vocal, guitar. Session for Ted Nugent (1979-80).

HULDANE, STEVE Bass. Member of the Andy Bown group.

HULL, DANNY Tenor saxophone. Member of Cold Blood.

HULL, DAVID Bass, vocal, keyboards. Member of the Dirty Angels, 1976-78, and the Joe Perry Project, 1980. Session for Ted Nugent (1978).

HULL, JAMES ALAN Vocal, guitar. Member of Lindisfarne, 1974-78.

HULLIN, GEORGE Drums, trumpet, vocal. Member of Redwing.

HULTGREEN, GEORGE Guitar, vocal. Member of Eclection, 1968.

HUMAN HOST AND THE HEAVY METAL KIDS See Hapshash and the Coloured Coat.

HUMAN LEAGUE Ian Craig Marsh—synthesizer, vocal; Phillip Oakey—synthesizer, vocal; Martin Ware—synthesizer, vocal. *Album:* Travelogue (VIR 2160) 1980.

HUMAN SEXUAL RESPONSE Larry Bangor—vocal; Casey Cameron—vocal; Windle Davis—vocal; Dini Lamot—vocal, percussion; Rich Gilbert—guitar; Chris Maclachlan—bass; Malcolm Travis—drums. *Album:* Figure 14 (PSS PB 9851) 1980.

HUMBLE, BILL Trombone. Session for J. J. Cale (1972).

HUMBLE PIE Steve Marriott—guitar, keyboards, vocals, writer (1969-75, 80); Jerry Shirley—drums, keyboards (1968-75, 80); Greg Ridley—bass, vocals (1969-75); Peter Frampton—guitar, writer (1969-71); Clem Clempson—guitar, keyboards (1971-75); Bobby Tench—vocal, guitar (1980); Anthony Jones—bass, vocal (1980). Much publicity resulted when Steve Marriott left the Small Faces to form Humble Pie in 1969 with Peter Frampton. Critically, they had a hard time trying to live up to their publicity until "Performance" was released in 1971. By then, Frampton, who had decided to pursue his own career, was already replaced by Clemson. Marriott and his distinctive vocals had taken control of the group, and his dancing supplied visual energy to their music. They disbanded in 1975. After Marriott's ill-fated reunion of the Small Faces, he re-formed Humble Pie in 1980. *Albums:* As Safe as Yesterday (AAM 3513) 1969; Town and Country (AAM 3513) 1969; Eat It (AAM 3701) 1970; Humble Pie (AAM 4270) 1970; Peformance (AAM 3506) 1971; Rock On (AAM 4301) 1971; Smoking (AAM 4342) 1972; Thunderbox (AAM 3611) 1974; On to Victory (ACO 38-122) 1980.

HUME, BRIAN Vocal, guitar. Member of Prelude, 1974.

HUME, IRENE Vocal. Voice of Prelude, 1974.

HUMMINGBIRD Bobby Tench—guitar, vocal; Clive Chaman—bass, harmonica, writer; Max Middleton—keyboards, moog, writer; Bernie Holland—guitar; Conrad Isidore—drums, writer (1975); Bernard Purdie—drums, percussion (1976). Formed from the remnants of the Jeff Beck Group, they banded together to pursue jazz-oriented rhythm and blues when Beck decided to branch into another field. *Albums:* Hummingbird (AAM SP 4536) 1975; We Can't Go On Meeting Like This (AAM 35P-4595) 1976; Diamond Nights (AAM SP 4661) 1977.

HUMMONS, DEAN Keyboards, percussion. Member of Dayton, 1980.

HUMPBACK WHALES A recording of the melodic communicative moans and squeaks of humpback whales. *Album:* Songs of the Humpback Whales (CAP ST 620) 1970.

HUMPHREY, RALPH Drums. Member of the Mothers of Invention, 1973-74, C.O.D., 1979, and In Transit, 1980. Session for Frank Zappa (1974).

HUMPHREYS, TONY Percussion. Session for Martin Mull (1974).

HUMPHRIES, GUY Session for Marianne Faithfull (1979); Roy Sundholm (1979).

HUMPHRIES, MITCH Keyboards. Member of the Rock Killough group, 1980. Session for Levon Helm (1980).

HUMPHRIES, PAUL Drums. Session for Joe Cocker (1968); Frank Zappa (1969); Tim Weisberg (1971).

HUMPHRIES, STEVE Bass. Member of Lion, 1980.

HUNGATE, DAVID Bass. Member of Toto since 1978. Session for Boz Scaggs (1976-80); Donovan (1976); John Sebastian (1976); Seals and Crofts (1976); Cher Bono (1976-79); Jimmy Webb (1977); Steve Kipner (1979); Adrian Gurvitz (1979).

HUNGER Bill Daffern—vocal; Steve Hansen; Mike Lane; Mike Parkinson; John Morton. Portland band that moved to Los Angeles. *Album:* Strictly from Hunger.

HUNGERFORT, GRANT Horns. Session for John Lennon (1980).

HUNT, JOE Drums. Member of Ars Nova, 1968-69.

HUNT, KIM Drums. Member of Zon, 1979.

HUNT, MIKE Saxophone. Session for the J. Geils Band (1973).

HUNT, PETE Drums. Member of the Jess Roden Band, 1976. Session for Jess Roden (1977).

HUNT Paul Dickinson—guitar, vocal; Brian Gagnon—bass, guitar, keyboards, vocal; Paul Kersey—drums, percussion. *Album:* Back on the Hunt (USA 7013) 1980.

HUNTER, CAROL Guitar. Former backup for Neil Diamond. Session for Bob Dylan (1973); Free Creek (1973).

HUNTER, CHRIS Horns. Session for the Jags (1980).

HUNTER, IAN Vocal, guitar, piano, percussion, writer, producer. Born 6/3/46. Co-founder of Mott the Hoople, 1969-74. After guitarist Mick Ralphs left to join Bad Company, he stayed through two more albums before embarking on his solo career in 1975. Produced Generation X (1979). Production and session for the Iron City Houserockers (1979). Session for Ellen Foley (1979). *Albums:* Ian Hunter (COL PC-33480) 1975; All American

Alien Boy (COL C-34142) 1976; You're Never Alone with a Schizophrenic (CYS 1214) 1979; Ian Hunter Live/Welcome to the Club (CYS 2-1269) 1980; Shades of Ian Hunter (COL C2-36251) 1980.

HUNTER, JIMMY Drums. Member of Paul Warren and Explorer, 1980.

HUNTER, LEE Bass. Member of Strider, 1973.

HUNTER, ROBERT Writer. Original member of the Grateful Dead, since 1967. Session for Jerry Garcia (1972). *Album:* Tales of the Great Rum Runners (GRT) 1974.

HUNTER, STEMSY Alto saxophone, vocal. Original member of the Electric Flag, 1967-68.

HUNTER, STEVE "DEACON" Guitar. Member of the Alice Cooper Show, 1977, and Ultra Latex, 1979. Session for Lou Reed (1973-74); Jack Bruce (1974); Dr. John (1975). *Album:* Swept Away (ACO 36-148) 1977.

HUNTLEY, GORDON Steel guitar. Member of Matthew's Southern Comfort. Session for Rod Stewart (1972); Pilot (1972).

HURD, BILL Piano, vocal. Member of the Rubettes.

HURDLE, LES Bass. Session for Elton John (1969); Lou Reed (1972); Rick Wakeman (1972); Olivia Newton–John (1976); Chris Spedding (1976); John Dawson Read (1976).

HURLEY, BILL Vocal. Member of the Inmates since 1979.

HURLEY, MICHAEL Vocal. Member of Arthur, Hurley and Gottlieb, 1975.

HURLEY, PETE Bass. Member of Lone Star, 1977.

HURT, MISSISSIPPI JOHN Guitar, vocal, writer. Born in 1892 in Mississippi, he began his recording career in Memphis in 1928, which the depression ended the following year. In 1963, blues collector Tom Hoskins remembered a line from a 1928 Hurt recording, "Avalon's My Home Town." He then journeyed to Avalon and rediscovered Hurt. Hurt appeared the next year at the Newport Folk Festival, with John Lee Hooker, Lightnin' Hopkins and others. His soft vocals and relaxing blues were an immediate hit. After television appearances (on the Tonight Show) and college tours through 1965, he returned to Mississippi, where he died. *Albums:* Mississippi John Hurt; Best of Mississippi John Hurt (VAN VSD 19/20) 1966; Today (VAN 79220) 1966; Immortal Mississippi John Hurt (VAN 79248) 1968; Last Sessions (VAN 79327) 1972; 1928 Sessions (YZO) 1965.

HURWITZ, MICHAEL Cello. Member of Centipede, 1971.

HUSKEY, ROY Bass. Session for Ringo Starr (1971); Waylon Jennings (1973).

HUSSAIN, ZAKIR Tabla. Member of Shanti, 1971, and the Dija Rhythm Band, 1976.

HUSTLER Steve Haynes—vocal; Micky Llewelyn—guitar, vocal; Tigger Lyons—bass, vocal; Kenny Daughters—keyboards; Henry Spinetti—drums. *Albums:* Play Loud (AAM SP 4556); High Street (AAM).

HUTCHCROFT, KIM Saxophone. Member of Seawind. Session for Dr. John (1979).

HUTCHINGS, ASHLEY Bass. Member of Fairport Convention until 1974.

HUTCHINSON, DAVE Bass, vocal. Member of the Jitters, 1980.

HUTCHINSON, JASPAR Drums. Member of Topaz, 1977.

HUTTER, RALF Vocal, electronics. Original member of Kraftwerk since 1975.

HUTTO, J. B. Guitar, vocal. Born 4/29/26, in Augusta, Georgia. Blues musician who recorded with his band, the Hawks. *Albums:* Hawk Squat (DEC DS 617); Sidewinder (DEL DS 636) 1973.

HUTTON, DANNY Vocal. Member of Three Dog Night. Session for Beck, Bogert and Appice (1973).

HUTTON, JEFF Keyboards, vocal. Member of Tatoo, 1976.

HUXLEY, RICK Guitar, banjo. Member of the Dave Clark 5, 1964-68.

HUYDTS, JAN Keyboards. Member of the Chris Hinze Combination, 1974.

HYDE, DICK Horns. Session for Neil Sedaka (1975); Arthur, Hurley and Gottleib (1975); Boz Scaggs (1976); Glen Campbell (1976); Steely Dan (1976); Jerry Corbetta (1978); Dick St. Nicklaus (1979); Adrian Gurvitz (1979).

HYDE, JON Drums. Member of Detective, 1977.

HYDRA Wayne Bruce—vocal, guitar, writer; Spencer Kirkpatrick—guitar, slide guitar, writer; Orville Davis—bass; Steve Pace—drums. *Albums:* Hydra (CPN 0130) 1975; Hydra II (CPN) 1975; Rock the World (POL PD 1-6096) 1977; Land of Money (CPN 0157) 1975.

HYLAND, BRIAN Vocal. Recorded "Itsy Bitsy Teenie Weenie Yellow Polka Dot Bikini" in 1960. Began a comeback in 1977. *Albums:* Bashful Blonde (KAP) 1960; Let Me Belong to You (ABC) 1961; Sealed with a Kiss (ABC) 1961; In a State of Bayou, 1977.

HYMAN, JERRY Trombone. Member of Blood, Sweat and Tears, 1968.

HYMAN, ROB Keyboards, vocal. Member of Baby Grand, 1977-78.

HYMAS, TONY Keyboards, vocal. Member of Prelude, 1976, and the Jack Bruce Band, 1977. Session for the Hollies (1979).

HYNDE, CHRISSIE Vocal, guitar. Member of the Pretenders, 1980.

HYNES, DAVE Drums, vocal. Replaced Pete York in the Spencer Davis Group, 1968. Session for the Small Faces (1977).

I

I THREES Rita Marley—vocal; Marcia Griffiths—vocal; Judy Mowati—vocal. Vocal trio backing Bob Marley and the Wailers.

IAN, JANIS Vocal. Prodigy singer/writer/performer whose "Society's Child" pushed her to the top of the female folk singing field in 1968. Session for Gene Simmons (1978). *Albums:* Janis Ian (POL 6058) 1967; For All the Seasons of Your Mind, 1968; Secret Life of J. Eddy Pink, 1968; Stars (COL PC-32857) 1974; Aftertones (COL PC-33919) 1975; Between the Lines (COL PC-33394) 1975; Miracle Row (COL PC-34440); Janis Ian (COL JC-35325) 1978; Night Rains (COL JC-36139) 1979; Present Company (CAP SM-683).

IAN AND SYLVIA Ian Tyson—guitar, vocal, writer; Sylvia Tyson—vocal, autoharp. Canadian duet of writers and singers who first appeared on a self-produced album in 1962. Basically a folk team, they wrote such classics as Canada's unofficial national anthem, "Four Strong Winds" (1965). *Albums:* Four Strong Winds (VAN 2149) 1962; Ian and Sylvia (VAN 79215) 1962; Best of Ian and Sylvia (COL F 32516); Northern Journey (VAN 79154) 1964; Play One More, 1966; Lovin' Sound, 1967; Full Circle, 1968; Best of Ian and Sylvia (VAN 79269) 1968; Nashville (VAN 79284) 1968; Greatest Hits (VAN VSD-5/6); Greatest Hits, Vol. 2 (VAN 23/24); Play One More (VAN VSD 79215); Early Morning Rain (VAN VSD 79175) 1965.

ICEBERG, MICHAEL Synthesizer. Session for Long John Baldry (1979).

IDES OF MARCH James Michael Peterik—guitar, vocal; Larry Millas—guitar, bass, flute, vocal; Mike Borch—drums, vibes, vocal; Bob Bergland—bass, vocal; Chuck Soumar—percussion, vocal, harmonica; Dave Arelland—keyboards. *Album:* Midnight Oil (VIC APLI-0143).

IDLE, ERIC Guitar, vocal, keyboards. Member of comedy troupe Monty Python's Flying Circus, and responsible for the Beatles parody, the Rutles, 1978, under the name Dirk McQuickly.

IDOL, BILLY Vocal. Member of Generation X, 1978-79.

IF John Mealing—keyboards, vocal; Terry Smith—guitar (1973); Jim Richardson—bass; Dennis Elliott—drums; Dick Morrissey—reeds; J. W. Hodgkinson—vocal, percussion; Dave Quincy—reeds (1973); Clive Davies—drums, synthesizer, vocal; Geoff Whitehorn—guitar, vocal (1974); Walt Monaghan—bass, vocal (1974); Gabriel Magno—keyboards. An underground hit, their first album was not enough to carry a following through If's changing personnel. *Albums:* If; Tea Break Over, 1974; Not Just Another Bunch of Pretty Faces (CAP).

IGUANA Arthur Bod—guitar, vocal; Shaw Hayes—guitar; Budge Witherspoon—guitar, vocal; Don Falk—guitar, bass, vocal. *Album:* The Winds of Alamar, 1977.

IIJIMA, YOSHIAKI Guitar. Original member of Creation, 1976.

ILLEGITIMATE JUG BAND Original name of the Nitty Gritty Dirt Band, which became the Dirt Band.

ILLINGSWORTH, GARY Keyboards. Session for Marc Benno.

ILLINOIS SPEED PRESS Paul Cotton—guitar; Kal David—guitar; Fred Page (1969); Michael Anthony (1969); Rob Lewine (1969). *Albums:* The Illinois Speed Press, 1969; Duet, 1970.

ILLSLEY, JOHN Bass, vocal. Member of Dire Straits since 1978.

ILLUSION John Vinci—vocal; Rick Cerniglia—guitar; Chuck Alder—bass; Mike Maniscalco—keyboards, guitar; Mike Ricciardella—drums, percussion. *Albums:* The Illusion, 1970; Together (As a Way of Life), 1971; If It's So, 1972.

ILLUSION John Hawken—keyboards; Louis Cennamo—bass; Jane Relf—vocal; Jim McCarty—vocal, guitar, percussion; John Knightsbridge—guitar; Eddie MacNeil—drums, percussion. *Album:* Out of the Mist (ISL 9489) 1977.

IMAGAWA, JIM Drums. Member of the Subhumans, 1979.

IMBODEN, TRIS Drums. Member of Honk, 1973-74. Session for Ian Matthews (1976); Paul Waroff (1980).

IMMER, DAVID Keyboards, vibes, percussion, vocal. Member of the Ron Gardner Group, 1974.

IMPELLITIER, KEITH Guitar, vocal. Member of Calico, 1975-76.

IMPRESSIONS Curtis Mayfield—vocal; Samuel Gooden—vocal; Fred Cash—vocal; Jerry Butler—vocal; Reggie Torian—vocal; Nate Evans—vocal. One of the historic soul groups in the history of the field, they began singing together in 1958. They were the starting places for future soloists Jerry Butler and Curtis Mayfield. *Albums:* Impressions (ABC 450) 1963; Best Impressions (CTM 8004); Best of Curtis Mayfield and the Impressions (SEP 8018); Check Out Your Mind (TM 8006); Curtis In Chicago (CTM 8018); Fabulous Impressions (ABC 606) 1963; Keep On Pushing (ABC 493)

1964; Never Ending Impressions (ABC 468) 1964; People Get Ready, 1965; Impressions Greatest Hits, 1965; One By One, 1965; Ridin' High (ABC 545) 1966; This Is My Country (CTM 8001) 1968; Three the Hard Way (CTM 8602); Times Have Changed (CTM 8012); Versatile Impressions (ABC 668); We're a Winner (ABC 635) 1968; Young Mod's Forgotten Story (CTM 8003) 1969; First Impressions (CTM 5003) 1975; It's About Time (CTL 9912) 1976; Loving Power (CTM 5009) 1976; Come to My Party (TWC 596) 1979; Funky Christmas (CTL 991); Vintage Years—Impressions Featuring Jerry Butler and Curtis Mayfield (SIR H-3717); Finally Got Myself Together (CTM 8019).

IN TRANSIT Bill Cuomo—keyboards, vocal; Clark Garman—guitar, vocal; Bob Siller—guitar, vocal; Don Dunn—vocal; Ralph Humphrey—drums, percussion; Bobby Lichtig—bass. *Album:* In Transit (VIC AFLI 3607) 1980.

INCREDIBLE STRING BAND Clive Palmer—vocal, guitar, keyboards (until 1968); Robin Williamson—vocal, guitar, keyboards, drums, percussion, harmonica; Mike Heron—vocal, guitar, keyboards, sitar, percussion, dulcimer (1968-69); Two Scottish eccentrics who, between playing assorted percussion and lead instruments, write lyrics heavily laden with mythological and personal images. *Albums:* U; Liquid Acrobat as Regards the Air; Spirits, 1967; Incredible String Band (ELK 7E-7322) 1967; Hangman's Beautiful Daughter (ELK 74021) 1968; Big Huge (ELK 74037) 1969; Wee Tam (ELK 74036) 1969; Changing Horses (ELK 74057) 1969; 5000 Spirits (ELK 74010); I Looked Up (ELK 74061); Incredible String Band (ELK 7E-2002) 1971.

INDOOR LIFE J. A. Deane—trombone, synthesizer; Bob Hoffnar—bass, vocal; Sabella—drums, synthesizer, percussion; Jorge Socarras—vocal. *Album:* Indoor Life (INL) 1980.

INFANTE, FRANK Guitar. Original member of Blondie, 1977-78.

INFLUENCE Louis McKelvey—guitar; Andrew Keiler—vocal; Dave Wynne—drums; Jack Gelsinger—bass; Walter Rossi—guitar; Bobo Island—keyboards. Canadian rock group that dissolved after moving to New York in 1968. *Album:* Influence, 1968.

INGBER, ELLIOT Guitar. Original member of the Mothers of Invention, 1966, and the Grandmothers, 1980.

INGBER, IRA Bass. Member of Captain Beefheart and His Magic Band, 1974.

INGLE, DOUG Organ, vocal, writer. Founder of Iron Butterfly, 1968-69, and author of "In-a-Gadda-da-Vida," rock's first heavy metal opus.

INGLE, STEVE Vocal, guitar. Member of the Creed, 1978.

INGLIS, DAVID Guitar. Replaced Dominic Troiano in the Guess Who.

INGRAHAM, BARBARA Vocal. Session for Elton John (1979).

INGRAHAM, CAROL Vocal. Session for Peter Green (1980).

INGRAHAM, GREG Guitar. Member of the Avengers, 1979.

INGRAM, ELISA "SKIP" Bass, vocal. Member of the Platinum Hook since 1979.

INGUI, CHARLES Vocal. Member of the Soul Explosion, 1966-68.

INGUI, RICHARD Vocal. Member of the Soul Explosion, 1966-68.

INHOFER, GREG Keyboards, guitar, vocal. Member of the Tremblers, 1980.

INMAN, DERRYL Guitar. Session for B. B. King (1974).

INMATES Peter Gunn—guitar, vocal; Bill Hurley—vocal; Ben Donnelly—bass; Tony Oliver—guitar; Jim Russell—drums, vocal. *Album:* First Offence (POL 1-6241) 1979; Shot In the Dark (POL 1-6302) 1980.

INMON, JOHN Guitar, mandolin, vocal. Member of the Lost Gonzo Band, 1978.

INNES, NEIL Percussion, piano, guitar. Original member of the Bonzo Dog Doo-Dah Band, and member of Grimms, 1973. Part of the Rutles, 1978, under the name Ron Nasty. Session for John Entwhistle (1971).

INTERIOR, LUX Vocal. Member of the Cramps, 1980.

INTERVIEW Jeff Stars—vocal; Pete Allerhand—guitar, vocal, keyboards; Alan Brain—guitar, vocal; Alfie Agius—bass, vocal; Manny Elias—drums, percussion. *Albums:* Big Oceans (VGN 13131) 1979; Interview (VGN 13141) 1980.

INVADERS Gerry Roslie—keyboards, vocal; James N. Busch—drums, percussion; George Crowe—bass, percussion; Michael Gone—guitar; Bill Shaw—drums, percussion, vocal; George Fencil-Wallace—guitar, keyboards, percussion, vocal. Roslie's attempt to recapture the fame he enjoyed as the head of the Sonics. *Album:* The Sonics (BMP LP 4011) 1980.

IOMMI, JIMMY Bass. Member of Riot, 1980.

IOMMI, TONY Guitar, keyboards. Original member of Black Sabbath, since 1970.

IOVINE, JIMMY Producer. Produced Patti Smith (1978); Tom Petty (1979); Golden Earring (1979); D.L. Byron (1980); the Motors (1980); Bruce Springsteen (1980); and others.

IPPOLITO, ADAM Keyboards, trumpet, vocal. Member of Pig Iron. Session for Yoko Ono and John Lennon.

IPSEN, MICHAEL Bass, vocal. Member of Bighorn, 1978.

IRISH AMERICANS Early name of the Beau Brummels.

IRON BUTTERFLY Doug Ingle—organ, vocal,

writer (1967-69); Eric Brann—guitar, writer, vocal (1967-69, 1974-75); Lee Dorman—bass (1967-69); Ron Bushy—drums (1967-69, 1974-75); Darryl de Loach (1967-68); Phil Kramer—bass, vocal (1974-75); Bill De Martinez—keyboards, vocal (1974); Howard Reitzes—keyboards, vocal (1975); Mike Pinera—guitar. In 1968, the definitive sound of heavy metal was not Cream or Led Zeppelin; but the Iron Butterfly, featuring Ingle's raunchy, deep vocals and spaced organ chords, and 17 year old guitarist, Brann. They made four albums in two years, including the heavy rock classic "In-a-Gadda-da-Vida" (translation: "In the Garden of Life") in 1968, the first rock song to last for the length of one side of an album (18:00). In 1969, Ingle left the group, and they disbanded (Dorman formed Captain Beyond). In 1974, in the midst of the nostalgia craze, Brann recalled Bushy and found Kramer (bass) and replacements for Ingle, while he absorbed the writing duties. "Scorching Beauty" (1974) was an embarrassment to the original group and "Sun and Steel" merited no better criticism. *Albums:* Best of the Iron Butterfly (ACO 369); In-a-Gadda-da-Vida (ACO 250) 1968; Heavy (ACO SD 33227) 1968; Iron Butterfly—Live (ACO 318) 1969; Ball (ACO SD 33280) 1969; Scorching Beauty (MCA) 1974; Sun and Steel (MCA) 1975; Metamorphosis (ATC).

IRON CITY HOUSEROCKERS Eddie Britt—guitar, vocal; Joe Grushecky—vocal, guitar; Gil Snyder—keyboards, vocal; Art Nardini—bass; Ned E. Rankin—drums; Marc Reisman—harmonica, vocal. *Albums:* Love's So Tough (MCA 3099); Have a Good Time (But Get Out Alive) (MCA) 1980.

IRON MAIDEN Paul Di Anne—vocal; Steve Harris—bass, vocal; Dennis Stratton—guitar, vocal; Dave Murray—guitar; Clive Burr—drums. *Album:* Iron Maiden, 1980.

IRONHORSE Randy Bachman—vocal, guitar, writer; Tom Sparks—vocal (1979); John Pierce—bass (1979); Ron Foos—bass (1980); Mike Baird—drums (1979); Frank Ludwig—vocal, keyboards (1980); Chris Leighton—drums (1980). After abandoning his Bachman-Turner Overdrive formula and an unsuccessful solo album, Bachman attempted a resurrection of the BTO sound in Ironhorse. *Albums:* Ironhorse (STB 7103) 1979; Everything Is Grey (STB 7108) 1980.

IRVIN, ZIP Saxophone, vocal. Member of the Bill Blue Band, 1980.

IRVINE, BRUCE Guitar. Member of the Tyla Gang, 1978-79.

IRVING, DAVE Drums, percussion, vocal. Member of Supercharge, 1976-77. Replaced Tony Cresswell in Sad Cafe, 1979.

IRWIN, BOBBY Drums. Member of the Sinceros, 1979.

IRWIN, CHARLES Vocal. Session for Boz Scaggs (1980).

IRWIN, TEDDY Guitar. Member of the Snakestretchers, 1972-73.

ISBELL, JIM Drums, percussion. Session for Tom Rapp (1972).

ISHAM, MARK Keyboards, trumpet, electronics. Member of Group 87, 1980. Session for Taj Mahal (1978).

ISIDORE, CONRAD Drums, writer. Member of Hummingbird, 1975. Session for Steve Stills (1970); Memphis Slim (1971); Joe Cocker (1972); Terry Reid (1973).

ISIDORE, REG Drums. Original member of Robin Trower's Group, 1973-74. Session for Richard Wright (1978); Peter Green (1979).

ISIDORE, SANDRA Vocal. Session for Hummingbird (1975).

ISIS Suzi Ghezzi—guitar; Stella Bass—bass, vocal; Liberty Mata—percussion; Jeannie Feinberg—saxophone, flute; Lauren Diaper—trumpet; Lolly Beinenfield—trombone, vocal; Carol MacDonald—guitar, vocal; Ginger Bianco—drums; *Albums:* I, I, I (BUD) 1974; Ain't No Backin' Up Now, (BUD) 1975.

ISLAND, BOBO Keyboards. Member of Influence, 1968.

ISLEY, ERNIE Guitar, drums, percussion. Member of the Isley Brothers.

ISLEY, MARVIN Bass, percussion. Member of the Isley Brothers.

ISLEY, O'KELLY Vocal. Member of the Isley Brothers.

ISLEY, RONALD Vocal. Member of the Isley Brothers.

ISLEY, RUDOLPH Vocal. Member of the Isley Brothers.

ISLEY BROTHERS Ronald Isley—vocal; Rudolph Isley—vocal; O'Kelly Isley—vocal; Ernie Isley—guitar, drums, percussion; Marvin Isley—bass, percussion; Chris Jasper—keyboards, drums. Recorded "Twist and Shout," 1964, before becoming stars of Motown with "This Old Heart of Mine," 1966. *Albums:* Best of the Isley Brothers (SEP 18005); Bitter End Years (ROX); Birth of Rock (SEP 5103); Rock On Brothers (CDN ACLI-0126); Twist and Shout; Take Some Time Out; Famous Isley Brothers, 1964; This Old Heart of Mine, 1966; Soul on the Rocks, 1968; Live It Up (TNK PZ-33070) 1974; Rock Around the Clock (CDN ACLI-0861) 1975; Harvest for the World (TNK PZ-33809) 1976; Showdown (TNK JZ-34930) 1978; Timeless (TNK KZ2-35650) 1978; Winner Takes All (TNK PZ2-36077) 1979; Go All the Way (TNK FZ-36305) 1980; Go For Your Guns (TNK PZ-34432); Heat Is On (TNK PZ-33536); 3 Plus (TNK PZ-32453).

ISOTOPE Gary Boyle—guitar; Nigel Morris—drums; Hugh Hopper—bass (1975); Laurence Scott—keyboards (1975); Jeff Clyne—bass (1974);

Brian Miller—keyboards (1974). *Albums:* Isotope (GLL) 1974; Illusion (GLL) 1975.

IT AND THEM Early name for the Black Plague, a Johnny and Edgar Winter band.

IT'S A BEAUTIFUL DAY David LaFlamme—violin, vocal, guitar, writer, producer; Linda La Flamme—keyboards, writer (1969); Hal Wagenett—guitar, vocal (1969-71); Michael Holman—bass, vocal (1969-71); Val Fuentes—drums, vocal; Pattie Santos—vocal, percussion; Fred Webb—keyboards, vocal, flugelhorn (1970-72); Billy Gregory—guitar (1971-72); Tom Fowler—bass (1971-72). The psychedelica inspired by bands like Santana at the Fillmore in the late 1960s was maintained by LaFlamme's electrified violin and group vocal harmonies. Their hit "White Bird," 1969, served testimony to their versatility and talent. Part of Fillmore, 1972. *Albums:* It's a Beautiful Day (COL CS 9768) 1969; Marrying Maiden (COL XSM 153159) 1970; Choice Quality Stuff/Anytime (COL KC 30734) 1971; At Carnegie Hall (COL) 1972.

IVAN, JOHN Guitar. Member of Off Broadway since 1979.

IVERS, PETER Vocal, harmonica. Namesake of the Peter Ivers Band, 1974.

PETER IVERS BAND Alice de Buhr—drums; Buell Neidlinger—bass; Paul Lenart—guitar; Marty Krystall—saxophone; Peter Ivers—vocal, harmonica. *Album:* Terminal Love (WBR BS 2804) 1974.

IVERSON, KEVIN Drums, percussion, vocal. Member of Junkyard Angel, 1972.

IVERSON, RUSS Horns. Member of the Numa Band, 1980.

IVES Original name for Badfinger.

IVEY, CLAYTON Keyboards, strings, arranger, producer. Session for Boz Scaggs (1972); Mike Harrison (1972); Roy Orbison (1979).

IZZO, AL Drums. Member of the Jeremy Spencer Band, 1979.

J. C. Guitar, vocal. Member of the Members, 1979-80.

J. W. G. Guitar, bass, vocal. Replaced Georg Kajamus in Sailor, 1980.

JAAP, MIKE Guitar. Session for Matthew Fisher (1974).

JABS, MATTHIAS Guitar. Member of the Scorpions, 1980.

JACK, DAVID Banjo. Member of the Dixie Flyers.

JACK, IAN Guitar, vocal. Member of the Naughty Sweeties, 1980.

JACKI Synthesizer. Credited as a member of the Silicon Teens, 1980.

JACKMAN, ANDREW PAYCE Keyboards. Session for Chris Squire (1975).

JACKMAN, BILL Saxophone. Session for Chick Churchill (1974).

JACKS, CHERYL MASON Vocal. Session for John Lennon (1980).

JACKS, RICK Guitar. Member of the Cowboys International, 1979.

JACKS, SUSAN Vocal. *Album:* Ghosts (EPC JE-36417) 1980.

JACKS, TERRY Guitar, vocal. *Album:* Seasons in the Sun (BLL 1307) 1974.

JACKS, TONY Guitar, vocal. Member of the Tigers, 1980.

JACKSON, AL Drums. Original member of Booker T. and the MGs, 1962-68. Died 1975. Session for Otis Redding; Freddie King (1972); Eric Clapton (1974); Leon Russell (1975); Rod Stewart (1975-76).

JACKSON, ANDREW Bass. Session for Paul Simon (1980).

JACKSON, ANTHONY Bass. Session for Martin Mull (1977); Steely Dan (1980).

JACKSON, BOB Keyboards, vocal, guitar. Member of Ross, and the Dodgers, 1978.

JACKSON, CHRIS Member of July.

JACKSON, CHUCK Vocal. Member of the Del Vikings.

JACKSON, CLYDENE Vocal. Session for the Climax Blues Band (1980). *Album:* Fresh (CRO 9002).

JACKSON, DAVID Saxophone. Member of Van der Graaf Generator, 1970-77, and Van der Graaf, 1978.

JACKSON, DAVID Bass. Member of the Dillard and Clark Expedition.

JACKSON, DAVID Keyboards, vocal. Member of the Naughty Sweeties, 1980.

JACKSON, DON Vocal. Member of the Del Vikings.

JACKSON, FRED Saxophone. Played with John Mayall, 1972. Session for the Mothers of Invention (1972); B. B. King (1977).

JACKSON, J. Member of the Crimson Tide, 1978-79.

JACKSON, JACKIE Bass. Session for Paul Simon (1972).

JACKSON, JOE Vocal, piano, harmonica, writer. *Albums:* I'm the Man (AAM 4794) 1979; Look Sharp (AAM 4743) 1979; Beat Crazy (AAM SP 4837) 1980.

JACKSON, JOHN Bass, vocal. Member of Johnny's Dance Band, 1977.

JACKSON, LEE Bass. Member of Blues Incorporated. Original member of the Nice until 1970. After the group disbanded, he formed Refugee, 1972, and Jackson Heights, 1974.

JACKSON, LEE Guitar. Member of J. B. Hutto's Hawks.

JACKSON, LINDSAY Vocal, mandolin, harmonica, percussion. Member of Lindisfarne, 1973-77.

JACKSON, MARTIN Drums. Member of Magazine, 1978.

JACKSON, MICHAEL Vocal. Session for Dave Mason (1980).

JACKSON, MICK Bass. Member of the Love Affair.

JACKSON, OSCAR Tenor saxophone. Session for the Marshall Tucker Band (1973-74); Hydra (1974).

JACKSON, PAUL Bass. Session for the Pointer Sisters (1974).

JACKSON, PYTHON LEE See Python Lee Jackson.

JACKSON, QUENTIN Trombone. Session for Martin Mull (1974).

JACKSON, RAY Mandolin. Session for Long John Baldry (1971); Rod Stewart (1974).

JACKSON, SHAWN Vocal. Session for Alice Cooper (1976); Long John Baldry (1980).

JACKSON, TALI Drums. Member of the Tidbits.

JACKSON, THOMAS Fiddle. Session for Waylon Jennings (1974).

JACKSON, TIM Drums. Member of Robin Lane and the Chartbusters, 1980.

JACKSON, TONY Original member of the Searchers, 1960-64.

JACKSON, WAYNE Trumpet, arranger. Leader of the Memphis Horns. Session for B. B. King (1973); Mike Harrison (1975); Joe Cocker (1978); Paul Butterfield (1980).

JACKSON HEIGHTS Lee Jackson—vocal, bass, guitar, harp; John McBurnie—vocal, guitar, keyboards; Brian Chatton—vocal, keyboards. *Album:* Jackson Heights (VRV) 1974.

JACKSON HIGHWAY Dennis Gulley—vocal, guitar, keyboards; Britt Meacham—guitar, vocal; Tommy Patterson—keyboards, vocal; Russel Gulley—bass, vocal; Ronnie Vance—drums, vocal. *Album:* Jackson Highway (CAP ST-12044).

JACOB, HECTOR Guitar. Member of the Lavender Hill Mob, 1977.

JACOBS, JACK Guitar. Member of Balcones Fault, 1977.

JACOBS, JEANNETTE Vocal. Member of Ginger Baker's Air Force, 1970-71.

JACOBS, KEN Bass. Session for Colin Winski (1980).

JACOBS, PAUL Keyboards, vocal. Session for Roy Buchanan (1980).

JACOBSEN, JACK Keyboards. Member of the Show of Hands, 1970.

JACQUEZ, AL Vocal, bass. Member of Savage Grace, 1970.

JADE WARRIOR Tony Duhig—guitar; Jon Field—flute, conga, percussion; Glyn Harvard—vocal, bass, guitar. Unique British jazz-rock trio. *Albums:* Jade Warrior (VTG 1007) 1971; Released (VTG 1009) 1971; Last Autumn's Dream (VTG 1012) 1972; Floating World (ISL 9290) 1974; Waves (ISL 9318) 1975; Kites (ISL 9393) 1976.

JAEGER, RICK Drums. Member of the Tim Weisberg Band, 1977. Session for Tim Weisberg (1973, 79); Dave Mason (1974, 80); Elvin Bishop (1978).

JAGGER, MICK Vocal, writer, harmonica. Born 7/26/43. The most famous rock singer/performer to appear since Elvis, he discarded the clean and sanitary look of the 1960s to gyrate on stage in animalistic, suggestive ways. He represents half of the Jagger/Richards writing team of the Rolling Stones since their inception, and his performances are largely responsible for the group's satanic image. Started in Blues, Incorporated. Session for Dr. John (1971); guitar for Leslie West (1975); Ron Wood (1979).

JAGGERZ Jimmy Ross—tuba, trombone, bass, vocal; Jim Pugliano—drums, vocal; Benny Faiella—guitar, bass, trumpet, vocal; Thom Davis—keyboards, trumpet; Billy Maybray—bass, drums, vocal. A variation of a legendary rock name does not make a successful band. *Albums:* We Went to Different Schools Together; Come Again (KST).

JAGS Nick Watkinson—vocal, guitar; John Alder—guitar, keyboards; Steve Prudence—bass; Alex Baird—drums. *Album:* Evening Standards (ISL 9603) 1980.

JAIMOE See Jai Johanny Johanson.

JAKUBOVIC, GAROSLAV Saxophone, keyboards, vocal. Member of Blast, 1979.

JAKUBOWSKI, DON JAKE Organ. Member of Cognition, 1971.

JAM Peter Weller—guitar, vocal; David Waller—drums; Bruce Foxton—vocal, bass; Rick Buckler—drums (1978-79). *Albums:* This Is the Modern World, 1977; All Mod Cons (POL 1-6188) 1978; Setting Sons (POL 1-6249) 1979.

JAMES, ALAN Bass, vocal. Member of July. Session for Cat Stevens (1972).

JAMES, BARNEY Drums. Member of Rick Wakeman's backup band, 1974.

JAMES, BOB Vocal. Replaced Sammy Hagar in Montrose, 1975-76.

JAMES, BOB Strings, horn arrangements. Session for Neil Diamond.

JAMES, BOB Guitar, reeds, vocal. Member of Skin Alley, 1973.

JAMES, BOBBY Keyboards. Session for Paul Simon (1973).

JAMES, CASEY Guitar, synthesizer. Session for Elton John (1979).

JAMES, CHARLIE Vocal. Member of the Cleftones.

JAMES, CHRIS Bass, vocal. Member of the Elektrics, 1980.

JAMES, DOUG Baritone saxophone. Member of the Roomful of Blues, 1977.

JAMES, EDDIE Guitar. Member of Harper's Bizarre, 1967-69.

JAMES, ELMORE Vocal, bottleneck guitar. The main popularizer of Mississippi Delta blues, bottleneck style, to such rock giants as the Beatles, Eric Clapton, Peter Green, and others. Died 5/23/63. *Albums:* History of Elmore James (TRP 8007); History of Elmore James, Vol. 2 (TRP X-9511); Elmore James (BEL 6037); Anthology of the Blues—Legend of Elmore James (KNT 9001); Resurrection of Elmore James (KNT 9010); Elmore James (KNT 522); Pure Soul (KNT 517); Street Talkin' (MUS 5087) 1975.

JAMES, HARVEY Guitar, vocal. Member of Sherbet, 1976-80.

JAMES, JAMIE Guitar, vocal. Member of the King Bees, 1980.

JAMES, JIMI Early recording name of Jimi Hendrix, as head of the Blue Flames.

JAMES, NICKY Vocal, percussion. Session with Ray Thomas (1975-76).

JAMES, ROBERT Vocal. Member of Magnet, 1979.

JAMES, RUBY Vocal. Session for Manfred Mann (1973).

JAMES, SKIP Guitar, piano, vocal. Bluesman born in 1902 in Mississippi. First began playing guitar at the age of seven, and taught himself to play the piano. *Albums:* Devil Got My Woman (VAN 79273); Skip James Today (VAN 79219).

JAMES, SPIT Guitar. Original member of the Keef Hartley Band, 1969.

JAMES, TOMMY Vocal, guitar. Organizer and star of Tommy James and the Shondells. *Albums:* My Head, My Bed, and My Red Guitar; In Touch (FSY 9509) 1976; Midnight Rider (FSY 9532) 1977; Three Times in Love (MLN BXLI-7748) 1980; Christian of the World (ROU 3001); Tommy James (ROU 42051).

TOMMY JAMES AND THE SHONDELLS Though organized after Tommy James's hit "Hanky Panky," the Shondells backed James through a variety of bubblegum hits, including "Mony, Mony," "Crimson and Clover," and others. *Albums:* Cellophane Symphony (ROU); Crimson and Clover (ROU 42023) 1969; Hanky Panky; It's Only Love; I Think We're Alone; Gettin Together; Shondells at the Saturday Hop; Mony, Mony (ROU 42005); Something Special (ROU 42005); Travelin' (ROU 42044); Best of Tommy James and the Shondells (ROU 42040).

JAMES, TONY Bass, vocal. Member of Generation X, 1978-79.

JAMES GANG Joe Walsh—guitar, keyboards, vocal, writer (1969-71); Tom Kriss—bass, percussion (1969); Jim Fox—drums, piano; Dale Peters—bass, guitar (1970-76); Tommy Bolin—guitar, synthesizer, vocal, writer (1973-74); Roy Kenner—vocal, percussion (1973-74); Bubba Keith—vocal, guitar (1975); Richard Shack—vocal, guitar (1975); Bob Webb—guitar, vocal (1976); Phil Giallombardo—keyboards, vocal (1976). One of rock's great trios, they emerged from the Midwest in 1969, produced by Bill Szymczyk. From the beginning, Joe Walsh's songs and guitars were the driving force of the group, specializing in hard rock. A large underground following built up and followed Walsh when he left in 1971. Fox and Peters regrouped with Tommy Bolin. Not popularly known, Bolin filled Walsh's shoes adroitly for two albums before leaving for a solo career, then to join Deep Purple. Undaunted, Fox and Peters replaced Bolin with Richard Shack and Bubba Keith for an enjoyable album in 1975, but too many personnel changes had diversified the group's following. *Albums:* Yer Album (ABC BLS 6094) 1969; James Gang Rides Again (MCA 711) 1970; Thirds (ABC ABCX 74-B) 1971; Live in Concert (ABC ABCX 733) 1971; James Gang Bang (ACO 7037) 1973; Miami (ACO SO 36102) 1974; Newborn (ACO 36-112) 1975; Jesse Come Home (ACO 36-141) 1976; Best of the James Gang (MCA X-774); 16 Greatest Hits (MCA X-801).

JAMESON, NICK Bass, keyboards, guitar, vocal, producer, drums. Produced Foghat, 1974, and joined the group the following year, replacing Tony Stevens. His solo debut in 1977 showed his versatility beyond the Foghat rock style. Session and production for Paul Butterfield's Better Days, 1973. Session for Tim Moore (1974). *Album:* Already Free (BSV 6F172) 1977.

JAMESON, PETER Guitar. Session for Nilsson (1976).

JAMISON, JIMI Vocal. Voice of Target, 1976-77.

JAMMER, JOE Guitar. Member of the Olympic Runners, 1974-79. Session for Mike Vernon; Jerry Lee Lewis (1973).

JAN AND DEAN Jan Berry—vocal, writer, producer; Dean Torrence—vocal. Early name: the Barons. Surf music began with Jan and Dean in 1958. Their two-part vocal harmonies sang of sunny California, sand, surf and "two girls for every boy." When surfing lyrics reached their limit, they became the leading exponents of drag (racing) music with "Drag City," "Dead Man's Curve" (both 1963), "Little Old Lady from Pasadena," (1964), and others. They continued as mainstays of their field until a car wreck in 1963 left Jan Berry severely injured. Dean attempted as a soloist in 1966 and 1968, but Jan's absence was an emotional and technical disappointment. *Albums:* Gotta Take That One Last Ride (UAR UALA 341-112); Jan and Dean Golden Hits (LIB 7417); Legendary Masters; Very Best of Jan and Dean, Vol. 1 (UAR UALA 433-E); Surf City; Jan and Dean Take Linda Surfin', 1963; Surf City, 1963; Drag City, 1963; Ride The Wild Surf, 1964; Little Old Lady from Pasadena, 1964; Command Performance, 1965; Folk 'n' Roll, 1965; Filet of Soul, 1966; Popsicle, 1966; Save for a Rainy Day (LIB) 1967; Deadman's Curve (UAR LT-999) 1964; Jan and Dean Anthology (UAR UAS 9961) 1971.

JANAHER, DARIUS Guitar. Member of the New Commander Cody Band, 1977.

JANKEL, CHAZ Guitar, keyboards. Member of Ian Dury's Blockheads, 1979.

JANS, TOM Piano, guitar, vocal. See Mimi Farina. *Albums:* Tom Jans (AAM) 1974; Eyes of an Only Child (COL PC 33699) 1975; Dark Blonde (COL PC-34292) 1976.

JANSCH, BERT Guitar, vocal, writer. Considered one of Britain's finest folk guitarists, he was an original member of Pentangle, 1968-72, which was more successful than his solo career. Session for Donovan. *Albums:* Lucky Thirteen (RPS) 1966; Stepping Stones (VAN 6506) 1969; Birthday Blues (RPS 6343); Jack Orion (VAN 6544); Rosemary Lane (RPS 6455) 1971.

JANSEN, STEVE Drums, percussion. Member of Japan since 1979.

JANSSEN, LUITJEN Bass. Member of Eloy, 1975.

JAPAN David Sylvian—vocal, guitar; Mick Karn—bass, saxophone; Steve Jansen—drums, percussion; Richard Barbieri—keyboards, synthesizer; Rob Dean—guitar. *Albums:* Adolescent Sex (ARA SW-50037); Obscure Alternatives (ARA SW-50047).

JAR, PETE Guitar. Session for Paul Simon (1975).

JARDINE, AL Guitar, vocal, writer. Born 9/3/42. Original member of the Pendletones who became the Beach Boys, 1962-present.

JARRE, JEAN MICHAEL Keyboards. *Albums:* Oxygene (POL 1-6112) 1976; Equinoxe (POL 1-6175) 1978.

JARRETT, DAVE Keyboards. Member of Mainstream, 1976. Session for Phil Manzanera (1975).

JARVIS, JAMES Vocal. Member of the Fugs Chorus.

JARVIS, JOHN Keyboards, vocal. Session for Art Garfunkel; Rod Stewart (1976-77); John Mayall (1979); the Marc Tanner Band (1979).

JASON, NEIL Bass. Member of the Jeremy Spencer Band, 1979. Session for Art Garfunkel (1979); Grace Slick (1980); Roxy Music (1980); Jimmy Maelen (1980).

JASPER Bass. Member of Battered Wives.

JASPER, CHRIS Keyboards, drums. Member of the Isley Brothers.

JAVAROO Barry Blue—vocal, guitar, bass, percussion; Paul Greedus—vocal, keyboards, guitar, percussion. *Album:* Out (CAP ST-12052).

JAY AND THE AMERICANS Jay Black—vocal; Kenny Vance—vocal; Sandy Deane—vocal; Marty Sanders—guitar; Howie Kane—vocal. Early names: the Harbor Lights; the Rockaways. Full vocal harmonies kept these New Yorkers on the charts through the Beatles invasion with such hits as "Come a Little Bit Closer" (1964), "Cara Mia" (1965), and others from 1962 to 1966. *Albums:* Try Some of This, 1962; She Cried, 1963; Jay and the Americans at the Copa, 1963; Come a Little Bit Closer, 1964; Blockbusters, 1965; Jay and the Americans Greatest Hits (UAR LM-1010) 1965; Sunday and Me, 1966; Livin' Above Your Head, 1966; Jay and the Americans Greatest Hits, Vol. 2, 1966.

JAY AND THE TECHNIQUES Jay Proctor—vocal; Karl Landis—vocal; Dante Dancho—guitar; Ronnie Goodly; John Walsh; George Lloyd; Chuck Crowl. Pennsylvanians who scored in 1967 with "Apples, Peaches, Pumpkin Pie." *Albums:* Apples, Peaches, Pumpkin Pie (SMA 1417) 1967; Love, Lost and Found, 1968; Keep the Ball Rollin' (SMA 1417).

JAYNE, MITCH Acoustic bass. Original member of the Dillards until 1977.

JDB See Nan Mancini and JDB.

JECKELL, FRANK Vocal, guitar. Member of the 1910 Fruitgum Company, 1968-69.

JEFFERSON, BLIND LEMON Guitar, vocal, writer. Texas blues troubadour who recorded from 1926 to 1929. An acquaintance of Leadbelly and influence on such guitarists as B. B. King. *Albums:* Black Snake Moan (MLS 32013) 1970; Immortal Blind Lemon Jefferson (MSL 32094); Immortal Blind Lemon Jefferson, Vol. 2 (MLS 32007); Jefferson; Blind Lemon Jefferson (MLS 47022) 1974.

JEFFERSON AIRPLANE Jorma Kaukonen—guitar, writer (1965-73); Jack Casady—bass (1965-73); Spencer Dryden—drums (1965-74); Paul Kanter—vocal, guitar, writer; Marty Balin—vocal, writer; Grace Slick—vocal, guitar, keyboards, writer; Skip Spence—drums; Signe Andersen—vocal (until 1965); Pete Sears—bass, keyboards (1974); Craig Chaquico—guitar (1974); Papa John Creach—violin (1974); Dave Freiberg—bass, keyboards, vocal (1974); John Barbata—drums, percussion (1974); Mark Ryan—bass, vocal; Dewey Dagreaze—drums, vocal; Vic Smith—guitar, vocal; Charlie Hickox—keyboards, vocal. Grace Slick's weaving of fantastic drug journeys and visions reflected the blooming culture of hippydom in 1965, and took the Airplane to national prominence. It also focused the rock industry on the sound from their native San Francisco. See Jefferson Starship. *Albums:* Jefferson Airplane Takes Off (VIC AFLI 3584) 1966; Surrealistic Pillow (VIC AFLI 3766) 1967; Crown of Creation (VIC AFLI 4058) 1968; After Bathing at Baxter's (VIC AFLI 4545) 1968; Volunteers (VIC AFLI 4238) 1969; Bless Its Pointed Little Head (VIC AFLI 4133) 1969; Worst of the Jefferson Airplane (VIC AYLI 3661) 1970; Bark (GNT FTR 1001) 1971; Thirty Seconds Over Winterland (GNT BXLI 0147) 1973; Baron Von Tollbooth and the Chrome Nun (GNT BXLI 0148) 1973; Early (GNT CYLI 0437) 1974; Bodacious; Flight Log 1966—1976 (GNT CYL2-1255).

JEFFERSON STARSHIP Marty Balin—vocal, writer; Grace Slick—piano, vocal, writer; Paul Kanter—guitar, vocal, writer; John Barbata—drums, percussion, vocal (1975-78); Craig Chaquico—guitar, vocal; Pete Sears—bass, keyboards, vocal; David Freiberg—bass, keyboards, vocal; Aynsley Dunbar—drums (1979-present); Mickey Thomas—vocal (1979-present). An image begun in the mid-'60s rock scene in San Francisco as Jefferson Airplane, they changed their name and altered their successful format slightly, replacing originals Jorma Kaukonen, Jack Casady and Spencer Dryden, who had gone on to other ventures. The new lineup featured songs with less social commentary, the previous Airplane trademark, and more melody, giving them their first #1 album since 1966, "Octopus." See Jefferson Airplane. *Albums:* Dragon Fly (GNT BLXI/BFDI 0717) 1974; Red Octopus (GNT AYLI 3660) 1975; Spitfire (GNT BXLI/BFDI 1557) 1976; Best of the Jefferson Starship (GNT BXLI 3247) 1977; Earth (GNT BXLI 215) 1978; Freedom at Point Zero (GNT BZLI 3452) 1979; Blows Against the Empire (VIC AFLI 4448); Gold (GNT BZLI 3247).

JEFFREYS, GARLAND Guitar, vocal. *Albums:* Ghost Writer (AAM 4629) 1977; One-Eyed Jack (AAM 4681) 1978; American Boy and Girl (AAM 4778) 1979.

JEFFRIES, MICHAEL Member of Tower of Power.

JEFFRIES, PAUL Bass. Member of Steve Harley's Cockney Rebel.

JELLY Fred Bliffert; Amy Madigan; Jesse Roe. *Album:* True Story (ASY 73-1096) 1977.

JENKINS, ARTHUR Percussion. Session for Barry Goldberg (1974); John Lennon (1974, 80); Dr. John (1978); John Mayall (1979).

JENKINS, BARRY Drums, percussion, vocal. Member of the Animals, 1967-68.

JENKINS, CARL Piano, saxophone. Member of the Soft Machine, 1973. Session on "Jesus Christ Superstar" (1970); Memphis Slim (1971).

JENKINS, CRYSTAL Vocal. Session for Bob Seger.

JENKINS, DAVID Guitar, vocal. Member of Pablo Cruise since 1975.

JENKINS, HAROLD Real name of Conway Twitty.

JENKINS, JOHNNY Guitar, vocal, harmonica. *Albums:* Star Eyes (SAV 1114); Jazz Eyes; Jazz We Heard Last Summer; Ton Ton Macoute (CPN 0136) 1970.

JENKINS, KARL Baritone, oboe. Member of Centipede, 1971.

JENKINS, LYLE Saxophone, flute. Session for the Keef Hartley Band (1970-71); Kevin Ayers (1973).

JENKINS, NIGEL Guitar. Session for Gerry Rafferty (1978).

JENNINGS, WAYLON Guitar, vocal, writer. Playing for Buddy Holly, he missed the fatal Feb. 3, 1959, airplane crash that claimed the lives of Holly, Ritchie Valens, and others. After that he switched from bass to guitar and began writing his own songs. Through the years, he has developed into a major western figure, with friend Willie Nelson. Sessions for Willie Nelson (1973-present). *Albums:* Singer of Sad Songs (VIC AFLI 4418) 1970; Heartaches by the Number (CDN 2556) 1972; Ladies Love Outlaws (VIC AFLI 4751) 1972; Honky Tonk Heroes (VIC AFLI 0240) 1973; Lonesome, On'ry and Mean (VIC AFLI 4854) 1973; Ruby, Don't Take Your Love to Town (CDN 2608) 1973; This Time (VIC AFLI 5039) 1974; Only Daddy That'll Walk the Line (CDN ACLI 0306) 1974; Dreaming My Dreams (VIC AFLI 1062) 1975; Are You Ready for the Country (VIC AYLI 3663) 1976; Dark Side of Fame (CDN ACL 7019) 1976; Waylon Live (VIC AFLI 1108) 1976; Ol' Waylon (VIC AFLI 2317) 1977; Best of Waylon Jennings (VIC AFLI 4341) 1978; Good Hearted Woman (VIC AFLI 4647) 1978; I've Always Been Crazy (VIC AHLI 3422) 1978; Taker/Tulsa (VIC AFLI 4487) 1978; White Mansions (AAM 6004) 1978; Banded Together (EPC JE-36177); Greatest Hits (VIC AHLI 3378) 1979; Honky Tonkin' (VIC AHLI 3422) 1979; Waylon Jennings (VOC 73873); Music Man (VIC AHLI 3602) 1980; The Outlaws (VIC AFLI 1321).

JENSEN, HANS Keyboards. Member of Spin, 1976.

JEREMIAH, KEN Vocal. Member of the Soul Explosion, 1966-68.

JEREMY AND THE SATYRS Jeremy Steig—flute; Donald McDonald; Edgar Gomez; Adrian Gulilleroy; Warren Bernhardt. First group of Jeremy Steig, bringing jazz to rock audiences, before going solo. *Album:* Jeremy and the Satyrs, 1968.

JERMOTT, JERRY Bass. Session for Wilson Pickett (1968); Barry Goldberg (1969); Aretha Franklin (1970); B. B. King (1969-70, 72); Pearls Before Swine (1971).

JERNIGAN, DOUG Steel guitar. Member of the Rio Grande Band.

JESUS CHRIST SUPERSTAR Cast: Judas Iscariot—Murray Head; Jesus Christ—Ian Gillan; Mary Magdalene—Yvonne Elliman; Priest—Paul Raven; Caiaphas—Victor Brox; Annas—Brian Keith; Simon—John Gustafson; Pontius—Barry Dennen; Maid—Annette Brox; Peter—Paul Davies; King Herod—Mike D'Abo; Bruce Rowland—drums, percussion; Alan Spenner—bass; Henry McCullough—guitar; Neil Hubbard—guitar; Peter Robinson—keyboards; Chris Mercer—tenor saxophone. The success of the Who's "Tommy" in 1968 led to this inevitable inspirational rock opera, initially performed in 1970. "Jesus Christ Superstar" was not the writers' first attempt; authors Anthony Lloyd Weber and Tim Rice had penned "Joseph and the Amazing Technicolor Dreamcoat" in 1967, a contemporary contata for full orchestra and pop choir that went virtually unnoticed. *Album:* Jesus Christ Superstar (MCA DXSA 7206) 1970.

JETER, REV. CLAUDE Vocal. Session for Paul Simon (1973).

JETHRO TULL Ian Anderson—saxophone, bass, guitar, mandolin, flute, piano, percussion, vocal, writer; Mick Abrahams—guitar, vocal, writer (1968); Clive Bunker—drums, percussion (1968-71); Glenn Cornick—bass (1968-71); Martin Barre—guitar, flute (1969-present); Jeffrey Hammond-Hammond—bass, vocal, recorder (1971-75); John Evan—keyboards (1971-79); Barriemore Barlow—drums, percussion (1971-80); John Glascock—bass, vocal (1976-80); David Palmer—keyboards (1977-79); Dave Pegg—bass (1980); Mark Craney—drums (1980). English rock group formed around Ian Anderson, who has become known as the premier flautist in rock music. His varied musical talents and controlled vocals are sometimes neglected for his concept compositions (begun with Aqualung in 1971), lasting through both sides of albums, and his hyperactive prancing and dancing. When he does settle down to his classic playing stance (standing on one leg), his imaginative flute work sets a fast and powerful pace for the rest of his talented group. His guitar virtuosity is equally competent. *Albums:* This Was (RPS 6336) 1968; Stand Up (RPS 6360) 1969; Benefit (RPS 6400)

1970; Aqualung (RPS 2035) 1971; War Child (CYS CH4-1067) 1971; Living in the Past (CYS 1035) 1972; Thick as a Brick (RPS 2072) 1972; Passion Play (CYS 1040) 1973; MU—The Best of Jethro Tull (CYS 1078) 1975; Minstrel in the Gallery (CYS 1082) 1975; Too Old To Rock 'N' Roll, Too Young to Die (CYS 1111) 1976; Repeat (CYS K-1135) 1977; Songs from the Wood (CYS 1132) 1977; Bursting Out (CYS 2-1201) 1978; Heavy Horses (CYS 1175) 1978; Stormwatch (CYS 1238) 1979; A (CYS 1301) 1980.

JETT, HARVEY Guitar, piano, banjo, vocal. Member of Black Oak Arkansas, 1971-77.

JETT, JOAN Guitar, vocal. Member of the Runaways before going solo. *Album:* Joan Jett (BST 99707) 1980.

JETT, JOHN Vocal. Session for Sean Tyla (1980).

JETTY, EARL Drums. Member of Duke Jupiter, 1978.

JEWELL, JIM Trumpet, saxophone. Member of the Keef Hartley Band horn section, 1969-70. Session for Lo and Behold (1972); the Hollies (1978).

JIGSAW Des Dyer—vocal, percussion; Clive Scott —keyboards, vocal; Tony Campbell—guitar; Barrie Bernard—bass. *Albums:* Sky High (CLS 509) 1975; Jigsaw (TWL T-545) 1977.

JIM Guitar. Member of the Five Americans, 1966.

JIMMY Vocal. Member of the Five Americans, 1966.

JIMENEZ, FLACO Accordion. Session for Ry Cooder (1977); Peter Rowan (1978).

JINK, PETER Bass. Member of Finch, 1975.

JITTERS P. K. Dwyer—guitar, vocal; Donna Beck, vocal; Pete Pendras—guitar, vocal; Dave Hutchinson—bass, vocal; Rick Tassin—drums, vocal; Joe Hadloc—piano; Bill Bagley—organ. *Album:* Jitters, 1980.

JIVA Michael Lanning—guitar, vocal; James Strauss —bass, vocal; Thomas Hilton—guitar, vocal; Mike Reed—drums, percussion. *Album:* Jiva (DKH) 1975.

JO JO GUNNE Jay Ferguson—keyboards, vocal, writer; Matthew Andes—guitar, vocal (1972-73); Mark Andes—bass, vocal; Curley Smith—drums, vocal; Jimmie Randall—bass, vocal (1973); John Staehely—guitar, vocal (1974). When Spirit came to a parting of the ways, Jay Ferguson took guitar player Matt Andes to form Jo Jo Gunne. Loud and proud with talent to spare, Gunne failed to catch on. Session for Johnny Winter (1973); Keith Moon (1975). *Albums:* Jo Jo Gunne (ASY 5053) 1972; Bite Down Hard (ASY SD 5056) 1973; Jumpin' the Gun (ASY SD 5071) 1973; So, Where's the Show (ASY 7E-1022) 1974.

JO JO ZEP AND THE FALCONS Gary Young—drums, percussion; Wilbur Wilde—saxophone, vocal; Jeff Burstin—guitar; Joe Camilleri—vocal, saxophone, guitar; Tony Faehse—guitar, vocal; John Power—bass, vocal. New wave Australian entry from ex-Daddy Cool member, Young. *Album:* Screaming Targets (COL JC-36442) 1980.

JO MAMA Joel O'Brien—drums, vibes; Ralph Shuckett—keyboards, vocal; Abigail Haness—vocal; Danny Kootch—guitar; Charles Larkey—bass. Collection of Carole King and James Taylor session men under their own steam. *Albums:* Jo Mama (ACO) 1970; J Is for Jump, 1971.

JOBE, RIVERS Bass. Replaced Ray Chappell in Savoy Brown, 1968-69.

JOBRIATH Billy Schwartz; Steve Love—guitar; John Siomos—drums; Andy Muson; Jobriath Boone; Jim Gregory; Hayden Wayne. *Albums:* Jobriath, 1973; Creatures of the Street (ELK) 1974.

JOBSON, EDDIE Violin, piano, synthesizer. Joined the Roxy lineup, 1974-78. Member of U.K., 1978-79. Session for Bryan Ferry (1974); John Entwhistle (1975); King Crimson (1975); Phil Manzanera (1975); Jethro Tull (1980).

JOBSON, RICHARD Vocal. Member of the Skids, 1979.

JOCHUM, MICHAEL Drums, percussion. Member of Kittyhawk, 1980.

JOEL, BILLY Keyboards, vocal. Session for Elliott Murphy (1976). *Albums:* Piano Man (COL PC-32544) 1973; Streetlife Serenade (COL PC-33146) 1974; Turnstiles (COL PC-33848) 1976; The Stranger (COL HC-34987) 1977; 52nd Street (COL FC-35609) 1978; Glass Houses (COL FC 36384) 1980.

JOFFE, RICHARD Vocal. Member of Sha Na Na, 1971.

JOHANSEN, DAVID Vocal, percussion. Member of the New York Dolls, 1973-74. *Albums:* David Johansen (BSK JZ-34926) 1978; In Style (BSK JZ-36082) 1979.

JOHANSON, JAI JOHANNY Congas, drums, percussion. Nickname: Jaimoe. Member of the Allman Brothers, 1970-76, 1979, and Sea Level, 1977-78. Session for Gregg Allman (1973); the Marshall Tucker Band (1973-74, 77); Bobby Whitlock (1975).

JOHN Member of the Five Americans, 1966.

JOHN, CLIVE Guitar, vocal. Member of Man.

JOHN, DEACON Bass. Original member of Queen since 1973.

JOHN, DELTON Early name used by John Lee Hooker.

JOHN, ELTON Keyboards, vocal. Real name: Reginald Dwight. Born 3/25/47. Following in the footsteps of Presley and the Beatles, John and lyricist Bernie Taupin seized control of rock publicity in 1969 when they released their first album in the States. The songs were moody and refreshingly well produced. The stage show, however, captured the public focus. *Time* magazine pictured John on its cover, long-haired, jumping at the keyboards like a wild man, a Hyde-like contrast to his studio Dr. Jekyll. In 1970, the long hair came off and the stage antics toned down, to be replaced by colorful costumes and what was to become his trademark, his eccentric collection of sunglasses, including an electrical pair that spelled E-L-T-O-N, at a reported price of $5,000. In 1971, he scored a movie, "Friends," after which rumors about his wildness ebbed. In the U.S., his albums turned gold, and better. He is the only person in recording history to have a #1 album on all three major trade magazine charts the same day it was released: "Captain Fantastic," 1975. But it took until 1976 before he had his first #1 single in his native England. Session and production for Long John Baldry (1971-72). Session for Rod Stewart (1974); John Lennon (1974); Ringo Starr (1974). *Albums:* Empty Sky (MCA 3008) 1969; Elton John (UNI 73090) 1970; Tumbleweed Connection (UNI 73096) 1970; 11/17/70 (MCA 3002) 1971; Madman Across the Water (UNI 94014) 1971; Friends (PAR PAS 6004) 1971; Don't Shoot Me, I'm Only the Piano Player (MCA 3005) 1972; Honky Chateau (UNI 93135) 1972; Goodbye Yellow Brick Road (MCA 2-10003) 1973; Caribou (MCA 3006) 1974; Captain Fantastic and the Brown Dirt Cowboy (MCA 3009) 1975; Rock of the Westies (MCA 3010) 1975; Blue Moves (MCA 2-110004) 1976; Here and There (MCA 3011) 1976; Greatest Hits (MCA 3007); Greatest Hits, Vol. 2 (MCA 3027) 1977; Single Man (MCA 3065) 1978; Victim of Love (MCA 5104) 1979; Thom Bell Sessions (MCA 13921) 1979; 21 at 33 (MCA 5104) 1980.

ELTON JOHN BAND Caleb Quaye—guitar (1969-71, 76); Dave Glover—bass (1969-71); Roger Pope—drums, percussion (1969-71, 76); Paul Buckmaster—orchestral arranger (1969-78); Davey Johnstone—guitar (1970-76); Dee Murray—bass (1970-75); Nigel Olsson—drums, percussion (1970-75); Ray Cooper—percussion (1974-78); Kenny Passarelli—bass (1976); James Newton Howard—synthesizer, organ (1975-77); Tim Renwick—guitar (1978); Steve Holly—drums (1978); Clive Franks—bass (1978). Elton John recorded with alternating studio musicians for the initial two years of his releases, but the most recurring names in the lineup were Quaye's, Glover's, and Pope's. In 1970, he selected a travelling band, consisting of Johnstone, Murray, and Olsson, which alternated with the other band in the studio before becoming a permanent fixture, 1971-76. Since 1978, John has used several studio musicians.

JOHN, PRAKASH Bass. Member of the Alice Cooper Show, 1977. Session for Lou Reed (1974); Alice Cooper (1975); Steve Hunter (1977).

JOHN, ROBERT Vocal. *Albums:* Robert John (EIA SW-17007) 1979; Back on the Street (EIA SW-17027) 1980.

JOHN LEE'S GROUNDHOGS See Groundhogs.

JOHNNY AND THE MOONDOGS Early name of the Beatles.

JOHNNY AND THE DISTRACTIONS Johnny Koonce—vocal, guitar, harmonica; Bill Feldman—guitar, vocal; Mark LaRue Todd—bass, vocal; Gregg Perry—keyboards, vocal, percussion; Kip Richardson—percussion, drums. *Album:* Johnny and the Distractions (KEM 5709) 1980.

JOHNNY'S DANCE BAND John Jackson—bass, vocal; Chris Darway—keyboards, vocal; Tony Juliano—vocal, percussion; Nanette Mancini—vocal, percussion; Bob Lenti—guitar; David Mohn—drums; Courtney Colletti—guitar, bass. *Album:* Johnny's Dance Band, 1977.

JOHNS, BOBBY Drums. Member of Exile, 1973-78, and Roadmaster since 1978.

JOHNS, GLYN Producer, engineer, guitar, percussion, vocal. Produced the Rolling Stones, and Lazy Racer, 1980. Production and session for Tim Renwick, 1980. Session for Steve Miller (1969-70); the Ozark Mountain Daredevils (1973-75); Marc Benno (1979).

JOHNS, ROBERT Member of Diamond Reo, 1979.

JOHNSGARD, RICK Guitar, flute, vocal. Member of Overland Stage, 1972.

JOHNSON, ALPHONZO Member of Weather Report, 1974.

JOHNSON, ART Guitar, vocal. Session for Tim Weisberg (1971, 74).

JOHNSON, BARRY Drums. Member of Acrobat.

JOHNSON, BRIAN Vocal. Member of Geordie, 1973, before replacing Bon Scott in AC/DC, 1980.

JOHNSON, CARL Guitar. Member of Rock Rose, 1979. Session for Tim Weisberg (1975).

JOHNSON, CHARLES "ICARUS" Guitar. Replaced Peter Leinheiser in Pages, 1979.

JOHNSON, CHRIS Drums. Member of Tucky Buzzard, 1973.

JOHNSON, CLIFF Vocal. Member of Off Broadway since 1979.

JOHNSON, CORIN Vocal. Member of the Del Vikings.

JOHNSON, DANNY Member of Axis, 1978.

JOHNSON, DAVE Bass, vocal. Member of Sweathog, 1973.

JOHNSON, DAVID EARL Percussion, vocal. Session for Blast (1979).

JOHNSON, DENNIS Bass, vocal. Member of Chase, 1971-73.

JOHNSON, DENNIS KEITH Bass. Member of Survivor, 1979.

JOHNSON, DOUG Keyboards. Member of Loverboy, 1980.

JOHNSON, DREW Drums. Member of the Righteous Brothers Band, 1966.

JOHNSON, EARL Guitar. Member of Moxy, 1976-78.

JOHNSON, ERIC Guitar. Session for Christopher Cross (1980).

JOHNSON, FLYNN J. Bass. Session for Mike Pindar (1976).

JOHNSON, GEORGE Guitar. Session for George Duke (1975).

JOHNSON, GERALD Bass. Replaced Ross Vallory in the Steve Miller Band, 1972-73. Session for Dave Mason; Crosby, Stills and Nash (1977); Les Dudek (1977-78); Steve Stills (1978).

JOHNSON, GORDON Bass. Session for Roy Buchanan (1980).

JOHNSON, HERMAN Vocal. Session for Ry Cooder (1979).

JOHNSON, HOWARD Baritone saxophone, tuba, euphonium. Session for the Fugs (1968); the Band (1972); B. B. King (1972); Paul Butterfield's Better Days (1973); Taj Mahal; John Lennon (1974, 80); Carly Simon (1974); Jaco Pastorius (1976); John Mayall (1979).

JOHNSON, HOWIE Drums. Original member of the Ventures, 1960-63.

JOHNSON, JAMES C. Vocal, guitar. Member of Gypsy, 1971-73.

JOHNSON, JAMES E. Organ. Session for Terry Reid (1979).

JOHNSON, JIMMY Guitar. Member of the Muscle Shoals Rhythm Section, and head of the Jimmy Johnson Band, 1977. Session for Clarence Carter (1967); Barry Goldberg (1968, 74); King Curtis (1969); John Hammond (1969); Boz Scaggs (1969, 72); Aretha Franklin (1970); Jim Capaldi (1971-73); Leon Russell (1971); Don Nix (1971); J. J. Cale (1972); Mike Harrison (1972); Bob Seger (1973, 75); Paul Simon (1973); Paul Kossoff (1974); Rod Stewart (1975); Richard Tate (1977); Art Garfunkel (1978); Joe Cocker (1978).

JIMMY JOHNSON BAND Jimmy Johnson—guitar, vocal; Carl Snyder—piano; Ike Anderson—bass; Dino Alvarez—drums. *Album:* Johnson's Whacks (DEL D5644) 1977.

JOHNSON, JOAN Vocal. Member of the Dixie Cups, 1964-65.

JOHNSON, JOHNNY Piano. Member of Chuck Berry and His Combo, 1955. Session for Chuck Berry (1957-61, 64-65).

JOHNSON, JOHNNY Bass. Member of the Dwight Twilley Band, 1976-78.

JOHNSON, JOHNNY LEE Drums, percussion. Session for Gregg Allman (1974).

JOHNSON, KEITH Trumpet, piano. Member of Paul Butterfield Blues Band, 1967-68.

JOHNSON, KENNY Drums. Session for the Steve Miller Band, 1976-77.

JOHNSON, KIRBY Keyboards. Session for Carly Simon (1972).

JOHNSON, LONNIE Guitar, vocal. New Orleans blues artist of the 1920s and 1930s reportedly born 1899. Entire family (14 in all) died of disease in 1922, except for himself. *Albums:* Finest of Lonnie Johnson — Folk Bluesmen (BET BCP-6017); Losing Game (PRS 7724); Tomorrow Night (KGO 1083) 1976.

JOHNSON, LUTHER Guitar. Nicknamed "Georgia Boy Snake" Johnson, his blues career was supported by such sideman as Otis Spann and Muddy Waters. *Album:* Chicken Shack (MUS 5021) 1974.

JOHNSON, MARK Horns. Session for Waylon Jennings (1976).

JOHNSON, MARTHA Vocal, keyboards. Member of Martha and the Muffins, 1980.

JOHNSON, PETER C. Vocal, guitar, keyboards, writer. *Album:* Peter C. Johnson (AAM 4723) 1980.

JOHNSON, PLAS Horns, reeds. Session for B. B. King (1972); Steely Dan (1974, 76); Ry Cooder (1974); Boz Scaggs (1976); Terry Reid (1976); Rod Stewart (1976); Dr. John (1979). *Albums:* After You've Gone (CCJ 6); The Blues (CCJ 15) 1976; Positively (CCJ 24) 1976.

JOHNSON, PRUDENCE Vocal. Member of Rio Nido, 1978.

JOHNSON, ROBERT Guitar, vocal. *Albums:* King of the Delta Blues Singers (COL CL-1654); Story of the Blues (COL CG-30008).

JOHNSON, ROBERT Guitar, vocal, drums, bass, writer, producer. Stax session man who went solo in 1978. Session for Isaac Hayes; Ann Pebbles; the Hot Dogs (1973). *Album:* Close Personal Friend (INF 9000) 1978.

JOHNSON, ROBERT Guitar. Member of Steeleye Span, 1972-74.

JOHNSON, ROD Drums. Member of Bruce Wooley and the Camera Club, 1980.

JOHNSON, ROGER Guitar. Member of the Sanford-Townsend Band, 1977-79.

JOHNSON, RON Bass. Session for Dr. John (1971); Carlos Santana and Buddy Miles (1972).

JOHNSON, RUSS Vocal, guitar. Member of Mississippi, 1973.

JOHNSON, TEX Congos. Session with Delaney and Bonnie.

JOHNSON, TOMMY Tuba. Session for Dr. John (1979).

JOHNSON, TONY Vocal, piano, drums. Member of the Moonlighters, 1977.

JOHNSON, WILCO Guitar. Member of Dr. Feelgood, 1975-80.

JOHNSTON, BOB Producer. Produced Bob Dylan, 1969-70.

JOHNSTON, BRUCE Vocal. Temporarily replaced Brian Wilson in the Beach Boys, 1964-65. Session for Elton John (1974, 80); Pink Floyd (1978). *Album:* Going Public (COL PC 34441) 1977.

JOHNSTON, TOM Guitar, harmonica, keyboards, vocal, writer. Co-founder of the Doobie Brothers, 1971-78. Session for the Doobie Brothers (1978). *Album:* Everything You've Heard Is True (WBR K-3304) 1979.

JOHNSTONE, DAVEY Guitar. Scottish guitarist who first became known alternating with Caleb Quaye in supporting Elton John, 1970, before becoming a member of John's permanent band, 1971-76. Member of Ultra Latex, 1979. Session for Long John Baldry (1972); Neil Sedaka (1976); Yvonne Elliman (1978); Elton John (1978); Alice Cooper (1979); Hilly Michaels (1980); the Tremblers (1980). *Album:* Smiling Face (MCA) 1975.

JOLLY, CHARLIE Tabla. Session for the Rolling Stones (1974).

JON AND THE NIGHTRIDERS John Blair—guitar; Eddy B. Gianni—guitar; Niki Syxx—bass; Dusty Watson—drums. Modern re-creation of the surf sound of the 1960s. *Album:* Surf Beat '80 (RMP 200-002) 1980.

JON AND VANGELIS Jon Anderson—vocal; Vangelis—keyboards, percussion, guitar. See individual listings. *Album:* Short Stories (POL I-6272) 1979.

JONES, ALAN Bass. Session for Brian Protheroe (1976).

JONES, ANDREW, JR. Guitar. Session for Freddie King (1975).

JONES, ANTHONY "SOOTY" Bass, vocal. Member of the re-formed Humble Pie, 1980.

JONES, BILLY Guitar, vocal. Member of Acrobat, 1972, and the Outlaws since 1975. Session for Freddie King (1975).

JONES, BOB Drums, percussion, vocal. Member of Love Sculpture, 1969-70.

JONES, BOB Guitar, writer, vocal. Chicago blues man, whose musical acquaintances include Barry Goldberg, Charlie Musselwhite, and others. Session for Harvey Mandel.

JONES, BOB Drums. Session for Mike Bloomfield (1977-79).

JONES, BOB Guitar. Member of the Demons, 1977.

JONES, BOBBY Vocal. Background vocal in Joe Cocker's Greatest Show on Earth, 1970. Session for the Sneakers (1980).

JONES, BOOKER T. See Booker T., and Booker T. and the MGs.

JONES, BRIAN Guitar, keyboards, sitar, dulcimer, vocal, harmonica, writer. Born 2/28/42. Early member of Blues Incorporated. Original member of Rolling Stones until his death 7/3/69, months after leaving the group to go solo.

JONES, "BUSTA CHERRY" Bass, vocal. Member of Sharks, 1974, and founder of White Lightnin', 1975.

JONES, CHRIS Drums. Member of Glass Moon, 1980.

JONES, CHRIS Vocal, trumpet, percussion. Member of Dayton, 1980.

JONES, CURT Vocal, guitar, percussion. Member of Aurra, 1980.

JONES, DAVEY Real name of David Bowie.

JONES, DAVEY Vocal, tambourine. Actor-turned-singer for the Monkees, 1966-69. Resurfaced as a member of Dolenz, Jones, Boyce and Hart, 1975.

JONES, DAVY Baritone saxophone, clarinet. Member of the Kinks, 1972.

JONES, ERNESTINE Vocal. Session for the Marshall Tucker Band, 1973.

JONES, GEORGE Vocal. Session for Dr. John (1978).

JONES, GLORIA RICHETTA Vocal. Session for Neil Young (1969); Ry Cooder (1970, 72); Elvin Bishop (1972); John Kay (1973).

JONES, JEFF Drums. Member of Man, and Wild Turkey, 1972.

JONES, JEFF Bass, vocal. Member of Red Rider, 1980.

JONES, JOHN Guitar, vocal. Session for Trapeze (1974); Ray Thomas (1975-76).

JONES, JOHN PAUL Keyboard, bass, vocal. Born 1946. Replaced Chris Dreja in the Yardbirds, 1966-69. Original member of Led Zeppelin, 1969-80. Session on Donovan's "Mellow Yellow," the Rolling Stones (1967); Jeff Beck (1968); Memphis Slim (1971); Roy Harper (1975); Wings (1979).

JONES, KENNY Drums, percussion. Original member of the Faces, 1967-68, and the Small Faces, 1967-78. Replaced Keith Moon in the Who, 1980. Session for Rod Stewart (1971-72, 74); Chuck Berry (1972); Jerry Lee Lewis (1973); the Rolling Stones (1974); Ron Wood (1976); Wings (1979); Pete Townshend (1980).

JONES, KENNY Drums. Member of Osiris, 1978.

JONES, MEL Drums, percussion. Session for Mike Berry (1976).

JONES, MICHAEL Guitar, vocal. Member of Man. Session for Peter Frampton (1972).

JONES, MICK Guitar, vocal. Member of the Clash since 1978.

JONES, MICK Guitar. Member of the Leslie West Band, 1975. Took over for Luther Grosvenor in the re-formed Spooky Tooth, 1974-75. Member of Foreigner, 1977-present. Session for Thomas F. Browne (1972); George Harrison (1974); Mike Harrison (1975); Leslie West (1976); Ian Lloyd (1979).

JONES, MICKIE Bass. Member of Bux, 1976, and the Angels, 1976-78.

JONES, MONROE, JR. Guitar. Session for John Littlejohn.

JONES, MOSE See Mose Jones.

JONES, PAUL Vocal, harmonica. Started in Blues Incorporated. Original member of Manfred Mann, until 1966. Started the Blues Band, 1979. Session for Gerry Rafferty (1978).

JONES, PERCY Bass. Member of Brand X, 1977-78.

JONES, PHALIN Vocal. Original member of the Bar-Kays. Died in the Otis Redding plane crash 12/10/67.

JONES, PRISCILLA Vocal. Wife of Booker T. Jones and sister of Rita Coolidge. Session for Steve Stills (1970); Rita Coolidge (1972); Bob Dylan (1973); Marc Benno.

JONES, QUINCY Keyboards, writer, arranger, producer. Born 3/14/33. String arrangements for Paul Simon, 1973. *Albums:* Mode (ABC X 782); My Fair Lady Loves Jazz (IPE 72); Ndeda (MER SRM Z-623); Quintessence (IPE 11); Jones Boys (EVR 270) 1957; Live at Newport (TRP 5554) 1961; You've Got It Bad, Girl (AAM 3041) 1973; Save the Children (MTN M7-800); Walking in Space (AAM 3023); Body Heat (AAM 3617) 1974; Birth of a Band (TRP 5596); Great Wide World of Quincy Jones (TRP 5514); Gula Matari (AAM 3030); Mellow Madness (AAM 4526) 1975; I Heard That (AAM 3705) 1976; In the Heat of the Night (UAR UA-LA290-G); Smackwater Jack (AAM 3037); Sounds . . . and Stuff Like That (AAM 4685) 1978.

JONES, RAY Bass. Member of Billy J. Kramer and the Dakotas, 1963-66.

JONES, RICHARD Bass. Original member of Climax Blues Band, 1968, 1975-77.

JONES, RICKIE LEE Guitar, keyboards, vocal, writer. *Album:* Rickie Lee Jones (WBR K-3296) 1979.

JONES, RONNIE Member of Blues Incorporated.

JONES, RONNY Vocal, guitar. Member of the Lavender Hill Mob, 1977-78.

JONES, ROYCE Vocal, percussion. Member of Ambrosia.

JONES, STEVE Piano. Session for the Avengers (1979).

JONES, STEVE Guitar, vocal. Member of the Sex Pistols, 1977. Session for Sean Tyla.

JONES, STEVEN Bass, vocal. Member of the Screams, 1980.

JONES, THAD Trumpet. Session for Martin Mull.

JONES, TOM Vocal. Real name: Thomas James Woodward. Recorded under the name Tiger Tom early in his career. Pop vocalist in the hip-shaking Elvis tradition who scored with "It's Not Unusual" (1965) with rock audiences before perfecting his lounge act. Sang the theme for the movie, "What's New Pussycat," 1965. *Albums:* Body and Soul of Tom Jones (PRR X-71060); Close Up (PRR X71055); Fever Zone (PRR X 71019) 1968; Help Yourself (PRR X-71025); I Who Have Nothing (PRR X-71039); Tom Jones' Greatest Hits (LON X 71062); Jones Live (PRR X 71014) 1967; Jones Live at Caesar's Palace (PRR ZXPA 71049); Jones Sings She's a Lady (PRR X 71046); Somethin' 'bout You Baby I Like (PRR X 71066); What's New Pussycat (UAR UA-LA278-G) 1965; It's Not Unusual, 1965; A-Tom-Ic Jones, 1965; Green Green Grass of Home, 1967; Funny Familiar Forgotten Feelings, 1967; Classic Tom Jones (EPC E-34383) 1977; Tom Jones Live in Las Vegas (PRR X-71031); London Collector—Tom Jones' Greatest Hits (LON LC-50002); Memories Don't Leave Like People Do (PRR 71068); Say You'll Stay Until Tomorrow (EPC PE-34468) 1977; This Is Tom Jones (PRR X-71028) 1977; What a Night (EPC JE 35023) 1977; Country Side of Tom Jones (LON PS-717) 1978.

JONES, TONY Bass. Member of Osiris, 1978.

JONES, TREVOR Bass, vocal. Session for Ray Thomas (1975-76).

JONES, URIEL Drums. Session for the Temptations (1973).

JONES, VICTOR Guitar, vocal. Member of Platinum Hook since 1979.

JONES, VIRGIL Trumpet. Session for Taj Mahal (1978); John Mayall (1979).

JONES, WORNELL Bass. Session for Nils Lofgren (1975-77); Leon Russell (1979); the Tears (1979). *Album:* Wornell Jones (PDS K-3308).

JONNIE, MICKIE LEE Vocal. Member of Root Boy Slim's Sex Change Band, 1978.

JONSSON, WILI Bass, keyboards, vocal. Member of Gasolin, 1974.

JONUTZ, LARRY Trumpet. Member of Cold Blood.

JONZ, JONI Vocal. Session for Dr. John (1971).

JOOLS Nickname for Julie Driscoll.

JOPLIN, JANIS Vocal, writer. Born 1/19/43, in Texas. Teamed up with Big Brother and the Holding Company, 1968. She left the group after two albums that same year to go solo. Backed by the Full Tilt Boogie Band, 1969. Perhaps the most popular female vocalist in rock history, she mesmerized audiences with her wrenching rendition of "Piece of My Heart," 1967. Died of a drug overdose on October 4, 1970. *Albums:* I Got Dem Ol' Kozmic Blues Again, Mama (COL PC-9913) 1969; Pearl (COL PC-30322) 1969; In Concert (COL CZX 31160) 1972; Janis (COL PG-33345) 1975; Janis Joplin's Greatest Hits (COL PC-32168).

JOPLING, LOUISE Violin. Member of Centipede, 1971.

JORDAN, CYRIL Guitar. Member of the Flamin Groovies, 1971-79.

JORDAN, DENE Bass, vocal. Member of Paul Warren and Explorer, 1980.

JORDAN, LONNIE Keyboards, percussion. Original member of War. *Album:* Different Moods of Me (MCA 2329) 1977.

JORDAN, MARC Keyboards, guitar. Member of the Edison Electric Band, 1970. Session for Dave Mason; Montrose (1974); Sammy Hagar (1979); Tom Johnston (1979). *Album:* Mannequin (WBR K-3143) 1978.

JORDAN, PERRY Guitar, vocal. Member of Heartsfield.

JORDAN, STEVE Drums. Session for Taj Mahal (1978); the Blues Brothers (1978-80); John Mayall

(1979).

JORDAN, VIC Guitar. Session for Neil Young (1978).

JOSEPH AND THE AMAZING TECHNICOLOR DREAMCOAT David Daltry—guitar, vocal; Terry Saunders—guitar, vocal; Malcolm Parry—bass, vocal; John Cook—organ, vocal; Brian Watson—drums, vocal. See "Jesus Christ Superstar." *Album:* Joseph and the Amazing Technicolor Dreamcoat (SPR SPS 588) 1971.

JOSEPH, DAVID Keyboards, synthesizer, vocal. Member of Hi Tension, 1978.

JOSEPH, JERRY Congas. Session for the Marshall Tucker Band (1974-76); Elvin Bishop (1974).

JOSEPH, KENNETH Bass, vocal. Member of Hi Tension, 1978.

JOSPE, BOB Drums. Member of Cosmology, 1977.

JOURARD, JEFF Guitar. Member of the Motels, 1979.

JOURARD, MARTIN LIFE Keyboards, saxophone. Member of the Motels, 1979-80.

JOURNEY Greg Rolie—keyboards, vocal (1975-80); Robert Fleischman—vocal (until 1975); Neal Schon—guitar, vocal, writer; Aynsley Dunbar—drums, percussion (1975-78); Ross Valory—guitar, bass, vocal; George Tickner—bass, piano, vocal (1975); Steve Perry—vocal (1978-present); Steve Smith—drums (1979-present). Greg Rolie, a key member of the early Santana sound, teamed up with former Santana guitarist Neal Schon and Englander Aynsley Dunbar in 1975 for a re-creation of the famous Santana sound that was so popular in the late 1960s. With Rolie at the helm, and Dunbar's driving rhythms, Schon finally got to display his lead talents, every bit as energetic and dominating as early Santana. The addition of Perry, 1978, added a more lyrical dimension to their sound. Rolie left for solo ventures in 1980. *Albums:* Journey (COL PC-33388) 1975; Look Into the Future (COL PC 33904) 1976; Next (COL PC-34311) 1977; Infinity (COL JC-34912) 1978; In the Beginning (COL C2-36324) 1979; Evolution (COL FC 35797) 1979; Departure (COL FC 36339) 1980.

JOY Toni Brown—piano, vocal; Terry Garthwaite—guitar, vocal; Reggie McBride—bass; James Gadson—drums. Abbreviated name for the Joy of Cooking after their reunion, following Garthwaite's less successful solo ventures. *Album:* The Joy (FSY 9538) 1977.

JOY DIVISION Ian Curtis—vocal; Norris Albrect—guitar; Peter Hook—bass; Stephen Morris—drums. English group who never released on a domestic label until 1981, a year after Curtis's suicide. *Albums:* Unknown Pleasures (FAC 1) 1979; Atmosphere (FAC 2) 1979; Closer (FAC 25) 1980; Love Will Tear Us Apart (FAC 12) 1980.

JOY OF COOKING Toni Brown—keyboards, steel guitar, vocal; David Garthwaite—bass, guitar; Terry Garthwaite—vocal, guitar, clarinet; Fritz Kasten—drums, alto saxophone; Ron Wilson—percussion. The lyrical vocal harmonies of a feminine duet lead brought Cooking brief notoriety. They ranged from rock to pop to blues, and to fame a little too fast, announcing solo careers that never really got off the ground. See Terry Garthwaite and Toni Brown, and Joy. *Albums:* Joy of Cooking (CAP ST-661) 1970; Closer to the Ground (CAP SMAS-828) 1971; Castles (CAP) 1972.

JOYCE, JOHN Vocal. Session for Pink Floyd (1979); Elton John (1980).

JTS BAND Jim Young—guitar, keyboards, flute, vocal; Jon Wild—guitar, vocal; Frank Heath—drums, vocal; Kevin Lillas—bass; Bill Goldiron—guitar, vocal. *Album:* Flyin, 1977.

JUBER, LAURENCE Guitar. Replaced Jimmy McCullough in Wings, 1979.

JUDAS PRIEST Ian Hill—bass; John Hinch—drums (1974); Bob Halford—vocal, harmonica; Glen Tipton—guitar, vocal, synthesizer; K. K. Downing—guitar; Les Binks—drums (1977-80); Alan Moore—drums (1974-76). *Albums:* Rock A Rolla (VSA IMP 7001) 1974; Sad Wings of Destiny (OVA 1751) 1975; Sin After Sin (COL PC-34787) 1977; Hell Bent for Leather (COL JC-35706) 1978; Stained Class (COL JC-35296); Unleashed in the East (COL JC-36179) 1979; British Steel (COL JC-36443) 1980.

JUDD, NICK Keyboards. Member of Sharks, 1974. Session for Audience (1972).

JUICY LUCY Glenn Ross Campbell—steel guitar, mandolin, percussion, vocal, writer; Ray Owen—vocal (1970); Chris Mercer—saxophone, keyboards; Neil Hubbard—guitar (1970); Keith Ellis—bass, vocal (1970); Pete Dobson—drums, percussion (1970); Paul Williams—vocal, percussion (1970-71); Mick Moody—guitar (1970-71); Rod Coombes—drums, percussion (1970-71); Jim Leverton—bass (1971). English hard rock group featuring American Campbell's writings and the raunchy sax work of former Bluesbreaker Chris Mercer, formed in 1969. Their changing personnel and uncommercial style failed to establish a consistent image for any following to grasp. *Albums:* Juicy Lucy (ACO SD 33-925) 1969; Lie Back and Enjoy It (ACO SD 33-345) 1970; Get a Whiff of This (ACO SD 33-367) 1971.

JUKE JOINT JIMMY Guitar, writer. Member of the J. Geils Band, 1970.

JUKIN BONE Joe Whiting—vocal; Mark Doyle—guitar; George Egosarian—guitar; John de Maso—bass; Tom Glaster—drums. *Album:* Whiskey Woman (VIC) 1972; Way Down East, 1972.

JULES AND THE POLAR BEARS Stephen Hague—keyboards; Jules Shear—vocal, guitar; Richard Bredice—guitar; David Beebe—drums. *Albums:*

Fenetiks (COL JC 36138) 1980; Got No Breeding (COL JC 35601) 1979.

JULIAN, IVAN Guitar, vocal. Member of Richard Hell and the Voidoids, 1977.

JULIAN, JO Synthesizer, vocal. Member of Berlin, 1980.

JULIANO, TONY Vocal, percussion. Member of Johnny's Dance Band, 1977.

JULLIEN, IVAN Trumpet. Session for Elton John (1972).

JULY Tony Duhig—guitar; Jon Field—flute, percussion; Alan James—bass; Tom Newman—vocal, guitar, mandolin, organ, percussion; Chris Jackson. English band that evolved into Jade Warrier. *Album:* July.

JUMONVILLE, JERRY Saxophone. Arranger for Captain Beefheart, 1972. Session for Delaney and Bonnie (1970); Dr. John (1971); Ry Cooder (1972); Freddie King (1975); Nilsson (1975); Rod Stewart (1976); Jules and the Polar Bears (1979); Tom Johnston (1979); the Doobie Brothers (1980).

JUMPERS Flasher—guitar, vocal; Gene Leppik—bass, vocal; Jimmie Mack—guitar, vocal; Steve Merola—drums; Roy Bittan—keyboards. Backup band for Jimmie Mack, 1980. *Album:* Jimmie Mack and the Jumpers (VIC AFLI 3698) 1980.

JUNIOR CADILLAC Ned Neltner—guitar, vocal; Jim Manolides—percussion, vocal; Buck Ormsby—bass, saxophone, vocal; Bob Hosko—saxophone; George Rudsker—drums; Larry Richstein—guitar; Tom Katila—keyboards, percussion, vocal; Les Clingingbeard—saxophone, percussion, vocal. Pacific Northwest stalwarts for over 10 years. *Albums:* Hamburgers to Go (GNW 003); Classics (GNW 005) 1979.

JUNIOR, MARVIN Vocal. Member of the Dells.

JUNKYARD ANGEL Kevin Iverson—drums, percussion, vocal; Peter Batey—bass, percussion; Ian Herbert—guitar, keyboards, vibes, vocal; Frank Kenyon—guitar, vocal. Backup band for Mike Harrison's solo debut. See Mike Harrison.

JURIC, TERRY Bass. Member of Moxy, 1976-78.

JUSTMAN, SETH Keyboards, vocal, writer. With Peter Wolf, nucleus of the J. Geils Band writing team since 1970.

JUSTO, RODNEY Vocal. Member of the Candymen, 1967-68.

JUSZKIEWICZ, KRZYSZTOR Keyboards, accordion. Member of Skin Alley, 1973.

KABAKA, REMI Percussion. Member of Ginger Baker's Air Force, 1970-71.

KABALLERO, KARLOS Drums. Member of the Dickies since 1978.

KABOODLESCHNITZER, FRED Drums, vocal. Member of the Skyhooks, 1975-77.

KABOR, JANOS Vocal, percussion. Member of Omega, 1975-78.

KAESCHNER, ROGER Bass. Member of Schloss, 1975.

KAFFINETTI, DAVE Piano. Member of Rare Bird, 1969-73. Session for Chuck Berry, 1972.

KAGAN, DAVID Vocal. Member of Baby Grand, 1977-78.

KAHAN, DOUG Bass, vocal. Member of Tilt, 1980.

KAHN, GEORGE Saxophone. Session for Arthur Brown, 1975.

KAHN, JOHN Bass. Session for Jerry Garcia and Howard Wales (1972); Super Session (1969); Merl Saunders (1973).

KAHNE, DAVID Keyboards, vocal. Half of the Voudouris and Kahne duet.

KAISER, GLENN Vocal, guitar. Member of the Resurrection Band, 1978.

KAISER, WENDY Vocal. Member of the Resurrection Band, 1978.

KAJANUS, GEORG Guitar. Member of Sailor since 1975.

KAK John Barg—guitar, vocal; Denner Patten—guitar, vocal; Gary Yoder—guitar, vocal, writer; Joseph Damrell—bass, sitar, percussion, vocal; Christopher Lockheed—drums, percussion, harpsichord, vocal. Little-known group of the late '60s with more commercial potential than exposure. *Album:* Kak (EPC BN 26429).

KAKOULLI, HARRY Bass. Original member of Squeeze, 1978-79.

KAKOULLI, KOULLA Vocal. Session for the Only Ones (1979).

KALAPANNA Malani Bilyea—guitar; Kirk Thompson—keyboards; Randy Aloya—bass; D. J. Pratt—guitar; Alvin Fejarang—drums; Mike Paulo—reeds. *Album:* 111, 1977.

KALB, DANNY Guitar. Considered one of New York's finest folk guitarists of the '60s. Original member of the Blues Project, 1966-67. Session for Judy Collins. *Album:* Blues Project (ELK 7264).

KALE, JIM Percussion, bass. Member of the Guess Who.

KALEIDOSCOPE David Lindley—guitar, violin, banjo, vocal; Solomon Feldthouse—guitar, oud, clarinet, vocal; Templeton Parcley—violin, organ, vocal; Paul Lagos—drums, vocal; Maxwell Buda—harmonica; Christopher Darrow—bass, vocal, mandolin (until 1968); John Vadican—drums (until 1968); Stuart Brotman—bass, oud, percussion. Synthesizing rock, folk, Eastern and Western music, they made their recording debut in 1967 but had been together for years. They headlined the 1968 Newport Folk Festival. For all their originality and talent, they failed to survive past four albums. An attempted comeback in 1977 went unnoticed. *Albums:* Side Trips (EPC) 1967; Beacon from Mars (EPC BN 26333) 1967; Kaleidoscope (EPC BN 26467) 1968; When Scopes Collide (PFA 102) 1976.

KALENSKY, HARRY Bass, vocal. Member of Trooper, 1975-79.

KALINOWSKI, JEAN-LOU Drums. Member of Shakin' Street, 1980.

KALOCHIE, VINNIE Guitar. Member of the Other Side.

KALSTEIN, RON Guitar, vocal. Member of the U.S. Radio Band, 1976.

KALTENECKER, HARALD Keyboards. Member of the Bullfrog, 1976.

KAMEN, MICHAEL Arp synthesizer, keyboards, clarinet, oboe, guitar, vocal, English horn. Original member of the New York Rock and Roll Ensemble, 1968-69. Session for Henry Gross (1973, 75).

KAMIN, IRA Keyboards. Session for Mike Bloomfield (1978-79).

KAMINSKY, MIK Violin, vocal. Member of the Electric Light Orchestra, 1974-78, and Violinski, 1979.

KAMMAN, ANDREW Drums. Member of the Sussman Lawrence Band, 1980.

KAMPF, CRAIG Drums, percussion, accordion. Member of Cherokee, 1971.

KANE, ARTHUR Bass. Member of the New York Dolls, 1973-74.

KANE, HOWIE Vocal. Former member of Jay and the Americans.

KANE, MIKE Bass, vocal. Added to the Youngbloods lineup, 1972.

KANE, PAUL Early recording name of Paul Simon.

KANE, WALTER Bass, clarinet. Session for Steely Dan (1980).

KANGA, SKAILA Harp. Session for Elton John (1969).

KANGAROO John Hall—bass; Teddy Speleos—guitar; Norman Smart—drums; Barbara Keith—vocal. *Album:* Kangaroo, 1968.

KANIA, ERWIN Keyboards. Member of Frumpy, 1973.

KANSAS Phil Ehart—drums; Steve Walsh—keyboards; Dave Hope—bass, vocal; Rich Williams—guitar, percussion, vocal; Kerry Livgren—guitar; Robbie Steinhardt—vocal, violin. Early names: White Clover; the Gimlets. Progressive rockers from Atlanta, GA. *Albums:* Kansas (KSH PZ-32817) 1974; Masque (KSH PZ-33806) 1975; Song for America (KSH PZ-33385); Leftoverture (KSH JZ-34224) 1976; Point of Know Return (KSH JZ-34929) 1977; Two for the Show (KSH PZ2-35660) 1978; Monolith (KSH FZ-36008) 1979; Audio Visions (KSH 36588) 1980.

KANT, RIP Baritone saxophone. Played with John Mayall, 1966.

KANTER, PAUL Guitar, writer. Born 3/12/42. Original member of Jefferson Airplane and Starship, since 1965. Session for David Crosby (1971).

KANTOR, GAIL Vocal. Session for Paul Butterfield (1975); Ian Hunter (1976).

KAPELL, DAVID Bass, piano, vocal. Member of the Tidbits.

KAPLAN, ARTIE Saxophone. Session for Grace Slick (1980).

KAPLAN, RORY Synthesizer. Session for Paul Waroff (1980).

KAPNER, MARK Keyboards. Member of Country Joe and the Fish, 1969.

KAPT. KOPTER AND THE FABULOUS TWIRLY BIRDS Randy California—guitar, vocal; Charlie Bundy—bass, vocal; Ed Cassidy—drums, percussion. Name of the album and group Randy California formed after the first dissolution of Spirit, dealing with experimental rock-jazz. *Album:* Kapt. Kopter and the Fabulous Twirly Birds (EPC I-31755) 1972.

KAPUSTIN, NATASHA Vocal, keyboards, synthesizer. Member of Black Russian, 1980.

KAPUSTIN, SERGE Keyboards, synthesizer, vocal, guitar. Member of Black Russian, 1980.

KARAN, CHRIS Congas. Session for Peter Frampton (1972); Mike Batt (1979).

KARAS, PAUL Member of Rare Bird, 1972. Member of Stackridge, 1974.

KARCZEWSKI, TED Guitar. Member of Flight, 1976-80.

KARER, CHRIS Vocal, guitar, banjo, violin. Member of Amon Duul.

KARLSA, KIM Vocal. Session for Peter C. Johnson (1980).

KARMELK, FERDIE Guitar. Member of Herman Brood and His Wild Romance since 1979.

KARN, MICK Bass, saxophone. Member of Japan since 1979.

KAROLI, MICHAEL Vocal, guitar. Member of Can, 1975.

KARPMAN, RON Drums. Member of the Flock.

KARSKI, LES Guitar, vocal, bass. Member of Supercharge, 1976-77, and Flash and the Pan since 1979.

KARSTEIN, JIMMY Drums. Session for Marc Benno; J. J. Cale (1972-79); the Rainbow Concert (1973); Joe Cocker (1974).

KARTHAGO Ingo Bischof—keyboards, vocal; Tomy Goldschmidt—percussion; Norbert Lehman—drums, percussion, vocal (1974); Gerald Luciano—bass, harmonica, vocal (1974); Glenn Cornick—bass (1974); Konni Bommarius—drums (1974-75); Reinhard Bopp—vocal, guitar (1976); Ringo Funk—drums (1976); Gerald Hartwig—bass (1976). *Albums:* Second Step (BSF) 1974; Rock 'N' Roll Testament, 1974; Live at the Roxy, 1976.

KARUSH, LARRY Tabla. Session for Steve Hillage (1976). *Album:* May 24, 1976 (ECM 1-1901) 1976.

KARWAN, PAT Vocal, guitar. Member of the 1910 Fruitgum Company, 1968-69.

KASKE, BETSY Vocal, guitar. Session for Snopek (1980). *Album:* Last Night in Town (MTR 52788) 1980.

KASTEN, FRITZ Drums, alto saxophone. Member of Joy of Cooking, 1970-73.

KASTNER, MATT Guitar, vocal. Member of Randy Burn's Sky Dog Band, 1973.

KASTNER, STANLEY Drums. Session for Peter C. Johnson (1980).

KASTRAN, DEAN Bass. Member of the Ohio Express, 1968-69.

KATAHN, MARTIN Violin. Session for Waylon Jennings.

KATH, TERRY Guitar, vocal. Born 1/31/45. Original member of Chicago from 1969 until his death in 1978.

KATICA, TOM Keyboards, percussion, vocal. Member of Junior Cadillac.

KATON, ROY Horns. Session for Jan and Dean, 1963.

KATONA, GABRIEL Keyboards, vocal. Member of Rare Earth, 1975, and Buckeye, 1979. Session for Richie Furay (1978); the Climax Blues Band (1980).

KATZ, DAVID String arranger. Session for Long John Baldry (1979).

KATZ, DIL Bass. Session for Matthew Fisher (1980).

KATZ, STEVE Harmonica, guitar, producer. Original member of the Blues Project, 1966-68, and Blood, Sweat and Tears, 1968-69. He began in the Even Dozen Jug Band. Produced Horslips (1979). Session for Lou Reed (1974).

KAUFMAN, AL Drums. Session for Martin Mull.

KAUFMAN, ERIC Keyboards. Member of Private Lightning, 1980.

KAUKONEN, JORMA Guitar, vocal, writer. An original member of the Jefferson Airplane, 1965-73, he was one of the first to leave for a successful career in Hot Tuna, 1970-79, before going solo.

Session for David Crosby (1971). *Albums:* Quah (GNT BXLI 0209) 1974; Jorma (VIC AFLI 3446) 1979.

KAUKONEN, PETER Guitar, vocal. Brother of Jorma Kaukonen. *Album:* Black Kangaroo (GNT FTR 1006) 1972.

KAVANAUGH, ANNIE Vocal. Voice of Fancy, 1975-76.

KAVANAUGH, KEVIN Keyboards, vocal. Member of Southside Johnny and the Asbury Jukes since 1976.

KAY, JOHN Vocal, guitar, dobro, writer. Born 4/12/44. Mastermind behind the Sparrow (1965), turned Steppenwolf in 1968. After the group disbanded in 1971, he did two blues albums, showing a depth beyond the Steppenwolf foundation. The group re-formed in 1974, synthesizing the old and the new, but did not last as dynamically or as long. See Steppenwolf. *Albums:* Forgotten Songs and Unsung Heroes (DHL DSX 50120) 1972; My Sportin' Life (DHL DSX 50147); All in Good Time (MER SRM 1-3715) 1978.

KAYAK Ton Scherpenzeel—keyboards, vocal; Pim Koopman—drums, vocal (1975-76); Max Werner—vocal; Bert Veldkamp—bass, vocal (1975-77); Johan Slager—guitar, vocal; Edward Reekers—vocal (1978-80); Irene Linders—vocal (1978-80); Peter Scherpenzeel—bass, vocal (1978-80); Katherine Lapthorn—vocal (1978-80); Theo de Jong—bass (1977); Charles Louis Schouten—drums (1980). Holland based band. *Albums:* Royal Bed Bouncer (JNS 7023) 1975; Starlight Dancer (JNS 7034) 1977; Phantom of the Night (JNS 7039) 1978; Periscope (MER SRM-1-3824) 1980.

KAYE, CAROL Bass. Session for Billy Strange; Joe Cocker (1968).

KAYE, LENNY Guitar. Member of the Patti Smith Group since 1975.

KAYE, THOMAS JEFFERSON Guitar, vocal, producer. Soloist and member of White Cloud, 1972. Produced Mistress (1979). *Album:* Thomas Jefferson Kaye (DHL).

KAYE, TONY Keyboards. Original member of Yes, 1970-72. Member of Detective, 1977.

KAYLAN, HOWARD Vocal, writer. Original member of the Turtles, 1965-69. Member of the Mothers of Invention, 1971. Eddie half of Flo and Eddie since 1971. See Flo and Eddie. Session for Steve Stills (1976).

KAZOOS, ELVIN ABDUL Kazoo. Half of the Kazoos Brothers, 1979.

KAZOOS, JACKSON "ACTION" Kazoo. Half of the Kazoos Brothers, 1979.

KAZOOS BROTHERS Elvin Abdul Kazoos—kazoo; Jackson "Action" Kazoos—kazoo. *Album:* Plate Full of Kazoos (RHI 504) 1979.

KAZOOSKI, TED Kazoo. Member of the Temple City Kazoo Orchestra, 1978.

KEACH, JAMES Vocal. Actor son of Stacy Keach. Session for Ry Cooder (1980).

KEAGGY, PHIL Guitar, vocal. Focal point of Glass Harp, 1970-72, before going solo. *Albums:* What A Day, 1973; Love Broke Through, 1976; Emerging, 1977; The Master and the Musician, 1978; Ph'Lip Sid, 1980.

KEALEY, DAVID Guitar. Member of Bloontz, 1973.

KEANE, BARRY Drums, percussion. Session for Bachman-Turner Overdrive (1973-74); Gordon Lightfoot (1972, 76, 80).

KEANE, SEAN Fiddle. Session for Art Garfunkel (1978).

KEARNEY, PETE Guitar. Member of the Fugs, 1966-67.

KEARNS, MICK Saxophone. Session for Bram Tchaikovsky (1980).

KEARSEY, J. MICHAEL Bass, vocal, percussion. Member of Upepo.

KECK, MIKE Keyboards. Member of Mothers Finest. Session for Elvin Bishop (1975).

KEEFER, JAMES BARRY Real name of Keith.

KEELEY, DAVID Guitar. Session for John "Rabbit" Bundrick (1974).

KEELEY, RON Drums. Member of Radio Birdman, 1978.

KEELS, BUNKY Piano. Session for Waylon Jennings (1974).

KEEN, JOHN "SPEEDY" Vocal, writer, drums. Member of Thunderclap Newman, 1973. Produced Motorhead, 1977. Session for Rod Stewart (1972). *Albums:* Previous Convictions (MCA) 1973; Y'Know Whot I Mean (ISL) 1975.

KEENAN, BRIAN Drums. Member of the Chambers Brothers, 1965-69, and Baby.

KEENE, BARRY Bass. Replaced Al Staehely in Spirit, 1975.

KEENE, MICKY Guitar. Member of Hudson-Ford.

KEENLYSIDE, TOM Saxophone. Session for Bachman-Turner Overdrive (1978).

KEFFORD, CHRIS Bass. Original member of the Move, 1969-72.

KEHR, MICHAEL Guitar, vocal. Member of Sterling, 1980.

KEHR, STEVE Drums, vocal. Member of Sterling, 1980.

KEILER, ANDREW Vocal. Member of Influence, 1968.

KEISTER, SHANE Keyboards. Session for Jimmy Hall (1980).

KEITH Vocal. In the era of bands with gimmicks, Philadelphian James Barry Keefer, with his soft vocals, hit the charts with "98.6" (1967). Following albums not received as popularly. *Albums:* Keith, 1967; Out of Crank, 1967; The Adventures of Keith (MER) 1968.

KEITH, BARBARA Vocal. Voice of Kangaroo, 1968.

KEITH, BEN Pedal steel guitar. Member of the

Stray Gators, 1972. Member of Crazy Horse, 1977. Session with Ringo Starr (1971); Paul Butterfield (1971-73, 75); Terry Reid (1976); Neil Young (1977-80).

KEITH, BILL Pedal steel guitar. Member of Orphan, 1974. Session for Jonathan Edwards (1971, 74); Maria Muldaur (1973); Martin Mull (1974).

KEITH, BRIAN Vocal, trombone. Played Annas in "Jesus Christ Superstar," 1970. Session for Lord Sutch.

KEITH, BUBBA Vocal, guitar. Replaced Roy Kenner in the James Gang, 1975.

KEITH, STEVE Bass. Member of Private Lightning, 1980.

KEITH AND DONNA Keith Godchaux—keyboards, vocal; Donna Godchaux—vocal. Duet venture of future Grateful Dead personnel. *Album:* Keith and Donna (RND 104) 1975.

KELL, TOM Guitar, vocal. Member of the Skyboys, 1979 to present.

KELLAWAY, ROGER Piano. Member of Tom Scott's L.A. Express, 1974-76.

KELLER, BOBBY Trombone. Member of the Buddy Rich Big Band. Session for Free Creek (1973).

KELLER, DANNY Drums. Session for Harvey Mandel (1974).

KELLER, DENNIS Vocal. Original member of Fever Tree, 1968-69.

KELLER, JIM Guitar, vocal. Member of Tommy Tutone, 1980.

KELLER, STEPHEN Saxophone. Session for Taj Mahal (1978).

KELLEY, KEVIN Drums. Session on John Fahey's "Requia."

KELLIE, MIKE Drums. Original member of Spooky Tooth, 1968-74, being replaced by Bryson Graham. Member of Three Man Army, 1971, and the Only Ones since 1978. Session for Joe Cocker (1968); Peter Frampton (1970); Gary Wright (1970); Jerry Lee Lewis (1973); Splinter (1974-75); Luther Grosvenor; Sean Tyla (1980).

KELLIS, RICHARD Saxophone, flute, vocal. Member of Sod, 1971.

KELLMAN, DON Horns. Session for the Heats (1980).

KELLOG Guitar. Member of Frut, 1972.

KELLOGG, RICK Harmonica. Session for Elvin Bishop (1975).

KELLY, BETTY Vocal. Original member of Martha and the Vandellas, 1962-64.

KELLY, BILL Guitar, vocal. Member of Dakota, 1980.

KELLY, DAVE Guitar, vocal. Noted British slide guitar soloist who joined the Blues Band, 1979. Session for Howlin' Wolf; John Lee Hooker.

KELLY, FRED Member of Rare Bird, 1972.

KELLY, JIM Guitar. Member of S.C.R.A., 1972.

KELLY, JOANNE Piano, vocal, writer. A blues and honky tonk pianist, she was part of the English blues wave of the 1960s.

KELLY, JOE Bass. Member of an early Gram Parsons band.

KELLY, KIM Vocal. Session for Long John Baldry (1979).

KELLY, MATTHEW Guitar, vocal. Member of Kingfish, 1976.

KELLY, PETE Piano. Session for Dave Edmunds (1978).

KELLY, PIERCE Drums. Session for John Weider (1976).

KELLY, ROGER Guitar, vocal. Member of the Streetband, 1980.

KELLY, TOM Guitar, vocal, bass. Member of Fools Gold, 1976. Session for Firefall (1980); the Ozark Mountain Daredevils (1980).

KELLY, WELLS Drums, percussion, vocal. Member of Orleans, 1973-76.

KELLY, WINSTON Keyboards, vocal. Member of Root Boy Slim's Sex Change Band, 1978. Session for Bill Blue (1980).

KELSO, JACKIE Saxophone. Session for Lee Michaels; Bangla Desh (1971); Dr. John (1979); Johnny Rivers (1980); Christopher Cross (1980).

KELTNER, JIM Drums. Member of Attitudes, 1976. Session for Marc Benno (1970, 79); Nilsson (1971, 74, 76); Leon Russell (1971); Bangla Desh (1971); B. B. King (1971); John Lennon (1971, 74); Gary Wright (1971, 75, 77); Russ Giguere (1971); Maria Muldaur (1971); Joe Cocker's Greatest Show On Earth (1970); Carly Simon (1972, 74); Henry Gross (1972); Ry Cooder (1972, 74, 79-80); Rita Coolidge (1972); the Steve Miller Band (1972); the Bee Gees (1973); Delaney and Bonnie; Bob Dylan (1973, 80); Art Garfunkel; Freddie King (1973); Yoko Ono and John Lennon; George Harrison (1973, 75); Ringo Starr (1973-74); Dave Mason; Splinter (1974); Jack Bruce (1974); Kim Carnes (1975); Hoyt Axton (1976); James Taylor (1976); Donovan (1976); Bill Wyman (1976); Firefall (1978); Tim Weisberg and Dan Fogelberg (1978); Tom Johnston (1979); Ron Wood (1979); Ian McLagen (1979).

KELTZ, PETER Guitar. Member of the Cats, 1980.

KEMP, BRIAN Keyboards, vocal. Member of Mark Andrews and the Gents, 1980.

KEMP, RICK Vocal, bass, guitar. Member of Steeleye Span until 1978. Session for Ian Matthews (1978).

KEMPER, DAVE Drums. Member of the Bernie Leadon-Mike Georgiades Band, 1977. Session for Elkie Brooks (1975).

KENDALL, ALAN Guitar. Member of the Bee Gees, 1971-79. Session for Andy Gibb (1980).

KENDRICK, DEREK Drums, percussion, vocal. Member of Moonquake, 1975.

KENDRICK, ROB Guitar. Added to the Trapeze lineup, 1974.

KENDRICKS, EDDIE Vocal, writer. Original member of the Temptations, 1964-70, before going solo. *Albums:* All By Myself (TML T5-309); People Hold On (TML T5-315) 1972; Eddie Kendricks (TML 3276) 1973; Boogie Down (TML T5-330) 1974; For You (TML 335-51) 1974; Hit Man (TML 76-338) 1975; Goin' Up in Smoke (T6 346-51) 1976; He's a Friend (T6 343-51) 1976; Vintage '78 (ARI 4170) 1978; Eddie Kendricks at His Best (TML T7-354) 1978.

KENDZOR, JIM Vocal, guitar. Member of Blue Ash, 1973.

KENFIELD, JAMES Bass. Member of the Dixon House Band, 1979.

KENMORE, DENNIS Drums, percussion, vocal. Member of Pollution, 1971, and the Goose Creek Symphony.

KENNEDY, DON Vocal, bass. Member of the Moonlighters, 1977.

KENNEDY, EMMETT Percussion. Session for Nilsson (1975).

KENNEDY, JIM Guitar, vocal. Member of the Numbers, 1980.

KENNEDY, JOYCE Vocal. Member of Mother's Finest since 1976.

KENNEDY, MARK Drums, percussion. Member of Ayers Rock, 1975-77.

KENNEDY, RAY Vocal. Member of KGB, 1975. *Album:* Ray Kennedy (COL NJC-36395) 1980.

KENNEDY, ZONDER Vocal, guitar. Member of the Elevators, 1980.

KENNELL, RICK Bass. Member of Happy the Man, 1977-78.

KENNEMORE, PHIL Bass, vocal. Member of Yesterday and Today, 1976.

KENNER, ROY Vocal, percussion. Member of Mandala, 1968, the James Gang, 1973-74, and Law, 1977.

KENNER, WILLIAM Mandolin. Session for Leon Russell (1974), J. J. Cale (1979).

KENNY, BERNARD Guitar. Session for D. L. Byron (1980).

KENNY, GERARD Keyboards, vocal. *Album:* Made It Thru the Rain (VIC APLI 3424) 1979.

KENNY, MICHAEL Vocal. Session for D. L. Byron (1980).

KENNY, MICK Trumpet. Member of S.C.R.A., 1972.

KENNY AND THE KASUALS Kenny Daniel—vocal, harmonica, guitar, bass; Rosebud—drums; Gregg Daniel—bass; Dan Green—guitar; Ron Mason—keyboards, percussion; Wally Wilson—keyboards, percussion; Max Ball—saxophone; Jerry Smith—slide guitar; Jack Morgan—slide guitar; Karl Tomorrow—keyboards; Tony Vinsey—violin. First appeared in 1965, but resurfaced in 1977. *Albums:* Garage Kings (MRK 7000); Impact (MRK 5000) 1977.

KENNY AND THE CADETS Early name for the Beach Boys.

KENSINGTON MARKET Alex Darou—bass; Luke Gibson—vocal; Gene Martynec—vocal, guitar, piano; Keith McKie—guitar, vocal; Jimmy Watson—drums, sitar. Canadian group whose talent was augmented by the production of Felix Pappalardi. *Albums:* Avenue Road, 1968; Aardvark, 1969.

KENT, BOB Keyboards. Member of Neil Norman's Cosmic Orchestra, 1975-80.

KENT, BRAD Guitar. Session for the Avengers (1979).

KENT, COTTON Keyboards. Member of Duke Williams and the Extremes, 1973. Session for the Catfish Hodge Band (1979).

KENT, JEFF Guitar, keyboards, vocal. Member of Dreams, 1970.

KENT, KLARK Keyboards, guitar, bass, percussion, vocal. *Albums:* Music Madness from the Kinetic Kid (IRS SP 70600) 1980.

KENT, MARTIN Bass. Replaced Pete Cruikshank in the Groundhogs, 1976.

KENT, ROGER Drums, percussion. Member of City Boy, 1976.

KENTON, RIK Bass. Original member of Roxy Music, 1973.

KENYON, FRANK Guitar, vocal. Member of Junkyard Angel, 1972.

KENZIE, PHIL Horns. Session for Rod Stewart (1977-78).

KEOUGH, PAUL Guitar. Session for Nilsson (1972); Carly Simon (1972).

KER, PETE Producer. Produced the Motors (1978); the Laughing Dogs (1980); the Elektrics (1980); and others.

KERANEN, CURLY Bass. Member of the Modern Lovers, 1977.

KERBER, RANDY Keyboards. Session for Robbie Robertson (1980).

KERMODE, RICHARD Keyboards. Member of Malo, 1972, and Santana, 1974. Session for Janis Joplin (1969).

KERR, DON Bass. Original member of Every Mother's Son, 1967.

KERR, JIM Vocal. Member of the Simple Minds since 1979.

KERR, JUNIOR Guitar, vocal. Member of the Keef Hartley Band, 1970.

KERSCHNER, CHUCK Drums. Member of the Other Side.

KERSEY, PAUL Drums, percussion. Member of the Hunt, 1980.

KERSEY, RON Keyboards. Session for B. B. King (1973-74).

KERSHAW, DOUG Fiddle, vocal, writer. As Johnny Cash brought Bob Dylan into the folk world, he introduced Doug Kershaw to the cajun world. Session for John Stewart. *Albums:* Doug Kershaw (WBR 1906) 1971; Devil's Elbow (WBR B-2649) 1972; Swamp Grass (WBR B-2581) 1972; Douglas James Kershaw (WBR B-2725) 1973; Mama Kershaw's Boy (WBR B-2793) 1973; Alive and Pickin' (WBR B-2851) 1975; Ragin' Cajun (WBR B-2581) 1976; Cajun Way (WBR 1820); Flip, Flop and Fly (WBR B-3025); Louisiana Man (WBR B-3166); Spanish Moss (WBR 1861).

KERSHAW, MARTIN Guitar. Member of Vigrass and Osborne, 1972. Session for Mike Batt (1979).

KERSLAKE, LEE Drums, percussion, vocal, writer. Began in the Gods, 1968. Replaced Ian Clark in Uriah Heep, 1972-78. Member of the Blizzard of Ozz, 1980.

KESH, ABE Producer. Produced Harvey Mandel; Blue Cheer.

KESKI, JOHN Bass. Member of One Hand Clapping, 1977. Session for Lee Michaels (1968).

KESTERSON, KIM Bass. Member of the Eric Burdon Band, 1975.

KETTNER, ALFONS Guitar. Session for Bobby Caldwell (1978).

KEWLEY, IAN Keyboards. Member of Strider, 1973.

KEYES, SONNY Keyboards, vocal. Member of the Kings, 1980.

KEYLON, DAN Bass. Replaced Johnny Fraga in the Rockets, 1979.

KEYS, BOBBY Saxophone. Member of the Rolling Stones, 1972, and Joe Cocker's Greatest Show on Earth, 1972. Session for Marc Benno; Delaney and Bonnie; the Rolling Stones (1970, 72-73, 80); Eric Clapton (1970); Sky (1970-71); Dr. John (1971); Nilsson (1971-72, 74, 76); B. B. King (1971); Gary Wright (1971); Carly Simon (1972); George Harrison (1972); the Audience (1972); Donovan (1973); Ringo Starr (1973-74); John Lennon (1974); Nicky Hopkins (1974); Country Joe McDonald (1975); Kate and Ann McGarrigle (1977); Joe Cocker (1978); Ron Wood (1979); Ian McLagen (1979); the Jim Carroll Band (1980).

KEYS, MARSHALL Saxophone. Member of Root Boy Slim's Sex Change Band, 1979.

KGB Carmine Appice—drums, vocal; Rick Grech—bass; Barry Goldberg—keyboards, vocal, writer; Mike Bloomfield—guitar; Ray Kennedy—vocal, writer. Auspicious, but unsuccessful, debut of Ray Kennedy. *Albums:* KGB (MCA 2166) 1975; Motion, 1976.

KHAN Steve Hillage—guitar, vocal; Nick Greenwood—bass, vocal; Eric Peachey—drums; Dave Stewart—keyboards. *Album:* Space Shanty (PVC 7902) 1972.

KHAN, ASHISH Sarod. Member of the Shanti, 1971.

KHAN, CHAKA Vocal. Featured vocalist of Rufus before going solo. Part of "No Nukes," 1979. Session for Ry Cooder (1979). *Albums:* Chaka (WBR K-3245); Naughty (WBR BSK 3385) 1980.

KHAN, NISAR AHMAD (GEORGE) Saxophone. Session for Formerly Fat Harry (1971); Annette Peacock (1979).

KHAN, STEVE Guitar. Session for Martin Mull (1977); Steely Dan (1980); Bette Midler; Billy Joel; Kenny Loggins; James Brown. *Albums:* Tightrope (TZC JC-34857) 1977; Blue Man (COL CG-36213) 1979; Individuals (COL CG-36213) 1979; Arrows (COL JC-36129) 1979; Best of Steve Khan (COL JC-36406) 1980; Evidence (ARI 3023) 1980; Two for the Road (ARI 4156).

KHAURY, HERBERT Real name of Tiny Tim.

KID DYNAMITE Dick Thompson—bass, keyboards, vocal; John King—drums; Mike Mallen—guitar, vocal; Val Garcia—vocal. *Album:* Kid Dynamite (CRE 1003) 1976.

KID SPIKE Guitar. Member of the Gears, 1980.

KID STRANGE Vocal, guitar, harmonica, saxophone. Member of the Doctors of Madness, 1977.

KIDD, ELLIOT Vocal. Member of the Demons, 1977.

KIDD, RONNIE Bass. Member of Wax, 1980.

KIDS Ronnie Thomas—bass, vocal; Keith Boyce—drums, percussion; Gary Holton—vocal; Danny Peyronnel—keyboards, vocal; Cosmo—guitar. *Album:* Anvil Chorus (ACO) 1975.

KIEFER, LEE Vocal. Session for Tommy Bolin, 1975.

KIEFFER, TOMMY Guitar, vocal. Member of Krokus, 1980.

KIELY, LARRY Bass. Member of Eden's Children, 1968.

KIEVIT, JEFF Trumpet. Member of the Boneroos, 1977.

KIHN, GREG Vocal, guitar. Namesake of the Greg Kihn Band, since 1975.

GREG KIHN BAND Greg Kihn—vocal, guitar; David Carpenter—guitar; Larry Lynch—drums; Steve Wright—bass. *Albums:* Greg Kihn (BES 0046) 1975; Greg Kihn Again (BES 0052) 1977; Next of Kihn (BES BZ-10063) 1978; With the Naked Eye (BES BZ-10063) 1979; Glass House Rock (BES BZ-10068) 1980.

KILBURN, DUNCAN Saxophone. Member of the Psychedelic Furs, 1980.

KILBURN, LEAH Vocal. Session for Ted Nugent (1979).

KILBURN, RICK Bass. Member of Cosmology, 1977.

KILBY, CRAIG Trombone. Session for Mike Bloomfield (1978).

KILLEN, BUDDY Percussion, producer. Session for Doug Kershaw (1972).

KILLOUGH, ROCK Guitar. Namesake of the Rock Killough group, 1980.

ROCK KILLOUGH GROUP Rock Killough—guitar; Mitch Humphries—piano; Billy Earl

McClelland—guitar; Eddie Bayers—drums; Michael Rhodes—bass; Rod Smarr—guitar. *Album:* Highway 31 (ELK 6E-260) 1980.

KILMER, DOUG Bass. Session for Mike Bloomfield (1978-79).

KILMISTER, LEMMY See Lemmy.

KIMBALL, BOBBY Vocal. Member of Toto since 1978.

KIMBROUGH, KERRY Trumpet. Member of Balcones Fault, 1977.

KIMMEL, BOB Guitar. Member of the Stone Poneys, 1967-68.

KIMPEL, LARRY Bass. Member of Captain Sky's Band since 1979.

KIMSEY, CHRIS Producer. Produced Peter Frampton (1975, 79).

KIMSEY, JEROME Drums. Member of the Hoodoo Rhythm Devils, and Halloween, 1979.

KINCAID, MARK Guitar, vocal. Replaced Weasel in the Electric Prunes, 1967.

KINCAID, RON Guitar, vocal. Member of Lance Romance.

KINDER, MICHAEL Drums, percussion. Member of Gabriel, 1975.

KINDRED, LISA Vocal, guitar. Member of U.F.O., 1966.

KING, ALAN "BAM" Guitar, vocal. Member of Ace, 1974-78. Session for Sean Tyla (1980).

KING, ALBERT Guitar, vocal. Basic blues played with the complacency of a master. King became popular in the blues explosion of the late 1960s. *Albums:* Born Under a Bad Sign, 1969; Door to Door (CSS 1538); I Wanna Get Funky (STX 5505); I'll Play the Blues for You (STX 3003); Jammed Together (STX 2020); King Does King's Things (STX 2015); King of the Blues Guitar (ATC 8213); Lovejoy (STX 2040); Albert (TMT 6004); Albert Live (TMT 2-7005); Chronicle (STX 4123); King Albert (TMT 6002); Live Wire/Blues Power (STX 4128); Montreaux Festival (STX 4132) 1974; New Orleans Heat (TMT 7022); The Pinch (STX 4101) 1977; Travelin' to California (KGO 1060); Truckload of Lovin' (TMT 6003) 1978.

KING, B. B. "BLUES BOY" Guitar, vocal, writer. Born 9/16/25. Most any guitarist of long-standing stature in rock, including greats like Eric Clapton, Jimmy Page, Alvin Lee and others, learned their initial blues licks from B. B. King. Born in 1925, King learned from Lightnin' Hopkins, Mississippi John Hurt, Son House and other traveling blues artists, and organized it into one of the most distinctive sounds in the history of blues. *Albums:* Mr. Blues (ABC 456) 1963; Confessin' the Blues (ABC 528) 1965; B. B. King Live at the Regal (MCA 724) 1965; Blues is King (ABC D-704) 1967; Blues on Top of Blues (ABC D-709) 1968; Completely Well (MCA D-868) 1969; Live and Well (MCA D-819) 1969; Indianola Mississippi Seeds (ABC 713) 1970; B. B. King in London (ABC X-730); L.A. Midnight (ABC XQ 743) 1972; To Know You Is To Love You (ABC 794) 1973; Lucille (ABC D712) 1974; Lucille Talks Back (ABC 898) 1975; Anthology of the Blues—B. B. King 1949/50 (KNT 9011); Back in the Alley (MCA D-878); Best of B. B. King (MCA XQ-767); Better Than Ever (KNT 561); Boss of the Blues (KNT 529); Doing My Thing, Lord (KNT 563); Electric B. B. King (MCA D-813); From The Beginning (KNT 533); Greatest Hits of B. B. King (KNT 552); Guitar Player (MCA 2-8012); Incredible Soul of B. B. King (KNT 539); The Jungle (KNT 521); B. B. King Live (KNT 565); B. B. King Live in Cook County Jail (MCA 723); Let Me Love You (KNT 513); Live, B. B. King on Stage (KNT 515); Live—"Now Appearing"—At Ole Miss (MCA 2-8016); Midnight Believer (MCA 1061); Original Sweet Sixteen (KNT 568); Pure Soul (KNT 517); Rhythm and Blues Christmas (UAR LW-654); Rock and Roll Festival, Vol. 1 (KNT 544); Rock Me Baby (KNT 512); Take It Home (MCA 3151); Together Again—Live (MCA 9317); Together for the First Time (B. B. King and B. Bland) (MCA 7-50190); Turn on with B. B. King (KNT 548); My King of Blues (VTD 7724); Soul of B. B. King (VTD 7714); I Love You So (VTD 7711); Easy Listening Blues (VTD 7705); Heart Full of Blues (VTD 7703); King Size (ABC 977) 1977.

KING, BEN E. Guitar, vocal. Replaced Rudy Lewis in the Drifters, 1963. Session with the Average White Band (1977). *Albums:* Ben E. King's Greatest Hits (ACO 165) 1966; Golden Soul (ATC 18198); I Had a Love (ACO SD 18169); Benny and Us (ATC 19105) 1977; Let Me Live in Your Life (ATC 19200) 1978; Music Trance (ATC 19269) 1980; Rough Edges (MXW 88001).

KING, BILL Trumpet. Member of the Righteous Brothers Band, 1966.

KING, BILLY Member of Small Wonder, 1976-77.

KING, BOBBY Vocal. Session for Ry Cooder (1979-80).

KING, CAROLE Piano, vocal, writer. Born 2/9/41. Half of the Goffin-King writing team of the 1960s. Went solo after receiving notoriety performing with James Taylor at the height of his career. Session for B. B. King (1970); Donovan (1973). *Albums:* Tapestry (EOD PE 34946) 1971; Rhymes and Reasons (EOD PE-34950) 1972; Fantasy (EOD PE-34962) 1973; Wrap Around Joy (EOD PE-34953) 1974; Really Rosie (EOD PE-34955) 1975; Thoroughbred (EOD PE-34963) 1975; Simple Things (CAP SMAS-11667) 1977; Welcome Home (CAP SW-11785) 1978; Her Greatest Hits (EOD JE-34967) 1978; Touch the Sky (CAP SWAK-11953) 1979; Pearls (CAP S00-12073)

1980; Music (EOD PE-34849); Writer (EOD PE-34944).

KING, CLYDIE Vocal. Member of the Nightingales, 1977, and the Orioles, 1977. Session for B. B. King (1970); Shuggie Otis (1971); Russ Giguere (1971); Steely Dan (1972, 76); the Rolling Stones (1972); Elvin Bishop (1972); Navasota (1972); Grin (1973); Joe Walsh (1973); Marc Benno; Joe Cocker (1974); Elton John (1974); Gene Clark (1974); Ringo Starr (1974); Neil Diamond (1976); Bill Wyman (1976); Bob Seger (1978); Great Southern (1978); Bob Dylan (1980).

KING, DON Vocal, guitar. *Album:* Lonely Hotel (EPC JC 36460) 1980.

KING, ED Guitar. Member of Strawberry Alarm Clock, 1968, and Lynyrd Skynyrd, 1973-77.

KING, FREDDIE Guitar, vocal. Born 9/3/34. Real name: Billy Myles. Blues song stylist brought to the rock world by Leon Russell and Don Nix. Specialized in boogie and rock renditions of old blues standards. Died as his popularity was beginning to grow, 1976. *Albums:* Getting Ready (SHE 8905) 1971; Texas Cannonball (SHE SW 8913) 1972; Woman Across the River (SHE SW 8919) 1973; Burglar (RSO 0698) 1974; Larger Than Life (SHE) 1975; Best of Freddie King (MCA 52021); Hideaway (KGO 1059); Freddie King—1934-1976 (RSO 1-3025); Freddie King Sings (KGO 762); All His Hits (FED 501 2X).

KING, GARY Bass. Member of Randall's Island, 1971-72.

KING, JACK Drums. Replaced Tim Davis in the Steve Miller Band, 1971.

KING, JAN Vocal, guitar, keyboards. Member of the Orchids, 1980.

KING, JEANNIE Vocal. Session for Mike Pindar (1976).

KING, JIM Harmonica. Original member of Family.

KING, JIMMY Vocal. Original member of the Bar-Kays. Died in the Otis Redding plane crash 12/10/67.

KING, JOHN Drums. Member of the Steve Miller Band, 1973, and Kid Dynamite, 1976.

KING, JON Drums. Member of the Gang of Four, 1980.

KING, JONATHAN Vocal. English college student who broke into the rock scene in 1965 with "Everyone's Gone to the Moon." He recorded through 1968, including the single "It's Good News Week" under the pseudonym Hedgehoppers Anonymous. *Album:* Jonathan King or Then Again, 1968.

KING, KIM Guitar. Member of Lothar and the Hand People, 1966-68. Session for Colin Winski (1980).

KING, MARK Bass, guitar, synthesizer, drums. Member of M, 1980.

KING, MARVIN "KINGFISH" Guitar. Member of Porrazzo, 1980.

KING, MIKE Piano. Original member of the Dharma Blues Band.

KING, PAT Replaced Colin Pattenden in Manfred Mann, 1978-present.

KING, PETER Saxophone. Session with Memphis Slim (1971).

KING, ROBBIE Keyboards. Member of the Hometown Band, 1976. Session for Chilliwack (1972).

KING, RONNIE Member of the Stampeders, 1973-76.

KING, SAUNDERS Vocal, guitar. Session for Santana (1979).

KING, SIMON Drums. Member of Hawkwind, and Hawklords, 1978 to present. Session for Steve Swindells (1980).

KING, TERRY Steel guitar, vocal. Member of the Cooper Brothers Band since 1978.

KING, WARREN Member of Diamond Reo, 1979.

KING COOL Guitar. Session for Free Creek (1973).

KING CRIMSON Robert Fripp—guitar, writer, mellotron; Ian McDonald—reeds, woodwind, vibes, keyboards, mellotron, vocal (1969); Greg Lake—bass, vocal (1969-70); Michael Giles—drums, percussion, vocal (1969-70); Peter Sinfield—lyrics (1969-72); Peter Giles—bass (1970); Keith Tippet—piano (1970); Mel Collins—saxophone, flute (1970-72); Gordon Haskell—bass, vocal (1971); Andy McCulloch—drums (1971); Ian Wallace—drums (1972); Boz—bass, vocal (1972); David Cross—violin, viola, mellotron (1973-75); John Wetton—bass, vocal (1973-75); Bill Bruford—drums (1973-75); Jamie Muir—percussion (1973). English experimental rock-jazz group formed by Robert Fripp in 1969. Each album had strange, colorful drawings on the cover and featured sound odysseys beginning at inaudible volumes and building to furious climaxes over periods of 5 to 15 minutes. Greg Lake began in this group and drew some attention to it after his later union with Emerson, Lake and Palmer. They disbanded officially in 1975. *Albums:* In the Court of the Crimson King (ATC 8245) 1969; In the Wake of Poseidon (ATC 8266) 1970; Lizard (ATC 8278) 1971; Islands (ATC 7212) 1972; Larks' Tongues in Aspic (ATC 7263) 1973; Starless and Bible Black (ATC 7296) 1974; Red (ACO SD 18110) 1974; USA (ATC 18136) 1975.

KINGBEES Jamie James—guitar, vocal; Michael Rummans—bass, vocal; Rex Roberts—drums, vocal. *Album:* The Kingbees (RSO 1-3075) 1980.

KINGDOM COME, ARTHUR BROWN'S Arthur Brown—vocal; Andy Dalby—guitar, vocal; Phil Shutt—bass, vocal; Slim Steer—drums (1973); Goodge Harris—keyboards, moog (1973); Victor Peraino—keyboards, vocal, percussion (1974). After the short-lived fame of the Crazy World of Arthur Brown (1968), Brown dropped from sight for several years. When he reappeared in 1972, it was as the head of Kingdom Come, an ethereal jazz-rock group specializing in electronic gadgetry, which lasted through 1974, when Brown went solo. See Arthur Brown. *Albums:* Kingdom Come (Import) 1973; Journey (PPT 0698) 1974.

KINGERY, PAUL Guitar. Session for Bob Seger (1975).

KINGFISH Bob Weir—guitar, vocal; Dave Torbert—bass, vocal; Matthew Kelly—guitar, vocal; Robby Hoddinott—guitar, slide guitar; Chris Herold—drums, percussion. Solo venture of the Grateful Dead's Bob Weir. *Albums:* Kingfish (RND) 1976; Live and Kickin' (RND) 1977; Trident (JET PZ 35479) 1978.

KINGS David Diamond—vocal, bass; Sonny Keyes—keyboards, vocal; Max Styles—drums; Aryan Zero—guitar, vocal. *Album:* Kings Are Here (ELK 6E-274) 1980.

KINGSTON TRIO Bob Shane; Dave Guard (1957-64); Nick Reynolds; John Hartford (1964-66). "Tom Dooley" (1959) marked the beginning of the folk era, and sounded the depths of a market yet untapped. The Kingston Trio were the fathers of folk for eight years, opening the door for Peter, Paul and Mary and others. *Albums:* Kingston Trio, 1958; Stereo Concert, 1959; At Large, 1959; Here We Go Again, 1959; Sold Out, 1960; String Along, 1960; Make Way, 1961; Goin' Places, 1961; Close Up, 1961; College Concert, 1962; Best of the Kingston Trio, 1962; Something Special, 1962; New Frontier, 1962; Number 16, 1963; Sunny Side, 1963; Sing a Song, 1963; Time To Think, 1964; Back in Town, 1964; Folk Era, 1964; Nick-Bob-John, 1964; Best of the Kingston Trio, Vol. 2, 1965; Stay Awhile, 1965; Somethin' Else, 1965; Children of the Morning, 1966; Best of the Kingston Trio, Vol. 3, 1966; From the Hungry I (CAP M-19968) 1958; Scarlet Ribbons (CAP STBB-513); Tom Dooley (CAP STBB 513).

KINKS Ray Davies—harmonica, vocal, writer, guitar; Dave Davies—vocal, guitar; Mick Avory—drums; Peter Quaife—bass, vocal (1964-70); John Dalton—bass (1970-79); John Gosling—keyboards (1970-79); John Beecham—trombone, tuba (1971-72); Mike Cotton—trumpet (1971-72); Davy Jones—baritone saxophone, clarinet (1972); Alan Holmes—baritone saxophone, clarinet (1972); Laurie Brown—vocal (1973-75); Ian Gibbons—keyboards, vocal (1980); Jim Rodford—bass (1980). Early name: the Ravens. While the Beatles were carving their initial reputation, Kinks' classics like "Well Respected Man," "Dedicated Follower of Fashion" (1966), "All Day and All of the Night" (1964), "Tired of Waiting" (1965), and "You Really Got Me" (1964) displayed more than competent musicianship and composition. The end of the 1960s saw the Kinks fade from the public eye, but they emerged in the early 1970s on RCA with a group featuring tubas and trombones, an unexpected innovation they handled superbly on "Muskwell Hillbillies" (1971). Ray Davies' concept albums then began to evolve, telling extremely detailed accounts of a Kinks' eye view of society in their distinctly original style. *Albums:* Kinks Album (RPS) 1963; Kinda Kinks (RPS) 1964; Kinkdom (RPS) 1966; Face to Face (RPS) 1967; Soap Opera (VIC LPLI 5081); Preservation Act II (VIC CPL2-5040) 1974; Preservation Act I (VIC LPLI 5002) 1973; Muskwell Hillbillies (VIC SP 4644) 1971; Arthur (RPS 6366) 1969; Everybody's in Showbiz (VIC VPS-6065) 1972; Kink Kronikles (RPS 2XS-6454) 1970; Kinks Are the Village Green Preservation Society (RPS 6327) 1969; Kinks Greatest—Celluloid Heroes (VIC AFLI-1743) 1976; Kinks Greatest Hits (RPS 6217) 1966; Kinks Size (RPS 6158) 1965; Kinks You Really Got Me (RPS 6143) 1964; Live Kinks (RPS 6260) 1967; Lola Vs. Powerman and the Moneyground (RPS 6423) 1970; Low Budget (ARI 4240) 1979; Misfits (ARI 4167) 1978; One for the Road (ARI 8401) 1980; Schoolboys in Disgrace (VIC AFLI-5102) 1975; Second Time Around (VIC AFLI-3620) 1980; Something Else (RPS 6279) 1968; Great Lost Kinks Album (REP MS 2127) 1973.

KINNEAR, KEN Producer. Producer of Heart (1976-80); TKO (1979); the Dixon House Band (1979); and other Seattle-based bands.

KINNEY, NORM Percussion. Session for George Harrison (1975).

KINSON, KEVIN Keyboards. Session for Sean Tyla (1980).

KIPNER, STEVE Vocal. *Album:* Knock the Walls Down (ELK 6E-202) 1979.

KIPPER, STAN Drums. Session for Jay Ferguson (1977-79).

KIRBY Guitar. Member of Elastique, 1976. Session for Danny Kirwan (1979).

KIRBY, DAVE Guitar. Member of Calico, 1975-76. Session for Doug Kershaw; Ringo Starr (1971); Waylon Jennings (1973).

KIRBY, STEVE Guitar. Member of Stretch, 1976.

KIRCHEN, BILL Guitar, vocal. Member of Commander Cody's Lost Planet Airmen, and the Moonlighters, 1977.

KIRCHER, PETE Drums. Member of the Original Mirrors, 1980.

KIRKE, SIMON Drums, percussion, writer. A member of the Black Cat Bones, where he met Paul Kossoff and formed Free, 1969-73. With Paul Rodgers, he left Free to form Bad Company, 1974-present. Session for Jim Capaldi (1979); Jess Roden (1974).

KIRKHAM, MILLIE Vocal. Session for Leon Russell (1973).

KIRKLAND, EDDIE Guitar, vocal, harmonica. American bluesman born 8/16/28 in Alabama. *Albums:* Anthology of the Blues—Detroit Blues (KNT 9006); Front and Center (TRX 3301) 1973;

The Devil (TRX 3308) 1972.

KIRKLAND, FRANK Drums. Member of J. B. Hutto's Hawks.

KIRKLAND, JERRY Vocal. Session for the Rolling Stones (1972).

KIRKLAND, JESSE Vocal. Session for Neil Diamond (1976).

KIRKLAND, KENNY Piano. Session for Steve Stills (1978).

KIRKLAND, ROBERT Vocal, guitar, percussion. Member of Arrogance, 1976-80.

KIRKMAN, TERRY Vocal, writer. Organizer of the Association.

KIRKPATRICK, JOHN Accordion, vocal. Member of Steeleye Span, 1977-78. Session for Gerry Rafferty (1979); Richard and Linda Thompson (1978).

KIRKPATRICK, SPENCER Guitar, slide guitar, writer. Member of Hydra, 1975-77.

KIRKWOOD, BRIAN Bass, vocal. Member of Sea Dog, 1972.

KIRSCHNER, SOOZIE Vocal. Session for Southside Johnny and the Asbury Jukes (1980).

KIRWAN, DANNY Guitar, vocal, writer. He left Boiler House to become an original member of Fleetwood Mac, 1968-72. The group's triple lead guitar format, with Peter Green handling the blues and jazz and Jeremy Spencer handling the rock, was augmented by Kirwan's commercial ear for both. Session for Christine McVie (1969); Jeremy Spencer (1970); Chris Youlden (1973). *Albums:* Second Chapter (DJM 1) 1975; Danny Kirwan (DJM 9) 1976; Hello There Big Boy (DJM 22) 1979.

KISS Gene Simmons (real name: Gene Klein)—bass, vocal; Peter Criss (real name: Chris Crisscoula)—drums, vocal (1973-80); Paul Stanley (real name: Stanley Eisen)—guitar; Ace Frehley (real name: Paul Frehley)—guitar, vocal. Early name: Bullfrog Bheer. Theatrical rock received a shot of new blood in 1973 when Kiss, in their makeup and black outfits, staged their debut. Simultaneous release of each member's solo album in 1978 showed their attentive eye on marketability. *Albums:* Alive (CAS 7020) 1975; Alive 2 (CAS 7076) 1977; Destroyer (CAS 7025) 1976; Double Platinum (CAS 7100) 1978; Dressed To Kill (CAS 7016) 1975; Dynasty (CAS 7152) 1979; Hotter Than Hell (CAS 7006) 1974; Kiss (CAS 7001) 1973; Kiss—The Originals (CAS 7032) 1976; Love Gun (CAS 7057) 1977; Rock and Roll Over (CAS 7037) 1976; Unmasked (CAS 7225) 1980.

KISSELL, DAVID Bass, vocal. Member of Sterling, 1980.

KISWINEY, DAVE Bass, vocal. Replaced Walt Monagham in Ted Nugent's backup band, 1980.

KITAJIMA, OSAMU Guitar, koto, biwa, vocal. Namesake of Osamu, 1977. Session for the Alpha Band (1977).

KITCHEN, KEVIN Piano. Session for Danny Kirwan (1979).

KITCHING, COLIN Violin. Member of Centipede, 1971.

KITHCART, GLENN Drums, percussion. Member of the Touch, 1980.

KITTYHAWK Daniel Bortz—guitar, cello; Paul Edwards—chapman stick, vocal; Michael Jochum—drums, percussion; Richard Elliot—lyricon, saxophone. *Album:* Kittyhawk (EIA SW-17029) 1980.

KJELDSEN, MARK Guitar, vocal, writer. Member of the Sinceros, 1979.

KLAASSE, BEER Drums. Member of Finch, 1975.

KLAATU John Woloschuk; Dee Long; Terry Draper. *Albums:* Endangered Species (CAP ST 12080) 1980; Hope (CAP ST 11633) 1977; Klaatu (CAP ST 11542) 1976; Sir Army Suite (CAP SW 11836) 1978.

KLAERS, HUGO Drums, percussion. Member of the Suburbs, 1980.

KLATKA, TOM Trumpet. Member of the re-formed Blood, Sweat and Tears.

KLAWON, DAN Bass. Member of Tatoo, 1976.

KLEBE, GARY Vocal, guitar. Member of the Shoes since 1979.

KLEIN, BETSY Vocal. Session for the Fugs (1966).

KLEIN, DANNY Bass, vocal. Member of the J. Geils Band since 1970.

KLEIN, GENE Real name of Kiss's Gene Simmons.

KLEIN, PAUL Vocal. Member of Wind in the Willows, 1968.

KLEIN, WARREN Guitar, slide guitar. Session for Kim Fowley (1972).

KLEINOW, PETE Steel guitar. See Sneaky Pete.

KLEINSCHMIDT, KIM Drums, percussion. Member of Viktor Koncept, 1979.

KLEMMER, JOHN Saxophone. Jazz soloist. Session for Ray Manzarek; Steely Dan (1976); Kittyhawk (1980). *Albums:* And We Were Lovers (CAD); Blowin' Gold (CDC 321); Eruptions (CDC 330); Impulsively (IPE Q-9266); No Energy Crisis (IPE Q-9267); Arabesque (MCA 1068) 1978; Barefoot Ballet (MCA D-950) 1976; Brazilia (MCA AA-1116); Constant Throb (MCA 9214) 1972; Cry (MCA AA-1106); Dedication—Vol. 14 (MCA 9354); Fresh Feathers (MCA D-836) 1974; Intensity (MCA 2-9244) 1973; Lifestyle (MCA 1007); Magic and Movement (MCA Q-9269); Magnificent Madness (ELK 6E-284) 1980; Mosaic (MCA 2-8014); Touch (MCA D-922) 1975; Waterfalls (MCA Q-9220) 1972.

KLIMACK, KEN Guitar. Session for Dr. John (1972).

KLIMAS, LARRY Saxophone, flute. Member of Puzzle.

KLINGBERG, JOHN Bass. Session for Van Morrison (1968-69).

KLINGMAN, MARK Piano. Session for Johnny Winter (1973).

KLINGMAN, MOOGY Keyboards, harmonica. Member of the Vagrants, and Utopia, 1974. Session for Free Creek (1973).

KLINKHAMMER, HANS D. Bass. Member of Ramses.

KLOETZKE, DON Vocal, keyboards. Member of White Duck, 1971.

KLUCHAR, JOEY Drums. Member of the Volunteers, 1976.

KNACK Doug Fieger—guitar, vocal; Berton Averre—guitar; Bruce Gary—drums; Prescott Niles—bass. *Albums:* But the Little Girls Understand (CAP SOO-12045); Get the Knack (CAP SO-11948) 1979.

KNAPE, SKIP Keyboards. Session for Bob Seger.

KNAPP, RANDY Bass, vocal. Member of Phaze Shifter, 1980.

KNAPP, TOM Kazoo. Member of the Temple City Kazoo Orchestra, 1978.

KNAUP, RENATE Vocal. Member of Amon Duul.

KNBIT, JEFF Played with John Mayall, 1962.

KNECHTEL, LARRY Keyboards, guitar, bass, vocal. Member of Bread, 1971-77. Session for Dave Mason; Lee Michaels (1968); Art Garfunkel (1979); Neil Diamond (1976); Jon Mark (1974); Paul Simon (1972); Tim Weisberg (1971-72); John Kay (1973); Simon and Garfunkel (1970); Russ Giguere (1971); Johnny Rivers (1980); Jimmy Webb (1976).

KNEPPER, JIMMY Trombone. Session for Martin Mull (1974).

KNICKERBOCKERS Recorded "Lies," 1965.

KNIGHT, GLADYS Vocal. Namesake and head of Gladys Knight and the Pips. *Albums:* Miss Gladys Knight (BUD 5714); Gladys Knight (COL JC-35704) 1979; About Love (COL JC-36387) 1980.

GLADYS KNIGHT AND THE PIPS Gladys Knight—vocal; Merald Knight—vocal; Edward Patten—vocal; William Guest—vocal. From "I Heard It Through The Grapevine" (1967) to "Midnight Train to Georgia" (1975), Gladys Knight and the Pips have been popular survivors of soul. *Albums:* Everybody Needs Love, 1967; Feelin' Bluesy, 1968; Anthology (MTN M7-792) 1973; Bless This House (BUD 5651) 1975; Early Hits (SPE 4035); Greatest Hits (SOL S7-723) 1970; I Feel a Song (BUD 5612) 1974; Imagination (BUD 5141); In Loving Memory (MTN M7-642); Gladys Knight and the Pips Greatest Hits (BUD 5653) 1968; Neither One of Us (SOL S7-737) 1973; One and Only (BUD 5701); Standing Ovation (SOL S7-736) 1971; Still Together (BUD 5689); At Last (CAS NBLP-7081) 1977; 2nd Anniversary (BUD 5639) 1975; Callin' (CAS NBLP 7113) 1978.

KNIGHT, HOLLY Keyboards, vocal. Member of Spider, 1980.

KNIGHT, JERRY Keyboards, percussion, vocal. *Album:* Jerry Knight (AAM SP 4788) 1980.

KNIGHT, LARRY Guitar, bass. Member of Spirit, 1979, and Phaze Shifter, 1980. Session for Randy California (1972).

KNIGHT, MERALD Vocal. Member of Gladys Knight and the Pips.

KNIGHT, PETER Violin, vocal. Member of Steeleye Span until 1977.

KNIGHT, STAN Guitar, organ, vocal. Member of Black Oak Arkansas, 1971-77.

KNIGHT, STEVE Keyboards. Original member of Mountain, 1968-73.

KNIGHT, TERRY Producer. Head of Terry Knight and the Pack and producer of Grand Funk Railroad.

KNIGHT, TONY Drums, percussion, vocal. Member of Skin Alley, 1973.

KNIGHTON, JOAN Vocal. Session for the Keef Hartley Band (1971).

KNIGHTON, REGGIE Guitar, vocal. Soloist and founder of the Reggie Knighton Band, 1978. Session for John Sebastian (1976). *Album:* Reggie Knighton (COL JC 34685) 1977.

REGGIE KNIGHTON BAND Reggie Knighton—guitar, vocal; Brian Ray—guitar; Glenn Simmonds—drums, vocal; Kurtis Teel—bass. *Album:* Reggie Knighton Band (COL JC 35286) 1978.

KNIGHTS, DAVID Bass. Original member of Procol Harum, 1966-70.

KNIGHTSBRIDGE, JOHN Guitar. Member of Illusion, 1977.

KNOPFLER, DAVID Guitar. Member of Dire Straits, 1978-79.

KNOPFLER, MARK Vocal, guitar. With brother, David, founder of Dire Straits, 1978-present. Session for Bob Dylan (1979); Steely Dan (1980).

KNOTT, RAY Bass. Replaced Dave Hewitt in Babe Ruth, 1976.

KNOWLES, GREG Guitar. Member of the Movies.

KNOWLES, KEITH Drums. Member of Marseille, 1980.

KNOWLES, WILLIE Vocal, guitar. Member of Arizona, 1976.

KNOWLING, RANSON Bass. Session for Tommy McClennan (1942).

KNOX Guitar, keyboards, vocal. Member of the Vibrators, 1977.

KNOX, NICK Drums. Member of the Cramps, 1980.

KNUCKLES, FREDDY Guitar. Member of the Group Image, 1968.

KNUDSEN, KEITH Drums. Backup drummer for Lee Michaels in the early 1970s before replacing Michael Hossock as the second drummer of the Doobie Brothers, 1974-77. Session for Tom Johnston (1979).

KNUDTSON, GORDY Drums. Member of the Jan Park Band, 1979.

KOBOR, JANOS Vocal, percussion. Member of Omega, 1975.

KOCK, PETER Percussion. Member of Supermax, 1979.

KODA, CUB Guitar, steel guitar, vocal. Member of Brownsville Station, 1972-77.

KOEHLER, TREVOR Horns. Session for Lou Reed (1974).

KOENIG, ART Bass. Member of Ars Nova, 1968-69.

KOGEL, MICHAEL Vocal. Voice of Los Bravos, 1966-68.

KOHL, MARTIN Bass. Session for Lord Sutch.

KOKOMO Washboard. Session with Poor Joe Williams (1935).

KOLLEN, HELMUT Bass, guitar, vocal. Original member of Triumvirat, 1973-75.

KOLOC, BONNIE Vocal, guitar. *Albums:* After All This Time (OVA QD-14-21); Bonnie At Her Best (OVA 1701); Hold On to Me (OVA QD-14-26) 1972; Bonnie Koloc (OVA QD-14-29) 1973; You're Gonna Love Yourself in the Morning (OVA QD-14-38) 1974; Close Up (EPC) 1976; Wild and Recluse (EPC 35254) 1978.

KOMANOFF, RUTH Percussion. Session for the Mothers of Invention (1968).

KONAS, JOE Guitar, vocal. Member of the Gods, 1968.

KONDOR, ROBBIE Piano. Session for John Hammond (1980).

KONGOS, JOHN Vocal, guitar, percussion, writer. The rise of Elton John brought attention to several lesser-known artists from the same producer, Gus Dudgeon. Most of these, including Kongos, made little to no impression in the United States. *Album:* Kongos (ELK) 1972.

KONIKOFF, SANDY Percussion. Member of Joe Cocker's Greatest Show on Earth, 1970. Session for Taj Mahal; B. B. King (1972).

KOONCE, JOHNNY Vocal, guitar, harmonica. Namesake of Johnny and the Distractions, 1980.

KOOPER, AL Keyboards, writer, vocal, guitar. First appeared as a member of the Blues Project, 1966-67, before forming Blood, Sweat and Tears, 1967-68. Formed and produced Four on the Floor, 1979. Production and session for Nils Lofgren (1976); Eddie and the Hot Rods (1980). Session for Bob Dylan (1970); Taj Mahal; the Rolling Stones (1970); Bill Wyman (1976); Rita Coolidge (1972); B. B. King (1969); the Paupers (1968); Ursa Major (1972); Moby Grape; Shuggie Otis (1970-71); the Alvin Lee Band (1980); Jimi Hendrix (1968). *Albums:* Kooper Session (COL CS-9951); Live Adventures of Mike Bloomfield and Al Kooper (COL PG-6) 1969; Super Session (COL CS-9701) 1968; I Stand Alone (COL); Unclaimed Freight (COL).

KOOPMAN, PIM Drums, vocal. Member of Kayak, 1975-77.

KOOTCH, DANNY Guitar. Real name: Danny Kortchmar. See Danny Kortchmar.

KOOYMANS, GEORGE Guitar, vocal, writer, producer. Co-founder of Golden Earring, 1968-present. Produced the New Adventures, 1980. *Album:* George Kooymans (Import) 1973.

KOPPEL, ANDERS Organ, vocal, writer. Member of Savage Rose, 1968-71.

KOPPEL, ILSE MARIA Harpsichord. Member of Savage Rose, 1968-69.

KOPPEL, THOMAS Piano, vocal, writer. Member of Savage Rose, 1968-71.

KORGIS Andy Davis—vocal, keyboards, mandolin, drums; James Warren—bass, vocal. *Albums:* Dumb Waiters (ASY 6E-290) 1980; The Korgis (WBR K-3349) 1979.

KORNER, ALEXIS Guitar, vocal. Played with Cyril Davies in a duet, 1952-64, before founding Blues Incorporated, featuring Long John Baldry and Dick Heckstall-Smith. Like John Mayall, he is considered a father of British blues. Also played in a duet with Robert Plant, 1968. Released an LP in 1972, backed by Snape, that failed to catch on popularly. Session for Otis Spann; Big Bill Broonzy; John Lee Hooker; Muddy Waters; Memphis Slim; Sonny Terry and Brownie McGee; Eric Burdon (1977); B. B. King (1971); *Albums:* Bootleg Him (WBR 265) 1966; Accidentally Born in New Orleans (with Snape) (WBR BJ-2647) 1972; Get Off My Cloud, 1977.

KORTCHMAR, DANNY Guitar, vocal, producer. First gained national recognition as a session musician for Carole King and James Taylor. Member of the Fugs, 1967, Jo Mama, 1970, the Section, 1972 and 1977, and Attitudes, 1976. Produced Louise Goffin, 1979. Session for Donovan (1973); Nilsson (1974-76); Neil Sedaka (1975); Bill Wyman (1974, 76); Gene Clark (1974); John Kay (1973); Crosby and Nash (1976); Jennifer Warnes (1976); Ringo Starr (1977); David Blue (1975); Yvonne Elliman (1978); Steve Stills (1978); Jackson Browne (1980). *Albums:* Kootch (WBR); Innuendo (ASY 6E-250) 1980.

KOSEK, KENNETH Fiddle, vocal. Member of the White Cloud, 1972.

KOSINSKI, RICHARD Keyboards, vocal. Original member of Big Wha-Koo, 1977.

KOSLEN, JONAH Vocal, guitar. Member of the Michael Stanley Band, 1977, and Breathless since 1979.

KOSMO, JOHN Bass. Member of Frut, 1970.

KOSOWSKI, EDDIE Guitar, vocal. Member of Arc, 1978.

KOSS, RON Vocal, guitar. Member of Savage Grace, 1970. Session for John Sebastian (1974-76).

KOSSOFF, PAUL Guitar. An original member of Free, 1969-73, and the Amazing Blondel, 1974. After a solo attempt, he formed Backstreet Crawler in 1975. His raunchy, free-form guitar style was gaining popularity until his untimely death in 1976.

See Backstreet Crawler. Session for Jim Capaldi (1971, 75-76); Champion Jack Dupree; Alexis Korner. *Albums:* Backstreet Crawler (ISL) 1973; Koss (DJM 2-300) 1979.

KOSSOFF, KIRKE, TETSU AND RABBIT See Free; also see John Bundrick.

KOTKE, LENNY Bass, vocal. Member of the Good Rats since 1978.

KOTKOV, RALPH Keyboards, vocal. Member of Chrysalis, 1968.

KOTTKE, LEO Guitar, vocal, writer. Acoustic guitarist from the John Fahey school. *Albums:* Balance (CYS 1234) 1979; The Best of Leo Kottke (CAP SWBC-11867) 1978; Burnt Lips (CYS 1191); Chewing Pine (CAP ST-11446) 1975; Did You Hear Me (CAP ST-11576) 1976; Dreams and All That Stuff (CAP ST-11335) 1974; John Fahey, Leo Kottke, Peter Lang (TKM 1040); Greenhouse (CAP ST-11000); Ice Water (CAP ST-11262) 1974; Leo Kottke (CYS 1106); Mudlark (CAP ST-682); My Feet Are Smiling (CAP ST-11164); Six and Twelve-String Guitar (TKM C-1024).

KOULOURIS, SILVER Guitar, percussion. Member of Aphrodite's Child.

KOUPAL, DAVE Bass. Member of the Wipers, 1980.

KOVAC, HERM Drums, percussion, synthesizer. Member of T.M.G., 1979.

KOVARIC, DENNIS Bass. Session for Elkie Brooks (1975); Steve Marriott (1976).

KOWALKIE, PETE Vocal, guitar. Member of Cowboy, 1971-73.

KOWALSKI, MIKE Drums. Session for Shuggie Otis (1971).

KOWALSKI, TED Vocal. Member of the Diamonds.

KOZAK, MIKE Drums, percussion. Member of Teaze, 1979.

KRAAN Peter Wolbradt—guitar, vocal; Jan Fride—drums; Helmut Hattler—bass; Johannes Pappert—saxophone; Ingo Bischof—keyboards. *Albums:* Let It Out, 1975; Andy Nogger, 1975.

KRAATZ, DOUG Violin, viola. Member of the Candle, 1972.

KRACKER Michael Stim—vocal, guitar; Steve Samsel—vocal, guitar, piano; Al Braun—bass; Dale Dunsmoor—drums. *Album:* Kracker (PRM) 1978.

KRAFT, KEN Guitar, vocal. Member of Snail, 1978-79.

KRAFTWERK Ralf Hutter—vocal, electronics; Florian Schneider—vocal, electronics; Klaus Roeder—violin, guitar (1974); Wolfgang Flur—percussion (1974-78); Karl Bartos—percussion (1975-78). The addition of electronics to rock was an exciting move in the late 1960s. It was carried to its extreme by Germany's Kraftwerk, an entirely electronic group. *Albums:* Autobahn (MER SRM-1-3704) 1974; Man Machine (CAP SW-11728) 1978; Radio-Activity (CAP ST-11457) 1975; Trans Europe Express (CAP SW-11603) 1977; Ralf and Florian (VTG VEL 2006) 1975.

KRAL, IVAN Guitar, bass. Member of the Patti Smith Group since 1975. Session for Iggy Pop (1980).

KRAMER, BILLY J. Vocal. Real name: William Howard Ashton. Born 8/14/43. Liverpool vocalist of 1963. Lasted to 1965 when he and his band, the Dakotas, vanished. His hits included "Do You Want To Know a Secret," 1963, and "Trains, Boats and Planes," 1965.

BILLY J. KRAMER AND THE DAKOTAS Mike Maxfield—guitar; Ray Jones—bass; Robin MacDonald—guitar; Tony Mansfield—drums; Billy J. Kramer—vocal. *Album:* Best of Billy J. Kramer and the Dakotas (CAP SM 11897) 1979.

KRAMER, EDDIE Keyboards, percussion, production. Session and production for Zephyr (1971).

KRAMER, IRVIN Guitar. Session for the Marc Tanner Band (1980).

KRAMER, JOEY Drums. Member of Aerosmith, 1971-79.

KRAMER, PHIL Bass, vocal. Member of Iron Butterfly, 1974-75.

KRAMER, TIMOTHY Cello. Member of Centipede, 1971.

KRAMER, WAYNE Guitar. Member of the MC 5, 1968-69.

KRAMPF, CRAIG Drums. Replaced Chet McCracken in Nick Gilder's backup band, 1978-79.

KRANENBURG, CEES Drums, percussion. Member of Spin, 1976.

KRANTZ, DALE Vocal. Member of the Rossington-Collins Band, 1980.

KRANTZ, JOEL Vocal. Session for Magnet (1979).

KRASINSKI, ANTONY Drums, percussion, flute. Member of Man.

KRASSENBURG, FRANZ Vocal. Original member of Golden Earring, until 1970.

KRAUSE, BERNARD Moog. Half of the Beaver and Krause duet of 1970-71. Session for John Mayall (1979). *Album:* Citadels (TKM 7074) 1979.

KRAUSS, SCOTT Drums. Member of Pere Ubu since 1979.

KRAVETZ, JEAN-JACQUES Keyboards. Member of Frumpy, 1973, and Randy Pie, 1975-77.

KRAWITZ, MICHAEL Piano. Session for Pearls Before Swine (1971).

KREIDER, MARK Bass, vocal, strings, percussion. Member of Tycoon.

KREIN, HENRY Accordion. Session for Nilsson (1971-72).

KRELL, LOTHAR Keyboards, vocal. Member of Supermax, 1979.

KRESS, CAREY Vocal. Member of Face Dancer,

1979.

KRETMER, DON Bass. Member of the Leslie West Band, 1975. Session for Leslie West (1975-76).

KREYER, SCOTT Keyboards. Member of Toronto, 1980.

KRIDLE, BOB Bass. Member of the Loading Zone, 1968.

KRIEGER, ROBBY Guitar. Born 1/8/46. Original member of the Doors, 1967-72, and the Butts Band. *Album:* Robby Krieger and Friends, 1977.

KRIKORIAN, STEVE Vocal. Voice of the Crickets, 1973.

KRISS, TOM Bass, percussion. Original member of the James Gang, 1969.

KRISTIAN, BILLY Bass. Member of Ian Carr's Nucleus, 1979, and Night.

KRISTINA, SONJA Vocal. Voice of Curved Air.

KRISTOPHERSON, KRIS Guitar, vocal, writer. A Rhodes scholar, country-folk singer Kristopherson maintains an acting career in addition to his recording career. See Kris Kristopherson and Rita Coolidge. *Albums:* Border Lord (COL PZ-31302) 1972; Easter Island (COL JZ-35310) 1978; Jesus Was a Capricorn (COL PZ-31909) 1972; Me and Bobby McGee (COL PC-30817) 1972; Ned Kelly (UAR LKAO-300); Shake Hands with the Devil (COL JZ-36135) 1979; Silver Tongued Devil and I (COL PZ-30679); Songs of Kristofferson (COL PZ-34687) 1977; Spooky Lady's Sideshow (COL PZ-32914) 1974; A Star Is Born (COL JS-34403); Surreal Thing (COL PZ-34254) 1976; Who's To Bless and Who's To Blame (COL ZX-33379) 1975.

KRIS KRISTOFFERSON AND RITA COOLIDGE See individual listings. *Albums:* Breakaway (COL PZ-33278) 1974; Gift of Song (POL 1-6214); Kris and Rita Full Moon (AAM 4403) 1973; Natural Act (AAM PR-4690) 1978.

KROKUS Tommy Kieffer—guitar, vocal; Marc Storace—vocal; Chris Von Rohr—bass, vocal; Fernando Von Arb—guitar, vocal; Juerg Naegeli—keyboards, vocal. *Album:* Metal Rendez-vous (ARA 1502) 1980.

KROON, STEVEN Drums, percussion. Session for Paul Butterfield (1975).

KRUEGER, JIM Guitar, vocal. Member of the Duedek-Finnigan-Krueger Band, 1980. Session for Dave Mason (1974-80); Tim Weisberg (1973-79); Les Dudek (1978); *Album:* Sweet Salvation (COL JC 35295) 1978.

KRUETZMAN, BILL Drums, percussion. Original member of the Grateful Dead, since 1967. Session for David Crosby (1971); Jerry Garcia (1972).

KRUGER, KEVIN Drums. Session for Trevor Rabin (1980).

KRUGER, KLAUS Drums. Session for Iggy Pop (1979-80).

KRUISMAN, ROB Saxophone, flute, guitar, vocal. Member of Ekseption.

KRYSTALL, MARTIN M. Tenor saxophone. Member of the Peter Ivers Band, 1974. Session for Nilsson (1975).

KRYSTI Vocal. Member of Nikki and the Corvettes, 1980.

KUBINEC, DAVID Guitar, piano, vocal. *Album:* Some Things Never Change (AAM 4766) 1979.

KUCH, PETE Drums. Member of Arizona, 1976.

KUEPPER, ED Guitar. Member of the Saints, 1977-78.

KUHN, JOACHIM Keyboards. Session for Jan Akkerman (1977).

KUIPERS, LESLIE Guitar. Member of the Christopher Morris Band, 1977.

KULBERG, ANDY Flute, bass, piano. Member of the Blues Project, 1966-68, before organizing Seatrain, 1968-70. *Album:* Blues Project (VRV 3069).

KULICK, BOB Guitar. Member of Blackjack, 1979-80. Session for Rozetta (1980); Billy Squier (1980).

KUNKEL, BRUCE Guitar, fiddle, banjo, mandolin. Original member of the Nitty Gritty Dirt Band, and the Section, 1972 and 1977. Session for the Rowans (1975); Tim Rose (1976); Jennifer Warnes (1976).

KUNKEL, LEAH Vocal. Session for Art Garfunkel (1978-79). *Albums:* I Run with Trouble (COL NJC 36398) 1980; Leah Kunkel (COL JC 35778) 1979.

KUNKEL, RUSS Drums, percussion. Member of the Section, 1972, 1977. Session for Tim Moore (1974); Donovan (1973); Bob Dylan (1970, 73); Doug Kershaw; Carole King; Steve Stills (1975); James Taylor; Art Garfunkel; Neil Diamond (1976); Neil Sedaka (1975-76); Gene Clark (1974); Rita Coolidge (1972); John Kay (1973); B. B. King (1970); Joe Walsh (1974); Crosby and Nash (1976); Russ Giguere (1971); Seals and Crofts (1971); Carly Simon (1974); Crosby, Stills and Nash (1977); David Blue (1971); Terence Boylan (1977); Karla Bonoff (1972); Richie Furay (1979); Jackson Browne (1980).

KUPERT, JOE Member of Mitch Ryder's Detroit Wheels.

KUPFERBERG, TULI Vocal, percussion, writer. Original member of the Fugs, 1965-70. Released one album of pop poetry. *Album:* No Deposit, No Return (ESP 1035).

KUPKA, STEPHEN Baritone saxophone. Member of the Tower of Power horn section. Session for Roy Buchanan (1974); Ron Gardner (1974); Bill Wyman.

KURAMOTO, DAN Reeds, vocal, percussion. Member of Hiroshima, 1980.

KURAMOTO, OKIDA Koto. Member of Hiroshima, 1980.

KURASH, BILL Violin. Session for Henry Gross (1972).

KURLAND, SHELDON Violin. Session for Waylon Jennings (1973-75); J. J. Cale (1979); Jimmy Hall (1980).

KURTZ, JOHN HENRY Vocal. *Album:* Reunion (ABC 742) 1972.

KUSTOW, DANNY Guitar. Member of the Tom Robinson Band, 1979.

KUSUMOTO, TERI Vocal, percussion. Member of Hiroshima, 1980.

KUTZ, DARRYL Vocal, guitar, harmonica. Member of Starbuck, 1977.

KUY, BILLY Guitar. Session for Mike Berry (1976).

KWESKIN, JIM Guitar, vocal. Founder and namesake of Jim Kweskin Jug Band, 1963-68. *Albums:* Jim Kweskin Lives Again (MTR 52782) 1977; Swing on a Star (MTR 52793) 1979.

JIM KWESKIN JUG BAND Jim Kweskin—guitar, vocal; Geoff Muldaur—guitar, vocal, percussion; Richard Greene—fiddle; Maria d'Amato—percussion, vocal; Bill Keith—banjo, pedal steel guitar, guitar; Fritz Richmond—bass, percussion. Good time jug band music thrived in New England in the early 1960s. Some, like Kweskin, survived; others, like the Even Dozen Jug Band, did not. *Albums:* Garden of Joy, 1967; Best of Jim Kweskin and the Jug Band, 1968; Happened to Those Good Old Days, 1968; Best of Jim Kweskin and the Jug Band (VAN 79270) 1968; Greatest Hits (VAN VSD-13/14); Jug Band Music (VAN 79163) 1965; Jump for Joy (VAN 79243) 1967; Jim Kweskin and Jug Band (VAN 2158) 1963; Jim Kweskin and Jug Band (VAN 79234) 1966; Relax Your Mind (VAN 79188) 1966.

L

L'ESTRANGE, LIAM Member of Starjets, 1980.

L.A. EXPRESS Tom Scott—horns, writer; Roger Kellaway—piano; Joan Guerin—drums; Max Bennet—bass; Robben Ford—guitar. See Tom Scott. Session for George Harrison (1974). *Albums:* Great Scott; Tom Scott in L.A., 1975; L.A. Express (CRB Z-33940); Shadow Play (CRB PZ-34355).

L.A. JETS Karen Lawrence—vocal; Silver Hanson—guitar, vocal; John Desautels—drums; Ron Cindrich—bass, vocal; Harlin McNees—guitar, vocal; James Lindsey—percussion, vocal; Wayne Cook—keyboards, vocal. *Album:* L.A. Jets (VIC) 1976.

LA BARGE, BERNIE Guitar. Session for Long John Baldry (1980).

LA BEEF, SLEEPY Guitar, vocal. Session for Preacher Jack (1980). *Albums:* Bull's Night Out (SUN 130); Down Home Rockabiily (SUN 1014); 1977 Rockabilly (SUN 1004); Souvenirs of Music City U.S.A. (PLN 506); 20 Great Hits (PLN 521); Western Gold (SUN 138).

LA BOSCHA, JOHN Piano. Session for Yoko Ono and John Lennon.

LA BOUNTY, BILL Vocal, keyboards. Member of Fat Chance, 1972.

LA BRANCHE, LEO Horns. Session for the Marshall Tucker Band, 1977.

LA CHAPPELLE, CHARLES Bass. Session for Martin Mull.

LA CROIX, JERRY Saxophone, vocal, harmonica. Member of Edgar Winter's White Trash, and replaced David Clayton-Thomas in the re-formed Blood, Sweat and Tears. Member of the re-formed Rare Earth, 1975. *Albums:* La Croix, 1972; Second Coming, 1974.

LA FLAMME, DAVID Violin, guitar, vocal, writer. Head of It's a Beautiful Day, 1969-72. *Albums:* Inside Out (AMH 1012) 1978; White Bird (AMH 1007) 1976.

LA FLAMME, LINDA Keyboards, writer. Original member of It's a Beautiful Day, 1969.

LA GRAND, JOHN Mouth harp. Session for the Golden Earring (1979).

LA KIND, BOBBY Congas. Session for the Doobie Brothers (1976, 78, 80).

LA MASTER, JOHN Guitar. Session for the Randle Chowning Band (1978).

LA MONICA, ARTHUR Guitar, vocal, keyboards. Member of the Shirts, 1978-80.

LA PIERE, CHERYL Maiden name of Cher.

LA PORTE, DEIRDRE Vocal. Original member of Stoneground, 1971.

LA RUE, D. C. Vocal, percussion, keyboards. *Album:* Star Baby (CAS NBLP 7244) 1980.

LA RUE, FLORENCE Vocal. Member of the Fifth Dimension.

LA TONDRE, TOM Piano, trumpet, percussion. Member of Cherokee, 1971.

LA VIE, JOE Guitar, vocal. Member of Bad Boy.

LABAT, M. FROG Keyboards. Member of Utopia, 1974. *Album:* M. Frog, 1974.

LABES, JEFF Keyboard. Session for Van Morrison (1968-69); Jonathan Edwards (1971).

LABORIEL, ABRAHAM Bass. Session for Andy Pratt (1973); Lee Ritenour (1978-79); Dr. John (1979).

LABOTZKE, ANN Harp. Session for Snopek (1980).

LABRITAIN, PABLO Drums, vocal. Member of 999, 1978-present.

LACEY, SEBIE Drums, vocal. Member of Stillwater, 1977.

LACKSMAN, DAN Member of Telex, 1980.

LADD, KERRY Bass. Session for Gus (1980).

LADEMACHER, DANNY Guitar. Member of Herman Brood and His Wild Romance since 1979.

LADLY, MARTHA Vocal, keyboards, trombone. Member of Martha and the Muffins, 1980.

LAFF, MARK Drums, vocal. Member of Generation X, 1978-79.

LAFFY, GERRY Guitar, vocal. Member of Girl, 1980.

LAFFY, SIMON Bass. Member of Girl, 1980.

LAGIN, NED Piano, keyboards, percussion, synthesizer. Member of the Seastones, 1976.

LAGOS, PAUL Drums. Replaced John Vadican in Kaleidoscope in June, 1968, and followed Harvey Mandel through Canned Heat into the Pure Food and Drug Act. Played with John Mayall, 1971. Session for Harvey Mandel; Don Sugarcane Harris.

LAGUNA, KENNY Keyboards. Session for Sean Tyla (1980).

LAHM, DAVID Piano. Session for Martin Mull (1974).

LAHTEINEN, KEITH Vocal, drums, percussion. Original member of Ultimate Spinach, 1968-69.

LAIDLAW, RAY Drums. Replaced Paul Nichols in Lindisfarne, 1978.

LAIER, TONY Drums. Member of Greezy Wheels, 1976.

LAINE, DENNY Guitar, vocal. Born 10/29/44. Original member of Wings, 1971-79, after being a member of Ginger Baker's Air Force, 1970-71, and the Moody Blues until 1966. *Albums:* Ah, Laine, 1974; Holly Days, 1977.

LAING, CORKY Drums, percussion. Original member of Mountain, 1969-71, where he developed a reputation as one of the hardest-driving drummers in rock. He left with guitarist Leslie West to form West, Bruce and Laing, 1971-74, and the Leslie West Band, 1975. Session for Mahogany Rush (1975). *Album:* Makin' It on the Street (ELK 7E-1097) 1977.

LAING, DENZIL Percussion. Session for Paul Simon (1972); Jackie DeShannon (1972).

LAIRD, CHRIS Drums. Member of the Rio Grande Band.

LAIRD, RICK Bass. Member of Treasure, 1977.

LAIRE, CHARLES Drums, percussion. Session for Peter C. Johnson (1980).

LAKE, GREG Vocal, bass, guitar, producer. Born 11/10/48. Member of King Crimson, 1969-70, before joining Keith Emerson and Carl Palmer in Emerson, Lake and Palmer, 1971-80. Produced Stray Dog (1973).

LAKE Martin Tiefensee—bass; James Hopkins Harrison—vocal; Alex Conti—guitar, vocal; Dieter Ahrendt—drums, percussion; Geoffrey Peacey—keyboards, bass, vocal, guitar; Detlef Petersen—keyboards, vocal (1979). *Albums:* Lake (COL PC-34763) 1977; Lake 2 (COL JC-35289) 1978; Paradise Island (COL JC-35817).

LAKELAND, CHRISTINE Vocal. Session for J. J. Cale (1979).

LAKOTAS, DEZSO Tenor saxophone. Session for the Marshall Tucker Band (1977).

LALA, JOE Percussion. Member of the Souther-Hillman-Furay Band, 1974-75, the Stills-Young Band, 1976, and McGuinn, Hillman and Clark, 1979. Session for Steve Stills (1975-76, 78); Firefall (1976, 78, 80); Neil Diamond (1976); Bill Wyman (1974); Gene Clark (1974); Rick Derringer (1973); Joe Walsh (1973); Pollution (1971); the Bee Gees (1977, 80); Rick Danko (1977); Brooklyn Dreams (1977); Tim Weisberg and Dan Fogelberg (1978); the Allman Brothers (1979); Jackson Browne (1980); the Henry Paul Band (1979); Andy Gibb (1980).

LALOU, DARI Vocal. Session for Pilot (1972).

LAMB, BILL Guitar, vocal. Member of Lazy Racer since 1979.

LAMB, BILL Trumpet, trombone, vocal. Session for John Mayall (1977); Elton John (1979); Rod Stewart (1980).

LAMB, BOB Drums. Member of the Steve Gibbons Band, 1977 to present.

LAMB, KEVIN Guitar, vocal, keyboards. Session for Lightnin' Slim (1978). *Album:* Sailing Down the Years (ARI 4166) 1978.

LAMB, RICK Keyboards, guitar, vocal. Member of Hellfield, 1978.

LAMB Barbara Mauritz—vocal, writer; Bob Swanson—vocal, writer. Folk duet born of the flower days of California and later augmented to a five-piece band. Part of Fillmore, 1972. *Album:* Cross Between (WBR) 1971.

LAMBERT, DAVE Guitar. Member of the Strawbs. Session for Rick Wakeman (1972). *Album:* Framed (POL 1-6193) 1979.

LAMBERT, DENNIS Producer. Produced Rock Rose (1979).

LAMBERT, JOHN Bass, vocal. Member of Pollution, 1971.

LAMBERT, KIT Producer. Original producer of the Who.

LAMBERT, MATT Guitar, vocal. Member of the Protector 4, 1980.

LAMM, ROBERT Keyboards, vocal, writer. Original member of Chicago, since 1969. *Album:* Skinny Boy (COL).

LAMOT, DINI Vocal, percussion. Member of Human Sexual Response, 1980.

LAMOTHE, MICHEL Bass, vocal. Member of Offenbach, 1976.

LAMP OF CHILDHOOD James Hendricks—guitar, vocal, writer; Fred Olson; Mick Tani; Billy Mundi—drums, percussion. Short-lived followup for the Mugwump's Hendricks, and starting point for Mundi.

LANCASTER, ALAN Bass, guitar. Original member of Status Quo, 1965-present.

LANCASTER, E. "LOCKER ROOM" Guitar. Member of Root Boy Slim's Sex Change Band, 1978-79.

LANCASTER, JACK Horns, saxophone, clarinet. Member of Mick Abrahams' Blodwyn Pig, 1969-70, the Mick Abrahams Band, 1972, and Aviator, 1978-80. See Jack Lancaster and Robin Lumley. Session for Alvin Lee (1975).

JACK LANCASTER AND ROBIN LUMLEY Jack Lancaster—horns, reeds; Robin Lumley—keyboards. See individual listings. *Album:* Marscape (RSO 1-3020).

LANCASTER, NEIL Vocal. Session for Chris Spedding, 1976-77.

LANCE ROMANCE Ron Kincaid—guitar, vocal; Keith Parmenter—drums; J. C. Rieck—piano, vocal; Dave Harmonson—guitar, vocal; Larry Pigott—bass. *Album:* Lance Romance.

LANCHA, FOFI Drums, percussion. Member of the Max Demian Band, 1979-80.

LAND, DAVID Bass, vocal. Member of the Racing Cars, 1976-78.

LANDER, JUDD Bagpipes, harmonica. Session for Nazareth (1972).

LANDERS, TIM Bass. Session for Rozetta (1980).

LANDES, ROB Keyboards, harmonica, flute, cello. Original member of Fever Tree, 1968-69.

LANDIS, JERRY Early recording name of Paul Simon.

LANDIS, KARL Vocal. Member of Jay and the

Techniques, 1967-68.

LANDON, MARK Guitar. Original member of the Music Machine, 1966.

LANDON, NEIL Vocal, writer. Original member of Fat Mattress, 1969-70.

LANDSBERG, NORMAN Piano. Member of Hammer, 1970. Session for Leslie West (1968); the Pointer Sisters (1973).

LANE, ERNST Piano. Session for Canned Heat (1969, 71).

LANE, JAMIE Drums. Member of the Movies.

LANE, MIKE Member of Hunger.

LANE, MILDRED Vocal. Session for Neil Diamond (1976).

LANE, RED Guitar. Session for Doug Kershaw; Willie Nelson (1973).

LANE, ROBIN Guitar, vocal. Namesake of Robin Lane and the Chartbusters, 1980.

ROBIN LANE AND THE CHARTBUSTERS Robin Lane—guitar, vocal; Tim Jackson—drums; Asa Brebner—guitar, vocal; Scott Baerenwald—bass, vocal; Leroy Radcliffe—guitar, vocal. *Albums:* Robin Lane and the Chartbusters (WBR K-3424) 1980; 5 Alive (WBR 3495) 1980.

LANE, RONNIE Bass, guitar, vocal, writer. Born 4/1/46. Original member of the Small Faces, 1967-68, 1977-78. Co-authored the movie soundtrack for "Mahoney's Last Stand" with Ron Wood, 1976. Teamed with Pete Townshend in 1977 on "Rough Mix" (MCA 2295). See Rough Mix. Session for Pete Townshend (1972); Wings (1979). *Albums:* Ronnie Lane's Slim Chance (AAM) 1975; Mahoney's Last Stand (ACO SD 36-126) 1976.

LANG, DAVE Drums. Member of the Numa Band, 1980.

LANG, JOHN Lyrics. Member of the Pages, 1978-79.

LANG, MIKE Keyboards. Session for Frank Zappa (1967); Robbie Robertson (1980).

LANG, STEVE Bass. Replaced Jim Clench in April Wine, 1975-79.

LANGE, ROBERT JOHN Producer. Produced the Motors (1977); Supercharge (1977); the Michael Stanley Band (1978); AC/DC (1979); the Records (1979); City Boy (1979); the Boomtown Rats (1979); Broken Home (1980); and others.

LANGE, STEVE Vocal. Session for Crawler (1977); Elton John (1978); Kevin Lamb (1978); Status Quo (1978).

LANGER, CLIVE Guitar. Member of the Deaf School, 1979-80.

LANGHORN, BRUCE Guitar. Session for Fred Neil (1968); John Sebastian (1970); Bob Dylan (1973).

LANGHORST, NORBERT Guitar. Member of Ramses.

LANGHORST, WINFRIED Keyboards, vocal. Member of Ramses.

LANGSTON, DAVE Guitar. Session for John Entwhistle (1972).

LANGSTON, DEL Vocal. Session for John Mayall (1979).

LANGSTON, LENNOX Congas, percussion. Member of Brian Auger's Oblivion Express, 1973-77. Session for Chris de Burgh (1975); Peter Green (1980).

LANHAM, JIM Vocal, bass. Member of Pure Prairie League, 1972-75.

LANIER, ALLEN Guitar, keyboards. Member of the Blue Oyster Cult, 1972-present. Session for the Jim Carroll Band (1980).

LANIGAN, DENNIS Vocal, reeds, keyboards. Member of the Ducks, 1973.

LANNING, MICHAEL Bass, guitar, vocal. Member of Jiva, 1975, and the Robbin Thompson Band, 1980.

LANSING, DENNIS Horns. Session for Howlin' Wolf (1972).

LANZETTI, BERNARDO Vocal, percussion. Member of P.F.M., 1973-77.

LANZON, PHIL Piano. Session for Chris Spedding (1980).

LAPLUME, HENRI Bass. Member of the Critical Mass, 1980.

LAPTHORN, KATHERINE Vocal. Added to the Kayak line-up, 1978-80.

LARAVEA, HUGH Keyboards. Member of El Roachos, 1973.

LARDEN, DENNIS Guitar, vocal. Member of Every Mother's Son, 1967-68, and the Stone Canyon Band.

LARDEN, LARRY Vocal, guitar. Member of Every Mother's Son, 1967-68.

LARKEY, CHARLES Bass. First gained national notoriety as session man for Carole King and James Taylor. Member of the Fugs, 1967-68, and Jo Mama, 1970. Session on the Doors' "Full Circle," 1972.

LARKIN, CARL Guitar. Session for Taj Mahal.

LARKINS, LUCIOUS Vocal. Member of Archie Bell and the Drells since 1976.

LARNYOH, GEORGE Horns. Session for John "Rabbit" Bundrick (1974).

LARRANCE, STEVE Percussion. Session for Spirit (1976).

LARRIVA, TITO Guitar, vocal. Member of the Plugz, 1979.

LARRY AND THE LEGENDS Early name of the Four Seasons.

LARSEN, DONI Bass. Member of Gypsy, 1971-72.

LARSEN, JAMIE Bass, vocal. Member of Hellfield, 1978.

LARSEN, KIM Vocal, guitar. Member of Gasolin, 1974.

LARSEN, NEIL Keyboards, percussion, arranger, writer. Member of Full Moon, 1972, the Gregg

Allman Band, 1977, and the Tim Weisberg Band, 1977. Session for Roy Buchanan (1974); Commander Cody (1978); Tim Weisberg and Dan Fogelberg (1978); Richard and Linda Thompson (1978); Dr. John (1979); Adam Mitchell (1979); Gary Wright (1979); George Harrison (1979). *Albums:* High Gear (AAM 738) 1979; Jungle Fever (AAM 733).

LARSEN, SCHUYLER Bass. Member of Every Mother's Son, 1968, replacing Don Keir.

LARSON, BILL Drums. Member of Missouri until 1978.

LARSON, JOEL Percussion. Session for Lee Michaels.

LARSON, NICOLETTE Vocal. Session for Hoyt Axton (1976); Neil Young (1977-78); Rodney Crowell (1978); Commander Cody (1978); the Doobie Brothers (1978-80); Tom Johnston (1979); Christopher Cross (1980). Part of "No Nukes," 1979. *Albums:* In the Nick of Time (WBR HS-3370) 1979; Nicolette (WBR K-3243); Radioland (WBR 3502) 1980.

LASLEY, DAVID Vocal. Member of Rosie, 1976-77. Session for Boz Scaggs (1980).

LAST Joe Nolte—guitar, vocal; Vitas Matare—keyboards, flute; Mike Nolte—bass; Jack Reynolds—drums. *Album:* L.A. Explosion (BMP 4004) 1979.

LASTIE, DAVID Saxophone. Session for Dr. John (1972).

LASTIE, MELVIN Coronet. Session for Dr. John (1972).

LATAILLE, RICHARD Alto saxophone. Member of Roomful of Blues, 1977.

LATHAM, BILLY RAY Banjo, guitar, vocal. Temporary replacement for Herb Pedersen in the Dillards, 1977.

LATHER, HENRY Trumpet. Session for Jack Bruce (1969).

LATIMER, ANDY Guitar, flute, vocal. Original member of Camel, 1975-77.

LATIMER, CARLTON Vocal. Member of Joey Dee and the Starlighters.

LATIMORE, BARRY Keyboards. Session for Bobby Caldwell (1978).

LATTISAW, JOSEPH, JR. Guitar, vocal, percussion. Member of Wax, 1980.

LAUBER, KEN Piano. Session for Area Code 615.

LAUBER, TERRY Guitar, pedal steel guitar, vocal. Member of Gabriel, 1975.

LAUGHING DOGS Moe Potts—drums, percussion, vocal; James Leonard—guitar, vocal; Carter Cathcart—keyboards, guitar, vocal. Ronnie Carle—bass, harmonica, vocal. *Albums:* Laughing Dogs (COL JC-36033) 1979; Laughing Dogs Meet Their Maker (COL JC-36429) 1980.

LAUGHTON, DENZIL Harp. Session for Nilsson (1975).

LAUPER, CYNDI Vocal. Member of Blue Angel, 1980.

LAURENCE, CHRIS Double string and acoustic bass. Session for Elton John (1971); Roxy Music (1974); Steve Howe (1975).

LAURIE, MARIE Real name of Lulu.

LAURIE AND THE SIGHS Laurie Beechman—vocal; Tony Salinas—guitar; Demo Ray Agcaoili—drums, percussion; David Wofford—bass; Derek Fox—piano. *Album:* Laurie and the Sighs (ATC 19268) 1980.

LAUX, JOSEPH Drums, percussion. Member of Locomotive GT, 1974-75.

LAVENDAR, SHORTY Fiddle. Session for J. J. Cale (1971); Ringo Starr (1971).

LAVENDER HILL MOB Chuck Chandler—vocal, keyboards; Ronny Jones—vocal, guitar; Gerald Hardy—vocal, reeds; Vito Fiory—drums, percussion; Nicky Prigeno—vocal, bass (1977); Hector Jacob—guitar (1977). *Albums:* Lavender Hill Mob (UAR UA-LA818-G) 1978; Lavender Hill Mob (UAR UA-LA719-G) 1977.

LAVIN, TOM Guitar. Member of Prism.

LAVIS, GILSON Drums. Member of the Squeeze since 1978.

LAVITZ, T. Keyboards. Member of the Dixie Dregs.

LAW Roy Kenner—vocal; Ron Cunningham—vocal, keyboards; John McIver—bass; Steve Acker—guitar; Steve Lawrence—drums (1977); Tom Pool—drums (1975). *Albums:* Hold On to It, 1977; Law (GRC 10017) 1975; Law, 1977; Breaking It (MCA 2240) 1977.

LAWAL, GASPAR Drums. Session for Steve Stills (1971); Jim Capaldi (1973).

LAWERENCE, RON Bass. Session for Dave Davies (1980).

LAWGOR, BARBARA Vocal. Member of White Lightnin', 1978.

LAWHORN, SAM Guitar. Session for Muddy Waters (1972).

LAWLER, MIKE Vocal, keyboards. Half of the Lawler and Cobb duet, 1980. Session for the Allman Brothers (1980).

LAWLER AND COBB Johnny Cobb—keyboards; Mike Lawler—vocal, keyboards. *Album:* Men from Nowhere (ASY 6E-279) 1980.

LAWLEY, LYNDA LEE Vocal. Member of the Thieves, 1979.

LAWRENCE, ARNIE Clarinet, flute. Session for Henry Gross (1973); Ian Hunter (1976).

LAWRENCE, CLAIRE Flute, saxophone, bass, organ, piano, writer. Original member of Chilliwack, 1971-73. Member of the Hometown Band, 1976. Session for Private Lines (1980).

LAWRENCE, GEORGE Drums. Replaced Russ Battelene in the Pages, 1979.

LAWRENCE, KAREN Vocal, piano. Voice of the L.A. Jets, 1976, and 1994, 1978-79. Session for the Mark Farner Band (1978).

LAWRENCE, LINDA Vocal. Session for Ringo Starr (1974).

LAWRENCE, MICHAEL Trumpet, flugelhorn. Member of Larry Coryell's Eleventh House, 1975-76.

LAWRENCE, ROB Mandolin. Session for the Babys (1978).

LAWRENCE, STEVE Drums. Replaced Tom Poole in Law, 1977.

LAWRENCE, TREVOR Tenor saxophone. Member of the Paul Butterfield Blues Band, 1969-71, and the Blacksmoke Horns, 1978. Session for B. B. King (1972); Nilsson (1974-75); Joe Cocker (1974); Country Joe McDonald (1975); Kate and Anna McGarrigle (1977). Arranger and session for Ringo Starr (1974).

LAWS, HUBERT Session for Jaco Pastorius (1976).

LAWS, KEN Drums, percussion. Member of Hudson-Ford.

LAWSON, DAVE Keyboards. Member of Greenslade.

LAWTON, APRIL Guitar. Member of Ramatam, 1972.

LAWTON, JOHN Vocal. Voice of Lucifer's Friend, 1974-76. Replaced David Byron as the voice of Uriah Heep, 1977-78.

LAY, SAM Drums. Member of the Paul Butterfield Blues Band, 1965-66. Member of Fathers and Sons, 1969.

LAYTON, JEFF Guitar. Session for John Mayall (1979).

LAZAROWITZ, BARRY Drums. Session for Peter C. Johnson (1980).

LAZY RACER Tim Renwick—vocal, guitar; Henry Spinetti—drums; Dave Markee—bass; Timothy Gorman—keyboards, vocal; Kelly Narland—keyboards, vocal; Bill Lamb—guitar, vocal. *Albums:* Formula (AAM 4808) 1980; Lazy Racer (AAM 4768) 1979.

LE BLANC, LENNY Vocal. Half of the Le Blanc and Carr duet, 1977. Session for Roy Orbison (1979). *Album:* Hound Dog Man (BIG 76003).

LE BLANC AND CARR Lenny Le Blanc—vocal; Pete Carr—guitar, vocal. *Albums:* Le Blanc and Carr (BGT 89521) 1977; Midnight Light (BGT 89521).

LE BOLT, DAVE Keyboards. Member of Spy, 1980.

LE FEVRE, JIM Keyboards, guitar, vocal. Member of the Max Demian Band, 1979-80.

LE FEVRE, MYLON Vocal, percussion, guitar, writer. White gospel singer discovered by Felix Pappalardi. Session with Alvin Lee (1974); Alias (1980); Kerry Livgren (1980). *Albums:* Mylon LeFevre and Holy Smoke; On the Road to Freedom (COL KC 32729) 1973; Love Rustler (WBR 3216); Rock and Roll Resurrection (MER SRM-1-3799) 1979; Weak at the Knees (WBR B-3070) 1977.

LE FLEUR, GLEN Drums. Member of Hanson, 1974, and Olympic Runners, 1974-79. Session for Ronnie Lane (1975); Pete Wingfield (1975); Gerry Rafferty (1978).

LE GRAND, CHRIS HANNE Vocal. Featured voice of the Swingle Singers. Session for Procol Harum (1973).

LE MAIRE, SONNY Bass, vocal. Replaced Kenny Wier in Exile, 1978-80.

LE MESURIER, ROBIN Guitar. Member of Lion, 1980.

LE PAGE, DENNIS Banjo. Member of the Dixie Flyers.

LE ROUX Leon Medica—bass; Jeff Pollard—guitar, vocal; Tony Haselden—guitar; Rod Roddy—keyboards, vocal; David Peters—drums; Bobby Campo—percussion, vocal. Session for Kerry Livgren (1980). *Albums:* Keep the Fire Burnin' (EMI SO 11926) 1979; Up (EMI ST 12092) 1980.

LEA, JIMMY Bass, vocal. Original member of Slade, 1972 to present.

LEA, LARRY Guitar, vocal. Member of Roy Loney and the Phantom Movers, 1979-80.

LEACH, ED Percussion. Session for the Rolling Stones (1974).

LEACH, JOHN Cimbalon, kantele. Session for the Alan Parsons Project (1976); the Vapors (1980).

LEACH, STEVE Vocal, bass. Member of the Shanti, 1971.

LEACOX, WILLIE Drums. Session for America (1977).

LEADBELLY Vocal, guitar, piano, accordion, bass, harmonica, 12-string guitar, writer. Reportedly born January 20, 1889, Huddie Ledbetter ran with Blind Lemon Jefferson around Dallas, Texas, before 1920. His first commercial recordings were made in 1935, after serving a ten-year term for murder at Angola State Prison in Louisiana. History has it he obtained his freedom by composing a song for the warden. (The same story is reported of a twenty-year term he was serving at Sugarland Prison Farm in Texas for another murder.) Equally at home on the 6-string and 12-string guitars, though he is more remembered for the latter, his repertoire included folk songs, prison ballads, and social-political songs. These were the tools he used when he moved to New York in 1935 with his wife, Martha. His temper bested him again in 1939, when he was arrested and convicted of third-degree assault, receiving a one year prison term. Following his release, he visited several recording studios, even moving to Hollywood in 1948, without much success. In 1949, after returning to New York, he died of polio, December 6. *Albums:* Leadbelly (PBY 119); Anthology of Folk Music (SQN 102); Anthology, Vol. 2 (SQN 126); Best of the Blues (SQN 103); Best of the Blues, Vol. 2 (SQN 124); Easy Rider (FLW 2034); Leadbelly (CAP SM-

1821); Leadbelly (COL C-30035); Leadbelly (EVR 202); Leadbelly (FSY 24715) 1973; Leadbelly, His Guitar, Voice and Piano (CAP SM-1821); Leadbelly's Last Sessions (FLW 2941) 1954; Leadbelly Legacy (FLW 2024); Leadbelly Library of Congress Recordings (ELK 301-2); Leadbelly Memorials (STI 317-19-48-51) 1962; Leadbelly Plays Party Songs (STI 39); Leadbelly Sings and Plays (STI 91) 1962; Leadbelly Sings Folk Songs (FLW 31006) 1968; Legend of Leadbelly (TRD 2093); Legendary Leadbelly (OLR 7103); Midnight Special (FLW 31046) 1976; Take This Hammer (FLW 31019) 1950; 12 String Guitar (FLW 8371); Shout On (FLW 31030) 1971; Tribute to Leadbelly (TOM Z-7003) 1977.

LEADON, BERNIE Guitar, vocal. Born 7/19/47. Member of the Flying Burrito Brothers, the Dillard and Clark Expedition, and Eagles, 1972-76. Co-namesake of the Bernie Leadon-Mike Georgiades Band, 1977. Session for Russ Giguere (1971); Rita Coolidge (1972); Free Creek (1973); Gram Parsons (1973-74).

BERNIE LEADON—MIKE GEOGIADES BAND Bernie Leadon—vocal, guitar, banjo; Mike Georgiades—vocal, guitar; Brian Garafolo—bass; Dave Kemper—drums; Steve Goldstein—keyboards. *Album:* Natural Progressions (ASY 7E-1107) 1977.

LEAHY, RON Keyboards. Replaced John McGinnis in Stone the Crows, 1972. Member of the Dukes, 1979. Session for Alvin Lee (1975); Chris de Burgh (1975); Donovan (1977).

LEAKE, LAFAYETTE Piano. Session for Chuck Berry (1957, 64); Howlin' Wolf (1972).

LEONARD, DEKE Vocal, guitar. Member of Man. *Album:* Deke Leonard (MAM).

LEAR, GRAHAM Drums, percussion. Member of Santana, 1977-present.

LEARY, S. P. Drums. Session for Fleetwood Mac (1969); "T-Bone" Walker (1973); Otis Spann.

LEARY, VINNY Guitar, vocal. Part of the Fugs musical backup, 1965-67.

LEATHERS, DAVE Saxophone. Session for Colin Winski (1980).

LEAVELL, CHUCK Piano, vibes. Member of the Allman Brothers Band, 1973-76. Original member of Sea Level, since 1977. Session for Martin Mull (1974); Richard Betts (1974); the Marshall Tucker Band (1976-77, 79); Missouri (1979); Bobby Whitlock (1975); Gregg Allman (1973-74); Tim Weisberg (1977); the Cooper Brothers Band (1979); the Rockets (1979).

LEAVES Recorded "Hey Joe" in the 1960s.

LEAVEY, TOM Bass. Session for Jimmy Carl Black and Bunk Gardner (1971).

LEAVITT, PHIL Vocal. Member of the Diamonds.

LECKENBY, DEREK Guitar. Member of Herman's Hermits, 1965-68.

LECKIE, JOHN Producer, engineer. Produced the Doctors of Madness (1977); Deaf School (1978); Magazine (1979); Simple Minds (1979); the Proof (1980); and others.

LED ZEPPELIN Jimmy Page—guitar, pedal steel guitar, vocal, writer, producer; Robert Plant—vocal, harmonica, writer; John Bonham—drums, percussion, vocal; John Paul Jones—bass, vocal, organ. Dissolving the Yardbirds, Page teamed up with Plant to form Zeppelin in 1969. Expectations for success were not high, as reflected in their name. A hard-rocking single, however, "Communication Breakdown" (1969), brought them AM exposure and led a following to their first album, a powerful debut of hard rock based in the blues. "Whole Lotta Love" (1969), on their second album, reinforced their image, featuring totally original material by the Plant/Page writing team. "Led Zeppelin III" saw a tribute to Roy Harper, and the beginning of a unique packaging design for their albums. A following had been established, strengthened by a lively stage performance. The classic "Stairway to Heaven" (1971) entrenched them in the superstar category and represented a solidification of style and sound. Bonham's death, 9/24/80, led to the group's retirement of their name. *Albums:* Houses of the Holy (ATC 19130) 1973; In Through the Out Door (SWN 16002) 1979; Led Zeppelin (ATC 19126) 1969; Led Zeppelin 2 (ATC 19127) 1969; Led Zeppelin 3 (ATC 19128) 1970; Led Zeppelin 4 (ATC 19129) 1971; Physical Graffiti (SWN 2-200) 1975; Presence (SWN 8416) 1976; Song Remains the Same (SWN 2-201) 1976.

LEDBETTER, HUDDIE Real name of Leadbelly. See Leadbelly.

LEDERER, LANE Bass, guitar, horn, percussion. Original member of Pearls Before Swine, 1967-69.

LEDESMA, ISH Guitar, vocal. Member of Foxy since 1978.

LEDFORD, LONNIE Bass. Member of FCC, 1980. Session for Roy Orbison (1979).

LEE, ALBERT Guitar. Member of Heads, Hands and Feet, 1970-71, and the Crickets, 1973. Session for Joe Cocker (1968, 76); Deep Purple; Jerry Lee Lewis (1973); Jonathan Edwards (1977); Rodney Crowell (1978); Marc Benno (1979); Dave Edmunds (1979); Gene Parsons (1979); Eric Clapton (1980). *Album:* Hiding (AAM 4750).

LEE, ALVIN Guitar, vocal, writer. Born 12/19/44. He arrived in the U.S. in 1968 with Ten Years After, playing the blues. By the time he struck out on his own in 1973, he had developed a distinct rock style, and began flirting more seriously with jazz. He formed Ten Years Later, 1978-79, which was poorly received, and the Alvin Lee Band, 1980. See Alvin Lee and Mylon LeFevre. Session for Splinter (1974-75); George Harrison (1974); Jerry Lee Lewis (1973). *Albums:* Rocket Fuel (RSO 1-3033) 1978; Pump Iron (COL PC 33796)

1975; In Flight, 1974.

ALVIN LEE BAND Alvin Lee—guitar, vocal; Steve Gould—guitar, vocal; Mickey Feat—bass; Tom Compton—drums. *Album:* Free Fall (ACO SD 19287) 1980.

ALVIN LEE AND MYLON LE FEVRE Alvin Lee —vocal, guitar; Mylon Le Fevre—vocal. *Album:* On the Road to Freedom (COL C-32729) 1973.

LEE, ARTHUR Guitar, keyboards, drums, harmonica, vocal, writer. Founder of Love, 1966-69, before dissolving the group for his solo career. *Album:* Vindicator.

LEE, BARBARA Vocal. Member of the Chiffons.

LEE, BRENDA Vocal. Bobby-soxer who matured through the years, but not beyond a 1960s nostalgia image. *Albums:* Brenda (MCA 305); Brenda Lee Now (MCA 433); New Sunrise (MCA 373); Sincerely Brenda Lee (MCA 477); Ten Golden Years (MCA 107); Brenda Lee, 1960; This Is Brenda, 1961; Emotions, 1961; Brenda Lee, All the Way, 1961; That's All Brenda, 1961; All Alone Am I, 1963; Let Me Sing, 1964; By Request, 1964; Top Teen Hits, 1965; Versatile, 1965; Too Many Rivers, 1965; Bye Bye Blues, 1966; Merry Christmas from Brenda Lee; Thanks a Lot; Coming On Strong, 1967; Reflections in Blue, 1967; For the First Time, 1968; Johnny One Time, 1969; Even Better (MCA 3211); Here's Brenda Lee (VOC 73795); Brenda Lee Story (MCA 4012); Let It Be Me (COR 20044).

LEE, DIANA Vocal. Session for the Babys (1978).

LEE, DIXIE Drums. Member of Lone Star, 1977.

LEE, GEDDY Bass, vocal. Member of Rush, 1972 to present.

LEE, JEANETTE Vocal. Member of the Public Image since 1979.

LEE, JIGGS Vocal, percussion. Member of Cain, 1975-77.

LEE, JOHN Drums, percussion. Member of Dirty Tricks, 1976, and the Catfish Hodge Band, 1979.

LEE, JOHN Bass. Member of the Chris Hinze Combination, 1974, Larry Coryell's Eleventh House, 1975-76, and Medusa, 1978.

LEE, LARRY Vocal, percussion, guitar, keyboards, drums, writer. Original member of the Ozark Mountain Daredevils, 1973-75, 1980.

LEE, LARRY Vocal, bass, keyboards, guitar. Member of the Scooters, 1980.

LEE, LARRY Guitar. Session for Jimi Hendrix (1969).

LEE, LAURA Vocal. Session for Rick Wakeman (1972).

LEE, LENNY Keyboards, vocal. Member of Sweathog, 1973.

LEE, PAUL Drums. Session for Steve Stills (1978).

LEE, PHIL Guitar. Member of Gilgamesh.

LEE, RIC Drums. Original member of Ten Years After, 1968-73. Session for Chick Churchill (1974); Mike Vernon.

LEE, ROBERT Synthesizer, keyboards. Member of the Other Side.

LEE, ROD Trumpet. Session for Chicken Shack.

LEE, RONI Guitar. Member of Venus and the Razor Blades, 1977.

LEE, SAUNDRA Vocal. Session for Martin Mull (1975).

LEE, SCOTT Bass. Member of the John Payne Band, 1976-77.

LEE, STAN Guitar, vocal. Member of the Dickies since 1978.

LEE, STEVE Bass. Member of Frut, 1972, replacing John Kozmo.

LEE, TONY Drums. Member of Texas, 1973.

LEE, WILL Bass. Session for Roy Buchanan (1977); the Mark and Clark Band (1977); Henry Gross (1977-78); Dr. John (1978); Mark-Almond (1978); Taj Mahal (1978); Ray Gomez (1980); Far Cry (1980).

LEE, WILLIAM Keyboards, vocal. Member of High Cotton, 1975.

LEECH, GEORDIE Bass. Member of Rose Tattoo, 1980.

LEECH, GREG Bass. Member of Morningstar, 1979.

LEECH, MIKE Bass. Session for Jackie DeShannon (1972); Tom Rapp (1972); Doug Kershaw (1974); J. J. Cale (1974).

LEEDS, GARY Drums. Member of the Walker Brothers, 1966-67.

LEEDS, STEVE Reeds. Session for Adrian Gurvitz (1979).

LEES, CAROL Keyboards. Member of the Floating Opera, 1974.

LEES, JOHN Guitar, vocal. Member of Barclay James Harvest.

LEESE, ERIC Guitar. Session for Donovan (1967).

LEESE, HOWARD Guitar, producer. Replaced Roger Fisher in Heart, 1980. Produced the Heats, 1980.

LEFT BANKE Rick Brand—banjo, mandolin; Steve Martin—vocal; Tom Finn—bass; Mike Brown—keyboards; George Cameron—vocal. *Album:* Walk Away, Renee, 1967.

LEGGETT, ARCHIE Bass, vocal. Session for Kevin Ayers (1973); John Cale (1974).

LEGS DIAMOND Michael Diamond—bass; Rick Sanford—vocal, flute; Mike Prince—keyboards, guitar, vocal; Roger Romeo—guitar, vocal; Jeff Poole—drums. *Albums:* Diamond is a Hard Rock (MER SRM-1-1191) 1977; Fire Power (CRE 1010) 1978; Legs Diamond (MER SRM-1-1136) 1977.

LEHMAN, NORBERT Drums, percussion, vocal. Member of Karthago, 1974.

LEHNERT, BOB Vocal, guitar. Member of Acrobat, 1972.

LEHNING, KYLE Piano. Session for Waylon Jennings (1974).

LEIB, GEOFFREY Keyboards, synthesizer, vocal. Member of the Pieces, 1979.

LEIGH, ANDY Bass. Member of Matthews Southern Comfort. Replaced Greg Ridley in Spooky Tooth, 1969.

LEIGH, GEOFF Saxophone, flute. Member of Henry Cow, 1973.

LEIGH, RICHARD Guitar, vocal. *Album:* Richard Leigh (UAR LT-1036) 1980.

LEIGHTON, CHRIS Drums. Replaced Mike Baird in Ironhorse, 1980.

LEIM, PAUL Drums. Member of Nitzinger, 1973-76.

LEINBACH, BOB Keyboards, trombone, vocal. Member of the Rhinestones, 1975.

LEINHEISER, PETER Guitar. Member of the Pages, 1978.

LEIROS, CORY Piano, vocal. Member of Pablo Cruise since 1975.

LEISZ, GREG Pedal steel guitar, guitar, vocal. Member of the Funky Kings, 1976.

LEITNER, SEBASTIAN Guitar. Member of the Bullfrog, 1976.

LEKA, PAUL Keyboards, producer, string arranger. Session for the Randle Chowning Band (1978).

LELAND, CHARLES Bass, vocal. Member of Susan, 1979.

LELAND, MIKE Drums, vocal. Member of Susan, 1979.

LEMER, PAUL Keyboards. Replaced John Norman Mitchell in the Baker-Gurvitz Army for "Elysian Encounter," 1975.

LEMMING, WAREEN Guitar, banjo, vocal. Member of Wilderness Road.

LEMMY Bass, vocal. Real name: Lemmy Kilmister. Member of Hawkwind until 1978, when he formed Motorhead, 1978 to present.

LEMOINE, PATRICK Keyboards. Member of the Gong since 1975.

LEMON PIPERS Bill Albaugh—drums; R. G. Nave—organ; Bill Bartlett—guitar; Steve Walmsley—bass; Ivan Browne—guitar, vocal. Though not intellectually inspiring, "Green Tambourine" contained enough psychedelic reverberation to become a hit in 1968. *Album:* Green Tambourine (BUD) 1968.

LEMORE, LAMONTE Vocal. Member of the Fifth Dimension.

LENART, PAUL Guitar. Member of the Peter Ivers Band, 1974, and the James Montgomery Band, 1976.

LENGYELL, MIKE Drums. Member of the Diodes, 1978.

LENNEAR, CLAUDIA Vocal. Member of Joe Cocker's Greatest Show on Earth, 1970. Session for Taj Mahal; Dave Mason; Steve Stills (1970); Freddie King (1971); Leon Russell (1971); Bangla Desh (1971); Don Nix (1971); Ry Cooder (1972); Gene Clark (1974); Nils Lofgren (1976).

LENNERS, RUDY Drums. Replaced Rudy Rarebell in the Scorpions, 1974-present.

LENNON, JEFF Member of the Now, 1979.

LENNON, JOHN WINSTON Harmonica, guitar, piano, vocal, writer. Born 10/9/40. In 1956, as head of the Quarrymen, Lennon met Paul McCartney, which led to the teaming of the greatest rock writers in the field of modern rock music. After a stormy split with McCartney which led to the demise of the Beatles in 1970, he continued recording with wife Yoko Ono. While still lyrically topical, his musical arrangements and production matured to a consistent level of professionalism. After a five year retirement, he returned to the studio in 1980. He was shot and killed outside his New York apartment 12/8/80. See John Lennon and Yoko Ono. Session and production for Nilsson (1974). Session for Ringo Starr (1974); David Bowie (1975); Yoko Ono. *Albums:* Pussycats (with Nilsson) (VIC CPLI-0570) 1974; Imagine (CAP SW-3379) 1971; John Lennon/Plastic Ono Band (CAP SW-3372) 1970; Mind Games (CAP SW-3414) 1973; Rock 'N' Roll (CAP SK 3419) 1975; Shaved Fish (CAP SW-3421) 1975; Walls and Bridges (CAP SW-3416) 1974; Double Fantasy (GEF GHS 2001) 1980; Sometime in New York City (APL) 1972; Wedding Album (APL SMAX 3361) 1969; Two Virgins (APL T 5001) 1968; Unfinished Music No 2: Life with the Lions (APL) 1969.

JOHN LENNON AND YOKO ONO See individual listings and the Plastic Ono Band. *Albums:* Sometime in New York City (CAP SVBB-3392) 1972; Two Virgins (APL T-5001) 1968; Wedding Album (APL SMAX 3361) 1969.

LENNON, PETE Guitar. Member of the Heroes, 1980.

LENNOX, ANN Vocal, keyboards. Member of the Tourists since 1980.

LENTI, BOB Guitar. Member of Johnny's Dance Band, 1977.

LENTIN, KEITH Guitar, vocal. Member of the Spider, 1980.

LENZ, JACK Keyboards. Session for Watson-Beasley (1980).

LEO, JOSH Guitar, vocal. Member of the Eddie Boy Band, 1975.

LEON, CRAIG Keyboards. Session for Moon Martin (1979).

LEON, DAVID Keyboards, guitar, vocal. Member of Helmet Boy, 1980.

LEONARD, DARRELL Trumpet, trombone. Session for Delaney and Bonnie (1970); Freddie King (1975); Jules and the Polar Bears (1979).

LEONARD, GLENN Vocal. Member of the Temptations.

LEONARD, JAMES Guitar, vocal. Member of the Laughing Dogs, 1979-present.

LEONARD, MICKEY Guitar. Member of the

Simms Brothers Band, 1979-80.

LEONARD, PAT Keyboards. Member of Trillion, 1978-80.

LEONARD, ROBERT Vocal. Original member of Sha Na Na, 1970.

LEONARD, STEVE Keyboards, vocal. Member of the Cretones, 1980.

LEONARDS, BOBBY Piano. Session for Mink de Ville, 1977.

LEONE, BOB Keyboards. Member of Flame, 1977.

LEONETTI, EDWARD Guitar, keyboards, producer. Member of the Soul Explosion, 1966-68. Session for Gus (1980).

LEOPOLD, JAMIE Acoustic bass. Member of Dan Hicks and His Hot Licks until 1974.

LEOPOLD, PETER Drums, percussion. Member of Amon Duul.

LEOPOLO, GLEN Vocal, guitar. Member of Gun Hill Road.

LEPPICK, GENE Bass, vocal. Member of Jimmie Mack and the Jumpers, 1980. Session for Jimmie Mack (1979).

LERCHEY, DAVID Vocal. Member of the Del Vikings.

LERNER, MIKE Drums, percussion. Member of the Eddie Boy Band, 1975.

LEROUX, CHRISTIAN Guitar, synthesizer. Member of the Transit Express, 1976.

LEROY, GREG Vocal, guitar. Member of Crazy Horse.

LESH, PHIL Bass, piano, writer. Original member of the Grateful Dead, since 1967, and Seastones, 1975. Session for David Crosby (1971).

LESKIW, GREG Guitar. Replaced Randy Bachman in the Guess Who, 1972.

LESLEY, JACK Vocal, keyboards. Member of Sam the Band.

LESPRON, MICKEY Guitar. Member of El Chicano, 1971-75.

LESS, JEFF Piano. Session for the Paley Brothers (1978).

LESTER, AL Fiddle. Session for Barry Goldberg (1974); Willie Nelson (1974).

LESTER, RAY Bass. Session for Harvey Mandel (1974).

LETANTE, DE PARIS Guitar, steel guitar. Session for Kaleidoscope (1977).

LETHBRIDGE, SUSAN Vocal. Member of Graham Shaw and the Sincere Serenaders, 1980.

LETSCH, GLEN Bass. Replaced Alan Fitzgerald in Gamma, 1980.

LETTERMEN Tony Butala—vocal; Gary Pike—vocal; Donny Pike—vocal; Bob Engemann—vocal; Jim Pike—vocal; Perry Botkin, Jr.—vocal; Dick Hazard—vocal; Jimmie Haskell—vocal. Wholesome vocal trio that began in 1961 and soared in the folk boom that followed. Since their inception, the trio has changed personnel completely. *Albums:* Alive Again, Naturally (CAP SW-11183) 1973; All Time Greatest Hits (CAP SW-11249) 1973; And I Love Her (CAP STBB-710); Best of the Lettermen, for Christmas (CAP STBB-2979); Best of the Lettermen, Vol. 2 (CAP SM-11834); Best of the Lettermen (CAP ST 2554); Best of the Lettermen, Vol. 2 (CAP SKAO-138); For Christmas This Year (CAP SM-2587); Goin' Out of My Head (CASP SM-11970); Hurt So Bad (CAP SM-11678); Kind of Country (CAP ST-11508) 1976; Let It Be Me (CAP STBB-710); Lettermen—and Live (CAP SM-11814); Love Book (CAP AST-836); Make a Time for Lovin' (CAP SW-11424) 1975; Now and Forever (CAP SW-11319); Put Your Head on My Shoulder (CAP SM-147); Spring (CAP SM-2711); There Is No Greater Love (CAP SW-11364); Feelings (CAP ST 781); Lettermen (CAP STCL 577); Kind of Love (CAP ST 2013); Lettermen I (CAP ST 11010); Peace on Earth (CAP STBB 585); Reflections (CAP ST 496); Spin Away (CAP SW 11124); Traces/Memories (CAP ST 390); You'll Never Walk Alone (CAP ST 2213).

LEVANT, GAYLE Harp. Session for John Sebastian (1970); Jon Mark (1974); Nilsson (1975); James Taylor (1976); George Harrison (1979); J. Michael Reed (1979); Gordon Lightfoot (1980).

LEVEL, DAVID Horns. Session for the Marshall Tucker Band (1979).

LEVENE, KEITH Guitar, synthesizer. Member of the Public Image since 1979.

LEVERTON, JIMMY Bass. After a brief outing as a member of Noel Redding's Fat Mattress, 1969-70, he replaced Keith Ellis in Juicy Lucy, 1971. A member of Savoy Brown's "Boogie Brothers," 1974.

LEVIEV, MILCHO Keyboards. Session for Airto (1974).

LEVIN, DANNY Fiddle, mandolin. Member of Asleep at the Wheel since 1973.

LEVIN, DRAKE Guitar. Member of Paul Revere and the Raiders. Session for Lee Michaels.

LEVIN, GEOFF Guitar. Member of Elephant, 1975. *Album:* Confederation (SLB 9).

LEVIN, LOUIS Keyboards. Member of the John Payne Band, 1975-76.

LEVIN, TONY Bass. Session for Lou Reed (1973); Paul Simon (1975-80); Alice Cooper (1975-76); Ringo Starr (1977); Henry Gross (1977); Kate and Anna McGarrigle (1977-78); Art Garfunkel (1978); Robert Fripp (1979); Randy Vanwarmer (1979); John Lennon (1980).

LEVINE, BURT Guitar, banjo, vocal. Member of Taos.

LEVINE, MARC Bass. Member of the Waves, 1977.

LEVINE, MIKE Bass, keyboards. Began with George Thorogood and the Destroyers, 1974, before becoming a member of Triumph, 1979-present.

LEVON AND THE HAWKS Early name of the Band.

LEVY, BOB String synthesizer. Session for Santana (1979).

LEVY, JAY Vocal, keyboards. Member of Melton, Levy and the Dey Brothers, 1972.

LEVY, JEFERY Guitar, bass, keyboards. Member of the Bottles, 1979.

LEVY, MARC Vocal, guitar. Member of Wild Oats, 1977.

LEVY, MARCY Vocal. Session for Bob Seger (1973); Leon Russell (1974); Eric Clapton (1975-78); Adam Mitchell (1979).

LEVY, RON Piano, synthesizer. Session for B. B. King (1972, 75).

LEWIE, JONAH *Album:* On the Other Hand, There's a Fist (STF USE 8) 1980.

LEWINE, ROB Member of the Illinois Speed Press, 1969.

LEWINTHAL, PAUL Synthesizer. Session for Pollution (1971).

LEWIS, ANDRE Organ, vocal. Session for Frank Zappa (1976).

LEWIS, DAVID Keyboards. Member of Ambrosia.

LEWIS, DAVID Guitar, vocal. Member of Atlantic Starr, 1978-79.

LEWIS, DIANA Synthesizer. Session for Elton John (1969, 71).

LEWIS, G. Bass. Member of the Wire, 1980.

LEWIS, GARY Guitar, vocal. Son of comedian Jerry Lewis and namesake of Gary Lewis and the Playboys.

GARY LEWIS AND THE PLAYBOYS Jerry Lewis's son, Gary, and his Playboys peppered the charts with hits like "This Diamond Ring," "Count Me Out," "Everybody Loves a Clown" (1965), "She's Just My Style" (1966), and others through 1968. *Albums:* A Session With Gary Lewis and the Playboys, 1965; Everybody Loves a Clown, 1965; She's Just My Style, 1966; Gary Lewis Hits Again, 1966; Paint Me a Picture, 1967; New Directions, 1967; Listen, 1967; Gary Lewis, Now, 1968; More Golden Hits (LIB) 1968; Golden Greats (LIB 4768) 1966; Greatest Hits of Gary Lewis and the Playboys (PPK 311); This Diamond Ring (UAR LM-1003) 1965.

LEWIS, HUEY Vocal, harmonica. Member of Clover, 1977, and head of Huey Lewis and the News, 1980. Session for Dave Edmunds (1979).

HUEY LEWIS AND THE NEWS Huey Lewis—vocal; Chris Hayes—guitar, vocal; Sean Hopper—keyboards, vocal; Bill Gibson—drums, vocal; Johnny Calla—guitar, saxophone, vocal; Mario Cipollina—bass. *Album:* Huey Lewis and the News (CYS 1292), 1980.

LEWIS, JAMES MINGO Congas. Member of Santana, 1972-74. Session for Carlos Santana-Buddy Miles "Live" (1972).

LEWIS, JERRY LEE Piano, vocal, writer. Born 2/29/35. Early names: the Hawk; the Killer. From the same studios as Elvis, Lewis released "Great Balls of Fire" and "Whole Lotta Shakin' Goin' On" (1957), and like Elvis, Lewis became a rock idol. His 1957 British tour was a disaster, however, due to his marriage to the 13-year-old daughter of his bass player (he was 22); he was received with total scorn, if he was not cancelled before hand. By 1968, foreign and domestic social pressure had eased to the point of recognition of his immense talent. *Albums:* All Country (SMA 67071); Another Place (SMA); Boogie Woogie Country Man (MER SRM 1-1030); Killer Rocks On (MER SRM 1-637); Sometimes a Memory Ain't Enough (MER SRM 1-677); Southern Roots (MER SRM 1-690); Sporting Club (BJD 95002); Return of Rock, 1965; Country Songs, 1965; By Request, 1966; Memphis Beat, 1968; The Session (MER SRM 2-803) 1973; Best of Jerry Lee Lewis (SMA 67131); Best of Jerry Lee Lewis, Vol. 2 (MER SRM 1-5006); Johnny Cash and Jerry Lee Lewis Sing Hank Williams (SUN 125); Country Memories (MER SRM 1-5004) 1977; Duets (SUN 1011) 1978; From the Vaults of the Sun (PPK 247); Golden Hits of Jerry Lee Lewis (SMA SL 7001); Golden Rock and Roll (SUN 1000); Greatest Hits, Vol. 1 (PPK 248); Greatest Hits, Vol. 2 (PPK 249); Harper Valley P.T.A. (PLN 700); Killer Country (ELK 6E-291); Jerry Lee Lewis (ELK 6E-184) 1979; Jerry Lee Lewis (EVR 298); Golden Cream of the Country (SUN 108); Jerry Lee Lewis Keeps Rockin' (MER SRM-1-5010); Jerry Lee Lewis Original Golden Hits, Vol. 1 (SUN 102); Jerry Lee Lewis Original Golden Hits, Vol. 2 (SUN 103); Jerry Lee Lewis Original Golden Hits, Vol. 3 (SUN 128); Jerry Lee Lewis Rockin' Rhythm and Blues (SUN 107); Memphis Country (SUN 120); Monsters (SUN 124); Old Time Country Music (SUN 121); Original Jerry Lee Lewis (SUN 1005); Original Memphis Rock and Roll (SUN 116); Rock and Roll Show (GUS 0002); Sunday Down South (SUN 119); Taste of Country (SUN 114); Trio Plus (SUN 1018); 20 Golden Souvenirs (PLN 533); When Two Worlds Collide (ELK 6E-254); I-40 Country (MER SRM 1710).

LEWIS, JIM Bass, drums. Replaced Johnny Johnson in the Dwight Twilley Band, 1978-79.

LEWIS, JIMMY Bass. Session for John Hammond (1964-65, 68).

LEWIS, JOHN Vocal, guitar. Part of the British blues invasion that did not make it to the U.S.

LEWIS, JONATHAN Trombone, percussion. Member of Atlantic Starr, since 1978-79.

LEWIS, KENNY LEE Bass, vocal. Member of the Pieces, 1979.

LEWIS, KENT Vocal, guitar, fiddle. Member of Liberty, 1975.

LEWIS, LINDA Vocal. Session for Cat Stevens

(1972); Hummingbird (1975).

LEWIS, LOU Guitar, vocal. Member of the Headboys, 1979.

LEWIS, MAXAYN Vocal. Session for Steve Marriott.

LEWIS, MIKE Horns, string arranger. Session for Steve Stills (1978); McGuinn, Hillman and Clark (1979).

LEWIS, PAT Congas. Member of Skin, Flesh and Bone, 1975.

LEWIS, PETER Guitar. Original member of Moby Grape, 1967-69.

LEWIS, PHILLIP Vocal. Member of Girl, 1980.

LEWIS, RANDY Bass, vocal. Member of Mose Jones, 1978.

LEWIS, RICHARD Trumpet, keyboards, vocal. Member of Pollution, 1971.

LEWIS, TWEKE Guitar. Member of Wild Turkey, 1971.

LEWIS, W. MICHAEL Synthesizer. Member of Passion, 1979.

LEWIS, WALTER "FURRY" Vocal, guitar. Born March 6, 1893. Mississippi blues man who first recorded in 1927. *Albums:* Back On My Feet Again (PRS 7810); Beale Street Messaround (RND 2006); Shake 'Em On Down (FSY 324703).

LEWIS, WAYNE Keyboards, vocal. Member of Atlantic Starr, 1978-79.

LEWISTON, CAL Trumpet. Session for Mike Bloomfield (1978).

LEYLAND, ALAN Drums, percussion. Member of Candlewick Green, 1974.

LEYNOR, JEFF Guitar, vocal. Member of the Stanky Brown Group, 1975-77.

LEYTON, MICKEY Vocal. Member of S.C.R.A., 1972.

LI PUMA, TOMMY Producer. Produced Dave Mason (1970); Mark-Almond (1971); Dr. John (1979); Seawind (1979); and others.

LI VIGNI, JOHN Drums, vocal, percussion. Member of Puzzle.

LIAR Clive Brooks—drums; Dave Burton—vocal, guitar; Dave Taylor—bass, vocal; Steve Mann—guitar, vocal, keyboards, percussion; Paul Travis—guitar, vocal. *Album:* Set the World on Fire (BSV K-6982) 1980.

LIBBY, BART Keyboards. Member of the Euphonius Wall, 1973.

LIBER, MICK Guitar. Member of Python Lee Jackson, 1972, and Medicine Head, 1973.

LIBERT, DAVE Organ. Member of the Happenings, 1966-68.

LIBERTY, BRUNO Keyboards. Member of Esperanto, 1975.

LIBERTY Dan Wheetman—vocal, guitar, fiddle; Vic Garrett—bass, vocal, guitar; Jan Camp Garrett—vocal, mandolin, piano, guitar; Kent Lewis—vocal, guitar, fiddle; Larry Gottlieb—bass, pedal steel guitar; Jerry Fletcher—vocal, piano. *Album:* Liberty (WGS) 1975.

LICHTIG, BOBBY Bass, flute, vocal. Member of Bonaroo, 1975, and In Transit, 1980. Session for Seals and Crofts (1971, 73).

LICKERT, MARTIN Bass. Replaced Roy Estrada in the Mothers of Invention, 1971.

LIDDLE, STEVE Percussion. Member of Fischer-Z since 1979.

LIEBER, RICHARD Percussion. Session for Jan and Dean (1963).

LIEBERMAN, LORI Vocal. *Album:* Letting Go (MLN 8005) 1978.

LIEBERMAN, TOM Vocal, guitar. Member of Rio Nido, 1978.

LIEBEZEIT, JACKI Drums. Member of the Can, 1975.

LIEBMAN, DAVE Saxophone, flute. Member of Ten Wheel Drive, 1970.

LIFE, T. Guitar. Session for Taj Mahal (1976).

LIFESONG, ALEX Guitar. Member of Rush, 1971 to present.

LIFETIME See Tony William's Lifetime.

LIGERTWOOD, ALEX Vocal, percussion. Member of Brian Auger's Oblivion Express, 1972-78, and Santana, 1979. Session for Billy Squier (1980).

LIGHTFOOT, GORDON Guitar, vocal, piano, writer. Born 11/17/38. Often called Canada's Bob Dylan (they shared the same manager), they are both storytellers, who have been performing their own songs since the 1960s. Peter, Paul and Mary's first hit, "For Loving Me," brought attention to his writing. His first single was released in 1968 ("Black Day in July"), and he received national attention with "Sundown" (1974). *Albums:* Very Best of Gordon Lightfoot (UAR UA-LA 381E); Sit Down Young Stranger, 1966; Did She Mention My Name; Back Here on Earth (UAR LW-6672); Best of Gordon Lightfoot (UAR LO-6754) 1980; Cold on the Shoulder (RPS M54-2206) 1975; Don Quixote (RPS 2056) 1972; Dream Street Rose (WBR HS-3426) 1980; Endless Wire (WBR K-3149) 1978; Gord's Gold (RPS 2RS-2237) 1975; If You Could Read My Mind (RPS 6392) 1970; Lightfoot (UAR LW-6487) 1966; Old Dan's Records (RPS 2037) 1971; Summer Side of Life (RPS 2116); Summertime Dream (RPS 2246) 1976; Sunday Concert (UAR LTAO-6714) 1969; Sundown (RPS MS4-2177) 1974; Way I Feel (UAR LW-6587); Lightfoot (UAR 6649) 1968.

LIGHTNIN' SLIM Guitar, vocal. Blues soloist. *Albums:* High and Low Down (EXC 8018) 1978; London Gumbo (EXC 8023) 1978.

LILJEDAHL, BOSSE Bass. Member of Blue Swede.

LILLAS, KEVIN Bass. Member of the JTS Band, 1977.

LILLJEQUIST, ERIC Guitar, vocal. Member of Orphan, 1971-74.

LILLY, KEITH Bass, vocal. Member of the Heats,

1980.

LILLYWHITE, ADRIAN Drums, percussion. Member of the Members, 1979-80.

LILLYWHITE, STEVE Producer. Produced Ultravox, 1977, Penetration, 1979, XTC, 1980, and others.

LIMOUSENE David Barnes—drums; David Bennett—guitar; John Cascella—keyboards, vocal; Mark Crawley—bass, vocal; Carl Storie—vocal. *Album:* Limousene (GSF) 1972.

LIND, BOB Vocal. Recorded "Elusive Butterfly" (1966). *Albums:* Don't Be Concerned, 1967; Elusive Bob Lind (VRV 3005); Bob Lind.

LIND, JOHN Vocal. Member of White Horse, 1977. Session for John Sebastian (1976).

LIND, ROB Saxophone, vocal. Original member of the Sonics.

LINDERMAN, ERIC Piano. Session for Don Preston.

LINDERS, IRENE Vocal. Added to Kayak lineup, 1978-80.

LINDES, HAL Guitar. Member of Darling, 1979.

LINDGREN, ALAN Moog, keyboards. Session for Neil Diamond (1976).

LINDISFARNE Lindsey Jackson—vocal, mandolin, harp, percussion; James Hull—vocal, guitar; Thomas Duffy—bass, vocal; Ken Cradock—keyboards, vocal; Keith Harcourt—guitar; Paul Nichols—drums (until 1974); Simon Lowe—guitar (1978); Ron Clements—bass (1978); Ray Laidlaw—drums (1978). *Albums:* Back and Fourth (ACO 38-108) 1978; Dingly Dell (ELK 75043); Fog on the Tyne (ELK 75021); Nicely Out of Tune (ELK 74099); Roll On, Ruby (ELK 75077) 1974; Happy Daze (ELK 7E1018) 1974.

LINDLEY, DAVID Guitar, violin, banjo, vocal. An original member of Kaleidoscope, 1967-68. Session for John Sebastian (1974); James Taylor (1976); Terry Reid (1973, 76); Neil Sedaka (1976); Crosby and Nash (1976); Ry Cooder (1978-80); Jackson Browne (1978-80); Warren Zevon (1980).

LINDO, EARL Keyboards. Member of Bob Marley's Wailers, 1980. Session for Taj Mahal.

LINDSAY, MARK Vocal, saxophone. Member of Paul Revere and the Raiders, 1965-69.

LINDSEY, JAMES Percussion, vocal. Member of the L.A. Jets, 1976.

LINDSEY, KEN Organ. Member of Rock Rose, 1979.

LINDSEY, MARY ANN Vocal. Member of Black Grass, 1972.

LINDSEY, PHYLLIS Vocal. Member of Black Grass, 1972.

LINDSEY, STEVE Keyboards, bass, drums, guitar, vocal. Member of the Planets, 1980.

LINDSEY, STEVE Bass. Member of the Deaf School, 1979-80.

LINE, KEITH Drums. Replaced Keith Boyce in Bram Tchaikovsky, 1980.

LINES, BARRY Guitar, vocal. Member of Mark Andrews and the Gents, 1980.

LINGLE, LARRY Guitar, vocal. Member of the Pieces, 1979.

LINGLE, MIKE Drums, vocal. Member of the Pieces, 1979.

LINGWOOD, JOHN Drums. Replaced Geoff Britton in Manfred Mann, 1980.

LINHART, BUZZ Vibes, vocal, guitar. New York folk singer and contemporary of Fred Neil, John Sebastian, etc. Session with Jimi Hendrix (1968); John Sebastian (1970); Zephyr (1971). *Albums:* Buzzy, 1969; Buzz Linhart Is Music; Pussy Cats Can Go Far; Best of Buzzy Linhart.

LINK, CRAIG Drums, percussion, vocal. Member of the Timberline, 1977.

LINK, GARY Bass. Session for Andy Pratt (1977).

LINK Ron Marrone—guitar, vocal; Burt Scheel—drums, percussion; Kevin Mazey—keyboards, synthesizer, vocal; Kent Mazey—bass, vocal; Roger Hatfield—reeds, keyboards. *Album:* All for You (MRS DGH 6601) 1980.

LINN, ROGER Guitar. Session for Leon Russell (1976-79); Adam Mitchell (1979).

LINN COUNTY Fred Walk—guitar, sitar; Larry Easter—woodwinds; Dino Long—bass; Stephen Miller—organ, vocal; Snake McAndrew—drums. *Albums:* Linn County, 1968; Fever Shot, 1969.

LINSCOTT, JODY Percussion. Session for John Mayall (1978); Nils Lofgren (1979).

LINSLEY, BRIAN Guitar. Member of the Jim Carroll Band, 1980.

LINSLEY, STEVE Bass. Member of the Jim Carroll Band, 1980.

LINTON, ROD Guitar. Session for John Lennon (1971).

LINVILLE, TERRY Bass. Member of 1994, 1979.

LION Gary Farr—vocal; Steve Webb—guitar, vocal; Robin Le Mesurier—guitar; Steve Humphries—bass; John Sinclair—keyboards, vocal; Eric Dillon—drums, vocal. *Album:* Running All Night (AAM 4755) 1980.

LIPSCOMB, MANCE Vocal, guitar. Born in Texas, April 9, 1895, the son of a fiddle player and farmer. *Albums:* Texas Sharecropper (ARH F1001); Texas Sharecropper, Vol. II (ARH F1023) 1964; Live Performance (ARH F1026) 1964; Volume IV (ARH F1033) 1967; Volume V (ARH 1049) 1968; Volume VI (ARH 1049) 1968; Blues Roots (TMT 2-7006).

LIPSIUS, FRED Horns. Member of Blood, Sweat and Tears, 1968. Session for Paul Simon (1972).

LISTON, DANNY Vocal, guitar. Member of Mama's Pride, 1975.

LISTON, PAT Vocal, guitar, organ. Member of Mama's Pride, 1975.

LITHERLAND, JAMES Guitar. Original member of Colosseum, 1968-70.

LITTLE BILL Keyboards, vocal. Member of the

Blue Jug, 1975.

LITTLE EVA Vocal. Made a hit of "Locomotion," 1962.

LITTLE FEAT Bill Payne—keyboards, vocal; Richie Hayward—drums, vocal; Lowell George—guitar, vocal, producer; Ken Gradney—bass; Sam Clayton—percussion, vocal; Paul Barre—guitar. *Albums:* Dixie Chicken (WBR 2686) 1972; Down on the Farm (WBR HS-3345) 1979; Feats Don't Fail Me Now (WBR B-2784) 1974; Last Record Album (WBR B-2884) 1975; Last Feat (WBR 1890) 1971; Over the Edge (WBR K-335); Sailin' Shoes (WBR B-2600) 1972; Time Loves a Hero (WBR B-3015) 1977; Waiting for Columbus (WBR 2B-3140) 1978.

LITTLE RICHARD Vocal, piano, writer. Born 12/25/32. Real name: Richard Penniman. Composer of rock classics like "Long Tall Sally," "Rip It Up," "Slippin' and Slidin'," "Lucille," "Good Golly Miss Molly," "Tutti Frutti," and many more. Indeed, he wrote the bible of rock 'n' roll for all hip shaking screamers that ever tried to get an audience on its feet to dance. His styled Pompadour and excessive make-up augment his effusive stage pressence. Session for Bachman-Turner Overdrive (1975). *Albums:* Cast a Long Shadow (EDC E4 30428); Rill Thing (RPS 6406); Second Coming (RPS 2107); Big Hits (CRS 9033); Fabulous Little Richard (SPE 2104) 1959; Little Richard (SPE 2103) 1958; Grooviest 17 Original Hits (SPE 2113); Pure Soul (KNT 517); This Is How It All Began, Vol. 2 (SPE 2118); King of Rock and Roll (RPS 6462); Let the Good Times Roll (BEL 9002); Little Richard (SPE 2111); Little Richard's Greatest Hits (TRP 8013) 1967.

LITTLE RIVER BAND Beeb Birtles—guitar, vocal; Graham Goble—guitar, vocal; Glenn Shorrock—vocal; Derek Pellicci—drums; David Briggs—guitar; George McArdle—bass. Australian rockers who made their U.S. debut in 1977. *Albums:* Backstage Pass (CAP SWBK-12061) 1980; Beginnings (CAP SN-11993); Beginnings, Vol. 2 (CAP SN-12056) 1980; Diamantina Cocktail (HAR SW-11645) 1977; First under the Wire (CAP SOO-11954) 1979; Little River Band (HAR ST-11512) 1979; Sleeper Catcher (HAR SW-11783) 1978; After Hours (HAR SN 16072) 1980.

LITTLE WALTER Harmonica. Muddy Water's harmonica man for 10 years (1950-60), he developed the electric harmonica sound that Junior Wells, Paul Butterfield and others later popularized. From Chicago, he died in 1968. *Albums:* Best of Little Walter, 1968; Boss Blues Harmonica; Confessin' to the Blues; Hate To See You Go; Super Blues.

LITTLE, CARLO Drums. Member of Cyril Davies and His All Stars. Session for Lord Sutch.

LITTLE, REEVE Vocal. Session for Peter C. Johnson (1980).

LITTLE, ROY Saxophone, drums, flute, bass. Member of the Alan Price Set, 1965-68.

LITTLEJOHN, JOHN Vocal, guitar, writer. Chicago blues man from Jackson, Mississippi, born 4/16/31. Did not start playing until 1951, and after six months he was playing professionally. *Albums:* Blues Roots (TMT 2-7006); Chicago Blues Star (ARH 1043) 1968.

LIVE ADVENTURES See Super Session.

LIVE WIRE Mike Edwards—vocal, guitar; Simon Boswell—guitar, vocal, keyboards (1980); Jeremy Meek—bass, vocal; German Gonzales—drums; Chris Cutler—guitar, vocal (1979). *Albums:* No Fright (AAM 4814) 1980; Pick It Up (AAM 4793) 1979.

LIVELEY, EDD Guitar, vocal. Member of the El Roachos, 1973.

LIVESLY, BILLY Keyboards. Session for Ronnie Lane (1975); Kevin Ayers (1977-78); Jess Roden (1977); Kevin Lamb (1978); Gerry Rafferty (1980).

LIVGREN, KERRY Guitar, keyboards, vocal. Born 9/18/49. Original member of Kansas, since 1974. *Album:* Seeds of Change (KSH JZ-36567) 1980.

LIVING, BERNIE Saxophone, flute. Member of Manfred Mann, 1971.

LIVINGSTON, DOUG Keyboards, guitar. Member of Fool's Gold, 1976.

LIVINGSTON, ROBERT Vocal, piano, guitar. Member of the Lost Gonzo Band, 1978.

LIZIK, BOB Member of Scott Wilk and the Walls, 1980.

LLEWELYN, MICKY Guitar, vocal. Member of Hustler.

LLOYD, CHARLES Flute, tenor saxophone. Established jazz soloist. Session for the Doors' "Full Circle" (1972); Harvey Mandel (1972); Canned Heat (1972). *Albums:* Best of Charles Lloyd (ATC 1556); Dream Weaver (ATC 1459) 1966; Flowering (of the Original) Charles Lloyd Quartet (ATC 1586); Discovery, 1964; Charles Lloyd at Monterey; Charles Lloyd in Europe; Journey Within; Of Course, of Course, 1966; Love-In; Big Sur Tapestry (PFA 139); Forest Flower (ATC 1473); Jazz Years (ATC 2-316); Weavings (PFA 123); Waves (AAM 3044) 1972; Nirvana (COL C5 9609).

LLOYD, DAVE Vocal, writer. Member of Nutz, 1974-77.

LLOYD, GEORGE Member of Jay and the Techniques, 1967-68.

LLOYD, IAN Vocal. Featured vocalist of Stories, 1972-73. Session for Foreigner (1977-78); Frank Carillo (1979). *Album:* Goose Bumps (STB 7104) 1979; 3WC (STB 7110) 1980.

LLOYD, RICHARD Guitar, vocal. Member of Television, 1977-78. *Album:* Alchemy (ELK 6E 245) 1979.

LLOYD-LANGTON, HUW Drums. Session for Steve Swindells (1980).

LO AND BEHOLD Dennis Coulson—vocal; Dixie Dean—bass, harmonica, percussion, coronet, vocal; Tom McGuinness—guitar, banjo, accordion, vocal; Hughie Flint—drums, percussion, vocal. Name of the album and the group, the remnants of McGuinness–Flint, featuring the same harmonies with Dylan material. *Album:* Lo and Behold (Import) 1972.

LOADING ZONE Paul Fauerso—vocal, keyboards; Linda Tillery—vocal, bass, drums, harmonica, bassoon; Peter Shapiro—guitar; Steve Dowler—guitar; Bob Kridle—bass; George Newcom—drums; Todd Anderson—reeds, piano, accordian; Patrick O'Hara—trombone. Multi-instrumental San Francisco rhythm and blues group. *Album:* Loading Zone, 1968.

LOBBETT, MIKE Keyboards, vocal. Member of Emperor, 1977.

LOCKE, JOHN Keyboards, writer. Original member of Spirit, 1968-71, 1976. Member of Simon Stoke's Black Whip Band, 1973.

LOCKE, SEAN Percussion. Member of the Blue Goose, 1975.

LOCKETT, PETER Vocal, guitar, violin. Member of Mainhorse, 1971.

LOCKHART, JIM Keyboards, flute, whistle, vocal. Original member of Horslips.

LOCKHEED, CHRISTOPHER Drums, percussion, harpsicord, vocal. Member of Kak.

LOCKIE, KEN Member of the Cowboys International, 1979.

LOCKMILLER, RICHARD Percussion. Member of Stone Country, 1968.

LOCKRIDGE, LES Guitar. Member of Buckacre, 1976.

LOCOMOTIVE GT Tamas Barta—guitar, harp, vocal; Joseph Laux—drums, percussion; Gabor Presser—piano; Thomas Somlo—bass, saxophone, violin, vocal. *Albums:* Locomotive GT, 1974; All Aboard (ABC) 1975.

LOCORRIERE, DENNIS Vocal, guitar, bass, harmonica. Member of Dr. Hook and the Medicine Show.

LODGE, JOHN Bass, cello, percussion, guitar, vocal, writer, producer. Original member of the Moody Blues, since 1965. Released a duet album, "Blue Jays," with group member Justin Hayward. Produced Trapeze (1974). *Album:* Natural Avenue (LON PS-683) 1973.

LOECKIE, RAY Saxophone. Session for Mike Bloomfield (1978).

LOFGREN, NILS Guitar, vocal, accordion, writer, keyboards. An original member of Crazy Horse, 1971, and founder of Grin, 1971-73. After Grin failed to catch the public's attention, he struck out on his solo career with greater success. Session for Steve Stills (1971); Neil Young (1970-75); the Tears (1979); Peter C. Johnson (1980). *Albums:* Best of Nils Lofgren (EPC PE-34247) 1976; Cry Tough (AAM 4573) 1976; I Came to Dance (AAM 4628) 1977; Nils Lofgren (AAM 4509) 1973; Night After Night (AAM 3707) 1977; Nils (AAM 4756) 1979.

LOFGREN, TOM Guitar. Brother of Nils Lofgren and member of Grin, 1971-73. Session for Nils Lofgren (1976, 77, 79).

LOGAN, ED Tenor saxophone. Session for the Memphis Horns.

LOGAN, JEFF Trombone, vocal. Member of High Cotton, 1975.

LOGAN, TODD Trumpet, vocal. Member of High Cotton, 1975. Session for Martin Mull (1974); the Marshall Tucker Band (1974); Gregg Allman (1974); Hydra (1974).

LOGGINS, DAVE Guitar, vocal. *Albums:* Apprentice (EPC KE- 32833) 1974; Country Suite (EPC PE-33946) 1975; David Loggins (EPC PE-35972) 1979; One Way Ticket to Paradise (EPC PE-34713) 1977; Personal Belongings (VAN 6580) 1972.

LOGGINS, KENNY Guitar, vocal. Half of the Loggins and Messina duet, 1972-77. Session for Jimmy Webb (1977); the Pages (1979). *Albums:* Celebrate Me Home (COL PC-34655) 1977; Keep The Fire (COL JC-36172) 1979; Nightwatch (COL JC-35387) 1978; Alive (COL C2X 36738) 1980.

LOGGINS AND MESSINA Kenny Loggins—guitar, vocal, writer; Jim Messina—guitar, vocal, writer, producer; Merle Bergante—drums; Al Garth—saxophone, clarinet, violin; Larry Sims—bass, vocal; Jon Clarke—saxophone, flute, oboe, clarinet. Testimony to the greatness of Buffalo Springfield is the talent that has become popular since that group's demise: Crosby, Stills, Nash and Young, Poco, and Loggins and Messina. After Springfield, Messina went to Hawaii and teamed up with writer/vocalist Kenny Loggins. *Albums:* Best of Loggins and Messina (COL PC-34388) 1976; Finale (COL JG-34167) 1977; Full Sail (COL PC-32540) 1973; Loggins and Messina (COL PC-31748) 1972; Kenny Loggins/Jim Messina Sittin' In (COL PC-31044) 1972; Mother Lode (COL PC-33175) 1974; Native Sons (COL PC-33578) 1976; On Stage (COL PC 32848) 1974; So Fine (COL PC-33810) 1975.

LOIZZO, GARY Member of the American Breed, 1965-68.

LOKEY, TOMMY Horns. Session for Leon Russell, 1974.

LOMAS, ROGER Guitar, bass, vocal. Member of the Dodgers, 1978.

LOMAX, JACKIE Vocal, writer. Having the Beatles' manager, Brian Epstein, meant a big thing in the 1960s, but when Epstein died, Lomax's future seemed bleak. Undaunted, the Beatles signed him to Apple, but he fell short of becoming a commercial success, despite his talent and the benefits of big name associations. Session for Rod Stewart (1980). *Albums:* Is This What You Want (APL) 1968; Home Is in My Head, 1969; Three, 1970; Did You Ever Get That Feeling?, 1977; Livin' for Lovin' (CAP ST 33558) 1976.

LOMAX ALLIANCE See Jackie Lomax.

LOMBAR, DRU Slide guitar, guitar, vocal. Member of Grinderswitch, 1974-75. Session for Bobby Whitlock (1975).

LONDON, JACK Bass. Session for James Taylor.

LONDON, JOHN Bass. Member of Michael Nesmith's First National Band. Session for Free Creek (1973).

LONDON, LARRY Drums. Session for Doug Kershaw (1974); Waylon Jennings (1973-74); Neil Young (1978); Frankie Miller (1980).

LONE STAR John Sloman—vocal; Paul Chapman—guitar; Tony Smith—vocal, guitar; Rik Worsnop—keyboards; Pete Hurley—bass; Dixie Lee—drums. *Album:* Firing on All Six (COL PC 34937) 1977.

LONELY BOYS Dermot Moughan—keyboards; Bob Wainright—bass; Steve Carroll—guitar; Terry Reece—drums; Tony Watson—vocal. *Album:* Lonely Boys (HAR ST-12030) 1979.

LONESOME DAVE See Dave Peverett.

LONEY, ROY Vocal. Voice of the Flamin' Groovies, 1969-78. Formed the Phantom Movers, 1979-80.

ROY LONEY AND THE PHANTOM MOVERS Roy Loney—vocal, guitar; James Ferrell—guitar; Larry Lea—guitar, vocal; Maurice Tani—bass, guitar, vocal; Danny Mihn—drums. Roy Loney's group venture after the Flamin' Groovies. *Albums:* Phantom Tracks (SSK 9002) 1980; Out After Dark (SSK 9001) 1979.

LONG, DEE Member of Klaatu since 1976.

LONG, DINO Bass. Member of Linn County, 1968-69. Session for Stephen Miller.

LONG, JOE Vocal. Original member of the Four Seasons.

LONG, STEVE Guitar. Member of Navasota, 1972.

LONGDANCER Brian Harrison—keyboards, guitar, bass, vocal; Steve Sproxton—guitar, vocal; Kai Olsson—guitar, vocal; Dave Stewart—bass, guitar, mandolin, vocal. *Album:* If It Was So Simple (RKT) 1973.

LONGMUIR, ALAN Vocal, bass, piano, accordion. Member of the Bay City Rollers, 1975-79.

LONGMUIR, DEREK Drums, percussion. Member of the Bay City Rollers, 1975-79.

LOOSIGIAN, BILLY Guitar, vocal. Member of Willie Alexander's Boom Boom Band, 1978-79.

LOPEZ, AMAURY Keyboards, percussion, vocal. Member of the Raices, 1975.

LOPEZ, DENNIS Percussion. Session for Elton John (1969).

LOPEZ, VINCENT Drums. Session for Bruce Springsteen (1973).

LORANGE, KIRK Bottleneck guitar. Session for Mike Harrison (1975).

LORD, JON Keyboards, vocal, writer. Born 6/9/41. Co-founder of Deep Purple, 1968-76. Also wrote and scored modern pieces, synthesizing rock instruments with classical orchestration, which met with moderate to minimal critical acclaim. Member of Paice Ashton Lord, 1977, and Whitesnake, since 1979. (See Deep Purple.)

LORD SUTCH Vocal. In 1968, his first album was released with the promotional ads saying, "He's Britain's answer to Little Richard." The session men on his albums included Noel Redding, Jeff Beck, Jimmy Page, Keith Moon, and a host of others. *Albums:* Lord Sutch and His Heavy Friends (COT) 1968; Hands of the Ripper (COT) 1969.

LORDAN, BILL Drums. Replaced Jay Epstein in Gypsy, 1972-73, and Reg Isidore in Robin Trower, 1975-present.

LORENZO, RANDY Vocal. Session for Ry Cooder (1979).

LORI Vocal. Member of Nikki and the Corvettes, 1980.

LORNA Member of the Germs, 1979.

LOS BRAVOS Michael Kogel—vocal; Manuel Fernandez—organ; Juan Pablo Sanllehi—drums; Antonio Martinez—guitar; Michael Luis Vicens Danus—bass. First Spanish group to hit rock noticeably. "Black is Black" was a big hit in 1966 and featured vocals reminiscent of Gene Pitney. *Albums:* Black is Black, 1966; Bring a Little Lovin', 1968.

LOSEKAMP, MIKE Keyboards. Member of the Cyrcle, 1966-67.

LOST GONZO BAND Gary Nunn—guitar, piano, vocal; Robert Livingston—vocal, piano, guitar; John Inmon—guitar, mandolin, vocal; Kelly Dunn—keyboards, vocal; Bobby Smith—bass, vocal; Michael J. Holleman—drums, percussion, vocal. *Album:* Lost Gonzo Band (MCA 487) 1978.

LOTHAR AND THE HAND PEOPLE John Emlin—theremin; Tom Flye—drums; Kim King—guitar; Paul Conly—guitar; Rusty Ford—bass. The electronic gadgetry responsible for horror movie sound effects, the theremin, was the star of Lothar and the Hand People from their beginnings, in 1966, to their recording debut in 1968 in New York. *Albums:* Lothar and the Hand People (CAP SM 2997) 1968; Space Hymn.

LOUGHMAN, COL Saxophone, flute, keyboards, vocal. Member of Ayer's Rock, 1975-77.

LOUGHNANE, LEE Trumpet, vocal. Born 10/21/46. Original member of Chicago, since 1968. Session for the Bee Gees (1979).

LOUIE, LOUIE Drums. Member of the Panic Squad, 1980.

LOUIS, DANIEL Drums, percussion. Member of Barrabas.

LOUIS, REBECCA Vocal. Member of the Nightingales, 1977.

LOUISIANA RED Guitar, vocal. Bluesman born in 1934 in Alabama. *Album:* Red's Dream (ROU GG-48).

LOUSEY, BRIAN Drums, percussion, vocal. Member of Stonebolt, 1978-80.

LOVE AFFAIR Rick Spina—vocal, keyboards; John Zdravecky—guitar, vocal; Wes Coolbaugh—guitar, vocal; Wayne Cukras—bass, vocal; Michael Hudak—drums, vocal. *Album:* Love Affair (RRD 2004) 1980.

LOVE AFFAIR Maurice Bacon—drums; Steve Ellis—vocal; Rex Brayley—guitar; Mick Jackson—bass; Lynton Guest—organ; Morgan Fisher—organ. English group noted for having spawned Steve Ellis, who formed the Steve Ellis Band, and Morgan Fisher who went on to join Mott the Hoople. *Album:* Love Affair (RAD 204).

LOVE OF LIFE ORCHESTRA Peter Gordon—keyboards, reeds; David Van Tiegham—percussion; Randy Gun—guitar, mandolin; Larry Saltzman—guitar; Al Scotti—bass (1980). *Albums:* Geneva (IFD JMB 233) 1980; Extended Niceties (IFD JMB 227) 1979.

LOVE SCULPTURE Dave Edmunds—guitar, keyboards, vocal, writer; Bob Jones—drums, percussion, vocal; John Williams—bass, vocal, piano. A late arrival of the British blues invasion of the 1960s, they were little known yet more talented than most. Behind Edmunds, who later became a self-sufficient band as a soloist, they played some of the most authentic and best-produced blues of the period. See Rockpile. *Albums:* Blues Helping (RRE RS 505) 1969; Forms and Feelings (PRT 71035).

LOVE Arthur Lee—guitar, keyboards, drums, harmonica, vocal, writer; John Echols—guitar; Bryan Maclean—guitar, vocal; Ken Forssi—bass; Michael Stuart—drums, percussion; Alban Pfisterer; T. Jay Cantrelli. A more appropriate name could not be thought of for a group in the psychedelic era of 1965. Their only big single, "My Little Red Book" (1966), obtained them an underground following that traced Arthur Lee's writing and arranging to and through his solo debut. *Albums:* Love (ELK) 1966; Da Capo (ELK) 1967; Love Four Sail (ELK) 1969; Reel to Real (RSO); Best of Love (RHI 800) 1980; Forever Changes (ELK 74013) 1967.

LOVE, ANDREW Tenor saxophone. Member of the Memphis Horns. Session for B. B. King (1973-74); the Doobie Brothers (1978); Tom Johnston (1979); Paul Butterfield (1980).

LOVE, BRAD Keyboards, vocal. Member of Aviary, 1979.

LOVE, MIKE Vocal. Born 3/15/41. Original member of the Pendletones, which became the Beachboys, 1962 to present.

LOVE, STEVE Guitar. Member of Stories, 1972-73, and Jobraith, 1973-74. Session for the Michael Zager Band; Jimmy Maelen (1980).

LOVECRAFT, H. P. George Edwards—guitar, bass, vocal, writer; Dave Michaels—keyboards, vocal; Tony Cavallari—vocal, guitar; Jerry Mc George—bass, vocal (1967); Michael Tegza—drums, percussion, vocal; Jeffery Boyan—bass (1968). Chicago based band whose originality went unnoticed. *Albums:* H. P. Lovecraft (PHL 252) 1967; H. P. Lovecraft, II (PHL 600279) 1968; Valley of the Moon (RPS) 1970.

LOVELACE, KENNETH Guitar. Session for Jerry Lee Lewis (1973).

LOVELESS, JIM Percussion. Member of the Dija Rhythm Band, 1976.

LOVELL, HERB Drums. Session for B. B. King (1969-70); Pearls Before Swine (1971); Muddy Waters (1972).

LOVERBOY Mike Reno—vocal; Paul Dean—guitar, vocal; Matt Frenette—drums; Doug Johnson—keyboards; Scott Smith—bass. *Album:* Loverboy (COL JC 36762) 1980.

LOVETRO, GARY Bass. Member of the Strawberry Alarm Clock, 1968.

LOVIN' SPOONFUL Zal Yanovsky—guitar; John Sebastian—guitar, harmonica, autoharp, vocal, writer; Steve Boone—bass; Joe Butler—drums; Jerry Yester—guitar (1968). "Do You Believe in Magic" (1965) was a touch of magic from New York, amidst the hordes of the British Invasion. Their casual good-time music (from years of jug band playing) fit their personalities and their talent, writing, and performing were superior. But a drug arrest in 1968 shattered their image. Yanovsky left for an unsuccessful solo career, to be replaced by Yester. The spell had been broken and the group dissolved in 1968. *Albums:* Once Upon a Time (KMS); Do You Believe in Magic (KMS 8050) 1965; Day Dream, 1966; What's Up Tiger Lily, 1966; Hums of the Lovin' Spoonful (KMS 5054) 1967; You're a Big Boy Now (KMS) 1967; Best of the Lovin' Spoonful, 1967; Everything Is Playing, 1967; Best of the Lovin' Spoonful, Vol. 2, 1968; Revelation Revolution, 1969; 24 Karat Hits (KMS 750-2); Best of the Lovin Spoonful (BUD 5706) 1977; What's Shakin' (ELK 74002).

LOVING AWARENESS Charlie Charles—drums; Norman Watt-Roy—drums; Michael Gallagher—guitar, vocal; John Turnbull—guitar, vocal. Formed from the nucleus of Glencoe. *Album:* Loving Awareness.

LOVING KIND First group organized by Noel Redding, who later became Jimi Hendrix's bass player. It disbanded in 1965.

LOW NUMBERS Harold Bronson—vocal; Louie Maxfield—guitar; Dave Dennard—bass; David Schneider—drums. *Albums:* Saturday Night Pogo (RHI 003); Twist Again with the Low Numbers (RHI 004) 1978.

LOWE, ALBERT Guitar. Session for Clarence Carter (1967).
LOWE, COLIN Bass, vocal. Member of Magnum, 1979.
LOWE, DANNY Guitar. Member of Painter, 1973, and Hammersmith, 1975-76.
LOWE, JIM Vocal, guitar, percussion. Original member of the Electric Prunes, 1967.
LOWE, MICK Pink Floyd's stage-light manager.
LOWE, NICK Bass, guitar, vocal, writer, producer. Member of Brinsley Schwartz before going solo. Teamed with Dave Edmunds in Rockpile, 1980. Session for Dave Edmunds (1975, 77); Frankie Miller (1977). *Albums:* Labour of Lust (COL JC-36087) 1979; Pure Pop for Now People (COL JC 35329) 1978.
LOWE, SIMON Guitar. Member of Lindisfarne, 1978.
LOWELL, JIMMY Bass, vocal. Member of the Spider, 1980. Session for Link Wray (1980).
LOWENTHAL, BARRY Drums. Member of the Tazmanian Devils, 1980.
LOWERY, ROBERT Vocal. Member of the Surprise Package, 1969, and American Eagle, 1970-71.
LOWTHER, HENRY Trumpet, violin, flugelhorn. Member of John Mayall's Bluesbreakers, 1968, and the Keef Hartley Band horn section, 1969-70. Session for Memphis Slim (1971); Bryan Ferry (1974); Elton John (1978).
LOZANES, EFREN Saxophone, keyboards. Member of Please, 1976.
LUBAHN, DOUGLAS Bass. Member of Clear Light, 1967-68. Occasional bass for the Doors, 1968-70. Member of Dreams, 1970.
LUCAFO, PHIL Guitar, vocal, pedal steel guitar. Member of Heartsfield, 1973-75.
LUCAS, ARNO Vocal, drums, percussion. Member of Crackin, 1975-78. Session for Randy Newman (1979); Adam Mitchell (1979).
LUCAS, BUDDY Harmonica. Played on the posthumous Hendrix album "Midnight Lightning," 1975.
LUCAS, GARY Guitar, french horn. Session for Captain Beefheart's Magic Band (1980).
LUCAS, KATE Flute. Session for the Wire (1980).
LUCAS, MIKE Drums. Member of Snopek since 1979.
LUCAS, PAULINA Vocal. Session for King Crimson (1972).
LUCAS, RAY Drums. Session for Jan Akkerman (1973).
LUCAS, TED Harmonica. Session for the Temptations (1973).
LUCAS, TREVOR Vocal, guitar, harmonica. Member of Eclection, 1968, and Fotheringay, 1971. Replaced Richard Thompson in Fairport Convention, 1975.
LUCE, AV Vocal. Member of Passion, 1979.
LUCERO, GENO Bass. Member of Growl, 1974.
LUCIANO, GERALD Bass, harmonica, vocal. Original member of Karthago, 1974.
LUCIFER'S FRIEND John Lawton—vocal; Peter Hesslein—guitar, vocal; Peter Hecht—keyboards; Dieter Horns—bass, vocal; Herbert Bornhold—drums: Adrien Askew—keyboards, vocal (1978-80); Mike Starbs—vocal (1978-80); Jochim Rietenbach—drums (1974-75). *Albums:* Banquet (PPT) 1974; Good Time Warrior (ELK 6E-159) 1978; Sneak Me In (ELK 6E-265) 1980; Where the Groupies Killed the Blues (PPT 98008) 1975.
LUCKEY, LENA Vocal. Session for Leon Russell (1979).
LUDWICK, REX Drums. Session for Leon Russell and Willie Nelson (1979); Willie Nelson (1976-79).
LUDWIG, FRANK Keyboards, vocal. Member of Trooper, 1976, and Ironhorse, 1980.
LUENING, WARREN Trumpet. Session for Dr. John (1975, 79).
LUEVANO, CARLOS Guitar. Member of A-440, 1978.
LUFRANO, TONY Mellotron. Session for the Screams (1980).
LUFT, LORNA Vocal. Session for Hilly Michaels (1980).
LUKATHER, STEVE Guitar, vocal. Member of Toto since 1978. Session for Steven T. (1978); Gary Wright (1979); John Mayall (1979); Adam Mitchell (1979); Elton John (1979-80); Boz Scaggs (1980).
LUKE Guitar, vocal. Member of the Fashion, 1979.
LUKE AND THE APOSTLES Early name of Kensington Market.
LUKENS, MALCOLM Keyboards. Session for Roy Buchanan (1974-77).
LUKYN, TONY Keyboard, vocal. Member of Tranquility, 1972.
LULEY, KLAUS Guitar, vocal. Member of Schloss, 1975.
LULU Vocal. Real name: Marie Laurie. Reviving memories of Brenda Lee, this Englander received a big boost to her career by singing the title cut to the movie "To Sir with Love," 1967. *Albums:* From Lulu with Love, 1967; Lulu Sings to Sir with Love, 1967; Don't Take Love for Granted (ROC BXLI-3073) 1978.
LUMLEY, ROBIN Keyboards, producer. Member of Brand X, 1977. See Jack Lancaster and Robin Lumley. Production for Aviator (1978); Bill Bruford (1977). Session for Wilding-Bonus (1978).
LUNCH, BRENDA Vocal. Session for Martin Mull.
LUNDGREN, ERIK Guitar. Member of the Johnny Van Zant Band, 1980.
LUNDGREN, KEN Bass. Session for Mike Berry (1976).
LUNDSTRUM, LARRY Bass, vocal. Replaced Ken Lyons in 38 Special, 1979-present.

LUPICA, FRANK Drums. Member of Shanti, 1971.

LUSHER, DON Trombone. Session for Savoy Brown (1969).

LUTHER, DONALD Vocal, bass. Member of the Ducks, 1973.

LUTTON, DAVE Drums. Member of Eire Apparent, 1969. Session for Chris Spedding (1978).

LUTTRELL, TERRY Vocal. Member of R.E.O. Speedwagon, and Starcastle, 1972-78.

LUTZ, MICHAEL Bass, guitar, vocal, keyboards. Member of Brownsville Station, 1972-77.

LUX, KAZ Vocal. Recorded a duet with Jan Akkerman, 1976. *Album:* Eli (ATC 18210) 1976.

LUXON, BILLY Vocal, percussion, trumpet. Member of Exile since 1973.

LYALL, WILLIAM C. Keyboards, flute, vocal, bass. Member of Pilot, 1974. Session for the Alan Parsons Project (1976); Runner (1979).

LYDON, JOHN Vocal, guitar. Real name of Johnny Rotten of the Sex Pistols. Member of Public Image since 1979.

LYGNSTAD, ANNIFRED Vocal. Member of Abba since 1974.

LYLE, BOBBY Keyboards. Session for Gary Wright (1975, 77, 79). *Albums:* New Warrior (CAP SW-11809); Night Fire (CAP ST-11956) 1979.

LYLE, GRAHAM Guitar, mandolin, bass, vocal, writer. Original member of McGuiness–Flint, and partner of Benny Gallagher in Gallagher and Lyle since 1973. Session for Ronnie Lane (1975).

LYLE, JOY Violin. Session for Barry Goudreau (1980).

LYLE, STEVE Keyboards. Session for the Marc Tanner Band (1980).

LYMAN, STEVE Guitar, vocal. Member of SRC.

FRANKIE LYMON AND THE TEENAGERS Lymon paved the way for teenage rock stars when he and his Teenagers made "Why Do Fools Fall in Love" (1956) and "I'm No Deliquent." Lymon died of a drug overdose in 1968. *Albums:* The Teenagers, 1956; Rock 'n' Soul, 1956.

LYNCH, BRUCE Bass. Session for Ken Tobias (1973); Cat Stevens (1975-76); Gary Brooker (1979); Rick Wakeman (1979).

LYNCH, CARL Guitar. Replaced Danny Kortchmar in the Fugs, 1968.

LYNCH, LARRY Drums. Member of the Greg Kihn Band since 1976.

LYNCH, STAN Drums. Member of Tom Petty's Heartbreakers, 1977-present. Session for the Tremblers (1980).

LYNCH, SUZANNE Vocal. Session for Chris Youlden (1974).

LYNCH, TIM Guitar. Member of the Flamin' Groovies, 1969-78.

LYNES, ROY Keyboards. Original member of Status Quo, 1965-68.

LYNN, CHERYL Vocal. Session for John Mayall (1979). *Albums:* In Love (COL JC-36145); Cheryl Lynn (COL JC-35486); Night at Studio 54 (CAS 2-7161).

LYNN, IAN Keyboards. Session for Runner (1979); Gerry Rafferty (1980).

LYNN, TAMI Vocal. Session for Dr. John (1971-72, 75, 78-79); the Rolling Stones (1972).

LYNNE, JEFF Vocal, piano, guitar, bass, percussion. Born 12/30/47. Member of the Move, 1969-72, and the Electric Light Orchestra since 1973.

LYNOTT, PHILIP Vocal. *Album:* Solo in Soho (WBR BSK-3405) 1980.

LYNTON, JACKIE Vocal. Assumed lead vocal duties from Dave Walker in Savoy Brown, 1973.

LYNYRD SKYNYRD Ronnie Van Zant—vocal; Gary Rossington—guitar; Allen Collins—guitar; Ed King—guitar; Billy Powell—keyboards; Leon Williams—bass; Bob Burns—drums; Steve Gaines—guitar; Artimus Pyle—drums. Southern rockers whose popularity was peaking until a tragic air crash, 10/20/77, claimed the lives of Van Zant, Gaines, and Cassie Gaines. Remaining band members retired the group name and formed the Rossington-Collins Band, 1980. *Albums:* Gimme Back My Bullets (MCA 3022) 1976; Gold and Platinum (MCA 2-11008) 1979; Nuthin' Fancy (MCA 3021) 1975; One More from the Road (MCA 2-8011) 1976; Pronounced Len-Herd Skin-Nerd (MCA 3019) 1973; Second Helping (MCA 23020) 1974; Skynard's First and Last (MCA 3047) 1978; Street Survivors (MCA 3029) 1977.

LYON, PETER Guitar. Member of the Ba-Fa Band, 1976.

LYONS, GARY Producer. Produced Gamma (1979-80).

LYONS, JAMIE Vocal. Started in the Music Explosion, 1967, before becoming the voice of the Capital City Rockets, 1973.

LYONS, JEFF Vocal, guitar. Member of Guns and Butter, 1972.

LYONS, JILL Acoustic bass. Member of Centipede, 1971.

LYONS, KEN Member of 38 Special since 1977.

LYONS, LEO Bass. Original member of Ten Years After, 1968-73. Session for Chick Churchill (1974); Mike Vernon.

LYONS, SEAN Guitar. Member of Metro, 1977.

LYONS, TIGGER Bass, vocal. Member of Hustler.

LYTTLE, FOGGY Guitar. Session for Chris Youlden (1973).

M Philip Gould—drums; Mark King—bass, guitar, synthesizer, drums; Julian Scott—bass; Robin Scott—guitar; David Vorhaus—synthesizer. *Album:* The Official Secrets Act (SIR 6099) 1980.

M'BOPO, JOSHUAH Guitar. Session for Long John Baldry (1971).

MG'S Steve Cropper—guitar; Al Jackson—drums; Donald "Duck" Dunn—bass; Willie Hall—drums. Backup band for Booker T. (Jones) since 1962, after originally traveling with Otis Redding. Initials stand for Memphis Group. See Booker T.

MAAT, FERRY Piano. Session for Jan Akkerman (1972).

MABEN, LUTHER Guitar. Member of the Creed, 1978.

MABEN, MICHAEL Guitar, vocal. Member of Texas, 1973.

MABRY, BILL Fiddle. Member of Asleep at the Wheel since 1973.

MABY, GRAHAM Bass. Session for Joe Jackson (1979).

MacAINSH, GREGG Bass. Member of the Skyhooks, 1975-77.

MacAULAY, JACKIE Guitar. Session for Jim Capaldi (1979).

MacCALLISTER, DON Bass. Member of the Barry Goldberg Reunion, 1968.

MacCORMICK, BILL Bass. Member of the Random Hold, 1980.

MacDONALD, CAROL Guitar, vocal. Member of Isis, 1974-75.

MacDONALD, IAN Alto saxophone. Member of Centipede, 1971. Session for Phil Manzanera (1975).

MacDONALD, RALPH Percussion. Session for Dr. John (1973); Art Garfunkel (1974-78); Barry Goldberg (1974); Carly Simon (1974); Splinter (1974); Mark-Almond (1978); Paul Simon (1980); Far Cry (1980). *Albums:* Counterpoint (MAR 2229); The Path (MAR 2210); Sound of a Drum (MAR 2202).

MacDONALD, ROBIN Guitar. Member of Billy J. Kramer and the Dakotas, 1968.

MacDOUGALL, AL Percussion. Session for the Richie Furay Band (1976).

MacGREGOR, CRAIG Bass, vocal. Replaced Nick Jameson in Foghat, 1976-present.

MacKAY, DUNCAN Keyboards. Replaced Milton Reame-James in Cockney Rebel. Member of 10 CC, 1980. Session for the Alan Parsons Project (1977-78).

MacKAY, IAN Bass, keyboards, vocal. Member of the Diodes, 1978.

MacKAY, STEVE Saxophone. Member of the Moonlighters, 1977.

MacKENZIE, MATTHEW Guitar, piano, vocal. Session for Richard Lloyd (1979).

MacKINNON, JAMIE Saxophone. Session for the Catfish Hodge Band (1979).

MacLEAN, GODFREY Drums, percussion. Replaced Robbie McIntosh in Brian Auger's Oblivion Express, 1973. Session for Hummingbird (1975).

MacLEOD, ALAN Bagpipes. Session for David Kubinec (1979).

MacLEOD, BRIAN Drums, keyboards, producer. Member of Chilliwack, 1978-80. Co-produced Toronto (1980).

MacLEOD, SEAN Half of the Phillips and MacLeod duet since 1979.

MacMILLAN, AL Piano. Session for Lou Reed (1973).

MacNEIL, EDDIE Drums, percussion. Member of Illusion, 1977.

MacVITTIE, BOB Drums. Original member of Sugarloaf.

MAC, TONY Drums, percussion. Session for Kim Fowley (1973).

MACALUSO, LENNY Guitar. Member of Herman Brood and His Wild Romance since 1979.

MACBETH, PETER Bass. Member of the Foundations, 1968.

MACHELL, TED Cello. Session for Gene Clark (1974).

MACHO, JOE Bass. Session for Henry Gross (1973).

MACK, JIMMIE Vocal, guitar. Member of the Slick Band, 1976-77, soloist, and head of the Jumpers, 1980. Session for Frank Carillo (1979). *Albums:* Jimmie Mack (BIG 76007) 1978; On the Corner (BIG 76014) 1979.

MACK, JOHN Drums. Member of Big Wha-Koo.

MACK, LONNIE Bass. Session for the Doors (1970). *Album:* Memphis Sound of Lonnie Mack.

MACKAY, ANDY Saxophone, oboe. Original member of Roxy, 1972-present. Session for Mott the Hoople (1973); Pavlov's Dog (1976); Phil Manzanera (1975).

MACLACHLAN, CHRIS Bass. Member of Human Sexual Response, 1980.

MACLEAN, BRYAN Guitar, vocal. Original member of Love.

MACLORE, RICHIE Guitar. Member of the Brooklyn Bridge.

MACOLINO, VIRGINIA Vocal. Member of Berlin,

1980.

MACRE, JOE Bass, vocal. Member of Crack the Sky, 1975-77.

MAD RIVER David Roberts—guitar; Rick Bochner—vocal, guitar; Lawrence Hammond—vocal, bass; Thomas Manning—vocal, drums, percussion, recorder. *Albums:* Mad River, 1968; Paradise Bar and Grill.

MADAIO, STEVE Trumpet. Member of the Paul Butterfield Blues Band, 1969-70, and the Blacksmoke Horns, 1978. Session for Joe Cocker (1974); James Taylor (1976); Nilsson (1976); the Marshall Tucker Band (1974-79); B. B. King (1972); Ringo Starr (1974); Carly Simon (1974); Country Joe McDonald (1975); Rod Stewart (1978); Richie Furay (1978); Bob Dylan (1978); Adrian Gurvitz (1979); Ian McLagen (1979); J. Michael Reed (1979); Jennifer Warnes (1976); Dick St. Nicklaus (1979).

MADAY, A. J. Drums. Session for Danny Spanos (1980).

MADAYAG, PHIL Drums. Member of Tierra, 1980.

MADDEN, PAUL Keyboards. Member of Aviary, 1979.

MADEY, BRYAN Drums, percussion. Member of Stories, 1972-73, and the Slick Band, 1976.

MADIGAN, AMY Member of Jelly, 1977.

MADISON, JIMMY Drums. Born 2/17/47. Session for Martin Mull (1974); Ellen McIlwaine (1973); Roland Kirk; Joe Farrell; James Brown; Chet Baker; Art Farmer. *Album:* Bumps on a Smooth Surface (ADP 5007) 1977.

MADLIN, PETE Dobro. Session for Kaleidoscope (1968).

MADNESS Mike Barson—keyboards; Chris Foreman—guitar; Graham McPherson—vocal; Mark Bedford—bass; Lee Thompson—saxophone, vocal; Dan Woodgate—drums, percussion. *Albums:* One Step Beyond (SIR SRK 6085) 1979; Absolutely (SIR SRK 6094) 1980.

MADU, CHYKE Percussion. Session for Phil Manzanera (1975).

MAEL, RON Keyboards. Member of Halfnelson, 1971, before forming Sparks with his brother, Russell, 1972-79.

MAEL, RUSSELL Vocal. Member of Halfnelson, 1971, before forming Sparks, 1972-79.

MAELEN, JIM Played on the posthumous Hendrix album "Crash Landing," 1975. Session for Alice Cooper (1976); Steve Hunter (1977); Mark Farner (1977); Henry Gross (1977-78); Magnet (1979); the Mark and Clark Band (1971); Pacific Gas and Electric (1973); Jimi Hendrix (1975); Stanky Brown (1977); Golden Earring (1978); Euclid Beach Band (1979); Ian Lloyd (1979); Grace Slick (1980).

MAERCKLEIN, KIP Bass. Member of the Elvin Bishop Band until 1972. Session for Stephen Miller.

MAESTRO, JOHNNY Vocal. Voice of the Brooklyn Bridge.

MAFFE, FRANK Vocal. Member of Danny and the Juniors.

MAGADINI, PETE Drums, percussion. Session for Tim Weisberg, 1971.

MAGAZINE Howard de Voto—vocal, writer; Barry Adamson—bass, vocal; Dave Formula—keyboards; Martin Jackson—drums (1978); John Doyle—drums (1979-present); John McGeoch—guitar, saxophone, keyboards; Robin Simon—guitar (1980). *Albums:* Real Life (VIR VA 2100) 1978; Secondhand Daylight (VIR VI 2121) 1979; The Correct Use of Soap (VIR VA 13144) 1980.

MAGGINI, PHIL Bass. Member of Shadowfax, 1976.

MAGIC BAND See Captain Beefheart and his Magic Band.

MAGIC DICK Harmonica. Real name: Richard Salwitz. Member of the J. Geils Band, 1970-present.

MAGLIA, BRENT Brent Maglia—vocal, guitar; Vito Giovanelli—bass, vocal; Dave Siebels—keyboards; Mel Steinberg—woodwinds; Steve Charles—drums, vocal. *Album:* Down at the Hardrock Cafe (FSY 9528) 1977.

MAGMA Christian Vander—drums, vocal, piano; Jannick Top—bass, cello, vocal, piano; Klaus Blasquiz—vocal; Gerald Bikialo—keyboards; Michel Graillier—piano; Stella Vander—vocal; Brian Godding—guitar; Bernard Paganotte—bass; Alan Hatot—flute. *Albums:* Attahk (TMT 7021); Magma Live (TMT 2-7008) 1978; Udu Wudu (TMT 6001) 1976; Kohntarkosz, 1974; Mekanik Destruktiw Kommandoh, 1975.

MAGNA CARTA Chris Simpson—vocal, guitar; Tom Hoy—vocal, guitar; Nigel Smith—vocal, bass, keyboards. *Albums:* Putting It Back Together (ARO ST 50014) 1976; Seasons.

MAGNESS, KERRY Bass. Session for the Doors (1968).

MAGNET Robert James—vocal; Michael Neville—bass, vocal; Les Nichol—guitar, vocal; Jerry Shirley—drums; Peter Wood—keyboards. *Album:* Worldwide Attraction (AAM 4740) 1979.

MAGNO, GABRIEL Keyboards. Replaced John Mealing in If.

MAGNUM, JEFF Bass. Member of the Dead Boys, 1977-78.

MAGNUM Tony Clarkin—guitar, vocal; Richard Bailey—keyboards, flute, vocal; Bob Catley—guitar, vocal; Rex Gorin—drums; Colin Lowe—bass, vocal. *Album:* Kingdom of Madness (JET JZ 35811) 1979.

MAGNUSSON, JACOB Synthesizer. Session for Long John Baldry (1980).

MAGRUDER, ROBBIE Drums. Session for Roy Buchanan (1973).

MAGUIRE, LES Piano. Member of Gerry and the

Pacemakers, 1962-65.

MAHAL, TAJ Vocal, guitar, harmonica, banjo, mandolin, keyboards, writer. Born 5/17/42. Real name: Henry Sainte Claire Fredericks Williams. In 1968, Taj Mahal quietly broke on the blues scene. He did not remain unknown for long. Though firmly rooted in the blues, he has experimented freely with Jamaican rhythms. Session on Fillmore (1972); B. B. King (1972). *Albums:* Sounder (COL S 31944); Satisfied and Tickled Too (COL PC 34103) 1976; Music Keeps Me Together (COL) 1975; Evolution (The Most Recent) (WBR K-3094) 1978; Happy Just to Be Like I Am (COL C-30767); Mo' Roots (COL KC 33051) 1974; Music Fuh Ya' (WBR B-2994) 1977; Natch'l Blues (COL CS 09698) 1968; Ooh So Good 'n Blues (COL C-32600) 1973; Real Thing (COL CG-30619); Recycling the Blues (COL C-31605) 1972; Taj Mahal (COL CG-18).

MAHER, GEORGE Guitar. Member of the Dirty Angels, 1976-78.

MAHER, JIMMY Drums, vocal. Member of the Dirty Angels, 1976-78.

MAHLER, JOHN Drums, vocal. Member of the Buzzcocks since 1977.

MAHOGANY RUSH Frank Marino—guitar, bass, vocal, writer, moog, mellotron, producer; James Ayoub—drums; Paul Harwood—bass. A Canadian heavy metal trio. Marino's voice, style, and writing are reminiscent of the late Hendrix. Yet despite the comparison, Marino can hold up as having an identity of his own. *Albums:* Live (COL JC-35257) 1978; Mahogany Rush IV (COL PC-34190) 1976; Tales of the Unexpected (COL JC-35753) 1979; What's Next (COL JC-36204) 1980; World Anthem (COL PC-34677) 1977; Child of the Novelty (TWC T-451) 1974; Strange Universe (TWC T-482) 1975; Maxoom (TWC) 1975.

MAHONEY, JIM Guitar. Member of Medusa, 1978.

MAIMONE, TONY Bass. Member of Pere Ubu since 1979.

MAINEGRA, RICHARD Guitar. Session for Doug Kershaw (1974).

MAINHORSE Patrick Moraz—keyboards; Peter Lockett—guitar, violin, vocal; Jean Ristori—bass, cello, vocal; Bryson Graham—drums. *Album:* Mainhorse (IMP 1001) 1971.

MAINIERI, MIKE Vibes. Session for Martin Mull (1977).

MAINSTREAM Charles Hayward—drums, percussion, keyboards, vocal; Dave Garrett—keyboards; Phil Manzanara—guitar; Bill MacCormick—bass. *Album:* Quiet Sun (ANT) 1976.

MAIR, ALAN Bass. Member of the Only Ones since 1978.

MAITLAND, ADAM Keyboards, saxophone. Session for the Only Ones (1979).

MAITLAND, GRAHAM Accordion, keyboards, vocal. Member of Glencoe, 1972. Session for Splinter (1974).

MAJOR, RAY Guitar, vocal. Replaced Ariel Bender in Mott the Hoople, 1975. Member of British Lions, 1978.

MAKI, SHIMMY Bass. Member of the Simms Brothers Band, 1979-80.

MALACH, BOB Tenor saxophone. Member of Southside Johnny and the Asbury Jukes until 1977.

MALCOLM, VIC Member of Geordie, 1973.

MALE, KERRILEE Vocal. Member of Eclection, 1968.

MALHERBE, DIDIER Saxophone, flute. Member of Gong.

MALKIN, AL Vocal. Session for Frank Zappa (1979).

MALKINE, SONJA Hurdy Gurdy. Session for Steve Hillage (1976).

MALLABER, GARY Drums, vibes. Member of the Steve Miller Band, 1972-73, 1976. Session for Van Morrison (1968-69); Kate and Anna McGarrigle (1977-78); Steve Miller (1977); Les Dudek (1978); Peter Frampton (1979); Ray Manzarek; the Marc Tanner Band (1979).

MALLEN, MIKE Guitar, vocal. Member of Kid Dynamite, 1976.

MALLORY, STEVE Saxophone. Session for Atlantic Starr (1979).

MALLSON, GINO Bass. Member of Esperanto, 1975.

MALLSON, TONY Drums. Member of Esperanto, 1975.

MALO Arcelio Garcia, Jr.—vocal; Jorge Santana—guitar; Abel Zarate—guitar, vocal; Pablo Tellez—bass; Richard Spremich—drums; Richard Kermode—keyboards; Luis Gasca—horns; Roy Murray—horns. *Albums:* Malo (WBR BS 2554) 1972; Dos (WBR BS 2652) 1972.

MALONE, KENNY Drums. Session for Doug Kershaw (1972, 74); J. J. Cale (1972); Waylon Jennings (1975).

MALONE, TOM Bass, trombone, trumpet, saxophone. Member of the Woody Herman Band. Session for Free Creek (1973); the Band (1977); the Blues Brothers (1978-80).

MALUCHNIK, DOUG Keyboards. Member of Shadowfax, 1976.

MAMA'S PRIDE Pat Liston—vocal, guitar, organ; Danny Liston—vocal, guitar; Kevin Saunders—drums; Max Baker—guitar, vocal; Joe Turek—bass, vocal; Frank Gagliano—keyboards. *Albums:* Mama's Pride (ACO) 1975; Uptown and Lowdown (ACO 36-146) 1977.

THE MAMAS AND THE PAPAS Denny Doherty—vocal; Cass Elliot—vocal; John Phillips—vocal, guitar, writer; Michelle Phillips—vocal. Vocal harmony was nothing new in 1965, but it was new to handle it in a commercial folk/rock format, the two predominant trends. They were the major musical influence of the times. *Albums:* Historic Performances at the Monterey Int'l Pop Festival (DHL X 50100); Mamas and Papas Deliver (DHL 50014) 1967; Mamas and the Papas Golden Era (DHL 50038) 1968; People Like Us (DHL X 50106); If You Believe Your Eyes and Ears (DHL) 1966; The Papas and Mamas Presents the Mamas and the Papas (DHL) 1968; Farewell to the First Golden Era (MCA 50025) 1967; Gathering of Flowers (MCA DSY-50073); Mamas and the Papas (MCA 50006); 16 of Their Greatest Hits (MCA 50064); 20 Golden Hits (MCA X-50145); Papas and the Mamas (MCA 50031) 1966.

MAMMOTH Early name of Van Halen.

MAN Michael Jones—guitar, vocal; Phil Ryan—keyboards, vocal; Clive John—keyboards, drums, percussion; Will Youatt—bass, vocal; John McKenzie—vocal, bass; Deke Leonard—vocal, guitar; Jeff Jones—drums. Welsh heavy rock group produced by Dave Edmunds. *Albums:* Welsh Connection (MCA 2190) 1976; Be Good to Yourself, 1973; Rhinos, Winos and Lunatics; Slow Motion; Back Into the Future (UAR LWB-179).

MAN Supa—guitar, vocal; Dennis Belline—guitar, piano, vocal; Richie Cardens—bass, vocal; Gilbert Slavin—keyboards, flute; Antony Krasinski—drums, percussion, flute. *Album:* Man (COL CS9803).

MANASA, RICK Keyboards. Original member of the Silver Bullet Band, 1974.

MANCHESTER, MELISSA Vocal. Session for Ringo Starr (1977); Martin Mull (1977-78); Bette Midler. *Albums:* Better Days and Happy Endings (ARI 4067) 1976; Bright Eyes (ARI 4011) 1974; Don't Cry Out Loud (ARI 4186) 1978; Help Is on the Way (ARI 4095) 1976; Home to Myself (ARI 4006) 1973; Melissa Manchester (ARI 9506) 1979; Melissa (ARI 4031) 1971; The Promise (MCA 3082); Singin' (ARI 4136) 1977; For the Working Girl (ARI 9533) 1980.

MANCHOVITZ, HENRY Drums. Session for Randy California (1972).

MANCINI, NANETTE Vocal, percussion. Member of Johnny's Dance Band, 1977, and Nan Mancini and JDB, 1979.

NAN MANCINI AND JDB Bobby Bunten; Chris Darway—keyboards, vocal; Nan Mancini—vocal, percussion; David Mohn—drums, vocal; Fran Smith, Jr. Reorganized Johnny's Dance Band with a new name. *Album:* It's a Man's World (WDS BXLI 3498) 1979.

MANCUSO, DONALD Guitar. Member of Black Sheep, 1975.

MANDALA BAND David Durant—vocal; Ashley Mulford—guitar; John Stimpson—bass, guitar; Tony Cresswell—drums; Vic Emerson—keyboards. *Album:* Mandala Band (CRS 1095) 1975.

MANDALA, JOHNNY Guitar. Replaced Steve Bolton in Atomic Rooster, 1973.

MANDALA George Olliver—vocal; Dominic Troiano—vocal, guitar; Joey Chirowski—organ; Don Elliott—bass; Whitney Glan—drums, percussion; Roy Kenner—vocal (1968); Hugh Sullivan—organ (1968). After this Canadian group disbanded, Troiano went to the Guess Who and Kenner became vocalist for the James Gang. *Album:* Soul Crusade, 1968.

MANDEL, FRED Keyboards. Member of the Alice Cooper Band, 1977-78, and Ultra-Latex, 1979.

MANDEL, HARVEY Guitar, writer. Received his training in Chicago with Barry Goldberg and Charlie Musselwhite in the early 1960s. He developed a unique jazz-blues style (shown in the Pure Food and Drug Act), which has influenced such greats as Jeff Beck. A member of Canned Heat, he became widely known in his later work with John Mayall. Session for Don "Sugercane" Harris; Free Creek (1973); the Rolling Stones (1976); Canned Heat (1979). *Albums:* Cristo Redentor (PHL 600 281); Games Guitars Play (PHL 600325); Feel the Sound (JNS 3064) 1974; Baby Batter (JNS 3017); Best of Harvey Mandel (JNS 7014) 1975; The Snake (JNS 3037) 1972; Shangrenade (JNS 3047) 1973.

MANDEL, MIKE Keyboards. Member of Larry Coryell's Eleventh House, 1975-76. Session for Larry Coryell. *Albums:* Sky Music (VAN 79409) 1978; Utopia Parkway (VAN 79437) 1980.

MANDEL, TOMMY Keyboards, vocal. Session for Ian Hunter (1980); Iron City Houserockers (1980); Hilly Michaels (1980).

MANFRED, JOHN Trombone. Session for Memphis Slim (1971).

MANFREDI, JERRY Bass. Member of the Pages, 1978-79.

MANGOLD, MARK Keyboards, vocal. Member of the American Tears, 1974-77, and Touch, 1980.

MANGONE, RICKY Drums, percussion, vocal. Member of Ursa Major, 1972.

MANGRUM, JIM "DANDY" Vocal. Born 3/30/48. Voice of Black Oak Arkansas, 1971-77.

MANHATTAN TRANSFER Alan Paul—vocal; Janis Siegel—vocal; Laurel Masse—vocal; Tim Hauser—vocal. Session for Dave Mason. *Albums:* Coming Out (ATC 18183) 1976; Extensions (ATC 19258); Junkin' (CAP ST-11405) 1971; Manhattan Transfer (ATC 18133) 1975; Pastiche (ATC 19163) 1978.

MANIERI, MIKE Vibes. Session for Paul Simon (1972).

MANILOW, BARRY Keyboards, vocal, writer. Writer-turned-performer with popular success. Session for Bette Midler (1973). *Albums:* Even Now (ARI 4164) 1978; Foul Play (ARI 9501); Greatest Hits (ARI 8601) 1978; Live (ARI 8500) 1977; Barry Manilow (ARI 4007) 1973; Barry Manilow (ARI 4016) 1974; One Voice (ARI 9505) 1980; This One's for You (ARI 4090) 1976; Tryin' to

Get the Feeling (ARI 4060) 1975.

MANION, EDDIE Baritone saxophone. Member of Southside Johnny and the Asbury Jukes.

MANISCALO, MIKE Keyboards, guitar. Member of Illusions, and Wiggy Bits.

MANITOBA, DICK Vocal. Member of the Dictators, 1977-78.

MANKEY, EARLE Guitar, producer. Member of Halfnelson, 1971, and Sparks, 1972. Produced the Pop (1979); 20/20 (1979); the Elevators (1980); Walter Egan (1980); and others.

MANKEY, JIM Bass, guitar. Member of Halfnelson, 1971, and Sparks, 1972.

MANLEY, COLIN Guitar, steel guitar. Session for George Harrison (1967).

MANN, BOB Guitar, keyboards. Member of Mountain, 1973.

MANN, BRIAN Keyboards. Session for the Vapour Trails (1980).

MANN, CHARLES Keyboards, vocal. Session for B. B. King (1973).

MANN, ED Percussion, vocal. Session for Frank Zappa (1979).

MANN, MANFRED Keyboards, producer. Born 10/21/40. Co-founder and namesake of Manfred Mann, 1963-present. Produced Lo and Behold (1972).

MANFRED MANN Manfred Mann—keyboards (1963-present); Mike Hugg—drums, percussion, vibes (1963-70); Michael D'abo—vocal (1963-66); Tom McGuinness—guitar (1963-66); Klaus Voorman—bass (1966); Mick Vickers—guitar, saxophone, flute, harmonica; Paul Jones—vocal (1963-66); Jack Bruce—bass; Bernie Living—saxophone, flute (1971); Craig Collinge—drums (1971); Mick Rogers—guitar, vocal (1972-75); Colin Pattenden—bass (1972-77); Chris Slade—drums, percussion (1972-78); Chris Thompson—vocal, guitar (1976-79); David Flett—guitar (1976-78); Geoff Britton—drums (1979); Steve Waller—guitar, vocal (1979); Pat King—bass (1979-80); John Lingwood—drums (1980). There were few alternatives to the Beatles' sound in 1964, but Manfred Mann's "Do Wah Diddy Diddy" was one. They developed a successful following in their native England and were constantly on the charts from 1964 through 1969 (including a movie sound track), ending with their version of Dylan's "Mighty Quinn." They dropped from sight shortly thereafter and emerged again in 1971 as Manfred Mann's Chapter Three, less pop-oriented with more jazz influences. Personnel changes were made in 1972, and the name was changed to Manfred Mann's Earth Band. *Albums:* Manfred Mann Chapter 3 (POL 24-4013) 1971; Manfred Mann Album, 1964; Five Faces of Manfred Mann, 1965; My Little Red Book of Winners, 1965; Mann Made, 1966; Manfred Mann's Greatest Hits, 1966; Up the Junction, 1967; Pretty Flamingo, 1966; Mighty Quinn, 1968; Angel Station (WBR K-3302) 1979; Best of Manfred Mann (CAP M-11688) 1977; Get Your Rocks Off (POL 5050) 1973; Glorified, Magnified (POL 5031) 1972; Good Earth (WBR B-2826); Manfred Mann's Earth Band (POL 5015) 1972; Nightingales and Bombers (WBR BK-3055) 1976; Solar Fire (POL 6019) 1973; Watch (WBR K-3157) 1978; Chance (WBR BSK 3498) 1980.

MANN, MONO Vocal, organ. Member of DMZ, 1978.

MANN, PAUL Vocal, bass. Member of Violinski, 1979.

MANN, STEVE Reeds. Member of the Marc Tanner Band since 1979.

MANN, STEVE Guitar, vocal, keyboards, percussion. Member of Liar, 1980.

MANNE, SHELLY Drums. Session for Frank Zappa (1967).

MANNING, TERRY Guitar, producer. Production and session for the Hot Dogs (1973).

MANNING, THOMAS Vocal, guitar, bass. Member of Mad River, 1968.

MANNINGS, LEO Drums. Original member of Savoy Brown, 1967.

MANOLIDES, JIM Percussion, vocal. Member of Junior Cadillac.

MANSEAU, MAURY Vocal, guitar, piano. Member of the Sunshine Company, 1967-69.

MANSFIELD, ALAN Guitar. Session for Robert Palmer (1980).

MANSFIELD, DARRELL Guitar, vocal. *Album:* Get Ready (POL 1-6288) 1980.

MANSFIELD, DAVID Violin, mandolin. Member of the Alpha Band, 1977. Session for Bob Dylan (1978-79).

MANSFIELD, DENNIS Drums. Session for Leon Russell (1976).

MANSFIELD, TONY Drums. Member of Billy J. Kramer and the Dakotas, 1963-66.

MANUEL, BOBBY Writer. Session for Leon Russell (1975).

MANUEL, RICHARD Vocal, keyboards. Born 4/3/43. Member of the Band, 1963-78.

MANUEL, VERNON Vocal. Session for Mylon LeFevre (1979).

MANUPUTI, RICHARD Vocal. Member of Growl, 1974.

MANZANERA, PHIL Guitar. Original member of Roxy, 1972-present, Mainstream, 1976, and Quiet Sun, 1975. Produced the Rockets (1980). Session for Nico (1974); Bryan Ferry (1974, 77); John Cale (1975). *Albums:* Diamond Head (ACO SD 36-113) 1975; 801 Live (POL 1-6148) 1976; K-Scope (POL 1-61787) 1979; Listen Now (POL 1-6147) 1977.

MANZAREK, RAY Keyboards, bass, vocal, writer. Born 2/22/55. Founding member of the Doors, who, after Jim Morrison's death in 1971, attempted to hold the group together through two mediocre albums before striking out on his own. Session and production for X (1980). *Albums:* The Golden Scarab (ELK); The Whole Thing Started with Rock 'n' Roll (ELK).

MARABUTO, RON Drums. Session for Country Joe McDonald (1975).

MARACLE, DON Guitar. Member of Duke Jupiter since 1978.

MARCANGELO, JOHN Keyboards. Member of Violinski, 1979.

MARCELLI, JOHN Bass. Member of Bad Boy.

MARCELLINO, DENNIS Tenor saxophone. Member of Rubicon, 1978-79. Session for Elvin Bishop (1972); Mike Bloomfield (1978).

MARCELLINO, GENE Vocal, bass. Member of Halloween, 1979.

MARCELLINO, JOHN Drums. Original member of Sha Na Na, since 1970.

MARCELLINO, MARK Keyboards. Member of Captain Beefheart and His Magic Band, 1974-75.

MARCELS Recorded "Blue Moon," 1961.

MARCHELLO, MICKY Guitar, vocal. Member of the Good Rats since 1978.

MARCHELLO, PEPPI Vocal. Member of the Good Rats since 1978.

MARCHESI, LEX Guitar, vocal. Member of Fotomaker, 1978-79.

MARCONI, MIKE Vocal, guitar. Member of the Billion Dollar Babies, 1977.

MARCOVITZ, DIANA Vocal, keyboards. *Album:* Horse of a Different Feather (COL KC 33063) 1974.

MARCUS HOOK ROLL BAND Harry Vanda—guitar, vocal; George Young—guitar, vocal. Formed from Haffy's Whiskey Sour, they lasted from 1973 to 1974 before evolving into Flash and the Pan. *Album:* Marcus Hook Roll Band (CAP SM 11991) 1973.

MARCUS, FLOYD Vocal, drums. Member of the 1910 Fruitgum Company, 1968-69.

MARCY, BOB Reeds, vocal. Member of Bighorn, 1978.

MARDIN, ARIF Arranger, producer, engineer. Worked with the Bee Gees (1975); the Rolling Stones (1976); Barry Goldberg (1974); the James Gang (1975); Jackie DeShannon (1972); Tony Joe White (1972); Roy Buchanan (1976); Willie Nelson (1973); Andy Pratt (1976-77); and others.

MARDONES, BENNY Vocal. *Albums:* Never Run Never Hide (POL 1-6263) 1980; Thank God for Girls (PST 7007) 1978.

MARGE, GEORGE Oboe, piccolo, bass, clarinet. Session for Airto (1971); Steely Dan (1980).

MARGEN, DAVE Bass. Member of Santana, 1977-present.

MARGOLIN, BOB Session for Muddy Waters (1978).

MARGOLIN, STUART Vocal. *Album:* And the Angel Sings (WBR K-3439) 1980.

MARGOLIS, SAMMY Clarinet. Session for Martin Mull (1974).

MARIAH Len Fogerty—guitar, vocal; Ed Burek—bass; Mark Ayers—keyboards; Wayne di Varco—drums; Frank Sullivan—guitar, vocal. *Album:* Mariah (UAR) 1976.

MARIER, DONN Vocal. Member of Citizen, 1980.

MARIMBA, ED Drums, percussion. Member of Captain Beefheart and His Magic Band, 1972.

MARINELLI, GEORGE, JR. Guitar. Member of Bobbidazzler, 1977, Osamu, 1977, and Photoglo, 1980.

MARINELLI, MICHAEL Drums. Session with Jerry Garcia and Howard Wales (1972).

MARINI, LOU Horns. Session for Lou Reed (1974); Randle Bramblett (1975); Henry Gross (1978); Magnet (1979); the Blues Brothers (1978-80).

MARINO, FRANK Guitar, bass, moog, mellotron, vocal, writer, producer. Founder and leader of Mahogany Rush, 1974-present.

MARINO, MICHAEL Bass, vocal. Member of Banchee, 1969.

MARINO, VINCE Guitar. Session for Mahogany Rush (1979).

MARINOS, JIMMY Member of the Romantics, 1980.

MARK AND CLARK BAND Mark Seymour—piano, vocal; Clark Seymour—piano, vocal; Scott Seymour—electronic keyboards. *Album:* Double Take (COL PC 34498) 1977.

MARK, DOUG Guitar, violin, vocal. Member of the Sunshine Company, 1967-69.

MARK, JON Guitar, vocal, writer. First became publicly known on John Mayall's "Turning Point" (1969), though he had backed Marianne Faithfull, 1965-66. A member of Sweet Thursday, 1970. With Johnny Almond, he formed Mark-Almond, 1970-73, 1976, a progressive rock-jazz combo. Session for John Mayall (1977). *Album:* Songs for a Friend (COL) 1974.

MARK-ALMOND Jon Mark—vocal, guitar; Johnny Almond—saxophone, flute, percussion, vocal; Roger Sutton—bass, vocal, cello, percussion (1970-71); Dannie Richmond—drums, percussion, vocal; Tommy Eyre—keyboards, flute, guitar, vocal (1971); Ken Craddock—keyboards, guitar, percussion, vocal (1972); Colin Gibson—bass, vocal (1972); Geoff Condon—horns, saxophone, flute, oboe, percussion (1972); Alun Davies—guitar, vocal, percussion (1973); Wolfgang Melz—bass, percussion (1973); Bobby Torres—percussion (1973). The dynamic "Turning Point" album by John Mayall in 1969 finally brought the due publicity to Mark and Almond, professional sidemen for years. They banded together in 1970 to pursue their unique guitar-reed alternating leads. Not aiming at commercialism, their sound was jazz-oriented and constantly changing through the years together. *Albums:* Mark-Almond II (BTH 32) 1971; Rising (COL C-31917) 1972; Mark-Almond 73 (COL KC 32486) 1973; Best of Mark-Almond (MCA 50) 1974; To the Heart (MCA D-945) 1976; Other Peoples' Rooms (AAM 730) 1978; Mark-Almond (BTH 8827) 1970.

MARKASKY, GARY Guitar. Member of the Michael Stanley Band since 1978.

MARKEE, DAVE Bass. Member of Centipede, 1971, and Lazy Racer since 1979. Session for Alan Price (1973); "Rough Mix" (1977); Eric Clapton (1980); the Who (1980).

MARKER, GARY Bass. Member of Rainbow Red Oxidizer, 1980.

MARKETTS Ben Benay—guitar; Mike Henderson—saxophone; Ray Pohlman—bass; Gene Pello—drums; Tom Hensley—piano; Richard Hobriaca—keyboards. *Album:* AM, FM, ETC. (MER) 1973.

MARKOWITZ, ROY Drums. Session for Free Creek (1973).

MARKS, LARRY Producer. Produced Lee Michaels, 1968.

MARKSMEN Early name of the Ventures.

MARLEY, BOB Vocal, guitar, percussion. Born 2/6/45. Leader of the Wailers. Died 5/11/81, of brain cancer.

BOB MARLEY AND THE WAILERS Bob Marley—vocal, guitar, percussion; Aston Barrett—bass, guitar, percussion; Carlton Barrett—drums, percussion; Tyrone Downie—keyboards, bass, percussion, vocal; Alvin Patterson—percussion; Earl Smith—guitar, percussion; I Threes—vocal (see separate listing); Junior Marvin—guitar, vocal (1978-80); Earl Lindo—keyboards (1980); Al Anderson—guitar (1980). Reggae artists thrust to the top of the heap in 1975 after several years of neglect. *Albums:* Babylon by Bus (ISL 11); Birth of a Legend (CLL ZX-34759); Burnin' (ISL 9256) 1973; Catch a Fire (ISL 9241) 1973; Early Music (CLL ZX-34760); Exodus (ISL 9498) 1977; Kaya (ISL 9517) 1978; Live (ISL 9376) 1975; Natty Dread (ISL 9281) 1974; Rastaman Vibrations (ISL 9383) 1976; Survival (ISL 9542) 1979; This Is—Reggae Music (ISL 9251); Uprising (ISL 9596) 1980; African Herbsman; Rasta Revolution.

MARLEY, RITA Vocal. Member of I Threes.

MARNELL, BRIAN Guitar, vocal. Member of SVT, 1980.

MAROTTA, RICK Drums. Member of Ronin, 1980. Session for Paul Simon (1973); Randle Bramblett (1975); Steely Dan (1976, 80); Henry Gross (1977-78); Bryan Ferry (1978); Baby Grand (1978); the Euclid Beach Band (1979); Night (1979); Annette Peacock (1979); Jackson Browne (1980); Warren Zevon (1980); Boz Scaggs (1980).

MARQUES, JOE Bass, vocal. Member of Emperor, 1977.

MARQUEZ, SAL Trumpet, vocal, writer. Member of the Mothers of Invention, 1972-74. Session for Frank Zappa (1972, 74).

MARRANO, LANA Vocal. Member of Rosie, 1976-77.

MARRERO, NICK Percussion. Session for Ringo Starr (1977).

MARRERO, NICHOLAS Percussion. Session for Steely Dan (1980).

MARRIOTT, STEVE Guitar, vocal, writer, harmonica. After co-writing "Itchycoo Park" with Ronnie Lane, Marriott left the Small Faces (1967-68), to form Humble Pie with Peter Frampton. Shooting to fame in 1971, Marriott became the trademark of the group with his high-pitched yelling and dancing on stage, after Frampton had left the group to pursue his solo career. Marriott dissolved the Pie in 1976 to pursue his solo career, with a sound not unlike Humble Pie. He re-formed the Small Faces, 1977-78, and Humble Pie, 1980. Session for B. B. King (1971); Snape (1972); Donovan (1973). *Album:* Marriott (AAM 4572) 1976.

MARRON, BOBBY Vocal. Member of the Atlantics since 1979.

MARRON, GORDON Violin, vocal. Member of the United States of America, 1968. Session for Nilsson (1975).

MARRONE, RON Guitar, vocal. Member of Link, 1980.

MARS, HEIN Bass. Member of Alquin, 1975.

MARS, TOMMY Keyboards, vocal. Session for Frank Zappa (1979).

MARS BARS Early name for Gerry and the Pacemakers until 1959.

MARSDEN, BERNIE Guitar. Member of Babe Ruth, 1977, Paice, Ashton, Lord, 1977, and Whitesnake since 1978. Session for Chick Churchill (1974).

MARSDEN, FREDDY Drums. Born 10/23/40. With his brother Gerry, original member of Gerry and the Pacemakers, 1959-65.

MARSDEN, GERRY Vocal. Born 9/24/42. Founder and namesake of Gerry and the Pacemakers, 1959-65.

MARSEILLE Paul Dale—vocal; Neil Buchanan—guitar; Andy Charter—guitar; Steve Dinwoodie—bass; Keith Knowles—drums. *Album:* Marseille (RCA AFL 1-3631) 1980.

MARSH, HENRY Keyboards, vocal, guitar. Member of Gringo, 1971, and Sailor.

MARSH, IAN CRAIG Synthesizer, vocal. Member of the Human League, 1980.

MARSH, OSIRIS Vocal. Member of Osiris, 1978.

MARSH, PETER Vocal. Session for Manfred Mann (1980).

MARSH, PHIL Guitar. Session for Country Joe McDonald (1975).

MARSH, RANDALL Drums, vocal. Member of Code Blue, 1980.

MARSH, TONY Piano. Session for Kim Fowley,

1973.

MARSHALL, ALAN Vocal. Member of Zzebra, 1975.

MARSHALL, ALLAN Bass, vocal. Member of the Wireless, 1979.

MARSHALL, BILL Drums, vocal. Member of Larry Rasberry and the Highsteppers.

MARSHALL, BOB Bass. Member of the John Miles Band since 1975.

MARSHALL, ED Drums. Session for the Pointer Sisters (1973).

MARSHALL, JAMES W. Drums. Replaced Don Murray in the Charlie Daniels Band, 1979-80.

MARSHALL, JOHN Drums. Member of Blues Incorporated, Centipede, 1971, and the Soft Machine, 1973. Session for Jack Bruce (1969, 71); "Jesus Christ Superstar" (1970).

MARSHALL, PETER Bass. Session for Martin Mull (1978).

MARSHALL TUCKER BAND Tom Caldwell—bass, percussion, vocal, drums (1973-80); Toy Caldwell—guitar, steel guitar, writer (1973-80); George McCorkle—guitar, percussion; Paul Riddle—drums; Doug Gray—vocal, percussion; Jerry Eubanks—saxophone, flute, percussion, vocal. The fame of the Allman Brothers brought national attention to their native state, Georgia, and the Marshall Tucker Band was on the spot immediately. Blending southern rock with jazz and country, the Marshall Tucker Band has established an identity of their own. *Albums:* Marshall Tucker Band (CPN 0112) 1973; A New Life (CPN 0124) 1974; Where We All Belong (CPN C-0145) 1974; Searchin' for a Rainbow (CPN 0161) 1975; Long Hard Ride (CPN 0170) 1976; Carolina Dreams (CPN 0180) 1977; Greatest Hits (CPN 0214) 1978; Together Forever (CPN 0205) 1978; Running Like the Wind (WBR K-3317) 1979; Tenth (WBR HS-3410) 1980; Stompin' Room Only (CPN 0228).

MARTELL, VINCENT Guitar. Original member of the Vanilla Fudge, 1967-69.

MARTER, JOHN Drums, percussion. Member of Voyager, 1979-80.

MARTHA AND THE MUFFINS Clark Finkle—bass; Mark Gane—guitar, synthesizer; Tim Gane—drums; Andy Haas—saxophone; Martha Johnson—vocal, keyboards; Martha Ladly—vocal, keyboards, trombone. *Album:* Metro Music (VIR 13145) 1980.

MARTHA AND THE VANDELLAS Martha Reeves—vocal; Rosalind Ashford—vocal; Betty Kelly—vocal (1962-65); Lois Reeves—vocal (1965). The Cinderella of Motown, Martha began as a secretary of that company before filling in at a recording session. From then on, it was stardom, beginning with "Heat Wave" (1963). *Albums:* Anthology (MTN M7-778); Come and Get These Memories, 1963; Heat Wave, 1963; Dance Party, 1965; Greatest Hits, 1966; Watch Out, 1966; Martha and the Vandellas Live, 1967; Ridin' High, 1968.

MARTIN, ALLAN Vocal. Session for Johnny Winter (1980).

MARTIN, CHARLIE Drums, percussion, vocal. Original member of the Silver Bullet Band, 1974-77.

MARTIN, CHIP Rhythm guitar. Session for Harvey Mandel.

MARTIN, DAVID "DEEZAL" Guitar. Member of No Dice, 1978-79.

MARTIN, DEWEY Drums, vocal, writer. Original member of Buffalo Springfield, 1966-68. When the group dissolved, he organized Dewey Martin's Medicine Ball, which despite Springfield's popularity, remained virtually unknown.

MARTIN, DINO, JR. Guitar. Original member of Dino, Desi and Billy, 1966-68.

MARTIN, DON Bass, vocal. Member of Mi-Sex, 1980.

MARTIN, GEORGE Producer. Producer of the Beatles from the beginnings of Beatlemania (1962), to the group's demise in 1970. Session and production for Jimmy Webb (1977). Also worked with Jeff Beck (1971-76); Gerry and the Pacemakers (1962); Billy J. Kramer and the Dakotas (1963-66); America (1971-79); Gary Brooker (1979); Cheap Trick (1980); and others.

MARTIN, GORDON Bass. Replaced Jim Mankey in Sparks, 1973-74.

MARTIN, GRADY Guitar. Session for Leon Russell (1973); J. J. Cale (1974).

MARTIN, JERRY Saxophone. Session for Mike Bloomfield (1978).

MARTIN, KEITH Tenor trombone. Session for Savoy Brown (1969).

MARTIN, LOU Keyboards. Session for Rory Gallagher (1974-75).

MARTIN, MEL Flute. Original member of the Sir Douglas Quartet, 1965-68. Session for Boz Scaggs (1972); Santana (1974).

MARTIN, MOON Guitar, vocal. Writer-turned-performer, backed by the Ravens. *Albums:* Escape from Domination (CAP ST-11933) 1979; Shots from a Cold Nightmare, 1978; Street Fever (CAP ST 12099) 1980.

MARTIN, PAT Bass, mandolin, vocal. Member of Unicorn, 1974-77.

MARTIN, PETER Guitar. Member of S.C.R.A., 1972.

MARTIN, RICCI Piano, vocal. *Album:* Beached (EPC PE 34834) 1977.

MARTIN, ROBERT Bass. Member of Curved Air.

MARTIN, ROY Vocal. Session for the Iron City Houserockers (1980).

MARTIN, SEAN Member of Starjets, 1980.

MARTIN, STEVE Vocal. Member of the Left Banke, 1967.

MARTIN, STEVE Comedian, banjo. Besides being

an excellent banjo player, Martin recorded "Let's Get Small," the first comedy album ever to go platinum (1 million sales). *Albums:* Let's Get Small (WBR K-3090) 1977; Wild and Crazy Guy (WBR HS-3238) 1978; Comedy Is Not Pretty (WBR HS-3392) 1979.

MARTINEZ, ANTONIO Guitar. Member of Los Bravos, 1966-68.

MARTINEZ, JOHNNY Bass, vocal. Member of Ruben and the Jets, 1973.

MARTINEZ, JOEL Drums. Member of the Pop, 1977-80.

MARTINEZ, PAUL Bass. Member of Paice, Ashton, Lord, 1977. Session for Cat Stevens (1974).

MARTINEZ, RAY Vocal, guitar, keyboards, horns. Member of Airwaves, 1978-79.

MARTINI, JERRY Saxophone, flute, piano, clarinet, accordion, percussion. Member of Sly and the Family Stone, and Rubicon, 1978-79.

MARTINS, J. P. Bass, guitar. Member of Elton Motello, 1980.

MARTYN, JOHN Guitar, vocal. Soloist and associate of Nick Drake. *Albums:* One World (ISL 9492); So Far So Good (ISL 9484).

MARTYNEC, GENE Guitar, moog, keyboards. Member of Kensington Market, 1968-69, and the Silver Tractors, 1976-77. Session for Gordon Lightfoot (1974, 76); Lou Reed (1973).

MARVELETTES Wanda Rogers—vocal; Katherin Schaffner—vocal; Gladys Horton—vocal; Ann Bogan—vocal. Vocal trio that led Motown to the top of the soul industry with "Don't Mess with Bill" and "Please Mr. Postman" (1961). *Albums:* Please Mr. Postman, 1961; Marvelous Marvelettes, 1963; Live on Stage, 1963; Marvelettes Sing, 1963; Playboy, 1963; Marvelettes Greatest Hits, 1966; Marvelettes, 1967; Sophisticated Soul, 1968; Anthology (MTN M7-827).

BRETT MARVIN AND THE THUNDERBOLTS Pete Gibson—vocal, trombone; Graham Hines—vocal, guitar; Jim Pitts—vocal, piano, mandolin; John Randall—percussion; Keith Truffell—percussion. Part of the British blues invasion of the late 1960s that did not make it to the United States.

MARVIN, HANK Guitar. Session for Wings (1979).

MARVIN, JUNIOR Guitar. Member of Bob Marley's Wailers, 1978-80. Session for Kevin Lamb (1978).

MARZULLA, FRED Trombone. Member of Mom's Apple Pie, 1973.

MAS, CAROLYNE Vocal, guitar, piano. *Albums:* Hold On (MER SRM-1-3841) 1980; Carolyne Mas (MER SRM-1-3783) 1979.

MASBIR, MICK Guitar. Session for Alice Cooper (1973).

MASCARA SNAKE Bass clarinet, vocal. Member of Captain Beefheart and His Magic Band, 1969-72.

MASCARO, DEBBIE Guitar. Member of Chichlids, 1980.

MASKED MARAUDERS Canadian group that appeared in the late 1960s. They received exceptional publicity due to the rumors that the group was a jam, including Bob Dylan and other great names. The sound was faintly similar to the rumors, but not to be mistaken for the originals. *Album:* The Masked Marauders (DTY 6378).

MASLIN, HARRY Percussion. Session for the Nervous Eaters (1980).

MASON, BOB Drums. Member of the Fugs, 1968.

MASON, BOBBY Guitar. Member of Starwood, 1976-77.

MASON, BONNIE JO Early recording name for Cher.

MASON, DAVE Guitar, vocal, writer. Born 5/10/45. Soloing after a stormy relationship with Traffic was no easy step, but Mason accomplished it with hard work and talent. Session with Delaney and Bonnie; Jim Capaldi (1971); George Harrison (1972); Wings (1975); Steve Stills (1978); Ron Wood (1979). *Albums:* Alone Together (MCA 19) 1970; Dave Mason Is Alive (MCA 54) 1971; Headkeeper (MCA 34) 1971; Dave Mason at His Very Best (MCA TD-880) 1972; Best of Dave Mason (MCA 6013) 1972; It's Like You Never Left (COL PC 31721) 1973; Dave Mason (COL PC 33096) 1974; Split Coconut (COL PC 33698) 1975; Certified Live (COL PG 34174) 1976; Let It Flow (COL PC 34680) 1977; Mariposa De Oro (COL JC 35285) 1978; Old Crest on a New Wave (COL JC 36144) 1980; Very Best of Dave Mason (MCA 6032).

MASON, DAVID Keyboards. Session for Joe Walsh (1976).

MASON, DAVID Vocal. Member of the Reels, 1980.

MASON, HARVEY Drums. Session for Martin Mull (1973); Seals and Crofts (1973); Phoebe Snow (1976); Lee Ritenour (1977); Jimmy Webb (1977); Gary Wright (1979); Santana (1980). *Albums:* Earthmover (ARI 4986); Funk in a Mason Jar (ARI 4157); Groovin' You (ARI 4227) 1979; Marching in the Street (ARI 4054).

MASON, LEE Drums, percussion. Member of Bagatelle, 1968.

MASON, LOL Vocal, percussion. Member of City Boy, 1976-present.

MASON, NICK Drums, percussion. Original member of Pink Floyd, since 1967.

MASON, ROBERT Synthesizer. Founder of Stardrive, 1974.

MASON, RON Keyboards, percussion. Member of Kenny and the Kasuals.

MASON, ROSS Bass. Session for Elvin Bishop (1975).

MASSE, LAUREL Vocal. Member of Manhattan Transfer since 1971.

MASSEURS, AD Drums. Member of the Tumbleweeds, 1975.

MASSEURS, BARRY Guitar. Member of the Tumbleweeds, 1975.

MASSEURS, INE Vocal. Voice of the Tumbleweeds, 1975.

MASSEURS, TON Guitar, pedal steel guitar. Member of the Tumbleweeds, 1975.

MASSEY, BARBARA Vocal. Worked on the posthumous Hendrix album "Crash Landing" (1975). Session for Johnny Winter (1973).

MASSEY, CURTIS Saxophone. Member of El Roachos, 1973.

MASTERS, BARRIE Vocal. Member of Eddie and the Hot Rods since 1976.

MASTERS, VANCE Vocal, drums. Member of the Guess Who, 1979.

MASTOS, NICK Member of Bill Haley and the Comets.

MASTRANGELO, CARLO Drums. Original member of Dion and the Belmonts.

MASTRO, JIM Guitar. Session for Richard Lloyd (1979).

MASUAK, CHRIS Guitar, piano. Member of Radio Birdman, 1978.

MATA, LIBERTY Percussion. Member of Isis, 1974-75.

MATARE, VITAS Keyboards, flute. Member of the Last, 1979.

MATCHBOX Graham Fenton—vocal; Steve Bloomfield—guitar, mandolin, harmonica, vocal; Fred Poke—bass, vocal; Gordon Scott—guitar, vocal; Jimmie Redhead—drums, percussion, vocal. *Album:* Rockabilly Rebel (SIR SRK 6087) 1979.

MATCHING MOLE David Sinclair—keyboards; Phil Miller—guitar; Robert Wyatt—drums, keyboards; Bill MacCormick—bass. *Album:* Matching Mole (COL).

MATHER, BILL Bass. Member of the James Montgomery Band, 1976.

MATHESON, BRANDON Drums, vocal. Member of the Rubber City Rebels, 1980.

MATHEWS, RICHARD Keyboards, synthesizer. Member of Hiroshima, 1980.

MATHEWS, SCOTT Member of the Durocs, 1979.

MATLOCK, GLEN Bass. Member of the Sex Pistols, 1976. Session for Iggy Pop (1980).

MATSUMOTO, SHIGERU Bass. Original member of Creation, 1976.

MATSUMURA, DANE Bass. Member of Hiroshima, 1980.

MATTACKS, DAVE Drums, percussion. Member of Fairport Convention until 1976, and Prelude, 1976. Session for the Sutherland Brothers (1973); Gay and Terry Woods (1976); the Babys (1978); Richard and Linda Thompson (1978); Red Noise (1979); Gary Brooker (1979); Matthew Fisher (1980); the Who (1980); Chris Spedding (1980); Peter Green (1980).

MATTHEW'S SOUTHERN COMFORT Gordon Huntley—pedal steel guitar; Mark Griffiths—guitar; Carl Barnwell—guitar; Roy Duffy—drums; Andy Leigh—bass; Ian Matthews—vocal. *Albums:* Southern Comfort; Frog City; Stir Don't Shake; Second Spring; Later that Same Year.

MATTHEWS, IAN Vocal, guitar. Namesake of Matthew's Southern Comfort, and soloist. Member of Hi-Fi, 1980. *Albums:* Go for Broke (COL PC-34102) 1976; Some Days You Eat the Bear (ELK 75078) 1974; Stealin' Home (MSH 5012) 1978; Valley Hi (ELK 75061) 1973; Spot of Interference (RSO 1-3092) 1980.

MATTHEWS, MYRNA Vocal. Session for the Richie Furay Band (1976); Seals and Crofts (1976); Christopher Cross (1980).

MATTHEWS, PAULINE Real name of Kiki Dee.

MATTHEWS, SCOTT Drums. Replaced Don Baldwin in the Elvin Bishop Band, 1978-79. Session for Rocky Sullivan (1978).

MATTHEWS, SHERLIE Vocal. Member of the Nightengales, 1977, and the Orioles, 1977. Session for John Kay (1973); B. B. King (1970); Navasota (1972); Seals and Crofts (1976); Neil Young (1969); Elton John (1974); Shuggie Otis (1971); Steely Dan (1972, 76); Joe Cocker (1974); Grin (1973); Elvin Bishop (1972); Gene Clark (1974); Rita Coolidge (1972); Country Joe McDonald (1975); Great Southern (1978); Bob Seger (1978); Gary Wright (1979); Nazareth (1980).

MATTHEWS, STANLEY Mandolin. Session for Rod Stewart (1971).

MATUTE, RAUL Piano, organ. Member of Cold Blood.

MAU, MICHAEL Drums. Original member of Stoneground, 1971.

MAUNN, PETER Guitar, keyboards, violin. Member of Group 87, 1980.

MAURITZ, BARBARA Vocal, writer. Half of the Lamb duet, 1971-72.

MAUS, JOHN Guitar, vocal. Member of the Walker Brothers, 1966-67.

MAVETY, JO Session for Marianne Faithfull (1979).

MAVLOIN, JOE B. Bass. Member of Buddy Holly's backup band, 1957-58.

MAX DEMIAN BAND Paul Rose—guitar, vocal; Jim LeFevre—keyboards, guitar, vocal; Dan Howe—keyboards, vocal; Kirt Pennebaker—bass, vocal; Fofi Lancha—drums, percussion. *Albums:* Call of the Wild (VIC AFLI 3525) 1980; Take It to the Max (VIC AFLI-3273) 1979.

MAXFIELD, LOUIE Guitar. Member of the Low Numbers, 1977-78, the Ravers, and the Wedge, 1980.

MAXFIELD, MIKE Guitar. Member of Billy J. Kramer and the Dakotas, 1963-66.

MAXWELL, DURIS Drums, keyboards. Member of Doucette, 1979.

MAXWELL, MARK Trombone. Member of the Band of Thieves, 1976.

MAXWELL, MICHAEL Bass. Member of the Panic Squad, 1980.

MAY, BRIAN Guitar, vocal, piano. Born 7/19/47. Original member of Queen, since 1973. Session for Ian Hunter (1976).

MAY, PHIL Vocal. Member of the Pretty Things.

MAY, TIM Guitar. Session for Martin Mull (1979).

MAYALL, JOHN Guitar, harmonica, keyboards, vocal, writer, producer. Born 11/29/43. The success of the blues invasion in the United States in the mid-1960s is due almost entirely to Mayall. He had been playing the blues in the Powerhouse Four and Blues Syndicate, before he formed the Bluesbreakers with Eric Clapton. Clapton left in 1967 to become famous with Cream, and was replaced by Peter Green, who in turn left that same year to form Fleetwood Mac. Undaunted, Mayall continued piecing together bands with such names as John McVie, Aynsley Dunbar, Keef Hartley, Mick Taylor, Dick Heckstall-Smith, Chris Mercer, and others. In 1969, he made a temporary split from his electric style, playing acoustic jazz-blues with Jon Mark and Johnny Almond without a drummer. The new sound was unexpected, but pleasant, which led to more experimentation, with Larry Taylor and Harvey Mandel (both from Canned Heat) and Don "Sugarcane" Harris on violin. In 1972, he made yet another shift to an all-black band, synthesizing his blues roots and jazz experimentation, with Blue Mitchell, Freddy Robinson, Ernie Watts, and Clifford Solomon. 1974 saw another change, this time with female vocalist Dee McKinney. Throughout his career, his "students" have returned to play with Mayall, many after carving their own reputations in the field of rock music. Popular music and blues owe no small debt to the "Father of English Blues." Produced Aynsley Dunbar's Retaliation (1970). Session for Sonny Terry and Brownie McGee (1973); Rod Stewart (1977). *Albums:* Down the Line (LON BP 618/9) 1964; Empty Rooms (POL 4010) 1971; Jazz-Blues Fusion (POL 5027) 1972; Live in Europe (LON PS 589) 1968; Memories (POL 5012) 1971; Moving On (POL 5036) 1972; New Year, New Band, New Company (BTM D-6019); Thru the Years (LON 2PS 600-1); Bare Wire (LON PS-537) 1968; Best of John Mayall (POL 2-3006); Blues Alone (LON PS-534) 1968; Blues from Laurel Canyon (LON PS-545) 1969; Bottom Line (DJM 23) 1979; Crusade (LON PS-529) 1968; Hard Core Package (MCA 1039) 1978; Hard Road (LON PS-502) 1967; Looking Back (LON PS-562) 1969; No More Interviews (DJM 29) 1979; Turning Point (POL 4004) 1969; Notice to Appear (ABC 926) 1976; Banquet in Blue (ABC) 1977; Lots of People (ABC) 1977; Back to the Roots (POL 3002) 1970; Blues Breakers (LON PS 570) 1967; Latest Edition (POL 6030); 10 Years Are Gone (POL 2-3050); USA Union (POL 4022) 1970; Last of the British Blues (MCA 1086) 1978; Live in Europe, Vol. 1 and Vol. 2 (LON) 1969.

JOHN MAYALL GROUPS John Mayall—vocal, guitar, keyboards, bass, moog, harmonica, writer; Jon Mark—guitar (1969); Steve Thompson—bass (1969); Johnny Almond—saxophone, flute (1969); Larry Taylor—bass (1969); Don "Sugarcane" Harris—violin (1970, 73, 75); Harvey Mandel—guitar (1970); Jerry McGee—guitar (1970); Blue Mitchell—trumpet (1972); Clifford Solomon—saxophone (1972); Ron Selico—bass (1972); Freddy Robinson—guitar (1972); Victor Gaskin—bass (1972); Fred Jackson—saxophone (1972); Ernie Watts—tenor saxophone (1972); Red Holloway—saxophone, flute (1973-74); Soko Richardson—drums (1974); Rick Vito—guitar (1974); Randy Resnick—guitar (1974); Hightide Harris—guitar (1974); Jay Spell—keyboards (1975); Dee McKinnie—vocal (1975). Though there is no "John Mayall Group" *per se,* this is to recount some of the different bands he has formed. See John Mayall, and John Mayall's Bluesbreakers.

JOHN MAYALL'S BLUESBREAKERS John Mayall—vocal, guitar, keyboards, writer; Eric Clapton—vocal, guitar (1966-67); John McVie—bass (1966-68); Hughie Flint—drums (1966-67); Aynsley Dunbar—drums (1967); Mick Taylor—guitar (1967); Keef Hartley—drums (1967-68); Chris Mercer—saxophone (1967); Rip Kent—saxophone (1967); Dick Heckstall-Smith—saxophone (1968); Jon Hiseman—drums (1968); Henry Lowther—coronet, violin (1968); Tony Reeves—bass (1968); Colin Allen—drums (1969); Stephen Thompson—bass (1969). See John Mayall.

MAYBRAY, BILLY Bass, drum, vocal. Member of the Jaggerz.

MAYES, FRANK Tenor saxophone. Session for Delaney and Bonnie (1970).

MAYFIELD, CURTIS Vocal, piano. Original member of the Impressions. *Albums:* Back to the World (CTM 8015) 1973; Curtis (CTM 8005); Curtis in Chicago (CTM 8018) 1973; Curtis Live (CTM 8008); Got to Find a Way (CTM 8604) 1974; His Early Years with the Impressions (ABC X-780); Super Fly (CTM 8014); There's No Place Like America Today, 1975; America Today (CTM 5001); Do It All Night (CTM K-5022) 1978; Give, Get, Take and Have (CTM 5007) 1976; Heartbeat (RSO 1-3053) 1979; Let's Do It Again (CTM 5005); Never Say You Can't Survive (CTM 5013); Short Eyes (CTM 5017); Something to Believe In (RSO 1-3077) 1980; Roots (CTM 8000); Save the Children (MTN M7-800); Sweet Exorcist (CTM 8601) 1974; Right Combination (RSO 1-3084) 1980; Got to Find a Way (BUD 8604) 1974.

MAYHEW, MICHAEL Guitar, writer. Member of Hapshash and the Coloured Coat.

MAYO, BOB Guitar, keyboards, vocal. Session for Peter Frampton (1976-present).

MAYORGA, LINCOLN Keyboards. Session for Doug Kershaw; Frank Zappa (1967); Ringo Starr (1974). *Album:* Lincoln Mayorga, Vol. 3 (SLB LAB-1).

MAYS, BILL Keyboards. Session for Dick St. Nicklaus (1979).

MAYS, WARREN Guitar, vocal. Member of Gambler since 1979.

MAZALAN, LARRY Bass, vocal. Member of Skafish, 1980.

MAZEY, KENT Bass, vocal. Member of the Link, 1980.

MAZEY, KEVIN Keyboards, synthesizer, vocal. Member of the Link, 1980.

MAZUR, BERNADETTE Vocal. Session for Johnny Winter (1980).

MAZUR, KENNY Guitar. Session for Robert Palmer (1980).

MAZZOCHI, DAVE Keyboards, vocal. Member of Mom's Apple Pie, 1973.

MC 5 Rob Tyner—vocal, saxophone; Fred Smith—guitar; Michael Davis—bass; Dennis Thompson—drums; Wayne Kramer—guitar. Heavy duty rockers from the Motor City, whose energy was matched only by their volume, and occasional off-color lyrics. *Album:* MC 5 (ELK) 1969; Back in the USA (ELK).

McALLISTER, JAMES Guitar. Member of Mitch Rider's Detroit Wheels. Session for Hilly Michaels (1980).

McALLISTER, LAURIE Bass, vocal. Member of the Orchids, 1980.

McALLISTER, MAYO JAMES Member of the Beckies, 1976.

McANALLY, MAC Guitar. Session for Roy Orbison (1979). *Albums:* Cuttin' Corners (VIC AFLI 3519) 1980; Mac McAnally (ARA 50019) 1977; No Problem Here (ARA SW-50029) 1978.

McANDREW, SNAKE Drums. Member of Linn County, 1968-69.

McARDLE, GEORGE Bass. Member of the Little River Band since 1977.

McAULEY, JOHN Drums, harmonica, piano. Original member of Them.

McAULIFF, VIVIAN Vocal. Session for Gerry Rafferty (1978, 80).

McAVOY, GERRY Bass. Session for Rory Gallagher (1971-present).

McBRIDE, BARRY Bass, vocal. Member of the Plugz, 1979.

McBRIDE, DANNY Drums. Member of Growl, 1974.

McBRIDE, MICHAEL Drums. Member of the Raspberries, 1972-74.

McBRIDE, REGGIE Bass. Member of Rare Earth, 1975-77, and Joy, 1977. Session for Phoebe Snow (1976); Steve Hillage (1977); Tim Weisberg (1977); John Palumbo (1978); Ry Cooder (1980).

McBRIDE, RICHIE Bass. Member of Hammer, 1970. Session for Elton John (1980).

McBURNIE, JOHN Vocal, guitar, keyboards. Member of Jackson Heights, 1974, and Vapour Trails, 1980. Session for Gerry Rafferty (1978).

McCABE, BRUCE Keyboards. Member of the Lamont Cranston Band, 1977.

McCAFFERTY, DAN Vocal, writer. Lead singer for Nazareth since 1972. *Album:* Dan McCafferty (AAM 4553) 1975.

McCALL, MARTI Vocal. Session for Sonny Terry and Brownie McGhee (1973); the Babys (1979); Christopher Cross (1980).

McCANN, JERRY Vocal, guitar, flute. Member of the Show of Hands, 1970.

McCANN, PETER Vocal, keyboards. *Album:* Peter McCann (TWC 544) 1979.

McCARL, SCOTT Guitar, bass, vocal. Member of the Raspberries, 1972-74, and Glider, 1977.

McCARTHY, JOHN Vocal. Session for Donovan (1973).

McCARTHY, KEVIN Guitar. Member of Tranquility, 1972.

McCARTNEY, JAMES PAUL Keyboards, vocal, bass, guitar, drums, writer, producer. Born 6/18/42. With partner John Lennon, with whom he had been writing since 1956, he began playing publicly in the Quarrymen, before picking up George Harrison in 1958. After several personnel changes, they adopted Ringo Starr in 1961, and became the Beatles. After the Beatles made history and disbanded, he continued as a soloist and then organized Wings, 1971-present, the closest sound to the Beatles since the legend's demise. See Wings. Session for Carly Simon (1972); Ringo Starr (1973); Denny Laine (1977). *Albums:* McCartney (COL JC-36478) 1970; McCartney 2 (COL FC 36511) 1980.

McCARTNEY, LINDA Piano, vocal, percussion, writer. Wife of Beatle Paul, and member of Wings, 1971-present. Session for Paul McCartney (1970); Carly Simon (1973); Ringo Starr (1973); Denny Laine (1977).

PAUL AND LINDA McCARTNEY Paul McCartney—keyboards, bass, guitar, vocal, drums, producer; Linda McCartney—piano, vocal, percussion. Joint venture of McCartney and his wife before forming Wings. *Album:* Ram (COL JC-36479) 1971.

McCARTHY, CHARLES, JR. Saxophone. Session for Taj Mahal (1978).

McCARTY, JIM Drums, percussion. Born 7/25/43. Original member of the Yardbirds, 1962-69, Renaissance, 1969-72, and Illusions, 1977.

McCARTY, JIM Vocal, keyboards, guitar. Member of Mitch Rider's Detroit Wheels, the Buddy Miles

Express, 1968-69, Cactus, 1970-72, Shoot, 1973, and the Rockets, 1977-present. Session for Jimi Hendrix (1969); Bob Seger (1974).

McCASLIN, MARY Vocal, guitar. *Albums:* Sunny California (MER SRM-1-3772) 1979; Old Friends (PHL 1046) 1977; Way Out West (PHL 1011) 1973; Prairie in the Sky (PHL 1024) 1975; The Bramble and the Rose (PHL 1055) 1978.

McCAULEY, MAVIS Vocal. Session for Ironhorse (1979).

McCLAIN, MARLON Guitar. Session for Taxxi (1980).

McCLAIN, VAN Vocal, guitar. Member of Shooting Star, 1979.

McCLAIN, WILLIAM Vocal. Member of the Cleftones.

McCLARTY, JIM Drums, percussion. Member of 707, 1980.

McCLELLAND, BILLY EARL Guitar. Member of the Rock Killough Group, 1980.

McCLENNAN, TOMMY Vocal, guitar. Chicago-based blues singer and guitarist whose recording career ran from 1939 until his death in 1942.

McCLURE, JOHN Keyboards. Member of Calico, 1975-76.

McCLURE, MATTHEW Drums. Member of Scargill, 1979.

McCLURE, PATRICK Guitar, vocal. Member of the Bones, 1973.

McCLURE, RON Bass. Replaced Jim Fielder in the re-formed Blood, Sweat and Tears. Session for the Pointer Sisters (1973).

McCLURE, SCOTT Bass. Member of Rich Mountain Tower, 1976.

McCLURE, TOMMY Bass. Session for Rita Coolidge (1972).

McCOLLUM, MICHAEL Guitar, vocal. Member of Scargill, 1979.

McCOO, MARILYN Vocal. Member of the Fifth Dimension and half of the McCoo/Davis duet.

MARILYN McCOO AND BILLY DAVIS, JR. Marilyn McCoo—vocal; Billy Davis, Jr.—vocal. Duet split from the Fifth Dimension. *Albums:* Marilyn and Billy (COL JC 35603).

McCORD, STEVE Guitar. Session for Tom Rapp (1972).

McCORKLE, GEORGE Guitar, percussion. Original member of the Marshall Tucker Band, 1973-present.

McCORKLE, LEWIS Drums. Member of Granmax, 1976.

McCORKLE, TIM Bass, vocal. Member of Granmax, 1976.

McCORMICK, BILL Bass, vocal. Member of Quiet Sun, 1975, and Mainstream, 1976. Session for Phil Manzanera (1975).

McCORMICK, GAYLE Vocal. Voice of Smith. *Album:* One More Hour (FSY).

McCORMICK, RANDY Keyboards. Member of the Muscle Shoals Rhythm Section, 1980. Session for Joe Cocker (1978); Watson-Beasley (1980).

McCOY, CHARLIE Guitar, dobro, vibes, keyboards, harmonica, vocal. Session for Tom Rapp (1972); Pearls Before Swine (1970); Waylon Jennings (1973, 75); Bob Seger (1974); Bob Dylan (1973); Doug Kershaw (1972); Leon Russell (1973); Paul Simon (1972); J. J. Cale (1972); Steve Miller (1970); Ringo Starr (1971). *Albums:* Christmas (MNT 2X-33176); Appalachian Fever (MNT MG-7632); Charlie My Boy (MNT MC-6628); Country Cookin' (MNT MG-7612); Fastest Harp in the South (MNT MC-6626); Good Time Charlie (MNT MC-6625); Harpin' the Blues (MNT 6629); Charlie McCoy (MNT MC-6624); Charlie McCoy's Christmas (MNT MG-7622); Charlie McCoy's Greatest Hits (MNT MG-7622); Nashville Hit Man (MNT MC-6627); Play It Again, Charlie (MNT MC-6630); Real McCoy (MNT MC-6623).

McCOY, JOE Imitation bass. Session for Arthur Crudup (1941).

McCOY, JOHN Bass. Member of Zzebra, 1974-75, and Gillan since 1979.

McCOYS Rick Derringer—guitar, vocal; Randy Zehringer—drums; Randy Hobbs—bass; Bobbie Peterson—organ. Pop rockers who hit the charts in 1965 with "Hang On Sloopy" and "You Make Me Feel So Good" (1966). Retrospectively acclaimed as the starting point for Johnny and Edgar Winter sidemen, Derringer and Hobbs. *Albums:* Infinite McCoys (BNG) 1968; Outside Stuff (BNG); Band and Shout Super Hits (BNG 220); Gang at Bang (BNG 215); Hang On Sloopy (BNG 212) 1965; You Make Me Feel So Good (BNG 213) 1966.

McCRACKEN, CHARLIE Bass. Session for Kim Fowley (1973); John Weider (1976); Kevin Ayers (1977-78).

McCRACKEN, CHET Drums. Member of Nick Gilder's backup band, 1977. Replaced John Hartman in the Doobie Brothers, 1980.

McCRACKEN, HUGH Guitar, producer. Produced Don Schlitz (1980). Production and session for Dr. John (1979). Session for Cognition (1971); Paul Simon (1975, 80); Henry Gross (1976); B. B. King (1969-70); Paul McCartney (1971); Gary Wright (1970-71, 79); Corbett and Hirsh (1971); Art Garfunkel (1978); Dr. John (1978); John Lennon (1980); the Mark and Clark Band (1977); Kate and Anna McGarrigle (1977); Steely Dan (1980).

McCRACKEN, RICH Guitar. Session for Mickey Thomas (1977).

McCRACKEN, RICHARD Drums. Original member of Taste, 1968.

McCRACKLIN, JIMMY Vocal. Recorded "The Walk," 1957.

McCRAE, DAVE Keyboards. Member of the Tiger,

1976.

McCREARY, LEW Trombone. Session for Nilsson (1975-76); Steely Dan (1974); Bangla Desh (1971); Ringo Starr (1974); Russ Giguere (1971); Austin Roberts (1973); Christopher Cross (1980).

McCREARY, MARY Vocal. Wife and recording partner of Leon Russell since 1975. See Leon and Mary Russell.

McCRORY, MARTHA Cello. Session for Waylon Jennings (1973, 75).

McCULLOCH, ANDY Drums. Replaced Michael Giles in King Crimson, 1971. Member of Greenslade. Session for Anthony Phillips (1980).

McCULLOCH, DANNY Bass, guitar, vocal. Member of the Animals, 1967-68, after which he released a little known solo album.

McCULLOUCH, IAN Vocal, guitar. Member of Echo and the Bunnymen, 1980.

McCULLOCH, JAMES Guitar. Member of Nick Gilder's backup band since 1977.

McCULLOUGH, HENRY Guitar, vocal, writer. Replaced Luther Grosvenor in Spooky Tooth, 1971, after being head of the Grease Band, 1971. A member of Wings, 1973, and the Frankie Miller Band, 1975. Session for "Jesus Christ Superstar" (1970); Joe Cocker (1976); Donovan (1973). *Album:* Henry McCullough (AAM) 1975.

McCULLOUGH, JIMMY Guitar. Replaced Les Harvey in Stone the Crows, 1972. Member of Thunderclap Newman, 1973, Wings, 1975-78, and the Dukes, 1979. Session for John Entwhistle (1972); Ricci Martin (1977); the Small Faces (1978).

McCULLOUGH, ULANDA Vocal. Session for John Mayall (1979); the Marshall Tucker Band (1980); Ray Gomez (1980); the Blues Brothers (1980).

McCUNE, SUSIE Vocal. Session for Gordon Lightfoot (1972).

McCURDY, JIM Drums. Member of the Stanley Steamer, 1973.

McCURDY, PAT Vocal, keyboards. Member of Yipes, 1979-80.

McCURDY, ROY Drums. Session for John Mayall (1977); Martin Mull (1978).

McDADE, DAVID "BUTCH" Drums, percussion, vocal. Member of Rich Mountain Tower, 1976, and the Amazing Rhythm Aces.

McDANIEL, BUDDY Tenor saxophone. Member of the Blacksmoke Horns, 1978. Session for John Mayall (1979).

McDANIEL, DAVE Bass. Session for Joe Cocker (1974); Jennifer Warnes (1976); Julie Tippets and Brian Auger (1978).

McDANIEL, DAVID Member of Gotham, 1979.

McDANIEL, ELLAS Real name of Bo Diddly.

McDIARMID, JOHNNY Organ. Session for Mahogany Rush (1975).

McDONALD, AL Mandolin. Session for the Marshall Tucker Band (1976).

McDONALD, CLARENCE Keyboards. Session for James Taylor (1976).

McDONALD, COUNTRY JOE Guitar, vocal, writer. Born 1/1/42. Founder of Country Joe and the Fish, 1965. After the group broke apart in 1969, he began his solo career, updating the social consciousness and arrangements of his songs. *Albums:* Country Joe (VAN 79348); Thinking of Woody (VAN 6546); Country Joe (VAN 79348) 1974; Essential (VAN VSD-85-86) 1976; Goodbye Blues (FSY 9525) 1977; Hold On It's Coming (VAN 79314); Incredible Live (VAN VSD 79316); Leisure Suite (FSY 9586) 1979; Love Is a Fire (FSY 9511) 1976; Paradise with an Ocean View (FSY 9495) 1975; Paris Sessions (VAN 79328) 1973; Quiet Days in Clichy (VAN 79303) 1970; Rock and Roll Music from the Planet Earth (FSY 9544) 1978; Tonight I'm Singing Just for You (VAN 6557); Tribute to Woody Guthrie (WBR 2W-3007); War, War, War (VAN 79315); Early Years (FAM 3309).

McDONALD, DONALD Member of Jeremy and the Satyrs, 1967-68.

McDONALD, FRANK Bass. Session for Mike Batt (1979).

McDONALD, HUGH Bass. Session for Willie Nelson (1973); Ringo Starr (1977).

McDONALD, IAN Woodwinds, horns, vibes, keyboards, guitar, mellotron, vocal. Original member of King Crimson, 1969, of McDonald and Giles, 1971, and Foreigner, 1977-80. Session for King Crimson (1974).

McDONALD, KATHI Vocal. Session for Freddie King (1971); Leon Russell (1971); the Rolling Stones (1972); Big Brother and the Holding Company; Don Nix (1971); Long John Baldry (1979-80). *Album:* Insane Asylum (ASY).

McDONALD, LARRY Congas. Session for Jackie DeShannon (1972); Taj Mahal (1977-78).

McDONALD, MIKE Keyboards, vocal, writer. Second member of Steely Dan to defect to the Doobie Brothers, 1976-present. Session for Gary Wright (1979); Tom Johnston (1979); Elton John (1979); Jackie DeShannon (1979); Stuart Margolin (1980); Christopher Cross (1980).

McDONALD, PETE Vocal. Voice of the Spiders from Mars, 1976.

McDONALD, SUSAN Harp. Session for Mike Pindar (1976).

McDONALD AND GILES Ian McDonald—woodwinds, vibes, keyboards, mellotron, vocal; Peter Giles—bass, vocal; Michael Giles—drums, percussion, vocal. King Crimson alumni who split from that group in 1971. *Album:* McDonald and Giles (CTL 9042) 1971.

McDONNELL, JIMMY Vocal. Member of the States, 1979.

McDOUGALL, DON Vocal, guitar. Member of

the Guess Who, 1979.

McDOWELL, HUGH Cello, vocal. Member of the Electric Light Orchestra.

McDOWELL, MISSISSIPPI FRED Bottleneck guitar, vocal. Born near Memphis, 1904, McDowell moved to Mississippi in 1928. Most noted for his bottleneck guitar style, he never relied on playing music for a living. *Albums:* Blues Roots (TMT 2-7006); I Do Not Play No Rock 'n' Roll (CAP ST-409); Long Way from Home (MSL 93003); Mississippi Fred McDowell (EVR 253); Mississippi Fred McDowell (ARH 1021) 1964.

McEUEN, JOHN Banjo, guitar, fiddle, mandolin, pedal steel guitar. Member of the Nitty Gritty Dirt Band, and the Dirt Band since 1978. Occasional session work with friend Steve Martin. Session for Bill Wyman (1974); the Marshall Tucker Band (1975).

McFADDEN, DUKE Keyboards, vocal. Member of 707, 1980.

McFADDEN, GEORGE Vocal. Session for Ry Cooder (1979).

McFARLAND, TIMMY Trombone, vocal. Member of Ballin' Jack.

McFARLANE, ELAINE Vocal, percussion. Nickname: Spanky. Namesake of Spanky and Our Gang, 1967-69.

McFEE, JOHN Guitar, fiddle, steel guitar. Member of Clover, 1977. Joined the Doobie Brothers, 1980. Session for Bill Wyman (1976); the Steve Miller Band (1976); Mistress (1979); Carlene Carter (1980).

McGARRIGLE, ANNA Piano, vocal, squeeze box. Duet with her sister Kate since 1975.

McGARRIGLE, KATE Piano, vocal, squeeze box. Duet with her sister Anna since 1975. Session for Gay and Terry Woods (1978).

KATE AND ANNA McGARRIGLE Kate McGarrigle—piano, vocal, squeeze box; Anna McGarrigle—piano, vocal, squeeze box. *Albums:* Dancer with Bruised Knees (WBR B 3014) 1977; Kate and Anna McGarrigle (WBR B 2862) 1975; Pronto Monto (WBR K 3248) 1978.

McGARY, DANNY Bass, vocal. Member of Piper, 1977.

McGEAR, MIKE Vocal, percussion. Brother of Paul McCartney. Member of Scaffold, 1968, and Grimms, 1973, before going solo in 1974. *Album:* McGear (WBR) 1974.

McGEE, BRIAN Drums, percussion, vocal. Member of the Simple Minds since 1979.

McGEE, EDWARD Vocal. Replaced Hubert Tubbs in Tower of Power, 1976.

McGEE, JERRY Guitar, dobro. He replaced Nokie Edwards as a member of the Ventures. Played with John Mayall, 1971-72. Session for Marc Benno; Delaney and Bonnie; Rita Coolidge (1972); Henry Gross (1972); Sonny Terry and Brownie McGhee (1973); Gene Clark (1974); Colin Winski (1980).

McGEE, MICKEY Drums. Member of Blue Steel since 1980.

McGEE, PARKER Guitar. Session for Splinter (1977). *Album:* Parker McGee (BIG 89520) 1976.

McGEENEY, ROSS Vocal, guitar. Member of Starry-Eyed and Laughing, 1975, and the Tigers, 1980.

McGEOGH, JOHN Guitar, saxophone, keyboards. Member of Magazine since 1978, and Visage, 1980.

McGEORGE, JERRY Bass, vocal. Original member of H. P. Lovecraft, 1967.

McGHEE, BILLY Bass. Member of R.A.F., 1980.

McGHEE, BROWNIE Vocal, guitar. Born 11/30/15. Country blues guitarist from Tennessee who teamed up with Sonny Terry in the 1930s. See Sonny Terry, Terry and McGhee. *Albums:* First Meeting (WPR 1817); Going Down Slow (MST 407); Home Town Blues (AST 308); Blues (FLW 3817); Blues Bash (OLR 7115); Blues by Brownie McGhee (FLW 2030); Brownie McGhee (FLW 3557); Brownie McGhee Sings the Blues (FLW 3557) 1957; Traditional Blues (FLW 2422) 1960; Traditional Blues (FLW 2421) 1951; Let's Have a Ball (MGP 1805) 1978; Carolina Blues (FRT 105).

McGILL, MIKE Vocal. Member of the Dells.

McGILLIVRAY, BILL Vocal, guitar, keyboards. Member of Tiger, 1976.

McGINN, SCOTT Bass, synthesizer, vocal. Member of Face Dancer since 1979.

McGINNIS, JOHN Keyboards. Member of Stone the Crows until 1972.

McGINNIS, SID Guitar. Session for John Mayall (1979).

McGOUGH, ROGER Vocal, percussion. Liverpool poet and member of Scaffold, 1968, and Grimms, 1973.

McGOVERN, MAUREEN Vocal. *Albums:* Morning After, 1973; Academy Award Performance, 1975; Nice To Be Around (1974); Gold; Towering Inferno (TWC); Maureen McGovern (WBR K-3327).

McGOVERN, TIM Drums, vocal, guitar. Member of Randy California's Kapt. Kopter and the Fabulous Twirly Birds, 1972, Neil Merryweather's Space Rangers, 1974-75, the Pop, 1977-79, and the Motels, 1979-80.

McGRATH, BAT Vocal. *Albums:* Blue Eagle (AMH 1005) 1976; The Spy (AMH 1011) 1978.

McGREARY, MIKE Drums, piano. Member of Balcones Fault, 1977.

McGREEVY, JAMES E., III Bass. Member of the Wazband, 1979.

McGROGGAN, HENRY Vocal. Session for Iggy Pop (1980).

McGRUDER, JUNE Vocal. Session for Gregg Allman (1973).

McGUFFIE, ROGER Bass. Session with Tony

Joe White (1971).

McGUFFY LANE Bob McNelly—guitar, vocal; Stephen Douglas—harmonica, keyboards, vocal; John Campigotto—percussion; Stephen Reis—bass, vocal; Terry Efaw—steel guitar, guitar; John Schwab—guitar, vocal. *Album:* McGuffy Lane (ACO SD 38-133) 1980.

McGUINESS, TOM Guitar, bass. Began with Eric Clapton in the Roosters before joining Manfred Mann until 1966. Co-namesake of McGuiness-Flint, and member of Lo and Behold, 1972. Member of the Blues Band, 1979.

McGUINESS-FLINT Graham Lyle—guitar, mandolin, vocal, bass, writer; Benny Gallagher—guitar, keyboards, vocal, bass, writer; Tom McGuiness—guitar, bass; Dennis Coulson—keyboards, vocal; Hughie Flint—drums, percussion. Two-part harmony (from writers Gallagher and Lyle) from England in the early 1970s. Though they disbanded after two albums, the group served as a starting point for Gallagher and Lyle, who continue today. *Albums:* McGuiness Flint (CAP SMAS 625); Happy Birthday Ruthie Baby (CAP).

McGUINN, ROGER Guitar, vocal, writer, keyboards, producer. Born 7/13/42. One of the original founders of the Byrds. Eventually, he shook off the changing band image and embarked on a semi-successful solo career. He regrouped with Byrd alumni Chris Hillman and Gene Clark for McGuinn, Hillman and Clark, 1979-80. Session for Bob Dylan (1973). *Albums:* Roger McGuinn (COL KC 31946) 1973; Roger McGuinn and Band (COL) 1975; Peace On You (COL) 1974; Cardiff Rose (COL) 1976; Thunderbird (COL PC 34656) 1977.

McGUINN, CLARK AND HILLMAN Roger McGuinn—guitar, vocal; Chris Hillman—guitar, mandolin, bass, banjo, vocal; Greg Thomas—drums; Gene Clark—guitar, vocal, keyboards; George Terry—guitar; Joe Lala—percussion; Paul Harris—keyboards. Byrds reunion begun in 1979. *Albums:* City (CAP AT-12043) 1980; McGuinn, Clark and Hillman (CAP SW-11910) 1979.

McGUIRE, BARRY Vocal. Originally from the New Christy Minstrels, McGuire's classic "Eve of Destruction" ran a healthy competition to Dylan's "Like a Rolling Stone" in 1965. *Albums:* Eve of Destruction, 1965; This Precious Time, 1966; World's Last Private Citizen (DHL) 1968; Jubilation (MYR A-6555); Jubilation, Too (MYR 6568); Lighten Up (MYR A-6531); Seeds (MYR A-6519); To the Bride (MYR X-6548).

McGUIRE, DUNCAN Bass. Member of Ayer's Rock, 1975-77.

McGUIRE, RA Vocal, harpsichord. Member of Trooper since 1975.

McHALE, BILL Bass, vocal. Member of Dakota, 1980.

McHUGH, PADDY Vocal. Session for Alvin Lee (1974); Bryan Ferry (1977).

McIAN, PETER Keyboards, vocal. *Album:* Playing Near the Edge (COL JC-36190) 1980.

McILWAINE, ELLEN Vocal, guitar, piano, writer. One of the few females in the blues field, and equally dexterous vocally and instrumentally. *Albums:* Honky Tonk Angel (POL); We the People (POL 5044) 1973; Ellen McIlwaine (UAR UA LA891) 1978.

McINTOSH, DANNY Guitar. Member of Bandit, 1976.

McINTOSH, ROBBIE Guitar. Member of Night, 1979.

McINTOSH, ROBBIE Drums. Original member of Brian Auger's Oblivion Express, 1971-73, and the Average White Band, 1974. Died in 1974. Session for Chuck Berry (1972); Manfred Mann (1980).

McINTYRE, EARL Trombone, tuba. Session for the Band (1972); Taj Mahal.

McINTYRE, MAURICE Saxophone. Member of J. B. Hutto's Hawks.

McINTYRE, OWEN Guitar. Member of the Average White Band since 1974. Session for Chuck Berry (1972).

McINTYRE, TIM Vocal, guitar, fiddle. Member of Fun Zone, 1977.

McIVER, DAVID Began in Blues Incorporated.

McIVER, JOHN Bass. Member of the Law, 1977.

McJOHN, GOLDY Keyboards. Born 5/2/45. Original member of Steppenwolf, 1965-74.

McKAY, AL Guitar. Session for Sonny Terry and Brownie McGhee (1973).

McKAY, STEVE Guitar. Member of the Stooges, 1969.

McKEEN, GARY Trumpet. Member of the Band of Thieves, 1976.

McKELVEY, LOUIS Guitar. Member of Influence, 1968.

McKENDREE, FRAN Vocal, guitar. Namesake of McKendree Spring.

McKENDREE SPRING Fran McKendree—vocal, guitar; Michael Dreyfuss—violin, viola; Martin Slutsky—guitar; Christopher Bishop—vocal, bass; Carson Michaels—vocal, drums. *Albums:* McKendree Spring (MCA 277); McKendree Spring (MCA 44) 1972; Too Young to Feel This Old (PYE 12124) 1976; Get Me to the Country (PYE 12108) 1975.

McKENNA, DANNY Member of Toby Beau since 1978.

McKENNA, HUGH Keyboards, percussion. Member of the Sensational Alex Harvey Band, and Sahb, 1976. Session for Dan McCafferty (1975).

McKENNA, TED Drums, percussion. Member of the Sensational Alex Harvey Band, 1972-78, and Sahb, 1976. Session for Dan McCafferty (1975); Rory Gallagher (1978-present).

McKENZIE, ALASTAIR Keyboards, mellotron,

vocal. Member of Suzi Quatro's Band, 1973-74.

McKENZIE, DON Bass, vocal. Member of Chuck and the Tigers, 1980.

McKENZIE, JOHN Bass. Member of Man. Session for Oxendale and Shephard (1979).

McKENZIE, SCOTT Vocal. Voice of the flower generation with his "San Francisco (Wear Some Flowers In Your Hair)," 1967. *Albums:* Voice of Scott McKenzie, 1967; Stained Glass Morning (ODE).

McKEOWN, LESLIE Vocal, guitar. Member of the Bay City Rollers.

McKERNAN, RON "PIG PEN" Percussion, harmonica, vocal. Original member of the Grateful Dead from 1967 until his death, 3/8/73.

McKIBBON, AL Bass. Session for Randy Newman.

McKIE, KEITH Guitar, vocal. Member of Kensington Market, 1968-69.

McKINLEY, JEANETTE Vocal. Session for Paice, Ashton, Lord (1977).

McKINLEY, MAURICE Drums. Chicago blues man of the mid-1960s who worked with Barry Goldberg and Harvey Mandel.

McKINLEY, SHEILA Vocal. Session for Paice, Ashton, Lord (1977).

McKINNEY, JERRY Saxophone, flute. Member of Larry Raspberry and the Highsteppers. Session for Elvin Bishop (1978).

McKINNIE, DEE Vocal. Played with John Mayall, 1973. Session for John Mayall (1977).

McKINNON, JAY Vocal. Session for Jorge Santana (1980).

McKNIGHT, CARL Percussion. Session for Nilsson (1975).

McKUEN, JERRY Guitar. Session for John Sebastian (1974).

McLAGEN, IAN Guitar, keyboards, vocal. Original member of the Faces, 1967-68. and the re-formed Small Faces, 1977-78, before going solo. Session for Rod Stewart (1971-76); Ron Wood (1975, 76, 78); Chuck Berry (1972); the Rolling Stones (1978). *Album:* Troublemaker (MER SRM-1-3786) 1979.

McLAIN, DAN Drums. Member of the Penetrators, 1980.

McLAUCHLAN, MURRAY Guitar, vocal, piano. Recorded with the Silver Tractors. See Silver Tractors. *Albums:* Boulevard, 1976; Hard Rock Town, 1977; Sweeping the Spotlight Away (COL TN 18).

McLAUGHLIN, JOHNNY "HAWK" Drums, vocal. Member of the Private Lines, 1980.

McLAUGHLIN, MAHAVISHNU JOHN Guitar, writer, piano. Noted jazz guitarist and co-author of "Love, Devotion and Surrender," with Carlos Santana, 1973. Session for Jack Bruce (1968); Carlos Santana (1974); Stanley Clarke (1975). *Albums:* Extrapolation (POL 5510); Where Fortune Smiles (PYE 12103); Electric Dreams (COL JC-35785) 1979; Apocalypse (COL KC-32957); Between Nothingness and Eternity (COL C-32766); Birds of Fire (COL PC-31996); Electric Guitarist (COL JC-35326) 1978; Handful of Beauty (COL PC-34372); Inner Mounting Flame (COL PC-31067); Love, Devotion, Surrender (COL C-32034) 1973; Natural Elements (COL JC-34980) 1977; Shakti (COL PC-34162) 1976; Spaces (VAN 79345); Visions of the Emerald Beyond (COL PC-33411) 1975.

McLEAN, DAVID Drums. Member of Willie Alexander's Boom Boom Band, 1978-79.

McLEAN, DON Vocal, guitar. His single, "American Pie," received enough air play to make it a classic in its own time. Though that hit was unfollowed, he established a loyal following. *Albums:* Don McLean; American Pie (UAR LO-5535); Chain Lightning (CAS 7173); Prime Time (ARI 4149) 1977; Solo, 1976; Tapestry, 1971; Playing Favorites, 1973; Homeless Brother, 1974.

McLEAN, ERNEST Guitar. Session for Fats Domino (1949-57).

McLEAN, PATRICK Saxophone. Member of Hi Tension, 1978.

McLEAN, PAUL Guitar, vocal. Member of Hi Tension, 1978.

McLEAN, RANCHE Guitar. Member of Skin, Flesh and Bone, 1975.

McLELLAN, MIKE Trumpet, vocal. Original member of White Trash.

McMAHON, ANDY Organ. Session for Waylon Jennings (1973). *Album:* Blueblood (DHM 4401).

McMAHON, GERARD Vocal. Session for Zephyr (1971).

McMANUS, DECLAN Real name of Elvis Costello.

McMASTER, ANDY Bass, keyboards, vocal. Member of the Ducks Deluxe, 1974-75, and the Motors, 1977-present.

McMORDIE, AL Bass. Member of the Stiff Little Fingers, 1980.

McMURRAY, STEVE Guitar. Member of the Wireless, 1979.

McNAB, MALCOLM Trumpet. Session for Nilsson (1975).

McNABB, JOANNE CALDWELL Woodwinds. Session for the Mothers of Invention (1972).

McNABB, KERRY Vocal. Session for Frank Zappa (1974).

McNAIR, HAROLD Flute. Member of Ginger Baker's Air Force, 1970-71. Session for Donovan (1967-68); Steamhammer (1969).

McNALLY, JOHN Guitar, vocal. Original member of the Searchers, 1960-64.

McNALLY, STEPHEN "MAC" Vocal. Member of Roadmaster since 1978.

McNAUGHT, MIKE Piano. Session for Chris Youlden (1973).

McNEES, HARLIN Guitar, vocal. Member of the L.A. Jets, 1976.

McNEIL, MICHAEL Keyboards, vocal. Member of the Simple Minds since 1979.

McNEILL, SYLVIA Vocal. Started in Blues Incorporated. Session for Rick Wakeman (1972).

McNELLY, BOB Guitar, vocal. Member of McGuffey Lane, 1980.

McPHATTER, CLYDE Vocal. Originally the head of the Drifters, McPhatter was a star of rock before Elvis was known. His "Money Honey" (1953) topped the charts, making him a contemporary equal to Fats Domino, Bill Haley, etc. He died in 1972. See the Drifters. *Albums:* Clyde McPhatter and the Drifters; Love Ballads, 1958; Clyde, 1959; Best of Clyde McPhatter, 1963; Songs of the Big City, 1964; Live at the Apollo; May I Sing for You.

McPHEARSON, BOB Tenor saxophone. Member of the Buddy Miles Express, 1968-69.

McPHEARSON, SAM Harmonica. Session for the Marshall Tucker Band (1974).

McPHEE, ANTHOHY CHARLES "TONY" Guitar, vocal, writer, producer. Born 3/23/44. Part of the English blues invasion of the 1960s that did not make it commercially in the United States. However, as founder of the Groundhogs, 1968-74, 1976, he enjoyed greater fame, with his progressive approach to rock. Session for Hapshash and the Coloured Coat; Mike Batt (1979).

McPHERSON, GRAHAM Vocal. Member of Madness, 1979.

McPOWELL, KEN Vocal. Replaced Van Morrison in Them.

McQUAIG, MIKE Guitar, vocal. Member of Potliquor, 1979.

McQUICKLY, DIRK Stage name of Eric Idle in the Rutles, 1978.

McRAUCH, JEFFREY Bass. Member of the Band of Thieves, 1976.

McRAY, STEVE Keyboards, vocal. Member of Mose Jones, 1978. Session for Ted Nugent (1975-76).

McREYNOLDS, JESSE Mandolin. Session for the Doors (1969).

McSHEE, JACQUI Vocal. Original member of Pentangle, 1968-72. Session for John Renbourn (1980).

McTELL, BLIND WILLIE Twelve string guitar, vocal, writer. Blind Georgia-born blues guitarist who recorded in the 1920s and 1930s. Also recorded under the names "Georgia Bill," "Barrelhouse Sammie," "Blind Sammie," "Blind Willie," "Red Hot Willie Glaze," and "Red Hot Willie." The coming of World War II saw him singing on the street corners of Atlanta, due to his disillusionment with the recording business. *Albums:* Bluebird Blues (VIC LPN 518); Cryin' in the Morning (MUS 5212); Last Session (PRS 7809).

McTELL, KATE Guitar, vocal. Session with Blind Willie McTell (1932).

McTELL, RALPH Guitar. Classical guitarist. *Album:* Live (FSY 9571).

McTORIUS, CLIT Bass. Session for Randy California (1972).

McVIE, CHRISTINE Vocal, piano. Born 7/12/43. Married name of Christine Perfect. See Christine Perfect. Session for Danny Douma (1979). *Album:* Legendary Christine Perfect (SIR 6022) 1976.

McVIE, JOHN Bass. Born 11/26/45. Member of John Mayall's Bluesbreakers, 1963-67. With Peter Green, he left the Bluesbreakers to form Fleetwood Mac, which developed into one of the finest British blues bands. He and drummer Mick Fleetwood survived the several personnel changes and continue to be the cornerstone of the group's ever-changing sound. Session for Duster Bennett (1968); Christine McVie (1969); Gordon Smith; Jeremy Spencer (1970); John Mayall (1977); Danny Douma (1979).

McWHIRTER, GEORGE Trombone. Session for the Catfish Hodge Band (1979).

MEACHAM, BRITT Guitar, vocal. Member of Jackson Highway.

MEACHAM, CRAIG Bass. Member of A-440, 1978.

MEADOR, SEAB Guitar. Member of the Werewolves, 1978.

MEADOW, PUNKY Guitar. Member of Bux, 1976, and the Angels, 1977.

MEADOWS, BUCKY Guitar, piano. Member of the Rio Grande Band. Session for Asleep at the Wheel (1976).

MEAGHER, RON Bass. Member of the Beau Brummels, 1966-68.

MEAKIN, ROGER Vocal. Member of Esperanto, 1975.

MEALING, JOHN Organ, piano. Original member of If, 1973. Session for Status Quo (1973); Long John Baldry (1975); John Entwhistle (1975).

MEATLOAF Vocal. Real name: Marvin Lee Aday. Session for Ted Nugent (1976). *Albums:* Bat Out of Hell (EPC PE-34974); Meatloaf (PRG P7-10029).

MECHAM, BRUCE Vocal, guitar. Member of Barooga, 1980.

MECHY, STEVE Guitar. Session for Bobby Caldwell (1978).

MEDICA, LEON Bass. Member of Le Roux since 1979.

MEDICINE HEAD John Fiddler—vocal, guitar, drums; Peter Hope-Evans—harmonica; Pat Donaldson—bass; Clive Thacker—drums; Roy Dyke—drums; Mick Liber—guitar; Brian Parish—guitar; Tony Ashton—keyboards. *Album:* One and One Is One (POL PD 5532) 1973.

MEDLEY, BILL Vocal, writer, producer. Half of the original Righteous Brothers, 1962-68, 1974-75. *Albums:* Someone Is Standing Outside (MGM); Song for You (AAM 3505); Lay a Little Lovin' on

Me (UAR LT-929) 1978; Sweet Thunder (UAR LT-1024); Wings (AAM 3503).

MEDLOCK, RICK Drums. Session for Lynard Skynard (1977).

MEDLOCKE, RICK Vocal, guitar. Member of Blackfoot, 1975-80.

MEDUSA John Lee—bass; Gerry Brown—drums, percussion; Darryl Thompson—guitar; Jim Mahoney—guitar; James Batton—keyboards, vocal; Cheryl Alexander—vocal; Eef Albers—guitar. *Album:* Medusa (COL JC-35357) 1978.

MEEK, JEREMY Bass, vocal. Member of the Live Wire since 1979.

MEEKER, BILL Drums. Member of the Elvin Bishop Band until 1972, and the Dudek-Finnigan-Kruger Band, 1980. Session for Elvin Bishop (1974).

MEERMAN, KEES Drums. Member of Herman Brood and His Wild Romance since 1979.

MEGGINSON, JOHN Piano, bass. Member of Grimms, 1973.

MEHLER, JOHN Drums. Member of Richie Furay Band, 1976. Session for Richie Furay (1978).

MEIGHAN, BOB Vocal. Namesake of the Bob Meighan Band, 1976.

BOB MEIGHAN BAND Bob Meighan—guitar, vocal; Dick Furlow—bass; Rodney Bryce—violin, mandolin, synthesizer; Milt Miller—drums; Richard Howard—keyboards; David Dodt—guitar. *Albums:* Bob Meighan Band (CAP) 1976; Dancer, 1976.

MEINE, KLAUS Vocal. Voice of the Scorpions since 1974.

MEISNER, RANDY Bass, vocal. Born 3/8/47. Member of the Stone Canyon Band, and original member of the Eagles, 1972-78. Session for James Taylor; Joe Walsh (1974); Richie Furay (1979). *Album:* Randy Meisner (ASY 6E-140) 1980.

MEKLER, GABRIEL Producer, organ. Production and session for Steppenwolf, 1968-71. Session for Janis Joplin (1969).

MELAMED, VINCE Keyboards, vocal. Session for Greg Sutton (1979).

MELANIE Vocal, guitar, writer. Real name: Melaine Safka. Played at Woodstock, 1969. *Albums:* Sunset and Other Beginnings, 1975; As I See It Now (NHD 5000); Candles in the Rain (BUD 5060); Four Sides of Melanie (BUD 95005); From the Beginning (ABC ND-379); Garden in the City (BUD 5095) 1971; Gather Me (NHD 47001); The Good Book (BUD 95000); Leftover Wine (BUD 5066); Madrugada (NHD 48001); Melanie (BUD 5041) 1973; Melanie at Carnegie Hall (NHD 4900); My First Album (BUD 5074); Please Love Me (BUD 5132); R.P.M. (BEL 1203); Stoneground Words (NHD 47005) 1972; Ballroom Streets (TOM 29003) 1978; Beautiful (BUD 16021) 1979.

MELENDEZ, CARLOS Guitar, vocal. Member of the Raices, 1975.

MELENDEZ, JUAN Flute, saxophone, clarinet, percussion, vocal. Member of the Raices, 1975.

MELOUNEY, VINCE Early member of the Bee Gees.

MELTON, BARRY Guitar, vocal, writer. Original member of Country Joe and the Fish, 1965-69, and Melton, Levy and the Dey Brothers, 1972. *Albums:* We Are Like the Ocean (FAM 9007) 1978; Level with Me (FAM 9014) 1978.

MELTON, BENNIE Vocal. Member of Wax, 1980.

MELTON, LEVY AND THE DEY BROTHERS Barry Melton—vocal, guitar, trombone; Jay Levy—vocal, keyboards; Rick Dey—vocal, bass; Tony Dey—vocal, drums. *Album:* Melton, Levy and the Dey Brothers (COL) 1972.

MELVOIN, MIKE Keyboards. Session for Donovan (1974); Tim Weisberg (1971, 73, 75); Martin Mull (1979).

MEMBERS Nicky Tesco—vocal; J. C.—guitar, vocal; Chris Payne—bass, vocal; Nigel Bennett—guitar, vocal; Adrian Lillywhite—drums, percussion. *Album:* At the Chelsea Night Club (VIR 2120) 1979.

MEMPHIS HORNS Andrew Love—tenor saxophone, flute; James Mitchell—baritone saxophone; Jack Hale—trombone; Lewis Collins—alto saxophone, flute; Jack Hale, Jr.—trumpet, flugelhorn (1978). Popular studio horn section. Session with the Doobie Brothers (1976); Dr. John (1971); Rod Stewart (1975); Mike Harrison (1975); B. B. King (1973-74); Tony Joe White (1971); Firefall (1977); Willie Nelson (1973); the Graeme Edge Band (1977); Tom Johnston (1979); Frankie Miller (1977). *Albums:* Welcome to Memphis (VIC AFLI-3221) 1979; Memphis Horns (VIC APLI 2643) 1978.

MEMPHIS SLIM Piano, vocal. Real name: L. C. Frazier. Tennessee-born blues piano player and singer who moved to Chicago in 1939, at the suggestion of Big Bill Broonzy. *Albums:* Memphis Slim, Vol. 2 (EVR 286); Raining the Blues (FSY 24705); Arbee's Blues (FLW 3824); Blues Is Everywhere (CRS 10002) 1973; Favorite Blues Singers (FLW 2387) 1973; Finest of Memphis Slim, Folk Bluesman (BET BCP-6017); Legacy of the Blues (CRS 10010); Legacy of the Blues, Vol. 7 (CRS 10017) 1976; Memphis Blues (OLR 7136); Memphis Slim (EVR 215); Memphis Slim and W. Dixon at the Village Gate (FLW 2386) 1962; Memphis Slim Chicago Boogie Woogie (FLW 3596); Memphis Slim with Lowell Fulsom (ICT 1011); Messin' Around with the Blues (KGO 1082); Raining the Blues (FSY 24705); Real Boogie Woogie of Memphis Slim (FLW 2385) 1960; Songs of Memphis Slim and Willie Dixon (FLW 2385); Sonny Boy Williamson/Memphis Slim in Paris (CRS 10003); Blue Memphis Suite (WBR 1892) 1971; Mother Earth (BUD 7505);

Right Now (TRP 2-8025).

MEN Early recording name of the Association.

MENAGE A TROIS Bunk Gardner—horns; Buzz Gardner—horns; John Backin—piano. Recording effort formed by former members of the Mothers of Invention.

MENDELSON, ANDY Vocal, keyboards, guitar, bass. *Album:* Maybe the Good Guy's Gonna Win (ARI 4207) 1978.

MENDOZA, MARK Bass. Member of the Dictators, 1977.

MENIKETTI, DAVE Guitar, vocal. Member of Yesterday and Today, 1976.

MENSAH, PAAPA Drums. Member of Hi Tension, 1978.

MENZA, DON Horns. Session for Neil Sedaka (1975). *Album:* First Flight (CLT 7617).

MEPHISTOPHELES Fred Tackett—guitar, piano, trumpet; Steven Simone—guitar, vocal; Bob Siller—guitar, vocal; Gordon Grant—keyboards; Skip Mosher—bass, flute; Daryl Burch—drums. *Album:* In Frustration I Hear Singing (RPS).

MERCER, CHRIS Saxophone. Member of John Mayall's Bluesbreakers, 1968, the Keef Hartley Band, 1969-70, and Juicy Lucy, 1970-71. Session for Chicken Shack (1973); Golden Earring (1976); Dr. John (1971); Freddie King (1974-75); "Jesus Christ Superstar" (1970); Bryan Ferry (1974, 76-77); Dan McCafferty (1975); Chris de Burgh (1975); Pete Wingfield (1975); Uriah Heep (1978); Elliott Murphy (1977); Gerry Rafferty (1980); Chris Spedding (1980).

MERCER, JERRY Drums. Replaced Ned Davis in the Snakestretchers, 1973, and Richie Henman in April Wine, 1976-79. Session for Ellen McIlwaine (1973).

MERCURY, ERIC Vocal. Session on Free Creek (1973).

MERCURY, FREDDIE Vocal, piano. Real name: Freddie Bulsara. Born 9/5/46. Original member of Queen, since 1973. Session for Ian Hunter (1976).

MEREDITH, LARRY Vocal. Half of the Pakalameredith duet, 1977.

MERING, SUMNER Vocal, guitar. Namesake of Sumner, 1980.

MERLIND, LOUIS Vocal. Member of Centaurus.

MEROLA, STEVE Drums. Member of Jimmie Mack and the Jumpers, 1980.

MERRIAM, CHARLIE Vocal. Session for Moon Martin (1978).

MERRILL, ALLAN Guitar, keyboards, vocal. Member of Runner, 1979.

MERRILL, JOHN Guitar. Member of the Peanut Butter Conspiracy, 1967-68.

MERRILL, WILLIAM Guitar. Member of the Group Image, 1968.

MERRIMAN, STEPHEN Piano. Session for Peter C. Johnson (1980).

MERRYWEATHER, NEIL Vocal, bass, guitar, producer. Namesake and founder of California heavy metal rockers, Neil Merryweather and the Space Rangers, 1974-75. *Album:* Neil Merryweather, John Richardson and Bores (KNT 546).

NEIL MERRYWEATHER AND THE SPACE RANGERS Neil Merryweather—vocal, bass, guitar, producer; Michael "Jeep" Willis—guitar; Tim McGovern—drums; Jaimie Herndon—keyboards, slide guitar. *Albums:* Space Rangers (MER SRM 1007) 1974; Kryptonite (SRM 1024) 1975.

MERSHON, NORMAN Vocal. Member of Tycoon.

MESQUITE, SKIP Saxophone, flute, vocal. Member of Tower of Power until 1972, and the Hoodoo Rhythm Devils, 1973. Session for Jennifer Warnes (1976).

MESSECAR, DEK Bass, vocal. Member of the Wolf, 1974.

MESSER, HOWARD Bass, vocal. Member of Couchois since 1979.

MESSICK, GORDON Trombone. Session for Lamb (1971); the Pointer Sisters (1974).

MESSINA, JIM Guitar, vocal, writer, producer. Cofounder of Poco with Richie Furay, he first met Furay after replacing Bruce Palmer in Buffalo Springfield, 1967-68. After the Springfield, he became half of the Loggins and Messina duet, 1972-77. Session for Stuart Margolin (1980). *Album:* Oasis (COL JC-36140) 1979.

MESSINA, JOE Guitar. Session for the Temptations (1973).

METEORS Hugo Sinzheimer—vocal; Ferdinand Bakker—guitar, vocal; John Vee—bass; Ake Danielson—keyboards; Eric de Zwaan—guitar, vocal; Job Tarenskeen—drums, vocal, saxophone. Formed from the Alquin Nucleus. *Album:* Teenage Heart (PVC 7911) 1980.

METER, WALTER Drums, vocal. Member of Elton Motello, 1980.

METERS Jeo Norcentelli—guitar; Arthur Neville—organ; George Porter—bass; Joseph Modeliste—drums. Backup group for Dr. John, 1973. *Albums:* Best of the Meters (VGO 12002); New Directions (WBR B-3042); Rejuvenation (RPS 2200); Trick Bag (RPS 2252).

METKE, BOB Drums. Session for Lord Sutch.

METRO Member of Quincy, 1980.

METRO Peter Godwin—vocal, saxophone, moog; Duncan Browne—vocal, guitar; Sean Lyons—guitar; John Giblin—bass; Simon Phillips—drums. *Album:* Metro (SIR 6401) 1977.

METROPOLIS BLUES BAND Early name of the Yardbirds.

METZER, DOUG Bass. Member of Country Joe and the Fish, 1969.

MEURER, ROB Keyboards. Session for Christopher Cross (1980).

MEURIS, PETER Drums. Member of the Tapes, 1980.

MEUSSDORFFER, JACK Vocal, guitar. Member of Sand, 1973-76.

MEYER, AUGIE Guitar. Session for Willie Nelson (1973).

MEYER, FRED Drums. Member of the New Commander Cody Band, 1977.

MEYER, GEORGE Keyboards, vocal. Session for Ian Hunter (1980).

MEYER, JEFFREY Drums. Member of the Charlie Daniels Band, 1972.

MEYER, SKIP Drums, vocal. Member of the Shoes since 1979.

MEYERS, CHRIS Drums. Member of the Sanford-Townsend Band, 1979.

MEYERS, RANDY Drums. Session for Bob Seger (1974).

MEYERS, STEVE Guitar, vocal. Member of Granmax, 1976.

MI-SEX Steve Gilpin—vocal; Kevin Stanton—guitar, vocal; Don Martin—bass, vocal; Murray Burns—keyboards, vocal; Richard Hodgkinson—drums, vocal. *Albums:* Computer Games (EPC JE-36349) 1980; Space Race (EPC JE 36744) 1980.

MICCOLI, DENNIS Organ. Original member of the Buckinghams, 1966-68.

MICELY, JOHN Drums. Member of John Fred and the Playboy Band.

MICHAEL Guitar. Original member of Fever Tree.

MICHAEL, DAVID Guitar. Member of the Mike Greene Band, 1975-76.

MICHAELS, CARSON Vocal, drums. Member of McKendree Spring.

MICHAELS, DAVE Keyboards, vocal. Original member of H. P. Lovecraft, 1967-68.

MICHAELS, HILLY Vocal, guitar, drums, percussion, synthesizer. *Album:* Calling All Girls (WBR BSK 3431) 1980.

MICHAELS, LEE Keyboards, guitar, bass, vocal, writer, producer. A pioneer of over-dubbing, Californian Michaels first began experimenting multitracking of his musical talents in 1968. He is also remembered for his dynamic traveling duet — Michaels on the keyboards and Bartholomew Smith-Frost on drums. Session for the Rockets (1980). *Albums:* Lee Michaels (AAM 4199) 1969; Barrel (AAM 4249); Carnival of Life (AAM 4210) 1968; 5th (AAM 4302); Lee Michaels Live (AAM); Nice Day for Something (COL); Recital (AAM 4152) 1968; Space and First Takes (AAM 4336); Tailface (COL KC 32846).

MICHAELS, ROY Banjo, guitar, bass. Member of Cat Mother and the All Night Newsboys, 1967-68.

MICHIE, CHRIS Guitar. Session for the Pointer Sisters (1974).

MICHLIN, SPENCER Member of Pacific Gas and Electric, 1973.

MICK Nickname of Michael Wilson. Member of Dave Dee, Dozy, Beaky, Mick and Tich.

MIDDLETON, MAX Piano. As a member of the re-formed Jeff Beck Group, 1971-72, he demonstrated a unique jazz flair which he continued in Hummingbird, 1975-76. Session for Jeff Beck (1975-76).

MIDDLETON, PAUL Steel guitar, bass. Member of Wally, 1974.

MIDLER, BETTE Vocal. "The Divine Miss M" became popular in 1972 with her unique song styling and lively stage show. Made her acting debut playing Janis Joplin in "The Rose," 1979. Session for Ringo Starr (1977). *Albums:* Broken Blossom (ATC 19151) 1977; Divine Miss M (ATC 7238) 1972; Live at Last (ATC 2-9000) 1977; Bette Midler (ATC 7270) 1973; The Rose (ATC 16010) 1979; Songs for the New Depression (ATC 18155) 1976; Thighs and Whispers (ATC 16004) 1979; Divine Madness (ATC 16022) 1980.

MIDNIGHTERS Hank Ballard; Henry Booth; Billy Davis; Clarence Green; Calvin Greene; Arthur Porter; Frank Sanford; Lawson Smith; Charles Sutton; Norman Thrasher; Sonny Woods. Backup group for Hank Ballard. See Hank Ballard.

MIELKE, GARY Keyboards. Session for Gary Wright (1977).

MIESSNER, BRIAN Bass, guitar, vocal. Member of Aeriel, 1978.

MIGHELL, NORMAN Tambourine. Session for Mick Taylor (1979).

MIGLIORI, JAY Horns, flute. Session for Jan and Dean (1963); Nilsson (1975).

MIGLIORI, TONY Keyboards. Session for Doug Kershaw. *Album:* Power (DDR 107).

MIHALY, THOMAS Bass, vocal. Member of the Flamin' Groovies, 1971-79, Omega, 1975-78, and Roy Looney and the Phantom Movers, 1979-80.

MIKE Keyboards. Member of Mother's Finest since 1976.

MIKE Guitar. Member of the Five Americans, 1966.

MIKENAS, ED Bass. Session for Scarlet Rivera (1978).

MILANO, FRED Piano. Original member of Dion and the Belmonts.

MILES, BUDDY Drums, vocal. Born 9/5/46. Original member of the Electric Flag, 1967-68, and founder of the Buddy Miles Express. An occasional member of the Jimi Hendrix Experience, 1970, he also recorded with Carlos Santana, 1972. Session for Nils Lofgren (1976). *Albums:* Buddy Miles Live; Buddy Miles; Carlos Santana and Buddy Miles Live (COL C-31308) 1972; Them Changes (MER 61280); Boogie Bear (COL KC 32694) 1973; Chapter VII (COL KC 32048) 1973; All the Faces (COL KC 33089) 1974; Bicentennial Gathering of Tribes (CAS NBLP 7024) 1976.

BUDDY MILES EXPRESS Jim McCarty—guitar;

Herbie Rich—organ; Virgil Gonsalves—baritone saxophone; Terry Clements—tenor saxophone; Marcus Doubleday—trumpet; Billy Rick—bass; Bob McPhearson—tenor saxophone; Ron Woods —drums; Buddy Miles—drums, vocal. Born from the ashes of Blood, Sweat and Tears, Miles carried the same format to his new group with lucrative success. *Albums:* Expressway to Your Skull, 1968; Electric Church, 1969.

MILES, GARY Bass. Member of Texas, 1973.

MILES, HELENE Vocal. Session for Gregg Allman (1973).

MILES, JOHN Vocal, guitar, keyboards. English soloist whose debut was produced by Alan Parsons. See John Miles Band. Session for the Alan Parsons Project (1976-78).

JOHN MILES BAND John Miles—vocal, guitar, keyboards; Barry Black—drums, percussion; Bob Marshall—bass. English rockers engineered by Alan Parsons. *Albums:* Rebel (LON 669) 1976; Sympathy (ARI 4261) 1980; Zaragon (ARI 4176); Stardiscs (LON BP-704/5).

MILES, LEE Bass. Session for Terry Reid (1973, 76, 79).

MILHIZER, BILL Member of the Fleshtones, 1980.

MILLAR, ROBERT Drums, harmonica. Original member of Supertramp, 1970.

MILLAS, LARRY Guitar, bass, flute, vocal. Member of the Ides of March.

MILLER, ADAM Vocal. Session for Nico (1970).

MILLER, BOB Guitar. Member of Mom's Apple Pie, 1973.

MILLER, BRIAN Keyboards. Original member of Isotope, 1974.

MILLER, BRIAN Guitar, vocal. Member of Zon, 1979.

MILLER, BYRON Bass. Session for George Duke (1975).

MILLER, CHARLES Saxophone, flute, vocal. Original member of War.

MILLER, CHARLIE Cornet. Session for Dr. John (1978-79).

MILLER, CHIP Drums. Replaced Tom Wynn in Cowboy, 1977.

MILLER, DAVE Bass, vocal. Member of Choice, 1980.

MILLER, DON Guitar. Member of the Overland Stage, 1972.

MILLER, FRANKIE Vocal, guitar. Soloist before forming the Frankie Miller Band, 1975. Backed by the Full House, 1977-78.

FRANKIE MILLER BAND Frankie Miller—guitar, vocal; Henry McCullough—guitar; Mick Weaver —keyboards; Chris Stewart—bass; Stu Perry—drums. *Albums:* Double Trouble (CYS 1174) 1978; Full House (CYS 1128) 1977; Frankie Miller's Highlife (CYS 1052) 1974; Once in a Blue Moon (CYS 1036) 1977; Perfect Fit (CYS 1220) 1979; The Rock (CYS 1088) 1975; Easy Money (CYS 1268) 1980.

MILLER, GENE Trumpet, trombone. Session for Clarence Carter (1967); Wilson Pickett (1968); Boz Scaggs (1969).

MILLER, GERI Vocal. Session for Free Creek (1973).

MILLER, GLENN Bass, vocal. Member of Chilliwack, 1972-78.

MILLER, HARRY Acoustic bass. Member of Centipede, 1971. Session for King Crimson (1972).

MILLER, JERRY Guitar. Original member of Moby Grape, 1967-69.

MILLER, JIM Guitar. Session for the Steve Miller Band (1970); Stanky Brown (1977).

MILLER, JIMMY Producer. Produced Traffic (1968-70); Spooky Tooth (1968-69); the Rolling Stones (1968-73); Blind Faith (1969); Savage Rose (1971); Sky (1970-71); Jim Capaldi (1979); Motorhead (1979); Trapeze (1980); and others.

MILLER, JOE Horns. Session for Howlin' Wolf (1972).

MILLER, KINCAID Keyboards, vocal. Session for Jorge Santana (1980).

MILLER, LEE Bass. Session for Waylon Jennings (1973).

MILLER, LESLIE Vocal. Session for Steely Dan (1980).

MILLER, MARCUS Bass. Session for Elton John (1979).

MILLER, MILT Drums. Member of the Bob Meighan Band, 1976.

MILLER, MRS. ELVA Vocal. She was the antithesis of music; unable to sing or carry a tune. It was ironic that her inability made her a temporary hit in 1966. *Albums:* Mrs. Miller's Greatest Hits, 1966; Will Success Spoil Mrs. Miller? 1966; Country Soul of Mrs. Miller, 1967.

MILLER, PERRY Real name of Jesse Colin Young.

MILLER, PETE Vocal. Session for Chris Spedding (1980).

MILLER, PHIL Guitar. Member of Matching Mole, and the National Health Band, 1977.

MILLER, RICE Real name of Sonny Boy Williamson. See Sonny Boy Williamson.

MILLER, ROBIN Oboe. Session for King Crimson (1971-72, 74).

MILLER, STAN Bass, vocal. Member of Earthquake since 1966.

MILLER, STEPHEN Keyboards, vocal. Member of Linn County, 1968-69, the Elvin Bishop Band, 1969-72, and Grinderswitch, 1977. Session for Harvey Mandel; Elvin Bishop (1974). *Album:* Stephen Miller (PHL 600-335).

MILLER, STEVE Guitar, keyboards, vocal, writer. Born 10/5/43. Founder and namesake of the Steve Miller Band since 1968. See the Steve Miller Band. Session for Ben Sidran.

STEVE MILLER BAND Steve Miller—guitar,

keyboards, harmonica, vocal; Curley Cooke—guitar (1968); Tim Davis—drums (1968-70); Lonnie Turner—bass (1968-70, 76); Jim Peterman—organ (1968); William "Boz" Scaggs—guitar, vocal (1968); Ben Sidran—keyboards, vocal (1969, 72); Jack King—drums (1971); Ross Vallory—bass (1971); Gerald Johnson—bass (1972-73); Gary Mallaber—drums (1972-73, 76); John King—drums (1973); Dickie Johnson—keyboards (1972-73). Inverting the British invasion, Miller and his band went to London to record their first album in 1968. Miller's soft sound was typically San Franciscan, refined to its most professional limits, and is still popular today. *Albums:* Anthology (CAP SVBB-11114) 1972; Book of Dreams (CAP SO-11630) 1977; Brave New World (CAP SKAO-184) 1969; Children of the Future (CAP SKAO-2920) 1968; Fly Like an Eagle (CAP SW-11497) 1976; The Joker (CAP SMAS-11235) 1973; Living in the U.S.A. (CAP STBB-717) 1969; Steve Miller Band Greatest Hits (CAP SOO-11872) 1978; Number 5 (CAP SKAO 436) 1970; Recall the Beginning (CAP SMAS-11022) 1972; Rock Love (CAP SW-748) 1971; Sailor (CAP ST-2984) 1968; Your Saving Grace (CAP SKAO-331) 1970.

MILLER, VERN, JR. Horns, guitar, bass. Member of the Remains, 1965-67.

MILLIKAN, BOB Trumpet. Session for Johnny Winter (1974).

MILLINGTON, JEAN Bass. Member of Fanny, 1974.

MILLIUS, MIKE Vocal, harmonica. Member of the Five Dollar Shoes, 1972.

MILLS, CHAS Vocal. Session for Chris Spedding (1976-77).

MILLS, JACK Guitar. Replaced Jim Mullen in Brian Auger's Oblivion Express, 1973-78. Session for Chris Youlden (1974).

MILLS, JERRY Mandolin. Member of the Ozark Mountain Daredevils, 1977.

MILNER, BRUCE Keyboards, vocal. Member of Every Mother's Son, 1967-68.

MILO, PETER Drums. Session for Country Joe McDonald (1975).

MILSAP, MICHAEL Piano, vocal, synthesizer. Member of Face Dancer, 1980.

MINDBENDERS Eric Stewart—piano, guitar, drums; Paul Hancox—guitar, drums; James O'Neill—guitar; Graham Gouldman—guitar; Wayne Fontana—vocal. Under the direction of Fontana, they scored with a "Groovy Kind of Love" in 1966, but failed to follow it up successfully. *Album:* A Groovy Kind of Love, 1966.

MINER, BILL Drums, vocal. Member of Calico, 1975-76.

MINER, DAVID Bass. Session for Leon Russell (1976); the Alpha Band (1977).

MINGLE, BRENT Guitar. Member of Osiris, 1978.

MINHINNET, RAY Guitar. Member of Frankie Miller's Full House, 1977.

MINK, BEN Mandolin, fiddle, vocal. Member of the Silver Tractors, 1976-77, and FM, 1979.

MINNEAR, KERRY Keyboards, cello, vocal. Member of Gentle Giant since 1971.

MINNELLI, LIZA Vocal. Actress/singer daughter of Judy Garland. Session for Alice Cooper (1973); Hilly Michaels (1980). *Albums:* The Act (DRG 6101); Cabaret (MCA D-752); Flora, the Red Menace (VIC CBLI-2760); It Amazes Me (CAP SM-2271); Live at the London Palladium (CAP ST-11191); Liza with a "Z" (COL KC-31762); Maybe This Time (CAP SM-11080); Liza Minnelli (AAM 4141); Minnelli Four-Sider (AAM 3524); New York, New York (UAR LKGL-750); There Is a Time (CAP SM-11803); The Singer (COL KC 32149); Live at the Wintergarden (COL PC 32854); Live at the Olympia in Paris (AAM); New Feelin' (AAM); Come Saturday Morning (AAM).

MINOR, DAVID Guitar. Member of the Great Society.

MINTER, LINDSEY Drums. Member of Navasota, 1972.

MINTER, PAUL Bass. Member of Navasota, 1972.

MINTZ, BILLY Drums. Member of Lowry Hamner and the Cryers, 1978.

MIRACLES See Smokey Robinson and the Miracles.

MIRANDA, BOB Vocal. Member of the Happenings, 1966-68.

MIRO, JENNIFER Vocal, keyboards. Member of the Nuns, 1980.

MIRONOV, JEFF Guitar. Played on the posthumous Hendrix albums "Crash Landing" and "Midnight Lightning," 1975. Session for Ringo Starr (1977); Martin Mull (1977); Kate and Anna McGarrigle (1977-78); the Euclid Beach Band (1979); Far Cry (1980); Paul Simon (1980).

MISCULIN, JOEY Accordion. Session for the Iron City Houserockers (1980).

MISENER, BILL Vocal. Session for Alice Cooper (1976).

MISSING LINK Group from which Mickey Dolenz of the Monkees began.

MISSISSIPPI Russ Johnson—vocal, guitar; Graham Goble—vocal; John Mower—vocal. *Album:* Mississippi (FSY 9438) 1973.

MISSOURI Ron West—guitar, keyboards, vocal; Lane Turner—guitar (until 1978); Alan Cohen—bass; Bill Larson—drums (until 1978); Web Waterman—vocal, guitar (1979); Randall Platt—keyboards (1979); Dan Billings—drums (1979). *Albums:* Missouri; Welcome Two Missouri (POL 1-6206) 1979.

MISTERIOSO, L'ANGELO Guitar. Session for Jack Bruce (1969).

MISTRESS Charlie Williams—vocal; Kenny Hopkins—guitar, vocal; Danny Chauncey—guitar, vocal; David Warner Brown—bass, vocal; Chris Paulsen—drums. *Album:* Mistress (RSO 1-3059) 1979.

MITCHELL, ADAM Keyboards, vocal, guitar, writer, producer. Original member of the Paupers, 1966-69. Reappeared as a soloist after a ten-year absence. Produced Manhattan Transfer (1971). *Album:* Redhead In Trouble (WBR K-3325) 1979.

MITCHELL, BILLY Tenor saxophone. Session for Martin Mull (1974). *Albums:* How's the Time (CTL 7611); Songs for Fun (DTN 212).

MITCHELL, BLUE Trumpet. Played with John Mayall, 1971-73. Member of Zulu. Session for Terry Reid (1976); John Mayall (1977). *Albums:* African Violet (MCA 9328); Blue Time (MLS 47055); Blue's Blues (MST 413); Doin' the Thing (BLN LT-84076); Graffiti Blues (MST 408); Jazz (MST 408); Last Tango Blues (MST 392); Many Shades of Blue (MST 402); Blue Mitchell (MST 315); Summer Soft (MCA 9347); Vital Blues (MST 343).

MITCHELL, DAN Drums. Member of the Moving Sidewalks.

MITCHELL, JAMES Baritone saxophone. Member of the Memphis Horns. Session for Clarence Carter (1967); Wilson Pickett (1968); Boz Scaggs (1969); Paul Butterfield (1980).

MITCHELL, JEFF Keyboards, vocal. Member of Dakota, 1980.

MITCHELL, JOHN NORMAN Keyboards, synthesizer, vibes. Member of the Baker-Gurvitz Army for their first album, 1975.

MITCHELL, JONI Guitar, keyboards, vocal, writer. Real name: Roberta Joan Anderson. Born 11/7/43. In 1969, her hit "Both Sides Now" gave her enough publicity to elevate her in the feminine folk singer hierarchy with Judy Collins and Buffy Ste. Marie. Over the years, her own material and talent have pushed her to the head of the field. Session for James Taylor; David Crosby (1971); David Blue (1975); the Band (1978). *Albums:* Blue (RPS 2038); Clouds (RPS 6341) 1969; Court and Spark (ASY 7E-1001); Don Juan's Reckless Daughter (ASY BB-701) 1977; For the Roses (ASY 5057) 1972); Hissing of Summer Lawns (ASY 7E-1051) 1975; Hejira (ASY 7E-1087); Ladies of the Canyon (RPS 6376); Miles of Aisles (ASY 202); Mingus (ASY 5E-505) 1979; Joni Mitchell (RPS 6293) 1968; Joni Mitchell and the L.A. Express (ASY) 1974; Shadows and Light (ASY BB 704) 1980.

MITCHELL, LINDSEY Guitar. Member of Prism, 1977. Session for Ian Lloyd (1979).

MITCHELL, MITCH Drums. Born 6/9/47. Original member of the Jimi Hendrix Experience, 1967-70, and Ramatam, 1972. Session for Mike Vernon; Muddy Waters (1972); Free Creek (1973).

MITCHELL, OLLIE Trumpet. Session for B. B. King (1971); Bangla Desh (1971); Steely Dan (1974).

MITCHELL, SAM Guitar, dobro, slide guitar. Session for Long John Baldry (1971-75).

MITCHELL, TONY Bass, vocal. Member of Sherbet, 1976-80.

MITCHELL, VINCE Vocal. Session for Janis Joplin (1969).

MITCHELL, WILLIE Horns, percussion. Session for Paul Butterfield (1980).

MITCHUM, SNAPPER Bass. Replaced John Riley in the Son Seals Blues Band, 1978-80.

MITTEREGGER, H. Drums, vocal, percussion. Member of Nina Hagen Band.

MIYASHTA, FUMIO Vocal, guitar, flute, keyboards. Member of the Far East Family Band, 1977.

MO, MOSES Guitar. Member of Mother's Finest since 1976.

MOANS Dutch rock group that spawned Jaap Van Eik of Trace.

MOBERLYS Jim Basnight—guitar, vocal; Bill Walters—drums, vocal; Steve Grindle—bass, vocal; Ernie Sapiro—guitar, vocal. Seattle-based band that broke up in 1979. *Album:* The Moberlys (SFR) 1979.

MOBY GRAPE Jerry Miller—guitar; Peter Lewis —guitar; Bob Mosley—bass; Don Stevenson—drums; Skip Spence—guitar (1967-68); Christian Powell—bass (1978); John Oxindine—drums (1978). San Franciscan group popular in the 1960s on the West Coast. Re-formed in 1978. *Albums:* Great Grape (COL C-31098); Moby Grape (COL CS-9498) 1967; Wow (COL CXS-3) 1968; Moby Grape '69 (COL); Truly Fine Citizen (COL) 1969; Live Grape (ESC SAIR) 1978.

MOCK, DON Guitar, vocal. Member of the Crosswinds.

MOCKINGBIRDS British group featuring Graham Gouldman, writer for the Hollies, before he formed 10 CC.

MODELISTE, JOSEPH Drums. Member of the Meters, 1972. Session for Jess Roden (1974); Ian McLagen (1979).

MODERN LOVERS Leroy Radcliffe—guitar, vocal; Jonathan Richman—vocal, guitar; D. Sharpe —drums, percussion, vocal; Curly Keranen—bass (1977); Asa Brebner—bass, vocal (1978). *Albums:* Rock 'n' Roll with the Modern Lovers (BSY 0053) 1977; Modern Lovers Live (BSY 0055) 1978.

MOELLER, DEE Vocal. Session for Willie Nelson (1973).

MOEN, ERIC Saxophone, vocal, guitar. Member of the Sussman Lawrence Band, 1980.

MOERBE, DAVID Drums. Member of Denim, 1977, and Traveler.

MOERLIN, PIERRE Drums, percussion. Member of Gong since 1975. Session for Mike Oldfield

(1975); Mick Taylor (1979).

MOERS, MICHAEL Member of Telex, 1980.

MOFFET, GARY Guitar, vocal. Replaced David Henman in April Wine.

MOHAWK, ESSRA Vocal. *Albums:* Essra (PVS 2024) 1976; Essra Mohawk (ELK 7E 1023) 1974.

MOHN, DAVID Drums, vocal. Member of Randy Burn's Sky Dog Band, 1973, Johnny's Dance Band, 1977, and Nan Mancini and JDB, 1979.

MOHN, MELINDA Vocal. Member of the Crosswinds.

MOIRE, DAVEY Vocal. Session for Frank Zappa (1976-79).

MOJO Vocal, guitar. Member of Sawbuck, 1971.

MOLE, JOHN Bass. Member of Colosseum II, 1977.

MOLELLAND, SAM Bass. Session for Taj Mahal (1976).

MOLINA, JOSEPH Keyboards, trumpet, percussion. Member of Sod, 1971.

MOLINA, RALPH Drums, vocal. Co-founder of Crazy Horse, 1971. Session for Neil Young (1969-70, 73, 75, 78-79); Nils Lofgren (1976).

MOLLINGER, MAX Drums, vocal. Member of Gruppo Sportivo, 1978.

MOLLY HATCHET Danny Joe Brown—vocal (1978-80); Jimmy Farrar—vocal (1980); Dave Hlubeck—guitar; Banner Thomas—bass; Steve Holland—guitar; Duane Roland—guitar; Bruce Crump—drums. Timely reincarnation of the Lynyrd Skynyrd formula. *Albums:* Flirtin' with Disaster (EPC JE-36110) 1979; Molly Hatchet (EPC JE-35347) 1978; Beatin' the Odds (EPC FE 36572) 1980.

MOLNAR, GYORGY Guitar. Member of Omega, 1975-78.

MOLONEY, PADDY Percussion, arranger. Session for Art Garfunkel (1978).

MOM'S APPLE PIE Bob Fiorno—vocal; Tony Gigliotti—vocal; Dave Mazzochi—keyboards, vocal; Bob Miller—guitar; Joe Ahladis—guitar; Pat Ahladis—drums; Greg Yochman—bass; Bob Pinti—trumpet; Fred Marzulla—trombone. *Album:* Music (BNB BB LA 073-F) 1973.

MOMAN, CHIPS Guitar. Session for Doug Kershaw (1974).

MONAGHAN, WALT Bass, vocal. Original member of the Mick Abrahams Band, 1971-72. Replaced Jim Richardson in If, 1974; replaced John Sauter in Ted Nugent's Group, 1979.

MONARCH, MICHAEL Guitar. Original member of the Sparrow, 1965, before the group changed its name to Steppenwolf. Member of Detective, 1977.

MONARDO, MECO Trombone. Session for Free Creek (1973).

MONETTE, RAY Guitar, vocal. Replaced Paul Warren in Rare Earth, 1975-77.

MONEY, EDDIE Vocal, keyboards, saxophone. *Albums:* Eddie Money (COL PC-34909) 1977; Life for the Taking (COL JC-35598) 1978; Playing for Keeps (COL FC-36514) 1980.

MONEY, ZOOT Keyboards, vocal. Real name: George Bruno. A member of Blues Incorporated, and the Animals, 1967-68, after which he released a little-known solo album. Member of Centipede, 1971, and Grimms, 1973. Session for Peter Green (1970); Snape (1972); Eric Burdon (1977).

MONKEES Mickey Dolenz—guitar, vocal, drums; Davy Jones—vocal, tambourine; Michael Nesmith—bass, guitar, vocal; Peter Tork—guitar, bass, vocal. The marriage of rock music and television situation comedy was consummated in 1966 by four actors who answered an ad in Variety and became the Monkees. Before playing their own music on television, they mimed the music of the Candystore Prophets. *Albums:* Monkees (CGM) 1967; Headquarters (CGM) 1967; Pisces, Aquarius, Capricorn and Jones, Ltd. (CGM) 1967; Birds, Bees and Monkees (CGM); Head (CGM) 1968; Instant Replay (CGM) 1969; Greatest Hits (ARI 4089) 1976.

MONKMAN, FRANCIS Keyboards, guitar. Member of Curved Air. Session for the Alan Parsons Project (1976).

MONOTONES Recorded "The Book of Love," 1958.

MONTALDO, BOB Piano. Session for John Hammond (1980).

MONTAN, CHRIS Vocal. *Album:* Any Minute Now (TWC 620) 1980.

MONTANA, VINCE Vibes. Session for B. B. King (1973-74).

MONTANEZ, VICTOR Drums. Session for Paul Simon (1972).

MONTGOMERY, DAVID Drums. Member of Python Lee Jackson, 1972.

MONTGOMERY, JAMES Harmonica, vocal. Namesake of the James Montgomery Band, 1976.

JAMES MONTGOMERY BAND James Montgomery—harmonica, vocal; Bill Mather—bass; David Case—keyboards; Peter Bell—guitar; Chuck Purro—drums, percussion; Paul Lenart—guitar; David Woodford—reeds. *Album:* James Montgomery Band (ISL 9419) 1976.

MONTGOMERY, LEE Vocal. Session for Commander Cody (1978).

MONTGOMERY, MELBA Vocal. Session for Leon Russell (1973). *Albums:* Greatest Gift of All (ELK CM-6) 1975; Aching, Breaking Heart (CAP SM 113); Being Together (ALR 3077); Big 16 Country and Western Favorites (MCR 3113); Duets (MCR 3079); Melba Toast (MCR 3113); Melba Montgomery (ELK 75069) 1973; No Charge (ELK 75079) 1974; Something to Brag About (CAP SM 686).

MONTGOMERY, MIKE Keyboards, vocal, writer. Member of Bloontz, 1974, and original member of Backstreet Crawler, 1975-76.

MONTGOMERY, ROBBIE Vocal. Session for Dr. John (1972-73, 75); Bryan Ferry (1974).

MONTROSE, RONNIE Guitar, vocal. First gained his reputation filling in for Rick Derringer behind Edgar Winter, before forming his own groups, Montrose, 1973-78, and Gamma, 1979-present. Session for Gary Wright (1975).

MONTROSE Ronnie Montrose—guitar, vocal; Sam Hagar—vocal; Denny Carmassi—drums; Bill Church—bass (1973); Alan Fitzgerald—bass, synthesizer (1974-75); James Alcivar—keyboards (1975); Bob James—vocal (1975). Montrose left Edgar Winter to form his own hard rock band in 1973. Featured vocalist Hagar went solo in 1975. *Albums:* Jump on It (WBR B-2963) 1976; Montrose (WBR K-3106) 1973; Montrose (WBR B-2892) 1975; Open Fire (WBR K-3134) 1978; Paper Money (WBR B-2823) 1974; Montrose (WBR 2740) 1973.

MOODY, MICK Guitar. Replaced Neil Hubbard in Juicy Lucy, 1970-71. Member of Snafu, 1973-75, the Young and Moody duet, 1977, and Whitesnake since 1978. Session for Gerry Rafferty (1978).

MOODY BLUES Justin Hayward—vocal, guitar, sitar, percussion, keyboards; Mike Pindar—keyboards, bass, guitar, vocal; John Lodge—bass, guitar, cello, percussion, vocal, drums; Ray Thomas—reeds, vocal; Graeme Edge—drums, percussion, keyboards, vocal; Denny Laine—guitar, vocal (until 1966); Clint Warwick—bass, vocal (until 1966). The Moody Blues arrived on the shirttails of the Beatles in 1965 with their hit "Go Now." Shortly thereafter, the group went into semiretirement because Laine had left to go solo. They returned in 1967 with a new orchestrated sound on their landmark album "Days of Future Passed." Repeating the same successful concept on later albums, the Moody Blues have achieved superstardom, also with success in their solo ventures. *Albums:* Days of Future Passed (DER 18012) 1967; Every Good Boy Deserves Favour (THS 5) 1971; In Search of the Lost Chord (DER 18017) 1968; Moody Blues No. 1 (LON PS-428) 1965; Octave (LON PS-708) 1978; On the Threshold of a Dream (DER 18025) 1969; Question of Balance (THS 3); Seventh Sojourn (THS 7) 1972; This is the Moody Blues (THS 2-12-13) 1974; To Our Children's Children's Children (THS 1); Caught Live and 5 (THS) 1977.

MOOG, PHIL Vocal. Voice of UFO since 1974.

MOON, DOUG Guitar. Session for Captain Beefheart and His Magic Band (1969).

MOON, KEITH Drums, percussion, vocal. Born 8/23/47. Wild man drummer for the legendary Who. Died 9/6/78. Session for Lord Sutch; John Entwhistle (1971); Nilsson (1974). *Album:* Two Sides of the Moon (MCA) 1975.

MOONEY, RALPH Steel guitar. Member of Waylon Jenning's Waylors, 1973-76.

MOONEY, THOM Drums. Member of the Nazz, 1968-69; Paris, 1975; and Tatoo, 1976.

MOONGLOWS Early name for the Spinners.

MOONLIGHTERS Bill Kirchen—vocal, guitar; Steve Fishell—pedal steel guitar; Steve MacKay—saxophone; Don Kennedy—vocal, bass; Rick Higginbotham—vocal, guitar; Rich Casanova—fiddle; Tony Johnson—vocal, piano, drums. *Album:* Moonlighters (AMH 1009) 1977.

MOONQUAKE Hovaness Hagopian—guitar, vocal; Jack August—bass, vocal; Derek Kendrick—drums, percussion, vocal. *Album:* Starstruck (FSY) 1975.

MOONRIDER Keith West—vocal, guitar; Chico Greenwood—drums; John Weider—guitar, vocal; Bruce Thomas—bass. Former Animal Weider's return to rock with partner West in 1975. *Album:* Moonrider (ANC 2010) 1975.

MOORE, ALAN Trombone. Session for Savoy Brown (1969).

MOORE, ALAN Drums. Replaced John Hinch in Judas Priest, 1974-76.

MOORE, ALBERT B. Flute, vocal. Member of Sweetwater.

MOORE, ANTHONY Guitar, producer. Session for Manfred Mann (1979); Kevin Ayers (1978).

MOORE, BOB Bass, vocal, guitar. Session for Harvey Mandel; Tom Rapp; Leon Russell (1973); Martin Mull (1975); Bill Medley (1978).

MOORE, BOBBYZIO Saxophone, keyboards, guitar, percussion. Member of the Nu Kats, 1980.

MOORE, DALE Keyboards. Session for No Dice (1979).

MOORE, DANIEL Vocal. With brother Matthew, part of Joe Cocker's Greatest Show On Earth, 1970. Session for Martin Mull (1973).

MOORE, DANNY Trumpet. Session for Taj Mahal (1978).

MOORE, DON Bass. Session for Ellen McIlwaine (1973).

MOORE, ERIC Bass. Original member of the Capital City Rockets, 1973, and the Godz, 1978-79.

MOORE, FREDDY Guitar, vocal, percussion. Member of the Nu Kats, 1980.

MOORE, GARY Guitar, vocal. Member of Colosseum II, 1977. Replaced Brian Robertson in Thin Lizzy, 1978-79. *Albums:* Back on the Streets (JET JZ-36187) 1978; Earth Will Sing (TEM 7091).

MOORE, GIL Drums, vocal. Member of Triumph since 1979.

MOORE, JERRY Keyboards. Member of Texas, 1973.

MOORE, KEVIN Guitar. Member of Zulu.

MOORE, KIM Vocal. Member of Esperanto, 1975.

MOORE, LINDSEY Vocal. Session for the Kinks (1975).

MOORE, MATTHEW Vocal, keyboards. With brother Dan, part of Joe Cocker's Greatest Show on Earth, 1970. Session for Martin Mull (1973); Jennifer Warnes (1976). *Albums:* Winged Horses (CBO JZ 35611) 1978; The Sport of Guessing (CBO JZ 36118) 1979.

MOORE, MIKE Bass. Session for Martin Mull (1974).

MOORE, MO Bass, vocal. Member of Nektar, 1972.

MOORE, NICKY Vocal. Member of the Tiger, 1976.

MOORE, PAT Bass. Member of the Goose Creek Symphony.

MOORE, PETE Vocal. Member of Smokey Robinson and the Miracles.

MOORE, SAM Vocal. Sam of Sam and Dave.

MOORE, TIM Drums, keyboards, guitar, bass, vocal. *Albums:* Behind the Eyes (ASY 7E-1042) 1975; High Contrast (ASY 6E-179) 1979; Tim Moore (ASY 7E-1019) 1974; White Shadows (ASY 7E-1088) 1977.

MOORE, TOM Keyboards. Member of the Moving Sidewalks.

MOORS, DON Vibes. Session for Taj Mahal (1976).

MOORSHEAD, JOHN Guitar. Original member of Aynsley Dunbar's Retaliation, 1968-70.

MORAIS, TREVOR Drums. Session for Jim Capaldi (1979); Mike Batt (1979).

MORALES, MIGUEL Guitar, bass. Member of Barrabas.

MORALES, RICKY Guitar. Member of Barrabas.

MORAN, GAYLE Vocal, keyboards. Member of Return to Forever, 1978.

MORAN, MIKE Vocal, guitar, percussion. Member of the Rockspurs, 1978-79.

MORAN, MIKE Keyboards, moog. Member of Howard Werth and the Moonbeams, 1975, and the Ian Gillan Band, 1976. Session for John Kongos (1972); Ray Thomas (1975-76); John Dawson Read (1976).

MORAZ, PATRICK Keyboards, synthesizer. Member of Mainhorse, 1971, and Refugee, 1972. Replaced Rick Wakeman in Yes, 1974-76. Session for Steve Howe (1975); Chris Squire (1975). *Albums:* Patrick Moraz (CMA 1-2201) 1975; Out in the Sun (IMP 1014) 1977.

MORDUE, EDDIE Baritone saxophone. Member of Candlestick Brass, 1977.

MOREING, JODY Vocal. Member of Giants, 1979.

MOREIRA, AIRTO Real name of Airto.

MORELAND, BRUCE Bass, piano. Member of the Wall of Voodoo, 1980.

MORELAND, MARC Guitar. Member of the Wall of Voodoo, 1980.

MORELLI, JOHN Drums. Member of the Tuff Darts, 1978, and Blue Angel, 1980.

MORETON, EVERETT Member of the English Beat, 1980.

MOREVE, JOHN Bass. Member of Steppenwolf.

MORFORD, GENE Vocal. Member of the Ron Hicklin Singers, 1979. Session for John Kay (1973).

MORGAN, BARRY Drums. Member of Blue Mink. Session for Elton John (1969, 71); Vigrass and Osbourne (1972); John Dawson Read (1976); Chris Spedding (1977).

MORGAN, CASSANDRA Member of Trout.

MORGAN, CHARLIE Drums, percussion, vocal. Member of Alibi, 1980.

MORGAN, CHRIS Guitar. Member of the reformed Canned Heat, 1979.

MORGAN, CHUCK Drums. Session for Delaney and Bonnie (1970).

MORGAN, JACK Slide guitar. Member of Kenny and the Kasuals.

MORGAN, JOHN RUSSELL Bass. Original member of the Sparrow, 1965, before the group became Steppenwolf in 1968.

MORGAN, PETER Bass. Session for "Jesus Christ Superstar" (1970); Vigrass and Osbourne (1972).

MORGAN, RON Guitar. Replaced Ken Williams in the Electric Prunes, 1967.

MORGAN, ROY Percussion. Member of Stackridge, 1974. Session for Mike Batt (1979).

MORGAN, TOMMY Harmonica. Session for Cashman and West (1972); the Bee Gees (1973); Neil Diamond (1976); Martin Mull (1978).

MORGAN, WARREN Keyboards. Member of Flash and the Pan since 1979.

MORGANFIELD, McKINLEY Real name of Muddy Waters.

MORGANSTEIN, ROD Drums, percussion. Member of the Dixie Dregs.

MORI, JOHNNY Percussion. Member of Hiroshima, 1980.

MORICE, ROYDEN Bass. Member of Hammersmith, 1975-77.

MORICE, WAYNE Bass, vocal. Member of Painter, 1973.

MORIN, BOB Drums. Session for B. B. King (1972).

MORIN, FRANK Horns. Original member of the Sir Douglas Quintet.

MORIN, JERRY Guitar, vocal. Member of the Small Wonder, 1976-77.

MORIN, MARTY Drums, percussion, vocal. Member of the Wireless, 1979.

MORITT, CHARLES Saxophone. Member of the Wax, 1980.

MORLEY, RICK Percussion. Member of the Crystal Mansion.

MORMAN, RALPH Vocal. Voice of Bux, 1976, and the Joe Perry Project, 1980.

MORNINGSTAR Rick Bacus—guitar, keyboards, chimes, vocal; Jerry Chambers—guitar, vocal; Michael Edmunds—guitar, vocal; Greg Harris—drums, percussion; Greg Leech—bass. *Album:*

Venus (COL JC 35713) 1979.

MOROUSE, DENNY Saxophone. Session for Taj Mahal (1978).

MOROVE, EDDIE Baritone saxophone. Member of the Candlestick Brass, 1977.

MORRELL, TOM Steel guitar. Member of Calico, 1975-76. Session for Willie Nelson (1976).

MORRESEY, DICKIE Saxophone. Session for Marc Benno (1979).

MORRILL, KENT Member of the Wailers.

MORRIS, CHRISTOPHER Guitar, vocal. Namesake of the Christopher Morris Band, 1977.

CHRISTOPHER MORRIS BAND Christopher Morris—guitar, vocal; Janet Morris—bass; Leslie Kuipers—guitar; Vince Colavita—drums. *Album:* Christopher Morris Band, 1977.

MORRIS, CLIFF Guitar. Session for Taj Mahal (1978); the Michael Zager Band.

MORRIS, FERREL Drums, congas. Member of the Coral Reefer Band. Session for J. J. Cale (1972, 74, 79); Neil Young (1978); Jimmie Hall (1980).

MORRIS, JANET Bass. Member of the Christopher Morris Band, 1977.

MORRIS, JEFF Guitar. Member of the Barbarians, 1979.

MORRIS, JIM Keyboards. Member of Trouble, 1977.

MORRIS, MARK Percussion. Session for the Allman Brothers (1980).

MORRIS, NIGEL Drums. Member of Isotope, 1974-75.

MORRIS, REX Tenor saxophone. Session for Savoy Brown (1969); Elton John (1971).

MORRIS, ROBERT Drums. Member of Whole Wheat, 1977, and the Johnny Van Zant Band, 1980.

MORRIS, ROGER Guitar. Member of the Psychedelic Furs, 1980.

MORRIS, STEPHEN Drums. Member of Joy Division, 1979-80.

MORRISON, JIM Vocal, writer. Born 12/8/43. Founder of the Doors, 1967-70. After over four years of recording, his macabre lyrics finally began receiving the attention they deserved only after his death, 7/3/71. Session with Jimi Hendrix (1968). *Album:* American Prayer (ELK 5E-502) 1978.

MORRISON, RICK Horns. Session for Long John Baldry (1980).

MORRISON, STERLING Guitar, bass. Original member of the Velvet Underground, 1967-70.

MORRISON, VAN Vocal, percussion, saxophone, harmonica, writer. Born 8/31/45. Former lead vocalist of Them. Began his solo career in 1968 and has built a large cult following. Session for Bill Wyman (1976); the Band (1978). *Albums:* Astral Weeks (WBR 1768) 1968; Best of Van Morrison (BNG 22); Blowin' Your Mind (BNG 218) 1968; Hard Nose the Highway (WBR 2712) 1973; Into the Music (WBR HS-3390) 1979; It's Too Late to Stop Now (WBR 2B-2760) 1974; Moondance (WBR K-3103); Van Morrison (WBR 1884); Period of Transition (WBR B-2987) 1977; Saint Dominic's Preview (WBR B-2633) 1972; T. B. Sheets (BNG 400); Them — Featuring Van Morrison (PRR BP-71053-54); Tupelo Honey (WBR 1950) 1971; Veedon Fleece (WBR B-2805) 1974; Wavelength (WBR K-3212) 1978; His Band and Street Choir (WBR WS 1884) 1970; Common One (WBR 3402) 1980.

MORRISON, WILLI Vocal, guitar. Member of Emigree, 1979.

MORRISSEY, DENNIS Reeds. Member of If.

MORRONGIELLO, TOMMY Guitar, vocal. Session for Jimmy Mack (1979); Ian Hunter (1980); D. L. Byron (1980).

MORSE, ELIZABETH Harp. Session for Martin Mull (1972).

MORSE, STEVE Guitar, banjo, pedal steel guitar. Member of the Dixie Dregs.

MORTON, GARTH Violin. Member of Centipede, 1971.

MORTON, JOHN Member of Hunger.

MORTON, RICHARD Guitar, keyboards, vocal. Member of Razmataz, 1972.

MORTON, ROCKETTE Bass, vocal, guitar. Member of Captain Beefheart and His Magic Band, 1969-72, 74.

MORTY Vocal, guitar. Member of the Racing Cars, 1976-78.

MOSE JONES Chris Seymour—drums, percussion; Marvin Taylor—guitar, vocal; Steve McRay—keyboards, vocal; Randy Lewis—bass, vocal. *Album:* Blackbird (VIC APLI 2793) 1978.

MOSES, BOBBY Drums. Replaced Roy Haynes in the Gary Burton Quartet. Session for Larry Coryell.

MOSES, CHUCK Bass, vocal. Member of Barooga, 1980.

MOSES, RICK Vocal. *Album:* Face the Music (TWC 575) 1979.

MOSHER, SKIP Bass, flute. Member of Mephistopheles.

MOSKOWITZ, DOROTHY Vocal. Member of the United States of America, 1968.

MOSLEY, BOB Bass. Member of Moby Grape, 1967-69.

MOSLEY, IAN Drums. Member of the Wolf, 1974. Replaced Pierre van der Linden in Trace, 1975.

MOSLEY, STEVE Drums. Session for Willie Nelson (1973).

MOSS, CECIL Trumpet. Session for Mike Vernon; Lightnin' Sam (1978).

MOSS, IAN Guitar, vocal. Member of the Cold Chisel, 1979.

MOSS, LARRY Member of Smith.

MOSS, PETER Banjo, mandolin, keyboards, vibes, violin, celeste, recorder. Session for Kim Fowley (1973).

MOSS, RALPH Percussion. Session for Creation (1976).

MOSS, RON Bass, vocal. Member of Player since 1977.

MOSS, WAYNE Guitar, percussion, engineer. Member of Area Code 615. Session for the Steve Miller Band (1970).

MOSSOTTI, ANDRE Bass. Member of the Coal Kitchen, 1977.

MOST, MICKIE Producer. Real name: Michael Haye. Produced Lulu; Donovan (1965-76); Terry Reid (1968-69); Jeff Beck (1968-69); Chris Spedding (1976, 80); and others.

MOSTERT, CHRISTIAAN Saxophone, flute, keyboards, vocal. Member of Pollution, 1971, and the Goose Creek Symphony. Session for John Mayall (1979).

MOTELLO, ELTON Vocal. Leader of the group that bears his name, 1980.

ELTON MOTELLO Elton Motello—vocal; Mike Burcher—guitar, vocal; Walter Meter—drums, vocal; Andrew Goldberg—keyboards, vocal; J. P. Martins—bass, guitar. *Album:* Pop Art (PPT 9846) 1980.

MOTELS Martha Davis—vocal, guitar; Jeff Jourard—guitar (1979); Martin Life Jourard—keyboards, saxophone; Michael Goodroe—bass; Brian Glascock—drums; Tim McGovern—guitar (1980). *Albums:* Careful (CAP ST 12070) 1980; The Motels (CAP ST-11996) 1979.

MOTHER EARTH Lonnie Castillo—drums; Powell St. John—harmonica; Tracy Nelson—vocal; Martin Fierro—saxophone. Texas-born Nelson's first group before going solo in 1969. *Album:* Living with the Animals, 1968.

MOTHER'S FINEST Joyce Kennedy—vocal; Glenn Murdock—vocal; Moses Mo—guitar; Wizzard—bass; B. B. Borden—drums; Mike—keyboards. *Albums:* Another Mother Further (EPC PE-34699) 1977; Mother Factor (EPC JE-35546) 1978; Mother's Finest (EPC PE-34179) 1976; Mother's Finest Live (EPC JE-35976) 1979.

MOTHERS OF INVENTION Frank Zappa—guitar, vocal, writer; Ray Collins—vocal, harmonica (1966-70); Roy Estrada—bass, vocal (1966-70); James William Guerico—guitar; Jimmy Carl Black—drums (1966-70); Elliot Ingber—guitar (1966); Billy Mundi—drums (1967-68); Don Preston—piano (1967-74); Bunk Gardner—saxophone, percussion (1967-70); Ian Underwood—keyboards (1967-74); James Sherwood—saxophone (1967-70); Buzz Gardner—trumpet (1968-70); Arthur Tripp—percussion (1968-70); Don "Sugarcane" Harris—violin (1969-70); Mark Volman—vocal (1971); Howard Kaylan—vocal (1971); Aynsley Dunbar—drums (1971-72); George Duke—keyboards (1971-75); Martin Lickert—bass (1971); Ruth Underwood—percussion (1971-75); Jim Pons—vocal (1971-72); Bob Harris—keyboards (1971); Tom Fowler—bass (1973-75); Jeff Simmonds—guitar, vocal (1974); Bruce Fowler—trombone (1973-74); Walt Fowler—trumpet (1974); Napoleon Murphy Brock—saxophone, flute, vocal (1974-75); Ralph Humphrey—drums (1973-74); Jean Luc Ponty—violin (1973); Chester Thompson—drums (1974-75); Sal Marquez—trumpet, vocal (1972-74). In 1966, when the clean cut image was a prerequisite in the recording business, Zappa appeared with his Mothers, the total antithesis to commercial success. Zappa openly satirized his culture, his group, his audience, and anything else he chose. If the jokes and stories wore thin, there was always an overabundance of musical talent in his group, which continues through today. Session for Yoko Ono. *Albums:* Absolutely Free (VRV V6-5013) 1967; Freak Out (VRV 5005-2) 1966; We're Only In It for the Money ((VRV V65045X) 1968; Bongo Fury (DSC 2234) 1975; Burnt Weeny Sandwich (BIZ 6370) 1969; Grand Wazoo (BIZ 2093) 1972; Just Another Band from L.A. (BIZ 2075) 1971; Mothers—Fillmore East—June, 1971 (BIZ 2042) 1971; One Size Fits All (DSC 2216) 1975; Over-Nite Sensation (DSC K-2288) 1973; Roxy and Elsewhere (DSC 2DS-2202) 1974; Uncle Meat (BIZ 2MS-2024) 1968; Weasels Ripped My Flesh (BIZ 1018) 1970; Mothermania; Worst of the Mothers; Cruising with Ruben and the Jets (VRV V6-5055X) 1968; 200 Motels (UAR UAS 9956) 1971.

MOTHERSBAUGH, MARK Vocal, guitar. Member of Devo since 1978.

MOTHERSBAUGH, BOB Guitar, vocal. Member of Devo since 1978.

MOTHLE, ERNEST African drums. Session for Mike Oldfield (1975).

MOTORHEAD Lemmy—bass, vocal; Larry Wallis—guitar (1978); Phil Taylor—drums; Eddie Clarke—guitar (1979-present). Though they were formed in 1978, Motorhead waited until 1980 to make their U.S. debut. *Album:* Ace of Spades (MER SRM 1-4011) 1980.

MOTORS Andy McMaster—bass, keyboards, vocal; Nick Garvey—vocal, bass, piano, guitar, percussion; Bram Tchiakovsky—guitar, vocal (1977-78); Ricky Slaughter—drums (1977-78). *Albums:* Motors (VIR) 1977; Tenement Steps (VGN 13139) 1980; Approved by the Motors (VIR) 1978.

MOTT THE HOOPLE Ian Hunter—piano, guitar, vocal, writer (1969-75); Mike Ralphs—guitar, vocal (1969-73); Overend Watts—bass, vocal; Dale "Buffin" Griffin—drums, vocal; Verden Allen—organ (1969-73); Ariel Bender—guitar, vocal (1974); Morgan Fisher—keyboards, vocal (1974-76); Ray Major—guitar, vocal (1974-76); Nigel Benjamin—vocal (1976). Heroes of the glitter rock set, they began in 1969 using a dual keyboard format. Hunter's voice and lyrics were compared to Dylan's. In 1973, Ralphs left to join super-group Bad Company and in 1975, Hunter also left to pursue his solo career. Watts and Griffin attempted to hold the group together, but with less success than their fans expected. *Albums:* Rock and Roll Queen (ATC 7297); Wildlife (ATC 8284) 1971; All the Young Dudes (COL PC-31750) 1972; Brain Capers (ATC 8304) 1972; Greatest Hits (COL PC-34368) 1976; Mott (COL PC-32425) 1973; Mott the Hoople (ATC 8258) 1969; Mott Live (COL PC-33282) 1974; Shades of Ian Hunter (COL C2-36251) 1979; Mad Shadows (ACO) 1970; The Hoople (COL PC 32871) 1974; Drive On (COL PC 33705) 1975; Shouting and Pointing (COL) 1976.

MOTTAU, EDDIE Guitar. Session for John Lennon (1974).

MOUGHAN, DERMOT Keyboards. Member of the Lonely Boys, 1979.

MOULDING, COLIN Bass, vocal. Member of XTC since 1979.

MOULIN, MARC Member of Telex, 1980.

MOULTON, VICTOR Drums. Member of the Barbarians, 1979.

MOUNSEY, ROB Keyboards. Session for Taj Mahal (1978); Art Garfunkel (1979); John Mayall (1979); Steely Dan (1980).

MOUNTAIN Leslie West—guitar, vocal; Felix Pappalardi—bass, vocal, guitar; Corky Laing—drums; Steve Knight—keyboards; Rob Mann—guitar, keyboards (1973); Alan Schwartzberg—drums (1973); Dave Perry—guitar (1974). For a moment in 1969, it seemed that Cream had been reincarnated. Masterminded by former Cream associate Pappalardi, Mountain featured guitarist West and the driving rhythms of Laing. At every point, Mountain was Cream's equal yet they never fared as well commercially. In 1974, the group disbanded. See West, Bruce and Laing. Played at Woodstock, 1969. *Albums:* Avalanche (COL C-33088) 1974; Best of Mountain (COL PC-32079) 1973; Twin Peaks (COL PG-32818) 1973; Climbing (WDF 4501) 1969; Nantucket Sleighride (WND 5500) 1970; Flowers of Evil (WND 5501) 1971; The Road Goes on Forever (WND 5502) 1972.

MOUZON, ALPHONSE Drums. Original member of Weather Report, 1971. *Albums:* Back Together Again (ATC 18220); Trilogue—Live (PAU 7055); Virtue (PAU 7054).

MOVE Bev Bevan—drums; Trevor Burton—vocal, guitar; Chris Kefford—bass; Carl Wayne—guitar, vocal; Roy Wood—guitar, vocal, banjo, sitar; Rick Price—bass (1969-72); Jeff Lynne—vocal, piano, guitar, percussion (1969-72). Avant garde British rockers who appeared in 1967. They did not fare well with U.S. audiences until they broke up. Bevan went to the Electric Light Orchestra and Roy Wocd formed Wizard. *Albums:* The Best of the Move; Shazam; Split Ends (UAR).

MOVIES Jamie Lane—drums; Colin Gibson—bass (1980); Greg Knowles—guitar; Julian Diggle—percussion; Jon Cole—guitar, slide guitar, vocal; Mike Parker—keyboards (1977); Dave Quinn—bass, vocals (1976). *Albums:* India (VIC AFLI 3552) 1980; Double A (GTO 026); Movies (ARI 4085) 1976.

MOVING SIDEWALKS Bill Gibbons—vocal, guitar, harmonica; Tom Moore—keyboards; Don Summers—bass; Dan Mitchell—drums. Psychedelic rock from Houston, Texas, in the late 1960s. *Album:* Flash.

MOWATI, JUDY Vocal. Member of I Threes.

MOWER, JOHN Vocal. Member of Mississippi, 1973.

MOXHAM, PHILLIP Bass. Member of the Young Marble Giants, 1980.

MOXHAM, STUART Guitar, organ. Member of the Young Marble Giants, 1980.

MOXY Buddy Caine—guitar; Bill Wade—drums, percussion (1976-77); Terry Juric—bass; Buzz Sherman—vocal (1976-77); Earl Johnson—guitar; Danny Bilan—drums (1978); Michael Rynoski—vocal (1978). *Albums:* Moxy (MER SRM-1-1087) 1976; Moxy II (MER SRM-1-1115) 1976; Ridin' High (MER SRM-1-1161) 1977; Under the Lights (MER SRM-1-3723) 1978.

MOYSE, DAVID Guitar, vocal. Member of Air Supply.

MR. BIG Dicken—vocal; Pete Crowther—bass, vocal; John Burnip—drums, percussion. *Album:* Sweet Silence (EMI 3101) 1975.

MR. PERSONALITY Nickname of Lloyd Price.

MUCKIN, BOB Trumpet, flugelhorn. Replaced Earl Gardner in Southside Johnny and the Asbury Jukes, 1979-present.

MUDFLAPS, RHINESTONE, III Saxophone, vocal. Member of Duke and the Drivers, 1975.

MUELLER, BILL Guitar. Session for Bob Seger (1973-74).

MUELLER, TEDDY Drums. Member of the Axe since 1979.

MUGGLETON, PAUL Vocal, guitar. Member of the Omaha Sheriff, 1977.

MUGWUMPS Cass Elliot—vocal; Denny Doherty—vocal; Zal Yanovsky—vocal, guitar; James Hendricks—vocal, guitar. Starting places for Elliot and Doherty, who formed the Mamas and Papas, and Yanovsky, who joined John Sebastian to form the Lovin' Spoonful.

MUHLFRIEDEL, MIKE Bass. Member of the Vivabeat, 1980.

MUHOBERAC, LARRY Keyboards. Session for Seals and Crofts (1971).

MUIR, JAMIE Percussion. Member of King Crimson, 1973.

MULDAUR, GEOFF Vocal, guitar, slide guitar, keyboards. Member of the Jim Kweskin Jug Band, 1962-68, and Paul Butterfield's Better Days, 1973. Session for John Cale (1975). *Album:* Motion (RPS) 1976; Having a Wonderful Time (RPS) 1975; Geoff Muldaur/Amos Garrett (FLF 061) 1978; Blues Boy (FLF 301) 1979.

MULDAUR, MARIA Vocal, fiddle. Named Maria Grazia Ross Domenica d'Amato until she married Geoff Muldaur. Sensuously voiced soloist who rose to stardom in 1973 with "Midnight at the Oasis." Session for Paul Butterfield's Better Days (1963); the Doobie Brothers (1976); Elvin Bishop (1978); Leon Russell and Willie Nelson (1979). *Albums:* Jug Band Music (EVR 339); Maria Muldaur (RPS 2148) 1973; Southern Winds (WBR K-3162) 1978; Sweet Harmony (RPS 2235) 1976; Waitress in the Donut Shop (RPS MS4-2194) 1974; Gospel Nights (TAK 7084) 1980; Open Your Eyes (WBR BSK 3305) 1979.

MULFORD, ASHLEY Guitar. Member of the Mandala Band, 1975, and Sad Cafe, 1978-79.

MULHERIN, JOE Trumpet. Member of Larry Raspberry and the Highsteppers.

MULHERN, A. J. Vocal, percussion. Member of Randy Burn's Sky Dog Band, 1973.

MULHOLLAND, KEITH Bass. Member of Nutz, 1974-77.

MULL, MARTIN Guitar, piano, vocal, writer. Mull lacks neither talent nor understanding, as displayed in his various musical satires of the straight life, hippy life, 1940s swing music, the blues, country and western music, and movies. *Albums:* Days of Wine and Neuroses (CPN 0155) 1975; I'm Everyone I Ever Loved (MCA 997) 1977; In the Soop (VAN 79338) 1974; Martin Mull (CPN 0106) 1972; Martin Mull and His Fabulous Furniture (CPN 0117) 1973; Near Perfect/Perfect (ELK 6E-200) 1979; No Hits, Four Errors (CPN 0195) 1976; Normal (CPN 0126) 1974; Sex and Violins (MCA 1064) 1978.

MULLANEY, JAN Keyboards. Session for Blackjack (1979-80); Frank Carillo (1978-79).

MULLEN, JIM Guitar, vocal. Original member of Brian Auger's Oblivion Express, 1971-73. Session for Annette Peacock (1979).

MULLEN, RICHARD Guitar. Member of Denim, 1977, and Traveler.

MULLIGAN Bass, synthesizer, vocal. Member of Fashion, 1979.

MULLIGAN, DELLON Member of the Beau Brummels.

MULLIGAN, TIM Vocal, producer. Member of Crazy Horse, 1978. Session for Neil Young (1975).

MULRY, TED Vocal, bass, piano. Member of T.M.G., 1979.

MUMFORD, JOHN Trombone. Member of Ox, 1975. Session for Jack Bruce (1969).

MUNCE, GARY Bass. Member of the Floating Opera, 1971.

MUNDEN, DAVE Drums. Member of the Tremloes.

MUNDI, BILLY Drums. Began in the Lamp of Childhood before joining the Mothers of Invention, 1967-68. Founder of Rhinoceros, 1968. Member of Razmataz, 1972, and the Johnny Average Dance Band, 1980. Session for Bob Dylan (1970); Pearls Before Swine (1971).

MUNOZ, CARLOS Vocal. Session for Henry Gross (1975).

MUNOZ, EDDIE Guitar. Member of the Plimsouls, 1980.

MUNSON, ART Guitar. Member of the Righteous Brothers Band, 1966.

MURAOKO, MINORU Japanese wooden flute. Session for Leon Russell (1975).

MURCIA, JOEY Guitar. Session for Bill Wyman (1974); Jay Ferguson (1976-77); the Bee Gees (1977); Mickey Thomas (1977); Steve Stills (1978); Joe Cocker (1978); Joe Walsh (1978); Andy Gibb (1980).

MURCIANO, CHARLIE Keyboards, woodwind, vocal, vibes. Member of Foxy, 1978-79.

MURDOCK, GLENN Vocal. Member of Mother's Finest since 1976.

MURE, GARY Drums. Session for Taj Mahal (1978).

MURPHY, ALAN Guitar. Session for Long John Baldry (1979-80).

MURPHY, ALEC Guitar. Member of the Vivabeat, 1980.

MURPHY, ELLIOTT Guitar, keyboards, vocal. *Albums:* Just a Story from America (COL 34653) 1977; Night Lights (VIC APLI 1318) 1976; Night Lights, II (VIC APLI 1318) 1976; Just a Little Story from America, II (COL PC 34653) 1977.

MURPHY, BRETT Trumpet. Session for Andy Gibb (1980).

MURPHY, GERRY Drums. Member of the Clinic, 1973, and the John Payne Band, 1976.

MURPHY, HUGH Percussion. Session for Gerry Rafferty (1978).

MURPHY, JEFF Vocal, guitar. Member of the Shoes since 1979.

MURPHY, JOHN Bass, vocal. Member of the Shoes since 1979.

MURPHY, MATT Guitar. Session for Chuck Berry (1960); the Blues Brothers (1978-80).

MURPHY, MICHAEL Guitar, keyboards, vocal. *Albums:* Blue Sky Night Thunder (EPC PE-33290) 1976; Cosmic Cowboy Souvenir (AAM 4388) 1973; Flowing Free Forever (EPC PE-34220) 1976; Geronimo's Cadillac (AAM 4358) 1972; Lonewolf (EPC JE-35013) 1978; Michael Murphy (EPC KE-32835) 1974; Peaks, Valleys, Honky-Tonks and Alleys (EPC JE 35742) 1979; Swans Against the Sun (EPC 33851) 1975.

MURPHY, PAT Percussion. Session for Nilsson

(1975); Les Dudek (1977-78).

MURPHY, PAT Bass, vocal. Member of Arizona, 1976.

MURPHY, PAUL Drums. Member of DMZ, 1978.

MURRAY, BILL Keyboards. Session for Phillip Walker (1977).

MURRAY, CINDY Vocal. Session for Johnny Winter (1980).

MURRAY, DAVE Guitar. Member of Iron Maiden, 1980.

MURRAY, DEE Bass. Replaced Muff Winwood in the Spencer Davis Group, 1968. Alternated with Roger Glover backing Elton John before becoming a member of John's backup band, 1971-75. Member of the Dinettes, 1976. Session for Alice Cooper; Jimmy Webb (1977).

MURRAY, DON Drums. Member of the Charlie Daniels Band, 1975-79.

MURRAY, GEORGE Bass. Session for David Bowie (1977).

MURRAY, NEIL Bass. Member of Hanson, 1974, the National Health Band, 1977, and Whitesnake since 1978.

MURRAY, PAULINE Member of the Penetration, 1979.

MURRAY, ROY Horns. Member of Malo, 1972.

MURREY, WILLY Drums. Member of the Amazing Blondel, 1974.

MUSAR, ANDY Bass. Original member of Seatrain, 1968.

MUSCLE SHOALS HORNS Harrison Calloway—trumpet; Charles Rose—trombone; Harvey Thompson—saxophone. Session for Ian Matthews (1976); Richard Tate (1977). *Albums:* Born to Get Down (BNG 403); Doin' It to the Bone (ARA ST-50021).

MUSCLE SHOALS RHYTHM SECTION Randy McCormick—organ (1980); Barry Beckett—keyboards; Jimmy Johnson—guitar; Roger Hawkins—drums; Pete Carr—guitar (1978); David Hood—bass. Studio backup band. Session for Kim Carnes (1976); Bob Seger (1977-present).

MUSE, DAVID Keyboards, flute, tenor saxophone, harmonica. Member of Boneroo, 1974-77, and Firefall, 1978-present. Session for Firefall (1976-77).

MUSIC EXPLOSION Jamie Lyons—vocal; Don Atkins—guitar; Rick Nesta—guitar; Butch Stahl—bass, organ; Bob Avery—drums, harmonica. Ohio-based rockers that scored in 1967 with "Little Bit o' Soul." *Album:* A Little Bit o' Soul, 1967.

MUSIC MACHINE Sean Bonniwell—guitar; Keith Olson—bass, vocal; Mark Landon—guitar; Ron Edgar—drums; Doug Rhodes—organ, vocal. The Music Machine enjoyed a brief period of popularity with their single, "Talk, Talk" (1966). *Album:* Turn On (OSD 8875) 1966.

MUSMANNO, SCOTT Vocal. Session for Roy Buchanan (1977).

MUSON, ANDY Member of Jobraith, 1973-74. Session for Randle Bramblett (1975).

MUSSELWHITE, CHARLES Harmonica, vocal. Early Chicago blues man who played with Harvey Mandel and Barry Goldberg in Barry Goldberg's Blues Band and the Barry Goldberg Reunion before organizing Charlie Musselwhite's Southside Band. Session for John Hammond (1965, 68); Harvey Mandel. *Albums:* Leave the Blues to Us (CAP SM-11450); Stand Back (VAN 79232); Stone Blues (VAN 79287); Tennessee Woman (VAN 6528); Takin' My Time (ARH 1056); Goin' Back Down South (ARH 1074) 1974; Harmonica According to Charlie Musselwhite (KKM 305) 1978.

MUSSIDA, FRANCO Guitar. Member of P.F.M., 1973-77.

MYALL, BRIAN Played with John Mayall, 1962.

MYERS, CHARLES Drums. Session for Freddie King (1971).

MYERS, DON Bass. Member of J. B. Hutto's Hawks.

MYERS, GEOFFERY Bass, vocal. Original member of Spanky and Our Gang, 1967-69.

MYERS, JACK Bass. Member of Junior Wells Chicago Blues Band.

MYERS, PHIL Drums. Member of High Cotton, 1975.

MYERS, RICK Alto saxophone. Session for Taj Mahal (1976).

MYERS, TOBY Bass, vocal. Member of Roadmaster since 1978.

MYERS, TOM Guitar, sitar, autoharp, percussion. Member of Glider, 1977.

MYERS, TOM Vocal, keyboards. Member of the Elevators, 1980.

MYHILL, RICHARD Vocal. Session for Gary Brooker (1979).

MYLES, BILLY Real name of Freddy King.

MYLETT, JOHN Drums. Member of Nutz, 1974-77.

MYRIC, WELDON Steel guitar. Member of Area Code 615. Session for J. J. Cale (1971-74); Tom Rapp (1972); Leon Russell (1973); the Pointer Sisters (1974).

MYRICK, GARY Head of Gary Myrick and the Figures, 1980.

GARY MYRICK AND THE FIGURES Jack White; Gary Myrick; David Dennard; Ed Beyer—keyboards. *Album:* Gary Myrick and the Figures (EPC).

MYROW, FREDRIC Organ. Session for Nilsson (1975).

MYSIOR, BERNIE Bass. Member of Starwood, 1976.

MYSLIWIEC, LARRY Drums, percussion. Member of Skafish, 1980.

NABONNE, SHARON Vocal. Session for Mylon LeFevre (1979).

NACHTSHEIM, BOBBY Saxophone, harmonica. Member of One Hand Clapping, 1977-79.

NAEGELI, JUERG Keyboards, vocal. Member of Krokus, 1980.

NAFTALIN, MARK Keyboards. Member of the Paul Butterfield Blues Band, 1965-68. Session for Bill Wyman (1976); Mike Bloomfield (1977-79).

NAGLE, RON Keyboards, percussion. Member of the Durocs, 1979. Session for Stoneground (1971).

NAGY, JOHN Bass, cello, mandocello. Member of Earth Opera, 1968-69. Session for Andy Pratt (1973); Peter C. Johnson (1980).

NAIFEN, JERRY Drums. Session for the Dwight Twilley Band (1979).

NAILS, TERRY Bass, vocal. Member of Tommy Tutone, 1980.

NAIN, NANCY Vocal. Member of Chrysalis, 1968.

NALLS, JIMMY Guitar. Original member of Sea Level, 1977-78. Session for Gregg Allman (1974); Missouri (1979).

NAMERDY, DAVID Guitar. Member of the Catfish Hodge Band, 1979.

NANCE, KEVIN Keyboards. Session for Golden Earring (1978).

NANCE, MARY Vocal, percussion. Member of the Sunshine Company, 1967-68.

NANINI, JOE Percussion. Member of the Wall of Voodoo, 1980.

NANTUCKET Larry Uzzell—vocal; Tommy Redd—guitar, vocal; Kenny Soule—drums; Mark Downing—guitar; Eddie Blair—saxophone, keyboards, vocal; Pee Wee Watson—bass, vocal; Mike Uzzell—bass, keyboards, vocal (1978-79). *Albums:* Long Way to the Top (EPC JE-36523) 1980; Nantucket (EPC JE-35253) 1978; Your Face or Mine (EPC JE-36023) 1979.

NAPIER, ALEX Drums. Original member of Uriah Heap, 1970-71.

NARDELLA, STEVE Guitar, vocal. *Album:* It's All Rock and Roll (BDP 879) 1979.

NARDINI, ART Bass. Member of the Iron City Houserockers since 1979.

NARDINI, NORM Member of Diamond Reo, 1979.

NARELL, ANDY Steel drums, keyboards. Member of the Candle, 1972. Session for the New Riders of the Purple Sage; Taj Mahal; Jon Mark (1974); Phoebe Snow (1976).

NARIZ, WAZMO Vocal, guitar. Soloist backed by the Wazband. *Album:* Things Aren't Right (IRS 005) 1979.

NARLAND, KELLY Keyboards, vocal. Member of Lazy Racer since 1979.

NARRAWAY, ROGER Percussion. Member of Wally, 1974.

NASH, DICK Trombone. Session for Robbie Robertson (1980).

NASH, EARL Percussion. Session for B. B. King (1977).

NASH, GRAHAM Vocal, piano, writer, producer. Founder and head of the Hollies, 1963-66, before becoming part of Crosby, Stills, Nash and Young, 1969-71. When the group dissolved, he went solo, and later teamed with David Crosby. Part of "No Nukes," 1979. Produced Terry Reid (1976). Session for Dave Mason; Steve Stills (1975); Neil Young (1972, 73, 75); James Taylor (1976); Art Garfunkel; Terry Reid (1976); David Crosby (1971); John Sebastian (1970); Joni Mitchell (1975); Gary Wright (1979). *Albums:* Graham Nash/David Crosby (ATC 72280) 1972; Earth and Sky (CAP SWAK-12014) 1980; Songs for Beginners (ATC 7204); Wild Tales (ATC 7288) 1973.

NASH, JOHNNY Vocal. *Albums:* I Can See Clearly Now (EPC KE 31607) 1972; Let's Go Dancing (EPC JE 36311) 1979.

NASH, PAT Drums. Member of the Woods Band.

NASH, RICHARD Trombone. Session for Nilsson (1976).

NASHVILLE TEENS Recorded "Tobacco Road," 1964.

NASTY, RON Stage name of Neil Innes in the Rutles, 1978.

NATHAN, STEVE Keyboards. Member of the Boatz, 1979.

NATHO, HERBERT Vocal. Member of Ramses.

NATIONAL HEALTH BAND Dave Stewart—keyboards; Phil Miller—guitar; Neil Murray—bass; Pip Pyle—drums; Jimmy Hastings—reeds; Amanda Parsons—vocal; Alan Gowen—keyboards. *Album:* National Health (USA IMP 7002) 1977.

NATTY, PAUL Keyboards. Session for George Kooymans (1973).

NATURAL GAS Mark Clarke—bass; Joey Molland—guitar; Jerry Shirley—drums; Peter Wood—keyboards. *Album:* Natural Gas (PVS 2011) 1976.

NAUGHTON, BRIAN Guitar. Member of the Rockicks, 1977.

NAUGHTY SWEETIES Ian Jack—guitar, vocal; Rollo Smith—guitar, vocal; David Jackson—keyboards, vocal; Simeon Pillich—bass; Bartholomew E. Smith-Frost—drums, vocal. *Album:* Chinatown (DTL DLS-1) 1980.

NAUSEEF, MARK Drums, percussion. Original member of the Ian Gillan Band, 1976.

NAVARETTE, BOBBY Reeds, vocal. Member of Tierra, 1980.

NAVARRA, TEX Percussion. Session for Elton John (1969).

NAVASOTA Ray Pawlik—guitar; Steve Long—guitar; Paul Minter—bass; Lindsey Minter—drums; Dicky Sony—vocal. Hard-rocking group with enough energy, talent, and session men to make it big, but no air play or publicity. *Album:* Rootin' (ABC X757) 1972.

NAVE, R. G. Organ, percussion. Member of the Lemon Pipers, 1968.

NAYLOR, TONY Guitar, vocal. Member of the Avalanche, 1976.

NAZARETH Dan McCafferty—vocal; Manuel Charlton—guitar, vocal; Pete Agnew—bass, vocal; Darrel Sweet—drums, vocal; Zal Cleminson—guitar (1979-80). Masters of hard rock and roll savored in a blues base. *Albums:* Close Enough for Rock 'N' Roll (AAM 4562) 1976; Expect No Mercy (AAM 4666) 1977; Hair of the Dog (AAM 4511) 1975; Hot Tracks (AAM 4643) 1977; Loud 'n' Proud (AAM 3609) 1974; Malice in Wonderland (AAM 4799) 1980; No Mean City (AAM 4741) 1979; Rampant (AAM 3641) 1975; Razamanaz (AAM 4396) 1973; Nazareth (WBR BS 2615) 1972; Exercises (WBR BS 2639) 1972.

NAZZ Robert Antoni—keyboards, vocal; Todd Rundgren—guitar, writer; Carson Van Osten—bass; Thom Mooney—drums. Philadelphia rock group that debuted an alternative style of rock to the Beatles, 1968-69, under the direction of Todd Rundgren. *Albums:* The Nazz, 1968; Nazz, Nazz, 1969; Nazz, III.

NDAGU See Leon Ndagu Chancler.

NEAL, DAVE Drums, percussion, vocal. Member of Suzi Quatro's band since 1974.

NEAL, JACK Bass. Member of Gene Vincent and His Hub Caps, 1956-61.

NEAO, JEFFREY Drums. Member of Taxxi, 1980.

NEARY, BRIAN Vocal. Member of Photoglo, 1980.

NECIOSUP, ALEXANDRO Percussion. Session for John Mayall (1979).

NEELY, TED Vocal. Member of A-440, 1978.

NEESON, DOC Vocal. Member of Angel City since 1977.

NEGRON, CHUCK Vocal. Member of Three Dog Night.

NEIDLINGER, BUELL Bass. Member of the Peter Ivers Band, 1974.

NEIL, FRED Guitar, vocal, writer. From Greenwich Village, Neil played with contemporaries John Sebastian and Felix Pappalardi, writing his own songs in the 1960s. His style, folksy and bluesy; his voice, melodic and full. *Albums:* Tear Down the Walls; Everybody's Talkin' (CAP SM-294); Little Bit of Rain (ELK 74073); Other Side of This Life (CAP ST 657); Down to Earth (PST 98005); Remember the Future (PST); Sessions (CAP ST 2862); Bleeker and McDougal; Fred Neil, 1967.

NEIL, LU ANN Harp. Session for Frank Zappa (1976).

NEILSON, ARTHUR Guitar. Member of Blue Angel, 1980.

NEIUWSTEDE, EVERT Vocal. Member of the Urban Heroes, 1980.

NEKTAR Roye Albrighton—guitar, vocal; Taff Freeman—keyboards, vocal; Ron Nowden—drums, percussion; Mo Moore—bass, vocal; Mick Brockett—lights. *Albums:* Recycles (PPT) 1975; A Tab in the Ocean (PPT) 1972; Down to Earth (PPT 98005) 1974; Magic Is a Child (POL PD 1-6115) 1977; Thru the Ears (IMP 9001) 1978.

NELSON, BILL Guitar, vocal, producer. Founder of Be Bop Deluxe, 1974-78, and Red Noise, 1979. Produced the Original Mirrors (1980).

NELSON, BOBBY Piano. Session for Willie Nelson (1973-79).

NELSON, DAVID Guitar, mandolin, vocal. Original member of the New Riders of the Purple Sage, and Spy, 1980.

NELSON, DAVID Saxophone, percussion, vocal. Member of Upepo.

NELSON, ERIC Bass. Member of Nick Gilder's backup band since 1977.

NELSON, ERROL Keyboards. Member of Skin, Flesh and Bone, 1975.

NELSON, IAN Saxophone, keyboards. Member of Red Noise, 1979.

NELSON, MARTY Vocal. Session for Henry Gross (1973, 75, 77).

NELSON, RICK Guitar, vocal, writer. Heart-throb of TV's "Ozzie and Harriet," Rick's popularity began in 1958 with "Poor Little Fool." Though not always on the charts, he was never far away. He recorded constantly through the 1960s, with large crowds appearing at his live appearances. In the 1970s he broke into rock again with his new sound and the Stone Canyon Band. Session for Keith Moon (1975). *Albums:* Ricky, 1958; Rick Nelson, 1958; Ricky Sings Again, 1959; Rick is 21; Rick Nelson, 1973; Rick Nelson Sings for You, 1964; Best Always, 1965; Love and Kisses, 1966; Rick Nelson, 1966; Bright Lights and Country Music, 1966; Spotlight on Rick, 1965; On the Flip Side, 1967; Country Fever, 1967; Another Side of Rick, 1968; Best Sellers by Rick (IMP 12218); Garden Party (MCA 62); Million Sellers by Rick Nelson (IMP); Rick Nelson Country (MCA 2-4004); Nelson in Concert (MCA 3); Rick Sings Nelson (MCA 20); Rudy the Fifth (MCA 37); Very Best of Rick Nelson (UAR LA 330-E);

Windfall (MCA 383); Ricky (UAR LM-1004) 1980; Long Vacation (IMP 12244); Intakes (EPC 34420) 1977; Ricky Nelson (UAR UAS 9960); Garden Party (DEC 7-5390) 1972.

NELSON, SANDY Drums. Rhythmic instrumentalist who recorded "Let There Be Drums" (1961). *Albums:* Let There Be Drums (IMP); Very Best of Sandy Nelson (UAR UALA 440-E); Big Bad Boss Beat (OSR 8871).

NELSON, STEVE Drums, vocal. Member of Earthquake since 1966.

NELSON, TERRY Percussion. Session for Jay Ferguson (1980).

NELSON, TRACY Vocal. Member of Mother Earth, 1968. Session for Boz Scaggs (1969). *Albums:* Sweet Soul Music, 1975; Tracy Nelson, 1974; Revolution; Time Is on My Side, 1976; Come See About Me (FLF 209) 1980; Deep Are the Roots (PRS 7726) 1969; Homemade Songs (FLF 052); Poor Man's Paradise (COL KC 31759) 1973; Sweet Soul Music (MCA 494) 1975.

NELSON, WALTER Guitar. Session for Fats Domino (1951-58).

NELSON, WILLIE Guitar, vocal, writer. Comrade of Waylon Jennings, he is considered an "outlaw" western artist and songwriter and is widely respected. Teamed with Leon Russell in 1979 for a double set of updated country hits. Made his motion picture debut in "Electric Horseman," 1979. Session for Leon Russell (1974); Rodney Crowell (1978). *Albums:* Banded Together (EPC JE-36177) 1979; Best of Willie Nelson (UAR LW-086) 1978; Columbus Stockade Blues (CDN 7018); Country Willie (UAR LW-410) 1975; Danny Davis and Willie Nelson/Nashville Brass (VIC AHLI-3549) 1980; Electric Horseman (COL JSA-36327) 1979; Face of a Fighter (LNS 4602) 1978; Honeysuckle Rose (COL S2-36752) 1980; Honky Tonkin' (VIC AHLI-3422); Willie Nelson and His Friends (PLN 24); Willie Nelson Live (VIC AFLI 1487) 1976; Willie Nelson Sings Kris Kristofferson (COL JC 36188) 1979; One for the Road (COL KC2-36064) 1979; The Outlaws (VIC AFLI 1321) 1976; Phases and Stages (ATC 7291) 1974; Pretty Paper (COL JC-36189); Red Headed Stranger (COL KC 33482) 1975; Redneck Mothers (VIC AYLI 3674); San Antonio Rose (COL JC-36476) 1980; Shotgun Willie (ATC 7262) 1973; Sound in Your Mind (COL PC-34092) 1975; Spotlight on Willie Nelson (CDN ACLI 0705) 1974; Stardust (COL JC 35305) 1978; Sweet Memories (VIC AHLI 3243) 1979; There'll Be No Teardrops Tonight (UAR LT-930); To Lefty from Willie (COL PC 34695) 1977; The Troublemaker (COL KC 34112) 1976; What Can You Do To Me Now (VIC AFLI 1234) 1975; Willie and Family Live (COL KC2 35642) 1978; Willie Before His Time (VIC AYLI 3671); Wishing You a Merry Christmas (VIC ANLI 1952); Yesterday's Wine (ANLI 1102) 1971.

NELTNER, NED Guitar, vocal. Member of Junior Cadillac.

NEMEROVSKI, JOHN Piano. Member of the Floating Opera, 1971.

NEOPOLITAN, RAY Bass. Session for the Doors (1970-71); John Sebastian (1970).

NERVOUS EATERS Steve Cataldo—vocal, guitar, writer; Jonathan Paley—guitar, vocal; Jeff Wilkinson—drums; Rob Skeen—bass, vocal. *Album:* Nervous Eaters (ELK 6E-282) 1980.

NERVUS REX Shaun Brighton—vocal, guitar; Lauren Agnelli—keyboards, vocal, guitar; Dianne Athey—bass; Jonathan Lee Gildersleeve—drums. *Album:* Nervus Rex (DML 1-5002) 1980.

NESBITT, PENELOPE Vocal. Session for Chris Spedding (1978).

NESE, RICHARD Bass. Original member of Ultimate Spinach, 1968-69.

NESMITH, MICHAEL Bass, guitar, vocal, writer. Singer-turned-actor for the Monkees, 1966-69. After the Monkees, he formed the First National Band before soloing. *Albums:* And the Hits Just Keep On Comin' (PAC 7-116); Pretty Much Your Standard Ranch Stash (PAC 7-117) 1973; Live at the Palais (PAC 7-118) 1978; Infinite Riders on the Big Dogma (PAC 7-130) 1979; The Prison (PAC 11-101A) 1974; Compilation (PAC 7-106) 1973.

NESTA, RICK Guitar. Member of the Music Explosion, 1967.

NETTO, LOZ Guitar. Member of Sniff 'n' the Tears, 1978-80.

NETWORK Michael Ricciardella—drums, vocal; Mike Coxton—keyboards; Howard Davidson—bass; Richie C.—guitar; Jean Paul Gaspar—percussion, vocal; George Bitzer—keyboards, vocal; John Vinvi—vocal. *Album:* Network (EPC PE 34979) 1977.

NEUMANN, JOHN Bass. Accompanied the Pointer Sisters, 1973-75.

NEUTRONS Will Youatt—bass, guitar, vocal; John Weathers—drums, vocal; Phil Ryan—keyboards; Taff Williams—guitar; Stuart Gordon—violin; Dave Charles—drums. *Album:* Black Hole Star (UAR Z9652) 1974.

NEVILLE, ARTHUR "RED" Organ. Member of the Meters, 1973.

NEVILLE, MICHAEL Bass, vocal. Member of Magnet, 1979.

NEVILLE-FERGUSON, JANET Vocal. Session for the Mothers of Invention (1972).

NEVINS, NANSI Vocal, guitar. Member of Sweetwater.

NEVITT, STUART Drums. Member of Shadowfax, 1976.

NEW, STEVE Session for Iggy Pop (1980).

NEW ADVENTURES Peter Bootsman—guitar,

vocal; Harry de Winter—bass, vocal, keyboards; Henk Torpedo—drums. Produced by Golden Earring's George Kooymans, New Adventure's debut album proved a nondescript name and bland cover photo can successfully hinder talent. *Album:* New Adventures (POL 1-6278) 1980.

NEW CACTUS BAND See Cactus.

NEW ENGLAND John Fannon—guitar, vocal; Hirsh Gardner—drums, vocal; Gary Shea—bass; Jimmy Waldo—keyboards, vocal. *Albums:* New England (INF 9007); Explorer Suite (ELK GE 307) 1980.

NEW LOST CITY RAMBLERS Mike Seeger—fiddle; Tom Paley—banjo (until 1968); John Cohen—guitar; Tracy Schwartz—vocal, percussion, fiddle, banjo (1968). Bluegrass-folkers who were playing their music to and through the folk explosion of the 1960s. *Albums:* American Moonshine and Prohibition (FLW 5263) 1963; Depression Songs (FLW 5264) 1960; Modern Times (FLW 31067) 1968; New Lost City Ramblers, Vol. I—V (FLW 2395-99); New Lost City Ramblers (FLW 2492) 1961; "New" New Lost City Ramblers (FLW 2491); On the Great Divide (FLW 31041) 1975; Remembrance of Things to Come (FLW 31035) 1973; 20 Years of Concert Performances (FLF 102); Moonshine and Prohibition (FLW 5263) 1962; Sing Songs (FLW 2494) 1961; Cousin Emmy (FLW 1015) 1968.

NEW RIDERS OF THE PURPLE SAGE Jim Dawson—guitar, vocal, writer; David Nelson—guitar, mandolin, vocal; Dave Torbert—bass, guitar, vocal; Spencer Dryden—drums, percussion; Skip Battin—bass, vocal, percussion; Buddy Cage—pedal steel guitar, vocal. San Francisco country vocal group that got their break as proteges of the Grateful Dead. Part of Fillmore, 1972. *Albums:* Adventures of Panama Red (COL PC-32450) 1973; Best of New Riders of the Purple Sage (COL PC 34367) 1976; Gypsy Cowboy (COL KC 31930) 1972; Home, Home on the Road (COL PC-32870) 1974; Marin County Line (MCA 2307) 1977; New Riders of the Purple Sage (COL PC-30888) 1971; Oh, What a Mighty Time (COL PC-33688) 1975; Powerglide (COL C 31284) 1972; Brujo (COL); New Riders (COL) 1976; Who Are Those Guys (COL) 1977.

NEW VAUDEVILLE BAND Pre-World War II music was given a humorous yet entertaining rock treatment by the New Vaudeville Band when "Winchester Cathedral" became their hit, complete with megaphone, 1966. *Albums:* Winchester Cathedral, 1966; New Vaudeville Band On Tour.

NEW YORK DOLLS Johnny Thunder—guitar, vocal; Sylvain Sylvain—guitar, piano, vocal; David Johansen—vocal, percussion; Arthur Kane—bass; Jerry Nolan—drums. Excessive publicity killed the Dolls before they were even heard. *Albums:* New York Dolls (MER) 1973; Too Much Too Soon (MER) 1974.

NEW YORK ELECTRIC STRING ENSEMBLE Bach on electric guitars? At least it was an untried angle yet to be exploited in 1967. *Album:* New York Electric String Ensemble, 1967.

NEW YORK ROCK AND ROLL ENSEMBLE Dorian Rudnytsky—piano, cello, guitar, bass, trumpet, French horn; Martin Fulterman—drums; Michael Kamen—keyboards, reeds, guitar, vocal; Brian Corrigan—guitar, vocal; Clifford Nivison—guitar. Classical baroque rock of 1968, but like the other novelty acts of the time, they were unable to survive. *Albums:* New York Rock and Roll Ensemble, 1968; Faithful Friends, 1969; Roll Over (COL 30033).

NEWBEATS Recorders of the pre-disco era hit "Bread and Butter," 1966. *Albums:* Big Beat Sounds, 1966; Bread and Butter, 1966; Run, Baby, Run, 1966.

NEWBERRY, MICKEY Vocal. *Albums:* Festival of Acoustic Music (FSY 79009); Frisco Mabel Joy (ELK 75055) 1973; Heaven Help the Child (ELK 74107) 1973; His Eye Is on the Sparrow (MCA 44011); I Came to Hear the Music (ELK 7E-1007) 1974; Live at Montezuma Hall/Looks Like Rain (ELK 7E-2007); Lovers (ELK 7E-1030) 1975; Rusty Tracks (MCA 44002); The Sailor (MCA HB-44017).

NEWCOM, GEORGE Drums. Member of the Loading Zone, 1968.

NEWELL, ALFRED Guitar. Session for Waylon Jennings (1974).

NEWELL, NICK Saxophone, flute, keyboards. Member of the Keef Hartley Band. Session for Chris Youlden (1974); Kinks (1975, 80).

NEWELL, ROGER Bass. Member of Rick Wakeman's backup band, 1974-77.

NEWHAM, COLIN Keyboards. Member of the Reels, 1980.

NEWHOUSE, ROB Guitar, vocal. Member of the Coal Kitchen, 1977.

NEWKIRK, LOREN Keyboards. Member of Aim, 1974.

NEWLON, JAMES Guitar. Member of Bux, 1976.

NEWMAN, ANDY Saxophone, keyboards. Namesake of Thunderclap Newman, 1973.

NEWMAN, COLIN Vocal. Member of the Wire, 1980.

NEWMAN, DALE Vocal. Session for Anthony Phillips (1979).

NEWMAN, DAVID "FATHEAD" Tenor saxophone. Session for Gregg Allman (1973); Freddie King (1975); Joe Cocker (1978). *Albums:* Concrete Jungle (PRS 10104) 1978; Front Money (WBR B-2984); Jazz Years (ATC 2-316); Keep the Dream Alive (PRS 10106) 1978; Scratch My Back (PRS 10108) 1979.

NEWMAN, DEL Strings, flute, percussion, producer. Produced Randy Vanwarmer (1979). Session for Donovan (1973); Art Garfunkel; Elton John (1973); Nilsson (1972-79); Paul Simon (1973); Cat Stevens (1971-72); Peter Frampton (1972); Mike Harrison (1975); Brian Protheroe (1976); George Harrison (1979); the Dukes (1979); Rod Stewart (1980).

NEWMAN, FLOYD Baritone saxophone. Member of the Memphis Horns. Session for Clarence Carter (1967); Wilson Pickett (1968); Boz Scaggs (1969).

NEWMAN, JOE Trumpet. Session for Muddy Waters (1972); Martin Mull (1974, 77). *Albums:* Blue Seven (PRS 7376); Echoes of An Era — Locking Horns (ROU RE-128); Main Stem (PRS 7236).

NEWMAN, JOEY Guitar, vocal. Member of Bandit, 1975.

NEWMAN, MICHAEL Guitar, vocal. Member of the Proof, 1980.

NEWMAN, NANETTE Vocal. Session for the Rolling Stones (1970); Gary Wright (1970-71).

NEWMAN, RANDY Vocal, piano, writer. Born 11/28/43. Los Angeles songwriter who first appeared in 1968. Highly regarded in the musical community by Judy Collins, Harry Nilsson, Long John Baldry, Alan Price and others who have recorded his songs. His "Short People," 1977, brought him AM exposure and overdue public recognition. Other popular songs he has written include "Yellow Man," "Let's Burn Down the Cornfields," and "Mama Told Me Not To Come." Session for Joe Cocker (1974). *Albums:* Born Again (WBR HS-3346) 1979; Good Old Boys (RPS MS4-2193) 1979; Little Criminals (WBR K-3079) 1977; Randy Newman (RPS 6286) 1968; Randy Newman Live (RPS 6459) 1971; Sail Away (RPS 2064) 1972; 12 Songs (RPS 6373).

NEWMAN, TOM Vocal, guitar, mandolin, organ, percussion. Member of July. *Album:* Fine Old Tom (ANT 7042) 1975.

NEWMAN, TONY Drums. Replaced Mick Waller in the Jeff Beck Group, 1969, and Mike Kelly in Three Man Army, 1972-74. Member of Boxer, 1975. Session for Long John Baldry (1975); Kevin Ayers (1977); Chris Spedding (1978).

NEWMAN, YOGI Percussion. Session for Jorge Santana (1980).

NEWMARK, ANDY Drums. Member of Duke Williams and the Extremes, 1973, and the Mark Farner Band, 1978. Session for Carole King; Rod Stewart (1974-76); Ron Wood (1975-76); Roy Buchanan (1976); George Harrison (1974-75, 79); Joe Walsh (1974); Gary Wright (1975, 79); Carly Simon (1972-74); Steve Winwood (1977); Richard and Linda Thompson (1978); Frank Carillo (1978); Tim Weisberg and Dan Fogelberg (1978); Randy Newman (1979); Firefall (1980); Roxy Music (1980); John Lennon (1980).

NEWSOME, GEORGE Drums. Original member of the Climax Blues Band, 1968-73.

NEWTON, JUICE Vocal. *Albums:* Well Kept Secret (CAP SW 11811) 1978; Come to Me (CAP ST 11662) 1977; Take Heart (CAP ST 12000) 1979.

NEWTON, KENNY Keyboards. Member of Nutz, 1977.

NEWTON, PAUL Bass, vocal. Original member of Uriah Heep, 1970-72.

NEWTON, TONY Bass, vocal. Member of the New Tony Williams Lifetime, 1975-77.

NEWTON-JOHN, OLIVIA Vocal. Born 9/26/47. The innocence behind "Have You Never Been Mellow" (1975) pushed Australian-born Newton-John to the top of the pop-rock and country charts at the same time, establishing her as a force to be reckoned with in both fields. Session for Andy Gibb (1980). *Albums:* Clearly Love (MCA 3015); Come On Over (MCA 3016) 1976; Don't Stop Believin' (MCA 3017); Gift of Song (POL 1-6214); Grease (RSO 2-4002); Greatest Hits (MCA 3028); Have You Never Been Mellow (MCA 3014) 1975; If You Love Me Let Me Know (MCA 3013) 1974; Let Me Be There (MCA 3012) 1973; Making a Good Thing Better (MCA 3018); Other Side of the Mountain (MCA 2086); Totally Hot (MCA 3067); Xanadu (MCA 6100).

NEY, MIKE Drums. Member of Clear Light, 1967-68.

NICE Brian Davison—drums; Keith Emerson—keyboards; Lee Jackson—bass; David O'List—guitar, vocal. Whipping each other on stage, burning American flags (for which they were banned from London's Royal Albert Hall for life in 1968), and other stage antics provided the basis for a very sensational career. But even that could not hide the virtuosity of the most talented keyboard man in the field of rock. When O'List left the group, the Nice blatantly continued without the essential rock ingredient, the electric guitar, and blazed into modern three-piece arrangements of Tchaikowsky and Bernstein. Disbanded in 1970. See Emerson, Lake and Palmer. *Albums:* Thoughts of Emerlist Davjack (IMD) 1968; Ars Longa Vita Brevis (IMD) 1967; Autumn to Spring (MER); Five Bridges (MER); Elegy (MER SRM 61324); Everything as Nice as Mother Makes It (IMD IMOCS 102) 1969; Greatest Hits (IMD 2003) 1977; The Immediate Story (IMD 3760-Z) 1975.

NICHOL, AL Guitar, vocal. Original member of the Turtles, 1965-69.

NICHOL, LES Guitar, vocal. Member of the Magnet, 1979.

NICHOLAS, SEAN Bass. Original member of the Crazy World of Arthur Brown, 1968.

NICHOLLS, BILLY Vocal, guitar. Member of White Horse, 1977. Session for Pete Townshend (1972); the Who (1980).

NICHOLLS, CHRIS Flute. Session for Donovan (1973).

NICHOLLS, GEOFF Keyboards. Session for Black Sabbath (1980).

NICHOLLS, MAGGIE Vocal. Member of Centipede, 1971.

NICHOLS, ALVIN Bass. Session for John Littlejohn.

NICHOLS, BILLY Bass. Session for John Hammond.

NICHOLS, NICK Vocal. Member of the Bizarros, 1979.

NICHOLS, PAUL Drums. Member of Lindisfarne until 1974, and Widowmaker, 1976.

NICHOLS, PENNY Vocal. Session for Art Garfunkel (1979).

NICHOLS, STEVE Drums. Member of Eddie and the Hot Rods since 1976.

NICHOLS, WARREN Bass. Session for Henry Gross (1971).

NICHOLSON, TIPPY Guitar. Session for Don Nix (1971).

NICKESON, THOMAS Guitar. Member of Pavlov's Dog, 1976.

NICKO Drums. Member of the Streetwalkers, 1975-77.

NICKS, STEVIE Vocal, writer. Born 5/26/48. With partner Lindsey Buckingham, she replaced Bob Welsh and Bob Weston in Fleetwood Mac, 1975-present. Session for Bob Welsh (1979).

NICO Vocal, writer. Originally an Andy Warhol superstar creation; he sponsored her in his Velvet Underground, with John Cale and Lou Reed in 1967. Shortly thereafter, Cale and Nico left, pursuing their solo careers, with Cale in charge of the musical arrangement behind Nico's sultry, mesmerizing voice and eerie lyrics. *Albums:* Chelsea Girl (VRV 5032) 1967; Marble Index (ELK 74029) 1968; Desert Shore (RPS 6424) 1970; The End (RPS) 1974.

NICOL, LES Guitar. Session for Pavlov's Dog (1976).

NICOL, SIMON Guitar. Member of Fairport Convention until 1974. Session for Cat Stevens (1976); David Swarbrick (1976); Richard and Linda Thompson (1978).

NIELSEN, REED Vocal, guitar, piano. Half of the Nielsen-Pearson duet, 1980.

NIELSEN, RICK Guitar, vocal, keyboards. Founder of Cheap Trick, 1977-present.

NIELSEN/PEARSON Reed Nielsen—vocal, guitar, piano; Mark Pearson—vocal, guitar, piano. *Album:* Nielsen/Pearson (CAP ST-12101) 1980.

NIEMAN, PAUL Trombone. Member of Centipede, 1971.

NIEUWSTEDE, EVERT Vocal. Member of the Urban Heroes, 1980.

NIEVE, STEVE Keyboards. Member of the Attractions.

NIGERA, TOM Bass, vocal. Member of the Trigger, 1978.

NIGHT Steve Lange—vocal; Chris Thompson—guitar; Robbie McIntosh—guitar; Billy Kristian—bass; Bob Guidotti—drums. *Album:* Night (PNT 3) 1979.

NIGHT SHIFT Original name of War.

NIGHTENGALES Sherlie Matthews—vocal; Rebecca Louis—vocal; Clydie King—vocal. Studio vocal backup trio. Session for Les Dudek (1977).

NIGHTHAWKS Mark Wenner—harmonica, vocal; Jan Zukowski—bass, vocal; Pete Ragusa—drums, vocal; Jimmy Thackery—guitar, vocal. *Albums:* Side Pocket Shot (ADP 4115) 1977; Jacks and Kings (ADP 4120) 1978; Jacks and Kings Full House (ADP 4125) 1979; The Nighthawks (MER SRM-1-3833) 1980.

NIGRA, TOM Bass, vocal. Member of Trigger, 1978.

NIKKI Vocal. Namesake of Nikki and the Corvettes, 1980.

NIKKI AND THE CORVETTES Lori—vocal; Krysti—vocal; Nikki—vocal. Recreation of the 1950s vocal trio style. *Album:* Nikki and the Corvettes (BMP 4012) 1980.

NILE, WILLIE Guitar, vocal, piano. *Album:* Willie Nile (ARI 4260) 1980.

NILES, PRESCOTT Bass. Member of the Knack since 1979.

NILSSON, HARRY Vocal, piano, writer. Songwriter from Los Angeles with extensive credits, including songs for the Ronettes, the Monkees, the Yardbirds, Blood, Sweat and Tears, the Turtles, Lulu, Jack Jones, and others. The scorer of movie soundtracks for "Everybody's Talking," "Midnight Cowboy," and "Son of Dracula," and TV ("The Point"), he first became widely known as a result of his friendship and session work for Beatles John Lennon and Ringo Starr. Session for Keith Moon (1975); John Lennon (1974); Ringo Starr (1973-74). *Albums:* Aerial Ballet (VIC LSP 3956) 1968; Aerial Ballet (VIC); Dui On Mon Dei (VIC AFLI 0817) 1975; Little Touch of Schmilsson in the Night (VIC APLI 0097) 1973; Nilsson, Schmilsson (VIC ANLI 3464) 1971; The Point (VIC AFLI 2593); 1971; Son of Schmilsson (VIC AFLI 4717) 1972; Knnillssonn (VIC AFLI 2276) 1977; Harry (VIC LSP 4197) 1969; Nilsson Sings Newman (VIC); Pandemonium Shadow Show (VIC) 1967; Pussy Cats (VIC CPL 0150) 1974; That's the Way It Is (VIC APLI-1119) 1976; Sandman (VIC ARLI 1031) 1975; Early Times (MER 2505) 1977.

999 Nick Cash—vocal, guitar; Guy Days—guitar, vocal; Jon Watson—bass, vocal; Pablo Labritain—drums, vocal; Ed Case—drums, vocal (1979-80). *Albums:* Biggest Prize in Sport (POL 1-6256) 1980; High Energy Plan (AVC 7999) 1979; The Biggest Tour in Sport (POL PD 1-6307) 1980.

1994 Karen Lawrence—vocal, piano; Rick Armand—guitar, vocal, piano (1979); Bill Rhodes—guitar, clarinet, bass; Terry Linville—bass (1979); John Desautels—drums; Steve Schiff—guitar (1978). *Albums:* 1994 (AAM 4709) 1978; Please Stand By (AAM 4769) 1979.

1910 FRUITGUM COMPANY Frank Jeckell—vocal, guitar; Pat Karwan—vocal, guitar; Mark Gutkowski—vocal, organ; Floyd Marcus—vocal, drums. Critics were not kindly receptive to bubble gum music, but few groups were as commercially successful as the Company with "Simon Says" and "1, 2, 3, Red Light." *Albums:* Simon Says (BUD) 1968; 1, 2, 3, Red Light (BUD) 1968; Indian River (BUD) 1968.

NITTY GRITTY DIRT BAND Ralph Barr—guitar, clarinet, banjo; Bruce Kunkel—guitar, fiddle, banjo, mandolin; Hanna—percussion, drums, trombone; Jeffrey Hanna—percussion, vocal, guitar, harmonica; Jackson Browne—guitar, banjo, piano, percussion; Les Thompson—guitar, banjo, mandolin, percussion; John McEuen—banjo, guitar, harmonica, piano, percussion; Jimmie Fadden—drums, percussion, trombone; Chris Darrow—fiddle, banjo, guitar, mandolin. Early name: the Illegitimate Jug Band. Goodtime shuffle and jug band music that started in 1966. They have survived and evolved into the Dirt Band, 1978. See the Dirt Band. *Albums:* All the Good Times (UAR 5553) 1971; Dirt, Silver and Gold (UAR LKCL-670) 1976; Dream (UAR LO-469) 1975; Uncle Charlie (LIB 7642); Stars and Stripes Forever (UAR LWB-184) 1974; Will the Circle Be Unbroken (UAR 9801) 1972.

NITZINGER, JOHN Guitar, vocal. Namesake of Nitzinger, 1973-76.

NITZINGER John Nitzinger—guitar, vocal; Paul Leim—drums; Jerry Harris—bass; Kenneth Whitfield—keyboards. *Albums:* Live Better Electrically (TWC) 1976; One Foot in History (TWC) 1973.

NITZSCHE, JACK Piano, vocal, percussion, producer. Co-founder of Crazy Horse, 1971. Member of Stray Gators, 1972. Has successfully branched into scoring movie soundtracks including "One Flew over the Cuckoo's Nest." String arrangements for the James Gang, 1970, and Ringo Starr, 1973. Produced Neil Young (1969-75); Buffy Sainte-Marie; Rick Nelson; Mink de Ville (1979); and Sumner (1980). Session for the Rolling Stones (1965-66); Buffalo Springfield (1967). *Albums:* Blue Collar (MCA 3034); One Flew over the Cuckoo's Nest (FSY 9500) 1975.

NIVEN, JAMES Keyboards, vocal. Member of the Sports since 1979.

NIVISON, CLIFFORD Guitar. Member of the New York Rock and Roll Ensemble, 1968-69.

NIX, DON Vocal, writer, producer, arranger. Author of the folk-rock classic "Goin' Down." Producer for John Mayall (1973). Session on Bangla Desh (1971). *Albums:* Living by the Days (ELK) 1971; Heroes and Street Corner Clowns (ELK); Alabama State Troopers (ELK); Gone Too Long (CRE 1001) 1976; Skyrider (CRE 1011) 1979.

NIX, ROBERT Drums. Member of the Atlanta Rhythm Section, 1972-78, and the Candymen.

NIXON, HAMMIE Harmonica. Partner and session man of Sleepy John Estes beginning in 1929. Session for Yank Rachel.

NO DICE Roger "Peaches" Ferris—vocal; Dave "Deezal" Martin—guitar; Gary Strange—bass; Kitty Wyles—drums. *Albums:* No Dice (CAP ST-11733) 1978; Two Faced (CAP ST-11925) 1979.

NO NUKES Benefit concert organized by Jackson Browne, Graham Nash, John Hall, and Bonnie Raitt, September 19-23, 1979, for the MUSE organization (Musicians United to Save Energy). Other guest artists included the Doobie Brothers, James Taylor, Carly Simon, Nicolette Larson, Ry Cooder, Sweet Honey in the Rock, Gil Scott-Heron, Jesse Colin Young, Chaka Khan, Poco, Tom Petty, Bruce Springsteen, and Crosby, Stills and Nash. *Album:* No Nukes (ASY ML 801) 1979.

NO SLACK Greg Calloway—bass, vocal; Tom Whitlock—drums, vocal; Terry Wilson—guitar, vocal; Jeff Grinnell—keyboards, vocal. *Album:* No Slack (MER SRM 1-3749) 1978.

NOAKES, RAB Vocal. Session for Gerry Rafferty (1978).

NOBLE, BOB Keyboards. Member of the Omaha Sheriff, 1977.

NOCENTELLI, LEO "BREEZE" Guitar. Member of the Meters, 1973. Session for Jess Roden (1974).

NOLAN, ALAN Guitar, vocal. Member of the Piper, 1977.

NOLAN, JERRY Drums. Member of the New York Dolls, 1973-74.

NOLTE, DAVID Bass. Member of the Last, 1979.

NOLTE, JOE Guitar, vocal. Member of the Last, 1979.

NOLTE, MIKE Vocal. Member of the Last, 1979.

NOONAN, STEVE Vocal, guitar, writer. California folk singer whose close affiliation with the Nitty Gritty Dirt Band brought attention to his solo debut in 1968. *Album:* Steve Noonan, 1968.

NOONAN, TERRY Trumpet. Session for Chicken Shack; the Keef Hartley Band (1971).

NOONE, JERRY Tenor saxophone, piano. Session for Daddy Cool (1972).

NOONE, PETER Piano, guitar, vocal. Herman of Herman's Hermits, 1965-68. Returned from retirement to form the Tremblers, 1980. Session for Elton John (1980).

NORMAL, NORMAN Guitar, vocal. Member of the Panic Squad, 1980.

NORMAN Bass. Member of the Five Americans, 1966.

NORMAN, CHRIS Vocal, guitar. Member of Smokie, 1975-79.

NORMAN, JIMMY Vocal. Session for Jimi Hendrix

(1965).

NORMAN, NEIL Guitar, synthesizer, theremin, vocal. Organizer of Neil Norman and his Cosmic Orchestra, 1975-80.

NEIL NORMAN AND HIS COSMIC ORCHESTRA Neil Norman—guitar, synthesizer, theremin, vocal; Les Baxter—keyboards; Hall Daniels—keyboards; Bob Kent—keyboards; John Guerin—drums; Max Bennett—bass. *Albums:* Not of This Earth (CSD 2111) 1975; Greatest Science Fiction Hits (CSD 2128) 1980.

NORMAND, BOOTSIE Guitar. Member of the Romeos, 1980.

NORRIS, CHRIS Vocal. Session for George Duke (1975).

NORRIS, JERRY Drums, vocal. Replaced Carmine Appice in the New Cactus Band, 1973.

NORRIS, JIM Drums, vocal. Member of Sea Dog, 1972.

NORRIS, PAT Vocal. Session for George Duke (1975).

NORRIS-ELYE, DAVE Horns. Session for Long John Baldry (1980).

NORTH, CHRISTOPHER Keyboards, vocal. Member of Ambrosia since 1975. Session for the Alan Parsons Project (1976).

NORTON, ROCKET Drums. Replaced Rod Higgs in Prism, 1979-80.

NOTTE, ROCCO Member of the A's, 1979.

NOVAG, NOVI See Novi.

NOVAK, JIM Drums. Member of the Lamont Cranston Band, 1977.

NOVEMBER, LINDA Vocal. Session for the posthumous Hendrix album "Crash Landing" (1975); Gregg Allman (1973).

NOVI Viola, synthesizer. Member of Chunky, Ernie and Novi, which evolved into Lauren Wood's backup band, 1979. Member of Sumner, 1980. Session for the Doobie Brothers (1974); Montrose (1975); John Mayall (1977).

NOVI, CARLO Saxophone. Member of Southside Johnny and the Asbury Jukes, 1976.

NOVIC, BILLY Saxophone. Session for Peter C. Johnson (1980).

NOW Bobby Ore; Robin Dee; Jeff Lennon; Mamie Francis. *Album:* The Now (MID 014) 1979.

NOWDEN, RON Drums, percussion. Member of Nektar, 1972-77.

NOYA, NEPPIE Percussion. Session for Jan Akkerman and Kaz Lux (1976); Golden Earring (1977); Jan Akkerman (1977).

NRBQ Terry Adams—keyboards, vocal; Al Anderson—guitar, vocal; Tom Ardolini—drums; Joe Spampinato—bass, guitar, vocal; Steve Ferguson—guitar, vocal, harmonica; Tom Staley—drums; Jody St. Nichols—bass, vocal; Frank Gadler—vocal, percussion. *Albums:* All Hopped Up (RND 3029) 1977; Boppin' the Blues (COL CS-9981); Kick Me Hard (RND 3030); NRBQ at Yankee Stadium (MER SRM-1-3712) 1978; Tiddly Winks (RDR 3048).

NU KATS Allen J. Galles—drums, percussion, vocal; Bobbyzio Moore—saxophone, keyboards, guitar, percussion; Freddy Moore—guitar, vocal, percussion; Dennis Peters—bass, vocal, percussion. *Album:* Plastic Facts (RHN 903) 1980.

NUANEZ, BUD Guitar. Member of Seawind.

NUCLEUS See Ian Carr.

NUGENT, TED Guitar, vocal, bass, writer. Founder and head of the Amboy Dukes, he dropped that name in favor of his own in 1975. Hard rock is his style and his heavy metal sound has remained unscathed by the fads and trends that vary weekly on the top 40 charts. See the Amboy Dukes. *Albums:* Cat Scratch Fever (EPC JE-34700) 1977; Double Live Gonzo (EPC KE2-35069) 1978; Free-For-All (EPC PE-34121) 1976; Ted Nugent (EPC PE-33692) 1975; Scream Dream (EPC FE-36404) 1980; State of Shock (EPC FE-36000) 1979; Weekend Warriors (EPC FE-35551) 1978.

TED NUGENT GROUP Ted Nugent—guitar, vocal; Derek St. Holmes—guitar, vocal (1975-78); Rob Grange—bass (1975-78); Cliff Davies—drums, percussion, producer; Charlie Huhn—vocal (1978-present); John Sauter—bass (1978); Walt Monaghan—bass (1979); Dave Kiswiney—bass, vocal (1980). Though not formally titled, these are members of Ted Nugent's backup band in his solo career.

NUMA BAND Russ Iverson—horns; Jack Baron—reeds; Bob Sutter—keyboards; Ernie Denov—guitar; Dave Lang—drums; Mitch Hennes—bass; Geraldo de Olivera—percussion. *Album:* Numa Band (OVA 1760) 1980.

NUMAN, GARY Vocal, keyboards, synthesizer. Session for Robert Palmer (1980). *Albums:* Pleasure Principle (ACO 38-120) 1979; Replicas (ACO 38-117) 1979; Telekon (ACO 32-103) 1980.

NUMBERS Coleman York—drums, vocal; Jim Kennedy—guitar, vocal; Ed Blockli—vocal, guitar, keyboards. *Album:* Add Up (BMT 6000) 1980.

NUNEZ, NESTOR Bass, vocal. Member of the Glass Moon, 1980.

NUNLEY, CHRIS Vocal. Member of the Royal Guardsmen, 1969.

NUNN, GARY Guitar, piano, vocal. Member of the Lost Gonzo Band, 1978.

NUNNEN, JIMMY Bass, vocal. Member of Candlewick Green, 1974.

NUNS Jennifer Miro—vocal, keyboards; Richie Detrick—vocal; Jeff Olener—vocal; Pat Ryan—guitar; Jeff Raphael—drums, percussion; Alejandro Escovedo—drums, percussion. *Album:* Nuns (BMP 4010) 1980.

NUTZ Dave Lloyd—vocal, guitar; Mick Devonport—vocal, guitar; Keith Mullholland—bass; John Mylett—drums; Kenny Newton—keyboards

(1976). *Albums:* Nutz (AAM SP 33699) 1974; Hard Nutz (AAM SP 4623) 1977; Nutz II (AAM) 1975; Nutz III (AAM) 1976.

NYE, STEVE Organ, piano, engineer. Session for Fleetwood Mac (1973); Gary Brooker (1974); Bryan Ferry (1978).

NYRO, LAURA Piano, vocal, writer. Pianist and vocalist whose original material is a curious and haunting blend of folk and jazz. She began recording in 1967 at the age of 20, and wrote "Stoned Soul Picnic" for the Fifth Dimension. *Albums:* More Than a Discovery (COL) 1967; Christmas and Beads of Sweat (COL PC-30259); Eli and the Thirteenth Confession (COL PC-9626) 1968; Gonna Take a Miracle (COL PC-30987); Nested (COL JC-35449) 1978; New York Tendaberry (COL PC-9737); Laura Nyro . . . The First Songs (COL C-31410) 1973; Smile (COL C-33912) 1976.

NYSTROM, JEFF Bass, vocal. Member of the Fist, 1980.

O'BRIEN, ANN HILLARY Vocal. Session for Neil Young (1980).

O'BRIEN, JACK Guitar. Member of the Hammer, 1970.

O'BRIEN, JOEL Drums, vibes. Member of Jo Mama, 1970.

O'BRIEN, MARY Real name of Dusty Springfield.

O'CONNELL, CHRIS Vocal, guitar. Member of Asleep at the Wheel since 1973.

O'CONNELL, MARSHALL Guitar. Member of Bagatelle, 1968.

O'CONNELL, MICHAEL Trombone. Member of the Downchild, 1979.

O'CONNELL, RICHARD Drums. Session for Steve Stills (1978).

O'CONNER, CHARLES Fiddle, mandolin, concertina, vocal. Original member of Horslips.

O'CONNER, GARY Guitar, bass, vocal. Member of Aeriel, 1978.

O'CONNER, KIERAN Drums, percussion, vocal. Member of the Seventh Wave, 1974-75.

O'CONNER, PATRICK Bass. Member of Aim, 1974.

O'DANIEL, JOHN Vocal. Voice of Point Blank, 1976.

O'DAY, ALAN Keyboards, vocal. Session for John Kay (1973). *Albums:* Appetizers (PAC 4300) 1977; Oh Johnny (PAC 4301) 1979.

O'DELL, ANN Keyboards, string arranger. Session for Pete Wingfield (1975); Shawn Phillips; the Baker-Gurvitz Army (1976); Bryan Ferry (1977-78); the Graeme Edge Band (1977).

O'DOHERTY, DEC Piano. Session for Horslips (1979).

O'DONNELL, JOE Violin, piano. Member of the Headstone, 1975.

O'FLYNN, DENNIS Violin, bass. Session for Rod Stewart (1971).

O'HARA, GEORGE Guitar, slide guitar. Session for Gary Wright (1971).

O'HARA, PATRICK Trombone. Member of the Loading Zone, 1968.

O'HARA, STIG Stage name of Ricky Fataar in the Rutles, 1978.

O'HEARN, PATRICK Bass. Member of Group 87, 1980. Session for Frank Zappa (1979).

O'KEEFE, DANNY Guitar, vocal. *Albums:* American Roulette (WBR B-3050); Breezy Stories (ATC 7264); Global Blues (WBR K-3314) 1979; Seattle Tapes (FSM 7700) 1977; So Long Harry Truman (ATC 18125) 1975; Danny O'Keefe (ATC); Seattle Tapes, Vol. II (FSM 7721) 1978.

O'KELLY, LEO Vocal, guitar, violin. Member of Tir Na Nog, 1973.

O'LIST, DAVID Guitar, vocal, writer. Original member of the Nice, until 1969. Session for Bryan Ferry (1974-76).

O'LOCHLAINN, RYAN Keyboards, saxophone. Session for Bryan Ferry (1974); Ronnie Lane (1975).

O'NEIL, MIKE Keyboards, vocal. Member of Heads, Hands and Feet, 1970-71.

O'NEILL, DAMIAN Guitar. Member of the Undertones, 1979.

O'NEILL, BOB Guitar, vocal. Member of the Snail, 1978-79.

O'NEILL, JAMES Guitar. Member of Fingerprintz, 1980. Session for Manfred Mann (1979).

O'NEILL, JAMES Guitar. Original member of the Mindbenders, 1966.

O'NEILL, JOHN Guitar. Member of the Undertones, 1979.

O'NEILL, MIKE Guitar, slide guitar. Session for Freddie King (1975).

O'ROURKE, JIMMY Guitar. Member of John Fred's Playboy Band, 1967-68.

O'SULLIVAN, GILBERT Piano, vocal. Recorded "Alone Again (Naturally)," 1972. *Album:* Back to Front (MAM 5) 1972.

O'SULLIVAN, HUGH Organ, vocal. Session for John Kay (1973).

OAK Scott Grover Weatherspoon—guitar, vocal; Rick Pinette—guitar, piano, vocal; Danny Caron—drums; George Weathers Borden, Jr.—bass, vocal; David Stone—keyboards, vocal; John Foster—bass (1980). *Albums:* Oak, 1980; Set the Night on Fire (MER SRM 1 4009) 1980.

OAKEY, PHILLIP Synthesizer, vocal. Member of the Human League, 1980.

OAKLEY, BERRY Bass. Born 4/4/48. Original member of the Allman Brothers Band until his death, 11/11/72. Session for Johnny Jenkins (1970).

OATES, JERRY Guitar, vocal. Member of Calico, 1975-76.

OATES, JOHN Vocal, guitar. Half of the Hall and Oates duet, since 1973.

OBERLE, DAVID Drums, vocal. Session for Steve Howe (1975).

OBERLE, MIKE Drums, percussion, vocal. Member of the Ian Thomas Band, 1976.

OBLASNEY, CATHERINE Vocal, percussion. Member of Polyrock, 1980.

OBLIVION EXPRESS Brian Auger—keyboards,

vocal; Barry Dean—bass, vocal (1971-74); Jim Mullen—guitar (1971-73); Robbie McIntosh—drums (1971-73); Alex Ligertwood—vocal, percussion (1972-77); Lennox Langston—congas (1973-77); Godfrey MacLean—drums, percussion (1973); Steve Ferrone—drums (1973-75); Lenny White—drums, percussion (1977); Jack Mills—guitar (1973-77); Clive Chaman—bass (1975-77); Dave Dowle—drums (1975). After a few years of the noticeable absence of his Trinity, Auger reappeared in California with the Oblivion Express in 1971. His obvious jazz inclinations became fully realized in his new group, which is accepted by both jazz and rock audiences. *Albums:* Brian Auger's Oblivion Express (VIC LSP 4462) 1971; Second Wind (VIC LSP 4703) 1972; A Better Land (VIC) 1973; Closer to It (VIC ALPI-0140) 1973; Straight Ahead (VIC APLI-0454) 1974; Live Oblivion, Vol. I (VIC) 1974; Live Oblivion, Vol. II (VIC) 1975; Reinforcements (VIC APLI-1210) 1975; Happiness Heartaches (WOR B-2981) 1977.

OCASEK, RIK Vocal, guitar, writer, producer. Founder of the Cars, 1978-present. Session for Ian Lloyd (1979).

OCEANS, LUCKY Pedal steel guitar. Member of Asleep at the Wheel since 1973.

OCHOA, MARIO Piano. Session for Santana (1971).

OCHS, HANS Guitar, vocal. Member of Supermax, 1979.

OCHS, PHIL Guitar, vocal, writer. Popular New York folk singer who began recording in 1964. His wry social conscience was ever-present in his topical, witty, and satirical songs. He was a significant force in preparing the audience Dylan was to conquer at a later date. Died in 1976. *Albums:* Rehearsals for Retirement (AAM) 1969; All the News That's Fit to Sing (ELK 7269) 1964; Chords of Fame (AAM 4599) 1974; I Ain't Marching Anymore (ELK 7287) 1965; Phil Ochs in Concert (ELK 7310) 1966; Pleasures of the Harbor (AAM 4133) 1967; Tape from California (AAM 4148) 1968; Phil Ochs Greatest Hits (PWK 3735) 1980; Phil Ochs Sings for Broadside (FLW 5320) 1976.

OCKER, DAVID Clarinet. Session for Frank Zappa (1979).

ODA, RANDY Guitar, keyboards, vocal. Member of Ruby, 1976.

ODDIE, BILL Vocal. Session for Rick Wakeman (1977-78).

ODETTA Vocal. A popular vocalist in the 1960s boom of folk singers. *Albums:* My Eyes Have Seen, 1959; Odetta Sings Dylan, 1965; Ballad for Americans, 1965; Odetta in Japan, 1965; Odetta Sings the Blues, 1968; Best of Odetta (TRD 2052) 1967; Essential, Vol. 1 (VAN VSD-43); Essential, Vol. 2 (VAN VSD 44); Odetta (EVR 273) 1963; Odetta at Carnegie Hall (VAN 73003) 1967; Odetta at the Gate of Horn (TRD 1025); Odetta at Town Hall (VAN 2109) 1962; Odetta Sings Ballads and Blues (TRD 1010); One Grain of Sand (VAN 2153) 1963.

ODGERS, BRIAN Bass, woodwinds, writer. Original member of Sweet Thursday, 1970. Session for Elton John (1971); Lou Reed (1972); Brian Protheroe (1976); Shawn Phillips.

ODUMOSA, MIKE Bass. Member of Osibisa.

OFF BROADWAY Cliff Johnson—vocal; John Ivan—guitar; Rob Harding—vocal, guitar; Ken Harck—drums; Mike Gorman—bass, vocal (1980); John Pazdan—bass, vocal (1979). *Albums:* Quick Turns (ATC SD 19286) 1980; On (ATC SD 19263) 1979.

OFFENBACH Gerry Boulet—vocal, keyboards, guitar; Jean Gravel—guitar, vocal; Michel Lamothe—bass, vocal; Roger Beval—drums, vocal. *Album:* Never Too Tender (AAM 4630) 1976.

OGAN, GARY Vocal. *Album:* Gary Ogan (PAR 3078) 1977.

OGDIN, BOBBY Keyboards. Session for Levon Helm (1980); Jimmy Hall (1980).

OGLETREE, MIKE Member of Cafe Jacques since 1977.

OHIO EXPRESS Douglas Grassel—guitar; Tim Corwin—drums; Dean Kastran—bass; Jim Pfayler—organ; Dale Powers—guitar. With the 1910 Fruitgum Company, they shared the throne of kings of bubble gum rock in 1968, with their hit "Yummy, Yummy, Yummy." *Albums:* Beg, Borrow and Steal, 1968; Yummy, Yummy, Yummy, 1968; Mercy, 1969; Very Best of the Ohio Express (BVD).

OJEDA, HENRY Bass. Session for Ry Cooder (1977).

OLDAKER, JAMIE Drums. Session for Bob Segar (1973); Freddie King (1974); Leon Russell (1974); Eric Clapton (1974-78); Peter Frampton (1979).

OLDFIELD, MIKE Guitar, bass, keyboards, mandolin, banjo, drums, percussion. The soundtrack to the film "The Exorcist" brought international fame to Oldfield, a one-man orchestra who recorded all of the tracks (over 15) himself, playing all of the instruments. Session for David Bedford (1974); Robert Wyatt (1974); Bram Tchaikovsky (1979). *Albums:* Airborn (VGN 13143) 1980; Tubular Bells (VGN 13135) 1973; Omanadawn (VGN 33913) 1975; Hergest Ridge (VGN 13-109) 1974; Exposed (Import) 1979.

OLDFIELD, SALLY Vocal, oboe. Session for Mike Oldfield (1973-75). *Albums:* Water Bearer (CYS 1211) 1978; Easy (Import) 1979.

OLDFIELD, TERRY Pan pipes. Session for Mike Oldfield (1975).

OLDHAM, ANDREW LOOG Producer. Early manager and producer of the Rolling Stones, 1964-67. Produced Donovan (1973); Bob Seger (1975); Marianne Faithful (1965-68); Benny Mardones (1978); the Werewolves (1978); and others.

OLDHAM, SPOONER Piano. Session for Aretha Franklin (1970); Russ Giguere (1971); Henry

Gross (1972); John Hammond (1975); Neil Young (1978); Bob Dylan (1980).

OLENER, JEFF Vocal. Member of the Nuns, 1980.

OLIVA, NICK Keyboards. Member of Gasmask, and Baby.

OLIVER, GRAHAM Guitar. Member of Saxon, 1980.

OLIVER, MICK Session for Chris Spedding (1978).

OLIVER, TONY Guitar. Member of the Inmates since 1979.

OLLIVER, GEORGE Vocal. Voice of Mandala, 1967-68.

OLNEY, DAVID Bass. Session for Maddy Prior (1980).

OLSCHESKY, STEVE Bass. Member of the Sunblind Lion, 1976.

OLSEN, KEITH Bass, vocal. Original member of the Music Machine, 1966.

OLSEN, MARQUIS Drums. Member of the Sneakers, 1980.

OLSEN, MICHAEL Guitar, keyboards, vocal. Session for Lee Michaels.

OLSEN, RICHARD Clarinet. Session for It's a Beautiful Day (1970); John Sebastian (1974).

OLSON, DAVID Drums. Member of the Robert Cray Band, 1980.

OLSON, MARK Keyboards, vocal. Member of Rare Earth, and Doucette, 1979.

OLSON, MARTY Keyboards. Member of the Thumbs, 1979.

OLSSON, KAI Guitar, vocal. Member of the Longdancer, 1973.

OLSSON, NIGEL Drums, percussion. First became known alternating with Roger Pope, supporting Elton John, 1970, before becoming a member of John's band, 1971-77. Member of the Dinettes, 1976. Session for Long John Baldry (1972); Rod Stewart (1975); Neil Sedaka (1975-76); Leon Russell (1976); the Tremblers (1980); Elton John (1980); Bob Wier (1978); Jimmy Webb (1977). *Albums:* Nigel (BNG JZ-35792) 1979; Nigel Olsson (COL JC 35048) 1978; Changing Tides (BNG JZ-36491) 1980.

OLSSON, OLLIE Drums. Session for Uriah Heep (1970).

OLYMPIC RUNNERS Joe Jammer—vocal, guitar; Pete Wingfield—vocal, keyboards; DeLisle Harper—vocal, bass; Glen LeFleur—drums, percussion, vocal; Mike Vernon—vocal, harmonica, percussion; George Chandler—vocal. *Albums:* Hot to Trot (LON PS 678) 1977; Dance a Lot (POL PD 1-6169) 1979; Put the Music Where Your Mouth Is (LON PS 654).

OLYMPICS Recorded "Hully Gully," 1960.

OMAHA SHERIFF Paul Muggelton—vocal, guitar; Bob Noble—keyboards; Chris Birkett—vocal, guitar; Tony Visconti—bass; Michael Spencer-Arscott—drums. *Album:* Come Hell or High Water, 1977.

OMARTIAN, MICHAEL Keyboards, producer. Session and production for Christopher Cross (1980). Session for Cashman and West (1972); Loggins and Messina (1972-76); Steely Dan (1974); Art Garfunkel; Glen Campbell (1976); John Sebastian (1976); the Richie Furay Band (1976); Hoyt Axton (1976); Code Blue (1980); the Vapour Trails (1980); Gordon Lightfoot (1980); Johnny Rivers (1980); Austin Roberts (1973); Roger Voudouris (1977). Produced Scott Wilk and the Walls (1980). *Albums:* Adam Again (MYR 6576) 1974; The Builder (MYR 6636); Great, Great Joy (MYR 6579); Jubilation, Too (MYR 6568); Power Music (MYR 6580); Seasons of the Soul (MYR B-6606).

OMARTIAN, STORMIE Vocal. Session for Christopher Cross (1980).

OMEGA Janos Kabor—vocal, percussion; Laszlo Benko—keyboards, vocal; Thomas Mihaly—bass, vocal; Gyorgy Molnar—guitar; Ferenc Debreceni—drums: *Albums:* Omega (PPT) 1975; Skyrover (FSY 9560) 1978.

ONDERISIN, JOSH Guitar. Member of the Ian Thomas Band, 1976.

ONE HAND CLAPPING Kirk Tuttle—drums, percussion; Bobby Nachtsheim—saxophone, harmonica; Mark Willett—bass; Richard Dean—keyboards, vocal; Red Erickson—vocal, guitar; Pat Hewett—bass (1977); Joel Eide—harmonica (1977); John Keski—bass (1977). *Albums:* Second Hand Clapping (TOR RED 1) 1979; Skidum, Skidum Doo-Wah, 1977.

ONLY ONES Mike Kellie—drums; Alan Mair—bass; Peter Perrett—vocal, guitar; John Perry—guitar. *Albums:* Baby's Got a Gun (EPC JE 36584) 1980; Special View (EPC JE-36199) 1979.

ONO, YOKO Vocal, percussion. Born 2/18/33. Widow of former Beatle John Lennon and sometime recording partner. Her political activism and idealism blended perfectly with Lennon's, but her less than melodic voice and interest in electronic experimentalism and avant garde poetry did not. See John Lennon, the Plastic Ono Band. *Album:* Feeling the Space (APL).

OPALISKY, GEORGE Horns. Session for Roy Buchanan (1976); John Lennon (1980).

OPPENHEIM, STEVE Guitar, keyboards, vocal. Member of Taos.

ORANGE, RICHARD Member of Zuider Zee, 1975.

ORBISON, ROY Guitar, vocal, writer. Orbison began in 1956 singing country music, but his distinctive vocals made him equally popular in the budding rock market. Like Buddy Holly, he did not have a pretty face; just an overabundance of talent. His string of hits, "Only The Lonely," "Crying," "Blue Angel," and others, led to a smash hit, "Oh Pretty Woman," in 1967, which re-cultivated interest in his past and solidified a following for the future. The tragic loss of his wife caused his self-imposed retirement, from which he emerged in 1979. *Albums:* There Is Only One Roy Orbison, 1965; Orbisongs, 1965; Orbison Way, 1966; Classic Roy Orbison, 1966; Roy Orbison Sings Don Gibson, 1967; Fastest Guitar Alive, 1967; Cry Softly, Lonely One, 1967; Roy Orbison at the Rock House; Early Orbison; Roy Orbison's Many Moods, 1969; In Dreams (MNT MC-6620) 1964; Laminar Flow (ASY 6E-198) 1979; Memphis Country (SUN 120); More of Roy Orbison's Greatest Hits (MTN MC-6619) 1962; Original Rock and Roll (PPK 251); Original Sounds (SUN 113); Regeneration (MNT MG-7600); Souvenirs of Music City, U.S.A. (PLN 506); Very Best of Roy Orbison (MNT MC-6622) 1966.

ORCHIDS Laurie Bell—drums, percussion, vocal; Jan King—vocal, guitar, keyboards; Laurie McAllister—bass, vocal; Sunbie Sinn—guitar, keyboards, vocal; Che Zuro—guitar, keyboards, vocal. *Album:* The Orchids (MCA 3235) 1980.

ORE, BOBBY Member of the Now, 1979.

OREJON Bass. Member of Captain Beefheart and His Magic Band, 1972.

ORIGINAL MIRRORS Steve Allen—vocal; Ian Broudie—guitar; Pete Kircher—drums; Jonathan Perkins—keyboards; Phil Spalding—bass. *Album:* Original Mirrors (ARI 4269) 1980.

ORILIO, DOUG Drums. Member of the Vivabeat, 1980.

ORIOLES Clydie King—vocal; Venetta Fields—vocal; Shirlee Matthews—vocal. Session for Firefall (1977); Gary Wright (1977).

ORLEANS John Hall—vocal, guitar, percussion, mandolin, piano; Larry Hoppen—vocal, keyboards, guitar, trumpet; Wells Kelly—drums, percussion, vocal; Lance Hoppen—bass, vocal. *Albums:* Before the Dance (MCA 1058); Forever (INF 9006); Let There Be Music (ASY 7E-1029) 1975; Orleans (MCA 5110) 1980; Waking and Dreaming (ASY 7E-1070) 1976; The ABC Collection (ABC AC 30011) 1976; Orleans (ABC X 795) 1973.

ORMSBY, BUCK Bass, saxophone, vocal. Member of the Wailers, and Junior Cadillac.

ORNELLAS, WILLY Drums. Member of Photoglo, 1980.

ORPHAN Stuart Schulman—bass, violin, piano, vocal; Bill Keith—pedal steel guitar, banjo; Bill Elliot—keyboards; Richard Adelman—drums; Eric Lilliejuist—guitar, vocal; Bob Chouinard—drums; Dave Conrad—bass. Backup band for Jonathan Edwards, 1971-74.

ORR, BENJAMIN Bass, vocal. Member of the Cars since 1978. Session for Ian Lloyd (1979).

ORSON, ANN Vocal. Session for Elton John (1975); Neil Sedaka (1975).

ORTEGA, TONY Woodwinds. Session for the Mothers of Invention (1972). *Albums:* Rain Dance (DCO 788) 1978; A Delanto (JCS 402) 1973; New Dance (REV M-3) 1967; Permutations (REV F) 1968.

OSAMU Osamu Kitajima—guitar, biwa, vocal; John Hug—guitar, harmonica, mandolin; Brian Whitcomb—keyboards; Geoffrey Hales—drums; Dennis Belfield—bass; Tatzuya Sano—nohkan, shakahachi; George Marinelli—guitar. *Album:* Osamu (ISL 9426) 1977.

OSBORN, JOE Bass. Original member of the Dillards. Session for Paul Simon (1972); B. W. Stevenson (1973); Art Garfunkel (1974-75); Simon and Garfunkel; Neil Young (1978); Johnny Rivers (1980).

OSBORNE, BILLY Piano. Session for Tim Weisberg (1975).

OSBORNE, BOBBY Vocal. Member of Gasmask.

OSBORNE, GARY Vocal. Half of the Vigrass and Osborne duet. Co-author of Elton John's "Single Man," 1978.

OSBORNE, MICHAEL Guitar. Member of Axe since 1979.

OSBORNE, RILEY Keyboards, guitar. Member of Balcones Fault, 1977.

OSBOURNE, JOHN "OZZIE" Vocal, harmonica. Born 12/3/48. Original member of Black Sabbath, 1970-80, and the Blizzard of Ozz, 1980.

OSBOURNE, JOE Bass. Session for Frankie Miller (1980).

OSEI, TEDDY Reeds, percussion, flute. Member of Osibisa.

OSFAR, TOM Drums. Member of the Tufana-Giammarese Band, 1973-77.

OSGOOD, CHRIS Guitar. Member of the Suicide Commandos, 1978.

OSIBISA Teddy Osei—reeds, percussion, flute; Mike Odumosa—bass; Kiki Gyan—keyboards, vocal; Wendell Richardson—guitar, vocal; Mac Tontoh—horns, percussion; Kofi Ayivor—congas, percussion; Sol Amarfio—drums, percussion. Session for Uriah Heep (1971). *Albums:* Ojah Awake (ISL 9411); Osibisa (MCA 32); Welcome Home (ISL 9355) 1975; Woyaya (MCA 43) 1971; Happy Children (WBR B-2732); Osibirock (WBR B-2802); Heads (MCA 55).

OSIER, GARY Drums. Member of Texas, 1973.

OSIRIS Osiris Marsh—vocal; Maceo Bond—keyboards; Tony Jones—bass; Kenny Jones—drums; Jimmy Stapleton—percussion; Tyrone Brunson—bass; Ron Holloway—saxophone; Brent Mingle—guitar. *Album:* Since Before Our Time (WBR K-3311) 1978.

OSKAR, LEE Harmonica. Born 3/24/48. Original member of War, and the first member of that group to release a solo album (1976). Member of Giants, 1978. *Albums:* Before the Rain (ELK 6E-150); Lee Oskar (UAR LW-594) 1976.

OSLAND, GORDON Drums. Member of Graham Shaw and the Sincere Serenaders, 1980.

OSSOLA, PAUL Bass. Member of the Yankees, 1978. Session for Donovan (1973).

OSTERBERG, JAMES Real name of Iggy Stooge.

OTHER SIDE Kim Burns—piano, vocal; Frank Avant—guitar; Chuck Kerschner—drums; Vinnie Kalochie—guitar; Jim Sibmanis—bass; Robert Lee—synthesizer, keyboards. *Album:* Rock-X-ing (DLT DSR-9503).

OTHER TIKIS Early name of Harper's Bizarre.

OTIS, CHARLES Drums. Session for John Hammond (1968, 1970).

OTIS, JOHNNY Vocal, percussion, guitar. Production and session for his son, Shuggie Otis. *Albums:* Live at Monterey (EPC EG 30473); Cold Shot (KNT 534); Guitar Slim Green's Stone Down Blues (KNT 549); Original Johnny Otis Show (SAV 32230) 1978; Roots of Rock 'N' Roll (SAV 32221).

OTIS, SHUGGIE Guitar, vocal, bass, keyboards, percussion, drums. Son of guitarist Johnny Otis, Shuggie made his debut in 1970, still a teenager, with Al Kooper. *Albums:* Freedom Flight (EPC E-30752) 1971; Guitar Slim Green's Stone Down Blues (KNT 549); Kooper Session (COL CS-9951) 1970; Love's Preston, Omaha Bar-B-Q (KNT 540); Here Comes Shuggie Otis (EPC 26511); Inspiration Information (EPC KE 33059); Live at Monterey (EPC EG 30473).

OTLEY, JAMES CHARLES, JR. Drums. Session for Taj Mahal.

OTTENHOFF, RONALD Saxophone, flute. Member of Alquin, 1975.

OTWAY, DAVE Drums. Session for Wreckless Eric.

OTWAY, JOHN Vocal. *Album:* Deep Thought (STF USE 5) 1980.

OUSLEY, CURTIS Real name of King Curtis.

OUTLAWS Harvey Arnold—bass, vocal; Billy Jones—guitar, vocal; Hughie Thomasson—guitar, banjo, vocal, pedal steel guitar; Henry Paul—guitar, vocal (1975-79); Monte Yoho—drums; David Dix—drums (1979-present); Freddie Salem—guitar, vocal (1979-present); Rick Cua—bass, vocal (1980). *Albums:* Bring It Back Alive (ARI 8300); Hurry Sundown (ARI 4135) 1977; In the Eye of the Storm (ARI 9507) 1979; Lady in Waiting (ARI 4070) 1976; Outlaws (ARI 4042) 1975; Playin' to Win (ARI 4205) 1978; Ghost Riders (ARI 9542) 1980.

OVERHOLT, ELAINE Vocal. Session for Triumph (1979).

OVERLAND STAGE Julian Elofson—vocal, percussion; Dave Hanson—drums, vocal; Jim Flint—keyboards; Steve Baldos—bass; Don Miller—guitar; Rick Johnsgard—guitar, flute, vocal. *Album:* Overland Stage (EPC) 1972.

OVERLY, MICHAEL Guitar, flute, vocal. Member of Aim, 1974.

OWEN, DAN Vocal. Session for Anthony Phillips (1979).

OWEN, DANNY "BONGO" Drums, percussion. Member of Porrazzo, 1980.

OWEN, DAVID Guitar. Member of the Critical Mass, 1980.

OWEN, RANDY Vocal, guitar. Member of Alabama, 1980.

OWEN, RAY Vocal. Voice of Juicy Lucy, 1970.

OWENS, CHARLES Flute. Played with John Mayall, 1972.

OWENS, FRANK Piano. Session for B. B. King (1972); the Mark and Clark Band (1977); Grace Slick (1980).

OWENS, JIMMY Trumpet, cornet. Member of Ars Nova, 1968-69.

OWENS, WILSON Drums. Backup for Mitch Ryder, 1978-79.

OX John Entwhistle—bass, vocal, synthesizer; Graham Deakin—drums, percussion; Tony Ashton—keyboards; Jim Ryan—guitar; Howie Casey—tenor saxophone; Dave Caswell—trumpet; John Mumford—trombone; Dick Parry—baritone saxophone. Traveling band for the Who's John Entwhistle on his solo tour of 1975. See John Entwhistle.

OXENDALE, PETER Keyboards. Half of the Oxendale and Shephard duet, 1979.

OXENDALE AND SHEPHARD Gerry Shephard—vocal, guitar; Peter Oxendale—keyboards. *Album:* Put Your Money Where Your Mouth Is (NMP JZ 36063) 1979.

OXIDIZER, RAINBOW RED Vocal. Head of Rainbow Red Oxidizer, 1980.

OXINDINE, JOHN Drums. Replaced Don Stevenson in the re-formed Moby Grape, 1978.

OZ, WILLIAM Vocal, harmonica. *Album:* William Oz (CAP ST-12015) 1980.

OZARK MOUNTAIN DAREDEVILS John Dillon—guitar, fiddle, mandolin, percussion, vocal, dulcimer, autoharp; Buddy Brayfield—keyboards, vocal, percussion; Steve Cash—vocal, harmonica, percussion; Randall Chowning—guitar, steel guitar, vocal, harmonica, mandolin (1973-75); Jerry Mills—mandolin (1977); Steve Cannady—guitar, drums, vocal (1977-78); Russell Chappell—keyboards, vocal (1977-78); Rune Walle—guitar, sitar, banjo, vocal (1977-78); Michael Granda—bass, vocal, percussion (1973-75, 80); Larry Lee—vocal, keyboards, guitar, percussion (1973-75, 80). With little fanfare, the Ozarks appeared in 1973 playing original country rock material. Besides being musically multi-faceted, they demonstrated their range in 1974 with the release of the pop hit "Jackie Blue." Personnel shifts resulted in their two-year sabbatical, 1978-80. *Albums:* Car Over the Lake Album (AAM 4549) 1975; It'll Shine When It Shines (AAM 3654) 1974; It's Alive (AAM 6006) 1978; Ozark Mountain Daredevils (AAM 4411) 1973; Men From Earth (AAM SP 4601) 1976; Don't Look Now (AAM) 1977.

OZZ Alex Tangel—vocal; Gregg Parker—guitar, vocal. Writing team who perform with a studio band. *Album:* No Prisoners (EPC JE-36198) 1980.

P.F.M. Franz di Cioccio—drums, percussion; Patrick Djavas—bass, moog; Bernardo Lanzetti—vocal, percussion; Gregory Bloch—violin (1977); Franco Mussida—guitar; Flavio Premoli—keyboards; Mauro Pagani—woodwinds (1976). Abbreviated name of Premiata Forneier Marconi. *Albums:* Chocolate Kings (ASY 7E-1071) 1976; Jet Lag (ASY 7E-1101) 1977; Cook (MCR 65025-1) 1974; Photos of Ghosts (MCR 66668) 1973.

PAAY, PATRICIA Vocal. Session for Golden Earring (1974-77); Barry Hay.

PABLO CRUISE Bud Cockrell—bass, vocal; David Jenkins—guitar, vocal; Cory Leiros—piano, vocal; Stephen Price—drums. *Albums:* Lifeline (AAM 4575) 1976; Nadia's Theme (AAM 3412); Pablo Cruise (AAM 4528) 1975; Place in the Sun (AAM 4625) 1977; Worlds Away (AAM 4697) 1978; Parts of the Game (AAM 3712) 1979.

PACE, MICHAEL Member of Gotham, 1979.

PACE, STEVE Drums. Member of Hydra, 1975-77.

PACE, THOM Vocal. *Album:* Maybe (CAP ST 12053) 1980.

PACEMAKERS See Gerry and the Pacemakers.

PACIFIC GAS AND ELECTRIC Charlie Allen—guitar, vocal; John Hill—guitar, keyboards, percussion; Spencer Michlin. *Album:* Get On It (KNT 547).

PACK, DAVID Guitar, vocal, keyboards. Member of Ambrosia since 1975. Session for the Alan Parsons Project (1976); Kerry Livgren (1980).

PACKARD, LARRY Violin. Member of Cat Mother and the All Night Newsboys. Session for Free Creek (1973); Henry Gross (1976); the Band (1977).

PACKER, MICHAEL Vocal, guitar, bass. Member of Free Beer, 1976.

PADDEN, PETER Vocal, drums, percussion. Member of the Straight Lines, 1980.

PADDY, KLAUS AND GIBSON Early band of Klaus Voorman.

PADRON, DAVID Trumpet. Member of Cold Blood.

PAGANI, MAURO Woodwinds. Member of P.F.M., 1976.

PAGANOTTE, BERNARD Bass. Member of Magma.

PAGE, FRED Member of the Illinois Speed Press, 1969.

PAGE, IAN Vocal, trumpet, keyboards. Member of the Secret Affair, 1980.

PAGE, JIM Guitar, vocal. Seattle-area street singer in the Dylan tradition. *Albums:* On the Street Again (WDI 02) 1976; Hot Times (WDI 03) 1978.

PAGE, JIMMY Guitar, pedal steel guitar, vocal, writer, producer. Born 1/8/44. Replaced Jeff Beck in the Yardbirds, 1967-69, before forming Led Zeppelin, 1969-80. Session for Joe Cocker (1968); Lord Sutch; the Kinks.

PAGE, RICHARD Vocal, keyboards, synthesizer. Namesake of the Pages, 1978-79.

PAGE, SID Violin, mandolin, vocal. Member of Dan Hicks and His Hot Licks until 1974.

PAGES Richard Page—vocal, keyboards, synthesizer; Steve George—keyboards, synthesizer, vocal; Charlie "Icarus" Johnson—guitar (1979); Jerry Manfredi—bass; George Lawrence—drums (1979); John Lang—lyrics; Russ Battelene—drums (1978); Peter Leinheiser—guitar (1978). *Albums:* Future Street (EPC JE 36209) 1979; Pages (EPC JE 35459) 1978.

PAHOA, DAVE Bass, vocal. Member of the Plimsouls, 1980.

PAICE, IAN Drums, writer. Co-founder of Deep Purple, 1968-75, and member of Paice, Ashton, Lord, 1977. Replaced Dave Dowle in Whitesnake, 1980.

PAICE, ASHTON, LORD Ian Paice—drums; Paul Martinez—bass; Jon Lord—keyboards, synthesizer; Tony Ashton—vocal, keyboards; Bernie Marsden—guitar, vocal. Deep Purple alumni Paice and Lord filling the Purple void. *Album:* Malice in Wonderland (WBR B-3038) 1977.

PAICH, DAVID Keyboards, producer. Member of Toto since 1978. Produced the Romeos (1980). String arranger for John Sebastian (1974). Session for Joe Cocker (1974); Boz Scaggs (1976, 80); Donovan (1976); Neil Diamond (1976); Nilsson (1976); Steely Dan (1974); Seals and Crofts (1973, 76); Glen Campbell (1976); Mickey Thomas (1977); Les Dudek (1977); Rick Danko (1977); Adrian Gurvitz (1979); Tom Johnston (1979); Elton John (1980); Bob Weir (1978); Jimmy Webb (1977).

PAINE, NICK Guitar. Member of Centaurus.

PAINE, RICHARD Drums, vocal. Member of the Twisters, 1980.

PAINTBOX The nucleus of the Easybeats, Harry Vanda and George Young, formed Paintbox in the early 1970s before becoming Haffy's Whiskey Sour, which became the Marcus Hook Roll Band and eventually Flash and the Pan, 1979-present.

PAINTER Danny Lowe—guitar; Dorian Beattie—

vocal; Wayne Morice—bass, vocal; Barry Allen—guitar, vocal; Bob Ego—drums. *Album:* Painter (ELK) 1973.

PAKALA, JIMMY Keyboards, vocal. Half of the Pakalameredith duet, 1977.

PAKALAMEREDITH Jimmy Pakala—keyboards, vocal; Larry Meredith—vocal. *Album:* Pakalameredith (ELK 7E-1106) 1977.

PAKULSKI, JAN MAREK Member of the Fleshtones, 1980.

PALEY, ANDY Guitar, organ, harmonica. Half of the Paley Brothers duet, 1978.

PALEY, ANN Keyboards. Session for the Nervous Eaters (1980).

PALEY, JONATHAN Guitar, vocal. Half of the Paley Brothers duet, 1978. Member of the Nervous Eaters, 1980.

PALEY, TOM Banjo. Member of the New Lost City Ramblers until 1968. *Albums:* Folk Banjo Styles (ELK 7217); Hard Luck Poppa (KML 201) 1976.

PALEY BROTHERS Andy Paley—guitar, organ, harmonica; Jonathan Paley—guitar. *Album:* Paley Brothers (SIR K-6052) 1978.

PALISELLI, BILLY Vocal. Voice of Artful Dodger, 1975-present.

PALMAR, WALLY Member of the Romantics, 1980.

PALMARO, CHRIS Keyboards, percussion. Session for Ray Gomez (1980); Blackjack (1980).

PALMER, BARRY Vocal. Voice of Triumvirat, 1976-79.

PALMER, BRAD Bass, vocal. Session for Bob Welch (1979).

PALMER, BRUCE Bass. Original member of Buffalo Springfield, 1966-67, with Steve Stills, Richie Furay and Neil Young.

PALMER, CARL Drums, percussion. Multifaceted jazz-rock drummer first appeared as co-founder of Atomic Rooster, 1971, with Vincent Crane, before leaving for greater success as one-third of Emerson, Lake and Palmer, 1971-80.

PALMER, CLIVE Vocal, guitar, keyboards, writer. Original member of the Incredible String Band.

PALMER, DAVE Drums. Member of the Amboy Dukes.

PALMER, DAVID Vocal. Original member of Steely Dan, 1972, Big Wha Koo, 1977, and Wha-Koo since 1979.

PALMER, DAVID Saxophone, keyboards, vocal, orchestral arranger. Worked with Jethro Tull since 1971, officially joining the group, 1977-79. Session for Maddy Prior (1980).

PALMER, EARL Drums. Session for Fats Domino (1949-57); Jan and Dean (1963).

PALMER, EARL Drums, percussion. Session for Donovan (1974); Taj Mahal (1969); Splinter (1975); B. B. King (1972).

PALMER, GEOFFERY Saxophone, keyboards. Member of the Sons of Champlin.

PALMER, KEN Mandolin. Member of the Dixie Flyers.

PALMER, PHIL Guitar, vocal. Member of the Bliss Band, 1977-78. Session for Ian Matthews (1978).

PALMER, POLI Vibes. Session for Peter Frampton (1975).

PALMER, ROBERT Vocal, guitar. *Albums:* Double Fun (ISL 9476) 1978; Pressure Drop (ISL 9372) 1975; Secrets (ISL 9544) 1979; Some People Can Do What They Like (ISL 9420) 1976; Sneakin' Sally Through the Alley (ISL 9294) 1974; Clues (ISL 9595) 1980.

PALMER, RON Guitar, vocal. Session for Harry Chapin.

PALUMBO, JOHN Keyboards, guitar, vocal. Member of Crack in the Sky, 1975-77. *Album:* Innocent Bystander (LIF JZ-35503) 1978.

PALUMBO, LARRY Vocal. Member of the Earls, 1959.

PANAMA RED Vocal. Member of Frut, 1970-72.

PANG, MAY Vocal. Session for John Lennon (1974).

PANIC SQUAD Norman Normal—guitar, vocal; Andy Gray—guitar, vocal; Louie Louie—drums; Michael Maxwell—bass; Billy Good—guitar, piano. *Album:* Panic Squad (WBR) 1980.

PANKOW, BILL Keyboards. Member of Private Lines, 1980.

PANKOW, JAMES Trombone. Original member of Chicago, since 1969. Session for the Bee Gees (1979).

PANKRATZ, PAT Guitar, vocal. Member of the Greezy Wheels, 1976.

PANOZZO, CHUCK Bass. Original member of Styx since 1970.

PANOZZO, JOHN Drums, percussion, vocal. Original member of Styx since 1970.

PANTOJA, VICTOR Conga. Member of Giants, 1978. Session for Carlos Santana-Buddy Miles "Live" (1972).

PAPA, ANDREW Drums. Member of the Elektrics, 1980.

PAPAGEORGE, BRIAN Vocal. Member of the Werewolves, 1978.

PAPALIA, GIOVANNI Member of Ars Nova, 1968-69.

PAPATHANASSIOU, VANGELIS Keyboards, flute, percussion, vibes, vocal, writer. Member of Aphrodite's Child, 1968-72, before going solo. See Vangelis.

PAPE, HANS Bass. Session for Triumvirat (1973).

PAPPALARDI, FELIX Bass, keyboards, vocal, producer. Session and producer for Cream. After leaving Cream (1969), he discovered Leslie West and formed Mountain, applying the Cream formula once again until 1974. He then left for Japan to organize a Japanese heavy metal group, Creation, 1975, which he also produced. He returned as a soloist, 1979. Production and session for Jack Bruce (1969); Leslie West (1968). Produced the Youngbloods (1967); Bo Grumpus (1968); Bedlam (1973); Fred Neil. *Album:* Don't Worry, Ma (AAM 4729) 1979.

PAPPERT, JOHANNES Saxophone. Member of Kraan, 1975.

PARAMOUNTS Early name for Procol Harum.

PARAMOURS Early name for the Righteous Brothers.

PARAZAIDER, WALTER Woodwinds, vocal. Original member of Chicago since 1969. Session for the Bee Gees (1979).

PARCLEY, TEMPLETON Violin, organ, vocal. Original member of Kaleidoscope, 1967-68, 76, and the Rank Strangers, 1977.

PARENTE, LOUIE Trombone. Member of Southside Johnny and the Asbury Jukes until 1977.

PARFITT, RICHARD Guitar, vocal, piano. Original member of Status Quo, 1965-present.

PARIS, JOHN Bass, guitar, harmonica, vocal. Session for Johnny Winter (1980).

PARIS Robert Welch—guitar, vocal, writer; Glenn Cornick—bass, keyboards; Thom Mooney—drums (1975); Hunt Sales—drums (1976). After his dramatic departure from Fleetwood Mac, Welch returned in 1975 with former Jethro Tull bassist Cornick in a heavy-metal trio. The overabundant volume, however, did not compensate for the lack of stimulating material. *Albums:* Paris (CAP) 1975; Big Towne 2061 (CAP ST 1156) 1976.

PARISH, BRIAN Guitar. Member of Medicine Head, 1973.

PARISI, DENNIS Trombone. Member of Ten Wheel Drive, 1970.

PARK, ALAN Keyboards. Replaced Dave McCraw in the Tiger, 1976. Member of the Bliss Band, 1978-79. Session for Brian Protheroe (1976).

PARK, JAN Vocal. Namesake of the Jan Park Band.

JAN PARK BAND Jan Park—vocal; John Bartle—guitar, vocal; Bill Barber—keyboards; Dick Hedlund—bass; Gordy Knudtson—drums; Mike Condon—guitar; Kent Saunders—guitar; Eric Holtze—guitar. *Album:* Jan Park Band (COL JC-35484) 1979.

PARK, RAY Fiddle. Session for New Riders of the Purple Sage.

PARK, SIMON Keyboards. *Album:* Venus Fly Trap (EMI ST 11581) 1975.

PARKER, ALAN Guitar. Member of Blue Mink. Session for Olivia Newton-John (1976); Mike Batt (1979).

PARKER, ANDY Drums. Member of UFO, 1974-75.

PARKER, ANDY Saxophone. Session for Bram Tchaikovsky (1980).

PARKER, BEAVER Drums, percussion, vocal. Member of Buckeye, 1979.

PARKER, CHRISTOPHER Drums. Part of Paul Butterfield's Better Days band, 1973. Session for Paul Butterfield (1975); Randle Bramblett (1975); Martin Mull (1977).

PARKER, DENNIS Bass. Session for Roy Buchanan (1977).

PARKER, ERIC Drums. Member of the Rhinestones, 1975. Session for Nick Jameson (1977); Randy Vanwarmer (1979); Ian Hunter (1980).

PARKER, GRAHAM Vocal, guitar. Soloist who teamed up with the Rumour, 1977-80. See Rumour. *Albums:* Heat Treatment (MER SRM 1-1117) 1976; Howlin' Wind (MER SRM-1-1095) 1976; The Parkerilla (MER SRM-2-100) 1978; Squeezing Out Sparks (ARI 4223); Stick to Me (SRM-1-3706) 1977; Up Escalator (ARI 9517) 1980.

PARKER, GREGG Guitar, vocal. Half of the Ozz duet, 1980.

PARKER, IAN Keyboards, vocal. Member of the Tom Robinson Band, 1979.

PARKER, JOHN Keyboards. Member of Zulu.

PARKER, JOHNNY Member of Blues Incorporated.

PARKER, RAY, JR. Guitar. Session for Joe Cocker (1974); Seals and Crofts (1976); Jim Capaldi (1978); Boz Scaggs (1980).

PARKER, KNOCKY Piano. Session for Sleepy John Estes (1962).

PARKER, LITTLE JUNIOR Vocal. Bluesman born in West Memphis, 1927. *Albums:* Anthology of the Blues—Memphis Blues (KNT 9002); Barefoot Rock and You Got Me (MCA DLDX-72); Best of Little Junior Parker (MCA 83); Driving Wheel (MCA 76).

PARKER, MAGGIE Vocal. Session for John Mayall (1979).

PARKER, MICHAEL Keyboards. Member of the Ba-Fa Band, 1976, and the Movies, 1977.

PARKER, PETER Drums, vocal. Member of Dirty Looks, 1980.

PARKER, SPARKIE Vocal. Session for Frank Zappa (1976); Phoebe Snow (1976); Lee Ritenour (1977).

PARKER, TOM Piano. Session for Status Quo (1976).

PARKES, PETER Trumpet. Member of Centipede, 1971.

PARKIN, IAN Guitar. Original member of Be Bop Deluxe, until 1975.

PARKINS, DONALD Guitar, bass. Member of the Bizarros, 1979.

PARKINS, GERALD Guitar. Member of the Bizarros, 1979.

PARKINSON, MIKE Member of Hunger.

PARKS, CHRIS Guitar. Member of Any Trouble, 1980.

PARKS, DEAN Guitar. Session for Carole King (1974); Art Garfunkel; Neil Sedaka (1975-76); Steely Dan (1974, 76); Arthur, Hurley, and Gottlieb; Glen Campbell (1976, 80); Kim Carnes (1976); Hoyt Axton (1976); Yvonne Elliman

(1978); Alan O'Day (1979); Chris Montan (1980); Jim Capaldi (1979); Johnny Rivers (1980); Austin Roberts (1973); Jimmy Webb (1977).

PARKS, LLOYD Bass. Member of Skin, Flesh, and Bone, 1975.

PARKS, RAY Fiddle. Member of the Dillards, 1979.

PARKS, VAN DYKE Piano, vocal, writer, arranger, producer. Compatriot of Brian Wilson. Produced Harpers Bizarre. Session and production for Ry Cooder (1970, 72). Session for Nilsson (1975-76). *Albums:* Clang of the Yankee Reaper (WBR B-2878); Song Cycle (WBR 1727) 1967.

PARLATO, CHRIS Drums. Session for Jimmy Carl Black and Bunk Gardner.

PARLATO, DAVE Acoustic bass. Session for Jimmy Carl Black and Bunk Gardner; Tim Weisberg (1972); Frank Zappa (1976); Martin Mull (1979).

PARMENTER, KEITH Drums. Member of Lance Romance.

PARNELL, RIC Drums, percussion. Replaced Paul Hammond in Atomic Rooster, 1972-73.

PARRAN, J. D. Saxophone. Session for the Band (1972); the Paul Butterfield Blues Band (1973); John Lennon (1980).

PARREN, CHRIS Keyboards. Member of Hudson-Ford, 1974-75, and the Contenders, 1979. Session for Ian Gomm (1979).

PARRISH, BRIAN Percussion. Half of the Parrish and Gurvitz duet, 1972. Session for Jerry Lee Lewis (1973).

PARRISH AND GURVITZ Brian Parrish—vocal, guitar; Paul Gurvitz—vocal, bass, guitar. *Album:* Parrish and Gurvitz, 1972.

PARRY, DICK Baritone saxophone. Member of Ox, 1975. Session for Pink Floyd (1973-75); Lightnin' Sam (1978).

PARRY, KEN Guitar. Session for Eric Burdon (1977).

PARRY, MALCOLM Bass, vocal. Played on "Joseph and the Amazing Technicolor Dreamcoat," 1967.

PARSONS, ALAN Guitar, keyboards, vocal, writer, engineer. After several years as an engineer (his credits include the Beatles' "Abbey Road," McCartney's "Wild Life" and "Red Rose Speedway," five Hollies albums, Pink Floyd's "Dark Side of the Moon," and others), he organized a group of friends for a concept album based on Poe stories in 1975. He has continued to the present as head of the Alan Parsons Project. Engineer for Formerly Fat Harry (1971); Hollies; John Miles (1980); and others. Produced Al Stewart (1978). Session for Roy Sundholm (1979).

ALAN PARSONS PROJECT Alan Parsons—guitar, keyboards, vocal, producer, engineer; Eric Woolfson—writer, keyboards; Andrew Powell—arranger, guitar; Ian Barinson—guitar; David Paton—bass, guitar, vocal. Studio musicians and technicians organized by producer Parsons. The tight production and concept album ideas are reminiscent of Pink Floyd. *Albums:* Eve (ARI 9504) 1979; I, Robot (ARI 7002) 1977; Pyramid (ARI 4180) 1978; Tales of Mystery and Imagination (TWC 539) 1975; The Turn of a Friendly Card (ARI 9518) 1980.

PARSONS, AMANDA Vocal. Member of the National Health Band, 1977.

PARSONS, DAVE Guitar. Member of Sham 69, 1978-80.

PARSONS, GENE Drums, guitar, vocal, banjo, harmonica. Born 4/9/44. Original member of the Byrds, 1965, and a member of the Flying Burrito Brothers. Session for Randy Newman. *Albums:* Kindling (WBR B-2687); Melodies (SIE 8703) 1979.

PARSONS, GRAM Guitar, vocal. Member of the Byrds for "Sweetheart of the Rodeo" and founder of the Flying Burrito Brothers. Died 1975. *Albums:* Early Years (SIE 8702) 1979; G.P. (RPS 2123) 1976; Grevious Angel (RPS 2171) 1974; Sleepless Nights (AAM 4578); Gram Parsons (SIL 4088) 1979.

PARSONS, SMOKEY Vocal. Session for the Alan Parsons Project (1976).

PARTRIDGE, ANDY Guitar, vocal. Member of XTC since 1979.

PARTRIDGE, JO Member of the Kiki Dee Band, 1973-74. Session for Justin Hayward (1980); the Who (1980).

PARUOLO, JOHN Keyboards, vocal. Member of the Eddie Boy Band, 1975.

PARYPA, ANDY Bass, vocal. Original member of the Sonics.

PARYPA, KEN Bass, vocal. Member of the Skyboys, 1979-present.

PARYPA, LARRY Guitar, vocal, writer. Original member of the Sonics.

PASEIRO, ARNOLD Bass. Member of Foxy since 1978.

PASH, JIM Saxophone, clarinet, guitar. Member of the Surfaris, 1963-65.

PASQUA, ALAN Keyboards. Member of the New Tony Williams Lifetime, 1975-77. Replaced Chris Rhyne in Santana, 1978-80. Session for Bob Dylan (1978-79).

PASSARELLI, KENNY Bass, vocal. Member of Joe Walsh's backup band, 1972-76. Joined the Elton John Band, 1976. Session for Rick Derringer (1973); Steve Stills (1975); Elton John (1975).

PASSION Av Luce—vocal; Jerry Field—bass; Nick Pepper—keyboards, vocal; Blair Anderson—drums, vocal; Mike Fleetwood—guitar, vocal; Lauren Rinder—percussion; W. Michael Lewis—synthesizer. Re-formed Whole Wheat backing featured vocalist Av Luce. *Album:* Passion (AVI 6059) 1979.

PASTERNAK, JOHN Bass, vocal. Original member of Bronco.

PASTORA, SERGIO Percussion. Session for Bob Seger (1973).

PASTORIUS, JACO Bass, guitar. Member of Weather Report, 1976-present. Session for Ian Hunter (1975); Joni Mitchell (1980); Flora Purim (1978).

PAT Member of the Germs, 1979.

PATE, SAM Bass. Member of the Rockicks, 1977. Session for Danny Spanos (1980).

PATILLO, LEON Vocal, keyboards. Member of Creation, 1974. Session with Santana (1974).

PATILLO, VAL Bass. Session for B. B. King (1969).

PATON, DAVID Bass, guitar, vocal. Member of Pilot, 1974, and the Alan Parsons Project, 1976-present. Session for Kate Bush (1978).

PATTEN, BRIAN Vocal, percussion. Member of Grimms, 1973.

PATTEN, DENNER Guitar, vocal. Member of Kak.

PATTEN, EDWARD Original member of Gladys Knight and the Pips.

PATTENDEN, COLIN Bass. Member of Manfred Mann's Earth Band, 1972-77.

PATTERSON, ALVIN Percussion. Member of Bob Marley's Wailers.

PATTERSON, ANN Reeds. Session for John Mayall (1977-78).

PATTERSON, BOB Guitar, vocal. Member of Elizabeth, 1968.

PATTERSON, BERMAN Vocal. Member of the Cleftones.

PATTERSON, BRENDA Vocal. Member of the Coon Elder Band, 1977.

PATTERSON, MICHAEL Piano. Member of the Righteous Brothers Band, 1966.

PATTERSON, TOMMY Keyboards, vocal. Member of Jackson Highway.

PATTINSON, LES Bass. Member of Echo and the Bunnymen, 1980.

PATTISON, DAVEY Vocal. Voice of Gamma since 1979.

PATTO, MIKE Vocal, keyboards, percussion. Member of Patto, 1970-72, and Centipede, 1971. Took over Mike Harrison's spot in Gary Wright's re-formed Spooky Tooth, 1974. Member of Boxer, 1975, and Timebox, 1976. Session for Alvin Lee (1973); Snape (1972).

PATTO Mike Patto—vocal; John Halsey—drums; Ollie Halsall—guitar, keyboards; Clive Griffiths—bass. *Albums:* Patto (VTG) 1970; Hold Your Fire, 1971; Roll 'Em, Smoke 'Em, Put Another Line Out, 1972.

PATUTO, MATTHEW "CHIPS" Drums, vocal. Member of Alda Reserve, 1979.

PAUL Percussion. Credited as a member of the Silicon Teens, 1980.

PAUL, ALLEN Vocal. Member of the Manhattan Transfer since 1971.

PAUL, DANA Keyboards, vocal. Member of Rich Mountain Tower, 1976.

PAUL, HENRY Guitar, vocal. Member of the Outlaws, 1975-79, and the Henry Paul Band since 1979.

HENRY PAUL BAND Henry Paul—guitar, vocal; Jim Fish—guitar, vocal (1979); Bill Crain—guitar; Barry Rapp—keyboards, vocal; Wally Dentz—bass, harmonica, vocal; Bill Hoffman—drums; David Fiester—guitar, vocal (1980); Monte Yoho—drums (1980). *Albums:* Feel the Heat (ATC 19273) 1980; Grey Ghost (ATC 19232) 1979.

PAUL, TERRY Bass. Session for Bob Dylan (1973).

PAUL AND PAULA Vocal duet responsible for "Hey Paula" (1963). Shortly afterward they were drowned in the British invasion.

PAULEN, KIP Bass, guitar. Member of Wild Oats, 1977.

PAULO, MIKE Reeds. Member of Kalapanna, 1977.

PAULSEN, CHRIS Drums. Member of Mistress, 1979.

PAULSON, ZEPH Drums, vocal. Member of the Scruffs, 1977.

PAUPERS Skip Prokop—vocal, drums, guitar, writer; Adam Mitchell—vocal, keyboards, guitar, writer; Chuck Beal—guitar, mandolin; Denny Gerrard—bass, drums, vocal (1966-67); Brad Campbell—bass, drums, vocals (1968-69). Formed in Canada in 1966, they were rumored to be a big up and coming group. They were signed by Dylan's manager, and the Mitchell-Prokop writing team began their work. But business problems led to the group's breakup after two albums in 1969. *Albums:* Magic People (VRV) 1967; Ellis Island (VRV 3051) 1968.

PAVEY, LEE Vocal. Session for the Kinks (1971).

PAVLOV'S DOG David Surkamp—vocal, guitar, writer; David Hamilton—keyboards; Doug Rayburn—mellotron, bass, flute, writer; Mike Safron—drums, percussion, writer (1975); Rick Stockton—bass; Siegfried Carver—violin, vitar, viola (1975); Steve Scorfina—guitar, writer; Thomas Nickeson—guitar (1976). Pavlov's Dog appeared in 1975, featuring the big band sound, including dual keyboards and Surkamp's tenor falsetto, which several critics found hard to accept. A second album brought little attention to this talented New York rock group. *Albums:* Pampered Menial (ABC 866) 1975; At the Sound of the Bell (ABC) 1976.

PAVONE, GLENN Guitar, vocal. Member of the Bill Blue Band, 1979.

PAWLETT, YVONNE Piano. Member of the Fall, 1979.

PAWLIK, RAY Guitar. Member of Navasota, 1972.

PAXON, MARK Keyboards, vocal. Member of the

Choice, 1980.

PAXTON, GARY S. Vocal. Member of the Hollywood Argyles, 1960. *Albums:* Astonishing, Outrageous, Amazing, Incredible, Unbelievable, Different World of Gary S. Paxton (NPX 33005); Christian Grit (NPX 33015); More from the Astonishing, Outrageous, Amazing, Incredible, Unbelievable Gary S. Paxton (NPX 33033).

PAXTON, TOM Guitar, vocal. In the Phil Ochs tradition, a topical folk singer who began in 1964. *Albums:* Compleat Tom Paxton (ELK 7E-2003) 1970; Heroes (VAN 79411) 1978; Morning Again (ELK 74019) 1968; New Songs from the Briarpatch (VAN 79395) 1977; Ramblin' Boy (ELK 7277) 1964; Things I Notice Now (ELK 74043); Ain't That News (ELK) 1965; Tom Paxton #6 (ELK); Something in My Life (ELK).

PAYNE, BILL Keyboards, vocal. Member of Little Feat, 1971-77. Session for the Doobie Brothers (1972, 74, 78); Jonathan Edwards (1976); Art Garfunkel (1974, 78); Carly Simon (1972); Martin Mull (1977); Andy Pratt (1973); Robert Palmer (1976); Pakalameredith (1977); Bob Seger (1978-80); Tom Johnston (1979); Rory Bloch (1979); Firefall (1980); Red Rider (1980); the Blues Brothers (1980); Jackson Browne (1980); the Marc Tanner Band (1980).

PAYNE, CHRIS Bass, vocal. Member of the Members, 1979-80.

PAYNE, COLIN Keyboards, vocal. Member of Taxxi, 1980.

PAYNE, DAVEY Saxophone. Member of Ian Dury's Blockheads, 1979.

PAYNE, DEVIN Vocal. *Album:* Excuse Me (CAS 7245) 1980.

PAYNE, DON Bass. Replaced Pete Van Allen in the Snakestretchers, 1973. Session for Ellen McIlwaine (1973); Henry Gross (1977); the Euclid Beach Band (1979). *Album:* Something Else (CTP 7551).

PAYNE, JODY Guitar. Session for Leon Russell (1979); Leon Russell and Willie Nelson (1979); Willie Nelson (1976, 79).

PAYNE, JOHN Saxophone, flute. Namesake and leader of the John Payne Band, 1976. Session for Peter C. Johnson (1980).

JOHN PAYNE BAND John Payne—saxophone, flute; Louis Levin—keyboards; Scott Lee—bass; Gerald Murphy—drums; Riccardo Torres—percussion. *Albums:* Bedtime Stories (ARI 1025); Razor's Edge (ARI 1036) 1976.

PAYNE, ODIE Drums. Session for Chuck Berry (1964).

PAYNE, PICO Vocal. Session for Ry Cooder (1979-80).

PAYNE, SHERRIE Vocal. Session for Bob Seger (1973).

PAYTON, DENNIS Saxophone, clarinet, guitar, harmonica. Member of the Dave Clark 5, 1964-68.

PAYTON, LAWRENCE Vocal. Original member of the Four Tops.

PAZDAN, JOHN Bass. Member of Off Broadway, 1979.

PEACEY, GEOFFREY Keyboards, bass, vocal, guitar. Member of Lake since 1977.

PEACHEY, ERIC Drums. Member of Khan, 1972.

PEACOCK, ANNETTE Vocal. Session for Chris Youlden (1974). *Albums:* Perfect Release (TMT 7044) 1979; X-dreams (TMT 7025) 1979.

PEACOCK, DAVE Bass. Session for Mike Berry (1976).

PEAKE, DON Guitar. Member of the Candle, 1972.

PEANUT BUTTER CONSPIRACY Al Brackett—bass; Lance Feat—guitar, harmonica; John Merrill—guitar; Sandi Robinson—vocal; Jim Voight—drums; Bill Wolff—guitar. The age of psychedelica brought names of abstractions for bands out of the closet. California's Peanut Butter Conspiracy was one of the first to come and go in 1967, but not one of the last. *Albums:* The Peanut Butter Conspiracy Is Spreading, 1967; The Great Conspiracy, 1967.

PEARL, DEBBIE Vocal. Half of the Pearl duet, 1977.

PEARL, LESLIE Vocal. Half of the Pearl duet, 1977.

PEARL, MICK Bass, vocal. Member of the Streetband, 1980.

PEARL Leslie Pearl—vocal; Debbie Pearl—vocal. *Album:* Pearl (LON PS 692) 1977.

PEARLS BEFORE SWINE Tom Rapp—guitar, vocal, writer; Wayne Harley—banjo, mandolin, percussion, vocal (1967-69); Lane Lederer—bass, guitar, horns, percussion (1967-69); Roger Crissinger—keyboards (1967); Warren Smith—drums, percussion (1967); Jim Bohannon—keyboards, percussion (1968); Elizabeth—vocal (1969); Jim Fairs—guitar, vocal, percussion (1969). From New York in 1967 came the Pearls' acid sound mixed with the social consciousness of folk music. Tom Rapp, head writer, mellowed his lyrics and the sound to develop into a major minor writer, and gain a cult following. With the dissolution of Pearls Before Swine, he continued as a soloist. *Albums:* These Things Too (RPS 6364) 1969; The Use of Ashes (RPS 6405) 1970; City of Gold (RPS 6442) 1971; Beautiful Lies You Could Live In (RPS 6467) 1971; Balaklava (ESP 1075) 1968; One Nation Underground (ESP 1054) 1967.

PEARSON, ARCH Bass. Replaced George Clark in Cowboy, 1977. Session for Robbie Robertson (1980).

PEARSON, CHARLES WOODS Vocal. Member of the Tears, 1979.

PEARSON, EUGENE Vocal. Member of the Cleftones.

PEARSON, KEN Organ. Member of the Full Tilt Boogie Band, 1969-70.

PEARSON, MARK Vocal, guitar, piano. Half of the Nielsen-Pearson duet, 1980.

PEARSON, STEVE Guitar, vocal. Member of the Heats, 1980.

PEART, NEIL Drums. Replaced John Rutsey in Rush, 1975-present.

PECCHIO, DANIEL Bass, vocal. Member of the Michael Stanley Band, 1977-79.

PECK, TOM Vocal. Member of the Crosswinds.

PEDDLER Kenny Wier—guitar, vocal; Russell Taylor—drums, vocal; Bo Gooliak—bass, piano. *Album:* Street Corner Stuff, 1976.

PEDERAST, CHAVO Vocal. Member of the Black Flag.

PEDERSON, HERB Guitar, banjo, vocal, writer. Original member of the Dillards, who altered the bluegrass formula to an electric country-folk format for his solo debut in 1976. Session for James Taylor (1976); Jonathan Edwards (1976-77); Russ Giguere (1971); the Doobie Brothers (1978); Adam Mitchell (1979); Gordon Lightfoot (1980); Jimmy Webb (1977). *Albums:* South By Southwest (EPC PE-34225); Herb Pederson (COL) 1976.

PEDRICK, CHRIS Drums. Member of the Fools, 1980.

PEDRICK, STACEY Guitar. Member of the Fools, 1980.

PEDRINI, TOM Bass. Session for Ry Cooder (1978).

PEEK, BILLY Guitar. Member of the Rod Stewart Band since 1978. Session for Rod Stewart (1976-77).

PEEK, DAN Guitar, vocal. Member of America, 1971-78. *Album:* All Things Are Possible (LLN 1040) 1978.

PEEL, DAVID Vocal. Voice of the Lower East Side.

DAVID PEEL AND THE LOWER EAST SIDE David Peel—vocal; Harold Black—percussion; Larry Adam—guitar; Billy Joe White—guitar; George Cori—washtub bass. An impromptu album including candid man-on-the-street conversations. *Album:* Have a Marijuana (ELK 74032) 1969.

PEEL, JERRY French horn. Session for Andy Gibb (1980).

PEGG, DAVE Bass. Replaced Ashley Hutchings in Fairport Convention, 1974, and John Glascock in Jethro Tull, 1980. Session for Gay and Terry Woods (1976); David Swarbuck (1976).

PEGRUN, NIGEL Drums. Member of Steeleye Span.

PELANDER, BOB Keyboards, synthesizer, percussion, vocal. Member of the Michael Stanley Band since 1977.

PELLICCI, DEREK Drums. Member of the Little River Band since 1977.

PELLINGER, MIKE Drums. Replaced Dave Hassinger in the Sunblind Lion, 1978.

PELLO, GENE Drums. Member of Captain Beefheart and His Magic Band, 1974.

PELOSI, JEFF Drums. Member of the Critters, 1966-67.

PELTIER, TOM Vocal. Session for Tim Weisberg (1974).

PEMBERTON, WARREN Drums. Member of Aim, 1974.

PENDARVIS, JANICE Vocal. Session for John Mayall (1979).

PENDARVIS, LEON Piano. Session for Martin Mull (1977); Taj Mahal (1978); Mark-Almond (1978); John Mayall (1979).

PENDERGRASS, BUDDY Keyboards. Member of the White Witch, 1973-74.

PENDLEBURY, ANDREW Guitar, vocal. Member of the Sports since 1979.

PENDLETONES Early name for the Beach Boys.

PENDRAS, PETE Guitar, vocal. Member of the Jitters, 1980.

PENDRITH, DENNIS Bass. Member of the Silver Tractors, 1976-77.

PENETRATION Neale Floyd; Fred Purser; Robert Blamire; Gary Smallman; Pauline Murray. *Album:* Coming Up for Air (VIR 2131) 1979.

PENETRATORS Dan McLain—drums; Chris Sullivan—bass, vocal; Chris Davies—guitar, vocal; Gary Heffern—vocal; Jim Call—keyboards. *Album:* Walk the Beat (EAM 1) 1980.

PENFIELD, HOLLY Vocal. *Album:* Full Grown Child (DML 1-5003) 1980.

PENNEBAKER, KIRT Bass, vocal. Member of the Max Demian Band, 1979-80.

PENNICK, CHRISTIEN Guitar. Member of Simon Stokes and the Black Whip Band, 1973.

PENNIMAN, RICHARD Real name of Little Richard.

PENNING, LESLIE Recorder. Session for Mike Oldfield (1975).

PENNINGTON, JIMMY Guitar, vocal. Member of Exile since 1973.

PENNINGTON, UNCLE MEAT Percussion. Member of George Thorogood and the Destroyers, 1978.

PENROD, JERRY Bass. Member of Rhinoceros, 1968.

PENSE, LYDIA Vocal. Member of Cold Blood before her less successful solo career.

PENTANGLE Terry Cox—drums; Bert Jansch—guitar; Jacqui McShee—vocal; John Renbourn—vocal, guitar; Danny Thompson—bass. Submerged behind the electricity and super-stardom images of the Beatles and other rockers aspiring in the Beatles' image, the Pentangle quietly began making records in 1968. Electricity was not their medium and rock 'n' roll was not their style. Traditional English ballads were their specialty. Their arrangements displayed the remarkable guitar talents of Jansch and Renbourn (both of whom have gone on to solo careers). *Albums:* Sweet Child (RPS 6334) 1968;

The Pentangle (RPS 6463) 1971; Basket of Light (RPS 6372) 1969; Cruel Sister (RPS 6430) 1970; Reflection (RPS 6463) 1971; Solomon's Seal (RPS 2100) 1972.

PENTIFALLO, KENNY Drums, vocal. Member of Southside Johnny and the Asbury Jukes, 1976-78.

PEPPER, CLAUDE Drums. Original member of Big Wha-Koo, 1977. Session for Danny Douma (1979).

PEPPER, JIM Flute. Session for Larry Coryell; the Fugs (1968).

PEPPER, NICK Vocal, keyboards. Member of Whole Wheat, 1977, and Passion, 1979.

PERAINO, VICTOR Keyboards, vocal, percussion. Replaced Goodge Harris in Arthur Brown's Kingdom Come, 1974.

PERATHONER, SERGE Keyboards. Member of the Transit Express, 1976, and the Rose, 1979.

PERAZA, ARMANDO Congas. Member of Santana since 1972. Session for Harvey Mandel.

PERE UBU Tom Herman—guitar, bass (1979); Scott Krauss—drums; Tony Maimone—bass; David Thomas—vocal; Allen Ravenstine—synthesizer; Mayo Thompson (1980). *Albums:* Dub Housing (CYS 1207) 1979; The Art of Walking (RTO 4) 1980.

PEREZ, JUAN Congas. Session for Jay Ferguson (1979).

PERFECT, CHRISTINE Vocal, piano. Married name: Christine McVie. Original member of Stan Webb's Chicken Shack in the late 1960s. She left that group and joined her husband, John McVie, in Fleetwood Mac, 1971-present. In 1969, she recorded a solo album, including her English hit, "I'd Rather Go Blind," which is one of the reasons she was voted most popular female vocalist in England two years running. Her album was not released in the United States until 1976. Session for Fleetwood Mac (1969). *Album:* The Legendary Christine Perfect Album (SIR 6022) 1976.

PERFECT, JOHN Saxophone. Session for Fleetwood Mac (1971).

PERKEY, CHRIS Drums. Member of the Blue Goose, 1975.

PERKINS, AL Pedal steel guitar, guitar, bass, dobro. Replaced Sneaky Pete in the Flying Burrito Brothers. Member of the Southern-Hillman-Furay Band, 1974-75. Session for Terry Reid (1976); the Rolling Stones (1972); Rita Coolidge (1972); Gram Parsons (1973-74); the Richie Furay Band (1976); the James Gang (1975); Joe Walsh (1972); Michael Nesmith (1978-79).

PERKINS, BILL Baritone saxophone, clarinet. Session for B. B. King (1971); Russ Giguere (1971). *Albums:* Confluence (ITP 7721) 1979; Jazz (PCJ LT-892).

PERKINS, DALE Member of the Crimson Tide, 1978-79.

PERKINS, JONATHAN Keyboards. Member of the Original Mirrors, 1980.

PERKINS, PINE TOP Piano. Session for Muddy Waters (1978).

PERKINS, TERRY Drums. Session for J. J. Cale (1974).

PERKINS, WAYNE Guitar. Member of the Crimson Tide, 1978-79. Session for Don Nix (1971); the Rolling Stones (1976); Mickey Thomas (1977).

PERLITCH, MICHAEL Keyboards, vocal, writer. Solo artist backing himself on multiple keyboards. His haunting tales of travel to far-off lands flowed from obscurity, but not into popularity. *Album:* Keyboard Tales (ATC SD 7230) 1972.

PEROSA, BRUNO Percussion. Member of the Bullfrog, 1976.

PERRETT, PETER Vocal, guitar. Member of the Only Ones since 1978.

PERRIER, PETE Drums, percussion, vocal. Member of the Unicorn, 1974-77.

PERRIN, BRIAN Tenor trombone. Session for Savoy Brown (1969).

PERRINE, PEP Drums, vocal. Original member of the Bob Seger System.

PERROTTET, DAVE Trombone. Member of Centipede, 1971.

PERRY, DAVID Guitar. Rhythm guitar for Leslie West in Mountain, 1974.

PERRY, DOANE Drums. Member of the Rivets, 1980.

PERRY, GEORGE Bass. Member of the Stills-Young Band, 1976. Session for Steve Stills (1975, 79); Jay Ferguson (1976); Crosby, Stills and Nash (1977); Bobby Caldwell (1978). *Album:* Chocolate Clay (CAT 2610).

PERRY, GREGG Keyboards, vocal, percussion. Member of Johnny and the Distractions, 1980.

PERRY, JOE Guitar. Member of Aerosmith, 1971-79, and head of the Joe Perry Project, 1979.

JOE PERRY PROJECT Joe Perry—guitar, vocal; Ralph Morman—vocal; David Hull—vocal, bass; Ronnie Stewart—drums. Spinoff from former Aerosmith member Perry. *Album:* Let the Music Do the Talking (COL JC-36388) 1980.

PERRY, JOHN Bass, vocal. Member of Gringo, 1971.

PERRY, JOHN G. Bass, vocal. Member of Aviator, 1978. Session for Dan McCafferty (1975); Danny Kirwan (1979); Anthony Phillips (1979).

PERRY, JOHN Guitar. Member of the Only Ones since 1978.

PERRY, RICHARD Percussion, producer. Session for Nilsson (1971-72); Ringo Starr (1973-74); Carly Simon (1972-74).

PERRY, STEVE Vocal. Member of Journey since 1978. Session for Sammy Hagar (1980).

PERRY, STU Drums. Member of the Frankie Miller Band, 1975.

PERSH, JOHN Bass, vocal. Member of Rare Earth.

PERT, MORRIS Percussion. Member of Brand X, 1977. Session for Bryan Ferry (1977); Elliott Murphy (1977); Kate Bush (1978); Wings (1979); Frankie Miller (1979); the Dukes (1979); Marianne Faithfull (1979); Peter Green (1980).

PESKIN, JOEL Woodwinds. Session for the Mothers of Invention (1972); Frank Zappa (1972); the Doobie Brothers (1980).

PETER AND GORDON Peter Asher—vocal; Gordon Waller—vocal. English coffeehouse duo who received their break when Peter's sister, Jane, dated Paul McCartney. They were given a Lennon/McCartney song to record, "World Without Love," 1964. Survived the mid-60s as hits, recording Del Shannon's "I Go to Pieces" but split up in 1968. *Albums:* World Without Love, 1964; I Don't Want to See You Again, 1964; I Go to Pieces, 1965; True Love Ways, 1965; Woman, 1966; Peter and Gordon Sing the Hits of Nashville, Tennessee, 1966; Lady Godiva, 1967; Knight in Rusty Armour, 1967; Peter and Gordon—In London for Tea, 1967; Hot, Cold, and Custard, 1968; Best of Peter and Gordon (CAP SM-2549) 1966.

PETER, PAUL AND MARY Peter Yarrow—vocal, guitar; Paul Stookey—vocal, bass; Mary Travers—vocal. Peter, Paul and Mary formed in 1962 in the hands of manager Albert Grossman. Their first single, "If I Had a Hammer," backed up by "Lemon Tree" (1962), was the beginning of their undisputed reign as the kings and queen of folk. *Albums:* Album 1700 (WBR 1700) 1967; Late Again (WBR 1751) 1968; Peter, Paul and Mary (WBR 1-1449) 1962; Peter, Paul and Mary Album (WBR 1648) 1966; Peter, Paul and Mary in Concert (WBR 1555) 1965; Peter, Paul and Mary in the Wind (WBR 1507) 1963; Peter, Paul and Mary Moving (WBR 1473) 1963; Peter, Paul and Mommy (WBR 1785) 1969; Reunion (WBR K-3231) 1965; See What Tomorrow Brings (WBR 1615) 1965; Song Will Rise (WBR 1589) 1965; Ten Years Together (WBR K-3105) 1970.

PETEREIT, DIETER Bass. Replaced Dick Frangenburg in Triumvirat, 1977.

PETERIK, JAMES MICHAEL Guitar, vocal. Member of the Ides of March.

PETERIK, JIM Guitar, vocal. Member of Survivor, 1979.

PETERMAN, JIM Organ. Original member of the Steve Miller Band, until 1968.

PETERS, BILL Guitar, vocal. Member of Pig Iron.

PETERS, DALE Bass, guitar. Replaced Tom Kriss in the James Gang, 1970-77.

PETERS, DAVE Saxophone, synthesizer. Member of Alexis, 1977.

PETERS, DAVID Drums. Member of Le Roux since 1979.

PETERS, DENNIS Bass, percussion. Member of the Nu Kats, 1980.

PETERS, JIM Bass. Member of the Reds, 1979.

PETERSEN, DETLEF Keyboards, vocal. Added to the Lake line-up, 1979.

PETERSEN, JOCHEN Guitar, saxophone, vocal. Member of Randy Pie, 1975-77.

PETERSON, BILL Percussion. Member of the White Witch, 1973-74.

PETERSON, BOBBIE Organ. Member of the McCoys, 1965-69.

PETERSON, CHARLES Baritone saxophone. Session for It's a Beautiful Day (1971).

PETERSON, CHRIS Vocal. Session for Frank Zappa (1972).

PETERSON, COLIN Member of Bee Gees early backup band.

PETERSON, DICK Bass, vocal, writer. Original member of Blue Cheer, 1968-69.

PETERSON, GARY Vocal, keyboards, guitar, percussion, writer. Member of Formerly Fat Harry, 1971.

PETERSON, GARY Member of the Guess Who until 1976.

PETERSON, GERRY Reeds. Member of the Creation, 1974.

PETERSON, JERRY Saxophone. Session for Jules and the Polar Bears (1979); Robbie Robertson (1980).

PETERSON, JOHN Member of the Beau Brummels.

PETERSON, JOHN Drums. Member of Harper's Bizarre, 1967-69.

PETERSON, RAY Vocal. Recorded "Tell Laura I Love Her," 1960.

PETERSON, SYLVIA Vocal. Member of the Chiffons.

PETERSON, TOM Reeds. Session for Mike Pindar (1976).

PETERSON, TOM Bass, vocal. Member of Cheap Trick, 1977-80.

PETTIS, JUNIOR Bass. Member of J. B. Hutto's Hawks.

PETTO, FRANK Keyboards, vocal. Member of the Fireballet, 1975-76.

PETTY, JOE DAN Bass, vocal. Member of the Grinderswitch, 1974-77.

PETTY, PHILLIP Bass. Member of Point Blank, 1976-79.

PETTY, TOM Guitar, vocal. His debut in 1977 with the Heartbreakers was often confused with the punk invasion, but Tom Petty's style of rock set him apart from the crowd. See Tom Petty and the Heartbreakers.

TOM PETTY AND THE HEARTBREAKERS Tom Petty—guitar, vocal; Mike Campbell—guitar; Stan Lynch—drums; Ron Blair—bass; Benmont Tench—keyboards. Part of "No Nukes," 1979. See Tom Petty. *Albums:* Damn the Torpedoes (BKS 5105) 1979; Tom Petty and the Heartbreakers (MCA 52006) 1977; You're Gonna Get It (MCA 52029) 1978.

PEVERETT, "LONESOME" DAVE Guitar, vocal,

writer. Replaced Marvin Stone as rhythm guitarist behind Kim Simmonds in Savoy Brown in 1968. From album to album he gradually progressed to an alternate lead guitar, and in 1971 he left with Brown drummer Roger Earle and bassist Tone Stevens to form Foghat, which he still heads.

PEYRONEL, DANNY Keyboards, vocal. Member of the Heavy Metal Kids, 1974, and UFO, 1974-75.

PEYTON, CARLA Vocal, percussion. Voice of the Coal Kitchen, 1977.

PEZBAND Mick Rain—drums; Mike Gorman—bass; Tommy Gauvenda—guitar; Mimi Betinis—vocal, guitar, piano. *Albums:* Cover to Cover (PST 9837) 1979; Laughing in the Dark (PST 9826) 1978; Pezband (PST 98021) 1977; Thirty Seconds over Schaumburg (PST 3901) 1978.

PEZIN, SLIM Vocal, guitar, percussion. Member of the Voyage.

PFAYLER, JIM Organ. Member of the Ohio Express, 1968-69.

PFISTERER, ALBAN Former member of Love.

PHANTOM MOVERS See Roy Loney and the Phantom Movers.

PHARAOHS See Sam the Sham and the Pharaohs.

PHAZE SHIFTER Randy Knapp—bass, vocal; Larry Knight—guitar; Elliot Thorne—drums, vocal; Jim Curnvite—guitar, keyboards, vocal. *Album:* Assassin of Silence (SHC 5002) 1980.

PHIL, GARY Guitar, vocal. Session for Sammy Hagar since 1977.

PHILBIN, GREGG Bass. Member of the R.E.O. Speedwagon.

PHILLIPS, ANTHONY Guitar, vocal, bass, keyboards, drums, percussion. Former guitarist for Genesis before going solo, 1977. *Albums:* Sides (PST 9834) 1979; Back to the Pavilion (PST 7913) 1980; Private Parts and Pieces (PST 7905) 1978; Wise After the Event (PST 9828) 1978; The Geese and the Ghost (PST 98020) 1977.

PHILLIPS, BILL Keyboards. Member of Cargoe, 1972.

PHILLIPS, BOB Trumpet. Session for J. J. Cale (1972).

PHILLIPS, BREWSTER Guitar. Member of Hound Dog Taylor's Houserockers.

PHILLIPS, COLINA Vocal. Session for Alice Cooper (1976); Triumph (1979); Nils Lofgren (1979); Long John Baldry (1980).

PHILLIPS, DON Guitar, vocal. Member of Sod, 1971.

PHILLIPS, HARRY Keyboards. Member of Catfish. Session for Ron Wood (1979).

PHILLIPS, JIMMY Keyboards, vocal. Member of the Small Wonder, 1976-77.

PHILLIPS, JOHN Guitar, vocal, writer, producer. Born 8/30/35. Co-founder of the Mamas and the Papas, 1966-68.

PHILLIPS, JOSEPH Percussion, flute. Member of the Atlantic Starr, 1978-79.

PHILLIPS, LEONARD GRAVES Vocal, keyboards. Member of the Dickies since 1978.

PHILLIPS, LYDIA Vocal. Original member of Stoneground, 1971.

PHILLIPS, MARC Guitar, keyboards, vocal. Member of Hotel since 1978.

PHILLIPS, MICHELLE Vocal. As John Phillips' wife, she was a member of the Mamas and the Papas, 1966-68. *Albums:* California Dreaming (AIR 3001); Victim of Romance (AAM 4651) 1977.

PHILLIPS, PAUL Guitar, vocal. Member of Hi Tension, 1978.

PHILLIPS, PETER Drums. Session for Oxendale and Shephard (1979).

PHILLIPS, RICKY Bass. Added to the Babys, 1980.

PHILLIPS, ROBERT Half of the Phillips and MacLeod duet since 1979.

PHILLIPS, SHAWN Guitar, vocal. *Albums:* Bright White (AAM 4402) 1973; Collaboration (AAM 4324); Faces (AAM 4363) 1972; Second Contribution (AAM 4282); Transcendence (VIC AFLI 3028) 1978; Spaced (AAM 4650) 1977; Do You Wonder (AAM 4539) 1975.

PHILLIPS, SID Tenor saxophone. Session for Lord Sutch.

PHILLIPS, SIMON Drums, tabla. Member of Metro, 1977, the Jack Bruce Band, 1977, and the Michael Schenker Group, 1980. Session for Nazareth (1975); Brian Protheroe (1976); Roger Glover (1978); Art Garfunkel (1979); Duncan Browne (1979); Pete Townshend (1980); Jeff Beck (1980); Roxy Music (1980).

PHILLIPS, TOM Guitar. Member of Redwing.

PHILLIPS AND MacLEOD Robert Phillips; Sean MacLeod. *Albums:* Le Partie Du Cocktail (POL 1-6198) 1979; Phillips/MacLeod (POL 1-6255) 1980.

PHILLPOTTS, TEX Saxophone, percussion. Member of the Greatest Show On Earth, 1970.

PHIPPS, PETER Drums. Member of the Random Hold, 1980.

PHISON, GENE Vocal. Member of the Cleftones.

PHOENIX John Verity—guitar, vocal, bass; Jim Rodford—bass, keyboards (1976); Robert Henrit—drums; Ray Minhinnet—guitar (1979). *Albums:* Phoenix (COL PC 34476) 1976; In Full View (CMA 1-2208) 1979.

PHOTOGLO, JIM Vocal. Namesake of Photoglo, 1980.

PHOTOGLO Jim Photoglo—vocal; Brian Neary—vocal; Dennis Belfield—bass; Bill Cuomo—keyboards; Willy Ornellas—drums; George Marinelli, Jr.—guitar. *Album:* Photoglo (TWC 604) 1980.

PHOTOS Wendy Wu—vocal; Steve Eagles—guitar, vocal; Dave Sparrow—bass, vocal; Olly Harrison—drums, percussion. *Album:* Photos (EPC NJE

36515) 1980.

PHYREWORK John Bryant—drums, percussion; Gerald Calhoun—bass, vocal; Bill Eden—reeds, vocal; Jim Foster—horns, vocal; Frank Hames—keyboards; Clarence Pitts—vocal, guitar; Willie Smith—guitar, vocal. *Album:* Phyrework (MER 1-3738) 1978.

PIANO, MICHAEL Vocal. Born 1944. Member of the Sandpipers.

PIAZZA, BOB Bass, vocal. Member of Ten Wheel Drive, 1970.

PIAZZA, SAMMY Drums, percussion. Member of Hot Tuna, 1971-73, and Stoneground, replacing Michael Mau.

PICARIELLO, FREDERICK ANTHONY Real name of Freddy Cannon.

PICCOLO, GREG Tenor saxophone. Member of the Roomful of Blues, 1977.

PICCOLO, JOHN Keyboards, guitar, vocal. Member of the Shirts, 1978-80.

PICKENS, LEE Guitar. Member of Bloodrock.

PICKERING, NIGEL Guitar, bass. Member of Spanky and Our Gang, 1967-69.

PICKET, BOBBY Bass. Member of Detective, 1977.

PICKETT, BOBBY "BORRIS" Vocal. He made the "Monster Mash" a hit in 1962. *Album:* Monster Mash (PRR X-71063).

PICKETT, LENNY Tenor saxophone. Member of the Tower of Power horn section. Session for Elton John (1974, 79); Roy Buchanan (1974); Ron Gardner (1974); Bill Wyman (1976).

PICKETT, PHIL Bass, piano, vocal. Member of Sailor, 1974-75.

PICKETT, STEVIE Guitar, synthesizer, vocal. Member of Sterling, 1980.

PICKETT, WILSON Vocal, writer. Born 3/18/41. The undisputed king of soul music in 1963, he left the Detroit Falcons to become a soloist. From that time, he began writing classic soul hits like "In the Midnight Hour" (1965), "Land of a Thousand Dances" (1966), "Mustang Sally" (1966), and many more. *Albums:* Best of Wilson Pickett (ATC 8751); Best of Wilson Pickett (SEP 18016); Miz Lena's Boy (VIC APLI 0312); Pickett in the Pocket (VIC PRLI 0495); In the Midnight Hour; Exciting Wilson Pickett; Wilson Pickett; Sound of Wilson Pickett; I'm in Love; Midnight Mover; Great Wilson Pickett Hits; Funky Situation (BIG 76011) 1978; Golden Soul (ATC 18198); I Want You (EIA SW-17019) 1979; Join Me and Let's Be Free (VIC ANLI-2149) 1975; Wilson Pickett's Greatest Hits (ATC 2-501) 1973; Super Hits (ATC 501); In Philadelphia (ATC 8270) 1970.

PICKFORD-HOPKINS, GARY Vocal. Member of Wild Turkey, 1972, and Rick Wakeman's backup band, 1974-75.

PIECES Geoffrey Leib—keyboards, synthesizer, vocal; Mike Lingle—drums, vocal; Larry Lingle—guitar, vocal; Kenny Lee Lewis—bass, vocal. *Album:* Pieces (UAR LW-966) 1979.

PIERCE, BABOO Percussion. Session for Ry Cooder (1980).

PIERCE, JOHN Bass, vocal. Member of Ironhorse, 1979, and Airborne, 1979. Session for Boz Scaggs (1980).

PIERCEFIELD, TED Trumpet, vocal. Member of Chase, 1971-73.

PIERSON, CLARK Drums. Member of the Full Tilt Boogie Band, 1969-70. Session for Stephen Miller.

PIERSON, JON Vocal, trombone. Original member of Ars Nova, 1968-69. Session for Lou Reed (1973).

PIERSON, KATE Vocal, keyboards, guitar. Member of the B-52's, 1980.

PIG IRON Paul Squire—trumpet; Gary Van Scyoc—bass, trumpet, vocal; Bill Peters—guitar, vocal; Adam Ippolito—keyboards, trumpet, vocal; Marty Fogel—saxophone; Alan Abrahams—drums, vocal. *Album:* Pig Iron (CS 1018).

PIG PEN Harmonica, vocal. Real name: Ron McKernan. Original member of the Grateful Dead, 1967 to his death, 3/8/73.

PIGEONS Early name of Vanilla Fudge.

PIGOTT, LARRY Bass. Member of Lance Romance.

PIKE, DONNY Vocal. Replaced his brother Jim in the Lettermen, 1971-present.

PIKE, GARY Vocal. Replaced Bob Engemann in the Lettermen.

PIKE, JIM Vocal. Member of the Lettermen, 1967-71.

PILKINGTON, FLORIAN Drums. Member of Curved Air.

PILLICH, SIMEON Bass. Member of the Naughty Sweeties, 1980.

PILLING, ED Vocal, percussion. Member of the Fludd, 1971.

PILLMORE, BILL Piano, guitar, vocal. Member of Cowboy, 1971-73.

PILNICK, PAUL Guitar. Member of Stealers Wheel, 1972-75, and the Deaf School, 1979.

PILOT, MIKE Guitar, vocal. Member of Stingray, 1979.

PILOT Bruce Stephens—vocal, guitar, keyboards; Mick Waller—drums; Martin Quittenton—guitar; Leigh Stephens—guitar; Neville Whitehead—bass. British studio musicians temporarily banded with San Franciscan Stephens, 1972. *Album:* Pilot (VIC LSP 4750) 1972.

PILOT Dave Paton—bass, guitar, vocal; Bill Lyall—keyboards, flute, vocal; Stuart Tosh—drums, percussion, vocal. *Album:* Pilot (EMI ST 11368) 1974.

PINCOTT, COLIN Guitar. Session for Eric Burdon (1977).

PINDAR, MIKE Keyboards, cello, guitar, bass, percussion, vocal, mellotron, synthesizer, writer.

Original member of the Moody Blues, 1965-81. Session for John Lennon (1971). *Album:* The Promise (THS 18) 1976.

PINDAR, MIKE Original member of the Searchers.

PINE, KEN Guitar, organ, percussion, vocal. Replaced Lee Crabtree in the Fugs, 1967-68.

PINEAU, FRED Guitar. Member of the Atlantics since 1979.

PINERA, MIKE Guitar, vocal. Member of Iron Butterfly and Ramatam, 1972. Replaced Werner Fritzschings in the New Cactus Band, 1973. Original member of Thee Image, 1975. *Album:* Forever (SPC SW-00001) 1979.

PINES, MARK Guitar. Session for Ray Manzarek.

PINETTE, RICK Guitar, piano, vocal. Member of Oak, 1980.

PINHAS, RICHARD Synthesizer, guitar, electronics. Member of Heldon, 1976. *Album:* Rhizosphere (ARX 5002) 1977.

PINI, GIL Guitar, vocal. Member of the Boyzz, 1978.

PINIZZOTTO, SHELE Guitar, vocal. Member of Birtha, 1973.

PINK FLOYD Rick Wright—keyboards, cello, fiddle; Nick Mason—drums, percussion; Roger Waters—bass, piano, percussion, vocal; Syd Barrett—guitar, vocal, writer (1967-68); Dave Gilmore—guitar, vocal (1968-present). After being the warm-up act for the Beatles' first European tour, Pink Floyd came to the U.S. from their native England in 1967 and produced the first quadrophonic rock concert. The undisputed masters of space rock, they carried an unseen fifth member, Mick Lowe, the producer of their stage shows. "Dark Side of the Moon" (1973) saw their first radio hit, which their already large underground following quickly accepted, giving them their due fame as innovators and survivors at the same time. They have two movie soundtracks to their credit: "More" and "Obscured by the Clouds." *Albums:* Saucerful of Secrets (TWR) 1968; Animals (COL KC-34474) 1977; Atom Heart Mother (HAR SMAS-382) 1970; Dark Side of the Moon (HAR SMAS 11163) 1973; Meddle (HAR SMAS 832) 1971; More (HAR SW 11198); Nice Pair (HAR SABB-11257); Obscured by the Clouds (HAR SW-11078) 1972; Relics (HAR SW 759) 1972; Ummagumma (HAR SKBB 388) 1969; The Wall (COL PC2-36183) 1979; Wish You Were Here (COL HC 33453) 1975; Piper at the Gates of Dawn (TWR ST 5093) 1967.

PINK SECTION Mic Todd—guitar, bass, vocal; Judy Gittlshon—vocal, synthesizer, keyboards; Stephen Wymore—bass, guitar, synthesizer, vocal; Carol Detweiler—drums, vocal. *Album:* Pink Section, 1980.

PINO, NATHAN Keyboards. Member of Simon Stokes and the Black Whip Band, 1973.

PINTI, BOB Trumpet. Member of Mom's Apple Pie, 1973.

PIPER Billy Squier—vocal, guitar, percussion; Alan Nolan—guitar, vocal; Tommy Gunn—guitar, vocal; Danny McGary—bass, vocal; Richie Fontana—drums, percussion, vocal. *Albums:* Piper (AAM 4615) 1977; Can't Wait (AAM 4654) 1977.

PIPPIN, BILL Flute, oboe. Session for Pearls Before Swine (1970).

PIPS See Gladys Knight and the Pips.

PIRATES Mick Green—guitar; Johnny Spence—bass, vocal; Frank Farley—drums. *Albums:* Out of Their Skulls (WBR K-3155); Skull Wars (WBR K-3224) 1978; Hard Ride (PAC 7-140) 1980.

PISANO, JOHN Guitar. Session for Tim Weisberg (1973).

PITCOCK, BILL Guitar. Member of the Dwight Twilley Band, 1976-79. Session for the Tremblers (1980). *Album:* Can't Keep My Eyes Off You (EGL 1153).

PITMAN, BILL Guitar. Session for Jan and Dean (1963).

PITMAN, LYNN Vocal. Member of Rosie, 1976-77.

PITNEY, GENE Vocal, writer. By the time the mid-60s rolled around, Pitney already had a string of hits longer than a top-100 chart. "Only Love Can Break a Heart," "The Man Who Shot Liberty Valance," "Angelique," "Looking Through the Eyes of Love," and many more had become standards on the oldies but goodies radio stations. With a rather stormy rise to the top, he wavered in and out of public favor with his "bad boy" image, but his melodic voice and styling made him impossible to keep off the air. *Albums:* Backstage (MCR 3095); Being Together (MCR 3077); Country Cousins (MCR 3053); Famous Country Duets (MCR 3079); Golden Greats (MCR 3134); Golden Hour of Gene Pitney (MCR 3233); Greatest Hits of Gene Pitney (MCR); I Must Be Seeing Things (MCR 3056); It Hurts To Be in Love (MCR 3019); It's Country Time Again (MCR 3065); Just One Smile (MCR 3117); George Jones and Gene Pitney (MCR 3044); Looking Through the Eyes of Love (MCR 3069); Many Sides of Gene Pitney (MCR 3861); Gene Pitney Big 16, Vol. 1 (MCR 3008); Vol. 2 (MCR 3043); Vol. 3 (MCR 3085); Country Side of Gene Pitney (MCR 3104); Greatest Hits of All Times (MCR); Only Love Can Break a Heart (MCR); Gene Pitney Sings Burt Bacharach and Others (MCR 5005); She's a Heartbreaker (MCR 3164); Ten Years Later (MCR 3206); This Is Gene Pitney Singing the Platters Golden Platters (MCR 3183); Tribute to Bacharach (SEP 5100).

PITTEL, HARVEY Saxophone. Session for Ry Cooder (1978).

PITTMAN, HERMAN Bass. Session for John Hammond (1968).

PITTS, CLARENCE Vocal, guitar. Member of Phyrework, 1978.

PITTS, JIM Vocal, piano, mandolin. Part of the British blues invasion of the late 1960s that did not make it to the U.S., as a soloist or as a member of Brett Marvin and the Thunderbolts.

PIZZARELLI, BUCKY Guitar. Session for Carly Simon (1974); Henry Gross (1976).

PLANETS Steve Lindsey—keyboards, bass, drums, guitar, vocal; Charlie Charles—drums, percussion; Mickey Gallagher—keyboard, vocal; John Turnbull—guitar. *Album:* The Planets (MTN M7-934) 1980.

PLANT, ROBERT Vocal, harmonica, writer. Born 8/20/48. After serving his apprenticeship in a blues duet with Alexis Korner in 1968, and replacing Keith Relf in the Yardbirds, 1969, he formed Led Zeppelin with Jimmy Page, 1969-80.

PLANT, TERRY String bass. Session with Alexis Korner and Cyril Davis (1954-61).

PLASMATICS Wendy Orlean Williams—vocal, saxophone, percussion; Richie Stotts—guitar; Wes Beech—guitar; Jean Beauvoir—bass; Stu Deutsch—drums. *Album:* New Hope for the Wretched (STF USE9) 1980.

PLASTIC BERTRAND Vocal. *Album:* Ca Plane Pour Moi (SIR 6061) 1977.

PLASTIC ONO BAND John Lennon—guitar, piano, vocal, writer; Yoko Ono—vocal, percussion; Ringo Starr—drums (1970); Klaus Voorman—bass (1969-73); Eric Clapton—guitar (1969); Alan White—drums, percussion (1969-71); Ken Asher—keyboards (1973); David Spinozza—guitar (1973); Gordon Edwards—bass (1973); Jim Keltner—drums (1973). Backup band for John Lennon and Yoko Ono, 1970-73. See John Lennon, Yoko Ono.

PLASTIC RHINO BAND Don Buchanan—guitar; Joe Stoddard—drums; Stuart Deal—bass. Backup band for Wild Man Fischer, 1977.

PLATANA, JOHN Guitar, vocal. Member of the Giants, 1976, and Baby. Session for Van Morrison (1968-69).

PLATES, DEXTER C. Bass. Member of the Hoodoo Rhythm Devils, 1973.

PLATINUM HOOK Robin David Corley—saxophone, vocal; Stephen Daniels—drums, percussion; Tina Renee Stanford—percussion, vocal; Robert Douglas—keyboards, vocal; Elisa "Skip" Ingram—bass, vocal; Victor Jones—guitar, vocal; Glenn Wallace—horns, vocal. *Albums:* Ecstasy Paradise (MTN M8-943); It's Time (MTN M7-918) 1979.

PLATSHON, DAVID Drums. Session for Nils Lofgren (1977).

PLATT, ALAN Drums. Session for Roy Sundholm (1979).

PLATT, RANDALL Keyboards. Added to the Missouri lineup, 1979.

PLAYBOY BAND See John Fred and the Playboy Band.

PLAYER J. C. Crowley—keyboards, vocal, guitar (1977-79); Peter Beckett—guitar, vocal; Ron Moss—bass, vocal; John Friesen—drums; Wayne Cook—keyboards. *Albums:* Danger Zone (RSO 1-3036); Player (RSO 1-3026) 1977; Room with a View (CAS 7217) 1980.

PLEASE Carlos David—guitar, vocal; Roy David—keyboards, vocal; Lito Cruz—horns, vocal; Manny St. Maria—guitar, trombone; Bobby Villegas—bass; Mike St. Maria—drums; Efren Lozanes—saxophone, keyboards. *Album:* Manilla Thriller, 1976.

PLEASURE FAIRE Early name of Bread.

PLIMSOULS Eddie Munoz—guitar; Lou Ramirez—drums; Peter Case—vocal, guitar; Dave Pahoa—bass, vocal. *Album:* Zero Hour (BET 1001) 1980.

PLOSS, RICHARD Saxophone, flute. Member of Guns and Butter, 1972.

PLOTEL, JON Bass. Member of the Streetwalkers, 1973-77.

PLUGZ Tito Larriva—guitar, vocal; Barry McBride—bass, vocal; Charlie Quintana—drums. *Album:* Electrify Me (PGZ PR001) 1979.

PLUMMER, BILL Upright bass. Session for Tim Weisberg (1971); the Rolling Stones (1972).

POCO Richie Furay—guitar, vocal, writer (until 1975); Jim Messina—guitar, vocal, writer, producer (until 1972); Timothy B. Schmidt—bass, vocal; Rusty Young—pedal steel guitar; George Grantham—drums, percussion; Paul Cotton—guitar, vocal. From the disbanded Buffalo Springfield, Furay and Messina formed Poco in 1968. Messina left to become half of the famous Loggins and Messina duet, while Furay continued until 1975 when he left for the Souther-Hillman-Furay Band. Part of "No Nukes," 1979. *Albums:* Cantamos (EPC PE 33192) 1974; Crazy Eyes (EPC KE 32354) 1973; Deliverin' (EPC KE-30208); From the Inside (EPC KE 38753); Pickin' Up the Pieces (EPC BXN 26460); Poco (EPC PKN 26522) 1974; Poco Seven (EPC KE 32895) 1974; Live (EPC PE 33336) 1976; Indian Summer (EPC) 1977; Very Best of Poco (EPC PEG 33537) 1975; Songs of Richie Furay (EPC JE 36211) 1979; Songs of Paul Cotton (EPC JE 36270) 1979.

PODOLOR, RICHARD Guitar. Session for John Kay (1973).

POHLMAN, RAY Bass. Member of the Marketts, 1973. Session for Jan and Dean (1963); Cashman and West (1972).

POINDEXTER, LEON Guitar. Session for Richard Betts (1974).

POINT BLANK Rusty Burns—guitar, vocal; Kim Davis—guitar, vocal; Peter Gruen—drums, percussion; John O'Daniel—vocal; Phillip Petty—bass (1976-79); Bill Randolph—bass (1979-present); Steve Hardin—keyboards, vocal (1979); Karl Berke—keyboards, vocal (1980). *Albums:* Airplay (MCA 3160) 1979; Hard Way (MCA 5114) 1980;

4137) 1977.

POINTER, ANITA Part of the Pointer Sisters since 1973. Session for the Rockets (1980).

POINTER, BONNIE Part of the Pointer Sisters, 1973-78, before going solo. *Albums:* Bonnie Pointer (MTN M7-911) 1978; Bonnie Pointer (MTN M7-929) 1979.

POINTER, JUNE Vocal. Part of the Pointer Sisters since 1973.

POINTER, RUTH Part of the Pointer Sisters since 1973. Session for the Rockets (1980).

POINTER SISTERS Anita Pointer—vocal, writer; Ruth Pointer—vocal, writer; Bonnie Pointer—vocal, writer (1973-78); June Pointer—vocal, writer. A female vocal quartet whose range seems to have no limits. Their songs range from pop and rhythm and blues to the swing of the 1920s and 1930s, to country-western, complete with costumes. They first appeared in 1973, and their talent justifies their publicity and popularity. Session for Alice Cooper (1973); John Sebastian (1974). *Albums:* Live at the Opera House (BTM 8002) 1974; Pointer Sisters (BTM 48) 1973; That's a Plenty (BTM 8009) 1974; Energy (PNT P-1) 1978; Priority (PNT 9003) 1979; Special Things (PNT P-9) 1980.

POISON IVY Guitar. Member of the Cramps, 1980.

POKE, FRED Bass, vocal. Member of the Matchbox, 1979.

POLICE Sting (Gordon Sumner)—vocal, bass; Andy Summers—guitar; Stewart Copeland—drums. *Albums:* Outlandos D' Amour (AAM 4753) 1979; Reggatta De Blanc (AAM 4792) 1979; Zenyatta Mondatta (AAM 4831) 1980; Ghost in the Machine (AAM SP-3730) 1981.

POLLARD, JEFF Guitar, vocal. Member of Le Roux since 1979.

POLLARD, PAM Vocal. Background vocals in Joe Cocker's Greatest Show On Earth, 1970.

POLLING, CHAN Keyboards, vocal. Member of the Suburbs, 1980.

POLLUTION John Lambert—bass, vocal; Richard Lewis—trumpet, keyboards, vocal; Christiaan Mostert—saxophone, flute, keyboards, vocal; Dennis Kenmore—drums, percussion, vocal; James Quill Smith—guitar, harmonica, vocal, producer; Dobie Gray—vocal, percussion; Tata—vocal, percussion. Los Angeles big band of 1971, featuring the vocal harmonies of Gray and Tata, and the production, writing, and arrangements of Smith. *Album:* Pollution (PSY) 1971.

POLYROCK Billy Robertson—guitar, vocal; Tommy Robertson—guitar, violin, electronics; Lenny Garon—keyboards; Curt Cosentino—bass, synthesizer; Joseph Yannell—drums, percussion, vocal; Catherine Oblasney—vocal, percussion. *Album:* Polyrock (VIC AFLI 3714) 1980.

POMBER, DONNIE Keyboards. Member of the Blend, 1978-79.

POMERANZ, DAVID Vocal, keyboards. Session for Gary Wright (1975); Phoebe Snow (1976). *Album:* The Truth of Us (PAC 4302) 1980.

POMPELLI, RUDY Member of Bill Haley and the Comets.

PONCE, JESSE Baso sexto. Session for Ry Cooder (1977); Peter Rowan (1978).

PONCER, DON Drums. Member of the Fun Zone, 1977. Session for Bobby Whitlock.

PONCIA, VINI Guitar, vocal, producer. Produced the Faragher Brothers (1980). Session for Ringo Starr (1973-74, 77); Martin Mull (1977).

PONCZEK, MICHAEL Keyboards. Member of Ethos, 1977.

PONDER, ED Drums. Replaced Michael Clarke in the Flying Burrito Brothers.

PONDER, JOHN Drums, vocal. Member of Tilt, 1980.

PONS, JIM Percussion, vocal, bass. Original member of the Leaves, the Turtles, 1965-69, and the Mothers of Invention, 1971-72.

PONTON, MIKE Saxophone. Session for Frut (1972).

PONTY, JEAN-LUC Violin. Experimental jazz violinist who became a member of the Mothers of Invention, 1972, popularizing his name in both jazz and rock fields. Session for Elton John (1972); Frank Zappa (1969-74). *Albums:* Electric Connection (PZZ 20156); King Kong (PZZ 20172); Open Strings (MPS 21288); Jean-Luc Ponty, Experience (PZZ); Aurora (ATC 19158); Canteloupe Island (BLN LW-632) 1976; Cosmic Messenger (ATC 19189); Enigmatic Ocean (ATC 19110) 1977; Experience (PAU 7065) 1980; Imaginary Voyage (ATC 19136) 1976; Jazz-60s, Vol. 2 (PCJ LT-895); Live (ATC 19229) 1979; Jean-Luc Ponty and Stephane Grappelli (ICT 1005) 1976; Sonata Erotica (ICT 1003); Sunday Walk (PAU 7033); Taste for Passion (ATC 19253) 1979; Upon the Wings of Music (ATC 18138) 1975; Violin Summit (EVR 355); Civilized Evil (ATC SD 16020) 1980.

POODLES See the Fabulous Poodles.

POOL, FREDDIE Vocal. Member of Giants, 1978.

POOL, TOM Drums. Member of the Law, 1975.

POOLE, BRIAN Vocal. Voice of the Tremeloes.

POOLE, DAVID Drums, vocal. Member of the Bill Blue Band, 1979.

POOLE, JEFF Drums. Member of Legs Diamond, 1977-78.

POOLE, MAC Drums. Original member of Broken Glass, 1976.

POP Tim Henderson—bass; Joel Martinez—drums; David Swanson—vocal, bass, guitar; Roger Prescott—vocal, guitar; Tim McGovern—guitar, vocal, drums. *Albums:* The Pop (AUT SA 101) 1977; Go (ARI AB 4243) 1979.

POP, IGGY Vocal. Real name: Jim Osterberg. Born

4/14/47. Formerly Iggy Stooge of the Stooges, Pop was rediscovered by David Bowie in 1977, showing the new wave rock generation bizarre, outrageous stage techniques he had developed over 10 years earlier. *Albums:* New Values (ARI 4237) 1979; Soldier (ARI 4259) 1980; Lust for Life (VIC) 1978; The Idiot (VIC) 1978; Kill City (BMP IMP 1018) 1977; TV Eye (VIC AFLI 2796) 1978; Metallic KO (IMP 1015) 1976.

POP GROUP Gareth Sager—guitar, horns; Bruce Smith—drums; Mark Stewart—vocal; Simon Underwood—bass; John Waddington—guitar. *Album:* For How Much Longer Do We Tolerate Mass Murder (RGA 192) 1980.

POPE, CAROL Vocal. Session for Steve Hunter (1977).

POPE, ROGER Drums. Member of Elton John's Band, 1970-71, 76, Hookfoot, 1972, the Kiki Dee Band, 1973-74, and Howard Werth and the Moonbeams, 1975. Session for Long John Baldry (1971); Nilsson (1971); John Kongos (1972); Elton John (1975); Kevin Ayers (1977); Mylon Le Fevre (1979).

POPER, ROY Trumpet. Session for B. B. King (1977).

POPPLE, TERRY Drums, percussion. Member of Snafu, 1973-75.

POPWELL, BOB Bass. Session for Les Dudek (1977-78); Ron Wood (1979).

PORCARO, JEFF Drums, producer. Member of Toto since 1978. Produced the Strand (1980). Session for Joe Cocker (1974); Boz Scaggs (1976, 80); Steely Dan (1974, 80); Tommy Bolin (1975); John Sebastian (1976); Seals and Crofts (1973, 76); Arthur, Hurley and Gottlieb; Mickey Thomas (1977); Les Dudek (1977-78); Robert Palmer (1976); Hoyt Axton (1976); Alan O'Day (1979); Steve Kipner (1979); Cher (1979); John Mayall (1979); Gary Wright (1979); Adrian Gurvitz (1979); Lee Ritenour (1977).

PORCARO, MIKE Session for Bob Weir (1976); Lee Ritenour (1977); Steven T. (1978).

PORCARO, STEVE Keyboards. Member of Toto since 1978. Session for Gary Wright (1977); Adrian Gurvitz (1979).

PORRAZZO, JOHNNY Vocal, piano. Member of Porrazzo, 1980. *Albums:* Country Side of Johnny Porrazzo (DMD 4003); Lighthouse (DMD 4004).

PORRAZZO Johnny Porrazzo—vocal, piano; David Bodenhamer—bass, vocal; Chuckie San Filippo—keyboards, vocal; Marvin "Kingfish" King—guitar; Danny "Bongo" Owen—drums, percussion; James Boro—guitar, vocal. *Album:* Porrazzo (POL 1-6277) 1980.

PORTER, ARTHUR Member of Hank Ballard's Midnighters.

PORTER, GARTH Keyboards, vocal. Member of Sherbet, 1976-80.

PORTER, GEORGE "FREAK MAN" Bass. Member of the Meters, 1973.

PORTER, JOHN Bass, guitar. Session for Long John Baldry (1972); Roxy (1973); Bryan Ferry (1974, 77).

PORTER, PHIL Keyboards. Member of Chase, 1971-73.

PORTER, ROBBIE Piano, steel guitar. Session for Daddy Cool (1971).

PORTER, TIRAN Vocal, bass. Replaced Dave Shogren in the Doobie Brothers, 1972-present.

PORTIUS, BRICE Vocal. Original member of Savoy Brown, 1967.

PORTMAN, ALLAN Guitar. Member of Chichlids, 1980.

PORTNOY, GARY Keyboards, vocal. *Album:* Gary Portnoy (COL NJC 36755) 1980.

POSA, FRANK Trumpet. Member of the Flock.

POST, JIM Guitar, vocal. *Albums:* Colorado Exile (FSY 9401); Slow to 20 (FSY 9408); Rattlesnake (FSY 9425) 1973; Looks Good to Me (FSY 9451) 1974; I Love My Life (MTN 52784) 1978; Magic (FLS 216) 1979.

POT Keyboards. Member of Randall's Island, 1971-72.

POTGER, KEITH Vocal. Member of the Seekers, 1965-67.

POTKIN, SHELLY Drums. Replaced Russ Chadwick in the Siegel-Schwall Band, 1970.

POTLIQUOR Jerry Amoroso—drums, percussion, vocal; Guy Schaeffer—bass, vocal; Mike McQuaig—guitar, vocal; Steve Sather—guitar, vocal. *Album:* Potliquor (CAP ST-11998) 1979.

POTSCHKA Guitar, vocal. Member of Nina Hagen Band.

POTTER, BRIAN Producer. Produced Rock Rose, 1979.

POTTER, NIC Bass. Member of Van der Graaf, 1978, and the Tigers, 1980. Session for Chuck Berry (1972); Steve Swindells (1980).

POTTER, ROBERT Vocal, guitar. Member of Free Beer, 1976.

POTTS, DAVE Drums. Session for Ray Thomas (1975).

POTTS, MOE Drums, percussion, vocal. Member of the Laughing Dogs, 1979-present.

POULAS, JON-JON Drums. Member of the Buckinghams, 1966-68.

POUSETTE-DART, JON Guitar. Namesake of the Pousette-Dart Band, 1976-79.

POUSETTE-DART BAND John Curtis—guitar; John Troy—bass; Jon Pousette-Dart—guitar; Allison Cook—drums (1976-77); Michael Dawe—drums (1978-79). *Albums:* Amnesia (CAP SW-11608) 1977; Never Enough (CAP ST-11935) 1979; Pousette-Dart Band (CAP ST-11507) 1976; Pousette-Dart Band 3 (CAP SW-11781) 1978.

POVEY, GAVIN Organ. Session for the Inmates (1979).

POVEY, JOHN Vocal, keyboards. Member of the

Pretty Things.

POWELL, ANDREW Guitar, arranger. Arranger whose credits include work from electronic musicians Stockhausen and Boulez to rock artists such as Donovan (1973), the Hollies, Humble Pie, and Leo Sayer. Recruited by Alan Parsons in 1975 to become part of the Alan Parsons Project.

POWELL, ANDY Guitar, vocal. Born 2/19/50. Replaced Ted Turner in Wishbone Ash, 1974-present.

POWELL, BENNY Trombone. Session for Nilsson (1976); John Mayall (1977); Dr. John (1979).

POWELL, BILLY Keyboards. Member of Lynyrd Skynyrd, 1973-77, and the Rosington-Collins Band, 1980. Session for Alias (1980).

POWELL, CHRISTIAN Bass. Replaced Bob Mosley in the reformed Moby Grape, 1978.

POWELL, COZY Drums. First became noticed as a member of the re-formed Jeff Beck Group, 1971-72, before forming the short-lived Bedlam in 1973. Replaced Gary Driscoll in Ritchie Blackmore's Rainbow, 1976-80. Session for Donovan (1973); Chick Churchill (1974).

POWELL, DAVE Drums. Member of the Heroes, 1980.

POWELL, DICK Violin. Session for Rod Stewart (1971-74).

POWELL, DON Drums. Original member of Slade, 1972-present.

POWELL, GEORGE Vocal, guitar. Member of Pure Prairie League since 1972.

POWELL, JANE Vocal. Session for the Alan Parsons Project (1976).

POWELL, JUDITH Vocal. Session for Steve Stills (1970); Rick Wakeman (1972); Lo and Behold (1972); Vigrass and Osborne (1972); Manfred Mann (1973).

POWELL, PETSYE Vocal. Session for Dr. John (1979).

POWELL, RANDE Drums. Member of the Mike Greene Band, 1975-76.

POWELL, RICK Drums. Member of the Boatz, 1979.

POWELL, ROGER Keyboards, synthesizer, producer, engineer. Member of Utopia, 1977-80. Session for Steve Hillage (1976). *Album:* Air Pocket (BSV 6994) 1980.

POWELL, SCOTT Vocal. Original member of Sha Na Na, 1970-71.

POWELL, SELDON Baritone and tenor saxophone. Session for Barry Goldberg (1969); Muddy Waters (1972); Martin Mull (1977); Taj Mahal (1978); John Lennon (1980).

POWER Early name for Stone the Crows.

POWER, DUFFY Harmonica. Early member of Blues Incorporated. Session for Bert Jansch; John Renbourn.

POWER, JOHN Bass, vocal. Member of Jo Jo Zep and the Falcons, 1980.

POWERHOUSE FOUR Early name for John Mayall's group, 1956.

POWERS, CHESTER Real name of Dino Valenti.

POWERS, DALE Guitar. Member of the Ohio Express, 1968-69.

POWERS, JIMMY Harmonica. Member of the Catfish Hodge Band, 1979.

POYRY, PEKKA Saxophone, flute, piano. Member of Tasavalian Presidenti, 1974.

POZAR, CLEVE Drums. Session for Roger Powell (1980).

PRAEKER, M. Bass, guitar, vocal. Member of Nina Hagen Band.

PRAIRIE PRINCE Drums. Member of the Tubes, 1975-79. Session for Tommy Bolin (1975).

PRATER, DAVE Vocal. Dave, of Sam and Dave.

PRATT, ANDY Vocal, guitar, keyboards, bass, sitar. Session for Peter C. Johnson (1980). *Albums:* Motives (NMP JZ 35781) 1979; Andy Pratt (COL PC 31722) 1973; Resolution (NMP 438) 1976; Shiver in the Night (NKP 443) 1977.

PRATT, D. J. Guitar. Member of Kalapanna.

PREACHER JACK Vocal, piano. Real name: Jack Lincoln Coughlin. Nicknamed the "Boogie Woogie Preacher," he was discovered by George Thorogood. He made his debut in 1980 with Thorogood sidemen Billy Blough (bass) and Jeff Simon (drums), and Sleepy La Beef (guitar) and Sal Spicola (saxophone). *Album:* Rock 'N' Roll Preacher (RND 3033) 1980.

PRELI, THOM Bass. Member of the Flying Island, 1976.

PRELUDE Irene Hume—vocal; Brian Hume—vocal, guitar; Ian Vardy—vocal, guitar. *Album:* After the Gold Rush (ISL) 1974.

PRELUDE Tony Hymas—keyboards; Hugh Burns—guitar; Dave Mattacks—drums; Alan Carney—bass. *Album:* Back into the Light (PYE 12139) 1976.

PREMIATA FORNEIR MARCONI Unabbreviated name of P.F.M.

PREMOLI, FLAVIO Keyboards. Member of P.F.M., 1973-77.

PRESCOTT, ROGER Vocal, guitar. Member of the Pop since 1977.

PRESKITT, GRAHAM Violin, arranger. Arranger for the Tourists (1980); Matthew Fisher (1980). Session for Ken Tobias (1973); Mott the Hoople (1973); Dan McCafferty (1975); Young Moody (1977); Roger Glover (1978); Gerry Rafferty (1978-79); Manfred Mann (1979).

PRESLEY, ELVIS Guitar, vocal, writer. Born 1/8/35. The Elvis story started in Memphis, with the future "Elvis the Pelvis" watching acts like Bo Diddley. In 1954, he made his first single, "Mystery Train." His fame grew on the country-western circuit until 1956, when he signed with RCA, who realized his rock and rhythm and blues potential with "Heartbreak Hotel." Hit after hit followed, then came movie after movie. The mere mention of his name caused girls to swoon. His live act, however, was his claim to fame and he guarded his career carefully. More than anyone else, he made music for the young, proving rock was a "marketable" business. With the dawn of the 1970s, Presley returned from his retirement, to just as large a crowd as when he left. He died 8/16/77. *Albums:* Elvis (VIC APLI 0283); Elvis' Christmas Album (CDN 2428); Good Times (VIC APLI 0475); Almost in Love (CDN 2440); Blue Hawaii (VIC AYLI-3683) 1961; Burning Love (CDN 2595) 1972; Clambake (VIC AFLI 2565) 1967; C'mon Everybody (CDN 2518); Date with Elvis (VIC AFLI 2011) 1959; Double Dynamite (CDN DL2-5001); Double Trouble (VIC AFLI 2564) 1967; Elvis (VIC AFMI 4088) 1968; Elvis (VIC AFLI 1382) 1956; Elvis, a Canadian Tribute (VIC KKLI 7065) 1978; Elvis Aloha From Hawaii (VIC CPD2-2642) 1972; Elvis as Recorded at Madison Square Garden (VIC AFLI 4776) 1972; Elvis Back in Memphis (VIC AFLI 3450) 1965; Elvis for Everyone (VIC AFLI 3450) 1965; Elvis Golden Records, Vol. 1 (VIC AFLI 1707) 1958; Elvis Golden Records, Vol. 2 (VIC AFLI 2075) 1959; Elvis Golden Records, Vol. 3 (VIC AFLI 2765) 1963; Elvis Golden Records, Vol. 4 (VIC AFLI 3921) 1968; Elvis Good Times (VIC AFLI 0475); Elvis in Concert (VIC APL2-2587) 1977; Elvis in Person (VIC AFLI 4428); Elvis Is Back (VIC AFLI 2231) 1960; Elvis—Legendary Performer, Vol. 1 (VIC CPLI 3078) 1973; Legendary Performer, Vol. 2 (VIC CPLI 1349) 1976; Legendary Performer, Vol. 3 (VIC CPLI 3082) 1978; Elvis Now (VIC AFLI 4671) 1972; On Stage (VIC AFMI 0818); Raised on Rock/For Ol' Times Sake (VIC AFLO 0388); Elvis Recorded Live on Stage at Memphis (VIC AFLI 0606) 1974; Elvis Sings "Flaming Star" (CDN 2304) 1969; Elvis Sings for Children (& Grownups Too) (VIC CPLI 2901) 1978; Elvis Sings Hits from His Movies (CDN 2567) 1972; Elvis Sings the Wonderful World of Christmas (VIC ANLI 1936) 1971; Elvis Sun Sessions (VIC AFMI 1675); Elvis That's the Way It Is (VIC AFLI 4445) 1970; Elvis Today (VIC APDI 1039) 1975; From Elvis in Memphis (VIC AFLI 4115); From Elvis Presley Boulevard, Memphis, Tennessee (VIC AFLI 1506) 1976; From Memphis to Vegas (VIC LSP 6020) 1967; Fun in Acapulco (VIC AFLI 2756) 1963; G.I. Blues (VIC AFLI 2256); Girl Happy (VIC AFLI 3338) 1965; Girls, Girls, Girls (VIC AFLI 2621) 1962; Harum Scarum (VIC AFLI 2558) 1965; He Touched Me (VICX AFLI 4690) 1972; He Walks Beside Me (VIC AFLO 2772); His Hand in Mine (VIC ANLI 1319) 1960; How Great Thou Art (VIC AFLI 3758) 1967; I Got Lucky (CDN 2533); I'm 10,000 Years Old (VIC AFLI 4460) 1971; It Happened at the World's Fair (VIC AFLI 2568) 1963; King Creole (VIC AFLI 1884) 1964; Kissin' Cousins (VIC AFL1 2894) 1964; Let's Be Friends (CDN 2408); Love Letters from Elvis (VIC AFLI 4530) 1971; Lovin' You (VIC AFLI 1515); Moody Blue (VIC AFLI 2428) 1977; On Stage (VIC AFL1 4362) 1970; Our Memories of Elvis (VIC AQL1 3279); Our Memories of Elvis, Vol. 2 (VIC AQL1 3448) 1979; Paradise Hawaiian Style (VIC AFL1 3643) 1966; Pot Luck (VIC AFL1 2523) 1962; Elvis Presley (VIC AFL1 1990); Elvis Presley for LP Fans Only (VIC AFLI 1254); Elvis Aron Presley (VIC CPL8 3699); Promised Land (VIC AFLI 0873) 1975; Pure Gold (VIC ANLI 0971) 1975; Roustabout (VIC AFL1 1999) 1964; Somethin' for Everybody (VIC AFL1 2370) 1961; Speedway (VIC AFLI 3989); Spinout (VIC AYL1 3684) 1977; Welcome to My World (VIC AFLI 2274) 1977; World Wide 50 Gold Award Hits, Vol. 1 (VIC LPM 6401); World Wide 50 Gold Award Hits, Vol. 2 (VIC LPM 6402); You'll Never Walk Alone (CDN 2472).

PRESLEY, REG Vocal, writer. Organized the Troggs.

PRESS, LINDA Vocal. Session for Neil Diamond (1976).

PRESSER, GABOR Piano. Member of Locomotive GT, 1974-75.

PRESTIA, FRANCIS Bass. Member of Tower of Power.

PRESTON, BILLY Keyboards, vocal, writer. Born 9/9/46. Session for Splinter (1974-75); Steve Stills (1971); the Beatles; the Rolling Stones (1972, 74, 76-77); Bangla Desh (1971); Peter Frampton (1972); George Harrison (1972, 74, 76); John Lennon (1970); Ringo Starr (1973-74); Doris Troy (1970); Joe Cocker (1978). *Albums:* Behold (MYR B-6605) 1978; Fastbreak (MTN M7-915); Gospel in My Soul (MCA 179); Late at Night (MTN M7-925); Original B. Preston—Soul'd Out (CRS 2-2071); Universal Love (MYR B-6607); A Whole New Thing, 1977; Billy's Bag (SPB 4012); Everybody Likes Some Kind of Music (AAM 3526) 1973; Goldfingers (TRP X 9506); I Wrote a Simple Song (AAM 3507); Kids and Me (AAM 3646) 1974; Music Is My Life (AAM 3516) 1972; Wildest Organ in Town (CAP SM-2532); It's My Pleasure (AAM 4532) 1975.

PRESTON, DON Guitar, vocal, dobro. Member of Joe Cocker's Greatest Show on Earth, 1970. Session for Dave Mason (1970); Freddie King (1971-73); Leon Russell (1971-72, 74-75); Bangla Desh (1971); Don Nix (1971). *Album:* I've Been Here All Along (SHL).

PRESTON, DON Piano, moog. Member of the Mothers of Invention, 1967-74, Raw Milk, 1970, and the Grandmothers, 1980. Part of the soundtrack for "Apocalypse Now." Session for Frank Zappa (1972).

PRESTON, JIM Drums, percussion, vocal. Member of the Sons of Champlin.

PRESTON, JOHNNY Vocal. Rose to fame in 1960 with "Running Bear."

PRESTON, LEROY Vocal, guitar. Member of Asleep at the Wheel since 1973.

PRESTOPINO, GREG Vocal, piano. Session for the Capital City Rockets (1973); Maria Muldaur (1973); Martin Mull (1975); Ry Cooder (1979).

PRESTOPINO, PAUL Banjo, mandolin, steel guitar. Session for Alice Cooper (1972-73); Pavlov's Dog (1976); Johnny Winter (1974).

PRESTWICH, STEVE Drums. Member of the Cold Chisel, 1979.

PRETENDERS Chrissie Hynde—vocal, guitar; Pete Farndon—bass, vocal; James Honeycutt Scott—guitar, keyboards, vocal; Martin Chambers—drums, vocal. *Album:* Pretenders (SIR K-6083) 1980.

PRETTY THINGS Phil May—vocal; Peter Tolson—guitar; John Povey—vocal, keyboards; Wally Waller—bass, guitar, vocal; Skip Allen—drums; Dick Taylor—guitar. First group to be recorded on Led Zepplin's Swan Song label. *Albums:* Cross Talk (WBR BSK 3466) 1980; Real Pretty (REH P7-549) 1976; Silk Torpedo (SWN 8411); Savage Eye (SWN 8414).

PREVOST, GERARD Bass, percussion. Member of the Rose, 1979.

PRICE, ALAN Piano, vocal, writer. Born 4/19/42. Member of the Alan Price Combo, until Eric Burdon joined him in 1962, and they became the Animals. He left shortly thereafter to continue his solo career with the Alan Price Set, 1965-68, but did not achieve any great degree of fame until his movie soundtrack, "O Lucky Man," 1973. Member of the re-formed Animals, 1977. *Albums:* Lucky Day (JET JC-35710) 1979; O Lucky Man (WBR B-2710) 1975; Rising Sun (JET JZ-36510) 1980; Alan Price (UAR JT LA809G) 1977; Alan Price and Rob Hoeke/Two of a Kind (Import) 1977.

ALAN PRICE SET Alan Price—vocal, keyboards, guitar, vibes, writer; Clive Burrows—saxophone, drums, flute; Steve Gregory—saxophone, flute; John Walters—trumpet; Rod Slade—bass; Little Roy—saxophone, drums, flute, bass. After Eric Burdon joined the Alan Price Combo, which became the Animals, and the smash hit "House of the Rising Sun" (1964), Price left to form the Alan Price Set, a return to lyrical rock, free of electric gadgetry. They were together through 1968, a consistently more popular group in England than in the United States. See Alan Price. *Album:* This Price Is Right.

PRICE, ALLAN Drums. Session for Jade Warrior (1971-72).

PRICE, BILL Moog. Session for Mott the Hoople (1973).

PRICE, BILLY Vocal. Session for Roy Buchanan (1973-74).

PRICE, CHRIS Vocal. Session for Roy Orbison (1979).

PRICE, CHUCK Guitar, vocal. Member of the Teaze, 1979.

PRICE, EARL LON Saxophone. Session for Adrian Gurvitz (1979); Rod Stewart (1980).

PRICE, JIM Trumpet, producer, organ. Member of the Rolling Stones, 1974, the Blacksmoke Horns, 1978, and Joe Cocker's Greatest Show on Earth, 1970. Producer of Joe Cocker's Greatest Show on Earth (1970). Session for Delaney and Bonnie; Nicky Hopkins (1974); Mott the Hoople (1972); Nilsson (1971-72, 75); Leon Russell (1971); the Rolling Stones (1972-73); Eric Clapton (1970); Peter Frampton (1972); George Harrison (1972); B. B. King (1971); Sky (1970-71); Gary Wright (1971); Audience (1972); Rod Stewart (1980); Jennifer Warnes (1976). *Album:* Kids Nowadays Ain't Got No Shame (AAM 4321).

PRICE, LLOYD Vocal. Nickname: Mr. Personality. Author of "Stagger Lee" and "Lawdy Miss Clawdy," Price laid the groundwork for rock of the future with his rhythmic arrangements and simple lyrics in the late 1950s. *Albums:* Exciting Lloyd Price; Mr. Personality; Mr. Personality Sings the Blues; Fantastic Lloyd Price; Mr. Personality's Big Fifteen; Lloyd Price Sings the Million Sellers; Lloyd Price Cookin'; Lloyd Swings for Sammy; Best of Lloyd Price; Sixteen Greatest Hits.

PRICE, LOUIS Vocal. Member of the Temptations.

PRICE, MARK Bass, vocal. Member of the Tin Huey, 1979.

PRICE, MARY ANN Vocal, percussion. Member of Dan Hicks and His Hot Licks until 1974.

PRICE, RICK Guitar, vocal. Member of the Brains, 1980.

PRICE, RICK Bass. Member of the Move, 1969-72.

PRICE, ROD Guitar, slide guitar. Alternating lead with Dave Peverett in Foghat, 1972-80.

PRICE, RONN Vocal, bass, guitar. Member of Buckeye, 1979.

PRICE, RONNIE Piano. Session for Kevin Ayers (1973).

PRICE, STEPHEN Drums. Member of Pablo Cruise since 1975.

PRICE, THOMMY Drums, vocal. Member of the Protector 4, 1980.

PRICE, TOPPER Harmonica. Member of Great Southern, 1978.

PRIEST, STEVE Bass, vocal, cello. Member of the Sweet since 1975.

PRIESTMAN, HENRY Keyboards, vocal. Member of the Yachts since 1979.

PRIGENO, NICKY Vocal, bass. Member of the Lavender Hill Mob, 1977.

PRIMES Early name for the Temptations.

PRIMETTES Early name of the Supremes.

PRINCE, MIKE Keyboards, guitar, vocal. Member of Legs Diamond, 1977-78.

PRINE, JOHN Vocal, guitar. *Albums:* Bruised Orange (ASY 6E-139) 1978; Common Sense (ATC 18127) 1975; Diamonds in the Rough (ATC 7240) 1972; Pink Cadillac (ASY 6E-222) 1979; Prime Prine (ATC 18202) 1976; John Prine (ATC 19156) 1971; Storm Windows (ASY 6E-286) 1980; Sweet Revenge (ATC 7274) 1973.

PRIOR, MADDY Vocal. Voice of Steeleye Span. Session for Jethro Tull (1976). *Albums:* Woman in the Wings (TKM 7078) 1980; Changing Winds (TKM 7079) 1980.

MADDY PRIOR AND JUNE TABOR Duet featuring Steeleye Span vocalist, Prior, with partner June Tabor. See individual listings. *Album:* Silly Sisters (TKM 7077) 1976.

PRISM Ron Tabak—vocal; Lindsey Mitchell—guitar; Tom Lavin—guitar; John Hall—keyboards; Ab Bryant—bass; Rod Higgs—drums; Allan Harlow—bass, vocal (1979-80); Rocket Norton—drums (1979-80). *Albums:* Armageddon (CAP ST-12051) 1979; Prism (ARA ST-50020) 1977; See Forever Eyes (ARA SW-50034) 1978; Young and Restless (CAP ST 12072) 1980.

PRITCHARD, MEL Drums, percussion. Member of the Barclay James Harvest.

PRITKIN, KITTY Vocal. Session for Steve Stills (1978).

PRIVATE LIGHTNING Steve Keith—bass; Paul Van Ness—guitar; Patty Van Ness—violin; Adam Sherman—vocal; Eric Kaufman—keyboards; Scott Woodman—drums. *Album:* Private Lightning (AAM 4791) 1980.

PRIVATE LINES Ryche Chlanda—guitar, vocal; Bill Pankow—keyboards; Spike Biglin—bass; Johnny "Hawk" McLaughlin—drums, vocal. *Album:* Trouble in School (PST 9848) 1980.

PROBY, P. J. "JIM" Vocal. *Albums:* Somewhere, 1965; P. J. Proby, 1965; Enigma, 1967; Phenomenon, 1967; What's Wrong With My World, 1968.

PROCOL HARUM Gary Brooker—vocal, piano, harmonica, percussion, writer; Keith Reid—lyrics; Matthew Fisher—organ, guitar, percussion, writer (1967-69); Robin Trower—guitar, vocal, percussion (1967-72); Dave Knights—bass (1966-70); B. J. Wilson—drums, percussion (1967-77); Chris Copping—bass, organ (1970-77); Dave Ball—guitar (1972); Mick Grabham—guitar (1973-77); Bobby Harrison—drums, percussion (1966); Ray Royer—guitar (1966); Alan Cartwright—bass (1972-77); Pete Solley—organ, synthesizer (1977). Procol Harum is Latin for "beyond these things." In 1967, they were using two keyboards, lyrics by an unseen sixth member of the group (Reid), and Bach themes, all of which together were alien to the rock scene. Their "Whiter Shade of Pale," 1967, sold 2½ million copies within weeks of its release and that was the turning point and subsequent foundation of their career. (They have been together since 1966.) The usual hassles of personnel and record company changes came after the hit, but a growing underground following allowed them comfortable success with no subsequent singles being released until 1974. Reid's lyrics bordered on the melancholy and fantastic. As sung by Brooker (and Robin Trower, before he left), they took on yet another mystical dimension. Known as the Paramounts, they backed Sandy Shaw before going solo. *Albums:* Best of Procol Harum (AAM 4401); Broken Barricade (AAM 4294) 1971; Exotic Birds and Fruit (CYS 1058) 1974; Grand Hotel (CYS 1037) 1973; Home (AAM 4261) 1970; Procol Harum (DER 18008) 1967; Procol Harum Live (AAM 4335) 1972; Procol's Ninth (CYS 1080) 1975; Salty Dog (AAM 4179) 1969; Shine On Brightly (AAM 4151) 1968; Something Magic (CYS 1130) 1977.

PROCTOR, JAY Vocal. Head of Jay and the Techniques, 1967-68.

PROFESSOR LONGHAIR Vocal, piano. *Albums:* New Orleans Piano (ATC 7225); Live on the Queen Mary (HAR SW 11790) 1978; Crawfish Fiesta (ALG 4718) 1980.

PROKOP, SKIP Drums, guitar, writer. Original member of the Paupers, 1966-69. Session for Super Session (1969).

PROOF Tom Cohen—vocal, guitar; Jeff Cohen—drums; Michael Hommel—bass, vocal; Michael Newman—guitar, vocal. *Album:* It's Safe (NMP JZ-36546) 1980.

PROSSER, SAMMY Played with John Mayall, 1961.

PROTECTOR 4 Thommy Price—drums, vocal; Joey Vasta—bass, vocal; Matt Lambert—guitar, vocal; Robert Salzo—guitar. Backup band for D. L. Byron, 1980.

PROTHEROE, BRIAN Vocal, keyboards. *Album:* I/You (CYS 1108) 1976.

PROTHEROE, DAN Bass. Member of Vance or Towers, 1975.

PROUTY, FRED Session for the Hot Dogs (1973).

PROVISOR, DENNIS Keyboards. Member of the Grass Roots.

PROVOST, GENE Guitar. Member of the Thundertrain, 1977.

PROVOST, RIC Bass. Member of the Thundertrain, 1977.

PRUDENCE, RON Percussion. Member of the Greatest Show on Earth, 1970.

PRUDENCE, STEVE Bass. Member of the Jags, 1980.

PRUETT, BILLY Saxophone. Session for J. J. Cale (1974).

PRUITT, JAN Keyboards. Session for B. W. Stevenson (1973).

PSYCHEDELIC FURS Tim Butler—bass; Richard Butler—lyrics; Vince Ely—drums; John Ashton—

guitar; Duncan Kilburn—saxophone; Roger Morris —guitar. *Album:* Psychedelic Furs (COL NJC 36791) 1980.

PSYCHEDELIC RANGERS Early name of the Doors.

PSYKA, RODNEY Percussion, vocal. Member of Breathless since 1979.

PUBLIC IMAGE John Lydon—vocal, guitar; Keith Levene—guitar, synthesizer; Jah Wobble—bass; Jeanette Lee—vocal; Dave Crowe—drums. *Album:* Second Edition (CSL 2WX 3288) 1979.

PUCKET, JERRY Guitar. Session for Paul Simon (1973).

PUCKETT, GARY Vocal. Voice of the Union Gap, 1967-68.

GARY PUCKET AND THE UNION GAP Gary Puckett—vocal; Dwight Bement—tenor saxophone; Kerry Chater—bass; Paul Wheatbread—drums; Gary Withem—piano. Their uniforms were cute, but the Union Gap's success was based on the powerful vocals of Gary Puckett. *Albums:* The Union Gap, 1968; Gary Puckett and the Union Gap, 1968; Incredible, 1968; Best of Gary Puckett and the Gap; Greatest Hits—Gary Puckett and the Union Gap; Lady Willpower (CSP EN-13093); Union Gap's Greatest Hits (COL CS-1042).

PUD Early name of the Doobie Brothers.

PUENTE, RICHIE Guitar, percussion. Member of Foxy since 1978.

PUERTA, JOE Bass, vocal. Member of Ambrosia since 1975. Session for the Alan Parsons Project (1976).

PUGH, JIMMY Member of Rubicon, 1978-79.

PUGH, MARTIN Guitar, writer. Original member of Steamhammer, 1969, and Armageddon, 1975. Session for Rod Stewart (1970).

PUGH, MIKE Bass. Member of Greezy Wheels, 1976.

PUGLESE, G. Harmonica. Session for the Doors (1970).

PUGLIANO, JIM Drums, vocal. Member of the Jaggerz.

PUKWANA, DUDU Alto saxophone. Member of Centipede, 1971.

PULLIAM, ROBERT Tenor saxophone. Session with John Littlejohn.

PULLMAN, BARRY Organ, moog. Member of the Ba-Fa Band, 1976.

PUNTER, JOHN Drums, producer. Produced Judy Tzuke, 1979, Marseilles, 1980, and Japan, 1980. Session for Bryan Ferry (1974); Sad Cafe (1978).

PURAS, ROBERTO Bass. Member of Raices, 1975.

PURDIE, BERNARD Drums, percussion, producer. Replaced Conrad Isidore in Hummingbird, 1976. Session and production for Felix Pappalardi (1979). Session for Tim Moore (1974); Paul Butterfield (1975); Joe Cocker (1974-78); Larry Coryell; Martin Mull (1974); Steely Dan (1976, 80); Cat Stevens (1974); B. B. King (1972); Kate and Anna McGarrigle (1977-78); Scarlet Rivera (1978).

PURE FOOD AND DRUG ACT Victor Conte—bass; Coleman Head—rhythm guitar; Paul Lagos —drums; Randy Resnick—rhythm guitar. Originally including Don "Sugarcane" Harris and Harvey Mandel, on violin and guitar respectively, the rhythm section of this group stayed together to back Mandel as a soloist. *Album:* Choice Cuts (EPC KE 31401).

PURE PRAIRIE LEAGUE Craig Fuller—vocal, guitar, bass; George Powell—vocal, guitar; William Hinds—drums (1975-present); Jim Caughlan—drums (1972-75); Jim Lanham—vocal, bass (1972-75); John Call—steel guitar (1972-78); Mike Conner—keyboards (1975-80); Larry Goshorn—guitar, vocal (1975-78); Tim Goshorn—guitar, vocal (1978); Mike Reilly—bass, vocal (1975-78); Vince Gill—guitar, banjo, dobro (1979); Patrick Bolen—guitar, vocal (1979); Jeff Wilson—guitar (1980). *Albums:* Bustin' Out (VIC AFLI 4769) 1972; Can't Hold Back (VIC AFLI 3335) 1979; Firin' Up (CAS 7212) 1980; If the Shoe Fits (VIC AFLI 1247) 1976; Just Fly (VIC AFLI 2590) 1978; Pure Prairie League (VIC AFLI 4650) 1972; Takin' the Stage (VIC CPL2-2404) 1977; Two Lane Highway (VIC AYL1 3669) 1976; Dance (VIC AYL1 2723) 1976.

PURIM, FLORA Vocal, percussion. Session for Santana (1974); George Duke (1975). *Albums:* Butterfly Dreams (MLS 9052); Carry On (WBR K-3344) 1979; Encounter (MLS 9077); Everyday, Everynight (WBR K 3168) 1978; 500 Miles High (MLS 9070); Nothing Will Be As It Was Tomorrow (WBR B 2985); Open Your Eyes, You Can Fly (MLS 9065); Stories to Tell (MLS 9058); That's What She Said (MLS 9081).

PURRO, CHUCK Drums, percussion. Member of the Colwell-Winfield Blues Band, 1968, and the James Montgomery Band, 1976.

PURSE, BILL Member of the Boneroo Horn Section, 1979.

PURSER, FRED Member of the Penetration, 1979.

PURSEY, JIMMY Vocal, writer, producer. Founder of Sham 69, 1978-80, before going solo. *Album:* Imagination Camouflage (Import) 1980.

PURVIS, BOBBY Vocal, writer. Half of the English duet, Splinter, 1974-77.

PUSTELNIK, KEN Drums. Original member of the Groundhogs, 1968-72.

PUTNAM, NORBERT Bass, producer. A member of Area Code 615. Session and production for Donovan (1974-76). Produced the Pousette-Dart Band (1976-79). Session for Pearls Before Swine (1970); Ian and Sylvia; Waylon Jennings (1973); the Pointer Sisters (1974); J. J. Cale (1971); Mike Harrison (1975); Splinter (1977); Ian Matthews (1976); Tim Weisberg and Dan Fogelberg (1978); Jimmy Hall (1980).

PUTNAM, WOODY Drums. Member of Baby, 1975.

PUTRELLO, MAURICE Drums. Member of the Sail.

PUTRELLO, PATRICK Trumpet, flugelhorn. Member of the Sail.

PUZZLE Larry Klimas—saxophone, flute; Bob Williams—trumpet; Ralf Richert—guitar, trumpet; Bobby Villalobos—guitar; Joseph Spinazola—keyboards; Anthony Siciliano—bass; John Li Vigne—drums, vocal, percussion. *Albums:* Second Puzzle, 1974; Puzzle (MTN); Puzzle (MCA 671).

PYE, FRANCIS Vocal. Session for Leon Russell (1979).

PYLE, ANDY Bass. Member of Mick Abraham's Blodwyn Pig, 1969-70. Replaced Andy Silvester in Savoy Brown, 1972-73. Session for Rod Stewart (1973); Alvin Lee (1975); the Kinks (1977).

PYLE, ARTEMIS Drums. Replaced Bob Burns in Lynyrd Skynyrd. Session for Alias (1980).

PYLE, PIP Drums. Member of the National Health Band, 1977.

PYNE, CHRIS Trombone. Session for Bryan Ferry (1974).

PYNE, MIKE Began in Blues Incorporated.

PYTHON LEE JACKSON Gary Boyle—guitar; Tony Cahill—bass; Mick Liber—guitar; David Montgomery—drums; David Bentley—keyboards; Rod Stewart—vocal. *Album:* In a Broken Dream (CRS 2066) 1972.

QUACKENBUSH, GARY Guitar. Member of SRC.

QUACKENBUSH, GLENN Organ. Member of SRC.

QUAIFE, PETER Bass, vocal. Original member of the Kinks, 1964-70.

QUANSAH, EDDY Horns. Session for John Bundrick (1974).

QUARRYMEN Pete Best—drums; George Harrison—guitar, vocal; John Lennon—piano, guitar, vocal; Paul McCartney—bass, piano, vocal. After leaving the Rebels, Harrison teamed up with Lennon and McCartney in 1958 to form the Quarrymen. The following year, they picked up Tony Sheridan and changed their name to the Silver Beatles.

QUATEMAN, BILL Vocal, guitar, piano. *Albums:* Shot in the Dark, 1977; Night After Night, 1977; Bill Quateman, 1973; Just Like You (VIC AFLI 2879) 1979.

QUATERMASS John Gustafson—vocal, bass; Pete Robinson—keyboards; Mick Underwood—drums. *Album:* Quatermass (HVT SKAO 314) 1970.

QUATRO, MICHAEL Keyboards. *Albums:* In Collaboration (UAR UR-1-9420 67) 1975; Michael Quatro (UAR) 1976.

QUATRO, PATTI Guitar. Member of Fanny, 1974.

QUATRO, SUZI Vocal, bass. Born 6/3/50. If crowds went wild over boys in black leather playing rock 'n' roll, why wouldn't they do the same for a girl? Suzi Quatro proved they would in 1974 with her band: Len Tucky—guitar; Alastaire McKenzie—keyboards; and Dave Neal—drums. Session for Donovan (1973). *Albums:* Quatro (BEL 1313) 1974; Suzi Quatro (BEL 1303) 1974; If You Knew Suzi (RSO 1-3044); Suzi (RSO 1-3064) 1979; Rock Hard (RSO 1-5006) 1980; Your Mama Won't Like Me (ARI 4035) 1975.

QUAYE, CALEB Guitar, piano. Original member of the Elton John band, 1969-71, 1975-76, and Hookfoot, 1972. Session for Long John Baldry (1971); Nilsson (1971); Lou Reed (1972); John Kongos (1972); Pete Townshend (1972); Vigrass and Osborne (1972); Mylon Le Fevre (1979).

QUEEN Freddie Mercury—vocal, piano; Brian May—guitar, vocal, piano; John Deacon—bass; Roger Meadows-Taylor—percussion, vocal. Early Name: Smile. The debut of Queen in 1973 was a fresh, new breeze into the world of rock. Fame scattered their brilliance and talent between pieces of commercially acceptable material without hindering their popularity. *Albums:* Day at the Races (ELK 6E-101) 1976; The Game (ELK 5E-513) 1980; Jazz (ELK 6E-166) 1978; News of the World (ELK 2E-112) 1977; Night at the Opera (ELK 7E-1053) 1975; Queen (ELK 75064) 1973; Queen 2 (ELK 75082) 1974; Queen Live Killers (ELK BB-702) 1979; Sheer Heart Attack (ELK 7E-1026) 1974; Flash Gordon (ELK 5E-518) 1980.

? AND THE MYSTERIANS Recorded "96 Tears," 1966.

QUICK Steve Hufsteter—guitar; Ian Ainsworth—bass; Danny Benair—drums; Billy Bizeau—keyboards, vocal; Danny Wilde—vocal. *Album:* Mondo Deco (MER SRM 1-1114) 1976.

QUICK, CLARENCE Vocal. Member of the Del Vikings.

QUICK, SCOTT Guitar. Session for Sammy Hagar (1975).

QUICKSILVER MESSENGER SERVICE John Cipollina—guitar, vocal; Gary Duncan—guitar; Dave Freiberg—bass, vocal; Gregory Elmore—drums; Nicky Hopkins—piano, percussion (1969); Mark Ryan—bass; Dino Valenti—vocal, guitar, percussion (from 1970). Quicksilver ushered in the flower age of the mid-1960s with the Jefferson Airplane, the Grateful Dead, and other San Francisco bands. In 1970, Valenti, a folk singer, joined the group. Under Valenti's direction, the group lost their identity in his lyrics. *Albums:* Comin' Through (CAP SMAS 4002); Just for Love (CAP SMAS 408); Anthology (CAP SVBB 11165); Happy Trails (CAP ST-120) 1969; Just for Love (CAP SN-16093); Quicksilver (CAP SW-819); Quicksilver Messenger Service (CAP ST-2904) 1967; Shady Grove (CAP SN-16094) 1969; Solid Silver (CAP SM-11820) 1975; What About Me (CAP SN-16092).

QUIET SUN Phil Manzanera—guitar; Dave Garrett—keyboards; Charles Hayward—drums; Bill McCormick—bass. *Album:* Mainstream, 1975.

QUINCEY, DAVE Reeds. Original member of If, and Zzebra, 1974.

QUINCY Brian Butler; Metro; Gerald Emerick; Steve Butler; Bob Holden. *Album:* Quincy (COL JC-36471) 1980.

QUINE, ROBERT Guitar, vocal. Member of Richard Hell and the Voidoids, 1977.

QUINN, DAVE Bass, vocals. Member of Movies, 1976.

QUINN, DEREK Member of Freddie and the Dreamers, 1962-66.

QUINN, LANCE Guitar. Session on Hendrix's

"Midnight Lightning" (1975).

QUINN, PAUL Guitar. Member of Saxon, 1980.

QUINTANA, CHARLIE Drums. Member of the Plugz, 1979.

QUINTON, DEREK Percussion. Member of the Tom Robinson Band since 1978.

QUITTENTON, MARTIN Guitar. Original member of Steamhammer, 1969, and Pilot, 1972. Session for Rod Stewart (1970-71).

QUIVER Tim Renwick—guitar, steel guitar; Bruce Thomas—bass (until 1975); Pete Wood—keyboards (until 1975); Willie Wilson—drums. Back-up band for the Sutherland Brothers. See the Sutherland Brothers.

R.A.F. David Valentine—vocal, keyboards; Douglas A. Bogie—guitar; Billy McGhee—bass; Tom Annan—drums. *Album:* R.A.F. (AAM 4816) 1980.

RABB, LUTHER Bass, vocal. Member of Ballin' Jack.

RABBIT Nickname of John Bundrick.

RABBITT Trevor Rabin—guitar, vocal, keyboards; Ronnie Robot—bass; Neil Cloud—drums; Duncan Faure—keyboards. *Albums:* Boys Will Be Boys, 1976; A Croak and Grunt in the Night, 1977.

RABIN, TREVOR Guitar, vocal, keyboards, bass, producer. Member of Rabbitt, 1976-77. Session for Manfred Mann (1980). *Albums:* Face to Face (CYS 1221) 1980; Trevor Rabin (CYS 1196) 1978.

RACHEL, JAMES "YANK" Mandolin, guitar. Born 1/16/08 in Tennessee. Session with Sonny Boy Williamson (1938); Walter Davis; Sleepy John Estes. *Albums:* Yank Rachell (BLG 2010) 1973; Mandolin Blues (DEL 606).

RACING CARS Graham Headley Williams—guitar, vocal; Ray Ennis—guitar, vocal; David Land—bass, vocal; Bob Wilding—drums, vocal; Morty—vocal, guitar. *Albums:* Bring on the Night (CYS 1178) 1978; Downtown Tonight (CYS 1099) 1976; Weekend Rendezvous (CYS 1149) 1977.

RACIOPPO, ROBERT Bass, vocal. Member of the Shirts, 1978-80.

RADCLIFFE, LEROY Guitar, vocal. Member of the Modern Lovers, 1977-78, and Robin Lane and the Chartbusters, 1980.

RADFORD, FLOYD Guitar. Original member of White Trash. Session for Johnny and Edgar Winter (1976).

RADFORD, ROLLO Bass. Replaced Jim Dawson in the Siegel-Schwall Band, 1970.

RADIATION, RODDY Guitar. Member of the Specials since 1979.

RADICE, MARK Keyboards. Session for Donovan (1974).

RADIO BIRDMAN Warwick Gilbert—bass; Ron Keeley—drums; Pip Hoyle—keyboards; Chris Masuak—guitar, piano; Deniz Tek—guitar; Rob Younger—vocal. *Album:* Radios Appear (SIR K-6050) 1978.

RADLE, CARL Bass. A member of Joe Cocker's Greatest Show on Earth, 1970, and Derek and the Dominoes, 1970-72. Session for Marc Benno (1979); Delaney and Bonnie; Donovan (1973); Dr. John (1971); Dave Mason; Art Garfunkel; Freddie King (1972-74); Leon Russell (1971-75); Bangla Desh (1971); J. J. Cale (1971, 79); Eric Clapton (1970, 74, 78); Rita Coolidge (1972); George Harrison (1972, 75).

RADNER, GILDA Vocal. Former "Saturday Night Live" star's comedy-music solo debut. *Album:* Live from New York (WBR HS-3320) 1979.

RAE, ANDY Bass, vocal. Replaced Jimmy Leverton in Savoy Brown, 1975.

RAE, TERRY Drums, vocal. Member of the Hollywood Stars, 1977.

RAFFEL, SCOTT Reeds, percussion. Member of Victor Koncept, 1979.

RAFFERTY, GERRY Vocal, piano, guitar, writer, producer. Member of Stealers Wheel, 1972-75, before making it big as a soloist with "Baker Street," 1978. Produced Jim Rafferty (1978). *Albums:* Gerry Rafferty (USA 7006) 1974; Can I Have My Money Back (MCA 6031); City to City (UAR LW-840) 1978; Night Owl (UAR LOO-958) 1979; Snakes and Ladders (UAR LOO 1039) 1980.

RAFFERTY, JIM Vocal. *Album:* Jim Rafferty (LON PS-722) 1978.

RAGIN, MELVIN Guitar. Session for Freddie King; the Temptations (1973).

RAGOVOY, JERRY Piano. Session for B. B. King (1971).

RAGUSA, PETE Drums. Member of the Nighthawks since 1976.

RAICES Roberto Puras—bass; Gonchi Sifre—drums, percussion, harmonica; Juan Melendez—flute, saxophone, clarinet, percussion, vocal; Amaury Lopez—keyboards, percussion, vocal; Carlos Melendez—guitar, vocal; Rafael Cruz—percussion; Sammy Figueroa—percussion, vocal. *Album:* Raices (NMR) 1975.

RAIDERS Paul Revere—keyboards; Mark Lindsay—vocal, saxophone; Mike Holiday—bass (until 1965); Drake Levin—guitar (until 1966); Mike Smith—drums (until 1966); Philip Volk—bass (1965); Freddie Weller—guitar (1966-69); Jim Valley—drums (1966-68); Charlie Coe—bass; Joe Correro—drums (1969). Idaho has spawned few superstars, but that was the starting point of Paul Revere and his Raiders, then known as the Downbeats. They moved to Portland, Oregon, for greener pastures in 1962. Then in 1965, their big break came as regulars on Dick Clark's "Where the Action Is." They survived the English invasion as financial and nostalgia successes due to the management of group leader, Paul Revere. *Albums:* Here They Come (COL 2307) 1965; Just Like Us

(COL 2451) 1966; Midnight Ride (COL) 1966; In the Beginning (COL) 1966; Spirit of '67 (COL) 1967; Revolution (COL) 1967; Going to Memphis (COL) 1968; Something Happening (COL) 1968; Christmas Present and Past (COL) 1967; Greatest Hits, Vol. 2 (COL C-30386); Indian Reservation (COL C-30768); All-Time Greatest Hits (COL CG-31464); Paul Revere and the Raiders Greatest Hits (COL C-35593) 1967.

RAILE, CARMEN Bass. Session for Kim Fowley.

RAIN, MICK Drums. Member of Pezband since 1977.

RAINBOW, CHRIS Vocal. Session for the Alan Parsons Project (1980).

RAINBOW, PHILIP Vocal. *Album:* Shooting Gallery (CAP ST 12074) 1979.

RAINBOW Ritchie Blackmore—guitar, writer; Ronnie James Dio—vocal, writer (1975-78); Gary Driscoll—drums (1975-76); Craig Gruber—bass; Mickey Lee Soule—keyboards (1975-76); Cozy Powell—drums (1976-80); Tony Carey—keyboards (1976-78); Mark Clarke—bass (1977); David Stone—keyboards (1978); Bob Daisley—bass (1978); Don Airey—keyboards (1979-present); Graham Bonnet—vocal (1979); Roger Glover—bass, producer (1979). Blackmore stepped down from Deep Purple to join Dio in 1975, forming Rainbow. The similarity of sound between the bands was no surprise and no disappointment. *Albums:* Down to Earth (POL 1-6221) 1979; Long Live Rock 'n' Roll (POL 1-6143) 1978; On Stage (OYS 2-1801) 1977; Rainbow Rising (OYS 1-1601) 1976; Richie Blackmore's Rainbow (POL PD 6049) 1975.

RAINBOW CONCERT Eric Clapton—guitar, vocal; Pete Townshend—guitar, vocal; Ronnie Wood—guitar, vocal; Rick Grech—bass; Steve Winwood—keyboards, vocal; Jim Capaldi—drums; Jimmy Karstein—drums; Reebop—percussion. One-time-only gala superstar concert-jam, recorded at the Rainbow Theater, London, 1/13/73. *Album:* Rainbow Concert (RSO SO 877) 1973.

RAINBOW RED OXIDIZER Mars Bonfire—guitar; Rainbow Red Oxidizer—vocal; Ed Cassidy—drums; Leon Rubinhold—guitar; Gary Marker—bass. *Album:* Recorded Lies (BMP Q-2) 1980.

RAINES, CHICK Vocal, guitar. Half of the Raines and Harris duet, 1977.

RAINES, JOHN Percussion. Member of C.O.D., 1979.

RAINES AND HARRIS Chick Raines—vocal, guitar; Greg Harris—guitar, mandolin, vocal. *Album:* Raines and Harris (VIC AFLI 2422) 1977.

RAINEY, CHUCK Bass. Namesake of Chuck Rainey's Coalition. Session for Paul Butterfield (1975); Larry Coryell; Dave Mason; Steely Dan (1974, 76, 80); Tim Weisberg (1973); Free Creek (1973); Nils Lofgren (1976); Joe Walsh (1972); Ringo Starr (1977); Les Dudek (1977); Martin Mull (1977).

RAINEY, MA Vocal. Born in 1886. Known as "the mother of the blues," she was the protege of Bessie Smith. *Albums:* Blame It On the Blues (MLS 2008) 1968; Down in the Basement (MLS 2017) 1971; Early Portrait (MLS 2010); Immortal Ma Rainey (MLS 2001) 1966; Jazz, Vol. 2 (FLW 2802); Jazz, Vol. 4 (FLW 2804); Jazz, Vol. 11 (FLW 2811); Ma Rainey (MLS 47021) 1974.

RAINFLOWERS Early group of Jimi Hendrix, which also included Randy California.

RAINS, GEORGE Drums. Original member of the Sir Douglas Quintet, 1965-68. Session for Boz Scaggs (1972); Arthur, Hurley and Gottlieb; Willie Nelson (1973); Shawn Phillips (1973); Robert Palmer (1976); Joe Cocker (1978); Felix Pappalardi (1979); Jim Capaldi (1979).

RAITT, BONNIE Vocal, guitar, writer. Country folk soloist. Session for James Taylor (1976); the Pointer Sisters (1974); Willie Nelson and Leon Russell (1979); Peter C. Johnson (1980). *Albums:* Give It Up (WBR 2643) 1972; The Glow (WBR HS-3369) 1979; Home Plate (WBRB-2864) 1975; Bonnie Raitt (WBR 1953) 1971; Streetlights (WBR B-2818) 1974; Sweet Forgiveness (WBR B-2990) 1977; Takin' My Time (WBR B-2729) 1973.

RAITTNEN, EERO Vocal. Member of Tasavallan Presidenti, 1974.

RAJA, ENRICO Trumpet. Member of Gasmask.

RALEIGH, KEVIN Vocal, keyboards, percussion. Member of the Michael Stanley Band.

RALPH, ALLAN Trombone. Session for John Mayall (1979).

RALPHS, MICK Guitar, keyboards, vocal, writer. Born 5/31/44. After gaining an international reputation as guitarist for Mott the Hoople (1969-73), he left to become part of Bad Company, 1973-present. Session for Luther Grosvenor.

RAM JAM Howie Blauvelt—bass; Jimmy Santoro—guitar (1978); Bill Bartlett—vocal, percussion; Peter Charles—drums; Myke Scavone—vocal, percussion. *Albums:* Ram Jam (EPC PE-34885) 1977; Portrait of the Artist as a Young Ram (EPC 35287) 1978.

RAMATAM April Lawton—guitar; Mitch Michell—drums; Mike Pinera—guitar, vocal; Russ Smith—bass, vocal; Tommy Sullivan—keyboards, vocal. *Albums:* Ramatam (ATC) 1972; In April Came the Dawning of the Red Sun (ACO SD 7261).

RAMEREZ, BOBBY Drums. Original member of White Trash.

RAMIREZ, LOU Drums. Member of the Plimsouls, 1980.

RAMIREZ, RAPHAEL Congas. Session for Taj Mahal.

RAMIREZ, RICK Guitar. Member of Striker, 1978.

RAMIREZ, THOMAS Saxophone. Session for

Christopher Cross (1980).

RAMISTELLA, JOHN Real name of Johnny Rivers.

RAMONE, DEE DEE Bass. Member of the Ramones since 1976.

RAMONE, JOEY Vocal. Voice of the Ramones since 1976.

RAMONE, JOHNNY Guitar. Member of the Ramones since 1976.

RAMONE, TOMMY Drums. Member of the Ramones since 1976.

RAMONES Johnny Ramone—guitar; Joey Ramone—vocal; Dee Dee Ramone—bass; Tommy Ramone—drums. *Albums:* End of the Century (SIR SRK-6077); Leave Home (SIR 6031) 1977; Over the Edge (WBR K-3335); Ramones (SIR 6020) 1976; Road to Ruin (SIR K-6063); Rocket to Russia (SIR 6042) 1977.

RAMPAGE, RANDY Bass. Member of D.O.A. since 1979.

RAMRODS Recorded "Ghost Riders in the Sky," 1961.

RAMSDEN Guitar. Session for Rick Wakeman (1979).

RAMSDEN, MICHAEL Vocal. Session for Hapshash and the Coloured Coat.

RAMSES Winfried Langhorst—keyboards, vocal; Hans D. Klinkhammer—bass; Norbert Langhorst—guitar; Herbert Natho—vocal; Reinhard Schroter—drums, percussion. *Album:* La Leyla (ANC 1002).

RAMSEY, PAT Harmonica. Session for Johnny Winter (1978).

RANCHIE Bass. Member of the Dillinger, 1976.

RANCID YEARS Early name of Chrysalis.

RANCIFER, RODERICK Keyboards, vocal. Member of Halloween, 1979.

RAND, BERTHA Vocal. Session for Leon Russell (1979).

RANDALL, ELLIOT Guitar. Member of Seatrain until forming Randall's Island, 1971-72. Session for Pavlov's Dog (1976); Steely Dan (1972-76); Free Creek (1973); Stanky Brown (1977); the Mark and Clark Band (1977); Far Cry (1980); the Blues Brothers (1980); Scarlet Rivera (1978). *Album:* Elliott Randall's New York (KRN 34351) 1977.

RANDALL, JIMMIE Bass, vocal. Member of Jo Jo Gunne, 1973-74.

RANDALL, JOHN Percussion. Member of Brett Marvin and the Thunderbolts.

RANDALL'S ISLAND Gary King—bass; Elliot Randall—guitar; Allen Herman—drums; Paul Fleischer—saxophone, vocal; Pot—keyboards. *Albums:* Rock and Roll City (POL) 1972; Randall's Island (POL) 1971.

RANDI, DON Piano. Session for Buffalo Springfield (1967).

RANDLE, RICK Vocal, guitar, keyboards. Member of Striker, 1978. Session for the Heats (1980).

RANDOLPH, BILL Bass. Replaced Phillip Petty in Point Blank, 1979-present.

RANDOM HOLD Random Hold—vocal; David Rhodes—guitar; David Ferguson—keyboards; Bill MacCormick—bass; Peter Phipps—drums. *Album:* Etceteraville (PST 9847) 1980.

RANDOW, FRITZ Drums, guitar, flute, percussion. Member of Eloy, 1975-76.

RANDY PIE Bernd Wippich—vocal, guitar; Werner Becker—keyboards, vocal; Jean-Jacques Kravetz—keyboards; Dicky Tarrach—drums, percussion; Jochen Petersen—guitar, saxophone, vocal; Thissy Theirs—bass, vocal. *Albums:* Kitsch (POL PD 6518); Fast Forward (PPD PD 1-6113) 1977; Randy Pie (POL PD 6515) 1975.

RANGE, GARY Bass. Member of No Dice, 1978-79.

RANK STRANGERS Templeton Parcley—violin; Chris Darrow—vocal, mandolin, dobro, Hawaiian guitar; Cindy Edwards—vocal; John Silk—bass, vocal; Robb Strondlund—vocal, guitar. *Album:* Rank Strangers (PFA 112) 1977.

RANKIN, BILLY Drums. Member of Brinsley Schwartz, and the Tiger, 1976. Session for Dave Edmunds (1977); Frankie Miller (1977).

RANKIN, KENNY Vocal, writer. Soft-spoken folk singer with jazz overtones. *Albums:* After the Roses (ATC 19271); Inside (LID 1009) 1975; Like a Seed (LID 1003) 1972; Kenny Rankin Album (LID 1013) 1977; Silver Morning (LID 3000) 1974; Mind Dusters, 1967; Clever Dogs.

RANKIN, NED E. Drums. Member of the Iron City Houserockers since 1979.

RANKINS, ROGER Member of the English Beat, 1980.

RANKU, LUCKY African drums. Session for Mike Oldfield (1975).

RANNO, RICHIE Guitar. Member of the Starz, 1976-78.

RANSOME, HANK Drums, bass, guitar. Member of Elizabeth, 1968.

RAO, JOHNNY Guitar. Session for Sylvain Sylvain (1979).

RAPH, ALAN Trombone. Session for Taj Mahal (1978).

RAPHAEL, JEFF Drums, percussion. Member of the Nuns, 1980.

RAPHAEL, MICKEY Harmonica. Member of the Tim Weisberg Band, 1977. Session for Leon Russell (1979); Leon Russell and Willie Nelson (1979).

RAPHAUEL, HOAGY Percussion. Member of Zulu. Session for Nils Lofgren, 1976.

RAPP, BARRY Keyboards, vocal. Member of the Henry Paul Band since 1979.

RAPP, DANNY Vocal. Member of Danny and the Juniors.

RAPP, MICHAEL Keyboards. Member of A-440, 1978.

RAPP, TOM Vocal, guitar, writer. Head writer and

mastermind for Pearls Before Swine, 1967-70. He dissolved the group to continue as a soloist. *Albums:* Familiar Songs (BTM) 1971; Sunforest (BTM) 1972; Stardancer (BTM 44) 1972.

RAPPA, BENNY Drums, vocal. Member of Whiteface, 1979.

RAPPONE, RONDO Vocal. Session for Henry Gross (1973).

RAPPOPORT, MIKE Drums. Member of the Demons, 1977.

RARE BIRD Fred Kelly; Dave Kaffinetti—piano; Ced Curtis; Paul Holland; Steve Gould—bass, vocal; Paul Karas; Graham Field—organ (1969); Mark Ashton—drums (1969). *Albums:* Epic Forest, 1972; Rare Bird, 1969; Somebody's Watching; Born Again, 1973; As Your Mind Flies By (POL).

RARE EARTH Pete Rivera—drums, percussion, vocal; Gil Bridges—woodwinds, percussion, vocal; John Persh—bass, vocal; Ray Monette—guitar (1975); Mark Olson—keyboards, vocal; Ed Guzman—conga, percussion; Mike Urso—bass, vocal (1975-77); Pete Hoorelbeke—drums, percussion, vocal (1975-77); Dan Ferguson—guitar (1977); Ron Franson—guitar (1977); Reggie McBride—bass (1975); Frank Westbrook—keyboards (1976-77); Jerry La Croix—vocal (1975); Paul Warren—guitar (1975); Barry Frost—drums (1975); Gabe Katona—keyboards, vocal (1975). A secondary favorite of the big band sounds, they enjoyed some success with their single "Hey Brother" (1970), but due to legal problems, the band was forced to break up. They have attempted two comebacks since their initial demise. *Albums:* Willie Remembers (REH 543L) 1972; Midnight Lady (REH) 1976; Rare Earth (PRD 1001651) 1977; Back To Earth (REH 54851) 1975; Ecology (REH R7-514) 1970; Get Ready (REH R7-507) 1969; Rare Earth in Concert (REH R7-534) 1971.

RAREBELL, HERMAN Drums. Member of the Scorpions.

RASCALS Eddie Brigati—vocal; Felix Cavaliere—organ, vocal, writer; Gene Cornish—guitar; Dino Danelli—drums. From Joey Dee's Starliners, they got together after the twist era and began kicking around New Jersey with their raunchy soul sound. They caught on, moved to New York in 1966, and released the blockbuster single, "Good Lovin'." They then toured England where they unleashed the black-sound-as-performed-by-white-artist sound. They survived the flower era with "Groovin'" (1967) and "People Got to Be Free" (1968), before dissolving. Cavaliere went on to a moderately received solo career. *Albums:* Young Rascals (ATC) 1966; Collection (ATC) 1966; Groovin' (ATC) 1967; Once Upon a Dream (ATC) 1968; Freedom Suite (ATC) 1969; Rascal's Greatest Hits (ATC 8190) 1968; Super Hits (ATC 2-501).

RASKIN, JONATHAN Member of Ars Nova, 1968-69.

RASPBERRIES Eric Carmen—guitar, keyboards, vocal; Wally Bryson—guitar, vocal; Scott McCarl—guitar, bass, vocal; Michael McBride—drums. Early name: the Choir. *Albums:* Starting Over (CAP) 1974; Raspberries (CAP) 1972; Fresh (CAP) 1973; Side 3 (CAP) 1973; Raspberries Best (CAP ST-11524).

RASPBERRY, LARRY Guitar, piano, vocal. Member of the Alamo, 1971, and namesake of Larry Raspberry and the Highsteppers, 1972-79.

LARRY RASPBERRY AND THE HIGHSTEPPERS Jerry McKinney—saxophone, flute; Bill Marshall—drums, vocal; Larry Raspberry—guitar, piano, vocal; Carol Ferrante—vocal, percussion, piano; Rocky Berretta—bass, vocal; Joe Mulherin—trumpet; Greg Taylor—harmonica, percussion, vocal. *Albums:* In the Pink (BKM) 1975; No Accident (MER SRM 1-37782) 1979.

RASSLER, J. Guitar. Member of DMZ, 1978.

RATHEL, GIL Horns. Session for Steppenwolf (1974).

RATHER, NICK Bass. Session for J. J. Cale (1979).

RATLEDGE, MICHAEL Keyboards. Original member of the Soft Machine. Session for Kevin Ayers (1973).

RATTI, MIKE Drums. Member of the Rex, 1977.

RATTLESNAKE RATTLES Bass. Member of Root Boy Slim's Sex Change Band, 1978.

RATZELOFF, ED Guitar, vocal. Member of the Blue Jug, 1975.

RAUCH, DOUGLAS Bass. Member of Santana, 1972-74, and the Giants, 1978.

RAVAN, GENYA Vocal, harmonica, percussion. Real name: Goldie Zelkowitz. Member of 10 Wheel Drive, 1970. See Goldie Zelkowitz. Session for Gamma (1980). *Albums:* Genya Ravan (COL C 31001); And I Mean It (TWC 595) 1979; Urban Desire (TWC 562) 1978.

RAVEN, KYLE Drums. Replaced Nick Beat in Venus and the Razor Blades, 1977.

RAVEN, PAUL Vocal. Played the Priest in "Jesus Christ Superstar," 1970.

RAVENS Early name for the Kinks.

RAVENS Jude Cole—guitar, vocal (1979); Dennis Croy—bass; Rick Croy—drums; Jeff Fargus—keyboards, vocal (1980). Backup group for Moon Martin.

RAVENSCROFT, RAPHAEL Saxophone. Session for Gerry Rafferty (1978-80); Red Rider (1980); the Alvin Lee Band (1980). *Album:* Her Father Didn't Like Me, Anyway (POR JR-35683).

RAVENSTINE, ALLEN Synthesizer. Member of Pere Ubu since 1979.

RAVERS Graham Daddy—vocal; Louie Maxfield—guitar; Dave Dennard—bass; Mike Campbell—drums. *Album:* Punk Rock Christmas (RHI 503).

RAW MILK Don Preston—vocal, keyboards, percussion; Sandy Reiner—drums; Christy Rundquist

—synthesizer; Phil Davis—synthesizer. Temporary group formed by former Mother of Invention, Preston.

RAWLINSON, ROB Bass. Original member of Broken Glass, 1976.

RAWLS, LOU Vocal. Injecting his soul into his jazz and blues, Rawls is a leader in his field. *Albums:* Black and Blue, 1962; Tobacco Road; Nobody But Lou, 1965; Lou Rawls and Strings; Pilgrim Travelers; Carryin' On, 1966; Too Much, 1967; That's Lou, 1967; Feelin' Good, 1968; You're Good For Me, 1968; Way It Was, the Way It Is, 1969; Natural Man; Lou Rawls at Century Plaza; She's Gone; Soul of Nigger Charley; All Things in Time (PHL PZ-33957) 1976; Best from Lou Rawls (CAP SKBB-11585) 1976; Best of Christmas (CAP SKBB-2979); Best of Lou Rawls (CAP SM 2948) 1968; Let Lou Be Good to You (PHL JZ 36006) 1979; Merry Xmas, Ho, Ho, Ho (CAP M-2790); Lou Rawls Live (CAP SM-2459) 1966; Lou Rawls Live (PHL PZ2-35517) 1978; Sit Down and Talk to Me (PHL JZ 36304) 1979; Soulin' (CAP SM-2566) 1966; Stormy Monday (CAP SM-1714); Unmistakably Lou (PHL PZ-34488) 1977; When You Hear Lou, You've Heard It All (PHL JZ-35036) 1977; Shades of Blue (COL JZ 36774) 1980.

RAY, BOB Bass. Session for J. J. Cale (1972).

RAY, BRIAN Guitar. Member of Crackin', 1978, and the Reggie Knighton Band, 1978.

RAY, JOHN Bass. Member of Flight, 1976-79.

RAY, NORM Baritone. Session for J. J. Cale (1972).

RAY, RITA Vocal. Member of the Darts since 1978.

RAY, WILLIE Accordion. Session for Gerry Rafferty (1978).

RAYBURN, DOUG Mellotron, flute, bass, percussion, writer. Original member of Pavlov's Dog, 1975-76.

RAYMOND, BOB Bass. Original member of Sugarloaf.

RAYMOND, BUTCH Drums. Member of the Edge, 1980.

RAYMOND, CAREY Guitar. Member of Trouble, 1977.

RAYMOND, DAN Member of Bill Haley and the Comets.

RAYMOND, MARGE Vocal. Member of the Flame, 1977.

RAYMOND, PAUL Keyboards, guitar, vocal, writer. Member of Stan Webb's Chicken Shack. Teamed up with Kim Simmonds in Savoy Brown in 1971, partly replacing Chris Youlden and partly adding a new dimension to the group, that of a keyboardist. He left in 1974, as Simmonds was experimenting with new group lineups, but returned, 1975-76. Member of UFO since 1977. Session for Danny Kirwan.

RAYNER, EDDIE Keyboards. Member of the Split Enz.

RAYS Recorded "Silhouettes," 1956.

RAZMATAZ Richard Morton—guitar, keyboards, vocal; Monc Blackburn—saxophone, flute, vocal; Peter Young—bass; Billy Mundi—drums. *Album:* The First Time (UAR) 1972.

RAZOR BLADES See Venus and the Razor Blades.

RCR Donna Rhodes—vocal, guitar; Charles Chalmers—vocal, saxophone; Sandra Rhodes—vocal, guitar. *Album:* Scandal (RDR G5-5001) 1980.

REA, CHRIS Producer. Produced Alibi (1980). *Albums:* Deltics (UAR LO 959) 1979; Tennis (COL JC-36435) 1980; Whatever Happened to Benny Santini (UAR LO-879) 1978.

READ, JOE Bass. Member of the Strapps, 1977.

READ, JOHN DAWSON Guitar, vocal. *Album:* Read On (CRS 1102) 1976.

READ, MICHAEL Keyboards, vocal. Member of Roadmaster since 1978.

READING, WARWICK Bass. Session for Jan Akkerman and Kaz Lux (1976).

REALE, MARK Guitar. Member of the Riot, 1980.

REAME-JAMES, MILTON Keyboards. Member of Steve Harley's Cockney Rebel.

REAY-SMITH, EDWARD Trombone. Session for Aynsley Dunbar (1970).

REBELS See Duane Eddy and the Rebels.

REBELS George Harrison's first group, 1958.

REBENNACK, MACK Real name of Dr. John.

REBILLOT, PATRICK Piano. Session for Steely Dan (1980).

RECORDS John Weeks—guitar, vocal; Huw Gower—vocal, guitar (1979); Jude Cole—guitar, vocal (1980); Phil Brown—bass, vocal; Will Birch—drums, vocal. *Albums:* Crashes (VGN 13140) 1980; The Records (VGN 13130) 1979.

RED HOT WILLIE See Blind Willie McTell.

RED HOT WILLIE GLAZE See Blind Willie McTell.

RED NOISE Bill Nelson—guitar, vocal, drums, keyboards, writer; Rick Ford—bass; Andrew Clark—keyboards, synthesizer; Ian Nelson—saxophone, keyboards. Dissolving the talented yet unrecognized Be Bop Deluxe in 1978, Nelson formed Red Noise in 1979, with as little success. *Album:* Sound on Sound (HAR ST-11931) 1979.

RED RIDER Ken Greer—vocal, guitar, keyboards; Tom Cochrane—vocal, guitar; Peter Boynston—vocal, keyboards; Rob Baker—drums; Jeff Jones—bass, vocal. *Album:* Don't Fight It (CAP ST-12028) 1980.

RED SOX Early name for Freddie and the Dreamers.

REDBONE Lolly Vegas—vocal, guitar, writer; Pat Vegas—vocal, bass; Tony Bellamy—vocal, guitar; Pete DePoe—drums; Butch Rillera—drums, vocal (1973). The promotion read, "America's first Indian rock group." A distinction, yes; a qualification, no. However, their steady rhythms were confident and the musicianship was competent. They enjoyed some notoriety in the late 1960s and survived into the 1970s. *Albums:* Redbone (EPC) 1970; Message From a Drum (EPC); Beaded Dreams Through Turquoise Eyes (EPC); Come and Get Your Redbone/The Best of (EPC) 1975; Cycles (VIC AFLI 2352) 1977; Wovoka (EPC E-32462) 1973.

REDBONE, LEON Guitar, vocal. *Albums:* Champagne Charlie (WBR K-3165) 1978; Double Time (WBR B-2971) 1972; On the Track (WBR B-2888); Leon Redbone (WBR) 1976.

REDD, SHARON Vocal. Session for Leslie West (1976); Boz Scaggs (1980).

REDD, TOMMY Guitar, vocal. Member of Nantucket since 1978.

REDDEN, MIKE Bass. Member of Calico, 1975-76.

REDDING, NOEL DAVID Bass, vocal, guitar, writer. Born 12/25/45. Being a member of Jimi Hendrix's Experience was not a good chance to showcase your talent, but it was worth trading your lead guitar for a bass (1967-69). He left Hendrix in 1969 to form Fat Mattress (until 1970), in which he returned to his lead guitar to play his own compositions. Following Fat Mattress came the Noel Redding Band, 1975-76. Session for Lord Sutch.

NOEL REDDING BAND Noel Redding—bass, guitar, vocal, writer; David Clarke—vocal, keyboards, writer; Eric Bell—guitar; L. T. Sampson—drums, percussion. The question concerning Noel Redding's disappearance after Fat Mattress was answered in 1975 with the appearance of the band bearing his name. The lyrics were a little risque and the music was mildly amusing, but not particularly inspiring. *Albums:* Clonakility Cowboys (VIC APLI 1237); Blowin' (VIC APLI 1863) 1976.

REDDING, OTIS Vocal. Born 9/9/41. Georgia-born Redding was perhaps the single most popular rhythm and blues soul singer in the soul and rock market. Whatever he sang generated energy, from Little Richard rockers to Sam Cooke ballads. His popularity was beginning to take on international proportions when he and the Bar Kays died in the crash of his plane, 12/10/67. *Albums:* Dictionary of Soul; Dock of the Bay; Great Otis Redding Sings Soul Ballads; Otis Blue; Pain in My Heart; Queen; In Person at the Whiskey-A-Go-Go, 1968; Otis Redding (Monterey Pop Festival); Best of Otis Redding (ACO 2-801); Golden Soul (ATC 18198); Here Comes Some Soul from Otis Redding and Joe Curtis (ALS 5082); History of Otis Redding (ACO 261); Immortal Otis Redding (ACO 252); Live in Europe (ACO 286); 1967; Otis Redding (RPS 2029); Soul Years (ATC 2-504); Otis Redding/Jimi Hendrix Experience (RPS 2029) 1970.

REDDY, HELEN Vocal. Number one contender in the pop female vocalist field, Reddy first appeared in the United States in 1966. *Albums:* Free and Easy (CAP ST 11348) 1974; Helen Reddy (CAP ST 857); Car Candy (CAP SO-11640) 1977; I am Woman (CAP ST-11068) 1972; I Don't Know How to Love Him (CAP ST-762); Live in London (CAP SKBO 11873) 1978; Long Hard Climb (CAP SMAS 11213) 1973; Love Song for Jeffrey (CAP S)-11284) 1974; Music, Music (CAP ST-11547) 1976; No Way to Treat a Lady (CAP ST-11418) 1975; Pete's Dragon (CAP SW-11704); Reddy (CAP SO-11949) 1979; Helen Reddy's Greatest Hits (CAP SW-11467); Take What You Find (CAP SOO-12068) 1980; We'll Sing in the Sunshine (CAP SW-11759) 1978; Helen Reddy (CAP ST 857).

REDHEAD, JIMMIE Drums, percussion, vocal. Member of the Matchbox, 1979.

REDING, GREG Piano, guitar, vocal. Half of the Hot Dogs duet, 1973.

REDMAN, JACK Trombone. Session for Richie Furay (1978).

REDMOND, JOHN Keyboards, vocal. Member of the Sea Dog, 1972.

REDS Bruce Cohen—keyboards; Rick Shaffer—guitar, vocal; Tommy Geddes—drums; Jim Peters—bass. *Album:* The Reds (AAM 4772) 1979.

REDUS, RICHARD Guitar, bass. Member of Captain Beefheart's Magic Band, 1978.

REDWING Ron Floegel—guitar, vocal; George Hullin—drums, trumpet, vocal; Tom Phillips—guitar; Andrew Samuels—guitar, vocal. *Albums:* What This Country Needs (FSY 9405); Beyond the Sun and Stars (FSY 9488) 1975.

REDZ, BRIAN Bass. Member of the Gears, 1980.

REEBOP Congas, percussion. Nickname of Reebop Kwaku Baah. First gained notice as a member of Traffic, 1971. Session for Joe Cocker (1972); Jim Capaldi (1971); Alvin Lee (1973); the Rolling Stones (1973); the Rainbow Concert (1973); the Graeme Edge Band (1977); Jess Roden (1974).

REECE, TERRY Drums. Member of the Lonely Boys, 1979.

REED, A. C. Saxophone. Member of Son Seal's Blues Band, 1978.

REED, BLIND ALFRED Vocal. Authentic American folk-blues recordings made between 1927 and 1929. *Album:* How Can a Poor Man Stand Such Times and Live (RND 1001).

REED, ALTO Saxophone, flute. Member of the Silver Bullet Band since 1973. Session for Foghat (1979).

REED, BILL Vocal. Member of the Diamonds.

REED, ERNIE Fiddle, viola, vocal. Member of the Rio Grande Band.

REED, J. MICHAEL Vocal. *Album:* J. Michael Reed (CAS 7177) 1979.

REED, JERRY Session for Ringo Starr (1971).

REED, JIMMY Vocal. Mississippi-born bluesman

who moved to Chicago to sing his country blues. *Albums:* New Jimmy Reed Album, 1967; Big Boss Man, 1968; History of Jimmy Reed; Greatest Hits of Jimmy Reed (KNT 553); Greatest Hits of Jimmy Reed, Vol. 2 (KNT 562); Jimmy Reed (EVR 234); Street Talkin' (MUS 5087); Wailin' the Blues (TRD 2069).

REED, LOU Vocal, guitar, writer, synthesizer, producer. Born 3/2/44. Original member of Andy Warhol's Velvet Underground, 1967-70. In 1972, his first solo LP came out. "Walk on the Wild Side" (1973), his only radio hit, proved his commercial potential, just as his double package of electronic music, "Metal Machine Music," showed his varied tastes. *Albums:* The Bells (ARI 4229) 1979; Coney Island Baby (VIC ANLI 2480) 1976; Growing Up in Public (ARI 9522) 1980; 1969 Velvet Underground Live (MER SRM-2-7504); Lou Reed Live (ARI 8502) 1979; Lou Reed Live (VIC AFLI 0959) 1975; Rock 'n' Roll Animal (VIC AYLI 3664) 1974; Rock and Roll Heart (ARI 4100) 1976; Street Hassle (ARI4169) 1972; Transformer (VIC AFLI 4807) 1972; Walk on the Wild Side (VIC AFLI 2001); Berlin (VIC APLI 0207) 1973; Lou Reed (VIC LSP 4701) 1972; Sally Can't Dance (VIC CPLI 0611) 1975; Metal Machine Music (VIC) 1975; Rock and Roll Diary, 1967-1980 (ARI 8603) 1980.

REED, MIKE Drums, percussion. Member of Jiva, 1975.

REED, SAM Vocal, percussion. Member of the Sunship, 1974.

REEDER, RANDY Drums. Member of Alexis, 1977.

REEKERS, EDWARD Vocal. Added to Kayak line-up, 1978-80.

REELS David Mason—vocal; Colin Newham—keyboards; John Bliss—drums; Paul Abrahams—bass; Craig Hooper—guitar. *Album:* The Reels (POL 1-6275) 1980.

REES-JONES, JOHN Cello. Member of Centipede, 1971.

REESE, AXXEL G. Vocals. Member of the Gears, 1980.

REESE, THAD Bass. Session for Mike Bloomfield (1978).

REEVES, ALAN Keyboards, vocal. Member of the Clinic, 1973.

REEVES, GREG Bass. Member of Crosby, Stills, Nash and Young, 1970-71. Session for Dave Mason; Neil Young (1970).

REEVES, LOIS Vocal. Sister of Martha, she replaced Betty Kelly in Martha and the Vandellas, 1964.

REEVES, MARTHA Vocal. Namesake and star of Martha and the Vandellas, 1962-77. Session for Ringo Starr (1973). *Albums:* Gotta Keep Moving (FSY 9591) 1980; We Meet Again (FSY 9549) 1978; Martha Reeves (MCA).

REEVES, TONY Bass. Member of John Mayall's Bluesbreakers, 1968, replacing John McVie. Original member of Colosseum, 1968-70, and Greenslade.

REFUGEE Lee Jackson—bass; Patrick Moraz—keyboards; Brian Davison—drums. *Album:* Refugee (CSM) 1974.

REGO, HOWARD Drums. Original member of Stardrive, 1974.

REHBEIN, STEVEN Percussion. Member of the Auracle, 1978-79.

REICHENBACH, BILL Trombone. Session for Elton John (1980).

REICHENBACH, GARY Bass. Session for the Marshall Tucker Band (1979).

REID, DAVID Drums. Member of Hi Tension, 1978.

REID, KEITH Lyrics. Co-founder, with Gary Brooker, of Procol Harum, 1966-77.

REID, MICHAEL Guitar, vocal. Member of the Hotel since 1978.

REID, ROGER Drums, vocal. Session for Jorge Santana (1980).

REID, TERRY Guitar, vocal, writer. Backup band: Keith Webb—drums (1968-69); Peter Shelley—organ (1968-69). Reid was still in his teens when he first appeared as head of a trio, 1967. Manager Mickie Most handled the publicity carefully and rumor had it he was the next "big talent" to appear. Just as the rumors looked as if they were true, he dropped out of sight. Graham Nash produced his comeback in 1976. Session for Hoyt Axton (1974). *Albums:* Bang, Bang, You're Terry Reid (EPC BN 26427) 1968; Terry Reid (EPC BN 26477); Seeds of Memory (ABC D 935) 1976; River (ACO) 1973; Rogue Waves (CAP SW-11857) 1979.

REID, WAYMAN Brass. Session for Martin Mull (1977).

REILICH, PETER Keyboards. Member of the Strand, 1980. Session for Gary Wright (1977).

REILLY, DAVE Vocal. Session for Gary Brooker (1979).

REILLY, JIM Drums. Member of the Stiff Little Fingers, 1980.

REILLY, MIKE Bass, vocal. Replaced Jim Lantham in Pure Prairie League, 1975-78.

REINER, SANDY Drums. Member of Raw Milk, 1980.

REINHARDT, LARRY Real name of Rhino.

REIS, STEPHEN Bass, vocal. Member of McGuffey Lane, 1980.

REISING, RICHARD Vocal, guitar, keyboards. Member of the Euclid Beach Band, 1979.

REISMAN, MARC Harmonica, vocal. Member of the Iron City Houserockers since 1979.

REITZES, HOWARD Keyboards, vocal. Member of Iron Butterfly, 1975.

REKOW, RAUL Percussion. Member of Santana, 1977-present.

RELF, JANE Vocal. Member of the Illusion, 1977.

RELF, KEITH Vocal, percussion, harmonica. Born 3/22/41. Original member of the Yardbirds, 1962-69; Renaissance, 1969; and Armageddon, 1975. Died in 1976.

RELLO, GENE Drums. Member of the Marketts, 1973.

REMAINS Barry Tashian—guitar, vocal; Chip Damiani—drums; Vern Miller, Jr.—trumpet, tuba, guitar, french horn, bass; William Briggs—keyboards. Popular New England rockers who failed to capture much renown outside of their homeland. *Album:* Remains, 1967.

REMINGTON, DEREK Drums, vocal. Member of the Trigger, 1978.

RENAISSANCE John Tout—keyboards, vocal; Annie Haslam—vocal (1976-78); Jon Camp—bass, vocal; Terrence Sullivan—drums, percussion; Michael Dunford—guitar, vocal; Jim McCarty—drums, percussion (1969-72); Keith Relf—vocal, harmonica. *Albums:* Ashes Are Burning (CAP ST-11216); Azure D'Or (SIR K-6068) 1979; Bacharach Baroque (RAN 8084); In the Beginning (CAP SWBC-11871) 1978; Live at Carnegie Hall (SIR 2XS 6029) 1976; Novella (SIR 6024) 1972; Prologue (CAP SMAS 11116) 1972; Scheherazade (SIR 6017) 1975; Song for All Seasons (SIR K-6049) 1978; Turn of the Cards (SIR 6015) 1974; Renaissance (TEM 7077).

RENBOURN, JOHN Guitar, vocal, writer. Original member of Pentangle, 1968-72. *Albums:* Lady and the Unicorn (RPS 6407) 1970; John Renbourn (RPS 2-6482); Sir Jon Alot of Merrie Englandes (RPS 6344); The Enchanted Garden (KKM 312) 1980; Stepping Stones (VAN 6506).

RENNIE, BILL Vocal, bass. Half of the Hot Dogs duet, 1973.

RENO, MIKE Vocal. Member of Loverboy, 1980.

RENTON, ANDY Drums. Session for Hapshash and the Coloured Coat.

RENTTE, DAMON Reeds. Member of the Atlantic Starr, 1978-79.

RENWICK, TIM Guitar, steel guitar. Member of Quiver until 1975, the Elton John backup band, 1978, and Lazy Racer since 1979. Session for Gary Brooker (1979); Frankie Miller (1979); Matthew Fisher (1980); Andy Gibb (1980). *Album:* Tim Renwick (Import) 1980.

R.E.O. SPEEDWAGON Gary Richrath—guitar; Gregg Philbin—bass; Alan Gratzer—drums; Terry Lutterell—vocal (1975); Neil Dougherty—keyboards; Kevin Cronin—vocal, guitar; Bruce Hall—bass. *Albums:* Decade of Rock and Roll (EPC KE2-36444) 1980; Lost in a Dream (EPC PE-32948) 1974; Nine Lives (EPC FE-35988) 1979; R.E.O. (EPC PE-34143) 1976; R.E.O. Speedwagon (EPC E-31089); R.E.O. Speedwagon—Live (EPC PEG-34494); R.E.O./T.W.O. (EPC PE-31745) 1972; Ridin' the Storm Out (EPC PE-32378) 1973; This Time We Mean It (EPC PE-3338) 1975; You Can Tune a Piano, But You Can't Tuna Fish (EPC JE-35082); You Get What You Play For (EPC); Hi Infidelity (EPC EE 36844) 1980.

RERRA, LOU Vocal. Member of the Flyer.

RESIDENTS Multimedia stage presentation loosely centered around music. *Albums:* Commercial Album (RLF 80521) 1980; Meet the Residents (RLF 0677) 1974; Not Available (RLF 1174) 1978; The Third Reich and Roll (RLF 1075) 1979; Fingerprince (RLF 1276) 1979; Duck Stab (RLF) 1978; Diskomo (RLF) 1980; Eskimo (RLF) 1979.

RESNICK, RANDY Guitar. Second guitarist to Harvey Mandel in the Pure Food and Drug Act. Played with John Mayall in 1973.

RESURRECTION BAND John Herrin—drums; Glenn Kaiser—vocal, guitar; Wendy Kaiser—vocal; Stu Heis—guitar, keyboards; Jim Denton—bass, guitar, vocal; Tom Cameron—harmonica. *Album:* Awaiting Your Reply (SRS 0011) 1978.

RETALIATION See Aynsley Dunbar's Retaliation.

RETTICK, ROGER Pedal steel guitar. Session for Carlene Carter (1980).

RETURN TO FOREVER Chick Corea—keyboards, percussion, vocal, writer; Stanley Clarke—bass, vocal; Lenny White—drums, percussion; Bill Conners—guitar (1973-74); Al Di Meola—guitar, percussion (1975-77); Joe Farrell—reeds (1978); Gayle Moran—vocal, keyboards (1978); Gerry Brown—drums (1978). Jazz was relatively alien to the rock community until 1973 when Corea organized Return. Corea was already a soloist of renown and each member of his group had played with countless other jazz recording artists. Their sound was very electric, tempered with acoustic interludes, and the combination bridged the gap between rock and jazz. *Albums:* Hymn of the Seventh Galaxy (POL 5536) 1973; Light as a Feather (POL 5525) 1972; No Mystery (POL 6512) 1975; Where Have I Known You Before (POL 6509) 1974; Return to Forever (ECM 1022); Musicmagic (COL PC-34682); Return to Forever Live (COL JC-35281) 1978; Return Live, the Complete Concert (COL C4X 35350); Romantic Warrior (COL PC-34076) 1976; Best of Return to Forever (COL JC 36359) 1980.

REV, MARTIN Electronics. Half of the electronic duet, Suicide, 1980. *Album:* Martin Rev (IFD) 1979.

REVERE, PAUL Piano, organ. Founder and namesake of Paul Revere and the Raiders, 1965-69.

REVEREND ETHER Piano. Session for Pollution (1971).

REVIS, RAY Percussion. Session for Dave Mason (1980).

REWIND, JOHN Guitar. Member of the Hoodoo Rhythm Devils, 1973.

REX Lars Hanson—guitar, keyboards, vocal; Orville

Davis—bass; Rex Smith—vocal; Lou Van Dora—guitar; Mike Ratti—drums. *Album:* Where Do We Go From Here, 1977.

REX, AL Member of Bill Haley and the Comets.

REY, SUZANNE Vocal, percussion. Member of the Euphonius Wall, 1973.

REYES, RICO Vocal, percussion. Member of the Giants, 1978. Session for Santana (1971).

REYMONDO Percussion. Session for Les Dudek (1977).

REYNOLDS, BARRY Session for Marianne Faithfull (1979).

REYNOLDS, BILLY Writer. Session for Waylon Jennings (1973-75); Alabama (1980).

REYNOLDS, EDDY Keyboards. Member of Cottonwood South, 1974.

REYNOLDS, JACK Drums. Member of the Last, 1979.

REYNOLDS, NICK Original member of the Kingston Trio, 1958-66.

REYNOLDS, RICKY Guitar, vocal. Member of Black Oak Arkansas, 1971-77.

REYNOLDS, TOM Original member of the T-Bones, and Hamilton, Joe Frank and Reynolds.

RHINESTONES Harvey Brooks—bass; Kal David—guitar, vocal; Bob Leinbach—keyboards, trombone, vocal; Arti Funard—guitar, vocal; Eric Parker—drums. Shortened name for the re-formed Fabulous Rhinestones, 1972-73. *Album:* The Rhinestones (TWC 489) 1975.

RHINO Guitar. Real name: Larry Reinhardt. Original member of Captain Beyond, 1972-73, 77.

RHINOCEROS John Finley—vocal; Michael Fonfara—organ; Alan Gerber—piano; Doug Hastings—guitar; Billy Mundi—drums; Danny Weiss—guitar; Jerry Penrod—bass. Talented group organized by the Doors' producer, Paul Rothchild, who could not live up to their publicity, despite their talent. *Album:* Rhinoceros (ELK 74056) 1968.

RHODES, BILL Guitar, clarinet, bass. Member of 1994, 1978-79.

RHODES, DAVID Guitar. Member of the Random Hold, 1980.

RHODES, DONNA Vocal, guitar. Member of RCR, 1980. Session for Jackie DeShannon (1972); Tony Joe White (1972); Andy Gibb (1980).

RHODES, DOUG Organ, vocal. Original member of the Music Machine, 1966.

RHODES, LEON Bass. Session for Waylon Jennings (1974).

RHODES, MICHAEL Bass. Member of the Rock Killough Group, 1980.

RHODES, ORVILLE "RED" Steel guitar. Member of the Byrds. Session for Doug Kershaw; Steve Marriott (1976); Nilsson (1972); Free Creek (1973); Kim Fowley; Hoyt Axton (1974); B. W. Stevenson (1973). *Albums:* Red Rhodes Steel Guitar (ALS 5370); Steel Guitar Favorites (ALS 5359).

RHODES, RANDY Guitar. Member of the Blizzard of Ozz, 1980.

RHODES, ROBERT Keyboards, brass. Member of the Beacon Street Union, 1968.

RHODES, RON Drums, vocal. Member of the Shakers.

RHODES, SANDRA Vocal, guitar. Member of RCR, 1980. Session for Jackie DeShannon (1972); Tony Joe White (1972); Firefall (1980); Andy Gibb (1980).

RHONDELLS Early name for the Cyrkle.

RHYNE, CHRIS Keyboards, synthesizer. Member of Santana, 1978. Session for Santana (1979).

RICCI, GEORGE Cello. Session for the James Gang (1975).

RICCIARDELLA, MIKE Drums, percussion. Member of the Illusions, the Wiggy Bits, and Network, 1977.

RICCO Drums. Member of Flash Cadillac.

RICE, JIM Member of Brush Arbor, 1977.

RICE, JOE Member of Brush Arbor, 1977.

RICE, RANDY Bass. Original member of the Eric Burdon Band, 1974.

RICE, TIM Composer. Co-author of "Jesus Christ Superstar," 1970.

RICH, BILLY Bass. Member of Paul Butterfield's Better Days Band. Session for Taj Mahal; Geoff Muldaur (1978).

RICH, BILLY Vocal, guitar. Member of the Sneakers, 1980.

RICH, EDDIE Bass. Session for Taj Mahal (1978).

RICH, HERBIE Organ. Member of the Buddy Miles Express, 1968-69.

RICH, JEFF Drums. Member of the Stretch, 1976-77.

RICH, LEWIS Vocal. Session for the Kinks (1971).

RICH MOUNTAIN TOWER David Carr—guitar; Dana Paul—keyboards, vocal; Bob Tuccillo—drums, percussion; Scott McClure—bass; Michael Fogerty—vocal; David "Butch" McDade—vocal. *Album:* Can't You Feel It (OVA 1709) 1976.

RICHARD, CLIFF Vocal. Real name: Harry Webb. Backed by the Shadows, Richard was an English idol of the late 1950s and 1960s whose popularity was confined mainly to his native land. *Albums:* Every Face Tells a Story, 1977; I'm Nearly Famous (RKT 2210) 1977; We Don't Talk Anymore (EIA SW-17018) 1979; Green Light (RKT BXLI 2958) 1979.

RICHARD, THADDEUS Horns. Session for Wings (1976, 79).

RICHARD, TOMMY Guitar. Member of Cargoe, 1972.

RICHARDS, CYNTHIA Percussion. Member of Skin, Flesh and Bone, 1975.

RICHARDS, EMIL Percussion. Session on the Doors' "Other Voices" (1971); Jimmy Carl Black and Bunk Gardner; Donovan (1976); Nilsson

(1975); George Duke (1975); George Harrison (1974, 76, 79); Nils Lofgren (1976); Frank Zappa (1967); Russ Giguere (1971); Gary Wright (1979).

RICHARDS, KEITH Vocal, guitar, bass, writer. Born 12/18/43. With Mick Jagger, co-author of the material for the Rolling Stones since 1964. Started in Blues Incorporated. Session for Ron Wood (1975-76); Ian McLagen (1979).

RICHARDS, MARK Drums, percussion. Member of Ethos, 1977.

RICHARDS, TERRY Vocal. Voice of Chase, 1971-73.

RICHARDS, TOM Guitar. Member of the Royal Guardsmen, 1969.

RICHARDSON, BILL Guitar. Member of T.I.M.E., 1968.

RICHARDSON, BUDDY Guitar. Member of the White Witch, 1973-74.

RICHARDSON, EDNA Vocal. Session for John Mayall (1978).

RICHARDSON, GEOFFREY Viola, guitar, flute. Member of Caravan, 1976. Session for Cafe Jacques (1977-79).

RICHARDSON, JEROME Flute, clarinet, saxophone. Session for the Bee Gees (1973); Steely Dan (1972-74); Neil Diamond (1976); B. B. King (1977).

RICHARDSON, JILES PERRY Real name of the Big Bopper.

RICHARDSON, JIM Bass. Original member of If, 1973.

RICHARDSON, JOHN Drums, vocal. Member of the Rubettes.

RICHARDSON, KARL Producer. Produced Andy Gibb (1977-present).

RICHARDSON, KIP Percussion, drums. Member of Johnny and the Distractions, 1980.

RICHARDSON, MARK Vocal. Session for the Brains (1980).

RICHARDSON, RALPH Steel drums. Session for Fleetwood Mac (1973); Jim Capaldi (1979).

RICHARDSON, SCOTT Vocal. Voice of S.R.C.

RICHARDSON, SOKO Drums. Played with John Mayall, 1973. Session for Terry Reid (1976); John Mayall (1977-78).

RICHARDSON, VERNA Session for Steve Stills (1978).

RICHARDSON, WENDELL Guitar, vocal. Member of Osibisa.

RICHERT, RALF Guitar, trumpet. Member of the Puzzle.

RICHMAN, SUE Vocal. Member of the Thieves, 1979.

RICHMAN, JONATHAN Vocal, guitar. Member of the Modern Lovers, 1977-78.

RICHMOND, BARD Bass. Session for Peter C. Johnson (1980).

RICHMOND, DANNIE Drums, percussion, vocal. Original member of Mark-Almond, 1970-73. *Album:* Mingus at Antibes (ATC 2-3001).

RICHMOND, DAVE Bass. Session for Elton John (1969).

RICHMOND, FRITZ Washtub bass, percussion. Original member of the Jim Kweskin Jug Band, 1963-68. Session for Ry Cooder (1972). *Album:* What Ever Happened (VAN 79278).

RICHMOND, HAM Piano. Session for Duster Bennett (1968).

RICHMOND, NEIL Electronics. Member of the Seventh Wave, 1975.

RICHRATH, GARY Guitar. Member of the R.E.O. Speedwagon.

RICHSTEIN, LARRY Guitar. Member of Junior Cadillac, using the name Rube Tubin.

RICK, BILLY Bass. Member of Buddy Miles Express, 1968-69.

RICK, RICK L. Vocal. Member of F-Word, 1978.

RICOTTI, FRANK Percussion. Session for Peter Frampton (1972); Trapeze (1972-73); Rick Wakeman (1972, 77-78); Status Quo (1978); Anthony Phillips (1979); Gerry Rafferty (1979-80); the Who (1980).

RIDDLE, PAUL Drums. Original member of the Marshall Tucker Band, 1973-present.

RIDGWAY, STANARD Vocal, organ. Member of the Wall of Voodoo, 1980.

RIDLEY, GREG Bass, vocal. Original member of Spooky Tooth, 1968-69, and Humble Pie, 1969-75. Session for B. B. King (1971); Steve Marriott (1976); the Small Faces (1977).

RIECK, J. C. Piano, vocal. Member of Lance Romance.

RIEFLIN, BILL Drums. Member of the Blackouts, 1980.

RIEL, ALEX Drums. Member of the Savage Rose, 1968-71.

RIETENBACH, JOCHIM Drums. Member of Lucifer's Friend, 1974-75.

RIFKIN, JOSH Member of the Even Dozen Jug Band, 1964.

RIGGS, DON Vocal, drums. Member of the Arthur Gee-Whiz Band, 1971-72.

RIGHTEOUS BROTHERS Bill Medley—vocal, producer; Bobby Hatfield—vocal; Jimmy Walker—vocal. Early name: the Paramours. Originators of "blue-eyed" soul, they began in 1962 with their infectious two-part vocal harmony and combination of jazz-gospel and rock-blues style, releasing hit after hit, including the classics "You've Lost That Lovin Feelin' " (1965), "Just Once in My Life," and "Unchained Melody" (1965). Produced by Phil Spector, they recorded together from 1962 through 1968 and had eighteen singles and over fifteen albums. Medley left in 1968 to go solo. Walker replaced him for a brief period before they disbanded. Hatfield then released a little-known solo LP and he, too, quickly disappeared. The originals teamed up again in 1974 for a comeback, but even they could not fill the void they had created. *Albums:* Give It to the People (HVN ST 9201) 1974; History of the Righteous Brothers (MGM 4845) 1972; Righteous Brothers Greatest Hits, Vol. 1 (VRV 6-5020) 1967; Righteous Brothers Greatest Hits, Vol. 2 (VRV 5-5071) 1967; Sons of Mrs. Righteous (HVN ST 9202) 1975; Soul and Inspiration (VRV 5001) 1966; Right Now, 1963; Some Blue Eyed Soul; This Is New; Best of the Righteous Brothers; You've Lost That Lovin' Feelin' (PHL 4007); Just Once in My Life (PHL 4008); Back to Back, 1966; Go Ahead and Cry, 1966; Sayin' Something, 1967; Souled Out, 1967; Righteous Brothers Standards, 1968; One for the Road, 1968.

RIGHTMER, JERRY Bass. Member of the Sanford-Townsend Band, 1977-79.

RILEY, DOUG Piano. Session for Bob Seger (1978-80); Nils Lofgren (1979).

RILEY, EDGAR, JR. Vocal. Member of the Axe since 1979.

RILEY, HERMAN Baritone saxophone. Session for Dr. John (1979).

RILEY, JOHN Bass. Member of Son Seal's Blues Band, 1973.

RILEY, JOHN Drums. Session for Joe Cocker (1978).

RILEY, MARC Bass. Member of the Fall, 1979.

RILEY, MICHAEL Drums. Member of Stone's Masonry, 1968.

RILEY, PAUL Bass. Session for Dave Edmunds (1977).

RILLERA, BUTCH Drums, vocal. Member of Redbone, 1973.

RIMSON, PAUL Bass. Replaced Phillip Chen in Headstone, 1975, and replaced Doni Harvey in Automatic Man, 1977.

RINDER, LAUREN Percussion. Member of Passion, 1979.

RIO GRANDE BAND Craig Chambers—guitar, vocal; Ben Brogan—bass, vocal; Ernie Reed—fiddle, viola, vocal; Hoot Hester—fiddle, vocal; Bucky Meadows—piano; Chris Laird—drums; Doug Jernigan—steel guitar. *Album:* Rio Grande Band (RND 0105).

RIO NIDO Tim Sparks—vocal, guitar; Prudence Johnson—vocal; Tom Lieberman—vocal, guitar. *Album:* I Like to Riff (SDW 3349) 1978.

RIOT Guy Speranza—vocal; Mark Reale—guitar; Jimmy Iommi—bass; Peter Bitelli—drums; Rick Ventura—guitar. *Album:* Narita (CAP ST-12081) 1980.

RIPPLE, MAX Keyboards. Member of the Deaf School, 1979-80.

RISHELL, PAUL Guitar. Session for Peter C. Johnson (1980).

RISTORI, JEAN Bass, cello, vocal. Member of Mainhorse, 1971.

RITCHIE, IAN Saxophone. Member of the Deaf School, 1979-80.

RITCHIE, JOHN Real name of Sid Vicious.

RITCHIE, JUNE Vocal. Session for the Kinks (1975).

RITENOUR, LEE Guitar. Session for George Duke (1975); Seals and Crofts (1976); Gavin Christopher (1976); Cher Bono (1976); B. B. King (1977); John Palumbo (1978); Flora Purim (1978); Art Garfunkel (1979); the Auracle (1979); John Mayall (1979). *Albums:* Captain Fingers (EPC PE 34426) 1977; Captain's Journey (ELK 6E 136) 1978; Feel the Night (ELK 6E 192) 1979; Guitar Player (MCA 2-6002); Guitar (MCA 2-8012); Friendship (ELK 6E-241) 1979; Best of Lee Ritenour (EPC JE 36527) 1980.

RITGEN, ULE Bass. Member of the Electric Sun, 1979.

RITTER, PRESTON Drums, percussion. Original member of Electric Prunes, 1967.

RITZ, LYLE Bass. Replaced Jamie Leopold in Dan Hicks' Hot Licks, 1978. Session for Russ Giguere (1971); Steven T. (1978); Austin Roberts (1973); Randy Newman; Nilsson (1975).

RIVERA, MARK Saxophone, percussion, vocal. Member of the Tycoon.

RIVERA, PETE Drums, percussion, vocal. Member of Rare Earth.

RIVERA, SCARLET Violin, guitar, vocal. Session for Bob Dylan (1975). *Albums:* Scarlet Rivera (WBR 3060); Scarlet Fever (WBR K-3174) 1978.

RIVERS, JOHNNY Guitar, vocal, writer. Rivers probably enjoyed the most fame of his career as the recorder of "Secret Agent Man," a 1960s television show theme. Other Rivers' hits included "Memphis" and "Poor Side of Town." *Albums:* And I Know You Wanna Dance (IMP 12307) 1971; Here We A-Go-Go Again (IMP 12274); Home Grown (UAR 5532); In Action (IMP 12280); L.A. Reggae (UAR 5650) 1972; Meanwhile Back at the Whiskey A-Go-Go (IMP 12284); Realization (IMP 12372); Rewind (IMP 12341); Rivers' Golden Hits (IMP 12324); Rivers Rocks the Folk (IMP 12293); Road (ATC 7301); Rockin' Rivers (UAR US-LA020-G); Slim, Slo, Slider (IMP 16001); New Lovers and Old Friends, 1975; Blue Suede Shoes (UAR LW-075) 1978; Changes (IMP 12334); Outside Help (SCT 76004) 1977; Johnny Rivers' Greatest Hits (IMP 12324); Touch of Gold (IMP 12427); Johnny Rivers (IMP 12264); Johnny Rivers (UAR USS-93) 1972; Very Best of Johnny Rivers (UAR US-LA387-E); Borrowed Time (RSO 1-3082) 1980; Wild Night (UAR UA-LA486-G) 1976.

RIVERS, TONY Vocal. Session for Dan McCafferty (1975); Danny Kirwan (1979).

RIVETS Jess Roden—vocal, drums, percussion; Peter Wood—keyboards, percusison, vocal; Steve Dwire—bass; Doane Perry—drums. *Album:* Multiplay (ANT 7072) 1980.

RIX, HARRY Drums. Replaced Bob Lamb in the Steve Gibbons Band, 1979-present.
RIX, LEON Drums. Member of the Group Image, 1968.
RIZZO, ANNA Vocal. Session for Mike Bloomfield (1977-78).
RIZZO, PAT Saxophone. Session for Ry Cooder (1978).
ROADMASTER Rick Benick—guitar, vocal; Toby Myers—bass, vocal; Michael Read—keyboards, vocal; Bobby Johns—drums; Stephen "Mac" McNally—vocal. *Albums:* Fortress (MER SRM-1-3814) 1980; Hey World (MER SRM-1-3774) 1979; Sweet Music (MER SRM-1-3760) 1978.
ROADY, TOM Percussion. Session for Art Garfunkel (1978); Roy Orbison (1979); Andy Gibb (1980).
ROBAY, TERRANCE Vocal. Member of the Vivabeat, 1980.
ROBB, TOM Bass. Session for Mylon Le Fevre (1979).
ROBBINS, DENNIS Guitar, vocal. Member of the Rockets since 1977.
ROBBINS, HARGUS Piano. Session for Harvey Mandel; Waylon Jennings (1973); Leon Russell (1973); J. J. Cale (1974); Bill Medley (1978); Levon Helm (1980). *Albums:* Country Instrumentalist of the Year (ELK 7E-1110) 1977; Pig in a Poke (ELK 6E-129) 1978; Unbreakable Hearts (ELK 6E-185) 1979.
ROBBINS, ROBYN Keyboards, vocal. Replaced Rick Manasa in the Silver Bullet Band, 1975-78.
ROBBINS, VERNIE Bass. Session for Paul Simon (1973).
ROBBS Dee Robb; Joe Robb; Bruce Robb; Craig Robb. Though they were never popular, they did not lack for work, backing such early greats as Del Shannon, Bobby Vinton, Gene Pitney, and others, including appearances on Dick Clark's "Where the Action Is." *Album:* The Robbs, 1967.
ROBERT, TONY Began in Blues, Incorporated.
ROBERTS, AL Vocal, bass, keyboards, writer. Original member of Stray Dog, 1973-74.
ROBERTS, ALUN Guitar. Replaced Chris Adams in the String Driven Thing, 1974-75.
ROBERTS, ANDY Guitar. Session for Kevin Ayers (1977); Maddy Prior (1980).
ROBERTS, AUSTIN Vocal. *Albums:* Rocky (PST 5000) 1975; The Last Thing on My Mind (CLS BCLI 0199) 1973.
ROBERTS, BRUCE Guitar, vocal. Member of the Jess Roden Band, 1976. *Albums:* Cool Fool (ELK 6E-262) 1980; Bruce Roberts (ELK 7E-1119) 1977.
ROBERTS, DAVID Guitar. Member of the Mad River, 1968.
ROBERTS, DON Saxophone. Session for Christopher Cross (1980).
ROBERTS, ELLIOT Session for David Crosby (1971).
ROBERTS, GARRY Member of the Boomtown Rats since 1977.
ROBERTS, JAMES Saxophone. Session for Nilsson (1976); John Mayall (1977).
ROBERTS, JIM Vocal. Original member of Seatrain.
ROBERTS, LISA Vocal. Session for Steve Stills (1978).
ROBERTS, PAUL Vocal, guitar. Member of Sniff 'n' the Tears, 1978-80.
ROBERTS, REX Drums, vocal. Member of the King Bees, 1980.
ROBERTS, RICHARD Percussion. Member of the Candle, 1972.
ROBERTS, RICK Guitar, vocal, writer. Replaced Gram Parsons in the Flying Burrito Brothers. Member of Firefall since 1976. Session for Steve Stills (1975); the Robbin Thompson Band (1980). *Albums:* She Is a Song (AAM) 1973; Windmills (AAM 4372) 1972; Best of Rick Roberts (AAM 4744) 1979.
ROBERTS, ROBERT Saxophone. Member of Ruben and the Jets, 1973.
ROBERTSON, BARNEY Piano. Session for Waylon Jennings (1976).
ROBERTSON, BILLY Guitar, vocal. Member of Polyrock, 1980.
ROBERTSON, BOB Saxophone, vocal. Member of Supercharge, 1976-77.
ROBERTSON, BRIAN Guitar, vocal. Member of Thin Lizzy, 1971-77.
ROBERTSON, CHARLES, III Flute, vocal. Member of the Cooper Brothers Band since 1979.
ROBERTSON, CLIFFORD Keyboards. Session for Levon Helm (1980).
ROBERTSON, KEITH Drums. Played with John Mayall, 1963.
ROBERTSON, RICHIE Bass, guitar, keyboards, percussion. Member of the Fabulous Poodles, 1978-79.
ROBERTSON, ROBBIE Guitar, keyboards, writer, producer. Born 7/5/43. Member of the Band, 1963-78. Starred in and produced the movie "Carny," 1980. Session and production for Neil Diamond (1976). Session for John Hammond (1965); Ringo Starr (1973-74); Carly Simon (1974); Rick Danko (1977).
ROBERTSON, TOMMY Guitar, violin, electronics. Member of Polyrock, 1980.
ROBERTSON, VELPO Guitar, vocal. Member of the Robbin Thompson Band, 1980.
ROBERTSON, WILLIAM Guitar, vocal. Georgia-born blues man. *Album:* South Georgia Blues (SLD 5) 1976.
ROBILLARD, DUKE Vocal, guitar. Member of the Roomful of Blues, 1977.
ROBINS, BUTCH Dobro. Session for Leon Russell (1973).
ROBINS, SUSAN Bass, organ. Member of Chichilds,

1980.

ROBINSON, ALBERT Vocal. Session for Bob Dylan (1970); Gregg Allman (1973).

ROBINSON, ALVIN Guitar, vocal. Session for Dr. John (1972, 75); Ringo Starr (1974). *Album:* Original New York Rock and Roll (SSS 6).

ROBINSON, ANDREA Vocal. Member of the Thieves, 1979.

ROBINSON, CHRIS Keyboards. Session for Link Wray (1979).

ROBINSON, CYNTHIA Trumpet, vocal. Member of Sly and the Family Stone.

ROBINSON, DAVID Producer. Producer for Santana (1977-80).

ROBINSON, DAVE Drums, percussion, vocal. Member of the Cars since 1978.

ROBINSON, DIANE Vocal. Session for Any Trouble (1980).

ROBINSON, FREDDY Guitar. Played with John Mayall, 1971-73.

ROBINSON, JANICE Brass. Session for Martin Mull (1977).

ROBINSON, JOHN Session for Dakota (1980).

ROBINSON, LARRY Vocal. Session for George Duke (1975).

ROBINSON, LEE Bass. Session for Arthur Brown (1975).

ROBINSON, PAUL Vocal. Member of the Diodes, 1978.

ROBINSON, PETER Keyboards. Member of Quatermass, 1970, the Hill, 1975, and Brand X, 1979-80. Session for Tim Weisberg (1971); "Jesus Christ Superstar" (1970); Carly Simon (1972); Bryan Ferry (1974).

ROBINSON, PERRY Clarinet. Session for Martin Mull (1974).

ROBINSON, PETE Drums, harmonica, vocal. Original member of Bronco. Session for Jerry Lee Lewis (1973); Shawn Phillips.

ROBINSON, RAY CHARLES Real name of Ray Charles.

ROBINSON, ROLAND Bass, vocal. Replaced Tim Bogert in the New Cactus Band, 1973. Session for Jimi Hendrix's "Nine to the Universe" (1979).

ROBINSON, SANDI Vocal. Member of the Peanut Butter Conspiracy, 1967-68.

ROBINSON, SMOKEY Vocal, writer, producer. Born 2/19/40. Head of the Miracles. *Albums:* Love Breeze (TML T7-359) 1978; Pops We Love You (MTN M7-921); Quiet Storm (TML T7-337); Smokin' (TML T9-363) 1978; Warm Thoughts (TML T8-367) 1980; Where There's Smoke . . . (TML T7-366) 1979; Pure Smokey; Smokey; I'll Try Something New (NTR 4009T1) 1978.

SMOKEY ROBINSON AND THE MIRACLES Ronnie White—vocal; Pete Moore—vocal; Bill Griffin—vocal; Bobby Rogers—vocal; Smokey Robinson—vocal. Rhythm and blues soulists organized by Smokey Robinson, singer, writer, and producer. *Albums:* Hi, We're the Miracles; Cookin' with the Miracles; I'll Try Something New; Fabulous Miracles; Miracles on Stage; Miracles Doin' Mickey's Monkey; Miracles Greatest Hits, 1966; Going to A-Go-Go, 1966; Away We A-Go-Go, 1967; Make It Happen, 1967; Miracles Greatest Hits with Smokey Robinson, 1968; Renaissance, 1973; Four in Blues, 1969; Do It Baby, 1974; Don't Cha Love Me, 1975; Flying High Together, 1972; In Loving Memory; Miracles Greatest Hits, Vol. 2; What Love Has Joined Together; City of Angels, 1975; Power of Music, 1976.

ROBINSON, TODD Guitar. Member of Tim Weisberg's backup group, 1974-78.

ROBINSON, TOM Guitar. Namesake of the Tom Robinson Band since 1978.

TOM ROBINSON BAND Tom Robinson—guitar; Jo Burt—bass; Stevie B.—guitar; Derek Quinton—percussion; Danny Kustow—guitar (1979); Ian Parker—keyboards, vocal (1979). *Albums:* Power in the Darkness (HAR STB 11778) 1978; TRB Two (HAR ST 11930) 1979; Sector 27 (IRS 70013) 1980.

ROBO Drums. Member of the Black Flag.

ROBOT, RONNIE Bass. Member of the Rabbitt, 1976.

ROCHE, MAGGIE Guitar, vocal. Member of the Roches since 1979. Session for Paul Simon (1973).

ROCHE, SUZZY Guitar, vocal. Member of the Roches since 1979.

ROCHE, TERRE Guitar, vocal. Member of the Roches since 1979. Session for Paul Simon (1973); Robert Fripp (1979).

ROCHES Maggie Roche—guitar, vocal; Suzzy Roche—guitar, vocal; Terre Roche—guitar, vocal. *Albums:* The Roches (WBR K-3298) 1979; Nurds (WBR K 3475) 1980.

ROCK ROSE Chris Barr—keyboards, guitar, vocal; Jack D'Amore—drums, vocal; Frank Demme—bass, vocal; Carl Johnson—guitar. *Album:* Rock Rose (COL JC-35819) 1979.

ROCKAWAYS Early name of Jay and the Americans.

ROCKETS Johnny Fraga—bass (1977); Dennis Robbins—guitar, vocal; Dave Gilbert—vocal; Jim McCarty—guitar, vocal; John Badanjek—drums, vocal; Dan Keylon—bass (1979); Donnie Backus—keyboards (1979-present); David Hood—bass (1979-present). *Albums:* Rockets (RSO 1-3047) 1979; No Ballads (RSO 1-3071) 1980; Love Transfusion, 1977.

ROCKICKS Jerry Zubal—guitar; Rick Altschuler—drums; Brian Naughton—guitar; Sam Pate—bass. *Album:* Rockicks (RSO 1-3012) 1977.

ROCKPILE Billy Bremner—guitar, vocal; Dave Edmunds—guitar, vocal, keyboards; Nick Lowe—bass; Terry Williams—drums. Backup band for Dave Edmunds since 1971, though they did not officially tour and record until 1980. See Dave Edmunds.

ROCKSPURS Rich Tannum—vocal, bass; Michael Festa—guitar, vocal, piano, pedal steel guitar; Mike Moran—vocal, guitar, percussion; Peter Brillion—drums, percussion. *Albums:* Getting Off (DJM 25); Rockspurs (DJM 15) 1978.

RODBY, JOHN Piano. Session for Ry Cooder (1978).

RODDY, ROD Keyboards, vocal. Member of Le Roux since 1979.

RODEN, JESS Vocal, guitar, percussion, writer, producer. Founder of Bronco, and the Jess Roden Band, 1976. Member of the Andy Bown group, the Keef Hartley Band, and Rivets, 1980. Session for Jim Capaldi (1975); Mott the Hoople (1971). *Albums:* Blowin' (ISL 9496) 1977; Keep Your Hat On (ISL 9349) 1976; Player Not the Game (ISL 9506) 1977; Stonechaser (ISL 9531) 1980; Jess Roden (ISL 9286) 1974.

JESS RODEN BAND Jess Roden—vocal; Ronnie Taylor—saxophone; Bruce Roberts—guitar, vocal; Steve Webb—guitar, vocal; Chris Gower—trombone; John Cartwright—bass; Pete Hunt—drums. See Jess Roden.

RODEN, SHIRLIE Vocal. Session for Kinks (1975).

RODFORD, JIM Bass, vocal. Original member of Argent, 1970-76, and Phoenix, 1976. Replaced Jim Dalton in the Kinks, 1980.

RODGER, MORT Played with John Mayall, 1961.

RODNEY, MARK Guitar, vocal. Half of the Batdorf and Rodney duet, 1971-75.

RODRIGUES, DENNIS Vocal. Member of the Growl, 1974.

RODRIGUES, DOUGLAS Guitar. Member of Mitch Ryder's backup band, and the Giants, 1978. Session for Santana (1972, 74); Free Creek (1973); Terry Reid (1979).

RODRIGUES, MARTY Drums, vocal. Member of Captain Beyond, 1973.

RODRIGUES, RICO Trombone. Member of the Specials since 1979.

ROE, JESSIE Member of Jelly, 1977.

ROE, TOMMY Vocal. Made "Sheila" a hit in 1962. *Albums:* Energy (MNT MG-7604); Full Bloom (MNT MG-7614) 1977.

ROEDER, KLAUS Violin, guitar. Original member of Kraftwerk, 1974.

ROESBERG, DIETER Guitar, reeds. Member of the Satin Whale, 1975.

ROESER, DONALD Guitar, vocal. Member of the Blue Oyster Cult since 1973.

ROETHLINGER, PAUL Vocal. Member of the Choice, 1980.

ROGERS, BARRY Horns. Member of Dreams, 1970. Session for Roy Buchanan (1976); Dr. John (1978); the Fabulous Rhinestones (1973); Randle Bramblett (1975).

ROGERS, BOBBY Vocal. Member of Smokey Robinson and the Miracles.

ROGERS, JIMMY Guitar. Session for Chuck Berry (1956); Muddy Waters (1978).

ROGERS, MAURICE Piano. Session for Sonny Terry and Brownie McGhee (1973).

ROGERS, MICK Guitar, vocal. Member of Manfred Mann's Earth Band, 1972-75, and Aviator, 1978. Session for Manfred Mann (1980).

ROGERS, PAUL Vocal, piano, guitar, writer. Born 12/12/48. Lead crooner for Free, 1968-73, he left that group to form Bad Company, 1973, under the auspices of Led Zeppelin's Swan Song records.

ROGERS, PHILLIP Bass. Session for George Harrison (1968).

ROGERS, VERLENE Vocal. Session for Neil Diamond (1976).

ROGERS, WANDA Vocal. Original member of the Marvelettes.

ROGERS, WILLIAM Keyboards. Session for the Platinum Hook (1979).

ROGNER, FALK Keyboards. Member of Amon Duul.

ROLAND, DUANE Guitar. Born 12/3/52. Member of Molly Hatchet since 1978.

ROLANDO, LARRY Guitar. Session for Art Garfunkel (1979).

ROLES, JOHN Guitar. Replaced Howard Froese in Chilliwack, 1980.

ROLIE, GREG Keyboards, vocal, writer. An original member of Santana, 1969-72, and Journey 1975-80. Also a member of the Giants, 1978. Session for David Crosby (1971); It's a Beautiful Day (1971).

ROLLING STONES Mick Jagger—vocal, harmonica, guitar; Keith Richard—vocal, guitar, bass; Brian Jones—keyboard, guitar, vocal, harmonica, sitar (1964-69); Bill Wyman—bass; Charlie Watts—drums, percussion; Mick Taylor—guitar (1970-75); Bobby Keys—saxophone (1972); Jim Price—trumpet, trombone (1972); Nicky Hopkins—piano (1972); Ron Wood—guitar (1976-present). While the Beatles brought Victorian rock lyrics to the people, the Stones were busy performing in dirty clothes, singing of drugs, sex, and destruction. Like the rest of the English invasion the Beatles had started in 1964, the base ingredient was the same: extrapolation of American blues. The Beatles had dressed it up for civilization, whereas the Stones played it from the streets. By 1966, the writing team of Jagger and Richards moved to the more melodic with "Aftermath," calming the brute force that existed prior to "Big Hits" (1965). "Their Satanic Majesty's Request" (1967), an answer to the Beatles' "Magical Mystery Tour," was not critically a success, but it confirmed Jagger's identity with hedonism and satanism, which was only a display until then. "Beggar's Banquet" (1968) showed a return to the roots, played with the knowledge of experience. In 1969, the seemingly solid personnel experienced a rift when Jones decided to go solo. Months later, he was found dead in his swimming pool. He was replaced by Mick Taylor, from John Mayall's Blues Breakers. "Let It Bleed" (1970) represented a continuation of the perfection of the early sound, with experimental expansions into country-western and classical choir accompaniment. Further refinement of lyrics was shown in their classic "You Can't Always Get What You Want." By 1972, the tempo had slowed down a bit, but the vocal harmonies and musical arrangements had matured for "Exile on Main Street." "Goat's Head Soup" (1973) was only a parody of themselves. "It's Only Rock 'n' Roll" (1974) and "Black and Blue" (1976) fit their already distinctive sound into a current framework of the disco fad, which no one doubted they could play, anyway. *Albums:* Aftermath (LON PS-476) 1966; Beggars Banquet (LON PS-539) 1968; Between the Buttons (LON PS-499) 1967; Big Hits—High Tide and Green Grass, Vol. 1 (LON NPS-1) 1966; Big Hits—Through the Past Darkly, Vol. 2, 1969; Black and Blue (RLS 79104) 1976; December's Children (LON PS-451) 1965; Emotional Rescue (RLS 2900) 1980; Flowers (LON PS-509) 1967; Get Yer Ya Yas Out (LON NPS-5); Goat's Head Soup (RLS 39106) 1973; Got Live If You Want It (LON PS-493) 1966; Hot Rocks 1964-71 (LON 2PS-606-7); It's Only Rock 'n' Roll (RLS 79101) 1974; Let It Bleed (LON NPS-4) 1970; Love You Live (RLS 2-9001) 1977; Made in the Shade (RLS 39107); More Hot Rocks (LON 2PS-626-27) 1972; Out of Our Heads (LON PS-429) 1965; Rolling Stones (LON PS-375) 1964; Rolling Stones Now (LON PS-420) 1965; Some Girls (RLS 39108) 1978; Sticky Fingers (RLS 39105) 1971; Their Satanic Majesties' Request (LON NPS-2) 1967.

ROLLINS, BILL Cello. Session for Tom Rapp.

ROLLO, ZOOT HORN Guitar, flute. Member of Captain Beefheart and His Magic Band, 1962-72, 74.

ROMAN, CLIFF Guitar. Member of the Wierdos, 1979-80.

ROMAN, GIL Bass, guitar, percussion. Member of Gun Hill Road.

ROMAN, JOE Vocal. Session for the Brains (1980).

ROMAN, JOHN Vocal. Vocalist for Lone Star, 1977.

ROMANTICS Rich Cole; Jimmy Marinos; Wally Palmar; Mike Skill. *Albums:* The Romantics (NMP JZ-36273) 1980; National Breakout (NEM JZ 36881) 1980.

ROMAO, DOM UM Percussion. Added to Weather Report in 1972. *Albums:* Hotmosphere (PAS 2310777) 1976; Om (ECM 19003) 1978; Percussion Profiles (ECM 19002); Dom Um Romao (MUS 5013) 1974; Spirit of the Times (MUS 5049) 1975.

ROME, RICHIE Keyboards, synthesizer, vocal. *Album:* Deep (ELK 6E-256) 1980.

ROMEO, FRANK Member of the Trout.

ROMEO, MAX Vocal. Session for the Rolling Stones (1980). *Albums:* This is Reggae Music, Vol. 3 (ISL 9391); War in Babylon (ISL 9392).

ROMEO, ROGER Guitar, vocal. Member of Legs Diamond, 1977-78.

ROMEO, TONY Member of the Trout.

ROMEOS Jerry Honigman—vocal, guitar; Bootsie Normand—guitar; Dan Diefenderfer—guitar, vocal; Dony Wynn—drums, percussion; Scott Chambers —bass, vocal. *Album:* Rock and Roll and Love and Death (COL WZ 36544) 1980.

ROMERSA, JOE Drums, percussion. Member of the Marc Tanner Band since 1979.

RONDOLONE, TONY Saxophone. Session for the Catfish Hodge Band (1979).

RONETTES A Phil Spector creation, they toured with the Beatles in 1966 and sang "Be My Baby" and "Do I Love You." *Albums:* Ronettes; Ronettes.

RONIN Waddy Wachtell—guitar; Dan Dugmore —guitar, pedal steel guitar; Stanley Sheldon—bass; Rick Marotta—drums. *Album:* Ronin (MER SRM-1-3832) 1980.

RONSON, MICK Guitar, piano, vocal, keyboards, bass, arranger, producer. Production and session for the Iron City Houserockers (1980). Session for David Bowie; Mott the Hoople (1972); Lou Reed (1972); Ian Hunter (1975, 79, 80); Ellen Foley (1979); Annette Peacock (1979).

RONSON, SUZIE Vocal. Session for Ian Hunter (1980).

RONSTADT, LINDA Vocal, guitar. Born 7/15/46. Her country-western vocals first became known in the Stone Poneys, 1967-68. Unofficial First Lady of California, she made her operatic debut in 1980. Session for Neil Young (1972-77); Free Creek (1973); Hoyt Axton (1974); Karla Bonoff (1977); Adam Mitchell (1979); Gram Parsons (1974); Warren Zevon (1980). *Albums:* Different Drum (CAP ST-11269) 1974; Don't Cry Now (ASY 5064); Greatest Hits (ASY 6E-106); Hand Sown (CAP ST-208); Hasten Down the Wind (ASY 7E-1072) 1976; Heart Like a Wheel (CAP SW-11358) 1974; Living in the U.S.A. (ASY 6E-155) 1978; Mad Love (ASY 5E-510) 1980; Prisoner in Disguise (ASY 7E-1045) 1975; Retrospective (CAP SKBB-11629); Linda Ronstadt (CAP SMAS-635); Silk Purse (CAP ST-407); Simple Dreams (ASY 6E-104) 1977; Stone Poneys, Featuring Linda Ronstadt (CAP ST-11383) 1967; Greatest Hits, Vol. 2 (ASY SE-516) 1980.

ROOMFUL OF BLUES Duke Robillard—vocal, guitar; Al Copely—piano; Preston Hubbard—bass, fiddle; John Rossi—drums; Richard Lataille—alto saxophone; Doug James—baritone saxophone; Greg Piccolo—tenor saxophone. *Album:* Roomful of Blues (ISL 9474) 1977.

ROOSHA Vocal. Voice of the Fox.

ROOSTERS Early name for the Impressions, 1958-63.

ROOT BOY SLIM Vocal, harmonica. Head of Root Boy Slim and the Sex Change Band since 1978.

ROOT BOY SLIM AND THE SEX CHANGE BAND Root Boy Slim—vocal, harmonica; E. "Locker Room" Lancaster—guitar; Rattlesnake Rattles—bass; Tommy Ruger—drums (1978); Cosmo Creek—pedal steel guitar (1978); Winston Kelly—keyboards; Ron Holloway—tenor saxophone; Cherie Grasso—vocal; Mickie Lee Jonnie —vocal; A. "Kung Fu" Basher—drums, percussion (1979); Flaco—percussion; Marshall Keys—saxophone (1979). *Albums:* Root Boy Slim and the Sex Change Band with the Rootettes (WBR K-3160) 1978; Zoom (IRS 006) 1979.

ROOVERS, IGOR Bass. Member of the Tapes, 1980.

ROPER, RAY Guitar, vocal. Member of the Stonebolt, 1978-80.

ROPER, TIM Drums. Member of the Ducks Deluxe, 1972-75. Session for Sean Tyla (1980).

ROSAS, RICHARD Bass. Member of Tango, 1974.

ROSBERG, SCOTT Bass, vocal, guitar. Member of Striker, 1978, and Randy Hansen's backup band, 1980.

ROSE David Rose—vocal, violin; Serge Perathoner —keyboards; Gerard Prevost—bass, percussion; Steve Shehan—percussion; Claude Salmieri—drums. *Album:* Worlds Apart (MLN BXLI 7749) 1979.

ROSE, BARRY Pipe organ. Session for Chris Squire (1975).

ROSE, BIFF Vocal. *Albums:* Roast Beef (PFA 108) 1978; Thee Messiah Album (PFA 127) 1978.

ROSE, CHARLES Trombone. Member of the Muscle Shoals Horns. Session for Mike Harrison (1972); Barry Goldberg (1974); Bob Seger (1975); Joe Cocker (1978); Roy Orbison (1979); the Boatz (1979).

ROSE, DAVE Keyboards. Session for Alan Price and Rob Hoeke (1977); the Vapour Trails (1980).

ROSE, DAVE Member of Brush Arbor, 1977.

ROSE, DAVID Violin, vocal. Member of the Transit Express, 1976, and the Rose, 1979.

ROSE, ERIC Guitar. Session for the Paley Brothers (1978).

ROSE, PAUL Guitar, vocal. Member of the Max Demian Band, 1979-80.

ROSE, ROBIN Member of the Urban Verbs, 1980.

ROSE, RON Member of Toby Beau since 1978.

ROSE, TIM Vocal, organ, writer. He began in the Big Three and it seemed that a writer who could co-author the much-recorded "Morning Dew" and the Jimi Hendrix classic "Hey Joe" would have nothing to fear in a solo venture, but he went virtually unnoticed. *Albums:* Tim Rose, 1967; Through Rose Colored Glasses; Unfinished Song (TGL 14052) 1976.

ROSE TATTOO Peter Wells—guitar, vocal; Angry Anderson—vocal; Dallas "Digger" Royall—drums; Geordie Leech—bass; Michael Cocks—guitar. Hard rock from Australia. *Album:* Rock 'n' Roll Outlaw (MIR WTG 19280) 1980.

ROSEBROUGH, RICHARD Drums. Member of the Alamo, 1971. Session for the Hot Dogs (1973).

ROSEBUD Drums. Member of Kenny and the Kasuals.

ROSEN, MICHAEL Guitar, vocal, bass. Member of Eclection, 1968.

ROSEN, MIKE Trumpet. Session for the Keef Hartley Band (1971).

ROSEN, SHELLY Bass. Member of the Sunship, 1974.

ROSENBAUM, ENRICO Vocal, guitar, percussion. Member of the Gypsy, 1971-73.

ROSENBERG, JOHN Horns. Session for Steppenwolf (1974).

ROSENBERG, RICHARD Trombone. Replaced Louie Parente in Southside Johnny and the Asbury Jukes, 1978-present.

ROSENBERG, ROGER Horns. Session for John Lennon (1980).

ROSENTHAL, JURGEN Drums. Replaced Rudy Lenners in the Scorpions.

ROSICA, JIMMY Bass, vocal. Member of the Brooklyn Bridge.

ROSIE David Lasley—vocal; Lynn Pitney—vocal; Lana Marrano—vocal. *Albums:* Last Dance, 1977; Better Late Than Never, 1976.

ROSLIE, GERRY Piano, vocal, writer. Original member of the Sonics, and the Invaders, 1980.

ROSS, ALAN Guitar. Namesake of Ross. Session for John Entwhistle (1972).

ROSS, ALLAN Reeds. Member of the Stanky Brown Group, 1975-76.

ROSS, DAN Steel guitar, guitar, vocal. Member of the Sand, 1973-76.

ROSS, DAVY Drums, vocal. Member of the Headboys, 1979.

ROSS, DIANA Vocal. Born 3/26/44. An original member of the Supremes, 1962-69, before becoming the pop-jazz queen of the 1970s and star of the movie "Lady Sings the Blues." See the Supremes. *Albums:* Last Time I Saw Him; Diana Ross Live at Caesar's Palace, 1974; Touch Me in the Morning; Diana Ross, 1976; The Boss (MTN M7-923) 1979; Diana (MTN M8-936) 1980; Lady Sings the Blues (MTN M7-758) 1972; Pops We Love You (MTN M7-921); Ross (MTN M7-907) 1978; Diana Ross' Greatest Hits (MTN M7-869) 1976; Diana and Marvin (MTN M7-803) 1973; Anthology (MTN 794A3) 1974.

ROSS, JIMMY Tuba, trombone, bass, vocal. Member of the Jaggerz.

ROSS, LEWIS Drums, percussion. Member of Wet Willie, 1972-79.

ROSS, RONNIE Baritone saxophone. Session for Lou Reed (1972); Bryan Ferry (1974).

ROSS Alan Ross—guitar, vocal; Steve Emery—bass, vocal; Bob Jackson—keyboards, vocal; Tony Fernandez—drums; Reuben White—percussion. *Albums:* Pit and the Pendulum (RSO) 1974; Ross (RSO).

ROSS THE BOSS Guitar, vocal. Member of the Dictators, 1977-78, and Shakin' Street, 1980.

ROSSA, DAVID DELLA Guitar, vocal. Member of the Bandit, 1975.

ROSSI, JOHN Drums. Member of the Roomful of Blues, 1977.

ROSSI, MIKE Guitar, vocal. Member of Slaughter, 1980.

ROSSI, MIKE Guitar, vocal. Original member of Status Quo, 1965-present.

ROSSI, WALTER Guitar. Member of the Influence, 1968.

ROSSINGTON, GARY Guitar. Member of Lynyrd Skynyrd, 1973-77, and the Rossington-Collins Band, 1980.

ROSSINGTON-COLLINS BAND Derek Hess—drums, percussion; Dale Krantz—vocal; Gary Rossington—guitar; Allen Collins—guitar; Barry Harwood—guitar, vocal; Billy Powell—keyboards; Leon Wilkeson—bass. Retiring the Lynyrd Skynyrd name after the tragic airplane crash in 1977, Rossington and Collins regrouped in 1980. *Album:* Anytime, Anyplace, Anywhere (MCA 5130) 1980.

ROTA, SAL Keyboards, vocal. Member of Crystal Mansion.

ROTARY CONNECTION Canadian answer to the Vanilla Fudge, 1968-69, specializing in heavy arrangements of then current rock material, rather than original writings. *Albums:* Rotary Connection, 1968; Rotary Connection, 1968; Peace at Last, 1968; Songs; Dinner Music.

ROTELLA, JOHNNY Woodwinds, horns. Session for the Mothers of Invention (1972); Nilsson (1975-76); Country Joe McDonald (1975).

ROTH, ARLEN Guitar, bass, vocal. *Albums:* Guitarists (RND 3022); Hot Pickups (RND 3044).

ROTH, DAVID LEE Vocal. Member of Van Halen since 1978.

ROTH, ULRICH Guitar, vocal. Member of the Scorpions, 1974-78, and Electric Sun, 1979.

ROTHCHILD, PAUL Producer. Produced the Doors (1967-71); Clear Light (1967); Fred Neil; and others.

ROTHERMEL, JIM Horns, clarinet. Session for Boz Scaggs (1972); the Pointer Sisters (1974).

ROTHSTEIN, DAN Guitar. Session for Rob Stoner (1980).

ROTTEN, JOHNNY Vocal. Real name: Johnny Lydon. Voice of the Sex Pistols, 1977. See John Lydon.

ROUGH DIAMOND David Byron—vocal; Clem Clempson—guitar; Geoff Britton—drums; Damon Butcher—keyboards; Willie Bath—bass. Formed by ex-Uriah Heep member Byron and Humble Pie's Clempson. *Album:* Rough Diamond (UL 9490) 1977.

ROUGH MIX Pete Townshend—guitar, vocal, keyboards, writer, producer; Ronnie Lane—guitar, vocal. The teaming of the Who's Townshend and the recently deposed Small Faces' Lane led to what was called the most enjoyable rock album of 1977, "Rough Mix." *Album:* Rough Mix (MCA 2295) 1977.

ROULETTE, FREDDIE Steel guitar. Session for Harvey Mandel (1972).

ROUSSEL, JEAN Keyboards. Member of the Keef Hartley Band. Session for Donovan (1973); Cat Stevens (1972-76); Ron Wood (1976); Trapeze (1974); Jim Capaldi (1973); Mick Taylor (1979).

ROUSSOS, DEMIS Bass, vocal. Member of Aphrodite's Child. *Album:* Demis Roussos (MER SRM-1-3724) 1978.

ROUTEN, IRMA Vocal. Session for Boz Scaggs (1969).

ROWAN, CHRIS Vocal, keyboards, guitar, flute. Member of the Rowans, 1975-77.

ROWAN, LORIN Vocal, guitar, piano. Member of the Rowans, 1975-77.

ROWAN, PETER Guitar, saxophone, vocal, writer. Member of the Earth Opera, 1968-69. Soloist after leaving Seatrain, and his brothers in the Rowans, 1975-77. *Albums:* Festival Tapes (FLF 068); Medicine Trail (FLF 205) 1980; Peter Rowan (FLF 071) 1978.

ROWANS Peter Rowan—vocal, guitar, mandolin, percussion; Chris Rowan—vocal, keyboards, guitar, flute; Lorin Rowan—vocal, guitar, piano. *Albums:* Jubilation (ASY 7E-1114) 1977; The Rowans (ASY 7E-1038) 1975; Sibling Rivalry (ASY 1073) 1976.

ROWBERRY, DAVE Organ. Member of the Animals until 1966.

ROWE, BOB Bass. Member of the Andy Fernbach Connexion.

ROWE, CHUCK Clarinet. Session for Flint (1978).

ROWE, EDWARD Trumpet. Session for B. B. King (1972-75).

ROWLAND, BRUCE Drums, percussion. Member of the Grease Band, 1971. Added to Fairport Convention, 1974. Session for Mike Vernon; "Jesus Christ Superstar" (1970); Bryan Ferry (1974); Chris Youlden (1973-74); Tim Renwick (1980); Dave Swarbrick (1976).

ROWLAND, PHIL Drums, percussion. Member of Slaughter, 1980.

ROWLANDSON, STEVE Violin. Member of Centipede, 1971. Session for Jerry Lee Lewis (1973).

ROWLES, GARY Guitar. Session for Leon Russell

(1976); John Mayall (1977).

ROWLEY, NICK Keyboards. Session for Kevin Ayers (1977).

ROWLEY, TERRY Synthesizer, keyboards, string arranger. Session for Trapeze (1973-74, 80).

ROXY MUSIC Phil Manzanera—guitar; Rik Kenton—bass (1972); Paul Thompson—drums (1972-78); Andrew Mackay—oboe, saxophone; Bryan Ferry—vocal; Eno—synthesizer (1972-73); Johnny Gustafson—bass (1974-77); Eddie Jobson—violin, keyboards, synthesizer (1974-78); Alan Spenner—bass (1978); Paul Carrack—keyboards, vocal (1979); Gary Tibbs—bass (1979). With Ferry's eerie, often macabre tales of love and frustration, Roxy is a band of originality and distinction. His mesmerizing vocals and Manzanera's arrangements set standards "New Wave" artists would follow years later. Adjusting personnel in 1979, Roxy settled to the nucleus of Ferry, Manzanera, and MacKay, with session support. *Albums:* Country Life (ACO 36-806) 1974; Flesh and Blood (ACO 32-102) 1980; For Your Pleasure (ACO 36-103) 1973; Manifesto (ACO 38-114) 1979; Roxy Music (ACO 36-133) 1972; Siren (ACO 36-127) 1975; Stranded (ACO 7045) 1974; Viva (ACO 36-139) 1976.

ROYAL, BILLY JOE Vocal. Recorded "Down in the Boondocks," 1965. *Album:* Billy Joe Royal (MER SRM-1-3837) 1980.

ROYAL, ERNIE Trumpet. Session for B. B. King (1972); Muddy Waters (1972).

ROYAL, WILBUR Trumpet. Session for Barry Goldberg (1969).

ROYAL GUARDSMEN Chris Nunley—vocal; Barry Winslow—vocal, guitar; Tom Richards—guitar; Bill Balough—guitar; Billy Taylor—organ; John Burdett—drums. Novelty rock was reaching its limits when the Guardsmen made a number one hit of the comic character Snoopy, in "Snoopy Versus the Red Baron" (1969). They attempted repeat performances on the same theme, but even their novelty lost its novelty. *Albums:* Return of the Red Baron (LAU 2039); Snoopy and His Friends (LAU 2042); Snoopy for President (LAU 2046); Snoopy Vs. the Red Baron (LAU 2038).

ROYAL TEENS Recorded "Short Shorts," 1957.

ROYALL, DALLAS "DIGGER" Drums. Member of the Rose Tattoo, 1980.

ROYER, RAY Guitar. Original member of Procol Harum in 1966, replaced by Robin Trower in 1967.

ROYER, ROB Original member of Bread, 1971.

ROZETTA Vocal. *Album:* Where's My Hero (TWC 602) 1980.

RUBBER CITY REBELS Rod Firestone—guitar, vocal; Buzz Clic—guitar, vocal; Johnny Bethesda—bass, vocal; Brandon Matheson—drums, vocal. *Album:* Rubber City Rebels (CAP ST-12100) 1980.

RUBEN AND THE JETS Ruben Guevera—vocal, percussion; Tony Duran—guitar, slide guitar, vocal; Robert Camarena—guitar, vocal; Johnny Martinez—bass, vocal; Robert Roberts—saxophone; Bill Wild—bass, vocal; Bob Zamora—drums; Jim Sherwood—saxophone, percussion. *Albums:* For Real (MER) 1973; Cow Safos (MER) 1973.

RUBETTES Pete Arnesen—piano, vocal; Bill Hurd—piano, vocal; Tony Thorpe—guitar, vocal; John Richardson—drums, vocal; Mick Clarke—bass, vocal; Alan Williams—guitar, vocal. *Album:* Wear It's At (POL).

RUBICON Greg Eckler; Dennis Marcellino—saxophone; Jack Baldes—bass; Jimmy Pugh; Jerry Martini—saxophone; Bradley Gillis; Max Haskett. *Albums:* Rubicon (TWC 552) 1978; America Dreams (TWC 577) 1979.

RUBIN, ALAN Trumpet. Member of Blood, Sweat and Tears. Session for Johnny Winter (1973); Jan Akkerman (1973); Free Creek (1973); Lou Reed (1974); the Blues Brothers (1978-80).

RUBIN, EDDIE Drums. Former backup for Neil Diamond.

RUBIN, JON Vocal, guitar. Member of the Rubinoos, 1977-79.

RUBIN, LYNN Vocal. Session for Gregg Allman (1974).

RUBINHOLD, LEON Guitar. Member of the Rainbow Red Oxidizer, 1980.

RUBINOOS Jon Rubin—vocal, guitar; Don Spindt—drums; Royse Ader—bass; Tommy Dunbar—guitar, keyboards. *Albums:* Rubinoos, 1977; Back to the Drawing Board (BSK 10061) 1979.

RUBINSTEIN, JOHN Keyboards, vocal. Member of the Fun Zone, 1977.

RUBY Tom Fogerty—guitar, vocal; Bobby Cochran—drums, vocal; Anthony Davis—bass, vocal; Randy Oda—guitar, keyboards, vocal. *Album:* Ruby (PBR 7001) 1976.

RUBY, FRANK Guitar. Member of the Flame, 1977.

RUBY, ROY Bass. Chicago blues man who played with Harvey Mandel and Charlie Musselwhite in the mid-1960s. Member of the Barry Goldberg Blues Band. Session for Barry McGuire.

RUCKER, KARL Bass, guitar. Member of the Giants, 1976.

RUDD, PHIL Drums. Member of AC/DC since 1977.

RUDES, JORDAN Keyboards. Member of Speedway Blvd., 1980.

RUDIGER, GEORGE Drums. Member of Junior Cadillac.

RUDNYTSKY, DORIAN Piano, cello, guitar, trumpet, french horn. Member of the New York Rock and Roll Ensemble, 1968-69.

RUEGER, GLENN Keyboards, vocal. Member of Upepo.

RUFF, CHUCK Drums, vocal. Member of Sawbuck, 1971, and the Edgar Winter Group. Session for Johnny and Edgar Winter (1976); Sammy Hagar

(1978-80).

RUFF, MICHAEL Keyboards. Session for Randy Vanwarmer (1979).

RUFF, WILLIE Acoustic bass. Session on the Doors' "Other Voices," 1971.

RUFFIN, DAVID Vocal. Original member of the Temptations, 1964-68. *Albums:* David Ruffin at His Best (MTN M7-895) 1977; So Soon We Change (WBR K-3306) 1979; Gentleman Ruffin (WBR K-3416) 1980; In My Stride (MTN M6-885) 1977.

RUFFY, DAVE Drums, percussion, vocal. Member of the Ruts, 1979.

RUGER, TOMMY Drums. Member of Root Boy Slim and the Sex Change Band, 1978.

RUGG, HAL Steel guitar. Session for Leon Russell (1973).

RUGSTED, JENS Bass, vocal. Member of the Savage Rose, 1968-71.

RUHL, GARY Bass. Member of Gabriel, 1975.

RUITER, BERT Bass. Member of Focus. Session for Jan Akkerman (1972).

RUIZ, MICHAEL Drums. Member of the Beat, 1979.

RUMMANS, MICHAEL Bass, vocal. Member of the Hollywood Stars, 1977, and the King Bees, 1980.

RUMOR BRASS SECTION John Earle—baritone saxophone; Dick Hanson—trumpet; Ray Beavis—tenor saxophone. Session for the Inmates (1979).

RUMOUR Brinsly Schwartz—guitar; Bob Andrews—keyboards; Martin Belmont—guitar; Steve Goulding—drums; Andrew Bodmar—bass. Gained notoriety backing Graham Parker. See Graham Parker. *Albums:* Frogs, Sprouts, Clogs and Krauts (ARI 4235) 1979; Squeezing Out Sparks (ARI 4223); Stick to Me (MER SRM-1-3706) 1977; Up Escalator (ARI 9517); Max (MER SRM 11174) 1977.

RUMPH, INGA Vocal, guitar. Member of Frumpy, 1973.

RUMPH, STEVE Drums. Original member of T.I.M.E., 1968.

RUNAWAYS John Jett—guitar, vocal; Lita Ford—guitar; Vicki Blue; Sandy West—drums, vocal; Jacki Fox—bass, vocal (1976); Cherie Currie—vocal, piano (1976). *Albums:* Queens of Noise (MER SRM I 1126); The Runaways (MER SRM I 1090) 1976; Waitin' for the Night (MER SRM I 3705) 1977.

RUNDGREN, TODD Mellotron, guitar, producer. Born 6/22/48. First appeared as head of Nazz, 1968-69. Also recorded under his nickname, "Runt." Head of Utopia, a multi-keyboard rock group since 1974. Produced Steve Hillage (1976); the Tom Robinson Band (1979); Patti Smith (1979); Shaun Cassidy (1980). Session for Flint (1978); Roger Powell (1980); Johnny Winter (1973); Free Creek (1973); Hall and Oates (1974). *Albums:* Back to the Bars (BSV 2BRX 6986) 1978; Faithful (BSV 6963) 1976; Hermit of Mink Hollow (BSV K6981) 1978; Initiation (BSV 6957) 1974; Something/Anything (BSV 2BX-2066) 1972; Todd (BSV 2B-6952) 1974; Wizard, a True Star (BSV 2133) 1972.

RUNDQUIST, CHRISTY Synthesizer. Member of Raw Milk, 1970.

RUNNER Steve Gould—vocal, guitar; Mickie Feat—bass, vocal; Dave Dowle—drums; Allan Merrill—guitar, keyboards, vocal. *Album:* Runner (ISL 9536) 1979.

RUNSWICK, DARRYL String bass. Session for the Alan Parsons Project (1976).

RUSH Alex Lifesong—guitar; Geddy Lee—bass, vocal; Neil Peart—drums (1975-present); John Rutsey—drums (1974). Canadian heavy metal rock trio that began in 1974. *Albums:* All the World's a Stage (MER SRM-2-7508); Archives (MER SRM-3-9200); Caress of Steel (MER SRM 1-1045); Farewell to Kings (MER SRM-1-1184) 1977; Fly by Night (MER SRM-1-1023) 1975; Hemispheres (MER SRM-1-3743) 1978; Permanent Waves (MER SRM-1-4001) 1980; Rush (MER SRM-1-1011) 1974; 2112 (MER SRM-1-1079.

RUSH, BILLY Guitar. Member of Southside Johnny and the Asbury Jukes since 1976.

RUSH, MERILEE Vocal. With her group, the Turnabouts, she sang "Angel of the Morning."

RUSH, OTIS Guitar, vocal. Chicago blues guitarist who first became known in 1956. *Albums:* Door to Door; Cold Day in Hell (DEL 638) 1975; So Many Roads (DEL 643) 1978.

RUSH, PAT Guitar. Member of the Thunderhead, 1976. Session for Johnny Winter (1978).

RUSH, TOM Vocal, guitar. Folk singer from Massachusetts whose fame did not grow as greatly as that of his contemporaries, Joan Baez and Joni Mitchell. *Albums:* Best of Tom Rush (COL PC-33907) 1976; Circle Game (ELK 74018) 1968; Classic Rush (ELK 74062) 1970; Ladies Love Outlaws (COL C-33054) 1974; Merrimack County (COL C-31306) 1963; Mind Rambling (PRS 7536) 1963; Tom Rush (COL CS 9972); Tom Rush (ELK 7288); Tom Rush (FSY 4709); Take a Little Walk with Me (ELK 7308); Wrong End of the Rainbow (COL C-30402) 1970; Got a Mind to Ramble (PRS 7536) 1963.

RUSHKENT, MARTIN Producer. Produced Generation X (1978); 999 (1980); and others.

RUSHTON, MICHAEL Drums. Original member of Steamhammer, 1969.

RUSSELL, BILL Bass. Member of Shoot, 1973.

RUSSELL, BRENDA Vocal. Session for Neil Sedaka (1975). *Album:* Brenda Russell (AAM 739) 1979.

RUSSELL, BRIAN Vocal. Session for Neil Sedaka (1975).

RUSSELL, GRAHAM Vocal. Member of Air Supply.

RUSSELL, JIM Drums, vocal. Member of the Inmates since 1979. Session for Danny Kirwan.

RUSSELL, KEVIN Guitar, vocal. Member of 707, 1980.

RUSSELL, LEON Keyboards, vocal, guitar, writer, producer. Founder of Shelter Records. First brought to the public's attention in a two-man band with Marc Benno, the Asylum Choir, in the late sixties. Before seriously embarking on his solo career, he worked with Joe Cocker's "Greatest Show on Earth," 1970, Delaney and Bonnie, and produced Bob Dylan. His raspy voice, styled after Dr. John, gave rise to the southern and country influences of rock today. In 1979, he teamed with Willie Nelson for a double set of updated country hits. See Leon and Mary Russell. Session and production for Freddie King (1971-73); Gary Ogan (1977). Session for Dave Mason; Nilsson (1975); Bill Wyman (1974); Bangla Desh (1971); Eric Clapton (1970); George Harrison (1975); Jan and Dean (1963); B. B. King (1970-71); the Ventures. Horn arrangements for the Rolling Stones (1970). *Albums:* Americana (PDS K-3172) 1978; Best of Leon Russell (MCA 52004); Carney (MCA 52011) 1972; Life and Love (PDS K-3341) 1979; Looking Back (OLR 7112); One for the Road (COL KC2-36064) 1979; Leon Russell (MCA 52007); Leon Russell and the Shelter People (MCA 52008); Will o' the Wisp (MCA 52020) 1975; Stop All That Jazz (SHL 2108) 1974; Hank Wilson's Back (SHL 8923) 1973.

RUSSELL, MARY Vocal. Wife of Leon Russell. See Leon and Mary Russell. *Album:* Heart of Fire (PDS K-3292) 1979.

LEON AND MARY RUSSELL Husband-wife recording team formed after the vows in 1976. See individual listings. *Albums:* Make Love to the Music (PDS 3066) 1977; Wedding Album (PDS 2943) 1976.

RUSSELL, RAY Guitar. Replaced Ray Minhinnet in Frankie Miller's Full House, 1978.

RUSSIA Larry Tuttle—bass, vocal; Richard Allyn White—keyboards, vocal; Thomas Richard Brighton—guitar, vocal; Jeff Swisstack—drums. *Album:* Russia (WBR K-3414) 1980.

RUTHERFORD, MICHAEL Guitar, bass, sitar. Born 12/2/50. Member of Genesis. Session for Anthony Phillips (1977). *Album:* Smallcreep's Day (CMA 1-2212) 1980.

RUTHERFORD, PAUL Trombone. Member of Centipede, 1971. Session for Lo and Behold (1972); Manfred Mann (1973).

RUTLEDGE, JIM Vocal. Replaced Warren Ham in Bloodrock, 1972.

RUTLES Dirk McQuickly (Eric Idle)—guitar, keyboards, vocal; Ron Nasty (Neil Innes)—guitar, keyboards, vocal; Stig O'Hara (Ricky Fataar)—guitar, bass, sitar, tabla, vocal; Barry Wom (John Halsey)—percussion. Parody of the Beatles written and produced by Eric Idle of Monty Python. *Album:* The Rutles (WBR 3151) 1978.

RUTLEY, TOM Acoustic bass. Session for Santana (1972).

RUTS Paul Fox—guitar, vocal, organ; Segs—bass, vocal; Malcolm Diven—vocal; Dave Ruffy—drums, percussion, vocal. *Album:* The Crack (VIR 2132) 1979.

RUTSEY, JOHN Drums. Member of Rush, 1974.

RUVIO, JOE Saxophone, vocal. Member of the Brooklyn Bridge.

RYAN, CHICO Bass. Replaced Bruce Clarke in Sha Na Na, 1973-present.

RYAN, CLINT Vocal. Session for Triumph (1979).

RYAN, JIM Guitar. Member of the Critters, 1966.

RYAN, JIM Bass, guitar. Member of Ox, 1975. Session for Carly Simon (1972-74); Matthew Fisher (1974); Cat Stevens (1975).

RYAN, JOHN Bass. Session for Cat Stevens (1970).

RYAN, MARK Bass. Member of Country Joe and the Fish, 1968, and Marty Balin's Jefferson Airplane on "Bodacious." Replaced David Freiberg in the Quicksilver Messenger Service. Session for Peter Kaukonen (1972).

RYAN, PAT Guitar. Member of the Nuns, 1980.

RYAN, PAUL Saxophone. Session for the Fingerprintz (1980).

RYAN, PHIL Keyboards, vocal. Replaced Clive John in Man. Member of the Neutrons, 1974.

RYAN, TERRY Keyboards. Member of the Eric Burdon Band, 1975.

RYDELL, BOBBY Vocal. Recorded "Volare," 1960. *Album:* Bye Bye Birdie (VIC LSO 1081).

RYDER, MITCH Vocal. Founder of Mitch Ryder and the Detroit Wheels. *Albums:* Naked But Not Dead (SAS 7804) 1979; How I Spent My Vacation (SAS 7801) 1978; The Detroit/Memphis Experiment (DOT 25963).

MITCH RYDER AND THE DETROIT WHEELS Mitch Ryder—vocal; James McCarty—vocal, keyboards, guitar; Johnny Bee Badanjek—drums, vocal; Joe Kubert; James McAllister. In 1967, Ryder's hits, "Jenny Take a Ride" and "Devil with a Blue Dress On/Good Golly Miss Molly," kept audiences dancing and screaming for more. *Albums:* Take a Ride, 1966; Breakout, 1967; Sock It to Me, 1967; What Now My Love, 1967; All Mitch Ryder Hits.

RYE, STEVE Guitar, vocal, writer. Soloist who was part of the British blues invasion of the 1960s that did not make it in the United States, except for a brief appearance as an original member of the Groundhogs, 1968.

RYNOSKI, MICHAEL Replaced Buzz Sherman in Moxy, 1978.

RYSER, SCOTT Synthesizer, vocal. Member of the Units, 1980.

S.C.R.A. Mickey Leyton—vocal; Sheryl Black—vocal; Ian Saxon—vocal; Peter Martin—guitar; Jim Kelly—guitar; Dave Ellis—bass; Russell Dunlop—drums; Ian Bloxsom—percussion; Mick Kenny—trumpet; Don Wright—reeds; Greg Foster—trombone, percussion. Initials stand for Southern Contemporary Rock Assembly. *Album:* The Ship Album (ATC 7235) 1972.

S-H-F BAND See Souther-Hillman-Furay Band.

SAAD, JIM Drums. Member of Vance or Towers, 1975.

SABELLA Drums, synthesizer, percussion. Member of the Indoor Life, 1980.

SABIN, JOHN Guitar. Member of Chrysalis, 1968.

SABINO, ROBERT Keyboards. Member of the Simms Brothers Band, 1979-80.

SAD CAFE Paul Young—vocal, percussion; Ashley Mulford—guitar; Vic Emerson—keyboards; John Stimpson—bass, guitar, vocal; Ian Wilson—guitar, vocal, percussion; Tony Cresswell—drums (1978); Dave Irving—drums (1979). *Albums:* Facades (AAM 4779) 1979; Misplaced Ideals (AAM 4737) 1978.

SADLER, SGT. BARRY Vocal. Romantic patriot who scored in 1966 with his single, "Ballad of the Green Berets."

SADLER, TIM Vocal. Session for Long John Baldry (1979).

SAFKA, MELANIE Real name of Melanie.

SAFRON, MIKE Drums, percussion. Original member of Pavlov's Dog, 1975.

SAGE, GREG Guitar, vocal. Member of the Wipers, 1980.

SAGE, PETE Violin, bass, mandolin. Member of Wally, 1974.

SAGE See the Paul Brett Sage.

SAGER, CAROLE BAYER Vocal. *Albums:* Carole Bayer Sager (ELK 7E 1100) 1977; Too (ELK 6E 151) 1978.

SAGER, GARETH Guitar, horns. Member of the Pop Group, 1980.

SAHB Zal Cleminson—guitar; Chris Glen—bass; Hugh McKenna—keyboards, vocal; Ted McKenna—drums, percussion. The Sensational Alex Harvey Band without Harvey. *Album:* Fourplay (MNT TOPC 5006) 1976.

SAHM, DOUG Guitar, fiddle, vocal. Founder of the Sir Douglas Quintet, 1965-68. Session for Willie Nelson (1973). *Album:* Hell of a Spell (TKM 7075) 1980.

SAIL Salvatore Alberico, Jr.—saxophone, clarinet; Paul Angerosa—guitar; Vincent C. Esposito—keyboards, vocal; Michael Della Gala—bass, vocal; Patrick Putrello—trumpet, flugelhorn; Maurice Putrello—drums; Duane C. Walker—percussion, vocal. *Album:* Steppin' Out on Saturday Night (UAR LT 906).

SAILOR Grant Serpell—drums, vocal; Phil Pickett—bass, piano, vocal (1974-75); Henry Marsh—keyboards, vocal; Georg Kajanus—guitar; Gavin David—vocal (1980); Virginia David—vocal (1980); J.W.G.—bass, guitar, vocal (1980); James Stroud—drums (1980). *Albums:* Sailor (EPC); Trouble (EPC) 1975; Dressed for Drowning (CRB NJZ 36746) 1980.

SAINTE GERMAIN, RONNIE Percussion. Session for Ray Gomez (1980).

SAINTE-MARIE, BUFFY Vocal, guitar. Born 2/20/41. One of the more vehement protesters in the folk era, Indian-born Sainte-Marie's hit, "Universal Soldier," established her immediately as a major force in the folk field of the early 1960s. *Albums:* Buffy (MCA 405); Performance (WBR B 2554); It's My Way (VAN 79142) 1964; Best of Buffy Sainte-Marie (VAN VSD 33/34); Festival of Acoustic Music (FSY 79009); Fire and Fleet and Candlelight (VAN 79250) 1967; Illuminations (VAN 79300); I'm Gonna Be a Country Girl Again (VAN 79280) 1968; Little Wheel Spin and Spin (VAN 79211) 1966; Many a Mile (VAN 79171) 1965; Moonshot (VAN 79312); Native North American Child (An Odyssey) (VAN 79340) 1974; Newport Folk Music Festival (VAN 79184); Quiet Places (VAN 79330) 1973; She Used to Wanna Be a Ballerina (VAN 79311); Sweet America (ABC 929) 1976.

SAINTS Chris Bailey—vocal; Ed Kuepper—guitar; Kym Bradshaw—bass; Ivor Hay—drums. *Albums:* I'm Stranded (SIR 6039) 1977; Eternally Yours (SIR K-6055) 1978.

SAKAMOTO, RYULCHI Keyboards, percussion. Member of the Yellow Magic Orchestra, 1979-80.

SALAMON, ROSS Drums. Session for Danny Spanos (1980).

SALAS, RUSTY Guitar, vocal. Member of the Tierra, 1980.

SALAS, STEVE Vocal, trombone, percussion. Member of the Tierra, 1980.

SALAZAR, VICTOR Percussion. Member of the Jeremy Spencer Band, 1979.

SALEM, FREDDIE Guitar, vocal. Replaced Henry Paul in the Outlaws, 1979-present.

SALEM, JEFF Guitar. Member of the Tuff Darts, 1978.

SALES, HUNT Drums. Replaced Thom Mooney in Paris, 1976. Member of Iggy Pop's backup band, 1977.

SALES, TONY Bass. Member of Iggy Pop's backup band, 1977.

SALESTROM, CHUCK Bass, vocal. Member of the Timberline, 1977.

SALESTROM, JIM Vocal, guitar, banjo. Member of the Timberline, 1977.

SALGADO, CURTIS Harmonica, vocal. Member of the Robert Cray Band, 1980.

SALINAS, TONY Guitar. Member of Laurie and the Sighs, 1980.

SALISBURY, TOM Keyboards, accordion. Accompanist of the Pointer Sisters, 1974-75.

SALLINGS, MARK Reeds, harmonica, vocal. Member of the Coon Elder Band, 1977.

SALMIERI, CLAUDE Drums. Member of the Rose, 1979.

SALMON, ANDY Bass. Session for Christopher Cross (1980).

SALONONSON, CHANNA Violin. Member of Centipede, 1971.

SALTER, BILL Bass. Session for Pearls Before Swine (1969).

SALTZMAN, LARRY Guitar. Member of the Love of Life Orchestra since 1979.

SALTZMAN, STAN Saxophone. Member of Savoy Brown, 1973. Session for Memphis Slim (1971); Brian Protheroe (1976).

SALVONI, LUIGI Drums, percussion. Member of Sniff 'n' the Tears, 1978-80.

SALWITZ, RICHARD Real name of Magic Dick.

SALZO, ROBERT Guitar. Member of the Protector 4, 1980.

SAM AND DAVE Sam Moore—vocal; Dave Prater—vocal. Vocal soul duet who struck it big in 1967 with "Soul Man." *Albums:* Hold On, I'm Coming (STX) 1965; Double Dynamite (STX) 1966; Soul Men (STX) 1967; I Thank You (STX) 1968; Best of Sam and Dave (ATC 8218) 1969; Back at 'Cha (STX) 1974; Golden Soul (ATC 18198); Super Hits (ATC 501).

SAM THE BAND Glenn Bell—vocal, guitar; Dennis Carmella—vocals, drums; Bernardo Dippolito—vocals, percussion; George Evers—vocal, bass; Jack Lesley—vocal, keyboards. *Album:* Play It Again Sam (CAS 7156).

SAM THE SHAM AND THE PHARAOHS Taking over in an already established band, Sam the Sham (real name: Domingo Samudio) renamed the band and swept the country with "Wooly Bully" (1965). The follow-ups, "Lil'l Red Riding Hood" and "My Chinny Chin Chin," though just as novel, were not as fresh, and the band quietly faded away. Sam attempted a solo comeback years later, with little success. *Albums:* Wooly Bully (MGM); Best of Sam the Sham and the Pharaohs (MGM SE 4422).

SAMARTINO, LEONARD Guitar. Session for the Plastic Rhino Band (1977).

SAMBATARO, JOHN Vocal. Session for Steve Stills (1978); McGuinn, Clark and Hillman (1979); Andy Gibb (1980).

SAMPEDRO, FRANK Guitar. Member of Crazy Horse, 1978-present. Session for Neil Young (1977-79).

SAMPLE, JOE Piano. Session for Joni Mitchell (1975); Seals and Crofts (1976); Steely Dan (1980). *Albums:* Carmel (MCA AA-1126); Rainbow Seeker (MCA 1050) 1978; The Three (ICT 6007) 1978.

SAMPSON, ANNIE Vocal. Original member of Stoneground, 1971. Session for Elvin Bishop (1974).

SAMPSON, LEE Drums, percussion. Original member of Stray Dog, 1973-74, and the Noel Redding Band, 1975-76.

SAMSEL, STEVE Vocal, guitar, piano. Member of the Kracker, 1978.

SAMSON, JACKIE Bass. Session for T-Bone Walker (1973).

SAMSON, JIM Bass. Member of Zon, 1979.

SAMSON, PAUL Guitar, vocal. Namesake of Samson, 1980.

SAMSON Bruce Bruce—vocal; Paul Samson—guitar, vocal; Thunderstick—percussion, vocal; Chris Aylmer—bass. *Album:* Head On (Import) 1980.

SAMUDIO, DOMINGO Organ, vocal. Alias Sam the Sham, he led the Pharaohs to number one in 1965 with "Wooly Bully." See Sam the Sham and the Pharaohs.

SAMUELS, ANDREW Guitar, vocal. Member of Redwing.

SAMUELS, BRUCE Bass, vocal. Member of Randy Burn's Sky Dog Band, 1973.

SAMUELS, CALVIN "FUZZY" Bass, percussion. Session for Mike Vernon; Dr. John (1971); Steve Stills (1970-71).

SAMWELL-SMITH, PAUL Bass, producer. Original member of the Yardbirds, 1962-66, before becoming a producer. Produced Cat Stevens (1970-76); Chris de Burgh (1975).

SAN FILIPPO, CHUCKIE Keyboards, vocal. Member of Porrazzo, 1980.

SANBORN, DAVID Saxophone. Member of the Paul Butterfield Blues Band, 1967-69. Session for B. B. King (1972); Henry Gross (1973, 76); Paul Butterfield's Better Days (1973, 75); the Fabulous Rhinestones (1973); Bruce Springsteen (1975); Tommy Bolin (1975); Cat Stevens (1976); Ian Hunter (1976); Jaco Pastorius (1976); Dr. John (1978); Scarlet Rivera (1978); the Euclid Beach Band (1979); Nils Lofgren (1979); the Eagles (1980); Steely Dan (1980). *Albums:* Beck and Sanborn (CTI 8002); Heart to Heart (WBR K-3189); Hideaway (WBR K-3379); Promise Me the Moon (WBR B-3051); Sanborn (WBR B-2957)

1976; Taking Off (WBR 2873) 1979; David Sanborn Band (WBR S-3051) 1977.

SANCHEZ, FREDDIE Vocal, bass. Member of El Chicano.

SANCHEZ, MARIO Conga, vocal. Member of the Crystal Mansion.

SANCIOUS, DAVID Guitar, keyboards. Session for Bruce Springsteen (1973, 75); Stanley Clarke (1975); Les Dudek (1977); Rozetta (1980); Ray Gomez (1980); Blackjack (1980); Jack Bruce (1980); Billy Squier (1980). *Albums:* Forest of Feelings (EPC KE-33441) 1975; Transformation (EPC PE 33939) 1976; True Stories (ARI 4201); Just As I Thought (ARI 4247) 1979.

SAND Jack Meussdorffer—vocal, guitar; Dan Ross—steel guitar, guitar, vocal; Dan Wilson—guitar, vocal; Rich Gooch—bass, vocal; Steve Williams—drums (1973); Atillo—synthesizer (1976); Ted Affolter—drums (1976). *Albums:* Sand, 1973; Head in the Sand, 1976.

SANDERS, ED Vocal, producer. Original member of the Fugs, 1965-70. *Album:* Beer Cans on the Moon (RPS) 1972.

SANDERS, MARK Drums. Member of Sumner, 1980.

SANDERS, MARTY Guitar. Member of Jay and the Americans, 1963-68.

SANDERS, ZACK Vocal. Session for Steely Dan (1980).

SANDFORD, BILLY Guitar, organ. Session for Leon Russell (1973); Waylon Jennings (1973); Doug Kershaw (1974); Bill Medley (1978); Levon Helm (1980).

SANDKE, JORDAN Horns. Session for Howlin' Wolf (1972).

SANDLIN, JOHNNY Percussion, bass, guitar, drums, producer. First gained recognition as a member of Hourglass, 1968, before moving into production. Production and session for Johnny Jenkins (1970); Elvin Bishop (1974-75). Production for the Allman Brothers; Alex Taylor (1972); Tim Weisberg (1977); the Rockets (1980); and others. Session for Gregg Allman (1973); Richard Betts (1974); Martin Mull (1974).

SANDOW, ALAN Drums, vocal. Member of Sherbet, 1976-80.

SANDPIPERS Jim Brady—vocal; Michael Piano—vocal; Richard Shoff—vocal. Early name: the Grads. Soft rock vocalists who recorded "Guantanamera," 1966. *Albums:* Sandpipers Greatest Hits (AAM 4246); Guantanamera (AAM 4117) 1966; Sandpipers Four Sider (AAM 3525); Softly (AAM 4147); Come Saturday Morning (PKW SPC 3710) 1970.

SANDRIDGE, SHAWN Vocal, guitar, keyboards, percussion. Member of Dayton, 1980.

SANDS, EVIE Vocal. *Albums:* Original New York Rock and Roll (SSS 6); Suspended Animation (VIC AFLI 2943) 1979.

SANDS, TOMMY Vocal. Elvis imitator of 1958 and idol of the Beach Blanket generation. *Album:* Tommy Sands (BRU 754216).

SANDVIG, PEGGY Piano. Session for Jennifer Warnes (1976).

SANFORD, ED Keyboards, vocal. Member of the Sanford-Townsend Band, 1977-79.

SANFORD, FRANK Member of Hank Ballard's Midnighters.

SANFORD, GARY Guitar. Session for Joe Jackson (1979).

SANFORD, RICK Vocal, flute. Member of Legs Diamond, 1977-78.

SANFORD-TOWNSEND BAND Ed Sanford—keyboards, vocal; John Townsend—vocal, keyboards; Roger Johnson—guitar; Jerry Rightmer—bass; Jim Varley—drums (1977); Chris Meyers—drums (1979). *Albums:* Duo Glide (WBR K-3081) 1977; Nail Me to the Wall (WBR K-3343) 1979; Smoke from a Distant Fire (WBR B-2966) 1977.

SANLLEHI, JUAN PABLO Drums. Member of Los Bravos, 1966-68.

SANO, TATZUYA Shakahachi, nohkan. Member of Osamu, 1977.

SANOIAN, PAUL Kazoo. Member of the Temple City Kazoo Orchestra, 1978.

SANTANA, DEVADIP CARLOS Guitar, vocal. Born 7/20/47. Founder and head of the San Francisco rock sensation of 1969, Santana. He developed through the years, taking his Latin rock into the area of jazz, making albums with John McLaughlin, Alice Coltrane, Billy Cobham, Stanley Clarke, and other popular jazz musicians. Member of the Giants, 1978. Session for Super Session (1969); Boz Scaggs (1980). *Albums:* Carlos Santana and Buddy Miles Live (COL C 31308) 1972; Love, Devotion, Surrender (COL C 32034) 1973; Illuminations (COL C32900) 1974; Oneness (COL JC 35686) 1979; The Swing of Delight (COL CZ 36590) 1980.

SANTANA, JORGE Guitar, vocal. Brother of Carlos Santana. Founded Malo, 1972. *Albums:* It's All About Love (TMT 7033) 1980; Jorge Santana (TMT 7020).

SANTANA Carlos Santana—guitar, vocal; Mike Carrabello—congas, percussion (1969-71); Dave Brown—bass (1974-76); Jose "Chepito" Areas—timbales, conga, percussion (1970-74); Mike Shrieve—drums (1969-74); Greg Rolie—keyboards, vocal (1969-72); Neal Schon—guitar (1971-72); Douglas Rauch—bass (1972-74); James Mingo Lewis—conga (1972-74); Armando Peraza—percussion (1972-present); Tom Coster—keyboards (1972-present); Richard Kermode—keyboards (1974); Leon "Ndugu" Chancler—drums (1976); Greg Walker—vocal (1976-78); Graham Lear—drums (1977-present); Paul Rekow—percussion (1977-present); David Margen—bass (1977-present); Chris Solberg—guitar (1978-80);

Pete Escovedo—percussion (1978); Chris Rhyne —keyboards (1978); Alan Pasqua—keyboards (1979-80); Alexander Ligertwood—guitar, vocal (1979). Their exciting debut album in 1969, featuring heavy Latin rhythms and the incredible guitar work of Carlos Santana, set a popular trend of Latin music through the 1970s. Many imitators followed, but none as jazz-oriented or with the imaginative guitar work of Santana. Part of Woodstock, 1969, and the Fillmore, 1972. See Devadip Carlos Santana. *Albums:* Santana (COL KCS 9781) 1969; Abraxas (COL KC 30130) 1970; Santana (COL KC 30595) 1971; Caravanserai (COL PC 31610) 1972; Borboletta (COL OC 33135) 1974; Santana's Greatest Hits (COL PC 33050) 1974; Welcome (COL PC 32445) 1974; Amigos (COL PC 33576) 1976; Festival (COL PC 34423) 1977; Moonflower (COL C2 34914) 1977; Inner Secrets (COL FC 35600) 1978; Marathon (COL VC 36154) 1979.

SANTANGELO, JOE Keyboards. Member of Brother Fox and the Tar Baby, 1969.

SANTIAGO, D. Bass. Member of the Wiggy Bits.

SANTINI, TONY Guitar. Replaced Vinnie Taylor in Sha Na Na, 1975-present.

SANTORO, JIMMY Guitar. Member of Ram Jam, 1978.

SANTOS Percussion. Member of Fandango.

SANTOS, PATTIE Vocal, percussion. Original member of It's a Beautiful Day, 1969-72.

SAPIRO, ERNIE Guitar, vocal. Member of the Moberlys, 1979.

SAPKO, RAY Guitar. Member of the Tantrum, 1978-79.

SARCH, HARVEY Guitar. Original member of Stardrive, 1974.

SARGENT, BOB Keyboards, guitar, mandolin, vocal. Original member of the Mick Abrahams Band, 1971-72.

SASSAFRAS Terry Bennett—vocal; Dai Shell—guitar; Ralph Evans—guitar, vocal; Steve Finn—bass, vocal; Chris Sharley—drums, vocal. *Album:* Wheelin' and Dealin' (CRS 1076) 1975.

SATHER, STEVE Guitar, vocal. Member of Potliquor, 1979.

SATIN WHALE Gerald Dellman—keyboards; Thomas Bruck—bass; Wolfgang Hieronymi—drums, percussion; Dieter Roesberg—guitar, reeds. *Album:* Lost Mankind (Import) 1975.

SATTEN, STEVE Horns, percussion. Member of Ten Wheel Drive, 1970.

SATYRS See Jeremy Steig.

SAUBER, TOM Banjo, guitar. Session for Ry Cooder (1980).

SAUDEK, PHILIP Violin. Member of Centipede, 1971.

SAUNDERS, BRAD Drums. Member of the Units, 1980.

SAUNDERS, KEVIN Drums. Member of Mama's Pride, 1975.

SAUNDERS, KENT Guitar. Member of the Jan Park Band, 1979.

SAUNDERS, MERLE Keyboards. Session for Taj Mahal; the Grateful Dead (1972). *Albums:* Fire Up (FSY 9421); Fritz the Cat (FSY 9406); Heavy Turbulence (FSY 8421); Live at Keystone (FSY 79002) 1973; You Can Leave Your Hat On (FSY 9503) 1976; Do I Move You (CCR 5006) 1979; Merle Saunders (FSY F 9460) 1974.

SAUNDERS, ROGER Guitar. Member of Freedom, 1971. Session for Kevin Ayers (1977).

SAUNDERS, TERRY Guitar, vocal. Played on "Joseph and the Amazing Technicolor Dreamcoat," 1967.

SAUTER, JOHN Bass. Replaced Rob Grange in Ted Nugent's backup band, 1978.

SAVAGE, JAN Guitar. Original member of the Seeds, 1966.

SAVAGE, RICK Bass. Member of Def Leppard, 1980

SAVAGE GRACE John Seanor—keyboards; Larry Zack—drums; Al Jacquez—vocal, bass; Ron Koss —vocal, guitar. *Album:* Savage Grace (REP S 6434) 1970.

SAVAGE ROSE Thomas Koppel—piano, vocal; Anders Koppel—organ, vocal; Ilse Maria Koppel —harpsichord (1968-69); Anisette—vocal; Alex Riel—drums; Jens Rugsted—bass, vocal; Nils Tuxen—guitar, steel guitar (1968-70); John Uribe —guitar (1971). Savage Rose was second in popularity only to the Beatles in their native Denmark in 1968. Lead vocalist Anisette could best be described as a Danish Janis Joplin who could scream the blues or croon love ballads with equal dexterity and range. The energy of the group was matched by their talent, but neither was given a chance in the United States. *Albums:* In the Plain (POL 24-6001) 1969; Your Daily Gift (GGR 103) 1970; Refugee (GGR 104) 1971.

SAVENE, BOBBY Bass, vocal. Member of Arc, 1978.

SAVIGAR, KEVIN Keyboards. Member of the Rod Stewart Band, 1980.

SAVOY BROWN Kim Simmonds—guitar, piano, harmonica, vocal; Brice Portious—vocal (1967); Martin Stone—guitar (1967); Ray Chappell—bass (1967); Leo Mannings—drums (1967); Bob Hall —piano (1968); Chris Youlden—vocal, piano (1968-70); Dave Peverett—guitar, vocal (1968-71); Rivers Jobe—bass (1968-69); Roger Earle—drums (1968-71); Tone Stevens—bass, vocal (1969-71); Andy Silvester—bass (1971-72); Dave Walker—vocal (1971-72); Dave Bidwell—drums (1971-73, 75); Paul Raymond—keyboards, vocal, guitar (1971-73, 75-76); Andy Pyle—bass (1972-73); Jackie Lynton—vocal (1973); Stan Saltzman —saxophone (1973); Ron Berg—drums (1973); Stan Webb—guitar, vocal (1974); Miller Anderson

—guitar, vocal (1974); Jimmy Leverton—bass (1974); Eric Dillon—drums (1974); Andy Rae—bass, vocal (1975); Tommy Farnell—drums, percussion (1976-78); Ian Ellis—bass, vocal (1976-78). Savoy Brown is a legend in the history of British blues and rock. Essentially, the group is the vehicle of Kim Simmonds, accompanied by some of the most competent musicians in the field. The first group (1967) did not release their first album in the United States, so the first taste of Savoy Brown, a totally different band from the 1967 group, came in 1968. "Getting to the Point" established a strong, cultish, blues and boogie following. In 1971, the group suddenly changed again when Stevens, Peverett, and Earle left to form Foghat. Savoy refined their sound, aiming at more commercial audiences, with even more success. In 1973, the band began to fall apart. "Jack the Toad" was a rather directionless attempt at holding their reputation. 1974 saw a super Savoy Brown, with Simmonds being joined by Stan Webb of Chicken Shack, Miller Anderson from the Keef Hartley Band, and Dillon and Leverton from Fat Mattress. Predictably, their reputations resulted in excessive publicity, which eclipsed their actual output as the Boogie Brothers. They dissolved that same year. In 1975, Simmonds returned to the success formula of 1973 with alumni from that same band. "Wire Fire" was an uncertain attempt at crystalizing the "old sound," which solidified in 1976 on "Skin 'n' Bone." *Albums:* Boogie Brothers (LON APS 638) 1974; Jack the Toad (PRR X 71059) 1973; Lion's Share (PRR X 71057) 1972; Shake Down (Import) 1967; Wire Fire (PRR) 1975; Skin 'n' Bone (PRR PS 670) 1976; Blue Matter (PRR 71027) 1969; Getting to the Point (PRR 71024) 1968; Hell Bound Train (PRR X 71052) 1972; London Collector—Best of Savoy Brown (LON LC 50000) 1977; Looking In (PRR 71042) 1970; Raw Sienna (PRR 71036) 1969; Savage Return (LON PS 718) 1978; Step Further (PRR 71029) 1969; Street Corner Talking (PRR 71047) 1971.

SAWBUCK Nine Year—bass; Starr Donaldson—guitar, vocal; Chuck Ruff—drums, vocal; Mojo—vocal, guitar. *Album:* Sawbuck (FMR) 1971.

SAWTELL, MARTIN Bass, vocal. Member of Mark Andrews and the Gents, 1980.

SAWYER, DAN Guitar. Session for Jennifer Warnes (1976).

SAWYER, KENNY Member of Wheatfield, 1980.

SAWYER, RAY Vocal, piano. Born 2/1/37. Namesake of Dr. Hook since 1971.

SAXA Member of the English Beat, 1980.

SAXON Biff—vocal, percussion; Paul Quinn—guitar; Graham Oliver—guitar; Steve Dawson—bass; Pete Gill—drums. *Album:* Wheels of Steel (CRR 38-126) 1980.

SAXON, IAN Vocal. Member of S.C.R.A., 1972.

SAXON, SKY Vocal. Founder of the Seeds, 1966-67, which was known as Sky Saxon's Blues Band until 1966.

SKY SAXON'S BLUES BAND See the Seeds.

SAXONS Original name of the Bay City Rollers.

SAYER, LEO Vocal, guitar. *Albums:* Another Year (WBR B 2885) 1975; Endless Flight (WBR K 3101) 1976; Here (WBR K 3374) 1979; Just a Boy (WBR B 2835) 1974; Leo Sayer (WBR K 3200) 1973; Silverbird (WBR B 2738); Thunder in My Heart (WBR K 3089) 1977; Living in a Fantasy (WBR K 3483) 1980.

SCABIES, RAT Drums, vocal, guitar. Member of the Damned, 1980.

SCAFFOLD Roger McGough—vocal, percussion; John Gorman—vocal, percussion; Mike McGear—vocal, percussion. Satiric rock group, including Paul McCartney's younger brother, Mike McGear. Despite their seeming built-in success factor, they remained an underground commodity in their native England. *Album:* Thank U Very Much, 1968.

SCAGGS, WILLIAM R. "BOZ" Guitar, vocal, producer. Born 6/8/44. An original member of the Steve Miller Band, 1968. He left the Miller Band in 1969, developing into an equally popular white soul solo artist. Part of Fillmore, 1972. Produced Les Dudek (1976). *Albums:* Down Two and Then Left (COL JC 34729) 1977; Middle Man (COL FC 36103) 1980; Moments (COL PC 30454); My Time (COL PC 31384) 1972; Boz Scaggs (ATC 8239) 1969; Boz Scaggs (COL C 30796); Silk Degrees (COL JC 33920) 1976; Slow Dancer (COL PC 32760) 1974; Greatest Hits (COL FC 36841) 1980.

SCALA, RALPH Vocal, organ. Member of the Blues Magoos.

SCARANGELLA, JACK Drums. Member of the Treasure, 1977.

SCARBOROUGH, ALLISON Bass. Member of Stillwater, 1977.

SCARGILL Max Paul Schwennsen—vocal, guitar, saxophone; Michael McCollum—guitar, vocal; Matthew McClure—drums; Brian Smith—bass. *Album:* Lessons from Love (FAM 7741) 1979.

SCARLETT, WILL Harmonica. Member of Hot Tuna, 1970-72.

SCAVONE, MYKE Vocal, percussion. Member of Ram Jam, 1977-78.

SCERBO, FRED Saxophone. Session for Joe Cocker (1972).

SCHACHER, MEL Bass. Original member of the Grand Funk Railroad, and Flint, 1978.

SCHACKLOCK, ALAN Guitar, moog, keyboards, vocal, percussion. Co-founder of Babe Ruth.

SCHAEFFER, GUY Bass, vocal. Member of Potliquor, 1979.

SCHAEFFER, JANNE Guitar. Member of Abba's backup band, 1974. Session for John "Rabbit" Bundrick (1974).

SCHAEFFER, STEVE Drums. Session for Dick

St. Nicklaus (1979); Levon Helm (1980).

SCHAFFNER, KATHERIN Vocal. Original member of the Marvelettes.

SCHALLOCK, DAVID Guitar. Session for Big Brother and the Holding Company.

SCHAMACH, RICHARD Guitar. Member of Eden's Children, 1968.

SCHARF, ROBBY Bass, vocal. Member of D. B. Cooper, 1980.

SCHECKEL, TOM Member of Scott Wilk and the Walls, 1980.

SCHEEL, BURT Drums, percussion. Member of the Link, 1980.

SCHEFF, JEFF Bass. Session for Ray Manzarek; Mark Benno; the Doors (1971); Jim Morrison's "American Prayer" (1978).

SCHEFF, JERRY Bass. Session for Bob Dylan (1978).

SCHEFRIN, ARAM Guitar, banjo, percussion, vocal. Member of Ten Wheel Drive, 1970.

SCHEIN, RICK Guitar. Backup for Mitch Ryder, 1978-79.

SCHELHAAS, JAN Keyboards. Replaced David Sinclair in Caravan, 1976.

SCHELL, JOHN LEE Guitar, organ, vocal. Member of Baby, 1975-76. Session for Ian McLagen (1979).

SCHENKER, MIKE Guitar. Member of UFO, 1974-79, and the Michael Schenker Group, 1980.

MICHAEL SCHENKER GROUP Michael Schenker—guitar, vocal; Gary Barden—vocal; Simon Phillips—drums; Mo Foster—bass; Don Airey—keyboards. *Album:* Michael Schenker Group (CYS 1302) 1980.

SCHERMIE, JOE Bass. Member of Three Dog Night. Session for Kim Fowley.

SCHERPENZEEL, PETER Bass, vocal. Replaced Theo de Jong in Kayak, 1978-80.

SCHERPENZEEL, TON Keyboards, vocal. Member of Kayak.

SCHERRER, ROLF Guitar. Session for Bo Hansson.

SCHERSTROM, DAVID Drums. Original member of Circus Maximus, 1967-68.

SCHERTZER, HYMIE Alto saxophone. Session for Martin Mull (1974).

SCHIFF, STEVE Guitar. Member of 1994, 1978.

SCHILDT, HERB Keyboards, synthesizer. Member of Starcastle, 1972-78.

SCHINDLER, ROBERT Keyboards. Member of the States, 1979.

SCHLINK, DOUG Guitar. Session for Donovan (1973).

SCHLITZ, DON Vocal. *Album:* Dreamer's Matinee (CAP ST 12086) 1980.

SCHLOSS Klaus Luley—guitar, vocal; Roger Kaeschner—bass; Willy Wald—drums. *Album:* Schloss (OAS) 1975.

SCHLOSSER, RICK Drums. Member of Montrose, 1978, and Four on the Floor, 1979. Session for Art Garfunkel; Andy Pratt (1973, 77); Rod Stewart (1976); Adrian Gurvitz (1979); Adam Mitchell (1979); Tom Johnston (1979); Rory Block (1979).

SCHMIDT, IRWIN Keyboards. Member of the Can, 1975.

SCHMIDT, KEN ROCLORD Keyboards. Member of the Bottles, 1979.

SCHMIDT, TIMOTHY B. Bass. Original member of Poco, and the Eagles, replacing Randy Meisner, 1978-present. Session for Gene Clark (1974); Steely Dan (1974, 76); Firefall (1977); Terrance Boylan (1977); Joe Walsh (1978); Richie Furay (1979); Bob Seger (1980); Elton John (1980); the Robbin Thompson Band (1980).

SCHMIERER, RICHIE Vocal. Session for Henry Gross (1975).

SCHNEE, BILL Percussion, producer. Produced Pablo Cruz (1979). Session for the Richie Furay Band (1976).

SCHNEIDER, DAVID Drums. Member of the Low Numbers, 1977-78.

SCHNEIDER, FRED Vocal, keyboards. Member of the B-52's, 1980.

SCHNEIDER, FLORIAN Vocal, electronics. Member of Kraftwerk since 1975.

SCHNEIDER, HELEN Vocal. *Albums:* Let It Be Now (WDS BXLI 2710) 1978; So Close (WDS BXLI 2037) 1977.

SCHOEN, JEFF Keyboards. Member of the Jeremy Spencer Band, 1979.

SCHOLZ, TOM Guitar, bass, keyboards. Born 3/10/47. Head of Boston, 1976-78. Session for Sammy Hagar (1980).

SCHON, NEAL Guitar. Member of Santana, 1971-72, and original member of Journey since 1975. Member of Giants, 1978. Session for Carlos Santana and Buddy Miles Live (1972); Sammy Hagar (1980).

SCHOTT, KARL-HEINZ Bass. Member of Frumpy, 1973.

SCHOUTEN, CHARLES LOUIS Drums. Replaced Pim Koopman in Kayak, 1978-80.

SCHRELL, STEVE Reeds. Member of Bagatelle, 1968.

SCHRODER, JACK Saxophone. Member of the Colwell-Winfield Band, 1968. Session for Van Morrison (1968-69); Art Garfunkel (1972, 74, 78); Paul Simon (1972); Boz Scaggs (1972).

SCHROTER, REINHARD Drums, percussion. Member of Ramses.

SCHUCKETT, RALPH Keyboards, vocal. Member of Clear Light, 1967-68, Jo Mama, 1970, and Todd Rundgren's Utopia since 1974. Session for David Blue (1971); Elliott Murphy (1976); Baby Grand (1978).

SCHULER, WILLIAM Vocal. Session for Elvin Bishop (1978).

SCHULMAN, JOY Percussion. Member of the Dija

Rhythm Band, 1976.

SCHULMAN, NEAL Half of the Aztec Two Step duet, 1972-79.

SCHULMAN, STUART Strings. Member of Orphan, 1971-74. Session for Martin Mull (1972, 74).

SCHULTZ, BOB Organ. Session for the Bob Seger System.

SCHULTZ, DUTCH Drums. Member of F-Word, 1978.

SCHULZE, KLAUS Electronics, producer, engineer. *Albums:* Go—Live From Paris (ISL 10) 1976; Body Love (ISL AN 7065) 1977.

SCHUSTER, STEVEN Horns. Session for the Jefferson Starship (1979).

SCHUURSMA, JOHN Guitar, bouzouki, bass. Session for Alan Price and Rob Hoeke (1977).

SCHWAB, JOHN Guitar, vocal. Member of McGuffey Lane, 1980.

SCHWALL, JIM Guitar, vocal. Member of the Siegel-Schwall Band.

SCHWARTZ, BILLY Member of Jobraith, 1973-74.

SCHWARTZ, BRINSLEY Guitar, percussion, vocal. Namesake of the group, Brinsley Schwartz. Member of the Rumour since 1977. Session for Frankie Miller.

BRINSLEY SCHWARTZ BAND Brinsley Schwartz —guitar, percussion, vocal; Nick Lowe—bass, guitar, vocal; Bill Rankin—drums, percussion; Bob Andrews—keyboards, bass, vocal. Session for Dave Edmunds (1975). *Albums:* Despite It All, 1970; Nervous on the Road; Silver Pistol; Brinsley Schwarz (CAP BC 11869) 1978.

SCHWARTZ, CHUCK Drums. Member of Gambler since 1979.

SCHWARTZ, DAVID Viola. Session for Barry Goudreau (1980).

SCHWARTZ, TRACY Vocal, percussion, fiddle, banjo. Replaced Tom Paley in the New Lost City Ramblers, 1968.

SCHWARTZ, WILLIE Clarinet. Session for Ry Cooder (1978).

SCHWARTZBERG, ALAN Drums, percussion. Replaced Corky Laing in Mountain, 1973. Session for Henry Gross (1973, 75-77); Pacific Gas and Electric (1973); Jimi Hendrix's "Crash Landing" (1975); Alice Cooper (1976); the Michael Zager Band; the Mark and Clark Band (1977); Tom Verlaine (1979); Nils Lofgren (1979); Grace Slick (1980); Roxy Music (1980).

SCHWEID, ELLIS Fiddle. Member of the Goose Creek Symphony.

SCHWENNSEN, MAX PAUL Vocal, guitar, saxophone. Member of Scargill, 1979. Session for Doug Kershaw.

SCIALFA, PATTI Vocal. Session for Southside Johnny and the Asbury Jukes (1980).

SCIUTO, TONY Vocal. *Album:* Island Nights (EPC NJE-36152) 1980.

SCOFIELD, JOHN Guitar. Session for the Blast (1979).

SCONCE, MIKE Bass, vocal. Member of the Two Guns, 1979.

SCONCE, PAT Drums. Member of the Two Guns, 1979.

SCOOTERS Larry Lee—vocal, bass, keyboards, guitar; Bobby Dean Wickland—drums, percussion; Luke Zamperini—vocal, guitar; Robert Ferrero—vocal, guitar. *Album:* Young Girls (EIA SW 17026) 1980.

SCOPPETTONE, DICK Guitar. Member of Harper's Bizarre, 1967-69.

SCORFINA, STEVE Guitar. Original member of Pavlov's Dog, 1975-76.

SCORPIONS Klaus Meine—vocal; Ulrich Roth—guitar, vocal (1974-79); Rudolph Shenker—guitar; Francis Buchholz—bass; Rudy Lenners—drums; Herman Rarebell—drums; Jurgen Rosenthal—drums; Matthias Jabs—guitar (1980). German heavy metal rock. *Albums:* Animal Magnetism (MER SRM 1-3825) 1980; Fly to the Rainbow (VIC AFLI 4025) 1974; In Trance (VIC AFLI 4128) 1976; Love Drive (MER SRM 1-3795); Tokyo Tapes (VIC CPL 2-3039) 1978; Virgin Killer (VIC AYL 1-3659) 1977; Taken by Force, 1977; Best of the Scorpions (VIC AFLI 1-3516) 1979.

SCOT, COLIN Vocal. *Album:* Colin Scot (USA 1009) 1971.

SCOTT, ANDY Guitar, vocal, cello, synthesizer. Member of the Sweet since 1975.

SCOTT, BARRY Guitar, vocal. Member of the States, 1979.

SCOTT, BOBBY Piano. Session for Paul Simon (1973). *Albums:* From Eden to Canaan (COL C 34324) 1976; Forecast: Rain With Sunny Skies (COL JC 35299) 1978.

SCOTT, BON Vocal. Voice of AC/DC, 1977, until his death, 1980.

SCOTT, CLIVE Keyboards, vocal. Member of Jigsaw, 1975-77.

SCOTT, DAVE Guitar. Member of Athletico Spizz 80, 1980.

SCOTT, GEORGE Bass, vocal. Session for John Cale (1979).

SCOTT, GORDON Guitar, vocal. Member of the Matchbox, 1979.

SCOTT, HAROLD Guitar, vocal. Original member of War.

SCOTT, JAMES HONEYCUTT Guitar, keyboards, vocal. Member of the Pretenders, 1980.

SCOTT, JOEL Guitar, vocal. Replaced Rick Roberts in the Flying Burrito Brothers.

SCOTT, JULIAN Bass. Member of M, 1980.

SCOTT, KEITH Member of Blues Incorporated.

SCOTT, KEN Guitar, vibes, percussion. Session for Kim Fowley (1973).

SCOTT, KERRY Vocal. Session for Kim Fowley (1973).

SCOTT, LAWRENCE Keyboards. Replaced Brian Miller in Isotope, 1975.

SCOTT, MARILYN Vocal. Session for John Mayall (1978).

SCOTT, MIKE Member of Blues Incorporated.

SCOTT, NOEL Keyboards. Member of the Strapps, 1977.

SCOTT, ROBIN Guitar. Member of M, 1980.

SCOTT, TOM Saxophone, synthesizer, cello, percussion, steel drums, producer. First gained national recognition as a session man for James Taylor and Carole King. In 1974, he gained even more notoriety backing George Harrison with the L.A. Express. Session for Harry Chapin; Jan and Dean (1963); Donovan (1973, 76); Ringo Starr (1973); Hoyt Axton (1974); George Harrison (1974-76); Splinter (1975); Steppenwolf (1975); Wings (1975); Boz Scaggs (1976); Neil Diamond (1976); Glen Campbell (1976); Bob Weir (1978); Rod Stewart (1978); the Blues Brothers (1978); Art Garfunkel (1979); Randy Newman (1979); Nielsen-Pearson (1980); the Vapour Trails (1980); Danny Spanos (1980); Steely Dan (1980). *Albums:* L.A. Express, 1976; Best of Tom Scott (COL JC 36352) 1980; Individuals (COL CG 36213); New York Connection (EOD PE 34959) 1973; Street Beat (COL JC 36137); Great Scott (AAM 4330); Intimate Strangers (COL JC 35557) 1978; Honeysuckle Breeze (IMP A 9163); Street Beat (COL JC 36237) 1979.

TOM SCOTT AND THE L.A. EXPRESS See individual listings. *Albums:* Blow It Out (EOD PE-34966) 1977; Tom Scott and the L.A. Express (EOD PER 34952) 1974; Tom Scott in L.A. (FLD BXLI 0833) 1975; L.A. Connection, 1975; Shadow Play (CBO 34355) 1976.

SCREAMS Steven Jones—bass, vocal; David Adams—vocal; Brad Steakley—drums; John Siegle—guitar, vocal. *Album:* Screams (INF 9009) 1980.

SCRIBNER, TOM Saw. Session for Neil Young (1980).

SCRUFFS Dave Branyan—guitar, vocal; Rick Branyan—bass, piano, vocal; Stephen Burns—guitar, vocal, piano, synthesizer; Zeph Paulson—drums, vocal. *Album:* Wanna Meet the Scruffs (PPR 5050) 1977.

SCUGGS, EDWIN Guitar. Session for Leon Russell (1974).

SEA DOG Paul Weston—guitar, vocal; John Redmond—keyboards, vocal; Brian Kirkwood—bass, vocal; Jim Norris—drums, vocal; Doug Varty—keyboards, vocal. *Album:* Sea Dog (BDH 5104) 1972.

SEA LEVEL Jai Johanny Johanson—congas, drums, percussion (1977-78); Chuck Leavell—keyboards, vocal; Jimmy Nalls—guitar, vocal (1977-78); Lamar Williams—bass, vocal; Joe English—drums (1978-present); Randall Bramblett—guitar, saxophone (1978-present); Davis Causey—guitar (1978-present); Matt Greely—percussion, vocal (1980). Formed from the ashes of the Allman Brothers, Sea Level uses the Allmans' familiar style in a jazz-oriented format. Though the Allman Brothers recalled some alumni for their reunion, Leavell and Williams continued on with Sea Level. *Albums:* Sea Level (CPN 0178) 1977; Cats on the Coast (CPN 0198) 1978; On the Edge (CPN 0212) 1978; Long Walk on a Short Pier (CPN 0227) 1979; Ball Room (ARI 9531) 1980.

SEAL, BOB Guitar. Member of Clear Light, 1967-68.

SEALS, ENGLAND DAN Saxophone, guitar, vocal. Brother of James Seals of Seals and Crofts. Half of the England Dan and John Ford Coley duet since 1974. *Album:* Stones (ATC 19257) 1980.

SEALS, JAMES Guitar, vocal. Half of the Seals and Crofts team since 1971.

SEALS, MELVIN Organ. Member of the Elvin Bishop group, 1977-78. Session for Mickey Thomas (1977).

SEALS, SON Guitar, vocal. Head of Son Seals Blues Band since 1973.

SON SEALS BLUES BAND Son Seals—guitar, vocal; A. C. Reed—saxophone (1978); Lacy Gibson—guitar (1978); Snapper Mitchum—bass (1978-80); Tony Gooden—drums (1978); Johnny "Big Moose" Walker—organ (1973); John Riley—bass (1973); Charles Caldwell—drums (1973); David D. Anderson—drums (1980); King Solomon—keyboards (1980); Mark Weaver—guitar (1980). *Albums:* Son Seals Blues Band (ALG 4703) 1973; Midnight Son (ALG 4708); Live and Burning (ALC 4712) 1978; Chicago Fire (ALC 4720) 1980.

SEALS, TROY Guitar. Session for Doug Kershaw (1972).

SEALS AND CROFTS James Seals—guitar, vocal; Dash Crofts—mandolin, vocal. The folk harmonies that were so popular in the 1960s were reincarnated in the 1970s by the writing/performing team of Seals and Crofts, augmented with more danceable arrangements. *Albums:* Compartments (VIC APDI 0141); Summer Breeze (WBR B-2629) 1972; Diamond Girl (WBR B-2699) 1973; Get Closer (WBR B-2907) 1976; I'll Play For You (WBR B-2848) 1975; Longest Road (WBR BSK-3365) 1980; One on One (WBR B-3076); Seals and Crofts Greatest Hits (WBR K-3109) 1975; Seals and Crofts — 1 & 2 (WBR 2WS-2809) 1974; Sudan Village (WBR B-2976) 1976; Takin' It Easy (WBR K-3163) 1978; Unborn Child (WBR 2761) 1974; Year of Sunday (WBR B-2568) 1971.

SEAMAN, PHIL Percussion. Member of Blues Incorporated, and Ginger Baker's Air Force, 1970-71.

SEAMONS, MARK Keyboards. Member of Whole Wheat, 1977.

SEANOR, JOHN Keyboards. Member of Savage Grace, 1970.

SEARCHERS John McNally—guitar, vocal; Tony Jackson; Chris Curtis; Billy Adamson—drums, percussion; Frank Allan—bass, vocal; Mike Pinder—guitar, vocal. Popular Liverpool group from 1960-64 specializing in the Mersey sound and responsible for the rock classic "Love Potion #9," 1964. *Album:* Searchers (SIR SRK 6082) 1979.

SEARLES, DAVID Percussion. Member of the Wax, 1980.

SEARS, PETE Bass, keyboards, vocal. Original member of Stoneground, 1971, and the Jefferson Starship, since 1974. Session for Steamhammer (1969); Rod Stewart (1971-74); Kim Fowley (1972); Tim Rose (1976).

SEASTONES Ned Lagin—piano, keyboards, percussion, synthesizer; Phil Lesh—bass; Jerry Garcia—guitar, vocal; David Crosby—vocal, guitar; Grace Slick—vocal; David Freiberg—vocal; Mickey Hart—gongs; Spencer Dryden—percussion. *Album:* Seastones (RND RX 106) 1975.

SEATRAIN Andy Kulberg—bass, flute; Roy Blumenfeld—drums; Richard Greene—violin, viola; John Gregory—vocal, guitar; Don Gretmar—saxophone, bass; Jim Roberts—vocal; Andy Musar—bass (1968); Lloyd Baskin—keyboards, vocal, percussion; Peter Atamanuik; Peter Rowan—guitar, saxophone, vocal; Julio Coronado. New Yorkers mourned the loss of the Blues Project in 1968. Strangely enough, however, they did not welcome the return of Project members Kulberg, Blumenfeld, Gregory, and Gretmar in their new group, Seatrain, later that same year. *Albums:* Seatrain (AAM 4171) 1968; Watch (AAM); Seatrain (CAP SMAS 659); Marblehead Messenger (CAP SN 16103).

SEAWIND Jerry Hey—horns; Kim Hutchcroft—reeds; Bud Nuanez—guitar; Ken Wild—bass; Larry Williams—keyboards, reeds; Bob Wilson—drums; Pauline Wilson—vocal. *Albums:* Light the Light (AAM 734) 1979; Seawind (AAM 4824) 1980; Seawind (CTI 5002); Window of a Child (CTI 5007).

SEBASTIAN, JOHN Guitar, vocal, harmonica. Born 3/17/44. Member of the Even Dozen Jug Band, 1964, founder of the Lovin' Spoonful, 1965-69, and soloist and session man since 1969. Recorded the theme song for television's "Welcome Back Kotter." Session for Fred Neil; Steve Stills (1970); Crosby, Stills, Nash and Young (1970); Rita Coolidge (1972); Keith Moon (1975). *Albums:* John B. Sebastian (RPS 6379) 1970; Four of Us (RPS 2041) 1971; Real Live (RPS 2036); John Sebastian Songbook (KMS 2011); Tarzana Kid (RPS 2187) 1974; Welcome Back (RPS 2249) 1976.

SECICH, FRANK Bass, vocal. Member of the Blue Ash, 1973.

SECOND COMING Florida band from which Richard Betts and Berry Oakley departed to join Duane Allman in the Allman Brothers Band.

SECRET AFFAIR Ian Page—vocal, trumpet, keyboards; David Cairns—guitar, vocal; Dennis Smith—bass, vocal; Seb Shelton—drums, percussion; Dave Winthrop—saxophone. *Album:* Secret Affair (SIR SRK 6089) 1980.

SECTION Danny Kortchmar—guitar; Russ Kunkel—drums, percussion; Leland Sklar—bass; Craig Doerge—keyboards. Group effort from James Taylor session men. *Albums:* Section (WBR BS 2714) 1972; Fork It Over (CAP ST 11656) 1977.

SEDAKA, NEIL Vocal, piano. Born 3/13/39. Author of the classic "Breaking Up Is Hard to Do," which was a hit in 1962 and 1976. A contemporary of Tommy Roe, Bobby Vinton, and others, he also penned such classics as "Oh Carol" (1959), "Happy Birthday Sweet Sixteen" (1961), and "Calendar Girl" (1961). He faded from the pop scene in the mid-1960s, but was rediscovered by Elton John in 1975. *Albums:* Neil Sedaka Sings His Greatest Hits (VIC ANLI 3465) 1962; Breaking Up Is Hard to Do (CDN ACL 7006); Solitare (VIC SFG 8324) 1972; Oh, Carol (VIC ANLI 0879) 1975; Sedaka's Back (MCA 463) 1975; The Hungry Years (RKT 2157) 1975; Pure Gold (VIC ANLI 1314) 1976; Steppin' Out (RKT 2195) 1976; Song (ELK 6E-102) 1977; Sedaka Back in the 60s (VIC APL 1-2254) 1977; All You Need Is the Music (ELK 6E-161) 1978; In the Pocket (ELK 6E-259) 1980.

SEEDS Sky Saxon—vocal, bass; Daryl Hooper—keyboards; Jan Savage—guitar; Rick Andridge—drums; Cooker—slide guitar. Originally known as Sky Saxon's Blues Band, they changed to the Seeds in 1966 in the midst of the Flower Power movement in Los Angeles. They were capable of playing good blues and rock, but not of generating a large following. *Albums:* Full Spoon of Seedy Blues (CRS 2040); Web of Sound (CRS 2033) 1966; Seeds (CRS 2023) 1966; Merlin's Music Box (CRS 2043) 1967; Future (CRS 2038) 1967; Fallin' off the Edge (CRS 2107) 1977.

SEEGER, MIKE Fiddle. Member of the New Lost City Ramblers, and soloist. Session for Peter Rowan (1978). *Albums:* American Folk Songs (FLW 32005); Feudin' Banjos (OLR 7105); Old Time Country Music (FLW 32325) 1962; Tipple, Loom and Rail (FLW 35273) 1966.

SEEGER, PETE Vocal, guitar. Born 5/3/19 in New York. Father of the "Hootenany," Seeger set the mood for younger folk artists to become stars in the folk boom of the 1950s and 1960s. Like Woodie Guthrie, Seeger was a traveling minstrel and author of such folk classics as "If I Had a Hammer" and "Where Have All the Flowers

Gone," made hits by Peter, Paul and Mary and the Kingston Trio respectively. Though never appearing on the charts himself, without him there would have been no folk boom at all. *Albums:* Bitter and the Sweet (COL CS 8716); Dangerous Songs (COL CS 9303); Rainbow Race (COL C 30739); 3 Saints, 4 Sinners and 6 Other People (ODY 32-16-02667); Waist Deep in the Big Muddy (COL); Young vs. Old (COL CS 9837); Abiyoyo (and Other Songs and Stories for Children) (FLW 31500); American Favorite Ballads (FLW 31017) 1957; American Folk Songs (FLW 32005); American Folk Songs for Children (FLW 37601); American Game and Activity Songs for Children (FLW 37002) 1962; America's Balladeer (OLR 7102); Banks of Marble (FLW 331040); Birds, Beasts, Bugs and Little Fishes (FLW 7610); Birds, Beasts, Bugs and Bigger Fishes (FLW 7611) 1955; Broadside Pete Seeger (FLW 5302) 1964; Brother, Can You Spare a Dime (NWD 270); Camp Songs (FLW 37628); Champlain Valley (FLW 35210); Circles and Seasons (WBR K-3329) 1979; Darling Corey (FLW 32003); Essential Pete Seeger (VAN VSD 97/98) 1978; Folk Songs for Young People (FLW 7532) 1960; Folk Songs and Ballads (STS 90) 1962; Frontier Ballads, Vol. 1 (FLW 32175); Frontier Ballads, Vol. 3 (FLW 32176); Gazette (FLW 32501, 32502) 1960; Gazette, Vol. II (FLW 2902) 1961; German Folk Songs (FLW 36843); God Bless the Grass (CSP ASC-9232); Golden Slumbers (CAE 1399); Goofing-Off Suite (FLW 32045); Guitar-Folksingers Guide (FLW 38354, CRB-1); Hootenanny at Carnegie Hall (FLW 32512); How To Play the 5 String Banjo (FLW 38303, CRB-2); Indian Summer (FLW 33851) 1961; Lonesome Valley (FLW 32010); Love Songs for Friends and Foes (FLW 32453); Nativity (FLW 335001); Old Time Fiddle Tunes (FLW 33531); Pete (STI 90); Rainbow Quest (FLW 32454); Pete Seeger (EVR 201); Pete Seeger and Sonny Terry (FLW 32412) 1958; Pete Seeger at the Village Gate (FLW 32451); Pete Seeger in Concert (STI 357); Pete Seeger Sampler (FLW 32043); Pete Seeger Sings and Answers Questions at Ford Forum Hall, Boston (FLW 35702) 1968; Pete Seeger Sings Folk Music of the World (TRD 2107); Pete Seeger Sings Leadbelly (FLW 31022) 1968; Pete Seeger Sings Woody Guthrie (FLW 31002) 1967; Pete Seeger's Greatest Hits (COL CS 9418); Sing Out with Pete (FLW 32455, 31018); Skip Rope (FLW 37649); Sleep Time (FLW 37525); Songs of Memphis Slim and Willie Dixon (FLW 32385); Songs of Struggle and Protest (FLW 35223) 1964; Songs of the Lincoln and International Brigade (STI 352); Songs of the Spanish Civil War; Songs of Lincoln Battalion (FLW 35436); Songs to Grow On, Vol. 2 (FLW 37020); Songs, Vol. 2 (FLW 37027); Together in Concert (Pete Seeger and Arlo Guthrie) (RPS 2R-2214) 1975; Traditional Christmas Carols (FLW 32311); Tribute to Woody Guthrie (WBR 2W 3007); Tribute to Leadbelly (TMT 2-7003); 12 String Guitar (FLW 38371, CRB-8) 1962; We Shall Overcome (COL CS 8901); Where Have All the Flowers Gone (FLW 31026) 1968; Wimoweh (FLW 31018) 1968; With Voices Together We Sing (FLW 32452); World of Pete Seeger (COL CG 31949).

SEEKERS Judith Durham—vocal; Athol Guy—vocal; Keith Potger—vocal; Bruce Woodley—vocal. A commercially popular folk group, the Seekers hailed from Australia, but did not become popular in the United States until "Georgy Girl," 1966. They disbanded in 1967. *Albums:* The New Seekers, 1965; A World of Our Own, 1965; Georgy Girl, 1967; Seekers Seen in Green, 1967; Best of the Seekers (CAP SM 2746) 1967.

SEGAL, GEORGE Banjo, vocal. Popular film star whose hobby is playing the banjo. Session for Ray Manzarek. *Album:* A Touch of Ragtime (SGN BSLI 0654-A) 1974.

SEGARINI, BOB Vocal, guitar. Member of the Dudes, 1975. Session for Ian Hunter (1976).

SEGEL, JAMIE Vocal. Session for Ian McLagen (1979).

SEGER, BOB Guitar, vocal, keyboards. Founder of the Beach Bums, the Bob Seger System, and a soloist, backed by the Silver Bullet Band, 1974-present. See the Bob Seger System, and the Silver Bullet Band. Session for Gene Simmons (1978). *Albums:* Back in '72 (PDM MS 2126) 1973; Seven (CAP ST 11748) 1974; Beautiful Loser (CAP ST 11378) 1975; Live Bullet (CAP SKBB 11523) 1976; Night Moves (CAP SW 11557) 1976; Stranger in Town (CAP SW 11698) 1978; Against the Wind (CAP SOO 12041) 1980; Mongrel (CAP SKAO 499); Ramblin' Gamblin' Man (CAP SM 172); Smokin' O.P.'s (CAP ST 11746).

BOB SEGER SYSTEM Bob Seger—guitar, keyboards, vocal; Dan Honaker—bass, vocal; Pep Perrine—drums, vocal; Dan Watson—keyboards, vocal. From the Midwest, Seger emerged in the late 1960s with the hit "Ramblin' Gamblin' Man." Though not a smash success, Seger continued making album after album without a hit. After dropping his System, Seger teamed up with the Silver Bullet Band in 1974 and won a large AM audience. See Bob Seger, and the Silver Bullet Band. *Albums:* Ramblin' Gamblin' Man (CAP SM 172); Mongrel (CAP SKAO 499).

SEGS Bass, vocal. Member of the Ruts, 1979.

SEIDEL, NEIL Guitar. Member of the Shanti, 1971.

SEIDENBERG, DANNY Violin. Member of the Spy, 1980.

SEITER, JOHN Drums. Member of Spanky and Our Gang, 1967-69.

SEITZ, JEFF Drums. Session for Long John Baldry

(1979).

SEIWELL, DANNY Drums. Member of Wings, 1971-75. Session for Art Garfunkel; Paul McCartney (1971); Donovan (1973).

SELDEN, FRED Tenor saxophone. Session for Tim Weisberg (1977); Jerry Corbetta (1978).

SELECTER Neal Davies—guitar; Pauline Black—vocal; Charley Anderson—bass; Charley Bembridge—drums; Compton Amanor—guitar; Arthur Hendrickson—vocal; Desmond Brown—keyboards. *Album:* Too Much Pressure (CYS 1274) 1980.

SELICO, RON Percussion. Played with John Mayall, 1971. Session for Frank Zappa (1969).

SELIGMAN, MATTHEW Bass. Member of Bruce Wooley and the Camera Club, 1980.

SELLAR, GORDON Bass, vocal. Replaced Chris Glen in the Sensational Alex Harvey Band.

SELLERS, DALE Guitar. Session for Waylon Jennings (1973); Neil Young (1978).

SELLERS, ROGER Drums. Member of Ian Carr's Nucleus since 1975.

SELVIDGE, MIKE Drums, percussion. Member of the Crosswinds.

SENAUKE, ALAN Guitar. Half of the Fiction Brothers since 1979.

SENNEVILLE, DON Guitar. Member of Simon Stoke's Black Whip Band, 1973.

SENSATIONS FIX Franco Falsini—vocal, guitar, synthesizer; Richard Ursillo—bass; Steve Head—drums, keyboards. *Album:* Vision's Fugitives (AER 11478).

SENTER, MEL Bass, piano, vocal. Member of the Acrobat, 1972.

SENTRYS Early name of Ambrosia.

SEOL, RANDY Drums. Member of the Strawberry Alarm Clock, 1968.

SERAPHINE, DANIEL Drums. Born 8/28/48. Original member of Chicago, since 1968.

SERGEANT, WILL Guitar. Member of Echo and the Bunnymen, 1980.

SERGEL, CRAIG Trombone. Member of the Stanley Steamer, 1973.

SERPELL, GRANT Drums, vocal. Member of Sailor until 1979.

SERRY, JERRY, JR. Keyboards. Member of the Auracle, 1978-79.

SERWA, AL Keyboards. Member of the Cooper Brothers band since 1978.

SESKIN, STEVE Vocal, guitar, piano. *Album:* This Good Tonight (BER 31452) 1979.

707 Phil Bryant—bass, vocal; Jim McClarty—drums, percussion; Duke McFadden—keyboards, vocal; Kevin Russell—guitar, vocal. *Album:* 707 (CAS NBLP 7213) 1980.

SEVENTH WAVE Kieran O'Conner—drums, percussion, vocal; Ken Elliott—keyboards, percussion; Neil Richmond—electronics (1975). *Albums:* Things to Come (JNS) 1974; Psi-Fi (JNS) 1975.

SEVILLA, MICKEY Drums. Member of Dr. Buzzard's Original Savannah Band.

SEX PISTOLS Steve Jones—guitar; Johnny Rotten (John Lydon)—vocal; Sid Vicious—bass; Paul Cook—drums; Glenn Matlock—bass (1976). Popularizers of the punk craze, they paved the way for lesser-talented groups to make it. Though they had only one domestic release, three additional British import albums were also recorded. *Album:* Never Mind the Bollocks (WBR K-3147) 1977.

SEYMOUR, CHRIS Drums, percussion. Member of Mose Jones, 1978.

SEYMOUR, CLARK Piano, vocal. Member of the Mark and Clark Band, 1977.

SEYMOUR, MARK Piano, vocal. Member of the Mark and Clark Band, 1977.

SEYMOUR, PHIL Drums, bass, vocal. Member of the Dwight Twilley Band, 1976-78. Session for Moon Martin (1978); Tom Petty (1978); 20/20 (1979); Dwight Twilley (1979).

SEYMOUR, SCOTT Electronic keyboards. Member of the Mark and Clark Band, 1977.

SFERRA, JOHN Drums, guitar, vocal. Member of the Glass Harp, 1970-72.

SHA NA NA Elliot Cahn—guitar, vocal (1970-71); Robert Leonard—vocal (1970); Scott Powell—vocal (1970-71); John Marcellino—drums (1970-present); Richard Joffe—vocal (1971); Frederick Green—vocal (1970-present); Alan Cooper—vocal (1970); Bruce Clarke—bass, vocal (1970-73); Henry Gross—guitar, vocal (1970); David Garrett—vocal (1970); Joseph Witkin—piano, vocal (1970); Donald York—vocal; Johnny Contardo—vocal (1971-present); Chris Donald—guitar (1971); Scott Simon—piano, vocal (1971-present); John Bauman—piano (1971); Lennie Baker—saxophone, vocal (1971-present); Bowzer—vocal (1972-present); Vinnie Taylor—guitar (1972-74); Chico Ryan—bass (1973-present); Tony Santini—guitar (1975-present). Early name: Eddie and the Evergreens. Unstuck in time, Sha Na Na is the closest artifact to 1950s music in the business today. Their musical arrangements are current, tight and concise, and their lead and background vocals are authentic, down to the choreography and tear drops in the eyes. The bulk of material they have to draw upon is virtually endless, and even the more obscure songs they perform take on new life in nostalgia and musical perfection. On the verge of breaking up, Sha Na Na landed a television contract in 1977, which kept them together. Performed at Woodstock, 1969. *Albums:* From the Streets of New York (KMS 2075) 1973; Golden Age of Rock 'n' Roll (KMS 2073-2) 1973; Hot Sox (KMS 2600) 1974; Night Is Still Young (KMS 2050) 1972; Sha Na Na (KMS 2034) 1971; Sha Na Now (KMS 2605) 1975; Rock and Roll Is Here to Stay (KMS 2010) 1970; Best of Sha Na Na (BUD 5703) 1977; Sha Na Na Is Here to Stay (BUD 5692) 1977.

SHAAR, DAHAUD Percussion. Member of Chrysalis, 1968.

SHACK, RICHARD Vocal, guitar. Replaced Tommy Bolin in the James Gang, 1975.

SHACKELFORD, EARL Vocal. Session for Iggy Pop (1979).

SHACKLOCK, ALAN Guitar, keyboards, vocal. Member of Babe Ruth until 1976.

SHACKMAN, AL Guitar. Session for Pearls Before Swine (1969).

SHADDICK, TERRY Guitar, vocal. Member of Tranquility, 1972.

SHADES See Pam Windo and the Shades.

SHADOWFAX Chuck Greenberg—saxophone, flute, clarinet; Phil Maggini—bass; Doug Maluchnik—keyboards; Stuart Nevitt—drums; Greg Stinson—guitar, vocal. *Album:* Watercourse Way (PST) 1976.

SHADOWS Instrumental English band that went solo after backing Cliff Richard. *Albums:* Surfing with the Shadows; The Shadows Know.

SHAFFER, GREG Keyboards, vocal. Member of the Highwind, 1980.

SHAFFER, NATHAN Vocal, guitar. Member of Gambler since 1979.

SHAFFER, PAUL Keyboards, drums. Session for the Mark and Clark Band (1977); the Blues Brothers (1978, 80); John Mayall (1979); Gilda Radner (1979); Jimmy Maelin (1980).

SHAFFER, RICK Guitar, vocal. Member of the Reds, 1979.

SHAFRAN, STAN Trumpet. Session for Paul Butterfield's Better Days (1973).

SHAGGS Dorothy Wiggin—guitar, vocal; Betty Wiggin—guitar, vocal; Helen Wiggin—drums. Claimed to be one of the most musically inept records ever recorded. *Album:* Philosophy of the World (RDR) 1969.

SHAKERS Ron Rhodes—drums, vocal; Don Fulton—bass, vocal; Bill Wallace—guitar, vocal; Chris Solberg—guitar, vocal; Janet Small—keyboards, vocal. *Albums:* Break It All (ASY); Yankee Reggae (ASY) 1976.

SHAKIN' STREET Fabienne Shine—vocal; Elewy—guitar; Ross the Boss—guitar; Mike Winter—bass; Jean-Lou Kalinowski—drums. *Album:* Shakin' Street (NJZ 36499) 1980.

SHALLOCK, DAVID Bass. Member of the Sons of Champlin.

SHAM 69 Jimmy Pursey—guitar, vocal; Dave Parsons—guitar; Dave "Kermit" Treganna—bass; Mark "Diode" Cain—drums (1978-79); Ricky Goldstein—drums (1979-80). *Albums:* Tell Us the Truth (SIR K 6060) 1978; That's Life (Import) 1978; Hersham Boys (Import) 1979; The Game (Import) 1980.

SHANAHAN, KELLY Drums. Member of the Strand, 1980. Session for John Sebastian (1974).

SHANAHAN, TONY Bass, vocal. Member of Alda Reserve, 1979.

SHANE, BOB Original member of the Kingston Trio, 1958-66.

SHANE, JAMES Bass, vocal, dobro, guitar. Replaced Antonio la Parreda in Canned Heat, 1973.

SHANGRI-LAS Rock had come a long way from "Venus in Blue Jeans" when the Shangri-Las, a white female trio, recorded "Leader of the Pack," 1965, complete with black leather jackets and motorcycles. *Albums:* Golden Hits of the Shangri-Las, 1966; Leader of the Pack, 1965; Shangri-Las, 1965.

SHANK, CLIFFORD "BUD" Horns. Session for Russ Giguere (1971); Nilsson (1975); Joni Mitchell (1975); Boz Scaggs (1976).

SHANKAR, RAVI Sitar, composer. One of the most unexplainable phenomena in rock music, Shankar enjoyed the benefits of rock audiences without playing rock music. In 1965, Beatle George Harrison played a sitar in "Norwegian Wood." His teacher had been Shankar. Rock audiences promptly picked up on sitar music, catapulting master Shankar into the limelight. Throughout 1967, he packed auditoriums and arenas wherever he traveled in the United States. Unfortunately, his music became a symbol of the pop cult. Publicity linked the cult to drugs, so Shankar gracefully eased from the spotlight. Part of Bangla Desh, 1971. *Albums:* At the Woodstock Festival (WPR 21467); Shankar Family and Friends (DKH 22002); Song of God (WPR 21466); Transmigration Macabre (SPK 06); Exotic Sitar and Sarod (CAP ST 10497); Genius of Ravi Shankar (COL CS 9560); Raga Parameshwari (CAP SP 10561); Ragas (FSY 24714) 1973; Ravi (CAP ST 10504); Six Ragas (CAP DT 10512); Sound of India (COL CS 9296); Two Raga Moods (CAP ST 10482).

SHANNON, DEL Vocal. Teen love was never more romantic than when Shannon sang "Runaway" in 1961. *Album:* In England (UAR UA LA151-F) 1973.

SHANNON, ORVILLE Guitar, vocal. Member of the Band of Thieves, 1976.

SHANNON, TOMMY Bass. Session for Johnny Winter (1969-70).

SHANTI Ashish Khan—sarod; Zakir Hussain—tabla; Neil Seidel—guitar; Steve Haehl—vocal, guitar; Steve Leach—vocal, bass; Frank Lupica—drums. The popularity of Indian music with folk and rock audiences led to this inevitable and short-lived incorporation in an electrified rock format in 1971. *Album:* Shanti (ATC) 1971.

SHAPIRO, DAVID Bass. Session for Peter C. Johnson (1980).

SHAPIRO, MICHAEL Vocal. Member of the Elephant's Memory.

SHAPIRO, PETER Guitar. Original member of the Loading Zone, 1968.

SHARBONO, DONI Drums. Member of Great

Southern, 1977-78.

SHARIF, MIRZA AL Timbales, percussion. Session for Brian Auger's Oblivion Express (1974).

SHARK, ERIC Vocal. Member of the Deaf School, 1979-80.

SHARK, NOAH Vocal, producer. Produced Tom Petty, 1978. Session for Dwight Twilley (1979).

SHARKEY, FEARGAL Vocal. Member of the Undertones, 1979.

SHARKEY, GEOFF Guitar, vocal. Member of the Alibi, 1980.

SHARKS Snips—vocal, guitar; Chris Spedding—guitar; Martin Simon—drums, vocal; Andy Fraser—bass, piano (1973); Nick Judd—keyboards (1974); Busta Cherry Jones—bass, vocal (1974). After leaving Free, Fraser formed Sharks with Battered Ornament's guitarist Spedding, introducing Snips, who later graduated to the Baker-Gurvitz Army. *Albums:* First Water (MCA 351) 1973; Jab It in Your Eye (MCA 415) 1974.

SHARLEY, CHRIS Drums, vocal. Member of Sassafras, 1975.

SHARP, CHRISTY Cello. Session for Henry Gross (1972).

SHARP, DEE DEE Vocal. Recorded "Do the Bird," 1963. *Albums:* Big Bad Boss Beat (ORS 8871); Happy 'Bout the Whole Thing (PHL PZ-33839) 1975; Gamble Dee/Dee (PHL JZ 36370) 1980.

SHARP, SID Violin. Session for Jan and Dean (1963); Henry Gross (1972); Barry Goudreau (1980).

SHARP, TODD Guitar. Session for Bob Welch (1979); Danny Douma (1979).

SHARP, WILL Guitar, vocal. Member of Ethos, 1977.

SHARPE, D. Drums, percussion, vocal. Member of the Modern Lovers, 1977-78.

SHARPE, TERRY Member of the Starjets, 1980.

SHAUGHNESSY, FRED Bass, vocal. Member of the Stanley Steamer, 1973.

SHAVER, DAVID Vocal, keyboards. Member of Starbuck, 1977-78.

SHAW, ADRIAN Bass. Replaced Lemmy in Hawkwind, 1975-present.

SHAW, BILL Drums, percussion, vocal. Member of the Invaders, 1980.

SHAW, ERMA Vocal. Session for Paul Butterfield (1980).

SHAW, GEORGE Trumpet. Session for John Mayall (1979).

SHAW, GRAHAM Guitar, piano, clarinet, harmonica, vocal. Head of Graham Shaw and the Sincere Serenaders, 1980.

GRAHAM SHAW AND THE SINCERE SERENADERS Ilena Zaramba—vocal; Gordon Osland—drums; Graham Shaw—guitar, piano, clarinet, harmonica, vocal; Susan Lethbridge—vocal; Gary Stefanink—bass; Danny Casavani—guitar. *Album:* Graham Shaw and the Sincere Serenaders (CAP ST 12065) 1980.

SHAW, JOCEYLN Vocal. Session for the Marshall Tucker Band (1980).

SHAW, KEN Guitar. Member of Ian Carr's Nucleus since 1975.

SHAW, SANDIE Vocal. English pop vocalist from the same school as Petula Clark, who recorded "Always Something There To Remind Me," 1965. *Albums:* Sandie Shaw, 1965; Me, 1966.

SHAW, STAN Keyboards. Member of the Hitmen, 1980.

SHAW, TOMMY Guitar, vocal. Replaced John Curulewski in Styx, 1976-present.

SHEA, BOBBY Percussion. Member of the White Witch, 1973-74.

SHEA, GARY Bass. Member of New England, 1980.

SHEA, RED Guitar, dobro. Gordon Lightfoot's recording partner since 1966.

SHEAR, JULES Vocal, guitar. Member of the Funky Kings, 1976, and namesake of Jules and the Polar Bears, 1978-present.

SHEARER, DICK Trombone. Member of the Righteous Brothers band, 1966.

SHEARS, STEVE Guitar. Member of Ultravox, 1977-78.

SHEBAR, STEVE Drums, vibes, vocal. Replaced Russell Dawber in Flight, 1980.

SHECK, GEORGE Bass. Original member of White Trash.

SHEEHAN, FRAN Bass. Born 3/26/49. Member of Boston, 1976-78.

SHEFFIELD, BILL Vocal. Session for Roy Buchanan (1974).

SHEFFIELD, DON Trumpet. Session for J. J. Cale (1972).

SHEFTS, CHRISSY Guitar. Member of the Dixon House Band, 1979.

SHEHAN, STEVE Percussion. Member of the Rose, 1979.

SHELDON, BOB Vocal. Session for the Nighthawks (1980).

SHELDON, STANLEY Bass. Member of Ronin, 1980. Session for Tommy Bolin (1975); Peter Frampton (1976-79).

SHELL, DAI Guitar. Member of Sassafras, 1975.

SHELLEY, BURKE Bass, vocal. Member of Budgie, 1975-77.

SHELLEY, PETER Organ, guitar, vocal. Member of Stone's Masonry, 1968, Terry Reid's trio, 1968-69, and the Buzzcocks, 1977-present.

SHELLY, SCOTT Guitar, vocal. Member of the Strand, 1980.

SHELTON, DONNIE Vocal. Session for Seals and Crofts (1976).

SHELTON, LOUIE Guitar, producer. Production and session for Seals and Crofts (1971, 73, 76); Art Garfunkel (1979). Session for Boz Scaggs

(1976).

SHELTON, SEB Drums, percussion. Member of the Secret Affair, 1980.

SHENKER, RUDOLPH Guitar. Member of the Scorpions since 1974.

SHENWELL, SYLVIA Vocal. Member of the Sweet Inspirations, 1967-69.

SHEPARD, SAM Drums. Member of the Holy Modal Rounders.

SHEPARD, THOMAS Trombone. Session for Nilsson (1975).

SHEPHARD, GERRY Vocal, guitar. Half of the Oxendale and Shephard duet, 1979.

SHEPHARD, KEN Vocal, guitar. Member of the Randle Chowning Band, 1978.

SHEPHERD, JIM Trombone. Session for Elton John (1978).

SHEPHERD, NEIL Piano, vocal. Session for Long John Baldry (1975); John Entwhistle (1975).

SHEPLEY, JOE Trumpet. Session for Eumir Deodato; Grace Slick (1980).

SHEPPARD, MIKE Bass, guitar, vocal. Member of Trickster, 1978.

SHERBET Daryl Braithwaite—vocal, percussion; Harvey James—guitar, vocal; Tony Mitchell—bass, vocal; Alan Sandow—drums, vocal; Garth Porter—keyboards, vocal. Australian rock band that debuted in the United States in 1976. *Albums:* Howzat (MCA 2226) 1976; Magazine (MCA 2304) 1977.

SHERIDAN, TONY Vocal. Lead singer for the Silver Beatles, 1961, which became the Beatles (without him) a year later.

SHERIFF, JAMIE Vocal. *Album:* No Heroes (POL 1-6280) 1980.

SHERMAN, ADAM Vocal. Member of the Private Lightning, 1980.

SHERMAN, BOBBY Vocal. Teen heart throb of television and records for the 1970s. *Albums:* Rock and Roll Is Here to Stay (GUS 0065); Just for You (MMD) 1972; With Cool Bobby (MMD); With Love, Bobby (MMD 1032).

SHERMAN, BUZZ Vocal. Voice of Moxy, 1976.

SHERMAN, FRED Horns. Member of Fat Chance, 1972.

SHERMAN, JOHN Guitar. Session for Hot Tuna (1975-76).

SHERMAN, MICHAEL Vocal. Session for Alice Cooper (1976).

SHERNOFF, ADNY Bass, keyboards, vocal. Member of the Dictators, 1977-78.

SHEROMAHN, JOE Bass. Member of the Lamont Cranston Band, 1977.

SHERR, DAVID Bass clarinet. Session for Ry Cooder (1978).

SHERWOOD, JAMES "MOTORHEAD" Saxophone. Member of the Mothers of Invention, 1967-70, Ruben and the Jets, 1973, and the Grandmothers, 1980.

SHIELDS, DAVID Bass. Session for Adrian Gurvitz (1979); Jim Capaldi (1979); John Mayall (1979); Randy Newman (1979).

SHIELDS, KENNY Vocal, percussion. Member of Streetheart, 1979.

SHIELDS, MARTYN Horns, vocal. Member of Rick Wakeman's backup band, 1976.

SHIKANY, JOE Guitar, vocal. Member of Bighorn, 1978.

SHILLING, BOB Drums. Member of the Fingerprintz, 1980.

SHINE, FABIENNE Vocal. Member of Shakin' Street, 1980.

SHINE, MICKEY Drums, percussion, vocal. Member of Tommy Tutone, 1980.

SHINES, JOHNNY Guitar, vocal. Born 4/26/15, in Tennessee. Mississippi-style bluesman influenced in his youth by Blind Lemon Jefferson, Lonnie Johnson, and others. *Album:* Hey Ba-Ba-Re-Bop (RDR 2020) 1978.

SHIPLEY, ELLEN Vocal. *Albums:* Ellen Shipley (NYR BXL 1-3428) 1979; Breaking Through the Ice Age (VIC AFL 1-3626) 1980.

SHIPLEY, TOM Guitar, vocal. Half of the Brewer and Shipley team.

SHIPSON, ROY Organ. Session for Peter Green (1980).

SHIRELLES Recorded "Will You Still Love Me Tomorrow," 1961, and "Soldier Boy," 1962.

SHIRLEY, JERRY Drums, vocal, keyboards. Born 2/4/52. Original member of Steve Marriott's Humble Pie, 1969-76, 80, Natural Gas, 1976, and Magnet, 1979. Session for Syd Barrett; John Entwhistle (1971); B. B. King (1971); Sammy Hagar (1975).

SHIRTS Arthur LaMonica—guitar, vocal, keyboards; Ronald Ardito—guitar, vocal, keyboards; Robert Racioppo—bass, vocal; Annie Golden—vocal; John Criscione—drums, vocal, percussion; John Piccolo—keyboards, guitar, vocal. *Albums:* The Shirts (CAP SW 11791) 1978; Street Light Shine (CAP ST 11986) 1979; Inner Sleeve (CAP ST 12085) 1980.

SHITHEAD, JOE Guitar. Member of D.O.A. since 1979.

SHNEIDER, VLADIMIR Vocal. Member of Black Russian, 1980.

SHOCKET, SAUL Saxophone. Session for Peter C. Johnson (1980).

SHOCKING BLUE Robby Van Leeuwen—guitar, sitar; Mariska Veres—vocal; Klaasje van der Wal—bass; Cornelius van der Beek—drums. Scandinavian rockers who hit the charts in 1970 with "Venus." *Album:* Shocking Blue.

SHOES Jeff Murphy—vocal, guitar; John Murphy—bass; Skip Meyer—drums, vocal; Gary Klebe—vocal, guitar. *Album:* Present Tense (ELK 6E-244) 1979.

SHOFF, RICHARD Vocal. Born 1944. Member

of the Sandpipers.

SHOGREN, DAVE Bass, keyboards, vocal. Original member of the Doobie Brothers, 1971-72, and the Ron Gardner Group, 1974.

SHONDELLS See Tommy James and the Shondells.

SHOOK, JERRY Guitar. Session for Neil Young (1978); Levon Helm (1980).

SHOOT Bill Russell—bass; Craig Collinge—drums, percussion; Dave Greene—vocal, guitar, banjo; Jim McCarty—vocal, keyboards. *Album:* On the Frontier (EMI) 1973.

SHOOTING STAR Steve Thomas—drums; Ron Verlin—bass; Bill Guffey—keyboards; Charles Waltz—vocal, violin, keyboards; Van McClain—vocal, guitar; Gary West—vocal, keyboards, guitar, drums, percussion. *Album:* Shooting Star (VGN 13133) 1979.

SHORE, HOWARD Saxophone, organ. Session for Gilda Radner (1979).

SHOREY, DAVID Bass. Session for Mike Bloomfield (1978).

SHORROCK, GLENN Vocal. Member of the Little River Band since 1977.

SHORT, DON Guitar, vocal. Member of the Heats, 1980.

SHORTER, WAYNE Reeds. Member of Weather Report since 1971. Session for Jaco Pastorius (1976); Santana (1980).

SHOTGUN EXPRESS British band featuring newcomers Rod Stewart and Mick Fleetwood in the early 1960s.

SHOW OF HANDS Rick Cutler—percussion; Jack Jacobsen—keyboards; Jerry McCann—vocal, guitar, flute. *Album:* Formerly Anthrax (ELK) 1970.

SHRELL, STEVE Reeds. Member of Bagatelle, 1968.

SHRIEVE, MIKE Drums, percussion. Original member of Santana, 1969-74, Yamashta, Winwood and Shrieve, 1976, and Automatic Man, 1976. Session for David Crosby (1971); Wilding-Bonus (1978); the Rolling Stones (1980).

SHROYER, KEN Trombone. Session for the Mothers of Invention (1972); Frank Zappa (1972).

SHULMAN, DEREK Vocal, saxophone. Member of the Gentle Giant, 1971-80.

SHULMAN, RAY Bass, vocal, violin. Member of the Gentle Giant, 1971-80.

SHUTE, WILLIAM D. Mandolin, guitar. Member of the Fifth Estate, 1967.

SHUTT, PHIL Bass, vocal. Member of Arthur Brown's Kingdom Come, 1973-74.

SIBMANIS, JIM Bass. Member of the Other Side.

SICILIANO, ANTHONY Bass. Member of the Puzzle.

SIDENER, WHIT Baritone saxophone, flute. Member of the Boneroos. Session for Firefall (1976); Steve Stills (1978).

SIDERAS, LUCAS Drums, vocal. Member of Aphrodite's Child.

SIDGRAVE, BOOKER Drums. Session for John Littlejohn.

SIDRAN, BEN Piano, vocal. First became known in the Steve Miller band, 1969, before developing as a soloist/writer on his own. The casual style of his vocal phrasing is reminiscent of Mose Allison. Session for Steve Miller (1970, 72). *Albums:* Don't Let Go (BTM 6012); I Lead a Life (BTM 40); Cat and the Hat (AAM 741); Little Kiss in the Night (ARI 4178); Live at Montreux (ARI 4218); Puttin' in Time on Planet Earth (MCA 55); Free in America (ARI) 1976.

SIEBELS, DAVE Keyboards. Member of Brent Maglia's backup band, 1977.

SIEGEL, CORKY Keyboards, vocal. Co-namesake of the Siegel-Schwall Band. *Album:* Corky Siegel (DHM 806).

SIEGEL, JANIS Vocal. Member of the Manhattan Transfer since 1971.

SIEGEL, PETE Member of the Even Dozen Jug Band, 1964.

SIEGEL-SCHWALL BAND Corky Siegel—keyboards, vocal; Jim Schwall—guitar, vocal; Rollo Radford—bass (1970); Shelly Potkin—drums (1970); Jim Dawson—bass; Russ Chadwick—drums. Jug and blues band contemporaries of the Lovin' Spoonful and others. *Albums:* Last Summer (WDN BWLI 0288); 953 West (WDN BWLI 0121); Siegel-Schwall Band; Three Pieces for a Blues Band; Best of Siegel-Schwall Band (VAN 79336); Say Siegel-Schwall (VAN 79249); Shake (VAN 79289); Siegel-Schwall Band (VAN 79235); Siegel-Schwall Band '70 (VAN 6562); R.I.P. Siegel-Schwall (WDN); Sleepy Hollow (WDN 1010).

SIEGLE, JOHN Guitar, vocal. Member of the Screams, 1980.

SIEGLER, JOHN Bass, cello. Member of Todd Rundgren's Utopia, 1974-76. Session for Hall and Oates (1974); Frank Carillo (1978).

SIFRE, GONCHI Drums, percussion, harmonica. Member of the Raices, 1975. Session for Roy Buchanan (1976).

SIGHS See Laurie and the Sighs.

SIGUENZA, RUBEN Bass. Backup for Mink DeVille, 1977.

SIKORSKI, JERRY Guitar. Session for Colin Winski (1980).

SILAGY, CHRIS Vocal, guitar, synthesizer. Member of 20/20, 1979.

SILENCERS No personnel listed. *Albums:* Rock 'n' Roll Enforcers (PRE JZ 36529) 1980.

SILENT DANCING Don Wilken—keyboards, vocal; John Berenzy—guitar, vocal; Mark Abel—bass, vocal; Leland Bobbe—drums, percussion. *Album:* City Lights (SIR) 1975.

SILICON TEENS Darryl—vocal; Jacki—synthesizer; Paul—percussion; Diane—synthesizer.

Album: Music for Parties (SIR SRK 6092) 1980.

SILK, JOHN Bass, vocal. Member of the Rank Strangers, 1977.

SILL, JUDEE Guitar, celeste, piano, vocal. Session for Russ Giguere (1971); Tim Weisberg (1974). *Albums:* Heart Food (ASY 5063); Judee Sill (ASY 5050).

SILLER, BOB Guitar, vocal. Member of Mephistopheles, and In Transit, 1980.

SILSON, ALAN Vocal, guitar. Member of Smokie, 1975-79.

SILVA, BLADE Vocal, guitar, harmonica. Founder of Toby Bean since 1978.

SILVA, STEVEN Guitar. Member of Thundertrain, 1977.

SILVER, KAREN Vocal. *Album:* Hold On, I'm Comin' (ARI 4248) 1979.

SILVER, MIKE Guitar, vocal. Session for Ray Thomas (1975).

SILVER APPLES Simeon—electronics, vocal; Dan Taylor—percussion, vocal. Ignoring the British invasion of the 1960s, this New York duet was experimenting with electronic music before Pink Floyd became popular. Enough variation existed in their arrangements to maintain listener interest, but not enough to inspire commercial success. *Albums:* Silver Apples (KAP 3562) 1968; Contact (KAP 3584) 1969.

SILVER BEATLES George Harrison—guitar; Paul McCartney—bass; John Lennon—guitar; Peter Best—drums; Stu Sutcliffe—guitar; Tony Sheridan—vocal. After Sheridan joined the Quarrymen in 1959, the group changed its name to the Silver Beatles. In 1961, Best was replaced by Ringo Starr, and Sutcliffe left the group. They then became known as the Beatles.

SILVER BULLET BAND Drew Abbott—guitar, vocal; Chris Campbell—bass, vocal; Rick Manasa—keyboards (1974); Charlie Martin—drums, vocal (1974-77); Alto Reed—saxophone, vocal, percussion (1976-present); Robyn Robbins—keyboards, vocal (1975-78); David Teegargen—drums (1978-present). Backup band for Bob Seger since 1974. See Bob Seger.

SILVER TRACTORS John Andersen—drums; Dennis Pendrith—bass; Ben Mink—mandolin, fiddle; Gene Martynec—guitar. Backup band for Murray McLaughlin, 1976-77. See Murray McLaughlin.

SILVERMAN, SHELLY Drums. Session for Peter Kaukonen (1972).

SILVESTER, ANDY Bass. Original member of Chicken Shack, and member of Savoy Brown, 1971-72, replacing Tone Stevens. Replaced Peter Freiberger in Big Wha-Koo, 1977. Session for Danny Kirwan; Mike Vernon; Christine McVie (1969); Chris Youlden (1973).

SILVIA, VICKY Vocal. Session for Nazareth (1975).

SIMEON Electronics, vocal. Co-founder of Silver Apples, 1968-69.

SIMMONDS, CLODAGH Vocal. Session for Mike Oldfield (1974).

SIMMONDS, JEFF Guitar, bass, vocal. Member of the Mothers of Invention, 1974. Session for Frank Zappa (1970, 72).

SIMMONDS, KIM Guitar, piano, harmonica, vocal. Founder of Savoy Brown, 1967-present.

SIMMONS, DEL Tenor saxophone, flute. Session for Captain Beefheart and His Magic Band (1974).

SIMMONS, GENE Bass, vocal. Real name: Gene Klein. Member of Kiss since 1973. *Album:* Kiss (CAS 7120, PIX-7120) 1978.

SIMMONS, "ANTENNAE" JIMMY Guitar. Original member of Captain Beefhart and His Magic Band, 1965-69.

SIMMONS, PAT Guitar, vocal. Co-founder of the Doobie Brothers, 1971-present. Session for Elton John (1979).

SIMMS, FRANK Vocal, guitar. With brother George, founder of the Simms Brothers Band, 1979-80.

SIMMS, GEORGE Vocal, percussion. With brother Frank, founder of the Simms Brothers Band, 1979-80.

SIMMS BROTHERS BAND George Simms—vocal, percussion; Frank Simms—vocal, guitar; Budd Tunick—drums; David Spinner—vocal, percussion; Robert Sabino—keyboards; Shimmy Maki—bass; Mickey Leonard—guitar. *Albums:* Simms Brothers Band (ELK 6E-220) 1979; Attitude (ELK 6E-289) 1980.

SIMON, CARLY Vocal, guitar. Born 6/25/45. Writer/singer whose solo career has gone from "Anticipation," 1971, to realization with a large following. Part of "No Nukes," 1979. Married to James Taylor. *Albums:* Another Passenger (ELK 7E-1064) 1976; Anticipation (ELK 75016) 1971; Best of Carly Simon (ELK 6E-109) 1975; Boys in the Trees (ELK 63-128) 1978; Come Upstairs (WBR BSK-3443) 1980; Hotcakes (ELK 7E-1002) 1974; No Secrets (ELK 75049) 1972; Playing Possum (ELK 7E-1033) 1975; Carly Simon (ELK 74082) 1976; Spy (ELK 5E-506) 1979; Carly Simon (ELK 4082) 1971.

SIMON, JEFF Drums. Member of George Thorogood and the Destroyers since 1975. Session for Preacher Jack (1980).

SIMON, JOHN Piano. Original member of the Electric Flag, 1967-68. Session for Taj Mahal; Dave Mason; Eric Clapton (1970); Howlin' Wolf (1972).

SIMON, JOHN Horns. Session for the Band (1977).

SIMON, LUCY Piano, vocal. *Album:* Lucy Simon (VIC APLI-1074) 1975.

SIMON, MARTIN Drums, vocal. Original member of Sharks, 1973-74.

SIMON, MARTY Piano. Session for Leslie West

(1975).

SIMON, PAUL Guitar, vocal. Early recording names: Paul Kane, Jerry Landis, True Taylor. Born 10/13/41. After leaving the famous Simon and Garfunkel duet that swept the 1960s, he continued as a soloist, at least matching the duo's popularity with his own. Made his acting debut in Woody Allen's *Annie Hall.* Produced, scored, and starred in *One Trick Pony,* 1980. Session for Art Garfunkel (1978). *Albums:* Paul Simon (COL KC 30750) 1972; Still Crazy After All These Years (COL PC 33540) 1975; Greatest Hits, Etc. (COL JC 35032) 1977; One Trick Pony (WBR HS 3472) 1980; There Goes Rhymin' Simon (COL KC 32280) 1973; Live Rhymin' (COL) 1974.

SIMON, ROBIN Guitar, vocal. Replaced Steve Shears in Ultravox, 1978-79, and John McGeogh in Magazine, 1980.

SIMON, SCOTT Piano, vocal. Replaced John Bauman in Sha Na Na, 1971-present.

SIMON AND GARFUNKEL Paul Simon—guitar, vocal; Art Garfunkel—vocal. Beginning in 1957 under the name of Tom and Jerry, they began perfecting their famous two-part harmonies in New York, despite the popularity of hip-shaking rock 'n' roll. By 1964, they had adopted their real names for their act, and constant air play of their first album made them stars of the pop-folk trend. "Sounds of Silence" became a classic in 1965, and was followed by "Feelin' Groovy." In 1968, they wrote and sang the soundtrack to Mike Nichols' film, *The Graduate.* By 1970, the partnership had reached the peak of its popularity. The two separated, not on unfriendly terms, to pursue their individual careers. *Albums:* Bookends (COL PC 9529) 1968; Bridge Over Troubled Water (COL JC 9914) 1970; The Graduate (COL JS 3180) 1968; Parsley, Sage, Rosemary and Thyme (COL PC 9363) 1966; Simon and Garfunkel's Greatest Hits (COL JC 31350); Sounds of Silence (COL JC 9269) 1966; Wednesday Morning, 3 A.M. (COL KCS 9049) 1964.

SIMONE, STEVEN Guitar, vocal. Member of Mephisopheles.

SIMONON, PAUL Bass, vocal. Member of the Clash since 1978.

SIMPER, NIC Bass, vocal. Original member of Deep Purple, 1968-70. Session for Lord Sutch.

SIMPLE MINDS Charles Burchill—guitar, violin, vocal; Derek Forbes—bass, vocal; Michael McNeil—keyboards, vocal; Brian McGee—drums, percussion, vocal; Jim Kerr—vocal. *Albums:* Life in a Day (PVC 7910) 1979; Empires and Dances (Import) 1980.

SIMPSON, CHRIS Vocal, guitar. Member of Magna Carta, 1976.

SIMPSON, GRAHAM Bass. Session for Roxy Music (1972).

SIMPSON, MEL Keyboards, vocal. Member of the Dog Soldier, 1975.

SIMPSON, MICHELLE Vocal. Session for John Lennon (1980).

SIMPSON, RICHIE Drums. Member of Acrobat, 1972.

SIMPSON, STEVE Guitar, violin, mandolin, harmonica. Session for Ronnie Lane (1975).

SIMPSON, VALERIE Vocal. Soloist and half of the husband-wife duet Ashford and Simpson since 1973. Session for Free Creek (1973); Steely Dan (1980). *Albums:* Keep It Comin' (TML T7-351); Smackwater Jack (AAM 3037).

SIMS, DICK Keyboards. Session for Bob Seger (1973); Eric Clapton (1974-75, 78); Marc Benno (1979).

SIMS, KAZOOT Kazoo. Member of the Temple City Kazoo Orchestra, 1978.

SIMS, LARRY Guitar, vocal. Member of the Sunshine Company, 1967-69. Member of Loggins and Messina's backup band, 1973-77.

SIMS, VON EVA Vocal. Session for Paul Simon (1972).

SIN, MARCO Bass, vocals. Member of the Dirty Looks, 1980.

SINATRA, NANCY Vocal. Daughter of Frank, she finally broke into the pop market with the aid of Lee Hazelwood with "These Boots Are Made for Walking," 1966. *Albums:* Boots (RPS) 1966; How Does That Grab You? (RPS) 1966; Nancy in London (RPS) 1966; Sugar (RPS) 1966; Country My Way (RPS) 1967; Movin' with Nancy and Lee (RPS) 1968; Speedway (VIC AFLI 3989); You Only Live Twice (UAR LT 289).

SINCERE SERENADERS See Graham Shaw and the Sincere Serenaders.

SINCEROS Ron Francois—bass, vocal; Mark Kjeldsen—guitar, vocal, writer; Don Snow—keyboards, vocal; Bobby Irwin—drums. *Album:* Sound of Sunbathing (COL JC-36134) 1979.

SINCLAIR, DAVID Keyboards, vocal, guitar. Member of the Caravan, and the Matching Mole. Session for Ian Lloyd.

SINCLAIR, DAVID Vocal, guitar. Member of the Straight Lines, 1980.

SINCLAIR, JOHN Synthesizer. Member of the Lion, 1980. Session for the Babys (1980).

SINCLAIR, RICHARD Bass, guitar, vocal. Member of the Caravan. Session for Robert Wyatt (1974).

SINFIELD, PETER Lyricist. Lyrical partner of Robert Fripp in King Crimson, 1969-72.

SINGER, HAL "CORNBREAD" Saxophone. Session for T-Bone Walker (1973); Brownie McGhee; Ray Charles; Joe Turner.

SINGER, MARC Drums, vocal. Member of the Waves, 1977.

SINN, SUNBIE Guitar, keyboards, vocal. Member of the Orchids, 1980.

SINNAEVE, SPIDER Bass, vocal. Member of

Streetheart, 1979.

SINNAMON, SHANDI Vocal. *Albums:* Shandi Sinnamon (ASY 7E-1054); Shandi (DML DL 5001) 1980.

SINZHEIMER, HUGO Vocal. Member of the Meteors, 1980.

SIOMOS, JOHN Drums, percussion. Member of Frampton's Camel, 1973, and Jobraith, 1973-74. Session for Corbett and Hirsch (1971); Peter Frampton (1975-77); Terry Reid (1979).

SIR DOUGLAS QUINTET Doug Sahm—guitar, fiddle, vocal, writer; George Rains—drums; Whitney Freeman—bass; Bill Atwood—trumpet; Terry Henry—trumpet; Mel Martin—trumpet; Frank Morin—trumpet; Martin Ferrio—trumpet; Wayne Talbert—piano. From Janis Joplin's home state of Texas, Sahm brought his group to San Francisco for his hit, "She's About a Mover," in 1966, before returning to his honky-blues roots. *Albums:* Best of Sir Douglas Quintet, 1966; Sir Douglas Quintet Plus 2 Equals Honky Blues, 1968.

SIXPENCE Early name for the Strawberry Alarm Clock.

SKAFISH, JIM Piano, vocal. Namesake of Skafish, 1980.

SKAFISH Jim Skafish—piano, vocal; Ken Bronowski—guitar, bugle, vocal; Javier Cruz—keyboards, synthesizer, vocal; Barbie Goodrich—guitar, vocal; Larry Mazalan—bass, vocal; Larry Mysliwiec—drums, percussion. *Album:* Skafish (IRS 008) 1980.

SKEAPING, RODDY Violin. Member of Centipede, 1971.

SKEEN, ROB Bass, vocal. Member of the Nervous Eaters, 1980.

SKEETON, JOHN Flute, vocal. Member of the Candle, 1972.

SKIDMORE, ALAN Tenor saxophone. Started in Blues Incorporated. Member of Centipede, 1971, and Candlestick Brass, 1977. Session for John Mayall's Bluesbreakers (1967); the Soft Machine (1970); Long John Baldry (1971); Bryan Ferry (1974).

SKIDS Richard Jobson—vocal; Stuart Adamson—guitar; Russell Webb; Mike Baillie. *Album:* Scared to Dance (VIR 2116) 1979.

SKIFS, BJORN Vocal. Member of the Blue Swede.

SKILL, MIKE Member of the Romantics, 1980.

SKIN ALLEY Nick Graham—bass, keyboards, flute, vocal; Tony Knight—drums, percussion, vocal; Bob James—guitar, reeds, vocal; Krzysztof Juszkiewicz—keyboards, accordion. *Album:* Two Quid Deal (STX 3013) 1973.

SKIN, FLESH AND BONE Ranche McLean—guitar; Errol Nelson—keyboards; Lloyd Parks—bass; Charley Dunbar—drums; Pat Lewis—congas; Cynthia Richards—percussion. Backup band for Arthur Brown, 1975.

SKINNER, DAVID Piano. Session for Bryan Ferry (1974, 77).

SKINNER, JACK Bass, vocal. Voice of Sundance, 1976. *Albums:* Confederation (SLB 9); Thriving Species (TKM 1065).

SKINNER, SANFORD Trumpet. Member of the Righteous Brothers Band, 1966.

SKLAR, LELAND Bass. Member of the Section, 1972, 77. Session for Carole King; James Taylor; the Doors (1972); Art Garfunkel; Rita Coolidge (1972); John Kay (1973); Donovan (1973, 76); Gene Clark (1974); Steve Stills (1975); Neil Sedaka (1975-76); Rod Stewart (1975-76); Glen Campbell (1976); Dick St. Nicklaus (1979); Hoyt Axton (1974); Kim Carnes (1975); Cher (1976, 79); Jelly (1977); Karla Bonoff (1977); Dave Lambert (1979); Alan O'Day (1979); Richie Furay (1979); Warren Zevon (1980); Billy Thorpe (1979); Roger Voudouris (1979); Steven T. (1978).

SKOLNIK, STEVE Keyboards. Member of Fischer-Z since 1979.

SKY, BOBBY BLUE Drums. Member of Duke and the Drivers, 1975.

SKY, PATRICK Guitar, harmonica, vocal. *Albums:* Patrick Sky (VAN 79179); Songs that Made America Famous (ADP 4101) 1973; Two Steps Forward, One Step Back (LEV).

SKY Doug Fieger—bass, guitar, vocal; John Coury—guitar, keyboards, flute, vocal; Rob Stawinski—drums, percussion. Multi-talented English trio that attracted Jimmy Miller, producer, for two dynamic albums (1970, 71) that included top-name session men. The more than adequate hit potential of each album was never realized and they faded into obscurity. *Albums:* Don't Hold Back (VIC LSP 4457) 1970; Sailor's Delight (VIC LSP 4514) 1971.

SKY DOG BAND See Randy Burns and the Sky Dog Band.

SKYBOYS Dudley Hill—guitar, vocal; Gaye Winsor—keyboards, vocal; Tom Kell—guitar, vocal; Leon Edwards Waldbauer—guitar, harmonica, vocal; Scott Smith—piano, guitar, vocal; Pat Bohle—drums; Ken Parypa—bass, vocal. Seattle-based country rock band. *Album:* Skyboys (FSM 7709) 1979.

SKYER, MARK Guitar, vocal. Session for Harvey Mandel (1974).

SKYHOOKS Graeme Strachan—vocal; Redmond Symons—guitar, vocal, piano; Bob Starkie—guitar; Fred Kaboodleschnitzer—drums, vocal; Greg Macainsh—bass. *Albums:* Livin' in the 70's (MER SRM 1-1124) 1977; Ego Is Not a Dirty Word, 1975.

SKYSCRAPER AND THE SNAKES Early band of XTC's Colin Moulding and Terry Chambers.

SLADE, CHRIS Drums, percussion. Member of Manfred Mann's Earth Band, 1972-78. Session for Frankie Miller (1979).

SLADE, ROD Bass. Member of the Alan Price

Set, 1965-68.

SLADE Noddy Holder—vocal, guitar; Dave Hill—guitar, vocal; Jimmy Lea—bass, vocal; Don Powell—drums. Masters of high volume, Slade featured the screaming Holder and attracted hordes of youths in the early 1970s. After their initial impact, Slade attempted to broaden their musical range and image with little success. *Albums:* Slade Alive (POL 5502) 1972; Slayed (POL 5524) 1972; Nobody's Fool (WBR 2936) 1976; Sladest (RPS 2173) 1973; Stomp Your Hands, Clap Your Feet, 1973.

SLAGER, JOHAN Guitar, vocal. Member of Kayak.

SLAIS, BILL Synthesizer, vocal. Session for Elvin Bishop (1975).

SLAMMER, MIKE Vocal, guitar, percussion. Member of the City Boy, 1976.

SLATER, CAROL Violin. Member of Centipede, 1971.

SLATER, GRANT Synthesizer. Session for Long John Baldry (1980).

SLATER, MUTTER Member of Stackridge, 1974.

SLATER, RODNEY Saxophone. Original member of the Bonzo Dog Doo-Dah Band.

SLAUGHTER, RICKY Drums. Member of the Motors, 1977-78.

SLAUGHTER Eddie Garrity—vocal; Howard Bates—bass, vocal; Phil Rowland—drums, percussion; Mike Rossi—guitar, vocal. *Album:* Bite Back (DJM 32) 1980.

SLAVEN, KEN Fiddle. Session for Ronnie Lane (1975).

SLAVEN, NEIL Guitar, producer. Production and session for Tony McPhee. Produced Chicken Shack; Savoy Brown (1971-73); Trapeze (1974); and others.

SLAVIN, GILBERT Keyboards, flute. Member of Man.

SLEDGE, PERCY Vocal. Soul sensation of 1966 with "When a Man Loves a Woman." *Albums:* When a Man Loves a Woman, 1966; Warm and Tender Soul, 1966; Percy Sledge Way, 1967; Take Time to Know Her; I'll Be Your Everything; Best of Percy Sledge (ATC 8210) 1969; Golden Soul (ATC 18198); Super-Hits (ATC 501).

SLICK, DARBY Guitar. Member of the Great Society.

SLICK, EARL Guitar. Namesake of the Slick Band, 1976. Session for Ian Hunter; John Lennon (1980).

SLICK, GRACE Vocal, guitar, keyboards. Born 10/30/43. From the Great Society, Slick replaced Signe Andersen in the Jefferson Airplane, 1966-72, and Starship, 1973-78. Her distinctive vocal style and lyrics were instrumental in the Airplane's and Starship's success. Member of Seastones, 1976. Session for David Crosby (1971). *Albums:* Dreams (VIC AFLI 3544) 1980; Manhole (GRT BFLI 0347) 1973.

SLICK, JERRY Drums. Member of the Great Society.

SLICK BAND Earl Slick—guitar; Jimmie Mack—vocal, guitar; Gene Ceppik—bass, vocal; Bryan Madey—drums, percussion. *Album:* Slick Band (CAP ST 11493) 1976.

SLOAN, ALLEN Violin, viola. Member of the Dixie Dregs.

SLOANE, MILTON Saxophone. Session for Joe Cocker (1972).

SLOMAN, JOHN Vocal. Voice of Lone Star, 1977.

SLUTSKY, MARTIN Guitar. Member of McKendree Spring.

SLY Drums. Member of Dillinger, 1976.

SLY AND THE FAMILY STONE Sly Stone—organ, vocal; Rose Stone—piano, vocal; Fred Stone—guitar, vocal; Larry Graham, Jr.—bass, vocal; Greg Errico—drums; Jerry Martini—reeds, piano, percussion, accordion; Cynthia Robinson—trumpet, vocal; Mark Davis—keyboards (1979); Alvin Taylor—drums (1979); Keni Burke—bass (1979); Hamp Banks—guitar (1979); Joseph Baker—guitar (1979). Sly first appeared in 1967, taking soul music and carrying it to its rocking extremes. Drawing from both audiences, he gathered a large, loyal following. Played at Woodstock, 1969. *Albums:* Small Talk (EPC PE 32936) 1974; Whole New Thing, 1967; High on You (COL PE 33835) 1975; High Energy, 1975; Greatest Hits (EPC PE 30325); There's a Riot Goin' On (EPC E 30986); Dance to the Music (EPC E 30334) 1968; Life (EPC E 30333) 1968; Stand (EPC 26456) 1969; Fresh (EPC KE 32134) 1973; Heard Ya Missed Me, Well I'm Back (COL PE 34348) 1976; Ten Years Too Soon (COL JE 35974) 1979; Back on the Right Track (WBR K 3033) 1979.

SMALL, GEORGE Keyboards. Session for John Lennon (1980).

SMALL, HENRY Violin, vocal, mandolin. Member of the Small Wonder, 1976-77. *Album:* California Dreaming (ARI 3001).

SMALL, JANET Keyboards, vocal. Member of the Shakers.

SMALL, LINDA Trombone. Session for Jules and the Polar Bears (1979).

SMALL, MICK Guitar. Member of the Growl, 1974.

SMALL, PHIL Bass. Member of the Cold Chisel, 1979.

SMALL FACES Steve Marriott—vocal, guitar, harpsichord (1967-68, 77-78), Ian McLagan—keyboards, vocal (1967-68, 77-78); Kenny Jones—drums, vocal (1966-67, 77-78); Rick Wills—bass, vocal (1977-78); Ronnie Lane—bass, guitar, vocal (1967-68). Original members of the group that recorded "Itchycoo Park" in 1968, Marriott, McLagan, and Jones re-formed in 1977 after their ventures in Humble Pie and the Faces. Wills, from

Frampton's Camel, was recruited to fill Ronnie Lane's place on bass. See the Faces. *Album:* Playmates (ATC S 19113) 1977; In the Shade (ATC S 19171) 1978.

SMALL WONDER Jimmy Phillips—keyboards, vocal; Jerry Morin—guitar, vocal; Henry Small—violin, vocal, mandolin; Billy King. *Albums:* Growin' (COL PC 34425) 1977; Small Wonder (COL PC 34100) 1976.

SMALLMAN, GARY Member of the Penetration, 1979.

SMARR, ROD Guitar. Replaced George Cummings in Dr. Hook and the Medicine Show, 1980. Member of the Rock Killough Group, 1980.

SMART, N. D. Drums. Session for Leslie West (1968).

SMILE Early name for Queen.

SMIT, FRANS Drums. Session for Jan Akkerman (1972).

SMITH, AARON Drums. Session for the Temptations (1973).

SMITH, ANDREW Drums. Session for the Temptations (1973).

SMITH, BILL Bass. Session for Long John Baldry (1972).

SMITH, BILL Vocal. Member of Hellfield, 1978.

SMITH, BOB Keyboards. Member of Cat Mother and All Night Newsboys. Session on Free Creek (1973).

SMITH, BOBBY Bass, vocal. Member of the Lost Gonzo Band, 1978.

SMITH, BRIAN Bass. Member of Scargill, 1979. Session for Watson-Beasley (1980).

SMITH, BRIAN Tenor saxophone. Began in Blues Incorporated. Member of Centipede, 1971, and Ian Carr's Nucleus, 1979. Session for Memphis Slim (1971).

SMITH, BRIAN Guitar, vocal. Member of Trooper since 1975.

SMITH, BRUCE Drums. Member of the Pop Group, 1980.

SMITH, CATHERINE Vocal. Session for Gordon Lightfoot (1974).

SMITH, CURLEY Drums, vocal. Original member of Jo Jo Gunne, 1972-74. Session for Jay Ferguson (1979-80).

SMITH, CURLEY Harmonica. Session for Danny Spanos (1980).

SMITH, DEAN Guitar. Member of Captain Beefheart's Magic Band, 1974.

SMITH, DENNIS Bass, vocal. Member of the Secret Affair, 1980.

SMITH, DON Bass. Session for Waylon Jennings (1973).

SMITH, DON Horns. Session for Paul Butterfield (1980).

SMITH, DUANE Piano. Session for Bill Wyman (1974).

SMITH, EARL Guitar, percussion. Member of Bob Marley's Wailers.

SMITH, ENRICO Castanets. Session for Arthur Brown (1975).

SMITH, FRAN, JR. Member of Nan Mancini and JDB, 1979.

SMITH, FRANK Bass. Session for Lee Michaels.

SMITH, FRED Drums. Session for John Cale (1975).

SMITH, FRED Guitar. Member of the MC 5, 1968-69.

SMITH, FRED Bass, vocal. Member of Television, 1977-78. Session for Tom Verlaine (1979); Richard Lloyd (1979); the Roches (1980).

SMITH, FREDDY Horns. Session for Jimi Hendrix (1968).

SMITH, G. Bass. Session for Chuck Berry (1958).

SMITH, G. E. Guitar. Session for Gilda Radner (1979).

SMITH, GARRY Harmonica. Session for Gary Brooker (1979).

SMITH, GARY Drums, percussion. Member of the Survivor, 1979.

SMITH, GEORGE Guitar. Session for the Blast (1979).

SMITH, GORDON Vocal, guitar. British blues soloist of the 1960s.

SMITH, GRAHAM Harmonica. Session for Ken Tobias (1973).

SMITH, GRAHAME Violin, viola. Member of the String Driven Thing, 1972-75, and Van Der Graaf, 1978.

SMITH, HOWARD Drums. Member of the Vapors, 1980.

SMITH, J. Keyboards. Session for Rod Stewart (1976).

SMITH, JAMES QUILL Guitar, harmonica, vocal, producer. Member of Pollution, 1971. Session with John Mayall (1977-79).

SMITH, JAMES "SMITTY" Guitar. Session for Dr. John (1975).

SMITH, JERRY Slide guitar. Member of Kenny and the Kasuals.

SMITH, JERRY Piano. Session for J. J. Cale (1974).

SMITH, JERRY Bass. Member of the Flock.

SMITH, JESSE MAY Vocal. Session for Dr. John (1972-73); Elton John (1974); Bryan Ferry (1974).

SMITH, JON Tenor saxophone, vocal. Original member of White Trash. Session for Johnny Winter (1973).

SMITH, KESTER "SMITTY" Drums, percussion. Session for Taj Mahal (1977).

SMITH, KEVIN Guitar, slide guitar. Member of the Unicorn, 1974-77, and Thumbs, 1979.

SMITH, LARRY Baritone saxophone, vocal. Member of Stanley Steamer, 1973.

SMITH, LARRY "LEGS" Drums. Original member of the Bonzo Dog Doo-Dah Band. Session for Elton John (1972); George Harrison (1975).

Album: Legs Larry Smith.

SMITH, LAWSON Member of Hank Ballard's Midnighters.

SMITH, LESLIE Vocal, percussion. Member of Crackin', 1975-78.

SMITH, LUKE Vocal. Session for Bob Seger (1973).

SMITH, MARK E. Vocal. Member of the Fall, 1979.

SMITH, MARTIN Vocal, guitar. Member of Charlie, 1976-79.

SMITH, MICHAEL LEE Vocal. Voice of Starz, 1976-77.

SMITH, MIKE Vocal, piano, vibes. Member of the Dave Clark 5, 1964-68.

SMITH, MIKE Drums. Member of Paul Revere and the Raiders, 1965.

SMITH, MYRNA Vocal. Member of the Sweet Inspirations, 1967-69.

SMITH, NEAL Drums. Member of the Alice Cooper Band, 1970-73, and the Billion Dollar Babies, 1977.

SMITH, NIGEL Vocal, bass, keyboards. Member of Magna Carta, 1976.

SMITH, NOLAN Trumpet. Session for John Mayall (1977).

SMITH, PAT Vocal. Session for Barry Goldberg (1974).

SMITH, PATTI Vocal. Born 12/31/46. Composer/performer head of the Patti Smith Group since 1975.

PATTI SMITH GROUP Ivan Kral—guitar, bass; Jay Dee Daugherty—drums; Lenny Kaye—guitar; Richard Sohl—piano; Patti Smith—vocal; Bruce Brodie—keyboards, synthesizer (1978). *Albums:* Easter (ARI 4171) 1978; Horses (ARI 4066) 1975; Radio Ethiopia (ARI 4097) 1976; Wave (ARI 4221) 1979.

SMITH, PATTY Vocal. Session for John Mayall (1977).

SMITH, PAUL Keyboards. Session for Frank Zappa (1967).

SMITH, RAY Guitar, vocal. Member of Heads, Hands and Feet, 1970-71, and Flying Island, 1976. Session for Jerry Lee Lewis (1973).

SMITH, REX Vocal. Voice of Rex, 1977, before going solo. *Albums:* Forever (COL JC 36275) 1979; Rex (COL PC 34399) 1976; Sooner or Later (COL JC 35813); Where Do We Go from Here (COL PC 34865) 1977.

SMITH, ROBERT Guitar, vocal. Member of the Cure, 1979.

SMITH, ROLLO Guitar, vocal. Member of the Naughty Sweeties, 1980.

SMITH, RON Guitar. Member of George Thorogood and the Destroyers, 1977.

SMITH, ROSCOE Drums. Session for Leon Russell (1974).

SMITH, RUSS Bass, vocal. Member of Ramatam, 1972.

SMITH, RUSSELL Guitar, harmonica, vocal. Member of the Amazing Rhythm Aces.

SMITH, SCOTT Piano, guitar, vocal. Member of the Skyboys, 1979-present.

SMITH, SCOTT Bass. Member of Loverboy, 1980.

SMITH, SKIP Drums. Member of the Blend, 1978-79.

SMITH, STERLING Organ. Session for Terry Reid (1979).

SMITH, STEVE Drums. Replaced Aynsley Dunbar in Journey, 1979-present.

SMITH, STEVE Guitar, keyboards. Session for the Hot Dogs (1973).

SMITH, STEVE Bass, vocal. Member of the Vapors, 1980.

SMITH, STEVEN MAXWELL Violin. Session for Waylon Jennings (1973).

SMITH, TERRY Guitar. Original member of If, 1973, and Zzebra, 1974.

SMITH, TIM Vocal. Session for Lynyrd Skynrd (1977).

SMITH, TONY Vocal, guitar. Member of the Lone Star, 1977.

SMITH, TONY Drums. Session for Santana (1974).

SMITH, VIC Guitar, vocal. Member of Marty Balin's Jefferson Airplane on "Bodacious."

SMITH, WALLY Trombone. Member of the Candlestick Brass, 1977.

SMITH, WARREN Drums. Original member of Pearls Before Swine, 1967.

SMITH, WILLIE Drums. Session for Muddy Waters (1978).

SMITH, WILLIE Organ, vocal. Session for Nilsson (1974); Bill Wyman (1974); Neil Sedaka (1975); Richie Furay (1979); the Vapour Trails (1980); Ry Cooder (1980).

SMITH, WILLIE Guitar, vocal. Member of the Phyrework, 1978.

SMITH Jerry Carter; James Cliburn; Gayle McCormick—vocal; Bob Evans; Larry Moss. Smith scored in the early 1970s with their arrangement of the Band's "The Weight" (which was used in the movie *Easy Rider*), before McCormick went solo. *Album:* A Group Called Smith (DHL).

SMITH-FROST, BARTHOLOMEW E. Drums, percussion. Head of Sweathog, 1973, and the Naughty Sweeties, 1980. Session for Lee Michaels (1968, 72).

SMITHWICK, BRYAN Bass. Member of the Brains, 1980.

SMOKEY HOGG Vocal, guitar. Country-influenced bluesman. *Albums:* Anthology of the Blues—Texas Blues (KNT 9005); Smokey Hogg (KNT 524); 20 Greatest Rhythm and Blues Hits (KNT 527).

SMOKIE Chris Norman—vocal, guitar; Alan Silson—vocal, guitar; Terry Utley—bass; Peter Spencer—drums. *Albums:* Smokie, 1975; Midnight Cafe

(RSO 1-3005) 1975; Bright Lights and Black Alley (RSO 1-3029) 1977; Montreux Album (RSO 1-3045) 1979.

SMOTHERMAN, MICHAEL Keyboards, vocal. Member of Captain Beefheart's Magic Band, 1974, and Buckwheat.

SMYTHE, DANNY Drums. Member of the Box Tops, 1965-68.

SNAFU Mick Moody—guitar, mandolin, harmonica; Bobby Harrison—vocal, percussion; Peter Solley—keyboards, fiddle; Terry Popple—drums, percussion; Colin Gibson—bass, percussion. *Albums:* Snafu (CAP) 1973; Situation Normal (CAP) 1975.

SNAIL Bob O'Neill—guitar, vocal; Ken Kraft—guitar, vocal; Brett Bloomfield—bass, vocal; Don Baldwin—drums, percussion, vocal. *Albums:* Flow (CRE 1012) 1979; Snail (CRE 1009) 1978.

SNAKEFINGER Guitar, vocal. Residents-styled soloist. *Albums:* Greener Postures (RLF 8053-L) 1980; Chewing Hides the Sound (RLF 7909).

SNAKESTRETCHERS Roy Buchanan—guitar, vocal; Ned Davis—drums (1972-73); Dick Heintze—keyboards; Teddy Irwin—guitar; Chuck Tilley—vocal; Pete Van Allen—bass (1972-73); Jerry Mercer—drums (1973); Don Payne—bass (1973). Backup group for Roy Buchanan, 1972-73.

SNAPE Alexis Korner—vocal, guitar; Peter Thorup—vocal, guitar, slide guitar; Ian Wallace—drums; Boz—bass, vocal; Mel Collins—saxophone, flute, piano. Session band for Alexis Korner, 1972.

SNARE, C. P. Drums. Member of Athletico Spizz 80, 1980.

SNARE, RICHIE Drums. Session for Nilsson (1972).

SNEAKERS D. Willy—vocal, guitar; Billy Rich—vocal, guitar; Johnny Zipgun—bass; C. Carr—keyboards, vocal; Marquis Olsen—drums, vocal. *Album:* Ear Cartoons (CLR 101) 1980.

SNEAKY PETE Steel guitar. Real name: Pete Kleinow. Original member of the Flying Burrito Brothers, 1969. Session for Crazy Horse; Arthur, Hurley and Gottlieb; Cherokee (1971); Frank Zappa (1972); Henry Gross (1972); Rita Coolidge (1972); the Bee Gees (1973); Martin Mull (1973); Gram Parsons (1973); John Lennon (1973); the Steve Miller Band (1973); Nilsson (1974); Neil Sedaka (1976).

SNEED, FLOYD Drums, percussion. Member of Three Dog Night.

SNIFF 'N' THE TEARS Paul Roberts—vocal, guitar; Mick Dyche—guitar; Luigi Salvoni—drums, percussion; Alan Fealdman—keyboards (1978); Chris Birkin—bass (1978); Loz Netto—guitar; Mike Taylor—keyboards (1980); Nick South—bass (1980). *Albums:* Fickle Heart (ATC 19242) 1978; The Game's Up (ATC 19272) 1980.

SNIPS Vocal. Lead singer for Sharks, 1973-74, before joining the Baker-Gurvitz Army, 1975-76. Session for Ginger Baker (1977).

SNOPEK, SIGMUND, III Vocal, synthesizer, keyboards, flute. Namesake of Snopek since 1979.

SNOPEK Sigmund Snopek III—vocal, synthesizer, keyboards, flute; Byron Wiemann III—vocal, guitar; Jim Gorton—vocal, bass; Mike Lucas—drums; Keith de Bolt—vocal (1980). *Albums:* Thinking Out Loud (MRR 52789) 1979; First Band on the Moon (MRR 52795) 1980.

SNOW, DON Keyboards, vocal. Member of the Sinceros, 1979.

SNOW, PHOEBE Vocal, guitar. Folk composer who introduced jazz to her audiences. *Albums:* Against the Grain (COL JC-35456) 1978; It Looks Like Snow (COL PC 34387) 1976; Never Letting Go (COL JC 34875) 1977; Second Childhood (COL PC 33952) 1976; Phoebe Snow (MCA 52017) 1974.

SNOW, SHERRY Vocal. Member of Dan Hicks and His Hot Licks.

SNYDER, AL Guitar, vocal. Member of the U.S. Radio Band, 1976.

SNYDER, CARL Piano. Member of the Jimmy Johnson Band, 1977.

SNYDER, CRAIG Guitar. Session for Elton John (1979).

SNYDER, GIL Keyboards, vocal. Member of the Iron City Houserockers since 1979.

SNYDER, MICHAEL Member of the A's, 1979.

SNYDER, STEVE Trumpet, trombone, vocal. Member of the Bill Blue Band, 1980.

SOBEL, PETE Bass. Session for the Private Lines (1980).

SOCARRAS, JORGE Vocal. Member of the Indoor Life, 1980.

SOD Robert Arnold—bass, tuba, percussion, vocal; Joseph Molina—keyboards, trumpet, percussion; Michael Green—horns, percussion, vocal; Larry Devers—drums, vocal; Richard Kellis—saxophone, vocal, flute; Don Phillips—guitar, vocal; Jay York—percussion, vocal. *Album:* Sod (COL) 1971.

SOFT MACHINE Michael Ratledge—keyboards; Robert Wyatt—vocal, drums, bass, piano, trumpet, cello; Kevin Ayers—vocal, guitar, bass; Roy Babbington—bass (1973); Hugh Hopper—bass (1970); Elton Dean—saxophone (1970); Karl Jenkins—reeds, piano (1973); John Marshall—drums (1973); David Allen—vocal, guitar. English experimental jazz-rock group that first appeared in 1968. *Albums:* Soft Machine 5 (COL KC 31604); Soft Machine (CMD 864) 1968; Soft Machine, Vol. 2, 1969; Bundles (EMH SHSP-4044); Fourth (COL C-30754) 1970; Soft Machine (COL C 32716) 1973; Softs (EMH SHSP 4056); Third (COL CG 30339); Triple Echo (EMH SHTW-800); The Progressives (COL); Six (COL KG 32260).

SOHL, RICHARD Piano. Member of the Patti Smith Group since 1975.

SOLAR, JIM Bass. Member of Athletico Spizz 80, 1980.

SOLBERG, CHRIS Guitar, vocal, organ. Member of the Shakers, and Santana, 1978-80.

SOLEM, PHIL Session for the Tremblers (1980).

SOLES, STEVEN Vocal, guitar, keyboards. Member of Tidbits, and the Alpha Band, 1977. Session for Bob Dylan (1975, 78, 79).

SOLLEY, PETE Keyboards, fiddle, vocal, producer. Member of Snafu, 1973-75, and Fox. Produced the Sports (1979); the Romantics (1980); Greg Clemmons (1980); and others. Session for Arthur Brown (1975); Whitesnake (1978).

SOLOFF, LEWIS Trumpet. Member of Blood, Sweat and Tears. Session for Free Creek (1973); Johnny Winter (1974); Randle Bramblett (1975); Ian Hunter (1976); John Mayall (1979).

SOLOMON, ANDY Keyboards. Member of the Amboy Dukes.

SOLOMON, CLIFFORD Tenor saxophone. Played with John Mayall, 1971-72. Session for Canned Heat (1972); Dr. John (1975); Terry Reid (1976).

SOLOMON, KING Keyboards. Member of Son Seal's Blues Band, 1980.

SOMA Bass. Session for Mike Bloomfield (1978).

SOMLO, THOMAS Bass, saxophone, violin, vocal. Member of Locomotive GT, 1974-75.

SOMMERS, ANDY Guitar, vocal. Replaced Vic Briggs in the Animals, 1968. Released a little-known solo attempt after the group disbanded. Session for Tim Rose (1976).

SOMMERS, BILL Drums. Born 4/17/46. Original member of the Grateful Dead, replaced by Mickey Hart.

SOMMERS, RONNIE Early recording name of Sonny Bono.

SOMMERVILLE, DAVE Vocal. Member of the Diamonds.

SONICS Gerry Roslie—piano, vocal; Andy Parypa—bass, vocal; Larry Parypa—guitar, vocal; Rob Lind—saxophone, vocal; Bob Bennett—drums, percussion. The Beatles may have invaded the country in the mid 1960s, but the Pacific Northwest's Sonics made a minor splash with their classic, "The Witch," and follow up "Psycho." *Albums:* Here are the Sonics (EQT); Boom (EQT); Original Northwest Punk (FSM 7715) 1977; Unreleased (FSM 7719) 1980; Sinderella (BMP 4011) 1980.

SONNY AND CHER Sonny Bono—vocal; Cher Bono—vocal. The union of folk and rock and the romance of a husband and wife made Sonny and Cher the pop rage of 1965 with "I Got You Babe." As hit after hit followed, including "Beat Goes On" (1966), "Baby Don't Go" (1965), and others, Cher developed as the performer and Sonny as the writer/manager. From pop-folk heroes to stalwarts of pop, older and less revolutionary, their divorce in 1976 did little to affect their separate recording and television careers. See individual listings. *Albums:* Look at Us, 1965; Wondrous World of Sonny and Cher, 1966; In Case You're in Love, 1967; Good Times, 1967; This Good Earth, 1968; All I Ever Need Is You; Live an Las Vegas; Greatest Hits; Mama Was a Rock 'n' Roll Singer; Beat Goes On (ACO 11000); Best of Sonny and Cher (ACO 219) 1967; Sonny and Cher "Live" (MCA 2009); Two of Us (ACO 2-804).

SONS OF CHAMPLIN Bill Champlin—vocal, keyboards, guitar; Terry Haggerty—guitar; Geoffery ,Palmer—saxophone, keyboards; Jim Preston—drums, percussion, vocal; Steve Frediana—saxophone, flute; David Shallock—bass. Part of Fillmore, 1972. *Albums:* Circle Filled with Love, 1976; Sons of Champlin, 1975; Loosen Up Naturally (CAP SWBB-200); Sons (CAP SM-332).

SONY, DICKY Vocal. Member of Navasota, 1972.

SOPWITH CAMEL Good-time San Francisco band in the Lovin' Spoonful tradition that appeared in 1967. *Albums:* Sopwith Camel, 1967; Hello, Hello; Miraculous Hump Returns from the Moon (RPS 2108).

SORENSON, LARS Horns. Session for the Heats (1980).

SORRENTO, MOOSE Vocal. Voice of the Colwell-Winfield Blues Band, 1968.

SORROWS Arthur Alexander—guitar; Ricky Street—bass; Jett Harris—drums; Joey Cola—guitar. *Album:* Teenage Heartbreak (PAV NJZ 36369) 1980.

SOUL GIANTS Early name for the Mothers of Invention.

SOUL SURVIVORS Ken Jeremiah—vocal; Richard Ingui—vocal; Charles Ingui—vocal; Paul Venturini—organ; Edward Leonetti—guitar; Joey Forgione—drums. White rhythm and blues group from New York that hit the charts in 1967 with "Expressway to Your Heart." *Album:* When the Whistle Blows, Anything Goes, 1967.

SOULE, GEORGE Drums, vocal. Session for J. J. Cale (1972); Tony Joe White (1972); Willie Nelson (1974).

SOULE, KENNY Drums. Member of Nantucket since 1978.

SOULE, MICKEY LEE Keyboards. Original member of Ritchie Blackmore's Rainbow, 1975-76. Session for Roger Glover (1978).

SOUMAR, CHUCK Percussion, vocal, harmonica. Member of the Ides of March.

SOUTH, ANGEL Guitar. Member of Chase, 1971-73, and Cottonwood South, 1974.

SOUTH, JOE Vocal. Recorded "Games People Play," 1969. *Albums:* Joe South's Greatest Hits (CAP SM 450); Midnight Rainbows (ISL 9328) 1975.

SOUTH, NICK Bass. Member of the Blue Goose, 1975. Replaced Chris Birkin in Sniff 'n' the Tears, 1980. Session for Mike Vernon; Donovan (1977).

SOUTHER, JOHN DAVID Guitar, vocal. After

starting as a soloist, he became popular in the Souther-Hillman-Furay Band, 1974-75, before continuing as a soloist again. Session for Joe Walsh (1974); Richie Furay (1979); Warren Zevon (1980); Christopher Cross (1980). *Albums:* John David Souther, 1974; Black Rose (ASY 74-1059) 1976; You're Only Lonely (COL JC-36093) 1979.

SOUTHER-HILLMAN-FURAY BAND John David Souther—guitar, vocal; Chris Hillman—guitar, bass, vocal, mandolin; Richie Furay—guitar, vocal; Al Perkins—steel guitar, bass, guitar, dobro; Joe Lala—percussion; Jim Gordon—drums, percussion (1974); Ron Grinel—drums (1975). After leaving Poco, Furay joined ex-Byrd Hillman, soloist Souther, and well-known session men Gordon, Perkins and Lala, in what could have been one of country rock's most impressive super-groups. A good first album was followed by a less appealing second album, that gave testimony to the adage "too many cooks spoil the broth." Within a year of their breakup, each namesake in the band's title had released solo albums. *Albums:* Souther-Hillman-Furay Band (ASY 7E-1006) 1974; Trouble in Paradise (ASY 7E-1036) 1975.

SOUTHERN COMFORT See Matthew's Southern Comfort.

SOUTHERN CONTEMPORARY ROCK ASSEMBLY See S.C.R.A.

SOUTHSIDE BAND Charley Musselwhite—harmonica, vocal; Harvey Mandel—guitar; Barry Goldberg—keyboards; Bob Anderson—bass; Fred Below, Jr.—drums. Backup band for Musselwhite from Chicago, playing the music of Muddy Waters, Howlin' Wolf, John Lee Hooker and other great blues artists to the post-World War II generation in the 1960s. See Charles Musselwhite.

SOUTHSIDE JOHNNY Harmonica, vocal. Born 12/4/48. Leader of Southside Johnny and the Asbury Jukes.

SOUTHSIDE JOHNNY AND THE ASBURY JUKES Southside Johnny—harmonica, vocal; Kenny Pentifallo—drums, vocal (1976-78); Kevin Kavanaugh—keyboards, vocal; Billy Rush—guitar; Alan Berger—bass (1976-79); Carlo Novi—saxophone (1976); Steve Buslowe—bass (1980); Rick Gasda—trumpet; Eddie Manion—baritone saxophone; Bob Malach—tenor saxophone (until 1977); Louie Parente—trombone (until 1977); Earl Gardner—trumpet (until 1977); Steve Becker—drums (1978-present); Richard Rosenberg—trombone (1978-present); Joel Gramolini—guitar, vocal (1979-present); Bob Muckin—trumpet, flugelhorn (1979-present); Stan Harrison—saxophone, flute (1979-present). *Albums:* Havin' A Party with Southside Johnny (EPC JE 36246) 1979; Hearts of Stone (EPC JE 35488) 1978; I Don't Want to Go Home (EPC PE 34180) 1976; The Jukes (MER SRM-1-3793) 1979; Love Is a Sacrifice (MER SRM-1-3836) 1980; This Time It's For Real (EPC PE 34668) 1977.

SOUTHWICK, LEONARD Harmonica. Session for Joe Walsh (1974).

SOUZA, CHARLIE Bass, percussion. Member of the White Witch, 1973-74.

SPACE RANGERS See Neil Merryweather and his Space Rangers.

SPAIN, DAVID Drums. Member of the Target, 1976-77.

SPALDING, PHIL Bass. Member of the Original Mirrors, 1980.

SPAMPINATO, JOE Bass, guitar, vocal. Member of NRBQ.

SPANGLER, MARK Guitar. Session for Johnny and the Distractions (1980).

SPANKY AND OUR GANG Elaine McFarlane—vocal, percussion; Nigel Pickering—guitar, bass; Malcolm Hale—guitar, trombone, vocal; John Seiter—drums; Geoffry Myers—bass; Lefty Baker—guitar, vocal. Combining soft rock and folk, Spanky and Our Gang's first hit, "Sunday Will Never Be the Same" (1967), was followed by "Like to Get to Know You" (1968), an even bigger hit, before they disbanded in 1969. *Albums:* Spanky and Our Gang, 1967; Like to Get to Know You, 1968; Spanky and Our Gang, 1969.

SPANN, OTIS Piano, vocal. Chicago has spawned countless blues artists, but when the subject of piano players comes to hand, few will dispute the supremacy of Spann in this field. Session for Fleetwood Mac (1969). *Albums:* Blues Never Die (PRS 7719) 1965; Cryin' Time (VAN 6514); Raw Blues (LON PS-543); Otis Spann (EVR 216).

SPANOS, DANNY Vocal. *Album:* Danny Spanos (WDS BXLI 3538) 1980.

SPARKS, JOHN B. Bass. Member of Dr. Feelgood, 1975.

SPARKS, TIM Vocal, guitar. Member of Rio Nido, 1978.

SPARKS, TOM Vocal, guitar. Member of Ironhorse, 1979. Session for Ironhorse (1980).

SPARKS Ron Mael—keyboards; Russell Mael—vocal; T. White—guitar; Ian Hampton—bass (1975-76); Dinky Diamond—drums; Adrian Fisher—guitar; Gordon Martin—bass (1973-74); Jim Mankey—bass, guitar (1972); Earl Mankey—guitar (1972); Harvey Feinstein—drums (1972); Ken Forsey—drums (1979). Most commercially successful effort of the Mael brothers' career. *Albums:* Sparks (BSV BV 2048) 1972; Propaganda (ISL 9312); Woofer in Tweeter's Clothing (BSV) 1975; Introducing, 1977; Kimono My House (ISL 9272) 1974; No. 1 in Heaven (ELK 6E-186) 1979; Indiscreet (12975).

SPARROW, DAVE Bass, vocal. Member of the Photos, 1980.

SPARROW, EDDIE Drums. Session for Kevin Ayers (1973).

SPARROW Early name for Steppenwolf.

SPEAR, ROGER RUSKIN Percussion. Original member of the Bonzo Dog Doo-Dah Band.

SPEARMAN, BOB Keyboards. Member of Stillwater, 1977.

SPEARS, DON "BEE" Bass. Member of the Waylors. Session for Waylon Jennings (1973); Willie Nelson (1973-79); Leon Russell and Willie Nelson (1979).

SPEARS, MAURICE Horns. Session for Waylon Jennings (1976).

SPECIALS Terry Hall—vocal; Neville Staples—vocal, percussion; Lynval Golding—guitar, vocal; Roddy Radiation—guitar; Jerry Dammers—keyboards, producer; Sir Horace Gentleman—bass; John Bradbury—drums; Rico Rodrigues—trombone; Dick Cuthell—flugelhorn, coronet. *Albums:* The Specials (CYS 1265) 1979; More Specials (CYS 1303) 1980.

SPECTOR, PHIL Producer. Born 12/25/40. Master producer for early groups such as the Shirells, the Crystals, the Ronettes and others before making superstars of the Righteous Brothers, 1963-65. Produced the Beatles (1970); John Lennon (1970); Leonard Cohen (1977); the Ramones (1980); and others. Session for the Rolling Stones (1965). *Album:* Phil Spector's Christmas Album (SPC 9103).

SPECTORS Early name for Status Quo.

SPEDDING, CHRIS Guitar, vocal, organ, producer. Co-founder of Battered Ornaments, before joining Sharks, 1973-74. Member of the Wildcats, 1979. Though a leader in the development of New Wave music, no American record company has elected to release his solo albums. Session for "Jesus Christ Superstar" (1970); Elton John (1971); Jack Bruce (1969, 71); Nilsson (1971-72); Memphis Slim (1971); Vigrass and Osbourne (1972); Donovan (1973); Chris Youlden (1973); Splinter (1975); Jim Capaldi (1975); Roy Harper (1975); John Cale (1975); Bryan Ferry (1976-77); Ginger Baker (1977); Frankie Miller (1977); David Kubinec (1979); Mike Batt (1979); Joan Armatrading (1979). *Albums:* Chris Spedding (Import) 1976; Hurt (Import) 1977; Guitar Grafitti (Import) 1976; Song Without Words (Import) 1970; I'm Not Like Everybody Else (Import) 1980.

SPEEDWAY BLVD. Greg Hoffman—guitar, vocal; Dennis Feldman—bass, vocal; Roy Herring, Jr.—vocal, percussion, piano; Glenn Dove—drums, percussion; Jordan Rudes—keyboards. *Album:* Speedway Blvd. (EPC NJZ 36523) 1980.

SPEEDY See John "Speedy" Keen.

SPEER, STEVE Bass. Member of the Gentrys.

SPELEOS, TEDDY Guitar. Member of the Kangaroo, 1968.

SPELL, JAY Keyboards. Session for John Mayall (1973, 75-77).

SPELLMORE, ABE Drums. Member of Fandango.

SPENCE, JOHNNY Bass, vocal. Member of the Pirates.

SPENCE, SKIP Drums. Original member of the Jefferson Airplane, replaced by Spencer Dryden. Member of Moby Grape, 1967-68. *Album:* Oar, 1969.

SPENCER, JEREMY Guitar, vocal, piano. Original member of Fleetwood Mac, 1967-71. A year after Peter Green's departure, he left the group to join the Children of God, a California-based religious group. Before leaving Fleetwood Mac, he developed a unique brand of rock, contrasting against Green's jazz and blues inclinations. Besides being musically talented, he does a humorous Elvis imitation. Formed the Jeremy Spencer Band, 1979. *Albums:* Jeremy Spencer (Import) 1970; Children of God (COL) 1971.

JEREMY SPENCER BAND Jeremy Spencer—guitar, vocal; Michael Fogarty—vocal, keyboards; Jeff Schoen—keyboards; Neal Jason—bass; Al Izzo—drums; Buz Buchanan—drums; Victor Salazar—percussion. Former Fleetwood Mac member, Spencer's return to rock music. *Album:* Flee (ATC 19236) 1979.

SPENCER, PETE Drums. Member of Smokie, 1975-79.

SPENCER, TREVOR Drums, percussion. Half of the Tarney and Spencer duet, 1978-79.

SPENCER-ARSCOTT, MICHAEL Drums. Member of the Omaha Sheriff, 1977.

SPENNER, ALAN Bass. Replaced Andy Leigh in Spooky Tooth, 1971, after leaving the Grease Band that same year. Replaced John Gustafson in Roxy Music, 1978-79. Session for "Jesus Christ Superstar" (1970); Joe Cocker (1972); Donovan (1973); Alvin Lee (1974); Steve Winwood (1977); Ted Nugent (1977); Bryan Ferry (1978); Jim Capaldi (1979); Mick Taylor (1979); Roxy Music (1980).

SPERANZA, GUY Vocal. Member of the Riot, 1980.

SPEVOCK, ED Drums, percussion. Original member of Babe Ruth.

SPHEERIS, JIMMY Guitar, vocal. *Albums:* The Original Tap Dancing Kid, 1973; The Dragon is Dancing (EPC PE 33565) 1975; Isle of View (COL C-30988) 1974.

SPICHER, BUDDY Fiddle, violin, viola. Member of Area Code 615. Session for the Steve Miller Band (1970); Pearls Before Swine (1970); J. J. Cale (1971); Tom Rapp (1972); the Pointer Sisters (1974); Waylon Jennings (1975). *Albums:* American Sampler (FLF 021) 1976; Buddies (FLF 041) 1977; Me and My Heroes (FLF 065) 1978; Nashville Jam (FLF 073); Buddy Spicher and Friends (DDR 102) 1977; Great American Fiddle (FLF 9025) 1980.

SPICOLA, SAL Saxophone. Session for Preacher Jack (1980); Oak (1980).

SPIDER Amanda Blue—vocal; Keith Lentin—

guitar, vocal; Jimmy Lowell—bass, vocal; Anton Fig—drums, vocal; Holly Knight—keyboards, vocal. *Album:* Spider (DML 1-5000).

SPIDER Saxophone. Member of Flash Cadillac.

SPIDERS FROM MARS Pete McDonald—vocal; Woody Woodmansey—drums; Dave Black—guitar; Trevor Bolder—bass. Originally gained fame as David Bowie's backup band. *Album:* Spiders from Mars (PIE) 1976.

SPIEGEL, RAY Vibes. Member of the Dija Rhythm Band, 1976.

SPIKE Vocal, guitar. Member of Flash Cadillac.

SPIN, CHARLIE Trumpet. Member of John Fred's Playboy Band, 1968.

SPIN Rein van der Broek—trumpet; Jan Vennick—reeds; Hans Jensen—keyboards; Jan Hollestelle—bass, synthesizer, piano; Hans Hollestelle—guitar, synthesizer; Cees Kranenburg—drums, percussion. *Album:* Spin (ARA) 1976.

SPINA, RICK Vocal, keyboards. Member of the Love Affair, 1980.

SPINAZOLA, JOSEPH Keyboards. Member of the Puzzle.

SPINDT, DON Drums. Member of the Rubinoos, 1977-79.

SPINELLA, BOB Organ. Member of the Critters.

SPINETTA, LUIS ALBERTO Vocal. Native Argentinian who began in the rock field composing and performing in Spanish. *Album:* Only Love Can Sustain (COL JC 36346) 1980.

SPINETTI, HENRY Drums. Member of Hustler, and Lazy Racer since 1979. Session for "Rough Mix" (1977); Gerry Rafferty (1978); Eric Clapton (1980); Tim Renwick (1980); Matthew Fisher (1980).

SPINNER, DAVID Vocal, percussion. Member of the Simms Brothers Band, 1979-80.

SPINOZZA, DAVID Guitar, producer. Produced Garland Jeffreys (1977-78). Session for Paul McCartney (1971); B. B. King (1971); Paul Simon (1972-73); the Plastic Ono Band (1973); Dr. John (1973); Richard Davis (1973); Carly Simon (1974); Steve Marriott (1976); Ringo Starr (1977); Kate and Anna McGarrigle (1977-78). *Album:* Spinozza (AAM 4677) 1978.

SPIRES, JACKSON Drums, vocal. Member of Blackfoot, 1975-79.

SPIRIT Mark Andes—bass, vocal (1967-72, 76); Randy California—guitar, vocal; Ed Cassidy—drums, percussion; Jay Ferguson—keyboards, vocal (1967-71); John Locke—keyboards (1967-71, 76); Al Staehely—bass, vocal (1972); J. Christopher Staehely—guitar, vocal (1972); Barry Keene—bass (1975); Matt Andes—guitar, vocal (1976); Larry Knight—bass (1976). One of the most talented, underexposed groups of the 1960s, Spirit came from California with "Mechanical World," (1968). Though displaying an innovative flair, combining jazz and rock, the record was not a dynamic hit. "I Got a Line On You" (1968) was a commercial rock number that followed "World" and started a loyal underground following. In 1971, Ferguson, Locke and Andes left (the latter to join his brother and Ferguson to form Jo Jo Gunne). California and his father-in-law, Cassidy, the nucleus of the group, did a brief stint as Kapt. Kopter and the Fabulous Twirly Birds, but California's writing was too esoterical to become commercial. In 1975, Spirit reformed. California's writing became more solid on "Son of Spirit," before he was joined by all of the original group (minus Ferguson, who went solo after working with Joe Walsh) for "Farther Along," 1976. *Albums:* Spirit (ODE 44004) 1968; Family That Plays Together (EPC E 31461) 1969; Clear (ODE 44016) 1970; Twelve Dreams of Dr. Sardonicus (EPC PE 30267) 1971; Feedback (EPC E 31175, BG 33761) 1972; Best of Spirit (EPC KE 3227) 1972; Spirit (EPC PEG 3147) 1973; Spirit of '76 (MER SRM 2-804) 1975; Son of Spirit (MER SRM 1-1053) 1975; Farther Along (MER SRM 1-1094) 1976; Live Spirit (FMR 2001) 1979.

SPIVEY, RED Session for J. J. Cale (1974).

SPIVEY, VICTORIA Vocal, keyboards. Born in Houston, Texas, 1926, before moving to St. Louis. Blues singer that made her recording debut at age 16. *Albums:* Blues Jam (BUD 7510); Blues Is Life (FLW 3541) 1976.

SPIZZ Vocal, guitar. Member of Athletico Spizz 80, 1980.

SPLINTER Bill Elliot—vocal; Bob Purvis—vocal. A vocal duet from England, featuring two-part harmonies behind George Harrison's full production with talented session men. They were the first group to record on Harrison's Dark Horse record label. *Albums:* The Place I Love (DKH 22001) 1974; Harder to Live, 1975; Two Man Band (DKH 3073) 1977.

SPLIT ENZ Tim Finn—vocal; Neil Finn—vocal, guitar; Eddie Rayner—keyboards; Noel Crombie—percussion; Malcolm Green—drums; Nigel Griggs—bass. Rock band from New Zealand. *Albums:* Dizrythmia (CYS 1145); Mental Notes (CYS 1131); True Colours (AAM 4822) 1980.

SPOELSTRA, MARK Guitar, vocal. *Albums:* Blues Project (ELK 7264); Mark Spoelstra (FLW 3572); The Songs of Mark Spoelstra (FLW 2444).

SPOOKY TOOTH Mike Harrison—keyboards, vocal (1968-74); Luther Grosvenor—guitar (1968-71); Greg Ridley—bass (1968-69); Michael Kellie—drums; Gary Wright—organ, vocal (1968-72); Andy Leigh—bass (1969); Henry McCulloch—guitar (1971); Chris Stainton—bass, keyboards, guitar (1971); Alan Spenner—bass (1971); Mick Jones—guitar (1974); Chris Stewart—bass (1974); Mike Patto—vocal, keyboards, percussion (1974); Val Burke—bass, vocal (1974); Bryson Graham—drums, percussion (1974). They first appeared in

England in 1967 as Art. In 1968, Wright joined the group and they became Spooky Tooth. Wright (the only American in the group) sang with a distinctive vibrato that contrasted with Harrison's raspy styling. A stormy relationship led to Wright's and Ridley's departure from the group after a progressive album, "Ceremony," with electronic musician Pierre Henri. Harrison and Grosvenor attempted to hold the group together through "The Last Puff" (1971), after which they too left to go solo. In 1974, the group re-formed with original members Wright, Harrison, and Kellie. Their comeback was eagerly anticipated, but short in realization. Kellie left after one album, soon to be followed by Harrison. Replacements Patto and company were talented and experienced, but not the originals. *Albums:* Spooky Tooth (Import) 1968; Ceremony (AAM SP 1225) 1969; Spooky Two (AAM 4194) 1969; Tobacco Road (AAM 4300) 1970; Last Puff (AAM 4266) 1971; You Broke My Heart So I Busted Your Jaw (AAM 4385) 1974; Witness (ISL 9387) 1974; The Mirror (ISL 9292) 1974.

SPOONER, WILLIAM Guitar, vocal. Member of the Tubes, 1975-present.

SPORTS Stephen Cummings—vocal; Andrew Pendlebury—guitar, vocal; Martin Armiger—guitar, vocal; Robert Glover—bass; Paul Hitchins—drums; James Niven—keyboards, vocal. *Albums:* Don't Throw Stones (ARI 4249) 1979; Suddenly (ARI 4266) 1980.

SPRADLIN, PAUL Vocal, guitar. Member of the Goose Creek Symphony.

SPREEN, GLEN Guitar, keyboards. Session for the Marc Tanner Band (1979).

SPREMICH, RICHARD Drums. Member of Malo, 1972.

SPRING, ALICE Vocal. Member of the Darling, 1979.

SPRING, KEITH Saxophone, percussion. Member of the Whole Wheat Horns. Session for Martin Mull (1972-73).

SPRINGER, JOHN Keyboards. Session for the Blues Brothers (1980).

SPRINGFIELD, DUSTY Vocal. Born 4/16/39. Real name: Mary O'Brien. English-born Springfield was initially a country-western singer, before converting to blue-eyed soul, as shown in her most famous hit, "Wishin' and Hopin'." In 1968, she immigrated to the United States to continue her career. Session for Elton John (1974). *Albums:* Cameo; Longing; Dusty Springfield's Tribute to Burt Bacharach; Look of Love, 1967; Stay Awhile, 1967; Dusty in Memphis, 1969; It Begins Again (UAR LW 791); Dusty Springfield's Golden Hits (PHI 600220) 1966; Living Without Your Love (UAR LT 936) 1978.

SPRINGFIELD, RICK Vocal. *Albums:* Working Class Dog (VIC AFLI 3697) 1980; Wait for the Night (CLS 515) 1976.

SPRINGSTEEN, BRUCE Guitar, vocal, harmonica. Born 9/23/49. Nickname: the Boss. Relatively unknown until 1975, he and his E Street Band were the victims of a massive publicity campaign, which labeled him the "next Bob Dylan" and superstar of the future. His tales of "Jungleland," New Jersey, and "Backstreets" are haunting, poetic, and irresistible with his moving arrangements around Clarence Clemon's wailing sax. The much-awaited "Darkness" album confirmed early speculation of his dynamism, while "The River" capped his claim to superstardom. Part of "No Nukes," 1979. *Albums:* Greetings from Asbury Park, N.J. (COL JC 31903) 1973; The Wild, the Innocent, and the E Street Shuffle (COL JC 32432) 1973; Born to Run (COL JC & HC 33795) 1975; Darkness on the Edge of Town (COL JC 35318) 1978; The River (COL PC 2-36854) 1980.

SPROXTON, STEVE Guitar, vocal. Member of Longdancer, 1973.

SPRUILL, JAMES Guitar. Session for John Hammond (1964-65).

SPRUILL, STEPHANIE Vocal. Session for Elton John (1979-80).

SPY Danny Seidenberg—violin; Michael Visceglia—bass; John Vislocky—vocal; David Nelson—guitar, vocal; Bob Goldman—drums; Dave LeBolt—keyboards. *Album:* Spy (KSH NJZ 36378) 1980.

SQUEEZE Glenn Tilbrook—guitar, keyboards, vocal; John Bentley—bass (1979-present); Jools Holland—vocal, keyboards; Chris Difford—guitar, vocal (1980); Gilson Lavis—drums; Harry Kakoulli—bass (1978-79). Catchy new wave/pop with a Farfisa beat. *Albums:* Argybargy (AAM 4802) 1980; Cool for Cats (AAM 4759) 1979; U.K. Squeeze (AAM 4687) 1978.

SQUIER, BILLY Vocal, guitar, percussion. Member of the Piper, 1977. *Album:* The Tale of the Tape (CAP ST 12062) 1980.

SQUIRE, CHRIS Bass, vocal. Born 3/4/48. Original member of Yes, since 1970. Session for Rick Wakeman (1972, 77-78). *Album:* Fish Out of Water (ATC 18159) 1975.

SQUIRE, PAUL Trumpet. Member of Pig Iron.

SRC Steve Lyman—guitar, vocal; Glenn Quackenbush—organ; Gary Quackenbush—guitar; Scott Richardson—vocal; E. G. Clawson—drums; Robin Dale—bass, vocal. American rockers from the late 1960s whose heaviness sank beneath the public's attention. *Albums:* SRC (CAP ST 2991); Milestones (CAP).

ST. CLAIRE, ALEX Guitar. Original member of Captain Beefheart's Magic Band, 1965-69, 74.

ST. CLAIRE-SHEETS, SCOTT Guitar. Member of Pat Benatar's backup band since 1979.

ST. HOLMES, DEREK Guitar. Second guitarist for Ted Nugent, 1975-78, before forming St. Paradise, 1979.

ST. JOHN, BARRY Vocal. Session for Gary Wright (1971); Long John Baldry (1972); Rick Wakeman (1972); Lo and Behold (1972); Vigrass and Osbourne (1972); Pink Floyd (1973); Kevin Ayers (1973); Bryan Ferry (1974); Dan McCafferty (1975); Ray Thomas (1976).

ST. JOHN, DENNIS Drums. Session for Neil Diamond (1976).

ST. JOHN, POWELL Harmonica. Member of Mother Earth, 1968-69.

ST. NICHOLAS, NICK Bass. Original member of T.I.M.E., 1968-69, before joining Steppenwolf.

ST. NICHOLS, JODY Bass, vocal. Replaced Joe Spampinato in NRBQ.

ST. NICKLAUS, DICK Keyboards, synthesizer, guitar. *Album:* Magic (EPC JE 36178).

ST. PARADISE Rob Grange—bass, vocal; Denny Carmassi—drums, vocal; Derek St. Holmes—guitar, vocal. Hard rock trio formed by Ted Nugent sidemen Grange and St. Holmes, with ex-Montrose member Carmassi. *Album:* St. Paradise (WBR K 3281) 1979.

ST. PETERS, CRISPIAN Vocal. English-born writer/singer whose lone hit, "The Pied Piper," was not enough to capture a commercial audience. *Album:* The Pied Piper (JAM 3027) 1966.

STA. MARIA, MANNY Guitar, trombone. Member of Please, 1976.

STA. MARIA, MIKE Drums. Member of Please, 1976.

STABBINS, LARRY Tenor saxophone. Member of Centipede, 1971.

STACEY, MIKE Trumpet. Session for Mike Harrison (1972).

STACKRIDGE Andy Davis—vocal, keyboards; Keith Gemmell—reeds; Rod Bowkett; Mike Evans; Roy Morgan; Mutter Slater; Paul Karas. *Album:* Pinafore Days (SIR 7509) 1974.

STAEBELL, BILL Bass. Member of the Auracle, 1978-79.

STAEHELY, AL Bass, vocal. Replaced Mark Andes in Spirit, 1972.

STAEHELY, JOHN CHRISTOPHER Guitar, vocal. Replaced Matt Andes in Spirit, 1972, and Jo Jo Gunne, 1974.

STAEHLE, FREDDY Drums, percussion. Session for Dr. John (1971-72, 79).

STAFFORD, RENELLE Vocal. Session for Jackie DeShannon (1972); Paul Simon (1972).

STAGG, ROSS Vocal, guitar. Member of the Strapps, 1977.

STAHL, BUTCH Bass, organ. Member of the Music Explosion, 1967.

STAINTON, CHRIS Keyboards, bass, guitar. Began with Joe Cocker, 1968, and grew with him through Cocker's Greatest Show on Earth, 1970, and the Grease Band, 1971, with Leon Russell. Member of Spooky Tooth, 1971. Session for Don Nix (1971); Leon Russell (1971); Ian Hunter (1975); Eric Clapton (1980).

STALEY, TOM Drums. Replaced Tom Ardolini in NRBQ.

STALLINGS, CAROL Violin, vocal. Member of the Creation, 1974.

STALLINGS, ORLANDO Guitar, vocal. Member of the Creation, 1974.

STALLINGS, RON Vocal, tenor saxophone. Session for Elvin Bishop (1972).

STALLWORTH, PAUL Bass. Member of the Attitudes, 1976. Session for Tommy Bolin (1975); George Harrison (1975); Nils Lofgren (1976); Tom Johnston (1979); Ian McLagen (1979).

STAMM, MARVIN Trumpet. Session for Eumir Deodato.

STAMPEDERS Rich Dodson; Kim Berly; Ronnie King. *Albums:* From the Fire (CAP) 1973; New Day (CAP) 1974; Hit the Road (CAP) 1976.

STAMPFEL, PETE Guitar, fiddle, harmonica, vocal. Member of the Fugs, 1965-66, and the Holy Modal Rounders since 1968.

STANFORD, TINA RENEE Percussion, vocal. Member of the Platinum Hook since 1979.

STANGER, NIGEL Saxophone. Started in Blues Incorporated. Session for John Mayall's Bluesbreakers (1967).

STANLEY, MICHAEL Vocal, guitar, percussion. Namesake of the Michael Stanley Band since 1977.

MICHAEL STANLEY BAND Bob Pelander—keyboards, synthesizer, percussion, vocal (1977-present); Tommy Dobek—drums, percussion (1977-present); Gary Markasky—guitar (1978-present); Michael Gismondi—bass, synthesizer (1980); Kevin Raleigh—vocal, keyboards, percussion; Michael Stanley—vocal, guitar, percussion; Jonah Koslen—guitar, vocal (1977); Daniel Pecchio—bass, vocal (1977-79). *Albums:* You Break It, You Bought It (EPC PE 33492) 1975; Stage Pass (EPC PEG 34661) 1977; Cabin Fever (ARI 4182) 1978; Friends and Legends (MCA 372); Greatest Hits (ARI 4236) 1979; Heartland (EIA SW 17040) 1980.

STANLEY, PAUL Guitar, vocal. Real name: Stanley Eisen. Member of Kiss since 1973. *Album:* Kiss (CAS 7123-PIX 7123) 1978.

STANLEY, PETE Banjo. Session for Long John Baldry (1975).

STANLEY STEAMER Warren Hartman—piano, harpsichord, vocal; Robert Eagle—guitar; Fred Shaughnessy—bass, vocal; Jim McCurdy—drums; Larry Smith—baritone saxophone; Tony Finocchiaro—tenor saxophone; Craig Sergel—trombone; Bob Dill—trumpet; Holly Vaughn—vocal. Big band sound produced by Kenny Rodgers in 1973. *Album:* Stanley Steamer (MGM) 1973.

STANNARD, TERRY Drums. Session for Long John Baldry (1972); Chris Youlden (1974); Young and Moody (1977); Marianne Faithfull (1979).

STANSHALL, VIV Percussion, vocal. Original

member of the Bonzo Dog Doo-Dah Band, 1968. Session for John Entwhistle (1971); Steve Winwood (1980).

STANTON, KEVIN Guitar, vocal. Member of Mi-Sex, 1980.

STANTON, LAURIE Drums. Member of the U.F.O.'s, 1966.

STAPLES, NEVILLE Vocal, percussion. Member of the Specials since 1979.

STAPLES, PETER Bass. Original member of the Troggs.

STAPLETON, JIMMY Percussion. Member of Osiris, 1978.

STAR PARK Early band of Colin Moulding and Terry Chambers of XTC.

STARBS, MIKE Vocal. Member of Lucifer's Friend, 1978-80.

STARBUCK Bruce Blackman—vocal, keyboards; Jimmy Cobb—vocal, bass; Ken Crysler—drums; Sloan Hayes—vocal, flute, keyboards (1977); Darryl Kutz—vocal, guitar, harmonica (1977); David Shaver—vocal, keyboards; Bo Wagner—percussion; John Frisde—vocal, guitar (1978); John Walker—vocal, guitar (1978). *Albums:* Rock 'n' Roll Rocket (PVS 2027) 1977; Searching for a Thrill (UAR LW 918) 1978.

STARCASTLE Terry Luttrell—vocal; Gary Strater—bass, vocal; Stephen Tassler—drums, percussion, vocal; Herb Schildt—keyboard, synthesizer; Matthew Stewart—guitar, vocal; Stephen Hagler—guitar, vocal. Though they had been together since 1972, six-piece Starcastle did not make their recording debut until 1976. *Albums:* Starcastle (EPC PE 33914) 1976; Citadel (EPC PE 34935) 1977; Fountains of Light (EPC PE-34375) 1977; Real to Reel (EPC JE 35441) 1978.

STARDRIVE Robert Mason—synthesizers; Howard Rego—drums; Harvey Sarch—guitar; Jaime Austria—bass. The funk craze of the early 1970s saw several combos trying to cash in on opportunity. Stardrive featured Mason's "funky synthesizer" and hip, space music. *Album:* Stardrive (COL) 1974.

STARGER, STEVE Keyboards. Member of the Sunship, 1974.

STARJETS Paul Bowen; Terry Sharpe; Sean Martin; Liam L'Estrange. *Album:* Starjets (POR JR-36245) 1980.

STARKEY, BARBARA Pump organ. Session for Ry Cooder (1978).

STARKEY, RICHARD Real name of Ringo Starr.

STARKIE, BOB Guitar. Member of the Skyhooks, 1975-77.

STARKS, JOHN Drums. Session for B. B. King (1975, 77).

STARLAND VOCAL BAND Bill Danoff—vocal; Taffy Danoff—vocal; Jon Carroll—guitar, vocal; Margot Chapman—vocal. *Albums:* 4 x 4 (WDS BXLI 2598) 1978; Late Nite Radio (WDS BXLI 2598) 1978; Starland Vocal Band (WDS BXLI 1351) 1976.

STARLITERS See Joey Dee and the Starlighters.

STARR, RINGO Drums, percussion, vocal. Born 7/7/40. After playing with Rory Storme and the Hurricanes, Starr met Brian Epstein in 1961, who had just become the manager of the Silver Beatles, later to be known as the Beatles. Through Epstein, Starr joined the Beatles, his rings and nose a contrast to the cuteness of McCartney, the political activism of Lennon, and the ethereal air about Harrison. Always overshadowed by the group's other super talents, it was surprising to find his solo career blossom after the group disbanded. His tastes ranged from the big band sound of "Sentimental Journey" to country and western ("Beaucoups of Blues"). Member of the Plastic Ono Band, 1970. Session for Bangla Desh (1971); B. B. King (1971); "Tommy" (1972); Peter Frampton (1972); George Harrison (1972-74); Nilsson (1974-75); Keith Moon (1975); the Alpha Band (1977); Doris Troy (1970); The Band (1978); Ian McLagen (1979). *Albums:* Bad Boy (POR JR 35378) 1978; Beaucoups of Blues (CAP SMAS 3368) 1971; Blasts from Your Past (CAP SW 3422) 1975; Concert for Bangla Desh (CAP STCX 3385); Goodnight Vienna (CAP SW 3417) 1974; Ringo (CAP SWAL 3413) 1973; The 4th Ringo (ATC 19108) 1977; Ringo's Rotogravure (ATC 18193) 1976; Sentimental Journey (CAP SW 3365) 1970.

STARR, RUBY Vocal. *Albums:* Smokey Places, 1977; Scene Stealer, 1976; Ruby Starr and Grey Ghost (CAP ST 11427) 1975.

STARRY EYED AND LAUGHING Tony Poole—vocal, guitar, organ, synthesizer; Ross McGeeney—vocal, guitar; Iain Whitmore—vocal, bass; Mike Wackford—drums. *Album:* Thought Talk, 1975.

STARS, JEFF Vocal. Member of the Interview since 1979.

STARWOOD Bob Carpenter—guitar, keyboards, vocal; Mike Buono—drums; David Holster—guitar; Bernie Mysior—bass; Bobby Mason—guitar. *Albums:* Homebrew, 1976; Starwood, 1977.

STARZ Dube—drums; Brenden Harkin—guitar; Richie Ranno—guitar; Peter Sweval—bass; Michael Lee Smith—vocal. *Albums:* Attention Shoppers (CAP ST 11730) 1978; Coliseum Rock (CAP ST 11861) 1978; Starz (CAP ST 11539) 1976; Violation (CAP SW 11617) 1977.

STATES, ANN Vocal. Session for the Brains (1980).

STATES Jimmy McDonnell—vocal; Dominic Germano—bass; Stephen Chandler—guitar, vocal; Barry Scott—guitar, vocal; Robert Schindler—keyboards; Jimmy Wilkins—drums. *Album:* The States (CYS 1229) 1979.

STATON, DAKOTA Vocal. *Albums:* In the Night (CAP M 1003); Late, Late Show (CAP SM 876).

STATON, JEFFERY Guitar. Session for Art Garfunkel (1979).

STATTON, ALISON Vocal. Member of the Young Marble Giants, 1980.

STATUS QUO Mike Rossi—guitar, vocal; Roy Lynes—keyboards, vocal (1968); Alan Lancaster —bass, guitar, vocal; John Coghlan—drums; Rick Parfitt—guitar, vocal, piano. Early names: the Spectors; Traffic Jam. Not many groups retain the same personnel for over ten years. If nothing else, it is a sign of devotion to the art form. But that is what Quo has done (with the exception of one original member dropping from the line-up in 1968). Though never a large commercial success, they are still playing the same music they originally played, raucous rock 'n' roll, with as much enthusiasm and energy as anyone in the business. *Albums:* Messages from Status Quo (CAP) 1968; On the Level (CAP ST 11381) 1975; Rockin' All Over the World (CAP ST 11749) 1977; Status Quo "Live" (CAP SKBB 11623) 1977; Status Quo, 1976; Hello (AAM SO 3615) 1973; Piledriver, 1972; Quo (AAM SP 3649) 1974; Dog of Two Heads (Import) 1971; If You Can't Stand the Heat (Import) 1978; 12 Gold Bars (Import) 1980; Now Hear This (RIV 7402) 1980.

STAWINSKI, ROB Drums, percussion. Original member of Sky, 1970-71.

STEADY, FREDDY Drums, vocal. Member of Krokus, 1980.

STEAKLEY, BRAD Drums. Member of the Screams, 1980.

STEALERS WHEEL Joe Egan—vocal, keyboards; Gerry Rafferty—vocal, guitar; Paul Pilnick—guitar; Tony Williams—bass; Rod Coombes—drums. *Albums:* Stealers Wheel (AAM) 1972; Ferguslie Park (SPC 3734) 1973; Right or Wrong (AAM) 1975; Stuck in the Middle with You (AAM 4708).

STEAM PACKET Brian Auger—keyboards, vocal; Julie Driscoll—vocal; Mick Waller—drums; Vic Briggs—guitar; Elton John—piano, vocal (1966); Neil Hubbard—guitar; Long John Baldry—vocal; Rod Stewart—vocal. Formed in 1965, they changed their name to Bluesology in 1966.

STEAMHAMMER Kieran White—vocal, harmonica, guitar; Martin Pugh—guitar; Martin Quittenton —guitar; Steve Davy—bass; Louis Cennamo—bass; Michael Rushton—drums. Like so many other British blues bands of the 1960s, they were more talented than publicized. After a dynamic first album, they released a lesser-known second album, after some of the personnel had left for greener pastures. *Album:* Steamhammer, 1969.

STEEL, JAN Alto saxophone, flute. Member of Centipede, 1971.

STEELE, ANDREW Drums. Member of the Herd, 1967. Session for Neil Sedaka (1976).

STEELE, DAVID Member of the English Beat, 1980.

STEELE, DREW Guitar, vocal, keyboards, synthesizer. Member of the Surf Punks, 1980.

STEELE, JOHN Drums. Member of the Animals, 1962-66, 77.

STEELE, LARRY Bass, vocal, percussion. Session for Steve Stills (1970); Memphis Slim (1971); Cat Stevens (1971); Elton John (1972); Richard Wright (1978).

STEELE, TOMMY Vocal. In 1956, the mere image of Elvis guaranteed a certain degree of success. Steele was one to capitalize upon this with his version of "Heartbreak Hotel." He was smart enough, however, to develop his other talents, branching out into acting. *Album:* Everything's Coming Up Broadway, 1967.

STEELE, WES Bass, cello. Member of the Touchstone, 1971.

STEELER, BOB Drums, percussion. Replaced Sammy Piazza in Hot Tuna, 1974-79.

STEELEYE SPAN Maddy Prior—vocal; Peter Knight—violin, vocal; Rick Kemp—vocal, bass, guitar; Nigel Pegrun—drums; Robert Johnson—guitar; Tim Hart—guitar, vocal; Martin Carthy—vocal, guitar, banjo, organ (1976-78); Gary Woods —vocal, percussion (1977); John Kirkpatrick—vocal (1977-78). *Albums:* All Around My Hat (CYS 1091) 1975; Below the Salt (CYS 1008) 1972; Commoner's Crown (CYS 1071) 1975; Hark the Village Wait (CYS 1120) 1976; Live at Last (CYS 1199) 1978; Now We Are Six (CYS 1053) 1974; Parcel of Rogues (CYS 1046) 1973; Please to See the King (CYS 1119) 1970; Rocket Cottage (CYS 1123) 1976; Steeleye Span Story—Original Masters (CYS 2-1136) 1977; Storm Force Ten (CYS 1151) 1977; Ten Man Mop (CYS 1121) 1976.

STEELY DAN Denny Dias—guitar (1972-76); Jeff "Skunk" Baxter—guitar, pedal steel guitar (1972-75); Walter Becker—bass, guitar, harmonica, vocal; Jim Hodder—drums, percussion, vocal (1972-75); Donald Fagen—keyboards, vocal; David Palmer —vocal (1972). In 1972, Steely Dan appeared with their fresh, introspective, satirical lyrics in a jazz-rock format. The lyrics of writing team Becker and Fagen were often obscure, but, as they illustrated with their single "Dirty Work" (1972), they could also be commercial. By 1975, Baxter had left to join the Doobie Brothers; by 1976, Dias had departed; and by 1977, only the core of Steely Dan remained, Becker and Fagen. Though lyrically self-conscious, often with obscure references, their production techniques remain first class and impressive. *Albums:* Aja (MCA 1006) 1977; Can't Buy a Thrill (MCA C-758) 1972; Countdown to Ecstasy (MCA C-779) 1973; Greatest Hits (MCA AK 1107); Katy Lied (MCA D 846) 1975; Pretzel Logic (MCA D 808) 1974; Royal Scam (MCA D 931) 1976; Gaucho (MCA 6102) 1980.

STEEN, ROGER Guitar, vocal. Member of the Tubes, 1975-present.

STEER, SLIM Drums. Member of Arthur Brown's

Kingdom Come, 1973.

STEFANINK, GARY Bass. Member of Graham Shaw and the Sincere Serenaders, 1980.

STEFFEN, DAVE Guitar. Member of the Sunblind Lion, 1976-78.

STEIG, JEREMY Flute. Founder of the jazz-rock group Jeremy and the Satyrs, 1967-68. Session for Johnny Winter (1973). *Albums:* Temple of Birth (COL KC 33297) 1975; This Is Jeremy Steig (SLS 18059); Wayfaring Stranger (BLN 84354); Firefly (CTI 7075) 1977; Outlaws (ICT 3015); Monium (COL KC 32579); What's New (VRV 6-8777); Jeremy Steig (AMR 6147) 1979.

STEIMONTS, KEN Bass, vocal. Member of the Aviary, 1979.

STEIN, ANDY Fiddle, saxophone. Member of Commander Cody's Lost Planet Airmen. Session for Alvin Lee (1973); Marshall Tucker Band (1974).

STEIN, CHRIS Guitar, bass. Member of Blondie since 1979, replacing Frank Infante.

STEIN, MARK Organ. Member of the Vanilla Fudge, 1967-69. Session for Dave Mason (1980).

STEINBERG, BRUCE Harmonica. Session for It's a Beautiful Day (1969, 71).

STEINBERG, MEL Woodwinds. Member of Brent Maglia's backup band, 1977.

STEINBERG, RICHARD Drums. Member of the Tycoon.

STEINHARDT, ROBBIE Vocal, violin. Born 5/25/50. Voice of Kansas since 1974.

STEKOL, RICHARD Vocal, guitar, piano. Member of Honk, 1973-74, and the Funky Kings, 1976.

STELLEY, PAT Vocal. Member of the Chiffons.

STEMBRIDGE, JERRY Guitar. Session for Waylon Jennings (1973).

STENSON, BOBO Piano. Session for Bo Hansson.

STEPHAN, STEFFI Bass. Session for Eric Burdon (1977).

STEPHENS, BRUCE Vocal, guitar, keyboards. Brother of Blue Cheer's Leigh Stephens, and member of Pilot, 1972.

STEPHENS, JODY Drums, vocal. Member of the Big Star.

STEPHENS, LEIGH Guitar, vocal. Original member of the Blue Cheer, and Pilot, 1972. *Albums:* Red Weather; Leigh Stephens and a Cast of Thousands, 1971.

STEPHENS, LENA Vocal. Session for Leon Russell (1974).

STEPHENS, LOUIS Piano. Session for Freddie King (1975).

STEPHENSON, BRAD Bass, vocal. Member of Ethos, 1977.

STEPHENSON, JAMES Real name of Guitar Slim Green.

STEPHENSON, TOM Organ. Session for Joe Walsh (1974).

STEPP, RICHARD Vocal. *Album:* Holiday in Hollywood (INF 9012) 1979.

STEPPENWOLF John Kay—vocal, guitar; Jerry Edmonton—drums; Goldy McJohn—organ (until 1974); Michael Monarch—guitar; John Russell Morgan—bass; John Moreve—bass; Nick St. Nicholas—bass; Mars Bonfire—guitar; Larry Byron—guitar (1970); Kent Henry—guitar (1971); George Biondo—bass (1971-76); Bobby Cochran —guitar, vocal (1974-76); Andy Chapin—keyboards (1975); Wayne Cook—keyboards (1976). After an ill-fated start as Sparrow in Toronto in 1965, Steppenwolf re-formed in 1968 with the rock classic "Born to Be Wild." They had traded their original blues sound for hard rock in Southern California. After three hit albums, it became obvious that Kay was a songwriter of no mean talent and a vocalist with range and depth. In 1971 the group disbanded. Kay recorded dynamic, yet unsuccessful solo albums until 1974, when Steppenwolf re-formed, proving again their mastery of rock. *Albums:* Hour of the Wolf (EPC PE-33583) 1975; 16 Great Performances (MCA D-4011); 16 Greatest Hits (MCA X-50135); Steppenwolf (DHL 50029) 1968; Steppenwolf Gold (DHL X-50099); Steppenwolf Live (MCA 50075); Steppenwolf Seven (MCA X-50090); Steppenwolf the Second (DHL 50037) 1968; At Your Birthday Party (DHL) 1969; Early Steppenwolf (DHL 50060) 1969; Monster (DNH 50066); For Ladies Only (DNH 50110) 1971; Rest in Peace (DHL); Slow Flux (MUM PZ 33093) 1974; Skullduggery (EPC RE 34120) 1976; Reborn to Be Wild (EPC PE 34382) 1976.

STERLING, JOHN Guitar. Member of the Eric Burdon Band, 1975.

STERLING, RANDY Bass. Member of Neil Diamond's backup band.

STERLING Stevie Pickett—guitar, synthesizer, vocal; Steve Kehr—drums, vocal; David Kissell—bass, vocal; Michael Kehr—guitar, vocal. *Album:* City Kids (AAM 4807) 1980.

STERN, HEIDI Vocal. *Album:* Heidi (FAM 9021) 1979.

STERNBERG, ANN Bass. Member of UFO, 1966.

STEVEN T. Vocal, guitar. Head of Venus and the Razor Blades, 1977, before going solo. *Album:* West Coast Confidential (DRM 3500) 1978.

STEVENS, CAT Guitar, keyboards, vocal, writer. Born 7/21/47. Supergroups had become passe by the 1970s and balladeers were once again in vogue. In the tradition established by Dylan and Donovan, came James Taylor, Carole King, and Cat Stevens. Produced by former Yardbird Paul Samwell-Smith and accompanied by Alun Davies, Stevens sang his repertoire of ballads with great success. *Albums:* Back to Earth (AAM 4735) 1978; Buddah and the Chocolate Box (AAM 3623) 1975; Catch Bull at Four (AAM 4365) 1972; Foreigner (AAM 4391) 1974; Izitso (AAM 4702) 1977; London Collector —Cat's Cradle (LON LC 50010); Mona Bone

Jakon (AAM 4260); Numbers (AAM 4555) 1976; Cat Stevens' Greatest Hits (AAM 4519) 1975; Tea for the Tillerman (AAM 4280) 1970; Teaser and the Firecat (AAM 4313) 1971.

STEVENS, DAVE Piano. Session for Cyril Davies and Alexis Korner, 1954-61, before graduating to Blues Incorporated.

STEVENS, GUY Producer. Produced the Clash (1980); and others.

STEVENS, LEAR Guitar. Member of the Storm, 1979.

STEVENS, LINDA Vocal. Member of the Marc Tanner Band since 1979.

STEVENS, MARK Drums. Session for Ry Cooder (1978).

STEVENS, MICHAEL Guitar, vocal. Member of Highway Robbery, 1972, and the Marc Tanner Band since 1979.

STEVENS, NICK Bass, vocal. Member of 3-D, 1980.

STEVENS, RAY Piano, vocal. Composer of fad songs like "Ahab the Arab" and "Bridget the Midget," 1971, Stevens also penned ballads like "Everything Is Beautiful," 1970. *Albums:* Be Your Own Best Friend (WBR K 3195); Best of Ray Stevens and Chet Atkins/Friends (VIC AHLI 1985); Feel the Music (WBR B 2997) 1977; Feeling's Not Right Again (WBR K 3332) 1979; Just for the Record (WBR B 2914); Shriner's Convention (VIC AHLI 3574) 1980; Nashville (BNB 5005) 1974; There Is Something on Your Mind (WBR 3098) 1978.

STEVENS, RICK Vocal. Featured vocalist of Tower of Power until 1972.

STEVENS, TONY "TONE" Bass. Replaced Rivers Jobe in Savoy Brown, 1969-71. Joined Foghat with Roger Earle and Dave Peverett, also of Savoy Brown, 1972-74.

STEVENSON, B. W. Guitar, vocal. *Albums:* Lifeline (MCA 3215); Lost Feeling (WBR B 3012); On the Christmas Night (MCA 3184); Calabasas (VIC APLI 0410) 1973.

STEVENSON, BILL Vibes, keyboards. Member of the Earth Opera, 1968.

STEVENSON, DON Drums. Member of Moby Grape, 1967-69.

STEVERS, RICH Drums, percussion. Member of Frijid Pink, 1970-71.

STEWARD, CRAIG Harmonica. Session for Frank Zappa (1979).

STEWART, AL Guitar, vocal. Soft vocalist who scored with "Year of the Cat," 1977. *Albums:* Past, Present and Future (JNS) 1974; Modern Times (PRI 9525) 1975; The Early Years, 1977; Time Passages (ARI 4190) 1978; 24 Carrots (ARI 9520) 1980; Year of the Cat (ARI 9503) 1976.

STEWART, BILL Drums, percussion. Member of the Gregg Allman Band, 1977, and the Tim Weisberg Band, 1977. Session for Roy Buchanan (1974); Martin Mull (1974); Randall Bramblett (1975); the Allman Brothers (1975); Robbie Robertson (1980).

STEWART, BOB Tuba, trumpet, flugelhorn. Session for Taj Mahal.

STEWART, CHRIS Bass. Member of Eire Apparent. Replaced Alan Spenner in Spooky Tooth, 1974. Member of the Frankie Miller Band, 1975, and Full House, 1977-78. Session for Joe Cocker (1974).

STEWART, DAVE Organ. Member of Egg, 1970, Khan, 1972, the National Health Band, 1977, and Bruford, 1979. Session for Nazareth (1972).

STEWART, DAVE Guitar, bass, mandolin, vocal. Member of Longdancer, 1973, and the Tourists since 1978.

STEWART, ERIC Guitar, vocal, piano. Original member of the Mindbenders, 1966, and 10 CC, 1973-present. Session for Neil Sedaka (1975).

STEWART, GAYNOR Vocal. Session for Donovan (1973).

STEWART, IAN Keyboards. Session for the Rolling Stones (1965-present); Sky (1971); Howlin' Wolf (1972); "Rough Mix" (1977).

STEWART, JOHN Xylophone. Session for Jackie DeShannon (1972).

STEWART, JOHN Guitar, vocal. *Albums:* California Bloodlines (CAP SN 11987); Signals through the Glass (CAP SN 11988); Willard (CAP SN 11989); In Concert (VIC AFLI 7513) 1980; Cannons in the Rain (VIC AFLI 4827) 1973; Phoenix Concerts—Live (VIC CPL 2-0265) 1974; Bombs Away Dream Baby (RSO 1-3051) 1979; Fire in the Wind (RSO 1-3027) 1977; Dream Babies Go to Hollywood (RSO 1-3074) 1980.

STEWART, KENNY Vocal. Voice of the Dirty Tricks, 1976.

STEWART, LARRY Vocal, guitar, keyboards, reeds. Member of Airborne, 1979.

STEWART, LOUIS Guitar. Session on "Jesus Christ Superstar" (1970).

STEWART, MAERETHA Vocal. Session for Bob Dylan (1970); Gregg Allman (1973); Free Creek (1973); Jimi Hendrix's "Midnight Lightning" (1973).

STEWART, MARK Vocal. Member of the Pop Group, 1980.

STEWART, MATTHEW Guitar, vocal. Member of Starcastle, 1972-78.

STEWART, ROD Vocal, banjo, guitar, harmonica. Born 1/10/45. Though not an immediate star as vocalist for the Steam Packet, Bluesology, Python Lee Jackson or original Jeff Beck Group, 1968-69, his distinctive raspy vocals developed into a trademark. After a solo album (1970), he replaced Steve Marriott in the Faces, 1971-76, and the group became an international sensation. Constantly maintaining a solo identity in addition to his group efforts has matured his writings and tempered the style of this true showman. Session for the Aynsley Dunbar's Retaliation; "Tommy" (1972). *Albums:* Atlantic Crossing (WBR K-3108) 1975; Best of Rod Stewart (MER SRM-2-7507); Best of Rod Stewart, Vol. 2 (MER SRM-2-7509); Blondes Have More Fun (WBR K 3261) 1978; Every Picture Tells a Story (MER SRM 1-609) 1973; Foot Loose and Fancy Free (WBR K-3092) 1977; Gasoline Alley (MER 61264) 1971; Gift of Song (POL 1-6214); In a Broken Dream (CRS 2066); London Collector — Rock Invasion (LON LC 50012); Never a Dull Moment (MER SRM-1-646) 1972; Night on the Town (WBR K-3116) 1976; Sing It Again Rod (MER SRM 1-680); Rod Stewart Album (MER ML-8001) 1970; Rod Stewart Greatest Hits (WBR HS-3373) 1979; Smiler (MER SRM 1-1017) 1974; A Shot of Rhythm and Blues (PRS 2021) 1976.

ROD STEWART BAND Carmine Appice—drums; Phil Chen—bass; Jim Cregan—guitar; Billy Peek —guitar; Gary Grainger—guitar; Kevin Savigar—keyboards (1980). Backup band for Rod Stewart since 1978. See Rod Stewart.

STEWART, RONNIE Drums. Member of the Joe Perry Project, 1980.

STEWART, SYLVESTER Real name of Sly Stone.

STEWART, TOMMY Drums, vocal. Member of the Trooper, 1975-80, and the Cats, 1980.

STEWART, WINSTON Member of the re-formed Bar-Kays.

STICKY Percussion. Member of Dillinger, 1976.

STIFANTAS, JEAN Drums. Session for Peter C. Johnson (1980).

STIFF LITTLE FINGERS Jake Burns—guitar, vocal; Henry Cluney—guitar, vocal; Jim Reilly—drums; Al McMordie—bass. *Albums:* Nobody's Heroes (CYS 1270) 1980; Flammable Material (RTR 5) 1980.

STIGWOOD, ROBERT Producer. Founder of the Robert Stigwood Organization. Production for the Bee Gees; Eric Clapton; and others.

STILETTO, JOHNNY Bass. Member of Ultra Latex, 1979.

STILL, DAVE Percussion. Session for Johnny Winter (1980).

STILLMAN, JEFF Vocal. Member of the Glider, 1977.

STILLS, STEPHEN Guitar, vocal, keyboards, bass, writer. Born 1/31/45. First appeared on the music scene as a member of Buffalo Springfield, 1966-68. From there he recorded a solo album before joining Crosby, Stills, and Nash (and later, Young), 1969-71. After the ebb of superstardom, he returned to a solo format, then the similar Springfield format, with Manassas. In 1976, a short-lived Stills-Young reunion went on tour. Session for "Super Session" (1968); the Jefferson Airplane (1969); John Sebastian (1970); Eric Clapton (1970); Neil Young (1970, 72, 75); Elvin Bishop (1975); Doris Troy (1970); Bill Withers (1971). *Albums:* Down the Road (ATC 7250) 1973; Illegal Stills (COL PC 34148) 1976; Manassas (ATC 2-903) 1972; Still Stills (ATC 18201); Stills (COL PC 33575) 1975; Stephen Stills (ATC 7202) 1970; Stephen Stills Live (ATC 18156) 1975; Stills 2 (ATC 7206) 1971; Super Session (COL CS 9701) 1968; Thoroughfare Gap (COL PC 35380) 1978; Best of Stephen Stills (ATC 18201) 1976.

STILLS-YOUNG BAND Neil Young—guitar, piano, vocal; Steve Stills—guitar, piano, vocal; Joe Lala —percussion, vocal; Jerry Aiello—keyboards; George Perry—bass, vocal; Joe Vitale—drums, vocal. Short-lived reunion of half of the Crosby, Stills, Nash, and Young supergroup. *Album:* Long May You Run (RPS 2253) 1976.

STILLWATER Mike Causey—guitar; Jim Hall—vocal; Bob Golden—guitar; Allison Scarborough —bass; Rob Walker—guitar; Bob Spearman—keyboards; Sebie Lacey—drums, vocal. *Albums:* I Reserve the Right (CPN 0210) 1978; Stillwater (CPN 0186) 1977.

STIM, MICHAEL Vocal, guitar. Member of the Kracker, 1978.

STIMPSON, JOHN Bass, guitar, vocal. Member of the Mandala Band, 1975, and the Sad Cafe, 1978-79.

STIMULUS, DEAN Bass. Member of Balcones Fault, 1977.

STING Vocal, bass. Real name: Gordon Sumner. Member of the Police since 1978.

STINGER, MARTY Drums. Member of Boulder, 1979.

STINGRAY Danny Anthill—organ; Shaun Wright —drums, percussion; Eddie Boyle—bass; Mike Pilot—guitar, vocal; Dennis East—vocal; Allan Goldswain—keyboards. *Album:* Stingray (CRR 38-127) 1979.

STINSON, ALBERT Bass. Session for Larry Coryell.

STINSON, GREG Guitar, vocal. Member of Shadowfax, 1976.

STINSON, HARRY Vocal. Session for Jay Ferguson (1980).

STIPE, TOM Keyboards, vocal. Member of the Richie Furay Band, 1976.

STIPS, ROBERT JAN Keyboards. Member of the Chris Hinze Connection, 1974, and Golden Earring, 1974-76. String arrangement and session for Golden Earring (1977-80). Session for Barry Hay.

STOCK, DAVID Drums, vocal. Member of the Edison Electric Band, 1970.

STOCKER, CAROL Vocal. Session for Manfred Mann (1980).

STOCKER, WALLY Guitar. Member of the Babys, 1976-present.

STOCKER, WOLFGANG Bass. Member of Eloy, replacing Luitjen Jansson, 1976.

STOCKFISH, JOHN Bass. Session for Gordon

Lightfoot (1974-75).

STOCKTON, RICK Bass. Original member of Pavlov's Dog, 1975-76.

STODDARD, JOE Drums. Member of the Plastic Rhino Band, 1977.

STOHL, BOB Lyricon. Session for the Randle Chowning Band (1978).

STOKELY, JIMMY Vocal. Member of Exile since 1973.

STOKES, O'DELL Guitar. Session for Leon Russell (1974).

STOKES, SIMON Vocal. Namesake of Simon Stokes and the Black Whip Band, 1973. *Album:* Buzzard of Love (UAR UA LA 769G) 1977.

SIMON STOKES AND THE BLACK WHIP BAND Simon Stokes—vocal; Don Senneville—guitar; Christian Pennick—guitar; Marty Tryon—bass; Billy Goodnick—drums; Harry Garfield—keyboards; John Locke—keyboards; Nathan Pino—keyboards. *Album:* Simon Stokes and the Black Whip Band (SDZ) 1973.

STONE, DAVID Keyboards. Replaced Tony Carey in Rainbow, 1978. Member of Oak, 1980.

STONE, FRED Guitar, vocal. Member of Sly and the Family Stone.

STONE, IVORY Vocal. Session for Santana (1976).

STONE, JOANNE Vocal. Session for Elton John (1978).

STONE, MARTIN Guitar. Original member of Savoy Brown, 1967, and founder of Stone's Masonry, 1968.

STONE, RONALD Session for David Crosby (1971).

STONE, ROSE Piano, vocal. Member of Sly and the Family Stone.

STONE, SLY Vocal, keyboards. Born 3/15/44. Real name: Sylvester Stewart. Founder of Sly and the Family Stone, 1967-present. Session for the New Riders of the Purple Sage; Elvin Bishop (1974).

STONE CANYON BAND Randy Meisner—guitar, vocal; Tom Brumley—steel guitar; Dennis Larden—guitar, vocal; J. DeWitt White—bass, vocal; Ty Grimes—drums. Backup band for Rick Nelson.

STONE COUNTRY Dan Barry—bass; Don Beck—banjo, guitar, mandolin, bass; Doug Brooks—guitar; Dennis Conway—drums, percussion; Steve Young—guitar; Richard Lockmiller—percussion. Versatile California group of 1968. *Album:* Stone Country, 1968.

STONE PONEYS Linda Ronstadt—guitar, vocal; Bob Kimmel—guitar; Ken Edwards—guitar. This Arizona folk trio served as the starting place for country-folk-rock singer Ronstadt. *Albums:* Stone Poneys, 1967; Evergreen, Vol. II, 1967; Stone Poneys, Vol. III, 1968; Stone Poneys, Featuring Linda Ronstadt (CAP ST 11383) 1967.

STONE THE CROWS Les Harvey—guitar; Jim Dewar—bass, vocal; Colin Allen—drums, percussion; John McGinnis—keyboards; Maggie Bell—vocal; Steve Thompson—bass (1972); Ron Leahy—keyboards (1972); Jimmy McCulloch—guitar (1972). Early name: Power. Parent group of soloists Bell, Robin Trower's Dewar, and ex-Wings member McCulloch. *Albums:* Stone the Crows (POL); Teenage Licks (POL) 1972; Continuous Performance (POL) 1972.

STONE'S MASONRY Martin Stone—guitar, vocal; Pete Shelley—organ; Keith Tillman—bass; Michael Riley—drums. British blues band formed by Martin Stone after he left Savoy Brown. They recorded only two cuts in the studio before retiring, 1968.

STONEBOLT Ray Roper—guitar, vocal; David Jay Wills—vocal; Dan Atchison—bass; John Webster—keyboards; Brian Lousey—drums, percussion, vocal. *Albums:* Keep It Alive (VIC KKLI 0357) 1980; New Set of Changes (VIC AFLI 3825) 1980; Stonebolt (PCT RRLP 9006) 1978.

STONEBRIDGE, LOU Keyboards. Teamed with Uriah Heep's David Byron for the latter's solo debut, 1975.

STONEGROUND Sal Valentino—guitar, vocal, percussion; Tim Barnes—guitar, bottleneck guitar, vocal; John Blakely—guitar, bass; Pete Sears—bass, keyboards; Michael Mau—drums; Luther Bildt—vocal, guitar; Lynne Hughes—vocal; Dierdre LaPorte—vocal; Annie Sampson—vocal; Lydia Phillips—vocal; Terry Davis—bass, vocal; Fred Webb—keyboards; Sammy Piazza—drums, percussion; Jo Baker—vocal; Lenny Lee Goldsmith—vocal, percussion. Originally a part of the Medicine Ball Caravan, a traveling group of San Franciscans, which featured the voice of former Beau Brummel, Valentino. Part of Fillmore, 1972. *Albums:* Stoneground (WBR 1895) 1971; Flat Out (FOR 001) 1976; Hearts of Stone (WBR K-3187) 1978.

STONER Bass. Member of the Doctors of Madness, 1977.

STONER, ROB Bass, vocal, piano, guitar, producer. Member of Topaz, 1977, and the Wildcats, 1979. Session for Bob Dylan (1977-79); Don McLean (1977); Moon Martin (1979); Link Wray (1979). *Album:* Patriotic Duty (MCA 5118) 1980.

STOOGE, IGGY Vocal. Real name: James Osterberg. Namesake of the Stooges, 1968-69. Later changed his name to Iggy Pop, when he was rediscovered in 1977 by David Bowie. He specializes in sado-masochistic live performances eliciting the "worst" from his audiences. See Iggy Pop.

STOOGES Iggy Stooge—vocal; Ron Asheton—guitar; Scott Asheton—drums; Dave Alexander—bass; Steve McKay—tenor saxophone (1969). Pioneers of punk rock, the Stooges were headed by Iggy Stooge. Totally hedonistic, Stooge demeaned society and his audience while he pranced on stage. *Albums:* The Stooges (ELK) 1968; Funhouse (ELK) 1969.

STOOKEY, PAUL Vocal, guitar. Paul of Peter,

Paul and Mary. *Album:* Paul And (WBR).

STORACE, MARC Vocal. Member of Krokus, 1980.

STORIE, CARL Vocal, harmonica. Voice of the Limousene, 1972. Member of the Faith Band, 1977-79.

STORIES Ian Lloyd—vocal; Steve Love—guitar; Kenneth Bichel—keyboards; Brian Madey—drums, percussion; Kenny Aaronson—bass. A minor sensation of 1972-73, due to vocalist Lloyd, a Rod Stewart soundalike. *Albums:* About Us (KMS 2068); Stories (KMS 2051); Traveling Underground (KMS 2078) 1973.

STORM Jeanette Chase—vocal; Lear Stevens—guitar; Ronni Hansen—bass; David Devon—drums. *Album:* Storm (MCA 3179) 1979.

STORM, SUZY Vocal. Session for Roy Orbison (1979).

RORY STORME AND THE HURRICANES Before joining the Silver Beatles, who later became the Beatles, Ringo Starr was a member of this group. They backed Gene Vincent in the 1950s.

STOTTS, RICHIE Guitar. Member of the Plasmatics, 1980.

STOUT, MARTY Keyboards. Member of Arrogance, 1976-present.

STRACHAN, GRAEME Vocal. Voice of the Skyhooks, 1975-77.

STRAIGHT LINES Daryl Burgess—drums, percussion; David Sinclair—vocal, guitar; Bob Buckley—keyboards, reeds; Peter Clarke—vocal, bass; Peter Padden—vocal, drums, percussion. *Album:* Straight Lines (EPC JE 36504) 1980.

STRAKER, PETER Vocal. Session for the Alan Parsons Project (1977).

STRAND Rick Calhoun—vocal; Scott Shelly—guitar, vocal; Peter Reilich—keyboards, vocal; Dean Cortez—bass, vocal; Kelly Shanahan—drums. *Album:* The Strand (ISL ILPS 9594) 1980.

STRAND, PETE Bass, vocal. Member of the Yipes, 1979-80.

STRANGE, BILLY Guitar. Strange shared an instrumental niche in rock with the Ventures and Duane Eddy. Each was guitar oriented, and each did other people's material. *Albums:* Anthology of the 12 String Guitar (TRD 2071); Best of Billy Strange (CRS 2037); Dyn-O-Mite Guitar (CRS 2094); 5 String Banjo (CRS 98); Folk Rock Hits (CRS 2016); Great Western Themes (CRS 2046); Guitar Greats (EVR 243); In the Mexican Bag (CRS 2022); James Bond Double Feature (CRS 2039); James Bond Theme (CRS 2004); Railroad Man (CRS 2041); Strange Country (TRD 2080); 12 String Guitar (CRS 94); Mr. Guitar (CRS 97); Goldfinger (CRS 2006); English Hits of '65 (CRS 2009); Billy Strange Plays the Hits (CRS 2012); Secret Agent File (CRS 2019); Billy Strange Plays Roger Miller (CRS 2024); Billy Strange and the Challengers (CRS 2030).

STRANGE, DAVID Cello. Session for Mike Oldfield (1975).

STRANGE, GARY Bass. Member of No Dice, 1978-79.

STRANGE, GILES Member of the Strangeloves.

STRANGE, MILES Member of the Strangeloves.

STRANGE, NILES Member of the Strangeloves.

STRANGE, STEVE Member of Visage, 1980.

STRANGELOVES Miles Strange; Niles Strange; Giles Strange. Reputed to be Feldman-Goldstein-Gottehrer, songwriters from Bang Records in the 1960s. *Albums:* Bang and Shout Super Hits (BNG 220); Gang at Bang (BNG 215); I Want Candy (BNG 21).

STRANGLERS Hugh Cornwell—guitar, vocal; Jean Jacques Burnel—bass, vocal; Dave Greenfield—keyboards, vocal. *Albums:* Black and White (AAM 4706) 1978; IV Rattus Norvegicus (AAM 4648); No More Heroes (AAM 4659) 1977; IV (IRS 70011) 1978.

STRAPPS Ross Stagg—vocal, guitar; Mick Underwood—drums; Joe Read—bass; Noel Scott—keyboards. *Album:* Secret Damage, 1977.

STRASSBURG, JAMES Drums. Member of Gasmask.

STRATER, GARY Bass, vocal. Member of Starcastle, 1972-78.

STRATON, STRAY Bass. Session for Richard Betts (1974).

STRATTON, DENNIS Guitar, vocal. Member of the Iron Maiden, 1980.

STRATTON, TED Organ. Session for Les Dudek (1977).

STRAUB, GREG Member of the Crimson Tide, 1978-79.

STRAUD, JAMES Drums. Session for Paul Simon (1973).

STRAUSS, JAMES Bass, vocal. Member of Jiva, 1975.

STRAWBERRY ALARM CLOCK Mark Weitz—organ; Lee Freeman—vocal, drums, flute, saxophone, harmonica; Ed King—guitar; Gary Lovetro—bass; George Bunnell—bass; Randy Seol—drums. Early name: Sixpence. Coupling their psychedelic name with hippy symbols in their debut, "Incense and Peppermint" (1968), the Strawberry Alarm Clock, from San Francisco, achieved some fame at the tail end of the psychedelic rock movement of the late 1960s. *Albums:* Psych-out; Incense and Peppermint; Wake Up, It's Tomorrow, 1968; World in a Sea Shell, 1968.

STRAWBS David Cousins—vocal, guitar; Dave Lambert—vocal, guitar; John Hawken—keyboards; Chas Cronk—bass, vocal; Rod Coombes—drums, percussion, vocal; John Ford—vocal, bass (1970-71); Tony Hooper—vocal, guitar (1970-72); Rick Wakeman—keyboards (1970-71); Rick Hudson—drums, percussion, sitar, vocal (1970-71); Blue Weaver—piano (1972). *Albums:* Best of Strawbs

(AAM 6005); Burning for You (OYS 1-1604) 1977; Bursting at the Seams (AAM 4383) 1973; Deep Cuts (OYS 1-1603) 1976; From the Witchwood (AAM 4304) 1971; Ghost (AAM 4506) 1974; Grave New World (AAM 3607) 1973; Just a Collection of Antiques and Curios (AAM 4288) 1970; Nomadness (AAM 4544) 1975; Early Years, 1970; Deadlines (ARI 4172) 1978.

STRAY Del Bromham—guitar, keyboards; Pete Dyer—vocal, guitar; Gary Giles—bass; Ritchie Cole—drums. English band that began recording in 1970. *Album:* Stand Up and Be Counted (PYE 12107) 1975.

STRAY DOG Snuffy Walden—guitar, vocal; Al Roberts—bass, vocal, keyboards; Lee Sampson—drums, percussion; Timmy Dulaine—guitar, vocal (1974); Luis Cabaza—keyboards, vocal (1974). Dog's appearance in 1973 reminded listeners of the early energy of such heavy metal specialists as Cream and Mountain, due to the guitar work of Walden. Their first album featured the basic trio format, which was augmented the following year. *Albums:* Stray Dog (MCR 66671) 1973; While You're Down There, 1974.

STRAY GATORS Ben Keith—steel guitar; Ken Buttery—drums; Tim Drummond—bass; Jack Nitzsche—piano, slide guitar. Session band for Neil Young's "Harvest," 1972.

STREET, RICHARD Vocal. Member of the Temptations.

STREET, RICKY Bass. Member of the Sorrows, 1980.

STREETBAND Paul Young—vocal, harmonica, percussion; John Gifford—guitar, vocal; Roger Kelly—guitar, vocal; Mick Pearl—bass, vocal; Chaulkie—drums, percussion. *Album:* Streetband, 1980.

STREETER, RIC Guitar, vocal. Member of D. B. Cooper, 1980.

STREETER, ROBERTA Real name of Bobbie Gentry.

STREETHEART Matthew Frenette—drums, vocal; Daryl Gutheil—keyboards, vocal; John Hannah—guitar, vocal; Kenny Shields—vocal, percussion; "Spider" Sinnaeve—bass, vocal. *Album:* Under Heaven Over Hell (ATC 19228) 1979.

STREETWALKERS Roger Chapman—vocal, percussion; Charlie Whitney—guitar; Bob Tench—vocal, guitar; Jon Plotel—bass; Nicko—drums. *Albums:* Vicious but Fair, 1977; Red (ARO MER SRMI-1053) 1973; Streetwalkers, 1975.

STRENG, KEITH Member of the Fleshtones, 1980.

STRETCH Elmer Gantry—guitar, vocal (1976); Steve Emery—bass; Jeff Rich—drums; Steve Kirby—guitar (1976); John Cook—piano (1977). Backup band for Danny Kirwan, 1977. *Album:* You Can't Beat Your Brain for Entertainment, 1976.

STRICKLAND, KEITH Drums. Member of the B-52's, 1980.

STRIDER Lee Hunter—bass; Gary Grainger—guitar; Ian Kewley—keyboards; Jimmy Hawkins—drums. *Album:* Exposed (WBR) 1973.

STRIKE, LIZA Vocal. Session for Steve Stills (1970); Gary Wright (1971); Long John Baldry (1971-72, 75); Carly Simon (1972); Vigrass and Osbourne (1972); Lo and Behold (1972); Rick Wakeman (1972); Elton John (1972); Pink Floyd (1973); Manfred Mann (1973); Kevin Ayers (1973); Bryan Ferry (1974); Dan McCafferty (1975); Ray Thomas (1976); Hummingbird (1976); Sad Cafe (1978); the Small Faces (1978); the Climax Blues Band (1978); Roger Glover (1978); Oxendale and Shephard (1979).

STRIKER Rick Taylor—drums, percussion, vocal; Scott Rosburg—vocal, bass, guitar; Rick Randle—vocal, guitar, keyboards; Rick Ramirez—guitar. *Album:* Striker (ARI 4165) 1978.

STRING DRIVEN THING James Exell—bass, vocal (1974-75); Grahame Smith—violin, viola; Kimberly Beacon—vocal (1974-75); Colin Fairley—drums, percussion, vocal; Alun Roberts—guitar (1974-75); Colin Wilson—bass (1972-73); Pauline Adams—vocal (1972-73); Chris Adams—vocal, guitar (1972-73). *Albums:* Please Mind Your Head (TWC) 1974; Keep Yer 'And on It (TWC T-503) 1975; The Machine That Cried, 1973; String Driven Thing.

STROHMAN, JOHN Saxophone. Session for Johnny Winter (1980).

STRONACH, JOHN Percussion, producer. Produced the Alvin Lee Band (1979). Session for Joe Walsh (1974).

STRONDLUND, ROBB Vocal, guitar. Member of the Rank Strangers, 1977.

STRONG, OLLIE Steel guitar. Session for Gordon Lightfoot (1972).

STROUD, JAMES Drums. Replaced Grant Serpell in Sailor, 1980.

STROZIER, FRANK Saxophone. Session for Martin Mull (1977).

STRUMMER, JOE Guitar, vocal. Member of the Clash since 1978.

STRUNZ, JORGE Guitar, percussion. Member of Caldera, 1976-78.

STRUZICK, EDDIE Vocal. Session for Roy Orbison (1979).

STRZELECKI, HENRY Bass, piano. Session for Waylon Jennings (1973); Levon Helm (1980).

STUART, CHAD Vocal, guitar, banjo, keyboards, sitar. Half of the English duet, Chad and Jeremy, 1963-68.

STUART, HAMISH Vocal, guitar, bass. Member of the Average White Band since 1974.

STUART, MICHAEL Drums, percussion. Member of Love.

STUART, ROLF Flute. Session for It's a Beautiful

Day (1971)

STUBBLEFIELD, CLYDE Drums. Session for Ben Sidran.

STUBBS, GEORGE Piano. Session for John Hammond (1968).

STUBBS, LEVI, JR. Vocal. Original member of the Four Tops.

STUBENHAUS, NEIL Bass. Member of Four on the Floor, 1979.

STUERMER, DUANE Bass, vocal. Member of Sweetbottom, 1978-79.

STUERNER, DARYL Guitar. Session for George Duke (1975).

STULL, BRUCE Drums, percussion, vocal. Member of the Highwind, 1980.

STUMUCK Bass saxophone. Session for Frank Zappa (1979).

STURMAN, JIMMY Drums. Member of Eden's Children, 1968.

STYLER, MARSHALL Keyboards, vocal. Member of Duke Jupiter since 1978.

STYLES, MARK Keyboards. Session for Roger Powell (1980).

STYLES, MAX Drums. Member of the Kings, 1980.

STYLES, MITCH Guitar. Member of Baby.

STYVERS, LAURIE Vocal. Born 8/3/51. *Album:* Spilt Milk (WBR 1946) 1971.

STYX Dennis de Young—keyboards, synthesizer, vocal; James Young—guitar, vocal; John Curulewski—guitar, vocal, synthesizer, autoharp (1970-75); Chuck Panozzo—bass; John Panozzo—drums, percussion, vocal; Tommy Shaw—guitar, vocal (1976-present). Early name: the Tradewinds (1964). "Lady," from their second album, put Styx on the charts in 1971. Since then, this Chicago band has built a loyal following around their interplay of synthesizer, organ, and guitar. *Albums:* Best of Styx (WDN AFLI-3116) 1980; Cornerstone (AAM 3711) 1979; Crystal Ball (AAM 4604) 1976; Equinox (AAM 4559) 1975; Grand Illusion (AAM 4637) 1977; Man of Miracles (WDN AFLI 3115) 1974; Pieces of Eight (AAM PR-4724) 1978; Serpent Is Rising (WDN BXLI 0287) 1973; Styx 2 (WDN AFLI 3111) 1971; Styx (WDN 1008) 1971; Styx I (WDN 3593) 1980; Styx Lady (WDN 3594) 1980.

SUALL, MARK Guitar, vocal. Member of Alda Reserve, 1979.

SUBHUMANS Wimpy Roy—vocal; Gerry Useless—bass, vocal: Jim Imagawa—drums; Mike Graham—guitar. *Album:* The Subhumans (QTS) 1979.

SUBURBS Hugo Klaers—drums, percussion; Bruce B. C. Allen—guitar, vocal; Michael Halliday—bass; Blain John Chaney—vocal, percussion; Chan Polling—keyboards, vocal. *Album:* In Combo (TWT TTR 8014) 1980.

SUCHORSKY, MICHAEL Drums. Session for Lou Reed (1976-present).

SUDANO, BRUCE Keyboards, vocal. Member of Brooklyn Dreams.

SUDDERTH, WILLIAM Trumpet. Member of Atlantic Starr.

SUGAR BLUE Harmonica. Session for the Rolling Stones (1980).

SUGARLOAF Jerry Corbetta—keyboards, vocal; Bob Webber—guitar, vocal; Bob Raymond—bass; Bob MacVittie—drums. Denver's Sugarloaf caused a minor sensation in the late 1960s with their pop-jazz hit, "Green Eyed Lady." Corbetta's organ work was the highlight of the group, and rumors circulated that they were destined to hit very big. The rumors, however, never became reality despite their attempted comeback in 1975 with "Don't Call Us, We'll Call You." *Albums:* Sugarloaf (LIB LST 7640); Don't Call Us, We'll Call You (CLA 1000) 1975.

SUICIDE Alan Vega—vocal; Martin Rev—electronics. *Albums:* Suicide (ANT 7080) 1980; Suicide (RSR 800) 1980.

SUICIDE COMMANDOS Dave Aitl—drums; Steve Almaas—bass; Chris Osgood—guitar. *Album:* Make a Record (BNK 002) 1978.

SULLIVAN, CHRIS Bass, vocal. Member of the Penetrators, 1980.

SULLIVAN, FRANK Guitar, vocal. Member of Mariah, 1976, and Survivor, 1979.

SULLIVAN, HUGH Organ. Replaced Joey Chirowski in Mandala, 1968.

SULLIVAN, JACQUIE Vocal. Session for Bryan Ferry (1977); Status Quo (1978).

SULLIVAN, JIM Guitar. Member of the Tiger, 1976.

SULLIVAN, NICK Guitar. Member of Buddy Holly's backup band, 1957-58.

SULLIVAN, PAT Vocal. Session for Martin Mull.

SULLIVAN, ROCKY Vocal. *Album:* Illegal Entry (BGL 6-5000) 1978.

SULLIVAN, TERRENCE Drums, percussion. Replaced Jim McCarty in Renaissance.

SULLIVAN, TOMMY Saxophone, flute, vocal. Member of the Brooklyn Bridge.

SULLIVAN, TOMMY Keyboards, vocal. Member of Ramatam, 1972.

SULTON, KASIM Bass. Replaced John Siegler in Utopia, 1977-80. Session for Steve Hillage (1976).

SULTZMANN, STAN Tenor saxophone. Member of the Candlestick Brass, 1977.

SUMLER, DIANE Vocal. Session for Roy Buchanan (1976).

SUMLIN, HUBERT Guitar. Session for Howlin' Wolf (1972).

SUMMERS, ANDY Guitar. Member of the Police since 1978. Session for Kevin Lamb (1978).

SUMMERS, BILL Percussion. Session for the Pointer Sisters (1974). *Albums:* Cayenne (PRS 10103) 1977; Feel the Heat (PRS 10102) 1977; On Sunshine (PRS 10107) 1979; Straight to the Bank (PRS 10105) 1978.

SUMMERS, DON Bass. Member of the Moving Sidewalks.

SUMNER Sumner Mering—vocal, guitar; Larry Treadwell—guitar, vocal; Novi—keyboards, viola; Robert Louis di Chiro—bass; Mark Sanders—drums. *Album:* Sumner (ASY 6E-266) 1980.

SUMNER, GORDON Real name of Sting.

SUNBLIND LION Dave Steffen—guitar; Larry Baldock—bass, vocal (1978); Keith Abler—guitar, vocal; Dick Colbath—piano (1978); Mike Pellger—drums (1978); Steve Olschesky—bass (1976); Dave Hassinger—percussion (1976); Duane Abler—keyboards (1976). *Albums:* Above and Beyond (HGN 5102) 1978; Observer, 1976.

SUNDANCE Byron Berline—fiddle, vocal; Jack Skinner—bass, vocal; Dan Crary—guitar; John Hickman—banjo; Allen Wald—guitar, pedal steel guitar, vocal. Upbeat country music with country master Byron Berline. *Album:* Byron Berline and Sundance (MCA 2217) 1976.

SUNDHOLM, ROY Vocal, guitar. *Album:* Chinese Method (POL 1-6233) 1979.

SUNNYLAND SLIM Vocal, piano. Mississippi bluesman, born 9/5/07. *Albums:* Cryin' in the Morning (MUS 5212); Legacy of the Blues (CRS 1001); Legacy of the Blues, Vol. II (CRS 10021); Rare Blues (TKM 7081); Slim's Shout (PRS 7723).

SUNSHINE COMPANY Mary Nance—vocal, percussion; Maury Manseau—vocal, guitar, piano; Larry Sims—guitar, vocal; Merle Bregante—drums, vocal; Doug Mark—guitar, violin, vocal; Dave Hodgkins—guitar (1968). Happy vocal harmonies were the feature of this California group, including the writings of Jackson Browne. *Albums:* Happy Is the Sunshine Company, 1967; The Sunshine Company, 1968; Sunshine and Shadows, 1968.

SUNSHIP Sam Reed—vocal, percussion; Bob Carabillo—saxophone, vocal; Peter Zummo—trombone, flute, vocal, synthesizer; Rik Albani—horns, vocal; Barry Grant—guitar; Ronnie Berger—drums, percussion; Shelly Rosen—bass; Steve Starger—keyboards. *Album:* Into the Sun (CAP) 1974.

SUPA, RICHARD Vocal, guitar. *Albums:* Life Lines (EPC PE 31277) 1976; Tall Tales (SCD 1-6155) 1978.

SUPER SESSION Albums featuring live and studio jams with the best rock-blues musicians in San Francisco, 1968-69. Included are Mike Bloomfield, Al Kooper, Steve Stills, Barry Goldberg, Elvin Bishop, Harvey Brooks, Eddie Hoh, Skip Prokop, Carlos Santana, and others. *Albums:* Super Session (COL C59701) 1968; Live Adventures (COL KGP-6) 1969.

SUPERCHARGE Albie Donnelly—saxophone, flute, vocal; Dave Irving—drums, percussion, vocal; Iain Bradshaw—keyboards; Les Karski—guitar, vocal; Ozzie Yue—guitar, vocal; Tony Dunmore—bass, vocal; Bob Robertson—saxophone, vocal. *Albums:* Supercharge (VIR) 1976; Horizontal Refreshment (VIR 34429) 1977.

SUPERMAX Kurt Havenstein—vocal, bass, keyboards, guitar; Peter Kock—percussion; Kenneth Taylor—bass; Lothar Krell—keyboards, vocal; Jurgen Zoller—drums, percussion; Hans Ochs—guitar, vocal. *Album:* Fly with Me (ELK 6E 193) 1979.

SUPERSTAR See Jesus Christ Superstar.

SUPERTRAMP Roger Hodgson—vocal, guitar, keyboards; Bob Benberg—drums; Doug Thomson—bass; John Helliwell—reeds, vocal; Richard Davies—vocal, keyboards; Richard Palmer—guitar, vocal (1970); Robert Millar—drums, harmonica (1970). *Albums:* Breakfast in America (AAM 3708) 1979; Crime of the Century (AAM 3647) 1974; Crisis, What Crisis (AAM 4560) 1975; Even in the Quietest Moments (AAM 4634) 1977; Supertramp (AAM 4665) 1977; Paris (AAM 6702) 1980.

SUPREMES Diana Ross—vocal; Mary Wilson—vocal; Florence Ballard—vocal; Cindy Birdsong—vocal. Originally called the Primettes. Organized in 1962, the Supremes have survived in the pop soul market because of their highly polished professionalism in person as well as on record. Through the years, Ross emerged as the star in the group and became the featured member of the trio before her solo debut in 1969. The Supremes continued on without her. *Albums:* Meet the Supremes, 1963; Where Did Our Love Go, 1964; A Bit of Liverpool, 1964; Country-Western and Pop, 1965; More Hits, 1965; We Remember Sam Cooke, 1965; Supremes at the Copa, 1965; Merry Christmas, 1965; I Hear a Symphony, 1966; Supremes Sing Holland, Dozier, Holland, 1967; Supremes Greatest Hits, 1967; Reflections, 1968; Funny Girl, 1968; Live at the Talk of the Town, 1968; Love Child, 1968; Without Diana Ross; Floy Joy; Supremes; In Loving Memory (MTN M7-642); Supremes Greatest Hits (MTN M7-663); Supremes (MTN M7-873); Anthology—Diana Ross and the Supremes (MTN M9-794) 1974; Supremes A-Go-Go (MTN) 1966; Supremes (MTN M6-828) 1975.

SURANOVICH, GEORGE Drums. Member of the Eric Burdon Band, 1975.

SURF PUNKS Dennis Dragon—drums, vocal, percussion, producer; Drew Steele—guitar, vocal, keyboards, synthesizer. *Album:* My Beach (EPC NJE 36500) 1980.

SURFARIS Pat Connolly—vocal, bass; Jim Fuller—guitar; Bob Berryhill—guitar; Ron Wilson—drums; Jim Pash—saxophone, clarinet, guitar. Mainly instrumental, the Surfaris rose to fame on the heels of the Beach Boys during the surf explosion. They were most noted for their 1963 hit, "Wipe Out." *Albums:* Wipe Out, 1963; Surfaris Play Wipe Out, 1963; It Ain't Me, Babe, 1965.

SURKAMP, DAVID Vocal, guitar. Original member of Pavlov's Dog, 1975-76, before teaming with Ian Matthews, 1980.

SURMAN, JOHN Saxophone. Member of Blues Incorporated. *Album:* Upon Reflection (ECM 1-1148).

SURPRISE PACKAGE Robert Lowery—vocal; Mike Rogers—organ; Fred Zeufeldt—drums; Greg Beck—guitar. Pacific Northwest band that regrouped in 1970 as American Eagle. *Album:* Free Up, 1969.

SURRAIT, PAUL Banjo. Member of Gram Parson's early band.

SURVIVOR Frankie Sullivan—guitar, vocal; Dave Bickler—vocal, keyboards; Jim Peterick—guitar, vocal; Gary Smith—drums, percussion; Dennis Keith Johnson—bass. *Album:* Survivor (STB 7107) 1979.

SUSAN Charles Leland—bass, vocal; Ricky Byrd—guitar, vocal; Tom Dickie—guitar, vocal; Mike Leland—drums, vocal. *Album:* Falling in Love Again (VIC BXL 1-3372) 1979.

SUSSMAN, RICHARD Keyboards. Member of Elephant's Memory.

SUSSMAN LAWRENCE BAND Peter Himmelman—guitar, vocal; Jeff Victor—keyboards, vocal; Al Wolovitch—bass; Andrew Kamman—drums; Eric Moen—saxophone, guitar, vocal. *Album:* Hail to the Modern Hero (RGR 80101) 1980.

SUSSWELL, JOHN Drums. Session for Steve Winwood (1977).

SUTCLIFFE, STU Guitar. Member of the Silver Beatles through 1961. Died 4/10/62.

SUTHERLAND, IAIN Vocal, guitar, harmonica. Half of the Sutherland Brothers, with brother Gavin, since 1973.

SUTHERLAND, GAVIN Vocal, guitar, steel guitar. With brother Iain, he formed the Sutherland Brothers band, 1973-present.

SUTHERLAND, STACY Member of the 13th Floor Elevators.

SUTHERLAND BROTHERS Iain Sutherland—vocal, guitar, harmonica; Gavin Sutherland—vocal, guitar, steel guitar. With their band, Quiver, this vocal duet flirts with commercial success effortlessly, but not as successfully as they might like. *Albums:* Dream Kid (ISL SW 9341); Lifeboat (ISL SW 9326); Reach for the Sky, 1975; Sutherland Brothers and Quiver, 1973; When the Night Comes Down (COL JC-35703) 1979; Slipstream (COL PC 34376) 1976; Down to Earth (COL NJ 35293) 1977.

SUTTER, BOB Keyboards. Member of the Numa Band, 1980.

SUTTON, ANN Vocal. Session for Gregg Allman (1974); Paul Butterfield (1975); Henry Gross (1975-76); Ian Hunter (1976).

SUTTON, CHARLES Member of Hank Ballard's Midnighters.

SUTTON, GREG Vocal. *Album:* Soft as a Sidewalk (COL JC 36036) 1975.

SUTTON, ROGER Guitar, bass, vocal, cello, percussion. Original member of Mark-Almond, 1970-71, and Ian Carr's Nucleus, 1975. Session for Aynsley Dunbar (1970).

SUTTON, STELLA Vocal. Session for Duster Bennett (1968).

SVT Nick Buck—keyboards, vocal; Jack Casady—bass; Paul Zahl—drums, vocal; Brian Marnell—guitar, vocal. *Album:* Extended Play, 1980.

SWALLOW, STEVE Bass. Original member of the Gary Burton Quartet.

SWAN, BILLY Vocal, keyboards. *Albums:* Billy Swan at His Best (MMT 7629) 1978; You're OK, I'm OK (PWK 3743) 1980.

SWANN, TOBY Guitar, vocal. Member of the Battered Wives.

SWANS Assumed name of James Brown and the Famous Flames. With Nat Kendrick, they recorded "Mashed Potatoes," 1960.

SWANSON, BOB Vocal. Half of the Lamb duet, 1970-72.

SWANSON, DAVE Vocal, keyboards. Member of Halloween, 1979.

SWANSON, DAVID Vocal, bass, guitar. Member of the Pop since 1977.

SWARBRICK, DAVE Violin, viola, vocal. Member of Fairport Convention, and soloist. *Albums:* Swarbrick (TAT 334) 1976; Swarbrick 2 (Import) 1978.

SWARTZ, STAN Piano, saxophone. Session for the Randle Chowning Band (1978).

SWEAT, I. P. Bass. Session for Johnny Winter (1978).

SWEATHOG Lenny Lee—keyboards, vocal; Frosty—drums, percussion; B. J.—guitar, vocal; Dave Johnson—bass, vocal. After his brief exposure as Lee Michaels' partner, Bartholomew Smith-Frost (Frosty) left for his less successful outing as leader of Sweathog, 1973. *Album:* Halleluja (COL) 1973.

SWEENEY, JOANN Vocal. Session for J. J. Cale (1972).

SWEENEY, VIC Drums. Member of the Andy Bown Band.

SWEET, BETTY Vocal. Session for Gary Wright (1975).

SWEET, DARRELL Drums, percussion, vocal. Original member of Nazareth since 1972.

SWEET, RACHEL Vocal. *Albums:* Fool Around (SFF JC 36101) 1979; Protect the Innocent (SFF JC 36337) 1980.

SWEET Andy Scott—guitar, vocal, cello, synthesizer; Steve Priest—bass, vocal, cello; Brian Connolly—vocal, keyboards; Mick Tucker—drums, percussion. *Albums:* Cut Above the Rest (CAP SO 11929) 1979; Desolation Boulevard (CAP ST 11395) 1975; Give Us a Wink (CAP ST 11496) 1975; Level Headed (CAP ST 11744)

1977; Off the Record (CAP STAO 11636) 1977; Sweet VI (CAP ST 12106) 1980.

SWEET INSPIRATIONS Cissy Drinkard Houston—vocal; Myrna Smith—vocal; Sylvia Shemwell—vocal; Estelle Brown—vocal; Gloria Brown—vocal. Originally a backup group, the Inspirations worked with Aretha Franklin before making their less spectacular solo debut in 1967. *Albums:* Sweet Inspirations, 1968; Songs of Faith and Inspiration; What the World Needs Now Is Love, 1968; Heavenly Stars; Disco-Trek (ATC 18158); Hot Butterfly (RSO 1-3058) 1979.

SWEET THURSDAY Brian Odgers—bass, woodwinds; Harvey Burns—drums, percussion; Jon Mark—vocal, guitar; Alun Davies—vocal, guitar; Nicky Hopkins—keyboards. The credits of the composite members of Thursday indicated that they had a chance at becoming a big group. But the financial difficulties of their recording label did not allow for adequate promotion of Thursday's debut album. Shortly after it appeared, the company folded and the band split up. *Album:* Sweet Thursday (TET T-112) 1970.

SWEETBOTTOM Warren Paul Wiegratz—keyboards, reeds, vocal; Mark Torroll—drums, percussion; Duane Stuermer—bass, vocal; Martin J. Appel—guitar. *Albums:* Angels of the Deep (ELK 6E 156) 1978; Turn Me Loose (ELK 6E 210) 1979.

SWEETENHAM, GEOFF Drums. Session for Matthew Fisher (1973).

SWEETWATER Fred Herrara—bass, vocal; Alex Del Zoppo—keyboards, harmonica, vocal; Albert B. Moore—flute, vocal; Nansi Nevins—vocal, guitar; August Burns—cello; Elpidio Cobain—percussion; Ricky Fataar—drums. *Albums:* Melon (RPS 6473); Sweetwater.

SWEVAL, PETER Bass. Member of the Starz since 1976.

SWINDELLS, STEVE Vocal, keyboards. Member of the Hawklords, 1978. *Album:* Fresh Blood (ACO 38-128) 1980.

SWISSTACK, JEFF Drums. Member of Russia, 1980.

SYED, ARSHAD Percussion. Member of the Dija Rhythm Band, 1976.

SYLVESTER, TERRY Vocal. Session for the Alan Parsons Project (1976).

SYLVAIN, SYLVAIN Guitar, piano, vocal. Member of the New York Dolls, 1973-74, before going solo. *Album:* Sylvain Sylvain (VIC AFLI 3475) 1979.

SYLVIAN, DAVID Vocal, guitar. Member of Japan since 1979.

SYME, HUGH Keyboards, vocal. Member of the Ian Thomas Band, 1976.

SYMMONDS, GLENN Drums. Replaced Michael Shrieve in Automatic Man, 1977. Member of the Reggie Knighton Band, 1978.

SYMONS, REDMOND Guitar, vocal, piano. Member of the Skyhooks, 1975-77.

SYNERGY Larry Fast—electronics. One-man electronic band. *Albums:* Cords (PST 6000) 1978; Electronic Realizations for Rock Orchestra (PST 6001) 1975; Games (PST 6003) 1979; Sequencer (PST 6002) 1976.

SYNGE, CASEY Vocal. Session for Pilot (1972).

SYNIAR, BILL Bass. Member of Tantrum, 1978-79.

SYXX, NIKI Bass. Member of Jon and the Nightriders, 1980.

SZCZESNAIK, STEVE Drums, vocal. Member of Arc, 1978.

SZYMCZYK, BILL Producer. Produced B. B. King (1969-70); the James Gang (1969-71); the J. Geils Band (1971, 73-74, 76); Joe Walsh (1972-73, 78); Jo Jo Gunne (1973); the Michael Stanley Band (1975); Jay Ferguson (1977-79); the Band (1979); the Eagles (1980); Bob Seger (1980); and others.

T

T., STEVEN See Steven T.

T-BONES Early name for Hamilton, Joe Frank and Reynold, when they recorded "No Matter What Shape," 1969.

T. C. Bass. Member of Eddie and the Hot Rods since 1976.

T.I.M.E. Larry Byron—guitar; Bill Richardson—guitar; Steve Rumph—drums; Nick St. Nicholas—bass; Pat Couchois—drums (1969). *Albums:* T.I.M.E., 1968; Smooth Ball, 1969.

T.M.G. Ted Mulry—vocal, bass, piano; Gary Dixon—vocal, guitar; Les Hall—guitar; Herm Kovac—drums, percussion, synthesizer. *Album:* Disturbing the Peace (ACO 38 115) 1979.

T. REX Marc Bolan—vocal, guitar; Steve Took—vocal. Originally an underground sensation, T. Rex's sound was so tightly produced that their commercial breakthrough was inevitable. Their popularity reached its peak in 1973 with "Get It On." *Albums:* Light of Love (CAS 7005); My People Were Fair (AAM); Prophets, Seers and Sages (AAM); Ride a Swan (RPS 6440); Tanx (RPS 2132); Electric Warrior (RPS 6466) 1971; The Slider (PRS 2095) 1972.

TABAK, RON Vocal. Voice of Prism, 1977.

TABET, PAUL Drums. Member of the White Duck, 1971.

TABOR, JUNE Vocal. Voted Melody Maker's top female singer of the year, 1976. *Album:* Airs and Graces (ANT 7043) 1976.

JUNE TABOR AND MADDY PRIOR Duet featuring Steeleye Span vocalist Prior, and Tabor. See individual listings. *Album:* Silly Sisters (TKM 7077) 1976.

TACKETT, FRED Guitar, piano, trumpet. Member of Mephistopheles. Session for Nilsson (1975-76); Rod Stewart (1975, 76, 78); Boz Scaggs (1976); Glen Campbell (1976); Jimmy Webb (1977); Gary Wright (1979); Adam Mitchell (1979); Rory Block (1979); Bob Dylan (1980).

TAFOYA, MIKE Guitar. Member of the Boyzz, 1978.

TAGG, ERIC Vocal. Member of Medusa, 1978.

TAK, BOBBY Drums. Member of the Chichlids, 1980.

TAKAHASHI, YUKIHIRO Drums, percussion, vocal. Member of the Yellow Magic Orchestra, 1979-80.

TAKEDA, KAZUO Guitar. Original member of Creation, 1976.

TALBERT, WAYNE Keyboards. Member of the Sir Douglas Quintet, 1966-68. Session for Kim Fowley.

TALBOT, BILLY Bass. Member of Crazy Horse, 1971-78. Session for Neil Young (1969, 70, 73, 75); Nils Lofgren (1976).

TALBOT, PHIL Guitar. Member of Tucky Buzzard, 1973.

TALBOT, RICHARD Vocal, slide guitar. Session for Hot Tuna (1972).

TALKING HEADS Martina Weymouth—bass; Jerry Harrison—guitar, keyboards, vocal; David Byrne—guitar, vocal; Chris Frantz—drums; Adrian Belew—guitar (1980). Rock minimalists and innovators, best known for their 1977 hit "Psycho Killer." *Albums:* Fear of Music (SIR K-6076) 1979; More Songs About Buildings and Food (SIR K-6058); Talking Heads '77 (SIR 6036) 1977; Remain in Light (SIR K 6095) 1980.

TALLENT, GARRY Bass. Member of the E Street Shuffle Band since 1973. Session for Ian Hunter (1979).

TALLEY, GARY Guitar. Member of the Box Tops, 1965-68.

TALTON, TOMMY Guitar, vocal, harmonica. Member of Cowboy, 1971-73. Session for the Allman Brothers (1973); Gregg Allman (1974); Richard Betts (1974); Martin Mull (1974).

TAMPA RED Bottleneck guitar. Real name: Hudson Woodbridge. Born between 1900 and 1908. (He gave varying dates.) Began recording in 1928 and reportedly released more 78-rpm discs in his 25-year career than any other blues performer. Session for Ma Rainey. *Album:* Guitar Wizard (VIC AXM2-5501) 1973.

TANDY, RICHARD Keyboards, guitar. Member of the Electric Light Orchestra since 1974.

TANGEL, ALEX Vocal. Half of the Ozz duet, 1980.

TANGERINE DREAM Edgar Froese—mellotron, guitar, bass, organ, synthesizer, electronics; Chris Franke—moog, keyboards, synthesizer; Peter Baumann—keyboards, flute, synthesizer, electronics. Tangerine Dream, from Germany, appeared in the early 1970s, using moog and electronic sound exclusively. Comprised of three members, the group sounded like a blend of Pink Floyd and John Cage. *Albums:* Phaedra (VIR) 1973; Live (WIR) 1977; Rubycorn.

TANGO Mark Guerrero—vocal, guitar, keyboards; Ernie Hernandez—drums, vocal; John Valenzuela—guitar, vocal; Richard Rosas—bass. *Album:* Tango (AAM SP 3612) 1974.

TANI, MAURICE Bass, guitar, piano. Member of

Roy Loney and the Phantom Movers, 1979-80.

TANNER, MARC Vocal, guitar, piano. Namesake of the Marc Tanner Band since 1979.

MARC TANNER BAND Marc Tanner—vocal, guitar, piano; Michael Stevens—guitar; Ron Edwards—bass; Joe Romersa—drums, percussion; Steve Mann—reeds; Linda Stevens—vocal. *Albums:* No Escape (ELK 6E 168) 1979; Temptation (ELK 6E 240) 1980.

TANNETTI, PETER Keyboards. Member of the Crystal Mansion.

TANNUM, RICH Vocal, bass. Member of the Rockspurs, 1978-79.

TANSIN, JOE Member of Badfinger, 1978.

TANTRUM Bill Syniar—bass; Barb Erber—vocal; Ray Sapko—guitar; Sandy Caulfield—vocal; Vern Wennerstron—percussion; Pam Bradley—vocal; Phil Balsano—keyboards. *Albums:* Rather Be Rockin' (OVA 1747) 1979; Tantrum (OVA 1735) 1978.

TAOS Albie Ciappa—drums, percussion, vocal; Burt Levine—guitar, banjo, vocal; Steve Oppenheim—guitar, keyboards, vocal; Jeff Baker—guitar, piano, harmonica, vocal; Kit Bedford—bass, piano, vocal. *Album:* Taos (MER SR 61257).

TAPES Peter Meuris—drums; Igor Roovers—bass; Michiel Brandes—guitar; Rolf Hermsen—vocal, guitar. *Album:* Tapes Party (PPT 9842) 1980.

TAPIA, ADRIAN Saxophone. Session for Boz Scaggs (1980).

TAPP, CHARLES Drums, vocal. Member of Randy Hansen's backup band, 1980.

TARBUTTON, JIMMY Guitar. Member of the Gentrys.

TARENSKEEN, JOB Drums, percussion, saxophone, vocal. Member of Alquin, 1975, and the Meteors, 1980.

TARGET Jimi Jamison—vocal; David Spain—drums; Tom Cathey—bass; Buddy Davis—guitar, organ; Paul Cannon—guitar. *Albums:* Target, 1976; Captured, 1977.

TARKESTY, ELI Guitar. Session for B. B. King (1973-74).

TARNEY, ALAN Guitar, keyboards, synthesizer, bass, vocal. Half of the Tarney and Spencer Duet, 1978-79. Session for Olivia Newton-John (1976).

TARNEY AND SPENCER Trevor Spencer—drums, percussion; Alan Tarney—guitar, keyboards, synthesizer, vocal. *Albums:* Run for Your Life (AAM 4757) 1979; Three's a Crowd (AAM 4692) 1978.

TARNOWER, HOWIE Mandolin. Half of the Fiction Brothers since 1979.

TARRACH, DICKY Drums, percussion. Member of Randy Pie, 1975-77.

TARRANT, ROBERT Congas. Session for J. J. Cale (1972).

TARTACHNY, PAUL Guitar, vocal. Member of the Beacon Street Union, 1968.

TASVALLAN PRESIDENTI Pekka Poyry—saxophone, piano; Eero Raittnen—vocal; Vesa Aaltonen—drums, percussion; Jukica Tolonen—guitar, keyboards; Heikka Virtanen—bass. *Album:* Milky Way Roses (JNS) 1974.

TASHIAN, BARRY Guitar, vocal. Head of the Remains, 1965-67.

TASSIN, RICK Drums, vocal. Member of the Jitters, 1980.

TASSLER, STEPHEN Drums, percussion, vocal. Member of Starcastle, 1972-76.

TASTE Rory Gallagher—guitar, vocal; John Wilson—drums; Richard McCracken—bass. Taste accompanied Blind Faith in 1969 on the latter's only U.S. tour. The group was the vehicle for red-haired Gallagher, who dissolved the group in 1971 for a more successful solo career. *Albums:* Taste (ATC) 1969; On the Boards (ATC 33-322); Live at the Isle of Wight (Import) 1972.

TATA Vocal, percussion. Member of Pollution, 1971.

TATANE, EDDIE African drums. Session for Mike Oldfield (1975).

TATE, GRADY Drums. Session for Pearls Before Swine (1969); Paul Simon (1973, 75). *Albums:* Jazz Gala Concert (ATC 1693); Multiplication Rock (CAP SJA 11174); Master Grady (ABC AS 9330) 1977.

TATE, RICHARD Guitar, bass, vocal. *Album:* Richard Tate (MCA 1016) 1977.

TATTOO Wally Bryson—guitar, vocal; David Thomas—guitar, vocal, percussion; Jeff Hutton—keyboards, vocal; Dan Klawon—bass; Thom Mooney—drums. *Album:* Tattoo (PDG) 1976.

TAUPIN, BERNIE Lyricist. Born 5/22/50. Silent members of rock groups rarely receive any publicity. Robert Hunter, of the Grateful Dead, and Keith Reid, of Procol Harum, were the most notable exceptions until the Elton John phenomenon of 1969. Taupin, partner of John, was an overnight star also. Since then, he has expanded into publishing and recording on his own. *Album:* He Who Rides the Tiger (ASY 6E 263) 1980.

TAVAGLIONE, STEVE Saxophone, flute, bass. Member of Caldera, 1976-78.

TAXXI David Cummins—guitar, vocal; Colin Payne—keyboards, vocal; Jeffrey Neao—drums. *Album:* Day for Night (FSY 9603) 1980.

TAYLOR, ALEX Vocal. Brother of James Taylor, who made an unsuccessful bid at a solo career in the wake of his brother's success. Session for James Taylor (1976). *Album:* Dinnertime (CPN 0101) 1972.

TAYLOR, ALVIN Drums, percussion. Original member of the Eric Burdon Band, 1974, and Sly and the Family Stone, 1979. Session for George Harrison (1976); Bob Welch (1977, 79); Eric Burdon (1977); Billy Thorpe (1979); Elton John (1980).

TAYLOR, BILLY Organ. Member of the Royal Guardsmen, 1969.

TAYLOR, BOB Drums. Session for Duane Eddy's Rebels (1961).

TAYLOR, BRIAN Vocal, guitar, percussion. *Album:* Brian Taylor (VIC APLI 2161) 1977.

TAYLOR, DALLAS Drums, percussion. Member of Clear Light, 1967-68, and Crosby, Stills, Nash and Young, 1969-70. Session for John Sebastian (1970-71); Steve Stills (1970-71, 75); Bill Wyman (1974, 76); Sammy Hagar (1975).

TAYLOR, DAN Drums, percussion, vocal. Cofounder of Silver Apples, 1968.

TAYLOR, DANNY Drums. Session for Gus (1980).

TAYLOR, DAVE Bass, vocal. Member of Liar, 1980.

TAYLOR, DAVID Horns. Session for Lou Reed (1974); Johnny Winter (1974).

TAYLOR, DICK Guitar. Member of the Pretty Things.

TAYLOR, GARY Guitar, bass, vocal. Member of the Herd, 1967, and Fox. Session for Jerry Lee Lewis (1973); Gerry Rafferty (1978-79).

TAYLOR, GRAEME Guitar. Session for Steve Howe (1975).

TAYLOR, GREG Harmonica, percussion, vocal. Member of Larry Raspberry and the Highsteppers. Session for Jimmy Hall (1980).

TAYLOR, HOUND DOG Guitar, vocal. Real name: Theodore Roosevelt Taylor. Born in 1915 in Mississippi. Died 12/17/75 in Chicago. See Hound Dog Taylor and the Houserockers.

HOUND DOG TAYLOR AND THE HOUSEROCKERS Hound Dog Taylor—guitar, vocal; Brewster Phillips—guitar; Ted Harvey—drums. *Albums:* Beware of Dog (ALG 4707) 1976; Natural Boogie (ALG 4704) 1974; Hound Dog Taylor and the Houserockers (ANG 4701).

TAYLOR, JAMES Guitar, vocal, writer. Born 3/12/48. Began on the Apple label as a folk artist, polishing his sound, growing into the 1970s as the foremost pop-folk singer in the business. His sound was new and fresh, and opened the door for others in his talented entourage, including Carole King and Carly Simon (whom he married), to share and expand his audiences. Session for Neil Young (1972); Carly Simon (1972-present); Joni Mitchell (1975); John Stewart. *Albums:* Banded Together (EPC JE 36177); Flag (COL FC 36058) 1979; Gorilla (WBR B 2866) 1976; In the Pocket (WBR B 2912) 1976; JT (COL JC 34811) 1977; Mud Slide Slim and the Blue Horizon (WBR B 2561); One Man Dog (WBR B 2660) 1972; Sweet Baby James (WBR 1843) 1970; James Taylor's Greatest Hits (WBR K 3113) 1976; Walking Man (WBR 2794) 1974.

TAYLOR, JANE Bassoon. Session for Airto (1974).

TAYLOR, JIM Piano. Session for Harvey Mandel (1972); Neil Merryweather's Space Rangers (1975).

TAYLOR, JOHN Keyboards. Session for Splinter (1975).

TAYLOR, KATE Vocal. *Album:* It's in There (COL JC 36034).

TAYLOR, KENNETH Bass. Member of Supermax, 1979.

TAYLOR, LARRY Bass. Original member of Canned Heat, 1965-70, before joining Harvey Mandel and moving to John Mayall's group, 1971-73, demonstrating his prowess in blues and jazz. Session for Don "Sugarcane" Harris; Free Creek (1973); John Mayall; Colin Winski (1980).

TAYLOR, LAURA Vocal. Session for Firefall (1978).

TAYLOR, LEROY Bass. Session for the Temptations (1973).

TAYLOR, LIVINGSTON Vocal. Another brother of James Taylor, who made a less successful bid at a solo career in the wake of his brother's success. *Albums:* Echoes (CPN 0220); 3-Way Mirror (EPC JE 35540) 1979; Man's Best Friend (EPC JE 36153) 1980.

TAYLOR, MARVIN Guitar, vocal. Member of Mose Jones, 1978.

TAYLOR, MARY ANN Vocal. Session for Mike Bloomfield (1977).

TAYLOR, MEL Drums. Replaced Howie Johnson in the Ventures, 1963-71.

TAYLOR, MICK Guitar, bass, vocal. Born 1/17/48. Member of John Mayall's Bluesbreakers, replacing Peter Green, 1967, and the Keef Hartley Band, 1969 and 1971. After Brian Jones died in 1969, Taylor took over in the Rolling Stones until 1974. Session for Nicky Hopkins (1974); Ron Wood (1976); Elliott Murphy (1977). *Album:* Mick Taylor (COL JC 35076) 1979.

TAYLOR, MIKE Keyboards. Replaced Alan Fealdman in Sniff 'n' the Tears, 1980.

TAYLOR, NICK Guitar. Member of Bloodrock.

TAYLOR, PHIL Drums. Member of Motorhead since 1978.

TAYLOR, RICK Drums, percussion, vocal. Member of Striker, 1978.

TAYLOR, ROGER MEADOWS Drums, percussion, vocal. Born 7/26/49. Original member of Queen since 1973. Session for Ian Hunter (1976).

TAYLOR, RON Guitar. Member of Tucky Buzzard, 1973.

TAYLOR, RONNIE Saxophone. Member of the Jess Roden Band, 1976.

TAYLOR, RUSSELL Drums, vocal. Member of Peddler, 1976.

TAYLOR, SAMMY Harmonica. Member of the Coral Reefer Band.

TAYLOR, SKIP Producer. Produced Canned Heat (1965-73).

TAYLOR, TERRY Guitar. Member of Tucky Buzzard, 1973.

TAYLOR, TOMMY Drums. Session for Christopher Cross (1980).

TAYLOR, TRUE Early recording name of Paul Simon.

TAYLOR, TUT Dobro. Session for Leon Russell (1973). *Albums:* Norman Blake and Tut Taylor (FLF 701); Critic's Choice (TKM 1062); Dobrolick Plectral Society (TKM 1050) 1976; Old Post Office (FLF 008); Walnut Valley Spring Thing (TKM 1054); Friar Tut (RDR 0111) 1971.

TAYLOR, VINNIE Guitar. Replaced Chris Donald in Sha Na Na in 1972. Died in 1974.

TAZMANIAN DEVILS David Carlson—guitar; Pat Craig—keyboards, vocal; Dennis Hogan—guitar, vocal; Barry Lowenthal—drums; Duane Van Deman—bass, vocal. *Album:* Tazmanian Devils (WBR K 3400) 1980.

TCHAIKOVSKY, BRAM Guitar, vocal, bass. Real name: Peter Bramall. Member of the Motors, 1977-78, before forming the group bearing his name, 1979-present.

BRAM TCHAIKOVSKY Bram Tchaikovsky—bass, guitar, vocal; Micky Broadbent—bass, guitar, keyboards, vocal; Keith Boyce—drums, percussion (1979); Keith Line—drums (1980); Dennis Forbes—bass, keyboards, vocal (1980). *Albums:* Pressure (POL 1-6273) 1980; Strange Man Changed Man (POL 1-6211) 1979.

TEARS Alan Adkins—vocal, guitar; Charles Woods Pearson—vocal; Eric Cartwright—guitar, vocal. *Album:* Tears (BKS 3172) 1979.

TEAZE Marc Bradac—guitar, vocal; Brian Danter—vocal, bass, moog; Mike Kozak—drums, percussion; Chuck Price—guitar, vocal. *Album:* One Night Stands (CAP ST 11919) 1979.

TEDDELL, SAUNDERS Real name of Sonny Terry.

TEDESCO, TOMMY Guitar, banjo. Session for Jan and Dean (1963); Billy Strange; Martin Mull (1978). *Albums:* Guitar Greats (EVR 243); When Do We Start (DCO 789).

TEE, RICHARD Keyboards. Member of the Fugs, 1968. Session for Joe Cocker (1975-76); Ringo Starr (1977); George Harrison (1976); Martin Mull (1977); Eric Gale (1977-79); the Randle Chowning Band (1978); Dr. John (1978); Joe Cocker (1978); Art Garfunkel (1978-79); Felix Pappalardi (1979); Paul Simon (1980); Andy Gibb (1980). *Albums:* Storkin' (TZC JC-35695) 1979; Natural Ingredients (TZC JC-36380) 1980.

TEEGARDEN, DAVID Drums, percussion. Replaced Charlie Martin in the Silver Bullet Band, 1978-present.

TEEL, KURTIS Bass. Member of the Reggie Knighton Band, 1978.

TEEN KING AND THE AMERICANS Early name for the Eagles.

TEENAGERS See Frankie Lymon and the Teenagers.

TEETER, RITCHIE Drums, vocal. Member of the Dictators, 1977-78.

TEGZA, MICHAEL Drums, percussion, vocal. Member of H. P. Lovecraft, 1967-70, and the Bangor Flying Circus.

TEJADA, JO Vocal. Voice of Barrabas.

TEK, DENIZ Guitar. Member of Radio Birdman, 1978.

TELEVISION Tom Verlaine—vocal, guitar, keyboards, writer; Richard Lloyd—guitar, vocal; Billy Ficca—drums; Fred Smith—bass, vocal. Short-lived talented New York rock group featuring the writing of Verlaine. *Albums:* Adventure (ELK 6E-133) 1978; Marquee Moon (ELK 7E-1098) 1977.

TELEX Dan Lacksman; Michael Moers; Marc Moulin. *Album:* Neurovision (SIR SRK 6090) 1980.

TELLEZ, PABLO Bass. Session for Santana (1977).

TELLONE, ALBANY Saxophone. Session for Bruce Springsteen (1973).

TEMPCHIN, JACK Vocal, guitar, harmonica. Member of the Funky Kings, 1976. *Album:* Jack Tempchin (ARI 4193).

TEMPEST Paul Williams—vocal, guitar, keyboards (1973); Alan Holdsworth—guitar, violin, vocal (1973); Mark Clark—bass, keyboards, vocal; Jon Hiseman—drums; Ollie Halsall—guitar, keyboards, vocal (1974). *Albums:* Tempest, 1973; Living in Fear, 1974.

TEMPLE, MICHAEL D. Mandolin. Session for Spirit (1976).

TEMPLE CITY KAZOO ORCHESTRA Jim Zane—kazoo; Richie Balance—kazoo; Kazoot Sims—kazoo; Glen Cobar—kazoo; Greg Gordon—kazoo; Tom Knapp—kazoo; Paul Sanoian—kazoo; Ted Kazooski—kazoo; Elija Goldstein—kazoo; David Andrews—kazoo; Jeff Ginsberg—kazoo. All kazoo renditions of Rolling Stones, Led Zeppelin, and Bee Gee hits. *Album:* Some Kazoos (RHI 501) 1978.

TEMPLEMAN, TED Producer, drums, vocal, trumpet. Member of Harper's Bizarre, 1967-69, before becoming a producer for the Doobie Brothers (1971-present); Captain Beefheart (1972); Montrose (1973-74); Van Halen (1978-present); Tom Johnston (1979); Nicholette Larson (1980); and others.

TEMPTATIONS Mel Franklin—vocal; Otis Williams—vocal; Eddie Kendricks—vocal (1964-70); Paul Williams—vocal; David Ruffin—vocal (1964-68); Dennis Edwards—vocal (1968); Richard Street—vocal; Glenn Leonard—vocal; Louis Price—vocal. One of the original soul groups to make it big and stay big through the years. They signed to Gordy records in 1964 and released their first hit, "The Way You Do the Things You Do." Their matched choreography and singing set the standards for imitators who have come and gone through the years. *Albums:* All Directions (GDR G5-962);

Gettin' Ready, 1966; House Party, 1975; I Wish It Would Rain, 1968; In a Mellow Mood (GDR G5-911) 1967; Live, 1967; Masterpiece (GDR G5-965) 1973; Meet the Temptations (GDR G5 911) 1964; 1990 (GDR G5 961) 1973; Puzzle People, 1969; Save the Children (MTN N7800); Solid Rock (GDR G5 961); Temptations Christmas Card (GDR); Temptations Sing Smokey (GDR 912) 1965; Temptations Temptin' (GDR G5 914) 1965; With a Lot of Soul, 1967; Anthology with Diana Ross/Supremes (MTN M9-7944); Anthology Temptations (MTN MO-782) 1973; Bare Back (ATC 19188) 1978; Cloud Nine (GOR G7-939); Do the Temptations (GOR G7-975) 1976; Hear to Tempt You (ATC 19143) 1977; In Loving Memory (MTN M7-642); Power (GOR G8-944) 1980; Song For You (GOR G7-969) 1975; Temptations Greatest Hits, Vol. 1 (GOR G7-919) 1966; Temptations Greatest Hits, Vol. 2 (GOR G7-954) 1970; All Directions (GOR G962-L) 1972; Wings of Love (GOR G6 971, S1) 1976.

10 CC Kevin Godley—drums, percussion (1974-76); Graham Gouldman—bass, guitar, vocal; Lol Creme—guitar (1974-76); Eric Stewart—guitar, vocal, piano; Rick Fenn—guitar, vocal (1980); Duncan MacKay—keyboards, vocal (1980); Paul Burgess—drums, percussion (1980); Stuart Tosh—vocal, percussion (1980). Early name: the Hot Legs. *Albums:* Bloody Tourists (POL 1-6161) 1978; Deceptive Bends (MER SRM 1-3702) 1977; Greatest Hits (POL 1-6244) 1979; How Dare You (MER SRM 1 1061) 1976; Live and Let Live (MER SRM 2 8600) 1977; Look Hear (WBR K 3442) 1980; 10 CC (UKR 53110) 1975; The Original Soundtrack (MER SRM 1 1029) 1975; Sheet Music (UKR 53107) 1974; 10 CC (UKR 53105) 1973.

TEN WHEEL DRIVE Bob Piazza—bass, vocal; Steve Satten—horns, percussion; Michael Zager—keyboards; John Gatchell—horns; Aram Schefrin—guitar, banjo, percussion, vocal; Dave Liebman—saxophone, flute; Genya Ravan—vocal, harmonica, percussion; John Eckert—trumpet; Allen Herman—drums, percussion, vibes; Dennis Parisi—trombone. Briefly popular big band of 1970 that spawned Ravan. *Album:* Brief Replies (POL 24 4024) 1970.

TEN YEARS AFTER Alvin Lee—guitar, vocal; Chick Churchill—keyboards; Leo Lyons—bass; Ric Lee—drums, percussion. They debuted in the United States in 1967, an average British blues band. But as they progressed through future albums, their talent and ability matured and expanded beyond their basic blues format into a unique style of rock. Alvin Lee was the focal point of the group, shaping the group's sound until they disbanded in 1973. He continued as a soloist, until forming Ten Years Later, 1978-79, and the Alvin Lee Band, 1980. Played at Woodstock, 1969. *Albums:* Classic Performances of Ten Years After (COL PC 34366) 1976; Alvin Lee and Company (DRM X 18064); Ten Years After (LON LC 50013); Positive Vibrations (COL C 32851) 1974; Rock and Roll Music to the World (COL C 31779) 1972; Space in Time (COL PC 30801); Ten Years After (DRM 18009) 1967; Ten Years After Recorded Live (COL C2X 32288) 1973; Undead (DMM 18016) 1968; Cricklewood Green (DRM 18038); Ssssh! (DRM 18029) 1969; Stonedhenge (DRM 18021) 1969; Watt (DRM X 18050).

TEN YEARS LATER Alvin Lee—guitar, vocal; Tom Compton—drums; Mick Hawksworth—bass; Bernie Clarke—keyboards (1978); Mick Weaver—keyboards (1979). Their name called to mind Lee's former group, Ten Years After, but they did not have the same high-quality music. *Albums:* Rocket Fuel, 1978; Ride On (RSO) 1979.

TENCH, BENMONT Keyboards. Member of Tom Petty's Heartbreakers since 1977. Session for Code Blue (1980).

TENCH, BOBBY Vocal, guitar. Original member of the re-formed Jeff Beck Group, 1971-72, before becoming the featured vocalist of Hummingbird, 1975-76. Member of the Streetwalkers, 1973-77, and the re-formed Humble Pie, 1980. Session for Freddie King.

TENILLE, TONI Vocal, keyboards. Wife of the Captain in the Captain and Tenille. Session for Elton John (1974, 76, 80); Pink Floyd (1979).

TEPP, JOEL Harmonica, guitar, woodwinds. Session for Crazy Horse; Leslie West (1975); Ian Matthews (1976); Jelly (1977).

TEPP, RICHARD Bass. Replaced Nick St. Nicholas in T.I.M.E., 1969.

TEPPER, JEFF MORRIS Guitar. Member of Captain Beefheart's Magic Band since 1978.

TERACE, DOMINIC Guitar, bass, trumpet, vocal. Member of the Jaggerz.

TERAN, ROGELIO Percussion. Session for Gilda Radner (1980).

TERESA, LINDA Vocal. Session for Magazine (1980).

TERRAN, TONY Trumpet. Session for Nilsson (1975-76).

TERRANORA, JOE Vocal. Member of Danny and the Juniors.

TERRELL, JEAN Vocal. Replaced Diana Ross in the Supremes.

TERROADE, KEN Flute. Session for Dr. John (1971).

TERRY, GEORGE Guitar. First became known as Eric Clapton's rhythm guitarist, 1974-76. Member of McGuinn, Hillman and Clark, 1979. Session for Barry Goldberg (1974); Freddie King (1974); Bill Wyman (1974, 76); Steve Stills (1975-76); Andy Gibb (1977); Joe Cocker (1978); the Bee Gees (1979).

TERRY, SONNY Harmonica, vocal. Born 10/24/13. Real name: Saunders Teddell. Lost his sight at age 11. Country blues vocalist and harmonica player who teamed up with Brownie McGhee in the 1930s and began recording in 1937. Their partnership has continued through the present day, as does their influence on countless folk, blues, and rock personalities. See Brownie McGhee, and Sonny Terry and Brownie McGhee. *Albums:* Goin' Down Slow (MST 407); Blues (FLW 33817); Blues Bash (OLR 7115); Chain Gang (STI 37); Blind Gary Davis (STI 356); Early Years (TRD 2988); Folksay, Vol. 1 (STI 35 39); From Spirituals to Swing (VAN VSD 47-48); Gotta Move Your Baby (PRS 7831); On the Road (FLW 32369); Pete Seeger and Sonny Terry (FLW 32412) 1958; Sonny Is King (PRS 7802); Sonny Terry (EVR 206); Sonny Terry and His Mouth Harp (STI 355); Sonny Terry Harmonica and Vocal Solos (FLW 32035); Sonny Terry New Sounds (FLW 33821); Sonny Terry Washboard Band (FLW 32006).

SONNY TERRY AND BROWNIE McGHEE Sonny Terry—harmonica, vocal; Brownie McGhee—guitar, vocal. Blues team from Tennessee who began in the 1930s and continue through today as a major influence in the blues field. See individual listings. *Albums:* Book of Numbers (BRR 6002); Down Home Blues (SAV 12218); Hometown Blues (MST 308); Best of Terry and McGhee (PRS 7715); Brownie and Sonny (EVR 242); Hootin' and Hollerin' (OLR 7108); Brownie McGhee and Sonny Terry (PRS 7803); Midnight Special (FSY 2471); Preachin' the Blues (FLW 31024) 1960; Sonny and Brownie (AAM 4379); Sonny and Brownie at Sugar Hill (FSY 8019); Back to New Orleans (FSY 24708); You Hear Me Talkin' (MUS 5131) 1978; Brownie McGhee and Sonny Terry Sing (FLW 2327) 1958.

TESCO, NICKY Vocal. Member of the Members, 1979-80.

TESTA, JIMMY Vocal. Member of Danny and the Juniors.

TETSU Bass. Real name: Tetsu Yamauchi. With John "Rabbit" Bundrick, he pieced together Free in 1972 under the heading Kossoff, Kirke, Tetsu and Rabbit, before becoming a member of the reformed Free in 1973, for their final album. Session for John "Rabbit" Bundrick (1974).

TEX, JOE Vocal. Soul artist influenced by country and western music. *Albums:* Turn Back the Hands; Best of Joe Tex, 1965; Hold On, 1965; Hold What You've Got; New Boss; Love You Save; I've Got to Do a Little Bit Better; Best of Joe Tex; Live and Lovely; Buying a Book; Gotcha; Another Woman's Man (PPK 305); Golden Soul (ATC 18198); He Who Is Without Funk Cast the First Stone (DIL 6100); Super Hits (ATC 501); Rub Down (TRE JC 35079) 1978.

TEXAS SLIM Early performing name of John Lee Hooker.

TEXAS Michael Maben—guitar, vocal; Gary Osier—drums; Gary Miles—bass; Jerry Moore—keyboards; Bob Anderson—saxophone, vocal; Wesley Harris—harmonica; Tony Lee—drums. *Album:* Texas (BLL 1128) 1973.

THACKER, ALAN Guitar, slide guitar. Member of Buckacre, 1976.

THACKER, CLIVE Drums. Member of Julie Driscoll, Brian Auger and the Trinity, 1968-69, and Medicine Head, 1973. Session for Alan Price (1973).

THACKERY, JIM Guitar, vocal. Member of the Nighthawks since 1976. Session for the Catfish Hodge Band (1979).

THAIN, GARY Bass. Original member of the Keef Hartley Band, 1969-71. Replaced Paul Newton in Uriah Heep, 1972-75.

THAMES Guitar, vocal. Member of the Flyboys, 1980.

THATCHER, DONNA Vocal. Session for Boz Scaggs (1969).

THATCHER, LES Guitar. Session for Elton John (1972); Nilsson (1972); Mike Batt (1979).

THEAKER, DRACHIAN Drums. Original member of the Crazy World of Arthur Brown, 1968. Session for Kim Fowley (1972); Arthur Brown (1975).

THEDFORD, BILI Vocal. Session for Boz Scaggs (1980).

THEE IMAGE Mike Pinera—guitar, vocal, producer; Duane Hitchings—keyboards, synthesizer, vocal; Donny Vosburgh—drums, vocal. Commercial trio formed from the remains of Son of Cactus. They exchanged the hard rock format of their parent group for popular rhythm and funk, which they handled capably, but not popularly. *Albums:* Thee Image (MCR MA6 50451) 1975; Inside the Triangle (MCR MA6 50651) 1975.

THEILMANS, JEAN "TOOTS" Harmonica. Session for Rick Derringer (1973); Henry Gross (1978). *Albums:* Jazz Gala Concert (ATC 1693); Love Me By Name (AAM 4563).

THEIRS, THISSY Bass, vocal. Member of Randy Pie, 1975-77,

THEM Van Morrison—vocal, harmonica, tenor saxophone; Billy Harrison—guitar; Alan Henderson—bass; John McAuley—drums, harmonica, vocal; Peter Bardens—organ; Jim Armstrong—guitar, sitar, drums; David Harvey—drums; Ray Elliot—organ; Ken McPowell—vocal. The first Irish group to receive international fame, Them gave the rock generation of the 1960s a national anthem with Van Morrison's "Gloria," 1965. Besides "Gloria," they are remembered for such rock classics as "Mystic Eyes" and "Here Comes the Night." Morrison's rough but controlled vocals were the trademark of the group until 1968, when he left to go solo. Them attempted to continue in his absence, but faded into obscurity. *Albums:* Them (PRR 71055) 1965; Now and Them (PRR) 1968; Time Out, Time In for Them (PRR) 1968; London Collector—Story of Them (LON LC 50001) 1977; Them Again (PRR 71008) 1967; Them Featuring Van Morrison (PRR BP 71053 54) 1972.

THEMEN, ART Soprano saxophone. Member of Blues Incorporated. Session for Jack Bruce (1969).

THIBODEAUX, RUFUS Fiddle. Session for Neil Young (1978, 80). *Albums:* Phyddle (PLN 516); 20 Golden Souvenirs (PLN 533).

THIELHELM, EMIL Vocal, guitar. Member of the Blues Magoos.

THIEVES Jerry Donahue—guitar, vocal; Lynda Lee Lawley—vocal; Sue Richman—vocal; Rusty Buchanan—vocal, bass, guitar; Gerry Conway—drums, percussion, vocal; Steve Goldstein—keyboards, synthesizer, vocal; Andrea Robinson—vocal. *Album:* Yucatan (ARI 4232) 1979.

THIN LIZZY Brian Downey—drums; Scott Gorham—guitar; Phillip Lynott—vocal, bass; Gary Moore—guitar, vocal (1978-79); Snowy White—guitar, vocal (1980); Brian Robertson—guitar, vocal (1971-77). *Albums:* Bad Reputation (MER SRM 1 1186) 1977; Black Rose/A Rock Legend (WBR K 3338) 1979; Fighting (MER SRM 1 1108) 1975; Jailbreak (MER SRM 1 1081); Live and Dangerous (WBR 2B 3213); London Collector: Rocker (LON LC 50004) 1977; Night Life (MER SRM 1 1107) 1974; Vagabonds of the Western World (LON PS 636) 1973; Thin Lizzy (LON PS 954) 1971; Johnny the Fox (MER SRM 1 1119) 1976; Chinatown (WBR BSK 3496) 1980.

13TH FLOOR ELEVATORS Rory Erickson—vocal; Stacy Sutherland; Tommy Hall; Dan Galindo; Danny Thomas. Acid rock from Austin, Texas, in the late 1960s. *Albums:* The Psychedelic Sounds of the 13th Floor Elevators; Easter Everywhere; Bull of the Woods.

31ST OF FEBRUARY Scott Boyer—guitar; David Brown—bass; Butch Trucks—drums. *Album:* The 31st of February, 1968.

38 SPECIAL Don Barnes—guitar, vocal; Jeff Carlisi—guitar; Steve Brookins—drums, percussion; Larry Lundstrum—bass, vocal (1979-present); Donnie Van Zant—vocal; Jack Grondin—drums, percussion; Ken Lyons—bass, vocal. *Albums:* Rockin' into the Night (AAM 4782) 1979; Special Delivery (AAM 4684) 1978; 38 Special (AAM 4638) 1977.

THOM, PETER Member of Far Cry, 1980.

THOMAS, B. J. Vocal. Pop vocalist from the 1960s whose sagging career was renewed when he sang "Raindrops Keep Falling on My Head" in the movie *Butch Cassidy and the Sundance Kid,* 1970. *Albums:* Songs (PMT); Help Me Make It to My Rocking Chair (ABC) 1975; Best of B. J. Thomas (SEP 18008); Greatest All Time Hits (SEP 5112); Greatest Hits, Vol. 1 (SEP 578); I'm So Lonesome I Could Cry (SEP 535); Longhorns and Londonbridges (PMT 1020); Most of All (SEP 586); Raindrops Keep Falling on My Head (SEP 580); B. J. Thomas Country (SEP 5108); B. J. Thomas Sings His Very Best (SPG 4005); Tribute to Burt Bacharach (SEP 5100); Very Best of B. J. Thomas (UAR UA LA389-E); Young and in Love (SEP 576); Best of B. J. Thomas (STR 992); Butch Cassidy and the Sundance Kid (AAM 4227) 1970; Everybody Loves a Rain Song (MCA 3035); For the Best (MCA 3231); Happy Man (MYR B 6593); Home Where I Belong (MYR 6580); On This Christmas Night (MCA 3184); Power Music (MYR 6580); B. J. Thomas (MCA 2286); You Gave Me Love (MYR 6633); Greatest Hits, Vol. II (SEP 597); On My Way (SEP 570); Reunion (ABC DP-858); Close to You (CBS Q 16038) 1979.

THOMAS, BANNER Bass. Born 9/6/54. Member of Molly Hatchet since 1978.

THOMAS, BRIGITTE Vocal. Session for Triumvirat (1973).

THOMAS, BRUCE Bass. Member of Quiver before joining Moonrider, 1975. Member of the Attractions. Session for Wings (1979).

THOMAS, CARLA Vocal. Popular soul singer of the 1960s who worked with Otis Redding. *Albums:* Gee Whiz, 1961; Comfort Me, 1966; Carla, 1966; King and Queen, 1966; Queen Alone, 1967; Chronicle (STX 4124).

THOMAS, CHIP Drums. Member of the Creed, 1978.

THOMAS, CHRIS Violin, keyboards, producer. Island Records producer. Produced Procol Harum (1970-74); Chris Spedding (1977); Wings (1979); the Pretenders (1980); Pete Townshend (1980); and others. Session for John Cale (1975).

THOMAS, DANNY Member of the 13th Floor Elevators.

THOMAS, DAVID Guitar, vocal, percussion. Member of the Tattoo, 1976.

THOMAS, DAVID Vocal. Member of Pere Ubu since 1979.

THOMAS, DAVID Vocal. Member of Bagatelle, 1968.

THOMAS, GLENN Guitar, mandolin. Member of Ballin' Jack.

THOMAS, GREG Drums. Member of McGuinn, Hillman and Clark, 1979. Session for Taj Mahal; Leon Russell (1976); Neil Young (1980).

THOMAS, GUTHRIE Guitar, vocal. *Albums:* Lies and Alibis (CAP ST 11519) 1976; Guthrie Thomas, 1975.

THOMAS, IAN Vocal, guitar, keyboards, mandolin, banjo. Soloist and head of the Ian Thomas Band, 1976. *Albums:* Ian Thomas (JNS 3058); Delights (GRT 1954).

IAN THOMAS BAND Ian Thomas—vocal, guitar, keyboards, mandolin, banjo; Mike Oberle—drums, percussion, vocal; Josh Onderisin—guitar; Hugh Syme—keyboards, vocal; Steve Hogg—bass, vocal. *Album:* Goodnight Mrs. Calabash (CVS 1126) 1976.

THOMAS, INGRID Vocal. Session for the Keef Hartley Band (1971).

THOMAS, JAMES Bass. Session for Taj Mahal (1968).

THOMAS, JASPER Drums. Member of Chuck Berry's Combo, 1955. Session for Chuck Berry (1964).

THOMAS, JIMMY Vocal. Session for Gary Wright (1971); Vigrass and Osborne (1972).

THOMAS, JOHN Trumpet. Session for Freddie King (1975).

THOMAS, "K. O." Piano. Session for Freddie King (1975); the Alpha Band (1977).

THOMAS, LEON Vocal. Session for Santana (1974).

THOMAS, MARVEL Organ. Session for Clarence Carter (1967); Wilson Pickett (1968).

THOMAS, MAX Vocal, keyboards, guitar, percussion. Member of City Boy since 1976.

THOMAS, MICKEY Vocal. Member of the Elvin Bishop Band, 1975-77, and the Jefferson Starship, 1979-present. Session for Elvin Bishop (1974). *Album:* As Long As You Love Me (MCA 2256) 1977.

THOMAS, PETE Drums. Member of the Attractions. Session for Sean Tyla (1980).

THOMAS, RAY Reeds, vocal. Original member of the Moody Blues since 1965. Teamed up with Nicky James for the release of his two solo albums. *Albums:* From Mighty Oaks (THS 16) 1975; Hopes, Wishes and Dreams (THS 17) 1976.

THOMAS, RAYMOND Imitation bass. Session for Sleepy John Estes (1941).

THOMAS, RONNIE Bass, vocal. Member of the Heavy Metal Kids, 1974, and Kids, 1975.

THOMAS, STEVE Drums. Member of the Shooting Star, 1979.

THOMAS, TASHA Vocal. Session for B. B. King (1971); Zephyr (1971); Full Moon (1972); Rick Derringer (1973); Pacific Gas and Electric (1973); Johnny Winter (1973-74); Henry Gross (1973, 75-76); Carly Simon (1974); Leslie West (1976); Martin Mull (1977). *Album:* Midnight Rendezvous (ATC 19223).

THOMAS, TRUMAN Piano. Session for Leon Russell (1976).

THOMASSIE, JOHN Drums. Session for Freddie King (1975).

THOMASSON, HUGHIE Guitar, banjo, vocal, pedal steel guitar. Member of the Outlaws since 1975.

THOMPSON, ALI Guitar, piano, vocal. *Album:* Take a Little Rhythm (AAM SP 4803) 1980.

THOMPSON, BARBARA Reeds. Member of the Keef Hartley Band horn section, 1969-71. Session for Colosseum (1970-71); Manfred Mann (1980).

THOMPSON, BOBBY Guitar, banjo. Member of Area Code 615. Session for Tom Rapp; the Steve Miller Band (1970); Leon Russell (1973); Doug Kershaw (1974); Waylon Jennings (1974); Buddy Spicher (1976); Frankie Miller (1980).

THOMPSON, CARRIE Vocal. *Album:* Carrie Thompson, 1980.

THOMPSON, CHESTER Drums. Member of the Mothers of Invention, 1974-75. Session for Frank Zappa (1975).

THOMPSON, CHESTER Keyboards, vocal. Member of Tower of Power, 1975-present. Session for Elton John (1974).

THOMPSON, CHRIS Vocal, guitar. Member of Manfred Mann, 1976-79, and Night, 1979. Session for Kevin Lamb (1978); Elton John (1978); Manfred Mann (1980).

THOMPSON, CHRISTOPHER Vocal. Session for the Doobie Brothers (1980).

THOMPSON, D. CLINTON Guitar. Session for the Ozark Mountain Daredevils (1980).

THOMPSON, DANNY Acoustic bass. Original member of Blues Incorporated, before Pentangle, 1968-72. Session for Bert Jansch; John Renbourn; Donovan (1968-73); Rod Stewart (1973).

THOMPSON, DARRYL Guitar. Member of Medusa, 1978.

THOMPSON, DAWN Vocal. Voice of Cosmology, 1977.

THOMPSON, DEBBIE Vocal. Session for the Brains (1980).

THOMPSON, DENNIS Drums. Member of the MC 5, 1968-69.

THOMPSON, DICK Bass, keyboards, vocal. Member of Kid Dynamite, 1976.

THOMPSON, DICK Keyboards. Member of the Steve Miller Band, 1972-73.

THOMPSON, GARY Guitar. Co-founder of Frijid Pink, 1970-71.

THOMPSON, HARRY Tenor saxophone. Member of the Muscle Shoal Horns. Session for Barry Goldberg (1974); Bob Seger (1975); Tim Weisberg (1977); Joe Cocker (1978); Roy Orbison (1979).

THOMPSON, JERRY Drums. Member of Great Southern (1977).

THOMPSON, JOHN Bass, vocal. Session for Jorge Santana (1980).

THOMPSON, KIRK Keyboards. Member of Kalapanna.

THOMPSON, LEE Saxophone, vocal. Member of the Madness, 1979.

THOMPSON, LES Guitar, banjo, mandolin, percussion. Original member of the Nitty Gritty Dirt Band.

THOMPSON, LINDA Vocal. Half of the Richard and Linda Thompson duet, 1978. Session for Gerry Rafferty (1979).

THOMPSON, MAYO Member of Pere Ubu since

1980.

THOMPSON, PAM Vocal. Session for Leon Russell (1974).

THOMPSON, PAUL Drums. Original member of Roxy, 1972-78. Session for Bryan Ferry (1974, 76-77); Phil Manzanera (1975).

THOMPSON, RICHARD Guitar, mandolin. Member of the Fairport Convention until 1974. Soloist and half of the Richard and Linda Thompson duet, 1978. Session for Gerry Rafferty (1979). *Album:* Live (More or Less) (ISL 9421).

RICHARD AND LINDA THOMPSON Linda Thompson—vocal; Richard Thompson—vocal, guitar, mandolin, synthesizer. See individual listings. *Album:* First Light (CYS 1177) 1978.

THOMPSON, ROBBIN Guitar, vocal. Soloist and head of the Robbin Thompson Band, 1980. *Album:* Robbin Thompson (NMP 440).

ROBBIN THOMPSON BAND Velpo Robertson —guitar, vocal; Robbin Thompson—guitar, vocal; Michael Lanning—bass, vocal; Eric Heiberg—keyboards, vocal; Bob Antonelli—drums, percussion, vocal. *Album:* Two B's Please (ONA 1759) 1980.

THOMPSON, ROBERT Guitar. Session for the Pointer Sisters (1975).

THOMPSON, RON Drums. Member of the Bugs Henderson Group, 1975.

THOMPSON, STEPHEN Bass. Replaced Tony Reeves in John Mayall's Bluesbreakers in 1969. Replaced Jim Dewar in Stone the Crows, 1972. Session for Memphis Slim (1971); Alvin Lee (1975); John Mayall (1977-78).

THOMPSON, THUMP Bass. Member of Darts since 1978.

THOMPSON, TOM Drums. Session for Tom Verlaine (1979).

THOMPSON, TREY Bass. Member of the Dudek, Finnigan, Kruger Band, 1980.

THOMS, PETER Trombone. Session for the Alvin Lee Band (1980).

THOMSON, DOUG Bass. Member of Supertramp.

THOMSON, MIKE Bass, guitar, vocal. Session for Donovan (1970).

THOMSON, PETE Drums. Session for David Byron (1975).

THORNBERG, LEE Trumpet, flugelhorn. Session for Jules and Polar Bears (1979); Rod Stewart (1980); the Doobie Brothers (1980).

THORNE, ELLIOT Drums, vocal. Member of Phaze Shifter, 1980.

THORNTON, BIG MAMA Vocal. *Albums:* Blues Roots (TMT 2-7006); Sassy Mama (VAN 79354) 1975; Jail (VAN 79351) 1975; She's Back (MCA 68).

THORNTON, BLAIR Guitar. Member of the Bachman-Turner Overdrive, 1974-79.

THORNTON, RANDY Vocal. Session for Frank Zappa (1979).

THORNTON-ODEN, BIANCA Vocal. Member of the Giants, 1978.

THOROGOOD, GEORGE Guitar, vocal. Head of George Thorogood and the Destroyers.

GEORGE THOROGOOD AND THE DESTROYERS George Thorogood—guitar, vocal; Jeff Simon—drums; Billy Blough—bass; Ron Smith—guitar (1977); Mark Levine—bass (1974); Hank Carter—saxophone (1980); Uncle Meat Pennington —percussion (1978). Originally called George Thorogood and the Delaware Destroyers, Thorogood brought Rounder Records to the public's attention with his authentic blues renditions. *Albums:* Better than the Rest (MCA 3091) 1979; Move It on Over (RND 3024) 1978; George Thorogood and the Destroyers (RND 3013) 1977; More George Thorogood and the Destroyers (RND 3045) 1980.

THORPE, BILLY Guitar, vocal. Australian who debuted in the U.S. with the Aztecs before going solo. *Albums:* Children of the Sun (CPN 0221) 1979; 21st Century Man (ELK 6E-294) 1980.

THORPE, TONY Guitar, vocal. Member of the Rubettes.

THORUP, PETER Vocal, guitar, slide guitar. Member of Snape, 1972.

THRALL, PAT Guitar, vocal. Member of the Automatic Man, 1976, and the Pat Travers Band, 1979-present.

THRASHER, NORMAN Member of Hank Ballard's Midnighters.

3-D Rick Zivic—vocal; Ken Ginsberg—vocal, guitar; Ted Wender—keyboards, vocal; Nick Stevens—bass, vocal; Mike Fink—drums, vocal. *Albums:* 3-D (POL 1-6254) 1980; See It Loud (POL 1-6297) 1980.

THREE DOG NIGHT Cory Wells—vocal; Chuck Negren—vocal; Danny Hutton—vocal; Jimmy Greenspoon—keyboards; Michael Allsup—guitar; Floyd Sneed—drums, percussion; Joe Schermie—bass. Early name: Redwood. Popular rock group that began in the late 1960s featuring a vocal trio in front of an electric rock format. *Albums:* Around the World (DHL Y 50138); Captured Live at the Forum (DHL 50068); Coming Down Your Way (ABC D-888) 1975; Hard Labor (DHL 50078); Joy to the World (DHL D 50778); Seven Separate Fools (DHL 50118); Cyan, 1973; Big Hits Now (DHL 50085); Golden Biscuits (DHL X-50098); Natural (DHL X 50086).

THREE MAN ARMY Adrian Gurvitz—guitar, organ, vocal; Paul Gurvitz—bass, vocal; Mike Kellie—drums, percussion (1971); Tony Newman —drums, percussion (1972). Hard rocking English trio formed by the Gurvitz brothers after Gun, 1968, and before the Baker-Gurvitz Army, 1975-76. *Albums:* A Third of a Lifetime (KMS 2044) 1971; Three Man Army (RPS 2150) 1973; Three Man Army II (RPS 2182) 1974.

THROCKMAN, BUZZ Drums. Original member of Angel City, 1977-78.

THULBORN, KATHERINE Cello. Member of Centipede, 1971.

THUMBS Kevin Smith—guitar, vocal; Karl Hoffman—bass, guitar; Marty Olson—keyboards; Mark Brennan—drums. *Album:* Thumbs (RRI) 1979.

THUNDER, THEO Drums, percussion. Session for Alan Price and Rob Hoeke (1977).

THUNDERBIRDS Name of the Hill, backup group for Chris Farlowe, before cello player Paul Buckmaster was added to the line-up.

THUNDERBOLTS See Brett Marvin and the Thunderbolts.

THUNDERCLAP NEWMAN Andy Newman—keyboards; Speedy Keen—drums; Jimmy McCulloch—guitar. *Album:* Hollywood Dream (MCA 354) 1973.

THUNDERHEAD Mike Dagger—vocal, flute; Pat Rush—guitar; Ronnie Dobbs—guitar; Otho Ware—bass; Bobby Torello—drums. *Album:* Thunderhead (ABC) 1976.

THUNDERS, JOHNNY Guitar, vocal. Member of the New York Dolls, 1973-74.

THUNDERSTICK Percussion, vocal. Member of Samson, 1980.

THUNDERTRAIN Mach Bell—vocal; Steven Silva—guitar; Bobby Edwards—drums; Gene Provost—guitar; Ric Provost—bass. Boston-based "new wave" band. *Album:* Teenage Suicide, 1977.

THURSTON, SCOTT Guitar, keyboards, synthesizer, vocal, harmonica. Session for Iggy Pop (1977-80).

TIANA, MAYO Trombone. Session for Joe Cocker (1974).

TIBBETTS, KENNY Bass. Member of Great Southern, 1977. Session for Bobby Whitlock; Gregg Allman (1974); Roy Buchanan (1974).

TIBBITS, BRUCE Vocal, guitar. Member of Edge, 1980.

TIBBS, GARY Bass. Member of Roxy Music, 1979, and Code Blue, 1980. Session for Roxy Music (1980).

TICH Nickname of Ian Amey. Member of Dave Dee, Dozy, Beaky, Mick and Tich.

TICHY, JOHN Guitar, vocal. Member of Commander Cody's Lost Planet Airmen.

TICKNER, GEORGE Bass, piano, vocal. Original member of Journey, 1975.

TIDBITS Steven Soles—guitar, organ, vocal; Ned Albright—keyboards, guitar, vocal; Tali Jackson—drums; David Kapell—bass, piano, vocal. *Album:* Greetings from Jamaica (FMY).

TIDWELL, GEORGE Trumpet. Session for J. J. Cale (1974); Jimmy Hall (1980).

TIEFENSEE, MARTIN Bass. Member of Lake, 1977.

TIERRA Rudy Salas—guitar, vocal; Steve Salas—vocal, trombone, percussion; Joey Guerra—keyboards, vocal; Bobby Navarette—reeds, vocal; Andre Baeza—percussion; Steve Falomir—bass; Phil Madayag—drums. *Album:* City Nights (BDW 36995) 1980.

TIGER Jim Sullivan—guitar; Nicky Moore—vocal; Les Walker—vocal; Ray Flacke—guitar; Phil Curtis—bass; Billy Rankin—drums; Dave McCrae—keyboards; Bill McGillivray—vocal, guitar, keyboards (1976); Alan Park—keyboards (1976); Andy Brown—bass (1976). *Albums:* Tiger (WBR B 2940) 1976; Goin' Down Laughing (EMI ST 11660) 1976.

TIGER TOM Early performing name for Tom Jones.

TIGERS Nick Cola—keyboards, vocal; Tony Jacks—guitar, vocal; Nic Potter—bass; Ross McGeeney—guitar, vocal; Pete Dobson—drums. *Album:* Savage Music (AAM SP 4817) 1980.

TILBROOK, GLEN Guitar, keyboards, vocal. Member of Squeeze since 1978.

TILL, JOHN Guitar. Member of the Full Tilt Boogie Band, 1969-70.

TILLERY, LINDA Vocal. Original member of the Loading Zone, 1968, and the Giants, 1978. Session for Santana (1971).

TILLEY, CHUCK Vocal. Member of the Snakestretchers, 1972-73.

TILLI, DENNIS Bass. Member of the Cats, 1980.

TILLMAN, JIMMY Drums. Session for the Steve Miller Band (1970).

TILLMAN, JULIA See Julia Tillman Waters.

TILLMAN, KEITH Bass. Played with John Mayall, 1967-68. Member of Stone's Masonry, 1968.

TILLMAN, WILLIAM Saxophone. Member of the re-formed Blood, Sweat and Tears.

TILT John Ponder—drums, vocal; Frank Ewing—guitar, bass, vocal; Mike Harner—guitar, vocal; Doug Kahan—bass, vocal. *Album:* Music (PCH 9008) 1980.

TILTON, COLIN Saxophone, flute. Member of the Colwell-Winfield Blues Band, 1968. Session for Van Morrison (1968-69); Ellen McIlwaine (1973).

TIMBERLINE Chuck Salestrom—bass, vocal; Craig Link—drums, percussion, vocal; Jim Salestrom—vocal, guitar, banjo; Dugg Duggan—guitar, mandolin, harmonica, vocal; Bill Howland—keyboards, vocal. *Album:* Timberline (EPC PE 34681) 1977.

TIMEBOX Mike Patto—vocal; Peter "Ollie" Halsall—guitar; Clive Griffiths—bass; John Halsey—drums; Clive Holmes—keyboards. *Album:* Moose on the Loose (DCL 9016) 1976.

TIN HUEY Harvey Gold—keyboards, guitar, vocal; Mark Price—bass, vocal; Michael Aylward—guitar, vocal; Chris Butler—guitar, vocal, percussion; Ralph Carney—reeds, keyboards, vocal, percussion; Stuart Austin—drums, vocal. *Album:* Contents Dislodged during Shipment (WBR BSK 3297) 1979.

TINDALL, T. J. Guitar. Member of the Edge, 1970,

and Duke Williams and the Extremes, 1973. Session for Martin Mull (1974); Bobby Whitlock (1975).

TINY TIM Vocal, ukelele. Real name: Herbert Khaury. He had been performing in New York's Greenwich Village since 1962, so his soprano falsetto was not a joke to those who knew him when Tim appeared on television, 1968. After the novelty of his record debut had faded, he recaptured headlines by marrying Miss Vicki on the Tonight Show. But even that was not enough to stimulate mass popularity, nor was the publicity of his divorce. *Albums:* God Bless Tiny Tim (RPS 6292) 1968; Tiny Tim's Second Album (RPS) 1968.

TIPPET, KEITH Piano. Member of King Crimson, 1970, and Centipede, 1971. Session for King Crimson (1971-72); Arthur Brown (1975).

TIPPETT, JULIE Vocal. Married name of Julie Driscoll. Member of Centipede, 1971. See Julie Driscoll. *Album:* Encore (WBR 3153) 1976.

TIPPINS, STAN Vocal. Session for Mott the Hoople (1971).

TIPTON, GLEN Guitar, vocal, synthesizer. Member of Judas Priest since 1974.

TIR NA NOG Sonny Caldwell—vocal, guitar, percussion; Leo O'Kelly—vocal, guitar, violin. *Album:* Strong in the Sun (CYS) 1973.

TISCHER, NANDO Vocal, guitar. Member of Amon Duul.

TITELMAN, RUSS Percussion, producer. Produced Gordon Lightfoot; Ry Cooder (1974); Randy Newman (1979); Adam Mitchell (1979); Code Blue (1980); and others. Session for Captain Beefheart (1972); James Taylor (1976).

TITUS, LIBBY Vocal. Session for Martin Mull (1972).

TIVEN, JOHN Vocal, guitar, saxophone. Member of the Yankees, 1978.

TOBIAS, KEN Vocal, guitar. Canadian folksinger. *Albums:* The Magic's in the Music (MGM 4917) 1973; Street Ballet (LAT 1033) 1977.

TOBIN, KAREN Vocal. Session for Hot Tuna (1976).

TOBY BEAU Balde Silva—vocal, guitar, harmonica; Rob Young; Danny McKenna; Steve Zipper; Ron Rose. *Albums:* More than a Love Song (VIC AFLI 3119) 1979; If You Believe (VIC AFLI 3575) 1980; Toby Beau (ACN AFLI 2771) 1978.

TODD, GRAHAM Keyboards. Session for Olivia Newton-John (1976).

TODD, LYN Vocal. *Album:* Lyn Todd (VAN 79436) 1980.

TODD, MARK LA RUE Bass, vocal. Member of Johnny and the Distractions, 1980.

TODD, MIC Guitar, bass, vocal. Member of the Pink Section, 1980.

TODD, PAM Vocal. Session for Bob Seger.

TOFANI, DAVE Saxophone. Session for Grace Slick (1980); John Lennon (1980); Steely Dan (1980).

TOKENS Early name: the Four Winds. Pop-soul vocalists who recorded "The Lion Sleeps Tonight" in 1961.

TOLER, DAN Guitar. Member of Great Southern, 1977, and the Allman Brothers since 1979.

TOLER, DAVID Drums, percussion. Replaced Jerry Thompson in Great Southern, 1978.

TOLES, MICHAEL Guitar, horns, vocal, synthesizer. Session for Paul Butterfield (1980).

TOLFREE, LARRY Drums. Member of Mark Andrews and the Gents, 1980.

TOLHURST, LOL Drums. Member of the Cure, 1979.

TOLLIN, LARRY Keyboards. Member of Wild Oats, 1977.

TOLMAN, GERRY Guitar. Session for Steve Stills (1978).

TOLONEN, JUKICA Guitar, keyboards. Member of Tasavallan Presidenti, 1974.

TOLSON, PETER Guitar. Member of the Pretty Things.

TOM AND JERRY Original name for Simon and Garfunkel, 1957.

TOMKINS, TREVOR Drums. Member of Gilgamesh.

TOMLINSON, MALCOLM Vocal, guitar, percussion. *Album:* Rock 'n' Roll Hermit (AAM SP 4765) 1979.

TOMLINSON, MARIE Vocal. Session for Roy Orbison (1979).

TOMMY After the recording success of the Who's "Tommy," a stage production was organized in 1972 with the London Symphony Orchestra, including Pete Townshend, Sandy Denny, Graham Bell, Steve Winwood, Maggie Bell, Richie Havens, Merry Clayton, Roger Daltry, John Entwhistle, Ringo Starr, Rod Stewart, and Richard Harris. Several members of the stage cast were also seen in the movie version by Ken Russell with actors Oliver Reed and Ann Margret, with the addition of Elton John and others. *Album:* Tommy (ODE SP 99001) 1972.

TOMMY TUTONE Tommy Heath—vocal, guitar, keyboards; Jim Keller—guitar, vocal; Terry Nails—bass, vocal; Mickey Shine—drums, percussion, vocal. *Album:* Tommy Tutone (COL NJC 36372) 1980.

TOMORROW, BUGS Guitar, vocal. Namesake of Bugs Tomorrow, 1980.

TOMORROW, KARL Keyboards. Member of Kenny and the Kasuals.

TOMPKINS, TIM Cello. Member of the Blue Jays, 1975.

TOMPKINS, TOM Viola. Member of the Blue Jays, 1975.

TONEY, JAMES Organ. Session for B. B. King (1975, 77).

TONIO, K. Vocal, guitar. *Albums:* Amerika (ARI

4271) 1980; Life in the Food Chain (EPC JE 35545) 1978.

TONTOH, MAC Horns, percussion. Member of Osibisa.

TONW, MEIKE Vocal. Member of Gruppo Sportivo, 1978.

TOOK, STEVE Vocal. Half of the Tyrannosaurus Rex duet, 1968-74.

TOOKER, HOLLY Vocal. Session for Martin Mull.

TOOKER, JON Guitar. Session for Pearls Before Swine (1971).

TOOLEY, RONALD Horns. Session for John Lennon (1980).

TOOMEY, JIM Drums. Member of the Tourists since 1980.

TOP, JANNICK Bass, cello, vocal, piano. Member of Magma.

TOP TEN Guitar, vocal. Member of the Dictators, 1977-78.

TOPAZ Rob Stoner—bass; Billy Cross—guitar; Jasper Hutchinson—drums. *Album:* Topaz, 1977.

TOPHAM, TOP Guitar. Original member of the Yardbirds, before joining Eric Clapton. Session for Christine Perfect (1969).

TOPPER, GREG Piano. Session for Canned Heat (1979).

TORANO, SANDY Vocal. Member of Tornader, 1977.

TORBERT, DAVE Bass, guitar, vocal. Original member of the New Riders of the Purple Sage, and Kingfish, 1976.

TORELLO, BOBBY Drums. Member of Thunderhead, 1976. Session for Johnny Winter (1975-80).

TORIAN, REGGIE Vocal. Member of the Impressions.

TORK, PETER Bass, guitar. Coffeehouse singer turned actor to join the Monkees, 1966-68.

TORME, BERNIE Guitar. Member of Gillan, 1979.

TORNADER Larry Alexander—vocal; Sandy Torano—vocal. *Album:* Hit It Again (POL PD 6098) 1977.

TORNQUIST, GREG Guitar, vocal, flute. Member of the Bones, 1973.

TORONTO Nick Costello—bass; Jimmy Fox—drums; Brian Allen—guitar; Sheron Alton—guitar; Holly Woods—vocal; Scott Kreyer—keyboards. *Album:* Lookin' for Trouble (AAM 4821) 1980.

TORPEDO, HENK Drums. Member of the New Adventures, 1980.

TORRANCE, RICHARD Vocal, guitar. Session for Leon Russell (1976). *Albums:* Anything's Possible (CAP SW 11860) 1978; Bareback (CAP SW 11610) 1977; Eureka (SHL 52022) 1973; Belle of the Ball (SHL 52019) 1975.

TORRENCE, DEAN Vocal. Half of the original surf sound of Jan and Dean, 1958-63. Session for the Beach Boys (1965).

TORRES, BOBBY Congas, percussion. Member of Joe Cocker's Greatest Show on Earth, 1970, and Mark-Almond, 1973. Session for Dr. John (1975); Tim Weisberg (1975).

TORRES, JOE Percussion. Session for Kim Fowley.

TORRES, RICCARDO Percussion. Member of the John Payne Band, 1976.

TORRICO, BILL Vocal. Member of the Flyer.

TORROLL, MARK Drums, percussion. Member of Sweetbottom, 1978-79.

TORY, CLAIRE Vocal. Session for Pink Floyd (1973); Olivia Newton-John (1976); Gary Brooker (1979).

TOSH, STUART Drums, percussion, vocal. Member of Pilot, 1974, and 10 CC, 1980. Session for the Alan Parsons Project (1976-77).

TOTESAUT, FRED Steel drums. Session for Fleetwood Mac (1973).

TOTO Steve Porcaro—keyboards, vocal; David Paich—keyboards, vocal; Steve Lukather—guitar; David Hungate—bass; Jeff Porcaro—drums; Bobby Kimball—vocal. *Albums:* Toto (COL JC 35317) 1978; Hydra (COL FC 36229) 1979.

TOUCH Craig Brooks—guitar, vocal; Mark Mangold—vocal, keyboards; Doug Howard—bass, vocal; Glenn Kithcart—drums, percussion. *Album:* Touch (ACO 38-123) 1980.

TOUCHSTONE Tom Constanten—keyboards; Paul Dresher—guitar, flute; Chicken Hirsh—drums; Wes Steele—bass, cello; Art Fayer—violin; Jim Byers—guitar. *Album:* Tarot (UAR) 1971.

TOUMAZIS, ANDREAS Bouzoukia. Session for Cat Stevens (1971-72).

TOURISTS Ann Lennox—vocal, keyboards; Peet Coombes—vocal, guitar; Dave Stewart—guitar, vocal; Eddie Chinn—bass; Jim Toomey—drums. *Album:* Reality Effect (EPC NJE-36386) 1980.

TOUSSAINT, ALLEN Keyboards, guitar, percussion, producer. Horn arranger for the Band (1972). Produced John Mayall; Joe Cocker (1978); and others. Session and production for John Mayall (1973); Mylon LeFevre (1979). Session for John Mayall (1975); Wings (1975); Jess Roden (1974). *Albums:* Motion (WBR 3142) 1978; Southern Nights (WBR 2186) 1975.

TOUT, JOHN Keyboards, vocal, guitar. Member of Renaissance. Session for John Lennon (1971).

TOWB, SUKI Cello. Member of Centipede, 1971.

TOWELS, SCOTT Bass, vocal. Member of the Flyboys, 1980.

TOWER OF POWER Lenny Pickett—tenor and soprano saxophones, clarinet; Stephen Kupka—baritone saxophone; Emilio Castillo—tenor saxophone, vocal; Mick Gillette—trumpet, trombone, vocal; Greg Adams—trumpet, piano, trombone, vocal, arranger; Rick Stevens—vocal (until 1972); Skip Mesquite—saxophone, flute, vocal (until 1972); David Garibaldi—drums (until 1975); Francis Prestia—bass; Lenny Williams—vocal (1973); Hubert Tubbs—vocal (1975); Bruce Conte

—guitar, vocal (1973-present); Chester Thompson —keyboards, vocal (1975-present); Edward McGhee—vocal (1976); Ronnie Beck—drums (1976); Brent Bryers—conga, vocal; Victor Conte—bass (1978); Michael Jeffries. Big band funk artists. Part of Fillmore, 1972. Horn section session for Elton John (1974); Peter Frampton (1979); Tom Johnston (1979); Jefferson Starship (1979); Chinga Chavin (1976). *Albums:* Ain't Nothin' Stoppin' Us Now (COL PC 34302) 1976; Back on the Streets (COL JC 35784) 1979; Back to Oakland (WBR B 2749); Bump City (WBR B-2616) 1972; In the Slot (WBR B 1880) 1975; Tower of Power (WBR B 2681) 1973; Live and in Living Color (WBR B 2924) 1976; Urban Renewal (WBR B 2834) 1974; We Came to Play (WL JC 34906) 1978.

TOWERS, MICHAEL Guitar, vocal. Member of Vance or Towers, 1975.

TOWNLEY, JOHN Vocal. *Album:* Townley (HAR ST 12007) 1979.

TOWNS, COLIN Keyboards. Replaced Mike Moran in the Ian Gillan Band, 1977. Member of Gillan since 1979.

TOWNSEND, DAVE Vocal. Session for the Alan Parsons Project (1977).

TOWNSEND, HENRY Guitar. Session for Poor Joe Williams (1935).

TOWNSEND, JOHN Vocal, keyboards. Member of the Sanford and Townsend Band, 1977-79.

TOWNSEND, LEE Vocal, guitar, keyboards, saxophone. Member of Lowry Hamner and the Cryers, 1978.

TOWNSEND, ROB Drums. Member of the Family. Session for Kevin Ayers (1977-78).

TOWNSHEND, PETE Guitar, vocal, keyboards, synthesizer, writer, producer. Born 5/1/45. Original member and head writer of the Who. He released his first solo album in 1972. Member of the Rainbow Concert, 1973, and "Tommy," 1972. Teamed with Ronnie Lane in 1977 on "Rough Mix." See Rough Mix. Produced John Otway (1980). Session for Wings (1979). *Albums:* Who Came First (DEC 79198) 1972; Secret Policeman's Ball (Import) 1980; Empty Glass (ACO 2-100) 1980; Rough Mix (MCA 2295) 1977; Tommy (POL 2-9502) 1972.

TOWNSON, RON Vocal. Member of the Fifth Dimension.

TOYS Recorded "A Lover's Concerto," 1965.

TRACE Rick van der Linden—keyboards, composer, arranger; Jaap van Eik—guitar, vocal; Pierre van der Linden—drums (1974); Ian Mosley—drums (1975); Darryl Way—violin (1975). Dutch rock group using the Emerson, Lake and Palmer trio formula, headed by Rick van der Linden. Though not particularly original in design or internationally known, each member has classical training and experience, resulting in memorable moments of particular identity beyond their formula. *Albums:* Trace (SIR) 1974; Birds (SIR 1975).

TRACY, STEVE Guitar, vocal. Member of the Euphonius Wall, 1973.

TRAFFIC Steve Winwood—keyboards, guitar, bass, vocal; Chris Wood—flute, saxophone, organ, percussion, vocal; Jim Capaldi—drums, percussion, vocal; Dave Mason—bass, sitar, guitar, vocal; Rick Grech—bass (1972); Jim Gordon—drums (1972); Reebop Kwaku Baah—percussion (1971-75); David Hood—bass (1973); Roger Hawkins—drums (1973); Barry Beckett—keyboards (1973). In 1967, Winwood left the Spencer Davis Group to start on his own. He retired to a private mansion with Wood and Capaldi and released "Paper Sun" in 1968. The "Mr. Fantasy—Heaven Is in Your Mind" album, featuring "Paper Sun," was an unusual trio combination, augmented by Mason on later albums as an occasional member of Traffic. Winwood's unique vocals and surreal lyrics gave the group a distinct trademark, while Wood's jazzy reed work gave a touch few groups had considered until their appearance. In 1969, the group disbanded for the first time; Winwood joined Blind Faith, while Capaldi and Mason pursued their individual solo careers. Without Mason, the group made a return in 1971, with an expanded rhythm section. After two albums, the lineup again shrank to the Winwood-Wood-Capaldi nucleus, with Reebop. *Albums:* Best of Traffic (UAR LO 5500) 1975; John Barleycorn Must Die (UAR LMAS 5504) 1971; Last Exit (UAR LO 6702); Low Spark of High Heeled Boys (ISL 9180) 1971; Mr. Fantasy (UAR LO 6651); Shoot Out at the Fantasy Factory (ISL 9224) 1973; Traffic (UAR LMAS 6676) 1968; Traffic on the Road (ISL 2) 1973; Welcome to the Canteen (UAR LO 5550) 1971; When the Eagle Flies (ASY 7E-1020) 1974; Heavy Traffic (UAR UA LA421-G).

TRAFFIC JAM Early name of Status Quo.

TRAINER, PHIL Bass, vocal. Member of Clinic, 1973.

TRAINOR, BILLY Drums. Member of Face Dancer since 1979.

TRAMMELL, DENISE Vocal. Session for Dr. John (1979).

TRANQUILITY Tony Lukyn—vocal, keyboards; Kevin McCarthy—guitar; Terry Shaddick—guitar, vocal; Bernard Hagley—guitar; Berkley Wright—guitar, vocal; Paul Francis—drums. *Album:* Tranquility (TEM 7801) 1972.

TRANSIT EXPRESS Dominique Bouvier—percussion; Jean-Claude Gusellit—bass; Christian Lerous—guitar, synthesizer; Serge Perathoner—keyboards; David Rose—violin. *Album:* Opus Progressif (PIR 9015) 1976.

TRAPEZE Glenn Hughes—bass, piano, vocal (until 1973); Mel Galley—guitar, vocal; Dave Holland—drums, percussion; Pete Wright—bass, vocal

(1974-present); Rob Kendrick—guitar (1974-75); Pete Goalby—vocal, guitar (1980). Initially a trio, they played for almost four years, receiving little attention until Hughes left to join Deep Purple in 1973. Retrospective interest was stimulated, however, though the group (now four pieces) is still less than well known. *Albums:* Final Swing (THS 11) 1974; Hot Wire (WBR B 2828) 1974; Medusa (THS 4); Trapeze (THS 2); You Are the Music, We're Just the Band (THS 8) 1972; Hold On (PAD 2003) 1980; Trapeze (WBR 2887) 1975.

TRAUM, HAPPY Bass, banjo, guitar, vocal. Session for Bob Dylan (1971).

TRAVELER Bill Browder—guitar, keyboards, vocal; David Moerbe—drums; Richard Mullen—guitar; Jerry Crow—bass. Reorganized Denim band. *Album:* Lost in the Late Late Show (MCA 1101).

TRAVERS, MARY Vocal. Born 11/9/36. Mary of Peter, Paul and Mary. *Album:* It's in Every One of Us (CYS 1168).

TRAVERS, PAT Guitar, vocal. Featured soloist of the band bearing his name.

PAT TRAVERS BAND Pat Travers—guitar, vocal; Pat Thrall—guitar, vocal (1979-present); Peter "Mars" Cowling—bass; Tommy Auldridge—drums. *Albums:* Crash and Run (POL I 6262) 1980; Go for What You Know (POL I 6202) 1979; Heat in the Street (POL I 6170) 1978; Makin' Magic (POL I 6103) 1977; Putting It Straight (POL I 6121) 1977; Pat Travers (POL I 6079) 1976.

TRAVIO, STEVE Bass. Session for Iggy Pop (1977).

TRAVIS, CHANDLER Percussion. Session for Jonathan Edwards (1972); Martin Mull (1974).

TRAVIS, MALCOLM Drums. Member of Human Sexual Response, 1980.

TRAVIS, PAMELA Vocal. Session for the Kinks (1973-75).

TRAVIS, PAUL Guitar, vocal. Member of Liar, 1980.

TRAX Pete Bellotte; Keith Forsey. *Albums:* Watch Out, 1977; Dancing in the Street (POL 1 6142) 1978.

TRAYNOR, JAY Vocal. Session for Leslie West (1975).

TREACHER, WENDY Violin. Member of Centipede, 1971.

TREADWELL, LARRY Guitar, vocal. Member of Sumner, 1980.

TREASURE Felix Cavaliere—vocal, keyboards; Vinnie Cusano—guitar, vocal; Jack Scarangella—drums; Rick Laird—bass. *Album:* Treasure, 1977.

TREE, ED Guitar. Session for the Marc Tanner Band (1980).

TREGANNA, DAVE "KERMIT" Bass. Member of Sham 69, 1978-80.

TREMBLERS Mark Browne—bass; Peter Noone—vocal, guitar, piano, bass, writer, producer; Greg Inhofer—keyboards, guitar, vocal; Robert Williams—drums, vocal; George Conner—guitar, vocal. Ex-Herman Hermit's vocalists return to rock after 10 years. *Album:* Twice Nightly (EPC NJZ 36532) 1980.

TREMELOES Ricky West—guitar; Len Hawkes—bass; Alan Blakely—guitar; Dave Munden—drums; Brian Poole—vocal. Straightforward rockers from England, originally led by Brian Poole until 1967. *Albums:* Here Comes My Baby, 1967; Tremeloes and Brian Poole Are Here, 1967; Even the Bad Times Are Good, 1968; Tremeloes 1958-69, World Explosion.

TREVISICK, NICK Drums. Session for Dave Davies (1980).

TRIBUNO, DIANE Guitar. Member of the U.F.O.s, 1966.

TRICKSTER Phil Bates—guitar, vocal; Colin Hewinson—keyboards, synthesizer, vocal; Mike Sheppard—bass, guitar, vocal (1978); Paul Elliott—drums, percussion; Michael Groth (1979); John Fincham (1979). *Albums:* Back to Zero (JET JZ 35968) 1979; Trickster (JET JZ 35478) 1978.

TRIFAN, DANNY Bass. Member of Larry Coryell's Eleventh House.

TRIGGER Jimmy Duggan—guitar, vocal; Richie House—guitar, vocal; Tom Nigera—bass, vocal; Derek Remington—drums, vocal. *Album:* Trigger (CAS 7092) 1978.

TRILLION Ron Anaman—bass, vocal; Frank Barbalace—guitar, vocal; Thom Griffin—guitar, vocal (1980); Pat Leonard—keyboards; Bill Wilkins—drums, percussion; Dennis Frederiksen—vocal (1978). *Albums:* Clear Approach (EPC NJE 36206) 1980; Trillion (EPC JE 35460) 1978.

TRINITY See Julie Driscoll, Brian Auger and the Trinity.

TRIPP, ARTHUR Drums, percussion. Member of the Mothers of Invention, 1968-70, and Captain Beefheart and His Magic Band, 1974. Session for Captain Beefheart (1978).

TRIPP, EDDIE String bass. Session for Hapshash and the Coloured Coat.

TRIUMPH Rik Emmett—guitar, vocal; Mike Levine—bass, keyboards; Gil Moore—drums, vocal. Hard rock Canadian trio that appeared internationally in 1979. *Albums:* Just a Game (VIC AFLI 3224) 1979; Progressions of Power (VIC AFLI 3524) 1980; Rock and Roll Machine (VIC AFLI 2982) 1979.

TRIUMVIRAT Helmut Kollen—bass, guitar, vocal (1973-75); Hans Bathelt—drums (1973-76); Jurgen Fritz—keyboards, synthesizer, vocal, writer, producer; Barry Palmer—vocal (1976-79); Dick Frangenberg—bass (1976); Curt Cress—drums (1977); Dieter Petereit—bass (1977). Members of the German invasion of 1973 (with Kraftwerk, Eloy, Camel, and others), simulating Emerson,

Lake and Palmer. *Albums:* A La Carte (CAP SAT 11862) 1979; Illusions on a Double Dimple (HAR ST 11311) 1973; Old Loves Die Hard (CAP ST 11551) 1976; Pompeii (CAP ST 11697) 1977; Spartacus (CAP ST 11392) 1975.

TRIUMVIRAT Mike Bloomfield—guitar, vocal; John Hammond—guitar, vocal; Dr. John—keyboards, vocal. *Album:* Triumvirat (COL).

TROCHIM, "KOOTCH" Bass. Member of the Dudes, 1975.

TROGGS Reg Presley—vocal; Chris Britton—guitar; Peter Staples—bass; Ronnie Bond—drums, percussion. The outrageousness of their name was a suitable match for the curious whining tone of lead singer Presley's voice. But not even the Beatles could rival their rock classic, "Wild Thing," when it appeared in 1966. Following that with "With a Girl Like You," the Troggs extended their novelty, but failed to survive into the 1970s. *Albums:* Wild Thing (FNA 27556); Troggs Tapes, 1976; Live at Max's (MKC 214) 1980.

TROIANO, DOMENIC Vocal, guitar. An original member of Mandala, 1968, he joined Burton Cummings in the Guess Who in 1972, replacing Greg Leskiw. *Albums:* Fret Fever (CAP ST 11932) 1979; Burnin' at the Stake (CAP ST 11669) 1977; The Joke's on Me (CAP SW 11772) 1978.

TROMBLY, RON Drums, vocal. Session for Flint (1978).

TROOPER Ra McGuire—vocal, harmonica; Brian Smith—guitar, vocal; Harry Kalensky—bass, vocal (1975-79); Tommy Stewart—drums, vocal; Frank Ludwig—keyboards, vocal (1976); Doni Underhill—bass, vocal (1980); Robert Deans—keyboards. *Albums:* Flying Colors (MCA 3173); Hot Shots (MCA 3222) 1979; Knock 'Em Dead Kid (MCA 2275) 1977; Thick as Thieves (MCA 2377) 1978; Trooper (MCA 2149) 1975; Two for the Show (MCA 2214) 1976; Trooper (MCA 5151) 1980.

TROPEA, JOHN Guitar. Session for Eumir Deodato; Paul Simon (1975); Alice Cooper (1976); Ringo Starr (1977); the Mark and Clark Band (1977); Mark-Almond (1978); Taj Mahal (1978); Dr. John (1978); the Randle Chowning Band (1978); John Mayall (1979); Jimmy Maelin (1980). *Albums:* Short Trip to Space (MAR 2204); To Touch You Again (MAR 2222); Tropea (MAR 2200) 1975.

TROST, VINCENT Bass. Member of the Bullfrog, 1976.

TROUBLE Rick Failla—vocal; Carey Raymond—guitar; John Higgerson—bass; Brian Glascock—drums; Jim Morris—keyboards. *Album:* Trouble, 1977.

TROUT Cassandra Morgan; Frank Romeo; Tony Romeo. *Album:* The Trout (MGM 4592).

TROUTNER, PETER Guitar, vocal. Original member of Circus Maximus, 1967-68.

TROWBRIDGE, FRANK Slide guitar. Session for Bachman-Turner Overdrive (1974).

TROWER, ROBIN Guitar, vocal. Born 3/9/45. An original member of Procol Harum, 1967-72, he left to embark on his solo career, being tagged by publicity as "the next Jimi Hendrix." Though in many ways his styling was comparable, he survived the publicity to enjoy an identity and following of his own. His backup band included James Dewar on bass and vocals (since 1973) and Bill Lordon on drums, who replaced Reg Isidore (1973-75). In 1977, Dewar attended to vocals full time while Rustee Allen took over on bass. *Albums:* Bridge of Sighs (CYS 1057) 1974; Caravan to Midnight (CYS 1148) 1977; For Earth Below (CYS 1073) 1975; In City Dreams (CYS 1148) 1977; Long Misty Days (CYS 1107) 1976; Robin Trower Live (CYS 1089) 1976; Twice Removed from Yesterday (CYS 1039) 1973; Victims of the Fury (CYS 1215) 1980.

TROXEL, GARY Vocal. Member of the Fleetwoods, 1959.

TROY, DORIS Vocal. Session for Gary Wright (1970-71); Sky (1970); the Rolling Stones (1970); Dr. John (1971); Long John Baldry (1971-72); Vigrass and Osbourne (1972); Carly Simon (1972); Pink Floyd (1973); Kevin Ayers (1973). *Album:* Doris Troy, 1970.

TROY, JOHN Bass. Member of the Pousette-Dart Band.

TROY, ROGER Bass. Session for Mike Bloomfield (1977-79).

TROYER, ERIC Vocal. Session for John Lennon (1980).

TRUAX, JAY Bass, vocal. Member of the Richie Furay Band, 1976.

TRUCKS, BUTCH Drums, percussion. Original member of the 31st of February, 1968, and the Allman Brothers Band, through the present. Session for Gregg Allman (1973); Gene Clark (1974).

TRUFFLE, KEITH Percussion. Member of Brett Marvin and the Thunderbolts.

TRUGMAN, PAUL Guitar, vocal. Member of Helmet Boy, 1980.

TRUJILLO, JAY Guitar. Session for the Pages (1979).

TRUNKHILL, MARYLS Vocal. Member of the Fugs Chorus.

TRUSSLER, JOHN Violin. Member of Centipede, 1971.

TRUSTY, SCOTT Member of the Beckies, 1976.

TRUTH John Gatti—keyboards, flute, vocal; Phil Girlando—guitar, vocal; Bob DeCaro—drums; Jerry White—vocal, percussion; Bill Zecker—bass, vocal. *Album:* Truth (ROU) 1975.

TRUTH, ROGER Drums. Session for Brian Protheroe (1976).

TRYON, MARTY Bass. Member of Simon Stoke's Black Whip Band, 1973.

TUBBS, HUBERT Vocal. Replaced Lenny Williams

in Tower of Power, 1975.

TUBBS, RUSSELL Reeds. Session for Santana (1980).

TUBES Rick Anderson—bass; Mike Cotten—synthesizer; Prairie Prince—drums; William Spooner—guitar, vocal; Roger Steen—guitar, vocal; Fee Waybill—vocal; Vincent Welnick—keyboards. *Albums:* Now (AAM 4632) 1977; Remote Control (AAM 4751) 1979; The Tubes (AAM 4534) 1975; What Do You Want From—Live (AAM 6003) 1978; Young and Rich (AAM 4580) 1976.

TUBIN, RUBE Recording name of Larry Richstein.

TUBRIDY, MICHAEL Flute. Session for Art Garfunkel (1978).

TUCCILLO, BOB Drums, percussion. Member of the Rich Mountain Tower, 1976.

TUCK, DEIRDRE Vocal. Session for Paul Simon (1972); Jacki DeShannon (1972).

TUCKER BAND, MARSHALL See Marshall Tucker Band.

TUCKER, JIM Guitar. Original member of the Turtles, 1965-69.

TUCKER, LUTHER Guitar. Original member of the James Cotton Blues Band.

TUCKER, MAUREEN Drums, percussion. Original member of the Velvet Underground, 1967-70.

TUCKER, MICK Drums, percussion. Member of the Sweet since 1973.

TUCKER, PETER Drums. Member of Guns and Butter, 1972.

TUCKER, TOMMY Vocal. Real name: Robert Higgenbotham. Recorded "High Heel Sneakers," 1964.

TUCKEY, LEN Guitar, slide guitar, vocal. Member of Suzi Quatro's band since 1974.

TUCKY BUZZARD Jimmy Henderson—vocal, harmonica; Terry Taylor—guitar; Ron Taylor—guitar; Dave Brown—guitar, bass; Chris Johnson—drums; Phil Talbot—guitar (1973). *Albums:* All Right on the Night, 1973; Buzzard, 1973.

TUDURI, EDDIE Drums. Member of Glider, 1977, and Wha-Koo since 1979.

TUFANO, DENNY Vocal, keyboards, guitar. Member of the Buckinghams before co-founding the Tufano-Giammarese Band, 1973-77.

TUFANO-GIAMMERESE BAND Dennis Tufano—vocal, keyboards, guitar; Carl Giammarese—guitar, vocal; John Forest—bass; Tom Osfar—drums; Darryl Warren—percussion; Marty Grebb—keyboards, saxophone. *Albums:* Tufano-Giammarese Band (OPE 77032) 1975; Long Playing (OPE 77017) 1973; The Other Side, 1977.

TUFF DARTS Tommy Frenzy—vocal; Jeff Salem—guitar; Bobby Butani—guitar; John De Salvo—bass; John Morelli—drums. *Album:* Tuff Darts (SIR K-6048) 1978.

TULIN, MARK Bass, keyboards. Original member of the Electric Prunes, 1967.

TULL, JETHRO See Jethro Tull.

TULLOCH, ALLISON Vocal. Session for Any Trouble (1980).

TUMAHAI, CHARLES Bass. Replaced Robert Bryan in Be Bop Deluxe, 1975-78. Member of the Dukes, 1979.

TUMBLEWEEDS Ine Masseurs—vocal; Ton Masseurs—guitar, pedal steel guitar; Barry Masseurs—guitar; Ad Masseurs—drums; Mickey de Boer—bass; Rudd Hermans—vocal, guitar. *Album:* Tumbleweeds (BSF 25551) 1975.

TUNICK, BUDD Drums. Member of the Simms Brothers Band, 1979-80.

TUNISON, JOHN Bass, vocal. Member of Highway Robbery, 1972.

TURBEVILLE, DAN Keyboards. Session for Hydra (1974); Cognition (1971).

TURBINTON, EARL, JR. Alto saxophone. Session for B. B. King (1972).

TUREK, JOE Bass, vocal. Member of Mama's Pride, 1975.

TURI, JOHN Keyboards, saxophone. Member of Blue Angel, 1980.

TURK, JOHN Keyboards. Session for Taj Mahal; B. B. King (1972).

TURNABOUTS See Merilee Rush.

TURNBULL, JOHN Guitar, vocal. Member of Glencoe, 1972, Loving Awareness, Ian Dury's Blockheads, 1979, and the Planets, 1980.

TURNER, BENNY Bass. Session for Freddie King (1975).

TURNER, C. F. Bass, vocal. Original member of Brave Belt, 1971, and Bachman-Turner Overdrive, 1973-79.

TURNER, IKE Guitar, vocal, arranger. See Ike and Tina Turner.

IKE AND TINA TURNER Ike Turner—guitar, vocal, arranger; Tina Turner—vocal. Though from the United States, Ike and Tina initially caught the British eye before taking their native land by storm with their version of "River Deep, Mountain High," in 1969. Featuring concise musical arrangements by guitarist Ike Turner, they also captured the public's attention with the physical impression of Tina and the Ikettes. The Turners' separation in 1977 left each to their individual careers. See Tina Turner. *Albums:* Best of Ike and Tina Turner (BTM 49); Come Together (LIB 7637); Feel Good (UAR 5598); Incredible Ike and Tina Turner (TRP); Let Me Touch Your Mind (UAR 5660); River Deep, Mountain High (AAM 4178) 1969; Too Hot to Hold (SPB 4011); Ike and Tina Turner of 1971 (UAR 6817); What You Hear Is What You Get (UAR); Working Together (LIB 7650); World of Ike and Tina Turner (UAR UA LA064-62); Ike and Tina Revue Live, 1965; Ike and Tina Turner Live, 1965; Ike and Tina Turner Show, 1966; Airwaves (UAR LT-917) 1978; The Edge (FSY 9597) 1980; Please, Please, Please (KNT 550); Soul of Ike and Tina (KNT 519); Ike and

Tina Turner's Festival of Live Performances (KNT 538); Gospel According to Ike and Tina (UAR UA LA 203-G); Nutbush City Limits (UAR UA LA 180-F); Sweet Rhode Island (UAR UA LA 312-G); Vibes (TRP 9520); Let Me Touch Your Mind (UAR UAS 5660) 1972; 'Nuff Said (UAR UAS 5530) 1971.

TURNER, JOE LYNN Vocal, guitar. Member of Fandango.

TURNER, "BIG" JOE Vocal, piano. Kansas City blues singer whose "Shake, Rattle and Roll" made stars of Bill Haley, Elvis, and others. Weighing over 300 pounds, Turner grew up in the 1920s and was still performing in 1978. *Albums:* Joe Turner; Rockin' the Blues, 1958; Big Joe Is Here, 1959; Big Joe Rides Again, 1960; Jumpin' the Blues, 1962; Best of Joe Turner, 1963; Joe Turner; Boss of the Blues; Careless Love; Singin' the Blues, 1967; His Great Recordings; Another Epoch Stride Piano (PAB 2310763); Blue Roots (TMT 2-7006); Effervescent (CLJ 138); Everyday I Have the Blues (PAB 2310818); From Spirituals to Swing (VAN VSD 47-48); In the Evening (PAB 2310776); Nobody in Mind (PAB 2310760); Story of the Blues (COL CG 30008); Things That I Used to Do (PAB 2310800); The Bosses (PAB 2310709); Have No Fear, "Big" Joe Is Here (SAV 32223); Singin' the Blues (MCA 2-4064); Big Joe Turner Turns On the Blues (KNT 542); Things That I Used to Do (PBL 800) 1977; Midnight Special (PBL 844) 1980; Everybody I Have the Blues (PBL 818) 1978.

TURNER, JOE Bass. Session for B. B. King (1977).

TURNER, JOHN "RED" Drums. Session for Johnny Winter (1969-70).

TURNER, LANE Guitar. Member of Missouri until 1978.

TURNER, LONNIE Bass. Member of the Steve Miller Band, 1968-70, 76. Session for Dave Mason; the Steve Miller Band (1973, 77).

TURNER, MARTIN Bass, vocal. Member of Wishbone Ash.

TURNER, NIK Saxophone, flute, oboe. Member of Hawkwind, 1978-present.

TURNER, RICK Guitar, banjo. Member of Autosalvage, 1968.

TURNER, SCOTTY Guitar. Member of the Wildcats, 1979.

TURNER, TED Guitar, vocal. Original member of Wishbone Ash until 1973. Session for John Lennon (1971).

TURNER, TINA Vocal. Real name: Annie May Bullock. *Albums:* Tina Turns the Country On (UAR UA LA200-G) 1974; Rough (UAR LTAO 919).

TURNEY, ROSS Drums, organ, percussion. Original member of Chilliwack, 1971-80.

TURPIN, MICHAEL Bass. Member of the Axe since 1979.

TURRE, STEVEN Horns. Session for Paul Simon.

TURRINGTON, BRIAN Bass. Member of the Tyla Gang, 1978. Session for Phil Manzanera (1978).

TURSON, BRUCE Bass. Member of the Black Sheep, 1975.

TURTLES Howard Kaylan—vocal; Mark Volman—vocal; John Barbata—drums; Jim Pons—bass, vocal; Al Nichol—guitar, vocal; Jim Tucker—guitar. Early name: the Crossfires. The Turtles entered the folk-rock race in 1965 with "It Ain't Me Babe," featuring the vocal harmonies of Kaylan and Volman. Though not always on the singles charts, they remained popular through 1967, when they released "Happy Together." They broke up in 1969. Kaylan and Volman continued as Flo and Eddie. *Albums:* It Ain't Me Babe, 1965; You Baby, 1966; Happy Together, 1967; Turtles Golden Hits, 1967; The Turtles Present a Battle of the Bands, 1968; Turtles—1968 (RHI 901) 1978.

TUTONE, TOMMY See Tommy Tutone.

TUTT, RONNIE Drums. Session for Gram Parsons (1973).

TUTTLE, JOHN Percussion. Original member of Fever Tree, 1968-69.

TUTTLE, KIRK Drums, percussion. Member of One Hand Clapping, 1977-79.

TUTTLE, LARRY Bass, vocal. Member of Russia, 1980.

TUXEN, NILS Guitar, steel guitar. Original member of the Savage Rose, 1968-70.

TW 4 Early name for Styx.

TWEEDY, DAVID Keyboards. Member of Randy Burn's Sky Dog Band, 1973.

20/20 Steve Allen—vocal, guitar; Ron Flynt—vocal, bass; Mike Gallo—drums; Chris Silagy—vocal, guitar, synthesizer. New wave rock produced by former Sparks member Earl Mankey. *Album:* 20/20 (POR JR-36205) 1979.

TWIGG, GARY Bass. Session for the Heroes (1980).

TWILLE, CARMEN Vocal. Session for Elton John (1980).

TWILLEY, DWIGHT Guitar, keyboards, vocal. Namesake of the Dwight Twilley Band, 1976-79.

DWIGHT TWILLEY BAND Dwight Twilley—guitar, harmonica, keyboards, vocal; Phil Seymour—drums, bass, vocal (1976-78); Bill Pitcock—guitar, vocal; Johnny Johnson—bass (1976-78); Jim Lewis—bass, drums (1978-79). *Albums:* Sincerely (SLT 52001) 1976; Twilley (ARI 4214) 1979; Twilley Don't Mind (ARI 4140) 1977.

TWISTERS Mike Wainwright—vocal, guitar; Jason Hickman—guitar, vocal; Fred Grabert—guitar, keyboards, vocal; Phil Gilbreth—bass, vocal; Richard Paine—drums, vocal. *Album:* Twisters (RHI 905) 1980.

TWITTY, CONWAY Vocal, guitar. Real name: Harold Jenkins. Currently a country-western singer and sometime partner of Loretta Lynn, Twitty began in 1956, achieving his initial fame as an Elvis imitator before establishing his own identity. *Albums:* Clinging to a Saving Hand/Steal Away (MCA 376); Fifteen Years Ago (MCA 128); How Much More Can She Stand (MCA 46); I Can't See Me Without You (MCA 30); I Love You More Today (MCA 130); I Wonder What She'll Think About Me Leavin' (MCA 34); I'm So Used to Loving You (COR 20000); She Needs Someone to Hold Her (MCA 303); To See My Angel Cry (MCA 18); I Can't Stop Loving You (MCA 53); Conway Twitty's Greatest Hits (MGM 3849) 1960; Conway Twitty Sings, 1966; Conway Twitty Country, 1968; Here's My Teardrops, 1968; Next in Line; Darling, You Know I Wouldn't Lie, 1969; Conway (MCA 3063); Cross Winds (MCA 3086); Georgia Keeps Pulling on My Ring (MCA 2328); Greatest Hits, Vol. 1 (MCA 2345); Greatest Hits, Vol. 2 (MCA 2235); Heart and Soul (MCA 3210); Hello Darlin' (MCA 19); High Priest of Country Music (MCA 2144); I'm Not Used to Loving You (MCA 441); I've Already Loved You in My Mind (MCA 2293); Linda on My Mind (MCA 469); Memphis Country (SUN 120); Now and Then (MCA 2206); Play, Guitar Play (MCA 2282); Twitty (MCA 2176); Twitty's Honky Tonk Angel (MCA 406); Very Best of Conway Twitty (MCA 3043); You've Never Been This Far Before (MCA 359).

TWO GUNS Kenny Barker—guitar, vocal; Bobby Williams—guitar, vocal; Mike Sconce—bass, vocal; Pat Sconce—drums. *Album:* Balls Out (CPN 0224) 1979.

TWYFORD, ROB Bass. Member of Demon, 1977.

TYCOON Mark Kreider—bass, vocal, strings, percussion; Norman Mershon—vocal; Michael Fonfara—keyboards, vocal; Mark Rivera—saxophone, percussion, vocal; Jon Gordon—guitar, synthesizer, strings; Richard Steinberg—drums. *Album:* Tycoon (ARI 4215).

TYLA, SEAN Guitar, keyboards, vocal. Member of the Ducks Deluxe, 1972-75, before forming the Tyla Gang, 1978-79. *Album:* Sean Tyla, Just Popped Out (POL I 6281) 1980.

TYLA GANG Sean Tyla—guitar, keyboards, vocal; Bruce Irvine—guitar; Michael Desmarias—drums, percussion; Brian Turrington—bass (1978); Ken Whaley—bass (1978-79). *Albums:* Yachtless, 1978; Moonproof, 1979.

TYLER, BONNIE Vocal, guitar. *Albums:* Diamond Cut (VIC AFLI 3072); It's a Heartache (VIC AFLI 2821) 1979; World Starts Tonight (CYS 1140) 1977.

TYLER, RICHARD Piano. Member of the Holy Modal Rounders.

TYLER, STEPHEN Session for Martin Mull (1975).

TYLER, STEVE Vocal. Voice of Aerosmith, 1971-79.

TYNER, ROB Vocal, saxophone. Voice of the MC 5, 1968-69.

TYRANNOSAURUS REX See T. Rex.

TYSON, IAN Guitar, vocal. Husband half of Canada's famous folk duo, Ian and Sylvia, since 1962. *Album:* One Jump Ahead of the Devil (BOO 7189).

TYSON, SYLVIA Autoharp, vocal. Wife half of Canada's famous folk duo, Ian and Sylvia, since 1962.

TZUKE, JUDIE Vocal. *Albums:* Sports Car (ROC 3249); Stay with Me Till Dawn (ROC 27001) 1979.

U

UFO Phil Moog—vocal; Andy Parker—drums (1974-75); Pete Way—bass; Mike Schenker—guitar (1974-79); Danny Peyronel—keyboards (1974-75); Paul Raymond—keyboards, guitar, vocal (1977-present); Paul Chapman—guitar (1980). *Albums:* Force It (CYS 1074) 1974; Lights Out (CYS 1127) 1977; No Heavy Petting (CYS 1103) 1975; No Place to Run (CYS 1239) 1980; Obsession (CYS 1182) 1978; Strangers in the Night (CYS 1209) 1979.

U.F.O. Ann Sternberg—bass; Lisa Kindred—vocal, guitar; Diane Tribuno—guitar; Laurie Stanton—drums. All-female rock quartet from the West Coast, 1966.

U.K. Eddie Jobson—violin, keyboards; John Wetton—vocal, bass; Terry Bozzio—drums, percussion (1979); Alan Holdsworth—guitar (1978); Bill Bruford—drums, percussion (1978). *Albums:* U.K. (POL 1-6146) 1978; Danger Money (POL 1-6194) 1979; Night After Night (POL 1-6234) 1979.

U.S. RADIO BAND Robert Dewald—bass, vocal; Ron Kalstein—guitar, vocal; Al Snyder—guitar, vocal; John Volturo—keyboards, vocal; Larry Freedman—drums, vocal. *Album:* Don't Touch That Dial (ABC) 1976.

ULAKY, WAYNE Bass, vocal. Member of the Beacon Street Union, 1968.

ULLIBARRI, EDDIE Vocal, keyboards. Member of Alexis, 1977.

ULRICH, SHARI Vocal, violin, flute. Member of the Hometown Band, 1976.

ULTIMATE SPINACH Ian Bruce-Douglas—vocal, bells, chimes; Barbara Hudson—vocal, guitar, percussion; Keith Lahteinen—vocal, drums, percussion; Richard Nese—bass; Geoffrey Winthrop—vocal, guitar, sitar. Spearhead of the "Boston Sound," 1968, with the Beacon Street Union and others. *Albums:* Ultimate Spinach (MGM) 1968; Behold and See (MGM 4570).

ULTRA LATEX Freddie Mandel—keyboards; Steve Hunter—guitar; Whitney Glan—drums; Davey Johnstone—guitar; Johnny Stiletto—bass. Alice Cooper's backup band for his *Welcome to My Nightmare* movie and tour.

ULTRAVOX John Foxx—vocal (1977-79); Steve Shears—guitar (1977-78); Warren Cann—drums, vocal; Billy Currie—violin, keyboards; Chris Cross—bass, vocal; Robin Simon—guitar, vocal (1978-79); Midge Ure—vocal, guitar, synthesizer (1980). *Albums:* Ultravox (ISL 9449) 1977; Vienna (CSY 1296) 1980; Systems of Romance (ANT 7069) 1978; Three into One (ANT 7079) 1979; Ha! Ha! Ha! (ISL 9505) 1977.

ULVAEUS, BJORN Guitar. Member of Abba since 1974.

UNDERHILL, DONI Bass, vocal. Replaced Harry Kalenski in Trooper, 1980.

UNDERTONES Feargal Sharkey—vocal; Damian O'Neill—guitar; Mickey Bradley—bass; Billy Doherty—drums; John O'Neill—guitar. *Album:* The Undertones (SIR K-6081) 1979.

UNDERWOOD, IAN Keyboards, woodwinds, percussion. Member of the Mothers of Invention, 1967-74. Session for Frank Zappa (1970, 74); George Duke (1975); Spirit (1976); Lee Ritenour (1977-78); Dick St. Nicklaus (1979); Robbie Robertson (1980).

UNDERWOOD, MARK Trumpet. Session for Jules and the Polar Bears (1979).

UNDERWOOD, MICK Drums, percussion. Member of Quatermass, 1970, Strapps, 1977, and Gillan, 1979-present.

UNDERWOOD, RUTH Percussion. Member of the Mothers of Invention, 1971-75. Session for Frank Zappa (1974, 76); George Duke (1975).

UNDERWOOD, SIMON Bass. Member of the Pop Group, 1980.

UNICORN Pat Martin—bass, mandolin, vocal; Pete Perrier—drums, percussion, vocal; Ken Baker—guitar, keyboards, vocal; Kevin Smith—guitar, slide guitar. *Albums:* Unicorn (CAP) 1974; Unicorn (CAP) 1976; One More Tomorrow (CAP ST 11692) 1977; Unicorn 2 (CAP ST 11493) 1976.

UNION GAP See Gary Puckett and the Union Gap.

UNITED STATES OF AMERICA Joseph Byrd—synthesizer; Dorothy Moskowitz—vocal; Craig Woodsen—drums, percussion; Gordon Marron—violin, vocal; Rand Forbes—bass. One of the first groups to experiment with commercial synthesized sound in a rock format. They failed to capture the attention of pop or underground audiences in 1968, despite their classically trained and talented personnel. *Album:* United States of America (COL) 1968.

UNITS Scott Ryser—synthesizer, vocal; Rachel Webber—synthesizer, vocal; Brad Saunders—drums. *Album:* Digital Simulation 1980.

UPCHURCH, PHIL Guitar, bass. Session for Ben Sidran; Howlin' Wolf (1972); Cat Stevens (1974). *Albums:* Phil Upchurch (CAO 826); Phil Upchurch /Tennyson Stephens (KDU 22); Feeling Blue (MLS 9010) 1967; Phil Upchurch (MAR 2209) 1978; Upchurch (CDT 826) 1969.

UPEPO Steven Bromberg—drums, percussion; Charles Croft—guitar, percussion, vocal; J. Michael Kearsey—bass, vocal, percussion; David Nelson—saxophone, percussion, vocal; Glenn Rueger—keyboards, vocal; Stanford Wood—congas. *Album:* International Ties (NEB 1051).

UPP Andy Clark—vocal, keyboards; James Copely—drums; Stephen Amazing—bass; David Bunce—guitar. *Albums:* Upp (EPC KE 33439) 1975; This Way (EPC) 1976.

UPSHUR, HIROSHI Keyboards. Session for Gary Wright (1977).

UPTON, STEVE Drums, percussion. Member of Wishbone Ash.

URBAN HEROES Evert Nieuwstede—vocal; Jaap De Jonckheere—guitar; Martin Zonderop—bass; Jerden Ernst—keyboards; Ad Van Der Ree—drums. *Album:* Who Said (FLT 36962) 1980.

URBAN VERBS Robin Rose; Roddy Frantz; Linda France; Robert Goldstein; Danny Frankel. *Album:* Urban Verbs (WBR K-3418) 1980.

URE, MIDGE Vocal, guitar, synthesizer. Replaced Robin Simon in Ultravox, 1980. Member of Visage, 1980. Session for Thin Lizzy (1980).

URIAH HEEP David Byron—vocal (1970-76); Ken Hensley—keyboards, guitar, vocal; Mick Box—guitar, vocal; Paul Newton—bass, vocal (1970-72); Alex Napier—drums (1970-71); Ian Clark—drums (1971); Lee Kerslake—drums, percussion (1972-78); Gary Thain—bass (1972-75); John Wetton—bass, keyboards, vocal (1975-76); John Lawton—vocal (1977-78); Trevor Bolder—bass (1977-78). When they first appeared in 1970, they were called "the Beach Boys of heavy metal," combining vocal harmonies with high-volume rock music. Hensley's screaming organ lines and Box's guitar work were the group's original trademark, but from album to album, Byron's vocal talents became more apparent. Both Hensley and Byron have recorded solo debuts. *Albums:* Best of Uriah Heep (MER SRM-1-1070) 1976; Demons and Wizards (MER SRM-1-603) 1972; Fallen Angel (CYS 1204) 1978; Firefly (WBR 3013) 1977; High and Mighty (WBR 2949) 1976; Innocent Victim (WBR K 3145) 1978; Look at Yourself (MER SRM-1-614) 1971; Magician's Birthday (MER SRM-1-652) 1972; Return to Fantasy (WBR B-2869) 1975; Salisbury (MER 61319) 1970; Sweet Freedom (WBR B-2724) 1973; Uriah Heep (MER ML-8004) 1970; Uriah Heep Live (MER SRM-2-7502) 1973; Wonderworld (WBR 2800) 1974.

URIBE, JOHN Guitar. Replaced Nils Tuxen in Savage Rose, 1971. Session for Sky (1971); B. B. King (1971); Nilsson (1971, 72).

URSA MAJOR Dick Wagner—guitar, vocal; Greg Arama—bass, vocal; Ricky Mangone—drums, percussion, vocal. Short-lived American trio that made their appearance in 1972, before Wagner left to work with Alice Cooper. *Album:* Ursa Major (VIC LJP 4777) 1972.

URSILLO, RICHARD Bass. Member of the Sensations Fix.

URSO, MIKE Vocal, bass. Replaced Reggie McBride in Rare Earth, 1975-77. Member of Hub, 1975.

USELESS, GERRY Bass, vocal. Member of the Subhumans, 1979.

UTLEY, MIKE Member of the Coral Reefer Band. Session for Marc Benno; Tony Joe White (1971); Rita Coolidge (1972); John Kay (1973); Gene Clark (1974); the Alpha Band (1977); Kim Carnes (1975); Geoff Muldaur (1978); Mistress (1979).

UTLEY, TERRY Bass. Member of Smokie, 1975-79.

UTOPIA Kevin Elliman—percussion; Moogy Klingman—keyboards; M. Frog Labat—synthesizer; Todd Rundgren—guitar; Ralph Shuckett—keyboards; John Siegler—bass, cello (1974-76); Roger Powell—synthesizer, piano (1977-80); John Wilcox—drums (1977-80); Kasim Sulton—bass (1977-80). *Albums:* Another Live (BSV 6961) 1975; Oops, Wrong Planet (BSV 6970) 1977; RA (BSV 6965) Todd Rundgren's Utopia (BSV 6954) 1974; Adventures in Utopia (BSV BRK 6991); Utopia (KNT 566); Deface the Music (BSV 3487) 1980.

UTTER, DAVID Guitar, vocal. Member of Face Dancer, 1979.

UTTING, JILL Vocal. Session for Donovan (1973).

UVENA, JAN Drums. Session for the Paley Brothers (1978).

UZZELL, LARRY Vocal. Member of Nantucket since 1978.

UZZELL, MIKE Bass, keyboards, vocal. Member of Nantucket, 1978-79.

V

VADICAN, JOHN Drums. Original member of Kaleidoscope, 1967-68.

VALDEZ, RUSSEL Steel drums. Session for Fleetwood Mac (1973).

VALDY Vocal, guitar. Canadian folk singer. *Albums:* See How the Years Have Gone By (AAM 4538) 1975; Valdy (AAM 4592) 1976.

VALENS, RITCHIE Vocal. Real name: Richard Valenzuela. One of the first Latin rock stars, Valens was a teen idol of the late 1950s at the age of nineteen. In 1959, under the name Arvee Allen, he recorded "Fast Freight." He was the author of "La Bamba," which made Trini Lopez a star, before his death in the plane crash that also killed Buddy Holly and the Big Bopper in 1959. *Albums:* Ritchie Valens; Ritchie; Ritchie Valens in Concert; Ritchie Valens Memorial Album.

VALENTI, DINO Vocal, guitar, percussion. Real name: Chester Powers. Joined Quicksilver Messenger Service in 1970 after soloing as a folk singer. Author of "Let's Get Together." *Album:* Dino, 1968.

VALENTINE, DAVID Vocal, keyboards. Member of R.A.F., 1980.

VALENTINE, GARY Bass, guitar. Replaced Nigel Harrison in Blondie, 1979-present. Session for Moon Martin (1978).

VALENTINE, HILTON Guitar. Born 5/2/43. A member of the Animals, 1964-66, 77. After his departure he released a solo album that remained virtually unknown. *Album:* Hole in My Head (MGM).

VALENTINE, KEVIN Drums. Member of Breathless since 1979.

VALENTINO, BOBBY Violin, vocal, mandolin. Member of the Fabulous Poodles, 1978-79.

VALENTINO, SAL Vocal. Original member of the Beau Brummels, and Stoneground, 1971.

VALENZUELA, JOHN Guitar, vocal. Member of Tango, 1974.

VALENZUELA, RICHARD Real name of Ritchie Valens.

VALERY, DANA Vocal. Session for Leslie West (1975).

VALESQUEZ, RICHIE Bass. Session for Bobby Caldwell (1978).

VALLANCE, JIMMY Drums, keyboards, guitar, bass. Session for Ian Lloyd (1979).

VALLEY, JIM Drums. Replaced Mike Smith in Paul Revere and the Raiders, 1966-68. *Album:* Dance Inside Your Heart (FAM 7710) 1977.

VALLI, FRANKIE Vocal. Head of the Four Seasons and soloist since 1967. *Albums:* Close Up; Frankie Valli Solo, 1967; Timeless, 1968; Frankie, Is the Word (WBR K-3233) 1978; Very Best of Frankie Valli (MCA 3198) 1979; Lady Put the Light Out (PRS 7002) 1972; Valli (PRS 2017); Closeup (PRS 2000) 1975; Inside You (MTN M6-85251) 1975; Our Day Will Come (PRS 2006) 1975.

VALLORY, ROSS Guitar, vocal, bass. Member of the Steve Miller Band, 1971, and Journey since 1975.

VAN ALLEN, PETE Member of the Snakestretchers, 1972-73.

VAN BLAIR, JARRY Trumpet, vocal. Member of Chase, 1971-73.

VAN DEMAN, DUANE Bass, vocal. Member of the Tazmanian Devils, 1980.

VAN DEN BROECK, ROB Piano. Member of the Chris Hinze Combination, 1974.

VAN DEN BROECK, REIN Trumpet. Member of Ekseption, and Spin, 1976.

VAN DER BEEK, CORNELIUS Drums. Member of the Shocking Blue.

VAN DER GRAAF Grahame Smith—violin; Charles Dickie—cello, piano, synthesizer; Nic Potter—bass; Guy Evans—drums, percussion; David Jackson—reeds, vocal. Abbreviated name for the re-formed Van der Graaf Generator, 1978. *Album:* Vital (PVC 9901) 1978.

VAN DER GRAAF GENERATOR Hugh Banton —keyboards, bass, vocal; Guy Evans—drums, percussion, piano; Peter Hammill—vocal, piano, guitar (1970-73); David Jackson—saxophone, flute, vocal. *Album:* Pawn Hearts, 1972; H to He Who Am the Only One; H to He, 1970; Still Life, 1976; Godbluff, 1976.

VAN DER KLOOT, FRANK Guitar. Session for Barry Hay.

VAN DER LAARSE, CEES Bass. Session for Jan Akkerman (1977).

VAN DER LINDEN, PIERRE Drums. Original member of Trace, 1974. Session for Jan Akkerman (1974, 77); Jan Akkerman and Kaz Lux (1976).

VAN DER LINDEN, RICK Keyboards, composer, arranger. Founder of Trace, 1974-75, after starting out in the Dutch band Ekseption. Session for Jan Akkerman and Kaz Lux (1976).

VAN DER REE, AD Drums. Member of the Urban Heroes, 1980.

VAN DER VEGT, HELMIG Keyboards. Session for George Kooymans.

VAN DER WAL, KLAASJE Bass. Member of the

Shocking Blue.

VAN DIJK, MICHAEL Vocal. Voice of Alquin, 1975.

VAN DORA, LOU Guitar. Member of the Rex, 1977.

VAN DYKE, EARL Piano. Session for the Temptations (1973).

VAN DYKE, MICHAEL Lyrics, vocal. Half of the Garrison and Van Dyke duet, 1979.

VAN EATON, DEREK Guitar, vocal. Half of the Lon and Derek Van Eaton brother team that had an early release on the Beatles' Apple records. Session for Ringo Starr (1973-74); George Harrison (1974); Nilsson (1976).

VAN EATON, LON Half of the Lon and Derek Van Eaton brother team. Session for Ringo Starr (1973-74, 77); George Harrision (1974); Art Garfunkel; Nilsson (1976).

LON AND DEREK VAN EATON See individual listings. *Album:* Who Do You Out Do (AAM SP 4507).

VAN EIK, JAAP Guitar, vocal. Original member of Trace, 1974-75, after starting in the Dutch band the Moans. Session for Jan Akkerman (1972).

VAN FLEET, LARRY Bass, vocal. Member of the Randle Chowning Band, 1978.

VAN GELDER, STEPHEN Vocal, guitar, keyboards, fiddle, banjo. Member of the Arthur Gee-Whizz Band, 1971-72.

VAN HALEN, ALEX Drums. Member of Van Halen since 1974.

VAN HALEN, EDWARD Guitar. Member of Van Halen since 1974.

VAN HALEN David Lee Roth—vocal; Edward Van Halen—guitar; Alex Van Halen—drums; Michael Anthony—bass. Originally formed in 1974 and called Mammoth, this brother-based hard rock band's success was as much a surprise to them as anyone. *Albums:* Over the Edge (WBR K-3335); Van Halen (WBR 1-3075) 1978; Van Halen II (WBR HS-3312) 1979; Women and Children First (WBR HS-3415) 1980.

VAN HOOF, HARRY Keyboards. Session for Barry Hay.

VAN HOOKE, PETER Drums. Replaced Chilli Charles in Headstone, 1975.

VAN HOY, RAFE Vocal. *Album:* Prisoner of the Sky (MCA 3207) 1980.

VAN IERSEL, JOSEE Vocal. Member of Gruppo Sportivo, 1978.

VAN KAMPEN, HUIB Guitar, saxophone. Member of Ekseption.

VAN LEER, THIJS Keyboards, flute, percussion. Member of Focus. *Album:* Introspection 2 (COL M 34510) 1977.

VAN LEEUWEN, ROBBY Guitar, sitar. Member of the Shocking Blue.

VAN MAARTH, NICK Guitar, production. Member of the Crickets, 1973, the Winters Brothers Band, 1977, and Big Wha-Koo, 1977. Session and production for Tonio K. Session for Danny Douma (1979).

VAN NESS, PATTY Violin. Member of Private Lightning, 1980.

VAN NESS, PAUL Guitar. Member of Private Lightning, 1980.

VAN NIMWEGEN, JOOP Guitar. Member of Finch, 1975.

VAN OSDALE, GARY Viola. Session for Waylon Jennings (1973).

VAN OSTEN, CARSON Bass. Member of Nazz, 1968-69.

VAN PATTEN, DAN Drums. Member of Berlin, 1980.

VAN RONK, DAVE Vocal, guitar. Country-folk singer who began recording in 1963. *Albums:* Just Dave Van Ronk (MER 60908); Songs for Aging Children; Dave Van Ronk (CAD 50044); Dave Van Ronk and the Ragtime Jug Stompers, 1964; No Dirty Names, 1966; Dave Van Ronk Sings Ballads, Blues and Spirituals; Dave Van Ronk Sings the Blues, 1965; Dave Van Ronk and the Hudson Dusters, 1968; Gamblers' Blues; Van Ronk Sings; Black Mountain Blues (FLW 31020) 1959; Blues Project (ELK 7264); In the Tradition (PRS 7800) 1964; Inside Dave Van Ronk (PRS 7716) 1964; Dave Van Ronk (FSY 24710); Dave Van Ronk, Folksinger (PRS 7527); Somebody Else, Not Me (PLO 1065) 1980; Sunday Street (PLO 1036) 1976.

VAN ROSS, LUTHER Vocal. Session for Roy Buchanan (1976).

VAN SCYOC, GARY Bass, trumpet, vocal. Member of Pig Iron. Session for Yoko Ono and John Lennon.

VAN TIEGHAM, DAVID Percussion. Member of the Love of Life Orchestra since 1979.

VAN VEEN, HERMAN Violin. Session for Barry Hay.

VAN VLIET, DON Vocal. Real name of Captain Beefheart, head of the Magic Band since 1968, and soloist. See Captain Beefheart.

VAN ZANDT, STEVE Vocal. Member of the E Street Band, 1978-present. Session for Bruce Springsteen (1975).

VAN ZANDT, TOWNES Guitar, vocal. *Albums:* Delta Momma Blues (TMT 7013) 1978; Flyin' Shoes (TMT 7017) 1978; High, Low and In Between (TMT 7012); Late, Great Townes Van Zandt (TMT 7011); Our Mother, the Mountain (TMT 7015) 1978; Townes Van Zandt (TMT 7014) 1978; Townes Van Zandt (TMT 2-7001).

VAN ZANT, DONNIE Vocal. Member of the 38 Special since 1977.

VAN ZANT, JOHNNY Vocal. Namesake of the Johnny Van Zant Band, 1980.

JOHNNY VAN ZANT BAND Johnny Van Zant—vocal; Robbie Morris—drums; Duncan Clausman

—bass; Erik Lundgren—guitar; Robbie Gay—guitar. *Album:* No More Dirty Deals (POL PDI 6289) 1980.

VAN ZANT, RONNIE Vocal. Born 1/15/49. Voice of Lynyrd Skynyrd, 1973-77. Died 10/20/77.

VAN'T HOF, JASPER Keyboards. Member of the Chris Hinze Combination, 1974.

VANCE, GLEN Keyboards, vocal. Member of Vance or Towers, 1975.

VANCE, KENNY Vocal. Member of Jay and the Americans, 1963-68.

VANCE, RONNIE Drums, vocal. Member of the Jackson Highway.

VANCE OR TOWERS Glen Vance—keyboards, vocal; Michael Towers—guitar, vocal; Dan Protheroe—bass; Jim Saad—drums. *Album:* Vance or Towers (AAM SP 4551) 1975.

VANDA, HARRY Guitar, vocal, producer. Cofounder of the Easybeats, Paintbox, Haffy's Whiskey Sour, the Marcus Hook Roll Band, 1973-74, and Flash and the Pan since 1979. With partner George Young, producer of Steve Wright (1974); John Paul Young (1976); AC/DC (since 1977); Angel City (since 1978); Flash and the Pan (since 1979); Rose Tattoo (1980); and others.

VANDEGILDER, PETER Bass. Member of the Great Society.

VANDENBURG, HANS Guitar, vocal. Member of Gruppo Sportivo, 1978.

VANDER, CHRISTIAN Drums, vocal, piano. Member of Magma.

VANDER, STELLA Vocal. Member of Magma.

VANDERKOOL, DAVID Cello. Session for Waylon Jennings (1973).

VANDERPUIJE, PETE Horns. Session for John "Rabbit" Bundrick (1974).

VANESS, THEO Vocal. *Album:* Theo Vaness (PLD 12173) 1979.

VANGELIS Keyboards, electronics. Real name: Vangelis Papathanassion. *Albums:* Albedo O. 39 (VIC AFLI 5136) 1976; Beaubourg (VIC AFLI 3020) 1978; China (POL 1-6199); Heaven and Hell (VIC AFLI 5110) 1975; Spiral (VIC AFLI 2627) 1977; Short Stories (POL 1-6372) 1979.

VANIAN, DAVID Vocal. Member of the Damned, 1980.

VANILLA FUDGE Carmine Appice—drums; Tim Bogert—bass; Mark Stein—organ; Vincent Martell—guitar. Early name: the Pigeons. Using proven material from the not-too-distant past, Vanilla Fudge rose to stardom as arrangers as well as performers. From the Supremes' "You Keep Me Hangin' On" (1967) to Donovan's "Season of the Witch," the Fudge, from New York, slowed the beats to stifling proportions and unleashed some of the most deafening guitar and organ work in rock. Bogert and Appice formed Cactus after the Vanilla Fudge disbanded in 1969. *Albums:* Near the Beginning (ACO 33-278) 1967; The Beat Goes On, 1968; Renaissance, 1968; Rock 'n' Roll, 1969; Best of the Vanilla Fudge; Vanilla Fudge (ACO 224).

VANNELLI, GINO Vocal. *Albums:* Brother to Brother (AAM 4722); Crazy Life (AAM 4395) 1973; Gist of the Gemini (AAM 4596) 1976; Pauper in Paradise (AAM 4664) 1977; Powerful People (AAM 3630) 1974; Storm at Sunup (AAM 4533) 1975.

VANWARMER, RANDY Vocal. *Albums:* Terraform (BSV BRK 6998) 1980; Warmer (BSV K 6988) 1979.

VAPORS David Fenton—guitar, vocal; Howard Smith—drums; Steve Smith—bass, vocal; Edward Bazalgette—guitar. *Album:* New Clear Days (UAR LT-1049) 1980.

VAPOUR TRAILS John McBurnie—vocal, guitar, keyboards; Andy Dalby—guitar; Phil Curtis—bass. *Album:* Vapour Trails (WBR K-3363) 1980.

VARDY, IAN Vocal, guitar. Member of Prelude, 1974.

VARLEY, JIM Drums. Member of the Sanford-Townsend Band, 1977.

VARLEY, PAUL Drums. Member of Darling, 1979.

VARNELL, AARON Tenor saxophone. Session for Clarence Carter (1967); Wilson Pickett (1968).

VARTY, DOUG Keyboards, vocal. Member of the Sea Dog, 1972.

VASEY, JANE Keyboards. Member of the Downchild, 1979.

VASQUEZ, JAMES Drums. Member of the Band of Thieves, 1976.

VASTA, JOEY Bass, vocal. Member of the Protector 4, 1980.

VAUGHN, HOLLY Vocal. Voice of Stanley Steamer, 1973.

VAUGHN, JIMMY Guitar. Member of the Fabulous Thunderbirds since 1979.

VAUGHN, ROLAND Tenor saxophone. Session for Fleetwood Mac (1969).

VAUGHN, STEVE Guitar. Session for "Jesus Christ Superstar," (1970).

VAUGHT, DAVID Bass. Member of Bugs Tomorrow, 1980.

VEE, BOBBY Vocal. Real name: Robert Velline. Popular teenage crooner of the early 1960s, who sang "Take Good Care of My Baby," 1961, and "Run to Him," 1961. *Albums:* Bobby Vee's Golden Greats, Vol. I (LIB); Bobby Vee's Golden Greats (UAR LM 1008); Bobby Vee's Golden Greats, Vol. II (LIB 7464).

VEE, JOHN Bass. Member of the Meteors, 1980.

VEEN, GERRIT Bass. Member of Herman Brood and His Wild Romance since 1979.

VEGA, ALAN Vocal. Half of the electronic duet, Suicide, 1980.

VEGA, CARLOS Drums, percussion. Member of Caldera, 1976-78.

VEGA, ROBERT Bass. Member of the Giants, 1978.

VEGAS, LOLLY Vocal, guitar. With brother Pat, he co-founded Redbone, 1970-77.

VEGAS, PAT With brother Lolly, he co-founded Redbone, 1970-77. Session for Danny Spanos (1980).

VEITCH, PETER Member of Cafe Jacques since 1977.

VELASCO, CHRIS Guitar, vocal. Member of Berlin, 1980.

VELDKAMP, BERT Bass, vocal. Member of Kayak, 1975-76.

VELEZ, MARTHA Vocal. *Albums:* American Heartbeat (SIR 6040) 1977; Matinee Weepers (SIR 7409); Hypnotized (POL 5034) 1972.

VELLINE, ROBERT Real name of Bobby Vee.

VELVET UNDERGROUND Lou Reed—guitar, vocal; John Cale—viola, keyboards, bass (1967-69); Nico—vocal (1967); Sterling Morrison—guitar, bass (1967-70); Maureen Tucker—drums, percussion (1967-70); Doug Yule—keyboards, bass, drums, guitar, vocal (1970); Bill Yule—drums (1970). Early name: the Falling Spikes. In the 1960s, Andy Warhol's name appeared in every major newspaper personality and/or art column. Naturally, when he decided to expand into the music world, it was inevitable that the vehicle he chose, the Velvet Underground, would receive large amounts of publicity. The group featured singer/writer Reed, who had studied piano since the age of five; Cale, a child prodigy in his native England where he was telecast performing his own musical compositions on the BBC at the age of eight; Morrison, a classical trumpeter since the age of ten; and female drummer, Tucker, a veteran of several years experience. Their debut album (1967) displayed a Warhol cover design and another Warhol discovery, vocalist Nico. Their music was the total antithesis of the current trends, including tales of drug addiction, sado-masochism, and bizarre tales of fantasy. Nico left after the first album for a solo career. By 1969, the group had developed musically and lyrically, fully cultivating their unnerving, eerie presence. Cale officially left in 1970, and shortly thereafter head writer Reed went out on his own. The Yule brothers attempted to hold the group together, but the dynamism had passed with the stars who had gone solo. *Albums:* The Velvet Underground and Nico (VRV V6 5008) 1967; White Light/White Heat (VRV V6 5046) 1968; The Velvet Underground (MGM 4617) 1969; Loaded (CTL 9034) 1970; 1969 Velvet Underground Live (MER SRM 2-7504); Velvet Underground Live (CTL 9600) 1970.

VENNICK, JAN Reeds. Member of Spin, 1976. Session for Barry Hay.

VENNIS, PETER Vocal, bass, synthesizer. Member of Freedom, 1971.

VENT, JOANNE Vocal, percussion. Member of White Cloud, 1972.

VENTURA, RICK Guitar. Member of the Riot, 1980.

VENTURES Bob Bogle—bass; Nokie Edwards—guitar; Don Wilson—guitar; Howie Johnson—drums (1960-63); Jerry McGee—guitar; Mel Taylor—drums (1963-71); John Durrill—keyboards. Early name: the Marksmen. The Ventures are unique in rock. Since their first hit in 1960, "Walk Don't Run," they have maintained exactly the same group sound, mainly recording instrumental versions of others' hit songs. *Albums:* Great Motion Picture Themes (UAR); Joy (UAR 5575); Let's Go (LIB 8024); One Million Dollar Weekend (LIB 8054); Ventures (UAR VXS 80) 1971; Ventures A Go-Go (LIB 8037); Ventures Knock Me Out (LIB 8033); Ventures on Stage (LIB 8035); Golden Greats by the Ventures (LIB 8053); Ventures Play Telstar—Lonely Bull (LIB 8019); 10th Aniversary Album (LIB 35000); Walk—Don't Run (LIB 8003) 1960; Another Smash (LIB 8006); Country Classics (LIB 8023); Jim Croce Song Book (UAR); Dance (LIB 8010); Hawaii Five-0 (LIB 8061); Only Hits (UAR LA147 G2); Play Guitar (LIB 17501); Play Guitar, Vol. II (LIB 17502); Play Guitar, Vol. III (LIB 17503); Play Guitar, Vol. VII (LIB 17504); Surfing (LIB 8022); Ventures in Space (LIB 8027); Rock and Roll Forever (UAR UAS 5649) 1972; New Ventures (UAR VA LA 586 G) 1975.

VENTURINI, PAUL Organ. Member of the Soul Survivors, 1966-68.

VENUS AND THE RAZOR BLADES Steven T.—vocal, guitar; Dyan Diamond—vocal, guitar; Danielle Faye—bass; Nicky Beat—drums; Vicki Razor Blade—vocal; Roni Lee—guitar; Kyle Raven—drums (1977). Kim Fowley directed and produced this band from Los Angeles. *Album:* Songs from the Sunshine Jungle (VSA 7004) 1977.

VERDISCO, DARRELL Drums, vocal. Replaced Billy Mintz in Lowry Hamner and the Cryers, 1979.

VERES, MARISKA Vocal. Voice of the Shocking Blue.

VERITY, JOHN Guitar, vocal. Replaced Russ Ballard in Argent, 1975. Member of Phoenix since 1976. Session for Matthew Fisher (1980).

VERLAINE, TOM Vocal, guitar, keyboards. Founder of Television, 1977-78, before his solo departure. *Album:* Tom Verlaine (ELK 6E 216) 1979.

VERLIN, RON Bass. Member of the Shooting Star, 1979.

VERNAZZA, JOHNNY Guitar, slide guitar. Member of the Elvin Bishop Band, 1974-76. Session for the Marshall Tucker Band (1974); Elvin Bishop (1978).

VERNE, ROBERT Guitar, vocal. Member of the

Candle, 1972.

VERNIERI, LARRY Vocal. Member of Joey Dee and the Starlighters.

VERNO, BUZZ Bass. Session for Sylvain Sylvain (1979).

VERNON, EDWARD Vocal. Member of the Dream, 1970.

VERNON, MIKE Vocal, percussion, producer. Probably the single most important producer responsible for bringing British blues stars of the 1960s and 1970s to the public's attention. He released a solo album in the early 1970s with some of the stars he made as session men. Member of the Olympic Runners, 1974-79, which he also produced. Production and session for Chicken Shack; Ten Years After (1967); Savoy Brown (1967-69); Fleetwood Mac (1968-69); John Mayall (1967-69); Christine McVie (1969); and Duster Bennett (1968-69). Session for Freddie King (1974-75); Lightnin' Slim (1978); Martha Velez. *Album:* Moment of Madness (SIR).

VERNON, TERRY Vocal. Session for Robert Gordon (1979).

VERNON, VIE Vocal. Wife of Mike Vernon, heard on his "Moment of Madness" album. Session for Freddie King (1974).

VERNON-KELL, PETER Piano, producer. Production and session for Peter Green (1980).

VERRUCHI, DICK Drums, percussion. Member of Buckacre, 1976.

VESTINE, HENRY Guitar. Original member of Canned Heat, 1965-69 and 1972-73. Got his start playing with Frank Zappa, prior to the Mothers of Invention.

VIBRATORS Knox—guitar, keyboards, vocal; John Ellis—guitar, vocal; Pat Collier—bass, vocal; Eddie—drums. *Album:* Pure Mania, 1977.

VICARI, FRANK Horns, reeds. Session for Leslie West (1975-76).

VICIOUS, SID Bass, vocal. Real name: John Ritchie. Member of the Sex Pistols, 1977. Arrested for murder, 1978. Died, 1979.

VICKERS, MIKE Guitar, saxophone, flute. Born 4/18/41. Member of Manfred Mann.

VICTOR, JEFF Keyboards, vocal. Member of the Sussman Lawrence Band, 1980.

VIDAL, JUAN Keyboards. Member of Barrabas.

VIDAS, PAT Bass, vocal. Member of Flight since 1976.

VIERTELL, JACK Slide guitar. Session for the Pointer Sisters (1974).

VIG, TOMMY Percussion. Session for Dr. John (1975); Art Garfunkel (1978); Rod Stewart (1978); the Marc Tanner Band (1979). *Album:* Encounter with Time (DCO 780).

VIGRASS, PAUL Vocal. Half of the Vigrass and Osborne team. Session for Magnet (1979).

VIGRASS AND OSBORNE Paul Vigrass—vocal; Gary Osborne—vocal. Lyrical folk duet from England that missed the mark despite the session work of Caleb Quaye, Chris Spedding, and others. *Albums:* Queues (UNI) 1972; Steppin' Out (UNI).

VIKTOR KONCEPT Scott Raffel—reeds, percussion; Kim Kleinschmidt—drums, percussion; Douglas P. Drake—reeds, piano, strings, percussion; Payles Boisen—guitar, saxophone, piano; Valerie Jean Fischer—vocal. *Album:* Viktor Koncept (RRR 009) 1979.

VILATO, ORESTEL Percussion. Session for Santana (1980).

VILICICH, JERRY Bass, vocal. Member of the Volunteers, 1976.

VILLALOBOS, BOBBY Guitar. Member of the Puzzle.

VILLARREAL, FRANK Alto saxophone. Session for Ry Cooder (1977).

VILLEGAS, BOBBY Bass. Member of Please, 1976.

VINCENT, GENE Vocal. Rocker of the 1950s, a contemporary of Elvis, backed by Rory Storme and the Hurricanes before forming Gene Vincent and his Hub Caps. Died 10/12/71.

GENE VINCENT AND HIS HUB CAPS Gene Vincent—guitar, vocal; Cliff Gallup—guitar; Jack Neal—bass; Willie Williams—guitar; Be-Bop Harrell—drums. *Albums:* Bop That Just Won't Stop (1956) (CAP SM 11826) 1974; Gene Vincent's Greatest (CAP SM-380); Forever (RLR 022) 1980.

VINCENT, JAMES Vocal. *Album:* Waiting for the Rain (CBO Z 34899) 1978.

VINCENT, "ROCKIN" REGGIE Vocal, guitar. Worked with Frijid Pink on "All Pink Inside," and guested on Alice Cooper's "School's Out," 1972.

VINCI, FRANKIE Keyboards, vocal. Member of Fotomaker, 1978-79.

VINCI, JOHN Vocal. Voice of the Illusions, and Network, 1977.

VINNEGAR, LEROY Acoustic bass. Session for the Doors (1968). *Albums:* Good Gravy (CTP 7292); Leroy Walks (CTP 7003); Leroy Again (CTP 7608); Shelly Manne, and His Friends (CTP 3525); Sonny Rollins and the Contemporary Leaders (CTP 7564); The Kid (PBR 6) 1974.

VINSEY, TONY Violin. Member of Kenny and the Kasuals.

VINTON, BOBBY Vocal. Pop vocalist who sang "Roses Are Red," 1962. *Albums:* Ev'ry Day of My Life (EPC KE 31286); Golden Decade of Love (EPC KEG 33468) Heart of Hearts (ABC D 891); Love Album (EPC EG 30431); Melodies of Love (ABC D 851); All-Time Greatest Hits (EPC PEG 31487) 1972; Autumn Memories (EPC JE 35605) 1978; Sealed with a Kiss (EPC E 31642) 1972; Spring Sensations (EPC JE 35998) 1979; Summer Serenade (EPC JE 35999) 1979; To All the Girls (TAP 100); Bobby Vinton's Greatest Hits (EPC 26098); Bobby Vinton's

Greatest Hits (EPC BG 33767); Vinton's Greatest Hits of Love (EPC 26517); Vinton's Greatest Hits of Love (EPC BG 33767); Serenade of Love (ABC D 957) 1976; Encore (TSY 1000) 1979; The Name Is Love (ABC 981) 1977; More of Bobby Vinton's Greatest Hits (EPC 2187); Blue Velvet (EPC 24068); Tell Me Why (EPC 24113); Drive In Movie Time (EPC 24170); Live at the Copa (EPC 24203); Songs for Lonely Nights (EPC 24154); Country Boy (EPC 24188); Roses Are Red (EPC 24020); There! I've Said It (EPC 24081); Mr. Lonely (EPC 24136); Satin Pillows (EPC 24182); With Love (EPC 32921) 1974.

VIOLETTI, GARY Bass, vocal. Member of the Euphonius Wall, 1973.

VIOLINSKI Mike De Albuquerque—vocal, guitar; Paul Mann—vocal, bass; Mik Kaminsky—violin; John Marcangelo—keyboards; John Hodgson—drums, percussion. *Album:* No Cause for Alarm (JET JZ 36133) 1979.

VIRTANEN, HEIKKA Bass. Member of Tasavallan Presidenti, 1974.

VISAGE Steve Strange; Midge Ure—vocal, guitar, synthesizer; Billy Currie—violin, keyboards; John McGeoch—guitar, saxophone, keyboards; Rusty Egan; Dave Formula—keyboards. *Album:* Visage (POL 1-6304).

VISCEGLIA, MICHAEL Bass. Member of the Spy, 1980.

VISCONTI, TONY Bass, guitar, engineer, producer. Member of Omaha Sheriff, 1977. Production, engineering, and session for Rick Wakeman (1979); David Bowie. Session for Joe Cocker (1968).

VISLOCKY, JOHN Vocal. Member of the Spy, 1980.

VITALE, JOE Drums, percussion, flute, keyboards, vocal. Part of Joe Walsh's backup band since 1972 and author of one solo album. Member of the Stills-Young Band, 1976. Session for Rick Derringer (1973); Steve Stills (1976, 79); Bill Wyman (1976); Jay Ferguson (1976, 79); Crosby, Stills and Nash (1977); the Henry Paul Band (1980); Peter Frampton (1979); Boz Scaggs (1980). *Album:* Roller Coaster (ATC) 1975.

VITO, RICK Guitar. Played with John Mayall, 1972. Session for Bobby Whitlock; John Mayall (1977, 79).

VITOUS, MIROSLAV Bass. Member of Weather Report, 1971-75. *Albums:* First Meeting (ECM I 1145) 1980; Miroslav (ARI 1040) 1977; Mountain in the Clouds (ATC 1622) 1972; Terje Rypdal-Miroslav Vitous-Jack De Johnette (ECM I 1125) 1979; Magical Shepherd (WBR 2925) 1976.

VITT, BILL Drums. Session for Jerry Garcia and Howard Wales (1972); Merle Saunders (1973).

VIVABEAT Alec Murphy—guitar; Consuelo De Silva—synthesizer; Doug Orilio—drums; Terrance Robay—vocal; Marina Del Ray—keyboards; Mike Muhlfriedel—bass. *Album:* Party in the War Zone (CSM 1-3102) 1980.

VOGUES Recorded "You're the One," 1965. *Albums:* Vogues' Greatest Hits (RPS 6371); Vogues' Greatest Hits (SSS 34).

VOICE, BOB Drums. Member of the Paul Brett Sage.

VOIGHT, JIM Drums. Member of the Peanut Butter Conspiracy, 1967-68.

VOLK, PHILLIP Bass. Replaced Mike Holiday in Paul Revere and the Raiders.

VOLLMER, SREDNI Harmonica. Session for Leslie West (1975-76); Scarlet Rivera (1978).

VOLMAN, MARK Guitar, vocal. Original member of the Turtles, 1965-69. Member of the Mothers of Invention, 1971, and Flo, of Flo and Eddie, since 1975. Session for Steve Stills (1976).

VOLTURO, JOHN Keyboards, vocal. Member of the U.S. Radio Band, 1976.

VOLUNTEERS Wayne Berry—guitar, vocal; Jerry Vilicich—bass, vocal; George Clinton—vocal, keyboards; Joey Kluchar—drums. *Album:* Volunteers, 1976.

VON ARB, FERNANDO Guitar, vocal. Member of Krokus since 1980.

VON ROHR, CHRIS Bass, vocal. Member of Krokus since 1980.

VON SCHMIDT, ERIC Vocal. Folk-blues singer of the early 1960s. *Albums:* Folk Blues, 1964; Eric Von Schmidt Sings, 1965; Rolf Cahn and Eric Von Schmidt (FLW 2417) 1967; Folk Blues of Eric Von Schmidt (PRS 7717); Cruel Family (PHL 1052) 1977.

VONK, HENRY Vocal. Voice of the Chris Hinze Combination, 1974.

VOORMAN, KLAUS Bass. Replaced Jack Bruce in Manfred Mann, 1966. Member of the Plastic Ono Band, 1969-74. Session for Long John Baldry (1972); Nicky Hopkins (1974-75); Splinter (1974-75); the Beatles; Donovan (1976); Art Garfunkel; Keith Moon (1975); Nilsson (1971-76); Lou Reed (1972); Bangla Desh (1971); Peter Frampton (1972); George Harrison (1972-75); B. B. King (1971); John Lennon (1974); Jerry Lee Lewis (1973); Ringo Starr (1971, 73-74); Howlin' Wolf (1972); Gary Wright (1970-71); Carly Simon (1972, 74); Hoyt Axton (1976).

VORHAUS, DAVID Synthesizer. Member of M, 1980.

VOSBURGH, DONNY Vocal. Original member of Thee Image, 1975. Session for Alice Cooper (1976).

VOUDOURIS, ROGER Guitar, vocal. Soloist, and part of the Voudouris and Kahne duet. *Albums:* Guy Like Me (WBR K 3401) 1980; Radio Dream (WBR K 3290) 1979; Roger Voudouris (WBR K 3154) 1980.

VOUDOURIS AND KAHNE Roger Voudouris—guitar, vocal; David Kahne—keyboards, vocal. *Albums:* Street Player (CAP SM 11959); There's a Secret Goin' On (CAP SM 11958).

VOYAGE Mark Chantereau—vocal, keyboards, percussion; Pierre-Alain Dahan—vocal, drums, percussion; Slim Pezin—vocal, guitar, percussion. *Albums:* Fly Away (MAR 2225); Night at Studio (CAS 2-7161); Voyage (MAR 2213); Sirocco (MAR 2-7161) 1980.

VOYAGER Paul French—vocal, keyboards, harmonica; Chris Hook—bass; Paul Hirsch—vocal, keyboards, guitar; John Marter—drums, percussion. *Albums:* Act of Love (VIC AFLI 3632) 1980; Halfway Hotel (ELK 6E-208) 1979.

WACHTEL, ROBERT "WADDY" Guitar, producer. Member of the Dinettes, 1976, and Ronin, 1980. Production and session for Warren Zevon (1979). Session for Splinter (1975); James Taylor (1976); Maria Muldaur; J. D. Souther; Jackson Browne; Rod Stewart; Karla Bonoff (1977); Bryan Ferry (1978); Randy Newman (1979); Adam Mitchell (1979); Richie Furay (1979); Bob Weir (1978).

WACKFORD, MIKE Drums. Member of Starry Eyed and Laughing, 1975.

WADDELL, BRUCE Bass. Member of the Hill, 1975.

WADDINGTON, JOHN Guitar. Member of the Pop Group, 1980.

WADE, BILL Drums, percussion. Member of Moxy, 1976-77.

WADE, BRETT Bass, flute, vocal. Replaced Mark Tulin in the Electric Prunes, 1967.

WADE, PETE Guitar. Session for Leon Russell (1973).

WADE, ROGER Saxophone. Session for the Keef Hartley Band (1971).

WADENIUS, GEORGE Guitar. Replaced Steve Katz in the re-formed Blood, Sweat and Tears. Session for Grace Slick (1980).

WADHAMS, WADS Keyboards. Member of the Fifth Estate, 1967.

WADSWORTH, DEREK Trombone. Member of the Candlestick Brass, 1977. Session for Savoy Brown (1969); the Keef Hartley Band (1971).

WAGENETT, HAL Guitar, vocal. Original member of It's a Beautiful Day, 1969-71.

WAGNER, BO Percussion. Member of Starbuck, 1977-78.

WAGNER, RICHARD Guitar, vocal. Original member of Ursa Major, 1972, member of the Alice Cooper Show, 1977. Production and session for Mark Farner (1977). Session for Alice Cooper (1972-76); Lou Reed (1974). *Album:* Richard Wagner (ATC 19172) 1978.

WAGNER, RON Drums. Member of the Auracle, 1978-79.

WAGNER, STEVE Drums. Member of the Wax, 1980.

WAGON, CHUCK Keyboards, guitar, saxophone, harmonica, percussion, vocal. Member of the Dickies since 1978.

WAILERS Ron Gardner—keyboards, vocal; Richard Dagnel; Kent Morrill; Mike Burk; Buck Ormsby—bass, saxophone, vocal. Pacific Northwest rockers of the 1960s.

WAILERS See Bob Marley and the Wailers.

WAINWRIGHT, BOB Bass. Member of the Lonely Boys, 1979.

WAINWRIGHT, LOUDON, III Guitar, vocal, banjo. *Albums:* Album 2 (ATC 8291) 1971; Album 3 (COL C-31462) 1972; Attempted Mustache (COL C-32710) 1973; T-Shirt (ARI 4063) 1976; Unrequited (COL PC-33369) 1975; Loudon Wainwright, III (ATC 8260) 1970; A Live One (RDR 3050) 1979.

WAINWRIGHT, MIKE Vocal, guitar. Member of the Twisters, 1980.

WAITE, JOHN Vocal, bass. Member of the Babys since 1976.

WAITROWSKI, ERNST Keyboards, vocal. Member of Citizen, 1980.

WAITS, TOM Vocal, piano, guitar. Gravelly voiced writer/performer from New York. *Albums:* Blue Valentine (ASY 6E-162) 1978; Closing Time (ASY 5061); Foreign Affairs (FSY 7E-1117) 1977; Heart of Saturday Night (ASY 7E-1015) 1974; Heartattack and Vine (ASY 6E-295) 1980; Nighthawks at the Diner (ASY 7E 2008) 1975; Small Change (ASY 7E 1078).

WAITZMAN, DANIEL Flute. Session for Jan Akkerman (1973).

WAKELING, DAVE Member of the English Beat, 1980.

WAKEMAN, RICK Keyboards. Born 5/18/49. Member of the Strawbs, 1970-71, and sometime member of Yes, 1972-73, 77-79. He made his mark as author of musical interpretations of classical stories, as the titles of his albums indicate, complete with orchestral and choral background. Session for Colin Scot (1971); Elton John (1971); Lou Reed (1972); Black Sabbath (1974). *Albums:* Journey to the Center of the Earth (AAM 3621) 1974; Myths and Legends of King Arthur (AAM 4515) 1975; No Earthly Connection (AAM 4583) 1976; Rhapsodies (AAM 6501) 1979; Six Wives of Henry VIII (AAM 4361) 1972; Rick Wakeman's Criminal Record (AAM 4660) 1977; White Rock (AAM 4614) 1977.

WALD, ALLEN Guitar, pedal steel guitar, vocal. Member of Sundance, 1976.

WALD, WILLY Drums. Member of Schloss, 1975.

WALDBAUER, LEON EDWARDS Guitar, harmonica, vocal. Member of the Skyboys, 1979-present.

WALDEN, NARADA MICHAEL Drums, vocal. Session for Tommy Bolin (1975); Jaco Pastorius (1976); Jeff Beck (1976); Roy Buchanan (1977);

Robert Fripp (1979); Santana (1979); Ray Gomez (1980). *Albums:* Awakening (ATC 19222) 1979; Dance of Life (ATC 19259) 1979; Garden of Love Light (ATC 18199) 1976; I Cry, I Smile (ATC 19141) 1977; Victory (ATC 19279) 1980.

WALDEN, SNUFFY Guitar, vocal. Founder and featured artist of Stray Dog, 1973-74. Session for John "Rabbit" Bundrick (1974); Free (1973); Brooklyn Dreams (1977).

WALDMAN, WENDY Vocal, guitar. Session for Jelly (1977). *Albums:* Gypsy Symphony (WBR 2792) 1974; Love Has Got Me (WBR B-2735); Main Refrain (WBR B 1974) 1976; Strange Company (WBR K 3178); Wendy Waldman (WBR B 2859).

WALDO, JIMMY Keyboards, vocal. Member of New England, 1980.

WALES, HOWARD Keyboards. Co-author of Jerry Garcia's solo debut in 1972. Session for Harvey Mandel. *Album:* Hooteroll (DGS 30859) 1972.

WALK, FRED Guitar, sitar. Member of Linn County, 1968-69. Session for Stephen Miller.

WALKER, AARON Real name of T-Bone Walker.

WALKER, CATO, III Alto saxophone. Session for B. B. King (1975).

WALKER, DAVE Keyboards, vocal. Member of Alexis, 1977.

WALKER, DAVE Vocal. Replaced Chris Youlden in Savoy Brown, 1971-72. In 1973, he joined Fleetwood Mac for one album, "Penguin."

WALKER, DENNIS Bass. Session for Phillip Walker (1977).

WALKER, DON Keyboards. Member of the Cold Chisel, 1979.

WALKER, DUANE C. Percussion, vocal. Member of the Sail.

WALKER, GARY Vocal. Member of Cottonwood South, 1974.

WALKER, GREG Vocal. Member of Santana, 1976-78. Session for Santana (1979).

WALKER, GREG Bass, vocal. Member of Blackfoot, 1976. Session for Lynyrd Skynyrd (1977).

WALKER, GREG Guitar, vocal. Member of Duke Jupiter since 1978.

WALKER, HERBIE Guitar. Member of Captain Sky's Band, 1980.

WALKER, JERRY JEFF Guitar, vocal. Born 3/16/42. Primarily a soloist, he was a member of Circus Maximus for one album, 1967, before returning to his country-folk style, as shown in his hit, "Mr. Bojangles" (1968). *Albums:* Contrary to Ordinary (MCA 3041); It's a Good Night for Singin' (MCA 2203) 1976; Jerry Jeff (ELK 6E 163) 1978; Man Must Carry On (MCA 2-8013); Ridin' High (MCA 2156) 1975; Too Old to Change (ELK 6E 239); Viva Terlingua (MCA 382); Jerry Jeff Walker (MCA 510) 1972; Walker's Collectibles (MCA 2355) 1974; Mr. Bojangles, 1978; Driftin' Way of Life (VAN 6521) 1969.

WALKER, JIMMY Vocal. Replaced Bill Medley in the Righteous Brothers, 1968, before the team disbanded that same year.

WALKER, JOHN Vocal, guitar. Member of Starbuck, 1978.

WALKER, JOHNNY "BIG MOOSE" Organ. Member of the Son Seals Blues Band (1973).

WALKER, LES Vocal. Member of Tiger, 1976.

WALKER, NELCY Vocal. Session for the Mothers of Invention (1968).

WALKER, PHILLIP Guitar, vocal. *Album:* Someday You'll Have These Blues (ALG 4715) 1977.

WALKER, ROB Guitar. Member of Stillwater, 1977.

WALKER, SCOTT Vocal. Recording name for Scott Engel. See the Walker Brothers. *Albums:* A Loner, 1968; Scott, Vol. II, 1968.

WALKER, T-BONE Guitar, vocal, piano. Texas-born Walker began recording the blues in 1929. Besides being a major influence in the development of blues artists like B. B. King, he is the co-author of the blues classic, "Stormy Monday." *Albums:* Singing the Blues; T-Bone Blues; Stormy Monday Blues; Funky Town; Fly Walker Airlines; Good Feelin'; The Truth (BRU 754126); T-Bone Walker (BLN LWB 533); I Want a Little Girl (DEL 633) 1973.

WALKER, TERRY Keyboards, viola, guitar, bass. Member of the Bizarros, 1979.

WALKER BROTHERS Gary Leeds—drums; Scott Engel—bass, vocal; John Maus—guitar, vocal. Not really brothers, these three Americans were a smash in England before disbanding in 1967 for their individual careers. *Albums:* Introducing the Walker Brothers, 1966; Nite Flights (GTO 033).

WALKLEY, PAUL Drums. Member of the Blue Jug, 1975.

WALKOE, TIM Bass, vocal. Member of the Eddie Boy Band, 1975.

WALL, ALWYN Guitar, vocal. Namesake of the Alwyn Wall Band, 1977.

ALWYN WALL BAND Alwyn Wall—guitar, vocal; Norman Barratt—guitar, vocal; Phil Holmes—keyboards, vocal; Tony Hudson—bass; Nick Brotherwood—drums. *Album:* The Prize (MYR MSB 6596) 1977.

WALL, DENNIS Bass. Session for Donovan (1973).

WALL OF VOODOO Stanard Ridgway—vocal, organ; Marc Moreland—guitar; Chas Gray—synthesizer; Bruce Moreland—bass, piano; Joe Nanini—percussion. *Album:* Wall of Voodoo (INX 4041) 1980.

WALLACE, BILL Guitar, vocal. Replaced Kurt Winter in the Guess Who, before becoming a member of the Shakers.

WALLACE, GLENN Horns, vocal. Member of the Platinum Hook since 1979.

WALLACE, IAN Drums. Replaced Andy McCulloch in King Crimson, 1972. Joined Snape later that same year. Session for Alvin Lee (1973-75); Steve Marriott (1976); Bob Dylan (1978-79); Tears (1979).

WALLACE, JOHN Bass, vocal. Member of Harry Chapin's backup group.

WALLE, RUNE Guitar, sitar, banjo, vocal. Joined the Ozark Mountain Daredevils, 1977-78. Session for the Ozark Mountain Daredevils (1980).

WALLER, DAVID Drums. Member of the Jam, 1977.

WALLER, GORDON Vocal. Half of the Peter and Gordon team, 1964-67. Less successful as a soloist, 1967.

WALLER, GRAHAM Piano. Session for Blodwyn Pig (1969).

WALLER, JERRY Keyboards. Session for Colin Winski (1980).

WALLER, MICK Drums, percussion. Began in Steam Packet, 1965. Original member of the Jeff Beck Group, 1968, and member of Pilot, 1972. Session for Rod Stewart (1970-76); Long John Baldry (1971-72); Andy Bown (1972).

WALLER, MICKEY Guitar. Member of the Heavy Metal Kids, 1974.

WALLER, STEVE Guitar, vocal. Replaced Dave Flett in Manfred Mann, 1979. Session for Manfred Mann (1980).

WALLER, WALLY Bass, guitar, vocal. Member of the Pretty Things.

WALLEY, DENNIS Slide guitar, vocal. Session for Jimmy Carl Black and Bunk Gardner (1971); Frank Zappa (1975-79).

WALLIS, BRIAN Bass, vocal. Member of the Heroes, 1980.

WALLIS, LARRY Guitar. Member of Motorhead, 1978.

WALLS See Scott Wilk and the Walls.

WALLY Vocal, percussion. Member of Flash Cadillac.

WALLY Pete Kosker—guitar, vocal, bass; Paul Gerret—keyboards, vocal; Paul Middleton—steel guitar, bass; Roger Narraway—drums; Pete Sage—violin, bass, mandolin; Roy Webber—vocal, guitar. *Album:* Wally (ATC) 1974.

WALMSLEY, STEVE Bass. Member of the Lemon Pipers, 1968.

WALMSLEY, TONY Guitar. Session for Shawn Phillips (1973).

WALRECHT, PETER Drums. Member of Herman Brood and His Wild Romance since 1979.

WALSH, DON Guitar, harmonica. Member of the Downchild, 1979.

WALSH, ED Synthesizer. Session for Grace Slick (1980); John Lennon (1980).

WALSH, JAMES Vocal, keyboards, percussion. Member of Gypsy, 1971-73.

WALSH, JOE Guitar, vocal. An original member of the James Gang, 1969-71. His solo career, with Joe Vitale and Kenny Passarelli, mellowed from the Gang's hard-rock reputation into his unique progressive style, which led to his union with the Eagles, 1976-present. Session for B. B. King (1970-72); Rick Derringer (1973); Ray Manzarek; Keith Moon (1975); Rod Stewart (1976); Bill Wyman (1976); Jay Ferguson (1976-77, 79-80); Randy Newman (1977); Emerson, Lake and Palmer (1977); Andy Gibb (1977); Warren Zevon (1980). *Albums:* Best of Joe Walsh (MCA AA-1083); But Seriously Folks (ASY 6E 141) 1978; Smoker You Drink, the Player You Get (MCA X 50140) 1973; So What (MCA D 50171) 1974; You Can't Argue with a Sick Mind (MCA D 932) 1976; Barnstorm (DHL 50130) 1972.

WALSH, JOHN Member of Jay and the Techniques.

WALSH, MARTY Guitar. Session for J. Michael Reed (1979).

WALSH, MICK Guitar. Member of the Fludd, 1971.

WALSH, RALPH Guitar. Member of the Paul Butterfield Blues Band, 1971.

WALSH, RICK Vocal. Member of the Downchild, 1979.

WALSH, STEVE Keyboards. Born 6/15/51. Original member of Kansas since 1970. *Album:* Schemer-Dreamer (KSH JZ-36320) 1980.

WALSHAW, DAVID Drums, percussion. Session for Richard Betts (1974); Elvin Bishop (1974).

WALTERS, BILL Drums, vocal. Member of the Moberlys, 1979.

WALTERS, BOB Trumpet. Session for the Climax Blues Band (1974).

WALTERS, JOHN Trumpet. Member of the Alan Price Set, 1965-68.

WALTZ, CHARLES Vocal, violin, keyboards. Member of Shooting Star, 1979.

WAMMACK, TRAVIS Guitar, vocal. *Album:* Travis Wammack (UAR FAS 1801) 1972.

WANKER, DIM Guitar. Member of the F-Word, 1978.

WAR Eric Burdon—vocal (1970); Harold Brown—drums, percussion; Dee Allen—conga, percussion, vocal; B. B. Dickerson—bass, vocal, percussion; Howard Scott—guitar, vocal, percussion; Lee Oskar—harmonica, percussion, vocal; Charles Miller—flute, saxophone; Lonnie Jordon—keyboards, percussion. Originally called Night Shift. After the demise of the Animals, Eric Burdon resurfaced in the early 1970s with an all-black band (except for Danish-born Oskar), War. They released two albums before Burdon slipped from sight again. War, however, continued without him, riding the first wave of the disco-funk fad of the 1970s. *Albums:* All Day Music (UAR LO 5546); Deliver the Word (UAR LO 128) 1973; Galaxy (MCA 3030); Greatest Hits (UAR LT 648); Music Band (MCA 3085); Music Band 2 (MCA 3193); Platinum Jazz (BLN LWB 193) 1972; Why Can't We Be Friends (UAR LW-441) 1975; World Is a

Ghetto (UAR LO 5652) 1972; Youngblood (UAR LO 904); Eric Burdon Declares War (MGM 4663); Black Man's Burdon (MGM 4710-2); Love Is All Around (ABC 988).

WARD, ANDY Drums, percussion. Original member of the Camel, 1975-77.

WARD, BILL Drums. Born 5/5/48. Original member of Black Sabbath since 1970.

WARD, CLIFFORD Vocal. Session for Bronco.

WARD, JACKIE Vocal. Session for Navasota (1972); Gordon Lightfoot (1975).

WARD, JOHN Bass. Original member of Elephant's Memory.

WARD, LAUREL Vocal. Session for Alice Cooper (1976).

WARD, PETER Played with John Mayall, 1962.

WARD, ROBERT Guitar. Session for the Temptations (1973).

WARE, ALLEN Trumpet. Member of Chase, 1971-73.

WARE, JOHN Drums. Member of Michael Nesmith's First National Band. Session for Free Creek (1973); Jonathan Edwards (1976-77); Kaleidoscope (1977); Michael Nesmith (1978-79).

WARE, MARTIN Synthesizer, vocal. Member of the Human League, 1980.

WARE, OTHO Bass. Member of the Thunderhead, 1976.

WARFORD, SUSAN Vocal. Session for Johnny Winter (1980).

WARLEIGH, RAY Flute. Started in Blues Incorporated. Session for John Mayall's Bluesbreakers (1967); the Keef Hartley Band (1969); Roy Harper (1975); Long John Baldry (1979); Bert Jansch; John Renbourn; Annette Peacock (1979).

WARLOCKS Early name for the Falling Spikes, before changing to the Velvet Underground. Also an early name for the Grateful Dead.

WARNER, ALLAN Guitar. Member of the Foundations, 1968.

WARNER, FLORENCE Vocal. Session for Tom Rapp (1972); Tim Weisberg and Dan Fogelberg (1978).

WARNER, MARK Guitar. Session for Cat Stevens (1975).

WARNER, MICHAEL Guitar, vocal. Member of the Capital City Rockets, 1973.

WARNES, JENNIFER Vocal. Session for Commander Cody (1978); Adam Mitchell (1979). *Albums:* Shot Through the Heart (ARI 4217) 1979; Jennifer Warnes (ARI 4062) 1976.

WAROFF, PAUL Vocal, guitar. *Album:* California Son (CSB 7235) 1980.

WARONKER, LENNY Producer. Produced Gordon Lightfoot; Ry Cooder (1970-74); James Taylor (1976); Randy Newman (1979); Code Blue (1980); and others.

WARREN, BILLY Drums. Member of Junior Wells' Chicago Blues Band.

WARREN, DARRYL Percussion. Member of the Tufana-Giammarese Band, 1973-77.

WARREN, JAMES Bass, vocal. Member of the Korgis since 1979.

WARREN, LEVI Drums. Session for Junior Wells.

WARREN, PAUL Guitar, vocal. Member of Rare Earth, 1975, and head of Paul Warren and Explorer, 1980. Session for the Temptations (1973).

PAUL WARREN AND EXPLORER Paul Warren—vocal, guitar; Steve Gornall—guitar, vocal; Jimmy Hunter—drums; Dene Jordan—bass, vocal. *Album:* One of the Kids (RSO 1 3076) 1980.

WARRICK, DIONNE Real name of Dionne Warwick.

WARWICK, DIONNE Vocal. A session singer in 1962, she went solo shortly thereafter, with the help of writers Burt Bacharach and Hal David, and became a major name on the pop-soul circuit. In 1968, she did the movie soundtrack for *Valley of the Dolls. Albums:* Anyone Who Had a Heart; Here I Am; Here Where There Is Love; Make Way for Dionne Warwick; Presenting Dionne Warwick; Sensitive Sound of Dionne Warwick, 1965; Valley of the Dolls and Others, 1968; Dionne Warwick; Dionne Warwick in Paris; Windows of the World; Magic of Believing; Soulful, 1969; Best of Dionne Warwick (SEP 18001); Forever Gold (SEP 25110); Golden Voice of Dionne Warwick (SPB 4001); I'll Never Fall in Love Again (SEP 581); Promises, Promises (SEP 571); Tribute to Burt Bacharach (SEP 5100); Very Best of Dionne Warwick (UAR UA LA 337 G); Very Dionne (SEP 587); Dionne Warwick Golden Hits, Vol. 1 (SEP 565); Greatest Motion Picture Hits (SEP 575); Dionne Warwick Sings Her Very Best (SPB 4002); Dionne Warwick Sings One Hit After Another (SPB 4003); Dionne Warwick Story (SEP 2 596); What's New Pussycat (UAR UA LA278-G); Dionne (ARI 4230); Dionne (WBR B 2585); Just Being Myself (WBR B 2658); Love at First Sight (WBR B 3119); Man and a Woman (MCA 2 10012); No Night So Long (ARI 9526); Pick of the Litter (ATC 18141); Then Came You (WBR B 2846); Track of the Cat (WBR B 2893) 1975; Winners (IAM 017); From Within (SEP 2 598); Dionne Warwick Golden Hits, Vol. II (SEP 577).

WASHBURN, DONNA Vocal. Member of Joe Cocker's Greatest Show On Earth, 1970. Session for Ry Cooder (1972); John Mayall (1978).

WASHINGTON, GENE Vocal. Member of the Giants, 1978.

WASHINGTON, LARRY Conga. Member of Duke Williams and the Extremes, 1973. Session for B. B. King (1973-74); Elton John (1979).

WASHINGTON, RICHARD "DIDIMUS" Percussion. Session for Dr. John (1972).

WASZEK, GORD Vocal. Session for Triumph (1979).

WATERMAN, WEB Vocal, guitar. Replaced Lane Turner in Missouri, 1979.

WATERS, JULIA TILLMAN Vocal. Session for Neil Diamond (1976); Harvey Mandel; Paul Butterfield (1975); Santana (1976); Mike Pindar (1976); Glen Campbell (1976); Julie Tippets and Brian Auger (1978); Elton John (1979); Jim Capaldi (1979); Peter Frampton (1979); the Climax Blues Band (1980); Boz Scaggs (1980).

WATERS, LUTHER Vocal. Session for Peter Frampton (1979).

WATERS, MAXINE WILLARD Vocal. Session for Santana (1976); Rita Coolidge (1972); Sonny Terry and Brownie McGhee (1973); Glen Campbell (1976); Mike Pindar (1976); Julie Tippets and Brian Auger (1978); Peter Frampton (1977); Terry Reid (1979); Elton John (1979); Jim Capaldi (1979); the Climax Blues Band (1980).

WATERS, MUDDY Guitar, vocal, slide guitar. Born 4/4/15. Born McKinley Morganfield in Clarksdale, Miss., Waters moved to Chicago to play his distinctive blues. His song "I Just Want to Make Love to You" was an early Rolling Stones single, and his talents were hailed by such younger blues stars as Mike Bloomfield, Eric Clapton, Peter Green, and others. Session for the Johnny Winters Band (1978). *Albums:* After the Rain (CSS 320); Blues—A Real Summit Meeting (BUD); Blues from Big Bill's (CSS 1933); Blues Jam (BUD 7510); Can't Get No Grindin' (CSS 50023); Electric Mud (CSS 314) 1968; Folk Singers (CSS 1483) 1964; London Muddy Waters Sessions (CSS 60013) 1972; London Revisited (CSS 60026); McKinley Morganfield (CSS 60006); Muddy Brass and the Blues (CSS 1507) 1967; Sail On (CSS 1539); Super Blues (CSS 3008) 1967; Super Super Blues Band (CSS 3010) 1968; They Call Me Muddy Waters (CSS 1553); Unk In Funk (CSS 60013); Muddy Waters at Newport (CSS 1449); Muddy Waters Live (CSS 50012); Real Folk Blues, 1966; More Real Folk Blues, 1967; Muddy Waters Sings Big Bill Broonzy; Best of Muddy Waters (CSS 1427); Woodstock Album, 1975; Chicken Shack (MUS 5021); Hard Again (BSK PZ 34449) 1977; I'm Ready (BSK JZ 34928) 1978; Mud in Your Ear (MUS 5008); Muddy Waters Mississippi Live (BSK JZ 35712) 1979.

WATERS, OREN Vocal. Session for Neil Diamond (1976); Peter Frampton (1979); Boz Scaggs (1980).

WATERS, ROGER Bass, piano, percussion, vocal. Born 9/6/47. Original member of Pink Floyd since 1966. Co-author of "Music from the Body" with Ron Geesin, 1970. *Album:* Music from the Body (IMP 1002) 1970.

WATKINS, BEN Vocal, guitar. Member of the Hitmen, 1980.

WATKINS, EDDIE Bass. Session for the Temptations (1973); Peter Frampton (1979).

WATKINS, JULIUS French horn. Session for the Fugs (1968); Martin Mull (1974).

WATKINS, KIM Keyboards. Member of Happy the Man, 1977-78.

WATKINS, PEPPER Vocal. Session for John Mayall (1977-79).

WATKINSON, NICK Vocal, guitar. Member of the Jags, 1980.

WATSON, BERNIE Guitar. Played with John Mayall, 1963.

WATSON, BRYAN Drums, vocal. Played on the soundtrack for "Joseph and the Amazing Technicolor Dreamcoat," 1967.

WATSON, DAN Keyboards, vocal. Member of the Bob Seger System.

WATSON, DUSTY Drums. Member of Jon and the Nightriders, 1980.

WATSON, GENE Bass. Member of the Winters Brothers Band.

WATSON, GINA Vocal, percussion. Half of the Watson-Beasley duet, 1980.

WATSON, JIMMY Drums, sitar. Member of Kensington Market, 1968-69.

WATSON, JOHNNY "GUITAR" Guitar, vocal, keyboards. Session for the Mothers of Invention (1975); George Duke (1975). *Albums:* Ain't That a Bitch (DJM 3); Anthology of the Blues — California Blues (KNT 9003); Funk Beyond the Call of Duty (DJM 714); Gangster of Love (PPK 306); Giant (DJM 19) 1978; I Don't Want To Be a Lone Ranger (FSY 9484) 1975; Listen (FSY 9437) 1973; Love Jones (DJM 31) 1980; Real Mother for Ya (DJM 7); What the Hell Is This (DJM 24) 1979; The Gangster Is Back (RLN 0013) 1976.

WATSON, JON Bass, vocal. Member of 999, 1978-present.

WATSON, MARTIN Guitar, vocal. Member of the Yachts since 1979.

WATSON, MARTYN Vocal. Session for Sean Tyla (1980).

WATSON, PEE WEE Bass, vocal. Member of Nantucket since 1978.

WATSON, TONY Vocal. Member of the Lonely Boys, 1979.

WATSON-BEASLEY Gina Watson—vocal, percussion; Alfred Beasley—vocal, percussion. *Album:* Watson-Beasley (WBR K 3445) 1980.

WATT, HAMILTON W. Guitar. Session for Lee Michaels (1968).

WATT-ROY, GARTH Vocal, guitar. Member of the Greatest Show on Earth, 1970.

WATT-ROY, NORMAN Bass, vocal. Member of the Greatest Show on Earth, 1970, Glencoe, 1972, Loving Awareness, and Ian Dury's Blockheads, 1979.

WATTS, CHARLIE Drums. Born 6/2/41. Started his career with Long John Baldry, Mick Jagger, and

Alex Korner in Blues Incorporated, 1961, before becoming an original member of the Rolling Stones, 1964-present. Session for Howlin' Wolf (1972); Ron Wood (1979).

WATTS, ERNIE Tenor saxophone. Played with John Mayall, 1972. Session for the Mothers of Invention (1972); Steely Dan (1974); Dr. John (1975); Greg Sutton (1975); James Taylor (1976); Steve Marriott (1976); Spirit (1976); B. B. King (1977); Jerry Corbetta (1978); Lee Ritenour (1978-79); Cher (1979); Dick St. Nicklaus (1979). *Album:* Look in Your Heart (ELK 6E 285) 1980.

WATTS, JOHN Guitar, vocal. Member of Fischer-Z since 1979.

WATTS, OVEREND Bass, vocal. Original member of Mott the Hoople, 1969-76, and British Lions, 1978.

WATTS, STEVE Drums, vocal. Member of the Emperor, 1977.

WAVES Marc Singer—drums, vocal; Mike Easley—guitar, vocal; Gene Holmes—guitar, vocal; Marc Levine—bass; Martie Echito—keyboards; K. Clanton—vocal. *Album:* Waves, 1977.

WAX Joseph Lattisaw, Jr.—guitar, vocal, percussion; Bennie Melton—vocal; James Claggett—keyboards; David Searles—percussion; Ronnie Kidd—bass; Steve Wagner—drums; Charles Moritt—saxophone. *Album:* Wax Attack (VIC AFLI 3608) 1980.

WAY, DARRYL Violin, vocal. Member of Curved Air, 1970-73, Wolf, 1974, and Trace, 1975. Session for Marianne Faithfull (1979).

WAY, PETE Bass. Member of UFO, 1974-present.

WAYBILL, FEE Vocal. Voice of the Tubes, 1975-present.

WAYCHESKO, RICK Horns. Session for Long John Baldry (1980).

WAYLON AND WILLIE Waylon Jennings—vocal, guitar; Willie Nelson—vocal, guitar. See individual listings. *Albums:* Outlaws (VIC AFLI 1321) 1976; Waylon and Willie (VIC AFLI 2686).

WAYLORS Jerry Gropp—guitar; Ralph Mooney—steel guitar; Bee Spears—bass; Don Brooks—harmonica; Richie Albright—drums. Backup group for Waylon Jennings.

WAYNE, CARL Guitar, vocal. Original member of the Move, until 1972.

WAYNE, HAYDEN Member of Jobraith, 1973-74.

WAYNE, JEFF Moog. Session for Vigrass and Osborne (1972); Justin Hayward (1980).

WAZBAND Jeff Boynton—keyboards; Jeff Hill—guitar, vocal; James E. McGreevy III—bass; Bruce Zelesnik—drums. Backup band for Wazmo Nariz, 1979.

WE FIVE Recorded "You Were on My Mind," 1966. *Albums:* Take Each Day As It Comes (AVI 6016); You Were on My Mind (AAM 4111).

WEASEL Guitar. Original member of the Electric Prunes, 1967.

WEATHER REPORT Josef Zawinul—keyboards; Wayne Shorter—reeds; Miroslav Vitous—bass; Eric Gravatt—drums (1972-76); Dom um Romao—percussion (1972); Alphonze Mouzon—drums (1971); Ismael Wilburn—percussion (1974); Alphonso Johnson (1974); Jaco Pastorius—bass, percussion (1976-present); Alex Acuna—drums. Jazz-rock group formed by Zawinul in 1971. *Albums:* Black Market (COL PC 34099) 1976; 8:30 (COL PC2 36030) 1979; Heavy Weather (COL PC 34418) 1977; Sing the Body Electric (COL PC 31352) 1972; Individuals (COL CG 36213); Mr. Gone (COL JC 35358) 1978; Mysterious Traveller (COL PC 32494) 1974; Sweetnighter (COL PD 32210) 1973; Tale Spinnin' (COL PC 30661) 1975; Weather Report (COL PC 30661) 1971; Night Passages (COL JC 36793) 1980.

WEATHERS, JOHN Drums, percussion, vocal. Member of the Neutrons, 1974, and Gentle Giant, 1971-80.

WEATHERSPOON, SCOTT GROVER Guitar, vocal. Member of Oak, 1980.

WEAVER, BLUE Keyboards, synthesizer. Member of the Strawbs, 1972. Session for Lou Reed (1973); Mott the Hoople (1974); the Bee Gees (1975, 77, 79); the Graeme Edge Band (1977); Andy Gibb (1980).

WEAVER, CURLEY Guitar. Session with Blind Willie McTell. *Album:* Cryin' in the Morning (MUS 5212).

WEAVER, DENNIS Guitar. Member of the Ron Gardner Group, 1974.

WEAVER, KEN Vocal, drums. Original member of the Fugs, 1965-70.

WEAVER, MARK Guitar. Replaced Lacy Gibson in the Son Seals Blues Band, 1980.

WEAVER, MICK Keyboards. Member of the Keef Hartley Band, 1969-71, the Frankie Miller Band, 1975, and Ten Years Later, 1979, replacing Bernie Clarke. Session for "Jesus Christ Superstar" (1970); Jess Roden (1974); David Gilmour (1978).

WEBB, BOB Guitar, vocal. Member of the James Gang, 1976. Session for Jay Ferguson (1977, 79, 80).

WEBB, CHAMP English horn. Session for the Doors (1969).

WEBB, CYNTHIA Percussion. Session for Nilsson/Lennon (1974); Ringo Starr (1974).

WEBB, DEAN Mandolin. Original member of the Dillards.

WEBB, FRED Keyboards, vocal, flugelhorn. Replaced Linda La Flamme in It's a Beautiful Day, 1970-72. Also a member of Stoneground.

WEBB, HARRY Real name of Cliff Richard.

WEBB, JIMMY Piano, vocal. Session for Nilsson (1971); Joe Cocker (1974). *Albums:* Land's End (ASY 5070); El Mirage (ATC 18218) 1977.

WEBB, KEITH Drums. Member of the Terry Reid

trio, 1968-69. Session for Donovan (1967).

WEBB, RUSSELL Member of the Skids, 1979.

WEBB, STAN Vocal, guitar, slide guitar. Originator of the British blues band Chicken Shack. Though talented and innovative, he has never made his burst into popularity, despite being a member of Savoy Brown's "Boogie Brothers" (1974). In 1976, he formed Broken Glass with Robbie Blunt.

WEBB, STEVE Guitar, vocal. Member of the Jess Roden Band, 1976, and Lion, 1980. Session for Jess Roden (1974-77).

WEBB, TERRY Vocal. Voice of Candlewick Green, 1974.

WEBB, TOM Saxophone. Member of the Flock.

WEBBER, ANDREW LLOYD Composer, keyboards, moog synthesizer. Co-author of "Jesus Christ Superstar," 1970. *Album:* Variations (MCA 3042).

WEBBER, BOB Guitar, vocal. Original member of Sugarloaf.

WEBBER, RACHEL Synthesizer, vocal. Member of the Units, 1980.

WEBBER, ROY Vocal, guitar. Member of Wally, 1974.

WEBBER, STEVE Guitar, vocal. Part of the Fugs' musical backup, 1965-66, and the Holy Modal Rounders.

WEBER, DON Guitar. Member of Dan Hicks and His Hot Licks.

WEBER, FRANK Vocal, keyboards. *Albums:* Frank Weber (VIC AFLI 3547) 1980; As Time Flies (VIC AFLI 2963) 1978.

WEBSTER, JOHN Keyboards. Member of Stonebolt, 1978-80.

WECK, HENRY Drums, percussion. Member of Brownsville Station, 1972-77.

WEDGE Tom Brown—drums; Fred Grabert—guitar; Lou Maxfield—guitar; Ace the Bass—bass. *Album:* Big, Bad, Boss Beat (RHN 509) 1980.

WEDGEWOOD, MIKE Bass, vocal, percussion. Member of Caravan, 1976.

WEEKS, JOHN Guitar, vocal. Member of the Records, 1979-present.

WEEKS, WILLIE Bass. Member of the Gregg Allman Band, 1977. Session for Splinter (1974); the Rolling Stones (1974); Rod Stewart (1974, 76); George Harrison (1974-76, 79); Ron Wood (1975-76); James Taylor (1976); Leon Russell (1976); Roy Buchanan (1976); Joe Walsh (1976, 78); Steve Winwood (1977); Tim Weisberg and Dan Fogelberg (1978); Richard and Linda Thompson (1978); Randy Newman (1979); Adam Mitchell (1979).

WEEMS, JERRY Guitar, vocal. Member of Bonaroo, 1975. Session for Ian Hunter (1976).

WEHRMEYER, ERIC Bass. Member of Gruppo Sportivo, 1978.

WEIDER, JOHN Violin, guitar. First became known with John Mayall, 1963. He was a member of the Animals, 1967-68, and founder of Moonrider, 1975. Session for John Entwhistle (1972). *Album:* John Weider (Import) 1976.

WEIGHILL, ALAN Bass. Session for Elton John (1969); "Jesus Christ Superstar" (1970).

WEINBERG, MAX Drums. Member of the E Street Band, 1973-present. Session for Ian Hunter (1979).

WEINGARTEN, STEVE Guitar, organ. Member of Elizabeth, 1968.

WEINSTOCK, MURRAY Piano. Session for John Sebastian (1976).

WEINZIERC, JOHN Guitar. Member of Amon Duul.

WEIR, BOB Guitar, vocal. Born 10/16/47. Original member of the Grateful Dead, since 1967. Member of Kingfish, 1976. *Albums:* Ace (WBR B 2627) 1975; Heaven Help the Fool (ARI 4155) 1978.

WEIR, CATHY Trumpet, vocal. Member of the Weirz, 1979.

WEIR, ESTELLE Keyboards. Member of the Weirz, 1979.

WEIR, JOAN Percussion. Member of the Weirz, 1979.

WEIR, KENNY Bass, vocal. Member of Exile, 1973-78.

WEIR, LARRY Guitar, vocal. Member of the Weirz, 1979.

WEIR, MARIA Bass, vocal. Member of the Weirz, 1979.

WEIR, MIKE Vibes, organ, vocal. Member of the Weirz, 1979.

WEIR, PIXIE Trombone, flute, vocal. Member of the Weirz, 1979.

WEIR, THERESA Saxophone, vocal. Member of the Weirz, 1979.

WEIR, TOM Drums. Member of the Weirz, 1979.

WEIRZ Larry Weir—guitar, vocal; Maria Weir—bass, vocal; Estelle Weir—keyboards; Tom Weir—drums; Pixie Weir—trombone, flute, vocal; Cathy Weir—trumpet, vocal; Theresa Weir—saxophone, vocal; Mike Weir—vibes, organ, vocal; Joan Weir—percussion. *Album:* The Weirz (PLL) 1979.

WEISBERG, LARRY Bass. Session for Peter Kaukonen (1972).

WEISBERG, RICHARD Drums. Member of the Beacon Street Union, 1968.

WEISBERG, TIM Flute, producer. Referred to as the "other flutist" in rock (the first being Ian Anderson), he is equally known to rock and jazz audiences. Since 1970, his reputation has been steadily growing without the aid of an AM hit. See the Tim Weisberg Group. Session for Dave Mason (1974); Terry Reid (1976). *Albums:* Dreamspeaker (AAM 3045) 1973; Hurtwood Edge (AAM 4352) 1972; Listen to the City (AAM 4545) 1975; Live at Last (AAM 4600) 1976; Night Rider (MCA 3084) 1979; Party of One (MCA 5125); Rotations

(UAR LW 857) 1978; Smile (AAM 4749) 1979; Twin Sons of Different Mothers (EPC JE 35339) 1978; Tim Weisberg (AAM 3039) 1971; Tim Weisberg Band (UAR LO 773) 1977; Tim Weisberg 4 (AAM 3658) 1974.

TIM WEISBERG GROUP Tim Weisberg—flute, synthesizer; Lynn Blessing—keyboards, vibes (1971-79); Doug Anderson—bass, guitar (1973-79); Todd Robinson—guitar (1974-78); Marty Foltz—drums, percussion (1975-76); Tom Dougherty—percussion; Neil Larsen—keyboards (1977-78); John Hug—guitar (1979); Rick Jaeger—drums (1977-79); Bill Stewart—drums (1977); Bobbye Hall—percussion (1977-79); Mickey Raphael—harmonica (1977). See Tim Weisberg.

WEISNER, BOB Drums. Member of the Flyer.

WEISNER, SKIP Trombone. Session for Jules and the Polar Bears (1979).

WEISS, DANNY Guitar. Member of Rhinoceros, 1968. Session for John Sebastian (1970); Lou Reed (1974).

WEISS, DONNA Vocal. Session for Rita Coolidge (1972); Ry Cooder (1972); Bob Dylan (1973).

WEISSBERG, ERIC Bass, guitar, violin, banjo. Gained notoriety with "Dueling Banjos," from the movie *Deliverance,* 1973. Session for Bob Dylan; Ian and Sylvia; Sha Na Na (1971); Willie Nelson (1974); Henry Gross (1975); Randall Bramblett (1975). *Albums:* Anthology of Folk Music, Vol. 2 (SQN 126); Banjo and Bluegrass (ELK 7238); Dueling Banjos from Deliverance (WBR B 2683) 1973; Folk Banjo Styles (ELK 7217).

WEITZ, MARK Organ. Member of the Strawberry Alarm Clock, 1967-68.

WELCH, BOB Guitar, vocal. Joined Fleetwood Mac in 1971, filling the position once held by three of the finest blues guitarists in the rock industry (Peter Green, Jeremy Spencer, and Danny Kirwan). Welch's rock influences blended well with the group's blues origins until his departure in 1974. He reappeared as the head of Paris, a heavy-metal trio, in 1975, with former Jethro Tull member Glenn Cornick. He went solo in 1977. Session for Sammy Hagar (1975); Bill Wyman (1976). *Albums:* French Kiss (CAP SW 11663) 1977; Other One (CAP SOO 12024) 1979; Three Hearts (CAP SO 11907) 1979; Man Overboard (CAP SOO 12107) 1980.

WELKOM, STEVE Guitar. Member of the Floating Opera, 1971.

WELLBELOVE, DAVE Guitar. Member of the Groundhogs, 1976.

WELLER, DON Reeds, vocal. Member of the Sensational Alex Harvey Band.

WELLER, FREDDIE Guitar. Replaced Drake Levin in Paul Revere and the Raiders, 1966-69.

WELLER, PAUL Guitar, vocal. Member of the Jam, 1977.

WELLS, AMOS Real name of Junior Wells.

WELLS, CORY Vocal. Born 2/5/42. Member of Three Dog Night. *Album:* Ahead of the Storm (AAM 4736).

WELLS, JUNIOR Harmonica, vocal. Real name: Amos Wells. Like Charlie Musselwhite, Wells is a second-generation blues harpist who learned from such teachers as Little Walter, Sonny Boy Williamson, Big Walter Horton, and others. In 1948, while still under age, he played in public for the first time, in a Chicago lounge. From there, he went to work for Muddy Waters before striking out on his own. *Albums:* Junior Wells Chicago Blues Band, 1966; You're Tuff Enough, 1968; Best of the Blues, Vol. 2 (SQN 124); Best of the Chicago Blues (VAN VSD 1/2); Chicago/The Blues/Today (VAN 79216) 1966; Comin' at You (VAN 79262) 1968; Great Blues Men (VAN VSD 25/26); It's My Life, Baby (VAN 79231) 1966; Hoodoo Man Blues (DEL 9612); On Tap (DEL 635) 1974.

WELLS, KEVIN Drums. Session for Carlene Carter (1980).

WELLS, MARY Vocal. Motown star responsible for "My Guy," 1964. *Albums:* Bye Bye Baby; One Who Really Loves You; Two Lovers; Mary Wells on Stage; Mary Wells Sings My Guy; Vintage Stock; Two Sides of Mary Wells; Love Songs to the Beatles; Marvin and Mary Together; Servin' Up Some Soul, 1968; Greatest Hits of Mary Wells (PPK 313); Mary Wells Greatest Hits (MTN) 1964.

MARY WELLS AND MARVIN GAYE Marvin Gaye—vocal; Mary Wells—vocal. See individual listings. *Album:* Anthology—Marvin Gaye (MTN M9-791).

WELLS, PETER Guitar, vocal. Member of the Rose Tattoo, 1980.

WELNICK, VINCENT Keyboards. Member of the Tubes, 1975-present.

WELSH, CHAUNCEY Trombone. Session for Dr. John (1975).

WELSH, PERRY Harmonica, vocal. Session for Elvin Bishop (1972).

WENDER, TENDY Keyboards, vocal. Member of the White Cloud, 1972, and 3-D, 1980.

WENDORF, MICHAEL Vocal. Session for Lou Reed (1976). *Album:* Kiss the World Goodbye (ARA 50030) 1978.

WENNER, MARK Harmonica, vocal. Member of the Nighthawks since 1976.

WENNERSTROM, VERN Percussion. Member of the Tantrum, 1978-79.

WEREWOLVES Kirk Brewster—vocal, guitar, bass; Buckner Ballard—vocal, guitar, bass; Brian Papageorge—vocal; Seab Meador—guitar; Bobby Barandwski—drums. *Albums:* Ship of Fools (VIC AFLI 3079) 1978; Werewolves (VIC AFLI 2746) 1978.

WERKMAN, TOM Percussion, producer. Production for Ted Nugent; Cheap Trick; Molly Hatchett (1978-80); and others. Session for Ted Nugent (1976-77).

WERNER, DAVID Vocal. *Album:* David Werner (EPC JE 36126) 1979.

WERNER, ERICH Vocal, guitar. Member of the Blackouts, 1980.

WERNER, MAX Vocal. Voice of Kayak since 1975.

WERSON, YVONNE Vocal. Member of A-440, 1978.

WERTH, HOWARD Vocal, guitar. Member of Audience, 1971, and head of Howard Werth and the Moonbeams, 1975.

HOWARD WERTH AND THE MOONBEAMS Howard Werth—vocal, guitar; Mike Moran—keyboards; Freddy Gandy—bass; Roger Pope—drums; Bob Weston—guitar. *Album:* King Brilliant (MCA 2180) 1975.

WERTZ, KENNY Member of the Flying Burrito Brothers.

WESLEY, FRED Horns. Session for Terry Reid (1976). *Albums:* Fred Wesley and the Horny Horns, 1977; Blow for Me, A Toot to You (ATC 182414); Say Blow by Blow Backwards (ATC 19254) 1979.

WEST, ANDY Bass. Member of the Dixie Dregs.

WEST, BOBBY Bass. Session for Buffalo Springfield (1967); Russ Giguere (1971); James Taylor; Captain Beefheart (1974).

WEST, GARY Vocal. Session for Missouri (1979).

WEST, GARY Vocal, keyboards, guitar, drums, percussion. Member of the Shooting Star, 1979.

WEST, KEITH Vocal, guitar. Original member of Moonrider, 1975.

WEST, LESLIE Guitar, vocal. Born 10/22/45. He first appeared in 1969 as the guitarist for Mountain, a group reminiscent of the late Cream. High volume and the use of feedback as melody were the group's trademarks, but West was equally dexterous on the acoustic guitar. With Mountain's demise, he became part of West, Bruce and Laing, 1972-73, with former Cream member Jack Bruce, which also failed to attract the attention that Cream attracted. Formed the Leslie West Band, 1975. *Albums:* Mountain (WDF 4500) 1968; The Great Fatsby (PTM BPLI 0954 1) 1975.

LESLIE WEST BAND Leslie West—guitar, vocal; Corky Laing—drums; Mick Jones—guitar; Don Kretmer—bass. *Album:* The Leslie West Band (PTM BPLI 1258) 1975.

WEST, PAUL Piano, vocal. Member of BLT, 1977.

WEST, RICKY Guitar. Member of the Tremloes, 1967-69.

WEST, RON Guitar, keyboards, vocal. Member of Missouri.

WEST, SANDY Drums, vocal. Member of the Runaways, 1976-77.

WEST, TOMMY Vocal, keyboards, guitar. Half of the Cashman and West vocal duet. Session for Henry Gross (1973, 75-78).

WEST, BRUCE AND LAING Leslie West—guitar, vocal; Jack Bruce—bass, vocal, keyboards; Corky Laing—drums, vocal. As the name indicates, the group was an assemblage of heavy rock classics, West and Laing from Mountain and Bruce from Cream, meant to be an alternative to the recently defunct Mountain. *Albums:* Whatever Turns You On (COL C 32216) 1973; Why Dontcha (CLO C31929) 1972; Live 'n' Kickin (COL) 1973.

WESTBROOK, FRANK Keyboards. Replaced Gabe Katona in Rare Earth, 1976-77.

WESTERBEEK, RON Organ. Session for Barry Hay.

WESTLAKE, KEVIN Guitar. Session for Ronnie Lane (1975).

WESTLEY, GEOFF Keyboards, string arranger. Session for the Bee Gees (1974, 77); the Hollies (1978); the Sweet (1979).

WESTON, DANNY Guitar. Member of the Cats, 1980.

WESTON, DAVE Bass. Session for the Blues Brothers (1980).

WESTON, PAUL Guitar, vocal. Member of the Sea Dog, 1972.

WESTON, ROBERT Guitar. Member of Fleetwood Mac, 1973, and Howard Werth and the Moonbeams, 1975. Session for Long John Baldry (1972); Danny Kirwan (1979).

WESTRATE, PAUL Drums, percussion. Member of Alquin, 1975.

WESTWOOD, PAUL Bass. Session for Matthew Fisher (1980); Peter Green (1980); Chris Spedding (1980).

WET WILLIE Jimmy Hall—vocal, harmonica, saxophone, percussion; Jack Hall—bass, vocal; Ricky Hirsh—guitar, vocal; John Anthony—guitar, keyboards; Lewis Ross—drums, percussion; Ella Avery—vocal (1974-79); Donna Hall—vocal (1974-79); Michael Duke—vocal, keyboards (1979). Early name: Fox. Southern rock 'n' roll from the Allman Brothers' Capricorn label. *Albums:* Drippin' Wet Live (CPN 0113) 1973; Manorisms (EPC JE 34983) 1977; Wet Willie's Greatest Hits (CPN 0200) 1977; Which One's Willie (EPC JE 35974) 1979; Wet Willie (CPN 0138); Wet Willie II (CPN 0109); Keep On Smilin' (CPN 0128) 1974; Dixie Rock (CPN 0149) 1975; Wetter the Better (CPN 0166) 1976; Left Coast Live (CPN 0182) 1977.

WETTON, JOHN Bass, vocal. Replaced Boz Burrell in King Crimson, 1973-75. Replaced Gary Thain in Uriah Heep, 1975-76, and John Gustafson in Roxy Music, 1976. Member of U.K., 1978-79. Session for David Byron (1975); Bryan Ferry (1974, 76-78); Phil Manzanera (1975).

WETZEL, GREG Piano. Session for Bill Blue (1980).

WEXLER, JERRY Producer, percussion. Early producer for Atlantic Records, who first recorded Ray Charles in 1954. Produced Willie Nelson (1974); Kim Carnes (1976); Gilda Radner (1979; Dire Straits (1979); Bob Dylan (1979-80); and others. Session for Barry Goldberg (1974).

WEYMOUTH, MARTINA Bass. Member of the Talking Heads since 1977.

WHA-KOO David Palmer—vocal, percussion; Ron Fransen—keyboards; Eddie Tuduri—drums; Eric Gotthelf. David Palmer's re-formed Big Wha-Koo. *Albums:* Berkshire (MCA 1043); Fragile Line (EPC JE 36173) 1979.

WHALEY, DON Bass. Member of Honk.

WHALEY, KEN Bass. Replaced Brian Turrington in the Tyla Gang, 1978-79.

WHEATBREAD, PAUL Drums. Member of Gary Puckett and the Union Gap, 1967-68.

WHEATFIELD Will Hobbs; Paul Douglas; Pete Wolfe; Kenny Sawyer; Kerry Canfield. *Album:* Wheatfield (OVL) 1980.

WHEELER, HAROLD Piano. Session for Bruce Springsteen (1973).

WHEELER, KENNY Trumpet. Session for Savoy Brown (1969); Memphis Slim (1971). *Albums:* Around Six (EMC I 1156) 1980; Azimuth (ECM I 1099) 1977; Deer Wan (ECM I 1102) 1978; Gnu High (ECM 1069).

WHEELOCK, MOSES Percussion. Member of the Eric Burdon Band, 1975.

WHEETMAN, DAN Vocal, guitar, fiddle. Member of Liberty, 1975.

WHELLER, BUDDY Bass. Session for Duane Eddy's Rebels (1961).

WHETSTONE, RICHARD Drums, guitar, vocal. Replaced Preston Ritter in the Electric Prunes, 1967-69.

WHIPLASH, SNIDELY Skins. Member of Frut, 1970-72.

WHITCOMB, BRIAN Keyboards. Member of Bobbidazzler, 1977, and Osamu, 1977.

WHITCOMB, IAN Vocal, piano. Born 7/10/41. Recorded "You Turn Me On," 1965. *Albums:* Crooner Tunes (FSM 7704); Red Hot Blue Heaven (FSM 7725) 1979; Treasures of Tin Pan Alley (ADF 115).

WHITE, ALAN Drums, percussion. Born 6/14/49. Member of Yes, 1972-present. Session for Sky (1970); Gary Wright (1970-71, 79); John Lennon (1969, 71); George Harrison (1972); Rick Wakeman (1972, 77-78); Joe Cocker (1972); Donovan (1973); Steve Howe (1975). *Album:* Ramshackled (ATC) 1976.

WHITE, ANDY Drums. Session for the Beatles.

WHITE, ANN Vocal. Session for the Richie Furay Band (1976).

WHITE, BILLY JOE Guitar. Member of David Peel's Lower East Side, 1969.

WHITE, BUBS Guitar. Session for Jim Capaldi (1973).

WHITE, BUKKA Vocal, guitar. Born 11/12/09, in Mississippi. Legendary country blues artist of the early 20th century. *Albums:* Bukka White, 1974; Bukka White, Vol. II, 1966; Blues Roots (TMT 2 7006); Legacy of the Blues (CRS 10010); Legacy of the Blues, Vol. I (CRS 10011) 1976; Story of the Blues (COL PG 30008); Big Daddy (BLO 12049) 1974; Sky Songs, Vol. I (ARH 1019) 1965; Sky Songs, Vol. II (ARH 1020) 1965.

WHITE, CHRIS Bass, vocal, producer. Member of the Zombies, 1965-68, with Rod Argent. When the group disbanded, he continued his partnership with Argent by producing Argent's new group, Argent.

WHITE, CLARENCE Guitar. Born 6/7/44. Original member of the Byrds, 1965. Died 1973. Session for Marc Benno; Randy Newman; Maria Muldaur (1973).

WHITE, DAVE Vocal. Member of Danny and the Juniors.

WHITE, DAVE Baritone, clarinet. Member of Centipede, 1971.

WHITE, DAVE Vocal, keyboards. Member of the Crystal Mansion.

WHITE, DAVID Bass, vocal. Session for Jay Ferguson (1980).

WHITE, GARY Bass, vocal. Original member of Circus Maximus, 1967-68.

WHITE, J. DEWITT Bass, vocal. Member of the Stone Canyon Band.

WHITE, JACK Member of Gary Myrick and the Figures, 1980.

WHITE, JERRY Vocal, percussion. Member of the Truth, 1975.

WHITE, JOSH Guitar, vocal. *Albums:* Anthology of Folk Music (SQN 102); Anthology, Vol. 2 (SQN 126); Best of the Blues (SQN 103); Decade of Jazz, Vol. 1 (BLN LWB 158); Empty Bed Blues (ELK 7211); Folksay, Vols. 1, 2, 3 & 4 (STI 5-9); House I Live In (ELK 7203); Leadbelly Sings and Plays (STI 91); Legend of Leadbelly (TRD 1093); Singin' the Blues (MCA 2 4064); Josh White (EVR 209); Josh White Sings (STI 15); Josh White Sings the Blues (STI 14).

WHITE, JOSH, JR. Guitar, vocal. *Albums:* The Dream Awake (SKN 1095); Josh White, Jr. (VAN 79406) 1978; Sing a Rainbow (MRR 52791) 1979.

WHITE, KIEREN Vocal, harmonica, guitar. Original member of Steamhammer, 1969.

WHITE, LENNY Drums, percussion. Original member of Return to Forever, 1973-77. Replaced Steve Ferrone in Brian Auger's Oblivion Express, 1977. Session for Santana (1972); Jaco Pastorius (1976). *Albums:* Adventures of Astral Pirates (ELK 6E 121) 1978; Big City (NMP 441); Streamline (ELK 6E 164) 1978; Venusian Summer (NMP 435) 1975; Twenny Nine (ELK 6E

304) 1980; Best of Friends (ELK 6E 223) 1979.

WHITE, PRICILLA Real name of Cilla Black.

WHITE, RICHARD ALLYN Keyboards, vocal. Member of Russia, 1980.

WHITE, RICKY Guitar, vocal. Replaced Glenn Pavone in Bill Blue's Band, 1980.

WHITE, ROBERT Guitar. Session for the Temptations (1973).

WHITE, RON Member of Smokey Robinson and the Miracles.

WHITE, REUBEN Percussion. Member of Ross.

WHITE, SNOWY Guitar. Replaced Gary Moore in Thin Lizzy, 1980. Session for Richard Wright (1978); Peter Green (1979).

WHITE, T. Guitar. Member of Sparks, 1972-77.

WHITE, TONY JOE Vocal, guitar, harmonica, percussion. Southern folk-rock artist with a touch of Elvis. He wrote "Polk Salad Annie," 1971. *Albums:* Tony Joe White (WBR) 1971; The Train I'm On (WBR) 1972.

WHITE CLOUD Thomas Jefferson Kaye—guitar, vocal; Joanne Vent—vocal, percussion; Richard Crooks—drums; Tendy Wender—keyboards, vocal; Kenneth Kosek—fiddle, vocal; Charlie Brown—guitar. *Album:* White Cloud (GDM) 1972.

WHITE CLOVER Early name for Kansas.

WHITE DUCK Lanny Fiel—guitar, horns, vocal; Rick Fel—guitar, vocal, keyboards; Don Kloetzke—vocal, keyboards; Paul Tabet—drums; Mario Friedel—bass, keyboards, guitar, vocal. *Album:* White Duck (UNI) 1971.

WHITE HORSE Jon Lind—vocal; Billy Nicholls—vocal, guitar; Kenny Altman—bass. *Album:* White Horse, 1977.

WHITE LIGHTNIN' Jana Giglio—vocal; Barbara Lawgor—vocal; Bonnie Guidry—vocal. Studio vocal trio. Session for Flint (1978).

WHITE WITCH Ron Goedert—vocal; Buddy Pendergrass—keyboards; Buddy Richardson—guitar; Bobby Shea—percussion; Bill Peterson—percussion; Charlie Souza—bass, percussion. *Albums:* Spiritual Greeting (CPN 0129) 1974; White Witch (CPN 0107) 1973.

WHITEFACE Steve Hardwick—guitar, vocal; Kyle Henderson—bass, vocal; Doug Bare—keyboards, vocal; Benny Rappa—drums, vocal. *Album:* Whiteface (MER SRM 1 3765) 1979.

WHITEHEAD, NEVILLE Bass. Member of the Pilot, 1972.

WHITEHORN, GEOFF Guitar, vocal. Replaced Terry Smith in If, 1974. Replaced Paul Kossoff in Crawler, formerly known as Backstreet Crawler, 1977. Session for Mike Berry (1976); Eric Burdon (1977); Manfred Mann (1980).

WHITEHURST, JERRY Piano. Session for J. J. Cale (1971, 74).

WHITESNAKE Bernie Marsden—guitar; David Coverdale—vocal; Mick Moody—guitar; Dave Dowle—drums (1978-79); Neil Murray—bass; Jon Lord—keyboards (1979-80); Ian Paice—drums (1980). *Albums:* Love Hunter (UAR LT 981) 1979; Ready An' Willing (MRG 19276) 1980; Trouble (UAR LT 937) 1979; Snakebite (UAR UA LA 915 H) 1978; Live — In the Heart of the City (MIR 19292) 1980.

WHITFIELD, KENNETH Keyboards. Member of Nitzinger, 1973-76.

WHITFORD, BRAD Guitar. Member of Aerosmith, 1971-79.

WHITING, JOE Vocal. Voice of Jukin' Bone, 1972.

WHITING, JUNE Oboe. Session for Mike Oldfield (1974).

WHITING, LEONARD Vocal. Session for the Alan Parsons Project (1976).

WHITLOCK, BOBBY Keyboards, vocal, guitar. First became known working with Delaney and Bonnie in the late 1960s and later with Leon Russell, Eric Clapton (in Derek and the Dominoes, 1970-72), and others before embarking on his solo career. Session for Dr. John (1971); George Harrison (1972); Donovan (1973). *Albums:* Bobby Whitlock (DHL); Raw Velvet (DHL 50131); One of a Kind (CPN); Rock Your Socks Off (CPN 0168) 1976.

WHITLOCK, TOM Drums, vocal. Member of No Slack, 1978.

WHITMAN, LARRY Guitar, vocal. Member of the Beat, 1979.

WHITMORE, IAIN Vocal, bass. Member of Starry Eyed and Laughing, 1975.

WHITMORE, LARRY Guitar. Session for Waylon Jennings (1973-75).

WHITNEY, CHARLIE Guitar. Member of the Streetwalkers, 1973-77.

WHITREN, JAKI Vocal. Session for the Alan Parsons Project (1977).

WHITSELL, GEORGE Vocal, cello, keyboards, harpsichord. Member of Crazy Horse.

WHITTAKER, JEFF Congas. Session for Steve Stills (1970).

WHITTAKER, STAN Guitar, vocal. Member of Happy the Man, 1977-78.

WHITTAKER, TIM Drums. Member of the Deaf School, 1979-80.

WHITTED, DENNIS Drums, vocal. Member of the Paul Butterfield Blues Band, 1971. Session for Paul Butterfield's Better Days (1973); Geoff Muldaur (1978).

WHITTEN, DANNY Guitar. Co-founder of Crazy Horse, 1971. Died 1972. Session for Neil Young (1969-70).

WHITWAM, BARRY Drums. Member of Herman's Hermits, 1965-68.

WHO Pete Townshend—guitar, vocal, keyboards; Roger Daltry—vocal; Keith Moon—drums, percussion (until 1979); John Entwhistle—bass, brass, vocal, piano; Kenny Jones—drums (1980). Even when they were called the High Numbers, the Who were strange: Townshend's windmill guitar strokes and bulbous nose, Daltry's curly blond hair and leather costumes, Moon's insanity behind the drums, and Entwhistle's catatonic normality. In the era when rock musicians were not paid well, it seemed even stranger when they destroyed their equipment at the end of each show. Yet they were the musical embodiment of the Marlon Brando image, in leather jackets and on motorcycles. "My Generation" (1966), consequently, received little airplay, as did "I Can See for Miles" and "Substitute." A large cult following began to build, however. When the classic "Tommy" appeared in 1969, the critics could no longer dismiss the genius of the Who. Besides their being talented musicians, Townshend's writing had matured by epic bounds. It was followed in 1971 by "Who's Next," another milestone album for the Who and rock music. Each member has his own solo career outside the Who, but the combination of their talents is without equal. Played at Woodstock, 1969. Drummer Moon died in 1979 and was replaced by Kenny Jones, formerly with the Faces. *Albums:* My Generation (MCA 2 1008) 1966; Odds and Sods (MCA 2126); Happy Jack (MCA 2 4067) 1967; The Kids Are Alright (MCA 2 11005) 1979; Magic Bus (MCA 4068) 1968; Meaty, Beaty, Big and Bouncy (MCA 3025) 1971; Quadrophenia (MCA 10004) 1973; Quardrophenia (POL 2 6235) 1979; Tommy (MCA 2 10005) 1969; Tommy (POL 2 9502); Who Are You (MCA 3050) 1978; Who by Numbers (MCA 3026) 1976; Who—Live at Leeds (MCA 3026) 1970; The Who Sell Out (MCA 4067) 1968; The Who Sings My Generation (MCA 2 4068); Who's Next (MCA 3024) 1971; McVicar (POL 1-6284) 1980.

WHOLE WHEAT Blair Anderson—vocal, drums; Mike Fleetwood—vocal, guitar; Jerry Field—bass; Nick Pepper—vocal, keyboards; Mark Seamons—keyboards; Robert Morris—drums. Evolved into a group called Passion, 1979. *Album:* 100% Whole Wheat, 1977.

WHOLE WHEAT HORNS Donn Adams—trombone; Keith Spring—tenor saxophone. Session for NRBQ.

WICKLAND, BOBBY DEAN Drums, percussion. Member of the Scooters, 1980.

WICKS, STUART Keyboards. Session for the Keef Hartley Band (1970).

WIDOWMAKER Steve Ellis—vocal; Paul Nichols—drums; Aeriel Bender—guitar, vocal; Bob Daisley—bass, vocal. *Albums:* Widowmaker (JET VA LA 642 G) 1976; Too Late To Cry (UAR) 1977.

WIECZORKE, MANFRED Keyboards, guitar, vocal, percussion. Member of Eloy, 1975-76.

WIEGRATZ, WARREN PAUL Keyboards, reeds, vocal. Member of Sweetbottom, 1978-79.

WIEMANN, BYRON, III Vocal, guitar. Member of Snopek since 1979.

WIENER, HARRIS Organ, vocal. Member of the Wind in the Willows, 1968.

WIER, KENNY Guitar, vocal. Member of Peddler, 1976.

WIERDOS John Denny—vocal; Dix Denney—guitar; Art Fox—drums; Cliff Roman—guitar; Willy Williams—bass. *Albums:* Action-Design EP (RHN 508) 1980; Who? What? When? Where? Why? (BMP W-3) 1979.

WIESNER, ULLA Vocal. Session for Triumvirat (1973).

WIESS, DONNA Vocal. Member of Joe Cocker's Greatest Show on Earth, 1970.

WIGGIN, HELEN Drums. Member of the Shaggs, 1969.

WIGGINS, BETTY Guitar, vocal. Member of the Shaggs.

WIGGINS, DOROTHY Guitar, vocal. Member of the Shaggs.

WIGGY BITS Peppy Castro—vocal, percussion; Rich Cerniglia—guitar; Mike Maniscalco—guitar, keyboards; Mike Ricciardella—drums; D. Santiago—bass. Short-lived spinoff from the Illusions. *Album:* Wiggy Bits.

WILBURN, ISHMAEL Percussion. Member of the Weather Report, 1974.

WILCOX, JOHN Drums. Replaced Kevin Elliman in Utopia, 1977-80. Session for Steve Hillage (1976).

WILD, BILL Bass, vocal. Member of Ruben and the Jets, 1973.

WILD, JON Guitar, vocal. Member of the JTS Band, 1977.

WILD, KEN Bass. Member of Seawind.

WILD OATS Joe Beshouri—drums; Marc Levy—vocal, guitar; Kip Paulen—bass, guitar; Larry Tollin—keyboards. *Albums:* Wild Oats (ALS 5235); Wild Oats (CLD 8803).

WILD ROMANCE See Herman Brood and His Wild Romance.

WILD TURKEY Gary Pickford-Hopkins—vocal; Mick Dyche—slide guitar, guitar, vocal; Tweke Lewis—guitar; Steve Gurl—piano; Glenn Cornick—bass; Jeff Jones—drums. *Album:* Turkey (CRS) 1972.

WILDCATS Chris Spedding—guitar; Rob Stoner—bass, piano; Howie Wyeth—drums, piano; Scotty Turner—guitar. Backup band for Robert Gordon, 1979.

WILDE, DANNY Vocal. Voice of Quick, 1976.

WILDE, WILBUR Saxophone, vocal. Member of Jo Jo Zep and the Falcons, 1980.

WILDER, JOE Trumpet. Session for Jan Akkerman (1973); Martin Mull (1974).

WILDERNESS ROAD Nate Herman—guitar, mandolin, dobro, vocal; Warren Lemming—guitar, banjo, vocal; Andy Haban—bass, vocal; Tom Haban—drums, oboe, vocal. *Album:* Wilderness

Road (COL).

WILDING, BOB Drums, vocal. Member of the Racing Cars, 1976-78.

WILDING, DANNY Flute. Half of the Wilding-Bonus duet of 1978.

WILDING-BONUS Danny Wilding—flute; Pete Bonus—guitar. *Album:* Pleasure Signals (USA 7003) 1978.

WILFERT, H. Trumpet. Session for Triumvirat (1973).

WILHELM, MIKE Guitar. Replaced Tim Lynch in the Flamin' Groovies, 1979.

WILK, SCOTT Head of Scott Wilk and the Walls, 1980.

SCOTT WILK AND THE WALLS Scott Wilk; Roger Ciszon; Bob Lizik; Tom Scheckel. *Album:* Scott Wilk and the Walls (WBR 3460) 1980.

WILKENS, DON Keyboards, vocal. Member of Silent Dancing, 1975.

WILKERSON, LEON Bass. Member of Lynyrd Skynyrd, 1973-77, and the Rossington-Collins Band, 1980. Session for Alias (1980).

WILKEY, DAVE Piano. Session for Peter Green (1980).

WILKIN, JOHN Guitar. Session for Waylon Jennings (1973-75).

WILKINS, BILL Drums, percussion. Member of Trillion, 1978-80.

WILKINS, JACK Guitar. Member of the Barry Miles Quartet. Session for Free Creek (1973). *Albums:* Guitar Players (MST 410); Windows (MST 396).

WILKINS, JIMMY Drums. Member of the States, 1979.

WILKINSON, B. Bass, vocal, keyboards. Member of the Atlantics since 1979.

WILKINSON, ED Bass. Session for Sleepy John Estes (1963).

WILKINSON, JEFF Drums. Member of the Nervous Eaters, 1980.

WILKINSON, SUE Vocal. Session for the Brains (1980).

WILKS, JAN Vocal, guitar, synthesizer. *Album:* Bombay Tears (MER SRM 1 3818) 1980.

WILLARD, LORNA Vocal. Session for Paul Butterfield (1975).

WILLARD, MAXINE See Maxine Willard Waters.

WILLETT, MARK Bass. Member of One Hand Clapping, 1977-79.

WILLIAMS, ADRIENNE Vocal, percussion. Member of Halloween, 1979.

WILLIAMS, ALAN Guitar, vocal. Member of the Rubettes.

WILLIAMS, BERNARD Percussion. Member of Baby.

WILLIAMS, BIG JOE Guitar, vocal. *Albums:* Classic Delta Blues (MLS 3001); Ramblin' on My Mind (MLS 3002); Rare Blues (TKM 7081); Blue Bash (OLR 7115); Dark Muddy Bottom Blues (SPE 2149); Hell Bound and Heaven Sent (FLW 31004); Legacy of the Blues (CRS 10010); Legacy of the Blues, Vol. 6 (CRS 10016) 1976; Mississippi's Big Joe Williams (FLW 33820); Story of the Blues (COL CG 30003); Big Joe Williams (EVR 218); Tough Times (ARH 1002) 1960; Thinking of What They Did to Me (ARH 1053).

WILLIAMS, BOB Trumpet. Member of the Puzzle.

WILLIAMS, BOBBY Guitar, vocal. Member of the Two Guns, 1979.

WILLIAMS, BRYAN Trombone. Session for John Entwhistle (1972).

WILLIAMS, BUDDY Drums. Session for the Blast (1979).

WILLIAMS, CARLENA Vocal. Session for Roy Buchanan (1974); Country Joe McDonald (1975); Steve Marriott (1976).

WILLIAMS, CHARLES Drums. Session for Fats Domino (1956).

WILLIAMS, CHARLIE Vocal. Member of Mistress, 1979.

WILLIAMS, CLIFF Bass. Member of Bandit, 1967-78. Replaced Mark Adams in AC/DC, 1978-present.

WILLIAMS, DENIECE Vocal. Half of the nucleus of the Michael Zager Band. Session for Terry Reid (1979).

WILLIAMS, DUKE Organ. Namesake of Duke Williams and the Extremes, 1973. Session for Martin Mull (1974).

DUKE WILLIAMS AND THE EXTREMES Duke Williams—vocal, organ, guitar; T. J. Tindal—vocal, guitar, bass; Bobby Hartnagle—guitar; Cotton Kent—keyboards; Andy Newmark—drums; Earl Young—drums; Larry Washington—percussion. *Album:* A Monkey in a Silk Suit Is Still a Monkey (CPN) 1973.

WILLIAMS, GRAHAM HEADLEY Guitar, vocal. Member of the Racing Cars, 1976-78.

WILLIAMS, HAROLD Baritone saxophone. Session for Martin Mull (1974); the Marshall Tucker Band (1974); Gregg Allman (1974); Elvin Bishop (1974).

WILLIAMS, IKE Horns. Session for Ry Cooder (1972).

WILLIAMS, JERRY Piano, vocal. Session for Ron Wood (1979).

WILLIAMS, JOHN Early performing name of John Lee Hooker.

WILLIAMS, JOHN Baritone, bass, soprano saxophone. Member of Love Sculpture, 1969-70, and Centipede, 1971. Session for Dave Edmunds (1971).

WILLIAMS, JOANNE Vocal. Session for Dan McCafferty (1975); Hummingbird (1976).

WILLIAMS, KEN Guitar. Original member of the Electric Prunes, 1967.

WILLIAMS, KENNETH Percussion. Session for

Mylon LeFevre (1979).

WILLIAMS, LAMAR Bass. Replaced Berry Oakley in the Allman Brothers Band, 1972-76. Original member of Sea Level, 1977-present.

WILLIAMS, LARRY Keyboards, saxophone, clarinet. Member of Seawind. Session for Mark-Almond (1978); Dr. John (1979); Elton John (1980).

WILLIAMS, LENNY Vocal. Replaced Rick Stevens in Tower of Power, 1973.

WILLIAMS, LEROY Percussion. Member of Hi Tension, 1978.

WILLIAMS, MASON Vocal, guitar, composer. Painter, author, poet, guitarist, and composer, Mason Williams released "Classical Gas" (1968) at approximately the same time he was a regular on the first Smothers Brothers' television show. *Albums:* Listening Matter; Anthology of the Banjo (TRD 2077); Anthology of the Twelve String Guitar (TRD 2071); Feudin' Banjos (OLR 105); Fresh Fish (FLF 059) 1975; Hand Made (WBR 1838); Mason Williams Listening Matter (EVR 3265); Mason Williams Listening Matter Phonograph Record (WBR 1729) 1968.

WILLIAMS, OTIS Vocal. Original member of the Temptations.

WILLIAMS, PATRICK Trumpet. Session for B. B. King (1969).

WILLIAMS, PAUL Vocal. Original member of the Tempations. Died 1973.

WILLIAMS, PAUL Piano, vocal. Composer/performer also noted for his movie scoring. *Albums:* Classics (AAM 4701) 1977; Here Comes Inspiration (AAM 3606) 1973; Just an Old Fashioned Love Song (AAM 4327); Life Goes On (AAM 4367) 1972; Little Bit of Love (AAM 3655) 1974; Little on the Windy Side (POR JR 35610) 1979; Phantom of the Paradise (AAM 3653); Wings (AAM 3503).

WILLIAMS, PAUL Piano. Session for Chuck Berry (1964).

WILLIAMS, PAUL Bass, vocal, percussion, guitar, keyboards. Started in Blues Incorporated before playing with John Mayall, 1969. Replaced Ray Owen in Juicy Lucy, 1970-71. Member of the Tempest, 1973. Session for Aynsley Dunbar (1970).

WILLIAMS, PIP Producer, synthesizer. Session and production for the Heroes (1980).

WILLIAMS, POOR JOE Guitar, vocal. Chicago-based blues man of the 1930s. Session for Sonny Boy Williamson (1938); Yank Rachel.

WILLIAMS, RICH Guitar, percussion, vocal. Born 2/1/50. Original member of Kansas, since 1974.

WILLIAMS, ROBERT Drums, vocal. Member of the Tremblers, 1980.

WILLIAMS, ROBERT ARTHUR Drums. Replaced Art Tripp in Captain Beefheart's Magic Band, 1978-present.

WILLIAMS, ROBERT PETE Guitar, vocal. Born 3/4/14. Louisiana-born bluesman. *Albums:* Free Again (PRS 7808); Great Blues Men (VAN VSD 25/26); Great Blues Men at Newport (VAN VSD 77/78); Legacy of the Blues (CRS 10019); Rural Blues (FSY 24716) 1973; Tenth Anniversary (FLF 099); When I Lay My Burden Down (SLD 4); Louisiana Blues (TAK 7011) 1980.

WILLIAMS, SAM Bass. Member of Zulu.

WILLIAMS, SHARON LEE Vocal. Session for Alice Cooper (1976); Long John Baldry (1980).

WILLIAMS, STEVE Drums. Member of the Sand, 1973, and Budgie, 1975-77.

WILLIAMS, TAFF Guitar. Member of the Neutrons, 1974.

WILLIAMS, TERRY Drums, percussion. Replaced Jeff Jones in Man. Member of Rockpile since 1971. Session for Dave Edmunds (1971-present); the Motors (1980); Carlene Carter (1980).

WILLIAMS, TOMMY Fiddle. Session for Waylon Jennings (1973).

WILLIAMS, TONY Bass. Member of Stealer's Wheel, 1972-75.

WILLIAMS, TONY Drums, percussion. Soloist and founder of the Tony Williams Lifetime and the New Tony Williams Lifetime, 1975-76. Session for Ben Sidran; Ray Manzarek; Stanley Clarke (1974); Les Dudek (1977); Santana (1980). *Albums:* Lifetime; Ego (POL 405); Emergency (POL 4010); Old Bum's Rush (POL 5040); Turn It Over (POL 4021).

TONY WILLIAMS LIFETIME Alan Holdsworth—guitar; Tony Newton—bass, vocal; Alan Pasqua—keyboards; Tony Williams—drums. *Albums:* Believe It (COL PC 33836) 1976; Million Dollar Legs (COL PC 34263) 1976; The Quintet (COL C2 34976); Joy of Flying (COL JC 35705).

WILLIAMS, TREVOR Bass. Member of the Audience, 1971.

WILLIAMS, WALTER Guitar. Session for Junior Wells.

WILLIAMS, WARREN Keyboards. Session for Watson-Beasley (1980).

WILLIAMS, WENDY ORLEAN Vocal, saxophone, percussion. Member of the Plasmatics since 1980.

WILLIAMS, WILLY Bass. Member of the Wierdos, 1979-80.

WILLIAMS, WILLIE Guitar. Member of Gene Vincent and His Hub Caps, 1956-61.

WILLIAMSON, BILLY Member of Bill Haley and the Comets.

WILLIAMSON, JOHN LEE Real name of Sonny Boy Williamson.

WILLIAMSON, ROBIN Vocal, guitar, keyboards, percussion, drums, harmonica. Member of the Incredible String Band, 1967, before going solo. *Albums:* American Stonehenge (FLF 062) 1978; Glint at the Kindling (FLF 096) 1979; Journey's

Edge (FLF 033) 1977.

WILLIAMSON, SONNY BOY Harmonica, vocal. Real name: John Lee Williamson. Blues vocalist and harmonica player who lived in Chicago until his murder in 1948. *Albums:* Bluebird Blues (VIC LPV 518); Story of the Blues (COL CG 30006).

WILLIAMSON, SONNY BOY Harmonica, vocal. Real name: Rice Miller. Often referred to as Sonny Boy Williamson II, he began as a one-man band before concentrating on the harmonica. He made a successful European tour in 1963. Many of his English followers, including the Yardbirds, saw and performed with him. *Albums:* Blues Jam (BUD 7510); Bummer Road (CSS 1536); This Is My Story (CSS 2CH 50027); Eric Clapton and the Yardbirds and Sonny Boy Williamson (MER ML 8003) 1963; Night Time Is the Right Time (SPB 4065); Special Early Works (SPB 4038); Sonny Boy Williamson and Memphis Slim in Paris (CRS 10003) 1973; Sonny Boy Williamson and the Yardbirds (MER 61071).

WILLIS, ANDREA Vocal. Session for Paul Butterfield, 1975.

WILLIS, CAROLYN Vocal. Session for Harvey Mandel; Neil Diamond (1976); Seals and Crofts (1976); the Richie Furay Band (1976).

WILLIS, EDDIE Guitar. Session for the Temptations (1973).

WILLIS, IKE Vocal. Session for Frank Zappa (1979).

WILLIS, LARRY Keyboards. Replaced Dick Halligan in the re-formed Blood, Sweat and Tears. Session for the Blues Brothers (1980).

WILLIS, MICHAEL Guitar. Member of Neil Merryweather's Space Rangers, 1974-75.

WILLIS, PETE Guitar. Member of Def Leppard, 1980.

WILLIS, VIOLA Vocal. Session for Joe Cocker (1972).

WILLISON, PETE Cello. Session for Chris Spedding (1980).

WILLS, DAVID JAY Vocal. Member of Stonebolt, 1978-80.

WILLS, RICK Bass. Member of Peter Frampton's Camel, 1973, and the re-formed Small Faces, 1977-78. Replaced Ed Gagliardi in Foreigner, 1980-present. Session for Kevin Ayers (1977); Peter Frampton (1972, 74); David Gilmour (1978).

WILLY, D. Vocal, guitar. Member of the Sneakers, 1980.

WILSEY, JOHN Bass, vocal. Member of the Avengers, 1979.

WILSON, ALAN Harmonica, vocal, guitar. Original member of Canned Heat, 1965, until his death in 1970. Called by John Lee Hooker, "the greatest harmonica player ever." Session for Son House.

WILSON, ANN Vocal, percussion. Born 6/19/51. Member of Heart since 1975.

WILSON, B. J. Drums, percussion. Real name: Barrie Wilson. Replaced Bobby Harrison in Procol Harum, 1967-77. Session for Joe Cocker (1968); Lou Reed (1972).

WILSON, BOB Drums. Member of the Seawind.

WILSON, BOB Piano. Session for Bob Dylan (1969); J. J. Cale (1971).

WILSON, BOB Guitar, vocal. Member of the Steve Gibbons Band, 1977. Session for Ken Tobias (1973).

WILSON, BRIAN Bass, keyboards, vocal. Born 6/20/42. Organized the Pendletones with brothers Carl and Dennis and high school friends Al Jardine and Mike Love; they became the Beach Boys in 1962.

WILSON, CARL Guitar, vocal. Born 12/21/46. Original member of the Beach Boys, since 1962. Session for Elton John (1974); Henry Gross (1975); Ricci Martin (1977); Lake (1978).

WILSON, CARY Vocal. Session for Donovan (1973).

WILSON, CHARLES Organ. Session for Leon Russell (1974).

WILSON, CHRIS Guitar, harpsichord. Replaced Cyril Jordan in the Flamin' Groovies, 1979.

WILSON, CINDY Vocal, percussion, guitar. Member of the B-52's, 1980.

WILSON, COLIN Bass. Original member of the String Driven Thing, 1972-73.

WILSON, DAN Guitar, vocal. Member of the Sand, 1973-76.

WILSON, DENNIS Drums, vocal. Born 12/4/44. Original member of the Beach Boys, since 1962. *Album:* Pacific Ocean Blue (CRB PZ 34354) 1977.

WILSON, DON Guitar. Original member of the Ventures.

WILSON, FRANK Drums. Session for John Mayall (1977).

WILSON, JACKIE Vocal. Pop-soul star of the 1950s and 1960s. *Albums:* Lonely Teardrops, 1958; Doggin' Around, 1959; Night, 1960; So Much, 1960; Try a Little Tenderness, 1961; You Ain't Heard Nothin' Less, 1961; By Special Request, 1961; Shake a Hand, 1962; Danny Boy, 1964; Something Else, 1964; No Pity, 1965; Higher and Higher, 1967; He's So Fine; Jackie Wilson at the Copa (BRU 754108); Hitsville; Jumpin' Jack; Millionairs; Jackie Wilson; Woman, a Lover, a Friend; Baby Workout (BRU 754110) 1963; Beautiful Day (BRU 754189); Body and Soul (BRU 754105) 1962; Do Your Thing (BRU 754154); 14 Original Greatest Hits (KGO 5007); I Get the Sweetest Feeling (BRU 754138) 1968; It's All a Part of Love (BRU 754158); Jackie Sings the Blues (BRU 754055) 1960; Merry Christmas from Jackie Wilson (BRU 754112); My Golden Favorites (BRU 754058); My Golden Favorites, Vol. 2 (BRU 754115); Nobody But

You (BRU 754212); Nowstalgia (BRU 754199); Soul Galore (BRU 754120) 1966; Soul Time (BRU 754118) 1965; Spotlight on Jackie Wilson (BRU 754119) 1965; This Love Is Real (BRU 754167); Whispers (BRU 754122) 1966; Jackie Wilson's Greatest Hits (BRU 754110) 1962; Jackie Wilson's Greatest Hits (BRU 754185); Jackie Wilson Sings the World's Greatest Melodies (BRU 754106) 1963; You Got Me Walking (BRU 754172).

WILSON, JEFF Guitar. Member of Pure Prairie League, 1980.

WILSON, JOHN Guitar, bass, vocal. Member of the Dodgers, 1978.

WILSON, JOHN Drums. Original member of Rory Gallagher's Taste, 1968-72.

WILSON, KELLY Vocal, guitar, keyboards. Half of the Wilson Brothers, 1979.

WILSON, KIM Vocal, harmonica. Member of the Fabulous Thunderbirds since 1979.

WILSON, MADRILE, JR. Percussion. Member of the Greezy Wheels, 1976.

WILSON, MARY Vocal. Original member of the Supremes.

WILSON, MICHAEL Mick, of Dave Dee, Dozy, Beaky, Mick and Tich, 1966-68.

WILSON, NANCY Guitar, vocal. Born 3/16/54. Member of Heart since 1975.

WILSON, PAULINE Vocal. Member of Seawind.

WILSON, PETE Keyboards, vocal, writer, engineer. Session for Sham 69 (1978-80).

WILSON, PHIL Drums, conga, trombone, percussion. Member of the Paul Butterfield Blues Band, 1967-69, and Full Moon, 1972. Session for Martin Mull (1972).

WILSON, RICKY Guitar. Member of the B-52's since 1980. Session for Tom Verlaine (1979).

WILSON, ROBERT Bass. Session for Leon Russell (1974); Freddie King (1975).

WILSON, RON Drums. Member of the Surfaris, 1963-65, and Joy of Cooking, 1970-72.

WILSON, RONNIE Horns. Session for Leon Russell (1974).

WILSON, RORY Guitar, vocal. Member of the Broken Home, 1980.

WILSON, ROSS Vocal, guitar, harmonica. Member of Daddy Cool, 1971-72.

WILSON, STEVE Vocal, guitar. Half of the Wilson Brothers, 1979.

WILSON, TERRY Bass. Member of Bloontz, 1973, Backstreet Crawler, 1975-76, and Crawler, 1977. Session for John "Rabbit" Bundrick.

WILSON, TERRY Guitar, vocal. Member of No Slack, 1978.

WILSON, TOM Producer. Produced the Animals; the Mothers of Invention (1966); the Velvet Underground (1967); and others.

WILSON, TONY Vocal. Session for Steve Stills (1970).

WILSON, WALLACE Guitar. Session for Paul Simon (1972).

WILSON, WALLY Keyboards, percussion. Member of Kenny and the Kasuals.

WILSON, WAYNE Drums. Member of the Downchild, 1979.

WILSON, WILLIE Drums. Member of Quiver. Session for David Gilmour (1978).

WILSON BROTHERS Steve Wilson—vocal, guitar; Kelly Wilson—vocal, guitar, keyboards. *Album:* Another Night (ATC 38-116) 1979.

WILSON-SLESSER, TERRY Vocal. Member of Backstreet Crawler, 1975-76, and Crawler, 1977.

WIMPY ROY Vocal. Member of the Subhumans, 1979.

WINCHESTER, JESSIE Guitar, keyboards, flute, vocal. *Albums:* Third Down, 110 to Go (BSV 2102) 1972; Learn to Love It (BSV 6953) 1974; Let the Rough Side Drag (BSV 6964) 1976; Nothing But a Breeze (BSV 6968) 1977; Touch on the Rainy Side (BSV K 6984) 1978.

WINCOTT, TERRY Guitar, vocal. Member of the Amazing Blondel, 1974.

WIND IN THE WILLOWS Gil Fields—drums; Harris Wiener—organ, vocal; Peter Brittain—guitar, vocal; Steve de Phillips—bass, vocal; Paul Klein—vocal; Deborah Harry—vocal; Ida Andrews—bassoon, flute, fife, vocal. *Album:* Wind in the Willows, 1968.

WINDING, JAI Keyboards, producer. Produced LeRou (1980). Production and session for the Currie Sisters (1979). Session for Dave Mason; Terence Boylan (1977); Steven T. (1978); the Pages (1978); Cheap Trick (1978-79); Gary Wright (1979); Molly Hatchett (1979-80); Adam Mitchell (1979); Cher (1979); the Ozark Mountain Daredevils (1980); Glen Campbell (1980).

WINDO, GARY Tenor saxophone. Member of Centipede, 1971, the Johnny Average Dance Band, 1980, and Pam Windo and the Shades, 1980. Session for Robert Wyatt (1974).

PAM WINDO AND THE SHADES Gary Windo—saxophone; Chris Grassi—drums; Charlie Brocco—guitar; Ian Bennett—saxophone; Ed Fitzgerald—bass. *Album:* It (BSV 3479) 1980.

WINE, TONY Vocal. Session for Steely Dan (1980).

WINFIELD, CHUCK Trumpet. Original member of Blood, Sweat and Tears, 1968-69.

WINFIELD, MIKE Bass. Member of the Colwell-Winfield Blues Band, 1968.

WINGFIELD, PETE Keyboards, vocal. Member of the Keef Hartley Band, 1970, and the Olympic Runners, 1974-79. Session for Memphis Slim (1971); B. B. King (1971); Nazareth (1972); Mike Vernon; Chris Youlden (1973-74); Freddie King (1974-75); Ian Matthews (1978); Lightnin' Slim (1978); the Hollies (1978-79); Phillip Rainbow (1979); Gerry Rafferty (1979-80).

WINGS Paul McCartney—guitar, vocal, bass, keyboards, producer; Linda McCartney—vocal, piano; Danny Seiwell—drums, percussion, vocal (1971-75); Denny Laine—guitar, vocal; Henry McCulloch—guitar, vocal (1973); Jimmy McCulloch—guitar, vocal (1975-78); Joe English—drums, vocal, percussion (1975-78); Laurence Juber—guitar (1979); Steve Holly—drums (1979). Post-Beatles band formed by Paul McCartney after the release of his solo album. Recorded the theme for the James Bond movie *Live and Let Die,* 1973. *Albums:* Back to the Egg (COL FC 36057) 1979; Band on the Run (COL JC 36482) 1973; Live and Let Die (UAR LMAS 100) 1973; London Town (CAP SW 11777) 1978; Red Rose Speedway (COL JC 36481) 1973; Venus and Mars (CAP SMAS 11419) 1975; Wild Life (COL JC 36480) 1971; Wings at the Speed of Sound (CAP SW 11525) 1976; Wings' Greatest (CAP SOO 11905) 1978; Wings Over America (CAP SWCO 11593) 1977.

WINKLEMAN, BOBBY Guitar, vocal. Member of Bonaroo, 1975.

WINN, TERRELL Guitar. Member of the Jim Carroll Band, 1980.

WINSKI, COLIN Guitar, vocal. *Album:* Rock Therapy (TKM 7083) 1980.

WINSKI, NINA Vocal. Session for Colin Winski (1980).

WINSLOW, BARRY Vocal, guitar. Member of the Royal Guardsmen, 1969.

WINSOR, GAYE Keyboards, vocal. Member of the Skyboys, 1979-present.

WINTER, DAVE Bass. Session for Rick Wakeman (1972).

WINTER, EDGAR Saxophone, keyboards, guitar, vocal. Born 12/28/47. Began with brother Johnny in Texas. After his initial exposure, he branched out as a soloist, then with White Trash, the Edgar Winter Group, and full circle to playing with his brother again in 1976. Though more jazz-oriented than his brother, he achieved commercial success with rock and blues. See Edgar Winter Group and White Trash. Session for Johnny Winter (1970-present); Rick Derringer (1973).

EDGAR WINTER GROUP Edgar Winter—keyboards, saxophone, vocal, percussion; Rick Derringer—guitar, vocal, bass, percussion; Dan Hartman—bass, vocal, guitar, percussion; Chuck Ruff—drums, percussion, vocal. See Edgar Winter. *Albums:* Entrance (EPC BG 33770); Roadwork (EPC PEG 31249); They Only Come Out at Night (EPC PE 31584) 1972; Edgar Winter Album (BSK JZ 35989) 1979; Edgar Winter's White Trash (EPC E 30512); Shock Treatment (BSK) 1974; Jasmine Nightdreams (BSK) 1975; Entrance /White Trash (EPC BG 33770); Edgar Winter Group with Rick Derringer (BSK) 1975; Recycled (BSK PZ 34858) 1977.

EDGAR WINTER'S WHITE TRASH Edgar Winter—vocal, keyboards, saxophone, percussion; Floyd Radford—guitar; Jerry LaCroix—vocal, saxophone, harmonica; Mike McLellan—trumpet, vocal; Jon Smith—tenor saxophone, vocal; Bobby Ramerez—drums; George Sheck—bass. After his less than successful solo debut, without brother Johnny, on "Entrance," Edgar Winter returned to the rock format by forming White Trash. It was a big band and slowly evolved into the Edgar Winter Group, a more commercial application of brother Johnny's style in the pop market. See the Edgar Winter Group.

WINTER, JOHNNY Guitar, slide guitar, vocal. Born 1/23/44. Rumor sent Steve Paul, a New York club owner, to Texas to discover Winter, a cross-eyed blues guitarist, in 1969. His talent afforded him an amazing six-figure contract before his first album was made. The publicity was tremendous and his name was constantly in the trade columns, resulting in huge record sales. Now that the novelty is gone, Winter's blues roots often reappear, contrasting his hard rock style that was originally his trademark in his rise to stardom. Production and session for Muddy Waters (1978). Session for Jimi Hendrix (1968); the Blast (1979); Muddy Waters (1979); Jeremy Steig (1975). *Albums:* About Blues (JNS 3008); Austin, Texas (VAR VA LA 139 E); Early Times (JNS 3023); John Dawson Winter III (COL PE 33292) 1974; Before the Storm; Progressive Blues Experiment (IMF 12431) 1969; Together Live, with Edgar Winter, 1976; Captured Live (BSK PZ 33944) 1975; Live (COL PC 30475); Nothin' But the Blues (BSK PZ 34813) 1977; Raisin' Cain (BSK JZ 36343) 1980; Saints and Sinners (COL PC 32715) 1974; Second Winter (COL KCS 9947); Still Alive and Well (COL KC 32188) 1973; White, Hot and Blue (BSK JZ 35475) 1978; Johnny Winter (COL CS 9826) 1969; Johnny Winter And (COL KC 30221).

JOHNNY WINTER AND Johnny Winter—vocal, guitar; Rick Derringer—vocal, guitar (1971-73); Randy Jo Hobbs—drums, percussion (1970-73); Richard Hughes—drums, percussion (1973-74). Johnny Winter's backup band, 1971-74. See Johnny Winter.

WINTER, KURT Member of the Guess Who.

WINTER, MIKE Bass. Member of Shakin' Street, 1980.

WINTERS, DENNIS Vocal, guitar. Member of the Winters Brothers Band.

WINTERS, DONNIE Vocal, guitar. Member of the Winters Brothers Band.

WINTERS, IAN Guitar. Member of Daddy Cool, 1972.

WINTERS BROTHERS BAND Donnie Winters—vocal, guitar; Dennis Winters—vocal, guitar; Gene Watson—bass; Kent Harris—drums; David Davis—keyboards. *Albums:* Coast to Coast (ACO

38 106); Winters Brothers Band (ACO 36 145) 1976.

WINTHROP, DAVE Saxophone. Member of the Secret Affair, 1980.

WINTHROP, GEOFFREY Vocal, guitar, sitar. Original member of the Ultimate Spinach, 1968-69.

WINTOUR, DAVID Bass. Session for Neil Sedaka (1976); Chinga Chavin (1976); Frankie Miller (1979); Tim Renwick (1980).

WINWOOD, MUFF Bass, producer. With brother Steve, an original member of the Spencer Davis Group, 1964-68. Produced the Sutherland Brothers (1973); Phillip Goodhand-Tait (1977); Dire Straits (1978); Sparks; and others.

WINWOOD, STEVE Guitar, keyboards, vocal, bass, drums, percussion, producer. Born 5/12/48. At the age of fifteen, in 1964, Winwood appeared as a member of the Spencer Davis Group (until 1967), playing and writing such rock classics as "I'm a Man" and "Gimme Some Lovin'." He was considered a prodigy, and his white-soul singing was both distinctive and popular. In 1967 he left to form his own group, which emerged the following year: Traffic, an unusual trio combination with a sometimes fourth member, Dave Mason. In 1969, the strife-torn group disbanded. Winwood joined Eric Clapton for the short-lived Blind Faith tour, 1969. The fall of Blind Faith led to his membership in Ginger Baker's Air Force (1970-71) and a dramatic reunion of Traffic, which again dissolved in 1975. In 1976, he was a member of Yamashta, Winwood and Shrieve, recording under the group name Go. Session for Joe Cocker (1968); Jimi Hendrix (1968, 70-71); McDonald and Giles (1971); Jim Capaldi (1971, 73, 75, 79); "Tommy" (1972); Muddy Waters (1972); Howlin' Wolf (1972); Alvin Lee (1973); Lou Reed (1973); the Rainbow Concert (1973); the Sutherland Brothers (1973); George Harrison (1979); Marianne Faithfull (1979). *Albums:* Go (ISL 9387) 1976; Go — Live From Paris (ISL 10) 1976; Stevie Winwood (ISL 9494) 1977; Arc of a Diver (ISL 9576) 1980.

WIPERS Dave Koupal—bass; Greg Sage—guitar, vocal; Sam Henry—drums. *Album:* Is This Real? (PKA 82801) 1980.

WIPPICH, BERND Vocal, guitar. Member of Randy Pie, 1975-77.

WIRE B. C. Gilbert—guitar; G. Lewis—bass; Colin Newman—vocal; Robert Gotobed—drums. *Albums:* 154 (WBR K-3398); Pink Flag (HAR ST-11757) 1980; Wire 154 (WBR BSK 3398) 1980.

WIRELESS Michael Crawford—guitar, vocal; Steve McMurray—guitar; Allan Marshall—bass, vocal; Marty Morin—drums, percussion, vocal. *Album:* Absotively Human Relatively Sane (MER SRM 1 3750) 1979.

WISE, EDDIE Keyboards, vocal. Session for Martin Mull (1974-79). *Album:* In the Soop (AN 79338) 1974.

WISE, FRED Fiddle. Session for the Marshall Tucker Band (1973).

WISE, JAMES Vocal. Member of Archie Bell and the Drells since 1976.

WISEFIELD, LAURIE Guitar, slide guitar, vocal. Member of Wishbone Ash.

WISELY, MAX Bass. Member of the Cargoe, 1972.

WISHBONE ASH Andy Powell—guitar, vocal (1974-present); Laurie Wisefield—guitar, slide guitar, vocal; Martin Turner—bass, vocal; Steve Upton—drums, percussion; Ted Turner—guitar, vocal (until 1973). Progressive rockers from England who first became known in 1970. *Albums:* Argus (MCA 2344); Front Page News (MCA 2311) 1977; Just Testing (MCA 3221) 1980; Live Dates (MCA 2 8006) 1973; Locked In (ATC 18164); New England (ATC 18200); No Smoke Without Fire (MCA 3060); Pilgrimage (MCA 36) 1971; Wishbone Ash (MCA 2343) 1970; Wishbone Four (MCA 2348); There's the Rub (MCA 464).

WISON, DAVEY Bass, vocal. Member of the Candle, 1972.

WITHEM, GARY Piano. Member of Gary Puckett and the Union Gap, 1967-68.

WITHERS, PICK Drums. Member of Dire Straits since 1978. Session for Dave Edmunds (1975); Bob Dylan (1979).

WITHERSPOON, BUDGE Guitar, vocal. Member of Iguana, 1977.

WITKEN, JOSEPH Piano, vocal. Original member of Sha Na Na, 1970.

WITKOWSKI, RICK Guitar, percussion. Member of Crack the Sky, 1975-77.

WITNEY, JOHN Guitar, sitar. Original member of Family.

WITSETT, CARSON Organ. Session for Paul Simon (1973).

WITTAKER, STAN Guitar, vocal. Member of Happy the Man, 1977-78.

WITTENBERG, JOHN Violin. Session for George Duke (1975).

WITTY, REGGIE Bass, vocal. Session for Van Wilks (1980).

WIZZARD Bass. Member of Mother's Finest since 1976.

WOBBLE, JAH Bass. Member of the Public Image since 1979.

WOFFORD, DAVID Bass. Member of Laurie and the Sighs, 1980.

WOLBRADT, PETER Guitar, vocal. Member of Kraan, 1975.

WOLF, BILL Bass. Replaced Charles Larkey in the Fugs, 1968.

WOLF, PETER Vocal. Born 3/6/46. Real name: Peter Blankenfield. Voice of the J. Geils Band since 1970. His stage antics and song styling resemble those of Mick Jagger.

WOLF, PETER Keyboards. Session for Frank Zappa (1979).

WOLF, RICHARD Member of the Crimson Tide, 1978-79.

WOLF Darryl Way—violin, viola, keyboards; Dek Messecar—bass, vocal; John Etheridge—guitar; Ian Mosley—drums. *Album:* Darryl Way's Wolf (DEC 644) 1974.

WOLFE, E. E. Bass. Original member of Fever Tree.

WOLFE, PETE Member of Wheatfield, 1980.

WOLFE, RANDY Guitar. Session for B. B. King (1972).

WOLFERT, DAVID Guitar, piano. Session for Nilsson (1976); Martin Mull (1977).

WOLFF, BILL Guitar. Replaced Lance Fent in the Peanut Butter Conspiracy, 1967.

WOLFF, CHARLES Drums, vocal. Member of the Brains, 1980.

WOLFF, DAVID Vocal, keyboards. *Album:* Aura (BUD 5725) 1979.

WOLINSKI, DAVID Keyboards, vocal, bass, percussion. Member of the Bangor Flying Circus.

WOLKEN, L. J. Accordion. Member of the Candle, 1972.

WOLOSCHUK, JOHN Member of Klaatu since 1976.

WOLOVITCH, AL Bass. Member of the Sussman Lawrence Band, 1980.

WOLSTENHOLME, WOOLY Keyboards, vocal. Member of the Barclay James Harvest.

WOLTERS, JOHN Drums, vocal. Member of Dr. Hook.

WOM, BARRY Stage name of John Halsey in the Rutles, 1978.

WOMACK, BOBBY Guitar, vocal. Session for Marc Benno; Janis Joplin (1969); Russ Giguere (1971); Leon Russell (1976). *Albums:* The Womack Live (UAR); My Prescription (UAR); Communication (UAR UAS 5539); Facts of Life (UAR) 1973; Looking for a Love Again (UAR) 1974; Greatest Hits (UAR UA LA 346 G); I Don't Know What the World Is Coming To (UAR); Safety Zones (UAR) 1975; Bobby Womack Goes Country Western (UAR) 1976; Roads of Life (ARI 4222) 1979; Understanding (UAR LM 1002) 1972; Pieces (COL JC 35083) 1978.

WONDER, STEVIE Harmonica, drums, vocal, keyboards, writer. Born 5/13/50. Real name: Steveland Morris Hardaway. From Detroit, Wonder made his debut at the age of twelve, in 1963, uniting soul and pop in his much respected writings and recordings. Session for Dave Mason; B. B. King (1973); James Taylor (1976); Peter Frampton (1977). *Albums:* Twelve Year Old Genius; Tribute to Uncle Ray; Jazz Soul; With a Song in My Heart; At the Beach; Uptight, 1966; Down to Earth, 1966; I Was Made to Love Her, 1967; Fulfillingness' First Finale (TML T7 332) 1974; In Loving Memory (MTN M7 642); Innervisions (TML T7 326); Journey Through the Secret Life of Plants (TML T13 371) 1979; Music of My Mind (TML T7 314) 1972; Someday at Christmas (TML T7 362) 1967; Songs in the Key of Life (TML T13 340) 1976; Talking Book (TML T7 3197) 1972; Stevie Wonder's Greatest Hits (TML T7 283) 1968; Stevie Wonder's Greatest Hits, Vol. 2 (TML T7 313); Hotter than July (TML T8 373) 1980.

WONDER WHO Early name for the Four Seasons.

WOOD, ANNAGH Vocal. Session for Nico (1974).

WOOD, ART Drums. Session for Gary Wright (1977).

WOOD, ARTHUR Keyboards. Original member of the Climax Blues Band, 1968-71.

WOOD, BOBBY Keyboards. Session for Tom Rapp (1972); Doug Kershaw (1972, 74).

WOOD, BRENTON Vocal. Soul vocalist in the Sam Cooke manner, who appeared in 1968. *Albums:* Oogum Boogum; Baby You Got It.

WOOD, CAROLYN Organ. Member of the Brooklyn Bridge.

WOOD, CHRIS Flute, saxophone, organ, percussion, vocal. Born 6/22/44. Original member of Traffic, 1967-75. His wailing sax and jazzy flute work matched his equally unique stage presence. Member of Ginger Baker's Air Force, 1970-71. Session for Fat Mattress (1969); Sky (1970); Jim Capaldi (1971); Free Creek (1973); Jimi Hendrix (1968-71); Crawler (1977).

WOOD, COLIN Keyboards. Session for Uriah Heep (1970).

WOOD, DON Percussion. Session for Jan and Dean (1963).

WOOD, LAUREN Vocal, keyboards. Member of Chunky, Ernie and Novi before the group re-formed under her name. See Chunky, Ernie and Novi. *Album:* Lauren Wood (WBR 3278) 1979.

WOOD, PETE Keyboards. Member of Quiver until 1975, Natural Gas, 1976, the Magnet, 1979, and the Rivets, 1980.

WOOD, RON Guitar, bass, vocal. Born 6/1/47. Wood was first noticed as one of Rod Stewart's session men when the latter started his solo career in 1969. It was no surprise when he joined the Faces with Stewart in 1970. As the group's reputation rose to superstardom through the years, so did the individual reputations of the members of the group. He left the Faces to replace Mick Taylor in the Rolling Stones, 1976-present. Session for Rod Stewart (1970-76); Long John Baldry (1971); Alvin Lee (1973); the Rainbow Concert (1973); George Harrison (1974); Bill Wyman (1976); Rick Danko (1977); the Band (1978); Ian McLagen (1979). *Albums:* Gimme Some Neck (COL JC 35702) 1979; I've Got My Own Album to Do (WBR B 2819) 1975; Mahoney's Last Stand

(ACO 36 126) 1976; Now Look (WBR B 2872) 1976.

WOOD, ROY Guitar, vocal, banjo, sitar. Born 11/8/46. Original member of the Move, 1969-72, and the Electric Light Orchestra, until 1974, when he formed the short-lived Wizzard. *Albums:* On the Road Again (WBR K 3247) 1979; Boulders (UAR UA LA 168 F) 1973.

WOOD, STANFORD Congas. Member of Upepo.

WOOD, STEVE Keyboards. Member of Honk. Session for Paul Waroff (1980).

WOOD, STUART Vocal, guitar, bass, piano. Member of the Congregation, and the Bay City Rollers. Session for Henry Gross (1973); Free Creek (1973); Annette Peacock (1979).

WOOD, VICKI Vocal. Session for Nico (1974).

WOODFORD, DAVID Reeds. Member of the James Montgomery Band, 1976.

WOODFORD, TERRY Vocal. Session for Roy Orbison (1979).

WOODGATE, DAN Drums, percussion. Member of Madness, 1979.

WOODHEAD, JOHN Guitar. Member of Ace, 1977.

WOODLEY, BRUCE Vocal. Member of the Seekers, 1965-67, and co-author of "Red Rubber Ball" with Paul Simon, a song made popular by the Cyrkle.

WOODLEY, KEN Organ, vocal. Member of the Alamo, 1971.

WOODMAN, SCOTT Drums. Member of the Private Lightning, 1980.

WOODMANSEY, WOODY Drums. Member of the Spiders from Mars, 1976.

WOODS, BOBBY Piano. Session for Jackie DeShannon (1972); J. J. Cale (1972); Bob Seger (1974).

WOODS, GARY Vocal, percussion. Member of Steeleye Span, 1977.

WOODS, GAY See Gay and Terry Woods; Woods Band.

GAY AND TERRY WOODS Terry Woods—guitar, autoharp, mandola, concertina, banjo, vocal; Gay Woods—dulcimer, autoharp, vocal. Nucleus of the Woods Band. *Albums:* The Time Is Right (ANT 7029) 1976; Tender Hooks (MLG 020) 1978.

WOODS, HOLLY Vocal. Member of Toronto, 1980.

WOODS, RON Percussion. Member of the Barry Goldberg Reunion and the Buddy Miles Express, 1968-69.

WOODS, SONNY Member of Hank Ballard's Midnighters.

WOODS, TERRY See Gay and Terry Woods; the Woods Band.

WOODS, WAYNE Drums. Member of the Jim Carroll Band, 1980.

WOODS BAND Terry Woods—mandola, concertina, bass, vocal; Gay Woods—concertina, autoharp, dulcimer, bodhran, vocal; Ed Deane—guitar, bass, harpsichord; Pat Nash—drums. *Album:* The Woods Band (MLG 015).

WOODSEN, CRAIG Drums, percussion. Member of the United States of America, 1968.

WOODSTOCK The pinnacle of the "hippy" movement's interrelationship with rock music was national news in 1969 when hordes of youths gathered at Max Yasgur's farm in Woodstock, New York, for the largest rock festival ever assembled to that date. It was headlined by artists Joan Baez, the Paul Butterfield Blues Band, Canned Heat, Joe Cocker, Country Joe and the Fish, Crosby, Stills, Nash and Young, Arlo Guthrie, Richie Havens, Jimi Hendrix, the Jefferson Airplane, Santana, John Sebastian, Sha Na Na, Sly and the Family Stone, Ten Years After, the Who, Melanie, Mountain, and others. *Albums:* Woodstock, Vol. 1 (COT SD 3500) 1970; Woodstock, Vol. II (COT SD2 400) 1971.

WOODWARD, THOMAS JAMES Real name of Tom Jones.

WOODWORTH, ZANE Trumpet. Session for Taj Mahal (1978).

WOODY, SCOTT Guitar, vocal. Member of the Five Dollar Shoes, 1972.

WOOLAM, STEVE Violin. Member of the Electric Light Orchestra.

WOOLEY, BRUCE Vocal. Head of the Buggles before going solo with Bruce Wooley and the Camera Club, 1980.

BRUCE WOOLEY AND THE CAMERA CLUB Bruce Wooley—vocal; David Birch—guitar; Rod Johnson—drums; Matthew Seligman—bass; Tom Dolby—keyboards. *Album:* Bruce Wooley Camera Club (COL JC 36301) 1980.

WOOLEY, SHEB Vocal. He and the "Purple People Eater" rose to fame in 1958 before he moved into the country/western field.

WOOLF, STEPHANIE Violin. Session for Waylon Jennings (1973-75).

WOOLFSON, ERIC Keyboards, writer. Inspiration for the concept behind the Alan Parsons Project "Tales of Mystery and Imagination" (1976), based on stories by Edgar Allan Poe, and for subsequent Project albums.

WOOTEN, CASSANDRA Vocal. Session for John Lennon (1980).

WORKMAN, FLAP Accordion. Session for Ian McLagen (1979).

WORKMAN, GEOFF Engineer, producer. Engineer for producer Roy Thomas Baker. Engineer and production for Reggie Knighton (1978); Ian McLagen (1979); and the Currie Sisters (1979). Engineer for Queen; the Cars (1978-79); Foreigner (1979); Ron Wood (1979); Sammy Hagar (1980); Journey (1980); and others.

WORKMAN, MICHAEL Keyboards. Replaced Tom Broome in Great Southern, 1978.

WORKMAN, NANETTE Vocal. Session for Mahogany Rush (1979).

WORNER, CARL Vocal. Member of the Elektrics, 1980.

WORSNOP, RIK Keyboards. Member of the Lone Star, 1977.

WORTH, CHRISTOPHER Keyboards, vocal. Member of Ambrosia, 1975-78.

WOTTON, AL Drums. Session for Mark Farner (1977).

WRATHER, STEVE Guitar. Session for Elton John (1980).

WRAY, BOB Bass. Session for Roy Orbison (1979).

WRAY, LINK Guitar, vocal. *Albums:* Bullshot (VSA 7009) 1979; Live at the Paradiso (VSA 7010) 1980; Robert Gordon/Link Wray (VIC AFLI 3296); Be What You Want To (POL 5047) 1973.

WRECKLESS ERIC Guitar, vocal, organ. *Albums:* Big Smash (SFF E2-36463); Whole Wide World (SFF 0798).

WRIGHT, BERKELY Guitar, vocal. Member of Tranquility, 1972.

WRIGHT, BOBBY Keyboards. Session for Tim Weisberg (1977).

WRIGHT, DAVID Drums. Replaced Danny Mihn in the Flamin' Groovies, 1979.

WRIGHT, DON Reeds. Member of S.C.R.A., 1972.

WRIGHT, EDNA Vocal. Session for Harvey Mandel.

WRIGHT, GARY Keyboards, vocal, writer. Founding member of Spooky Tooth, 1968-72, he left to go solo, finally achieving the fame both he and the group deserved years beforehand with his album "Dreamweaver," 1976. Session for Sky (1970); Nilsson (1971); B. B. King (1971); George Harrison (1972, 76, 79) Thomas F. Browne (1972); Jerry Lee Lewis (1973); Splinter (1974); Leslie West (1975); the Platinum Hook (1979). *Albums:* Dream Weaver (WBR 2868) 1976; Headin' Home (WBR K 3244) 1979; Light of Smiles (WBR B 2951) 1977; Touch and Gone (WBR K 3137) 1977; Extractions (AAM SP 4277) 1970; Footprint (AAM) 1971.

WRIGHT, GAVYN Violin. Session for Pavlov's Dog (1976).

WRIGHT, HOSHAL Guitar. Session for Taj Mahal.

WRIGHT, JOHN Vocal, percussion. Member of the Beacon Street Union, 1968.

WRIGHT, JOSEPH Guitar. Session for Pete Wingfield (1975).

WRIGHT, LORNA Vocal. Session for Gary Wright (1975-79).

WRIGHT, NORMAN Vocal. Member of the Del Vikings.

WRIGHT, PETE Bass, vocal. Replaced Glenn Hughes in Trapeze, 1974-present.

WRIGHT, RICHARD Keyboards, vocal. Born 7/28/45. An original member of Pink Floyd since 1966. Session for Syd Barrett; B. B. King (1971). *Album:* Wet Dream (COL JC 35559) 1978.

WRIGHT, SHAUN Drums, percussion. Member of the Stingray, 1979.

WRIGHT, STEVE Bass. Member of the Greg Kihn Band since 1976.

WRIGHT, STEVE Vocal. Voice of the Easybeats. *Album:* Hard Road (ATC 36 109) 1974.

WRIGLEY, JOE Guitar. Member of Gram Parsons' early band.

WU, WENDY Vocal. Member of the Photos, 1980.

WYATT, FRANK Keyboards, reeds. Member of Happy the Man, 1977-78.

WYATT, ROBERT Vocal, keyboards, drums, producer. Original member of the Soft Machine, and Matching Mole before going solo in 1974. Session for Eno; Kevin Ayers (1973); Phil Manzanera (1975). *Album:* Rock Bottom (VIR 2017).

WYETH, HOWIE Keyboards, mellotron, drums. Member of the Wildcats, 1979. Session for Leslie West (1975); Bob Dylan (1975); Don McLean (1977); Moon Martin (1979); Link Wray (1979); Rob Stoner (1980).

WYLES, KITTY Drums. Member of No Dice, 1978-79.

WYMAN, BILL Bass, vocal, guitar, piano. Born 10/24/36. Original member of the Rolling Stones, since 1964. Session for Howlin' Wolf (1972). *Albums:* Monkey Grip (SFS 79100) 1974; Stone Alone, 1976.

WYMORE, STEPHEN Bass, guitar, synthesizer, vocal. Member of the Pink Section, 1980.

WYNANS, REESE Piano. Member of Captain Beyond, 1973. Session for Great Southern (1978).

WYNN, DONY Bass, vocal. Member of the Romeos, 1980.

WYNN, TOM Drums. Member of Cowboy, 1971-73.

MICHAEL WYNN BAND No personnel listed. *Album:* Queen of the Night (ARA SW 50027) 1978.

WYNNE, DAVE Drums. Member of the Influence, 1968.

WYRICH, BARBARA Vocal. Session for Roy Orbison (1979).

X Billy Zoom—guitar; John Doe—bass, vocal; Exene—vocal; D. J. Bonebrake—drums. *Album:* Los Angeles (SLS 104) 1980.

XTC Barry Andrews—keyboards (1976-78); Andy Partridge—guitar, vocal, synthesizer, percussion; Colin Moulding—bass, vocal; Dave Gregory—guitar, vocal; Terry Chambers—drums. Early names: Star Park, the Helium Kids, and Skyscraper and the Snakes. Became XTC in 1976. *Album:* Drums and Wires (VGN 13134) 1980.

YACHTS Martin Watson—guitar, vocal; Henry Priestman—keyboards, vocal; Martin Dempsey—bass, vocal; Bob Bellis—drums, vocal. *Albums:* Yachts (POL 1 6220) 1979; Yachts Without Radar (POL 1 6270) 1980.

YAKUS, SHELLY Engineer. Engineer for Tom Petty (1979); D. L. Byron (1980); and the Motors (1980).

YAMAMOTO, DANNY Drums. Member of Hiroshima, 1980.

YAMASHTA, STOMU Percussion, conductor. Cofounder, with Steve Winwood and Michael Shrieve, of the experimental rock group Go, 1976. *Albums:* Go (ISL 9387) 1976; Go — Live from Paris (ISL 10) 1976; Red Buddha (VAN 79343).

YAMASHTA-WINWOOD-SHRIEVE Stomu Yamashta—percussion, conductor; Steve Winwood—keyboards, vocal; Michael Shrieve—drums, percussion. An East-West experimental jazz-rock venture of 1976. *Albums:* Go (ISL 9387) 1976; Go — Live from Paris (ISL 10) 1976.

YAMAUCHI, TETSU See Tetsu.

YANCE, BOB Flute. Session for Santana (1974).

YANCEY, RAY Bass, vocal. Member of the Highwind, 1980.

YANKEES John Tiven—vocal, guitar, saxophone; Sally Young—guitar, vocal; Paul Ossola—keyboards, bass; Mickey Curry—drums. *Album:* High 'n' Inside (BSD 037) 1978.

YANKEL, JOE Harmonica, percussion. Session for Neil Young (1973).

YANNELL, JOSEPH Drums, percussion, vocal. Member of Polyrock, 1980.

YANOVSKY, ZAL Guitar, vocal. Starting as a member of the Mugwumps, he joined John Sebastian in 1965 to form the Lovin' Spoonful. He attempted a solo career in 1967, with dubious success. *Albums:* Beyond a Dream; Unconditional Love; Free Me; There's a New Wind Blowin'.

YARBOROUGH, RULE Banjo. Session for Barry Goldberg (1974).

YARDBIRDS Keith Relf—vocal, percussion, harmonica (1962-69); Chris Dreja—guitar, percussion, piano, bass (1962-69); Paul Samwell-Smith—bass, producer (1962-66); Eric Clapton—guitar (1962-64); Jim McCarty—drums, percussion (1962-69); John Paul Jones—bass (1966-69); Jeff Beck—guitar (1964-67); Jimmy Page—guitar (1967-69); Robert Plant—vocal (1969); John Bonham—drums, percussion (1969). Formerly the Metropolis Blues Quartet, they changed their name in 1962 when Eric "Slowhand" Clapton joined the group. Clapton left to join John Mayall's Bluesbreakers before the Yardbirds released their first album in the U.S., and was replaced by Jeff Beck. Their first U.S. single, "For Your Love" (1966), was an underground success and represented the new rock music, based in the blues. Hit followed hit, "Shapes of Things" (1966), "Heart Full of Soul" (1965), "Over, Under, Sideways, Down" (1966), but the Yardbirds were pushed into the background by more commercial bands of the time like the Dave Clark 5, the Beatles, and Herman's Hermits. Not even the guitar work of Beck's replacement, Jimmy Page (1967), salvaged the popularity of the group. Relf, McCarty, and Dreja left in 1969 to form Renaissance, and their replacements, Plant and Bonham, dissolved the old name to become Led Zeppelin. *Albums:* For Your Love (EPC 24167) 1965; A Rave Up with the Yardbirds (EPC 24177) 1965; Over, Under, Sideways, Down (EPC 26210) 1966; Yardbirds Greatest Hits (EPC 26313) 1967; Live (EPC 30615) 1968; Favorites, 1977; Eric Clapton and Yardbirds (MER 61271) 1966; The Yardbirds (EPC EG 30135).

YARROW, PETER Guitar, vocal. Peter of Peter, Paul and Mary. Session for Jim Capaldi (1975). *Album:* That's Enough for Me (WBR).

YATES, JOY Vocal. Session for Chris Youlden; the Climax Blues Band (1978); Status Quo (1978).

YAW, BRUCE Bass. Session for Lou Reed (1976).

YEADON, GUS Keyboards, flute, guitar, vocal. Member of Zzebra, 1974.

YEAGER, ROY Drums. Replaced Robert Nix in the Atlanta Rhythm Section, 1979-present.

YEAR, NINE Bass. Member of Sawbuck, 1971.

YELLOW MAGIC ORCHESTRA Ryulchi Sakamoto—keyboards, percussion; Yukihiro Takahashi—drums, percussion, vocal; Harjomi Hosono—bass, keyboards. *Albums:* Yellow Magic Orchestra (ALF SP 736) 1979; X 00 Multiplies (AAM SP 4813) 1980.

YELLOW PAYGES Dan Hortter—vocal, harmonica; Dan Gorman—drums; Bill Ham—guitar; Bob Barnes—bass. The inevitable connection of this band's name to the phone company was built into their planned obsolescence. *Album:* The Yellow Payges, 1969.

YES Jon Anderson—vocal, percussion (1970-80); Chris Squire—bass, vocal; Bill Bruford—drums, percussion (1970-72); Tony Kaye—keyboards (1970-72); Peter Banks—guitar, vocal (1970-71); Steve Howe—guitar, vocal (1971-79); Rick Wakeman—keyboards (1972-73, 77-79); Alan

White—drums (1972-present); Patrick Moraz—keyboards (1974-76); Geoff Downes—keyboards, vocal (1980); Trevor Horn—vocal, bass (1980). Yes's new sound appeared on the rock scene in 1970. Anderson's lyrics extended for sides of albums, varied with ever-changing instrumental melodies, and were as space-oriented as the cover drawings. Their commercial success with underground audiences has allowed each of the members to release solo efforts. *Albums:* Close to the Edge (ATC 19133) 1972; Fragile (ATC 19132) 1971; Going for the One (ATC 19106) 1977; Relayer (ATC 19135) 1974; Tales from Topographic Oceans (ATC SD2 908) 1973; Tormato (ATC 19202) 1978; Time and Word (ATC 8273) 1970; Yes (ATC 8243) 1970; Yes Album (ATC 19131) 1971; Yessongs (ATC 3 100) 1973; Yesterdays (ATC 19134) 1974; Drama (ATC 16019) 1980; Yesshows (ATC 2 510) 1980.

YESTER, JERRY Guitar, vocal. Replaced Zal Yanovsky in the Lovin' Spoonful, 1968. Session for Russ Giguere.

YESTER, JIM Vocal, guitar. Original member of the Association.

YESTERDAY AND TODAY Dave Meniketti—guitar, vocal; Joey Alves—guitar, vocal; Phil Kennemore—bass, vocal; Leonard Haze—drums, vocal. *Album:* Yesterday and Today (LON PS 677) 1976.

YIPES Pat McCurdy—vocal, keyboards; Andy Bartel—guitar, vocal; Michael Hoffman—guitar, vocal, percussion; Pete Strand—bass, vocal; Teddy Freese—drums. *Albums:* Bit Irrational (MLN BXLI 7750) 1980; Yipes (MLN BXLI 7745) 1979.

YOCHMAN, GREG Bass. Member of Mom's Apple Pie, 1973.

YODER, GARY Vocal, guitar. Member of Kak.

YOHO, MONTE Drums. Member of the Outlaws, 1975-79, and the Henry Paul Band, 1980.

YORK, COLEMAN Drums, vocal. Member of the Numbers, 1980.

YORK, DON Keyboards. Session for Hall and Oates (1974).

YORK, DONALD Vocal. Original member of Sha Na Na, since 1970.

YORK, JAY Bass, percussion, vocal. Original member of the Byrds, 1965, and Sod, 1971.

YORK, PAUL Drums. Member of the Dillards.

YORK, PETE Drums, percussion. Member of the Spencer Davis Group, 1964-68. Session for the Keef Hartley Band (1971); Nazareth (1972).

YORK, STEVE Bass. Member of Manfred Mann, 1971. Session for Dr. John (1971); Arthur Brown (1975); Marianne Faithfull (1979).

YOUATT, WILL Bass, vocal. Member of Man, and the Neutrons, 1974.

YOULDEN, CHRIS Vocal, piano. Replaced Brian Portius in Savoy Brown, 1968-70, before starting his solo career. His husky vocals became a trademark of the group (with Kim Simmonds' guitar work) and helped the band gain its initial cult following. His solo career saw a departure from rock for bluesier roots and ballads. *Albums:* Nowhere Road (LON 633) 1973; City Child (LON 642) 1974.

YOUMAN, JAMES Bass. Session for the Mothers of Invention (1975).

YOUNG, ANGUS Guitar. Member of AC/DC since 1977.

YOUNG, BOB Harmonica. Member of Young and Moody, 1977. Session for Status Quo (1974-75, 77, 79).

YOUNG, CHIP Guitar. Session for Tom Rapp; Leon Russell (1973).

YOUNG, DENTON Vocal, percussion. Member of Zon, 1979.

YOUNG, EARL Drums. Member of Duke Williams and the Extremes, 1973. Session for B. B. King (1973-74).

YOUNG, GARY Drums, vocal. Original member of Daddy Cool, 1971-72, and Jo Jo Zep and the Falcons, 1980.

YOUNG, GEORGE Saxophone, flute. Session for Dr. John (1978); Ian Hunter (1979); John Mayall (1979); Ray Gomez (1980); Hilly Michaels (1980).

YOUNG, GEORGE Guitar, vocal, producer. With Harry Vanda, co-founder of the Easybeats. Brother of Angus and Malcolm Young of AC/DC, and their producer, he was also a member of Paintbox, Haffy's Whiskey Sour, and the Marcus Hook Roll Band before forming Flash and the Pan, 1979-present. See Harry Vanda for production credits.

YOUNG, JAMES Guitar, vocal. Original member of Styx, since 1970.

YOUNG, JESSE COLIN Guitar, vocal. In 1967, the Youngbloods were hailed as the greatest country-folk group since the Lovin' Spoonful. Young assumed leadership of the group after Jerry Corbitt left, demonstrating his more than adequate songwriting and singing talents. As a soloist since 1972, he has achieved even more fame and a loyal following. Part of "No Nukes," 1979. *Albums:* American Dreams (ELK 6E 157) 1978; Light Shine (WBR B 2790) 1974; Love on the Wing (WBR B 3033) 1977; On the Road (WBR B 2913) 1976; Songbird (WBR B 2845) 1975; Song for Juli (WBR B 2734) 1973; The Soul of a City Boy (CAP ST 11267) 1974; Together (WBR B 2588) 1972.

YOUNG, JIM Drums. Session for the Mark and Clark Band (1977).

YOUNG, JIM Guitar, keyboards, flute, vocal. Member of the JTS Band, 1977.

YOUNG, JOACHIM Keyboards. Session for Taj Mahal; Boz Scaggs (1972); Steve Miller (1976-77); Les Dudek (1977).

YOUNG, JOHN PAUL Vocal. *Albums:* Love Is in

the Air (SCB 7101) 1978; John Paul Young (MDG BKLI 2535) 1977.

YOUNG, JOHNNY Vocal, guitar. *Albums:* Best of the Chicago Blues (VAN VSD 1/2); Blues Roots (TMT 2 7006); Chicago/The Blues/Today (VAN 79216); Great Blues Men (VAN VSD 25/26); Ramblin' on My Mind (MLS 3002).

YOUNG, KERRY Guitar, vocal. Member of the Fox.

YOUNG, LARRY Organ. Session for Carlos Santana and John McLaughlin (1973); Jimi Hendrix (1969). *Album:* Mother Ship (BLN LT-1038) 1980.

YOUNG, MALCOLM Guitar. Member of AC/DC, since 1977.

YOUNG, MICHAEL Guitar, synthesizer. Session for Richard Lloyd (1979).

YOUNG, MIGHTY JOE Guitar, vocal. Born 9/23/27. Louisiana-born bluesman who moved to Cleveland. *Albums:* Chicken Heads (OVA QD 1437); Legacy of the Blues (CRS 10010); Legacy, Vol. 4 (CRS 10014); Mighty Joe Young (OVA 1706).

YOUNG, MONA LISA Vocal. Session for Bob Dylan (1980).

YOUNG, NEIL Guitar, piano, vocal, harmonica, vibes, writer. Born 11/12/45. In 1966, Young met Steve Stills and Richie Furay and formed Buffalo Springfield, perhaps the most versatile group to grace the American rock scene. Each member of the band displayed a distinct songwriting style. Young specialized in the country field, branching into folk. After the Springfield dissolved in 1968, he coupled his talents with Stills, David Crosby, and Graham Nash to form America's most successful supergroup, Crosby, Stills, Nash and Young (1970-71), which boosted the popularity of each of their solo careers. In 1976, he formed the short-lived Stills-Young Band. Session for David Crosby (1971); the Band (1978). *Albums:* After the Gold Rush (RPS K 2283) 1970; American Stars 'n' Bars (RPS 2261) 1977; Comes a Time (RPS K 2266) 1978; Decade (RPS 3RS 2257) 1976; Everybody Knows This Is Nowhere (RPS K 2282) 1969; Harvest (RPS K 2277) 1972; Journey Through the Past (RPS 2KS 6480) 1972; Live Rust (RPS 2RX 2296) 1979; On the Beach (RPS 2180) 1973; Rust Never Sleeps (RPS HS 2295) 1979; Time Fades Away (RPS 2151) 1973; Tonight's the Night (RPS 2221) 1975; Where the Buffalo Roam (BKS 5126) 1980; Neil Young (RPS 6317) 1969; Zuma (RPS 2242) 1975; Hawks and Doves (RPS 2297) 1980.

YOUNG, PAUL Vocal, percussion, harmonica. Member of Sad Cafe, 1978-79, and the Streetband, 1980.

YOUNG, PETER Bass. Member of Razmataz, 1972.

YOUNG, REGGIE Guitar. Member of the Coral Reefer Band. Session for Jackie DeShannon (1972); Waylon Jennings (1973); Tom Rapp (1972); J. J. Cale (1974); Doug Kershaw (1974); Donovan (1974, 76); Bill Medley (1978); Frankie Miller (1980).

YOUNG, ROB Member of Toby Beau since 1978.

YOUNG, RODNEY Drums, percussion, vocal. Member of Bagatelle, 1968.

YOUNG, ROY Piano. Session for Long John Baldry (1979).

YOUNG, RUSTY Pedal steel guitar, dobro. Member of Poco since 1968. Session for the James Gang (1970).

YOUNG, SALLY Guitar, vocal. Member of the Yankees, 1978.

YOUNG, SNOOKY Trumpet, flugelhorn. Session for Barry Goldberg (1969); the Band (1972); Steely Dan (1972). *Albums:* Horn of Plenty (CCJ 91) 1979; Snooky and Marshal's Album (CCJ 55) 1978.

YOUNG, STARLEANA Vocal. Member of the Aurra, 1980.

YOUNG, STEVE Guitar, vocal. Member of Stone Country, 1968. Session for Waylon Jennings (1973). *Albums:* Redneck Mothers (VIC AYLI 3674); Seven Bridges Road (BCR 505); No Place to Fall (VIC AHLI 2510) 1978; Renegade Picker (VIC APLI 1759) 1976.

YOUNG, TERRY Keyboards, vocal. Session for Bob Dylan (1980).

YOUNG, WILLIE Tenor saxophone. Session for John Littlejohn.

YOUNG AND MOODY Bob Young—vocal, harmonica; Mick Moody—guitar, mandolin, vocal. *Album:* Young and Moody (UAR UA LA 759 G) 1977.

YOUNG MARBLE GIANTS Alison Statton—vocal; Phillip Moxham—bass; Stuart Moxham—guitar, organ. *Album:* Colossal Youth (RTD US 6) 1980.

YOUNG RASCALS See Rascals.

YOUNGBLOODS Jerry Corbitt—guitar, bass (1967-68); Jesse Colin Young—guitar, bass, vocal (1967-72); Joe Bauer—drums; Banana—piano, guitar, vocal; Mike Kane—bass, vocal (1972). Like the Lovin' Spoonful, they hailed from New York. With their melodic version of "Get Together" (1967), they established themselves as heirs to the country-folk throne of the Lovin' Spoonful. Corbitt left the group in 1968 and Young assumed the lead of the trio. As the albums progressed, so did their music. Banana's electric piano lines reached closer into jazz areas. But as "Ridgetop" (1972) showed, they had not forgotten their roots. They disbanded in 1972. *Albums:* High on a Ridge Top (WBR 2653) 1972; Ride the Wind (WBR B 2563); Rock Festival (WBR 1878) 1970; Best of the Youngbloods (VIC AYLI 3680) 1970; This Is the Youngbloods (VIC VPS 6051) 1972; Youngbloods (VIC

AFLI 4150) 1967; Earth Music (VIC) 1967; Elephant Mountain (VIC LSP 4150) 1969.

YOUNGER, ROB Vocal. Member of Radio Birdman, 1978.

YOUNT, DICK Guitar. Member of Harper's Bizarre, 1967-69.

YUE, OZZIE Guitar, vocal. Member of Supercharge, 1976-77.

YULE, BILL Drums. Replaced Maureen Tucker in the Velvet Underground, 1970.

YULE, DOUG Keyboards, bass, guitar, drums, vocal. Replaced John Cale in the Velvet Underground, 1970. Session for Lou Reed (1974); Elliott Murphy (1976).

YULES, MYRON Bass trombone. Member of Elephant's Memory.

Z

Z Z TOP Billy Gibbons—guitar, vocal, harmonica; Dusty Hill—bass, vocal; Frank Beard—drums. Hard rock trio from Texas. *Albums:* Best of Z Z Top (WBR K 3273) 1977; Deguello (WBR HS 3361); Fandango (WBR K 3271) 1975; First Album (WBR K 3268); Rio Grande Mud (WBR K 3269) 1972; Tejas (WBR K 3272) 1976; Tres Hombres (WBR K 3270) 1973.

ZACK, LARRY Drums. Member of Savage Grace, 1970.

ZAGER, MICHAEL Keyboards. Member of Ten Wheel Drive, 1970, and namesake of the Michael Zager Band, 1978-80.

MICHAEL ZAGER BAND Michael Zager—keyboards; Deniece Williams—vocal. *Albums:* Life's a Party (COL JC 35771) 1978; Night at Studio 54 (CAS 2 7161); Zager (COL JC 36348) 1980.

ZAGNI, IVAN Guitar. Session for Aynsley Dunbar (1970).

ZAHL, PAUL Drums, vocal. Member of SVT, 1980.

ZAKATEK, LENNY Vocal. Session for the Alan Parsons Project (1977, 78, 80).

ZAKSEN, LENNI Saxophone. Session for Sad Cafe (1978-79).

ZAMORA, BOB Drums. Member of Ruben and the Jets, 1973.

ZAMPERINI, LUKE Vocal, guitar. Member of the Scooters, 1980.

ZANDER, ROBIN Vocal, guitar. Voice of Cheap Trick since 1977.

ZANE, JIM Kazoo. Member of the Temple City Kazoo Orchestra, 1978.

ZANGRANDO, JOHN Saxophone. Session for Taj Mahal (1978).

ZAPPA, FRANK Guitar, vocal, producer. Born 12/21/40. Founder and driving force of the Mothers of Invention since 1966. See the Mothers of Invention. Session for Yoko Ono; Flint (1978). Session and production for the G.T.O.'s; Alice Cooper; Captain Beefheart (1969); Wild Man Fisher (1968); Grand Funk Railroad (1976). *Albums:* Apostrophe (DSC K 2289) 1974; Bongo Fury (DSC 2234) 1976; Chunga's Revenge (BIZ 2030) 1970; Hot Rats (BIZ 6356) 1969; Joe's Garage, Act 1 (ZPA SRZ 1 1603) 1978; Joe's Garage, Acts 2 & 3 (ZPA SRZ 2 1502) 1979; One Size Fits All (DSC 2216) 1975; Orchestral Favorites (DSC K 2294) 1979; Roxy and Elsewhere (DSC 2DS 2202) 1974; Sheik Yerbouti (ZPA SRZ 2 1501) 1979; Sleep Dirt (DSC X 2292) 1979; Studio Tan (DSC K 2291) 1978; Waka/Jawaka (BIZ 2094) 1972; Zappa in New York (DSC 2D 2290) 1978; Zoot Allures (WBR B 2970) 1976; Lumpy Gravy (VRV V6 8741) 1967.

ZARAMBA, ILENA Vocal. Member of Graham Shaw and the Sincere Serenaders, 1980.

ZARATE, ABEL Guitar, vocal. Member of Malo, 1972.

ZAREMBA, PETER Member of the Fleshtones, 1980.

ZARRA, FRED Keyboards, vocal. Member of the Cats, 1980.

ZAWINUL, JOSEF Keyboards. Founder of Weather Report, 1971-present. *Albums:* Piano Giants (PRS 24052); Trav'lin' Light (MLS 47056); Zawinul (ATC 1579) 1971; Concerto Retitled (ATC 1694) 1976.

ZAZA, JACK Recorder, English horn. Session for Gordon Lightfoot (1974).

ZDRAVECKY, JOHN Guitar, vocal. Member of the Love Affair, 1980.

ZEBULON, DANIEL BEN Congas. Session for the Bee Gees (1979); Andy Gibb (1980).

ZECKER, BILL Bass, vocal. Member of the Truth, 1975.

ZEHRINGER, RANDY Drums. Member of the McCoys, 1965-69. Session for Jimi Hendrix (1968).

ZEHRINGER, RICKY Real name of Rick Derringer.

ZELESNIK, BRUCE Drums. Member of the Wazband, 1979.

ZELKOWITZ, GOLDIE Vocal. Real name of Genya Ravan. See Genya Ravan. *Album:* Goldie Zelkowitz (JNS 3060) 1974.

ZELLER, JIM Harmonica. Session for Mahogany Rush (1979).

ZEPHYR David Givens—bass, vocal; Bobby Berge—drums; Tommy Bolin—guitar; Candy Givens—keyboards, vocal, harmonica; John Faris—keyboards, reeds, vocal. *Album:* Going Back to Colorado (WBR WS 1897) 1971.

ZERO, ARYAN Guitar, vocal. Member of the Kings, 1980.

ZERO, JIMMY Guitar. Member of the Dead Boys, 1977-78.

ZEUFELDT, FRED Drums. Member of the Surprise Package, 1969, American Eagle, 1970-71, and the Dixon House Band, 1979.

ZEVON, WARREN Piano, vocal. *Albums:* Bad Luck Streak in Dancing School (ASY 5E 509) 1980; Excitable Boy (ASY 6E 118) 1979; Warren Zevon (ASY 7E 1060) 1976; Stand in the Fire

(ASY 53 519) 1980.

ZIEGLER, RON Drums. Member of Elephant, 1975. Session for Andy Gibb (1980).

ZIEGLER, TUBBY Drums. Session for Steve Stills (1975-76).

ZIMMERMAN, ROBERT Real name of Bob Dylan.

ZIMMITTI, BOB Percussion. Session for the Mothers of Invention (1972).

ZINCAN, JOE Bass. Session for J. J. Cale (1972); Leon Russell (1973).

ZIPGUN, JOHNNY Bass. Member of the Sneakers, 1980.

ZIPPER, STEVE Member of Toby Beau since 1978.

ZIRNGIEBEL, ZEKE Guitar, bass, vocal. Member of Boulder, 1979.

ZITO, RICHIE Guitar, producer. Produced the Dukes (1979). Session for Neil Sedaka (1976); Chinga Chavin (1976); Yvonne Elliman (1978); Art Garfunkel (1979); the Marc Tanner Band (1979-80); Elton John (1980).

ZITO, SCOTT Guitar. Session for Grace Slick (1980).

ZIVIC, RICK Vocal. Member of 3-D, 1980.

ZOLLER, JURGEN Drums, percussion. Member of Supermax, 1979.

ZOMBIES Rod Argent—keyboards, violin, vocal, clarinet; Hugh Grundy—drums; Paul Atkinson—guitar, violin, harmonica; Chris White—bass, vocal; Colin Blunstone—guitar, percussion, vocal. Responsible for such hits as "Tell Her No" (1965), "She's Not There" (1964), and "Time of the Season," the Zombies survived the 1960s to become Argent. *Albums:* Zombies, 1965; Odyssey and Oracle, 1968; Early Days (LON PS 557); Time of the Zombies (EPC PEG 32861).

ZON Denton Young—vocal, percussion; Howard Helm—keyboards, vocal; Brian Miller—guitar, vocal; Kim Hunt—drums; Jim Samson—bass. *Album:* Back Down to Earth (EPC JE 36022) 1979.

ZONDEROP, MARTIN Bass. Member of the Urban Heroes, 1980.

ZOOM, BILLY Guitar. Member of X, 1980.

ZORILUK, DAVID Bass. Member of the Dixie Flyers.

ZORN, PETE Bass, vocal. Session for Gerry Rafferty (1980); Matthew Fisher (1980).

ZUBAL, JERRY Guitar. Member of the Rockicks, 1977.

ZUIDER ZEE John Bonar; Robert Hall; Kim Foreman; Richard Orange. *Album:* Zuider Zee, 1975.

ZUIDERWIJK, CESAR Drums, percussion. Member of the Golden Earring, 1970-present. Session for George Kooymans.

ZUKOWSKI, JAN Bass, vocal. Member of the Nighthawks since 1976.

ZULU Carl Byrd—drums; Kevin Moore—guitar; John Parker—keyboards; Hoagy Raphauel—percussion; Sam Williams—bass; Blue Mitchell—trumpet. Released one album as the backup band for Papa John Creach.

ZUMMO, PETER Trombone, flute, vocal, synthesizer. Member of the Sunship, 1974.

ZURI, FRANK Member of Diamond Reo, 1979.

ZURO, CHE Guitar, keyboards, vocal. Member of the Orchids, 1980.

ZWOL, WALTER Vocal. *Albums:* Effective Immediately (EMI 17014) 1979; Zwol (EMI 17005) 1978.

ZYCHEK, DAVID Vocal, guitar. Member of Airborne, 1979.

ZZEBRA Terry Smith—guitar (1974); Dave Quincey—saxophone, keyboards; Loughty Amao—percussion, reeds, vocal; Gus Yeadon—keyboards, flute, guitar, vocal (1974); Liam Genockey—drums, vocal; John McCoy—bass; Alan Marshall—vocal (1975); Tommy Eyre—keyboards, flute, vocal (1975); Steve Byrd—guitar (1975). *Albums:* Zzebra, 1974; Panic, 1975.

APPENDIX

Record Label Abbreviations

AAM—A & M Records
1416 No. LaBrea
Los Angeles, CA 90028

ABC—See MCA

ABQ—Arabesque Recordings
1995 Broadway
New York, NY 10023

ACC—Accent Records
71906 Highway 111
Rancho Mirage, CA 92270

ACO—ATCO Records
75 Rockefeller Plaza
New York, NY 10019

ADP—Adelphi Records
P.O. Box 288
Silver Spring, MD 20907

AIR—American Int'l. Records
c/o Casablanca Records
8255 Sunset Blvd.
Los Angeles, CA 90046

AKO—Abkco Records
1700 Broadway
New York, NY 10019

ALG—Alligator Records
P.O. Box 60234
Chicago, IL 60611

ALS—Alshire Records
P.O. Box 7107
Burbank, CA 91510

AMH—Amherst Records
355 Harlem Road
Buffalo, NY 14224

APL—Apple Records
Distributed by Capitol Records

ARA—Ariola America
c/o Arista Records
6 West 57th Street
New York, NY 10019

ARC—Arcano Records
c/o Caytronics Corp.
401 5th Avenue
New York, NY 10016

ARI—Arista Records
6 West 57th Street
New York, NY 10019

ASY—Asylum Records
c/o Elektra/Asylum
962 N. La Cienega
Los Angeles, CA 90069

ATC—Atlantic Recording Corp.
75 Rockefeller Plaza
New York, NY 10019

AUF—Audio Fidelity
Audio Fidelity Enterprises, Inc.
221 West 57th Street
New York, NY 10019

AVD—Avant Garde Records, Inc.
250 West 57th Street
New York, NY 10019

AVI—AVI Records
American Variety International
7060 Hollywood Blvd.
Hollywood, CA 90028

BDP—Blind Pig Records
208 South First Street
Ann Arbor, MI 48103

BIG—Big Tree
c/o Atlantic Recording Corp.
75 Rockefeller Plaza
New York, NY 10019

BIZ—Bizarre Records
c/o Warner Bros.
3300 Warner Blvd.
Burbank, CA 91510

BKS—Backstreet Records
c/o MCA Records
70 Universal City Plaza
Universal City, CA 91608

BLN—Blue Note Records
c/o EMI-A/United Artists
6920 Sunset Blvd.
Hollywood, CA 90028

BNG—Bang Records
4488 N. Shallowford Road N.W.
Suite 1000
Atlanta, GA 30338

BOO—Boot Records
P.O. Box 120478
Nashville, TN 37212

BRI—Briar Records
c/o Sierra/Briar Records
11312 Santa Monica Blvd., Suite 7
Los Angeles, CA 90025

BRU—Brunswick Records
888 Seventh Avenue
New York, NY 10019

BSK—Blue Sky Records
c/o CBS Records
51 West 52nd Street
New York, NY 10019

BSV—Bearsville Records
c/o Warner Bros.
3300 Warner Blvd.
Burbank, CA 91510

BTF—Butterfly Records
c/o MCA Records
70 Universal City Plaza
Universal City, CA 91608
BTM—Blue Thumb Records
See MCA
BUD—Buddah Records
c/o Arista Records, Inc.
6 West 57th Street
New York, NY 10019
BUL—Bullet Records
c/o Bang/Bullet Records
4488 N. Shallowford Road N.W.
Suite 1000
Atlanta, GA 30338
CAP—Capitol Records, Inc.
1750 North Vine Street
Hollywood, CA 90028
CAS—Casablanca Records
8255 Sunset Blvd.
Hollywood, CA 90046
CDN—Camden Records
c/o Pickwick Int'l., Inc
7500 Excelsior Blvd.
Minneapolis, MN 55426
CEN—Century 21 Records
6760 Selma Ave., Suite 1422
Hollywood, CA 90028
CHA—Charta Records
c/o Nationwide Sound Dist.
P.O. Box 23262
Nashville, TN 37202
CHC—Chocolate City Records
c/o Casablanca Records
8255 Sunset Blvd.
Los Angeles, CA 90046
CHT—Chute Records
P.O. Box 24272
Nashville, TN 37202
CHU—Churchill Records
535 N. Michigan Ave., Suite 611
Chicago, IL 60611
CIN—Cinnamon Records
c/o Int'l. Rec. Dist. Assocs.
260 W. Main, Suite 107
Hendersonville, TN 37075
CLD—Clouds Records
c/o T.K. Productions Inc.
495 S.E. 10th Court
Hialeah, FL 33010
CLL—Calla Records
c/o Epic Records
51 West 52nd Street
New York, NY 10019
CLT—Catalyst Records
c/o Vee-Jay Int'l. Records
131 East Magnolia Boulevard
Burbank, CA 91502
CLV—Cleveland International
c/o CBS Records
51 West 52nd Street
New York, NY 10019
CMA—Charisma Records
c/o Polygram Dist., Inc.
810 Seventh Avenue
New York, NY 10019
CMS—CMS Records, Inc.
14 Warren Street
New York, NY 10007
COL—Colombia Records
CBS Records
51 West 52nd Street
New York, NY 10019
COR—Coral Records
c/o MCA Records
70 Universal City Plaza
Universal City, CA 91608
CPM—Copper Mountain Records
49 Music Square West, Suite 403
Nashville, TN 37203
CPN—Capricorn Records
535 Cotton Avenue
Macon, GA 31201
CRB—Caribou Records
c/o Epic Records
51 West 52nd Street
New York, NY 10019
CRE—Cream Records
8025 Melrose Avenue
Los Angeles, CA 90046
CRK—Cricket Records
c/o Pickwick Int'l., Inc.
7500 Excelsior Blvd.
Minneapolis, MN 55426
CRO—Crossover Records
2107 W. Washington Blvd.
Los Angeles, CA 90018
CRS—Crescendo Records
c/o GNP-Crescendo Records, Inc.
8560 Sunset Blvd., Suite 603
Los Angeles, CA 90069
CRY—Crystal Records, Inc.
2235 Willida Lane
Sedro Woolley, WA 98294
CSA—Country Showcase America
11350 Baltimore Avenue
Beltsville, MD 20705
CSW—Casablanca West Records
c/o Casablanca Records
8255 Sunset Blvd.
Los Angeles, CA 90046
CTI—CTI Records
Division of Creed Taylor, Inc.
1 Rockefeller Plaza
New York, NY 10020
OR
c/o Motown Records
6255 Sunset Blvd.

Hollywood, CA 90028
OR
c/o CBS Records
51 West 52nd Street
New York, NY 10019

CTL—Cotillion Records
c/o Atlantic Records
75 Rockefeller Plaza
New York, NY 10019

CTM—Custom Records
c/o RSO Records
8335 Sunset Blvd.
Los Angeles, CA 90069
OR
c/o Warner Bros.
3300 Warner Blvd.
Burbank, CA 91510

CTP—Contemporary Records
8481 Melrose Place
Los Angeles, CA 90069

CUR—Curb Records
c/o CBS Records
51 West 52nd Street
New York, NY 10019

CYC—Cyclone Records
9000 Sunset Blvd., Suite 1010
Los Angeles, CA 90069

CYS—Chrysalis Records
9255 Sunset Blvd., Suite 212
Los Angeles, CA 90069

DDR—Direct Disk Records
16 Music Circle South
Nashville, TN 37203

DER—Deram Records
c/o London Records
137 West 55th Street
New York, NY 10019
OR
c/o Polygram Dist., Inc.
810 Seventh Avenue
New York, NY 10019

DHL—Dunhill Records
See MCA

DHM—Dharma Records
Division of Saturn Industries
117 W. Rockland Road, Box 615
Libertyville, IL 60048

DIS—Disneyland Records
350 S. Buena Vista Street
Burbank, CA 91521

DJM—DJM Records
c/o Polygram Dist., Inc.
810 Seventh Avenue
New York, NY 10019

DKH—Dark Horse Records
c/o Warner Brothers Records
3300 Warner Blvd.
Burbank, CA 91510

DLS—Delos Records, Inc.
855 Via De La Paz
Pacific Palisades, CA 90272

DLT—De Lite Records
c/o Polygram Dist., Inc.
810 Seventh Avenue
New York, NY 10019

DML—Dreamland Records
c/o RSO Records
8335 Sunset Blvd.
Los Angeles, CA 90069

DOR—Dore Records
1608 Argyle
Hollywood, CA 90028

DOT—Dot Records
See MCA

DPW—Deepwater Records
12506 Edgewater Drive
Cleveland, OH 44107

DRG—DRG Records
200 W. 57th Street
New York, NY 10019
OR
c/o RCA Records
1133 Avenue of the Americas
New York, NY 10036

DSC—Discreet Records
c/o Warner Bros.
3300 Warner Blvd.
Burbank, CA 91510

DSH—Dash Records
c/o TK Productions
495 S.E. 10th Court
Hialeah, FL 33010

DTA—Delta Records
P.O. Box 225
Nacogdoches, TX 75961

ECM—ECM Records
c/o Warner Bros. Records
3300 Warner Blvd.
Burbank, CA 91510

EIA—EMI America
6920 Sunset Blvd.
Hollywood, CA 90028

ELK—Elektra Records
Elektra/Asylum
962 N. La Cienega
Los Angeles, CA 90069

EOD—Epic/Ode Records
c/o Epic Records
51 West 52nd Street
New York, NY 10019

EPC—Epic Records
51 West 52nd Street
New York, NY 10019

ESP—ESP-Disk Records
Acorn Hill Road
Krumville, NY 12447

FFL—Free Flight Records
c/o RCA Records

1133 Avenue of the Americas
New York, NY 10036
FIE—Fiesta Records
1619 Broadway
New York, NY 10019
FLD—Flying Dutchman
c/o RCA Records
1133 Avenue of the Americas
New York, NY 10036
FLF—Flying Fish Records
1304 Schubert Street
Chicago, IL 60614
FLN—Frontline Records
6515 Sunset Blvd., Suite 204
Hollywood, CA 90028
FLW—Folkways/Scholastic
43 West 61st Street
New York, NY 10023
FON—Fontana Records
c/o Polygram Dist., Inc.
810 Seventh Avenue
New York, NY 10019
FSA—First Artists Records
4000 Warner Blvd.
Burbank, CA 91522
FSM—First American Records
65 Marion Street
Seattle, WA 98104
FSR—Fidelity Sound Recordings
23 Don Court
Redwood City, CA 94062
FSY—Fantasy Records
Tenth & Parker Streets
Berkeley, CA 94710
GFN—Geffen Records
c/o Warner Bros. Records
3300 Warner Blvd.
Burbank, CA 91510
GNT—Grunt Records
c/o RCA Records
1133 Avenue of the Americas
New York, NY 10036
GOR—Gordy Records
c/o Motown Records
6255 Sunset Blvd.
Hollywood, CA 90028
GRD—Grateful Dead Records
c/o United Artists
6920 Sunset Blvd.
Hollywood, CA 90028
GRP—GRP Records
c/o Arista Records
6 West 57th Street
New York, NY 10019
GRT—GRT Records
Reported Inactive
HAR—Harvest Records
c/o Capitol Records
1750 North Vine Street
Hollywood, CA 90028
HDS—Handshake Records
c/o CBS Records
51 West 52nd Street
New York, NY 10019
HTK—Hilltak Records
c/o Atlantic Recording Corp.
75 Rockefeller Plaza
New York, NY 10019
ICT—Inner City Records
c/o Music Minus One Records
423 West 55th Street
New York, NY 10023
IMP—Imperial Records
c/o United Artists Records
6920 Sunset Blvd.
Hollywood, CA 90028
INE—Inergi Records
1300 Texas Avenue
Houston, TX 77002
INF—Infinity Records
10 East 53rd Street
New York, NY 10022
OR
c/o MCA Records
70 Universal City Plaza
Universal City, CA 91608
INP—Inphasion Records
c/o T.K. Productions
495 S.E. Ten Court
Hialeah, FL 33010
IRS—Int'l. Record Syndicate
c/o A&M Records
1416 N. LaBrea Avenue
Hollywood, CA 90028
ISL—Island Records
444 Madison Avenue
New York, NY 10022
OR
c/o Warner Bros.
3300 Warner Blvd.
Burbank, CA 91510
JAM—Jamie Records
919 North Broad Street
Philadelphia, PA 19123
JDC—JDC Records
610 S. Venice Blvd., Suite 4284
Marina Del Rey, CA 90291
JET—Jet Records
c/o CBS Records
51 West 52nd Street
New York, NY 10019
JNS—Janus Records
1633 Broadway
New York, N.Y. 10019
KEY—Key Records
P.O. Box 46728
Hollywood, CA 90046
KLD—Kaleidoscope Records

c/o Flying Fish Records
1304 W. Schubert Street
Chicago, IL 60614

KNT—Kent Records
5810 S. Normandie Avenue
Los Angeles, CA 90044

KSH—Kirshner Records
c/o CBS Records
51 West 52nd Street
New York, NY 10019

KWD—Kenwood Records
c/o Nashboro Records
1011 Woodland Street
Nashville, TN 37206

LAF—Laff Records
4218 W. Jefferson Blvd.
Los Angeles, CA 90016

LAU—Laurie Records
20 F. Robert Pitt Drive
Monsey, NY 10952

LAX—LAX Records
c/o Mac Records
70 Universal City Plaza
Universal City, CA 91608

LIB—Liberty Records
c/o United Artists Records
6920 Sunset Blvd.
Hollywood, CA 90028

LIM—Limelight Records
c/o Polygram Dist., Inc.
810 Seventh Avenue
New York, NY 10019

LNS—Lone Star Records
c/o Polygram Dist., Inc.
810 Seventh Avenue
New York, NY 10019

LON—London Records
137 West 55th Street
New York, NY 10019

MAR—Marlin Records
c/o T.K. Productions
495 S.E. 10th Court
Hialeah, FL 33010

MCA—MCA Records
70 Universal City Plaza
Universal City, CA 91608

MCR—Musicor Records
Reported Inactive

MER—Mercury Records
c/o Polygram Dist., Inc.
810 Seventh Avenue
New York, NY 10019

MGM—MGM Records
c/o Polydor Inc.
810 Seventh Avenue
New York, NY 10019

MID—Midsong Int'l.
Midsong Int'l. Recording Co.
1650 Broadway
New York, NY 10019

MLN—Millennium Records
c/o Casablanca Records
8255 Sunset Blvd.
Los Angeles, CA 90046

MLS—Milestone Records
10th & Parker Streets
Berkeley, CA 94710

MMG—Moss Music Group
48 West 38th Street
New York, NY 10018

MNC—Manticore Records
c/o Motown Records
6255 Sunset Blvd.
Hollywood, CA 90028

MNT—Monument Records
21 Music Square East
Nashville, TN 37203

MRG—Mirage Records
c/o Atlantic Records
75 Rockefeller Plaza
New York, NY 10019

MSH—Mushroom Records
9000 Sunset Blvd., Suite 710
Los Angeles, CA 90069

MTN—Motown Records
6255 Sunset Blvd.
Los Angeles, CA 90028

MUS—Muse Records
160 West 71st Street
New York, NY 10023

MYR—Myrrh Records
c/o Word Records, Inc.
4800 W. Waco Drive
Waco, TX 76703

NMP—Nemperor Records
c/o CBS Records
51 West 52nd Street
New York, NY 10019

OAS—Oasis Records
c/o Casablanca Records
8255 Sunset Blvd.
Los Angeles, CA 90046

ODE—See EOD

OLR—Olympic Records
c/o Everest Group
2020 Avenue of the Stars
Concourse Level
Century City, CA 90067

OSR—Original Sound
7120 Sunset Blvd.
Los Angeles, CA 90046

OVA—Ovation Records
1249 Waukegan Road
Glenview, IL 60025

OYS—Oyster Records
c/o Polydor Records
810 Seventh Avenue
New York, NY 10019

PAB—Pablo Records
c/o RCA Records
1133 Avenue of the Americas
New York, NY 10036
PAC—Pacific Records
c/o Atlantic Recording Corp.
75 Rockefeller Plaza
New York, NY 10019
PAD—Paid Records
50 Music Square West, Suite 306
Nashville, TN 37203
PBY—Playboy Records
c/o CBS Records
51 West 52nd Street
New York, NY 10019
PCH—Parachute Records
c/o Casablanca Records
8255 Sunset Blvd.
Los Angeles, CA 90046
PCJ—Pacific Jazz Records
c/o United Artists Records
6920 Sunset Blvd.
Los Angeles, CA 90028
PDS—Paradise Records
c/o Warner Bros.
3300 Warner Blvd.
Burbank, CA 91510
PHI—Philips Records
c/o Polygram Dist., Inc.
810 Seventh Avenue
New York, NY 10019
PHN—Phantom Records
See VIC
PLN—Plantation
c/o SSS International
3106 Belmont Avenue
Nashville, TN 37212
PNT—Planet Records
c/o Elektra/Asylum Records
962 N. La Cienega Blvd.
Los Angeles, CA 90069
POL—Polydor Records
810 Seventh Avenue
New York, NY 10019
POR—Portrait Records
c/o CBS Records
51 West 52nd Street
New York, NY 10019
PRE—Precision Records
c/o CBS Records
51 W. 52nd Street
New York, NY 10019
PRG—Prodigal Records
c/o Motown Records
6255 Sunset Blvd.
Hollywood, CA 90028
PRL—Prelude Records
200 West 57th Street
New York, NY 10019
PRR—Parrot Records
c/o London Records
137 West 55th Street
New York, NY 10019
PRS—Prestige Records
10th & Parker Streets
Berkeley, CA 94710
PSM—Prism Records
636 11th Avenue
New York, NY 10036
PST—Passport Records
3619 Kennedy Road
South Plainfield, NJ 07080
PVS—Private Stock
Reported Inactive
PYR—Pyramid Records
c/o Roulette Records
1790 Broadway
New York, NY 10019
QUA—Quality Records
40 West 57th Street
New York, NY 10023
QUI—Quintessence Records
c/o Pickwick Int'l. Records
7500 Excelsior Blvd.
Minneapolis, MN 55426
RCA—See VIC
REH—Rare Earth Records
c/o Motown Records
6255 Sunset Blvd.
Hollywood, CA 90028
RGT—Ridgetop Records
c/o Curtis Wood Dist.
1010 17th Avenue South
Nashville, TN 37212
RHI—Rhino Records
11609 W. Pico Blvd.
Los Angeles, CA 90064
RLS—Rolling Stones Records
c/o Atlantic Recording Corp.
75 Rockefeller Plaza
New York, NY 10019
RMP—Rampart Records
255 North New Hampshire
Los Angeles, CA 90004
RND—Rounder Records
186 Willow Avenue
Somerville, MA 02144
ROC—Rocket Records
c/o MCA Records
70 Universal City Plaza
Universal City, CA 91608
ROU—Roulette Records
1790 Broadway
New York, NY 10019
RPS—Reprise Records
3300 Warner Blvd.
Burbank, CA 91510
RSO—RSO Records

810 Seventh Ave.
New York, NY 10019
SBD—Sunbird Records
c/o Capitol Records
1750 North Vine Street
Hollywood, CA 90028
SCT—Soul City Records
c/o Atlantic Recording Corp.
75 Rockefeller Plaza
New York, NY 10019
SER—Seraphim Records
c/o Capitol Records, Inc.
1750 North Vine Street
Hollywood, CA 90028
SFF—Stiff Records
c/o CBS Records
51 West 52nd Street
New York, NY 10019
SHE—She Records
c/o Atlantic Recording Corp.
75 Rockefeller Plaza
New York, NY 10019
SIR—Sire Records
c/o Warner Bros. Records
3300 Warner Blvd.
Burbank, CA 91510
SLD—Southland Records
c/o Jazzology Records
3008 Wadsworth Mill Place
Decatur, GA 30032
SLT—Shelter Records
c/o MCA Records
70 Universal City Plaza
Universal City, CA 91608
SMA—Smash Records
c/o Polygram Dist., Inc.
810 Seventh Avenue
New York, NY 10019
SNW—Soundwaves Records
c/o Nationwide Sound Dist.
P.O. Box 23262
Nashville, TN 37202
SOG—Solid Gold Records
c/o Bang/Bullet Records
4488 N. Shallowford Road N.W.
Suite 1000
Atlanta, GA 30338
SOL—Soul Records
c/o Motown Records
6255 Sunset Blvd.
Hollywood, CA 90028
SOZ—Spindizzy Records
See CBS
SPC—Spector Records
c/o Capitol Records
1750 North Vine Street
Hollywood, CA 90028
SPG—Spring Records
c/o Polydor, Inc.
810 Seventh Avenue
New York, NY 10019
SRF—Surfside Records
c/o Hula Records
1020 Auahi Street
Honolulu, HI 96814
SSL—Salsoul Records
c/o RCA Records
1133 Avenue of the Americas
New York, NY 10036
SSS—SSS International
Shelby Singleton Corp.
3106 Belmont Blvd.
Nashville, TN 37212
STB—Scotti Bros. Records
c/o Atlantic Recording Corp.
75 Rockefeller Plaza
New York, NY 10019
STF—Starflite Records
c/o Epic Records
51 West 52nd Street
New York, NY 10019
STX—Stax Records
c/o Fantasy Records
10th & Parker Streets
Berkeley, CA 94710
SUN—Sun Records
c/o SSS International
3106 Belmont Blvd.
Nashville, TN 37212
SWN—Swan Song Records
c/o Atlantic Records
75 Rockefeller Plaza
New York, NY 10019
TAP—Tapestry Records
12011 San Vicente Blvd., Suite 502
Los Angeles, CA 90049
TAT—Tattoo Records
c/o RCA Records
1133 Avenue of the Americas
New York, NY 10036
THS—Threshold Records
c/o London Records
137 West 55th Street
New York, NY 10019
TKM—Takoma Records
c/o Chrysalis Records
9255 Sunset Blvd.
Los Angeles, CA 90069
TML—Tamla Records
c/o Motown Records
6255 Sunset Blvd.
Hollywood, CA 90028
TMT—Tomato Records
611 Broadway
New York, NY 10012
TWC—20th Century Records
8544 Sunset Blvd.
Los Angeles, CA 90069

UAR—EMI-A/United Artists
6920 Sunset Blvd.
Hollywood, CA 90028
VAN—Vanguard Recording Soc., Inc.
71 West 23rd Street
New York, NY 10010
VGN—Virgin Records
c/o Atlantic Records
75 Rockefeller Plaza
New York, NY 10019
OR
c/o RSO Records
8355 Sunset Blvd.
Los Angeles, CA 90069
VIC—Victor Records
RCA Records
1133 Avenue of the Americas
New York, NY 10036
VIS—Vista Records
350 S. Buena Vista Street
Burbank, CA 91521
VRV—Verve Records
c/o Polydor Inc.
810 Seventh Ave.
New York, NY 10019
VSA—Visa Records
c/o Jem Records, Inc.
3619 Kennedy Road
South Plainsfield, NJ 07080
VTG—Vertigo Records
c/o Polygram Dist., Inc.
810 Seventh Avenue
New York, NY 10019
WBF—Warner Bros./RFC Records
c/o Warner Bros.
3300 Warner Blvd.
Burbank, CA 91510
WBR—Warner Bros. Records
3300 Warner Blvd.
Burbank, CA 91510
WDN—Wooden Nickel
c/o RCA Records
1133 Avenue of the Americas
New York, NY 10036
WDS—Windsong Records
c/o RCA Victor
1133 Avenue of the Americas
New York, NY 10036
WSB—Westbound Records
19631 W. Eight Mile Road
Detroit, MI 48219
WTH—Waterhouse Records
100 N. 7th Street
Minneapolis, MN 55403
ZPA—Zappa Records
c/o Polygram Dist., Inc.
810 Seventh Avenue
New York, NY 10019